Literature Criticism from 1400 to 1800

Guide to Gale Literary Criticism Series

For criticism on	Consult these Gale series
Authors now living or who died after December 31, 1959	*CONTEMPORARY LITERARY CRITICISM (CLC)*
Authors who died between 1900 and 1959	*TWENTIETH-CENTURY LITERARY CRITICISM (TCLC)*
Authors who died between 1800 and 1899	*NINETEENTH-CENTURY LITERATURE CRITICISM (NCLC)*
Authors who died between 1400 and 1799	*LITERATURE CRITICISM FROM 1400 TO 1800 (LC)* *SHAKESPEAREAN CRITICISM (SC)*
Authors who died before 1400	*CLASSICAL AND MEDIEVAL LITERATURE CRITICISM (CMLC)*
Authors of books for children and young adults	*CHILDREN'S LITERATURE REVIEW (CLR)*
Dramatists	*DRAMA CRITICISM (DC)*
Poets	*POETRY CRITICISM (PC)*
Short story writers	*SHORT STORY CRITICISM (SSC)*
Black writers of the past two hundred years	*BLACK LITERATURE CRITICISM (BLC)*
Hispanic writers of the late nineteenth and twentieth centuries	*HISPANIC LITERATURE CRITICISM (HLC)*
Native North American writers and orators of the eighteenth, nineteenth, and twentieth centuries	*NATIVE NORTH AMERICAN LITERATURE (NNAL)*
Major authors from the Renaissance to the present	*WORLD LITERATURE CRITICISM, 1500 TO THE PRESENT (WLC)*

ISSN 0740-2880

Volume 52

Literature Criticism from 1400 to 1800

Critical Discussion of the Works of Fifteenth-, Sixteenth-, Seventeenth-, and Eighteenth-Century Novelists, Poets, Playwrights, Philosophers, and Other Creative Writers

Marie Lazzari

Editor

GALE GROUP

Detroit
San Francisco
London
Boston
Woodbridge, CT

STAFF

Marie Lazzari, *Editor*
Jelena O. Krstović , *Contributing Editor*
Pam Revitzer, *Associate Editor*
Lynn Spampinato, Janet Witalec, *Managing Editors*

Maria Franklin, *Permissions Manager*
Kimberly F. Smilay, *Permissions Specialist*
Kelly A. Quin, *Permissions Associate*
Sandra K. Gore, *Permissions Assistant*

Victoria B. Cariappa, *Research Manager*
Patricia T. Ballard, Tamara C. Nott, Tracie A. Richardson,
Corrine Stocker, Cheryl L. Warnock, *Research Associates*

Gary Leach, *Graphic Artist*
Randy Bassett, *Image Database Supervisor*
Mike Logusz, Robert Duncan, *Imaging Specialists*
Pamela A. Reed, *Imaging Coordinator*

This book is printed on acid-free paper that meets the minimum requirements of American National Standard for Information Sciences—Permanence Paper for Printed Library Materials, ANSI Z39.48-1984.

Library of Congress Catalog Card Number 94-29718
ISBN 0-7876-3267-8
ISSN 0740-2880
Printed in the United States of America

10 9 8 7 6 5 4 3 2 1

Contents

Preface vii

Acknowledgments xi

Preface

*L*iterature Criticism from 1400 to 1800 (LC) presents critical discussion of world literature from the fifteenth through the eighteenth centuries. The literature of this period is especially vital: the years 1400 to 1800 saw the rise of modern European drama, the birth of the novel and personal essay forms, the emergence of newspapers and periodicals, and major achievements in poetry and philosophy. *LC* provides valuable insight into the art, life, thought, and cultural transformations that took place during these centuries.

Scope of the Series

LC provides an introduction to the great poets, dramatists, novelists, essayists, and philosophers of the fifteenth through eighteenth centuries, and to the most significant interpretations of these authors' works. Because criticism of this literature spans nearly six hundred years, an overwhelming amount of scholarship confronts the student. *LC* organizes this material concisely and logically. Every attempt is made to reprint the most noteworthy, relevant, and educationally valuable essays available.

A separate Gale reference series, *Shakespearean Criticism,* is devoted exclusively to Shakespearean studies. Although properly belonging to the period covered in *LC,* William Shakespeare has inspired such a tremendous and ever-growing body of secondary material that a separate series was deemed essential.

Each entry in *LC* presents a representative selection of critical response to an author, a literary topic, or to a single important work of literature. Early commentary is offered to indicate initial responses, later selections document changes in literary reputations, and retrospective analyses provide the reader with modern views. The size of each author entry is a relative reflection of the scope of criticism available in English. Every attempt has been made to identify and include the seminal essays on each author's work and to include recent commentary providing modern perspectives.

Volumes 1 through 12 of the series feature author entries arranged alphabetically by author. Volumes 13 through 47 of the series feature a thematic arrangement. Each volume includes an entry devoted to the general study of a specific literary or philosophical movement, writings surrounding important political and historical events, the philosophy and art associated with eras of cultural transformation, or the literature of specific social or ethnic groups. Each of these volumes also includes several author entries devoted to major representatives of the featured period, genre, or national literature. With Volume 48, the series returns to a standard author approach, with occasional entries devoted to a single important work of world literature. One volume annually is devoted wholly to literary topics.

Organization of the Book

Each entry consists of a heading, an introduction, a list of principal works, annotated works of criticism, each preceded by a bibliographical citation, and a bibliography of recommended further reading. Many of the entries include illustrations.

- The **Author Heading** consists of the most commonly used form of the author's name, followed by birth and death dates. Also located here are any name variations under which an author wrote, including transliterated forms for authors whose native languages use nonroman alphabets. Uncertain birth or death dates are indicated by question marks. Topic entries are preceded by a **Thematic Heading,** which simply states the subject of the entry. Single-work entries are preceded by the title of the work and its date of publication.

- The **Introduction** contains background information that concisely introduces the reader to the author, work, or topic that is the subject of the entry.

- The list of **Principal Works** is ordered chronologically by date of first publication. The genre and publication date of each work is given. In the case of foreign authors whose works have been translated into English, the title and date (if available) of the first English-language edition is given in brackets following the original title. Unless otherwise indicated, dramas are dated by first performance, not first publication. Lists of **Representative Works** by different authors appear with topic entries.

- Reprinted **Criticism** is arranged chronologically in each entry to provide a useful perspective on changes in critical evaluation over time. The critic's name and the date of composition or publication of the critical work are given at the beginning of each piece of criticism. Unsigned criticism is preceded by the title of the source in which it appeared. All titles by the author featured in the text are printed in boldface type. Footnotes are reprinted at the end of each essay or excerpt. In the case of excerpted criticism, only those footnotes that pertain to the excerpted text are included. Criticism in topic entries is arranged chronologically under a variety of subheadings to facilitate the study of different aspects of the topic.

- Critical essays are prefaced by brief **Annotations** explicating each piece.

- A complete **Bibliographical Citation** of the original essay or book precedes each piece of criticism.

- An annotated bibliography of **Further Reading** appears at the end of each entry and suggests resources for additional study. In some cases, significant essays for which the editors could not obtain reprint rights are included here.

Cumulative Indexes

Each volume of *LC* includes a series-specific cumulative **Nationality Index** in which author names are arranged alphabetically by nationality. The volume or volumes of *LC* in which each author appears are also listed.

Each volume of *LC* includes a cumulative **Author Index** listing all of the authors that appear in a wide variety of reference sources published by The Gale Group, including *LC*. A complete list of these sources is found facing the first page of the Author Index. The index also includes birth and death dates and cross references between pseudonyms and actual names.

LC includes a cumulative **Topic Index** that lists the literary themes and topics treated in the series as well as in *Nineteenth-Century Literature Criticism*, *Twentieth-Century Literary Criticism*, and the *Contemporary Literature Criticism* Yearbook.

Each volume of *LC* also includes a cumulative **Title Index,** an alphabetical listing of all the literary works discussed in the series. Each title listing includes the corresponding volume and page numbers where criticism may be located. Foreign-language titles that have been translated into English followed by the tiles of the translation—for example, *El ingenioso hidalgo Don Quixote de la Mancha (Don Quixote)*. Page numbers following these translated titles refer to all pages on which any form of the titles, either foreign-language or translated, appear. Titles of novels, dramas, nonfiction books, and poetry, short story, or essay collections are printed in italics, while individual poems, short stories, and essays are printed in roman type within quotation marks.

A Note to the Reader

When writing papers, students who quote directly from any volume in the Literary Criticism Series may use the following general format to footnote reprinted criticism. The first example pertains to material drawn from periodicals, the second to material reprinted from books.

Eileen Reeves, "Daniel 5 and the *Assayer*: Galileo Reads the Handwriting on the Wall," *The Journal of Medieval and Renaissance Studies,* Vol. 21, No. 1, Spring, 1991, pp. 1-27; reprinted in *Literature Criticism from 1400 to 1800,* Vol. 45, ed. Jelena O. Krstović and Marie Lazzari, Farmington Hills, Mich.: The Gale Group, 1999, pp. 297-310.

Margaret Anne Doody, *A Natural Passion: A Study of the Novels of Samuel Richardson*, Oxford University Press, 1974, pp. 17-22, 132-35, excerpted and reprinted in *Literature Criticism from 1400 to 1800,* Vol. 46, ed. Jelena O. Krstović and Marie Lazzari. Farmington Hills, Mich.: The Gale Group, 1999, pp. 20-2.

Suggestions Are Welcome

Readers who wish to suggest new features, topics, or authors to appear in future volumes, or who have other suggestions or comments are cordially invited to call, write, or fax the editor:

Editor, *Literature Criticism from 1400 to 1800*
The Gale Group
27500 Drake Road
Farmington Hills, MI 48133-3535
1-800-347-4253
fax: 248-699-8049

Acknowledgments

The editors wish to thank the copyright holders of the reprinted criticism included in this volume and the permissions managers of many book and magazine publishing companies for assisting us in securing reproduction rights. We are also grateful to the staffs of the Detroit Public Library, the Library of Congress, the University of Detroit Mercy Library, Wayne State University Purdy/Kresge Library Complex, and the University of Michigan Libraries for making their resources available to us. Following is a list of the copyright holders who have granted us permission to reproduce material in this volume of *LC*. Every effort has been made to trace copyright, but if omissions have been made, please let us know.

COPYRIGHTED MATERIAL IN *LC*, VOLUME 52, WAS REPRODUCED FROM THE FOLLOWING PERIODICALS:

—*Ball State University Forum*, v. VIII, Summer, 1967; v. XIX, Summer, 1978. Copyright 1967, 1978 by Ball State University. Both reproduced by permission.—*The British Library Journal*, v. 18, Autumn, 1992. Reproduced by permission.—*English Studies*, v. 6, 1985. © 1985, Swets & Zeitlinger. Reproduced by permission.—*Enlightenment Essays*, v. V, Summer, 1974 for "Idea and Art in Prior's Dialogues of the Dead" by John Higby. Reproduced by permission of the author.—*The Explicator*, v. 51, Winter, 1993. Copyright © 1993 by Helen Dwight Reid Educational Foundation. Reproduced with permission of the Helen Dwight Reid Educational Foundation, published by Heldref Publications, 1319 18th Street, NW, Washington, DC 20036-1802.—*Grand Street*, v. 9, Autumn, 1989. Reproduced by permission.—*The Historical Journal*, v. 37, December, 1994. Copyright © 1994 Cambridge University Press. Reproduced with the permission of Cambridge University Press.—*The Journal of Ecclesiastical History*, v. 39, April, 1988. © Cambridge University Press 1988. Reproduced with the permission of Cambridge University Press.—*Journal of the History of Ideas*, v. XXVI, January-March, 1965. Copyright 1965 Journal of the History of Ideas, Inc. Reproduced by permission of The Johns Hopkins University Press.—*MLN*, v. 87, November, 1972; v. 106, September, 1991. © copyright 1972, 1991 by The Johns Hopkins University Press. All rights reserved. Both reproduced by permission.—*Papers on Language & Literature*, v. 28, Winter, 1992; v. 33, Fall, 1997. Copyright © 1992, 1997 by the Board of Trustees Southern Illinois University. Both reproduced by permission.—*Philological Quarterly*, v. XLVIII, January, 1969 for "More Light on Rasselas: The Background of the Egyptian Episodes" by Arthur J. Weitzman. Reproduced by permission of the author.—*The Review of English Studies*, v. XVIII, November, 1967 for "The Artistic Form of Rasselas" by Emrys Jones; v. XXVIII, February, 1977 for "Julian of Norwich and Her Audience" by B. A. Windeatt. Both reproduced by permission of Oxford University Press and the respective authors.—*The Romantic Review*, v. LXXXI, January, 1990; v. 83, November, 1992. Both reproduced by permission.—*The Seventeenth Century*, v. VI, Autumn, 1991. Reproduced by permission.—*The Sixteenth Century Journal*, v. XXVII, Fall, 1996. Copyright © 1996 by The Sixteenth Century Journal Publishers, Inc., Kirksville, Missouri. All rights reserved. Reproduced by permission.—*Studies in English Literature, 1500-1900*, v. 28, Summer, 1988; v. 29, Summer, 1989; v. 35, Summer, 1995; v. 36, Summer, 1996. © William Marsh Rice University 1988, 1989, 1995, 1996. All reproduced by permission of The Johns Hopkins University Press.—*Studies in Philology*, v. XC, Fall, 1993. Copyright © 1993 The University of North Carolina Press. Used by permission of the publisher.—*Studies on Voltaire and the Eighteenth Century*, v. 304 1992. Reproduced by permission.

COPYRIGHTED MATERIAL IN *LC*, VOLUME 52, WAS REPRODUCED FROM THE FOLLOWING BOOKS:

—Baker, Denise Nowakowski. From *Julian of Norwich's "Showings": From Vision to Book*. Princeton University Press, 1994. Copyright © 1994 by Princeton University Press. All rights reserved. Reproduced by permission. —Bate, Walter Jackson. From *The Achievement of Samuel Johnson*. Oxford University Press, 1955. Copyright 1955 by Oxford University Press, Inc. Renewed 1983 by Walter J. Bate. Reproduced by permission of the Literary Estate of Walter Jackson Bate. —Bradley, Ritamary. From "Julian of Norwich: Writer and Mystic" in *An Introduction to The Medieval Mystics of Europe*. Edited by Paul E. Szarmach. State University of New York Press, 1984. © 1984 State University of New York. All rights reserved. Reproduced by permission of the State University of New York Press. —Brailsford, H. N. From "The True Levellers" in *The Levellers and the English Revolution*. Edited by Christopher

PHOTOGRAPHS AND ILLUSTRATIONS APPEARING IN *LC*, VOLUME 52, WERE RECEIVED FROM THE FOLLOWING SOURCES:

The History of Rasselas, Prince of Abyssinia

Samuel Johnson

The following entry presents criticism of Johnson's novel *The History of Rasselas, Prince of Abyssinia* (1759). For information on Johnson's complete career, see *LC,* Volume 15.

INTRODUCTION

Rasselas remains one of the most popular works by the esteemed and prolific Johnson. Supposedly written in just seven days, *Rasselas* is alternately considered a novelistic rendering of the pessimism evinced in his poem *The Vanity of Human Wishes* (1749) or as an optimistic philosophical argument for the limitless potential of humankind. The ambiguous genre and tone of *Rasselas,* neither novel nor essay, neither moral tale nor satire, make it a crucial text in the history of both prose fiction and Enlightenment philosophy.

Biographical Information

Johnson was born in Lichfield in 1709 to Sarah Ford and Michael Johnson, a bookseller. Though the young Johnson's formal schooling was cut short by his family's poverty, he continued to read extensively in his father's bookshop. He eventually developed a reputation in literary circles as a translator, commended by one of the greatest poets of the day, Alexander Pope. Johnson's first book, published anonymously in 1735, was a translation of the French *Voyage to Abyssinia,* by Father Jerome Lobo, an important historical source for *Rasselas.* That same year Johnson married, and with money from the marriage settlement opened a boarding school. When the school failed Johnson went to London, accompanied by a former student, David Garrick, who would soon become the most important actor of the eighteenth century. For the next twenty-five years Johnson worked as a journalist, initially writing for *Gentleman's Magazine,* and eventually launching his own publication, *The Rambler,* for which he wrote several essays exploring themes he would develop at greater length in *Rasselas.*

When Johnson's wife died in 1752, he ceased publishing *The Rambler,* working on his *Dictionary,* a project that firmly established his contemporary reputation. He also contributed essays to such periodicals as *The Adventurer* and *The Universal Chronicle,* the latter of which published his series of essays as "The Idler." In 1759, Johnson published *Rasselas.* His biographer James Boswell reported that Johnson wrote it hurriedly in the hope "that with the profits he might defray

the expense of his mother's funeral and pay some little debts that she had left." Johnson requested that the book be published anonymously, although he assumed that its authorship would eventually be known. In 1764, he became a member of what would later be known as The Literary Club; other illustrious members included Edmund Burke, Oliver Goldsmith, Edward Gibbon, and Boswell. Johnson spent much of the last part of his life traveling, documented in *A Journey to the Western Islands of Scotland* and other travel essays. In 1777, Johnson began writing biographical prefaces for editions of English poets; these were published together in 1781 as the ten-volume *Lives of the English Poets,* an important resource for scholars and, according to Johnson himself, one of his favorite writing projects. He died in 1784.

Major Works

Johnson's literary output is substantial and encompasses a wide variety of genres. His first major poems were imitations of classical satire, a genre popular at the time, especially after Alexander Pope's imitations of Horatian epistles. *London,* an imitation of Juvenal's third satire, was a modest success in 1738. In it Johnson attacked the prime minister Horace Walpole and denounced the poverty and corruption that afflicted lower-class Londoners, such as Johnson himself. Though his work was favorably compared with that of Pope, Johnson did not continue writing poetry; instead, he turned to journalism and essays, not publishing his second major poem until 1749. Entitled *The Vanity of Human Wishes (in Imitation of the Tenth Satire of Juvenal),* the popular, well-received poem details the futility of human pursuits, deflating the hopes and ambitions of monarchs, soldiers, and scholars alike, and points toward the miserable deaths of those most successful in life. The year 1749 also saw the production of Johnson's only drama, *Irene.* His former student Garrick produced the play as the manager of the Drury Lane theatre, but by most accounts the production was not a great success. In 1747, Johnson had proposed to the Earl of Chesterfield the necessity of a dictionary of the English language; Johnson subsequently spent the early part of the 1750s working on the project, finally completing the forty-thousand-word volume in 1755. Such authors as John Dryden, Jonathan Swift, and Pope himself had long complained about the rapid, uncontrolled innovations in English grammar and vocabulary; Johnson's attempt to gather together the many variances in the language and to bend the lexicon to the authority of classical precedent made him an instant literary hero. He also continued writing his moral essays for *The Adventurer, The Literary Magazine,* and *The Universal Chronicle;* his review of Soame Jenyns' *A Free Inquiry into the Nature and Origin of Evil,* published in 1757, is among his most famous. Two years later, when *Rasselas* was published, it was virtually assured success based on the identity of its popular author. The book went through several editions in its first year and eventually inspired a sequel, penned by the daughter of one of Johnson's friends, entitled *Dinarbas* (1790), which enjoyed short-term popularity and eight printings due to its connection to Johnson's highly esteemed work. *Rasselas* tells the story of the title character, the eponymous prince of Abyssinia (or Ethiopia), and his growing dissatisfaction with the unceasing pleasures of his utopian home in the Happy Valley. According to Ethiopian tradition, the children of royalty were confined to an edenic valley, secluded from the harsh realities of the outside world. Happy Valley, though, rather than being seen as a paradise by Rasselas, is instead considered by him to be a prison, harboring boredom and tediousness. So Rasselas, accompanied by his teacher Imlac, his sister Nekayah, and her lady-in-waiting Pekuah, escapes his idyllic homeland to experience the outside world and search out the one way of life most likely to lead to lasting happiness on earth. After a series of comic misadventures, brushes with danger, and repeated dis-

appointments, the travelers determine that, in the words of Nekayah, "the choice of life is become less important; I hope hereafter to think only on the choice of eternity."

Johnson's next major project was an edition of Shakespeare's plays (1765), generally considered by critics as the best edition of Shakespeare that had yet been published, and distinguished by Johnson's prior work as a lexicographer and his very personal, opinionated commentary on the plays. Johnson also remained a staunch critic of English politics, publishing a series of controversial essays, many supporting the policies of his friend M. P. Henry Thrale, Hester Thrale's husband before Piozzi. Johnson's attack on American colonists in *Taxation No Tyranny* (1775) is especially blistering; in it he mocked their pretensions to "freedom of conscience" and condemned the hypocrisy of slave-holders fighting for "liberty." The pamphlet won him an honorary doctorate from Oxford. His last major work published during his lifetime was the impressive biographical scholarship in *Lives of the English Poets,* published collectively in 1781. His *Prayers and Meditations,* a reflection of his sincere and searching practice of Christianity, was published in 1785, within a year of his death.

Critical Reception

Rasselas was published to general acclaim: although it must be acknowledged that many early reviewers were friends and admirers of Johnson, their praise is validated by the generations of later critics who have also held the book in high esteem. Early commentary, particularly from Johnson's first biographers, focused on the work's reflection of Johnson's personal life and beliefs; Boswell, for example, noted that the "gloomy picture" Johnson painted in *Rasselas* was possibly a result of Johnson's own "melancholy constitution." Sir Walter Raleigh, too, called the work "the most melancholy of fables." The dark nature of *Rasselas* is a point of concern even for those who admire the book, and the debate over whether the work is finally optimistic or pessimistic has continued throughout its entire critical history. Closely linked to this argument is the debate over the moral value of *Rasselas.* Boswell, for instance, stated that Johnson emphasized the vanity of life on earth in order to instruct mankind to look to eternal life for happiness. In this way, according to Boswell, Johnson offered his readers hope that, rather than like "beasts who perish," humankind could achieve everlasting happiness through their immortality. Indeed, in the view of many commentators, *Rasselas* presents an essentially moral and Christian outlook, with its emphasis on the afterlife rather than on temporal concerns. Many modern critics, however, have seen *Rasselas* as neither moral nor optimistic but simply as a form of entertainment. Claiming that Johnson himself did not direct his readers to consider the moral value of his work, Duane H. Smith has asserted that the author knowingly offered *Rasselas* as merely a form of amusement for his audience. Commenting also on *Rasselas* as a form of diversion, Catherine N. Parke has focused on the "psychology of boredom" as evidenced in the piece. According to Parke, Johnson saw "historical thinking"—the ability to look beyond the immediate present to the past—as a way for a bored mind to express and stimulate itself. Looking at the power of the human imagination in the work, Walter Jackson Bate, too, has studied how *Rasselas* exhibits a typical Johnsonian investigation into the "human craving for 'novelty'." According to Bate, the title character, though all his wants and needs are fulfilled in Happy Valley, desires a life where unsatisfied needs would force him into activity to stimulate his unoccupied mind.

The style and genre of *Rasselas* has also remained a point of critical contention. Raleigh included it in his history of the English novel, despite its distinctly un-novel-like characterization and structure; Sheridan Baker has called it an ironic adaptation of oriental romance; and more recent critics, such as James F. Woodruff, have considered it a variation on classical satire. Other modern critics have labeled it a philosophical discourse, a comedy, a philosophical romance, and a quest romance, among other classifications. The structure of *Rasselas* has also prompted critical discussions. Refuting the claims of many earlier critics who found *Rasselas* "structureless" with no beginning, middle, or end, Gwin J. Kolb has argued that the structure of *Rasselas,* in the form of a tale, is vital to its message, or "thesis"—that happiness is not achievable in earthly life but is attainable in eternal life. Other twentieth-century critics have continued this focus on *Rasselas* as a literary achievement. Commenting on *Rasselas* as a work of art rather than as a philosophical piece, Emrys Jones has maintained that *Rasselas* shows Johnson's wit and artistic power, particularly in its "inconclusive conclusion." In Jones's view, there can be no ending to the work because life itself cannot be contained within a neat literary piece. Critics have been virtually unanimous, however, in acknowledging Johnson's acute perception of the nature of life and the capacity of the human soul in *Rasselas*. Marlene R. Hansen has praised Johnson's positive, progressive portrayal of the equality of women, and several scholars—including J. P. Hardy, Carey McIntosh, and Robert Walker—have noted Johnson's emphasis on the need for hope.

CRITICISM

Sir Walter Raleigh (essay date 1894)

SOURCE: "The Novels of the Eighteenth Century," in *The English Novel: A Short Sketch of Its History from the Earliest Times to the Appearance of "Waverly",* John Murray, 1894, pp. 180-215.

[*In the following excerpt, Raleigh considers whether* Rasselas *belongs to the novel genre.*]

The contributions of Johnson and Goldsmith to prose fiction are examples of pure eighteenth-century work. It was in the year 1759, some months before the publication of the earliest instalment of *Tristram Shandy,* that the great Cham descended into the arena of the novelists with his moral apologue called **The History of Rasselas, Prince of Abissinia.** His immediate object in writing it was, as the printer told Boswell, "that with the profits he might defray the expense of his mother's funeral and pay some little debts that she had left." There could be no doubt that a novel by the great lexicographer would be eagerly bought by the public, and, in seeking for a framework for his story, it is possible that Johnson was directed to Abyssinia by the memory of his labours, twenty-five years earlier, on the translation of Father Lobo's *Voyage to Abyssinia.* However this may be, the theme of the story was all his own. The natural gloom of his temperament, deepened by the sadness of the occasion, finds fuller and stronger expression in **Rasselas** than in the poem that treats the same subject, **The Vanity of Human Wishes.**

It has been doubted whether **Rasselas** may justly be considered as a novel at all. The conversations held between the characters, it has been pointed out, are to be criticized, not in relation to circumstance and verisimilitude, but after the manner of an essay, in relation to truth. And certainly the strong moral and didactic purpose cannot be gainsaid. But the youth of the modern novel was a season of experiment, no rules of form had been determined, and a moral directly inculcated had never been disallowed. Far later in the century a noted literary critic, out of compliment to Richardson, refused to his works the title of novels, preferring to class them as excursions in "imaginative ethics." The sermon has played its part, as well as the drama, the epic, and the narrative poem, in shaping the form of the novel.

Sermon or novel, **Rasselas** was written at a time when Johnson had first attained his full command of literary expression. In the essays of **The Rambler,** begun some nine years earlier, his inversions, abstractions, monotonous sentences, and long words seem almost to exhibit, if the thought be not heresy, an imperfectly educated person struggling to acquire a polite diction. They certainly make his style as unsuitable for narrative as for the light ridicule of social foibles. **The Rambler** is not easy to read; or rather, to speak as the case demands, the otiose prolongation of the periods and the superabundance of polysyllabic vocables render the task of the intrepid adventurer who shall endeavour to peruse the earlier performances of this writer an undertaking of no inconsiderable magnitude. On the other hand, the later highly finished and effective style of the *Lives of the Poets* has an epigrammatic quality, a studied balance of phrase and a dogmatic ring, like the stroke of a hammer, that would infallibly interrupt the flow of imaginative narrative. In *Rasselas* the merits of both manners are combined to produce that ease of narration and those memorable and weighty turns of phrase which give it its principal distinction.

The main theme is never forgotten. The prince, educated in the happy valley, and taken with his sister into the world, is acquainted with human aims and human enjoyments, only that their futility and insufficiency may be demonstrated, and the verdict again and again recorded with merciless severity. The "choice of life" is indeed difficult. The pastoral life is marred by ignorance, discontent, and stupid malevolence. Prosperity means disquiet and danger. Is happiness to be found in solitude? "The life of a solitary man will be certainly miserable, but not certainly devout." Is marriage to be preferred? "I know not whether marriage be more than one of the innumerable modes of human misery." Will varied pleasures serve to wile away the time? "Pleasures never can be so multiplied and continued as not to leave much of life unemployed." May the true solution be found in the pursuit of virtue? "All that virtue can afford is quietness of conscience, a steady prospect of a happier state; this may enable us to endure calamity with patience; but remember that patience must suppose pain."

All the sterner traits of Johnson's character, his uncompromising rectitude, his steadiness of outlook on unrelieved gloom, his hatred of sentimental and unthinking optimism, have left their mark on *Rasselas.* What was perhaps less to be expected, the structure of the plot is masterly, the events are arranged in a skilful climax, culminating in the story of the mad astronomer, whose delusions supply the picture with a shade darker than death itself. "Few can attain this man's knowledge," says Imlac, "and few practise his virtues, but all may suffer his calamities. Of the uncertainties of our present state the most dreadful and alarming is the uncertain continuance of reason." And a note of personal sadness is struck towards the close in the declaration of the virtuous sage, who confesses that praise has become to him an empty sound. "I have neither mother to be delighted with the reputation of her son, nor wife to partake the honours of her husband." The words recall a similar phrase in the famous letter to Lord Chesterfield, but the defiant strain that they there introduce is exchanged for a subdued and deepened melancholy. Taken as a whole, *Rasselas* is one of the most powerful of moral fables to be found in any literature, and the lighter and wittier passages, such as those on the functions of a poet and on the definition of a life "according to nature," relieve its

inspissated tenebrosity with something like an air of comedy. . . .

Gwin J. Kolb (essay date 1951)

SOURCE: "The Structure of *Rasselas*," in *PMLA*, Vol. LXVI, No. 5, September, 1951, pp. 698-717.

[*In the following essay, Kolb discusses the relationship of structure to meaning in* Rasselas. *Kolb argues that Johnson's story is structurally distinct from the generic eighteenth-century oriental tale, and suggests that the common practice of viewing* Rasselas *as an oriental tale is misleading and results in an incomplete understanding of the work.*]

I

In beginning a discussion of the structure of *Rasselas* one need not spend much time clearing the ground of previous arguments before advancing one's own. What the new commentator must face—and this is perhaps more disturbing than arguments would be—is the almost universal opinion[1] that *Rasselas* has only the slightest structure and that the little it does have results from Johnson's not too successful effort to write an ordinary novel or "oriental tale."[2] The narrative is "episodic," unimportant, dull, say some critics; the ending concludes nothing, the work merely stops. The action—and some of the characters—say others,[3] lack dramatic power. At the same time that they thus observe, either directly or indirectly, the tale's failure to conform to their notions of what the structure should be, most commentators recognize a fundamental difference between Johnson's piece and those works in the light of which they attempt to judge *Rasselas.* Wishing to make the difference clear and to do justice to what they feel is a manifest accomplishment, they praise the wisdom set forth in the book and the skill and power displayed in individual chapters.[4]

The result of this persistent tendency to talk of the work as though it were really several distinct pieces is perhaps best illustrated both by the most recent discussion of the book, which calls it Johnson's "greatest comic work,"[5] and, more generally, by the equivocal position it occupies in histories of English literature: on the one hand, it has found a place in surveys of the eighteenth-century novel; on the other, it has been treated as a composition designed to enforce a moral lesson. *Rasselas* the novel has elicited no admiration,[6] *Rasselas* the moral work has been called the wisest book in English literature.[7] Yet, with the exceptions already noted, its admirers, although more or less aware of the end presumably sought by Johnson, have not attempted really to argue the adequacy of the structure of *Rasselas* in relation to that end. They have been content to praise the wisdom and ignore the narrative.

Certainly, however, this relationship must be considered before one can make a complete estimate of *Rasselas* as a literary achievement. In addition, this kind of examination may help to clarify the connections between *Rasselas* and earlier "oriental tales" and between it and Johnson's other writings and opinions.

The most cursory reading is enough to convince anyone that, as most critics have pointed out, *Rasselas* is no ordinary "eastern" tale. For either the work shows Johnson to have been an incredibly inept writer of the *Arabian Nights* type of story or else one must conclude that the tale as tale is not the principle which best explains what the book contains. And the facts in the case support the latter alternative. Unhappy in an earthly paradise, a young prince, accompanied by other discontented persons, escapes into the outside world, where he investigates modes of life supposedly conducive to happiness until, persuaded of the futility of the search, he and his party decide to return to the "happy valley." Clearly, the problem of happiness rather than the element of "story" emerges from this recital as the determinant by reference to which questions about the book's structure may be most adequately answered. On this hypothesis, *Rasselas* may be labelled an apologue—which, indeed, many commentators have dubbed it—and the narrative about the prince may be considered as a device[8] for presenting certain notions concerning happiness and the moral and emotional attitudes to be drawn thence by the reader. What, briefly, Johnson seems to be urging upon us is this: human limitations make happiness in this world ephemeral, accidental, the product of hope rather than reality, and almost as nothing compared to the miseries of life; consequently, searches for permanent enjoyment, although inevitable to man as man, are bound to end in failure. The wise man, therefore, will accept submissively the essential grimness of life, seek no more lasting felicity than is given by a quiet conscience, and live with an eye on eternity, in which he may perhaps find, through the mercy of God, the complete happiness unattainable on earth.

Similar opinions about happiness aimed at establishing similar attitudes in the reader play equally important roles in several of Johnson's earlier works, notably *The Vanity of Human Wishes* and *Rambler* Nos. 204-205,[9] and the techniques of presentation used in these pieces illuminate, by comparison and contrast, the method employed later in *Rasselas.* In *The Vanity of Human Wishes,* for example, Johnson stresses the insufficiency of human pursuits as a means to happiness and encourages the reader to pray for internal "goods" attained through religion—"a healthful mind," "a will resign'd," "obedient passions," "love," "patience," and that "faith" which looks forward to a "happier seat" after death. This summary of the moral suggests the organization of the poem: Johnson first considers various supposedly desirable "goods" representative of both public and private life (riches, political and military power, learning, etc.) and applicable to women as well as men (e.g., in the case of beauty), points up the vanity of all of them by the use of direct statements and examples drawn from history, and finally directs "Hope and Fear" to the proper objects listed above.

In the *Rambler* Nos. 204-205, however, the positive aspect of Johnson's counsel is missing; he concentrates on emphasizing the futility of a person's decision to be happy. "No man," we are told, should "presume to say, 'This day shall be a day of happiness'"; for not only is a man's happiness far overshadowed by his miseries but the small amount of happiness he actually obtains is the result of circumstances over which he has practically no control. As the medium for this somber instruction Johnson devises the narrative of Seged, the "lord of Ethiopia," who, resolving to be completely happy for ten days, withdraws to an island where he practices without success various schemes designed to produce happiness until the sickness of his daughter on the eighth day puts an end to his plans. The account of Seged clearly anticipates *Rasselas* in several important respects. For instance, the monarch's change of place in his search for felicity corresponds to Rasselas' departure from the happy valley and his entrance into the ordinary world. However, Seged's specific transfer is, in a sense, exactly the opposite of Rasselas'; for he seeks happiness by escaping from everyday life to a "happy" island. Nonetheless, in both cases the same two kinds of places are visited by the royal searchers, although Seged concentrates his efforts to find happiness in an earthly paradise; and Rasselas, miserable in such a paradise, examines the possibilities for pleasure in the outside world. Again, the monarch's various schemes to induce happiness parallel the prince's investigations into those modes of life praised for their ability to produce contentment. Finally, in the history of Seged, Johnson uses an Abyssinian background in much the same way as in *Rasselas.* Specifically, "Sultan Segued" and "Rassela Christos" were actual members of Ethiopian royalty ("Rassela Christos" served "Sultan Segued" as lieutenant); the group of islands in Lake Dambea, to oneof which Seged retires, is mentioned, like the royal prison in Amhara, in various historical accounts of Abyssinia,[10] and, so far as Seged's palace is concerned, at least one early author states that "about the middle of [Lake Dambea] is an island, wherein stands one of the Emperor's palaces, which, though not so large as that of Gondar, is yet equally beautiful and magnificent."[11]

Having decided to write another work embodying the same moral, generally, as that expressed in *The Vanity of Human Wishes* and *Rambler* Nos. 204-205, and aiming, explicitly, at the end I have suggested earlier, Johnson was again faced with the problem of selecting a vehicle for pointing the moral. How could he demonstrate the prevailing unhappiness of life in a lively, telling manner? How lead his reader to accept the consolation offered by the prospect of eternity? If he followed the customary—and perhaps more effective—way of presenting such a "lesson," the first question would have to be dealt with before he could proceed to a more positive conclusion. How, in any case, could he represent the paucity of happiness so as to interest and impress the reader? Obviously, one method that might have occurred to Johnson would be to show the comparative lack of happiness among persons who might be expected to be happy. Such persons would consist of (1) those who possess all material ingredients for happiness, (2) those who follow particular schemes designed to produce happiness, and (3) those who occupy certain positions in ordinary life usually thought to afford happiness. If members of all three groups were shown to be discontented, that would do much to prove his "thesis" and would help to direct the reader's attention to the hereafter. And how, he might have asked himself, could he more effectively present this discontent than by repeating the narrative device he had used in the **Rambler** Nos. 204-205, and writing a story about a man who, surrounded by every possible luxury, is nevertheless dissatisfied and whose search for contentment reveals only misery and unhappiness. Thus the reader's interest might be maintained and the author's "text" illustrated and amplified. From the posing of various solutions to problems of representation, Johnson, one may suppose, finally decided to write the tale of the Abyssinian prince.

Rasselas falls into two general parts. Part one, dealing with life in the happy valley, reveals the absence of happiness in an earthly paradise. Part two discloses the same condition in the outside world. Since the only remaining locale with respect to happiness would be a spot completely lacking in means to pleasure—a spot in which perhaps no one could imagine happiness possible—these two parts achieve, in effect, an exhaustive survey of the kinds of places where happiness might be found.

Life in an earthly paradise presents perhaps the most widespread notion of perfect bliss and it is with a narrative treatment of this conception that Johnson begins **Rasselas.** If the paradise is to seem a paradise to the readers addressed in the opening sentence, it must be situated and characterized, and so in Chapter i he describes the happy valley, employing for the purpose the "romantic" tradition of the imprisonment of Abyssinian royalty and endowing the spot with all the remoteness, delights, and luxuries usually attributed to paradises. The reasons for Johnson's use of an oriental setting, in general, and of Abyssinia, in particular, may be considered under two headings, (1) structural and (2) non-structural. Among those of the first sort proposed by various critics are the statements that "scene plays an important rôle in the story, both in the

reënforcement it lends to ideas, and in the background of vague, exotic beauty which it provides for the action"; and that "the novel . . . was set deliberately in a non-Christian part of the world, like many of the didactic tales of its time, so that Johnson could deal with man on a purely naturalistic level and feel free to discuss the issues he had in mind unimpeded by other considerations."[12] Additional functions which the eastern background serves may be mentioned briefly: it provides for the reader the aura of strange and distant lands where human happiness is commonly thought to be complete and lasting; by reminding us of the superficial likenesses and essential differences between *Rasselas* and ordinary oriental tales with their happy-ever-after conclusions, it tends to heighten the skeptical attitude toward earthly happiness which Johnson seeks to inculcate in the reader;[13] and, finally, the employment of the romantic legend surrounding the imprisonment of the children of Abyssinian monarchs affords a ready means of examining in an exhaustive fashion the places in which men might be presumed happy.

Seeking what I have called "extra-structural" causes for the setting of the tale, most writers invoke Johnson's translation of Lobo's *Voyage to Abyssinia* and the vogue of oriental tales in England during the eighteenth century. A few have linked Johnson's location of the happy valley in Abyssinia with the descriptions of terrestrial paradises made by other authors who also drew upon material about Abyssinia.[14] But not enough emphasis has been placed on the latter attempt at explanation. For the practice of Milton and Coleridge—to name only the best known examples—in utilizing data about Abyssinia in their descriptions of Eden and Mount Abora,[15] added to Johnson's setting for *Rasselas,* would seem to indicate that, at least from the seventeenth to the nineteenth century, English writers usually drew upon the rich store of fact and fancy about Abyssinia contained in numerous travel-books whenever they decided to depict earthly paradises.

Still, although it qualifies as one of these earthly paradises, Johnson's happy valley is not perfect, for, ironically enough, it is a prison; its palace is built "as if suspicion herself had dictated the plan," and, once obtained, admission therein is, with rare exceptions, permanent. Unblemished joy, Johnson intimates, may not always dwell even in paradise. And he shortly introduces us to the unhappy prince of Abyssinia.

Rasselas is a young man in his twenty-sixth year, well past the age when the novelty of the world is enough to make life pleasant and exciting. His character as a serious, high-minded, discontented, rather naive person is eminently adapted to the functioning of the apologue. Were he less serious and high-minded he would probably be less likely to interest himself in the question of happiness, and were he more sophisticated and perceptive he would not perhaps be so persistent in his search for enduring happiness. Bored with the luxuries of the valley he recognizes that the proper happiness of man is different from animal contentment and he regrets his lack of this happiness. His attempt to obtain it by finding a man who can tell him the recipe for happiness makes up the principal "story" in the book. For the search to begin, however, Rasselas must believe that something he does will bring him happiness. Consequently, the sage who wants to persuade him that he has no cause for uneasiness says, "If you had seen the miseries of the world, you would know how to value your present state." And the prince promptly expresses a wish to see the world, "since the sight of [its miseries] is necessary to happiness." In addition to serving the purpose of the narrative, the sage's remark provides the first of many testimonials to the predominance of misery in the world, while the dissatisfaction he expresses over Rasselas' reaction to his statement enlarges the scope of the unhappiness in the happy valley.

The prince, possessed of a new subject for thought, i.e., his actions in the regions beyond the valley, is satisfied to let many months pass without trying to see the outside world. His pleasure in this extended procrastination offers a striking contrast to the increasing impatience he might have been expected to feel until he had actually entered the world. Content and discontent, Johnson seems to be telling us, are not subject to the rules of logic.

When Rasselas is finally roused to action, his endeavors to escape from the valley involve a trial-and-elimination of possible means of exit. He enjoys his explorations but they are unsuccessful. Next he meets the artist who proposes to fly over the mountains to freedom. Skeptical because of his failure, Rasselas still entertains some hope for the success of the flying scheme, but it too is a disappointment.[16] So far, then, the prince's investigations of the possibilities of escape have kept the narrative in motion as a narrative. They have also served to embroider Johnson's notions about happiness. For the contrast between Rasselas' impatience to leave the valley and the ten months cheerfully spent in searching for an exit is pronounced. Again, the artist's willingness to accompany the prince is a significant commentary on the happiness prevailing in the valley. Moreover, the vast difference between the enthusiasm and self-assurance with which the artist undertakes the aerial experiment and his terror and vexation at its dismal conclusion exemplifies the strange disparity which, as Johnson suggests, always operates where happiness is concerned. And, again, his remarks on the need for secrecy about the art of flying furnish added if indirect evidence of the evil and misery in the world outside the valley: "If men were all virtuous," he says, "I should with great alacrity teach them all to fly. But what would be the security of the good, if the bad could at pleasure invade them from the sky?"

In Chapter vii, Rasselas, restless and forced by the rainy season to remain indoors, hears Imlac read a poem on "the various conditions of humanity," and entering into talk with him is delighted with his company. Days later he commands the poet to tell the story of his life but being called to a concert is obliged to delay the story until evening. Thus is the narrative continued and simultaneously the accidental quality of happiness delicately underscored: the rainy season is responsible for Rasselas' meeting Imlac; the summons to the concert (intended to give pleasure) actually prevents him from enjoying the poet's history immediately.

Imlac's account of his life, besides showing him to be a person possibly clever enough to help Rasselas escape from the valley and certainly experienced enough to direct him in his choice of life, contributes materially to the case Johnson is making against faith in earthly happiness. To begin with, it is the history of a more versatile Rasselas, grown old and wise—but not happy. Imlac has done much more than Rasselas will do when he enters the world. The son of a rich man, he early indulged a thirst for travel and knowledge (his joy in learning and subsequent attitude toward his teachers parallel Rasselas' similar pleasure in knowledge and contempt for the old sage who could tell him nothing new). Later, determined to be a poet, a profession demanding the highest and most varied knowledge, he intensified his studies of nature and men. Finally, after years of traveling and observing the customs of many nations, he arrived back in Abyssinia, to find all his fond expectations changed into bitter disappointments. Weary, he resolved to retire from the world and succeeded in being admitted to the happy valley. Thus, Imlac in a sense may be said to have ended his search for contentment where Rasselas begins. The inference is inescapable: no permanent happiness for young or old anywhere. But Rasselas, strong in the hope of youth, has yet to learn this disagreeable truth.

In the second place, Imlac's history represents the final and most detailed picture of the world's unhappiness painted for Rasselas while he remains in the valley. The sage and the artist had mentioned the misery and wickedness of men; now the poet particularizes their statements by reference to his own life. Rasselas' interruptions during the account reveal his inexperience and idealism and at the same time afford Imlac an opportunity to emphasize the absence of enduring peace and contentment in the world. His father, a wealthy merchant, wanted his son to be still richer, though he himself lived in fear of being "spoiled by the governours of the province." Observing his teachers Imlac "did not find them wiser or better than common men." When he joined a trade caravan during his travels, his companions, envious of his wealth, "exposed [him] to the theft of servants, . . . and saw [him] plundered upon false pretences"; yet afterwards they sought his help in selling their goods. Estimating for Rasselas the contentment he found among Europeans, he remarks that they are less miserable than other people but that they are not happy. "Human life is every where a state in which much is to be endured, and little to be enjoyed." At the end of his story, on hearing Rasselas' decision to escape and make a free choice of life, he warns him that he will find the world "a sea foaming with tempests, and boiling with whirlpools," and that "amidst wrongs and frauds, competitions and anxieties, [he] will wish a thousand times for these seats of quiet, and willingly quit hope to be free from fear." This declaration, added to Imlac's record of his life, suggests persuasively the fruitlessness of Rasselas' resolution to seek happiness outside the valley. The only stronger evidence would involve the prince's own experiences in the world. And such evidence is shortly forthcoming.

Again, the poet's remarks regarding felicity in the royal prison expand the number of miserable persons to include almost everyone in the valley. At first Johnson introduces us to the dissatisfied prince; later he makes clear the discontent (though it is only temporary) of the sage and the artist; then he allows Imlac to declare flatly to Rasselas: "I know not one of all your attendants who does not lament the hour when he entered this retreat . . . They envy the liberty which their folly has forfeited, and would gladly see all mankind imprisoned like themselves." Prince and servant, young and old, male and female (as is soon apparent)—none are happy in the happy valley. Imlac is less unhappy than the rest of the servants because he has "a mind replete with images, which [he] can vary and combine at pleasure." But he regrets the uselessness of his acquirements.

In the last place, Imlac's history (and, indeed, much of *Rasselas*) produces a result perfectly consonant with Johnson's purpose by virtue of the fact that, although modelled on the story-within-a-story device common in conventional oriental tales,[17] it contrasts sharply with such tales. That is to say, it possesses enough points of contact to make us more or less aware of the model but reminds us constantly that it has nothing to do with exciting adventures, beautiful women, romance, and the happy conclusions inoriental tales. For example, Imlac was introduced to the Mogul: he might have fallen in love with his daughter, perhaps become his heir, and enjoyed a long life and many children. But what actually happens? Nothing—except that he can remember not a word the Mogul uttered "above the power of a common man." The difference between what might have been and what is, thus underlines the grave tenor of Imlac's history.

The poet finishes his account, Rasselas confides to him his longing to break prison, and Imlac, despite the counsel noted above, agrees to help him. In Chapter xiii he proposes the single means of exit untried by the prince and the two set to work. Nekayah, Rasselas' sister, who is also weary of "tasteless tranquility," and her favorite Pekuah join the men when they escape from the valley. By the addition of the women to the party, Johnson, as indicated earlier, achieves a group whose members represent all the inhabitants of the valley: prince and princess, male and female subordinates—the list is complete. Their willingness to leave offers weighty testimony to the dissatisfaction prevailing there. As types, too, the four provide an inclusive means for sampling and commenting on modes of life in the ordinary world—the wise Imlac to direct the search and interpret the findings, the naive prince to be gradually disillusioned as he pursues the will-o'-the-wisp of happiness, and Nekayah and the maid for investigations into the distaff domain.

If, as I have said, Johnson seeks to impress upon the reader of *Rasselas* the vanity of believing in permanent earthly happiness, he may logically be expected to make the same comprehensive survey with respect to normal life that he made in treating the happy valley. What he does bears out this expectation. Imlac conducts the prince to Cairo, a place in which Rasselas will be able to "see all the conditions of humanity." Here, if anywhere, one would think, a happy man might be found. And at first it seems to Rasselas that everyone is happy—except himself. His uneasiness, contrasted with the rapture he anticipated on looking at the new world from the mountain top of the prison, offers another pointed example of the failure of reality to fulfill one's hopes. It also parallels his position when, at the beginning of the book, he appears for a short time to be the only unhappy person in the royal retreat. Rasselas confesses his sadness to Imlac, who declares that his condition is the condition of mankind. "We are long," he says, "before we are convinced that happiness is never to be found, and each believes it possessed by others, to keep alive the hope of obtaining it for himself." But the prince insists that "one condition is more happy than another"; and heedless of Imlac's remarks on the futility of making a choice of life, resolves to examine various conditions with a view to choosing one for himself.

He associates first with "young men of spirit and gaiety," whosepleasures, "gross and sensual," soon convince Rasselas "that he should never be happy in a course of life of which he was ashamed." He is next attracted to the doctrine of stoicism as expounded by an eloquent sage whose life he proposes to imitate until he discovers that the teacher, notwithstanding the cogency of his arguments, is in practice subject to the miseries of ordinary men.

Plainly, the prince's investigations thus far display considerably more method than critics have usually been ready to admit. He begins by examining two extreme—and opposing—avenues to happiness, one below, the second above, the level on which human beings are capable of sustained pleasure. Mere gratification of sensual appetites, Rasselas recognizes, cannot be called human happiness because it fails to satisfy peculiarly human capacities. Stoicism, on the other hand, with its insistence on the suppression of passions, aims at a state of mind (or contentment) beyond the reach of men as men; witness the sage's grief over his daughter's death. Neither from it nor from gross sensuality springs human felicity, and the prince is forced to continue his search.

Moving from the city to the country (another case of procedure by division), he and his companions inquire into three modes of rural life—those followed by the shepherds, the rich man, and the hermit—that seem to offer possibilities for permanent happiness. Like the previous conditions investigated, these form an orderly treatment designed to enforce the same general theme. Of the three groups the shepherds possess fewest potentialities for happiness: they are "envious savages," "so rude and ignorant, so little able to compare the good with the evil of the occupation, and so indistinct in their narratives and descriptions, that very little could be learned from them." The country gentleman represents the brighter side of country life: the shepherds are stupid, he is intelligent; they are comparatively poor, he is wealthy. But he is not happy, for his "prosperity puts [his] life in danger." The hermit presents still a third possibility: he is even more intelligent than the gentleman but, somewhat like the shepherds, he enjoys few material comforts. In contrast to them both, he has renounced all contact with society in an effort "to close [his] life in peace." The effort, however, he confesses, has not brought him peace; for, by withdrawing into solitude, he has cut himself off from the relaxations and diversions necessary to his happiness as a human being. Digging up "a considerable treasure"—what a neat touch that is!—he accompanies the prince's party back to Cairo.

The last special formula for happiness which Rasselas explores is the declaration made by the "philosopher" that to live according to nature is to live happily. When the young man asks "what it is to live according to nature," the philosopher's reply shows him "that this was one of the sages whom he should understand less as he heard him longer." From him one could not begin to learn the secret of happiness. The modes of life inspected earlier were at least intelligible; the trouble with them was that they did not attain happiness, chiefly because, as has been noted, they tried to leap over the hard fact of human nature in the chase. The pat advice, to cooperate with the present system and be happy, also ignores the limits of human comprehension by being wholly unintelligible. Neither it nor any of the other projects gives Rasselas (or the reader) the slightest hope of finding contentment via schemes specifically fashioned to produce it.

In the next chapter Johnson begins a different kind of survey but one directed to the same end as the first. Rasselas and Nekayah decide to look into "the private recesses of domestick peace." Considering the three possible areas for investigation, "high stations," middle, and low, they discard the last, believing that "ease" could not be found "among the poor," and concentrate their inquiries on the first, which Rasselas is to examine, and the second, assigned to Nekayah. Once again Johnson has achieved a completeness in approach which, viewed in relation to his purpose, can scarcely be called accidental.

After a vain search for a happy person in "courts" and "private houses," the prince and princess discuss the results of their searches in Chapters xxv-xxviii. The conversation consists of a discourse on the evils incident to "greatness" and private life, broken up between brother and sister whose roles shift back and forth from that of a lecturer to that of a listener who, by comments and questions, serves to vary and guide the other's speech. Thus, as a result of their inquiries and, still more, of their conversation, Rasselas and Nekayah are used to demonstrate the lesson of the book: neither in high stations and moderate, married and single life, early and late marriages, nor in virtuous conduct can one hope to discover a full measure of happiness. Moreover, the comprehensiveness of the survey is emphasized by the tiff between brother and sister during their talk. What they do points up what they have found in their searches and what they say about them.

So far Rasselas and his party have moved in the world largely as observers of other people's lives. Next, however, with the areas for pure observation pretty well explored, they become more active participants by taking a trip to the pyramids. When they arrive Pekuah is afraid to go inside and the princess allows her to stay in the tent until they return. On coming out they learn that Pekuah and her maids have been captured by Arabs. They go back to Cairo and begin unsuccessful attempts to locate the maid of honor, whose abduction has made Nekayah inconsolable. Slowly, however, she becomes reconciled to the loss.

These are the facts of the narrative. How do they promote the end sought by Johnson? The circumstances of the abduction itself supply a partial answer. In the conversation with Rasselas about domestic happiness, Nekayah had said that a virtuous life does not always mean a happy life. Pekuah's seizure is an example of that dictum calculated to impress the reader as much as possible by affecting the main characters in the narrative. As Imlac says, Nekayah had shown kindness and generosity in allowing the maid to remain outside the pyramid; yet the result is sorrow for her and misery, as she thinks, for Pekuah. At the same time the abduction affords Imlac an occasion to tell what, if not happiness, may be gained from virtuous actions: "that no unlucky consequences can oblige us to repent it" is its "present reward"; for the future, we have the hope of "recompense" to "console our miscarriage"—a hope based on the belief that He "by whose laws our actions are governed, . . . will suffer none to be finally punished for obedience." Furthermore, Imlac's earlier remarks concerning Pekuah's fear of ghosts in the pyramid provide a kind of justification for extending one's view of existence beyond earthly life, while his comment on the vanity represented by the pyramids reminds the reader that among the "royal magnificence" of the past men were also discontented. Again, the description of the progression of Nekayah's grief reveals her illogical but human tendency to think change of place will decrease one's misery; although she has heard the hermit's story, she vows to retire from the world and "hide [herself] in solitude," a resolution Imlac opposes with the argument that loss "of one pleasure is no very good reason for rejection of the rest" and that in time she "will wish to return into the world." And gradually, of course, she does return to normal life, wondering, however, what may "be expected from our persuit of happiness, when we find the state of life to be such, that happiness itself is the cause of misery."

From Nekayah Johnson turns to Pekuah, who, being discovered and ransomed, tells the story of her capture to her friends. Even more than Imlac's history of his life, her tale presents a sharp contrast to many oriental adventure stories, in which a noble lady's abduction often initiates or continues a series of marvelous happenings. The beginning is the only mildly exciting part of the whole adventure; the remainder consists, by and large, of Pekuah's efforts to prevent ennui. All potentially "romantic" aspects of the affair are made flat and prosaic. The Arab chieftain, who might have been dashing and handsome, an ardent lover, is avaricious; the time Pekuah might have spent in listening to his addresses, she actually spends "observing the manners of the vagrant nations, and . . . viewing remains of ancient edifices." At the Arab's stronghold, where she might have met another captive—say, a young man—and plotted with him to escape, she begins the study of astronomy under the captor's guidance as a means of beguiling "the tediousness of time," and when he leaves on his expeditions, her "only pleasure was to talk with my maids about the accident by which we were carried away, and the happiness that we should all enjoy at the end of our captivity." Clearly, the captivity itself offers none of that bliss, frequently romantic in nature, which the heroines in oriental tales usually enjoy in the course of their adventures.

But more than this. Pekuah's account is not only a deflation of the ordinary eastern tale; it also enables Johnson to document his thesis concerning happiness by reference to an area hitherto unexplored—the life of a sheik and of his harem (representing, in a sense, the reverse of marriage, discussed earlier by Rasselas and Nekayah). As indicated above, Pekuah finds no happiness in this life; her principal reaction, once the pleasure of seeing new sights is gone, is tedium. The Arab chief is a greedy man, though "far from illiterate"; the pleasures he enjoys among the members of his seraglio are "not those of friendship or society." He prefers the company of Pekuah but when offered the ransom gold "he hastened to prepare for our journey hither." As for his women they possess scarcely any of the qualifications requisite for happiness: "they had no ideas but of the few things that were within their view, and had hardly names for any thing but their cloaths and their food." Decidedly, this mode of life produces no more happiness than the conditions already examined.

After the party's return to Cairo, Rasselas, who begins "to love learning," declares that he intends to "pass the rest of his days in literary solitude." Imlac replies that he first "ought to examine its hazards" and he tells the prince the history of the astronomer. Beginning with a description of his many admirable qualities, Imlac slowly unfolds the astronomer's fixation concerning his power to control the weather and distribute the seasons. Instead of being happy, as the princess assumes he must be when Imlac begins the story, he is actually a victim of "the heaviest of human afflictions." The poet declares, "Of the uncertainties of our present state, the most dreadful and alarming is the uncertain continuance of reason"; and prompted by Rasselas he generalizes on the frequency and causes of insanity. Impressed by Imlac's remarks, Pekuah, Nekayah, and the prince confess and renounce visionary projects, thoughts of which have pleased their solitary hours: the maid resolves to stop imagining herself in a position of great power, the princess (in contrast) to cease dreams of pastoral obscurity, and Rasselas to repress utopian visions of "a perfect government." One cannot rely on day-dreaming for happiness, Johnson seems to be warning us.

With his repudiation of the delights of day-dreaming and the conversation with the "old man" in the following chapter, Rasselas reaches a terminal point in his search for the best choice of life. Taken together his inquiries form a broad survey of possible avenues to happiness arranged to cover the principal "ages" (fromyouth to old age) and parallel interests of man. He began by investigating the life of young men engaged in sensual pleasure, moved to examinations of other special recipes for happiness, explored (with Nekayah) private life on various levels, witnessed the princess' sorrow over her maid's abduction, heard Pekuah's account of her adventures, and, lastly, hears the history of the mad astronomer. Although it is apparently removed from the woes of the world, a life of learning offers no more hope for permanent happiness than the other conditions he has surveyed. Indeed, it may number among its evils the worst of misfortunes—loss of one's sanity; for, the prince discovers, the exercise of the mind itself, the indulgence of the imagination to compensate for the deficiencies of reality, may eventually prevent one from enjoying any human happiness.

Finally, the old man's remarks in Chapter xliv serve to round out an investigation which association with youth began. To the sage "the world has lost its novelty . . . . Nothing is now of much importance . . ." He tries to be tranquil and looks forward to possessing "in a better state that happiness" which he has not found in life. The young people refuse to accept this estimate of long life and console themselves in various ways, and Imlac remembers "that at the same age, he was equally" optimistic.

The astronomer joins the prince's party, recovers his reason by mingling "in the gay tumults of life," and when questioned about the best choice of life, answers only that he has "chosen wrong." Then, Rasselas' quest for happiness completed, Johnson develops the positive side of his argument, i.e., the prospect of eternal happiness, which has been mentioned but not discussed previously by Nekayah, Imlac, and, most recently, by the old man. In Chapter xlvi "the prince enters and brings a new topick," the life of the monks of St. Anthony. "Those men," Imlac declares, "are less wretched . . . than the Abissinian princes in their prison of pleasure. Whatever is done by the monks is incited by an adequate and reasonable motive . . . Their devotion prepares them for another state, and reminds them of its approach, while it fits them for it." To live well in the world is better than to live well in a monastery, he continues; the important thing, however, is not where a man lives but his constancy, as evinced by action, in remembering that this state is "transient and probatory" and that the future state will contain "pleasure without danger, and security without restraint."

The intellectual reasons which support such a conduct of life Imlac presents in his discourse on the nature of the soul. He argues the absolute separation of mind and matter, says that "immateriality seems to imply a natural power of perpetual duration as a consequence of exemption from all causes of decay," but acknowledges that the Author of the soul can destroy it. "That it will not perish by any inherent cause of decay . . . may be shown by philosophy; but philosophy can tell no more. That it will not be annihilated by him that made it, we must humbly learn from higher authority." Nekayah's reaction to the discourse points up Johnson's moral and brings the book to a close: "To me," she says, "the choice of life is become less important; I

hope hereafter to think only on the choice of eternity." Being young she, Pekuah, and Rasselas still entertain schemes of happiness, but they know that their wishes cannot "be obtained" and so they decide "to return to Abissinia." Their decision is at once a sign of the inevitable human desire for change in life and, more significant, impressive evidence of the futility of searches for lasting happiness on earth.

II

From the beginning the status of **Rasselas** as an oriental tale has troubled commentators. Practically everyone has recognized that the tale is not a tale of the sort represented by (say) those in the *Arabian Nights,* yet an early critic somehow felt bound to judge it as though it were the same (or a similar) kind of work.[18] More than a century later another, while considering it an oriental tale, esteemed it primarily for its reflection of the author's lofty character.[19] And recently still another has argued that **Rasselas** owes its "subject and outline" to a certain group of eastern stories.[20]

In view of this uncertainty about the book's relationship to the larger group of writings with which it has traditionally been associated, we may examine the nature of the connection with more particularity than has been employed heretofore. And first of all we are faced with the problem of connecting **Rasselas** to a body of heterogeneous compositions, over which the term "oriental tale" has been spread like a cover only poorly equipped to hide the variety of objects within. These objects consist of at least two clearly defined kinds of literature, with many pieces occupying intermediate positions between the two extremes.[21] On the one hand are such collections as the *Arabian Nights Entertainments,* the *Persian Tales,* the *Chinese Tales,* etc.—identical works in the sense that the stories they contain are all unified, more or less successfully, by the element of plot. In works of the second type, though a thread of narrative may still remain, the "story" has been replaced by another organizing principle, the exact nature of which depends on the end—satiric, moral, etc.—to be achieved in individual pieces. Representing this group are Marana's *Letters of a Turkish Spy* (and other volumes of "letters"), Brown's *Amusements Serious and Comical,* various papers in the *Spectator, Guardian, Rambler, Adventurer,* etc. **Rasselas** also has been thought to belong to this latter group. But it is labelled a "tale" on the title page; the prince and his companions have definite characters; and they engage in a series of actions possessing at least a superficial resemblance to the parts of a real story. That the work appears most impressive when these features are treated as means to a didactic end has become clear, I hope, from an examination of its structure. Recognizing the general nature of the operations of the features, however, we may discuss the similarities between them and particular aspects of those oriental tales in which story or plot is the controlling determinant of what they contain.

Perhaps the most striking likenesses between the narrative in *Rasselas* and the first group of stories are to be found in a long section of the *Persian Tales,* englished from the French early in the century by Ambrose Philips, whose translation reached a sixth edition in 1750.[22] Philips' preface to the translation explains that "the design of these feigned histories"—related by a nurse—"is to reduce a young princess to reason, who had conceived an unaccountable aversion to men, and would not be persuaded to marry. In order to this, each story furnishes a shining instance of some faithful lover, or affectionate husband: and though every tale pursues the same drift, yet they are all diversified with so much art, and interwoven with so great a variety of events, that the very last appears as new as the first." As the nurse finishes one tale the princess finds fault with the behavior of the lover depicted in it, and this leads the nurse to begin another story (or sequence of stories). Among the yarns she spins is a group dealing with the experiences of certain constant lovers made permanently unhappy by the loss of their mistresses. Bedreddin, King of Damascus (so the nurse informs us), while admitting that he himself is not fully "content"—the main cause of his discontent, we learn later, arises from a tragic love affair—asserts, in opposition to his "Sorrowful Vizier's" opinion, that somewhere in the world are persons whose joy is unmixed with "disquiet" (p. 131). Whereupon the vizier tells the exciting story of his life; his sorrow is caused by the mysterious disappearance of his beloved princess. The king then turns to his favorite. His "history," filled with wild adventures, reveals that he, too, has been unfortunate in love; he is attached to the picture of "a lady who is not in being" (p. 163). Bedreddin inquires further in the city and his court. Everywhere the result is the same: the "happy weaver," for instance, who tells his tale to the king is miserable because of love; the courtiers and officers of his household, none of whom tell stories, are also dissatisfied for various reasons—envy, ambition, domestic troubles, etc. Disregarding the vizier's counsel to "judge of every body by yourself" (p. 175), the king decides to travel until he finds a happy man. In disguise and accompanied by his adviser and the favorite, he begins an unsuccessful journey. He meets many persons who are apparently contented and hears many marvelous tales, but all the narrators confess an unhappiness arising from disappointment of one sort or another in their love affairs. Concluding, finally, that everyone "has something or otherto trouble him," Bedreddin returns with his comrades to Damascus; "if we three are not entirely contented," says the ruler, "let us consider that there are others more unhappy" (p. 257).

The principal similarities between Bedreddin's "history" and *Rasselas* are obvious. Two members of eastern royalty undertake searches for a happy man first in the immediate vicinity, then in the outside world, and, unable to find one, return (Rasselas only decides to return) to the place from which they set out. Neither is happy, both travel incognito and are accompanied by wiser men who foresee the failure of the mission, and both hear stories during their searches. In addition, a few similar remarks about happiness are included in both pieces. On the other hand, fundamental differences between the two leave scant grounds for assuming that the works are of the same kind, and make, I think, highly doubtful the statement that *Rasselas* is indebted to the *Persian Tales* for its "subject and outline."[23] For in the latter the story is the thing: Bedreddin's inquiries afford a convenient entry into the realm of the adventure tale—replete with handsome princes, lovely ladies (and some not so lovely), hairbreadth escapes, enchanted castles, magic chests, powerful genii, and so on. Only when a tale is finished is the narrator's unhappiness really mentioned and this slight emphasis is necessitated, not by a desire to point a moral, but by the nurse's pretext of telling in this series experiences of unhappy lovers in order to persuade the princess that certain men, although deprived of their loved ones, are forever faithful and miserable. Unlike Rasselas, Bedreddin is not intent on making a wise choice of life and little is said about his personal dissatisfaction; he simply believes that some persons are completely happy and tries to find at least one. Clearly, he cannot discover such a person unless the nurse's stories are to cease being what they presumably are—adventure tales of men who say they are unhappy lovers. And no one has ever offered this as an accurate description of *Rasselas.*

Once Bedreddin's search for a happy man is seen to be primarily a device for telling a group of stories within the framework of a larger collection, the parallels between it and *Rasselas* lose much of their impressiveness as evidence of Johnson's supposed borrowings from the *Tales.* Numerous partial resemblances remain, however, and a listing of these may throw light on the relationship of certain aspects of *Rasselas* both to the *Persian Tales* and, more important, to the whole genre comprising the "true" (as I have called it) oriental tale.[24] First of all, the prince of Abyssinia shares with the king of Damascus—and many characters in earlier stories of the same kind—the distinction of being a royal personage who, born and bred in one oriental country, leaves his home, wanders in another part of the east, and finally returns (Rasselas only decides to return) home. Rasselas and Bedreddin conceal their identity during their travels; so do many of the heroes in otheroriental tales. Older, wiser men go with them; trusted advisers not infrequently accompany other royal travellers. Again, the princess and maid in *Rasselas* correspond to the beautiful women who crowd the pages of the *Persian* and most other oriental tales. Furthermore, like all such collections, *Rasselas* consists, in part, of so-called "stories within a story." Of these Imlac's history and Pekuah's tale of her abduction parallel (roughly) more eventful stories told by heroes and heroines in many oriental tales. Finally, the *Persian Tales* and others contain scattered remarks about the miseries of life, the brevity of happiness, etc., which resemble, though only in a general way, observations in **Rasselas.**

The characteristics listed above obviously do not place **Rasselas** in the classification of the real oriental tale. With the possible exception of the eastern setting, not one is peculiarly "oriental"; each has been put to use in many different writings. Still, all of them, including the oriental trappings, are found most commonly, perhaps, in works of which the *Arabian Nights* is the best known example; and the fact that they also appear in **Rasselas** suggests the only reason for calling it an oriental tale and for considering its structure in terms of what such a tale frequently or ordinarily contains. But as long as the work is criticized in these terms it will remain a relatively unsuccessful composition. On the other hand, as has been argued above, an examination which begins with a fairly precise notion of the end sought in **Rasselas** and then moves to a discussion of the elements incorporated in the work for the purpose of attaining that end discloses more pertinent reasons for the inclusion of the "oriental" traits than the mere statement that they are oriental or the assertion that Johnson borrowed them from earlier tales.

Notes

[1] Perhaps the most positive statement of the minority opinion is made by Sir Walter Raleigh, who, in *The English Novel* (London, 1894), after admitting that *Rasselas* may be a "sermon" rather than a "novel," declares that "the structure of the plot is masterly, the events are arranged in a skilful climax, culminating in the story of the mad astronomer . . ." (p. 206). O. F. Emerson's discussion in the introduction to his edition of *Rasselas* (New York, 1895) indicates that he, too, credits it with a rather systematic organization (pp. xxxvii-xl).

[2] E.g., Thomas Seccombe, *The Age of Johnson,* 3rd ed. (London, 1907), p. 12; D. Nichol Smith's remarks in the *CHEL* [*Cambridge History of English Literature*], x, 201.

[3] See, e.g., G. B. Hill, ed. *Rasselas* (Oxford, 1887), p. 31; Leslie Stephen, *Hours in a Library* (New York, 1899), II, 17; D. Nichol Smith's comment in the *CHEL*, x, 201; Louis Cazamian, *A History ofEnglish Literature* (New York, 1939), p. 834; George Sherburn in *A Literary History of England* (New York & London, 1948), pp. 994-995.

[4] See, e.g., the writers and works cited in the preceding note.

[5] C. R. Tracy, "Democritus, Arise!: A study of Dr. Johnson's Humor," *Yale Rev.,* XXXIX (1950), 305. The prince, according to Tracy, is "the antithesis of the man of common sense of the eighteenth century, and a stubborn rationalist who makes himself ridiculous by refusing to comply with the *modus vivendi* that has been worked out by the men of good sense of his age" (p. 309). Although no one, I suppose, would deny that certain incidents in the book are humorous and amusing and that Rasselas himself is mildly ridiculous at times, Tracy's argument about the form of the work as a whole remains unconvincing. Its essential weakness, as it seems to me, lies in the arbitrary limitation of the kinds of works which *Rasselas* might represent; for Tracy the choice is between tragedy and comedy, and not unnaturally he chooses comedy. As I hope to demonstrate in the course of this paper, the contents of *Rasselas* appear to best advantage if the book is viewed (as most critics have thought it should be considered) as a didactic work, of the same general sort as *The Vanity of Human Wishes* and *Rambler* Nos. 204-205. . . . Tracy acknowledges that *Rasselas* "is a kind of 'Vanity of Human Wishes'" (p. 310) but apparently fails to see anything incongruous between this admission and his insistence that *Rasselas* is a comic work.

[6] See, e.g., William Lyon Phelps, *Advance of the English Novel* (New York, 1916), p. 71. Other historians of the novel suggest that the tale is an "Oriental apologue"—Robert M. Lovett and Helen S. Hughes, *The History of the Novel in England* (Boston, 1932), p. 124—or "the longest and most sustained of [Johnson's] sermons on the vanity of human wishes"—Ernest A. Baker, *The History of the English Novel* (London, 1934), IV, 61.

[7] George Saintsbury, *The Peace of the Augustans* (London, 1916), p. 190. Saintsbury says, "Except *Ecclesiastes, Rasselas* is probably the wisest, though with that same exception it is almost the saddest book ever written."

[8] In the remarks on *Rasselas* in his *Samuel Johnson* (New York, 1944), Joseph Wood Krutch says that part of the story "would seem to be no more than a device for introducing a survey of some of the various conditions of life . . ." (p. 176). But Krutch does not extend his comment to cover the whole narrative nor does he concern himself with an analysis of the book's organization (see pp. 175 ff.).

[9] Practically all discussions of *Rasselas* note the similarity in ideas between it and *The Vanity of Human Wishes,* and severalmention the likenesses between it and these two *Rambler* papers; see, e.g., Emerson's ed., pp. xvii, xxxi, and Miss Martha Conant, *The Ori-*

ental Tale in England in the Eighteenth Century (New York, 1908), pp. 123-124.

[10] See Johnson's translation of F. Jerome Lobo's *Voyage to Abyssinia* (London, 1735), pp. 102, 118.

[11] Charles Jacques Poncet, *Journey to Abyssinia*, in *Pinkerton's Collection of Voyages* (London, 1814), xv, 89.

[12] Lovett and Hughes, *Hist. of the Novel*, p. 125; Tracy (see n. 5), p. 310.

[13] For further discussion of this point, see [text following note 17]

[14] See, e.g., Emerson (n. 1, above), pp. xxvi, xxviii-xxix.

[15] For evidence of their use of this material, see, e.g., Evert Mordecai Clark, "Milton's Abyssinian Paradise," *Studies in English* (Austin, Texas, 1950), XXIX, 129-150; Lane Cooper, "The Abyssinian Paradise in Coleridge and Milton," *MP* [Modern Philology], III (1906), 327-332.

[16] For a more detailed discussion of the "Dissertation on Flying," see my article on "Johnson's 'Dissertation on Flying' and John Wilkins' *Mathematical Magick*," *MP*, XLVII (1949), 24-31.

[17] In this connection, see [the last two paragraphs of this essay].

[18] Owen Ruffhead—*Monthly Review*, xx (May 1759), 428-438—having admitted the great usefulness of "fiction or romance" in making the "dictates of morality agreeable to mankind," insists that "*tale-telling* is not the talent" of the author of *Rasselas*. He also objects to the "matter" of the work: "the topics" have been handled until they are "threadbare"; most of the "sentiments" are to be found "in the Persian and Turkish tales, and other books of the like sort; wherein they are delivered to better purpose, and cloathed in a more agreeable garb" (p. 428).

[19] *Rasselas* "may be regarded," Martha Conant says in *The Oriental Tale in England*, "as the best type of the serious English oriental tale" (p. 140), being raised to this height by Johnson's "earnestness and dignity" (p. 153).

[20] Geoffrey Tillotson, "*Rasselas* and the *Persian Tales*," *Essays in Criticism and Research* (Cambridge, 1942), pp. 111-116.

[21] See Conant, pp. 267-283, for a list and approximate dates of the "more important oriental tales published in English" before 1759.

[22] See Tillotson, p. 112, for information about the date of Philips' translation; it may have been done in 1714. Another translation, by "Dr. *King*, and several other Hands," was definitely published in 1714. My quotations are taken from the 1783 ed. *The Novelists' Magazine*, Vol. XIII (London, 1784).

[23] Tillotson, p. 114. Moreover, no evidence has been produced to show that Johnson had read the *Tales* before—or even after—he wrote *Rasselas*. Tillotson acknowledges that "he does not seem to have mentioned the 'Persian Tales' in writing or conversation, except in the 'Life of Philips,' when he wrote bibliographically of the book in a way suggesting that he had handled it." The passage Tillotson refers to reads: "[Philips] was reduced to translate the Persian Tales for Tonson, for which he was afterwards reproached, with this addition of contempt, that he worked for half-a-crown. The book is divided into many sections, for each of which, if he received half-a-crown, his reward, as writers then were paid, was very liberal; but half-a-crown had a mean sound." Certainly, this comment tells us little about the date or the nature of Johnson's acquaintance with the *Tales*.

[24] The *Arabian Nights*, the *Persian Tales* (exclusive of the group in which Bedreddin figures), the *Peruvian Tales*, and the *Chinese Tales* all include stories which contain one or more of the partial similarities listed below in the text.

Walter Jackson Bate (essay date 1955)

SOURCE: "The Hunger of Imagination," in *The Achievement of Samuel Johnson*, Oxford University Press, 1955, pp. 63-91.

[*In the following essay, Bate, a leading scholar of the eighteenth century, explores Johnson's view of the mind as a aspect of the human organism that should be constantly stimulated and diverted with intellectual pursuits and conscious reflection.*]

In *Rasselas*, the little group, which has been traveling about in search of a fuller understanding of human nature and destiny, is taken by the philosopher, Imlac, to see the pyramids. Neither Rasselas nor his sister is excited by the prospect of the visit. They state, rather pretentiously, that their 'business is with *man*'—with human manners and customs—not with 'piles of stones' or 'fragments of temples.' Imlac replies that in order to know anything we must also know the products and traces it leaves behind: to understand men, we must see what they did 'that we may learn what reason has dictated or passion incited, and find what are the most powerful motives of action. To judge rightly of the present, we must oppose it to the past; for all judgment is comparative . . . ' The travelers enter the Great

Pyramid, and descend to the tomb. As they sit to rest awhile before returning, Imlac, in an altogether Johnsonian way, starts to speculate why the pyramid was ever built in the first place, and why a king, 'whose power is unlimited, and whose treasures surmount all real and imaginary wants,' should be compelled to 'amuse the tediousness of declining life, by seeing thousands labouring without end.' Secrecy for a tomb or treasure could have easily been secured by less costly and more effective means:

> It seems to have been erected only in compliance with that *hunger of imagination which preys incessantly upon life* . . . Those who have already all that they can enjoy, must enlarge their desires. He that has built for use, till use is supplied, must begin to build for vanity . . . *I consider this mighty structure as a monument of the insufficiency of human enjoyments.*[1]

The 'hunger of imagination,' or what he elsewhere calls the 'hunger of mind,' puts in a strong metaphor a perception almost constantly present in Johnson's writing: that 'few of the hours of life are filled up with objects *adequate to the mind of man,*' since the mind of man can conceive so much more than the present can ever supply. We are therefore 'forced to have recourse, every moment, to the past and future for *supplemental* satisfactions.'[2] The recognition appears in the phrasing of almost every page, sometimes with comic impatience and more usually with charity: riches fail to '*fill up* the vacuities of life'; '*fill* the day with petty business'; the recourses of people at summer resorts to 'rid themselves of the day'; '*filling the vacuities* of his mind with the news of the day'; literary quarreling gratifies the malignity of readers or 'relieves the vacancies of life' for them. 'The *vacuity* of life,' said Mrs. Thrale, 'had at some early period of his life struck so forcibly' on Johnson's mind that it appeared in every context, even in casual talk; and she cites some instances. For example, a rake noted for gaming and sensuality was mentioned: 'Why, life must be *filled up* (says Johnson), and the man who is not capable of intellectual pleasures must content himself with such as his senses can afford.' Another is mentioned as a hoarder: 'Why, a fellow must do something; and what so easy to a narrow mind as hoarding halfpence till they turn into sixpences.'[3]

'The truth is,' said Imlac, 'that no mind is much employed upon the present: recollection and anticipation fill up almost all our moments.' Our emotions, he goes on, take some form of love, hate, fear, or hope. In all of these, we find ourselves glancing back to what occurred five minutes, five days, or five years ago. Or we flit ahead into the future in the same way. In fact, as Johnson says elsewhere, we can hardly think at all except in terms of the past and future. For 'the present is in perpetual motion, leaves us as soon as it arrives,'

and is hardly felt for what it is until we note 'the effects which it leaves behind. The greatest part of our ideas arises, therefore, from the view *before* or *behind* us'; and we are happy or miserable as we are affected by what we believe has happened or is to come.[4] The context of Imlac's remark that 'recollection and anticipation fill up almost all our moments' is the defense of the study of history that he makes before the group visits the pyramids. To employ the mind by studying the different forms that men's motives and desires have taken is itself a way of satisfying the restless appetite of 'looking before and after'; and it is a method that is valuable and self-enlightening. The ironic corollary is that the Great Pyramid itself, which the group then visits, is still another result of the constant need to find 'supplemental satisfaction,' but a result that takes a very different form. When fed with objective knowledge the 'hunger of imagination' may be turned to profit and lead to growth. But if this awareness is lacking, as is generally the case, the imagination will seek to fill itself in some other way, or will uneasily begin to prey upon itself. In doing so, it can only too often transform man's state into one 'in which many of his faculties can serve only for his torment.'

2

If we take into consideration the sheer amount of time spent in 'recollection and anticipation,' the appetite for novelty as a means of 'disburdening the day' or inciting new interest is perhaps man's most constant and pervasive desire. The term 'novelty,' as Johnson uses it, suggests the whole seductive vista of everything we desire, do not actually need, and do not have at the moment. It includes the desire for possessions, of course, whether we want more of the same or something different. Considering the lack of vivid enjoyment we feel once we possess them, novelty also provides much of the attraction we feel in our hunger for reputation or fame, for learning, for possessing the love of others, our desire for seeing a task completed, or even—once it is finished—to have it brought back in order to keep ourselves occupied. With that leap of the imagination which is 'always breaking away from the present,' the novelty desired may even be the wish that we ourselves should be able to feel differently, just as emotional or passionate people envy the calm and serene, or as those who feel they cannot love envy those they think able to love. Even Rasselas, in the Happy Valley, where all desires are gratified, envies an existence where active and unsatisfied desires would stimulate him to some sort of activity. Infants, as we know, cry more frequently from mere boredom than from pain. When they toss away their toys in spite or weariness, they cry to have them back—not because the toys are really prized, but because to have them again will be different from the present moment when they are lacking. Nor do we live down the desire for novelty and difference as we grow older, though it may take subtler forms and use a more elaborate vocabulary. The sheer capacity to desire is so much greater than any possible satisfactions that can be wrung from attaining what we want that satiety, as we all know abstractly, provides no joy or durable contentment. Nor does satiety, as a general state at least, last very long. 'We desire, we pursue, we obtain, we are satiated; we desire something else, and begin a new pursuit.'[5]

Even when we cling to familiar memories of the past in an imaginary hope for security, we are often indirectly responding to the tug of novelty. The nostalgia for lost childhood in Wordsworth's *Ode on Intimations of Immortality* ('Whither is fled the visionary gleam? Where is it now, the glory and the dream?'), the garden and the lost pool of sunlight in Eliot's *Burnt Norton*, bring back the haunting memory of circumstances in our past that were once graphic and fresh. They look back to a time when, as Johnson said, the 'diversity of nature *pours* ideas in,' when neither search nor labor is necessary to gratify the imagination, and 'we have nothing more to do than to open our eyes.' The contrast with Wordsworth's *Immortality Ode* is singularly pointed: what is now going on about Wordsworth ('The young lambs bound . . . The cataracts blow their trumpets from the steep') lacks the visionary splendor it once had. Johnson, a half century before, states that 'we all remember a time when nature . . . gave delight which can now be found no longer, when the noise of a torrent, the rustle of a wood . . . or the play of lambs, *had power to fill the attention, and suspend all perception of the course of time.*[6]

Few classical moralists are closer to Freud than Johnson, or have so uncanny a sense of what repression can mean. Yet in the nostalgic pull backward to one's childhood, whether with Wordsworth's sense of vision or simply Proust's absorption in early impressions, the attraction, from Johnson's point of view, is not simply to security in the ordinary sense. What we really want is a security that includes more than mere safety; we want to recapture a keener, fresher fullness of impression than we now feel. However tamed or circumscribed they may now be beneath the proscenium arch of memory and familiarity, the luster of what was once an eager newness still floods these recollected scenes. The situation is comparable to the occasional envy of the single by the married, who sometimes describe 'the happiness of their earlier years,' and, at least secretly, 'blame the rashness of their own choice.' But they forget that the days they wish to call back 'are the days not only of celibacy but of *youth,* the days of *novelty* and . . . of hope.' Sheer novelty, in fact, explains much of the vivid impact that sexual love makes on us in youth; and the memory of this creates the nostalgia in later years for those infatuations that could once *fill* the attention,' and stirs the vicarious interests of those' who employ themselves in promoting matrimony, and . . . without any discoverable impulse of malice or benevolence, without any reason, but that they *want objects of attention* and topics of conversation, are incessantly busy in procuring wives and husbands.'[7] Yet, in this remembered vividness, we forget that there were fears as well as hopes, and that not everything that 'fills the attention' through freshness or novelty does so in an agreeable way. The pleasures that we recall may actually have been outweighed by disadvantages we now forget. We should remember how rarely we look back with painful longing on any past circumstances that closely parallel our present state. But when once the past has become irretrieveable, and the portcullis closed, the liabilities and disadvantages of former conditions more easily lapse from memory; and recollected novelties and attractions blend without hindrance into a simpler and denser unit of pleasure than had ever really existed.

3

Nothing is so typical of the dynamic character of Johnson's thinking as the way in which he follows the human craving for 'novelty' and immediately recognizes it despite its agile, Proteus-like ability to take any form. He is always getting directly to the activity of 'looking before and after.' The procedure contrasts with the optical illusions of naïve naturalism, which lead us to interpret or at least label instincts or desires in terms merely of the particular objects on which they happen to fix. It is, in fact, this clear-eyed ability to brush aside the clutter of labels, and to seize on the actual process of desiring itself, that enables Johnson's moral thought to avoid the egocentric determinism of Thomas Hobbes and of moralists or psychologists who have repeated or refined on Hobbes for the past three centuries. Johnson does not, like Shaftesbury, Rousseau, or other romantics, simply deny Hobbes's arguments that man is basically selfish. Instead, he takes them for granted. Where Johnson differs from Hobbes is in supplementing these arguments with other considerations which Hobbes overlooks or disregards. He does this especially by recurring always to the nature of desire itself, as an activity inherent in a living creature 'whose motions are gradual.' Those only, said Coleridge, 'can acquire the *philosophic imagination* . . . who within themselves can interpret and understand the symbol, that the wings of the air-sylph are forming within the skin of the caterpillar. . . . They know and feel that the *potential* works in them, even as the *actual* works on them.'[8] Exactly this sense of process is immanent throughout all of Johnson's writing on human nature. By reaching down to the active function of desire itself, Johnson's thought touches a greater generality than that of Hobbes. Indeed, from this standpoint, the naturalism of Hobbes and his modern descendants is just another side of the coin to the romantic temptation to glorify the particular objects of desire. In either case, what we have is a confusion of a process with a static concept: a confusion of the instinct—

of the desiring mechanism, so to speak—with particular images or objects on which desire happens to fasten. Both of them mirror—one in a poetic, the other in an analytic way—the common tendency of the imagination to simplify its own wants and then to mistake the objects to which it happens to turn for actual *ends*—as ends that are somehow able, because of nature or one's own personal character, to serve as permanent sources of satisfaction once we get them. Precisely this mistake—a variety of Whitehead's 'fallacy of misplaced concreteness'—is, as Johnson conceives it, the source of most of the chronic dissatisfaction we feel when, once our basic physical needs are met, 'we begin to form wants in consequence of our wishes.'

The insight is that of Ecclesiastes: 'All the rivers flow into the sea; yet the sea is not full . . . the eye is not satisfied with seeing, nor the ear filled with hearing.' Of course, general wishes have to localize themselves into definite wants. Human existence could hardly continue otherwise. Also the objects of what we desire may vary in value. Some may satisfy a greater range of human needs, and some may offer a more enduring satisfaction. The protest, in Johnson's case, is only against the quick answer, against the flat, two-dimensional interpretation, whether in philosophy, in the criticism of literature, or in daily ambitions. Increasingly, as we look back on the great series of reflections on human nature that begin with the **Rambler** and continue through **Rasselas,** one of their prevailing themes appears to be the paradox of the human imagination itself. It is the paradox that the human imagination is potentially boundless in what it desires, and yet will fix itself hypnotically on a single aim or object. For what Swift called the 'converting imagination,' or the 'mechanical operation of the spirit,' has a frightening way of over-simplifying or restricting its field of interest for the moment. Hence its slap-dash tendency, as Swift says, 'to reduce all Things into *Types,*' to pluck out of context, interpret according to one aim, engross itself in only one object or aspect, and conveniently remove other elements or else twist them around to this immediate concern. But the paradox appears less extreme when we recall that the tendency to over-simplify—at least as far as our hopes for happiness are concerned—is only one more by-product of the fact that the 'capacity of the imagination' is so 'much larger than actual enjoyment.' Finding the present moment inadequate, the imagination bounds ahead to something else that contrasts with it. Naturally, the future, not yet being experienced, is 'pliant and ductile,' and will be imperceptibly molded by our wishes. The past, too, once it is safely removed, becomes 'ductile' in our memories. For the 'hope of happiness . . . is so strongly impressed, that the longest experience is not able to efface it. Of the present state, whatever it be, we *feel* . . . the misery; yet, *when the same state is against a distance,* imagination paints it as desirable.*[9]*

4

'The general remedy,' said Johnson, 'of those, who are uneasy without knowing the cause, is *change of place,*' or of condition generally: 'they are willing to imagine that their pain is the consequence of some *local* inconvenience, and endeavour to fly from it . . . '[10] To the extent that it snatches at whatever seems to contrast with the present, hope, like nostalgia for the past, also simplifies outlines and blots out the probable context. Hence, in our 'anticipation of change' to other conditions and different possessions, too often 'the change itself is nothing; when we have made it, the next wish is to change again.' The hard-driven merchant, chained down by a lifetime of routine, will naturally have periods when he looks forward to retirement from 'the fatigues of business, and the confinement of a shop'; it may even become an obsession; and then we find, when the looked-for retirement is attained, that he relieves the 'vacuity' of life in his country retreat by watching carriages from his window, and eagerly hoping he will be interrupted. Johnson himself, in his own reactions, certainly provides examples. The difference is that he cannot refrain from thinking about them. So, after writing the long series of the **Rambler,** the occasion of the next to the last issue suggests its own subject, in which he notes—and he was still at work on the **Dictionary**—that 'When once our labour has begun, the comfort that enables us to endure it is the prospect of its end.' Pleasing intervals may occur, as he goes on to say, during which we day-dream about the work in its completed form. But these intervals are short-lived. The mind is pitched to getting the thing done, and to being able to look back on the finished work as a whole. Yet like Gibbon, who had so long looked forward to the 'freedom' he would possess when he completed the *Decline and Fall of the Roman Empire,* we find the experience of this freedom does not fill the imagination with the vivid pleasure we expected; and the liberty quickly proves empty, until some further desire charges this vacant freedom with uneasiness and stimulates us to start something new. One thinks of Johnson, himself, while he was writing, impatiently running his finger down the margin to see how many verses were completed and how many were yet to be written, and at the same time seeing exactly what he was doing.

'Every man recounts the inconveniences of his own station, and thinks those of any other less, because he has not felt them. Thus the married praise the ease and freedom of a single state, and the single fly to marriage from the weariness of solitude. . . . *Whoever feels great pain, naturally hopes for ease from change of posture . . . '[11]* Indeed, Johnson seems to become most light-hearted and amusing in the **Rambler** and **Idler** sketches when he is discussing either marriage, the pursuit of wealth, or the hopes we place in retirement to country retreats. The expectations we feel, in all three cases, also serve for Johnson as recurring symbols of the way in which the imagination, in common and daily life, is always simplifying the endless desires of the heart into specific wants, and then finding them insufficient. To interpret the sprightly essays on marriage, or the debates about it in *Rasselas,* as an expression or rationalization of Johnson's own disillusionment about "Tetty' only suggests the limitations and projections of the interpreter. It is on a par with interpreting the great *Preface to Shakespeare,* with its massive plea for sanity of outlook, as a compensatory recoiling from Johnson's own distress of mind in the 1760's. Moreover, Johnson's point of view is generally that 'Marriage has many pains, but celibacy has few pleasures'; that much of the pain simply results from that tendency by which 'every animal *revenges his pain upon those who happen to be near';* and that 'we see the same discontent at every other part of life which we cannot change.' Again, it is plain that marriage is far from being really miserable, if for no other reason than that we find 'such numbers, whom the death of their partners has set free from it, entering it again.' In fact, he himself, after the death of 'Tetty,' was apparently thinking of marrying again, even though, on hearing of another's remarriage, he referred to it as 'the triumph of hope over experience.'

Indeed, whatever is subjective in Johnson's own experience he generally uses in an opposite way from rationalization. That is not to say that he automatically swings away from it through simple compensation. Instead, the immediately personal in Johnson remains openly and honestly present, serving as a bond, as a basis for charitable sympathy with the illusion he is dispelling. And if we at times find him cutting through the illusion with phrasing that seems too vigorous, we also find him equally able to turn against the next level—against psychological compensation in practically every temptation to it that he experienced (and his range of susceptibility was large)—and then qualifying the compensation itself with equal vigor. We know how strongly Johnson clung to religious orthodoxy, for example (and there may be an element of compensation here, in reaction from his own disturbing doubts), and that he had misgivings about the work of the brilliant Samuel Clarke. But when the Reverend Hector Maclean said that 'Clarke was very wicked for going so much into the Arian system,' 'I will not say he was *wicked,'* answered Johnson; 'he *might be mistaken.'* And when Maclean blandly asserted that 'worthy men since, in England, have confuted him to all intents and purposes,' Johnson burst out, 'I know not *who* has confuted him *to all intents and purposes.'*[12]

5

When we recall Johnson's poverty during the years before he wrote the *Rambler,* his enlightened treatment there of the hunger for wealth or possessions provides an especially graphic example of the balance and purity of his thinking—of his ability to resist not merely the temptation to rationalize the bitterness of poverty but also the temptation to compensate for it by a sour-grapes attitude toward wealth. True enough, he later admitted that 'When I was running about this town a very poor fellow, I was a great arguer for the advantages of poverty; but I was, at the same time, very sorry to be poor.' Yet the spectrum of his thinking in the *Rambler* ranges from 'that *false estimation* of the value of wealth, which poverty, long continued, always produces,' to the balancing reminder of how few desires 'can be formed which riches do not *assist* to gratify.'[13] Even the 'art of pleasing,' of being sympathetically receptive to others, is made very difficult by poverty; for 'by what means can the man please whose *attention is engrossed* by his distresses?' Moreover, defensive pride, even if it does not turn into truculence or freeze into awkward reserve, may still incite too aggressive and eager a desire to excel and 'attract notice.' Here indeed Johnson was speaking from his own experience. He admitted to Mrs. Thrale that he was thinking of himself when he wrote the story of the poor scholar in *Idler,* No. 75, who tried to fight his way by his learning and wit, and who found that wherever 'he had remarkably excelled, he was seldom invited a second time.'

These essays persuade because nothing that can attract the human imagination or bias judgment is ever lightly or easily dismissed. In fact, any such quick dismissals of the desire for wealth are themselves anticipated and exposed as simply another variety of over-simplification. Once a man attains wealth, and finds himself in a state of 'imagination operating on luxury,' where other desires begin to spawn 'in numberless directions,' he who wishes 'to become a philosopher at a cheap rate' can only too easily gratify himself by speaking lightly of poverty 'when he does not feel it, and by boasting his contempt of riches when he has already more than he enjoys.' Years later, when the wealthy Mrs. Thrale 'dwelt with peculiar pleasure' on David Garrick's line, 'I'd smile with the simple, and feed with the poor,' he at once interrupted: 'Nay, my dear Lady, this will never do. Poor David! Smile with the simple! What folly is that! *And who would feed with the poor that can help it?* No, no; let me smile with the wise, and feed with the rich.'[14] But if Johnson undercuts cant in this he is not satirizing it. Instead there is charity in seeing it as being itself one more instance of man's 'dream of happiness in *novelty'*—of happiness from different circumstances. Again, almost everyone values 'esteem and influence,' and 'whoever has found the art of securing them without the help of money, ought, in reality, to be accounted rich, since he has all that riches can purchase to a wise man.' Even the monk, though he is living an ascetic life, is not entitled to brush aside too quickly the powerful desire of the human heart for possessions, which convinces us that, 'Whatever is the *remote or ultimate* design, the *immediate* care is to be rich,' with no 'disagreement but about the use.' For if the monk resides in a monastery, he ought to remember that 'he converses only with men whose condition is the same with his own.' He should recall that 'the munificence of the founder' saves him from that destitution which is an 'impediment to virtue' simply because it does not allow 'the mind to *admit any other care.*' Temptations to 'envy and competition' are kept down: he is not exposed to the same range of 'pains and insults' as others; and if 'he wanders abroad, the sanctity of his character amply compensates all other distinctions.' Nor, lastly, are we to forget that many who neglect opportunities to amass wealth do so not because 'they value riches *less,* but that they dread labour or danger more than others.' Practically none would refuse 'to be rich, when to be rich was in his power.'[15] Hence the confidence inspired by Johnson as he illuminates the 'fallacies of imagination' that attach themselves to the image of wealth or possessions. We simplify reality when we dispose of the powerful appeal of wealth after we ourselves have attained it and found it inadequate. We do so when we cannot attain wealth, and therefore, by compensation, dismiss it as unimportant. We do so, thirdly, when the imagination narrows itself by confusing one means—the possession of wealth—with the end, and creates an image of possessions without which happiness is deemed impossible. Especially in the light of the other realizations, we can accept this final perception as something more than an abstract moral cliché.

Thus Johnson describes the hope of an entire family, waiting for the death of three wealthy, elderly aunts, and governing every action in this expectation. When snubbed or out-shone by their neighbors, the family has always the solace of the future before them. They dream of putting their neighbors in their place, and chalk up 'every act of civility and rudeness.' As the years pass, the nerves of the father of the family become more edgy, and he occasionally barks out that no creature has 'so many lives as a cat and an old maid.' Finally, when one of the aunts recovers from a severe illness, the father begins to pine away and dies. The family continues in the *'shackles of expectation,'* meeting together

> only to contrive how our approaching fortune should be enjoyed; for in this our conversation always ended, on whatever subject it began. *We had none of the collateral interests which diversify the life of others with joys and hopes,* but had turned our whole attention on one event, which we could neither hasten nor retard.

Finally, the two eldest aunts die, but leave their for-

tunes to their younger sister. She, in turn, plunges the remaining family into dismay by contemplating marriage now in her old age. In time this panic subsides. The nephew consoles himself with the undeniable truth that 'all are mortal,' without making the obvious application back to himself; for he is fast moving into middle age. When the remaining aunt dies at ninety-three, he now finds himself *'accustomed to give the future full power over my mind,* and to start away from the scene before me to some *expected* enjoyment.'[16]

Yet the almost savage irony of this brief satiric sketch is at once crossed by the large sadness through which Johnson's range of perception is always passing. For the 'shackles of expectation' have, as the aging nephew finds, now chained and reduced his own mind to 'an *inveterate disease of wishing . . .* unable to think on anything but *wants.*' Elsewhere, with more pity, Johnson can stress that 'Of riches, as of everything else, *the hope is more than the enjoyment . . .* no sooner do we sit down to enjoy our acquisitions, than we find them insufficient to fill up the vacuities of life.'[17] Hence the blind attempt, when we do have money, to 'fill our houses with useless ornaments, only to shew that we can buy them,' and to show not only others but principally ourselves;—or else we congratulate ourselves upon now dismissing the belief that money is a good, and turn instead to other ends. Turning to other ends is desirable, even though the self-congratulation and lapse of sympathy are to be avoided.

Our motives, as Johnson continually reminds us, can rarely be completely pure. But they are not for that reason to be left unused. The value is to be judged by the *final* degree of purity. This is one of the ways in which Johnson goes beyond Swift, who so frequently darkens his interpretation by recurring to original motives. If 'poverty long continued' leads to a 'false estimation' of the importance of wealth, then one of the advantages of wealth is certainly that it can help free us, though it does not do so automatically, from stumbling into this false estimate. If Johnson's treatment of the hope of riches is viewed as a self-protective method of reminding himself and of keeping his own mind clear, the fact remains that we can tell ourselves what is true and desirable while we are also telling others, particularly if we are emphasizing not one but two or more different aspects of a matter. Indeed, we may question whether what we are telling others will have the desired persuasiveness unless we are also telling ourselves. With what we know too well, as with what we already possess too abundantly, the difficulty of attaining it and the pressures that once underlay our desire for it may be forgotten. In his moral writing as in his criticism of literature, Johnson never writes in the closet or the study as one who has lived through an experience and forgotten the details but as one who is again reliving it.

6

Macaulay is largely responsible for the strange notion that, because Johnson praised the variety of London life as compared with that of a village or a hermitage, he therefore disliked traveling; that, in fact, he dismissed travel 'with the fierce and boisterous contempt of ignorance.' Macaulay seems to have forgotten Johnson's financial condition; his constant reading of books of travel; his pathetic hope that he could make a trip to Iceland; the arduous trip over the Scottish mountain-paths that he made with Boswell; the visits that he restlessly made to Lichfield, Oxford, and Ashbourne; his snatching at the opportunity to go to France with the Thrales; his final resurgence of hope while dying—which he dared not speak out, for he was dependent on another's bounty—that he might at last go to Italy.

If he had money, he once wrote to Mrs. Thrale, the very first use to which he would put it would be to travel extensively through the Orient. 'He loved indeed the very act of travelling,' said Mrs. Thrale, and was 'an admirable companion on the road, as he piqued himself upon feeling no inconvenience, and on despising no accommodations.' There are also the various remarks about the height of felicity consisting of riding rapidly in a postchaise. In fact, any inconvenience seemed so trifling compared with the enormous advantages and interest of travel that he regarded the complaints of others about 'the rain, the sun, or the dust,' about 'long confinement in a carriage' or meagerness of comfort at inns, as 'proofs of an empty head, and a *tongue desirous to talk without materials of conversation.* "A mill that goes without grist (said he) is as good a companion as such creatures." 'And when a visitor at the Thrales' who had traveled through Bohemia seemed uninterested in taking part in any sort of conversation, 'Surely,' said Johnson afterward, 'the man who has seen Prague might tell us something new and something strange, and not sit silent for want of matter to put his lips in motion.'[18]

Hence the shallowness of viewing his discussions of the restless desire for travel or for rural retreat as a rationalization of his own physical near-sightedness, his deafness, or his insensibility to those 'natural' objects to which the nineteenth century automatically assumed that the eighteenth century was oblivious, as though the neo-classic ideal of bliss were to sit at the court of George II or in the midst of Fleet Street. Instead, the impulsive hopes of travel, or of flying to rural retreats, are only one more instance, in daily life, of both the insatiability and self-defeating simplicity of the human heart. **Rambler,** No. 6, comes as close to satire as Johnson generally permitted himself. Its theme

is the much advertised assertion of the poet, Abraham Cowley, that, since fame had brought him everything but rest, he now intended to sail overseas to a plantation, and '*foresake this world forever,* with all the vanities and vexations of it, and to bury myself there in some obscure retreat.' He could easily have buried himself, says Johnson, within his own country: "There is prideenough in the human heart to prevent much desire of acquaintance with a man, by whom we are sure to be neglected . . . Even those to, whom he has formerly been known, will very patiently support his absence when they have tried a little to live without him.' But Cowley, when he was interrupted or fatigued in his present state, 'conceived it impossible to be far enough from [what he thought] the cause of his uneasiness,' and picturing by contrast an idyllic state of leisure and retreat, he

> determined to enjoy them for the future without interuption . . . He forgot, in the vehemence of desire, that solitude and quiet owe their pleasures to those miseries, which he was so studious to obviate . . . that *day and night, labour and rest, hurry and retirement, endear each other* . . . we desire, we pursue, we obtain, we are satiated; we desire something else, and begin a new pursuit.

> If he had proceeded in his project . . . it may be doubted, whether his distance from the *vanities* of life, would have enabled him to keep away the *vexations. It is common for a man, who feels pain, to fancy that he could bear it better in any other part.* Cowley, having known the troubles and perplexities of a particular condition, readily persuaded himself that nothing worse was to be found, and that every alteration would bring some improvement; *he never suspected that the cause of his unhappiness was within* . . .

'He that travels in theory,' as Johnson says elsewhere, 'has no incovenience: he has shade and sunshine at his disposal.' In its recoil from one's present state, the imagination selects only those advantages which seem most attractive, and then unites them into an impossible expectation that is 'indulged till the day of departure arrives.' A few miles then teach the traveler the 'fallacies of imagination': the road is dusty, and the horses slow; he 'longs for the time of dinner, that he may eat and rest,' and finds the inn crowded; while the people he has looked forward to visiting turn out to be cool, occupied with their affairs, or burdened with private sorrow. If 'Pleasure is very seldom found where it is sought'—where it is imagined and then deliberately searched for—it is because we seldom

> find either men or places such as we *expect* them. He that has pictured a prospect upon his fancy, will receive little pleasure from his eyes; he that has anticipated the conversation of a wit, will wonder to what prejudice he owes his reputation. *Yet it is*

necessary to hope, though hope should always be deluded; for hope itself is happiness, and its frustrations, however frequent, are less dreadful than its extinction.[19]

The recurring theme of the 'vanity of human wishes,' then, from the poem through the great prose of the following decade, isnot merely that we give ourselves unnecessary pain by desiring what is unattainable, and thus become inevitably frustrated. Least of all is it some vague, pessimistic assertion that all wishes are vain. The theme is rather that, in the very activity or process of wishing, there are inherent liabilities that are able to undercut the wish itself—the liabilities that the 'capacity of the imagination' is always so 'much larger than actual enjoyment,' and that nevertheless it tends to simplify, to fix on a specific object, if only by contrast, and to dwell 'attentively upon it, till it has wholly engrossed the imagination, and permits us not to conceive any happiness but its attainment, or any misery but its loss.'[20] But 'since life is uncertain, nothing which has life as its basis can boast much stability.'

Even if the external objects we want proved to be stable, yet we ourselves, in our ability to enjoy them, would not be. The sense of process, and the awareness of what lies beyond the horizon of the moment, is indigenous and continual in Johnson, habitually modifying fears as well as hopes; even casual conversational remarks reveal it. Not long after meeting Johnson, Boswell planned a dinner for several guests; a quarrel with his landlord left him without a house; and he was worried about the impression this would give. Johnson's immediate response is typical: 'Consider . . . how insignificant this will appear a twelvemonth hence.' Or again, in Boswell's *Tour to the Hebrides,* when Johnson was sixty-four, some young women were discussing among themselves how ugly he was. One of them took a bet to go over, sit on Johnson's knees, and kiss him. Even in this little incident, Johnson's amused awareness of the situation and his unsleeping, almost Shakespearean realization of the transitoriness of things come at once into focus, in a healthful and comic sanity of statement, entirely characteristic of him when once uttered, and yet completely unpredictable: *'Do it again,'* he said, *'and let us see who will tire first.'*[21]

7

If Johnson comes closest to comedy when he is dealing with the disappointments of what we expect in ordinary experience—expectations of happiness from riches, marriage or single life, travel or country retreats—it is because, for most of us, these disappointments have been tamed by familiarity. We are all so used to them that we feel we have such expectations—or could have them—fairly well under control. As such, they remain comparatively innocent. Of course, the frustrations that result, like any other disappointment,

can arouse in us a hidden tendency to revenge ourselves on those with whom we spend our lives or whom we imagine to possess what we lack. Generally, however, we learn to take them for granted, and try to proceed to other matters, if not in our actual lives at least in what we think is reputable to discuss.

But Johnson's vigorous grip on the principal weakness of human nature has subtlety as well as range. He reaches vertically, so to speak, as well as horizontally. With shrewd perception, he discloses the motives, hopes, and frustrations that reach to the philosopher's desk, seeing them not as special reactions, cut off from more familiar desires and fears, but as refinements of them. The underlying sense of community contrasts refreshingly with the usual belief of the sophisticated that they have escaped or lived through the temptations of the unsophisticated. For while they verbally dispose of the hunger for riches, and of the more obvious desires for change of scene and condition—or even, as academic moralists, pin such desires down and describe them—we know very well that exactly these compulsions and others like them are at work within themselves.

The needless demands and the delight in machinery for its own sake that clutter up the pursuit of learning and trivialize it are seen as the product of the same simplicity and 'fallacy of the imagination,' the same confusing of the means with the end, that leads the miser to concentrate on his coins.[22] Usually Johnson cites the way in which scholars dig intently and single-mindedly in what he calls the 'secondary' fields of learning, glorify what they are doing as an end in itself, make a vested interest of it, and self-defensively fight others who seek greater generality. Now, the writer of the **English Dictionary** can hardly be charged with dismissing detailed scholarship lightly. In fact, those who do dismiss it, as Johnson implies, are rarely invigorated by any impelling concern for human values. Johnson's protest is not against labor that requires only 'sluggish resolution' but against a flatness of mind that confuses this with the end. Even more, the protest is against the habit—by which everyone seeks to 'conceal his own unimportance from himself'—of identifying ourselves too exclusively with what we are doing. For we bog down, in our habitual feeling and judgments, into a self-protective and therefore intolerant defense, which is really more of a defense of ourselves than of what we are doing. Since man's powers are limited, 'he must use *means* for the attainment of his ends.'[23] But the immediate end, when attained, is—and should be—found to be 'only one of the means to some remoter end. *The natural flights of the human mind are not from pleasure to pleasure, but from hope to hope.*'[24] Unless we feel what we are doing is important, we should neglect it—and neglect it, in all probability, not for something better but for something worse. The weakness is that, in learning as in other human activities, we institutionalize, and then seal and arm this fortress instead of keeping it open by trying constantly to generalize, to extend our vision, and to see what 'can be put to use' for daily human needs. Too often the aim is merely to keep or 'advance reputation' within a specialized groove. At the very least there is the temptation to use knowledge rather to '*diversify conversation* than to *regulate life.*' Johnson could say this while maintaining that curiosity is, 'in great and generous minds, the first passion and the last; and perhaps always predominates in proportion to the strength of the contemplative faculties.'[25] One of the **Ramblers** (No. 61) describes a rustic who, after returning from London to his native village, took care to crowd his talk with 'names of streets, squares, and buildings' with which he knew his hearers to be 'unacquainted,' and 'when any of his phrases were unintelligible, he could not suppress the joy of confessed superiority.' In the eighteenth century, polite conversation was more frequently sprinkled with historical allusions to antiquity than the more compartmentalized talk of today. The Punic Wars became a stock symbol to Johnson of talk that 'carried one away from common life' without really extending 'ideas':

> He never (as he expressed it) desired to hear of the *Punic war* while he lived: such conversation was *lost time* (he said) . . . I asked him once [Mrs. Thrale goes on] concerning the conversation powers of a gentleman [Charles James Fox] . . . 'He talked to me at club one day . . . concerning Cataline's conspiracy—so I withdrew my attention and thought about *Tom Thumb.*'[26]

The use of knowledge for the sake of learned allusions—knowledge to impress others, 'advance reputation,' or make the day less 'vacuous' for oneself—is so obvious an example of devoting the mind to 'employments that *engross,* but do not improve it' that few people fail to recognize it. Less innocent, perhaps, is the openly analytic thinking about human values—in life, literature, or anything else—continued solely for its own sake apart from the end that gives it relevance and dignity. This has its own obvious and comic side, of course. While the moralist is analyzing the emptiness of ambition, we can only too often find him swelling 'with the applause he has gained by proving that applause is of no value'[27] (we may contrast Johnson's honest reminder that 'the applause of a single human being is of great consequence'). But the real danger is that it subtly encourages ourselves and others to believe that analysis for its own sake is the proper aim and indication of intelligence. The potential hypocrisy is greater if only because such analysis seems intellectually more respectable. It satisfies the imagination more quickly that something is being done which is immediately relevant to human values. Johnson's own greatest pleasure, as Mrs. Thrale said, was in 'metaphysical reasoning.' The delight in an incisive analytic thinking

that could 'fill the mind,' even when pursued for its own sake, had a powerful attraction for him, as his literary criticism especially shows. But there is always the swing back to remember that, in technical analysis or incisive ingenuity when pursued apart from the broad concern of actual human development, there is just as much pedantry, just as much a sidetracking of effort into means, as in collecting and redistributing brute knowledge. It is the light verbalizing—however sharply analytic—about human ends and conduct that Imlac has in mind when he cautions Rasselas that the philosophers lecturing on ethics 'discourse like angels, but they live like men.' And when Rasselas himself visits a learned society, he finds that, however the members differ in other ways, 'every one was pleased to hear the genius or knowledge of another depreciated.'[28]

8

Even when our motives are as pure as human nature is able to attain, an inevitable simplification follows the process of *idealizing*—the process of plucking out from experience an ideal, a pattern, or a form. For we then find that details do not precisely fit it. 'He that has abilities to conceive perfection, will not easily be content without it'; and since perfection cannot be reached, he may neglect the chance of doing anything in the hope of impossible excellence.[29] Not that we are for this reason to throw over ideals, or become embittered like Swift. Rather, it follows that we should nuance and inform our ideals with practical judgment, and watch lest we narrow charity and even our own experience by prematurely recoiling from what fails to fit exactly into our ideals. Yet almost any ideal, however objectively based, is bound to be somewhat smoothed out and simplified by the human imagination. It will be at best an abbreviation of reality. Hence, as Johnson notes, the disappointment or irritability of so many scholars, critics, or philosophers, when they are faced with all the concrete problems and exceptions which they have previously hoped to settle or iron out by clean-shaped theory. Hence also their love of system and definition, and the tendency of some of them to eulogize the past; for all the accomplishments of a lengthy past are blended together in their imagination with such density as to make the smaller unit of the present seem, by contrast, hopelessly sterile. The habit of idealizing, although no development is possible without it, can still create states of expectation and anxiety that are a mixed blessing; and the problem becomes acute when it turns on ourselves, creating a self-expectation that intimidates our inventive originality. This, as Johnson recognizes, is a real problem in literature as it becomes more self-conscious. Also, in what we talk or write about, we become afraid to deal with what is most important, as he says, because we feel we can add so little to it, and show ourselves to advantage. We start worrying about frills, occupy ourselves with minor qualifications or embellishments, and, either as a pose or a form of despair, become the victims of our ideal of 'elegance refined into impatience.' But Johnson also touches on other examples, from the stagefright of lecturing to self-consciousness in social gatherings. Bishop Sanderson, anxiously preparing his lectures, 'hesitated so much, and rejected so often,' that when thetime came to deliver them he had to present not what was best but what he had at hand. Again, the lecturer who imagines an audience of admirers

> panting with expectation, and hushed with attention, easily terrifies himself with the dread of disappointing them, and strains . . . [to] show his reputation was not gained by chance. He considers that what he shall say or do will never be forgotten; that renown or infamy is suspended on every syllable; and that nothing ought to fall from him which will not bear the test of time. Under such solicitude, who can wonder that the mind is overwhelmed . . . ? Those who are *oppressed by their own reputation,* will, perhaps, not be comforted by hearing that their cares are unnecessary. . . . While we see multitudes passing before us . . . we should remember, that we are likewise lost in the same throng; that the eye which happens to glance on us is turned in a moment on him that follows . . . [30]

'Nothing is more hopeless,' said Johnson, 'than a *scheme of merriment.*' He seems to have found irresistibly amusing the way in which we form a precarious image of ourselves—or the image we imagine others to have of ourselves—and the paralysis we then feel because of our dread of disappointing it. There is the story of the wit who is invited by a friend to dinner and told how many people will be present who have heard of his reputation.[31] Instead of quickening his eagerness, the mere thought of the high expectation with which the company awaits him fills him with anxiety. Lying sleepless all night, he plans out to himself 'the conversation of the coming day,' recollects 'all my topics of raillery,' makes up 'answers to imaginary repartees,' and then shows up at dinner the next day, completely exhausted and 'sunk under the weight of expectation.' Forgetting that mirth cannot operate in a vacuum but needs 'objects,' and that most people are gay or serious by infection, the company is hushed with expectation. Dinner gives only a temporary relief. There is no real context within which his wit can get a start, especially any context like that he had imagined the night before. A few desperate efforts produce 'neither applause nor opposition.' The contagious atmosphere of expectation became so general that, if others uttered remarks 'with timidity and hesitation, there was none ready to make any reply. All our faculties were frozen, and *every minute took away our capacity of pleasing, and disposition to be pleased.*' The effect of self-consciousness, as Johnson returns to this fascinating subject, is seen to apply to all aspects

of social and intellectual life arranged by 'preconcerted invitation.' To know that a thing is expected can often stimulate us, particularly in carrying out physical or mechanical actions, where an obvious or clear-cut course of action is indicated. But it can also chill invention, unless we already possess a confidence firmly grounded in experience and habit. The imagination, instead of flowing out tomeet new and unexpected objects, recoils into taut or frozen self-defense. And this pause of spirits is then all the more difficult to overcome except through awkward and self-conscious jerks of effort. Johnson mentions how fortunate we are to have set conventions for beginning and ending letters. There would be an appalling loss of time if we had to decide, in every case, the most appropriate method of beginning and closing every letter. He contrasts with this the unfortunate situation of the writer, paralyzed before the blank page, searching for a beginning that will at once ensnare attention, or suggest, with impressive impact, the sum total of all he feels he can later unfold. Again, Johnson pictures a group of wits, invited together for an evening, 'with admirers prepared to laugh and applaud.' But they 'gaze awhile on each other, ashamed to be silent, and *afraid to speak.*' They become discontented both with themselves and each other, and later 'retire to vent their indignation in safer places, where they are heard with attention; their *importance is restored,*' and they 'recover their good humour.'[32]

9

On matters about which we really care, we are not usually convinced until we have seen for ourselves. The relevance of Johnson is not simply that he touches directly on so much that we care about. It is especially to be found in the way his thought proceeds, which is like that of experience itself. For his thinking goes first through everything that will not work, minimizing nothing, sharing in the attraction felt by the human heart, and even expressing that appeal memorably. And only gradually, as one thing after another gives way, do we find left a citadel of unshaken results that have withstood the test. Too often the abstract systems of the philosopher, as Sir Philip Sidney said, teach only those who are 'already taught,' appearing thin, irrelevant, or even visionary to others; while the dramatist can concretely show what happens to human beings under certain conditions, leading us to identify ourselves with them and to take in their experience as our own.

Johnson's own procedure, in other words, is ultimately dramatic, evoking personal sympathies and tapping the reader's own experience. The real actors are not, it is true, individual characters. Even in **Rasselas** the particular characters are only incidental. Instead, the motives and persuasions within this drama are always being gathered up into the great generalizations that rise from its pages. Like characters in dialogue, they give dramatic expression and even dignity to widely different motives and hopes; or, like brief asides or longer soliloquies, they serve as pauses in which human actions break out into reflection or self-knowledge. That the final outline of the action does not emerge easily or mechanically, that it is not cut to order, is a tribute to its genuineness. Like the close of **Rasselas**—a 'Conclusion in which Nothing is Concluded'—the results cannot be put into a rigid, air-tight formula, if only because every new experience will always be somewhat different. The drama, in short, is that of life itself, which is rarely neat in the answers it provides, and in which honest doubts and perplexities still persist. But when conviction does follow, it is the massive conviction that our own experience gives.

Notes

1 *Rasselas,* chs. 30-32.

2 *Rambler,* No. 41.

3 Piozzi, *Anecdotes,* I, 251.

4 *Rambler,* No. 41.

5 No. 6.

6 *Idler,* No. 44.

7 *Rambler,* Nos. 45, 115.

8 *Biographia Literaria* (ed. Shawcross, 1907), I, 167.

9 *Rasselas,* ch. 22.

10 *Rambler,* No. 6.

11 No. 45.

12 [Boswell, James,] *Tour to the Hebrides,* [New York, 1936] pp. 256-7.

13 *Rambler,* Nos. 170, 131.

14 No. 202; Boswell, *Life [of Johnson* (Oxford, 1934-50)], II, 79.

15 *Rambler,* Nos. 202, 58, 48, 131.

16 No. 73.

17 *Idler,* No. 73.

18 *Anecdotes, J.M.,* I, 263, 329-30; Boswell, *Life,* III, 459.

19 *Idler,* No. 58.

20 *Rambler,* No. 17.

21 *Tour to the Hebrides,* p. 226.

22 Cf. *Rambler,* Nos. 82-3, 103, 177.

23 No. 2.

24 Loc. cit.

25 No. 150.

26 *Anecdotes, J.M.,* I, 202.

27 *Rambler,* No. 54.

28 *Rasselas,* ch. 22.

29 *Rambler,* No. 134.

30 Nos. 19, 159.

31 No. 101.

32 *Idler,* No. 58.

George Sherburn (essay date 1959)

SOURCE: "Rasselas Returns—To What?," in *Philological Quarterly,* Vol. XXXVIII, No. 3, July, 1959, pp. 383-84.

[*In the following essay, Sherburn argues that, contrary to the assumption of earlier critics, Rasselas and his party do not end their journey with an optimistic return to the Happy Valley. Instead, according to Sherburn, the travellers return to Abissinia only to find the Happy Valley closed to them forever.*]

Since **Rasselas** is this year two hundred years old, it is natural for us all to write about it. But it is painful to find people misinterpreting one important fact of the work. In *Philological Quarterly* for January, 1959, William Kenney optimistically represents the travellers, Rasselas, Imlac, *et al.* as returning improved, and even hopeful, to the Happy Valley. Such an interpretation—and Kenney is not alone in the error—is totally unwarranted and contrary to Dr. Johnson's intention. The travellers return *to Abissinia,* but not under the circumstances represented. They do not return to the Happy Valley.

The abrupt conclusion of the book is carefully prepared for in its first chapters. In Chapter I Dr. Johnson tells us that "those, on whom the iron gate [of the Valley] had once closed, were never suffered to return" (Chapman ed. [1927], p. 10). Added preparation for an unhappy ending is found in Chapters VIII to XII in which Imlac tells of his own travels—and his return to Abissinia. His barren return, prophetic for Rasselas, is described (Chapter XII) as follows:

> My father had been dead fourteen years, having divided his wealth among my brothers, who were removed to some other provinces. Of my companions the greater part was in the grave, and of the rest some could with difficulty remember me, and some considered me as one corrupted by foreign manners. (*ed. cit.,* p. 60)

It was a cold Abissinia and not the Happy Valley in which returning Rasselas could, as Kenney incisively suggests, "begin the practice of orderly diversification" (*PQ,* XXXVIII [1959], 89). The work ends in almost complete frustration. The travellers are now in the condition in which Imlac had formerly found himself before he achieved the Happy Valley, now closed to him and his companions. In the Valley, he had told Rasselas, "I am less unhappy than the rest because I have a mind replete with images. . . . " So Rasselas and his sister will have to fortify themselves with memories, but not with the now forbidden delights of the Happy Valley. One may regret Dr. Johnson's pessimism, but must face it.

Emrys Jones (essay date 1967)

SOURCE: "The Artistic Form of *Rasselas,*" in *The Review of English Studies,* n.s., Vol. XVIII, No. 72, November, 1967, pp. 387-401.

[*In the following essay, Jones argues that a three-part structure, rather than the usual division of* Rasselas *into two unequal parts, reflects more accurately Johnson's original intent for this work.*]

Johnson's powers as a poet are more readily appreciated than they were fifty years ago. But the artistry of **Rasselas** is still too little recognized. The traditional reading of the book speaks of it as a species of sober discourse, and finds its unity—if it has one—in its mood or temper, that of a philosophical pessimism. To approach **Rasselas** in terms of its apparent sentiments may be misleading; for where a work has the degree of organization that, I suggest, may be found in **Rasselas,** the bearing of its statements cannot be clear until their context is ascertained. The tone of **Rasselas** will be misunderstood, in fact, if its artistic form is neglected.

I

'That most melancholy of fables' is how Walter Raleigh described **Rasselas.** That is all he had to say about it in his book on Johnson,[1] and in using such a phrase he was no doubt assenting to the traditional way of reading it. The gloom of **Rasselas** has long been a critical commonplace. Boswell's short account of it in the *Life,*[2] although conventional and perfunctory, serves to indicate how the book was usually read until close to our time. He first recounts the circumstances in which **Rasselas** was written: 'The late Mr. Strahan the printer told me, that Johnson wrote it, that with the profits he might defray the expense of his mother's funeral, and pay some little debts which she had left. He told Sir Joshua Reynolds that he composed it in the evenings of one week. . . . ' Boswell remarks: 'This Tale, with all the charms of oriental imagery, and all the force and beauty of which the English language is capable, leads us through the most important scenes of human life, and shews us that this stage of our being is full of "vanity and vexation of spirit".' And he goes on to quote the observation of a 'very accomplished lady' that **Rasselas** was 'a more enlarged and more deeply philosophical discourse in prose, upon the interesting truth, which in his *Vanity of Human Wishes* he had so successfully enforced in verse'. Boswell's three main points: that **Rasselas** was associated with the funeral of Johnson's mother; that it was a philosophical discourse, a prose counterpart of *The Vanity of Human Wishes;* and that its aim was to enforce the moral of *Ecclesiastes,* that in this life 'all is vanity and vexation of spirit': these three points have all become critical commonplaces. Professor Nichol Smith, for example, observes of **Rasselas** that 'the gloom is heavy', and for him 'The book ends in resignation to the futility of searching for happiness, and in resolution to pursue life as it is found'.[3] Nearer our own time, in his biography of Johnson, Professor Krutch finds the term 'pessimism' appropriate to **Rasselas,** although he adds: 'It was, indeed, the pessimism which is more properly called the tragic sense of life.'[4] 'Gloom', 'melancholy', 'vanity and vexation of spirit', 'resignation', 'pessimism', 'the tragic sense of life': it is in such terms as these that **Rasselas** has traditionally been interpreted. And Imlac's undeniably gloomy remark has been the sentence most readily quoted to justify such a reading: 'Human life is every where a state in which much is to be endured, and little to be enjoyed.'[5]

The term 'tragic', used by Professor Krutch, may serve to introduce, by way of contrast, a fairly recent and very different way of reading **Rasselas.** I am referring to a fresh and stimulating article by Mr. Alvin Whitley which he provocatively named 'The Comedy of *Rasselas*'.[6] He claims that what he calls 'the ponderous school' of critics has been mistaken in its views, and that the right way to read **Rasselas** is to see it as a 'critical comedy'. He insists on the 'dramatic' structure of the book;[7] he argues that its moral is implicit, not explicit; that we cannot, or should not, tear maxims out of their context and interpret them as unqualified assertions of the author; for even Imlac is not Johnson, even if Imlac is closer to him than Pekuah. Finally, in *The Rhetorical World of Augustan Human-*

ism (London, 1965), Mr. Paul Fussell describes an eighteenth-century literary form, or set of motifs, which he calls 'the salutary moral comedy of disappointment' (p. 270), and as an example of this kind—this comic kind—he confidently cites *Rasselas.*

Here are two ways of reading the same book. The first sees *Rasselas* as a work of heavy gloom; it tends to stress the moral, a detachable moral, or (to use Nichol Smith's term) the 'lesson'. The second, which sees the book as belonging to a species of comic narrative, neglects the moral—or at least does not look for a detachable one—but instead attends to its sardonic or rueful wit. It insists on Johnson's deliberate control of his material, his freedom to choose, his artistry. In particular it calls attention to certain structural features of *Rasselas.* The first school, by contrast, is not interested in the book's structure. Indeed, Boswell and Nichol Smith, for example (others could be found saying much the same thing), do not merely fail to give attention to the book's structure, they positively suggest that there would not be very much structure if they looked for it. Boswell sees it as a philosophical discourse in prose on the same subject as *The Vanity of Human Wishes,* while Nichol Smith remarks: 'There is little or no story, no crisis, no conclusion: there is little more than a succession of discussions and disquisitions on the limitations of life.' And he goes on to call it 'an expanded essay'.[8] The second school of critics, who argue for an essentially comic *Rasselas,* do not deny its moralistic intentions, but they see them as working through a set of literary contrivances; and so for them a careful attention to the structure of *Rasselas* is necessary. Far from being a philosophical discourse or an 'expanded essay', which might well be carelessly assembled, *Rasselas* is properly to be viewed as an arrangement of effects, a patterned sequence, in short a work of art.

Of course some critics, among them the most perceptive, can be said to belong to neither school. Among these are Dr. F. R. Leavis[9] and Miss Mary Lascelles,[10] who have both noted in *Rasselas* certain affinities with Jane Austen. And in general the critical situation is more complicated and more untidy than this simplified account would suggest. For not all those who have examined the structure of *Rasselas* believe it to be a comic work. In his article 'The Structure of *Rasselas*'[11] Professor Gwin Kolb rejects a comic interpretation. His summing-up firmly allies him to the school of gloom:

> What, briefly, Johnson seems to be urging upon us is this:human limitations make happiness in this world ephemeral, accidental, the product of hope rather than reality, and almost as nothing compared to the miseries of life; consequently, searches for permanent enjoyment, although inevitable to man as man, are bound to end in failure. The wise man, therefore, will accept submissively the essential

grimness of life, seek no more lasting felicity than is given by a quiet conscience, and live with an eye upon eternity, in which he may perhaps find, through the mercy of God, the complete happiness unattainable on earth.

So for Professor Kolb, as for Professor Raleigh, *Rasselas* could be described, in summary phrase, as 'that most melancholy of fables'.

It is not my purpose to try to adjudicate between the two approaches. It is, after all, not altogether unknown for works of art of exceptional vitality to be interpreted in similarly diverse ways. Some of Shakespeare's plays have provoked this kind of disagreement, and in Johnson's own century, among Mozart's operas for example, *Don Giovanni* and *Così fan Tutte* have been tugged, now in the direction of comedy, now of tragedy, by critics of opposed views. One might, in an attempt to reconcile them, quote Horace Walpole's dictum: 'This world is a comedy to those who think, a tragedy to those who feel.' However, there is this to be said for those critics who interpret *Rasselas* as a fundamentally comic work, that they seem to be those most willing to credit Johnson with the powers and the intentions of an artist; and it is as a work of art, a deliberately shaped sequence, that *Rasselas* deserves to be considered, and has perhaps been insufficiently so considered in the past.

In the first place, the book needs to be released from the bonds laid on it by an otherwise justifiable interest in Johnson's biography. Mr. Whitley says of *Rasselas* (perhaps rather extravagantly): 'It would be hard to name another literary work which has been so completely transformed . . . by bringing extraneous knowledge to bear upon it'[12]. The foremost item of extraneous knowledge is undoubtedly that concerning the death of Johnson's mother.[13] So far as we can determine them, the circumstances in which Johnson sat down to write *Rasselas* were certainly melancholy; but in traditional accounts of the book too easy or too direct a transition has been made from these circumstances to the state of Johnson's mind while he actually composed. It has been too hastily assumed that because these circumstances were gloomy, therefore *Rasselas* must be gloomy. But the circumstances in which a work of art was composed are seldom if ever a safe guide to the meaning of the work itself. We could hardly have guessed from listening to Mozart's *Così fan Tutte* that it was composed in circumstances of increasingly desperate financial hardship. Mozart and Johnson make an odd pair. Yet in onerespect they are comparable: in the facility and extraordinary competence with which each practised in his chosen medium. The facility and fecundity of Mozart are famous, while *Rasselas* was composed in the evenings of a week. I doubt if one could have inferred from *Rasselas* itself that Johnson had very recently suffered a severe bereavement. The subject of bereavement does indeed occur in it, but it is treated with a fine comic irony. Johnson the writer is unmistakably in control of his material; there is no suggestion that he is struggling to subdue a painful pressure of emotion. The incident in question is Nekayah's grief after the abduction of her handmaid Pekuah. Nekayah, we are told,

> sat from morning to evening recollecting all that had been done or said by her Pekuah, treasured up with care every trifle on which Pekuah had set an accidental value, and which might recall to mind any little incident or careless conversation. The sentiments of her whom she now expected to see no more, were treasured in her memory as rules of life, and she deliberated to no other end than to conjecture, on any occasion, what would have been the opinion and counsel of Pekuah. (p. 118)

She determines to go into a permanent retreat from the world, until dissuaded by Imlac and Rasselas; and the following chapter (xxxvi) has for its title 'Pekuah is still remembered. The Progress of Sorrow.' And the progress of sorrow is shown to be in fact its abatement:

> She rejoiced without her own consent at the suspension of her sorrows, and sometimes caught herself with indignation in the act of turning away her mind from the remembrance of her, whom yet she resolved never to forget.

As Imlac had said, 'sorrow is never long without a dawn of ease' (p. 120). The writing in this episode is masterly in its mature equilibrium. Nekayah engages our sympathies, but Johnson sees to it that we can also afford to smile.

It is possible then that *Rasselas* has been seen too restrictively within the context of Johnson's private life. It is also possible that it has been seen too restrictively, and prejudicially, within the context of Johnson's other writings. Johnson the writer was seen by his own contemporaries primarily as a moralist, one who habitually spoke as if in the first person, and also as one distinguished from other men by a habitual sincerity of utterance. The literary form most congenial to him was felt to be the essay, the form that most closely approximated to his conversation. So Boswell, in the passage already quoted, thinks of *Rasselas* as a 'philosophical discourse'; later, Nichol Smith speaks of it as an 'expanded essay' (and he later quotes it for what he calls Johnson's 'perfect sincerity'). In keeping with these assumptions *Rasselas* is commonly said to be not very much more than a series of *Rambler*-type papers. The association of *Rasselas* with the *Rambler* and the other periodical essays is perhaps another restrictive bond that needs to be loosened. Of course there are good reasons for comparing some of the episodes in

Rasselas to certain of the periodical essays: reasons of style, presentation, and length as well as substance. A clear example is *Rambler* 6, whose subject is 'Happiness not Local', which is, of course, the thought underlying Johnson's ironical invention of the Happy Valley. But interesting and indeed inescapable as are such affinities between the periodical essays and *Rasselas,* it is perhaps now more desirable to insist on the differences. In her essay on *Rasselas* Miss Lascelles has urged some of the greater opportunities awaiting Johnson in the long fable as opposed to the short essay. 'Johnson', she remarks, 'liked, and needed, more room to turn in than a single periodical number allowed him.' And moreover: 'whereas the essays forming a series in a periodical must be all of a length, these episodes [in *Rasselas*] vary both in bulk and density.' And she goes on to point out the greater complexity in attitude allowed Johnson by the long narrative form:

> *Rasselas* expresses such a tension of contrarieties as no other medium could sustain. It urges, with equal cogency, the necessity, and the danger, of hope. For moderation in both, a *Rambler* paper could offer a sufficient plea. But for a stronger and subtler tension; for the presentation of contrary states of mind alike valid; for the annihilation of distinction between successive and simultaneous phases of experience—only this will serve.[14]

This is admirably put; but one may argue for an even greater degree of liberation from the directly instructive, hortatory mode of the periodical essay, a liberation into the freer, more open-minded, more inconclusive mode of imaginative fiction. *Rasselas* is not, in short, a few periodical essays stitched together and given a flimsy fictional envelope—for this would suggest that the relation between its episodes were merely additive, as if the whole were merely the sum of its parts, as it would be in a series of *Rambler* papers. The whole of *Rasselas* is really more than this: the parts merge together, they work accumulatively, to form a whole larger and more interesting than the parts themselves.

II

If we want a wider setting, outside the context of Johnson's own life and writings, we have only to consider the time when he started writing *Rasselas.* This seems to have been January 1759.[15] In exactly the same month another writer was starting on *his* novel: one who at first glance has very little to do with Johnson. This was Laurence Sterne, who was just embarking on *Tristram Shandy.*[16] Sterne's novel would also seem to have little in common with *Rasselas.* The differences need hardly be dwelt on, they are sufficiently striking. But is it true that they have nothing whatever in common? *Rasselas* is often described as a philosophical romance; and Miss Lascelles has adopted a term used by Gibbon: 'philosophical fiction'. (Critics of **Rasselas** have tended to stress the philosophy at the expense of the fiction.) But *Tristram Shandy* might also—without unduly stretching the term—be described as philosophical fiction. It is not exactly a straight novel in the course of narrating incidents in the lives of Mr. Shandy, Uncle Toby, and the rest, it raises large questions about time and the self, as well as some especially radical questions about literary form. This point has been well put in a recent essay on Sterne by Mr. Christopher Ricks. He notices that one of the questions that initially perplexed Sterne was, Where to begin? And he remarks: 'The innovation and the value of *Tristram Shandy . . .* are that it reminds us of what novelists are tempted to let us forget. That there is no such thing as a beginning, middle, and end.'[17] Now **Rasselas** has also been thought formless: 'There is little or no story, no crisis, no conclusion', says Nichol Smith—he might almost be talking about *Tristram Shandy*. And its inconclusiveness is something that Johnson pointedly draws our attention to: the last chapter is 'A Conclusion in which Nothing is Concluded'. His intention here has been variously interpreted, and I shall return to it later. But apart from their apparent formlessness, what else have the two books in common? It can be said of Sterne and Johnson that they both have a subversive attitude to certain kinds of theory and certain kinds of form. Both are hostile to certain kinds of philosophical system, to ready-made formulas of all kinds; both in their different ways are enemies of the rigid, the prescriptive, the thoughtlessly mechanical or theoretical: mere custom, mere cant. Johnson's remark in his **Preface to Shakespeare,** 'there is always an appeal open from criticism to nature' might, suitably adapted, have been made by Sterne. And Johnson's attack on Soame Jenyns's callow cosmic optimism shows another aspect of what is the same general policy. In *Tristram Shandy* much of the comedy arises of course from a collision between theory and practice: Mr. Shandy, we are told, is 'the most philosophical man who ever lived'; he is the slave of theory, he plans his life minutely, he tries to apply his learning to daily domestic experience and is always thwarted by Nature, by the irrepressibly unexpected, by what happens to happen. Rasselas is a youthful example of the same philosophical or theoretical tendency. He wants to make the right *'choice of life'*. (And Johnson usually prints the phrase *'choice of life'* in italics, as if to bring out its ludicrously theoretical nature. As is well known, he originally planned to call his story *The Choice of Life*.) Rasselas wants to make the *'choice of life'* that will bring him perfect happiness; he wants to choose his life in the same way as one chooses a pair of shoes: something that will fit properly and give perfect satisfaction. He is like Mr. Walter Shandy in that he desires something unattainable: a perfectly regulated life. This is brought out by, for example, the finely comic debate on marriage (chs. xxviii-xxix). Rasselas hopes to choose

the perfect wife, he wants to be *certain* in his choice of a marriage partner. He is fully aware of the dangers of choosing hastily but, he says: 'Surely all these evils may be avoided by that deliberation and delay which prudence prescribes to irrevocable choice.' Nekayah remonstrates with him on the insurmountable difficulties, but still he persists: 'Whenever I shall seek a wife, it shall be my first question, whether she be willing to be led by reason.' Nekayah's next reply has a convincing resonance:

> 'Thus it is', said Nekayah, 'that philosophers are deceived. There are a thousand familiar disputes which reason never can decide; questions that elude investigation, and make logic ridiculous; cases where something must be done, and where little can be said. Consider the state of mankind, and inquire how few can be supposed to act upon any occasions, whether small or great, with all the reasons of action present to their minds. Wretched would be the pair above all names of wretchedness, who should be doomed to adjust by reason, every morning, all the minute detail of a domestic day. (p. 106)

Everything Nekayah says here could be applied, with little modification, to Mr. Walter Shandy who does the same: 'adjust by reason . . . all the minute detail of a domestic day'.

One should not, of course, exaggerate the similarities between Johnson and Sterne. It is true that Johnson had very different allegiances from Sterne both as a moralist and as a critic. But the books they both wrote testify to a similar impatience with closed systems, whether in philosophy or in literature. In literary matters both question the validity of the concept of form in terms of beginning, middle, and end. Johnson's defence of tragi-comedy (in his **Preface to Shakespeare**) is perhaps relevant here: he favoured a form more inclusive than either tragedy or comedy. And similarly, his fondness for biography seems also to indicate a preference for the all-inclusive, for something approaching the amorphous all-inclusiveness of life itself. He preferred truth to fiction, for the imaginative mode was perhaps felt to be constraining to the mind compared with the liberating wide spaces of actuality. Like Sterne to some extent, Johnson—or one side of him—felt that theory could never catch up with practice; closed systems of thought would eventually be burst from within; the prescriptive critic will inevitably lag behind the innovating artist.

Part of the tension of Johnson's thought comes from two opposed impulses in him. He was at once a dogmatist and a sceptic. He loved to generalize, but he also saw the futility of generalization. A reading of Johnson will make one aware not only of the uniformity of life but of its endless diversity, all that part of it which resists generalization. His **Rambler** 184 gives strong statement to this aspect of his thinking. In the course of this essay he turns to the reader: 'Let him that peruses this paper review the series of his life, and inquire how he was placed in his present condition. He will find that, of the good and ill which he has experienced, a great part came unexpected, without any visible gradations of approach; that every event has been influenced by causes acting without his intervention; and that, whenever he pretended to the prerogative of foresight, he was mortified with conviction of the shortness of his views.' He goes on: 'No course of life is so prescribed and limited, but that many actions must result from arbitrary election . . . it is necessary to act, but impossible to know the consequences of action, or to discuss all the reasons which offer themselves on every part to inquisitiveness and solicitude.' He concludes: 'Since life itself is uncertain, nothing which has life for its basis can boast much stability.'

Such remarks as these show where Johnson's thought comes closest to Sterne's in an intense awareness of arbitrariness, ignorance, uncertainty, flux. 'Our minds, like our bodies', says Imlac, 'are in continual flux; something is hourly lost, and something acquired.' (p. 121.) And in *Rasselas* our attention is repeatedly drawn to the passage of time,[18] it flows ceaselessly, like the Nile. If we give due weight to this side of Johnson's mind—his concern with that part of life which eludes prescription and planning, his concern with the unforeseeable and unrepeatable movement of things—then we will hardly expect to find in *Rasselas* a simple definitive moral of the kind which Professor Kolb and others offer us. For although there are scores of generalizations about life in *Rasselas,* it seems unwise to assume that we have in any one of them Johnson's considered philosophy—and this applies even to Imlac's often quoted (surely too often quoted) 'Human life is every where a state in which much is to be endured, and little to be enjoyed'.

It has often been said that the four travellers in *Rasselas* all speak with Johnson's voice. It needs to be said just as often that none of them speaks with his voice: they are all partial, including Imlac. Indeed, when Johnson himself speaks with his own voice in a very obvious sense, as in the essays or in conversation, even in his most generalized and dogmatic utterances, he must know that he is being partial since nothing worth saying can possibly embrace the whole truth. Hence, Imlac's observation: 'Inconsistencies cannot both be right, but, imputed to man, they may both be true' (p. 56). At one point in the debate on marriage Rasselas accuses his sister of inconsistency. Her reply has an emphasis and a depth of reflectiveness that should be taken into account if we are to do justice to Johnson's full meaning in *Rasselas:*

'I did not expect', answered the princess, 'to hear that imputed to falsehood which is the consequence only of frailty. To the mind, as to the eye, it is

difficult to compare with exactness objects vast in their extent, and various in their parts. Where we see or conceive the whole at once, we readily note the discriminations, and decide the preference; but of two systems, of which neither can be surveyed by any human being in its full compass of magnitude and multiplicity of complication, where is the wonder, that, judging of the whole by parts, I am alternately affected by one and the other, as either presses on my memory or fancy? We differ from ourselves, just as we differ from each other, when we see only part of the question, as in the multifarious relations of politics and morality; but when we perceive the whole at once, as in numerical computations, all agree in one judgment, and none ever varies his opinion.' (p. 103)

Two phrases here seem particularly striking: 'in its full compass of magnitude and multiplicity of complication', and 'the multifarious relations of politics and morality'. Both phrases indicate Johnson's considered awareness of an almost bewildering heterogeneity in the varied scenes of human life; just as Nekayah's speech as a whole argues for an undogmatic position with regard to questions of politics and morality because no one can know enough.

This sense of life's multifariousness is of prime importance in *Rasselas* for it not only gives the book its subject; in large part it determines the structure. The book is organized in such a way as to show life in its 'multiplicity of complication' and 'multifarious relations' resisting and defeating the narrow theories which men (in this case the young travellers) mistakenly desire to impose on it. The structure of *Rasselas* must now be considered.

III

In their analyses of *Rasselas* Professor Kolb and Mr. Whitley divide it into two parts: (1) in the Happy Valley; (2) in the World. In Mr. Whitley's scheme the division between the two parts occurs after chapter xiv. But this division into two unequal parts does not, I think, bring out the real shape—indeed the shapeliness—of the book. If we disregard for the moment the final chapter, *Rasselas* can be said to fall into three movements; each of these movements has an equal number of chapters, namely sixteen.[19] The first sixteen chapters set the scene in the Happy Valley and state the main subject: Rasselas's wish to make the *'choice of life'*. The sixteenth chapter shows the four travellers arrived in Cairo and ends with the prince's emphatic declaration: 'I have here the world before me,[20] I will review it at leisure: surely happiness is somewhere to be found.' And the next chapter opens: 'Rasselas rose next day, and resolved to begin his experiments upon life.' We have here a clear indication that the narrative is entering on a new phase. This second, or middle, phase also occupies sixteen chapters. In it the travellers survey mankind: they investigate different walks of life (hedonists, stoics, hermits, shepherds, etc.); they discuss public and private life; and the movement ends with the visit to the Pyramids which itself culminates in Imlac's sombre apostrophe:

> Whoever thou art that, not content with a moderate condition, imaginest happiness in royal magnificence, and dreamest that command or riches can feed the appetite of novelty with perpetual gratifications, survey the Pyramids, and confess thy folly! (p. 114)

This sonorous utterance brings the second movement of **Rasselas** to a close. At the beginning of the next chapter (ch. xxxiii) the narrative takes a new turn: the chapter itself is entitled 'The Princess Meets with an Unexpected Misfortune'. The misfortune is, of course, the abduction of Pekuah. As a result of this sudden emergency the quest for the *'choice of life'* is tacitly abandoned, and this last phase or movement of the book (the sixteen chapters from xxxiii to xlviii) is occupied with, on the face of it, a haphazard series of happenings: Nekayah's grief, Pekuah's return and her account of her adventures, the meeting with the mad astronomer, and his recovery to sanity, the brief meeting with the old man, and finally the visit to the Catacombs.

If **Rasselas** is considered with this tripartite arrangement in mind, it will be seen to be far from formless: on the contrary it can be said to have a regular and significant design. The first movement shows us Rasselas, driven by a restless impulse he hardly understands, determining to make the *'choice of life'*. He witnesses the artist's abortive attempt to fly, meets Imlac and hears his life story, and, finally, accompanied by Imlac, Nekayah, and Pekuah, escapes to the outside world. The second movement is given to the 'experiments upon life' which Rasselas carries out; and he discovers that no actual case will fit his theory—no one can be said to possess perfect happiness. The third movement, from Pekuah's abduction to the visit to the Catacombs, shows the travellers living fully in the world, no longer at leisure to contemplate the spectacle of life, but buffeted by circumstances, and themselves becoming actively involved with other men. Seen in this way, the whole narrative exhibits the breakdown of untested theory in the face of actual experience. Rasselas loses his insularity, his state of innocent isolation from ordinary living; he becomes fruitfully involved in life—but it is a life which refuses to be planned and which can no longer be called a series of 'experiments'.

That this scheme was deliberately planned by Johnson may be borne out by the following suggestion. The first two movements in this three-movement structure stand in marked opposition to each other. There is a good deal of local complication in each, but this does not obscure the general design of the two movements. Their relationship is like that of the two parts of an antithesis: the Happy Valley and Lower Egypt, innocence and experience, hope and disappointment, idealistic theory and frustrating particularity. This antithetical relation between the two parts—that between a largely misplaced hope and an apparently definitive disappointment ('expectation and disgust'[21])—may be seen as a structural parallel to that favourite figure of eighteenth-century rhetoric, the antithetical epigram. This figure, amusing in its succinctness and apparently conclusive in its wisdom, occurs perhaps more frequently in **Rasselas** than in any other of Johnson's writings. The way we take these epigrams may help to determine how we interpret the antithetical structure of the narrative in these first two movements of **Rasselas**. These epigrams (e.g. 'Marriage has many pains, but celibacy has no pleasures') are often, perhaps usually, taken 'straight', as if they were Johnson's weighty conclusions on life. They should surely be more guardedly interpreted, enjoyed as wit rather than prized as nuggets of explicit wisdom. For Johnson often uses them in such a way that one is made to see, even while enjoying them, how comically insufficient to the true purposes of life such rhetorical devices really are. If they seem, often, to lead us into a baffling cul-de-sac, this is their precise intention; they lead us there because we follow too innocently the false premiss upon which they are based and which they are designed to undermine. This can be illustrated from one of the most amusing of the episodes: the debate on marriage.

Rasselas has taken as his theme the unhappiness that arises from early marriages:

> From those early marriages proceeds likewise the rivalry of parents and children. The son is eager to enjoy the world before the father is willing to forsake it, and there is hardly room at once for two generations. The daughter begins to bloom before the mother can be content to fade, and neither can forbear to wish for the absence of the other. (p. 105)

A little later in this conversation Nekayah concludes: 'I believe it will be found, that those who marry late are best pleased with their children, and those who marry early, with their partners.' 'The union of these two affections' (answers Rasselas soberly) 'would produce all that could be wished. Perhaps there is a time when marriage might unite them, a time neither too early for the father, nor too late for the husband.'[22] This neat antithesis comes as the climax of a systematic categorization; it proclaims the mastery of reason and theory over the obstreperousness of existence. Rasselas's sentiments may seem grave and admirable, but they have one flaw: the abstract 'time' he speaks of does not exist—or does not exist in dissociation from the particular 'husband' or 'father', or rather the particular *man,* who must 'make the happiness he does not find'. The premises on which the young travellers argue are exquisitely innocent, and false; and the very form of the limiting, stylishly neat antithesis declares its own insufficiency. In short, Johnson can use the antithetical epigram much as Swift uses his ironical formulas (although with far more sympathy towards his characters than Swift ever shows), as a way of arousing the reader to detached reflection and self-criticism.

It is necessary to bear this in mind when we return to the structural antithesis formed by the first two movements of *Rasselas.* Our first impulse should not be, I think, to take as a simple statement this large antithesis of hope and disappointment and argue whether or not it suggests pessimism in Johnson. We should rather see in it the underlying structural device: the posited closed system of false hope and false disappointment which is to be broken down. This process of breaking down is to be shown in the important third movement of the book (chs. xxxiii-xlviii).

The third movement, announced by the title of chapter xxxiii ('The Princess Meets with an Unexpected Misfortune'), opens with a marked change of *tempo* and incorporates a new kind of material. Imlac's calm and gravely detached oration on the Pyramids (his theme, 'that hunger of imagination which preys incessantly upon life') is rapidly succeeded—indeed almost interrupted—by a scene of tumultuous activity.

> What had happened they did not try to conjecture, but immediately inquired. 'You had scarcely entered into the Pyramid,' said one of the attendants, 'when a troop of Arabs rushed upon us . . . ' (p. 114)

There follows the first of the two extended episodes which give the third movement its character and meaning. In this first episode, Pekuah's abduction, the travellers become for the first time the passive ones, feeling the full weight of the unplannable and unlooked-for in human life. They had expected the world—other people—to lie passive before their inspection; instead, their philosophical reflections are cut short, and they emerge from the Pyramid to find themselves the victims of others. The member of the party who is lost and must be ransomed back seems to be the least important; yet it is she, Pekuah, who provides a link, albeit a tenuous one, with the next episode: she plays a prominent part in leading the astronomer back to sanity. Indeed, Rasselas himself plays a comparatively subordinate role in this third movement. The curing of the astronomer constitutes the second extended episode of this last movement; and it is given a peculiar emphasis. (The episode fills five chapters; one may suspect that, as well as stressing its importance, Johnson

perhaps had an eye to the number of chapters he was required by his scheme to supply. Chapter xli, for example, is exceptionally brief and its two paragraphs seem to gain little by being detached from what follows.) In the context of *Rasselas* as a whole, the astronomer, virtuous and learned as he is, illustrates in an extreme and disturbing form the tendency of the young travellers to impose theories upon life.[23] He has moved beyond the understandable desire to regulate one's own life into the further reaches of delusion: he is burdened with the god-like task of regulating the weather. The travellers are moved by his case, and actively help him in a simple and humane way; they win him back to sanity by offering him their friendship and admitting him to their society. So for the second time in this third movement of the book the actual number of the party of travellers has changed: they were first reduced to three by the loss of Pekuah, and now, after her return, have gained a fifth member, the astronomer. Both incidents show the travellers engaged in some real give and take with life, some natural reciprocity. By means of these two extended episodes the baffling cul-de-sac formed by the first two movements yields to a more promising way forward.

The last chapter stands outside the tripartite scheme, and Johnson's purpose in it has often been debated. Its witty title, 'A Conclusion in which Nothing is Concluded', contains a multiple word-play that suggests the theme of the whole work. It is an ending in which the *'choice of life'* is not decided, a decision that nothing can end here, a decision that nothing can be simply decided, and an ending that acknowledges the seeming endlessness of things. Moreover, the chapter makes a further point that concerns the artistic structure of the book. From a conventional point of view the book, with its trailing coda, has now become structurally defective. But at a second glance one sees originality and aesthetic purpose in this new asymmetrical design in which the neat tripartite form is given a brief extension that at once fractures and fulfils it. The book therefore contrives to be both a closed and an open system; the demands of literary form and the demands of life are both met.

Johnson's intentions here in the last chapter, and indeed in the book as a whole, may be elucidated by a Shakespearian analogy. Shakespeare's comedy *Love's Labour's Lost* also ends with an ending which is no conclusion. The philosophical young men do not win their ladies, but are made to do penance for a year and a day, at the end of which period they may try again. Their unnatural vows, their artificial behaviour, and their clever wit are rebuked by the supremely natural, indeed banally unavoidable fact of death—the death of the princess's father, the King of France. And so the play's ending is also a 'Conclusion in which Nothing is Concluded':

Berowne: Our wooing doth not end like an
old play:

Jack hath not Jill. These ladies'
courtesy

Might well have made our sport a
comedy.

King: Come, sir, it wants a twelvemonth
and a day,

And then 'twill end.

Berowne: That's too long for
a play.

(v. ii. 862-4)

Rasselas, like Shakespeare's comedy, is about 'labour
lost': 'Of these wishes that they had formed they
well knew that none could be obtained' (p. 158).
Both Shakespeare's comedy and Johnson's tale are concerned with wisdom and folly; their leading characters
are 'wise' or clever fools. And both have a similar
structural feature, the inconclusive conclusion. Shakespeare's characters take their leave with a curiously
effective realism: 'You that way: we this way', and
Johnson's simple resolve, for all their plans, to return
to the place where they began. This last feature—the
inconclusive conclusion—may in both cases be interpreted as Nature making a *critique* on Art. Nature
exposes the insufficiency of Art by calling in question
the very form of the work of art itself—by suggesting
that an ending is not possible because there are no
endings in nature. The flow of life cannot be checked;
life refuses to be contained within a neat literary form.
In **Rasselas** Johnson has created a form in which this
perception can be artistically conveyed in his own terms
and for his own age. To have done so is evidence of
an artistic power with which he has been too little
credited.

Notes

[1] Walter Raleigh, *Six Essays on Johnson* (Oxford,
1910), p. 33.

[2] Ed. G. B. Hill, revised L. F. Powell (Oxford, 1934),
i. 341-2.

[3] [Nicole Smith,] *Cambridge History of English Literature,* x (1913), 179.

[4] J. W. Krutch, *Samuel Johnson* (New York, 1944), p.
163.

[5] Ch. xi, p. 67. Quotations are taken from *Rasselas,* ed.
G. B. Hill (Oxford, 1887).

[6] [Alvin Whitley,] *E.L.H.,* xxiii (1956), 48-70.

[7] Cf. the remarks on Johnson's 'dramatic' procedure in

Rasselas in W. J. Bate's *The Achievement of Samuel
Johnson* (New York, 1955), pp. 90-91.

[8] Loc. cit., p. 179 [Nicole Smith].

[9] 'Johnson and Augustanism' in *The Common Pursuit*
(London, 1952), p. 115.

[10] [Mary Lascelles,] 'Rasselas Reconsidered' in *Essays
and Studies* (1951), p. 51.

[11] *P.M.L.A.,* lxvi (1951), 698-717.

[12] Loc. cit., p. 49 [Alvin Whitley].

[13] In '"The Fourth Son of the Mighty Emperor": The
Ethiopian Background of Johnson's *Rasselas*',
P.M.L.A., lxxviii (1963), 516-28, D. M. Lockhart
establishes that Johnson's Ethiopian research for
Rasselas was probably completed at least seven
years before he wrote *Rasselas.* It may thus be con-
jectured that Johnson had conceived the idea of the
book long before the occasion of its writing and publication.

[14] Loc. cit., pp. 44-45 [Mary Lascelles].

[15] See *Rasselas,* ed. R. W. Chapman (Oxford, 1927), p.
xv.

[16] See W. L. Cross, *The Life and Times of Laurence
Sterne* (New Haven, 1929), p. 189.

[17] *The Listener,* 11 Feb. 1965; reprinted in *The Novelist as Innovator* (London, 1965).

[18] Cf. Geoffrey Tillotson, 'Time in Rasselas', in *Augustan Studies* (London, 1961).

[19] This scheme would perhaps have been obscured on
the book's first publication by its division into two
volumes, the first volume ending with chapter xxv.

[20] The echo of the ending of *Paradise Lost* is unmistakable: 'The World was all before them, where to
choose'.

[21] Ch. xlix, p. 157.

[22] p. 107.

[23] In the astronomer himself Johnson uses the traditional opposition between astronomy, or star-knowledge,
and self-knowledge; astronomy was traditionally cited
as an example of knowledge remote from use, as opposed to the supremely useful study of ethics. Cf. John
Hardy, 'Johnson and Raphael's Counsel to Adam' in
*Johnson, Boswell, and their Circle: Essays presented
to L. F. Powell* (Oxford, 1965), pp. 122-36.

Arthur J. Weitzman (essay date 1969)

SOURCE: "More Light on *Rasselas:* The Background of the Egyptian Episodes," in *Philological Quarterly,* Vol. XLVIII, No. 1, January, 1969, pp. 42-58.

[*In the following essay, Weitzman identifies sources Johnson probably used for the Egyptian settings in* Rasselas, *arguing that the sources reflect Johnson's intent in incorporating Cairo, the pyramids, and other Eastern elements into his story. The critic adds that sources further support the hypothesis that Johnson did not simply compose* Rasselas *in seven days without any prior preparation, as is often claimed.*]

Recent scholarly investigations of Johnson's **Rasselas** have tended to focus on the Abyssinian setting of the tale to the neglect of the second half of the book, the Egyptian setting. In the past two decades numerous articles[1] have appeared detailing the sources which Johnson either consulted for the Abyssinian portion of the tale or recollected from memory in the week Boswell claimed[2] Johnson wrote **Rasselas.** In a recent study Donald Lockhart made an exhaustive survey of the accounts of Ethiopia which Johnson conceivably may have consulted in order to describe the Happy Valley. Lockhart's very close examination of all pre-1759 descriptive works and histories of Ethiopia led him to the conclusion that Johnson's sources were so numerous and so accurately utilized as to invalidate Boswell's implication that Johnson wrote **Rasselas** in the space of a week without prior preparation. From the evidence he uncovered Lockhart contends that Johnson's research for the Ethiopian background of **Rasselas** "must have been in progress and may even have been completed before 29 February 1752."[3] More support for the theory of Johnson's gradually developing interest in writing such a book may be adduced by an examination of the Egyptian background of the story.

As Professor Gwin Kolb has pointed out in his study of "The Structure of **Rasselas,**"[4] the tale falls into two parts. In the first Johnson depicts an Edenic world of pleasure, free from sordid cares, where the princely hero has no other responsibility but to please himself. As he matures, the prince discovers that "pleasure has ceased to please," and guided by Imlac he escapes from the Happy Valley for the greater experience of the outside world, which in the book is represented by Cairo in Egypt. In contrast to the first world of pleasure, innocence, simplicity and retirement in Abyssinia, the second world of Cairo is a modern metropolis of jostling crowds composed of different races; a city dedicated to trade, with its corrupt officials and gay ostentation of wealth—a very different way of life from that to which the prince had beenaccustomed. In accordance with the design of the tale, Cairo and Egypt were not meant to represent a romantic setting, even though Europeans had long regarded the Near East in a romantic light. Rasselas' excursion into Egypt is a journey into the variety and confusion characteristic of an urban world.

Yet the question may be raised, why choose Cairo and Egypt?[5] To put the question in another form, what did Johnson know about Egypt of his time that he should have picked it as a setting for Rasselas to pursue his education? Johnson had never been to the East; whatever, therefore, he describes or asserts of Egypt he must have picked up in books. It will not do to say—as I shall presently show—that his knowledge of Egypt is commonplace even for the eighteenth century. True, the settings of **Rasselas** are not its paramount feature, but Johnson has given enough suggestions and references for us to recognize the landmarks of Egypt. Almost all of these references are quite accurate and show that Johnson must have read widely in European travel and geography books dealing with Egypt and the Near East, besides what he may have read of ancient Egypt by Greek and Roman historians. That he knew of contemporary travel books is evinced by Pekuah's remark about European travelers to the Nile. She says to her Arab captor that she "expected to see mermaids and tritons . . . stationed in the Nile" (II, 87-88),[6] which Imlac had told her were reported by European travelers. For this fabulous report of tritons and mermaids Lockhart has shown that Johnson was referring to a specific work on Ethiopia.[7] It is also likely that Johnson consulted travel accounts of Cairo, Egypt, the pyramids at Gizeh, the catacombs at Saccara and the customs of the Moslem inhabitants.

One of the most important sources drawn upon for the Egyptian adventure in **Rasselas** is Aaron Hill's *A Full and Just Account of the Present State of the Ottoman Empire* (London, 1709). A youthful work, *The Present State of the Ottoman Empire* was Hill's recollection of his travels in the Middle East during the years 1700-1703. While we have no external evidence that Johnson read Hill's travel book, it is certainly possible that Johnson had access to *The Present State of the Ottoman Empire,* which enjoyed a second edition in 1710. That Johnson knew of Hill and may even have been personally acquainted with him is attested by the warm and intimate way he refers to this traveler and poet in the life of Savage.[8] Savage, who had submitted a play to Hill for correction, had been his friend and may have introduced the elder poet to Johnson before or during 1738, the year Hill retired to Essex, where he lived until his death in 1750. Moreover, one of the subscribers to Hill's *Collected Works,* which appeared in 1753, was one "Samuel Johnson, Esq." Could this have been the future Dr. Johnson? While Hill's *Collected Works* do not contain his early travel book, it is not inconceivable that Johnson may have been sufficiently interested in Hill to have taken the trouble to read one of his earliest published works.[9]

The evidence that Johnson drew upon Hill's *Present State* lies in the striking similarity between Hill's adventure in the catacombs and Pekuah's abduction by the Arab rover. Hill's remarkably similar experience occurred when he descended into the catacombs of Saccara, visited also by Rasselas' party. Hill describes vividly his descent with a servant into the caverns where the mummies were located.[10] Once inside he discovered the bodies of two Europeans, who had died from lack of water and food, imprisoned by Arabs who had blocked the entrance. Hill immediately realized his danger and tried to get above ground again but found the entrance blocked by a large rock. Looking for another exit, Hill encountered six Arab assailants hiding in the caverns ready to pounce on him and his servant. He drew his pistol and fired upon them, whereupon they fled through a secret narrow passage to the open daylight. Hot in pursuit Hill gained the upper air and saw the Arab gang of horsemen plundering what they could of his goods. They were interrupted, however, by an approaching squad of Janissaries, who immediately gave chase to the now-fleeing Arabs. Finding the Turks too close for comfort, the Arabs released the mules they had stolen from Hill's campsite and made good their escape. In a few minutes the Janissaries returned to the catacomb entrance and calmed Hill by their presence. With the help of the new guard he returned to the caverns in search of his Moslem servant, who had hidden among the mummies in fear of his life. The episode ends on an amusing note when Hill discovers his servant, who in excessive gratitude hugs and kisses his master, much to Hill's annoyance. Added to this account of his escape is an etched plate in the book, showing the sequence of events described. The inside of the catacomb is displayed with the dead Europeans and Hill firing his pistol at the Arabs. Above ground the picture reveals the Arabs fleeing and the Janissaries coming to the rescue in the distance.

The similarity of Hill's adventure to Pekuah's abduction is noteworthy. In both accounts a band of Arab horsemen has taken sightseers unaware and attempted to carry off anything of value. Just as the Arabs were about to escape with the travelers' goods, a troop of Janissaries appeared and chased unsuccessfully the Arab band. In Johnson's account the Arabs were able to carry off Pekuah and her maids but nothing else. Hill's mules were for the moment stolen, but the Arabs had to free them to escape from their swift pursuers; Hill therefore lost no equipment. Immediately afterwards the Janissaries returned to the campsite of both parties, their lack of success apparent.

These similarities, moreover, do not exhaust Johnson's probable indebtedness to Hill's and other European travel accounts. Pekuah's abduction takes place at the pyramids, presumably the most famous grouping at Gizeh, a short distance from Cairo. Since the prince's journey is described as a day's jaunt, Johnson probably had them visit the three most important pyramids of Egypt: Cheops, Chephren and Mycerinus, all first described in Herodotus' account of Egyptian history,[11] the most ancient of Western commentaries on these monuments. While Herodotus' speculations on the history of the pyramids are seminal historical evidence for succeeding writers, ancient historians and geographers besides Herodotus had visited and described this wonder of the ancient world. The most important of the ancient commentators on the pyramids were Strabo, Diodorus Siculus and Pliny the Younger.[12] Of these Johnson had in his library editions of Strabo and Pliny.[13] Johnson was acquainted with at least some of the accounts of these historians, for Imlac says of the pyramids that they are "fabrics raised before the time of history, and of which the earliest narratives afford us only uncertain traditions" (II, 37-38). Hieroglyphics not having been deciphered in Johnson's time, he can only have referred to the classical histories.

Johnson must have also read contemporary European discriptions of the pyramids, since he has his characters explore the inside of the Great Pyramid of Cheops. None of the historians and geographers of antiquity mentioned above ever described the passageways and chambers of the pyramids of which Johnson writes so knowingly. The depiction of the inside of Cheops, brief as it is in *Rasselas,* is too exact to have been imagined. Among travel books describing the pyramids both inside and outside, the most readily available accounts were those of Hill (already cited), Richard Pococke's *A Description of the East,* 2 vols. (London, 1743-45), John Greaves's *Pyramidographia* in *The Miscellaneous Works of John Greaves,* 2 vols. (London, 1737), and Thomas Shaw's *Travel Observations Relating to Several Parts of Barbary and the Levant* (Oxford, 1738); the latter two books were in Johnson's library.[14] According to Boswell, Johnson knew Pococke's travel account, for in a reported conversation[15] Johnson judged it inferior to some other contemporary travels. Other travel books dealing with Egypt which Johnson may have been acquainted with are Charles Perry's *A View of the Levant* (London, 1743) and perhaps Fredrick L. Norden's *Travels in Egypt and Nubia,* 2 vols. (London, 1757). Johnson, however, seems to have relied mainly on Hill, Greaves and Pococke for his description of the inside of the pyramid.

Only one short paragraph of *Rasselas* is devoted to description of the interior explorations of the pyramid.

> Pekuah descended to the tents, and the rest entered the pyramid: they passed through galleries, surveyed the vaults of marble, and examined the chest in which the body of the founder is supposed to have been reposited. They then sat down in one of the most spacious chambers to rest a while before they attempted to return. (II, 44)

All of these elements with a great many more details were mentioned by both Hill and Greaves, both of whom believed they were the first Europeans to describe the interior of the Cheops Pyramid. Actually Greaves came first. The result of his investigation was *Pyramidographia* (1646), a learned treatise on the pyramids, which remained the fullest and most exact until the archeological expeditions of the nineteenth century.

Most of what Johnson said of the interior of the pyramid can be fully documented in Greaves's explorations. The galleries or passageways mentioned by Johnson were described in detail by Greaves. Of one of them the explorer says, "This gallery or corridor, or whatsoever else I may call it, is built of white and polished marble, the which is very evenly cut in spacious squares or tables.[16] He investigated what he called "a little chamber," one of which Johnson may have included in his general descriptive term of "vaults of marble."

> This rich and spacious chamber, in which art may seem to have contended with nature, the curious work being not inferior to the rich materials, stands as it were in the heart and center of the Pyramid . . . The floor, the sides, the roof of it, are all made of vast and exquisite tables of *Thebaick* marble. (I, 125)

Greaves explored and reported on the other chambers of the pyramid, which like the little chamber were sheathed in marble.

Johnson was quite aware that the pyramid did not contain the body of its illustrious founder Cheops. Rasselas and his party examined a "chest in which the body of the founder is supposed to have been reposited." The empty "chest" to which Johnson refers was probably the sarcophagus described by Greaves: a hollow sepulcher made of marble in which he believed once lay the king who commanded the construction of the burial monument. The explorer called the sarcophagus "the monument of Cheops or Chemmis" (I, 127), and described the inside: "a narrow space, yet large enough to contain a most potent and dreadful monarch being dead" (I, 131). Johnson's debt to Greaves and others may perhaps go even deeper. Imlac's speculation that the pyramids are "monument[s] of the insufficiency of human enjoyments," built "to amuse the tediousness of declining life" echoes Greaves's paraphrase of Pliny's comment on the pyramids: "he [Pliny] judges them *to be an idle, and vaine ostentation of the wealth of Kings*" (I, iii). Johnson may have of course recalled Pliny's judgment in the original. Since Imlac's opinion is not very far from Pliny's, perhaps the ancient historian ought to be quoted in full:

Regum pecuniae otiosa ac stulta ostentatio quippe cum faciendi eas causa a plerisque tradatur, ne pecuniam successoribus aut aemulis insidiantibus praeberent aut ne plebs esset otiosa.Multa circa hoc vanitas hominum illorum fuit. (XXXVI.16)

Johnson's belief that the pyramids were built from vanity is also adumbrated in Hill's observation that the pyramids "have so long amus'd the World, with strange Reflections on the strong *Ambition,* and vainglorious *Aim* of their aspiring *Founders*" (p. 245).

Like Greaves, Hill measured the pyramids, as did most travelers who visited the monuments. It may be recalled that Mr. Spectator as reported in Addison's first number of *The Spectator* had also measured the pyramids in his travels in the East. It is not very suprising therefore that Rasselas' party "measured all its [the pyramid's] dimensions" (II, 40); that was the tourist's traditional act. Hill's description of the inside of the Cheops Pyramid, while not quite so thorough as Greaves's, certainly could have provided Johnson with all the necessary details that are in **Rasselas.** Hill also observed the galleries and chambers, the white marble walls and the marble sarcophagus which Rasselas examined. Furthermore, Pekuah's refusal to enter the pyramid for fear of ghosts and "the dreadful gloom" can be well understood in the light of Hill's exploration of the inside of the edifice. When Hill visited Egypt—as was true in the time of Greaves's examination—the pyramids were not open to casual tourists; for, as Hill explains, the Egyptian natives were fearful that if the pyramids, which kept within them the plague, were thrown open, the contagion would spread throughout the land. However, the reigning bassa (or pasha) disdaining this superstition, determined to explore the inside of the Great Pyramid, and he allowed Hill to accompany him and his servants through the galleries and chambers. Once inside Hill was struck by the foul and musty air, the numerous bats and general gloom of the corridors, which were difficult to light with torches (p. 250). Pekuah's fear is therefore not altogether the product of a morbid imagination. Nekayah's preparation for her favorite of "a long narrative of dark labyrinths" is well documented in both Greaves's and Hill's accounts of the inside of the largest pyramid.

While neither Greaves nor Hill used the word "chest" in connection with the sarcophagus, Richard Pococke's *Description of the East* may have provided Johnson with the term. For his description of the interior of the Great Pyramid, Pococke relied upon the account of a French explorer named Benoit Maillet, who published his *Description de l'Egypte* in 1735, of which portions were translated and inserted into Pococke's travel book. Pococke translated Maillet's description of the sarcophagus in these words:

> This chest, no doubt, contain'd the body of the King enclosed in three or four chests of fine wood, as

was usual among the great people: It is likewise probable, that this room contain'd several other chests besides that of the Prince, especially thosethat belong'd to the people, who were shut up with him in his tomb, to keep him company.[17]

The discovery of one word does not necessarily constitute a source, yet the evidence is strong that Johnson had read extensively in the contemporary books dealing with Egypt. Greaves's and Hill's accounts and perhaps even Pococke's volumes Johnson must have examined either leisurely or deliberately with an eye to writing Rasselas' trip to the pyramids.

The visit to the catacombs at Saccara, upon which episode the tale draws to a close, is probably based on Hill's adventure in the ancient burial caves. Judging that the prince has nothing more to learn of the living, Imlac suggests a visit to the catacombs, where Rasselas may contemplate the dead. Imlac calls these tombs "the wonders of this country . . . , or the ancient repositories, in which the bodies of the earliest generations were lodged, and where, by the virtue of the gums which embalmed them, they yet remain without corruption." (II, 151). Hill says of the catacombs: "The Old *Egyptians* were Embalm'd and Buried, and whose Black, horrid Wombs do yet contain a formidable Proof, how long our Humane Bodies may preserve their Substance, when defended by the help of *Art,* from the destructive Power of a *Natural* Corruption" (p. 264). Further echoes of Hill's description may perhaps be perceived in Johnson's depiction of the caves. Hill speaks of a "gloomy *Labyrinth* of Death and Horrour." Johnson: "the labyrinth of subterraneous passages, where bodies were laid in rows on either side" (II, 153). The bodies in Hill's description "on either side, lie rang'd in *measur'd* Order." The prince's question why the Egyptians preserved bodies did not seem to have occurred to Hill, for he made no inquiries into the matter, though he did distinguish the mummies according to their sumptuous adornments. The question, however, was long a subject of controversy, which Greaves attempted to answer by summoning the testimony of the ancient historians (I, 66-80). Imlac's supposition that "only the rich or honourable were secured from corruption" is justified by Greaves's paraphrase of Herodotus, that "when any man of quality of the family is dead" (I, 66) the body is then embalmed. In support of this thesis Greaves also quotes Diodorus Siculus, whom he translates: "The manner of their [Egyptian] burial is three-fold: the one is very costly, the second less, the third very mean" (I, 71).[18] Johnson, however, may have gone directly to the ancient commentaries for this information.

Another aspect of *Rasselas* for which Johnson was indebted to European travelers was Pekuah's adventure with the Arab Rover and the description of her abductor's "seraglio." Yet in one respect Johnson's depiction of the Arab and his household is clearly at variance with the available contemporary accounts of desert Arabs. And perhaps this episode is the only one in the tale in which Johnson took liberties with his setting, but for good reason. Pekuah's sojourn with the Arab in his island fortress was inserted primarily to give Johnson an opportunity to destroy the hedonistic and romantic notion of the voluptuous lives led by Moslem men, which had become a staple of Oriental fiction in the eighteenth century. European readers had been alternately shocked, titillated and amused by the numerous accounts both in travel books and fiction of Moslem marriage customs and the image of the Moslem as a man of enormous sexual appetites, of a jealous and passionate nature. Few European travelers to the Middle East refrained from inquiring into and describing in as much detail as they could (some of it perforce fanciful) women of the harems and their eunuch guards.[19] Many writers used this material for its sensational effect in their fiction, the most notable example being Montesquieu's *Persian Letters.* Johnson had relied upon this image of the Moslem earlier in his career when he wrote his only play **Irene** (performed 1749). But by 1759, either because of his maturity or the thematic demands of **Rasselas** or perhaps both, Johnson in the narrative of Pekuah's imprisonment impugned the popular conception of the rich Mussulman.

Johnson's treatment of life in the harem should be viewed as an antidote to the "Oriental" infection in storytelling which made the most of the exotic and erotic elements of Moslem marriage and concubinage. In accordance with his dictum that life is "a state in which much is to be endured, and little to be enjoyed" (I, 79), he shows the Arab sheik far from happy in Sybaritic bliss. Pekuah informs us that the Arab could not find friendship or society from "his seraglio" and that he often turned away from his women in disgust; his ladies could neither exalt nor amuse him with engaging conversation. Seeing in Pekuah a woman of intelligence and rank, the Arab delays her departure but finally gives her up when his vice of avarice overcomes his love for the lady. Johnson's characterization of the Arab and his situation diverges indeed from the romantic tales of high passion, extreme jealously and violent action in order to satisfy the power of lust. Unsatisfied with his harem, the Arab is made even more unhappy in his futile love for Pekuah; at her departure he appears "like a man delivered from the pain of an intestine conflict" (II, 97). Thus this episode affords Johnson the chance to destroy another illusion of happiness by his searching realism.

Johnson's picture of the Arab disaccords with what travelers had described of the desert Arabs or Bedouin tribesmen. Nothing in Hill's account of the Bedouin (pp. 325-27) or any other description of roving Arabs which I have examined provides an analogy to the fortress seraglio in Johnson's tale. The kind of seraglio Johnson used as a model for his description was the household of a rich Turk or bey, perhaps the Ottoman Sultan. The Arab Rover in *Rasselas* is characterized as "a man of more than common accomplishments,"who has a keen interest in astronomy and who knows "the rules of civil life"; he makes "professions of honour and sincerity" and shows a lively concern for Pekuah, in whom he recognizes a well-bred young woman. This is certainly not a description of a Bedouin chieftain, but rather a picture of an aristocratic Turk. The fortress with its apartments and many dependent women is more like a grand seigneur's harem than the tents of a roving shiek. Johnson has brought together two modes of life, the life of a robber whose ruling passion is greed and the life of a rich Moslem who is bored with his household of decorative women. By this economy of means the author impugns both modes of life showing how unsatisfactory both are.

Johnson had anticipated the tedium of life in a harem in his play *Irene.* Aspasia, prudent friend of the heroine, warns Irene against becoming the mistress to Mahomet, the Ottoman Sultan in the play. She freely expatiates on the boredom of her future life with the sultan.

> When soft security shall prompt the Sultan,
> Freed from the tumults of unsettled conquest,
> To fix his court, and regulate his pleasures,
> Soon shall the dire seraglio's horrid gates
> Close like th'eternal bars of death upon thee.
> Immur'd, and buried in perpetual sloth,
> That gloomy slumber of the stagnant soul,
> There shalt thou view from far the quiet
>   cottage,
> And sigh for cheerful poverty in vain;
> There wear the tedious hours of life away,
> Beneath each curse of unrelenting Heav'n,
> Despair and slav'ry, solitude and guilt.[20]

Although Aspasia's prediction is gloomier than Pekuah's report on the life of the Arab's ladies, both passages bear out the tedium, sloth and stagnation of a harem.

Johnson had read of harems in Alexander Russell's *The Natural History of Aleppo* (London, 1756), which he had reviewed in June, 1756 in the *Literary Magazine or Universal Review.*[21] Russell had reported that he had known opulent men in Aleppo (where Russell had spent thirteen years as a physician) to have as many as forty women in their harems. "It may be appear strange," Russell adds, "how such a number should agree tolerably well together; and in fact the master of the family hath very frequently enough to do to keep the peace among them."[22] Russell thought that because Moslem women are servile and a man can easily divorce them and sell his slaves, "it will appear not so

extraordinary that they live together in a tolerable degree of harmony." Johnson in his review of this book said, "Yet the author [Russell] has known 40 [women] kept by some of the wealthy. This multitude of rivals sometimes gives the master disturbance, but trained up in servile obedience, they commonly live well together."[23] While Pekuah's account of the Arab's women does not indicate any disturbance among them, a disposition toward competition may be seen when Pekuah is first introduced into the "seraglio"; but harmony is soon restored when the ladies realize that she is not a competitor for their master's favors. Whatever harmony there was in the Arab's household, the ladies' lives were far from enviable, as Pekuah makes quite clear.

Johnson's knowledge of harem life could have come from a variety of sources other than Russell's book. For *Irene* Johnson probably drew his material from Richard Knolles's *Generall Historie of the Turkes* (1603),[24] which Johnson evidently read with keen appreciation, judging from his praise of the historian in *Rambler* No. 122. Besides his *Pyramidographia* John Greaves wrote a book about the Ottoman Sultan's palace, *Description of the Grand Seignor's Seraglio* (1650), which was included in his two-volume collected works which Johnson had in his library. Relevant information about the seclusion of women may have been got from that detailed description. Aaron Hill devoted, in addition to so much other information about Moslem domestic life, a long passage to the particulars of the ladies' apartments in the sultan's seraglio (pp. 159-169). He even mentions their pastime making "Embroidery in various colours," (p. 162) a detail echoed in Pekuah's report that the ladies' only activity was needlework embroidering "silken flowers." Even more strikingly similar is Hill's sober view of the life of the sultan. After describing the manner of life in the harem, Hill says that such a life of pleasure (that is, for the sultan) might be thought to lead to happiness. But no, the sultan is made unhappy by "a thousand little Anxietys [which] torment and vex him" (p. 169) in the regulation of the women he maintains. The traveler then adds sententiously: "THUS can no Condition of our Life be fully happy, *Celibacy* has its Inconveniences, and so has *Matrimony;* we oft change sides like Men in *Fevers,* yet can never reach the ease we aim at" (p. 169). Johnson could not help agreeing with a sentiment so central to his own pessimism and which after all is the moral of *Rasselas.* Yet similar attitudes do not necessarily imply an influence; Johnson undoubtedly came to his pessimism independently of Hill and long before he wrote *Rasselas* or thought of gathering materials for his tale. But could not such congeniality of sentiment have disposed Johnson to regard Hill's travel book—assuming he read it—with particular favor? The appeal may have been irresistible. There are too many details common to both works to ascribe the similarities to mere coincidence.

Other details of the Egyptian setting may also be traced to the sources cited here. Imlac's description of Cairo is based on solid fact. Recounting his experiences before retiring to the Happy Valley, he relates how he "found in Cairo a mixture of all nations; some brought thither by the love of knowledge, some by the hope ofgain and many by the desire of living after their own manner without observation and lying hid in the obscurity of multitudes: for in a city, populous as Cairo, it is possible to obtain at the same time the gratifications of society, and the secrecy of solitude" (I, 82-83). Hill devoted a whole chapter in his book to Cairo, describing the immensity and variety of the city: "THIS famous City is so very *Populous,* tho' of so vast a Magnitude, that as we rode along the Streets, about the *Center* we were . . . extreamly *Crowded*" (p. 240). In this chapter he told in some detail of the rich and the poor, their places of trade and amusement, the public buildings and private homes, giving in capsule the heterogeneity of Cairo in the early eighteenth century. Pococke corroborates what Imlac says of the diversities of peoples residing in Cairo. A catalogue of the nationalities of the inhabitants include such diverse peoples as the Copts, Arabians, Berberines of Nubia, Turks, Mamelukes, Greeks, Armenians, Jews and natives of Barbary. European merchants, French, Italian and English were also listed.[25]

As the small group of Abyssinian travelers led by Imlac is about to enter the city, the poet informs them that Cairo is a "place where travellers and merchants assemble from all the corners of the earth. You will find men of every character and every occupation. Commerce is here honourable" (I, 106). So Hill described the inhabitants: "I shou'd mention the *Condition* of the People, now inhabiting Grand *Cairo,* whom we found in *rolling Plenty,* and the blest Possession of the richest Smiles of Providential Nature; Trading greatly, and encreasing *Wealth* with wonderful Dexterity; nor can *Provisions* of all kinds be any where, more reasonably Sold than in the well-stor'd *Markets* of this spacious City" (p. 241). Pococke remarked that "the conveniency of water of carriage makes Cairo a place of great trade"; and because the Turks cannot be trusted in money matters, "this always occasions a great conflux of people to Grand Cairo; so that probably near a quarter of the souls in the city not being fix'd inhabitants."[26] Johnson no doubt had London in mind when he set his tale in Cairo, and he was careful to choose a city which was an Eastern counterpart to his own varied metropolis. The information on Cairo which he gathered from these travel books thus gave him the opportunity to suggest London but yet keep the Eastern milieu. By keeping the setting remote and yet familiar enough to the experiences of his readers, Johnson provided a universal backdrop to the scenes of Rasselas' search for happiness. Cairo of the eighteenth century, a great trading center with a diverse population, was the best possible choice as the school for Rasselas' education.

The introduction of the astronomer as an example of excesses of learning is also consistent with the setting of Egypt. As Imlac explains, Egypt was "a country famous among the earliest monarchies for the power and wisdom of its inhabitants; a country where the sciences first dawned that illuminate the world, and beyond which the arts cannot be traced of civil society or domestick life" (II, 32). And in his ***Dictionary*** under the heading "Astronomy" Johnson asserted that "from Egypt it travelled into Greece, where Pythagoras was the first European who taught that the earth and planets turn around the sun, which stands immoveable in the center, as he himself had been instructed by the Egyptian priests. . . . It [astronomy] was revived by the Ptolemys, the kings of Egypt and the Saracens."[27] The ancient city of Heliopolis (located a few miles northeast of modern Cairo) had been the center of Egyptian astronomy and philosophy in the days of Plato. The Greek geographer Strabo had mentioned Heliopolis, in decline in his day, as a center of learning and as the place where Plato and Eudouxus had applied to learn of these sciences but found the priests reluctant to reveal their secrets. "Since these priests," Strabo informs us, "excelled in their knowledge of the heavenly bodies, albeit secretive and slow to impart it, Plato and Eudoxus prevailed upon them in time and by courting their favour to let them learn some of the principles of their doctrine; but the barbarians concealed most things."[28] While Johnson's astronomer is not nearly so reticent as these ancient priests, he might be, according to Imlac, reluctant "to repeat the elements of [his] art." (II, 133). In the tradition of the ancient Egyptian wise men, the sage is characterized as secretive and retiring, which as Johnson shows is partly the cause of his folly.

In Chapter XXIV of ***Rasselas*** the happiness of those in high station is examined. Rasselas visits the governing bassa of Egypt, thinking that among the great he will find contentment, but he soon discovers cabals, intrigue and finally that those in high station like everybody else are at the mercy of the wheel of fortune. In swift succession two bassas are deposed and the Turkish sultan murdered by the Janissaries. The author once again asserts the uncertainty of human happiness, in this case in the lives of those who govern others. Knowledge of the extremely unsettled nature of Middle Eastern politics, upon which this chapter is based, may be found in innumerable accounts of the region. By the middle of the eighteenth century the uneasiness of the crowned head of the Ottoman Empire and his viceroys had become a commonplace of political discourse to Europeans, who often cited Turkish politics as an example of the dangers of the lack of stable government. The most immediate source that leaps to mind where Johnson may have learned of deposed bassas and murdering Janissaries is Knolles's *Historie of the Turks,* which is filled with the bloody events associated with the Ottoman court. Hill also investigated the administration of the empire and discovered how the sultan disposed of his viceroys when they displeased him (pp. 14-15). Hill reported of Egypt that the "first *Bashaw* of all the *Turkish Empire* [that is, the plenipotentiary of Egypt] continues seldom in his Government above three Years" (p. 228).

Other details of the setting of *Rasselas* are less easily attributable. The volumes which Imlac claims "are suspended in the mosque of Mecca" (I, 66) remain a mystery. While many European travelers described Mecca, none had actually visited the shrine for the reason that nonbelievers are forbidden to enter the holy city. No travel book which I have examined mentioned these suspended volumes. Johnson's statement that the Monastery of St. Anthony (where Pekuah is restored to her friend's emissary) is located in the deserts of Upper Egypt is at worst a geographical exaggeration. It is found near the Gulf of Suez, not more than eighty miles south of the city of Suez. Pococke, who visited the Coptic monastery and described it, declared that it is "in the deserts near the Red Sea,"[29] and according to his accompanying map in the beginning of the first volume, it is in Lower Egypt.

The results of this investigation, if they do not disprove, at least lead us to regard with skepticism Boswell's assertion that *Rasselas* was composed "in the evenings of one week." Too much evidence of Johnson's indebtedness to Ethiopian and Egyptian travel books has been presented for us to be comfortable with the traditional account of the time spent writing the tale or the preparation for it, which Boswell would have us believe was nil. That Johnson wrote *Rasselas* and did all the reading of all the books on Ethiopia and Egypt cited here and elsewhere in the evenings of a week is scarcely credible. Oliver Emerson, also doubtful of Boswell's assertion, cited several of Johnson's contemporaries and the author himself for contrary evidence. Sir John Hawkins, whom Boswell took to task for inaccuracy, claimed that Johnson "had been for some time meditating a fictitous history, . . . which might serve as a vehicle to convey to the world his sentiments of human life and the dispensations of Providence; and having digested his thoughts on the subject, he obeyed the spur of that necessity [his mother's funeral] which now pressed him."[30] Edmund Malone's report of Baretti's account of the incident would have Johnson finished with *Rasselas* before his mother died.[31] And according to a letter Johnson wrote William Strahan, the publisher, on January 20, 1759, the book was either completed or well under way.[32] His mother's death occurred on the twentieth or the next day, but the news did not reach Johnson until January 23. Emerson opines that Boswell tried "to make out, as he might be expected to with his unbounded admiration for Johnson, that the writing of *Rasselas* was something wholly remarkable, both as to the conception of the tale and as to the time of composition."[33] We have

good grounds, therefore, for regarding Boswell's implication that there was no prior preparation to the composition of the tale with great skepticism, even if we accept the fact that the actual writing of the book may have been done in the space of a week.

In his study of the Abyssinian setting of the book, Lockhart hypothesized the existence of notes on Ethiopia, which Johnson began accumulating "at least seven years before that week in January 1759."[34] This is certainly a tempting thesis, especially considering Hawkins' statement. The existing evidence as presented in my study of the Egyptian background demonstrates that the information contained in these hypothetical notes would also include Johnson's researches into Egyptian travel books as well as Ethiopian accounts. Brought out of his usual lethargy by the demands of paying for his mother's funeral, Johnson may have turned to these notes and written *Rasselas* in the evenings of a week as Boswell asserts. This is certainly more reasonable than to suppose that all of Johnson's friends were wrong; Lockhart's hypothesis does less violence to the facts as we know them.

Lockhart's theory of these notes can never be fully proved until the external evidence of their existence is presented to the scholarly world. Yet the strong suspicion of their use must remain in the light of such evidence of Johnson's indebtedness to a variety of books on Ethiopia and Egypt for the setting of *Rasselas.*

Notes

[1] Harold D. Jenkins, "Some Aspects of the Background of *Rasselas,*" *Humanistic Studies of the University of Kansas,* VI, no. 4 (1940), 8-14; John R. Moore, "*Rasselas* and the Early Travelers to Abyssinia," *MLQ,* XV (1954), 36-41; Ellen D. Leyburn, "'No Romantick Absurdities or Incredible Fictions': The Relation of Johnson's *Rasselas* to Lobo's *Voyage to Abyssinia,*" *PMLA,* LXX (1955), 1059-67; Gwin J. Kolb, "The 'Paradise' in Abyssinia and the 'Happy Valley' in *Rasselas,*" *MP,* LVI (1958), 10-16. One of the first speculations on sources other than Lobo's work is by Oliver F. Emerson, "Introduction," *History of Rasselas* (New York, 1895), pp. xix-xxxi.

[2] *Life of Johnson,* ed. G. B. Hill and L. F. Powell (Oxford, 1934), I, 341.

[3] Donald M. Lockhart, "'The Fourth Son of the Mighty Emperor': The Ethiopian Background of Johnson's *Rasselas,*" *PMLA,* LXXVIII (1963), 516-28.

[4] *PMLA,* LXVI (1951), 702. See also Kolb's article cited above.

[5] Louis E. Goodyear's "Rasselas' Journey from Amhara to Cairo Viewed from Arabia" in *Bicentenary*

Essays on Rasselas, ed. Magdi Wahba (Cairo, 1959), pp. 21-29 is of no real help. In fact Goodyear only confuses the issue, since his essay speculates on what the journey from Amhara to the Red Sea and the sea voyage to Suez and thence overland to Cairo must have been like in the eighteenth century. Needless to say, Johnson could not have known the details of geography, the state of roads and the sea traffic comprehende-din Goodyear's article. Moreover, the profusion of geographical details offered here are quite irrelevant to the purposes of the tale.

[6] *The Prince of Abissinia,* 2 vols. (London, 1759). All page citations in the text refer to this, the first edition of *Rasselas.*

[7] Lockhart, p. 524.

[8] *Lives of the English Poets,* ed. G. B. Hill (Oxford, 1905), II, 339 passim. Aaron Hill is also mentioned in the life of Mallet, III, 402; in the life of Pope, III, 151 and 213; and in connection with Thomson, III, 284 passim.

[9] In the life of Savage, Johnson shows enough of a familiarity with Hill's writings to say that Hill "is remarkable for singularity of sentiment and bold experiments in language," *Lives of the English Poets,* II, 339.

[10] *The Present State of the Ottoman Empire* (London, 1709), pp. 265-68.

[11] II, 124-36.

[12] The following portions of their work are devoted to the pyramids: Strabo, XVII.i.33-34; Diodorus Siculus, I.63-64; Pliny, XXVI.16-17.

[13] *Sale Catalogue of Dr. Johnson's Library,* ed. A. Edward Newton (Philadelphia, 1925).

[14] *Sale Catalogue,* items no. 38 and 67. Item no. 38 is "Greave's tracts, 2 v," which I take to refer to Greaves's two-volume collected works (of which the first volume contains the tracts) published in 1737; *Pyramidographia* is in volume one. No. 67 is "Shaw's travels."

[15] *Life of Johnson,* II, 346.

[16] *Greaves's Miscellaneous Works* (London, 1737), I, 122.

[17] Pococke, I, 239. Norden also used the word "chest" in his description, I, 122-23.

[18] Norden also discussed the various methods of embalming, I, 124.

[19] See my "The Influence of the Middle East on English Prose Fiction, 1600-1725," unpub. diss. (New York University, 1963), pp. 51-54.

[20] *Works of Samuel Johnson,* ed. Arthur Murphy (London, 1801), I, 80.

[21] Reprinted with Lobo's *A Voyage to Abyssinia,* ed. George Gleig (London, 1789), pp. 403-20—hereafter cited as Gleig.

[22] *Natural History of Aleppo,* p. 110.

[23] Gleig, p. 409. Johnson in this review used the word "harum" (p. 410), which is the more exact designation of the women's apartments of the Moslem household. A seraglio, which the author used in *Rasselas,* is properly speaking a palace with all its grounds and buildings. In his *Dictionary* Johnson defined seraglio as a "house of women kept for debauchery." Either Johnson was not aware of the distinction meant by these terms, or he meant to convey the popular meaning of seraglio in both the dictionary and the tale.

[24] See Berna Moran, "The Irene Story and Dr. Johnson's Sources," *MLN,* LXXI (1956), 87-91.

[25] Pococke, I, 38.

[26] Pococke, I, 39.

[27] (London, 1755).

[28] *The Geography of Strabo,* trans. H. L. Jones, Loeb Classical Library (London, 1932), VIII, 85 (XVII.i.29).

[29] Pococke, I, 128.

[30] *The Life of Samuel Johnson,* 2nd ed. (London, 1787), p. 367. I am indebted for this quotation and the following references to Emerson's "Introduction," *op. cit.,* pp. x-xii.

[31] James Prior, *Life of Edmund Malone* (London, 1860), pp. 160-61.

[32] *The Letters of Samuel Johnson,* ed. R. W. Chapman (Oxford, 1952), I, 117-18.

[33] *Op. cit.,* p. xvi. Emerson's skepticism of Boswell's account is further suggested by his statement that "If Johnson without previous purpose, wrote *Rasselas* in a single week, he must have composed it with unusual rapidity. . . . The writing of *Rasselas* in the time specified would be exceptionally rapid" (p. xvi).

[34] Lockhart, p. 527.

James F. Woodruff (essay date 1984)

SOURCE: "*Rasselas* and the Traditions of 'Menippean Satire'," in *Samuel Johnson: New Critical Essays*, edited by Isobel Grundy, Vision Press and Barnes & Noble, 1984, pp. 158-85.

[*In the following essay, Woodruff considers* Rasselas *within the context of classical satiric traditions, suggesting that such a view makes clearer Johnson's efforts to create a Christian philosophy founded on realism.*]

As Carey McIntosh has pointed out, **Rasselas** is 'the most problematic' of Johnson's narrative works.[1] Disagreement exists about its genre and about the effect of its style, moral, structure, plot and characterization. My aim is to suggest a context of discussion that I hope will contribute to the clarification of at least some of these controversies.

Most of the extensive and valuable discussion of the literary backgrounds of **Rasselas** has been in a biblical or relatively modern context. Occasionally Cicero and the Stoics are cited, but, as far as I am aware, the book has rarely been associated with ancient literary traditions. Earl R. Wasserman, however, has connected **Rasselas** with two Greek allegories, well known in the eighteenth century if not today: Prodicus's *Choice of Hercules* and the *Tablet* of Cebes.[2] Wasserman uses his suggestion to work out implications of a fundamental insight about **Rasselas** and its period: 'the eighteenth century . . . produced a literature that . . . questions, transforms, and undermines the established norms themselves' (3). Though Johnson must certainly have known the allegories of Prodicus and Cebes and even have been influenced by them at certain points in his work as a whole, it is hard not to share some of Irvin Ehrenpreis's scepticism about the degree to which we should see their influence operating in **Rasselas**.[3] Yet the validity of the insight about the book's essentially subversive nature remains.

Ehrenpreis, in the concluding part of his essay, makes a series of statements that formulate precisely and elegantly many of the essential characteristics of **Rasselas** and develop the argument about the critical and ironic nature of Johnson's book. A selection of them should provide a sound starting point for further discussion.

> Rather than call the work a novel, I agree with those who classify it as a philosophical romance like More's *Utopia* and Voltaire's *Candide*. The action seems intended to illustrate a set of doctrines. What holds the reader is the author's playful substitution of ironically framed argument for exciting incident. . . . He invites us to identify ourselves with Imlac or Rasselas but then detaches himself from the person in order to smile sympathetically at him and us. . . . [Johnson] gives us a mock-romance. The story of Rasselas moves through ironic contrasts between the fantasies of traditional romance and the realities of earthly experience. (111) . . . Consistency and depth of characterization do not [lend themselves to the author's purpose of creating 'an impression that [he] has confronted all the possibilities of sublunary existence'.] (112) . . . If Johnson provides us with the superficial features of the oriental romance, he frustrates the expectations aroused by them. . . . The method is deliberate and works as comic irony. (113) . . . In the style of the speeches (as also in much of the narrative) Johnson recalls the distinctive manner of the oriental tale, but he does so in a delicate parody. . . . Even when the style is straightforward, and wisdom is offered such as the author might recommend as his peculiar teaching, it may be set in an ironic frame. (116)

These statements formulate sharply some real but difficult qualities of **Rasselas** which are certainly, as Ehrenpreis suggests, well suited to Johnson's habits as a writer, but which I propose in the following essay to associate with a somewhat wider and more enduring literary tradition than he or other writers on **Rasselas** mention.

1

A discussion has been developing in recent years, mainly outside the field of eighteenth-century studies, about a literary kind variously referred to as the anatomy, the menippea, and Menippean satire. While the genre is referred to by earlier writers, the mention is usually brief. The detailed conception of this literary kind recently developed, however, allows a new historical and critical understanding of the form of many 'problematic' works, from the eighteenth century as well as from other times. **Rasselas,** I think, is one of them, along with such a likely companion as *Candide* and such less likely associates as *Gulliver's Travels* and *Tristram Shandy*.[4] Indeed, the eighteenth-century philosophic tale may be seen as a sub-class of the genre.

To some the identification may only need to be asserted to be evident. To others one of the main focuses of objection to such a description is the word 'satire' itself. While several writers have called **Rasselas** satiric, the description has also been vigorously denied.[5] Part of the problem in using the term may lie in the conception of the Menippean genre, but part lies in the way the basic characteristics of satire *per se* are viewed. Many 'Menippean' works such as *Gulliver's Travels, A Tale of a Tub,* Erasmus's *Praise of Folly,* and some of Lucian's dialogues like the *Icaromenippus* or the *Vitarum auctio* are by common consent and usage 'satiric'.[6] Others, such as Boethius's *Consolation of Philosophy,* are not. It is this difficulty that has led Northrop Frye to suggest that the term 'anatomy' be substituted for the cumbersome and misleading 'Menippean satire', and Mikhail Bakhtin generally shortens the term to 'menippea'. The substitution, however, has been rejected by other writers such as Eugene Kirk and F. Anne Payne, who insist on the genre's basically satiric nature.

In the seventeenth and eighteenth centuries most attempts to understand the essential quality of satire involved placing it in an antithesis of praise and invective. Dryden uses this approach in his 'Discourse Concerning the Original and Progress of Satire' in a sentence that Johnson slightly misquotes in his *Dictionary* under the first meaning of 'invective' as a noun: 'If we take satire in the general signification of the word, as it is used in all modern languages, for an invective, 'tis certain that it is almost as old as verse.[7] The problem, however, as Dryden recognizes, is that satire in becoming an art form becomes much more complex than its primitive original or its common modern meaning would allow. He echoes Dacier in observing

> that the word *satire* is of a more general signification in Latin than in French or English. For amongst the Romans it was not only used for those discourses which decried vice, or exposed folly, but for others also, where virtue was recommended. (II, 116)

Like most writers in the period he sees true satire as achieving general moral significance rather than remaining mere personal abuse. Johnson sums up this view in the definition of 'satire' in his *Dictionary:*

> A poem in which wickedness or folly is censured. Proper *satire* is distinguished, by the generality of the reflections, from a lampoon which is aimed against a particular person; but they are too frequently confounded.[8]

This extended conception of satire implied certain things about the satirist's character, as many writers in the eighteenth century were certainly aware.[9] An indulgence in invective can easily lead to the image of the satirist as a mean-spirited and vindictive creature who cares little for truth and real virtue in his attempts to mount an attack on his victims. Yet some satirists would rather think of themselves as noble moralists willing to suffer if necessary for the good of mankind. Pope as seen by his enemies and by himself is a good example of both images. Such a perceived conflict or tension could in turn have implications for the character satire was allowed to develop. The more scrupulous the satirist about truth and general morality the less likely he might be to indulge in violence and personal invective. But the farther the writer moves towards moral nobility and away from mere invective the less like satire his work will appear to many readers, though he may still think of himself as working withinsatiric traditions. In the end it comes to a matter both of the real

character of the writer and of the rhetorical character he wishes to project in his works. It has been observed, most notably by W. Jackson Bate in his influential discussion of 'Johnson and Satire Manqué', that Johnson seems to have felt acutely both the impulse of the satirist and the need to mute that impulse because of compassion and, one might add, a concern for truth.[10] Several of the illustrative quotations he gives for 'satire' and its derivatives in the *Dictionary,* particularly for the word 'satirist' itself, reiterate a need to mute the violence of satire and to stress positive moral concerns. They bring out the tension we have noted between the character of satire and that of the good satirist. Two examples must serve, though at least eight out of the sixteen quotations used to illustrate these words have a similar thrust.

> Wycherly, in his writings, is the sharpest *satyrist* of his time; but, in his nature, he has all the softness of the tenderest dispositions: in his writings he is severe, bold, undertaking; in his nature gentle, modest, inoffensive.
>
> *Granville.*

> Yet soft his nature, though severe his lay;
> His anger moral, and his wisdom gay:
> Blest *satyrist!* who touch'd the mean so true,
> As show'd vice had his hate and pity too.
>
> *Pope.*

Taken together, the quotations Johnson selects bring out the responsibilities of the satirist and the dangers inherent in using a powerful weapon irresponsibly, the sort of points that Addison before him had reiterated many times. They caution by implication against the temptation satire too readily offers of indulging ill nature, and they suggest the controls we should expect to find operating when Johnson himself worked in a satiric mode or genre.

The complex nature of satire, involving tensions between the personal and the general, invective and exposure, raillery and morality, makes it difficult to simplify its definition in terms of a single characteristic such as attack or ridicule. A satiric writer experiencing the compunctions just suggested would be likely, I think, to de-emphasize the more personal, more violent aspects—the mere decrying of vice—and to emphasize the exposure of folly and the recommending of virtue. When this aspect of satire is stressed it begins to sound more and more like one of Johnson's usual modes. This stripping bare from the encrustations of pretence- and wish-fantasy is perhaps satire's most universal though not its sole aim. The fictions of satire force the fresh look that leads to such exposure. Satire intends not only to rob the shameless of honour but, in a famous phrase, to clear the mind of cant, of what we take for granted and mindlessly repeat. Satire is the mode of 'reality', of the actual, of things as they are. At base it is the opposite of romance, which is the mode of wishes and their fulfilment and of the ideal rather than the actual. Sometimes to show or suggest this difference satire stresses the anti-romantic.

Irony becomes another way of establishing the actual through implied contrast, for it is a trope that is constantly bringing out a sense of difference. In the most general sense irony depends on a perception of discrepancy within moral structures. In itself it does not necessarily imply moral judgement, only difference. Though such judgement is frequent in satire and the ironic discrepancy is between an actual and an ideal (as in Juvenal), there may be ironies where right (and wrong) rests on both sides and our primary awareness is of the discrepancy between different perspectives. This latter kind of irony is, in fact, frequent in Johnson's writing. Other kinds of irony, like 'dramatic irony' or even much 'tragic' or 'comic irony', depend on discrepancies in knowledge or in point of view—between different characters, between audience and characters, or even between knowledge of a part and of the whole. Irony, then, can be employed as a ready means to the satiric end of exposure. Similarly, ridicule in satire is perhaps more means than end. In a good deal of satire at least, the underlying intention, as we have noted, is to expose a truth or reality concealed or ignored by the assumptions or fictions or wilful misrepresentations of everyday living and converse. The ridicule is one of the techniques used to effect the exposure of falsity and discovery of truth.[11]

When satire is viewed thus *Rasselas* appears much more convincingly to belong within the mode. The point has already been made succinctly by Arieh Sachs:

> The method of *Rasselas* is the method of satire, in the sense that it involves an ironical exposé of human delusions which is intended to make us confront unpleasant realities. By means of its irony, it makes us see the absurdity of many 'luscious falsehoods' and feeds us the salutary 'bitterness of truth'.[12]

The conception of the 'Menippean satire' allows a good deal more to be said about *Rasselas* seen in this way and also allows us to incorporate into our view many of the characteristics of the book noted by Ehrenpreis and others.

2

Not only does it make sense to see *Rasselas* as Menippean satire in a modern critical context, but there is a good possibility that Johnson himself might have looked on it as connected with that kind of work. Thus

there is some point in looking both at how the genre was viewed in Johnson's time and how it has been described by recent critics. The principal source of theoretical and historical knowledge about Menippean satire in the seventeenth and eighteenth centuries was Isaac Casaubon's *De Satyrica Graecorum Poesi et Romanorum Satira* originally published in 1605.[13] Later writers who touch on the genre, such as Dacier, Dryden (in his 'Discourse . . . ' prefixed to the translation of Juvenal and Persius, 1693[14]), and Joseph Trapp add very little. Dryden's few pages are a good summary from an important writer who saw his own 'MacFlecknoe' and 'Absalom and Achitophel' as being of this kind.[15] He follows Casaubon in preferring the term 'Varronian satire', though he notes that the Roman satirist Varro himself, whose works survive only in fragments, called it Menippean after the Cynic philosopher Menippus of Gadara, who later appears as a character in the dialogues of Lucian. One essential characteristic of Menippean satire for these writers rests in the root meaning of satire in *satura,* a mixture, a point first established by Casaubon. Dryden notes: 'This sort of satire was not only composed of several sorts of verse, like those of Ennius, but was also mixed with prose; and Greek was sprinkled amongst the Latin' (113). Varro, 'one of those writers whom they called *spoudogeloioi,* studious of laughter' (114), had commented on the mixture of mirth and philosophy in his own writings. Dryden observes Menippus's reputation for cynical impudence, obscenity, and parody, but notes that 'Varro, in imitating him, avoids his impudence and filthiness, and only expresses his witty pleasantry. . . . As [Varro's] subjects were various, so most of them were tales or stories of his own invention' (115). The writers and works that for Dryden define the continuation of this tradition are the *Satyricon* of Petronius Arbiter, many of Lucian's dialogues, particularly his *Vera Historia,* the *Golden Ass* of Apuleius, the *Apocolocyntosis* of Seneca, the *Symposium* of the Emperor Julian the Apostate, Erasmus's *Praise of Folly,* John Barclay's *Euphormionis Lusinini Satyricon,* a German work (probably, according to W. P. Ker, the *Epistolae Obscurorum Virorum*), Spenser's *Mother Hubbard's Tale,* and his own works mentioned above. In these remarks, many of the characteristics listed in recent accounts of the genre are already present, thought its satiric ethos is assumed rather than explicitly articulated. Central to Dryden's and the seventeenth-century view is a notion of medley that breaks through ordinary literary decorums, brings together mirth and philosophic seriousness, and is usually embodied in dialogue or at least quasi-narrative forms, often fragmentary and digressive.

Modern criticism spells out much more fully the notion of medley central to older views, and often seeks the *raison d'être* behind the mixtures. Considerable scholarship has touched on the subject of Menippean satire in classical literature. A rather full summary in relation to Lucian is given by J. Bompaire in his *Lucien Ecrivain,* and Eugene P. Kirk has recently published *Menippean Satire: An Annotated Catalogue of Texts and Criticism,* a useful account of texts and scholarship that follows the genre to 1660.[16] Kirk emphasizes the genre's Protean character, how writers looking to the same models can be led by their own concerns to emphasize very different characteristics so that both Boethius and Erasmus can be seen as imitators of Lucian. Such diversity makes definition difficult. Kirk arrives at a statement of 'family resemblances' that appears to grow from a sense of the genre similar to Dryden's, and emphasizes diversity of language, variety of structure, and a concentration in theme on subjects dealing with problems of right learning or right belief.

Even more suggestive of aspects of Johnson's work are the analyses of this genre by Northrop Frye, Mikhail Bakhtin and F. Anne Payne. Frye outlined his view in *Anatomy of Criticism.*[17] He distinguishes the kind of characterization typically found in these works from more 'novel-centred' conceptions.

> The Menippean satire deals less with people as such than with mental attitudes. Pedants, bigots, cranks, parvenus, virtuosi, enthusiasts, rapacious and incompetent professional men of all kinds, are handled in terms of their occupational approach to life as distinct from their social behaviour. . . . [Its characterization] is stylized rather than naturalistic, and presents people as mouthpieces of the ideas they represent. . . . A constant theme in the tradition is the ridicule of the *philosophus gloriosus.* . . . The novelist sees evil and folly as social diseases, but the Menippean satirist sees them as diseases of the intellect, as a kind of maddened pedantry which the *philosophus gloriosus* at once symbolizes and defines. (309)

The characterization in **Rasselas,** frequently described as wooden yet in context somehow right, is suggested by such an account. The book also contains a whole procession of *philosophi gloriosi* from the would-be flyer to the astronomer. Many other characteristics of Menippean satire noted by Frye could readily be illustrated from **Rasselas:** its loose-jointed narrative is often confused with romance but differs significantly from it; 'at its most concentrated the Menippean satire presents us with a vision of the world in terms of a single intellectual pattern' (310)[18]; 'the form is not invariably satiric in attitude, but shades off into more purely fanciful or moral discussions' (310); the dialogue and the *cena* or symposium often appear; piling up of erudition and jargon are common and authors of this sort of work have frequently been encyclopaedic compilers. Frye adds to writers and works already mentioned not only Rabelais and Swift but Burton's *Anatomy of Melancholy,* the work which Johnson said 'was the only book that ever took

him out of bed two hours sooner than he wished to rise'.[19]

Before Frye wrote, the Russian scholar Mikhail Bakhtin had analysed the menippea in his book *Problems of Dostoevsky's Poetics,* which originally appeared in the late 1920s but was not widely known in the West until recent years.[20] For Bakhtin the concept of the menippea is deeply connected with his notion of the carnivalization of literature. He sees the 'carnival spirit' holding together and making coherent the disparate characteristics of the genre. Bakhtin posits a large class of ancient serio-comical literature including 'Menippean satire' and 'Socratic dialogue' with several other forms, and notes the difficulties of establishing distinct and stable boundaries within its realm. He suggests three basic characteristics for all the serio-comic genres. (1) 'Their starting point for understanding, evaluating, and formulating reality is the *present*' (88). I understand this to mean that they make a sense of things-as-they-are reality their basis rather than introducing a vision of epic or tragic distance. (2) These genres are *consciously* based on *experience* and on *free imagination* rather than on *legend.* They are often explicitly critical of previous formulations of experience such as are found in myth. (3) They exhibit deliberate multifariousness and discordance. Stylistically self-conscious, they reject the stylistic unity of the established genres. Bakhtin proceeds next to the Socratic dialogue, pointing out how it is set up to undermine the claims of those who profess to possess the truth, which 'does not reside in the head of an individual person; it is born of the dialogical intercourse *between people* in the collective search for the truth' (90). Thus juxtaposed points of view are characteristic of the serio-comic genres.

Bakhtin's listing of specific traits of the menippea is also relevant to **Rasselas.** The weight and nature of the comic element can vary widely from the burlesque of Varro and Lucian to the contemplative irony and 'reduced laughter' of Boethius.[21] Recent writers, beginning with Clarence Tracy and Alvin Whitley, have found a comic element in **Rasselas,** though the precise way to read it remains a problem.[22] The genre also shows great freedom of invention and fantasy. However, it creates

> *extraordinary situations* in which to provoke and test a philosophical idea—the word or the *truth,* embodied in the image of the wise man, the seeker after this truth. We emphasize that the fantastic serves here not in the positive *embodiment* of the truth, but in the search after the truth, its provocation and, most importantly, its *testing.* (94)

Rather than developing complex argument like the Socratic dialogue, the Menippean dialogue tests ultimate philosophical positions, and makes us aware of the human dimensions of ideas.These are the characteristics of **Rasselas.**

Bakhtin's statement is a precise formulation of the way in which **Rasselas** differs from the simple, Aesop's-fable type of apologue or from allegory as conventionally conceived; many passages such as the encounter with the stoic in Chapter 18 or with the philosopher of nature in Chapter 22 show the testing of ultimate positions in their human terms. The positions tested are characteristically of an 'ethico-practical inclination' rather than more clearly 'academic' ones. Characteristic too is the juxtaposition of stripped-bare positions (for example, the happiness of solitude set against the happiness of various kinds of society, or the sensual indulgence of young men set against the stoic denial of an old man). There are only hints in **Rasselas** of the tri-level construction (heaven, earth, hell) often found, but they may be important, as is the characteristic of observation from an unusual point of view—here wealthy outsiders from the happy valley look at the ordinary world. Significantly, Johnson brings his characters to the level of the real world for most of their work of observation. The whole element of the fantastic is muted in **Rasselas** compared with many works in the genre. However, 'the representation of man's unusual, abnormal moral and psychic states—insanity of all sorts . . . unrestrained daydreaming . . . etc.' (96) appears in the astronomer or the daydreaming of Rasselas and later of all the young people. Of other elements identified by Bakhtin, **Rasselas** includes sharp contrasts and oxymoronic combinations (the happy valley as paradise and prison, for example), elements of a social Utopia usually involving a journey to another land (the happy valley again, and perhaps the Arab's harem, but with some interesting—though not unprecedented—reversals), inserted genres intensifying the variety of styles and tones, parody, etc. (the elements of anti-romance and of the oriental tale, as well as summaries of several philosophical positions, dissertations, dialogues, etc. and various life stories which are in a way mock-aretology, another ancient aspect of the genre), and finally a topical quality (not prominent in Johnson though he does address some current philosophical issues). The element most obviously omitted from **Rasselas** is the scandalous, the 'underworld naturalism' that has given so many Menippean works the reputation of dirty books. The omission is typical of Johnson. But Boethius omits it too and in so doing, as Casaubon pointed out, emulates Varro who effectively established the genre.[23]

F. Anne Payne offers the most extensive and probing analysis of Menippean satire I have yet encountered.[24] Her discussions of Lucian and Boethius are extremely suggestive in relation to Johnson's work, though eighteenth-century literature is not her concern. She maintains that the genre should continue to be viewed in the context of satire, but that it is satire of a special kind whose ultimate aim is to set the mind free. While ordinary satire isfrequently seen as setting up some ideal standard and criticising deviations, she sees at this genre's centre a questioning of the very possibility of ideal standards.[25] Consequently interest centres on freedom of will and the dominance of choice in human action as well as in thought. The conventions found in the satires are 'merely aids to the dramatization of this fundamental assumption' (6). Johnson's exploration of the 'choice of life' obviously has this kind of focus, and the end, if seen only as a demonstration that the travellers should abandon their search for the answer to an impossible question and get on 'with living an ordinary life in an everyday world' (202), sounds very much like one of Lucian's terminal positions. Johnson, however, superimposes the Christian perspective of eternity on the position typically taken by the pagan writer, thus transforming its meaning.

Several of the characteristics Payne adds to Bakhtin's list have an obvious applicability to **Rasselas:** a central dialogue between a 'know-it-all' and a 'neophyte'; one character involved in an endless quest, 'helped' by the comments of the other, but with any norm which tries to provide an end satirized; freedom to think, frequently imaged as freedom of action, seen as a gift and a burden; characters who 'exhibit a courteous intention to continue conversing no matter what happens and no matter what must be given up'; and the radiation of 'an unquenchable hope and titanic energy for whatever the problem is' (10). Payne stresses that the genre is to be recognized not by the occurrence of particular characteristics—many occur at least singly in other kinds of work—but by the totality and by the domination of themes like freedom of will, choice, and the questioning of the possibility of ideal standards.

To consider **Rasselas**'s affinities to this genre leads to certain emphases, especially on the anti-establishment dimension which it shares with most of Johnson's writings. The genre works towards questioning things. It lets nothing rest easy. Ultimately a grasp on reality is aimed at—just the opposite of the world of wishes that dominates in romance. In **Rasselas** the stress is always on the presence of alternatives and the uncertainty of final answers. All truths except the final and ultimately unknowable divine truth are partial, but the undercurrent of hope and elation which many readers sense in this book as in other Menippean works (despite the temptation rationally to label the book pessimistic) comes from the vision of the world without forced answers, the emphasis on discovery and on the continuing effort to know rather than the subsidence into easy decision or agnosticism. The Menippean satirist is 'too restless for settled schools'.[26] Johnsonians will surely echo with 'Nullius addictus jurare in verba magistri . . . '.[27] In **Rasselas** Johnson has created frequent difficulties for readers by undercutting in some way speakers of obvious wisdom, as he does with Imlac at the end of Chapter 10. This does not mean that we are to reject the speaker. It is part of the creation of a dialogical way of thinking. We are neither to accept or reject on the basis of authority but to weigh thoughtfully in context. Above all Johnson does not want his readers to relax into merely following authority in earthly matters. Only in the other dimension which Robert G. Walker has argued lies behind most of **Rasselas,** that dimension of spiritual immortality suggested by the mind's unsatisfiable yearning and which in its fullness always keeps behind the surface of the work, is there a prospect of certainty.[28] In this respect Johnson has modified some of the genre's tendency as described by Payne. While he questions the possibility of ideal earthly and temporal standards he holds out the possibility of eternity where the hope for enduring happiness may be fulfilled. The constant irony remains, however, of the separation between this dimension and the temporal, living and changing world where inevitably unsatisfied human beings find themselves.

3

Having established the relationship of **Rasselas** to Menippean satire, we are left with two further lines of questioning: what was Johnson's likely knowledge of and attitude to works of this kind, and what are the significant affinities between **Rasselas** and major earlier works from the genre?

Johnson's acquaintance throughout his life with works from this tradition can be demonstrated. Often he can be shown not merely to have known them but to have liked and admired them. During his first interview as a new undergraduate at Pembroke College, Oxford, he quoted Macrobius, and, though this could have been the *Commentary on the Dream of Scipio,* Charles G. Osgood has suggested that it may have been the *Saturnalia,* a compendium of learning in the Menippean tradition.[29] Other Menippean works appear in the list of his undergraduate library left behind at Oxford in 1729: More's *Utopia,* the *Colloquies* of Erasmus, and the *Satyricon* of John Barclay, the early-seventeenth-century Franco-Scottish neo-Latin writer, whose allegorical romance *Argenis* was also in Johnson's collection. The works of Seneca are included in the list too.[30]

Works of this kind are part of the schemes of education Johnson drew up during the 1730s.[31] Among Greek authors for pre-University study (along with the allegory of Cebes, mentioned by Wasserman) is 'Lucian by Leeds', a collection of the dialogues prepared for school use originally published in the mid-1670s.[32] Its motto from Horace's *De Arte Poetica* (ll. 343-44), 'Omne tulit punctum, qui miscuit utile dulci/ Lectorem delectando pariterque movendo [*sic*]', a significant hint of Johnson's and the eighteenth century's dominant attitude towards this kind of work, is close in senti-

ment to the passage from Phaedrus that Johnson used as a motto for the collected *Idlers.* Leedes's collection contained several of thedialogues of the gods along with some of the other shorter dialogues and the *Judicium Dearum, Somnium sive Gallus,* and *Vitarum Auctio.* The sale catalogue of Johnson's library (far from a complete listing, of course, of the books he owned) includes works by several Menippean authors: the Emperor Julian, Boethius, Lucian (three editions), Macrobius, Erasmus, More, Cervantes (two editions), Swift, Burton, Seneca and Lipsius.[33]

Other connections with writers whose works have at least sometimes been looked on as Menippean appear throughout Johnson's life. We have evidence of his admiring Chaucer, Burton, Cervantes and Boileau.[34] Lucian was not only included in his scheme of education (a usual thing at the time) but was once noticed as his reading during a stagecoach journey, and in 1776 he alluded to the *Juppiter Tragoedus* in a way suggesting he had been struck by how Lucian shows a sense of character and emotion operating in 'intellectual' argument.[35] His interest in Boethius was also enduring. On several occasions he was involved with the *Consolation of Philosophy* in the context of translation, and he drew from it in the **Rambler** and **Adventurer.**[36] Not all these writers and works are equally relevant to **Rasselas.** In many of them, however, are found a tone or stance that seems to be echoed or deliberately built on by Johnson. The sense many of them try to establish of the value, even the necessity, of giving up attractive but ultimately impossible delusions and resting content with freshly apprehended ordinary reality is in harmony with one dominant strain in Johnson's own thought, as is the rather consistent strain of anti-romance that runs through them. The odd mixtures and complex ironies characteristic of much of this work suggest another important side of his writing.

The connection of Johnson's work with the traditions of Menippean satire is not simple. It is often a good example of what is now fashionably referred to as intertextuality, a condition where works 'have meaning in relation to other texts which they take up, cite, parody, refute, or generally transform'.[37] Sometimes the affinities between **Rasselas** and earlier works connected with this tradition go so far that they suggest an association specific as well as general; here I can only present a few of these. Some works already mentioned offer one striking point of resemblance—Barclay's *Euphormio* presents the story of a young man who comes from a Utopia to the ordinary world and in the course of his adventures exhaustively surveys it—as well as some general stylistic resemblance in the use of balance and parallel. Similarities of vision occur fairly often in other works, and similarities of design can be found. However, some of the writings of Lucian of Samosata and Boethius's *Consolation of Philosophy* are of particular interest.

4

Evidence of Johnson's knowledge of Lucian has already been mentioned. Like Johnson Lucian is fundamentally devoted to getting at the basic realities which lie under the structure of human illusions, though as a pagan he rests, unlike Johnson, in the here and now. Lucian sometimes uses allegories rather like those Johnson included in his periodical essays, reminding us that Prodicus and Cebes are not the only classical models for allegory.[38] An element of anti-romance also runs throughout Lucian, most apparent perhaps in the *Vera historia* but more directly reminiscent of Johnson in *De morte Peregrini* or *Alexander,* whose mock-aretology deflates, by realistic presentation, the forms and illusion of exemplary biography. Beyond general similarities of vision and treatment particular works by Lucian more closely resemble **Rasselas.** For example, the *Vitarum auctio* presents the weakness in practice of all philosophies through an auction of their founders or practitioners, and the *Somnium sive Gallus* contains a kind of Pythagorean 'choice of life' in the cock's accounts of the various transmigrations he has lived through from high to low, male to female, human to animal.[39] The stimulus to the survey is Micyllus's desire to find out the relative happiness of the different lives (21), and on the whole animals come out best. As the cock says, 'there is no existence that did not seem to me more care-free than that of man, since the others are conformed to natural desires and needs alone' (27; II, 227). The perception is like the one that Rasselas arrives at in Chapter 2.

Anyone who reads through the works of Lucian will find, I think, more interesting points of contact with Johnson's work. Obviously it is Lucian the moralist, 'Lucian, severe, but in a gay disguise[40] as seen in the seventeenth and eighteenth centuries, rather than Lucian the entertainer of modern scholarship, that engages Johnson. Johnson's Lucian is not the Lucian of Fielding or even of Swift. In some respects it is as if Johnson sees him through Boethius's eyes. But the Greek writer provides many examples of ways to embody brilliantly an ironic, questioning world view that in important respects is consonant with Johnson's own, and poses issues that Johnson engages in his turn. Two of Lucian's dialogues in particular show interesting affinities with **Rasselas.**

The first is the *Navigium seu vota.* In this dialogue a trip to see a ship that had landed at Piraeus after a peculiarly trouble-ridden voyage suggests the perception that human wishes are as uncertain and as subject to misfortune and fatality as the voyage. Each of three companions tells of his wishes during their walk back to Athens, and in turn the Lucian figure helps show the vanity of these wishes for wealth, for power, and for more than man's mortal and imperfect bodily state allows. The themes, of course, are favourites with

Johnson. The final wish, particularly, suggests **Rasselas** and is what the would-be flier in Chapter 6 tries to put into practice. One of the Navigium's wishes, in fact, involves themagically granted ability to fly. 'I alone would know the source of the Nile and how much of the earth is uninhabited and if people live head-downwards in the southern half of the world', says Lucian's Timolaus (44; VI, 483). 'How easily shall we then trace the Nile through all his passage; pass over to distant regions, and examine the face of nature from one extremity of the earth to the other!' says Johnson's philosopher.[41] A desire to fly is a recurrent symbol in Lucian of aspiration to more than the human state permits,[42] and this could easily have been a source for Johnson's similar use of the image, along with all the more modern contexts so illuminatingly set out by Gwin Kolb and Louis Landa.[43] Johnson certainly modifies the motif in introducing it into 'realistic' action, but the essential point is the same.

Lucian's long dialogue *Hermotimus* also suggests **Rasselas** in certain ways. Its subject is the failings of all specialized philosophies as guides to happiness, with particular reference to Hermotimus's Stoic master but with the moral extended to other philosophies as well. Like **Rasselas,** it contains in passing the deflation of a Stoic who acts passionately in response to the ordinary contingencies of life (though on a different scale of magnitude from the calamity Johnson introduces). But it is focused throughout on an obsessive pursuit of happiness and the single philosophical way of life that will be most likely to lead to it. One of the problems considered is how, with limited experience, to make an intelligent choice of such a philosophy. Choice can only be valid if the full range of choices is known. Lycinus imagines the problem posed this way:

> Tell me this, Lycinus: suppose an Ethiopian, a man who had never seen other men like us, because he had never been abroad at all, should state and assert in some assembly of the Ethiopians that nowhere in the world were there any men white or yellow or of any other colour than black, would he be believed by them? Or would one of the older Ethiopians say to him: "Come now, you are very bold. How do you know this? You have never left us to go anywhere else, and indeed you have never seen what things are like among other peoples?" . . .

> 'Let us make a comparison, Lycinus, and posit a man who knows only the Stoic tenets, like this friend of yours, Hermotimus; he has never gone abroad to Plato's country or stayed with Epicurus or in short with anyone else. Now, if he said that there was nothing in these many lands as beautiful or as true as the tenets and assertions of Stoicism, would you not with good reason think him bold in giving his opinion at all, and that when he knows only one, and has never put one foot outside Ethiopa?' (31-2; VI, 317-19)

One can imagine that such a passage may have jogged Johnson's imagination towards the construction of his own tale. 'What if wewere to examine the experience of an Ethiopian who does examine all the choices of life open?', Johnson may have asked himself. At least the passage strongly suggests the situation in Chapter 3 of **Rasselas** where the old man's reminder that he has not seen the miseries of the world gives the prince a motive for wanting to escape the happy valley.[44]

Other details in *Hermotimus* also resemble elements of Johnson's book. One passage (71), for example, elaborates on the seductiveness of daydreaming and the difficulty of coming back to reality afterwards—a mental state noted in both Chapters 4 and 43 of **Rasselas.** Throughout Lucian's dialogue one observes a constant concern more with the human factor than with the philosophical doctrine. There is, moreover, a basic perception, as Lycinus says, 'that virtue lies in action, in acting justly and wisely and bravely' (79; VI, 405). His final advice is 'you will do better in the future to make up your mind to join in the common life. Share in the city life of everyday, and give up your hopes of the strange and puffed-up' (84; VI, 413). There are also ironic dimensions to the work's ending, though Hermotimus's final response recalls Gulliver more clearly than **Rasselas.** In throwing off what he now calls his madness he proposes to change his appearance as much as his mind. Unlike Imlac and the astronomer who are content 'to be driven along the stream of life' he thanks Lycinus for coming and pulling him out 'when I was being carried away by a rough, turbid torrent, giving myself to it and going with the stream' (86; VI, 415). These elements, some though not all specific to *Hermotimus,* suggest a special relationship between it and **Rasselas** that is more than the merely generic and may even be genetic.

Johnson reinterprets and goes beyond positions found in Lucian, but in many respects he seems in **Rasselas** to be carrying on a dialogue with him. They work over the same themes and subjects with similar aims and techniques. In his analysis of Lucian's satires Ronald Paulson makes statements that could up to a point apply to Johnson.[45]

> Aristophanes focused on the solution; Lucian focuses on the quest and on the witnesses and their testimony. He is interested in the separate encounters, knowing that there is no solution but only the people who offer false solutions. (32)

Paulson analyses Lucian's basic techniques as a writer of anti-romance and shows how he works to expose the evil of illusion and reduce things to the plane of reality which if not ideal is at least real. Lucian's 'purpose', he concludes, 'is the very general one of discomfiting his reader, shaking up his cherished values, disrupting his orthodoxy' (41). Johnson is also concerned with disrupting the orthodoxies of a too easy optimism. But always in Johnson behind this view of man's earthly life is a Christian senseof the immortality of the soul and of the new perspective that the prospect of eternity can give to the inconclusiveness and ordinariness of terrestrial and temporal life.

5

Boethius's *Consolation of Philosophy,* Menippean though not obviously comic or satiric, engages, like the works by Lucian just discussed, some of the same central themes as **Rasselas;** it leads to a specifically Christian conclusion; and to a greater extent than Lucian, I think, its style frequently suggests Johnson's strikingly balanced, ironic dignity. In many respects it is very different from **Rasselas.** It is not a tale but a dialogue between the imprisoned Boethius and the allegorical figure of the Lady Philosophy, its passages of prose alternate with passages of verse, and much of the time it is concerned less with practical moral problems than with rather technical questions of philosophy and theology. The search for happiness becomes an exploration of the problem of the *summum bonum.* Yet there are underlying similarities that suggest Johnson may have been transferring some of Boethius's problems and themes to another context. The two works complement each other; Boethius treats at length the philosophical and theological issues that Johnson mutes and Johnson brings into the foreground the practical moral dimensions unexplored in Boethius. Most of the ground they share is covered in the first three books of the *Consolation,* particularly the second, the book of fortune (which examines and rejects worldly conditions, such as wealth, power and fame, as possible sources of enduring happiness), and the third, the book of the *summum bonum* (which examines the nature of happiness). It is, by the way, from these two books especially that Johnson drew mottoes and quotations for the **Rambler** and **Adventurer,** and it was mainly the metres from these two books that Johnson and Mrs. Thrale translated week by week.

The underlying thematic structure of the *Consolation* is in broad outline like that used by Johnson. It begins with one who is disillusioned with what had been taken to be happiness (I, i). Boethius is concerned that righting wrongs and doing good in a position of power (one of Rasselas's favourite aspirations) has not brought him earthly happiness (I, iv). In this first book a strong image of man's condition as imprisonment is developed, just as Johnson develops the image of the happy valley as an imprisonment, mental as well as physical, from which Rasselas seeks to escape. Also developed in this first book is a sense of human alienation. Man finds himself surrounded by the order in God's natural world expressed in ordered and balanced images and statements. Only man's acts do not seem to participate in this order (I, v). Rasselas too finds himself in the happy valley in a natural world (expressed in its completeness in a highly ordered set of images), from which he apprehends his difference (9; 14-16; 23-4).

Boethius proceeds in the second book to consider the constant vicissitudes of fortune. The deepest poetic sense of this part lies perhaps in a realization of the inevitable transience and change of things in this world and of man's yearning in such a context for permanence, a quality of vision shared with *Rasselas.* After the refutation of false ideas of how happiness may be obtained, the third book proceeds to an exploration of what constitutes true happiness and the supreme good, concluding that God is happiness itself. These books are close to the middle section of *Rasselas.* The final conclusion is also the same, that man is led by the immortality of his soul, the yearning of the mind to find again its proper place which it cannot quite locate in the order of nature, to realize that true and lasting happiness is only to be found with God in the realm of eternity.[46] Although Johnson's presentation of a 'choice of life' gives his work a different emphasis, its wisdom is consonant with that of Boethius.

Boethius's fourth and fifth books go on among other things to explore the rôle of evil in the scheme proposed and to affirm the freedom of the human will, the final freedom of the mind that transcends the imprisonment of the body. Only in the most general terms are these parts echoed by Johnson. More akin to the tone of *Rasselas* is the ironic view of human weaknesses and insufficiencies in the face of the cosmic scheme perceptible in the verses that conclude the books of the *Consolation,* the account of Orpheus in III, xii, for instance, where the power of human love leads to disaster on the upward way and the sense of ironic discrepancy is perhaps at its strongest and most poignant,[47] or the distinctly ambiguous accounts of ancient heroes in IV, vii.

Boethius's Menippean dialogue takes up some of the commonplaces which Lucian treated ironically—the vain pursuit of happiness, the vanity of wishes, the power of fortune—with a heightened sense of the discrepancy between the position of the human sufferer and the transcendent capabilities personified in Philosophy which though still human are able to lead man to the divine. He goes beyond Lucian's here-and-now reality to focus on the status of the human mind and the affirmation of its freedom. While Johnson shares this central interest in the mind, he recognizes more clearly the delusions to which reason can be subject. He also affirms the value of a grasp on here-and-now reality, but with the important qualification that while freed from delusion it must be put in the perspective of the transcendent.

This perspective is in Boethius especially the gift of Philosophy. It does not take away melancholy or im-

perfection, but allows it to be seen in a larger context and thus transformed in significance. A similar gift of perspective occurs at the end of *Rasselas.* The wishing mortals continue with their wishing though now they know they will not get what they want. It is only those without such perspective who fall prey to disillusion or even madness. The difference is that between Swift and the Gulliver at the end of the fourth voyage[48]; with considerable variations of tone, the ends of many Menippean satires present something similar. This gift of perspective is an important reason why, I think, *Rasselas* does not seem ultimately to most readers a sad or nihilistic book. As Philosophy says, 'Talia sunt quippe quae restant, ut degustata quidem mordeant, interius autem recepta dulcescant.'[49]

6

The affiliation of *Rasselas* with the tradition of Menippean satire and with specific works from that tradition suggests an important dimension of the environment within which Johnson's imagination was operating when he wrote the book. Much recent scholarship on *Rasselas* deals, in fact, with aspects of its 'Menippean' character, even though the term is not used.[50] The 'Lucianic' strain in Johnson is not confined to *Rasselas.* This quality of vision has for long been recognized as part of the essential Johnson even if this name has not been applied to it, and it is strong in the periodical essays. I have argued elsewhere that the *Idler,* written at the same time as *Rasselas,* can profitably be associated with works of this kind.[51] In *Rasselas* Johnson takes up themes basic to Lucian and Boethius and seems even to engage specific works and passages by them, but he transforms the ancient commonplaces into something Johnsonian and of the eighteenth century. There is no single 'source' for *Rasselas* (like the undiscovered source of the Nile), but a confluence of many streams. He goes beyond Lucian in a specifically Christian way and gives to Boethius a more directly practical, here-and-now thrust. He casts his work as a 'tale' in compliance, no doubt, with the taste of his time and the model of the contemporary *conte philosophique* (though narrative of one kind or another had always been common enough in the genre), and he brings in not only Abyssinian and Biblical background but suggestions of a popular genre, the oriental tale, and elements of other forms and genres. He gives every indication of writing with awareness not only of a vast philosophic and theological background which he distills to its essentials but also of how things were done in this *kind* of work and of the sort of emphases it usually gave.

At the core of *Rasselas* is an exploration of the psychology and environment of choice, which is equally important with the idea of the search for happiness as the controlling principle of the book (though the two can scarcely be separated). Johnson produced a work which generates all sorts of meaningful patterning in terms not only of ideas *per se* but of structures of thought, imagery and human situation. It is a technique and a structure calculated to raise questions, stimulate thought, and undermine orthodox illusions rather than to provide answers. Truths always exist inhuman contexts. A reader needs consequently to cultivate an awareness not only of obvious pattern but, as Ehrenpreis suggests, a sensitivity to variations in tone and style and to complex and subtle ironies which, while they do not undercut the main thrust of the work, may qualify it. This constant possibility of irony and allusion means that a reader must further cultivate an awareness of the impact of differences as well as similarities within the larger controlling patterns which he perceives in the book. In this context the final direction of the book is not to the disillusioning proof of a thesis but to a satiric sense that we should discover reality by whatever means and learn to rest with the impossibilities and imperfections of the world in the context of a larger knowledge that inoculates us against disillusion and in Christian terms sanctifies and transforms the ordinary.

Notes

[1] *The Choice of Life* (New Haven: Yale University Press, 1973), p. 163.

[2] 'Johnson's *Rasselas:* Implicit Contexts', *Journal of English and Germanic Philology,* LXXIV (1975), 1-25. Page references to this and other works cited will after the first citation be included in parentheses in the text.

[3] Irvin Ehrenpreis, '*Rasselas* and Some Meanings of "Structure" in Literary Criticism', *Novel,* XIV (1981), 101-17. See pp. 112-13.

[4] Johnson himself in 1778 observed to Boswell the similarity in plan and conduct between *Candide* and *Rasselas.* See [James Boswell, *The Life of Samuel Johnson, LL.D.,* edited by George Birkbeck Hill, revised by L.F. Powell, 6 vols. (Oxford: Clarendon Press, 1934)], Vol. 1, p. 342. For a comparison see James L. Clifford, 'Some Remarks on *Candide* and *Rasselas'* in *Bicentenary Essays on* Rasselas, ed. Magdi Wahba, Supplement to *Cairo Studies in English,* 1959, pp. 7-14, and McIntosh, pp. 209-12.

[5] E.g. see Alvin Whitley, 'The Comedy of *Rasselas*', *E.L.H.,* XXIII (1956), 48-70 (who blunts his argument by making little distinction between satire and comedy); Arieh Sachs, *Passionate Intelligence* (Baltimore: Johns Hopkins Press, 1967), pp. 98-9; Clifford, p. 10; George F. Butterick, 'The Comedy of Johnson's *Rasselas*', *Studies in the Humanities,* II (1971), 25-31. Vs. Sheldon Sacks, *Fiction and the Shape of Belief* (Berkeley and Los Angeles: University of California Press,

1964), especially pp. 49-60; Patrick O'Flaherty, 'Dr. Johnson as Equivocator: The Meaning of *Rasselas*', *Modern Language Quarterly,* XXXI (1970), 195-208.

[6] In the absence of agreed-on English names I follow the convention of referring to Lucian's works by the Latin names common since theRenaissance. A table of equivalent names appears in Christopher Robinson, *Lucian and His Influence in Europe* (London: Duckworth, 1979), pp. 239-41.

[7] John Dryden, *Of Dramatic Poesy and Other Critical Essays,* ed. George Watson (London: Everyman, 1962), Vol. 2, p. 97.

[8] In this and other citations I refer to the fourth edition of Johnson's *Dictionary* (London, 1773), two volumes folio. For an extended discussion of meanings of and attitudes to satire in this period see P. K. Elkin, *The Augustan Defence of Satire* (Oxford: Clarendon Press, 1973).

[9] See Elkin, Chapters 6 and 7.

[10] Originally in *Eighteenth-Century Studies in Honor of Donald F. Hyde,* ed. W. H. Bond (New York: Grolier Club, 1970), pp. 145-60. The argument is repeated in Bate's *Samuel Johnson* (New York: Harcourt Brace Jovanovich, 1977), pp. 489-97. Cf. Johnson's 'Life of Akenside', para. 7 (*Lives of the English Poets,* edited by George Birkbeck Hill, 3 vols. (Oxford: Clarendon, 1905)], Vol. 3, p. 413).

[11] It will be noted that in this discussion I have in mind the treatments of satire by Edward W. Rosenheim, *Swift and the Satirist's Art* (Chicago: University of Chicago Press, 1963), especially pp. 11-13, and Sheldon Sacks, especially pp. 7 and 26. The latter uses his definition of satire to differentiate it from the apologue, of which he uses *Rasselas* as an example. While I respect the theoretical rigour and literary perception of these writers I cannot completely accept their arguments on this point.

[12] Sachs, pp. 98-9.

[13] *De Satyrica Graecorum Poesi et Romanorum Satira* (1605; rept. Delmar, N.Y.: Scholar's Facsimiles and Reprints, 1973, intro. Peter E. Medine). Parts of Casaubon's discussion are translated in Eugene P. Kirk, *Menippean Satire: An Annotated Catalogue of Texts and Criticism* (New York: Garland, 1980), pp. 231-33.

[14] This book was in Johnson's undergraduate library. See Aleyn Lyell Reade, *Johnsonian Gleanings: Part V. The Doctor's Life 1728-1735* (1928; repr. New York: Octagon, 1968), p. 225.

[15] Dryden, Vol. 2, pp. 113-15.

[16] J. Bompaire, *Lucien Ecrivain* (Paris: Boccard, 1958), pp. 550-62; Kirk, n. 13, above, especially his description of the genre, p. xi.

[17] N. Fyre, *Anatomy of Criticism* (Princeton, N.J.: Princeton University Press, 1957), pp. 308-12.

[18] Cf. the tendency of most recent discussions of structure in *Rasselas*. See, for example, Gwin J. Kolb, 'The Structure of *Rasselas*', *P.M.L.A.,* LXVI (1951), 698-717; Emrys Jones, 'The Artistic Form of *Rasselas*', *Review of English Studies,* n.s. XVIII (1967), 387-401; and Eric Rothstein, *Systems of Order and Inquiry in Later Eighteenth-Century Fiction* (Berkeley and Los Angeles: University of California Press, 1975), pp. 23-61. Rothstein lists other studies on p. 37.

[19] Boswell, *Life,* Vol. 2, p. 121.

[20] M. Bakhtin, *Problems of Dostoevsky's Poetics,* tr. R. W. Rotsel (Ann Arbor: Ardis, 1973). See Ch. 4, especially pp. 87-113.

[21] See ibid., p. 296 n. 91.

[22] Tracy, 'Democritus, Arise! A Study of Johnson's Humour', *Yale Review,* XXXIX (1950), 294-310; Whitley, 'The Comedy of *Rasselas*'; Butterick, 'The Comedy of Johnson's *Rasselas*'.

[23] Casaubon, *De . . . Satira,* p. 270. A translation is in Kirk, p. 233.

[24] *Chaucer and Menippean Satire* (Madison: University of Wisconsin Press, 1981). See especially Chapters 1-3.

[25] Cf. Ronald Paulson's contrast of Juvenal and Lucian, *The Fictions of Satire* (Baltimore: Johns Hopkins Press, 1967), p. 32.

[26] In this paragraph I paraphrase Payne, p. 11.

[27] Motto of the *Rambler* from Horace, *Epistles,* I, i, 14.

[28] *Eighteenth-Century Arguments for Immortality and Johnson's 'Rasselas',* English Literary Studies Monograph Series No. 9 (Victoria, B.C.: University of Victoria, 1977).

[29] Charles G. Osgood, 'Johnson and Macrobius'. *Modern Language Notes,* LXIX (1954), 246. Osgood associates the text he proposes from Macrobius with *Rasselas.*

[30] See Reade, *Johnsonian Gleanings,* Part V, Appendix K, pp. 213-29.

[31] Boswell, *Life,* Vol. 1, pp. 99-100.

[32] *Nonnuli e Luciani Dialogis selecti, Et Scholiis illustrati ab Edwardo Leedes . . . In usum eorum, Qui dum Graecari student, non metuunt interim ridere* (London, 1678). There were later editions.

[33] Donald Greene, *Samuel Johnson's Library: An Annotated Guide,* andJ. D. Fleeman (ed.), *The Sale Catalogue of Samuel Johnson's Library: A Facsimile Edition,* English Literary Studies Monograph Series Nos. 1 and 2 (Victoria, B.C.: University of Victoria, 1975).

[34] For Chaucer, *Life,* Vol. 4, p. 381. For Cervantes and Boileau, William Shaw and Hester Lynch Piozzi, *Memoirs and Anecdotes of Dr. Johnson,* ed. Arthur Sherbo (London: Oxford University Press, 1974), pp. 152-53. See also Johnson's 'Life of Butler', paras. 22, 23, 25 (*Lives,* Vol. 1, pp. 209-10). Cf. Stuart Tave's account of eighteenth-century readings of *Don Quixote* as primarily satiric, *The Amiable Humorist* (Chicago: University of Chicago Press, 1960), pp. 151-63.

[35] Anecdote from Croker's Boswell in *Johnsonian Miscellanies,* ed. G. B. Hill (1897; rept. New York: Barnes and Noble, 1966), Vol. 2, p. 405; *Life,* Vol. 3, p. 10.

[36] He suggested a translation to Elizabeth Carter, 1738 (*Life,* Vol. 1, p. 102) and undertook one with Mrs. Thrale in the mid-1760s (Samuel Johnson, *Poems,* ed. David Nichol Smith and Edward L. McAdam, 2nd edn. (Oxford: Clarendon Press, 1974), pp. 169-77). See also *Idler* 69 (11 August 1759) on previous English translations. See *Ramblers* 6, 7, 96, 143, 178, *Adventurer* 10.

[37] Jonathan Culler, *The Pursuit of Signs* (Ithaca, N.Y.: Cornell University Press, 1981), p. 38.

[38] See e.g. *De mercede conductis,* 42; *Somnium sive vita,* 5-16; *Prometheus es in verbis,* 6. The extended metaphor of scaling the heights in *Hermotimus* 5 is also reminiscent of one of Johnson's allegorical images. Parenthetical references in the text will be to the marginal chapter numbers in the Loeb edition (as above in this note) followed by volume and page for quotations. Lucian, ed. with English transl. by A. M. Harmon, K. Kilburn, and M. D. Macleod (London: Heinemann, 1913-67), 8 vols.

[39] Cf. also *Menippus* and perhaps *Charon, Icaromenippus,* and *Piscator.*

[40] Walter Harte, *An Essay on Satire, Particularly on the Dunciad* (1730), Augustan Reprint Society, Publication Number 132 (Los Angeles, 1968), p. 18.

[41] *The History of Rasselas Prince of Abissinia,* ed. R. W. Chapman (Oxford: Clarendon Press, 1927), p. 30.

[42] Cf. not only *Navigium* and *Icaromenippus* but *Somnium sive Gallus,* 23, and *Hermotimus, 71.*

[43] Gwin J. Kolb, 'Johnson's "Dissertation on Flying" and John Wilkins' *Mathematical Magick*', *Modern Philology,* XLVII (1949), 24-31; Louis Landa, 'Johnson's Feathered Man: "A Dissertation on the Art of Flying" Considered' in *Eighteenth-Century Studies in Honor of Donald F. Hyde,* ed. W. H. Bond (New York: Grolier Club, 1970), pp. 161-78.

[44] In the original the elder addresses the one of limited experience as *thrasutate,* a noun formation related to the adjective *thrasus* meaning in a good sense 'bold, spirited, resolute' and in a bad sense 'rash, venturous, presumptuous', and it is tempting to speculate that some residual memory of the word may have influenced Johnson's choice of an Abyssinian name for his prince, whose character its meaning certainly touches. Johnson had formed many names in the *Rambler* on Greek roots. One may add that *'Nekuia'* is the title of a dialogue by the real Menippus thought to lie behind Lucian's *Menippus* and apparently involving a descent to the underworld and an exploration of the vanity of human wishes. Does Pekuah suggest *peko* meaning to comb or to card wool, perhaps the occupations of a lady's companion? Or does Imlac, another real Abyssinian name, suggest *elake,* 'he spoke loud, shouted forth' or 'he sang', activities not inappropriate to a rhetorician and poet? It may be added that the subtitle of *Hermotimus* is *'peri hairese n',* translated in the Loeb as 'concerning the Sects [of philosophy]'. It could also be translated 'concerning choices'. *Rasselas,* of course, in Johnson's letter to William Strahan of 20 January 1759, was titled 'The Choice of Life'. The title of *Vitarum auctio* (Philosophies for Sale) is *'Bi n prasis',* 'the sale of lives', or, as the Loeb editor points out, 'of various types of the philosophic life' as they are embodied in their practitioners—a meaning close to Johnson's usage here. Cf. also J. P. Hardy's note on the 'choice of life' topos in ancient literature in his edition of *Rasselas* (London: Oxford University Press, 1968), pp. 141-42.

[45] *The Fictions of Satire,* pp. 31-42.

[46] The pattern may be a frequent Menippean one in so far as there is a final movement to the divine.

[47] Johnson not only translated these verses with Mrs. Thrale but alluded to them in *Ramblers* 143 and 178. The lines he quotes in the latter are not far in tone (and even form), especially in the Latin, from the opening paragraph of *Rasselas,* and the paragraph following in *Rambler* 178 suggests the context of the search for happiness and its relation to the life of faith. Cf. especially ll. 52-4.

[48] Cf. Swift's letter to Pope, 26 November 1725: 'I tell you after all that I do not hate Mankind, it is vous autres who hate them because you would have them reasonable Animals, and are Angry for being disappointed' (*Correspondence,* ed. Harold Williams (Oxford: Clarendon Press, 1963), Vol. 3, p. 118).

[49] 'Those remedies that are left now are like those that sting on the tongue, but sweeten once taken within' (III, i: *The Theological Tractates and The Consolation of Philosophy,* ed. H. F. Stewart, E. K. Rand, and S. J. Tester, Loeb Classical Library (Cambridge, Mass.: Harvard University Press, 1973), pp. 228-29).

[50] Among critical discussions, for example, Carey McIntosh anticipates several Menippean qualities in his description of the form of *Rasselas.* See *The Choice of Life,* e.g. pp. 201, 206, and other parts of his discussion. Among others see also Ehrenpreis, '*Rasselas* and Some Meanings of "Structure" in Literary Criticism'; Whitley, 'The Comedy of *Rasselas*'; Sheridan Baker, '*Rasselas:* Psychological Irony and Romance', in *Essays in English Neoclassicism in Memory of Charles B. Woods: Philological Quarterly,* XLV (1966), 249-61. The need for studies of large and complex backgrounds is typical of Menippean works. There are many of the backgrounds of *Rasselas.*

[51] James F. Woodruff, 'Johnson's *Idler* and the Anatomy of Idleness', *English Studies in Canada,* VI (1980), 21-38, especially 36-7.

Marlene R. Hansen (essay date 1985)

SOURCE: "Sex and Love, Marriage and Friendship: A Feminist Reading of the Quest for Happiness in *Rasselas,*" in *English Studies,* Vol. 6, 1985, pp. 513-25.

[*In the following essay, Hansen argues that Johnson portrays friendship as the way to happiness in* Rasselas. *Hansen also suggests that Johnson's depiction of friendship suggests his view that women and men share an equal humanity.*]

In this article I intend to argue that happiness is not shown to be unobtainable in ***Rasselas,*** although it is not connected with any particular way of life. Happiness arises from friendship, that is, from equal and affectionate relationships, which may break down the barriers of social, generational and gender differences. I call it a feminist reading because I place special emphasis on the role played by the female characters, whom I examine in relation to the preconceptions of eighteenth century literature and the contemporary attitudes. It will be seen that my methods are eclectic: I start with a thematic analysis of the text and proceed to a consideration of current ideas about the nature of women, ending up with some remarks on Johnson's own attitudes to women.

Rasselas is not a sexy book. There is not even much romantic interest; and perhaps only the force of Johnson's prose style keeps us from finding it incongruous that the search for happiness circumvents any serious consideration of sexual relationships. It is true that there is a protracted debate on marriage, but it is largely concerned with the family as an institution, with its intergenerational problems. Despite these obvious discouragements, I intend to consider the presentation of sexuality in *Rasselas.*

One notable point is that none of the characters falls in love, or even seriously anticipates the possibility of doing so. The nearest we get to a love-affair is the warm regard which grows up between Pekuah and the unnamed astronomer, which restores his sanity. This, however, is soon assimilated into the general good fellowship of the sociable group, and it is clearly not envisaged that their relationship should become official and permanent: in fact, we are informed the Pekuah's whim at the end of the tale is to embrace religion, as 'she was weary of expectation and disgust, and would gladly be fixed in some unvariable state'[1]— in a *female* community; while the astronomer, like Imlac, was content to drift aimlessly through life 'without directing their course to any particular port'.[2] After twenty years of travel, apparently without any notice of the opposite sex worth mentioning, Imlac decides to marry and 'sit down in the quiet of domestick life',[3] but being rejected on his first offer gives up the attempt. The nearest Rasselas himself comes to contemplating a sexual relationship is summed up in his pronouncement, 'Whenever I shall seek a wife, it shall be my first question, whether she be willing to be led by reason?'[4] His 'whenever' is as inconclusive as his premises are naive. Nekayah shows equal detachment when, in reply to her brother's moralising observation that 'the world must be peopled by marriage, or peopled without it.' 'How the world is to be peopled, returned Nekayah, is not my care, and needs not be yours. I see no danger that the present generation should omit to leave successors behind them.'[5]

The only significant figure in the tale who actually has sex is the desert chieftain, that gloomy, noble alienated figure, who kidnaps Pekuah and holds her for ransom. Her terrors on being captured are soon alleviated when she learns that 'the Arab ranged the country merely to get riches',[6] and his sexual needs are satisfied within the confines of his seraglio. Pekuah is left to the society of these women, but finds them no company for her:

> The diversions of the women . . . were only childish play, by which the mind accustomed to stronger operations could not be kept busy. I could do all which they delighted in doing by powers merely sensitive, while my intellectual faculties were flown to Cairo. They ran from room to room as a bird

hops from wire to wire in his cage. They danced for the sake of motion, as lambs frisk in the meadow. One sometimes pretended to be hurt that the others might be alarmed, or hid herself that the others might seek her. Part of their time passed in watching the progress of light bodies that floated on the river, and part in marking the various forms into which the clouds broke in the sky.

> Their business was only needlework, in which I and my maids sometimes helped them; but you know that the mind will easily straggle from the fingers, nor will you suspect that captivity and absence from Nekayah could receive solace from silken flowers.

> Nor was much satisfaction to be hoped from their conversation: for of what could they be expected to talk? They had seen nothing; for they had lived from their earliest youth in that narrow spot: of what they had not seen they could have no knowledge, for they could not read. They had no ideas but of the few things that were within their view, and had hardly names for any thing but their cloaths and their food. As I bore a superiour character, I was often called to terminate their quarrels, which I decided as equitably as I could. If it could have amused me to hear the complaints of each against the rest, I might have been often detained by long stories, but the motives of their animosity were so small that I could not listen without intercepting the tale.[7]

I have quoted at such length because this will be a key passage in my argument. Pekuah is here giving information not only about the Arab women but also about herself by way of contrast. At this point she embodies the Johnsonian concept of the mature human personality, whose mind is never fully at rest, who seeks satisfaction beyond the inadequacies of the present moment, and for whom physical existence is insubstantial beside the moral and intellectual. The Arab women, on the other hand, are compared to children and to animals, and are by implication neither truly adult nor indeed truly human. They are unconscious spiritual prisoners, occupied with the same inevitable songs and motions, their minds and bodies integrated in an eternal present, like Shelley's skylark or Keats's nightingale. They lack the alienation that makes us human; and while Pekuah's intellectual faculties were flown to Cairo, a neo-Platonic bird of the divine intellectual soul, they ran from room to room as a cage-bird hops from wire to wire. Their condition is that to which human nature can sink without the stimulation of responsibility and education.[8]

These are the Arab's bedfellows, but scarcely his loves or companions; for him, the delights of eroticism are not entangled with the solemn burden of self-awareness. He separates his true self from his sexual nature, and the beauty of the women who gratify his lust is only a flower to pluck and throw away, whereas his true delight is the conversation of Pekuah. Before he knew her, his attitude to women had been the one generated by patriarchal societies, which confine the minds and bodies of women, turning them into auxiliary persons whose function is to minister to the needs of their fully human menfolk. Pekuah, by being interesting as a person, cannot become a sex-object and as such implicitly degraded. Knowing her, the Arab becomes aware of a quality of companionship which could mitigate his loneliness, and he understands enough not to seduce her: the divisiveness of patriarchy makes sexuality a barrier rather than a bridge between the sexes which must be excluded from honourable relationships. It is also apparent that the Arab is spiritually as unmarried as Rasselas and his companions, and shares with them an awareness of the complexities of existence that is so oppressive that one can scarcely imagine them abandoning themselves to passion. Some of these complexities arise from the conflict between the doctrine of human equality and the various kinds of subordination found in society.

But certainly, both love and happiness exist within the framework of the story; indeed, it is shown that in the end there can be no possibility of lasting happiness without love. There is, however, a delusive happiness, an ecstatic, explosive experience which cannot settle into a prolonged state, a kind of epiphany akin to Keats's 'Joy, whose hand is ever at his lip / Bidding adieu'. In *Rasselas* it functions as a release from tension, whether confinement or deprivation, a kind of emotional orgasm whose euphoria soon collapses into some such negative affect as ennui or panic. One may cite Imlac's reactions to finding himself free of his father's repressive authority and embarked upon the sublime ocean:

> When I first entered upon the world of waters, and lost sight of land, I looked round with pleasing terrour, and thinking my soul enlarged by the boundless prospect, imagined that I could gaze round forever without satiety; but, in a short time, I grew weary of looking on barren uniformity, where I could only see again what I had already seen.[9]

When he first beholds the world beyond the Happy Valley Rasselas experiences a similar elation, though in this case the deflation is communicated indirectly and ironically, via the reactions of other characters:

> The prince looked round with rapture, anticipated all the pleasures of travel, and in thought was already transported beyond his father's dominions. Imlac, though very joyful at his escape, had less expectation of pleasure in the world, which he had before tried, and of which he had been weary. . . . The princess and her maid turned their eyes towards every part, and, seeing nothing to bound their prospect,

considered themselves as in danger of being lost in boundless vacuity.[10]

In both cases, the joy of hope is fallacious as it lacks an adequate object. Furthermore, Johnson characteristically brings his pragmatism to bear on the sublimity of natural scenery, which he tended to regard as boring once its initial impact has faded, and morally irrelevant.[11]

The third instance of ecstatic happiness is of a different nature and proceeds in a more auspicious direction. Again, it is a release from tension, in this case the tension resulting from deprivation: the reunion of Nekayah with her friend Pekuah, whom she thought she had lost forever:

> The princess and her favourite embraced each other with a transport too violent to be expressed, and went out together to pour the tears of tenderness in secret, and exchange professions of kindness and gratitude.[12]

In this case there is no deflation or defection of the emotion, but it simply spreads out genially into a settled state. And this must be because friendship is one of the few positive values of the book, and perhaps the only one not to operate on the purely spiritual level: as such, it is the only unambiguous good. Affectionate mutual regard does not disappoint; in fact, it is the precondition of other kinds of happiness. When Pekuah is abducted, and seems irrevocably lost, Nekayah resolves 'to retire from the world with all its flatteries and deceits'; however, Imlac advises her:

> 'That you have been deprived of one pleasure is no very good reason for rejection of the rest.' 'Since Pekuah was taken from me, said the princess, I have no pleasure to reject or to retain. She that has no one to love or trust has little to hope. She wants the radical principle of happiness . . . Wealth is nothing but as it is bestowed, and knowledge nothing but as it is communicated: they must be imparted to others, and to whom could I now delight to impart them?'[13]

Sad words of wisdom; and not merely the transient sentiments of a shocked and bereaved woman, for they are reiterated in the discourse of the sage whom the company fall in with one evening on the banks of the Nile. They are impressed with his immense learning and his comprehensive grasp of the causes of things, and congratulate him on possessing this unfailing source of pleasure; but he too is bored and disillusioned, and strives to correct their misconceptions:

> Let the gay and the vigorous expect pleasure in their excursions, it is enough that age can obtain ease. To me the world has lost its novelty: I look round, and see what I remember to have seen in happier

days. I rest against a tree, and consider, that in the same shade I once disputed upon the annual overflow of the Nile with a friend who is now silent in the grave . . . I have neither mother to be delighted with the reputation of her son, nor wife to partake the honours of her husband. I have outlived my friends and my rivals. Nothing is now of much importance; for I cannot extend my interest beyond myself.[14]

It is certain that love is necessary to happiness, love that has to do with communication and sharing, with the dignified concept of mutual regard. Everywhere in the book there is the quiet insistence that people need objects of affection to give their endeavours meaning—their *secular* endeavours, at least; and I find that the solitary religious quest which seems to receive the final accolade is thrown into ironic perspective by much of the realistic psychological investigation. Remember also that the grandiloquent systems of the stoic philosopher are immediately discredited when his daughter dies and he is left alone.

Sexuality does not figure at all as a means to happiness. Perhaps this is one aspect of Johnson's concern to define the human in contrast to the animal, for it is unlikely that he consciously held views about the nature of sexuality under patriarchy, whatever his observation of life may have taught him. It is certainly a concomitant of Johnson's rationalistic separation of matter and spirit. His rationalism and basically empirical attitudes would never permit him to regard conjugal sexuality as divine, as Milton does. However, Milton's doctrine of marriage was patriarchal, as was that of the majority of Johnson's contemporaries, while **Rasselas** is certainly not a male chauvinistic document. If we look at it in its contemporary context, we will realize that it is constructed around an ideal of freedom and equality which is surprisingly advanced, and this includes the element of sexual equality. The prince and his sister, his tutor, her maid, and the learned astronomer form a group of individuals who have freely chosen each other's company, who come to respect and care for each other, practise mutual tolerance and co-operation, and receive pleasure and happiness from this voluntary association.

Friendship, indeed, seems to be presented as a humanistic quality, the potential for which distinguishes humankind from the other creatures; but like language and reason, the primary human characteristics, it is a quality which can be abused, or deteriorate, or fail to develop properly without proper nurture and education. **Rasselas** provides examples of people who have not developed their full human potential. There are, for instance, the celibate, who are further characterized as misanthropic recluses who

dream away their time without friendship, without fondness, and are driven to rid themselves of the day, for which they have nouse, by childish amusements, or vicious delights. They act as beings under the constant sense of some known inferiority, that fills their minds with rancour, and their tongues with censure. They are peevish at home, and malevolent abroad; and, as the outlaws of human nature, make it their business and their pleasure to disturb that society which debars them from its privileges. To live without feeling or exciting sympathy, to be ·fortunate without adding to the felicity of others, or afflicted without tasting the balm of pity, is a state more gloomy than solitude: it is not retreat but exclusion from mankind.[15]

This, we may protest, is not entirely fair to the single state: after all, the speaker and her friends are themselves unmarried.[16] Nekayah seems to regard celibacy as indicative of a general refusal, or inability, to form connections and accept responsibility. Marriage here means the highest form of friendship, and the deprivations of celibacy are primarily social, not sexual. Indeed, the refusal to involve one's fate with anyone else amounts to 'exclusion from mankind'.

The two other important instances of groups who fail to develop their human faculties are specifically female: the women of the seraglio, mentioned above, and the daughters of the middle-class families visited by Nekayah in her investigations of 'private life'. Though nominally Egyptian, these girls are certainly modelled on English young ladies of the time and function as a familiar counterpart to the more exotic Arab women, as if to drive the point home:

The daughters of many houses were airy and cheerful, but Nekayah had been too long accustomed to the conversation of Imlac and her brother to be much pleased with childish levity and prattle which had no meaning. She found their thoughts narrow, their wishes low, and their merriment often artificial. Their pleasures, poor as they were, could not be preserved pure, but were embittered by petty competitions and worthless emulation. They were always jealous of the beauty of each other; of a quality to which solicitude can add nothing, and from which detraction can take nothing away. Many were in love with triflers like themselves, and many fancied they were in love when in truth they were only idle. Their affection was seldom fixed on sense or virtue, and therefore seldom ended but in vexation. Their grief, however, like their joy, was transient; every thing floated in their mind unconnected with the past or future, so that one desire easily gave way to another, as a second stone cast into the water effaces and confounds the circles of the first.

With these girls she played as with inoffensive animals, and found them proud of her countenance, and weary of her company.[17]

There are several points here that are relevant to Johnson's humanistic preoccupations: the girls are compared to 'inoffensive animals', their levity is 'childish' and their conversation 'prattle which had no meaning'. Their concerns are not rational: the present moment for them is 'unconnected with the past or future', and their emotions are transient and superficial, mere reflex responses without a moral basis. Nor are they capable of appreciating Nekayah's superior character, except from the point of view of social prestige. In this they are not superior to Pekuah's companions in the harem, who can only make use of the captive lady's education and experience to help them settle their silly differences. Such girls are not capable of friendship: their relationships are 'embittered by petty competitions and worthless emulation', as will commonly be the case with women brought up to regard their own worth as dependent on the favour they find in men's eyes.

I do not think that the foolishness, giddiness and immaturity of these girls is stressed in order to argue the natural inferiority of women, as the princess and her maid are by way of contrast two young women who undergo the same process as the prince, an educational adventure towards full humanity begun equally in restlessness and discontent.[18] Rasselas, who at first imagines that only he is dissatisfied with life in the Happy Valley, learns that in fact he is not alone: most of the attendants and entertainers curse the day they first entered the place, especially those who are unlike Imlac in that their memories are not stocked with images. These, 'whose minds have no impressions but of the present moment, are either corroded by malignant passions, or sit stupid in the gloom of perpetual vacancy'.[19] The only one to attempt escape is the projector who designs the wings, but his hatred of the place has become so fervent that it distorts his intellectual ability, causing him to reason illogically and disregard essential objections. Unvaried security and pleasure do not apparently make for satisfying human lives.

When the prince and Imlac have half finished work on the secret tunnel they receive a secret visit from Nekayah, who informs them:

> I am equally weary of confinement with yourself, and not less desirous of knowing what is done or suffered in the world. Permit me to fly with you from this tasteless tranquillity, which will yet grow more loathsome when you have left me.[20]

Nekayah's plea is a departure from the convention, most familiar and probably most representative in *Genesis* in the Bible and in *Paradise Lost,* in *Hamlet* and in various Faust stories, that the male is the quintessentially human figure, while women are simply one of the problems he encounters, the most serious temptation of the flesh, the motive for deserting reason and virtue. It is significant that Nekayah is not the mistress of Rasselas but his sister; as such, her motives cannot be sensual and presented as an obstacle to the male. She is his female counterpart. The princess demands the right to accompany her brother as her quest is the same as his.

She and her lady-in-waiting come to represent one of the important human qualities, friendship,[21] and thus function as a contrast to the class of celibates (the wilfully alone) and to the flighty middle-class girls (the uneducated and undeveloped personalities), at the same time refuting the misogynistic dictum, still sometimes heard, that women are incapable of friendship. This may well have had some substance in an age when women's minds were generally uncultivated and when, as marriage was usually their only approved aim in life, being decisive for their security and social position, rivalry with other women was encouraged. In 1727, a generation before *Rasselas* was written, Swift comments in 'A letter to a young lady on her marriage': 'I advise that your Company at home should consist of Men rather than Women. To say the Truth, I never yet knew a tolerable Woman to be fond of her own Sex.'[22] He clearly cannot envisage that a woman might receive any benefit, either of instruction, intellectual stimulation or affection from the company of her own sex. Johnson, who was acquainted with the letters of Katherine Philips,[23] the High Priestess of friendship, knew better; furthermore, by the mid-century, thanks in part to the enormous expansion of the publishing industry, there were more, and more noticeable, 'tolerable' women in England. Swift's views, indeed, were not unreasonable, given the state of society in the early eighteenth century. Furthermore, his misogyny is merely a subsection of his cynical misanthropy, his refusal to expect too much of the human race; he never gives evidence of the rabid hatred of women evinced by true misogynists[24] like the unspeakable author of *Man Superior to Woman* (1739), a specious and condescending reaction to feminine 'wit'. Swift is a conservative who, though he may seem to agree with 'Sophia' that the apparent inferiority of women is the result of practices dictated by custom and interest,[25] can give his young lady no more radical advice than that she must submissively learn from her husband and his friends. Thirty years later, *Rasselas* presents serious, educated female characters who do not define themselves in relation to men.

But this was exceptional. Popular fiction aimed at a female readership has from the earliest times concerned itself chiefly with romance and marriage and portrayed female excellence almost exclusively as it functioned as a bait for Prince Charming, and this was certainly true in Johnson's day, even of the better quality writers. Richardson, who was probably the most popular of all with women, shows both the comic and tragic aspect of this world-view, but does not challenge it.

The only considerable eighteenth century novelist to depart substantially from these stereotypes is Defoe, who is much more interested in the money side of sexual relationships and whose major female protagonist, Moll Flanders, while endowed with wit and beauty, is far from a paragon of virtue and perfectly aware of the economic aspects of her sexuality. Defoe, incidentally, also held moderate feminist views more than half a century before the publication of *Rasselas:* as his essay on the education of women demonstrates, he realized that lack of educational opportunities was one significant cause of the inferior status of women. In this essay, however, despite his evident wish to think justly of the other sex, Defoe betrays by his linguistic usage that he cannot avoid regarding the masculine half of our species as 'man', and hence by association as 'the human race':

> And, without partiality, a woman of sense and manners is the finest and most delicate part of GOD's Creation, the glory of Her Maker, and the great instance of His singular regard to man, His darling creature: to whom He gave the best gift either GOD could bestow or man receive.[26]

Such slight, casual usage is indicative of deeper attitudes which the writer must have shared with the greater part of his contemporaries, probably female as well as male. We can cite by contrast this sentence from the opening chapter of *Rasselas:*

> According to the custom which has descended from age to age among the monarchs of the torrid zone, Rasselas was confined in a private palace, with the other sons and daughters of Abissinian royalty, till the order of succession should call him to the throne.[27]

It is significant that both 'sons and daughters' are specified, not simply 'sons' or 'heirs': from the very first page of *Rasselas,* women are visible members of the human race. Whether this indicates a general change of sensibility in the half century since *An Essay on Projects* is not to be decided here, but his Eastern tale does show Johnson's individual consciousness of women's equal humanity. This can further be seen in the context of the rather voluptuous and sensational genre which provides the literary background to the work.

We are all familiar with the fantastic adventures and romantic sexuality of the Oriental stories, and also with their gender stereotypes, later to become part of our popular culture through the success of 'Gothic' orientalism and Byron's metrical romances. The genre became known in England in the first half of the eighteenth century largely from Ambrose Philips's translated *Persian Tales* (1714). It has been supposed that the second and third volumes of this collection, which relate the search for a happy man, could be a primary source

for *Rasselas.* However, as Geoffrey Tillotson observes,[28] each of the *Tales* provides an example of true love. The one dramatic incident in *Rasselas,* the episode which effects the travellers' transition from observation of life to involvement, concerns loss and reunion in friendship, not in romantic love. My contention is that in avoiding romance and eroticism and instead emphasizing friendship in this way, Johnson manages to avoid the polarization of the sexes. It is also significant that in the debate on marriage the main consideration is relative maturity and compatibility of temperament, and the question of sovereignty is circumvented: that is, the relations between the sexes are depicted as based on equality, not subordination.

Johnson had several advantages over his more genteel male contemporaries, whose literary education was limited to the prescribed syllabus at school and university and whose knowledge of society was equally superficial and restricted. He had read voraciously in his father's bookshop during his formative years, so that at Oxford he astounded his tutors with his extensive knowledge. During much of his early manhood he struggled in poverty and among the poor, an experience which taught him to respect human worth wherever he found it: his **'Elegy on the Death of Levet'** reminds us of this. I believe that both his reading and his wide acquaintance with life led him to regard the achievements of women seriously and sympathetically. In preparing his edition of Shakespeare his knowledge of the sources of the plays was probably obtained chiefly from Charlotte Lennox's *Shakespeare Illustrated,* and he had read the critical writings of Elizabeth Montagu, the Queen of the Blues;[29] the Blue-Stockings, indeed, were his conversational companions, with Elizabeth Carter, for whom he had a special respect, having her own chair in his house. Of the long *Rambler* series only four numbers are not by Johnson, and three of these he deputised to women (no. 30 to Catherine Talbot, nos. 44 and 100 to Elizabeth Carter; no. 97 is by Samuel Richardson). A glance through Boswell's *Life of Johnson* will suffice to show how important female acquaintances were in his social and intellectual life. One thinks also of his encouragement of Fanny Burney and his delight in her success. At the end of his life he writes approvingly, in the *Life of Addison,* of the general intellectual improvement of women in the course of the century.[30]

I cannot find any proof that Johnson may have read Mary Astell's *A Serious Proposal to the Ladies* (1694), the most important feminist essay on education before Mary Wollstonecraft; but, as A. D. Atkinson remarks:

> the reading record of a man who lived two centuries ago is bound to be deficient. We will never know every detail of his book-borrowing, his browsing in book-shops, or his reading in the King's library or on his visits to Oxford. What books he dipped into

while helping to compile the *Harleian Catalogue* can never be more than a matter of speculation.[31]

One may permit oneself to feel that the account of Nekayah's last ambition sounds like a reminiscence of Mary Astell's proposal for a female seminary:

> The princess thought, that of all sublunary things, knowledge was the best: she desired first to learn all sciences, and then purposed to found a college of learned women, in which she would preside, that, by conversing with the old, and educating the young, she might divide her time between the acquisition and communication of wisdom, and raise up for the next age models of *prudence,* and patterns of *piety.*[32] [my italics]

Mary Astell called her proposed seminary a 'Monastery or Religious Retirement' and envisaged it as

> a Type or Antepast of Heav'n, where your Employments will be, as there, to magnify God, to love one another, and to communicate that useful Knowledge which by the due improvement of your time in Study and Contemplation you will obtain. [It will be] a Seminary to stock the Kingdom with *pious* and *prudent* Ladies, and is to expel that cloud of Ignorance which Custom has involv'd us in . . . and to furnish our minds with a stock of solid and useful Knowledge, that the Souls of Women may no longer be the only unadorn'd and neglected things.[33] [my italics]

This passage partakes so much of the serious and dignified spirit of **Rasselas** that I cannot help conjecturing that, even if he had not read the work that it is taken from, Johnson would have been in agreement with the philosophy behind it. Nekayah's college is not so thoroughly a religious foundation as Astell's seminary, but it is immediately preceded in the text by Pekuah's ambition to fill the convent of St. Anthony with pious maidens and be made prioress of the order, so the work ends with the two ladies resolving to dedicate themselves to learning and piety. What **Rasselas** adds to *A Serious Proposal* is irony. It is characteristic that Nekayah must first learn *all* sciences, and that she and Pekuah automatically envisage themselves as the leaders of their respective institutions. But the two ladies have high and worthy ambitions, and should not be judged too harshly for sharing in the weaknesses of humanity.

In 1755, writing to her daughter, Lady Bute, about the education of girls, Lady Mary Wortley Montagu, who had known Mary Astell personally, remarks: 'I have already told you that I look on my Grand Daughters as Lay Nuns'.[34] It is interesting that two years previously her earnest recommendation that Lady Bute should provide a thorough scholarly education for her eldest daughter was followed by the caution that the girl should

> conceal whatever Learning she attains, with as much solicitude as she would hide crookedness and lameness. The parade of it can only serve to draw on her the envy, and consequently the most inveterate Hatred, of all he and she Fools, which will certainly be at least three parts in four of all her Aquaintance.[35]

This is a useful indication of the attitude to the educated woman prevalent in the highest circles in the decade in which **Rasselas** was written. It is also significant that Lady Bute rejected her mother's advice and brought up her daughters in the conventional manner. We might therefore conjecture that Johnson's serious-minded female characters could only win acceptance because they were dressed in Eastern costume. He uses the exoticism of his chosen genre not, as later writers were to do, to create divisive Romantic stereotypes, but to portray a world of the imagination where the destructive divisions are far less extreme than they were in the England of his day.

Imlac's discourse on the nature of the soul, as well as making explicit the body/soul dualism which seems intrinsic to Johnson's conception of sexuality, is also potential evidence for a doctrine of human equality and as such a suitable transition to the conclusion of a book whose main theme has been human nature. It is interesting that a similar rationalistic definition of the soul, as an immaterial entity which necessarily lacks physical attributes and distinctions, had been adduced in *Woman not inferior to Man* (1739):

> It is a known truth, that the difference of sexes regards only the body, and That merely as it relates to the propagation of human nature. But the soul, concurring to it only by consent, actuates all after the same manner; so that in *this* there is *no sex* at all. There is no more difference to be discern'd between the souls of a dunce, and a man of wit, or of an illiterate person and an experienced one, than between a boy of four and a man of forty years of age. And since there is not at most any greater difference between the souls of *Women* and *Men,* there can be no real diversity contracted from the body: All the diversity then must come from *education, exercise* and the *impressions* of those external objects which surround us in different circumstances.[36]

'Sophia' lacks Imlac's elegance of exposition and rigorous logic, but one gets the point.

It would not be true to say that Johnson's protestant belief in the equality of souls was entirely free of the patriarchal emphasis of the Civil War radicals. His views on male inheritance are wellknown, as indeed is his doctrine of subordination in society. His life and practice are not always easy to reconcile with his stated views; indeed, he is also a notorious master of inconsistency and of talking for effect. His outrageous remarks about female preachers, women who know Greek, and Mrs. Carter's skill in making puddings are also celebrated, though the last story is not necessarily sexist: Johnson did not despise female occupations like cooking and needlework, and may only have meant to imply that Mrs. Carter was no narrow pedant. But even today, only the most humourless feminists fail to find drag-shows amusing, and we all make jokes based on outmoded stereotypes: humour has its own enclosed universe, which is largely linguistic. Furthermore, there is no figure whose everyday conversation is so fully recorded as Johnson, and few people would think it fair to have their every observation handed down to posterity, often by a far from impartial recorder, and subjected to the scrutiny of scholars two hundred years later. The published works must have their own autonomy.

I believe that Johnson avoids romance and sexuality in **Rasselas** while providing admirable female characters because he wished to depict women as potentially equal to men, with similar problems and aims, and not as the supporting cast in a drama of humanity in which men play all the important roles. In many ways it is the work of a traditional humanist, but one whose humanism includes the whole human race. Although the book sometimes seems to communicate a vision of human futility its tone is lofty and sympathetic. The irony is not harsh and damaging, and the possibility of human dignity is never lost sight of. It depicts a group of people who need and respect each other, for whom incidental differences of age, sex and fortune are not important. Perhaps the noblest achievement of Prince Rasselas is his acceptance on equal terms of women and social inferiors, including his admiration and sympathy for the deluded astronomer. The dignity of the human ideal is not consistent with social or sexual prejudice.

Notes

1 Samuel Johnson, *The History of Rasselas, Prince of Abissinia,* ed. D. J. Enright, Penguin, 1976, p. 149. The text is based on the revised second edition of 1759 (see Note on the Text, p. 35).

2 Ibid p. 150.

3 Ibid p. 67.

4 Ibid p. 102.

5 Ibid pp. 99-100.

6 Ibid p. 122.

7 Ibid pp. 124-5.

8 I have developed this theme in my earlier article, *'Rasselas,* Milton, and Humanism', *English Studies,* vol. 60, no. 1 (Feb. 1979), pp. 14-22. Rasselas himself, at the beginning of the tale, is aware that his discontent sets him apart from the animals of the valley, but his humanity is undeveloped and at this stage expresses itself in play and make-believe rather than conscious moral action. Johnson, of course, contends here and in his essays that truly adult status is strenuous to achieve and maintain, and that most of us do in fact play and dream our way through life most of the time.

9 *Rasselas,* p. 57.

10 Ibid p. 73.

11 For my previous remarks on Johnson's ambiguous response to sublimity, see *'Rasselas,* Milton, and Humanism', p. 17.

12 *Rasselas* p. 118.

13 Ibid. p. 114.

14 Ibid. p. 136.

15 Ibid. p. 95.

16 In this context, it is well to remember that there are strong indications that unmarried women were generally despised and mistrusted in the eighteenth century, cf: 'there can be no doubt that the spinster in the early eighteenth century, when the problem first became of serious proportions, enjoyed a reputation for malice and ill-temper, "If an old maid should bite anybody, it would certainly be as mortal as the bite of a mad dog", remarked Defoe in 1723, and from then onward the ill-natured old maid became a feature of the English novel, and a subject of hostile comment by all writers of domestic handbooks'. Lawrence Stone, *The Family, Sex and Marriage in England 1500-1800,* Penguin Books, 1979, pp. 244-5. See also: 'Among the unmarried *Women,* what numberless Tribes of useless Things are there not, whose Pride, Avarice, Fickleness or icy Constitutions, rob human Nature of the Individuals they were intended to bear; and by not answering the Use they were given to him for, become a dead Weight upon *Man?* Indeed, if there are some among them less squeamish than the rest, who atone out of Wedlock for their Slowness to engage in it; how few of them is human Nature the better for? How many of them stifle the Fruit of their Pleasures before it is ripe! Not to speak of those Disgraces to the soft Shape they wear, who only delay Destruction to make it morecruel'. *Man Superior to* woman; *or a* vindication *of* man's *Natural Right of Sovereign Authority over the Woman,* London, 1739, p. 21. Need we suppose that this author

was alone in his contempt of women? This excerpt also demonstrates that the generalised term 'man' could commonly be used to denote the male sex rather than the entire human race. In *Rasselas,* women are portrayed as having the same potential and responsibilities as men: they are not mere breeding machines.

[17] *Rasselas,* pp. 91-2.

[18] I am not trying to persuade the reader that the behaviour of the two women shows no weak, 'feminine' traits. They are, for example, initially more fearful than the men, and Pekuah is superstitious, but the course of the action educates them away from these failings. They also display mirth when they first hear of the astronomer's madness; however, their triviality is soon corrected by Imlac's reprimand (p. 132). Characteristic female weaknesses are not presented as intrinsic but as the result of convention and upbringing and thus susceptible of cure.

[19] *Rasselas,* p. 68.

[20] Ibid. p. 72.

[21] I am using this term in a very generalized sense. Johnson's first definition of 'friendship' in his *Dictionary* is: 'The state of minds united in mutual benevolence', and as such the word can be applied to groups and social units as well as to pairs of friends, who thus represent a heightened form of the general social tie.

[22] Swift, *Works,* vol. IX, ed. Herbert Davis, p. 88, Oxford, 1968.

[23] A. D. Atkinson, 'Dr. Johnson's English Prose Reading', *N & Q,* 1953, p. 108.

[24] I do not see poems like 'The lady's Dressing-Room' as misogynistic, though they are certainly misanthropic. In them, men are wilfully deluded and then driven to madness because they are as unprepared as women to face the truth about physical existence.

[25] See, passim, *Woman not Inferior to Man: or, A short and modest Vindication of the natural Right of the FAIR-SEX to a perfect Equality of Power, Dignity, and Esteem, with the Men,* by SOPHIA, A Person of Quality, London, 1739 (2nd ed., which I have consulted, 1740).

[26] Daniel Defoe, 'The Education of Women', from *An Essay upon Projects,* written about 1692 but first published 1697. Quoted from *An English Garner,* ed. Edward Arber, Westminster, 1897, vol. II, p.267.

[27] *Rasselas,* p. 39.

[28] Geoffrey Tillotson, '*Rasselas* and the "Persian Tales",

T. L. S., Aug. 29, 1935, p. 534.

[29] Atkinson, p. 110.

[30] 'That general knowledge which now circulates in common talk, was in his time rarely to be found. Men not professing learning were not ashamed of ignorance; and, in the female world, any acquaintance with books was distinguished only to be censured.' *Lives of the English Poets,* vol. I, p. 366, Everyman's Library, 1925 (1964).

[31] Atkinson, p. 60.

[32] *Rasselas,* pp. 149-50.

[33] [Mary Astell], *A Serious Proposal to the Ladies for the Advancement of their True and Greatest Interest,* in two parts, by a Lover of her Sex, 1697. Quoted in Dorothy Gardiner, *English Girlhood at School,* p. 222, Oxford, 1929.

[34] *The Complete Letters of Lady Mary Wortley Montague,* ed. Robert Halsband, Oxford, 1967, vol. III, p. 83.

[35] Ibid. p. 22.

[36] 'Sophia', p. 23.

Catherine N. Parke (essay date 1987)

SOURCE: "*Rasselas* and the Conversation of History," in *The Age of Johnson: A Scholarly Annual,* Vol. 1, edited by Paul J. Korshin, AMS Press, Inc., 1987, pp. 79-109.

[*In the following essay, Parke proposes that in* Rasselas, *Johnson elaborated on the thesis that history—as a reflection on the past and an awareness of the continuity of time—is both the antidote to life's natural boredom and a precondition for understanding the future.*]

The travellers who escape from the Happy Valley to make their world tour in search of the happy choice of life experience on their trip many feelings: terror, disappointment, pleasure, curiosity, suspicion, perplexity, grief, sympathy, joy. But markedly absent,and notably so both in the context of life in the Happy Valley and the subsequent motive of their escape, is the feeling of boredom. And thus their journey in this basic sense, despite its disappointments, succeeds. The psychology of boredom, its meaning and antidotes, is central to an understanding of Johnson's distinctive approach as critic and moralist to literature and to life. Aspects of this psychology of boredom in *Rasselas,* particularly "the hunger of the imagination" that can never be satisfied by finite earthly activity, have been richly considered by several Johnsonians.[1] And this subject repays our returning to consider it again when a new angle strikes us as promising. In this essay I want to consider how Johnson in *Rasselas* sizes up the situation of boredom and comes to see history as the strategic solution to this problem. By strategic solution I mean what Johnson means—not a recipe or prescription for avoiding boredom, but rather a way of identifying the problem, of naming it, and by that very naming to draft the terms that, when achieved, will be recognized to constitute an adequate solution. Such a distinction is nice, but not small. By history I have in mind neither a mere chronology or sequence of events nor a specialized professional undertaking, but rather a natural interest and function of our minds "to push back the narrow confines of the fleeting present moment and so fashion for ourselves a more spacious world than that of the immediately practical."[2]

1

The Happy Valley is an experiment in creating a society without history. Its protective and imprisoning geography, its constant schedule of delights, and the ideal pleasures built into its very architecture embody a scheme for felicity that attempts a statistical approach toward overturning the human fate of dissatisfaction with whatever our current state happens to be. The presumed equation here is: the more pleasures, the more likelihood of happiness. So few of the hours of life are filled with objects adequate to our imaginations and so frequently do we lack sufficient present pleasure or employment, that we habitually refer to past and future for supplemental satisfactions in order to relieve the vacuities of our being. Such a condition does sound like a liability. But Johnson would agree with William James and Kenneth Burke that one of the measures of good sense and a healthy mind is our capacity to convert liabilities into assets. And *Rasselas* is a study in the principle that informs such transformations. The Happy Valley attempts to provide an adequate sequence of present pleasures and thus to leave no such imaginative vacuities. This experiment in living without history aims to relieve us of our constant craving and dissatisfaction with being creatures who live in time, a condition often mistaken for longings that can be literally or even figuratively satisfied. For none of the inhabitants, however, does an additive approach toward achieving happiness succeed; all are unhappy. And it is particularly disturbing to think of the Happy Valley as an antechamber to the throne for young Abissinian royalty who await their call to service here in a place that excludes history and which, by its very presuppositions, would allow no *History of Rasselas, Prince Abissinia* to be written. As Imlac observes late in the tale:

If we act only for ourselves, to neglect the study of

history is not prudent: if we are entrusted with the care of others, it is not just.[3]

The ethos of the Happy Valley could only produce inadequate rulers deprived of the important qualification of historical thinking.

This place, then, is a prison of pleasure which attempts to minimize the fear of life (and death) by simulating an eternal present. But this attempt results in the inhabitants being treated like the daughters of the families in Cairo whom Nekayah interviews. She discovers that "their grief, however, like their joy, was transient; everything floated in their mind unconnected with the past or future" (pp. 63-64). Such an attempt offers, of course, perfectly obvious attractions. Its distinctive logic that reduces the uncertainty of the drama of history, that cooperative competition for which the model is good conversation, has a definite, if specious, appeal.[4] But surely it is no accident that what young Prince Rasselas most hungers for in the Happy Valley is good conversation. Johnson's work implicitly asks how the liability of our fear of agonistic development through history (and the personal drama of history in the form of conversation) can be turned into an asset. Assuredly one of the negative answers is that we should not reduce the uncertainty and fearfulness of conversation with its risks and vulnerabilities. For in so doing, according to Johnson, we come up against an unanswerable opponent: our own avoidance of participating in history. And this opponent is resolutely and dangerously mute.

The implications of the foregoing perceptions are serious no less for the education of a prince than for that of any other man or woman. For insofar as a totalitarian state attempts to eradicate history and historical thinking, that state cannot generate a description adequate to the real circumstances it aims to encompass. And by silencing the opponent, it deprives itself of that mature collective revelation to which vocal opposition radically contributes (paraphrase from *PLF,* pp. 107-108). What begins to establish itself when Rasselas determines to leave the Happy Valley is a renewed drama of history occurring as self-renewing conversation. A second passage from *The Philosophy of Literary Form* will aptly serve to identify this new model of history as an unending conversation:

Where does the drama [of history] get its materials? From the "unending conversation" that is going on at the point in history when we are born. Imagine that you enter a parlor. You come late. When you arrive, others have long preceded you, and they are engaged in a heated discussion, a discussion too heated for them to pause and tell you exactly what it is about. In fact, the discussion had already begun long before any of them got there, so that no one present is qualified to retrace for you all the steps that had gone before. You listen for a while, until you decide that you have caught the tenor of the argument; then you put in your oar. Someone answers; you answer him; another comes to your defense; another aligns himself against you, to either the embarrassment or gratification of your opponent, depending upon the quality of your ally's assistance. However, the discussion is interminable. The hour grows late, you must depart. And you do depart, with the discussion still vigorously in progress. (pp. 110-11)

But the Happy Valley contradicts such a model of history and the politics of conversation. The royal palace, for instance, was "built as if suspicion herself had dictated the plan," the inhabitants closed within the valley by an iron gate and isolated in the present moment by the valley's round of delightful, but covertly repressive, activities. There is pleasure, but pleasure occurring solely in the present is totalitarianism, for it denies the imagination's freedom. Here Johnson anticipates modern analyses of the totalitarian state in his perception that the exclusion of history tyrannizes the mind because it disallows one of the mind's natural functions, historical thinking. And historical thinking is, indeed, a subversive act because it leads one to ask questions.

If the inhabitants of the Happy Valley passage should read: experience "vacancies of attention" and suffer "the tediousness of time," only some of them feel the motivation to inquire into the reason for the paradox that a place rationally calculated to give pleasure does not always please. Such an inquiry, which we will shortly be examining, would discover the distinction between the specious repetition of pleasure directed toward the end of maintaining the subjects and suppressing the fear of difference in the perpetual present, on the one hand, and genuine repetition of pleasure, on the other. The former fails because it is mere redundancy; the latter, which the travellers in *Rasselas* regularly enjoy, succeeds because it affirms what Heidegger calls "the connectedness of life."[5] This connectedness, in turn, serves as the basis of historical thinking which values genuine repetition. And genuine repetition is, in turn, grounded in a healthy attitude toward both difference and similarity. A subtle but significant transformation of false into genuine repetition throughout *Rasselas* dramatizes Johnson's definition of historical thinking, a complex activity for which we are all naturally equipped, responsible, and in which we take instinctive pleasure. Johnson would agree with Carl Becker's adage, "every man his own historian." Historical thinking is a means of understanding rather more than it is a way of explaining the world and ourselves in that world. And to say this is to argue that historical thinking considered as equipment for living, functions in a way similar to the drama we refer to when we speak of one person knowing or becoming acquainted with another.[6]

2

Rasselas is not a narrative of character in the usual sense of that term. But it is a tale about human acquaintance, about how people understand one another, about what familiarity with another person means and involves. And further, this fiction is about how the activity of acquaintance serves as a model for historical thinking. Biography in *Rasselas* is the form that embodies the acts of such acquaintance, as people tell and listen to their own and other people's lives. The distinctive complexity of one person's understanding another is accounted for by the fact that such understanding depends upon operations of the imaginative intelligence. These operations function in the continuum of history and cannot be directly translated from one person to another. Rather they must be made in greater or lesser degree a personal possession before they can be communicated. The drama of education is the central drama in *Rasselas,* but teaching and learning are not shown to be related as mere cause and effect. They occur in unpredictable, but not incomprehensible, ways through time.

The activity of acquaintance as a model for understanding that combines the imaginative procedures of projection and identification contrasts with the method of science that values explanation as its aim and proceeds by causal analysis. This method of acquaintance is identified early in *Rasselas* as the primary strategy for sizing up a situation. And the method proceeds by de-emphasizing subject matter and concurrently emphasizing the maintenance and encouragement of a reliable circuit of communication. This re-emphasis is predicted in the opening lines of the tale, a monitory aphorism that has no conclusion of a conclusive sort and that thereby opens the narrative with an invitation to our repeatedly different interpretations:

> Ye who listen with credulity to the whispers of fancy, and pursue with eagerness the phantoms of hope; who expect that age will perform the promises of youth, and that the deficiencies of the present day will be supplied by the morrow; attend to the history of Rasselas prince of Abissinia. (p. 1)

One could say that the conclusion is implicit in the syntax and that to express this meaning one need only insert negatives into each of the parallel phrases. But *Rasselas* is more resilient of meaning and offers more possibilities for genuine repetition than such a reading would suggest. Furthermore, we have for comparison other aphorisms in the story which do have explicit conclusions, such as the maid's comment about the broken cup: "What cannot be repaired is not to be regretted"; or Imlac's observation on choices, that "one cannot drink at once from the mouth and source of the Nile." These suggest, by contrast, that the opening aphorism offers us an invitation to invent our own interpretations over time. Thus it is appropriate that the narrative begins, as it ends, without simple closure.

Implicit in this diction is a stance that withholds itself from telling the reader what to think, for to do so would deny the possibility of genuinely returning to the story. The search in **Rasselas** is indeed for something like the pleasing captivity, a circuit of pleasing repetition, that is embodied with insufficient complexity in the Happy Valley. But the search for a version of such captivity in the form of true repetition is not wrong if it is neither literalized nor used to control the minds and imaginations of others. This opening movement toward identifying repetition that is healthful and interesting continues when Rasselas meets his former teacher who, concerned and perplexed by Rasselas's incomprehensible refusal to participate in the happiness of the Happy Valley, asks the Prince what is disturbing him. The scene is a familiar one, but well worth reconsidering for the way it establishes several key subjects that the rest of the tale elaborates. The old teacher's approach at first annoys Rasselas:

> Why, said he, does this man thus intrude upon me; shall I be never suffered to forget those lectures which pleased only while they were new, and to become new again must be forgotten.

(p. 7)

The first issue introduced is the tedium of one kind of repetition—the repetition of rote instruction. The lectures in the schoolroom are of use substantively. But they are of no interest the second time around by contrast with subjects or approaches that admit of genuine repetition. Such interest requires neither forgetting nor artificial incitement for its motivation. The events that follow examine in detail how genuine repetition in investigation avoids such tedium.

Learning through investigation, by contrast with rote study, (which Johnson knows also has its appropriate uses), takes its origin inthe investigator's own agenda of inquiry. Such learning comes in a sense from the inside out, unlike the reception of learning to which Rasselas refers in the preceding passage. However uninteresting certain repetitions may be, however much one owes it to oneself to avoid boredom, other obligations, so Johnson dramatizes in this scene, may sometimes compete for and even override the personal responsibility to seek out genuine repetition. In this instance the competing responsibility Rasselas feels is to respect and love his former teacher. The prince puts aside an annoyance that is rendered legitimate only because it can temporarily abdicate its natural authority. Instead he offers his dutiful respect to the man who seemingly now can teach him nothing more. Such improvisatory flexibility testifies to a healthy mind that can shift agilely from its own concerns and appetites to those of another. And if this seems to be a small matter, one should remember that Johnson urges us throughout his work to remember how the presence or absence of such acts collectively over a lifetime determines the general emotional tenor of our lives.

In the course of their conversation the teacher finds himself "surprized at this new species of affliction." How can anyone be unhappy in the Happy Valley? Attempting to correct his former pupil's mistaken view and, no doubt, wishing to make himself once again useful to the student whose reverence he once commanded, he lectures the prince on his comparative pleasures and security. If Rasselas knew the dangers and afflictions of the world, his teacher remarks rhetorically, he would appreciate his present state. In a manner he could not have predicted, the teacher's observation helps Rasselas to define his discontent: "I have already enjoyed too much, give me something to desire." This discovery is the first in a series that goes to show how insights may be motivated by surprising circumstances and how the drama of conversation, as Socrates well knew, is the midwife, though sometimes the inadvertent midwife, of ideas. The teacher's words, against their intention, give Rasselas the insight he needs to define his discontent and to devise a strategy for answering its demands.

The scene has comic qualities and the comedy is complex. No one completely fails, but success is difficult to define and requires a keen eye for revising expectation and seeing useful information where none was expected. Such is Johnson's distinctive definition of a healthy intelligence. Each member of the dialogue has succeeded to some degree in ways that require both to revise their measures of success in order to see emerging a new economy of education. Rasselas's teacher has unwittingly made himself once again useful to his student. He has given him a new lecture, quite to Rasselas's surprise. And thus what began as an unwanted intrusion has become for the prince a happy accident. Furthermore, Rasselas's interpretation of the practical implication of his teacher's lesson, quite against its intended meaning to teachcontentment in one's present circumstances, illustrates a simple but important fact about education: it occurs between people in a particular scene of circumstances, wherein more meaning can be generated than any single participant could anticipate or account for. Rasselas has not changed the meaning *per se* of his teacher's remarks, but rather has altered their implications for practical action. Yet such a transformation makes all the difference. And here it has occurred in the transaction of conversation. The intention and reception are not always identical. The effects of the words we speak are not always calculable in simple ways. They fall on the ears of others who have their own histories of experience and expectation through which they interpret what they hear. These autobiographical aspects of conversation, education, and history interest Johnson in the ways they may be liabilities in communication, if used wrongly, but assets, if used well. They are, as he understands them, the bases of creativity. And in writing **Rasselas** Johnson wrote a parable to dramatize these interrelated issues.

To make the foregoing claims does not transform Johnson into a relativist. Communication is not, as he sees it, subject to infinite vagaries. But it is difficult and also promising in ways that no merely rational schema can fully account for. Rather than being amazed at misunderstanding, Johnson would agree with Bertrand Russell that, given the complications attendant on communication, our relatively high degree of success in understanding one another is remarkable. But this success, in turn, cannot be measured by any single person's standards. Meaning, then, as we have seen that meaning unfold in the exchange between Rasselas and his teacher, is made according to the various agendas of interests that members of conversation bring to the episode. In the course of their conversation, Rasselas once again learns from his teacher or, perhaps, rather learns through the intermediation of his teacher. But now he is learning in a way which sets him on a course of genuine repetition because he has established his own distinctive stance toward the meaning of the lesson. To earn meaning in this way may take some of its energy from contradiction. The majority of the pleasure and energy that Rasselas experiences after this conversation which so discouraged him in prospect comes from its meaning now connected with a decision and a plan.

The conclusion of this episode focuses on the old teacher's discontent in finding his intentions quite reversed. But once again the frame shifts from the narrowly personal to something larger that seems to be as significant as the comic scene of successfully, but accidentally, renewed teaching. As Rasselas moves from annoyance to thoughtfulness to curiosity and finally to delight, the old man moves quickly from discontent to resignation. This trajectory that characterizes their respective ages illustrates how our thinking and feeling unfold distinctively over the historicalcontinuum of our lives. Rasselas's circumstances have not changed, but he now imagines the world differently, thanks simply to a new thought that organizes his prospects differently. To be sure, hope may be a feeling, but that feeling arises from one's view of things. And here hope replaces the imaginative configuration of boredom that can see no future.[7] Rasselas's hope at this stage, however, is incomplete because it is hope only for himself. As Imlac will comment later, describing the effect on his imagination of determining to be a poet, "I saw every thing with a new purpose; my sphere of attention was suddenly magnified: no kind of knowledge was to be overlooked" (p. 27). Such kaleidoscopic conversions fascinate Johnson as instances of the mind's capacity

radically to reconceive and reperceive reality by shifting its viewpoint, by looking on the world from different angles over time. But these different angles remain incomplete until they can be shared with and used by others, which is to say, until they become the subject of conversation. For, as one remembers, Imlac's greatest unhappiness in the Happy Valley is realizing that his knowledge is no longer of use.

Pleased by his discovery of a possibility for happiness in seeing the world's affliction, Rasselas now considers himself to be the "master of a secret stock of happiness, which he could enjoy only by concealing it" (p. 10). Such a response is in keeping with the condition of secrecy that informs the politics, the architecture, and the pattern of human relations in the Happy Valley. Totalitarianism may be achieved in any number of ways that reduce the temporal and thereby the moral and emotional complexity of the operations of the human imagination. At this point in the story, when Rasselas discovers his "secret stock of happiness," he becomes guilty of a version of the dramatic pretense that characterizes the other inhabitants of the Happy Valley who, melancholy and idle, entice others to join them in the valley simply in order to spread their misery. Without revealing his own discovery, the prince encourages his fellow prisoners to enjoy their condition. Rasselas is not so actively culpable, for he offers his companions relatively harmless pleasure; although his encouraging their enjoyment of the eternal present hardly seems worthy of a future ruler of Abissinia. These motifs of secrecy and pretense which Johnson introduces early in the tale to exemplify the valley's mistaken politics recur throughout the journey to come.

3

To consider the psychology of this complex of pretenses, lies, and secrecy takes us directly to the heart of Johnson's thinking about the possibility for succeeding in our relations with others in the private or the public realm. Such consideration also contributes to defining our understanding of Johnson's view of the uses of history. For history does not merely attempt to gather truth,restore accuracy, enlighten secrecy. Rather the very condition of its possibility is predicated on a reliance on the general currency of intended truth and accuracy in human communication. As Sissela Bok argues in *Lying: Moral Choice in Public and Private Life* (New York: Pantheon Books, 1978), physical violence and lying are the two forms of harm that we perform against one another. Both threaten the very possibility of society's continuing to function. Johnson, like Bok, identifies the violence of the lie as a fundamentally antisocial act.

Rasselas's concern with secrecy is mirrored by such other figures as the mechanic flyer who is designing wings to lift him above the turmoil of earthly life. The man swears Rasselas to secrecy, fearful that the invention he is preparing will fall into the wrong hands. He advises the prince of the dangers to which they would be vulnerable if this should happen:

> If men were all virtuous, returned the artist, I should with great alacrity teach them all to fly. But what would be the security of the good, if the bad could at pleasure invade them from the sky? Against an army sailing through the clouds neither walls, nor mountains, nor seas, could afford security. A flight of northern savages might hover in the wind, and light at once with irresistible violence upon the capital of a fruitful region that was rolling under them. (p. 17)

Rasselas's vow of secrecy proves comically unnecessary when the flyer's wings fail to support him. But the accidental equilibrium is achieved as his wings unpredictably ballast him in the water and save his life. This comic success recalls the earlier incident of Rasselas's conversation with his old teacher whose unwillingness to be silent led inadvertently to his becoming once again useful to his student. The intention behind the flyer's wings, like the lesson intended by the teacher, miscarries. But each turns out to have an overdetermined usefulness that could not have been predicted. There remains, however, the fact that both the teacher and the flyer express the distinctive ethos of the Happy Valley with its emphasis on isolation and safety to be achieved by suspending time. The teacher would have had Rasselas take delight in his comparative good fortune behind the gates of the valley. The flyer would have offered the prince a similar isolation and protection literally suspended above the earth. This episodic punning prepares us for the entrance of Imlac who restores the prince's imagination to healthy movement by reciting his poetry and then telling his life story. In each of the prince's first two conversations one of the speakers has invoked fear to manipulate Rasselas—the teacher in order to encourage Rasselas to appreciate the virtues of his current situation, and the mechanic flyer in order to gain the prince's conspiratorial silence. But Imlac, who also mentions the fears and dangers of the world, does so in quitea different way that marks a significant new direction for the drama of education to follow throughout the remainder of the tale.[8]

Instead of using accounts of danger as a means of evoking fear and thereby manipulating his subject, Imlac discusses the psychology of crime, envy, and other abuses of power in a way that empowers the listener actively to comprehend rather than merely to react to fearful information. While the flyer and the teacher give Rasselas information, but would have him trust passively to them for its interpretation, Imlac's tale conditions the possibility for true education by building into its very structure the possibility for the listener to disagree. Imlac achieves this openness by combining narrative with analysis. Thus he offers Rasselas his first lesson in naming fearful circumstances and allows him to make the first entries in, to borrow Kenneth Burke's phrase, "a dictionary of pivotal terms" that will become the ongoing, collective composition of the travellers who will soon gather for their extended tour.

The remainder of the tale can be read as a search for happiness that takes the form of a search for ways of naming fearful and disturbing circumstances. This naming in itself constitutes and directs the attitudes toward and strategies for encompassing the situations they encounter on their way. Here is a sample from Imlac's first vocabulary lesson:

> *Subordination* supposes *power* on one part and *subjection* on the other; and if power be in the hands of men, it will sometimes be abused. The vigilance of the supreme magistrate may do much, but much will still remain undone. He can never know all the crimes that are committed, and can seldom punish all that he knows. (p. 21, italics mine)

For the first time in the tale figures have a real conversation. Their conversation is real, not according to the conventions of verisimilitude, but rather according to an understanding of conversation as a cooperative undertaking. Here a speaker and listener, one of whom obviously has more experience than the other and thus both a certain advantage and degree of power, enjoy a wholesome measure of emotional equality in the drama of conversation. Neither participant takes advantage either of his knowledge or of the other's ignorance.

The discrepancy measured here between Rasselas's untested logic and the drama of human contingency to which he is applying it serves to identify the young man's inexperience. But Johnson in this scene as elsewhere in **Rasselas** and throughout his work is less interested in exposing naiveté or inexperience than he is in exploring the service that the drama of conversation may perform in bringing to light the different ways different people think. If this sounds like a simple, perhaps even an over-simple, observation, it is also one which, as Johnson well understood, we often forget or neglect in terms of its implications for our self-identification in history. The drama of history is that of conversation as a cooperative competition, the agonistic development of viewpoints that differ through time from one person to another and also within the individual.

Rasselas is indebted to Imlac for this initiation into the unending conversation of history. It is interesting to note how this first true conversation develops. Beginning in disagreement, the discussion ends with Rasselas feeling a flicker of recognition based on his own experience. This fleeting recognition gives the prince a clue about how to enter Imlac's thinking and at the same time makes that entry desirable. To Imlac's comment about how desires, either real or fanciful, are necessary to keep life in motion, Rasselas gives an understated reply: "This I can in some measure conceive. I repent that I interrupted thee." (p. 22). Such a connection is crucial to preserving the pre-condition of trust and belief necessary to an ongoing conversation of any significance. Whereas Rasselas's meeting with his former teacher was motivated by his sense of obligation to honor the man he formerly reverenced and his meetings with the flyer by the lack of any better prospect for locating his hopes (neither of these a negligible reason), his genuine conversation with Imlac is differently motivated. He hears Imlac recite a poem about his world travels. This motivation is distinct from the earlier two because of the active nature and the equal relationship between the poet and his listener. Johnson would not have us simplistically deem this conversation better than its predecessors, for circumstances indeed contribute to the definitions of virtue and goodness. But he understands how improvisatory skill is required of us all along the way in the practice of virtue. Hence, as the dialogue between the prince and the poet continues, Johnson dramatizes the importance of improvisation to keep a conversation going in the right direction.

In his first long conversation with Rasselas, Imlac offers the prince a set of strategic definitions that suggest the contours of a larger chart of meaning adequate to describe a scene in the world. Rasselas has sufficient experience only to begin to understand part of the poet's chart of meanings. But this understanding, at least for the moment, is less important than his simple exposure to a new way of thinking about the world—to kinds of categories and distinctions useful for assessing circumstances that the prince has never before had an opportunity to consider. Rasselas is able to learn this new way of sizing up the world precisely, if ironically, because it resembles a fictional strategy that he had already experimented with before meeting Imlac. After the meeting with his old teacher, Rasselas begins to spend his time picturing the world he has yet to visit. In the familiar scene where he fantasizes about saving an orphan virgin robbed by a faithless lover he finds himself so powerfully under the sway of his fiction which, as Johnson observes in *Rambler* 4, moves directly to the heart without passing through the mind, that he literally rises and runs to save his sentimental heroine. Catching himself in this uncontrolled literalizing of a fiction, Rasselas proceeds to calculate sternly how much time he has lost in not having already entered the world.

This pair of incidents dramatizes Johnson's notions about the stages of the mind's maturing, from visionary bustle to critical mapping. The stages do not coin-

cide simply with one's age, nor does visionary bustle completely disappear when the critical mapping establishes itself as the predominant mode. But critical mapping is requisite for adulthood and for that degree of analytical mastery of the world which may not be synonymous either with complete accuracy or success, but which is synonymous with grounds for a feeling of probable competence. Both Rasselas's fiction and Imlac's tactical vocabulary are strategies that the mind applies to understand its circumstances, accomplish its yearnings, and discharge its responsibilities. We should not blur the distinctions between these two ways of thinking, for we must recognize that they are both modes of thought which, if sometimes antagonistic, are precisely for this reason useful to one another.

The strength of both imaginative and rational thought— thought that pictures and figures forth and thought that analyzes and creates schema—and the quality which makes them natural allies, lies in what Imlac later in the story names the "indiscerptible power of thought." While the travellers contemplate mortality and immortality in the catacombs, he observes:

> Consider your own conceptions, . . . and the difficulty will be less. You will find substance without extension. An ideal form is no less real than material bulk: yet an ideal form has no extension. It is no less certain, when you think on a pyramid, that your mind possesses the idea of a pyramid, than that the pyramid itself is standing. . . . As is the effect such is the cause; as thought is, such is the power that thinks; a power impassive and indiscerptible. (pp. 131-32)

Thought is real and the world is real. Their joint reality, as conceived and dramatized collectively through time while each contributes to the conversation of history, is one of the significant subjects of *Rasselas.*

4

The drama of knowledge as ongoing conversation that emerges early in the travellers' journey becomes their priority, beginning with Rasselas's fascination with Imlac's autobiography and continuing through the young travellers' interviews in the search for the happy choice of life. Although they are interested in each other's subject matter, they come to recognize that communication is a circuit as well as the subject matter thereof and that the continuity of conversation both testifies to and constitutes the ground of connection among its participants. Therefore that continuity must be respected and thoughtfully conserved. There are several moments in the story when the continuity of conversation threatens to break down. These points are well worth our considering in detail for their implications regarding Johnson's view of the benefits and dangers inherent in conversation. Imlac is an exemplary guardian of conversational continuity, not to be mistaken for simple agreement, ease, or even necessarily mutual comprehension, who so values continuing a conversation that he will even swallow his pride in the face of an exasperated student. When, for instance, Rasselas interrupts his speech on the education of the poet, remarking, "Enough! thou hast convinced me, that no human being can ever be a poet," Imlac is more interested in continuing the dialogue than in defending himself. So he answers understatedly in a way that encourages the listener to reenter the conversation: "To be a poet is indeed very difficult" (p. 29).

Later in the journey Nekayah expresses her serious suspicion of their teacher in a remark that threatens their educational conversation with complete breakdown. She remarks to her brother that Imlac seems not to favor their search for the happy choice of life, "lest we should in time find him mistaken" (p. 61). For a student thus to suspect a teacher is serious indeed since learning requires trust. Students must be able to believe that their teachers unselfishly wish them well. And such trust includes accepting the possibility that students may sometimes find their teachers to be wrong. Where there is no trust there can be no learning. And the motive and intention behind the teaching are crucial to the exchange of trust that underwrites education.

Although Johnson understands such trust to be a precondition for education, he does not thereby take its existence for granted. Here in *Rasselas* he dramatizes a moment of critical suspicion between student and teacher that could put a stop to their conversation. Later in the story, on several occasions, Johnson shows the students affirming Imlac's teaching. These affirmations do not merely show that Imlac was right all along, but rather demonstrate that the students now trust him. The teacher's trustworthiness is far more crucial to education than being right, for error, unlike untrustworthiness, does not undermine the entire activity and put an end to the conversation. If we add to the effects of suspicion the two motives that Johnson notes in the *Life of Sir Thomas Browne* which account for good minds often never making public their discoveries, namely the sense that little is of sufficient interest to publish and the feeling of greater pleasure taken ininvestigation than in publication, we can begin better to take the measure of the importance of conversation in *Rasselas*. Conversation in this story functions as an active assertion of meaning and exchange in the present against the many temptations to silence.

The recentering of the journey's formal significance in the establishment of a safe, ongoing conversation in which the participants come, though not without difficulty, to trust one another, is also anticipated by Rasselas's particular interest in the European postal system which, among all the various details that Imlac mentions in his account of the world, pleases the prince most. His interest in this circuitry by which distant friends may come together gives a glimmer of what Rasselas will come to insist upon later in the story when he alone urges the Princess and Pekuah not to disguise themselves in order to meet the mad astronomer. The women's intentions are kindly: they want to cure the astronomer's madness. But Rasselas rightly perceives the serious mistake in their plan:

> I have always considered it as treason against the great republick of human nature, to make any man's virtues the means of deceiving him, whether on great or little occasions. All imposture weakens confidence and chills benevolence. (p. 120)

To weaken confidence and chill benevolence are crimes against the very community of trust upon which the possibility of communication depends.

This latter passage also sends us back to recall with added emphasis the scene before the travellers escape when Nekayah, the Prince's sister, discovers her brother and Imlac digging their way out of the valley—a scene which also anticipates the tale's increasing emphasis on the circuit rather than on the subject matter of communication:

> He started and stood confused, afraid to tell his design, and yet hopeless to conceal it. A few moments determined him to repose on her fidelity, and secure her secrecy by a declaration without reserve. . . .

> The prince, who loved Nekayah above his other sisters, had no inclination to refuse her request, and grieved that he had lost an opportunity of shewing his confidence by a voluntary communication. (pp. 40-41)

This passage offers a complex portrait of mixed emotions that arise from the drama of fear and regret. The drama is all the more emphatic and compelling because it involves family relations whose trust and mutual benevolence we instinctively feel should serve as a model for the ideal operations of these virtues. Rasselas findshimself, as Johnson describes his experience, "afraid to tell his design, and yet hopeless to conceal it." His training to secrecy in the Happy Valley has had its effects. When Nekayah makes her case, she identifies precisely the elements of his fear and her good will that epitomize the theme of *Rasselas:* "Do not imagine that I came hither as a *spy*. . . . not *suspicion* but *fondness* has detected you" (p. 40, italics mine). And the prince's response, which combines public action with private recognition of his lost opportunity is a simple but characteristically subtle mark of Johnson's way of demonstrating how profoundly in trust and confidence are the very possibilities of human communication.

In an essay on lying in **Adventurer** 50, Johnson cites Sir Thomas Browne's observation that "the devils do not tell lies to one another; for truth is necessary to all societies; nor can the society of hell subsist without it."[9] Rasselas has not exactly lied, but by acting out of suspicion and fear, by failing to trust and share knowledge with one whom he loves, he misses an opportunity to contribute to the community of mutual reliance in a world of so many unavoidable divisions and disappointments. And as the force of the story will cumulatively suggest, to let such an opportunity pass is always unfortunate. Rasselas's failure with his sister identifies how profoundly we are at risk with our intimates, an issue which recurs throughout the tale and to which Johnson gives extended treatment in a later scene between Nekayah and her brother. After Nekayah has completed her inquiry into married life, she reports to her brother, "if those whom nature has thus closely united are the torments of each other, where shall we look for tenderness and consolation?" (p. 68). The very fact of such disappointment, however, locates a source of particular energy, for in his characteristic way Johnson would have us recognize a vulnerability as a potential strength. But more precisely he would have us recognize what kinds of useful evidence about the interrelated operations of mind and feeling we may gain from examining the precise terms of such vulnerability.

5

The longest discussion in **Rasselas** is the debate on family life. And the length and subtlety of the section measure the degree of Johnson's interest. Nekayah's account to Rasselas ends with her reporting contradictory findings on whether it is better to marry early or later and whether celibacy or marriage is preferable. Rasselas points out his sister's self-contradiction:

> "You seem to forget," replied Rasselas, "that you have, even now, represented celibacy as less happy than marriage. Both conditions may be bad, but they cannot both be worst. Thus it happens, when wrong opinions are entertained, that they mutually destroy each other, and leave the mind open to truth." (p. 74)

Though speciously accurate, Rasselas's criticism is certainly hurtful and, when examined by standards more complex and appropriate to the matters being discussed than those which he applies, mistaken. Nekayah then points out to her brother his two interlinked errors in a manner which offers a kind but firm corrective to his mistaken enthusiasm for logic. Each of Rasselas's errors involves a failure to accommodate ends to means aptly and economically.

The prince's quickness to point out his sister's error of logic phrased in absolutist terms expresses a philosophical attitude that sees the search for truth as a search for explanation only. If one considers a motive not to be something that lies "behind" an act, but something that every act embodies in its structure—in the way events and values are put together (paraphrase from *PLF,* p. 20)—then we can analyze the structure of Rasselas's criticism formally. He begins with forensic condescension ("You seem to forget . . ."), followed by the short sentences and the brusquely confident use of parallel structure ("Both conditions may be bad . . ."), and the case-clinching use of cause-and-effect logic ("Thus it happens . . ."), that includes a disturbingly violent expression ("mutually destroy each other"). The prince's rhetoric enacts a view of truth that values explanation absolutely as the acceptable terms of its success. His method sees explanation (the charting of cause-and-effect relationships) as the only legitimate form of knowledge. Truth, in the pragmatist perspective of William James, is the name we give to whatever serves us well to believe. And Rasselas here represents a point of view that narrowly values what will serve him well.

Nekayah's answer critiques her brother's attack by noting the usefulness of another mode of knowledge, knowledge by understanding, for the purposes of the kind of inquiry she has just undertaken. Knowledge by understanding proceeds according to a model of inquiry based on the drama of human acquaintance. The very style of her rebuttal, quite different from her brother's, enacts the attitudes that characterize understanding as attempting to come to know and to be known by another person. She replies:

> I did not expect, . . . to hear that imputed to falshood which is the consequence only of frailty. To the mind, as to the eye, it is difficult to compare with exactness objects vast in their extent, and various in their parts. Where we see or conceive the whole at once we readily note the discriminations and decide the preference: but of two systems, of which neither can be surveyed by any human being in its full compass of magnitude and multiplicity of complication, where is the wonder, that judging of the whole by parts, I am alternately affected by one and the other as either presses on my memory or fancy? We differ from ourselves just as we differ from each other, when we see only part of thequestion, as in the multifarious relations of politicks and morality: but when we perceive the whole at once, as in numerical computations, all agree in one judgment, and none ever varies his opinion. (p. 74)

Unlike Rasselas, Nekayah does not open with an accusation of error, but rather with a first person expression of surprise that introduces the philosophical issue she will now proceed to elaborate. Her response introduces the logic of counterargument. But the shape of the princess's thinking is distinctively different from her brother's in the way it includes an element of subjectivity as an avowed part of its method.

In her opening words, "I did not expect to hear . . . ," Nekayah speaks not out of narrowly private subjectivity but from a perspective that the rest of her speech will dramatize as a coherent manner of thinking appropriate to certain kinds of inquiries. This manner of thinking we might call "perspectival," quite different from Rasselas's earlier criticism that assumed as stance and aim the ideal of objectivity. Nekayah's thinking capitalizes on precisely what would seem to be losses in a world that prizes objective (explanation-based) thinking. Opening with her own reaction, rather than with a direct rebuttal, Nekayah introduces an invitational style that characterizes her acquaintance model of thinking. Her aim is not, like her brother's, solely to clear the mind of contradictory opinions, thus leaving it open to truth. Rather, she draws a different picture of the mind that emphasizes, not the spatial, but rather the temporal qualities of thinking. Her investigations of married and single life occurred over time. And hence the contradictions in her findings. These qualities are an admitted frailty in the search for certain kinds of surety. But as Nekayah proceeds to suggest, by identifying this admitted frailty of temporal thinking, we provide ourselves with valuable information that bears upon distinguishing the different forms of evidence and shapes of answers we can expect to find on different kinds of searches.

Nekayah's style exemplifies her counterclaims, increasingly complex, always controlled. Beginning with the initial use of "I," she moves from the first person singular to the plural. Rasselas's remarks, by contrast, portray a drama of thought markedly different. It appears less directly associated with the speaker's "I" or the speaker's and audience's "we." The pivots of her invitational style, those places where she corrects her brother in a manner that encourages their conversation to continue, contrast with his flat-footed correction. Her gentle but acute question—introduced in the phrase, "where is the wonder?"—characterizes a stance at once confident and generous. Her tactic is astute in the way it allows her listener a dignity that he did not formerly grant her, by giving Rasselas some genteelleeway in the drama of correction. This maneuver is not merely a personal kindness, although for Johnson such would be no negligible act. Rather, in its form as personal kindness this act serves as a synecdoche for the operations of understanding through acquaintance.

The "frailty" of the mind, when considered from the perspective of the attempt to make use of our liabilities and to apply our burdens as a basis of insight, leads to a view of the function of time not only in our thinking, but also in our relations with others in that drama of communication over time that we call history. The measure of Nekayah's success in introducing a new mode of thought is evident in her brother's reply that takes up the tone she has introduced as the vehicle for her thought:

> Let us not add, said the prince, to the other evils of life, the bitterness of controversy, nor endeavour to vie with each other in subtilties of argument. We are employed in a search, of which both are equally to enjoy the success, or suffer by the miscarriage. It is therefore fit that we assist each other. You surely conclude too hastily from the infelicity of marriage against its institution; will not the misery of life prove equally that life cannot be the gift of heaven? (p. 74)

This scene dramatizes a vision of a cooperative endeavor and its economy with the corollary that together we all will gain or lose equally. Hence our individual success is linked to our success in group relations. The episode serves neither as a rebuttal nor an alternative to, but rather a substantial enrichment of, Rasselas's position. The scene began as confrontation between a spatial model of truth that values explanation as the only form that satisfies the inquiring mind and a temporal model of truth as acquaintance. It ends as a cooperative drama that admits and uses the differences expressed by each speaker.

The episode, as we can begin to see, serves an important retrospective function: from this new collaborative perspective we find ourselves in possession of new concepts in the growing dictionary of pivotal terms that *Rasselas* as a whole composes. These terms allow us retrospectively to identify the shapes of several earlier scenes in ways that clarify their importance. The exchange between Nekayah and Rasselas identifies how much is at stake emotionally in performing our mode of thought. Thinking and attempting to communicate that way of thinking are risky business. They can easily break down. And the participants' ultimate success in keeping their conversation going is no small achievement.

From the vantage point of this scene with its efficient and happy resolution we can return to the scene where Imlac discussed the ideal education of the poet, and more precisely appreciate thesignificance of his turning the conversation back toward the listener at the crucial moment when the conversation threatens to break off. It is unrealistic to hope always for such successes. Nor should we assume that continuing conversation is always the better course. Some conversations should end, if only for the moment, as Johnson instances halfway through the journey when Rasselas begins to feel uneasy with Imlac's scepticism. The prince has just repeated to the poet the results of his interview with some shepherds whose life he expected to be ideal, but whom he found no happier than anyone else. He shares his uneasiness with Imlac that he may never find any who have made the happy choice of life. From Imlac he hears in return "new doubts, and remarks that gave him no comfort." The narrative continues to describe Rasselas's response:

> He therefore discoursed more frequently and freely with his sister, who had yet the same hope with himself, and always assisted him to give some reasons why, though he had been hitherto frustrated, he might succeed at last. (p. 61)

The prince's instinctive response to retreat from Imlac's doubt may contain from our perspective as readers a degree of comic self-deception. But it is also a natural and not unhealthy response, a kind of emotional and intellectual survival instinct. For in order to continue, one must guard and nurture one's hopes.

Youth is, as Johnson regularly observes throughout his writings, the season for hopeful perseverance, as Nekayah discovers from her inquiries into domestic happiness:

> The colours of life in youth and age appear different, as the face of nature in spring and winter. And how can children credit the assertions of parents, which their own eyes show them to be false? (p. 67)

The difference here defined is so often treated as a problem, which indeed not infrequently it may be, that an opportunity is lost for converting a liability into an asset. The misuse of that difference usually results in a difference being mistaken for a problem. One notable example in *Rasselas* of the artful use of such a difference occurs when Imlac decides to leave the Happy Valley and tour the world with young travellers. Imlac has already seen the world and withdrawn from it. He has no hopes for finding happiness there the second time around. But he can take pleasure in watching the young travellers on their search. Their "repetition" of his earlier journey is an example of genuine repetition. For them it is a first attempt, for Imlac a diverting variation of his first tour. Here we see an artful and efficient conversion of difference into a ground of interest, rather than of suspicion or of fear.

Placing the line between premature suspicion and naive receptivity is, for Johnson, a subtle business. Indeed, the project of its delineation turns out to be more a fabrication of a semi-permeable membrane than the building of a firm wall. Johnson's persistent attempts to maintain conversation in *Rasselas* are the dramatic enactment of the fabrication and functioning of such a membrane. The aim of conversation is to avoid both mere self-protection and the maintenance of personal territoriality, on the one hand, and injudicious acceptance, on the other. Johnson locates the model for cultivating such an ideal semi-permeability in Nekayah's recommendation that we recognize how "we differ from ourselves as we differ from each other." Autobiography and biography thus become the basis of epistemology.

This use of the example of one's own self-differing over time serves to familiarize us with the possibility that differing from others is not always dangerous. There remains the fact that since we generally learn from others or through their intermediation, we often find ourselves in situations where, as Johnson notes in *Rambler* 3, we must become "reconciled to [our] guide" and "must not only confess [our] ignorance, but, what is still less pleasing, must allow that he from whom they are to learn is more knowing than ourselves."[10] Hence we often learn less uneasily and perhaps more successfully from books or from other advice that does not come from living individuals. Such sources reduce the uneasiness of confrontation and humiliation which are the most unavoidable liabilities of personal teaching. But where there are liabilities there are potential assets. One of the benefits of the travellers' tour is precisely and simply their being together. For all their difficulties throughout the journey, they still discover, when they return together to Cairo after ransoming Pekuah from the sheik, that they "were so well pleased at finding themselves together, that none of them went much abroad" (p. 107). Given the strains, suspicions, and failures that chronically plague human relationships, this single sentence implies success against heavy odds.

However, the participants in such a gathering will predictably tire of one another's company and wish to move on to something else. It is thus significant that *Rasselas* ends with just such a gathering. The travellers repeat their ideal wishes now set in a notably more complex setting of the dramatic construction throughout the tale of psychology of creativity—that delicate relationship among hope, perseverance, disappointment, and the semi-permeability of the boundary between self and other. The expression of their wishes followed by the seeming contradiction, "Of these wishes that they had formed they well knew that none could be obtained. . . . and resolved, when the inundation should cease, to return to Abissinia" (p. 134), seems to function as a fairly straightforward comic deflation. And yet we remember the mechanic flyer's accurate reply to Rasselas's criticism of his project, "Nothing will ever be attempted, if all possible objections must be first overcome" (p. 17). Of course, the man's project fails. But this fact does not invalidate the truth of his earlier remark although it sets off the remark comically and shows once again that useful information may come at surprising times and from surprising sources. Indeed, given their circumstances and resources, Rasselas, Nekayah and Pekuah are more likely to succeed than the flyer.

Johnson seems to have two related aims in mind here. One is a kind of criss-crossed structure of logic on the architectural analogy of balancing stresses, strengths, and weaknesses. He places a useful general principle, a kind of sceptic's optimism, in the mouth of a figure involved in a wild project and an optimist's pessimism in the minds of those with less unreasonable goals. Thus the general principles and projected practice cross over to produce a buttressing effect that offers a complex support that enables our imaginations to move in seemingly destabilizing oppositions. *Rambler* 2 offers a useful gloss on this matter:

> He that directs his steps to a certain point, must frequently turn his eyes to that place which he strives to reach; he that undergoes the fatigue of labour, must solace his weariness with the contemplation of its reward. In agriculture, one of the most simple and necessary employments, no man turns up the ground but because he thinks of the harvest, that harvest which blights may intercept, which inundations may sweep away, or which death or calamity may hinder from reappearing. (III,10)

The idea of an imagined future, like the idea of a pyramid, is no less real than the acts we perform to achieve that future or the actual pyramid, though each reality is differently constituted. By noting how Johnson identifies such ordinary acts of the imagination that accompany, motivate, and solace our physical movement into the future, we can better discern the distinctive quality of his insight into the sheer wonder of human accomplishment, however ordinary. Every individual human act lies on a continuum of the imaginative and the marvelous. Such a sense of the marvelous underwrites all the activity in *Rasselas.* That we manage to do as much as we do never ceases to amaze Johnson because this achievement testifies to the active and precise interrelationship between imagining a future and acting in the present. And, as *Rasselas* repeatedly illustrates, this interrelationship can never be taken for granted.

As human beings we seem to be so constructed that this interrelationship of imaginative cause and physical effect is a natural principle in our existence. But this principle often fails for any number of reasons. Foremost among them is our wrongly categorizing an event. When, for instance, Imlac and Rasselas are digging a tunnel out of the Happy Valley, they work along slowly with no perceptible progress for some time. When Rasselas begins to feel discouraged, Imlac offers the following advice:

> . . . mark, however, how far we have advanced, and you will find that our toil will some time have an end. Great works are performed, not by strength, but perseverance: yonder place was raised by single stones, yet you see its height and spaciousness. He

that shall walk with vigour three hours a day will pass in seven years a space equal to the circumference of the globe. (p. 39)

This calculation, based on the certainty of their invisible efforts to date, which is to say its history, Imlac then extrapolates probabilistically into the future. And such a calculation is tonic for a mind that always questions itself. The image of the palace complements the exercise in projecting past certainty into future success by giving a future image and analyzing this image back into its constituent parts. Thus the present is defined from both directions by way of this two-part exercise that encourages the prince's current project. The present now has a lively meaning, indeed the only meaning it can have by its relationship to past and future.

When the pair begin to make some faster headway, Rasselas interprets this event as "a good omen." Imlac now offers another revision of terms:

> "Do not disturb your mind," said Imlac, "with other hopes or fears than reason may suggest: if you are pleased with prognosticks of good, you will be terrified likewise with tokens of evil, and your whole life will be a prey to superstition. Whatever facilitates our work is more than an omen, it is a cause of success." (p. 40)

This and the preceding correction are both directed toward exercising Rasselas's imagination in enacting a healthy stance toward the future and in understanding that such a stance is a function of our present being. As Johnson writes in *Rambler* 2:

> This quality of looking forward into futurity seems the unavoidable condition of a being, whose motions are gradual, and whose life is progressive: as his powers are limited, he must use means for the attainment of his ends, and intend what he performs last. . . . (*Y,* III, 10)

Yet we seem to need constantly to rediscover the implications for thought and action that this natural imperative, suggested by the very condition of our being, represents.

The first computational exercise gives Rasselas a basis for the closest thing to certainty one can hope for in the future (certainty, except in demonstrable reasoning, is a function of history, an *ex post facto* determination), namely probable projection. The second exercise also similarly contributes to a degree of stability and, like the first, requires accurate evaluation—in this case, naming of the past or writing its history. Imlac works systematically to keep Rasselas's imagination working within an historical framework. Undue discouragement flies in the face of present evidence of other large accomplishments. And "omens of good" do not, by definition, occur within the historical framework, which admits "causes," not omens. The question of what to name that evidence which goes toward both actually achieving future ends and encouraging one to continue work is important for the reason that Johnson defines in the ***Rambler*** essay just cited.

As beings whose movement toward the future is gradual and progressive and who must use ends to accomplish means, our choice of whether to call something an "omen" or a "cause" distinguishes two quite different ways of sizing up the reality we are living in and working with. Appropriate naming is important in and of itself, and Johnson is a product of an age that valued accurate denomination. But the implications of naming are yet more important for action itself. In the manner of William James's notion that not all true answers are worth our time, only those that make a practical difference, Johnson believes that our accent must fall upon the naming that makes a difference. Clearly for Rasselas, susceptible as he is to fantasy regarding his escape from the Happy Valley, to name his means accurately does make an important difference. What underlies the pervasive interest with people's actions in ***Rasselas,*** with how they come to be doing what they are now doing or why they gave up what they used to do or why they have resumed what they formerly abandoned, is Johnson's profound and wondering fascination with how things are done in this world, with how we accomplish what we accomplish. Such things for him never go without saying. They always require being thought through and talked out.

W. J. Bate has identified how Johnson withheld himself from Swiftian irony, and has argued that this characteristic act derives from his refusal not to implicate himself in the collective condition of human error.[11] To this we might add an observation that takes into account a more positive force in Johnson's imagination, one that directs him to maintain a stance of surprise and pleasure toward all achievement. I might here turn briefly to ***Rambler*** 9 for a concluding perspective on this complex of issues I have been defining. The essay observes:

> And it might contribute to dispose us to a kinder regard for the labours of one another, if we were to consider from what unpromising beginnings the most useful productions of art haveprobably arisen. Who, when he saw the first sand or ashes, by the casual intenseness of heat melted into a metalline form, rugged with exerescences, and clouded with impurities, would have imagined, that in this shapeless lump lay concealed so many conveniencies of life, as would in time constitute a great part of the happiness of the world? (*Y,* III, 49)

Here Johnson notes how the study of history and in particular the study of the evidence of past success

from modest beginnings define the good sense of a stance of decent receptivity toward the work of others. The historical record directs us probabilistically not to dismiss work we do not as yet understand and to be receptive toward new ways of seeing the present and imagining the future of our situations. The precondition for such a stance is ensured by our being wary of boredom and from this preliminary alertness thereafter to allow the mind to exercise its natural fascination with history and to find for this fascination a full and accurate expression, like the travellers in ***Rasselas*** who repeat the stories of their own and other people's lives genuinely and with pleasure.

Notes

[1] One thinks particularly of the work of W. J. Bate in *The Achievement of Samuel Johnson* (New York: Oxford Univ. Press, 1961) and *Samuel Johnson* (New York and London: Harcourt, Brace, Jovanovich, 1975) particularly pp. 297-316; and John Wain in *Samuel Johnson: A Biography* (New York: Viking Press, 1976), particularly pp. 209-15. This essay places itself within the critical conversation among most notably these Johnsonians: Mary Lascelles, "*Rasselas* Reconsidered," *Essays and Studies by Members of the English Associations,* n.s., 4 (1951), 37-52; Geoffrey Tillotson, "Time in *Rasselas,*" in *Bicentenary Essays on Rasselas,* ed. Magdi Wahba, supplement to *Cairo Studies in English* (Cairo: 1959), pp. 97-103; W. K. Wimsatt, "In Praise of *Rasselas:* Four Notes (Converging)," in *Imagined Worlds: Essays on Some English Novels and Novelists in Honor of John Butt,* ed. Maynard Mack and Ian Gregor (London: Methuen, 1968), pp. 111-36; Cary McIntosh, *The Choice of Life: Samuel Johnson and the World of Fiction* (New Haven: Yale Univ. Press, 1973); Patrick O'Flaherty, "Dr. Johnson as Equivocator: The Meaning of *Rasselas,*" *Modern Language Quarterly,* 31 (1970), 195-206; Gloria Sybil Gross "Sanity, Madness, and the Family in Samuel Johnson's *Rasselas,*" *Psychocultural Review,* 1 (1977), 152-59; Edward Tomarken, "Travels into the Unknown: *Rasselas* and *A Journey to the Western Islands*" in *The Unknown Samuel Johnson,* ed. John J. Burke and Donald Kay (Madison: University of Wisconsin Press, 1983), pp. 150-65; Leopold Damrosch, Jr., *The Uses of Johnson's Criticism* (Charlottesville: Univ. Press of Virginia, 1976), especially the discussion of genius and the nature of human achievement, pp. 135-48; and John A. Vance, *Samuel Johnson and the Sense of History* (Athens, Georgia: Univ. of Georgia Press, 1984), particularly the discussion of the kind of participatory thinking that good historical writing requires of the reader, pp. 112-17. The work of W. R. Keast in, for instance, "Johnson and Intellectual History," in *New Light on Dr. Johnson: Essays on the Occasion of his 250th Birthday,* ed. Frederick W. Hilles (New Haven: Yale Univ. Press 1959), pp. 247-57; and "The Theoretical Foundations of Johnson's Criticism" in *Critics*

and Criticism: Ancients and Moderns, ed. R. S. Crane and others (Chicago: Univ. of Chicago Press, 1952), pp. 389-408, has become central to the way I think about Johnson in a way that makes specific acknowledgment no longer possible. And finally, William F. Lynch's *Images of Faith: An Exploration of the Ironic Imagination* (Notre Dame and London: Univ. of Notre Dame Press, 1973) offers a fascinating book-length discussion of boredom. Lynch characterizes boredom as a failure to embody thought and to comprehend irony. I have discussed other aspects and implications of the psychology of boredom in the essay, "Johnson, Imlac, and Biographical Thinking," in *Domestick Privacies: Samual Johnson and the Art of Biography,* ed. David G. Wheeler (Lexington: Univ. of Kentucky Press, 1987) pp. 85-106.

[2] From Carl Becker's "Every Man his own Historian," *American Historical Review,* 37 (1932), 227.

[3] *The History of Rasselas, Prince of Abissinia,* ed. Geoffrey Tillotson and Brian Jenkins (London and New York: Oxford Univ. Press, 1971), p. 80. Future citations from *Rasselas* in the body of the essay will refer to this edition by page number.

[4] For a discussion of conversation as a model for philosophy, see particularly Richard Rorty's *Philosophy and the Mirror of Nature* (Princeton: Princeton Univ. Press, 1979), especially Chapter VIII, "Philosophy Without Mirrors," section 5, "Philosophy in the Conversation of Mankind," pp. 389-95; and Kenneth Burke's *The Philosophy of Literary Form,* 3rd ed. (Berkeley and Los Angeles: Univ. of California Press, 1973), p. 107. Future citations from *The Philosophy of Literary Form* in the body of the essay will refer to this edition as *PLF.*

[5] Joel Weinsheimer, in his notable essay, "Writing about Literature and Through It," *Boundary 2,* X, 3 (Spring 1985), 69-91, uses this Heideggerian notion as the basis for distinguishing specious from genuine repetition in criticism. Genuine repetition, Weinsheimer argues, values the unity of discontinuity that makes possible relation to rather than identity with history.

[6] James Noxon makes this argument in his essay "Human Nature: General Theory and Individual Lives," *Biography in the 18th Century,* ed. J. D. Browning (New York and London: Garland Publishing, 1980), p. 16.

[7] A notable discussion of the psychology of hope through an evocation of archetypal pathology appears in James Hillman's *Re-Visioning Psychology* (New York and London: Harper and Row, 1975), passim, but particularly in Chapter 2, "Pathologizing or Falling Apart," and Chapter 4, "Dehumanizing or Soul-making."

[8] I have discussed some aspects of Imlac's abilities as a teacher, particularly his good sense of timing, and also the importance of trust in the drama of education, a subject addressed later in this essay, in "Imlac and Autobiography," *SECC,* 6 (1977), 183-198.

[9] *The Idler and The Adventurer,* Vol. II of The Yale Edition of the Works of Samuel Johnson, ed. W. J. Bate, J. M. Bullitt, and L. F. Powell (New Haven and London: Yale Univ. Press, 1963), p. 362.

[10] *The Rambler,* Vols. III-V of The Yale Edition of the Works of Samuel Johnson, ed. W. J. Bate and Albrecht B. Strauss (New Haven: Yale Univ. Press, 1969), I, 15. Future citations from *The Rambler* in the body of the essay will refer to this edition.

[11] W. J. Bate makes this argument in "Johnson and Satire Manqué," *Eighteenth-Century Studies in Honor of Donald Hyde* ed. W. H. Bond (New York: The Grolier Club, 1970), pp. 154-61.

Richard Braverman (essay date 1990)

SOURCE: "The Narrative Architecture of *Rasselas,*" in *The Age of Johnson: A Scholarly Annual,* Vol. 3, edited by Paul J. Korshin, AMS Press, Inc., 1990, pp. 91-111.

[*In the following essay, Braverman examines the significance of architectural structures as well as interior and spiritual spaces in* Rasselas.]

More than twenty years ago, Paul Fussell noted the prevalence of architectural imagery in the writing of the major Augustan humanists. Writers from Swift to Burke, he observed, had found in the "architectural image-system" a way of expressing "the role of forethought, arrangement, will, and order in the self-construction of the human imagination . . ." Fussell went on from there to suggest that

> If we could learn to pay less attention to what eighteenth-century writers say they are doing and more to what they actually do, I think we should find that instead of being devoted to the Horatian formula *ut pictura poesis,* as they sometimes say they are, they really are much more profoundly committed to the premise *ut architectura poesis.*[1]

Given the prevalence of the "architectural image-system" in what Fussell termed the "rhetorical world" of the major Augustan writers, it is not surprising that architectural monuments find an important place in Samuel Johnson's ***Rasselas.*** In this work, Johnson's best known narrative, prominent architectural spaces—the palace of Abyssinia, the Egyptian pyramids, and the catacombs—serve to objectify thematic complexities by providing a correlative to the travelers' moral progress as they seek to resolve the paradox inherent in their quest.[2]

Rasselas is a quest romance whose narrative object is the redeeming knowledge that human experience promises but fails to deliver.[3] The narrative is itself generated by a fundamental hermeneutical activity as the various characters who travel through its fictive landscape are continually engaged in acts of interpretation. Most acts of interpretation are fruitless because the travelers, armed with the wrong questions until the final chapters, cannot properly "read" the true nature of their quest. In fact, enlightened insight is possible only at a few critical junctures where interpretation might permit the appropriation of redeeming knowledge and power. Those critical junctures—points at which the temporal and noumenal intersect—are situated within the architectural monuments through which the travelers pass; those monuments, the palace of Abyssinia, the Egyptian pyramids, and the catacombs, are, in fact, the only spaces in the narrative where the travelers can gain access to an interpretive code denied them elsewhere. However, only in the final architectural space, the catacombs—a place that confronts them with their own mortality—do the travelers pose questions and answer them in ways that suggest that they comprehend the contradictory nature of their quest. Their realization, however, comes with a price, because it calls for a kind of moral discipline that undermines the autonomy they so ardently desire. When Rasselas and his companions recant their lost illusions and decide to travel back to Abyssinia, their quest is appropriately concluded. But it cannot be resolved, even though the narrative architecture, a fundamental trope for the narrative itself, is demystified. In spite of their disillusionment, however, their progress through the architectural monuments permits them to comprehend the terms of their journey so that they may return to Abyssinia with a deeper understanding of human resignation and hope.

The story of Rasselas begins in a "spacious valley in the kingdom of Amhara, which is surrounded on every side by mountains."[4] This place, called the "Happy Valley," is one where "All the diversities of the world were brought together, the blessings of nature were collected, and its evils extracted and excluded" (p. 74). Above the floor of the fertile valley which "supplied its inhabitants with the necessaries of life," stands a palace, a masterpiece of architectural intricacy:

> The palace stood on an eminence raised about thirty paces above the surface of the lake. It was divided into many squares or courts, built with greater or less magnificence according to the rank of those for whom they were designed. The roofs were turned into arches of massy stone joined with cement that grew harder by time, and the building stood from century to century, deriding the solstitial rains and equinoctial hurricanes, without need of reparation. (p. 74)

The palace, designed to withstand the ravages of time, is a monument that symbolizes the immutability of the social order it houses; even the material that bonds the massive arches supporting the "roofs" grows "harder," meaning stabler, with time. However, this monument to stability contains within it—in surprising contrast to its implacable exterior—a suspiciously intricate plan whose purpose is described at length in the concluding paragraph of the first chapter.

> This house, which was so large as to be fully known to none but some ancient officers who successively inherited the secrets of the place, was built as if suspicion herself had dictated the plan. To every room there was an open and secret passage, every square had a communication with the rest, either from the upper stories by private galleries, or by subterranean passages from the lower apartments. Many of the columns had unsuspected cavities, in which a long race of monarchs had reposited their treasures. They then closed up the opening with marble, which was never to be removed but in the utmost exigencies of the kingdom; and recorded their accumulations in a book which was itself concealed in a tower not entered but by the emperour, attended by the prince who stood next in succession. (pp. 74-75)

The palace, "built as if suspicion herself had dictated the plan," clearly contains more than the "treasures" accumulated within its secret cavities. In fact, the treasures themselves, concealed within the columns that support the structure, seem to possess a significance beyond the mere riches that they apparently represent. Their whereabouts, after all, are denied to all but the royal inhabitants of the Happy Valley, whose general population, already amply provided for by the emperor, does not, we presume, seem likely to take them. And it is just as unlikely—given the monumental construction of the palace and the equally impregnable mountains that surround the Happy Valley—that the emperor fears their expropriation by hostile invaders. It seems more likely, I think, that Johnson intends for us to see the treasures in a different sense, a sense that serves to establish a fundamental problem posed by the text, namely the respective legacies of the royal sons. First of all, the very fact that the "prince who stood next in succession" is not permitted to enter the tower and presumably read the contents of the "book of treasures" *except* when accompanied by the emperor his father, suggests that the tower is a space of initiation and the book a critical instrument of that process. But what sort of initiation? And what importance might the initiation of the heir hold for the narrative? The initiation process of which the book appears to be an integral part is the royal succession, the means by which the emperor elevates the heir apparent. However, if power will presumably fall to the next in line upon the death of the emperor, why does Johnson introduce the royal succession in a work that altogether avoids practical politics? He does so because, I think, he is principally concerned with the theme of education, and the revelation of the contents of the book form part of the special education intended specifically for the heir apparent but denied to younger sons like Rasselas. Given the special nature of the initiation, what secrets does the book contain? Surely not the royal accounts. In fact, whatever it contains, it is far less important *what* secrets it holds than what the process of initiation itself represents in the context of the narrative; and in that regard the book in the tower is, I will argue, a sign for something conferred and something denied. What is conferred, I think, is the knowledge and concomitant authority that paternal nomination carries. Such knowledge and authority are, furthermore, legitimate only through inheritance, and Rasselas, we know, is *not* the heir apparent, nor is he ever likely to succeed to power. Having only the remotest chance of being initiated into the secrets of the palace through the special dispensation of the emperor his father, he will consequently seek compensation ("happiness") in the "worldly" education of a younger son. And in so doing he will find himself caught in the moral tensions that the text generates over and over again, tensions owing to the basic conflict between the available alternatives to the problem of succession.[5]

Johnson gives narrative form to the moral tensions generated by the presence of the book in the tower by posing questions of authority and succession in the form of two alternative readings of experience, one based on the principles of what I will call "secular" narrative, the other on those of what I will call "divine" narrative, which is introduced as the privileged point of view. These two fundamentally different versions of narrative (and interpretation) are based on contrary notions of time. Secular narrative is based on the logic of sequence related by discursive motions proceeding in the perpetual present, while divine narrative is based on the ritual logic of the eternal return. The distinction between secular and divine narrative is essentially one between *chronos,* time as it is ordinarily apprehended, and *kairos,* time comprehended under the aspect of eternity. In contrast to the tick-tock time that we experience from moment to moment, *kairos* generally signifies a divine moment, "an event in time significant because of the [divine] presence in it."[6] Such events, which permit access to knowledge beyond the limits of ordinary temporal experience, are available only in specially sanctioned places. In ***Rasselas,*** such places (in which the temporal and eternal intersect) are associated with architectural monuments. However, the secrets of the first such monument, the royal palace, are denied to Rasselas, who thinks he can

find the answers he seeks beyond the Happy Valley. But in so doing he falls prey to a way of interpreting experience (via secular narrative) that will not allow him to transcend the limitations inherent in his quest—until, that is, he descends into the catacombs in Chapter 48.

The quest upon which Rasselas will embark with his companions outside the Happy Valley takes place for the most part within the framework of secular narrative. But in the tale it is the framework of divine narrative that is introduced first, through the succession theme that is brought up in the second paragraph of the first chapter. It is there that we learn that Rasselas is not the immediate heir to the throne of Abyssinia, but "the fourth son of the mighty emperour, in whose dominions the Father of waters begins his course; whose bounty pours down streams of plenty, and scatters over half the world the harvests of Egypt" (p. 73). Like all the princes of Abyssinia, Rasselas must remain in the Happy Valley until the time of his accession:

> According to the custom which has descended from age to age among the monarchs of the torrid zone, Rasselas was confined in a private palace, with the other sons and daughters of Abyssinian royalty, till the order of succession should call him to the throne. (p. 73)

Given his status as the "fourth son of the mighty emperour," the chances that Rasselas will become the heir apparent who will be initiated into the secrets of the tower and the book are quite slim. But if Rasselas will never get to read the book, why does Johnson mention it? Because, as I said above, what is denied to Rasselas, an inheritance, is as critical as what is available to him as a younger son, experience. The difference between the paths available to the emperor's sons takes form in the tale as the difference between the narrative possibilities that shape their respective legacies. This becomes clear in the construction of the narrative, in which the book, stored in a tower which is itself in a palace that stands unperturbed "from century to century . . . without need of reparation," represents the discourse that royal sons desire of their fathers. Not only do its contents reveal the riches of the palace of Abyssinia, but its possession confers mastery over the imperial palace, whose passages and corridors very much resemble the kind of narrative labyrinth that Rasselas will soon discover outside the Happy Valley. While learning how to decipher the labyrinth—the space of the palace by means of the book—is the goal and the responsibility of the royal heir, Rasselas, as a younger son, has little hope of being initiated into the knowledge that would permit him to decipher and possess the secrets of the palatial labyrinth. And as he seeks to gain through experience what is denied him by inheritance—by the "grace" of his father—Rasselas registers his dissatisfaction with his predicament by expressing his boredom with the pleasures of the Happy Valley.

The Happy Valley is a world of pastoral ease that is isolated in space by impenetrable mountains and in time by an absence of temporality beyond the natural rhythm of the seasons.[7] In contrast to Milton's Eden, where Adam and Eve work contentedly as a sign of their obedience, Johnson's Happy Valley is a place where members of the court find peace in refined leisure. Made aware of the miserable world beyond the mountains by "the sages who instructed them," the "sons and daughters of Abyssinia lived only to know the soft vicissitudes of pleasure and repose, attended by all that were skilful to delight, and gratified with whatever the senses can enjoy" (p. 75). Furthermore, on the occasion of the emperor's annual visit, "all delights and superfluities were added. . . . Every desire was immediately granted" (p. 74). Rasselas, however, grows cloyed with his diversions and discontented with his world. In contrast to what his teachers have told him, he believes that man must have desires in addition to, yet distinct from, those equated with the satisfaction of appetite: "Man surely has some latent sense for which this place affords no gratification, or he has some desires distinct from sense which must be satisfied before he can be happy" (p. 76). Imlac, however, reminds him that he is in "full possession of all that the emperour of Abyssinia can bestow" (p. 77). But what of the book in the tower?

The book in the tower—the symbol of the knowledge and power he wants but cannot have—underlies Rasselas's compulsion to undertake his quest. The book, which contains the secret of interpretation, the *a priori* code, holds the interpretive knowledge that Rasselas seeks but is denied.[8] And it will be continually denied him unless he regulates his will and desire according to the prescript of a divine authority that operates according to a higher order of succession. He can do this, in narrative terms, when his quest for happiness is made to signify a quest for felicity; for as progress in space and time is not coextensive with spiritual progress, only through the substitution of eternal felicity for temporal happiness as the object of narrative desire can the secular discourse signify the sacred.[9] To accomplish this end, Rasselas must, to borrow a Miltonic phrase, "stand and wait," that is, substitute spiritual for temporal progress.[10] The opportunities to comprehend this axiom outside the Happy Valley occur within the architectural spaces of funerary monuments, the Egyptian pyramids and the monastic catacombs, spaces where the spiritual and temporal intersect. At these junctures, the opportunity to interpret, a kind of training,makes available the means to transcend the labyrinth of the narrative. Yet the outcome of the inquiry is in each case governed by the immediately preceding events. In the Happy Valley those events, which include Rasselas's plans to escape and Imlac's account of events beyond the Happy Valley, prepare Rasselas for his subsequent fall into fictive narrative itself.

In the Happy Valley, Rasselas cannot escape the desires emblematized by the labyrinthine corridors of the palace, whose secrets are denied him. In fact, he only exacerbates his predicament by acting out romantic fictions that permit him to transcend only through his imagination the filial limitations implied by the laws of succession. Giving in to his impetuosity, he figures himself as a romantic hero, and in that guise he even chases an imaginary "treacherous lover" who has robbed an equally illusory "orphan virgin": "So strongly was the image impressed upon his mind, that he started up in the maid's defence, and ran forward to seize the plunder with all the eagerness of real pursuit" (p. 79). When the spectre passes, Rasselas realizes his "useless impetuosity" in chasing it, for confronting his "fatal obstacle," the mountains surrounding the Happy Valley, he concludes: "How long is it that my hopes and wishes have flown beyond this boundary of my life, which yet I never have attempted to surmount!" (p. 79). But the mountains, the natural boundary surrounding the Happy Valley, do not represent his real obstacle. His true impediment is internal; it is his implacable desire to transcend the filial limitations inherent in the laws of succession. Rasselas's limitation, like Oedipus' club foot, is the defect that he cannot outdistance, and Johnson uses his complaint to illustrate an almost Augustinian attitude to fortune. As Walter Jackson Bate has written, Johnson believed quite firmly that misfortune was less the result of external circumstances than internal disposition:

> Johnson traces the inevitable "doom of man" to inward and psychological causes . . . and the confused jostle he depicts in the outer world finds an analogy in the nature of man himself . . . [11]

If it is not external circumstances, namely the mountains that entangle Rasselas and lead him to undertake his quest, but an internal cause, his flight from the Happy Valley can only be an escape into bondage, a point that is later reenforced by the place where he seeks his first adventures, Egypt. In his ardor to escape the Happy Valley Rasselas therefore overlooks the truths that "lie open before him," and his "fall" into experience will carry him into the space and time of secular narrative. It is significant that narrative itself is the means of the fall, narrative that takes the form of the tempting story that Imlac tells. But Imlac is only the *instrument* of theodicy, because it is the word he bears—the narrative of the younger son that he presents—rather thanthe man himself that is the origin of Rasselas's desire to circumvent the filial limitations necessitated by the laws of succession and seek through experience what is denied him through inheritance.

Once Rasselas and his companions are outside the Happy Valley, the main action of the narrative, the search for the happy man, begins. At first (Ch. 17), Rasselas searches for happiness among the Epicureans, but he rejects their frivolity for he thought it "unsuitable to a reasonable being to act without a plan, and to be sad or cheerful only by chance" (p. 102). Next, the stoic philosopher with whom he is impressed violates the principles of his philosophy when he mourns uncontrollably the death of his daughter. In their "Glimpse of the Pastoral Life," Rasselas and his companions are dismayed to learn that shepherds do not lament their lost loves but their lost labors, for "they considered themselves as condemned to labor for the luxury of the rich" (p. 104). Similarly, the life of the country gentleman who represents the prevalent Horatian ideal of the happy man is only apparently idyllic. Though a man of many possessions, he is a prisoner of his wealth, fearing expropriation by the tyrannical Bassa of Egypt. The travelers' hopeful expectations are also disappointed by the hermit, who admits to having been "impelled by resentment, rather than by devotion, into solitude" (p. 107). In every case the happy man Rasselas searches for is fundamentally flawed because he represents a secular *topos;* and a quest without a transcendent goal can only fail the test of experience. Despite these disappointments, Rasselas, "almost discouraged from further search," sets out on a new adventure, resisting the stasis of which Imlac accuses him: "You wander about a single city, which, however large and diversified, can now afford few novelties, and forget you are in a country, famous among the earliest monarchies for the power and wisdom of its inhabitants . . ." (p. 120). Rasselas's curiosity leads him and his companions to the pyramids, those monuments which, according to Imlac, contain the secrets of their era.

The pyramids are funerary monuments in which the temporal and noumenal intersect. "Raised before the time of human history," they were designed to permit their sacred inhabitants eternal life.[12] In the narrative architecture of **Rasselas,** however, the pyramids are emblematic of the pilgrims' own interpretive blindness. Although the travelers listen to a philosophical meditation on the nature of human desire while in the great pyramid, the visit, preceded as it is by the fruitless search for the happy man in Egypt, does not permit comprehension of their quest. In fact, the significance of the pyramids is understood only retrospectively, after the pilgrims descend into the labyrinthine spaces of the catacombs in Chapter 48. In the "discourse on the nature of the soul" in the catacombs (Chapter 48), Rasselas tells Imlac that "it is commonly supposed that the Egyptians believed the soul to live as long as the body continued undissolved, and therefore tried this method of eluding death" (p. 151). The pyramids are, at last, understood as monuments representing a version of redemption in which the physical condition of the body

and the status of its possessor determine the nature and duration of the afterlife. But the travelers cannot recognize this notion at first (in Chapters 31 and 32), nor can they apply it to their own circumstances, namely their search for the happy man, because until they visit the catacombs, they remain ignorant of the nature of what they are searching for.

As the party are leaving the great pyramid, the Princess, Rasselas's sister, prepares "for her favourite a long narrative of dark labyrinths, and costly rooms, and of the different impressions which the varieties of the way had made upon her" (p. 124). But upon meeting those who stayed behind, they discover that the favourite, Pekuah, has been abducted. The subsequent chapters, which tell the story of the abduction and its happy conclusion, mark a change in the tale's focus because, as Emrys Jones points out, it shows the travelers "living fully in the world" for the first time: "they no longer . . . contemplate the spectacle of life [but] become fruitfully involved in [it]."[13] The sequence leads to a turning point in their interpretive education, which comes in Chapters 40 through 46 in the episode of the astronomer.[14] It is in this sequence that they prepare themselves for their final opportunity to comprehend their quest, which will culminate shortly after the discussion of their visit to the monastery of St. Anthony.

In Chapter 44, after his visit with the astronomer, Imlac delivers his famous discourse upon "the dangerous prevalence of the imagination." At the end of this lecture, an admonition both to Rasselas and to the readers of his quest, Imlac warns of the dangers when "fictions begin to operate as realities, false opinions fasten upon the mind, and life passes in dreams of raptures or of anguish" (pp. 141-142). Thereafter, Rasselas and his companions vow to recant their temporal desires: the favourite will no longer act the part of queen of Abyssinia; the princess will no longer play shepherdess; and Rasselas will no longer seek the role of philosopher-king. However, only after they have cured the astronomer of his madness do the travelers demonstrate that they possess useful knowledge, because their action is self-curative. Suffering from the "disease" of narrative, theirs is truly an affliction of the imagination: just as the astronomer cannot control the weather, they cannot control their destiny, or choice of life. Before he is cured, the astronomer believes that he has appropriated divine authority, for having effectively removed God from the universe, he thinks that he can impart the knowledge of His control, the legacy of the providential will, to Imlac: "The care of appointing a successor has long disturbed me; the night andthe day have been spent in comparisons of all the characters which have come to my knowledge, and I have yet found none so worthy as thyself" (p. 140). Believing his authority to be divine in nature, the astronomer—in a way that evokes the themes of succession and secret knowledge—presumes he can pass on his power to Imlac through the authority of his word. His condition is clearly an analogue of the travelers', for his belief in the control of the future, signalled by the conventional symbol of destiny, the heavens, reflects the desire of the wanderers in their quest for happiness. In relieving the astronomer of the fictions of his imagination, the pilgrims prepare to remove themselves from their own. This transformation occurs with the lessons of the monks of the monastery of St. Anthony, which is followed by the descent into the catacombs.

Critics have often noted the shift in subject and tone that comes over the narrative after the travelers discuss their visit to the monastery of St. Anthony. But none, I think, has sufficiently stressed just how in these chapters Johnson works within the conceptual and narrative context of Christian heroism.[15] Christian heroism, in contrast to heroic virtue, usually takes the form of vigilance: it is a kind of heroic or "standing." To take one example, standing is the "action" that Christ commends to the angelic band before the conclusion of the war in heaven in Book VI of *Paradise Lost:*

> Stand still in bright array ye Saints, here stand
> Ye Angels arm'd, this day from Battle rest;
> Faithful hath been your Warfare, and of God
> Accepted, fearless in his righteous Cause,
> And as ye have receiv'd, so have ye done
> Invincibly . . .
>
> (VI. 801-806)

With Christ as their vanguard, the angelic band win an easy rout, but as the Son explains, they win merely by standing, that is, by the conviction of their faith. If heroic resolution is the essence of Christian heroism, its prelude is the humble submission that prepares one for temptation and conflict. Expressed in high heroic fashion in Milton's poem, this axiom is conveyed in a much more sober fashion by Johnson, who in a prayer that he wrote later in his life, espoused a quiet yet resolute heroism. Striving to submit himself to the will of the heavenly father, Johnson vowed to stand steadfastly in the "patient expectation" of his own spiritual illumination: "Let me rejoice in the light which Thou hast imparted, let me serve Thee with active zeal and humble confidence, and wait with patient expectation for the time in which the soul which Thou receivest shall be satisfied with Knowledge."[16] Stressing the need to wait for the *time* when he might be satisfied with the knowledge and the certainty he desires, Johnson can be "active" only in his "zeal," that is, in his obedience. In *Rasselas,* likewise, a son must come to recognize his filial obligations: he must learn, that is, to stand and "wait with patient expectation" for the paternal word that holds the key to the mystery of the book in the tower. So do the monks of the monastery of St. Anthony stand and wait, as Imlac observes: " . . . their toils are cheerful, because they consider them as acts of piety, by which they are always advancing towards

endless felicity" (p. 149). While they remain in their monastic enclosures they are *advancing,* because they possess the interpretive code Rasselas is denied: "Their devotion prepares them for another state, and reminds them of its approach, while it fits them for it" (p. 148). Imlac's earlier articulation of this paradox of progress in the Happy Valley becomes, retrospectively, a gloss on the pilgrims' progress heretofore: "Change of place is no natural cause of the increase of piety . . ." (pp. 91-92). Pilgrims of a sort like Rasselas and his companions, the monks, however, accept their filial obligations and resist the temptation of narrative. And they are able to transcend its labyrinthine elaborations because they know that felicity (spiritual succession) is made possible only through submission. Such is the paradox of progress, which can be achieved only when the secular narrative signifies the sacred—when one makes the proper choice of eternity.[17] For once the *a priori* code is grasped, they labyrinth of narrative is demystified and appropriated.

In bringing the pilgrims to the order of St. Anthony, the oldest in Christendom, Johnson may simply have chosen a Christian analogue available in Egypt. Yet I think there is reason to suspect that he may have had in mind one of the most famous passages from St. Augustine's *Confessions.* In Book VIII, Augustine, tormented by his sinful nature, took refuge beneath a fig tree where he sought in vain for a way to escape his contemptible condition. Paralyzed by self-recrimination and "with bitter sorrow in his heart," Augustine "all at once heard the sing-song voice of a child in a nearby house." Again and again the child repeated the refrain "Take it and read, take it and read." Augustine, telling himself that "this could only be a divine command to open my book of Scripture and read the first passage on which my eyes should fall," remembered the miraculous story he had recently heard concerning St. Anthony:

> For I had heard the story of Antony, and I remembered how he had happened to go into a church while the Gospel was being read and had taken it as a counsel addressed to himself when he heard the words *Go home and sell all that belongs to you. Give it to the poor, and so the treasure you have shall be in heaven; then come back and follow me.*[18]

In the *Confessions,* it is Augustine's recognition of St. Anthony's miraculous experience that put him on the path to conversion and which provided him with a new way of interpreting. Augustine's text, "Spend no more thought on nature and nature's appetites" (Romans 13.13-14), certainly resonates in Johnson's text, and in *Rasselas* the travelers come to recognize the limited nature of their quest after their discussion of the monks of St. Anthony, a discussion that is followed by their descent into the catacombs. In this final monument of the narrative architecture of **Rasselas,** the party will come at last to understand the true nature of their quest, and they will be able to because their discussion is preceded by their recognition of the paradox of progress.

Upon entering the catacombs, the travelers rove "with wonder through the labyrinth of subterraneous passages where the bodies were laid in rows on either side" (p. 150). Their visit to this "labyrinth" recalls the descent by which the epic hero receives the legacy of the future that he will fulfill as the agent of the paternal will. Although a number of analogues of epic descent were available to Johnson, I think that he may very well have had in mind Aeneas's descent in Book VI of Virgil's poem.[19] In that book, Aeneas, having captured the golden bough that permits him to cross the threshold of mortality, receives a prophetic vision of Rome from his father, Anchises. But before the revelation of empire, he receives a lesson that draws upon Lucretian cosmology and stoic religious dogma. Anchises tells his son about the elemental fire that links the soul to the divine spirit that imbues the universal mind, instructing Aeneas on the path by which all souls seek to return to the "fiery energy" that forged them:

> First, then, the sky and lands and sheets of
>   water,
> The bright moon's globe, the Titan sun and
>   stars,
> Are fed within by Spirit, and a Mind
> Infused through all the members of the world
> Makes one great living body of the mass.
> From Spirit come the races of man and beast,
> The life of birds, odd creatures the deep sea
> Contains beneath her sparkling surfaces,
> And fiery energy from a heavenly source
> Belongs to the generative seeds of these,
> So far as they are not poisoned or clogged
> By mortal bodies, their free essence dimmed
> By earthiness and deathliness of flesh.[20]

Anchises continues his lecture by explaining that the soul, after passing through successive incarnations, finally returns to its elemental point of rest in the eternal fire from which it was born. While most have to undergo numerous incarnations, some, like Anchises, are free:

> We are sent
> Through wide Elysium, where a few abide
> In happy lands, till the long day, the round
> Of Time fulfilled, has worn our stains away,
> Leaving the soul's heaven-sent perception
>   clear,
> The fire from heaven pure.

In Virgil's text, Anchises's speech serves as a kind of prelude to the prophecies to follow, prophecies that link past, present, and future through the legacy of pious Aeneas. In Johnson's text, Rasselas and his companions do not receive such an inspiring vision. But in their symbolic descent into the underworld, they come to appreciate the paradoxical nature of transcendent knowledge in a fallen world. And in the lecture they receive from Imlac, who, like Anchises, discourses on the nature of the soul, they come to reflect upon their own condition from the prospect of eternity.

In their discussion in the catacombs, the travelers dispute the nature of the soul, at last fixing their quest upon its proper object. At first they cannot determine whether the soul is material or immortal. But as Imlac explains, it is both, despite the apparent contradiction of the example he provides: "It is no limitation of omnipotence . . . to suppose that one thing is not consistent with another, that the same proposition cannot be at once true and false, that the same number cannot be even and odd, that cogitation cannot be conferred on that which is created incapable of cogitation" (pp. 151-52). Imlac's explanation leads Rasselas to understand the intersection of the noumenal and the temporal in the *internal* architectural space of the soul, for as the travelers prepare to leave the catacombs, he at last hits upon a potential interpretive code when he remarks: "How gloomy would be these mansions of the dead to him who did not know that he shall never die" (p. 152). Soon after Rasselas's revelation, the travelers at last comprehend the nature of narrative and recognize the limitations of their understanding. Although they make ambitious plans for more useful lives than they have lead heretofore, they recognize that in constructing such plans they have once again been seduced by their irrepressible desires. As a result, they plan almost immediately to return to Abyssinia. But in so doing they show that they can decipher the labyrinth of narrative even though they cannot so easily discipline their desires. And when Rasselas and the pilgrims resolve to return to Abyssinia, it is in tacit recognition that the privileged discourse, symbolized by the book in the tower, is not the preserve of the privileged; on the contrary, anyone who learns how to interpret its contents may decipher the mystery of the labyrinth and appropriate the riches of the palaces of Abyssinia, and of eternity.[21] However, judging from the conclusion in which nothing is concluded, it is clear that the knowledge and potential power the book represents are not at all easily obtained, their elusive possession being the subtler lesson of the monastic visit. For while Johnson depicts the monks of St. Anthony advancing towards spiritual accession because they humbly submit to the rigors of the religious life, he implies at the same time that such rigor may not be possible beyond the monastic enclosure. But the life of discipline is both a desirable goal and a moral challenge, especially in light of the appetite for experience that characterizes both Johnson and his fictional characters. Johnson, of course, was continually troubled about his own moral discipline, and he may have wondered whether such obedience as he hoped to attain was possible beyond the monastic life. But in spite of his doubts, he nonetheless continued to rededicate himself to the quest for spiritual peace, hoping to transcend his inherent limitations through diligent labor, the same labor for which Rasselas, the "fourth son of the mighty emperour," must prepare himself as well:

> To give the heart to God, and to give the whole heart, is very difficult; the last, the great effort of long labour, fervent prayer, and diligent meditation.—Many resolutions are made, and many relapses lamented, and many conflicts with our own desires, with the powers of this world, and the powers of darkness, must be sustained, before the will of man is made wholly obedient to the will of God.[22]

Notes

[1] Paul Fussell, *The Rhetorical World of Augustan Humanism* (Oxford: Clarendon Press, 1965), p. 189.

[2] Of the numerous critical studies of *Rasselas,* those that I have found most useful for my purposes are Earl R. Wasserman, "Johnson's *Rasselas:* Implicit Contexts," *JEGP,* 74 (1975), 1-25; Eric Rothstein, *"Rasselas,"* in *Systems of Order and Inquiry in Later Eighteenth-Century Fiction* (Berkeley and Los Angeles: Univ. of California Press, 1975), pp. 23-61; Emrys Jones, "The Artistic Form of *Rasselas,"* *Review of English Studies,* 18 (1967), 387-401; Gwin Kolb, "The Structure of *Rasselas,"* *PMLA,* 66 (1951), 698-717; and Carey McIntosh, *The Choice of Life: Samuel Johnson and the World of Fiction* (New Haven: Yale Univ. Press, 1973), pp. 163-212. Also, Bertrand Bronson's footnote to the description of the palace (in chapter one) in his edition of *Rasselas* initially aroused my interest in the narrative's architecture: "The description here seems 'planted' for future narrative development. Johnson never exploits it, however, having his mind on events of a different order." *Rasselas, Poems, and Selected Prose* (New York: Rinehart, 1952), p. 507. My disagreement with Bronson's footnote generates the central thesis of this essay.

[3] Though "redeeming" has unmistakable theological overtones, I also want to stress its narrative sense, which emphasizes recovery and fulfillment. Recovery and fulfillment, denied to the travelers in narrative time, can only be glimpsed at privileged moments (such as the monastery of St. Anthony and the catacombs) when they approach without crossing the threshold that promises access to transcendent knowledge. Of the many critical works on the theory of romance, I have found Patricia Parker's *Inescapable Romance* (Princeton: Princeton Univ. Press, 1979) particularly helpful.

Parker defines romance as a form which "simultaneously quests for and postpones a particular end, objective, or object" (p. 4). In her subsequent elaborations, Parker shows how romance, operating as a narrative strategy deferring the anticipated moment of revelation, dilates the threshold before the promised end, word, or name is disclosed. In a generalization pertinent to *Rasselas* as well, she remarks: "For poets for whom the recovery of identity of the attainment of an end is problematic, or impossible, the focus may be less on arrival or completion than on the strategy of delay" (p. 5). The historical background on Johnson's use of romance can be found in Martha P. Conant, *The Oriental Tale in England* (New York, 1908); and Geoffrey Tillotson, "Rasselas and the Persian Tales," *Essays in Criticism and Research* (Cambridge, 1942), pp. 111-16.

[4] Samuel Johnson, *Rasselas* in *Samuel Johnson, Selected Poetry and Prose,* ed. Frank Brady and W. K. Wimsatt (Berkeley and Los Angeles: Univ. of California Press, 1977), p. 73. Subsequent citations, given parenthetically in the text by page, are to this edition.

[5] Johnson, I think, uses succession as a trope for the transmission of privileged knowledge. Rasselas therefore desires to circumvent his filial obligations by means of an alternative "succession" through experience. The ultimate failure of such alternative schemes (of a younger son) is foreshadowed in the attempted flight from the Happy Valley in chapter 6, a flight that ends in Icarian bathos. On Johnson's thinking on succession in general, see Adam Potkay, "Johnson and the Terms of Succession," *SEL,* 26 (1986), 497-509.

[6] Edward W. Tayler, *Milton's Poetry, Its Development in Time* (Pittsburgh: Duquesne Univ. Press, 1979), p. 128. On the distinction, see also Henri-Charles Puech, *Man and Time* (New York, 1957), pp. 40-41.

[7] On the debatable Edenic status of the Happy Valley, see Gwin J. Kolb, "The 'Paradise' in Abyssinia and the 'Happy Valley' in *Rasselas,"* *Modern Philology,* 56 (1958), 10-16; and D. M. Lockhart, "'The Fourth Son of the Mighty Emperour': The Ethopian Background of Johnson's *Rasselas,"* *PMLA,* 78 (1963), 516-28.

[8] In *The Poetics of Prose,* trans. Richard Howard (Ithaca: CornellUniv. Press, 1977), p. 129, Tzvetan Todorov explains the nature of the quest narrative: "The quest of the Grail is the quest of a code. To find the Grail is to learn how to decipher the divine language, which means . . . to appropriate the *a priori* aspects of the system." It is also worth noting that in *Rasselas* the knowledge that the book in the tower contains applies to a realm of experience outside the Happy Valley, because the emperor does not live there but only visits once a year.

[9] John Freccero elaborates this connection between narrative and desire: "The theology of the Word binds together language and desire by ordering both to God, in Whom they are grounded. From a naturalistic standpoint, it is impossible to say whether human discourse is a reflection of the Word or whether the idea of God is simply a metaphoric application of linguistic theory." "The Fig Tree and the Laurel: Petrarch's Poetics," *Diacritics,* 5 (1975), 35. In *Rasselas,* Johnson's "theology of the Word" emphasizes the difference between happiness and felicity. In the *Dictionary,* Johnson defines "happiness" as the "state in which desires are satisfied." He defined "felicity" as "blissfulness, blessedness," giving as an illustration lines from Spenser's Amoretti 78: "The joyous day, dear Lord, with joy begin, / And grant that we, for whom thou did'st die / Being with thy dear blood clean wash'd from sin, / May live for ever in *felicitie.*"

[10] The phrase concludes sonnet 19: "God doth not need / Either man's work or his own gifts, who best / Bear his mild yoak, they serve him best, his State / Is Kingly. Thousands at his bidding speed / And post O're land and ocean without rest; / They also serve who only stand and wait."

[11] W. Jackson Bate, *Samuel Johnson* (New York: Harcourt, Brace, Jovanovich, 1977), p. 281. The influence of the church fathers on Johnson's thought was first remarked upon by Hawkins: "To speak of . . . his religion, it had a tincture of enthusiasm, arising from the fervour of his imagination, and the perusal of St. Augustine and others of the fathers, and the writings of Kempis and the ascetics" (pp. 162-63). Johnson's relation to the church fathers has been considered by Katherine C. Balderston in "Dr. Johnson and William Law," *PMLA,* 75 (1960), 382-94, who argues that Johnson may have gotten such ideas from William Law. Nevertheless, given the evidence of Johnson's library, it seems clear that he knew the church fathers first hand. On Johnson's relationship to Augustinian theology, see Donald Greene, "Johnson's Late Conversion: A Reconsideration," in *Johnsonian Studies,* ed. Magdi Wahba (Cairo, 1962), pp. 61-92.

[12] Eric Rothstein notes that contemporary sources "treat the pyramid . . . positively, with reference to immortality or eternity." (*Systems of Order and Inquiry,* p. 45). In *The Pyramids of Egypt* (Harmondsworth, 1977), I. E. S. Edwards notes that "the possession of the Pyramid" enables the king to "mount up to heaven at will and return to his tomb" (p. 288).

[13] Emrys Jones, "The Artistic Form of *Rasselas,*" p. 397.

[14] The way in which these chapters fit into later temporal patterns whereby characters try to control past, present, and future is treated by Geoffrey Tillotson in "Time and *Rasselas,*" in *Bicentenary Essays on Rasselas,* ed. Magdi Wahba (Cairo: S.O.P. Press, 1959), pp. 97-103. A recent account of these chapters is Leonard Orr, "The Structural and Thematic Importance of the Astronomer in *Rasselas,*" *Recovering Literature,* 9 (1981), 15-21.

[15] For an extended discussion of Christian heroism in Milton, see Stanley Fish, *Surprised by Sin* (London: Macmillan, 1967), pp. 180-207. Contrasting it to heroic achievement, Fish writes that Christian heroism is "the willingness to rest easily and happily on days when there are no battles" (p. 196). What underlies Christian heroism is a post-Reformation conceptualization of man's temporal experience that, according to Georges Poulet, is based on the belief of "God the redeemer" rather than "God-the-creator-and-preserver," and which empowers the hero by joining "the particular moment . . . to an eternal moment." *Studies in Human Time,* trans. Elliot Coleman (Baltimore: Johns Hopkins Univ. Press, 1956), p. 11.

[16] *Diaries, Prayers, and Annals,* ed. E. L. McAdam, Jr., in The Yale Edition of the Works (New Haven: Yale Univ. Press, 1958), I, 384.

[17] Saint Anthony of Egypt, who died *ca.* 355, was the founder of Christian monasticism. By fasting and other ascetic practices, St. Anthony repeatedly overcame the devil, who appeared to him in the form of various visual and auditory temptations. See *Butler's Lives of the Saints,* ed. Herbert Thurston and Donald Atwater (New York: P. J. Kennedy, 1956), I, 104-109.

[18] *Confessions,* ed. R. S. Pine-Coffin (Harmondworth: Penguin, 1961), p. 177.

[19] Although the allegorization of the classical epic was of greater importance to the later middle ages and Renaissance, in the eighteenth century, observes Wasserman, "Homer's epics and especially Virgil's Aeneid were still read as allegorical journeys of the prince (such as Prince Rasselas)" (p. 16). Johnson frequently cited passages from Aeneid VI in his periodical essays. He was apparently keen on lines 126-29, the descent into the nether world, which he cites on five occasions: *Rambler* 16, 64, 155; *Idler* 27, and *Adventurer* 34. Here are the lines in Dryden's translation: "The gates of Hell are open night and day; / Smooth the descent, and easy is the way: / But, to return, and view the chearful skies; / In this, the task and mighty labour lies."

[20] *The Aeneid,* trans. Robert Fitzgerald (New York: Random, 1985), p. 185. While the afterlife first appears "localized and final," writes R. G. Austin, "now [VI.724-51], astonishingly, all is changed and a new prospect opens. The underworld spirit-existence, in its various forms, is replaced by a cosmic system of the

origin and progress of the soul in its connection with the body; after death it is gradually purged of the contaminations that have become ingrained during its bodily imprisonment, and with a lapse in time, depending on individual circumstance, it ascends in purity to the fiery element that gave it birth." *Aeneis: Book VI* (Oxford: Clarendon Press, 1977), p. 220.

[21] There has always been disagreement concerning the ultimate destination of the pilgrims. See George Sherburn, "Rasselas Returns—To What?" *Philological Quarterly*, 38 (1959), 383-84; Wasserman, op. cit., 20-21; and Gwin Kolb, "Textual Cruxes in *Rasselas*," *Johnsonian Studies*, ed. Magdi Wahba (Cairo, 1962), pp. 257-66. I interpret the ending according to Johnson's own uncertainties about divine election. Reflecting the emotional urgency under which it was produced, *Rasselas* affirms Johnson's belief that the individual can only "stand and wait" for the intervening grace of the father.

[22] Samuel Johnson, *Sermons,* ed. Jean Hagstrum and James Gray, in The Yale Edition of the Works (New Haven: Yale Univ. Press, 1978), XIV, 143.

Duane H. Smith (essay date 1996)

SOURCE: "Repetitive Patterns in Samuel Johnson's *Rasselas*," in *Studies in English Literature, 1500-1900,* Vol. 36, No. 3, Summer, 1996, pp. 623-39.

[*In the following essay, Smith examines the use and function of repetitive narrative structures in* Rasselas.]

> Ye who would listen with credulity to the whispers of fancy, and pursue with eagerness the phantoms of hope; who expect that age will perform the promises of youth, and that the deficiencies of the present day will be supplied by the morrow; attend to the history of Rasselas prince of Abissinia.

Thus, Samuel Johnson begins *The History of Rasselas, Prince of Abissinia,* raising the expectation that attention to thenarrative which follows will somehow dispel "the whispers of fancy," "the phantoms of hope," or help one to understand whether "the deficiencies of the present day will be supplied by the morrow."[1] Whether and how the narrative actually does this has been debated almost ever since. On the one side, James Boswell argues that *Rasselas* "leads us through the most important scenes of human life, and shews us that this stage of our being is full of 'vanity and vexations of spirit'" and that "Johnson meant, by shewing the unsatisfactory nature of things temporal, to direct the hopes of man to things eternal."[2] On the other hand, Johnson's earlier biographer, Sir John Hawkins, asserts that *Rasselas* "is rendered, by its obvious moral, of little benefit to the reader" and that "it cannot be said that it vindicates the ways of God to man."[3] These essentially hopeful and hopeless interpretations have continued into the realms of modern criticism in the work of such figures as Irvin Ehrenpreis and Patrick O'Flaherty, respectively.[4]

The apparent contradiction between the hopeless and hopeful interpretations arises from Johnson's attempt to assert a particular belief or meaning in a context which negates the meaning he would like to convey.[5] This is immediately apparent even in the work's title, *The History of Rasselas, Prince of Abissinia. A Tale,* especially when the key terms "history" and "tale" are viewed in light of Johnson's definitions. Johnson's primary definition of "history" is "a narration of events and facts delivered with dignity." The difficulty that arises for modern readers with the use of the word "history" defined as such to describe an obvious fiction seems not to have been a problem for Johnson, as he indicates in *The Rambler* No. 4, where he writes: "The works of fiction, with which the present generation seems more particularly delighted, are such as exhibit life in its true state, diversified only by accidents that daily happen in the world, and influenced by passions and qualities which are really to be found in conversing with mankind."[6] But Johnson's own definition of "tale" subverts the very idea of "events and facts delivered with dignity," for his primary definition of "tale" reads "a narrative; a story. Commonly a slight or petty account of some trifling or fabulous incident." By focusing on repetitions in the narrative, I argue that the two aspects of the text, meaning and facts, are not contradictory, but complementary, and that Johnson affirms the value of the narrative as entertainment even as he denies its value as a moral tale. In other words, rather than directing our attention to eternal life or pointing out the essential nihilism of life, as critics have repeatedly argued, Johnson presents a narrative that functions for us as readers in much the same way as the many activities of Rasselas and Nekayah: they divert attention from fear and boredom and provide some measure of entertainment.

The fundamental question posed by *Rasselas* may be formulated in a variety of ways: What is the meaning of life? What is the correctchoice or path in life? What makes for human happiness? For critics such as Boswell and Ehrenpreis, *Rasselas* posits that the meaning of life is found ultimately in the next world, not in this, that the correct choice leads one to the preceding revelation, and that human happiness can be found only in eternal life. On the other hand, for critics such as Hawkins and O'Flaherty, the work posits that life has no meaning, there are no correct choices, and human happiness is illusory. The contradictory nature of these answers arises more from the critic's emphasis of or preference for different aspects of the same narrative, but such an emphasis or preference may have a direct relation to the reader's expectations, expectations that are central to any reading experience, particularly narrative. As Roland Barthes argues:

> Expectation . . . becomes the basic condition for truth: truth, these narratives tell us, is what is *at the end* of expectation. This design . . . implies a return to order, for expectation is a disorder: disorder is supplementary, it is what is forever added on without solving anything, without finishing anything; order is complementary, it completes, fills up, saturates, and dismisses everything that risks adding on: truth is what completes, what closes . . . To narrate (in the classic fashion) is to raise the question as if it were a subject which one delays predicating; and when the predicate (truth) arrives, the sentence, the narrative, are over, the world is adjectivized (after we had feared it would not be).[7]

Rasselas presents a question-answer structure similar to that suggested by Barthes. The questions raised by the narrative concern human happiness—what it is and how it is to be attained—and the reader expects that some answer (for Barthes, Truth) will be provided in response to these questions. But at the end of *Rasselas,* the reader encounters not answers or truth, or closure, but a chapter entitled, "The Conclusion in which Nothing is Concluded." This lack of closure certainly frustrates the reader's expectations, and to counter such frustrations, critics such as Boswell and Ehrenpreis suggest that Johnson provides the reader with another Truth, that is, that the text points to a transcendental Truth: happiness lies in a hope for eternal life. These critics thus satisfy expectations by resorting to extrinsic themes, by imposing transcendental meaning on a text that deliberately thwarts such an imposition. However, as I hope to demonstrate, the affirmation of such a transcendental "Truth" is invariably undercut in *Rasselas* by the repetition of a particular pattern within the text.

An example of the fundamental pattern in *Rasselas,* and one which, interestingly, has similarities to the narrative described at length by Barthes, can be found in Imlac's narrative. At the end of chapter 7, Rasselas commands Imlac "to relate his history" (p. 30)but, just as Imlac is about to begin, Rasselas is called to a concert, and the fulfillment of the narrative contract is delayed until the evening. Then, it is partially fulfilled as Imlac tells his history. But just when Imlac reaches an "enthusiastic fit" and begins "to aggrandize his own profession," that is, being a poet, Rasselas interrupts, saying "that no human being can ever be a poet" (p. 46). Rasselas's comment renders Imlac's narrative meaningless while not rendering it unentertaining, for Rasselas immediately requests that Imlac resume the narrative. While Imlac is telling Rasselas the story as a means of diverting him from his melancholic disquiet, he is also rendering an account of himself, explaining his profession, what it entails, demands; in short, Imlac gives utterance to his very being, a being which

Rasselas immediately invalidates, thus rendering the narrative itself meaningless. Rasselas, in other words, creates a double irony: he affirms the value of Imlac's narrative as entertainment even as he denies its value as a moral tale. This, I contend, is essentially what Johnson does on the level of the general narrative. He both affirms and denies his text; he both arouses and thwarts expectations. But this arousal and thwarting are ultimately complementary rather than contradictory.

Indeed, the repetition of a pattern of unfulfilled expectations so permeates the narrative that it extends to and applies to any final answers, especially those suggested by Ehrenpreis and Boswell as available in an after life. That *Rasselas* depends to some extent on repetitions has not gone unnoticed. For example, Geoffrey Tillotson underscores important aspects of repetition and sameness when he asks, "could the interest be maintained among experiments which, as forecast, are all at bottom the same?" and when he states that "the use to which the material is to be put is, from the reader's point of view, identical, and therefore at bottom likely to be boring," and finally when he writes of "the simpler arrangements that defeat the effect of monotony where materials are discernible as sameish at bottom."[8] A more convincing argument is mounted by J. Hillis Miller, who, on the other hand, argues for the fundamental importance of repetition in all narrative structures, especially the novel: "Any novel is a complex tissue of repetitions and of repetitions within repetitions, or of repetitions linked in chain fashion to other repetitions."[9]

Miller identifies the two kinds of repetition as Platonic and Nietzschean, terms which by Miller's definition bear some similarity to the eighteenth-century terms "imitation" and "originality." Miller argues that the difference between the two kinds of repetition is similar to the "distinction . . . between the rational, willed, intentional remembering of the daytime, and that kind of involuntary memory which [Walter] Benjamin calls forgetting."[10] The first of these corresponds to Miller's Platonic repetition which is "grounded in a solid archetypal model which is untouched by the effects of repetition. All the other examples are copies of this model."[11] The second type of remembering corresponds to Miller's Nietzschean repetition which "is not grounded. It arises out of the interplay of the opaquely similar things, opaque in the sense of riddling." Similarities are important to both types of repetition: in Platonic repetition, "similarities . . . are seen as identities, one thing repeating another and grounded in a concept on the basis of which their likeness may be understood"; in Nietzschean repetition, the similarities are dream-like, that is, "one thing is experienced as repeating something which is quite different from it and which it strangely resembles."[12] And finally, Miller insists on the intertwining of these two types of repetition: "Another necessity of the second form of repetition . . . is its dependence on the first, grounded, logical form. Each form of repetition calls up the other, by an inevitable compulsion. The second is not the negation or opposite of the first, but its 'counterpart,' in a strange relation whereby the second is the subversive ghost of the first, always already present within it as a possibility which hollows it out."[13] For Miller, "all modes of repetition represent one form or another of the contradictory intertwining of the two kinds of repetition."[14] *Rasselas* provides a vivid illustration of the fundamental relationship between repetition and the narrative mode; this relationship remains crucial in understanding the fundamental questions posed by *Rasselas* as an entertaining diversion.

II

In *Rasselas,* the Platonic mode of repetition, the mode that is "grounded in a solid archetypal model," can be seen in the way that the plot repeats, or imitates, the Christian archetype of man's origins, a fall from innocence in paradise, a search for that lost innocence in the world, and a return to paradise. Rasselas is introduced to the reader in the Happy Valley where he has lived blissfully innocent for some years; that innocence is lost and Rasselas becomes discontented; he leaves the Happy Valley and searches unsuccessfully in the world for happiness, and at the end resolves to return to Abyssinia. There are, of course, some obvious differences between the biblical archetype and Johnson's repetition—for example, Rasselas desires to leave the Happy Valley, but Adam and Eve are driven from Eden; it is unclear whether Rasselas re-enters the Happy Valley, but the Christian archetype provides for the re-establishment of paradise. Minor differences aside, the archetypal repetition confirms the reading favored by those who see the meaning of *Rasselas* contained in Nekayah's statement: "'the choice of life is become less important; I hope hereafter to think only on the choice of eternity'" (p. 175).

Within this Platonic repetition, a number of repetitions occur, which, as they subvert the reading suggested above, correspond towhat Miller calls the Nietzschean mode of repetition. The first instance of this mode, and therefore the model for later repetitions, occurs at the close of the first chapter, where the narrator describes the palace situated in the Happy Valley:

> This house, which was so large as to be fully known to none but some ancient officers who successively inherited the secrets of the place, was built as if suspicion herself had dictated the plan. To every room there was an open and secret passage, every square had a communication with the rest, either from the upper stories by private galleries, or by subterranean passages from the lower apartments. Many of the columns had unsuspected cavities, in

which a long race of monarchs had reposited their treasures. They then closed up the opening with marble, which was never to be removed but in the utmost exigencies of the kingdom; and recorded their accumulations in a book which was itself concealed in a tower not entered but by the emperour attended by the prince who stood next in succession. (pp. 10-1)

The palace, we are told, contains a treasure just as the book, we believe (at the outset, anyway, given our general expectations), contains a truth. But the treasure of the palace is locked away and its whereabouts known only to those who never take an active part in the narrative, and the truth of the book—truth in the sense of predication or closure—is also withheld when we as readers finally reach that place where we expect it, the conclusion. Citing the description of the palace and the treasures as examples, Ehrenpreis claims that "It would be absurd to claim that Johnson carefully foresaw the course of his narrative."[15] But the frustrations aroused by the apparently inconsequential description of the palace opaquely parallels the frustrations aroused by the narrative that poses questions concerning human happiness, promises the fulfillment of those expectations, and simply fails on one level at least to answer these questions. The possibility that Johnson did not foresee "the course of his narrative" in no way prevents us from regarding the description of the palace as the prototype for the Nietzschean repetition, an initial example, perhaps, of Walter Benjamin's "forgetting memory."

Indeed, at a number of points in the narrative, events transpire that can be regarded as opaquely similar to the pattern suggested by the description of the palace. The palace contains riches beyond belief, yet without the key (that is, access to the *sanctum sanctorum*), they are useless. The Happy Valley itself is described as a place where "All the diversities of the world were brought together, the blessings of nature were collected, and its evils extracted and excluded" (p. 9). Yet, both the palace with all its treasures and the Valley itself with all evil excluded are found wanting. The pattern that emerges might be stated: potential panacea, test, failure. The repetition of this Nietzschean patternintertwines with and ultimately subverts the traditional Christian repetition on the narrative's Platonic level. Thus, the description presents an extension of the Platonic archetype at the infrastructure of the work, and at the same time repels this archetype by subverting its essential meaning.

The recurrence of this subversive pattern permeates the narrative. While still in the Happy Valley, after he has resolved to leave in some way, Rasselas makes the acquaintance of the artist skilled in mechanical arts. He raises Rasselas's hopes of leaving the Happy Valley by telling him that it is possible for men to swim through the air as the fish swims through the water. Initially, Rasselas maintains a degree of skepticism, being "not wholly hopeless of success," but as the artist himself becomes daily more confident, "the contagion of his confidence seized upon the prince." But after a year of waiting, on the day of the test, the artist's attempt to use artificial wings to soar beyond the confines of the surrounding mountains fails: "he waved his pinions a while to gather air, then leaped from his stand, and in an instant dropped into the lake" (p. 28). Clearly, the pattern emerges here: panacea, test, failure.

The only instance where such a pattern does not emerge occurs when Rasselas and Imlac tunnel their way through the mountain and escape the confines of the Happy Valley. But once the travelers, including Nekayah and Pekuah, enter the outside world, nearly every encounter they have suggests the pattern of potential panacea (or correct choice of life), test, and failure. Indeed, their very entrance into the world suggests the ultimate failure of their endeavor. Once outside, "The princess and her maid turned their eyes towards every part, and, seeing nothing to bound their prospect, considered themselves as in danger of being lost in a dreary vacuity." The princess, Nekayah, says that she is "'almost afraid . . . to begin a journey of which [she] cannot perceive an end.'" Rasselas, too, we are told, "felt nearly the same emotions, though he thought it more manly to conceal them" (p. 61). The reactions of Nekayah and Rasselas seem opaquely similar to the reaction Imlac had as a young man when he set out on his own exploration of the world. As he recounts when telling his history to Rasselas:

> When I first entered upon the world of waters, and lost sight of land, I looked round about me with pleasing terror, and thinking my soul enlarged by the boundless prospect, imagined that I could gaze round for ever without satiety; but, in a short time, I grew weary of looking on barren uniformity, where I could only see again what I had already seen. I then descended into the ship, and doubted for a while whether all my future pleasures would not end like this in disgust and disappointment. "Yet, surely," said I, "the ocean and the land are very different; the only variety of water is rest and motion, but the earth has mountains and vallies, desarts and cities: it is inhabited by men of different customs andcontrary opinions; and I may hope to find variety in life, though I should miss it in nature." (p. 35)

Imlac ultimately does not find that variety in life; rather, he finds just the sort of dreary vacuity that Nekayah fears, for he tells Rasselas his history after he has found only dreary vacuity or barren uniformity in life. He describes his decision thus: "Wearied at last with solicitation and repulses, I resolved to hide myself forever from the world, and depend no longer on the opinion or caprice of others. I waited for the time when the gate of the Happy Valley should open, that I might bid farewell to hope and fear: the day came; my performance was distinguished with favour, and I resigned myself with joy to perpetual confinement" (p. 54). Imlac's experience in the world and ultimate decision to withdraw from the world finds a parallel in Rasselas's, Nekayah's, and Pekuah's final resolutions to return to Abyssinia, a similar withdrawal from hope and fear and desire for perpetual confinement.

Another example of the subversive pattern of potential panacea, test, and failure occurs when Rasselas and his party seek out a hermit who they believe has found the correct choice of life. It seems immediately ironic that they should seek a solution in the life of the hermit at all. After all, Rasselas's dissatisfaction arose in part, he believes, from being confined in a place isolated from the rest of the world. Rasselas, therefore, leaves a quiet place, the Happy Valley, because of internal disquiet and seeks internal quiet in an unquiet place, the world. The hermit's life initially inverts this pattern. He withdrew from the disquiet of the world to seek quiet in the wilderness; there, he found disquiet; therefore, he is ready to return to the disquiet of the world to find quiet. In addition to the internal disquiet he feels living apart from the rest of the world, the hermit's situation parallels Rasselas's situation in the Happy Valley in three other ways. First, the hermit's cell was "at such a distance from the cataract, that nothing more was heard than a gentle uniform murmur" (p. 80). In the Happy Valley, the "lake discharged its superfluities by a stream which entered a dark cleft of the mountain on the northern side, and fell with dreadful noise from precipice to precipice till it was heard no more" (p. 8). Second, in response to the question posed by Rasselas and his sister, Nekayah, as to the proper *"choice of life,"* the hermit responds: "'To him that lives well . . . every form of life is good; nor can I give any other rule for choice, than to remove from all apparent evil'" (p. 81). The second half of his advice here might be taken as a sign that the seekers after life should return to the Happy Valley, for it is there that "All the diversities of the world were brought together, the blessings of nature were collected, and its evils extracted and excluded" (p. 9). And finally, after he has announced his intention to return to Cairo and the travelers have offered to conduct him, the hermit "dug up a considerable treasurewhich he had hid among the rocks" (p. 83). The parallel in the Happy Valley can be found in the passage already cited which describes the hidden treasure. Thus, the parallels between the Happy Valley and the hermit's life—the water, the absence of evil, and the buried treasure—in addition to the similarity between Rasselas's frustrations with life in the Happy Valley and the hermit's with his own reclusive life—he calls his occupation "tasteless and irksome" and feels "unsettled and distracted" (p. 82)—suggest the opaque similarity of these two aspects of the narrative. Furthermore, when

Rasselas returns to Cairo and relates the hermit's story to an assembly of learned men, one responds that he thinks it "likely, that the hermit would, in a few years, go back to his retreat, and, perhaps, if shame did not restrain, or death intercept him, return once more from his retreat into the world" (p. 85).

Such behavior can be seen also to some extent in Imlac, who entered the world, retreated from the world when he entered the Happy Valley, and re-entered the world when he led Rasselas, Nekayah, and Pekuah to Cairo. Rasselas's and his sister's actions also mirror this pattern of behavior. They, however, move from being separate from the world to being a part of the world, to being separate again at the end, that is, if their resolution to return to Abyssinia at the narrative's end is read as a retreat to enclosure. To explain this behavior on the part of the hermit, an explanation which can certainly apply equally to Imlac, Rasselas, and Nekayah, the one who predicted the behavior in the hermit comments that "'the hope of happiness . . . is so strongly impressed, that the longest experience is not able to efface it. Of the present state, whatever it be, we feel, and are forced to confess, the misery, yet, when the same state is again at a distance, imagination paints it as desirable'" (p. 85). This conclusion resembles that drawn by Nekayah at the end of the marriage debate: "Those conditions which flatter hope and attract desire, are so constituted, that, as we approach one, we recede from another" (p. 110). Fundamental truisms such as these guarantee the pattern outlined above: potential panacea or choice of life, test, failure.

Numerous incidents throughout **Rasselas** illustrate this pattern. For example, there is Rasselas among the youths, then later among the splendor of the court, and Nekayah among the people of middle station. At one point, Rasselas meets a philosopher who espouses a philosophy which he claims will enable one to deal with the vicissitudes of the world, but when that philosophy is tested by the death of the philosopher's daughter, it turns out to be ineffectual. Another philosopher claims that living according to nature is the correct choice of life, but when he is pressed by Rasselas to explain what he means, he is unable, and again, the correct choice becomes unattainable. Thus, the disquiet Rasselas felt in the Happy Valley, the disquiet that provoked his escape tosearch for the choice of life, is never dispelled during the course of the narrative. This lack of success at finding the correct choice of life, coupled with the visit to the catacombs, provokes Nekayah into saying: "'To me . . . the choice of life is become less important; I hope hereafter to think only on the choice of eternity'" (p. 175). This apparent solution, however, is subverted by the Nietzschean repetitions, for its emergence also follows the pattern of potential panacea (eternal life or the soul's salvation), test (death), and failure (lack of knowledge).

On another level, too, the text ends on an ambivalent note, a note sounded by the repeated images of confinement suggested by Rasselas, Nekayah, and Pekuah. At the narrative's beginning, the disquiet felt by Rasselas seems to have its origin in the sense of enclosure he feels. Indeed, references to confinement abound in the opening chapter. We learn that "Rasselas was *confined* in a private palace," that the valley was "surrounded on every side by mountains," and that "the valley was closed with gates of iron . . . so massy that no man could, without the help of engines, open or shut them" (p. 8; emphasis added). Every year during the emperor's annual visit, various artists and musicians compete for the "blissful captivity," and every year there are "new competitors for imprisonment" (p. 10). And Rasselas identifies this sense of imprisonment as the source of his disquiet when he looks at the mountain and sees it as "'the fatal obstacle that hinders at once the enjoyment of pleasure and the exercise of virtue'" (p. 18).

Yet, it is just such a desire for enclosure that marks the ending of the narrative. Each of the travelers, Rasselas, Nekayah, and Pekuah, still desires enclosure, and the hope for happiness, depicted as illusory by the incidents in the narrative, continues to be fostered in the final paragraphs. Pekuah desires a place similar to "the convent of St. Anthony," where she can be "fixed in some unvariable state." Nekayah desires "to found a college of learned women," where she can "raise up for the next age models of prudence, and patterns of piety" (p. 175). And Rasselas desires "a little kingdom," where he can "administer justice . . . and see all parts of government with his own eyes" (pp. 175-6). Each desires some small space of confinement where happiness can be found (or manufactured), yet the subversive pattern established by the text suggests that these desires, modest as they are, are not likely to be any more obtainable than the other choices of life. The closing paragraphs suggest one other possibility in the characters of Imlac and the astronomer, who are content "to be driven along the stream of life without directing their course to any particular port" (p. 176). Thus, the narrative offers two possible answers to its fundamental question, what is the correct choice of life: one, that the individual can continue to invest hope in unobtainable desires, or two, that one can drift with the current of life. Neither provides a satisfactory answer, yet both promise sufficientdiversion or entertainment to help one avoid boredom and fear, the two scourges of human life.

III

Thus, while on one level Johnson confirms traditional moral values and truth, the pattern of repetition on another level denies the very possibility of truth. The problem for the reader is somehow to negotiate this apparent contradiction. The meaning conveyed on the text's Platonic level is throughout subverted by the facts conveyed through the Nietzschean repetitions of Johnson's involuntary memory. It is possible in an act of interpretation to emphasize one or the other as Ehrenpreis and O'Flaherty do, but doing so undoes the complex intertwining of the two modes of repetition that gives Johnson's *Rasselas* its unique character.

Ehrenpreis argues that "Johnson's true doctrine seems to be that if there is no best way to live, there are good ways to pass limited parts of one's life," and he provides as examples of these good ways, "doing good for others, increasing our store of useful knowledge, practicing the fine and applied arts—these are some of the occupations that let us ignore the lapse of hours while we wait for eternity." But Ehrenpreis cites no examples of doing good for others, increasing one's store of useful knowledge, or practicing the fine and applied arts from *Rasselas* as occupations which allow one to ignore the lapse of hours; instead, the occupations he cites as "proper occupations" which allow one to ignore the lapse of hours occur when Rasselas "amuses himself by imagining" the "bleak world outside"; when he "seeks a means of escape without finding one"; when he passes months "cheerfully" continuing "his fruitless but absorbing researches"; when he is involved in another attempt to escape, "the digging of the tunnel by which the travelers leave the valley"; and finally, the endless and fruitless attempt "for the best choice of life."[16] The "proper occupation," therefore, involves key terms which negate rather than affirm: "imagining," "escape," "fruitless." In short, while the outer structure of the work affirms the notion of the quest, its thematic concerns deny any promise of fulfillment, both for the characters within the work and for the reader who participates vicariously in a similar quest for truth. But, if Johnson's *Rasselas* affirms neither a traditional Christian otherworldliness nor a "proper occupation," what prevents it from being essentially nihilistic, a result of the subversive Nietzschean repetitions overwhelming the Platonic repetition? As suggested earlier, Johnson asserts the value of his work as entertainment even as he denies its value as a moral tale, positive or negative, and indeed, *Rasselas* provides example after example of the positive power of entertainment or diversion.

The most striking incident which demonstrates the value of diversion occurs towards the end of the narrative in Nekayah's reaction to the abduction of Pekuah. Nekayah's initial reaction seems quite typical: she retires to her chamber accompanied by her women who try to comfort her. But she is not to be comforted. For some time, the efforts made to recover Pekuah help keep some hope alive in Nekayah. As each new attempt brings no more success than the last, the princess sinks into "hopeless dejection" (p. 122), and she upbraids herself for having let the abduction take place. Imlac eventually convinces her that had she exercised

her authority and made Pekuah accompany her into the pyramid, Pekuah might have died, an outcome Nekayah sees as unforgivable. Thus, somewhat reconciled, Nekayah becomes obsessed with the memory of Pekuah: "She sat from morning to evening recollecting all that had been done or said by her Pekuah, treasured up with care every trifle on which Pekuah had set an accidental value, and which might recall to mind any little incident or careless conversation. The sentiments of her, whom she now expected to see no more, were treasured in her memory as rules of life, and she deliberated to no other end than to conjecture on any occasion what would have been the opinion and counsel of Pekuah." Nekayah, like the astronomer, keeps these thoughts private from the others; "The women, by whom she was attended, knew nothing of her real condition" (p. 124). Her condition attracts the attention of her brother:

> Rasselas endeavoured first to comfort and afterwards to divert her; he hired musicians, to whom she seemed to listen, but did not hear them, and procured masters to instruct her in various arts, whose lectures, when they visited her again, were again to be repeated. She had lost her taste of pleasure and her ambition of excellence. And her mind, though forced into short excursions, always recurred to the image of her friend. (p. 124)

Interestingly, Rasselas repeats for Nekayah essentially what was done for him when he found the pleasures of the Happy Valley no longer pleasing. But clearly, here, Nekayah's constant thinking on Pekuah, what she said, and what she might have said, has a dangerous potential. This danger seems close to realization when Nekayah resolves to retire from the world, so she can devote herself to "'a constant succession of innocent occupations'" until she dies and can rejoin again "'the friendship of Pekuah'" (p. 125). But Nekayah does not retire from the world, for Imlac convinces her that experiencing or seeking novelty is the natural state of life. Imlac argues that

> Our minds, like our bodies, are in continual flux; something is hourly lost, and something acquired. To lose much at once is inconvenient to either, but while the vital powers remain uninjured, nature will find the means of reparation. Distance has the same effect on the mind as on the eye, and while we glide along the stream of time, whatever we leave behind us is always lessening, and that which we approach increasing in magnitude. Do not suffer life to stagnate; it will grow muddy for want of motion: commit yourself again to the current of the world; Pekuah will vanish by degrees; you will meet in your way some other favourite, or learn to diffuse yourself in general conversation. (p. 127)

Nekayah commits herself "again to the current of the world," and with the most positive of results. Assured that the search for Pekuah will continue and that her desire to retire from the world at the end of a year will be respected, she "began imperceptibly to return to common cares and common pleasures." For some time, she keeps an appointed hour of mourning, but "By degrees she grew less scrupulous, and suffered any important and pressing avocation to delay the tribute of daily tears" (p. 128). In time, she yields "to less occasions; sometimes forgot what she was indeed afraid to remember, and, at last, wholly released herself from the duty of periodical affliction" (pp. 128-9). Thus, involvement with the "current of the world," finding a means of entertainment or diversion, keeps Nekayah from becoming fixed upon one particular idea and running the risk of the dangerous prevalence of the imagination. The fates of Rasselas, Imlac, the Astronomer, and numerous other characters in the narrative also illustrate the same point, the value of diversion and entertainment.

Interestingly, Johnson's own state of mind at the time that he composed *Rasselas* might be compared to Nekayah's state of mourning for the lost Pekuah. As his early biographers point out, Johnson wrote *Rasselas* soon after his mother's death in January 1759. Her death, Boswell points out, was "an event which deeply affected him."[17] Sir John Hawkins's account is much more explicit about how deeply Johnson felt his mother's death. While Hawkins praises Johnson for the filial piety and depth of feeling expressed in *Rasselas,* he also comments that "he, whose mind acquired no firmness by the contemplation of mortality, was as little able to sustain the shock as he would have been had this loss befallen him in his nonage."[18] Hawkins suggests that in *Rasselas,* Johnson "poured out his sorrow in gloomy reflection, and being destitute of comfort himself, described the world as nearly without it."[19] Hawkins ends his discussion of *Rasselas* with a warning to young readers who might be swayed by Johnson's nihilism that they should "remember that he saw through the medium of adversity."[20] But while recognizing that Johnson did perhaps see through the medium of adversity, we do not have to conclude that he saw the world as "destitute of comfort," nor need we take recourse in the other extreme, that Johnson wrote to "direct the hopes of man to things eternal," as Boswell suggests. Instead, we might see Johnson, in the act of writing *Rasselas,* doing for himself what Rasselas and Imlac do for Nekayah when she became melancholy for her lost Pekuah, or what Nekayah and Pekuah later do for the astronomer: provide a means of diversion or entertainment.

Thus, the reader also experiences the narrative as a diversion, an entertainment, which surveys the possibilities of the human endeavor from the artist to the poet, from the philosopher to the astronomer. Though the narrative denies any absolute ability in these endeavors to convey happiness, it does suggest that while our attention, Rasselas's attention, or Johnson's attention, is temporarily absorbed in these diversions, it is possible to forget about failure, hopelessness, and boredom. Finally, on a practical level, just as there is little to distinguish life in the Happy Valley from life in the world, there is little to distinguish the decision of Rasselas, Nekayah, and Pekuah to return to places of confinement in Abyssinia from Imlac's and the astronomer's decision "to be driven along the stream of life without directing their course to any particular port" (p. 176). Both are simply different forms of entertainment or diversion. It is in this sense, as a text which directs our attention to the value of diversion and entertainment, that the narrative's importance as a "tale" supplements rather than subverts its pretensions to "history."

Notes

[1] Samuel Johnson, *The History of Rasselas, Prince of Abissinia,* in *Rasselas and Other Tales,* ed. Gwin J. Kolb (New Haven: Yale Univ. Press, 1990), p. 7. All references to the text will be to this edition and page numbers will be cited parenthetically.

[2] James Boswell, *Life of Johnson,* ed. R. W. Chapman (New York: Oxford Univ. Press, 1980), pp. 241 and 242.

[3] Sir John Hawkins, *The Life of Samuel Johnson, LL.D.,* ed. Bertram H. Davis (New York: Macmillan, 1961), p. 156.

[4] See Irvin Ehrenpreis, "*Rasselas* and Some Meanings of 'Structure' in Literary Criticism," *Novel* 14, 2 (Winter 1981): 101-17, and Patrick O'Flaherty, "Dr. Johnson as Equivocator: The Meaning of *Rasselas,*" *MLQ* 31, 2 (June 1970): 195-208. More recently, in *Johnson, "Rasselas," and the Choice of Criticism* (Lexington: Univ. of Kentucky Press, 1989), Edward Tomarken has provided an extensive summary of *Rasselas* criticism in his attempt to reconcile these two trends; Tomarken argues that *Rasselas* "manipulates generic and formal literary characteristics . . . to show how man's religious impulse leads to an understanding of how the literary process applies to the human world" and that "the theoretical dilemma posed by *Rasselas* can only be resolved when the hermeneutic and structuralist conceptions are seen in dialectical relationship to one another" (p. 37).

[5] Interestingly, this apparent contradiction between the text's hopeless and hopeful outlooks receives textual endorsement in the depiction of Imlac's father, who, though he has much, continues to desire more. During Imlac's historical narrative, Rasselas asks why Imlac's father desired "'the increase of his wealth when it was already greater than he durst discover or enjoy?'" Imlac responds: "'Inconsistencies . . . cannot both be

right, but, imputed to man, they may both be true. Yet diversity is not inconsistency. My father might expect a time of greater security. However, some desire is necessary to keep life in motion, and he, whose real wants are supplied, must admit those of fancy'" (p. 33). Thus, though Imlac's father hopes to increase his wealth, that time of greater security seems impossible. But as Imlac explains, this constitutes not an inconsistency, but a diversity, just one in a text devoted to cataloguing life's diversities, especially their underlying similarity.

[6] Samuel Johnson, *The Rambler,* ed. W. J. Bate and Albrecht B. Strauss (New Haven: Yale U. Press, 1969), p. 19.

[7] Roland Barthes, *S/Z,* trans. Richard Miller (New York: Farrar, Strauss, and Giroux, 1974), p. 76. Barthes is not alone in stressing the importance of closure or predication to the fulfillment of expectations. For example, Peter Brooks, in *Reading for the Plot,* suggests that "meanings are developed over temporal succession in a suspense of final predication" and that "what animates us as readers of narrative is *la passion du sens* . . . : the active quest of the reader for those shaping ends that, terminating the dynamic process of reading, promise to bestow meaning and significance on the beginning and middle" ([New York: Random House, 1984], p. 19). And Frank Kermode, in *The Sense of an Ending,* claims that "all such plotting presupposes and requires that an end will bestow upon the whole duration and meaning" ([New York: Oxford Univ. Press, 1967], p. 46).

[8] Geoffrey Tillotson, *Augustan Studies* (London: Athlone Press, 1961), pp. 241 and 245.

[9] J. Hillis Miller, *Fiction and Repetition: Seven English Novels* (Cambridge MA: Harvard Univ. Press, 1982), pp. 2-3.

[10] Miller, p. 7.

[11] Miller, p. 6.

[12] Miller, p. 8.

[13] Miller, p. 9.

[14] Miller, p. 4.

[15] Ehrenpreis, p. 111.

[16] Ehrenpreis, p. 115.

[17] Boswell, p. 240.

[18] Hawkins, p. 154.

[19] Hawkins, p. 155.

[20] Hawkins, p. 156.

FURTHER READING

Bibliography

Clifford, James L., and Donald J. Greene. "*Rasselas* and Other Prose Fiction." In *Samuel Johnson: A Survey and Bibliography of Critical Studies,* pp. 225-33. Minneapolis: University of Minnesota Press, 1970.

Includes a bibliography of primary editions of *Rasselas* and secondary sources.

Criticism

Baker, Sheridan. "*Rasselas:* Psychological Irony and Romance." *Philological Quarterly* 45, No. 1 (January 1966): 249-61.

Examines *Rasselas* as an ironic form of the popular eighteenth-century genre of oriental romance, suggesting that it reflects Johnson's ironic views of human nature.

Chapman, R. W. Introduction to *The History of Rasselas, Prince of Abissinia: A Tale by Samuel Johnson,* pp. ix-xxi. Oxford: Clarendon Press, 1927.

Provides a thorough textual history of *Rasselas,* including the circumstances under which it was written.

Hardy, J. P. "*Rasselas.*" In *Samuel Johnson: A Critical Study,* pp. 127-48. London: Routledge & Kegan Paul, 1979.

Offers an essentially positive reading of *Rasselas,* finding that the repeated diversions and constant motion of the narrative reflect the need for both hope and continuous movement in human life.

Joost, Nicholas. "Whispers of Fancy; or, The Meaning of *Rasselas.*" *Modern Age: A Conservative Review* 1, No. 2 (Fall 1957): 166-73.

Focuses on *Rasselas* as both a moral and religious work, finding its basic assumptions grounded in Christianity and a "faith in authority," rather than in rational proof.

Kenney, William. "*Rasselas* and the Theme of Diversification." *Philological Quarterly* 38, No. 1 (January 1959): 84-89.

Argues that the diverse and sundry activities engaged in by the principal characters in *Rasselas* illustrate that "life in familiar surroundings can be made tolerable if the right principles are followed."

Kolb, Gwin J. Introduction to *The Yale Edition of the Works of Samuel Johnson,* Vol. XVI: *Rasselas and Other Tales,* edited by Gwin J. Kolb, pp. xix-lxx. New Haven,

Conn.: Yale University Press, 1990.
> Discusses the work's publication history and reviews its orientalist sources, generic precedents, and contemporary critical reception.

———. "Sir Walter Scott, 'Editor' of *Rasselas*." *Modern Philology* 89, No. 4 (May 1992): 515-18.
> Attempts to demonstrate Scott's link to 1805 and 1819 editions of *Rasselas*.

Lockhart, Donald M. "'The Fourth Son of the Mighty Emperor': The Ethiopian Background of Johnson's *Rasselas*." *PMLA* 78 (December 1963): 516-28.
> Details Johnson's likely sources for the Abyssinian settings of *Rasselas;* also includes an appendix listing pre-1759 European works containing information on Ethiopia.

Mace, Nancy A. "What Was Johnson Paid for *Rasselas?*" *Modern Philology* 91, No. 4 (May 1994): 455-58.
> Uses evidence from an eighteenth-century copyright lawsuit to explore the publication history of *Rasselas*.

McIntosh, Carey. *"Rasselas."* In *The Choice of Life: Samuel Johnson and the World of Fiction,* pp. 163-212. New Haven, Conn.: Yale University Press, 1973.
> Delineates the diverse modes of fiction in *Rasselas* and considers them in the context of related Enlightenment texts, including Voltaire's *Candide* and the philosophy of Isaac Newton.

Munns, Jessica. "The Interested Heart and the Absent Mind: Samuel Johnson and Thomas Otway's *The Orphan*." *ELH* 60, No. 3 (Fall 1993): 611-23.
> Compares themes of desire in *Rasselas* and the cited Restoration tragedy by Otway, finding that Johnson's later text reflects a gloomy, more "modern" alienation from life.

Peake, Charles. Introduction to *'Rasselas' and Essays,* edited by Charles Peake, pp. xxix-xxxvii. London: Routledge & Kegan Paul, 1967.
> Describes *Rasselas* as an "argument," suggesting that thework is pessimistic only for those who do not share Johnson's belief in immortality.

Walker, Robert G. "A Reading of *Rasselas*." In *Eighteenth-Century Arguments for Immortality and Johnson's Rasselas,* pp. 35-63. Victoria, B.C.: English Literary Studies, 1977.
> Agrees with Boswell's contention that Johnson attempted to instill hope in his readers by pointing them toward eternal, rather than earthly, happiness. Walker finds that in *Rasselas* desire is seen as insatiable on earth, which leads one to look toward immortality for everlasting happiness.

Additional coverage of Johnson's life and career is contained in the following sources published by Gale: *Literature Criticism from 1400 to 1800,* Vol. 15; *DISCovering Authors; World Literature Criticism, 1500 to the Present;* and *Dictionary of Literary Biography,* Vols. 39, 95, 104, and 142.

Julian of Norwich

1342(?)-1416(?)

(Also known as Mother Juliana of Norwich, Dame Julian, Lady Julian, and Dame Jelyan.) English devotional writer. For information on Julian's complete career, see *LC*, Volume 6.

INTRODUCTION

Julian was the first woman writer of extended English prose. Her *Revelations of Divine Love*, in which she details the spiritual insights she derived from a series of sixteen visions, is considered an outstanding document of medieval religious experience. In it she considers the mysteries of Christian faith, commenting on predestination, the nature of sin, and other matters of traditional theology. *Revelations of Divine Love* has been praised for its freshness, simplicity, sincerity, and vigor, and it reveals the author as one endowed with an uncommon intellect and a profound faith.

Biographical Information

Julian was careful to ensure that no materials for her biography remained after her death. She asked readers of *Revelations* to forget the work's earthly author, and evidently she died in the obscurity she sought. Nothing is known of Julian's origin and little is known with reasonable certainty of her later life, although some facts do appear in *Revelations*, in scribal commentary, and in contemporary documents. That she was for some time an anchoress—a religious contemplative living a solitary life of meditation and prayer—is confirmed by a bequest in a 1404 will to "Julian an anchoress at St. Julian's Church" and by a record in Archbishop Henry Chichele's 1416 register of a legacy to "Julian, recluse at Norwich," who was, according to the register, then alive at age seventy-four. This information, considered along with Julian's age at the time of the events described in her book, points to about 1342 as her birth date. Little else is known about Julian except that she was attended by her mother during the illness described in *Revelations*.

Major Works

Revelations of Divine Love, Julian's only known work, is a prose account of visions she experienced while seriously ill in May of 1373. She later described these events in a short version of *Revelations of Divine Love*, believed to have been written soon after its author's recovery, and a longer, more reflective version, written probably about twenty years later. She recounts that while she contemplated a crucifix held before her by a curate, she was suddenly freed from pain. She reports that the crucifix before her eyes seemed to come to life and the visions began. The first fifteen "ghostly shewings" followed continuously for several hours, but then Julian's illness returned, causing her to lose faith in what she has seen. Falling asleep, she dreamed of the Devil trying to strangle her, and awoke to experience smoke, heat, and a "foul stench" apparent to no one in the room but herself. She then blessed God, and immediately lost all sense of sickness. Julian's faith in her visions returned, and that same night she experienced her sixteenth and, as far as can be gathered, final revelation. The following fifteen years she devoted to inquiry into the meaning of her visions, but her understanding was not made complete, she explains in the later version of *Revelations*, until nearly twenty years had passed.

Critical Reception

Julian and her work have not always been widely known and esteemed. There is no convincing evidence that there was any appreciable cult attached to her during her life; her present reputation for holiness is based on two sources only, *Revelations of Divine Love* and a reference to her by the fifteenth-century contemplative Margery Kempe, who visited Julian and described her as an expert in giving good counsel. The manuscript tradition for Julian's work indicates that in its author's day the *Revelations* enjoyed only limited circulation. In contrast with the plethora of surviving copies of the writings of such fourteenth-century English mystics as Richard Rolle, Walter Hilton, and the anonymous author of *The Cloud of Unknowing*, of Julian's work there are singularly few—perhaps, scholars have suggested, owing to its profundity and difficulty. *Revelations* was rescued in the mid-seventeenth century by Augustine Baker, whose spiritual school, located among the exiled English Benedictines of France and the Low Countries, transcribed the long text and provided the copy-text for the first printing of *Revelations of Divine Love*. Since that time, interest in Julian's work has remained slight, although at different times in the nineteenth and twentieth centuriess such issues as the text's language, prose style, and theological content have led in turn to inquiry into the extent of Julian's learning, the nature of her illness, her place among her contemporaries, and the relationship of the two versions of her account.

For the most part, contemporary critics have given *Revelations of Divine Love* and its author almost unqualified praise. Near the beginning of the twentieth century, William Ralph Inge described Julian's work as a "fragrant little book," and Evelyn Underhill labelled Julian "the most attractive, if not the greatest, of the English mystics." Concentrating on the work's literary style, T. W. Coleman characterized Julian's writing as "a moorland stream flowing gently along with crystalline cleanness and a sweet musical murmur," while others have acknowledged Julian's important position in the evolution of English prose. Touching on his subject's personal qualities, David Knowles called Julian "a generous and loving woman with an extraordinary delicacy of feeling," and E. I. Watkin wrote of Julian that "she comes to us with the credentials of a personal experience whose authenticity we cannot doubt." More recently, Edmund Colledge and James Walsh, in marked contrast to some earlier critics who approached Julian as a simple, untutored devotee miraculously endowed by the Holy Spirit, have seen Julian as a great writer and scholar: "Julian became such a master of rhetorical art as to merit comparison with Geoffrey Chaucer. . . . In adapting the rhetorician's figures and modes of thought to the needs of English prose, Julian was herself a pioneer."Outside of the critical mainstream, Julian's work has in this century been modernized, condensed, anthologized, and "interpreted" for contemporary readers, and the work's most celebrated messages, "All shall be well . . ." and "Love was His meaning," have been widely imitated and embraced, most notably the former saying in T. S. Eliot's 1943 poem "Little Gidding."

Julian is celebrated for her fundamental outlook of optimism and as a spiritual teacher of the first order. Her *Revelations of Divine Love* is recognized as a sound and consoling spiritual document, offering its readers a rich source of instruction impressive for its stylistic virtues and sober piety. Its message once nearly lost, Julian's *Revelations of Divine Love* has found an audience, and Julian is admired today as a woman of intellect and faith.

PRINCIPAL WORKS

XVI Revelations of Divine Love, Shewed to a Devout Servant of Our Lord, Called Mother Juliana, an Anchorete of Norwich, Who Lived in the Days of King Edward the Third (meditation) 1670

Comfortable Words for Christ's Lovers, Being the Visions and Voices Vouchsafed to Lady Julian (meditation) 1911

A Shewing of God's Love: The Shorter Version of Sixteen Revelations of Divine Love by Julian of Norwich (meditation) 1958

A Book of Showings to the Anchoress Julian of Norwich. 2 vols. (meditation) 1978

Showings meditation (meditation) 1978

CRITICISM

Robert H. Thouless (essay date 1924)

SOURCE: "Some Characteristics of Julian's Thought" in *The Lady Julian: A Psychological Study,* Society for Promoting Christian Knowledge, 1924, pp. 51-65.

[*Considering Julian's mystical experiences within a psychoanalytic framework, Thouless speculates on the psychic sources and meanings of her imagery.*]

Before passing to a consideration of particular teachings embodied in the shewings of the Lady Julian, we may notice two characteristics of her thought which must strike at once her most casual reader. These are the rich content of imagery in her thinking, and her almost repellent insistence on the physical awfulness of the crucifixion. The former is a point of psychological interest upon which we may dwell a little; the second is one which we shall be forced to consider, for it would be indeeduseless to commend a mediæval religious writer to the average reader of the present day unless some defence could be made for her against the charge of morbidity.

The plentifulness of the imaginal content of Julian's thought is shown not only by the corporeal and other visions of her revelation. She seems at other times to think in pictures. An example of the ease with which her thought expressed itself in imagery may be found in her tenth chapter. Her mind was occupied with the abstract idea that a man or woman in any situation "if he might have sight of God so as God is with a man continually, he should be safe in body and soul, and take no harm: and overpassing, he should have more solace and comfort than all this world can tell."[1] This thought expressed itself in a visual image of "the sea-ground, and there I saw hills and dales green, seeming as it were moss-begrown, with wrack and gravel."[2]

And later, when she received the locution, *"I thank thee for thy travail, and especially for thy youth,"* the thought contained in this shewing presented itself in the following visual image: "I saw our Lord as a lord in his own house, which hath called all his dearworthy servants and friends to a stately feast. Then I saw the Lord take no place in His own house, but I saw Him royally reign in His house, fulfilling it with joy and mirth, Himself endlessly to gladden and to solace His dearworthy friends, full homely and full courteously, with marvellous melody of endless love, in His own fair blessed countenance."[3] It should be noticed that this picture of our Lord in Heaven is not described as a shewing. It did not appear to Julian to have come from outside herself, as did the words of thanks. It was simply the way in which she thought of the idea of God thanking those who have served Him.

The significance of these observations for an appreciation of Julian's methods of thought may best be appreciated if we examine shortly the process of thinking as it goes on in different minds. Probably the most primitive elements in our thinking are *images*. These are pictures seen before the mind's eye, sounds heard, movements felt in the mind, or reproductions of sensations from other senses (smell, taste, etc.). They may be simple reproductions of the past, or new combinations of imagined impressions—the work of the creative imagination. Such images form an undercurrent in most of our thinking, attaining a more important position in the condition of reverie, and becoming dominant in dreams. Dreams seem to be the expression in images of primitive levels of thought of which we are not conscious when, in waking life, we are dominated by our environment with its demand for action.

A later acquired element of our mental life is our habit of thinking in words. Words, when we think them, are of course also images (we must either image the movements of pronouncing them, ortheir sound, or their appearance), so the kinds of imagery mentioned in the previous paragraph may be distinguished by giving them the name of *concrete images*. It is mainly the use of words in thinking, under conscious direction and control, which makes up intellectual processes of thought—processes which stand at the opposite pole to mere dreaming.

In addition, however, to words and concrete images, there appear to be elements in our thought of a more elusive character which have been given the somewhat clumsy name of "imageless thought." These are immediate grasps of meanings—of relationships or of references to fact—without any appearance of a mental intermediary in the form of a word or other image. Such imageless thoughts are much more difficult to speak of clearly, since they are less tangible than concrete images and words; but they are probably no less important for the full understanding of the thinking process.

Galton was the first person to draw attention to the importance of the differences between the types of thinking in different minds.[4] He found that, while most

persons have more or less rich and vivid imagery of things seen, such visual imagery may be completely absent from the minds of other persons, particularly of those who have devoted themselves to abstract thought. It is difficult for the person with vivid visual imagery to imagine what a barren waste would appear to him the mind of the person without visual images; while the verbal thinker is shocked if he discovers that the intellectual processes of the visualiser are accompanied by what seem to him to be merely a logically irrelevant riot of mental pictures. Differences of outlook are often determined by such profound differences in the contents of different peoples' minds, and the adherents of different schools of philosophy may have their views determined in this way.[5]

It is a very important peculiarity of our thinking in words that we can distinguish between valid and invalid trains of thought by logical rules. Of course, we can reach conclusions (and correct conclusions) by using images and imageless thoughts without going through a logical process of reasoning. Indeed, it is probable that generally most of us reach our conclusions in this way; but we can only be sure whether such conclusions are right or wrong when they are put to the test of experience. It is only when our steps to the conclusion have taken logical verbal form that we can assure ourselves that they are right and can convince other people of their rightness before they have been tested by experience.

Most persons will agree to one limitation of verbal thinking—that it is powerless, by itself, to give us new knowledge. We may be able by the use of words to draw correct conclusions from our experience, but no manipulation of words alone can tell us anything except what those words mean in the current use of language. It cantell us nothing about facts. The belief that manipulation of words can give us new knowledge about facts is the fallacy underlying certain ambitious metaphysical theories by which men have tried to gain knowledge about the universe by *a priori* construction of theories.

Possibly there is another limitation. The biological end of our intelligence is to enable us to modify our environment for our advantage. Verbal thinking is the last and most efficient weapon for this end. Professor Bergson suggests, however, that it is not an effective method of discovering what is ultimately true. Philosophic thought was not the end for which the intelligence was designed in the course of evolution. There are conditions known to the student of religion in which verbal thinking is reduced to a minimum and its place is taken by images and the processes of imageless thought. These may be called conditions of intuitional knowledge. Such knowledge, whether true or false, may be very convincing to the person experiencing it. He cannot demonstrate to us that it is true, for it cannot be put into logical verbal form without losing its character; but we must bear in mind the possibility of such intuitional conditions giving a real insight into reality, possibly even an insight which cannot be gained by verbal thinking. Such states certainly occur in mysticism, and their occurrence produces the note of subjective certainty which was mentioned in the first chapter as a characteristic mark of mystical writings. A more detailed examination of such states would take us too far into fields which we must not explore now. Enough has, I hope, been said to indicate how a knowledge of the psychology of normal thinking can help us to an understanding of such conditions.

The predominant use of concrete imagery, which we have seen to be so characteristic of Julian's writing, is found very commonly (but by no means universally), in the thinking processes of mystics. It is characteristic of the type of mind most sharply opposed to the logical and mathematical, which thinks mainly in words. The person with the logical-mathematical kind of mind is inclined to call the imaginal mind primitive or infantile. Thinking in concrete images has certainly its own peculiar pitfalls. There is, for example, the danger of passing from a perceived loose analogy between two things to a tacit assumption of their identity. An image which serves well for the illustration of an abstract thought becomes a danger if new facts about the object of the thought are deduced from the properties of the image. Examples of such misuse of imaginal illustrations abound in the loose thinking of both popular theology and psychology. The word *subliminal*, for example, was coined for mental processes which seemed not to appear in consciousness. The word, of course, means "below the threshold," and suggests the image of a threshold beneath which something is buried. An improper use of the illustration was made as soon as people began to attach a different metaphorical meaning to the "below," and inferred that what was below the threshold was in some ethical respect inferior to what was present in consciousness.

While such dangers are ever present to the thought of the imaginal thinker, there are others to which he is less exposed than the thinker in words. He is, for example, generally more clearly conscious of the inadequacy of his means of expression. Julian, seeing God in a point, was not likely to be misled into thinking that she had obtained an adequate expression of the immanence of God. The religious philosopher, on the other hand, who has obtained a conception of the Absolute by the manipulation of thoughts expressed in words (as in the Hegelian dialectic), is less inclined to be modest about the adequacy of his formulæ.

One result of the predominance of imagery in Julian's thinking is the concreteness of the objects of her devotion. We may take, as an example, the rhapsody on the blood of Jesus at the end of the Fourth Revelation.

"Behold and see!" she exclaims, "the precious plenty of His dearworthy blood descended down into Hell and burst her bands and delivered all that were there which belonged to the Court of Heaven. The precious plenty of His dearworthy blood overfloweth all Earth, and is ready to wash all creatures of sin, which be of good-will, have been, and shall be. The precious plenty of His dearworthy blood ascended up into Heaven to the blessed body of our Lord Jesus Christ, and there is in Him, bleeding and praying for us to the Father,—and is, and shall be as long as it needeth;—and ever shall be as long as it needeth. And evermore it floweth in all Heavens enjoying the salvation of all mankind, that are there, and shall be—fulfilling the number that faileth."[6] Here it is to the blood of Christ, a concrete imaginable thing, that she gives the emotional significance which to a theological mind would appear properly to belong to the notion (unimaginable and expressed inadequately in words), of Christ's Atonement. We are reminded of the devotion of St. Francis to the Christmas crib as a pictorial representation of the mystery of the Nativity. Consideration of the differences between the kind of thinking which goes on in different types of mind—one of the most striking and significant discoveries of the empirical psychology of the end of the last century—should prepare us to view with understanding the highly concrete devotions which have grown up in Roman piety which seem often to the uncomprehending intellectual mind to savour of idolatry.

The worst that the intellectually disposed can think of Julian's imaginal thinking is that it is childlike. But what are we to think of the content of her terribly vivid visions of the crucifixion? The spirit in which she broods over the sufferings of Jesus on the Cross is one with which we moderns are strangely out of sympathy. We do not hesitate to call it morbid. We no longer wish to think of such things as death and misery, but prefer to saturate our minds with wholesome ideas of health and beauty. The agonising Christ on the roadside crucifix shocks us by its cruel emotional contradiction to the beauty of the sunlit Tirolese mountain and valley in which it is set. We love living too well to wish to be reminded of death at every turn.

But it may be doubted whether our rejection of "morbidity" is entirely a gain. Death, failure, and misery become no less real because we have lost our feeling of reality about them. We may "healthy-mindedly" refuse to face the fact, but fact it remains, that the end of all our earthly struggles, hopes, and loves is death and bodily decay. We have attained "healthy-mindedness" by thrusting these facts out of the region of conscious recognition. In the rare moments of realisation when they force themselves into consciousness they are an unresolved terror before which we quail until we can again attain confidence by the redirection of our energy towards the business of living. Julian's method of dealing with the ultimate horror of existence was the opposite of this. She saturated her mind with pictures of this side of life, trying not to banish the morbid from consciousness but rather to attain the fullest possible consciousness of it, with the object of developing an attitude towards existence which should include it but in which it should be robbed of its power to terrify. This she succeeded in doing. If we do not believe in Julian's religion we shall probably say that she attained mental harmony by the construction of a delusional system. But at least we must admit that she did attain a harmony, and a harmony which was stable because it included all the facts; while the harmony of "healthy-mindedness" is essentially unstable because it refuses to face a wide range of facts, which, as life advances, it becomes more difficult and finally impossible to continue to ignore.

Such a complete view of the universe as is contained in a religion like that of Julian is also attained by those who face the facts of pain, desolation, and hopelessness, and who find them so to predominate that any belief in a benevolent God appears to them to be impossible. Thus a modern philosopher writes: "Brief and powerless is man's life; on him and all his race the slow, sure doom falls pitiless and dark. Blind to good and evil, reckless of destruction, omnipotent matter rolls on its relentless way; for man, condemned to-day to lose his dearest, to-morrow himself to pass through the gate of darkness, it remains only to cherish, ere yet the blow falls, the lofty thoughts that ennoble his little day."[7] It is true that such a view of the universe leads to a despairing resignation instead of to the hope of Lady Julian, but both are alike in their "morbidity"—in their fearless facing of unpleasant facts—and both are equally far removed from the shallow cheerfulness which results from the repressions of "healthy-mindedness."

In a later chapter I shall try to demonstrate that there is a further purpose in this close affective touch with suffering. This purpose is that it may take the place, in the life of the mystic, of the pain which the love for other persons brings to one whose affections have remained in the world. The love which seeks the sky may too easily be lost in the self. Christ in agony on the Cross is the object calling out in sympathetic pain all the love of Julian, thus saving her from the dangers of self-love.

It is probably true also that the sufferings of Christ, on which Julian's mind dwelt, themselves served to strengthen the bond of her love for Him. There is a primitive element in the sex instinct which finds itself attracted by the pain, physical or mental, of the beloved. Even this element is made to serve, by devotion to Christ's Passion, a useful purpose in the building up of Julian's religious sentiment. Sympathetic pain, which is the sharing of the pain of a loved one, strengthens

love as no other relationship can. From the psycho-pathological side, it is no more a really effective criticism of religious devotion of this kind to say that it is sadism, than to say that other forms of devotion are disguised sexuality. All the elements in our instinctive make-up can be used and transmuted for the ends of the religious sentiment, and the more perfectly God-directed is a person's character, the more certain it is that they will be so used.

One must not omit to notice, also, her diabolical visitations. These were two in number: the first when the Fiend set him on her throat while she was sleeping on the night following the first fifteen revelations; the other the noise of mocking jangling after the Sixteenth Revelation. It is customary amongst writers on this subject to apologise for the entry of such elements in mystical revelations and to judge the worth of a religious mystic by the smallness of such *pathological* elements. I prefer to regard such phenomena as integral parts of the mystical processes, as little pathological as the formation of sediment in the process of maturing good wine. In any case, such terms as *pathological* appear to be abusive epithets which do not at all help towards understanding any psychological fact.

Let us consider the forces we may suppose to be at work in mysticism on the human side to see if this study supplies us with any better understanding of the diabolical element in mystical experience. The mechanism suggested by modern psychological knowledge is that of primitive instincts evolved for primitive biological ends—the ego instincts for the preservation of the individual in a largely hostile environment, the herd instincts for welding him into communities and so preserving the existence of social groups, and the sex and parental instincts for securing the continuance of the race. We see how, in the mystic's purgation each of these instincts is denied its natural outlet so that its energy may be given wholly to the religious sentiment. Julian fasted and probably practised other austerities so that her desires might be detached from her own earthly comfort and be directed entirely towards God. She lived the life of a celibate and solitary, so that neither her love for husband or children nor even her desire for human intercourse of a less intimate kind might distract her from an undivided love of God. But, since the material from which her mysticism grew was human nature with instinctive desires craving their natural biological end, these suppressed elements in her mental make-up (particularly when control was weakened by illness) tended to break through their restraint and to exhibit themselves in their simple and natural forms. These forms were to her evil because they were opposed to the supernatural redirection of her instinctive energies which was dominant in her character. Thus, primitive sexual desire remained a suppressed but not destroyed element in her psyche, and expressed itself in the vision of the young man who set him on her throat and thrust near her face a visage which was long and wondrous lean. The other elements—his red hair, his paws, and his malicious grin—which made this vision a horrible one—may be regarded as the reaction of her "higher" nature against the primitive and suppressed desires which were obtruding into her consciousness. Similarly, we may regard the noise of mockery at gabbled prayers as the expression of that part of her own nature which remained in revolt against her subjugation to the demands of the exclusive love of God. The mechanism of this visitation may well have been the same as that of the compulsions to blasphemous speech and acts which have often been the torment of persons of saintly life.

Instead of regarding these diabolical visitations as in themselves evidences of something unhealthy in the mysticism of those in whose lives they are found, we may consider that they show the clear-sightedness with which the mystic recognises the character of the impulses surging up from his suppressed instincts. It is an unhealthy symptom when such impulses are not recognised in their true character; when, for example, an impulse of primitive eroticism, instead of appearing as a diabolical visitation, undergoes a merely sentimental transformation into an apparently religious experience. Such transformation is, for example, probably to be found in the stories (which offended the good sense of William James) of nuns whose spiritual experiences seem to have contained amatory embraces and expressions of personal preferences of Jesus Christ for themselves.[8] It seems reasonable to suppose that the same mental events would have led to some other (perhaps diabolical) experiences in persons more alive to their real source. Diabolical visitations, then, can be regarded as the occasional activity of parts of the whole mental make-up which have been rejected by a mind dominated by the desire for the exclusive love of God. They are diabolical, not because they are evil in themselves (though indeed they may be), but because they are rejected, and are thus evil from the point of view of the mystic. Their occurrence is no measure of the unhealthiness of Julian's mysticism; rather they are a natural by-product of the whole mystical process.

Notes

[1] *Revelations of Divine Love,* ed. Grace Warrack (London: Methuen and Co., 1901). P. 22.

[2] Ibid.

[3] P. 33.

[4] *Inquiries into Human Faculty,* by Galton; see also *Remembering and Forgetting,* by Professor T. H. Pear (London, 1922).

[5] It is probable, for example, that the difference between the nominalists and the conceptualists in the seventeenth and eighteenth senturies was essentially the difference between predominantly visual and predominantly verbal thinkers.

[6] P. 30.

[7] "The Free Man's Worship," by the Hon. Bertrand Russell, reprinted in *Philosophical Essays* (London, 1910), p. 70.

[8] *The Varieties of Religious Experience,* chapter on "The Value of Saintliness."

Evelyn Underhill (essay date 1925)

SOURCE: "English Medieval Mystics" in *The Mystics of the Church,* James Clarke & Co., 1925, 11. 110-32.

[*In the excerpt that follows, Underhill emphasizes Julian's skill as a writer, noting especially her ability to fuse "feeling and expression" and "soaring philosophy with homely simplicity."*]

[Julian of Norwich] stands out with peculiar distinctness. As the first real English woman of letters, she has special interest for us: the more so when we consider the beauty of character, depth of thought, and poetic feeling which her one book displays. In her mingled homeliness and philosophic instinct, her passion for Nature, her profound devotion to the Holy Name, she represents all the best elements of English mysticism. We feel in her the literary culmination of the Gothic spirit: the sense of mystery, delicate beauty, and robust contact with the common life, which meet us in the cathedrals; the vivid human sympathy with the mysteries of the Passion, yet the natural gaiety and homeliness, which inspired those miniature painters of the thirteenth and fourteenth centuries who form part of the cultural surroundings in which her genius flowered.

Apparently the most subjective, Julian is really the most philosophic of our early mystics: an attractive and also an astonishing figure. Internal evidence proves that she was a Norfolk gentlewoman of considerable education, though she humbly describes herself as simple and unlettered. She was born about 1343, in the reign of Edward III. In spite of the wonderful atmosphere of joy which transfigures her writing, her invulnerable conviction that the universe, when we come to understand it, will be found to be good and rational through and through, her early life was not happy. She says she often desired death because "for sloth and weakness I liked not to live and travail, as fell me to do." As a girl she prayed that she might have an illness at thirty years of age, and closer understanding of the Passion. The illness came at the right time: a fact which indicates Julian's psychic suggestibility. At its crisis she fell into a trance lasting five hours, and in this received the visions of the Passion and the spiritual revelations which form the foundation of her book. All that she afterwards wrote was the result of meditation on this experience; in which she found ever more meaning with the passing years, and her own growth in insight and knowledge.

It is a mistake to regard Julian's book as the mere outpouring of an ecstatic, the uncriticized record of the working of her subconscious mind. Like her predecessors, St. Hildegarde and Angela of Foligno, she was intelligent and well-informed, and pondered much upon her mystical experience. Her **Revelations of Divine Love** exist in two forms: a short version, perhaps written soon after the visions were received, a long version, composed twenty years after this experience. Analysis shows how greatly Julian's outlook had developed in the interval; how numerous the literary sources drawn upon in order to explicate the meanings she had discovered in the "ghostly words" heard long before in her mind. The difference between the first experience and the finished product is much like the difference we must presume between St. Augustine's highly finished *Confessions* and the actual events they record. As an anchoress, she was obliged by her rule to spend part of each day in such reading as her education allowed; and it is clear that from such reading, sermons, or conversation she had learned a considerable amount of that Christian Platonism which came through St. Augustine into the mediæval Church. She obviously knew Hilton's work, and sometimes reminds us of her great contemporaries, Suso, Tauler and Ruysbroeck.

In her combination of soaring philosophy with homely simplicity Julian resembles and excels the great Franciscan mystics. She istruly Christian in her power of including transcendence and humanity in her sweep, and this she is able to do because of her peculiar and vivid consciousness of the changeless, all-penetrative, yet simple action of God.

> In this same time our Lord showed me a ghostly sight of His homely loving. I saw that He is to us everything that is good and comfortable for us; He is our clothing that for love wrappeth us, claspeth us and all becloseth us for tender love, that He may never leave us; being to us all-thing that is good, as to mine understanding. . . . And after this I saw God in a point, that is to say in mine understanding, by which sight I saw that He is in all things. . . . Wherefore me behoveth needs to grant that all-thing that is done, it is well done: for our Lord God doeth all. For in this time the working of creatures was not shewed, but of our Lord God in the creature: for He is the mid-point of all thing and all He doth. . . . God is nature in His being,

that is to say, the goodness that is in nature, this is God. He is the ground, He is the substance, He is the same thing that is Naturehood.

In such passages we are with the philosophers. But it is a vivid picture of home life, not the lofty speculations of Christian metaphysic, which Julian gives us when she says:

> A child, when it is a-hurt or adread, it runneth hastily to the mother for help, with all its might. So willeth He that we do, as a meek child saying thus, "My kind mother, my gracious mother, my dearworthy mother, have mercy on me! I have made myself foul and unlike thee, and I nor may nor can amend it but with thy help!

This sweet and homely sense that most men are spiritual babies, and that human sins and mistakes are best dealt with from this point of view, is found in Julian again and again. It is part of her tender-hearted and generous sense of humanity. Men, she thinks, are all thoroughly lovable, in spite of their weaknesses and sins. A "saint" is not, to her seeing, an anæmic, thin creature, the amateur of an impossible perfection; but a real human being who has often done real bad things, yet whose sins and imperfections have been transcended, and become in her paradoxical phrase "not wounds but honours." "Mine understanding," she says, "was lifted up into heaven, and then God brought merrily to my mind David and others in the old law without number"—personages, we must agree, not distinguished by a prudish moral sense. It was a great joy to Julian to feel that heaven was as wide and tolerant as her own great heart. Yet she never minimizes evil or descends to a merely sentimental optimism. "Our failing," she says, "is dreadful, our falling is shameful, and our dying is sorrowful. But in all this the sweet eye of pity and love cometh never off us, nor the working of mercy ceaseth not." In this last quotation we have anexample of the perfect fusion of feeling and expression which Julian displays in her best passages. She is a great stylist, in spite of the fact that we see in her that passion for significant numbers which is so often allied with the mystical temperament. Her arguments and images always fall into threes. "For all our life," she says, "is in three. In the first we have our being, in the second we have our increasing, and in the third we have our fulfilling. The first is Nature, the second is Mercy, and the third is Grace." And in her culminating vision of reality she declares its properties to be three: Life, Love and Light.

> In life is marvellous homeliness, and in love is gentle courtesy and in light is endless Nature-hood. These properties were in the Goodness: unto which Goodness my reason would be oned, and cleave to it with all my might.

Julian's work forms a fitting crown to the golden period of English mysticism. Though she seems, and indeed is, so strongly individual, yet she is also in the best sense fully traditional. Even her loftiest flights do not represent an escape from the common religious environment, but rather the artist's power of feeding on it and discovering in it more and more beauty, reality and depth.

"From the beginning to the end," she says in a passage which well describes the classic relation of the mystic to the Church, "I had two manners of beholding. The one was endless, continuant love, with secureness of keeping and blissful salvation, for of this was all the shewing. The other was of the common teaching of Holy Church in which I was afore informed and grounded, and with all my will having in use and understanding. And the beholding of this went not from me: for by the shewing I was not stirred nor led therefrom in no manner of point, but I had therein teaching to love it and like it: whereby I might, by the help of our Lord and His grace, increase and rise to more heavenly knowing and higher loving."

David Knowles (essay date 1927)

SOURCE: "Margery Kempe and Dame Julian" in *The English Mystics,* Burns Oates & Washbourne Ltd., 1927, pp. 128-49.

[*In the following excerpt, Knowles examines Julian's work in order to characterize her qualities as a writer and as a mystic. In both capacities, he contends, her sincerity of feeling and natural style set her apart from her contemporaries.*]

We have already in an earlier chapter considered a spiritual writing which had for its end the direction of ancresses. We have now to examine the writings of two holy women who followed this life of solitude, Margery Kempe of Lynn and Dame Julian of Norwich; and though we have only a few pages to tell us of the first, whereas the second has left us a book of considerable length, there is a very striking agreement of spirit between them.

Of Margery Kempe little need be said. All that survives of her "Book" is a small number of selections, preserved for us in one of Wynkyn de Worde's printed books, and we know nothing of her besides. It is, however, usually assumed that she lived early in the fourteenth century. Her little treatise for the most part takes the form of a dialogue between herself and our Lord speaking "in her mind." Several passages remind us of Dame Julian.

"I assure thee in thy mind," says our Lord, "if it were possible for me to suffer pain again, as I have

done before, me were lever to suffer as much pain as ever I did for thy soul alone, rather than thou shouldest depart from me everlastingly."[1]

And it is clear from others that she was advanced in contemplative prayer.

Daughter, for to bid many beads, it is good to them that can not better do, and yet it is not perfection. . . . I have often told thee, daughter, that thinking, weeping, and high contemplation is the best life in earth, and thou shalt have more merit in heaven for one year thinking in thy mind than for an hundred year of praying with thy mouth.[2]

In her devotion to the Passion of our Lord she is a true daughter of her century.

When she saw the Crucifix, or if she saw a man had a wound, or a beast, or if a man beat a child before her, or smote a horse or another beast with a whip . . . she thought she saw our Lord beaten or wounded.[3]

We are more fortunate in possessing the whole book of her sister in East Anglia, for Dame Julian of Norwich reveals herself to us as a singularly lovable personality. As we shall see, besides her eloquent presentation of the divine goodness, she has much to say on moral questions, and her thoughts on the problems of predestination and the nature of evil show a depth of speculation greater than is found in any other English mystical writer before the Reformation. Nevertheless, the impression she leaves with us is not that of a powerful mind, nor of an original and elusive personality, but of a heart that has loved much and that has succeeded well in the hard task of showing to others fresh beauty in the object of its love.

At the outset of any examination of Dame Julian's **Revelations,** the reader has to make up his mind upon a very important point of interpretation. The other English mystics of our review, though they treat of unusual ways in the spiritual life, do not speak of their experiences as having any source outside themselves beyond the invisible and inaudible touching of the soul by the grace of God. Dame Julian, on the other hand, clearly reveals a type of sanctity which has probably always existed in the Church, and which has attracted a great deal of attention among devotional writers and hostile critics. The characteristics of this type, which perhaps is more common among women than men, are certain morbid conditions of body combined with a claim to have heard or seen supernatural manifestations. In the words of Catholic practice, they have seen visions, heard locutions, and fallen into ecstasies quite distinct from the *alienatio mentis* of such a mystical experience as is hinted at by the author of the *Cloud.*

As we have seen, once granted the possibility of such supernatural manifestation, there still remains the task of judging in each particular case whether the individual is to be believed in his assertion that he has experienced this touch of the finger of God. In the case of many of the saints, the Church, in the person of her rulers and theologians, has pronounced a verdict of credibility, but her decisions can be based on nothing but an estimate of the character of the subject, the purport of the communications, and their moral effect on the soul. For this purpose, the testimony of contemporaries is of the highest value. Consequently, Dame Julian can never hope to be erected to a place beside her great sisters, the two St Catherines, of Siena and of Genoa, and St Teresa. Their actions, their conversation, their prayer even, was watched and judged by competent witnesses who were often the chief authorities of the Church; they themselves have received the supreme stamp of the Church's approval, and their doctrine has passed into common use. In the case of Dame Julian, we have nothing on which to base a judgement save her one piece of writing.

Yet probably all who read the **Revelations** will be convinced, not only of the virtue and sincerity of their author, but of her sanity and orthodox faith. Even if we allow, as most of her editors are unwilling to allow, that she was possessed of considerable culture, she was certainly no professional theologian, nor is there any reason to suppose her well read in theology; yet she passes with a step that is almost always unerring through some of the most pathless tracts of thought, and while she is as original as a Christian writer well can be, yet she is entirely without a touch of that self-assertive and rebellious spirit which is so common in those who claim to be seers of visions when in reality they are but dreamers of dreams. Her **Revelations** do not present new truths to a chosen few; they impress the truth and meaning of old teaching upon her mind and heart and, through her, on the minds and hearts ofothers.

We know nothing of Dame Julian beyond what she tells us herself and what the early copyists of her manuscript tell us. From the latter we learn her name and dwelling-place and condition of life (which is also apparent from her writing), and the interesting fact that she was still alive when an unknown scribe was writing in 1413.[4] From herself we learn that on the eighth day of May, 1373,[5] she was thirty and a half years old, thus giving the date of her birth as 1342. Of her station in life we know nothing directly, but it is surely not absurd to conjecture that she was born of prosperous, if not gentle, parents. Ancresses, and in particular those, like her, who entered upon the life when still young, were in general girls of the upper class, for only these could easily obtain the permission, promise of support, and lodging which were necessary. Besides this, in spite of her self-depreciation the book is not that of a totally uneducated mind. The cell in which she lived was built against the Church of St Julian in Norwich; its foundations may still be seen, and the window through which she could watch the priest at Mass. This anchorage was in the gift, so to say, of the neighbouring Benedictine nunnery of Carrow, and this fact has given rise to a suggestion that Dame Julian was originally a nun of that convent. Such a suggestion is, of course, based on no positive evidence, but it is worth remarking that the only clear citation of a known author by Dame Julian is a passage from St Gregory's *Life of St Benedict*.

Her motive in writing was to relate a spiritual experience which she clearly regarded as a crisis of her life. This experience was not primarily a union of her will with God, but the communication of knowledge on certain spiritual matters. The communication took three forms, as Dame Julian herself tells us.[6] First, there was bodily—that is, sensible or seemingly sensible—sight; secondly, there were comprehensible words spoken, as if to her ears; thirdly, there was a formless intellectual enlightenment.[7] This last is very similar to that described by St Teresa and other contemplatives, and took the form of an illumination on some deep point of doctrine which is made clear to the recipient, but which cannot readily be comprehended in words, and which therefore may be more fully explained according as fresh grace or natural acquisition of knowledge assists. In Dame Julian's case, the visions and locutions took place on a single day, but her meditation on them lasted for many years—twenty at least[8]—and in some cases was assisted by lights and locutions similar to the original ones. Her book in its fullest form was written at least twenty years after her great experience, but a shorter form exists containing little but an account of the first visions. This latter has been taken to be either an abbreviation from the longer account, or an earlier version written before she had evolved her final thoughts. The latter alternative was chosen by the first editor of this manuscript,[9] and he is surely right. All the "showings" except one are in the shorter version, and that one may most probably have been omitted for reasons to be suggested below. This version stops at points where no abbreviator could have had any reason for stopping; there is no mention of the exceedingly beautiful "word" which would surely have commended itself to an anthologist, but which we know to have been spoken fifteen years after the great day of revelation. The long and complicated Fourteenth Revelation is omitted altogether, and on the supposition that the short version is the earlier this can easily be explained. This particular revelation, as Dame Julian tells us, was not understood by her till supplemented twenty years after; it would therefore be natural to omit it when writing before the further revelation had been received. Finally, there are several minute personal details in the shorter version which do not occur in the longer. We are told that the priest who came to assist Dame Julian was accompanied by a "child," and that Dame Julian's mother was present in the cell with her.[10]

The experience of the eighth of May is told at some length. Dame Julian had some years before desired three things—a "bodilie sight" of our Lord's sufferings, that her compassion might be the greater; a painful bodily sickness, even unto death, which might help her to realize the last truths and act upon them afterwards; and "a wilful longing to God." The first two, as she tells us with extreme sanity, she asked for "with a condition" that they might be the will of God. The third she asked "mightilie without any condition." She also tells us, and we must believe her, that the two first desires passed from her mind.[11]

At the age of thirty she was visited by a sickness of the kind she desired. Some of the most sympathetic of her admirers have taken this as a proof that the illness was produced by auto-suggestion. Such a line of argument is clearly based, not on any critical reasoning, but on an assumption that the supernatural or rather the miraculous, in the Christian sense, does not exist. Dame Julian's original prayer had been strictly conditional; it was not the whole-hearted persuasion of suggestion. During her illness she had no refuge against the fear of death in the thought that her illness would pass. She even seems to have forgotten that she had ever prayed for an illness. It is useless to speculate on the nature of her disease. Those who attribute it to suggestion have set it down as primarily mental, whereas Julian herself, almost significantly, always alludes to her "bodilie sickness." Whatever its nature, it lasted a week, and both herself and her attendants thought her on the point of death. She says:

> On the fourth night, I tooke all my Rites of Holy Church, and weened not to have liven till daie. And after this I lingered on two daies and two nights, and on the third night I weened oftentimes to have passed, and so weened they that were with me.[12] . . . And they that were with me sent for the parson my curate to be at mine ending. He came, and a child with him, and brought a cross.[13]

She looked upon the cross, but for the moment there was no change in her state. The first unusual symptom was a sudden feeling of ease, and it occurred to her to desire the wound of compassion for our Lord's sufferings. She expressly tells us that she desired no vision, but suddenly the crucifix held before her eyes changed.

> And in this, sodeinlie I saw the red blood trickling down from under the garland [of thorns] hott and freshly and right plenteouslie . . . like to the drops of water that fall off the eaves of an house after a great shower of rain . . . and for the roundness, they were like to the scale of herring.[14]

Henceforth, the "showings" succeeded one another; as far as we can gather from her words, the sight of our Lord's head on the crucifix was present to her all the time, while to her mind came "words" and "ghostly showings" or illuminations. These revelations took a considerable time.

> The first began early in the morning about the hour of four; and it lasted showing by process full fair and steadily, each following other till it was nine of the day overpassed.[15]

The last revelation took place in the following night, and when it ended her feeling of illness returned. The return of pain weakened her mind, and for a moment she lost faith in the reality of what she had seen.

> Then came a religious person to me, and asked me how I fared. I said I had raved that day.[16]

She fell asleep, and while asleep saw, or dreamed, that she was assaulted by the devil. It is noticeable that she distinguishes the manner of this from the other visions.

> And in my sleep *methought* the fiend, etc. . . . This ugly showing was made sleeping, and so was none other.[17]

We might put this down as a dream, were it not for what follows. After she waked,

> Anon a light smoke came in the door, with a great heat and a foul stench; I said, "Benedicite Dominus, it is all on fire that is here!" And I weened it had been a bodily fire. I asked them that were with me if they felt any stench; they said nay, they felt none; I said, "Blessed be God," for that I wist well it was the fiend that was come.[18]

This also, it is to be noticed, she saw in a different way from the showings. Though invisible to others, it appeared to her as visible smoke, whereas the showings impressed themselves upon her mind at once as supernatural. Needless to say, this diabolical visitation is not to the taste of modern non-Catholic writers. It has been explained as a valueless working of auto-suggestion, and as the emergence of old desires into the mind's consciousness, clothed in terrifying images.[19] Yet it is hard to see how Dame Julian could have been clearer in her account, and if we distrust her testimony here, there seems no valid reason for trusting it elsewhere.

Immediately after this visitation she made an act of faith in the revelations which had been made to her, and which she had for a time doubted. On the same evening she had the final vision, and it was followed by more diabolical assaults, which lasted for most of the night and till about nine in the morning. Then the supernatural showings ceased, though she was confirmed in the truth of what she had seen.

> On the same day that it was showed . . . as a
> wretch I forsook it. . . . Then our Lord Jesu of his
> mercy . . . showed it all again within my soul with
> more fulness, saying . . ."Wit it now well, it was no
> raving that thou sawest this day."[20]

As far as we can gather from her writing, Dame Julian had no further visions. We are, however, told that her questioning as to the meaning of one of the showings was answered fifteen years later "in ghostly understanding," and one of the visions, the fourteenth and hardest, was made clear to her twenty years less three months from the original revelation. These two passing references show that the happenings of the eighth of May were for her an abiding and unreplaced source of meditation—one more indication of their external and non-subjective nature. She herself says:

> As for the bodily sight, I have said as I saw, as truly
> as I can. And as for the words formed, I have said
> them right, as our Lord showed me them. And as
> for the ghostly sight, I have said somewhat; but I
> may never fully tell it.[21]

When we are thus addressed by one who claims to have had communications from another world, it is natural for us to ask what was the content of those communications, and to judge the genuineness of the revelation by the weight of what has been revealed. We cannot at times banish a feeling that even the greatest seers of things hidden—St Teresa or St Catherine—have told us nothing new, nothing that we might not have discovered by the light of ordinary reason assisted by grace and working on thecontent of the revelation. It is only a step further to debate the need for such useless revelations. Yet perhaps such a method of argument is unsound. It would undoubtedly be a cogent method in certain circumstances, as, for instance, when the claims of spiritualism or other occult religious practices were being canvassed. The supporters of such practices claim that they are worthy to supplant or supplement Christianity; Christians are therefore justified in asking what the new teaching may be that is derived from such sources. If it is occupied entirely with trivialities, or contains nothing that was not previously known and realized, we may reasonably doubt both the value and the authenticity of the revelation. The case is different with revelations within the Christian body. Even if it were lawful for Christians to look for a further revelation than that given in the New Testament, it would not seem *a priori* likely that the Divine Founder, who so copiously taught his apostles and who has spoken at such length by the Holy Spirit, would reserve a momentous pronouncement for centuries, and then make it to a private person. There are, indeed, many speculative points of theology of which the human mind has always longed for a fuller knowledge, but they are precisely the points upon which the silence of revelation and tradition is most significant of the divine will. Further, if it be objected that the words of our Lord to St Teresa or Dame Julian are moral exhortations, conveying little or nothing that is new, the objection may be returned by pointing out that by far the greater part of our Lord's words, recorded or unrecorded, taken merely as so many words, are neither new nor methodical. Their value lies in the unique force and spirit which they convey, not as isolated sayings, but as a body of teaching of a unique personality, and just as they have exerted a boundless influence over the world, so the kindred words spoken to saints have had a great influence for good over fields very varying in extent. Once again, if a "revelation" be considered as a development of the touch of grace in the soul, many of the difficulties which the common view of its nature causes will disappear.[22]

The revelations of Dame Julian may be divided into two classes. In the one she saw the sufferings of our Lord on the Cross, and occasionally heard words, and the result of these was to deepen her realization of our Lord's sufferings.[23] As the passages about to be quoted show, the "bodily showing" in these cases was very vivid, and she is perfectly clear that the words were not her own. She says:

> This showing was quick and lively, and hideous
> and dreadful, sweet, and lovely.[24] . . . I saw his
> sweet face as it were dry and bloodless, with pale
> dying, and later more pale, dead, languoring, and
> then turned more dead unto blue . . . also his nose
> clogged and dried to my sight.[25] And St John of
> Beverley our Lord showed him full highly in comfort
> to us for homeliness and countrey sake: andbrought
> to my mind how he is a kind neighbour, and of our
> knowing: and God called him plainly St John of
> Beverley, as we do.[26]

At the same time, the vision does not seem to have conveyed to Dame Julian the impression that she was watching the Crucifixion.

> The hot blood ran out so plenteously . . . and when
> it came where it should have fallen down, then it
> vanished.[27]

In this respect—and it is an important one—she differs from many medieval and modern ecstatics, such as Catherine Emmerich. Their visions derive what value they may possess from their claim to be glimpses of the Crucifixion; with Dame Julian the material showing is no more than a taking-off point for the words and meditations.

The other class of vision is different.[28] In these the showing was concerned with some abstract point of theology, and was often far more inexpressible. Thus she relates:

> And after this, I saw God in a point; that is to say, in my understanding: by which sight I saw that he is in all thing.[29] . . .

Occasionally we are told the three stages of a vision.

> And in this he showed a little thing, the quantitie of a hazel-nutt, lying in the palme of my hand. . . . I thought, "What may this be?" and it was answered . . ."It is all that is made!" In this little thing I saw three properties. The first is that God made it: the second, is that God loveth it: the third is that God keepeth it.[30]

It was for visions such as these that the meditation of years was employed to draw out their meaning, and it is these that constitute for many the chief interest of the book. We may, indeed, wonder at the deep things that filled the mind of this secluded woman, and at the strength of intellect which strives to explain them.

Among the speculative problems that have occupied the minds of thinkers in the Christian centuries, perhaps none has caused greater difficulty than the problem of the existence of evil. It has always pressed peculiarly hard on mystics, for the mystical temperament naturally desires to see unity and goodness in all things. Consequently, mystics both within and without the Church have tended towards Monism, and have ignored evil or considered it a quality of an inferior state of being. In the case of Dame Julian, we can see this tendency at work, though it is checked both by her extreme deference to orthodox teaching and by her strong practical sense. She is throughout a strong optimist, and passages such as the following abound:

> And then [in heaven] shall verily be made known to us his meaning in those sweet words, where he saith, "All shall be well; and thou shalt see thyself that all manner thing shall be well." . . . Then shall none of us be stirred to say in any wise, "Lord, if it had been thus, it had been full well." But we shall say all with one voice, "Lord, blessed mote thou be, for it is thus: thus it is well."[31]

In the face of this belief in the ultimate goodness of all that is, there rises up the problem of the existence of sin, which may at the last resort be taken as the origin of all evil. She puts this problem herself.

> Methought, if sin had not been, we should all have been clean and like to our Lord as he made us. And thus, in my folly . . . often I wondered why, by the great foreseeing wisdom of God, the beginning of

sin was not letted, for then methought all should have been well.[32]

Her answer to it is as follows, in part an insistence on sin as being nothing positive, in part a submission to God's wisdom.

> But I saw not sin; for I believe it had no manner of substance, nor no part of being, nor could it be known but by the pain that it is cause of. Jesu . . . answered . . . and said, "Sin is behovely, but all shall be well, and all shall be well, and all manner of thing shall be well."[33]

But there remains the further difficulty of the origin of sin. She says:

> "Ah, good Lord, how might all be well for the great hurt that is come by sin?" . . . To this our blessed Lord answered . . . that Adam's sin was the most harm that ever was done, or ever shall be . . . [and said] "sithen that I have made well the most harm; then it is my will that thou know thereby that I shall make well all that is less."[34]

That is to say, the power and goodness of God could not be shown to better effect than by his ability to take Adam's sin as an occasion for bringing about a greater good. That he did this in the Incarnation and Passion of his Son is generally taught by theologians, and the Church exclaims in her liturgy, "O felix culpa!"

> This atonement-making is more pleasing to God, and moreworshipful, without comparison, than ever was the sin of Adam harmful.[35]

So far, Dame Julian stands in the common way. More original is her mystical identification, somewhat after the manner of St Paul, of our Lord with Adam, and her vision that our Lord's suffering is so closely bound up with Adam's sin, that the latter is lost sight of in the joy with which God regards the former. This part of the *Revelations* is exceedingly deep, and may be recommended to a most careful meditation. Beyond this, Dame Julian goes perhaps as far as human thought may in explaining the anger of God at sin, and how *a parte Dei* there is not, and cannot be, change. It is we who change, and depart from him.

Having thus dealt with the metaphysical aspect of sin, she proceeds to examine the process of sin. Here it should be noted that Dame Julian holds—in common with some other mystics[36]—a view which is, at least as it stands and if words are to have their usual meaning, unorthodox. This is the opinion that there is a supreme point in the soul that never sins, or, as Dame Julian puts it, that the predestined never really sin.[37] Her utterance on this subject is not very clear. Thus she says once, recording a vision,

In which showing I saw and understood full surely, that in every soul that shall be saved is a godly will that never assented to sin, nor ever shall.[38]

This is dangerous doctrine, and it is interesting to see that when she is giving her own reflections she modifies it.

We shall verily see in heaven without end, that we have grievously sinned in this life. And notwithstanding this, we shall see that we were never hurt in his love, nor were never the less of price in his sight.[39]

Later, this is still further explained.

And thus [in sin] we are dead for the time from the very sight of our blissful life. But in all this I saw soothfastly that we be not dead in the sight of God . . . but he shall never have his full bliss in us till we have our full bliss in him. . . . Thus I saw how sin is deadly for a short time in the blessed creatures of endless life.[40]

Akin to this is her manner of speaking of sin as if it were an accident; thus St John of Beverley is spoken of as having more joys in heaven than if he had never sinned; and in the "showing" of Adam,

The servant not only he goeth, but suddenly he starteth, andrunneth in great haste for love to do his lord's will. And anon he falleth in a slade, and taketh full great hurt . . . then saith this courteous lord . . ."Lo, lo, my beloved servant, what harm and disease he hath taken in my service for my love, yea, and for his good will. Is it not reason that I reward him, his frey and his dread, his hurt and his maim, and all his woe?[41]

Of such language it may be remarked, first, that such words should probably not be taken *au pied de la lettre*, but as the words of love welcoming back the Prodigal, or the greater joy in heaven for one sinner doing penance; and secondly, that even if from the sinner's point of view a mortal sin in St Mary Magdalen is the same as one in Judas, yet from the point of view of God, so to speak, there is all the difference between a sin that will be cancelled and one that will remain for ever. Further than this we cannot go, nor can we admit that, all else being equal, a sinner will be more rewarded than one who has preserved his innocence, as a wounded man might be rewarded more than his fellow who had fought the campaign without a scratch. This Dame Julian herself realizes elsewhere.

If any man think, "If this be true, then were it good to sin, to have more meed" . . . beware of this stirring, for truly, if it come, it is untrue, and of the enemy.[42]

So far optimism has been triumphant, even if at times strict theological accuracy has suffered. Sin is merely the absence of God; Adam's sin brought a greater good into the world; the sins of the predestined are not fully sins. There remains the supreme problem of the eternally lost. How can they be all well? Here at last Dame Julian is silent. She never doubts the existence of evil spirits, but she does not explain it. The damned she has tried to compass, but in vain.

What time that we by our folly turn us to the beholding of the reproved, tenderly our Lord toucheth us, and blissedfully calleth us, saying in our soul, "Let me alone, my dear worthy child; intend to me, I am enough to thee."[43] And yet in this I desired as I durst, that I might have full sight of hell and purgatory. . . . And for aught that I could desire, I could see of this right naught[44]

It has been suggested that some inaccuracies of language in the ***Revelations*** may be explained by reading Dame Julian's words as the language of love. This is, indeed, the ground of all her words, and in her eager, almost passionate response to the divine love, and in the extraordinary delicacy of her perception of the depths and shades of feeling, she is unique among English spiritual writers. Probably some who have little sympathy with her faith, and little interest in her perplexities, will have been moved almost to tears by the tender grace of her words, fragrant as ointment poured out.

What? wouldest thou wit thy Lord's meaning in this thing? Wit it well: love was his meaning. Who showeth it thee? Love. What showed he thee? Love. Wherefore showeth he it thee? For love.[45]

These words she heard "in ghostly understanding" fifteen years after her great vision, but they told her nothing new. In the first revelation she had said:

There is no creature that is made, that may wit how much, and how sweetly, and how tenderly our Maker loveth us.[46]

And already she returned the love.

Then had I a proffer in my reason. . . . "Look up to heaven" [away from the crucifix]. . . . I answered inwardly with all the might of my soul, and said, "Nay, I may not; for thou art my heaven."[47]

Indeed, many of the words of our Lord which she records are of an exquisite and piercing beauty.

Then said our good Lord Jesus Christ, "Art thou well apaid that I suffered for thee?" I said, "Yea, good Lord, gramercy; yea, good Lord, blessed mote thou be." Then said Jesu our kind Lord, "If thou art apaid, I am apaid: it is a joy, a bliss, an endless liking to me, that ever I suffered passion for thee: and if I might suffer more, I would suffer more."[48]

And again:

"My dear darling, I am glad thou art come to me in all thy woe; I have ever been with thee, and now seest thou me loving, and we be oned in bliss."[49]

These passages may have served to show not only the warmth of Dame Julian's love, but also the simplicity and absence of all that is false or artificial in her expression of it. It is also worth remarking, that her solitary life, her lonely meditations, and the closeness of her communion with God in no way emancipate her either from obedience to the Church or from an abiding sympathy with her neighbour. Her submission to the Church is apparent throughout. The Church is the test of her revelations and must be believed where private revelation ceases. The sacraments and devotion to our Lady and the saints are taken for granted. Still more clear is her love for her neighbour, and here she is at one with the apostles and early Christians in feeling that the whole Church is the body of Christ, and we, members of each other.

If any man or woman depart his love from any of his even-Christians, he loves right naught, for he loves not all. And so at that time he is not safe, for he is not in peace.[50]

What may make me more to love mine even-Christian, than to see in God that he loveth all that shall be saved, as it were all one soul?[51]

For if I look singularly to myself, I am right naught; but in general I am in hope, in one-head of charity with all my even-Christians; for in this one-head standeth the life of all manking that shall be saved.[52]

The extracts given in this chapter have, perhaps, sufficiently illustrated the style of the **Revelations.** Two passages may be added to show Dame Julian's command of words; the one is from her vision of God and Adam, the other her conclusion.

[The Lord's] clothing was wide and side, and full seemly, as falleth to a lord: the colour of the clothing was blue as azure, most sad and fair: his cheer was merciful; the colour of his face was fair, brown, white, with full seemly countenance; his eyes were black, most fair and seemly showing, full of lovely pity. . . . [The servant's] clothing was a white kirtle, single, old, and all defaced, dyed with sweat of his body; strait-sitting to him, and short as it were an handful beneath the knee; bare, seeming as it should soon be worn out, ready to be ragged and rent.[53]

And I saw full surely in this and in all, that ere God made us, he loved us; which love was never slacked, nor ever shall be. And in this love he hath done all his works: and in this love he hath made all things profitable to us; and in this love our life is everlasting; in our making we had beginning: but the love wherein he made us was in him from without beginning. In which love we have our beginning. And all this shall we see in God without end. Which may Jesus grant us.[54]

Notes

[1] *Cell of Self Knowledge,* ed. Gardner, p. 51.

[2] *Cell of Self Knowledge,* ed. Gardner, p. 52.

[3] *Ibid.,* p. 54.

[4] Introduction to Amherst MS.

[5] The MSS. disagree as to the date of the month. Dom Meunier (*Révélations de l'Amour Divin,* footnote, p. 6) points out that the Feast of St John of Beverley fell on the seventh of the month. Thismakes the eighth the most likely date.

[6] *Dame Julian,* ed. Dom Hudleston, ch. ix: Burns Oates and Washbourne. The references throughout this chapter are to this edition. The division of chapters is not entirely in agreement with previous editions.

[7] It is perhaps worth noting that this third kind of vision usually accompanies a very high degree of mystical prayer. We have thus indirect evidence that Dame Julian's visions were not isolated favours, but were intimately bound up with her spiritual progress.

[8] *Revelations,* ch. li, p. 135.

[9] *Comfortable Words for Christ's Lovers,* ed. Rev. D. Harford, 1911.

[10] *Comfortable Words,* ch. x.

[11] *Revelations,* ch. ii.

[12] *Revelations,* ch. iii.

[13] *Comfortable Words,* ch. ii.

[14] *Revelations,* chs. iv and vii.

[15] Ch. lxv.

[16] Ch. lxvi.

[17] *Ibid.*

[18] *Ibid.*

[19] So Thouless, *The Lady Julian.*

[20] Ch. lxx.

[21] *Comfortable Words,* ch. xxiii.

[22] We must remember that mystics insist that what has been revealed is ineffable. Their words are pale shadows of reality.

[23] I have here treated together the corporeal and imaginative visions of theologians.

[24] *Revelations,* ch. vii.

[25] Ch. xvi.

[26] Ch. xxxviii. Dame Julian was picturing heaven to herself before this showing, and it was natural that she should think of St John, whose feast had fallen on the previous day.

[27] Ch. xii.

[28] This is the class of vision known to theologians as intellectual—*i.e.,* not produced in the senses, but by an infusion into the intellect.

[29] Ch. xi.

[30] Ch. v

[31] Chs. lxiii and lxxxv.

[32] Ch. xxvii.

[33] Ch. xxvii. Behovely=it behoved there should be sin.

[34] Ch. xxix.

[35] *Ibid.*

[36] Above all, the great Eckhart (1260-1327). It is hard to believe that this passage does not reflect his teaching.

[37] Dom Hudleston, *op. cit.,* pp. xxxiii and 251, has excellent notes on this passage, in which he asserts Dame Julian's fundamental orthodoxy. He quotes a striking parallel from St Bernard, which I had not seen when I wrote my chapter on Dame Julian.

[38] Ch. liii.

[39] Ch. lxi.

[40] Ch. lxxii.

[41] Ch. li (slade=ravine; frey=fright).

[42] Ch. xl.

[43] Ch. xxxvi. I here follow Father Cressy's reading.

[44] Ch. xxxiii.

[45] Ch. lxxxvi.

[46] Ch. vi.

[47] Ch. xix.

[48] Ch. xxii.

[49] Ch. xl (quoted from Cressy's version).

[50] *Comfortable Words,* ch. vi.

[51] *Revelations,* ch. xxxvii.

[52] Ch. ix.

[53] Ch. li.

[54] Ch. lxxxvi.

Conrad Pepler (essay date 1958)

SOURCE: "Mother Julian and Visions" in *The English Religious Heritage,* B. Herder Book Co., 1958, pp. 305-20.

[*In the excerpt that follows, Pepler discusses the often controversial matter of whether Julian's visions were authentic spiritual events. He concludes that even her confessed moment of doubt does not detract from what he considers evidence that her revelations were divinely inspired.*]

The *Riwle* written at the very end of the twelfth century for two or three sisters, anchoresses, was designed to train its readers in the more perfect life of contemplation. But it was treating of the first stages of the spiritual life, and, as we have seen, it only rises above the humdrum of the purgative way in its final section. Now we are to consider the doctrine of a woman who had no doubt been trained by that or a similar Rule, and had so far profited by it as to have first been favoured by a series of visions in which she was passive in her acceptance of the 'Revelations', and finally to have reached the highest forms of prayer. We are thus given the opportunity of studying the effects of the *Ancren Riwle* in their perfect stages; we are here taught the outcome of the natural growth of the spirit if it follows the straight lines of an authorised rule.

We have called this 'The Way of Wisdom' and placed Mother Julian firmly in the Unitive Way, because of the main theme of her visions. Doubtless some of these appearances are imaginative and 'sensible', but that is accidental to the main theme of the ***Revelation of Divine Love.*** Her knowledge and sight come, as her own title informs us, from the touch of love, from affinity with divine things. Her knowledge is an affective knowledge; she has been led to see things in their highest causes. Mother Julian is not concerned with her growth in the spiritual life; she does not consider her own prayer. All that may be found in *The Cloud of Unknowing* and *Epistle of Privy Counsel,* works which provide a thorough companion to the Revelations. *The Cloud,* almost anti-intellectualist in tone, considers the unseeing way of prayer in which the soul is established in the Unitive Way. Mother Julian on the other hand, describes the vision of all things in the love of God which should be the counterpart of the 'unknowing' side of union. For in this third way the vision of infused contemplation begins to flower in unusual and wonderful ways.

Thus Mother Julian sets forth a cosmic view of all things and all happenings in relation to God, and in particular to the love of God. Her outlook has the deeply metaphysical style of *The Epistle of Privy Counsel,* but whereas the latter is still limited to the relationship of the individual soul with God, her mystic eye brings all things into focus with the Trinity down to the very uttermost, the problem of evil.

> For the Trinity is God: God is the Trinity; the Trinity is our Maker and Keeper, the Trinity is our everlasting love and everlasting joy and bliss, by our Lord Jesus Christ. And this was shewed in the First Shewing and in all; for where Jesus appeareth, the blessed Trinity is understood, as to my sight (c. 4).[1]

It is as though she had been a student of St Thomas's *Prima Pars* for the greater part of her life. She conveys her meaning in a dialectical form, searching for the truth of her visions. She does not give us any moral exhortation, but sets forth simply what has been revealed to her of the mystery of Divine Love as a far greater direction to prayer than any analytical discussion of states of prayer. 'Though the three Persons in the Trinity be all even in itself, the soul took most understanding in Love; yea, and he willeth that in all things we have our beholding and our enjoying in Love' (c. 73). For fifteen years this anchoress of Norwich meditated on what had been revealed to her, and finally our Lord speaks to her once again to make all clear: 'Love was his meaning. . . . Hold thee therein and thou shalt learn and know more in the same. But thou shalt never know nor learn therein other thing without end' (c. 86).

In the world of today her message is needed far more than any other, for we are in danger of being crushed under a lethal pessimism which derives from the decline and degeneracy of our age, and which in its turn contributes to hasten that same decline. It leads us to wars and to individual human catastrophes of all sorts. Mother Julian should give us new heart by showing the ultimate explanation, the events of the world in their highest cause. She insists on a more passive approach to the love of God, which might be summed up in the words of Mme Maritain: 'You are for ever seeking what you must do. You have only to love God and serve him with all your heart!' But the doctrine of this theological recluse must be taken as a whole and no part of it isolated for one's convenience. The words of the scribe who wrote out the ***Revelations*** early in the fifteenth century are to be borne in mind: 'I pray Almyty God that this booke com not but to the hands of them that will be his faithfull lovers. . . . And beware thou take not one thing after the affection and liking, and leve another. . . . '[2]

The anchorites of the fourteenth century were approaching their dissolution. One century more and they would have died out. By the time the Church came to be despoiled of her property in the sixteenth century, there seem to have been none, or very few, left in England. The anchoress might be leading a more lax life, than that described in the *Ancren Riwle,* but it is unlikely that the majority were in any serious sense relaxed. For the English spiritual writings of the period—the *Scale, The Cloud of Unknowing* and its companions—were addressed mainly to recluses of this sort, and they presuppose a fairly advanced and fervent life of prayer. And then here is Mother Julian herself in the full stream of holiness and mystic prayer flowing out from Eckhart through Tauler to the Flemish Mystics, and from them across the North Sea to East Anglia and up to Yorkshire. The original MS of the ***Revelations*** seems to have been written in a combination of East Anglian and Northern Dialects which suggests a connection with the mystics of Yorkshire, and lends colour to the hypothesis that this stream of mysticism was carried back and forth in the traffic of merchants. The wool of Yorkshire was carried to East Anglia and over to Flanders, and so established this intimate connection with the prayers of the continent. Mother Julian herself is a contemporary of St Catherine of Siena, whom she resembles in a most remarkable way. But she does not appear to have known of the great Italian Dominican, though one of St Catherine's most faithful followers was William Fleet from Lincoln, who was himself in contact with his English Augustinian brethren, including certainly Master Walter Hilton.[3] Mother Julian's Revelations of Divine Love are comparable in many ways with the Dialogue of the great Siennese.

In the heart of Norwich, there stood, until the Germans destroyed it in 1942, a church with a round Norman tower and other early features, dedicated to St Julian. It belonged in the fourteenth century to the large nunnery on the outskirts of the town, the Benedictine Abbey of Carrow. It was in a cell outside this church that Mother Julian established herself. It has been suggested that like many recluses of that time she began life in a regular community. (In the eyes of Cassian and the early Fathers, a successful community life was a necessary prerequisite to the higher form of solitude—the hermit must learn first to live with his brethren.) And where else if not at Carrow, in whose gift the cell lay? She may have chosen the church of her patron saint and obtained the necessary permissions from Carrow, but it is likely that she was Benedictine trained in her early years. She was probably well-to-do, her family being able to provide for her anchorhold; but on her own admission she was unlettered, 'cowde no letter'[4] (c. 2). She was born towards the end of 1342.

She cannot have spent many years in community for she was only in her thirty-first year when the events she describes took place. And our Lord himself draws attention to this fact: 'I thank thee for thy travail, and especially for thy youth,' he says; and she, meditating on this: 'And specially the age of them that willingly and freely offer their youth unto God, passingly is rewarded and wonderfully is thanked' (c. 14). It was on the eighth day of May in the year 1373, the day after England had been celebrating the feast of St John of Beverley, at four o'clock in the morning that the visions came to Mother Julian. She was very sick at the time and she and her neighbours thought she was at death's door. So her own mother was there, the local curate (c. 3), and others as well. And the showings lasted until nine o'clock in the morning. It is natural that St John of Beverley should appear to her, and she remarks on his English character (c. 38 and cf. Warrack's footnote to p. 78). She was surrounded thus by her natural neighbours, both saints and sinners, a young English woman apparently delirious and dying in the heart of Norwich.

But she recovered suddenly at the first vision and was apparently quite well by the morning when she had had fifteen of these showings. Then the following night came the final, sixteenth, showing to summarise and conclude them all. She seems to have had these revelations written down fairly soon without any explanation or commentary, for the earliest MS, the Amherst MS, appears in this form. But her mind could not rest with such vivid representations stored in her memory, and for twenty years she puzzled over, meditated on and drew deep theological conclusions from what she had seen. She explains how these sights are preserved: 'when the Showing which is given in a time is passed and hid, then the faith keepeth it by grace of the Holy Ghost unto our life's end' (c. 7). But before her life's end, after twenty years

pondering, she has further light from the Holy Spirit:

> The first (of the three properties) is the beginning of teaching that I understood therein, in the same time; the second is the inward teaching that I have understood therein afterward; the third, all the whole Revelation from the beginning to the end (that is to say of this Book) which our Lord God of his goodness bringeth oftentimes freely to the sight of mine understanding. . . . For, twenty years after the time of the Shewing, save three months, I had teaching inwardly. . . . (c. 51).[5]

That was in 1392 or 1393, and it must have been after that date when the explanation and commentary were finally set down. She was still alive in 1413, but we hear nothing more of her. Until *The Book of Margery Kempe* was discovered, there were no traces of contemporary references to her and there are few extant MSS of the **Revelations,** showing that she was no outstanding figure in her day. But Margery did go to see her in Norwich, and she was evidently at that time of some local fame for the meeting between these two was not a chance affair (cf. *The Book of Margery Kempe,* c. 18).

There is little more to know of her outward life. Her book gives little indication of her surroundings or upbringing. The Scriptures which she must have heard expounded from her tenderest youth, and which must have been frequently on the lips of the clergy who came to visit her, hardly put in an appearance, except incidentally, as when she understands the Annunciation and the words of our Lady, 'Lo me, God's handmaid' (c. 4). Once she quotes St Gregory's life of St Benedict and once she refers to the legend of the pseudo-Denis (c. 18). Yet her outlook has a Dominican flavour, for although her insistence is naturally all upon Love, she sees it always in terms of understanding and she looks forward constantly to the *vision* of heaven (cf. cc. 36 and 44). She may have had a Dominican confessor or director. Before she entered religion she would certainly have heard the Dominicans preaching in the Norfolk pulpits, as we may understand in reading *The Book of Margery Kempe*. But nothing more can yet be ascertained of the biography of this holy maid.

Let us now scrutinise more closely the happenings on that celebrated eighth of May. Were these showings historical facts of divine origin or merely the dreams of a sick woman? This raises the question of the natural basis of mystical experience. In the heights of the spiritual life, as at every other level, natural temperament and physical predispositions play an important, if material, part. If we accept, *ex hypothesi,* the view that Plotinus or the Arabian Mystics were without grace and therefore not in the supernatural plane of Christian prayer, we can explain a great deal of the nature of their utterances in terms of psychological and even pathological factors. Socrates' philosophical trance which lasted so many hours and was very comparable with a Christian ecstasy, would make an interesting study for a neuropathologist. The super-being, super-essential Unity which Plotinus reaches may be reached by a man with a poetic vision tempered by metaphysical insight, a man of great natural vigour of mind. In spite of many similarities with the phraseology of St John of the Cross all he says can be explained in natural terms. That is why these natural mystics who have experienced something of the Socratic ecstasy are usually so optimistic—nature is good and the author of nature is super-good. The Christian mystics are never optimistic without the Cross. But the noteworthy fact is that when God works on anaturally mystical and poetic temperament, he leads him to a special type of unitive way which holds strong connection with these natural states. Had God raised Plotinus, again *ex hypothesi,* to a state of grace, he would in fact have been the earliest Christian mystic. These extraordinary graces do not descend on souls like some ready-made thunderbolt. Grace is received and modified according to the nature of the recipient. A child receives the same faith as an adult at baptism but in a different way according to his natural capacities. The literal-minded man of rosary beads and charitable institutions will receive the same graces but in a different mould from the natural mystic who will himself easily be moved by divine locutions and other manifestations.

Mother Julian must have had natural dispositions to mystical experiences. But she was evidently unaccustomed to them. This was probably her first experience. For she is not credulous and does not accept them without question. She goes so far as to say she had been merely dreaming or 'seeing things' under the influence of a neurotic illness. 'Then came a Religious person to me and asked me how I fared. I said I had raved today. And he laughed loud and heartily' (c. 66). She quickly repented of this infidelity; but there is no doubt that her illness had played some part in the experience. She had been ailing for about a week; her kinsfolk thought she was on the threshold of death, and arranged for her to receive the Last Sacraments. Some sort of paralysis then attacks her; her body is 'dead from the middle downwards'. She is propped up in bed and by the time the curate arrives is speechless and finds it difficult to raise her eyes. Everything then goes dark; all she can see is the Crucifix held before her. There is a sense of great evil, as of 'fiends', in the darkness about her; and then the paralysis begins to creep upwards, leaving her almost breathless and insensible. It is in the sudden, apparently miraculous, release from this extreme pathological state that the visions begin, woven round that crucifix and continuing for five hours while she is without sensation of pain. Five of the Showings were directly concerned with what she had before her eyes, the others were derived from that—as when our Lord on the Cross leads her to look into the wound in his side and see the delectable place and the heart cloven in twain (c. 24). And after they have ceased the pain returns though she is in fact cured of the paralysis and very painful feeling returns to her body. She sleeps a bit, and in the evening suffers from violent dreams of the arch-fiend throttling her, his red, lean face, freckled with black spots, pressed close to her own (c. 66). This, as she declares, was the only vision that came in a dream.

All this suggests an acute neurosis, induced perhaps by an over-enthusiastic life of penance and solitude. But she appears to have retained consciousness throughout, except in the final dream. She is aware of those around her during the visions. It must, however, be admitted that extreme forms of physical weakness induced either by long illness or exceptional penances, fasting and bodily sufferings, are often the occasion of, and the physical predisposition for the extraordinary forms of religious experience. That is why the Church demands great care in ascertaining the genuineness of such revelations. St Thomas points out that imaginary apparitions may be induced by animal spirits and moods (I, 111, 3). But in the end hysterical neurosis can be detected by the unbalanced state of the subject. St Teresa, who has been accused of hysteria, could distinguish between the unbalanced hysterical state and the states of ecstasy and true 'showings'. The body is often a more fitting instrument for the increased perceptivity of the sanctified soul when it has been thoroughly subjected by austerities and sickness. The true balance may at times only be achieved in such physical weakness. This may be confirmed by the lives of almost all the Christian visionaries. There is a final test in the nature and message of the visions: for many of them are their own justification. No one thought that Mother Julian had raved, and the religious person who laughed when she told him that, became serious and impressed the instant she told him the content of her 'raving'.

It remains now to consider the exact nature of these revelations. Granting that they are not purely neurotic ravings, were they objective manifestations, or purely in the imagination of this sickly Norwich nun? From St Augustine to St Teresa, mystical writers have drawn clear distinctions among the various types of visionary phenomena. There have been lights and voices such as struck St Paul to earth on his way to Damascus. There have been secret and inexpressible touchings of the soul by God, as experienced by St John of the Cross, and there are many types between. St Thomas has drawn up a handy and rational scheme in which to fit them all. Beginning with the most objective, there is the external, corporeal apparition *mediante sensu exterius . . . formae sensibiles* impressing themselves on the external senses. (Apparitions that affect surrounding material things, leaving footprints or bending bushes, may be judged as external.) Then there are the visions which are subjective, residing within the imagination of the visionary. These may occur in sleep or while awake, and may be new forms, not experienced before and impressed by a divine agency, as perhaps the apparition to Bernadette at Lourdes, or forms already seen in real life and used by God to instruct the soul, as the appearance of St Scholastica to her brother St Benedict at the moment of her death. St Thomas remarks here that words are more perfect than images for they are more spiritual and not so bound up with sense. So that the final and most perfect vision is the intellectual one, independent of the senses, either external or internal, and impressed directly on the human mind by God; and this either by a special light on a truth already known in a larger way, or by a new species (*species impressa*). Such an intellectual vision is evidently possible only in the advanced stages of the spiritual life when the gifts of the Holy Spirit are free to influence the soul.[6]

Mother Julian's revelations are not restricted to any one of these types; she seems to have experienced them all during the course of these sixteen showings. She is not unaware of the distinction and this is one of the many indications of her thorough grounding in theology. 'All this was showed by three ways; that is to say, by bodily sight, and by word formed in my understanding, and by spiritual sight' (c. 9, cf. c. 73).

In so far as the showings begin in the figure of the crucifix held before her, she considers them to be 'bodily' and external. What she sees is very vivid and very material.

> I saw the bodily sight lasting of the plenteous bleeding of the Head. The great drops of blood fell down from under the Garland like pellots, seeming as it had come out of the veins; and in the coming out they were brown-red, for the blood was full thick; and in the spreading-abroad they were bright-red; and when they came to the brows, then they vanished (c. 7).

The vision was as she says, 'quick and life-like, and horrifying and dreadful, sweet and lovely' (id.); and its realism would almost incline us to believe it was in fact external. But at other times the showing was not so clear, it was 'so low and so little' (c. 10); so that we may conclude that they were all, however vivid and clearly defined, subjective images, conjured up by some means, natural or supernatural, in her 'mind's eye'.

In the imaginative visions St Thomas says that the forms may be naturally induced, accepted from what one has experienced, in one's natural life. And these are disposed by God for his own purpose, to convey his own meaning. Or they may be divinely induced, coming

directly from his agency. In this way the natural predispositions may play a considerable part. It would be no argument to deny the significance of a man's dreams merely because he had caviare for dinner and was naturally dyspeptic. The important fact was not that there were dreams, but what the dreams meant. God uses natural secondary causes universally; he dispenses with them only by way of exception. He can dispose the material of dreams or imaginings to bring about his own designs; and is more likely to do that than to insert entirely new images from without. Mother Julian's bodily showings, therefore, may be derived partly from her psychological state; partly from what she had read or imagined about the Passion; and partly from her intense desire to know more of the Passion and to suffer more with our Lord, which was the occasion of the whole affair (c. 2). It matters little where these images came from; God at least ordered and disposed them for his own divine purposes.

Some literal-minded people have asked whether her visions were true to fact, whether they represented what actually happened on the Cross. They have been impressed by the apparent accuracy of such revelations as those of Catherine Emmerich who saw all the details of the Holy Land though she had never been there. They then turn to the very literal description of our Lord's dying body in the Eighth Showing (cc. 16 and 17), and wonder whether these also represent the truth of fact. Some are inclined to deny their historicity. Such discussions are more futile than any hair-splitting of decadent scholasticism. Even had these visions been thoroughly external, taking place objectively on the Crucifix before Mother Julian, it was and is quite irrelevant whether they show what happened on Calvary or not. The meaning of these Showings, as of any genuine revelation in dreams, imaginations or ghostly forms, is not literal in a material sense but spiritual. The Mexican of Guadalupe does not ask: Does this figure before me show our Lady as she really was at Bethlehem or Nazareth? As though a photographer ought to have been introduced to let us know the exact truth. Our Lady appears as a Mexican lass to tell him truths about herself and her Son—the spiritual meaning. Mother Julian understands this quite clearly.

The bodily sights are not given to teach a literal historic truth that may be found with as much clarity as necessary in the gospels themselves. The 'spiritual sight' to which the bodily sight leads her is the important feature. The question always uppermost in her mind is not: What do I see? But: What does it mean? The external things of religion in all its aspects are always signs of internal grace, be they scriptures, sacraments, miracles or private revelations. The clearest example of the relationship of these two 'senses' of her visions is in the celebrated showing of the Lord and the Servant.

Which sight was shewed doubly in the Lord and doubly in the Servant: one part was shewed spiritually in bodily likeness, and the other part was shewed more spiritually without bodily likeness. For the first sight, thus, I saw two persons in bodily likeness . . . and therewith God gave me spiritual understanding (c. 51).

The Lord takes her into the inner sense of what she sees, not leaving her simply to stand and marvel at it as a fact without significance. The spiritual meaning of what she sees in our Lady comes out very clearly too.

In this Shewing he brought our blessed Lady to my understanding. I saw her ghostly, in bodily likeness; a simple maid and a meek, young of age and little waxen above a child, in the stature that she was when she conceived. Also God shewed in part the wisdom and the truth of her soul. . . . (c. 4).

The purely physical sight of the crucifix and the passion, or of our Lady, is never left to stand on its own; it always stands for something deeply hidden. For visions are symbols.

Many of these Showings do not come from imaginative pictures at all, but have the more perfect form of words spoken. Here in fact it may be we pass over from the imaginative locution to the intellectual vision which is impressed directly on the mind itself, or which comes in the form of a new light in which the mind sees what has been presented. For Mother Julian tells us that the words often were formed in her understanding without any humanly-formed locution, exterior or interior:

And after this, ere God shewed any words, he suffered me for a convenient time to give heed unto him and all that I had seen, and all intellect that was therein, as the simplicity of the soul might take it. Then he, without voice and opening of lips, formed in my soul these words: *Herewith is the Fiend overcome* (c. 13, cf. c. 68).

When she is anxious for a clearer bodily sight of what was before her, she is answered in her reason: 'If God will show thee more, he shall be thy light; thee needeth none but him' (c. 10). Although she still uses the terminology of words, she is very emphatic that the showing comes rather by impression on the soul itself which is led to understand. There are occasions when she understands in this way properties of God and virtues of our Lady's soul. 'Christ showed me his Father; in no bodily likeness, but in his property and in his working. That is to say, I saw in Christ that the Father is.' (c. 22, cf. c. 25) She calls this often 'ghostly sight', and she speaks of the Lord opening her spiritual eye. All this would suggest some direct intuition of truth resulting from infused contemplation.

Père Garrigou-Lagrange writes of the extraordinary graces which sometimes accompany this infused contemplation, and among these graces stands out the *simplex intuitus veritatis*, the divine touch on the very substance of the soul. We learn of this most strikingly from St John of the Cross who also uses the terminology of words—substantial words impressed substantially on the soul.[7] Mother Julian's language is closely allied with that of the mystic doctor: 'All this was showed in a touch' (c. 27); 'I had in partie touching and it is grounded in kynd: that is to sey, our reson is groundid in God, which is substantial kyndhede'—which Warrack edits as 'I had, in part, experience of the Touching of God in the soul, and it is grounded in Nature' (c. 56). However we may explain some of these individual experiences, there can be little doubt that several of these visions were of that extraordinary type of substantial touch which reveals the Gift of Wisdom and Understanding operating in a very special manner.

The difficulty in analysing the nature of these showings lies, not in her own description which is unwontedly explicit, but in the transition of years between the first visions and her final understanding of them. Much of what she saw was at first quite beyond her, they passed her wit and all her understanding and all her powers (c. 26). There were obstacles in the way of her visions, either by sins or by an untoward anxiety over their meaning. Reason is a good faculty and she never despises it; but reason can be impatient of the truths which are beyond its reach, and can fuss in an arrogant manner, thinking to analyse all truth. 'The more we busy us to know his secret counsels in this or any other thing, the farther shall we be from the knowing thereof' (c. 33). The blindness and ignorance that prevent our knowing the hidden things of God (c. 34) will often arise from this busy-ness of reason, when we should be aligning ourselves to divine truth by love and submission. The whole style of the revelations, however, suggests that the mysteries were presented precisely as mysteries that the soul might always be seeking more understanding, or, becoming more passive, might be open to further manifestation. Often the Lord leads forth her understanding to greater perception, but still 'every Showing is full of secret things left hid' (c. 51 near the beginning). They make the letters of an alphabet, which, when put together in different ways, can teach all manner of truth (id. and c. 80). So with the advance in holiness, and the purification of her sins, Mother Julian learns to see more and more in what was revealed to her. Quite clearly the Holy Ghost is at work, leading her forth into the understanding proper to the Unitive Way.

Her progress is in fact quite marked in what she tells us of her experiences. She had set out on the quest of the contemplative life, which she describes in terms of 'the creatures that have given them to serve our

Lord with inward beholding of his blessed Goodness' (c. 76). Like many beginners who are too idealistic and impatient to be at the End before they have taken the means thereto, she was anxious to die to escape the world and to find her Lover. The world is full of woe, heaven is bliss, so why wait here: 'This made me to mourn and eagerly to long' (c. 64). She was evidently overflowing with holy desires, but they needed to be purified. And the beginning of that final purification came with her sickness and her Showings.

Some people may be inclined to think that visions and the like are evidences of sanctity. They recognise that so often these heavenly manifestations have been granted to those afterwards raised to the altars of the Church, such as St Catherine or St Bernadette. But though there is a close connection between the holiness of the subject and the divine revelations, not infrequently it marks the beginning of real progress, as with St Bernadette who could lay noclaim to sanctity when our Lady appeared to her. Mother Julian is humbly conscious of this: 'Because of the Showing I am not good but if I love God the better . . . for I am certain that there be many that never had Showing nor sight but of the common teaching of Holy Church, that love God better than I' (c. 9). At the very end she seems to be conscious that what had been begun by heavenly visitation was still incomplete. 'This book is begun by God's gift and his grace, but it is not yet performed, as to my sight' (c. 86). She is conscious of her shortcomings, and in particular is she constantly sorrowing over her infidelity when, for a brief moment, she spurned these revelations, saying she had raved. But our Lord seems not to have upbraided her for her doubts, but later comforts her and assures her that the Showings were of God. At another time she seems to have regretted having asked for the gace to suffer with Christ (c. 17). But these are brief infidelities due more to the first movement of nature than to any deliberate choice, and it must be admitted that the evidence of the book suggests she had already reached a fairly high state of perfection when that eighth day of May dawned in 1373. The intellectual visions and understandings of what she had seen could only come to one already experiencing infused contemplation. And we have her witness that the Lord never really left her, in spite of her infidelity.

> In all this blessed Shewing our good Lord gave understanding that the Sight should pass: which blessed Shewing the Faith keepeth, with his own good will and his grace. For he left me with neither sign nor token whereby I might know it, but he left me with his own blessed word in true understanding (c. 70).

So the holy maid grounded in faith, learnt to grow always more responsive to the Gifts of the Holy Ghost, growing into the Life of Union.

Notes

[1] I here use Grace Warrack's edition of the *Revelations,* first published by Methuen in 1901. It is a convenient and readable edition.

[2] Page 204 in the Warrack edition. The whole postscript should be read.

[3] Cf. Aubrey Gwynn S.J. *The English Austin Friars in the time of Wyclif* (Oxford, 1940), pp. 150-205.

[4] It is argued that this remark contains more of humility than truth as she appears throughout to be a well-instructed woman and of some culture.

[5] The same sort of divine locution had occurred fifteen years afterthe visions as she explains in the last chapter (c. 86).

[6] Cf. II-II. 173, 2; 174, 3. St Thomas discusses a little later (177, 1 and 2) the nature of the *Gratia Sermonis,* and asks particularly whether this is able to be received by womenfolk!

[7] Cf. Garrigou-Lagrange, *Perfection Chrétienne* II 459; St John of the Cross, *Ascent of Mount Carmel* II 31; *Living Flame,* st. I vi-2. st. II v. 4.

B. A. Windeatt (essay date 1977)

SOURCE: "Julian of Norwich and Her Audience," *The Review of English Studies,* n.s. Vol. xxviii, No. 109, February 1977, pp. 1-17.

[*In the following essay, Windeatt compares the early, shorter version of* Revelations *with the later and longer edition in order to demonstrate the sense of authority and control over her material and awareness of her audience that Julian developed during the years between the two works.*]

It is an unusual opportunity, but in the manuscript situation of the **Revelations** of Julian of Norwich there is indeed a chance to see a mystic's literary revision of her account of her experience and of her interpretation of it.

Julian's text in its usually read form is extant in three manuscripts of post-medieval date.[1] But a shorter form of the text, apparently complete in itself, survives in a fifteenth-century manuscript.[2] Critics of Julian generally accept that this *A* (Amherst)[3] text is shorter because it is the author's earlier work, rather than a scribal abbreviation of the longer *S* (Sloane) text.[4] It is certain differences between this *A* version and the *S* text which indicate the development in Julian's understanding and presentation of her material during her lifetime.

A clue to this development is the omission from *S* of some vivid details of the events at Julian's sickbed, which are present in *A* and support its status as a genuine witness of the shewings.[5] After long years of meditation on the content of the revelations the mystic herself considers these original circumstantial details less relevant to what she has to say in her later *S* text. When Julian feels herself dying from the middle downwards she is in *S* 'stered to be sett upright underlenand with helpe' (ch. 3; 2ᵛ), to have more freedom of the heart to be at God's will. But the *A* text pictures Julian's position somewhat differently: 'than was I styrrede to be sette vppe ryghttes lenande *with clothes to myheede*' (ch. II; f. 98ʳ).[1] This detail, characteristic of a memoir near to the event, disappears from the polished text of *S,* and comparable changes occur between the accounts of the curate's visit. Divergences in both syntax and content reflect the texts' different approaches. In *S,* Julian—mainly concerned with the spiritual results of this visit—states simply 'My curate was sent for' (ch. 3; f. 2ᵛ). But the *A* text is still interested in the circumstances of the sickroom: 'and thay that were with me Sente for the Persou*n* my curette' (ch. II; f. 98ʳ). While the more considered *S* account places the curate's coming and Julian's own progress in parallel ('and by than he cam I had sett my eyen and might not speke', ch. 3; f. 2ᵛ); the *A* text records consecutively a simple narrative of events:

> he come and a childe with hym and brought A crosse
> & be than*n*e I hadde sette myne eyen And myght
> nought speke. (ch. II; f. 98ʳ)

In *A,* Julian is still interested in the details of the visit: the child, unnecessary to the spiritual import of the scene but retained by the sick woman's memory in *A,* disappears from *S;* and only in *A* does the curate call Julian 'dowgh*ter*' as he sets the Crucifix before her eyes. When the upper body begins to die the *A* text again has vivid observed detail. *S* simply says the body died 'so ferforth that onethys I had ony feleing with shortness of winde' (ch. 3; f. 3ʳ). But the *A* text continues 'myne handdys felle downe on Aythere syde And also for vnpowere my heede satylde downe On syde' (ch. II; ff. 98ʳ-98ᵛ). When *S* comes to be written this expressive account of Julian's dying gestures in *A* is felt to be expendable. Julian, then, selects and omits in the later text details of the original account of her experience. In the 8th Revelation, after she sees Christ's agony, Julian feels great pain (ch. 27), but the later text omits the description from Julian's first account of this scene in *A* of how her mother

> that stode emangys othere and behelde me lyftyd
> vppe hir hande before me face to lokke myn eyen
> for sche wenyd I had bene dede. (ch. X; f. 103ᵛ)

Julian's heightened sense of the scene round the sickbed gives immediacy to her recollected experience, but she drops these personal details from the later text as extraneous to her meditative response to the shewing.

A and *S* reflect very different stages in Julian's life as a contemplative, and their distinct characters are represented in the openings of the two texts. *A* begins, after the biographical colophon about Julian, a recluse at Norwich who 'ys on lyfe' (f. 97ʳ), with Julian's direct utterance: 'I desyrede thre graces be the gyfte of god'. But *S* opens with a 'table ofcontents', a chapter sketching what is to follow. This manner of beginning with a formal summary characterizes the more consciously presented and arranged nature of the *S* text, written later in Julian's life and showing some adjustment of attitude and presentation. To Julian's desire in *A* for a bodily sickness, *S* adds the detail that she desired this 'in youth at xxx yeeres of age' (ch. 2; f. 1ᵛ). Although in her sickness *A* has the remark 'Botte in this I was ryght sarye & lothe thought for to dye' (ch. II; f. 97ᵛ), the *S* text explains this was because she was still in youth (ch. 3). In such touches the text of *S* looks back reflectively on an experience more distant than it was to *A.*

These autobiographical changes distinguishing *S* from *A* are part of a wider pattern of differences between the manuscripts involving the position of the author in her work. Between *A* and *S* Julian's presentation of herself is modified, and the emphasis of her approach to her readers is altered, reflecting the mystic's development from the newness and insecurity of her position at the time of writing *A* towards the meditative assurance of *S.* In *A* Julian tends to be more conscious of herself and of her own position than in *S.* From this comes a sense of the otherness of other people and of their frailties, and also an anxiousness about the correct understanding of her material. Julian's realization through meditation of the meaning of her original shewings brings transformation of the author's position in the later text. In *S* the sense of self is comparatively reduced, and the occasional aloofness is forgotten in the author's perception of oneness with all men. This move towards a more universalist position, realizing in *S* the implicit meaning of *A,* is a recurrent pattern of change between the two texts.

The opening chapters show these characteristic adaptations of the author's presentation of her own position. Insecurity leads in *A* to an assertive tone. The *A* text declares the first of the three desires 'come to my mynde *with devocoun*' (ch. I; f. 97ʳ), but between *A* and *S* Julian drops the mention of her own devotion. Similarly, *A* says confidently 'I hadde *grete* felynge in the passyou*n*' (f. 97ʳ), but *S* says only 'I had *sume* feleing in the passion' (ch. 2; f. 1ᵛ). This modification of her position between *A* and *S* appears in changes in Julian's confidence in her perceptions. In *S* Julian says that our Lord may never leave us 'being to us althing that is gode' (ch. 5; f. 4ʳ). But with this she rephrases what she had declared in *A* ('And so in this syght *y sawe sothelye* that he ys alle thynge that ys goode', ch. 4; f. 99ʳ). With a similar change in the assuredness of her perceptions, Julian writes in *S* of her response to the 15th shewing: 'And thus I vnderstode' (ch. 65; f. 47ʳ). But in *A* she was more emphatic: 'In this blyssed revelacio*u*n *I was trewly taught*' (ch. XX; f. 111ʳ). Again, *A* had declared:

Other syght of gode ne schewynge desyrede I never none tylle atte the sawlle wer departyd frome the bodye *for I trayste Sothfastlye that I schulde be safe and this was my menynge.* (ch. I; f. 97ʳ)

But the confident words in italics do not reappear in the *S* text. It is a change, natural after years of reflection, in the presentation of her own worthiness to perceive, and also in her view of her own position, represented by the remarks on her safety. In ch. 9 ('ffor the shewing I am not gode but if I love god the better', f. 7ᵛ), Julian shows this same tendency to remove from *S* a sense of assurance too closely linked with personal optimism. In *A* she declares:

And thus wille I love & thus I love and thus I am safe. ffor y mene in the perso*u*n of myne evyncrystene. And the more I love of this lovynge whiles I Am here the mare I Am lyke to the blysse that I schalle have in hevene withowten ende. (ch. VI; ff. 100ᵛ-101ʳ)

But Julian omits this from *S*. Finally, in the 15th shewing, where Julian in both texts 'had gret longyng . . . to be deliverid of this world', it is only *A* which explains: 'for I schulde be with my god in blysse whare I hope sikerlye thurgh his m*e*rcye to be with owten ende' (ch. XX; f. 110ᵛ). Such individual authorial confidence disappears from *S*. Julian moves away from the personal context of revelation towards a more generally based assuredness. This is seen in her changes in the manner of address towards the audience of reader or hearer:

she that hyerys and sees this visio*u*n and this techynge that is of I*hesu* cryste to edificacou*n* of thoure saule *it is goddys wille* & my desyrere *that the take it with als grete ioye and lykynge as Ihesu hadde schewyd it thowe* as he dyd to me. (ch. VI; f. 100ᵛ)

Quite simply, only the italicized words are left in *S* (ch. 8). The changes excise the personal framework of reference, and with accumulated trust in the worth of her shewings Julian can later drop the concern with her authenticity.

This is a marked trend between *A* and *S* in the presentation of the author. Manuscript differences show how Julian removes some 'defensive' passages in which

the first text had carefully countered possible objections. Concerning the second desire, Julian represents herself in *S* 'frely desireing that sekenesse so herde as to deth' (ch. 2; f. 2ʳ). But *A* is much more cautiously phrased:

frelye *with owtyn Any sekynge* a wylfull desyre to hafe *of goddys gyfte* a bodelye syekenes and I wolde th*a*t this bodylye syekenes myght have beene so harde as to the dede. (ch. I; f. 97ʳ)

Apart from difference in *A*'s looser syntax, reflecting the untidied nature of the record in *A* as against the literary presentation in *S,* the italicized words in *A* aim to forestall objections to the divine nature of the shewings. Again, in the 13th shewing, the shewn material at first strikes Julian in *A* as in need of some qualified presentation in relation to the role of the mystic herself. Only the italicized words survive into *S:*

& Neuerthe-lesse ihesu in this visioun enfourmede me of alle that me neded. I saye nought that me nedes na mare techynge for oure lorde with the schewynge of this hase lefte me to haly kyrke, and I Am hungery and thyrstye and nedy and synfulle and freele & wilfully Submyttes me to the techynge of haly kyrke with alle myne euencrysten into the ende of my lyfe. *He aunswerde be this worde and sayde: Synne is behouelye.* (ch. XIII; f. 106ʳ)

So uncompromisingly complete is the shewn matter's claim to be all that is needed, that in *A* the mystic feels she must stress that this 'sufficing' does not come from her own merits. But meditation has evidently vindicated that original uncompromising force of expression, for the outcome of rewriting is the removal of the early defensiveness. In short, just as a certain self-awareness generated in the mystic by a sense of her material's importance is found out of keeping as the original is fully understood in the *S* text, so too Julian's corresponding defensive attitude in *A* in the face of the potential of her visions becomes irrelevant as meditation vindicates those shewings.[2]

A third important divergence between the texts concerning the author lies in the differing position taken up by Julian in relation to her audience.[3] The change of tone is represented in the 16th shewing: *A* states directly 'for man is harde in slepe of syn he is nought able . . . ' to feel the comfort of the Holy Ghost (ch. VII; f. 114ᵛ). But *S* has simply *He* is not able. Again, Julian explains in *A* 'ffor this es the cause why thaye th*a*t er occupyede wylfullye in er-thelye besynes & eu*er*mare sekes warldlye wele er nought here of his in herte and in sawlle' (ch. IV; f. 99ᵛ). But in *S* Julian rewrites the passage: 'For this is the cause why we be not all in ease of herete & soule' (ch. 5; f. 4ʳ).

A clue to the change in the author's position, with consequent omission of her sense of the otherness of sinners, lies in this shift from the third-person address of *they* or *he* in *A* towards the predominant *we* of the *S* text. Such changes recur throughout the texts: where *A* had said 'if a man be in so mekylle payne' (ch. XX; f. 111ʳ), the *S* text will say 'thow we be . . . '; or again, where *A* said 'for many men and women leues' (ch. XXIV; f. 114ʳ), the *S* text will develop this to 'ffor som of us leven' (ch. 73; f. 51ʳ). The emotional effectiveness of this change of attitude towards the audience derives from the simplicity and humility with which by a grammatical change of person the author casts aside aloof distinctness to be united with every reader or hearer. After stressing that she is not good because of the shewing unless she loves God better, *A* continues:

> and so may and so schulde ylke man do that sees it & heres it with goode will and trewe menynge. And so ys my desyre that it schulde be to euery like manne the same profytte that I desyrede to my selfe & therto was styrryd of god in the fyrste tyme when I sawe itte for yt comoun & generale as we ar alle ane. And I Am sekere I sawe it for the profytte of many oder (ch. VI; f. 100ᵛ) . . . and so motte it be for we are all one in loove. (f. 101ʳ)

But in contrast the *S* text rewrites:

> In as much as ye love God the better it is more to you than to me. I sey not this to hem that be wise for thei wote it wele, but I sey it to you that be simple for ese & comfort, for we arn al one in comfort. (ch. 9; f. 7ᵛ)

The earlier text's characteristic concerns distinguish *A:* a sense of its importance to others, and unease about communication, for other people cannot be relied on to understand what Julian intends. The tone of *S* is transformed. *A*'s didactic aim towards the reader is modified by the author's humility in explicitly limiting herself to the simple and including herself among them. The dynamic possibility of *profit* becomes the resigned calm of *ease and comfort.* Any zealous stridency, any distancing awareness of the specialness of the author's role in the revelation, is replaced by an inclusive and accepting attitude towards the reader.

This shift in attitude towards the audience is seen most specifically in several cases where the *S* text replaces the inclination of *A* to address itself to *contemplatives.* Discussing the 'hazlenut' shewing in *A*, Julian remarks 'Of this nedes like man & woman to hafe knawynge that desyres to lyeve contemplatyfelye' (ch. IV; f. 99ᵛ), but *S* continues its discussion without this limitation of its address. This same shift is seen in the 12th shewing away from the specialized third-person in *A*. *A* has: 'and in this was I lerede that like saule contemplatyfe

to whilke es gyffen to luke and seke god schalle se hir and passe vnto god by contemplacioun' (ch. XIII; f. 106ʳ). This is replaced and reduced in *S* to 'wherin I was lernyd that our soule shal never have rest til it comith to hym' (ch. 26; f. 18ᵛ). The move from a detached third-person address to 'each soul contemplative' towards the involved and involving address to 'our soul' is a striking instance of Julian's adapted position as author between the texts. The allusions to contemplation have become dispensable because they represent a specific, limiting address for the matter of the shewings. That universalism which upon meditation Julian perceives as one of the great themes of her shewings could not be fully expressed if the text continued to be so narrowly directed. Julian's original perceptive experience was unique, of a strange, intensely individual quality. But with long reflection Julian comes to see its general significance and application. Manuscript divergences between *A* and *S* show how she accordingly develops the presentation and interpretation of her original matter to influence the reader's response to it.

These manuscript differences enable us to appreciate to what extent *S* is a consciously 'presented' and arranged text, a literary redaction of the original account of experience, which through its expansions sets the shewings within a wider frame of reference. The manuscript divergences show that Julian was prepared to make radical changes in the presentation of material in *S,* changes which altered the sequence of historical events to improve the effect of the over-all account. Between the writing of the two texts Julian shifts forwards her first vision of the Virgin. In *S* this vision comes *after* the first shewing of the trickling red blood and the following meditation, which concludes that the Passion is strength enough against all the fiends of hell. *S* now has the Mary passage, which forms an appropriate sign of encouragement at this point.[4] But in *A* the situation is different, and its order of material more awkward. After Julian concludes that the Passion is strength enough, the *A* text passes straight on to the 'hazelnut' vision and the meditation on its three properties. Only after the lesson of this does the Mary passage follow in *A*. The order of material in *A* is stylistically inferior to that in *S,* not merely in that the vision of Mary does not follow very obviously here, but most of all because the meditation on the 'hazelnut' is not finished in *A* before the Mary passage starts (f. 99ᵛ). Accordingly, Julian must somehow return in *A* to the nut theme, and this she does in a transitional passage which a little clumsily repeats the very same observations she made when the hazelnut vision first appeared.[5] However, although the rearrangement in *S* is a literary improvement of a badly organized passage, the fact remains that in the earlier account of experience the vision of Mary comes after that of the hazelnut, whereas in *S* it comes before. In the historical experience it cannot have come in both places, and if the awkwardness of the *A* order indeed represents that of life, then the manuscript differences show Julian's preparedness to rearrange the presentation of her account.

II

Willing to reorganize her material for greater effect, Julian in *S* sets about influencing the reader's response to the shewings. The first form of the revelations and much of the subsequent adaptation of the reader's perception of them is in intensely visual terms. Julian has a way of thinking which progresses naturally in terms of pictures and the development within pictures.[6] A 'defensive' passage in *A* about her reasons for writing—later omitted from *S*—artlessly preserves a hint of Julian's original indebtedness to the stimulus of visual representations of the Passion.[7] The omission occurs just before (in both texts) Julian desires a bodily sight of the Passion (ch. 2). In the passage in *A* Julian insists she believes Holy Church's teaching on Christ's pains, but further declares that she accepts:

> also the Payntyngys of Crucyfexes that er made be the grace of god after the techynge of halykyrke to the lyknes of Crystes passyou*n* als farfurthe as manys witte maye reche. (ch. I; f. 97ʳ)

This cancelled autobiographical remark on her own original motivation in seeking the shewings indicates that Julian looks on her visions as in some relation to the devotional effects of artistic representations. She regards the form of the shewings as a special further stage which enables her to progress beyond the visual arts, but when she comes to express her interior 'shewings' her form and method are much influenced by such visual aids to devotion.

Between *A* and *S* Julian quite literally alters her way of looking at her original shewings, and these developments of the given visual matter are among the most striking evidence of the author's shift of approach towards her material. In the nature of the shewings many of these changes—made on manuscript evidence long after the event of revelation—concern the Passion descriptions. In the third phase of the 1st shewing, when Julian's attention returns to the bleeding head, *A* has this stark observation and response: 'I saye the body-lye syght lastande of the plentyuouse bledynge of the hede. And als longe as y sawe that syght y sayde Oftyn tymes Benedicite Dominus' (ch. V; f. 100ʳ). But in *S* Julian adds the vividly detailed description (as she says 'quick & lively & hidouse & dredfull, swete & lovely') of those 'grete dropis', which were like 'pellots . . . in the comeing out . . . browne rede; . . . in the spredeing abrode . . . bright rede; . . . & for the roundhede it were like to the scale of heryng in the spreadeing on the forehead' (ch. 7; f. 6ʳ). From the intimacy of this physical detail Julian takes comfort that the awesome

and dreadful Lord is also so homely and courteous to us. The precision of description in this inserted account is almost photographic, and so too is its concentration on a particular part of the Passion. The beholder is conscious of a sharp edge to the picture: '& whan it come to the browes than it vanyshid . . . The plenteoushede is like to the dropys of water that fallen of the evys after a greate showre of reyne'. Beyond the edge of this area where her vision is sharply focused on the movement and quality of the blood is a blankness with which Julian is not here concerned. The powerful idea of the rain pouring over the eaves, while intended to evoke the profusion of blood, compounds this sense of a clearly defined edge to Julian's field of concentrated vision, over which the blood, her main concern, flows away out of sight. The vision is at once very precisely delineated yet so imaginatively forceful as to appear curiously both fervent and dispassionate. This is part of the distinctive approach of *S*. The details of colour, quality, and extent reflect an emotional response in Julian and summon a corresponding reponse from the reader. But the picture is also carefully framed, and its minutely dissecting attention to detail presents an image focused to heightened, unnatural effect. Julian expresses the suffering of Christ in recognizable human terms, but also conveys to the reader by this added, distancing strangeness the unique quality of that suffering.

An added visual detail in the 2nd shewing is very comparable in effect. *A* notices briefly 'alle his blyssede face Atyme closede in dry blode' (ch. VIII; f. 101ᵛ). But Julian in *S* examines the particular stages of the process observed:

> And one time I saw how halfe the face begyning at the ere over rede with drie blode til it be closid to the mid face. And after that the tother halfe be closyd on the same wise & there whiles in this party even as it came. (ch. 10; f. 8ʳ)

This inserted detail consolidates the meditation also added to this shewing in *S*, to the effect that the awful appearance of the dying Christ (as with the disconcerting ugliness of the face in the Vernicle relic) reflects the dark, sinful state of man in which the Lord has for a while come to dwell. In method, this visual amplification resembles the 1st shewing in concentrated observation. Both passages rigidly control the zone of vision, and the alternating divisions of Christ's suffering stylize the shewing of His suffering. Added visual detail of Christ's blood in the 4th shewing sustains the later text's trend to alter the approach to the visual matter of the original shewing. *A*'s brief observation of bleeding 'hate & freschlye and lyfelye' (ch. VIII; f. 101ᵛ) is refashioned into a more effectively detailed passage in *S*, suggesting the process of Christ's pain by added emphatic language ('faire skyn*ne* . . . brokyn ful depe into the tender flesh with sharpe smyting al about the sweete body', ch. 12; f. 10ᵛ). The later description has a hyperbolical, non-naturalistic quality ('there was neither sene skyn*n*e ne wound but as it were al blode'). In both *A* and *S* Julian thinks the blood was so plenteous that if the vision had been in 'kind' and in substance it would have flowed down over her bed. But *S* adds on reflection that when the blood 'come wher it should a fallen downe than it vanyshid . . . The bleding continued a while til it migt be sene with Avisement' (f. 11ʳ). This recalls Julian's comment on the 1st shewing ('the bleding continuid till many things were seene & understondyn', ch. 7; f. 6ʳ). The physical forcefulness of both accounts is much increased, but so too is the sense of frame and focus with which the vision is presented. The potential of the vision is stressed to be not such as can cross that observational frame into the world of Julian's bedchamber. It remains an image for consideration, for *avisement*.

Essentially visual detail added in the 8th shewing brings to a climax this trend in *S* to see the original *A* shewing in a rather different perspective. The ideas underlying the addition ('the blyssyd bodye dryede alle ane lange tyme with wryngy*n*ge of the nayles and paysyn-ge of the hede', ch. X; f. 103ᵛ) were all along present in *A*. The added matter again consists of selected physical details, together with a very individual perception of the processes of suffering through the focus brought to bear upon them. The passage in part concerns itself with the skin of His head which is somehow raised away from the skull, and then shifts its focus to the strange process by which the congealing blood forms another 'garland' in addition to the Crown of Thorns ('I saw it was for it began tò dreyen & stynte a party of the weyte & sette abute the garland. And thus it envyronyd al aboute as it were garland upo*n* garland', ch. 17; f. 14ʳ). Intense concern for these detailed processes of change creates a tension as to whether the loose skin will fall off. Again, the strength of emotional involvement in Julian almost suggests a crossing of the frame into the picture ('ffor me thowte I wold not for my life asen it fallen', f. 14ʳ). But Julian's way of looking also contains within itself a sense that the picture and its developments are upon another, distinct plane ('How it was don I saw not but understode it was with the sharpe thornys . . .', f. 14ʳ). Her description has power to evoke a fresh response of feeling to this most familiar of icons, through the unusualness of its attention to details of the extraordinary violation of Christ's body in the Passion. Further, manuscript differences indicate that the most striking use of colour detail to represent the process of Christ's dying in this shewing is added in *S*. Where *S* says Christ turned pale, then 'more dede into blew & sithen more browne blew as the flesh turnyd more depe dede' (ch. 16; f. 13ʳ), *A* does not have the unusual compound 'browne blew', but simply repeats 'blew'. This may be scribal omission, but a comparable passage a little later is also lacking in *A*: 'The swete body was brown & blak al

turnyd oute of faire lifely colour of hymselfe on to drye deyeng' (f. 13ᵛ). These apparently later additions show how Julian in *S* wishes to present a conception of the Passion which through strikingly individual, imaginative insights represents the extremity of Christ's unique pain and sacrifice.[8]

This more intense way of looking at the shewn material in itself in the later text is part of the same cast of mind which produces the passages of meditation on those shewings in *S*. Julian relies on picture, on developments in visual and spatial terms, to represent the transforming of perception in response to the implications of the shewings. Julian's recasting between *A* and *S* of the 10th shewing confirms her tendency to rearrange in the later text the way the original, very individual narrative of experience in *A* is regarded, in order to introduce more universal perspectives. The opening visual idea of the shewing ('our Lord looked into His side and beheld') is common to *A* and *S*. But the manner of perceiving the shewing alters between the texts. The revelation in *A* is brief:

> [He] sayde this worde, 'Loo how I lovyd the', as ʒyf he hadde sayde, 'my childe, ʒyf thow kan nought loke in my godhede see heere howe I lette opyn my syde and my herte be clovene in twa and lette oute blude and watere.' (ch. XIII; f. 105ᵛ)

Here *A* preserves an early stage in Julian's conception of her shewing. She responds to a pregnant locution as an injunction to visualize aspects of the Passion ('*as if He said . . . See here*'). The Man of Sorrows speaks out directly and points to his wounds. But *S* casts its account of the same experience into a more literary mould:

> He browte to mende his dereworthy blode & pretious water which he lete poure al oute for love. And with the swete beholdyng he shewid his blisful herte even cloven on two. (ch. 24; f. 17ᵛ)

The picture is still affective, yet presented so that it may be seen with 'avisement'. But the *S* text also differs in containing within itself the outcome of that consideration. The *A* injunction *See heere howe I lette opyn my syde* becomes in *S*:

> With his swete lokyng he led forth the under-stondyng of his creture be the same wound into hys syde withinne. And than he shewid a faire delectabil place & large enow for al mankynd that shal be save to resten in pece & in love. (f. 17ᵛ)

Through this striking, non-naturalistic idea of Christ's side, Julian represents by a visual development of her detailed attention to the Crucifixion an understanding of the universal significance of the shewing. Comparable developments of her visual concern with the

Passion recur in the added passages of meditative re-action to the shewings, and draw their strength from the reader's feeling of oneness—instilled by the mode of the Revelations—with the sufferings of Christ. While *A* has the germ of an idea that the change of Christ's *chere* changes Julian's mood to one of joy, in the added meditation in *S*

> we wilfully abydyng in the same Cross with his helpe & his grace into the last poynte, sodenly he shall chonge his chere to us & we shal be with hym in hevyn. Betwix that one & that other shal be no tyme & than shal al be browte to joy. (ch. 21; f. 16ʳ)

Imaginative closeness of association between aspects of Christ's body on the Cross and the mystic's percep-tions allow this striking figure of the extension of perception. Addition to the 4th shewing places in its larger context Julian's interest in the blood of the Passion shewings, by representing that blood's meta-physical significance in visual terms. The original sh-ewing of the plenteous bleeding of the body is with meditation supplemented by a dynamic visualizing ('Be-holde & se!') of that blood streaming through and trans-figuring hell and earth, and ascending to heaven back into Christ's body, and 'there is in him, bleeding & praying for us to the father' (ch. 12; f. 11ʳ). By such an addition the later text extends through a vividly expressed, though traditionally based, visualization the reader's understanding of the universal implications of the original shewing.

A passage in *A* which Julian later omits from *S* indi-cates the role played by traditional religious patterns and images in shaping her way of thinking about spir-itual developments. The context is Julian's third de-sire. In *S* she states simply the origin of her desire: 'By the grace of God and teachyng of holy church I con-ceived a mighty desire to receive iii wounds in my life' (ch. 2; f. 2ʳ). But in *A* Julian gave a fuller account of how the desire came to her:

> I harde A man telle of halye kyrke of the Storye of Saynte Cecylle, In the whilke schewynge I vnderstode that sche hadde thre woundys with A swerde In the nekke with the whilke sche pynede to the dede. By the styrrynge of this I conseyvede a myghty desyre, Prayande oure lorde god that he wolde grawnte me thre woundys in my lyfe tyme. (ch. I; f. 97ᵛ)

The three wounds in the hagiographical account of St. Cecilia have a formative influence on the idea of a pattern of three wounds in Julian's own spiritual life. This passage in *A* offers a glimpse into what stimu-lated Julian's imagination and devotion before she provides a more conventional explanation in the *S* redaction.

Julian's adapted way of looking at her shewings through the medium of the *S* text makes comparable use of allusions to familiar saints, which emphasizes certain points by drawing on a parallel between patterns in the argument and in the saint's life. In the 8th shewing *A* has a hint of the later addition in *S* ('thaye that knewe hym nought this was thare payne: that alle creatures, sonne & the mone, withdrewe thare seruyce and so ware thaye alle lefte in sorowe for the tyme', ch. X; f. 104ʳ). But in *S* this is replaced by an allusion to the story of 'St. Dyonise', who is moved by the phenom-ena accompanying the Passion to set up an altar to the Unknown God. In the 13th shewing, where Julian dis-cusses her faith that God rewards the sins of the saved soul, she adds in confirmation in *S* a vision of St. John of Beverley, whom God allowed to fall but rewarded the more. Such added allusions confirm thematically the trend of the argument, and Julian relies on the visual element in their presentation to make her point. The story of Dyonise achieves its impact through the idea of the altar with its inscription, and although the legend of John's fall is not in itself visual, the sense of marvel in that reward is presented in visual terms be-cause the saint is shown being favoured with great courtesy in the sight of God.[9]

By a comparable use of a traditional iconographical idea in the later text of the 15th shewing, Julian rep-resents the new understanding generated by her shewn material. The original shewing has a declaration 'Sun-danly thowe schalle be takene fra alle thy payne . . . & thowe schalle comen vp abouen' (*A*, f. 110ᵛ). But in *S* Julian adds a passage visualizing this. She first sees a hideous and shapeless rotting corpse; then follows a sudden vision of a healthy, graceful child 'whiter than lilly' who springs from the body and 'sharply glode up on to hevyn' (ch. 64; f. 46ᵛ). The contrast of worlds could scarcely be more strongly presented in terms of form and movement. Inspiration for the idea stems from the visual arts, where the soul is often of course so represented. Julian adds the familiar representa-tional idea to bring out in emphatic visual terms the change of perception implicit in the original shewing. How-ever, Julian's imagination is not at all confined to use of traditional images. In the 2nd shewing, from the theme 'He shal be thy light thee nedith none but him' (ch. 10; f. 8ʳ) Julian moves in her later text into a remarkable visual representation of a change of plane in her perceptions: 'Mine understondyng was led downe into the see ground & there I saw hill & dalis grene semand as it were mosse begrowne with wrekke & with gravel' (f. 8ᵛ). For the woman recluse this idea of movement into an alien environment conveys by an imaginative leap of understanding that 'if a man or a woman were under the broade watyr if he might have sight of god so as god is with a man continually he should be save in body & soule' (f. 8ᵛ). Julian represents visually and imaginatively in her addition the change of awareness to which, as in other meditative expansions, an understanding of the general significance contained in the original shewing gives rise.

III

A passage present only in *A,* in which Julian discusses her role in the communication of the shewings, indicates her own understanding of this movement in the later text towards a more general interpretation of the meaning of these individual shewings. In *A* she disclaims forcefully the position of instructor of her audience: 'Botte god for-bede that the schulde saye or take it so that I am a techere, for I meene nought soo, no, I mente nevere so' (ch. VI; f. 101ʳ). The self-conscious insecurity of herposition in *A* emerges at this omitted passage in Julian's defensiveness about the unusualness of publication by one of her sex ('for I am a woman schulde I therfore leve that I schulde nought telle howe the goodenes of god, Syne that I sawe in that same tyme that is his wille that it be knawen?' f. 101ʳ). But the understanding that the shewings should be given the widest possible application overcomes her hesitation, and is an indication in *A* of the future development of *S.* In this early passage Julian already envisages that a general understanding of the shewings involves a diminishing of her position as medium: 'Thane schalle the sone forgette me that am a wrecche and dose so that I lette howe nought & be-halde Ih*esu* that ys techare of alle' (f. 101ʳ).

This section about Julian's view of her position towards her audience disappears from *S,* because the later text represents in the very changes in its form from *A* that development in understanding of the original shewings which Julian had hinted in the omitted passage was the way forward from *A.* For *A* the movement towards a wider understanding of the shewings will occur in the reader's mind in response to the text. But in additions to *S* Julian herself sets out that response to the shewings as it developed through her meditations. The later text provides its frame of comment on the original experience, and so contains within itself the development beyond the individual into general significance hinted in *A.* In the 1st shewing of the trickling blood the visual impression is 'placed' by Julian's insertion just afterwards ('And in the same sheweing sodenly the trinite fullfilled the herte most of joy . . . for where Jesus appereith the blissid trinite is understond as to my sight', ch. 4; ff. 3ʳ-3ᵛ). Similarly, Julian's rephrased accounts of perception reflect the adaptation of *S* into a text where the first experience of revelation is seen through the medium of subsequent reflection: a comment in *A* such as 'Thus chese I Ih*esu* for my heuen' (ch. XI; f. 104ʳ), becomes in *S* 'Thus was I lerid to chose Jesus to my hevyn' (ch. 19; f. 15ʳ), and such a direct report of perception as 'Luffe was moste schewed to me' (ch. XXIV; f. 114ʳ), is set within the more general frame of "The soule toke most vnderstonding in love' (ch. 73; f. 51ʳ). It is largely Julian's addition of meditative passages which achieves the more universalist outlook of *S,* and this redirection of her text appears in the development between *A* and *S* of Julian's use of language.

Most of what is now best known in Julian's style and language is the work of *S.* While *A* relates a narrative of experience with relatively simple diction and syntax, Julian's reflective approach in *S* leads to inclusion of more abstract terms and construction of more complex, various sentences, reflecting the optimism of the later text. Where Julian in *A* represents man's obligation to God by the idea of an individual bond between the soul and God, who is felt to have done for the individual soul everything that He has done, *S* will go beyond this with the comment: 'that is to seyn,the Charite of God makyth in us such a Unite that whan it is trewly seen no man can partin himsilfe fro other' (ch. 65; f. 47ᵛ). Julian's extension in these terms of the idea of the individual bond develops the reader's understanding of its universal implication. Stylistic pattern as reflection of the nature of God marks the meditations. Through devices of balance and symmetry, and her recurrent patterns of triads, Julian's syntax represents her perception of the stable order of God's dispositions. But alongside symmetrical patterns reflecting God's ordinance, Julian deploys in the later additions rolling, cumulative patterns of repetition to convey to the reader an understanding of the original experience of revelation which can only be expressed in terms of a swelling of reverent, incantatory affirmation.[10] In wavelike movements long sentences gain momentum from attempts to evoke the indescribable. Key words which acclaim aspects of God ring through meditative passages, giving thematic unity by incantatory repetition ('mervelous homlyhede . . . joy of the grete homlyhede . . . homlyest & curteysest . . . this mervelous joy . . . the mervelous Curtesie & homlyhede of our fader . . . this Mervelous homlyhede', ch. 7; f. 6ᵛ). Such additions represent through syntax and diction the ripple of reflective response which moves out from the original experience in *S.* In this later writing too, Julian conveys by use of superlatives her sense of the universal application of her shewings: ideas of highest and lowest, of endlessness, and of *overpassing* are the contribution of *S.* But the manuscript divergences most dramatically indicating the later text's movement towards more emphatic use of language involve those instances where Julian's meditative expansions paraphrase the original divine words (*as if He said* . . .) to achieve more expansive, incantatory effect, or present direct utterances by God not appearing in the *A* text to bring passages to a climax by confirming the meditation.[11] It is by such drawing out and emphasis of the implications of the original shewing through the language of the meditative expansions in *S* that Julian moves the reader— at least to a much greater extent than in *A*—to 'forgette me that am a wrecche . . . & be-halde Ihe*su* that ys techare of alle'.

Julian's reorganization of the first ending of her text in *A* provides a pointer to her developing approach between the writing of the two texts. Comparison of the contexts involves comparison of imagery, and indeed, more generally, Julian's development of her imagery reflects the progress between *A* and *S:* the extension in *S* of her original potent image of fulfilment through being *enclosed* in God;[12] or again, her recurrent addition of the idea of the Lord and Servant relationship, emphasizing in the later text the progress and reward of the soul.[13] In the ending of *A* Julian is concerned to distinguish between the reverent and false types of dread. It is characteristic that the more uncertain, earlier text should end on this note, for discussion of dreads shows Julian again close to questions about her own role in the shewings, andbeset by the possibility of an evil, deceiving revelation ('Knawe tham bath & refuse the fals, righte as we walde do a wikkyd spiritte that schewed hym in liknes of a goode Angell', ch. XXV; f. 114*v*). Julian's presentation of this deluding spirit shows an author still near to the experience of revelation and its immediate responses ('thowgh he com vnder the coloure and the liknes of a goode angell, his daliaunce & his wirkynge thowgh he schewe neu*er* so fayre, fyrst he travayles & tempes & trubles the p*er*sou*n* that he spekes with and lettes hym and lefeth hym alle in vnreste', ff. 114*v*-115*r*). The change Julian makes in her later discussion of the dreads shows in its development in imagery the development in the mystic's commitment to the validity of her original experience as vindicated by subsequent meditation. The idea of the bad angel, and with it the possibility of an uncertain or delusive shewing, has disappeared. Instead, Julian inserts an idea of reverent dread which causes us to 'fleen fro*m* all that is not good & fallen into our Lords brest as the Child into the Modir barme *with all our entent & with all our mynd*' (ch. 74; f. 52*r*). Doubts and insecurity of position in the early text are replaced by an image of absolute trust and commitment. As Julian knew in her additions elsewhere on the theme of Jesus Our Mother,[14] the Mother and Child idea is the most emotionally evocative way of expressing the rightness and completeness of the soul's trust in God, while the italicized words carefully tying the later text's confident, emotive image into relation with the interior actions which it is to signify, underline the greater sensitivity in accounting for the inward movements which her meditative years have brought to Julian in *S.*

Like the 14th shewing, the ending of this 16th Revelation in *A* proves a growth point from which Julian in *S* develops a series of chapters of refined spiritual reflections on the original theme. The contrast between the terse, parting moralization in *A* after its bad angel idea, and the chapters of illumination which have grown out from and beyond it in the later text, represents

through differences of literary form the progress and enhancement of the spiritual understanding Julian is able to offer her reader. The survival of both these texts gives a precious opportunity to perceive how in a person of rare sensibility spiritual understanding and its literary expression have developed. In one text we seem to have an account very close to what happened on that eighth day of May in 1373, and in the other we have a text representing Julian's position later in life. But such written texts can only mirror forth to us stages in an ongoing spiritual progression ('He will that we be occupied in knoweing and loveing til the tyme that we shall be fulfilled in hevyn & therefore was this lesson of love shewid', ch. 6; f. 5*v*). For Julian, even the achievement of her later text was but a development in a spiritual response to those unique shewings which would occupy her soul continually, and accordingly, on opening her last chapter of thatlater text she stresses its still provisional position within the ceaseless process of reflection and understanding: 'This booke is begun*ne* be gods gift & his grace but it is not yet performid as to my syte' (ch. 86, f. 57*r*).

Notes

[1] Bib. Nat., Paris, Fonds Anglais No. 40 (late 16th c.); B.L. Sloane MS. 2499 (17th c.); B.L. Sloane MS. 3705 (late 17th c. or early 18th c.).

[2] B.L. Add. MS. 37790; formerly owned by Lord Amherst.

[3] Hereafter, MS. Add. 37790 is termed *A,* and the later state of the text is termed *S,* after Sloane MS. 2499. In the absence of scholarly editions of either text citations are from these two manuscripts, with minimal added punctuation and capitalization. In quoting from the *A* MS., which is not divided into chapters, chapter divisions are given (in roman numerals) for ease of reference to the modernizations by the Revd. Dundas Harford (*Comfortable Words for Christ's Lovers* (London, 1911)) and by Sister Anna Maria Reynolds (*A Shewing of God's Love: The Shorter Version of 'Sixteen Revelations of Divine Love' by Julian of Norwich* (London, 1958)). Chapter divisions of *S* are those of MS. Sloane 2499 itself. Grace Warrack modernizes this manuscript tactfully in *Revelations of Divine Love* (London, 14th edn., 1952).

[4] For critical opinion on the standing of *A* and *S:* John Lawlor sets out the earlier views in 'A Note on the *Revelations* of Julian of Norwich', *R.E.S.,* N.S. ii (1951), 255-8; P. Molinari also discusses the problem and summarizes opinions in *Julian of Norwich: The Teaching of a 14th Century Mystic* (London, 1958), pp. 4-6; Sister Reynolds discusses the manuscript situation, op. cit., pp. xii-xiii and on p. 199 of 'Julian of Norwich' in *Pre-Reformation English Spirituality,* ed. J. Walsh (London, 1966).

[5] The fact of the omissions is noted by E. I. Watkin, *Poets and Mystics* (London, 1953), p. 81, and by a Benedictine of Stanbrook in 'Dame Julian of Norwich' (*English Spiritual Writers*, ed. C. Davis (London, 1961), pp. 59-61).

[1] All italics in quotations from Julian are of course my own.

[2] Watkin (op. cit., pp. 90, 96) comments on Julian's apparent revision of her first 'bold' ideas on sin, which could have been misunderstood. She omits from *S* her apostrophe upon sin in *A* ('A, wriched synne whate ert th*ou*? thowe er nought, for I sawe that god is alle thynge; I sawe nought the . . . ' f. 113[r]). The rather isolated *A* allusion to Philippians 2: 5 is also omitted from *S* ('botte ylke saule aftere the sayinge of saynte Pawle schulde feelein hym in *c*riste I*h*esu', ch. X; f. 103[v]). For Julian's use of biblical material see Sister A. M. Reynolds, 'Some Literary Influences in the *Revelations* of Julian of Norwich', *Leeds Studies in English and Kindred Languages,* vii-viii (1952), 18-28.

[3] Julian's omitted reference in *A* to 'ye that hear and see this vision and this teaching' (ch. VI; cited above, p. 4), seems to indicate that she thought of both a readership and of some kind of oral delivery for her work, perhaps among small groups of religious.

[4] In *S*, ch. 4.

[5] 'This lytill thynge that es made that es benethe oure ladye Saynt marye, god schewyd it vnto me als litill as it hadde beene a hasylle notte. Me thought it myght hafe fallene for litille' (ch. IV; f. 99[v]). No longer needed, this repetition is swept away in *S*.

[6] Cf. the *S* addition on the Lord in blue and his servant.

[7] For an impression of Norwich as a medieval artistic centre see *Medieval Art in East Anglia 1300-1520,* ed. P. Lasko and N. J. Morgan (Norwich, 1973).

[8] For Julian's more vivid sense of colour in the later text, cf. description of the Fiend's appearance added in *S* text of ch. 66: 'The color was rede like the tilestone whan it is new brent with blak spots therin like blak freknes fouler than the tile stone' (f. 48[r]).

[9] 'Our Lord shewid hym ful heyly in comfort to us for homlyhed . . . And God called hy*m* Sey*n*t John of Beverley pleynly as we doe with a full glad swete chere shewyng that he is a ful hey seynt in hevyn in his syght' (ch. 38; f. 25[r]).

[10] What Geoffrey Shepherd has succinctly called 'making melos out of memory'. Cf. his most penetrating discussion of Julian in 'The Nature of Alliterative

Poetry in Late Medieval England', *Proceedings of the British Academy,* lvi (1970), pp. 69-70.

[11] e.g. Sloane ch. 11; ch. 36; or in the *S* amplification on the words 'Lo how I loved thee' in the 10th shewing (ch. 24).

[12] e.g. the reference to *enclosing* in ch. 5 is present in *A* and *S*, but the use of the idea in ch. 6 is added in the later text.

[13] Opening the 6th shewing *A* reads: 'Aftyr this oure lorde sayde: I thanke the of thy servyce & of thy trauayle & na*m*ly in though' (f. 102[v]; ch. VIII in Harford, ch. IX in Reynolds). In *S* the mention of *servyce* is omitted, but replaced with an idea of the Lord and servant relationship: 'After this our Good Lord seid: I thanke the of thy travel & namely of thy youthe. And in this myn understondyng was lifted up into hevyn where I saw our Lord as a Lord in his owne house which hath clepid al his derworthy servants & freinds to a solemne feste' (ch. 14; f. 12[r]).

[14] Ch. 59 ff. For a general discussion see A. Cabassut, 'Une dévotion médiévale peu connue', *Revue d' Ascétique et de Mystique,* XXV (1949), 234-45.

Jennifer P. Heimmel (essay date 1982)

SOURCE: "Culmination of the Tradition in Julian and her *Revelations*" in *"God Is Our Mother": Julian of Norwich and the Medieval Image of Christian Feminine Divinity,* pp. 46-69, Institut für Anglistik und Amerikanistik Universitat Salzburg, 1982, pp. 46-69.

[*In the following excerpt, Heimmel credits Julian with being the first Christian writer to synthesize a cohesive image of "God the mother" from the suggestions of feminine divinity scattered throughout the Bible and other traditional sources.*]

It was not until approximately 1393 that the medieval image of a Christian feminine divinity reached its culmination in the single work of an English anchoress and mystic. Despite the setting of the concept of the motherhood of God by numerous preceding and contemporary authors in an already established tradition, it is Julian of Norwich who gives this idea a full birth in the way no other writer had. She does so in her revised version of the **Revelations of Divine Love**.

Four manuscripts are extant today of Julian's **Revelations.** This is a relatively small amount when compared to the number of surviving copies of the writings of other great mystics of the day. Walter Hilton's *Scale of Perfection* has over forty extant manuscripts for Book I and at least twenty-four for Book II.[1] There are twenty-six extant manuscripts in England of

Richard Rolle's *Incendium Amoris.*[2] There also still survive seventeen different texts of the *Cloud of Unknowing.*[3]

The oldest of the four manuscripts of the *Revelations* is the fifteenth century Amherst MS in the British Museum. It is of a shorter version which was apparently written immediately after the visions were received. The other three manuscripts record a longer version of the same revelations written some twenty years after the experience and incorporating the insights derived from thosesubsequent years of meditation. Of these, there is one from the seventeenth century in the Bibliothèque Nationale in Paris. The other two are Sloane Manuscripts No. 2499 and No. 3705 of the seventeenth and eighteenth centuries, respectively, and both are presently located in the British Museum. These surviving manuscripts contain much of what is known of the author of the **Revelations.**

External references to Julian of Norwich include four wills of the years 1393/4, 1404, 1415, and 1416, in which money was left to the anchoress at St. Julian's Church. In each of these a Julian is mentioned by name and the third also makes reference to an Alice, her serving maid.[4] In the *Book of Margery Kempe,* as earlier mentioned, there is a record of Margery's visit and conversation with Julian at Norwich when Julian was approximately seventy-one years of age. Also, in 1413 the scribe of the shorter version prefaced the work with the information that this was a vision shown by the goodness of God to "a deuoute Woman and her Name is Iulyan that is recluse atte Norwyche and ʒitt on lyfe."[5] Beyond these, there is no further external record of Julian's life.

From the surviving manuscripts come Julian's own words concerning the specific experience which was the basis for her writings. She reveals that in her youth she had asked for three gifts from God: first, she wanted to share in Christ's passion; second, to suffer physically a serious illness almost to the point of death at the age of thirty; and third, to receive the three wounds of contrition, compassion, and longing for God. On a Friday morning, May 13, 1373 at the age of thirty and a half, her prayers were answered. She was struck with an acute illness which grew steadily worse. Three days later she received the last rites and three days after that she became paralyzed from the waist down, her sight began to fail, and she was unable to speak. Her priest came and brought a crucifix which he placed before her fixed eyes. As she gazed on it and believed she was about to die, suddenly all her pain disappeared. She remembered her youthful petitions and as she gazed at the crucifix it appeared to come to life with blood streaming down from the crown of thorns. For the next five hours, from approximately four o'clock till past nine of that morning, she experienced fifteen visions in sequence. At that point Julian's own sufferings re-

turned and caused a temporary lack of faith in what she had seen. While asleep, she dreamed of the devil attempting to strangle her. After awakening and experiencing smoke, heat, and stench apparent to no one else, she lost all sense of illness. Her faith in the truth of her visions returned and that night Julian experienced the sixteenth and last revelation. The short text includes the additional information that her mother was present along with the others at her bedside.

Of other details beyond this central experience of her life, Julianwrites very little. She begins the second chapter of the long text with the curious statement that: "This reuelation was made to a symple creature vnlettryde" (II, Ch. 2, p. 285). However, there is nothing definitely known of her place of birth, family, upbringing, or education beyond the knowledge reflected in the **Revelations.** The existing evidence of the wills reveals that she was enclosed in the cell attached to the parish church of St. Julian at Norwich, which belonged to the Benedictine monastery at Carrow. Therefore, much of the manner of her subsequent solitary life can be deduced from the pattern set down in the *Ancrene Riwle.* In 1670, Serenus Cressy published the first printed edition of Julian's work. In his own introduction, however, he admits his inability even at that time to discover anything concerning Julian further than what is in the book itself.

Despite the lack of any extensive external knowledge into more precise information on Julian's life and background, this woman must stand out clearly beyond all her predecessors and contemporaries as well when it comes to the feminine representation of a Christian God in literature. What singles Julian of Norwich out from the other mystics of the Middle Ages who have spoken of the maternal aspects of Christ's love is not simply the concept itself, but the encompassing, developed, and integral image that she makes of it. She exceeds all others by her development of the idea in the **Revelations** with new length, innovation, and directness.

For Julian the statement of God's maternity is no simple invocation or comparison, but a repeated insistent reality. It is clearly a form of relationship which finds a natural and essential place in her thoughts and expression. Although there is no explicit evidence other than the one reference which singles out her own mother who stands among the others attentive by her sick bed, one can realize from the **Revelations** the lasting and positive impression that the mother-child relationship must have had on her. This is evidenced in such statements as, "To the properte of moderhede longyth kynd, loue, wysdom and knowyng" (II, Ch. 60, pp. 598-99) and "The moders seruyce is nerest, rediest and suerest: nerest for it is most of kynd, redyest for it is most of loue, and sekerest for it is most of trewth" (II, Ch. 60, p. 595). The portrayed image of the mother-child relationship is one of the most prevalent found in the *Revelations* and one which she applies to church, Mary, and natural mothers, as well as to her divinity. For Julian, there is ultimately no human relationship able to give an idea more exact and complete of the love of God than feminine maternal love.

Julian strikes clearly away from the traditional at the outset. Her concept of the motherhood of God is the first among her many predecessors and contemporaries which is not limited to one, or several brief passages, or even to a lengthy but single prayer.Rather, shortly following the pivotal and central chapter of her work, Julian devotes some four chapters almost exclusively to the development of this idea. These are chapter 58 through 61. Moreover, there are preceding and subsequent references throughout the work which lead up to, reecho, and reenforce the divine and maternal image as found in these chapters.

In addition, in contrast to such as Anselm and Marguerite who would restrict the title to the second person of the Trinity, or even Mechtilde who would include the third person, Julian seems to find in the title "mother" a more encompassing symbolic association. The very word seems to have been special to her. Julian uses the word "moder" with some few variations such as "moderhede" or "moderly" some eighty-three times throughout the *Revelations.* Of this amount Julian attributes the title nine times to Mary and four times to Holy Church. She also uses it not as a title but simply to refer to natural human mothers and the general idea of motherhood. The overwhelming majority of her references, however, attribute the title to none other than her God in all the persons. Over thirty of these references she specifically associates with Jesus Christ as the second person of the Trinity. Julian's numerical division of her use of the title accords well with her expressed belief, "Thys feyer louely worde: Moder, it is so swete and so kynde in it selfe that it may not verely be seyde of none ne to none but of hym and to hym that is very mother of lyfe and of alle" (II, Ch. 60, p. 598).

Another difference which distinguishes Julian in the original treatment she gives to this concept is her directness. No other orthodox Christian writer in this tradition has been as explicit or emphatic in the expression of God's maternity. To Julian, God is never simply "like" a mother. For her, he is a mother and the most ultimate of mothers. In her use of this title, Julian passes beyond the more typical similes of Biblical, patristic, and other mystical writers to the far more vivid and equating forms of metaphoric relationship. That Julian was capable of creating striking similes is evident from numerous examples in her work such as: "Holy chyrch shalle be shakyd in sorow and anguyssch and trybulacion in this worlde as men shakyth a cloth

in the wynde" (II, Ch. 28, p. 408). This makes it all the more astounding that Julian never states anywhere that God is "like" a mother, or does things "as" a mother would. Julian has deliberately chosen metaphor over simile for this image.

Julian employs three forms to express this relationship. The most common link between the two concepts of God and mother in Julian's prose is the direct and equating verb "is" as in "god is oure mother" (II, Ch. 59, p. 591), or "oure savyoure is oure very moder" (II, Ch. 57, p. 580). The relationship is also drawn through the use of the appositive as in "very moder Jhesu" (II, Ch. 63, p.616), or "oure moder, Cryst" (II, Ch. 83, p. 724). Julian's final method is to substitute the title of mother in place of God when she implies a clear reference to the divinity as in "oure mother werkyth" (II, Ch. 59, p. 591) or "prayeng to oure moder of mercy and pytte" (II, Ch. 59, p. 592).

There are only two apparent exceptions to this direct and equating style that Julian uses for the image, in "wyll he that we done as the meke chylde" (II, Ch. 61, pp. 605-606) and "dreed that makyth vs hastely to fle fro alle that is nott goode and falle in to oure lordes brest, as the chylde in to the moders arme" (II, Ch. 74, p. 675). On closer investigation, however, one discovers that in these instances the "as" refers not to God but to the "we" of the relationship and is concerned with our role as child rather than God's as mother.

The final and most important distinction through which Julian must stand out from the earlier tradition of feminine and maternal God is in the completeness which she gives to her vision. For the first time all facets of the earlier examples come together in a single author. It is as though Julian herself had sought out this form and deliberately chosen to incorporate each within her own work. There is but one exception. The *Revelations* does not have a single reference to God as the mother hen of Matthew's gospel. This is all the more interesting since this example is second in frequency throughout all the earlier sources of the tradition only to the picture of a nursing mother-God. Apparently, Julian had no interest in the image which likened God to a feminine maternal bird. In contrast, the portrait of God as a human mother can be easily seen in the *Revelations* to have fascinated her from every aspect.

Within the longer .text of her writings Julian includes nearly every previously encountered form and variation of this tradition. The extensiveness of her usage ranges from the standard images, such as that of a nursing mother-God found in almost every earlier Biblical, patristic, and mystrical writer, to the less common image, such as that of the mother-God who feeds the child with the sacrament of the Eucharist which was found earlier only in St. John Chrysostom. Julian states: "oure precyous moder Jhesu, he may fede vs wyth hym selfe, and doth full curtesly and full tendyrly with the blessyd sacrament, that is precyous fode of very lyfe" (II, Ch. 60, pp. 596-97).

In the manner established by the Bible, St. Augustine, St. Bonaventure, Albert the Great and others, Julian also repeatedly declares that the wisdom of God is our mother, as in "the depe wysdome of \??\e trynyte is our moder" (II, Ch. 54, p. 563). Unlike many of her predecessors as found in this tradition, however, Julian goes well beyond the more conventional expression of God's femininity as limited only to the role of divine wisdom.

In the manner of the apocryphal *Acts of Peter,* Mechtild von Hackeborn, and the anonymous English litany, Julian further includes not one but three passages which formally list God as mother among the other human family roles. One example of this is: "god enjoyeth that he is our fader, and god enjoyeth that he is our moder, and god enjoyeth that he is our very spouse" (II, Ch. 52, p. 546). Another example is: "He is oure moder, broder and savyoure" (II, Ch. 58, p. 584).

Julian also follows in the terminology of the Bible, Albert the Great, the Monk of Farne, and Marguerite d'Oyngt, by asserting God as more a mother than our human parent, as in "though oure erthly moder may suffer hyr chylde to peryssch, oure hevynly moder Jhesu may nevyr suffer vs that be his chyldren to peryssch" (II, Ch. 61, pp. 604-605). Although in this assertion Julian is following earlier tradition, her emphasis is singularly more positive than some of her predecessors. She does not, like Marguerite d'Oyngt, emphasize the inferiority of the earthly mother who is rejected for Christ as mother. Julian equally knows and affirms the superiority of God. Yet Julian's love of the superior mother, God, does not cause her to reject but rather to incorporate and confirm her continued love of earthly mother and world as integral parts of that same God's creation.

The extensive thoroughness with which Julian has followed and gathered the earlier examples of this tradition is clear from the ***Revelations.*** Julian, however, has done far more in her book than to merely lump all her source examples together. In many cases she progresses beyond a simplistic statement or idea with a richer development and innovation than previously encountered.

In the ***Revelations*** Julian presents her vision of God in the feminine maternal role not in the isolated fragments of the tradition but in a complete connected cycle of life from before birth through after death. Julian's majestic vision proceeds through all the various stages of: enclosure and growth within the womb; the trauma of labor and birth; the suckling of the infant and feeding of the child; the care and education of the older child; the setting of examples and disciplining of the child; the washing, healing, forgiving, and comforting of the child as it matures; and the continual loving, touching, and guiding of the child even to the point of its own death which becomes in turn a rebirth and return to the original womb.

The imagery begins with our original placement and growth within God which is envisioned in terms of the child within the womb. Julian goes beyond the single womb references of Saint Ambrose and the Monk of Farne to create her own vivid picture through repeated suggestive wording. Julian many times in her work echoes the Biblical phrasing of Saint Paul who tells how the children arerooted and built up in God when she speaks of the maternal God's children who are "so depe growndyd in god" (II, Ch. 56, p. 570) and "kyndely rotyd in god" (II, Ch. 56, p. 571), whose "lyfe is alle grounded and rotyd in loue" (II, Ch. 49, p. 505), and of the mother "Crist, in whom oure hyer party is groundyd and rotyd" (II, Ch. 57, p. 578) and "oure moder" who is "the / seconde person of the trynyte" and "in whom we be groundyd and rotyd" (II, Ch. 58, p. 586). Another favorite wording Julian employs to evoke the womb-like description is her repetition of the mother-God in whom the children are enclosed. Examples of this are: "our moder, in whom we be closyd" (II, Ch. 54, p. 563), "Crist, vs alle havyng in hym that shall be savyd" (II, Ch. 55, p. 565), "we be all mercyfully beclosyd in the myldehed of god" (II, Ch. 49, p. 507), "oure god verely, that hath vs all in hym selfe beclosyde" (II, Ch. 6, p. 306), "out of whom we be all come, in whom we be alle enclosyd" (II, Ch. 53, pp. 557-58), "he vs all havyng beclosyd in hym" (II, Ch. 57, p. 580), and others.

Still further descriptive of the child's development within the womb, Julian speaks of the children who are "beclosyd in hym in to the tyme that we be waxyn and growyn" (II, Ch. 55, p. 567), and of "oure very moder Jhesu" who "susteyneth vs with in hym in loue and traveyle, in to the full tyme" (II, Ch. 60, pp. 595-96). God is further the mother to whom the child is "so fastned to him that ther be right nought that is made betweene my god and me" (II, Ch. 5, p. 300), to whom the child is "knytt to hym in the makyng" (II, Ch. 53, p. 560), and to whom the child comes "naked" (II, Ch. 5, p. 302), as well as the one within whom the child was "tresured in god and hyd" (II, Ch. 53, p. 560), and from whom "we haue oure beyng of hym, where the ground of moderhed begynnyth" (II, Ch. 59, p. 589).

The imagery of God as mother continues from the womb into labor and birth. Her references to the maternal God who endures labor pains to give birth surpass in their directness the comparative example of the Bible. As with Saint Anselm and Marguerite d'Oyngt, Julian equates Christ's suffering and death on the cross with the labor necessary for the maternal God to give birth.

While Julian adds more detail to this image than Anselm, she does not give as gruesome a picture of the suffering as Marguerite and chooses rather to emphasize the unceasing love which motivates the maternal God to endure. Of Christ's labor, Julian writes, "he abydyth / vs, monyng" (II, Ch. 80, p. 710) and "it passyth nevyr fro Crist tylle what tyme he hath brought vs oute" (II, Ch. 80, p. 711). Again Julian compares the crucifixion to the pains of labor when she writes that Christ sustains us within himself:

> . . . in to the full tyme he wolde suffer the sharpyst thornes and grevous paynes that evyr were or evyr shalle be, and dyed at the last. And whan he had done, and so borne vs to blysse, yett myght nott all thys make a seeth to his mervelousloue. And that shewd he in theyse hye ovyrpassyng wordes of loue: If I myght suffer more I wold suffer more. He myght no more dye, but he wolde nott stynte werkyng.

> (II, Ch. 60, p. 596)

Julian also composes a striking paradoxical statement which envisions the subsequent process of birth in both a stasis and perpetual production: "oure savyoure is oure very moder, in whome we be endlessly borne and nevyr shall come out of hym" (II, Ch. 57, p. 580). Our mother, Christ, is further the one who has "borne vs to blysse" (II, Ch. 60, p. 596), the one who "quyckyd vs, and in his blessyd dyeng vppon the crosse he bare vs to endlesse lyfe" (II, Ch. 63, pp. 616-17), the "god in whome we haue oure beyng" (II, Ch. 59, p. 592), and "oure very moder Jhesu, he alone beryth vs to joye and to endlesse levyng" (II, Ch. 60, p. 595). In reference to "oure bodely forthbryngyng" Julian adds that "it is he that doth it" (II, Ch. 60, p. 599), that "all his blessyd chyldren whych be come out of hym by kynd shulde be brougt agayne in to hym by grace" (II, Ch. 64, p. 619), and that "of this swete feyer werkyng / he shalle nevyr ceese nor stynte, tylle all his deerwurthy chyldren be borne and brought forth" (II, Ch. 63, p. 616).

After labor and birth, as the mother provides nourishment for the infant, so too does Julian's image develop in this manner. She presents an image of God who, from the time of the labor of the death on the cross and our birth to life, has continually fed us as a mother should:

> And from that tyme, and now and evyr shall in to domysday, he fedyth vs and fordreth vs, ryght as the hye souereyne kyndnesse of moderhed wylle, and as the kyndly nede of chyldhed askyth.

> (II, Ch. 63, p. 617)

This same maternal God is also the one who feeds the children since "hym behovyth to fynde vs, for the deerworthy loue of moderhed hath made hym dettour to vs" (II, Ch. 60, p. 596).

Julian more specifically approaches the tradition's popular image of a nursing mother-God when she speaks of the children who obtain nourishment from God by "hym swetly swelwyng" (II, Ch. 43, p. 481) and from the "dyversytes flowyng oute of hym" so that of all the children "none shalle be perysschyd" (II, Ch. 57, p. 577). Julianalso uses the still more particular image in which the nursing child drinks not the milk but the blood of Christ as nourishment as found earlier in St. John Chrysostom, St. Bonaventure, the Blessed Angela de Foligno, the Monk of Farne, and the treatise entitled, "A talkyng of þe loue of God." Julian speaks of Christ's "blessyd / blode . . . ther is no lycour that is made that lykyth hym so wele to yeue vs. For it is most plentuous, as it is most precious" (II, Ch. 12, p. 343).

In two further passages Julian deliberately deviates from the more common from of her many predecessors in this tradition who have already spoken vividly of the nursing breasts of Christ by branching out into new and more significant directions. Julian portrays our mother, Jesus, who does not simply give the child suck of milk, but rather feeds us still more directly with God's own flesh and with the food of very life in the sacraments:

> The moder may geue her chylde sucke hyr mylke, but oure precyous moder Jhesu, he may fede vs / wyth hym selfe, and doth full curtesly and full tendyrly with the blessyd sacrament, that is precyous fode of very lyfe; and with all the swete sacramentes he systeynyth vs full mercyfully and graciously.

> (II, Ch. 60, pp. 596-97)

Julian again pictures our mother, Jesus, who does not merely lay the child to the breast, but rather more intensely leads us actually within his breast through the blessed wound of his open side:

> The moder may ley hyr chylde tenderly to hyr brest, but oure tender mother Jhesu, he may homely lede vs in to his blessyd brest by his swet opyn syde.

> (II, Ch. 60, p. 598)

In this cycle of God as mother, Julian further continues and develops the image past infancy. In what is a new development for the tradition, she describes her divinity in terms of a mother who sets a good and virtuous example for the child as it grows, who cares for and teaches the young child right from wrong, and who expects obedience as it grows and begins to learn.

God is therefore a mother who far beyond carrying, giving birth, and feeding the child, is always "to vs dyverse manner werkyng" (II, Ch. 58, p. 586). This is a mother who ever "woot and knowyth the neyde of hyr chylde, she kepyth it full tenderly, as the kynde and condycion of moderhed wyll" (II, Ch. 60, p. 599): who fosters in the child:

> . . . myldnesse and mekenesse and all þe feyer vertuse that long to chyldren in kynde. For kyndly the chylde dysperyreth nott of the moders loue, kyndely the chylde presumyth nott of it selfe, kyndely the chylde louyth the moder and eche one of them other. Theyse be as feyer vertues with alle other that be lyke, wher with oure hevynly moder is servyd and plesyd.
>
> (II, Ch. 63, p. 617)

and who:

> . . . kyndelyth oure vnderstondyng . . . prepareth oure weyes . . . esyth oure consciens . . . conforntyth oure soule . . . lyghteth oure harte and gevyth vs in party knowyng and louyng . . . with curtesse mervelyng . . . and makyth us to loue all that he louyth for his loue, and to be well apayde with hym and with alle his werkes.
>
> (II, Ch. 61, pp. 601-602)

A number of passages in the **Revelations** refer to Christ, whom Julian has consistently identified with the maternal image, in the role of teacher. This is evident in: "Crist hym selfe is ground of alle the lawes . . . he taught vs to do good not evylle" (II, Ch. 40, pp. 458-59), "he / wylle we be his helpers, gevyng to hym alle oure entent, lernyng his lawes, kepyng his lore, desyeryng that alle be done that he doth, truly trustyng in hym" (II, Ch. 57, p. 581), and "And yf we wett nott how we shall do alle this, desyer we of oure lorde, and he shalle lerne vs" (II, Ch. 77, p. 695). This is a teacher who does not merely speak, but sets the clear precedent for the child to follow, as in: our mother Christ who "doyth to vs as he techyth vs to do; for he wylle that we be lyke hym" (II, Ch. 40, p. 459), and "And the blessyd creatures þat shalle be in hevyn with hym with out / ende, he wylle haue them lyke vnto hym selfe in alle thing" (II, Ch. 77, p. 695). Julian frequently refers to this exemplary mother as "all wysdom" and she explicitly states: "Thus workyth oure moder in mercy to all his belovyd chyldren whych be to hym buxom and obedyent" (II, Ch. 58, p. 586).

Yet another avenue of maternal care which the **Revelations** includes is that of the mother's washing of the child. A single earlier example is in the lyric "Ihesu, thi swetnes wha moghte it se" where the poet in two lines speaks of the mother who even before the child's birth washed it clean of Adam's sin through baptism. Julian speaks more extensively of "oure moder" whose "deerworthy blode and precious water is plentuous to make

vs feyer and clene" (II, Ch. 61, pp. 607-608); of the "precious plenty of his dereworthy blode" which "ovyrflowyth all erth, and is redy to wash / all creatures of synne" (II, Ch. 12, p. 344); of the unclean soul which "oure derewurthy mother" shall make clean when "he shall all besprynkyl vs in his precious blode" (II, Ch. 63, pp. 615-16); and of the mother, Christ, whom we need but to "touch" and "we shalle be made cleene" (II, Ch. 77, p. 694).

The cycle of maternal imagery continues on as the child grows still older and Julian's divine mother changes tactics, but not love. Julian both incorporates the attributes of the maternal God found in the earlier *Ancrene Riwle* and expands upon them. In the *Ancrene Riwle,* the mother indulged in playful games of hide and seek with the young child, so that the child seemed left alone and the grace and comfort of the mother was apparently withdrawn. Yet this was actually done out of love for the child rather than through a lack of it. In a similar manner Julian's image of God as mother of the growing child also with-draws out of love and concern for the child's development. This mother further allows the child to deal with some mishaps apparently on its own while she remains ever ready in the background in case the child should come to any real harm.

When the child is "wexid of more age" Julian, therefore, reveals God as mother who at times "sufferyth / it that it be cha(s)tised in brekyng downe of vicis, to make the chylde receyve vertues and grace" (II, Ch. 60, p. 599). Of this same mother, Julian further states: "By hys sufferannce we falle . . . and by mercy and grace we be reysyd to manyfolde more joy" (II, Ch. 35, p. 435) as well as:

> And yett aftyr thys he sufferyth some of vs to falle more hard and more grevously then evyr we dyd before, as vs thyngkyth. / And than ween we that be nott alle wyse that all were such that we haue begonne. But it is nott so, for it nedyth vs to falle, and it nedyth vs to see it; for yf we felle nott, we shulde nott knowe how febyll and how wrechyd we be of oure selfe, nor also we shulde not so fulsomly know þe mervelous loue of oure maker.
>
> For we shalle verely see in hevyn without ende þat we haue grevously synned in this lyfe; and not withstondyng this we shalle verely see that we were nevyr hurt in his loue, nor we were nevyr the lesse of pryce in his syght. And by the assey of this fallyng we shalle haue an hygh and a mervelous knowyng of loue in god without ende; for hard and mervelous is that loue whych may nottnor wyll not be broken for trespas.
>
> (II, Ch. 61, pp. 602-603)

In regard to mercy which "longyth to moderhode in tender loue" Julian adds that it "sufferyth vs to feyle"

but "in all this the swet eye of pytte and of loue dep-
erteth nevyr from vs, ne the werkyng of mercy cesyth
nott" (II, Ch. 48, pp. 501-502). Although this process
of falling is for the child's own good, Julian makes
clear that the heavenly mother never really abandons
the child as in:

> The moder may suffer the chylde to fall some tyme
> and be dyssesed on dyuerse manner, for the one
> profyte, but she may nevyr suffer that ony manner
> of perell come to her chylde for loue. And though
> oure erthly moder may suffer hyr chylde to peryssch,
> oure hevynly moder Jhesu may nevyr suffer vs that
> be his chyldren to peryssch.

(II, Ch. 61, pp. 604-605)

Always the motivation of Julian's maternal God remains constant since:

And if we feele vs nott than esyd, as sone be we suer
that he vsyth the condycion of a wyse moder. For yf he
see that it be for profyte to vs to morne and to wepe,
he sufferyth with ruth and pytte in to the best tyme for
loue.

(II, Ch. 61, pp. 606-607)

When the child in the process of growing up involves
itself in more serious difficulties, Julian reveals other
aspects of this image of God as mother. In the *Revelations* God is also a mother who forgives the child for
wrongdoing, who listens attentively to the problems,
questions, and apologies of the child and gives comfort; and who, through an imagery of healing, assists
when the child has hurt itself and restores it to a healthful life.

An earlier example of the maternal God who is ready
to forgive and comfort the child who has done wrong
is in the treatise "A talkyng of the loue of God." Here
the author describes the widespread arms of Christ on
the cross ever ready to comfort the sinful child. This
mother needs but to hear the child crying in distress
and shewill take it in her arms, kiss and console it, ask
it the nature of the problem, and then give it her breast
to still its tears. In the *Ancrene Riwle* there is this same
picture of the mother who will run to the crying child,
hug it, kiss it, and wipe its eyes.

Julian expands on this pattern when her divine mother
gives "vnderstandyng" through "swet worde" (II,
Ch. 60, p. 598); when the mother "reformyth vs
and restoryth" (II, Ch. 58, p. 586); and when the
mother in the time of "oure fraylte and oure fallyng"
continues to "kepyth vs in this tyme as tendyrly and as
swetely . . . as / he doth when we be in most solace

and comfort" (II, Ch. 62, p. 610). This is the mother
from whom we must ask forgiveness "myghtly prayeng
to oure moder of mercy and pytte" (II, Ch. 59, p. 592),
and the one to whom in times of trouble "mekely make
we oure mone to oure derewurthy mother" (II, Ch. 63,
p. 615). This mother does not wish the child to run
away out of dread and shame for his failings, but rather wishes the child to quickly run towards the mother
for help and to trust in her love as in: "That dreed that
makyth vs hastely to fle fro alle that is nott goode and
falle in to oure lordes brest, as the chylde in to the
moders arme" (II, Ch. 74, p. 675) and:

> But oft tymes when oure fallyng and oure
> wrechydnes is shewde vs, we be so sore adred and
> so gretly ashamyd of oure selfe that vnne this we
> witt wher we may holde vs. But then wylle nott
> oure curtesse moder that we flee away, for hym
> were nothing lother; but he wyll than that we vse
> the condicion of a chylde. For when it is dissesyd
> and a feerd, it rynnyth hastely to the moder; and if
> it may do no more, it cryeth on the mother for helpe
> with alle myghtes. So wyll he that we done as the
> meke chylde, seyeng thus: My kynd moder, my
> gracyous moder, my deerworthy moder, haue mercy
> on me. I haue made my selfe foule and vnlyke to
> thee, and I may not nor canne amende it but with
> thyne helpe and grace . . . And he wylle then \??\at
> we vse the properte of a chylde, that evyr / more
> kyndly trustyth to the loue of the moder in wele and
> in woo.

(II, Ch. 61, pp. 605-607)

Although the mother may punish the child, it will be
tempered rather than severe since "he is all wysdom,
and can ponyssch me wysely" yet "whan we wyll
wylfully and gladly take the skorgyng and the
cha(s)tyssyng" then "it shalle be fulle tendyr and fulle
esy" (II, Ch. 77, pp. 691-92). Julian's maternal God
clearly takes greater delight in forgiving and comforting the child as in: "My dere darlyng, I am glad thou
arte come to me in alle thy woe. I haue evyr ben with
the, and now seest thou me louyng, and we be onyd in
blysse. Thus are synnes forgevyn" (II, Ch. 40, p.
455);"And when we be fallen by freelte or blyndnes,
than oure curtesse lord touchyng vs steryth vs and
kepyth vs . . . but he wylle nott that we abyde ther-
with . . . he hath haste to haue vs to hym, for we are
his joy and his delyght" (II, Ch. 79, pp. 705-706); and
"yf we see verely that oure synne deserve it, 3ett hys
loue excusyth vs. And of hys gret curtesy he doth away
alle / oure blame, and beholdeth vs with ruth and pytte,
as children innocens and vnlothfulle" (II, Ch. 28, p.
411).

After forgiving and comforting the child who has fall-
en, Julian's divine mother has the equally important
task of restoring the child back to the healthy state of
a sinless life. Other than the Biblical allusions to this

maternal role, the one earlier reference in the tradition is that of St. Catherine of Siena where the nursing mother-God drinks the bitter medicine so that it may be transmitted to the child through her milk. In the *Revelations,* the mother-God is not only "oure medycyne" (II, Ch. 82, p. 718), but also "oure salue" (II, Ch. 79, p. 706), "the remedy" (II, Ch. 77, p. 693), and "the helth and the lyfe" (II, Ch. 60, p. 597) of the child. After the child has fallen into the hard injury of sin, it is this mother who will "make oure soule full softe and fulle mylde, and heele vs fulle feyer by processe of tyme" (II, Ch. 63, p. 616); who "thorow contrycion and grace" shall "perfetely cure vs" (II, Ch. 78, pp. 698-99); who "vsyth the very office of a kynde norysse, that hath not elles to done but to entende about the saluation of hyr chylde" (II, Ch. 61, p. 608); and whose "blessed woundes . . . be opyn and enjoye to hele vs" (II, Ch. 61, p. 608). As a result of this "helyng" (II, Ch. 48, p. 503) and of the "swete werkyng" of the mother, the children are ever "strenthyd" (II, Ch. 61, p. 602).

Julian further describes God in the **Revelations** as repeatedly expressing love for humanity through touch much as a mother does with her child. God is the one who: "touchyth vs fulle prevely" (II, Ch. 40, p. 454); "wylle geve vs grace to loue hym and cleve to hym" (II, Ch. 86, p. 732); "tendyrly . . . towchyth vs and blyssydfully callyth vs, seyeng in our soule: Lett me aloone, my derwurdy chylde" (II, Ch. 36, p. 439); "colleth vs and beclosyth vs for tendyr loue, that he may nevyr leue vs, and is more nere to vs than tonge may telle or harte may thyngke" (II, Ch. 72, pp. 661-62); "touchyng vs steryth vs and kepyth vs" (II, Ch. 79, p. 705); and "hastely . . . reysyth vs by his louely beclepyng and his gracyous touchyng" (II, Ch. 61, p. 602). God's children, in turn: "cleue to hym" (II, Ch. 34, p. 431, etc.): "reverently cleue to god" (II, Ch. 52, p. 551): "clevyng to his loue and to his goodnesse" (II, Ch. 82, p. 718); "clevyng to with feythfulle trust" (II, Ch. 74, p. 675); and need only to "Touch we hym, and we shalle be made cleene. Cleve we to hym, and we shalle be suer and safe from alle manner of peryllys" (II, Ch. 77, p. 694). Julian further makes this imagery more explicit when she speaks of the "swetgracious handes of oure moder" which always "be redy and diligent a bout vs" (II, Ch. 61, p. 608).

The **Revelations** further shows the cycle of the maternal God's activity throughout the child's life through an imagery suggestive of mother as unceasing guide for the child. God as the one who leads the child repeatedly along the safe and proper way is expressed in such examples as: "oure good lord contynually ledyth vs" (II, Ch. 48, p. 500); "he is with vs in erth, vs ledyng" (II, Ch. 52, p. 549); "oure tender mother Jhesu, he may homely lede vs in to his blessyd brest" (II, Ch. 60, p. 598); "Crist is oure wey, vs suerly ledyng" (II, Ch. 55, p. 565); "he is here with vs ledyng vs" (II,

Ch. 81, p. 714); "oure lorde is with vs, kepyng vs and ledyng in to fulhed of joy" (II, Ch. 77, p. 694); and "In whych endlesse loue we be ledde and / kepte of god, and nevyr shalle be lost" (II, Ch. 53, p. 559). There is an additional passage which is reminiscent of the tradition's earlier homily "An Bispel" in its use of light and dark imagery used to express God's guiding maternal care:

> Oure feyth is a lyght, kyndly comyng of oure endlesse day . . . in whych lyght oure moder, Cryst, and oure good lorde the holy gost ledyth vs in this passyng lyfe. This lyght is mesuryd dyscretly, nedfully stondy(ng) to vs in the nyght. The lyghte is cause of oure lyfe, the nyght is cause of oure payne and alle oure woo . . . Thus I sawe and vnderstode that oure feyth is oure lyght in oure nyght, whych lyght is god, oure endlesse day.

(II, Ch. 83, pp. 723-25)

No matter whether teaching, guiding, healing, touching, cleansing, feeding, or laboring to give birth, God is most significantly envisioned in the work by Julian as an ultimately loving mother. This love, just as it is the answerer of all at the end of the **Revelations,** through Julian's imagery extends even to the point of death and beyond. Through wording often recalling the scattered references of the Bible, Julian envisions a God who is not angry or powerful, but rather throughout the cycle found to be continually loving, sweet, and gentle. Julian states: "I saw no manner of wrath in / god" (II, Ch. 49, p. 506). Rather, Julian repeatedly attributes to God the title of "all loue" and speaks of the "endlesse loue" God has for the children. She further describes God with such terminology as: "lowest and mekest, hamlyest and curtysest" (II, Ch. 7, p. 314); "gentylle, curteyse, fulle swete" (II, Ch. 74, p. 676): and "Feyer and swete is our hevenly moder in \??\e syght of oure soule" (II, Ch. 63, p. 617). Julian's maternal God is one whose love is so great that: "we be endlesly onyd to hym in loue" (II, Ch. 49, p. 505): "we be brought agayne by themotherhed of mercy and grace in to oure kyndly stede, where we ware in, made by \??\e moderhed of kynd loue, whych kynde loue nevyr leevyth vs" (II, Ch. 60, p. 594); "he wylle haue alle oure loue fastenyd to hym" (II, Ch. 60, p. 600); and in this mother "alle the swete kepyng of loue . . . endlesly folowyth" (II, Ch. 59, p. 589). This marvelous love continues beyond death whether it be the death of the mother as in, "He myght no more dye, but he wolde nott stynte werkyng" (II, Ch. 60, p. 596), or the death of the child who is ultimately borne to bliss when at the end of life "oure very moder Jhesu, he alone beryth vs to joye and to endlesse levyng" (II, Ch. 60, p. 595).

Julian has drawn the cycle of active motherhood so perfectly that it becomes joined at the identical point of beginning and conclusion so that there is no beginning or end and the death and birth of the child become as one. Julian has pictured this in her work a number of times: in "all his blessyd chyldren whych be come out" of the divine maternal womb and yet must eventually return within that same womb when they shall "be brought agayne in to hym by grace" (II, Ch. 64, p. 619): in the mother in whom the children are "endlesly borne and nevyr shall come out" (II, Ch. 57, p. 580): and in that same mother "out of whom we be all come, in whom we be alle enclosyd, in to whom we shall all goo, in hym fyndyng oure full hevyn in everlastyng joy by the forseyeng purpose of alle the blessyd trynyte fro without begynnyng" (II, Ch. 53, pp. 557-58). Thus the image comes full circle to its completion, which viewed through Julian's eyes must be seen not as a conclusion but as a continually new beginning: "And than shall \??\e blysse of oure moderheed in Crist be new to begynne in / the joyes of oure fader god, whych new begynnyng shall last, without end new begynnyng" (II, Ch. 63, p. 618).

There is no single previous example which even begins to approach the depth with which Julian has explored the varied potentials of the image of a Christian maternal God. Only by combining the scattered suggestive examples of the Bible on the guiding, teaching, washing, healing, etc., as well as the more common nursing mother, can the reader establish a pattern for the complete maternal cycle of love and caring that Julian has created. But these diverse examples as earlier evidenced are not easily found within the more common image of the Old Testament male father-God, unless one is actively looking for them or receptive to them. That Julian had read the Bible in this searching receptive manner and been strongly influenced by these examples seems the logical conclusion, particularly when considering the many passages in the ***Revelations*** which echo Biblical wording and ideas.

In addition to the Bible, Julian clearly seems to have been influenced by at least some if not all of the earlier examples of this tradition. She seems further to have well used that earliertradition as a basis upon which to add her own length, elaboration, and new development. In an unprecedented manner she combines all of the tradition's divided fragments into a unified cohesive picture of active motherhood from birth until death. The result is her unique cyclical vision which powerfully presents the image of God as a mother to the read-er so throughly and naturally as to be readily accepted.

For reasons of her own, Julian chose to devote a great deal of her creative talent to this particular image. She developed the image not only through four main chapters, but further through echoing references forwards and backwards in her work. She strove with her innovatively direct and expansive style to reveal God as mother from every aspect of the human role. Her inter-

est and energy in this achievement enabled the centuries old tradition of a Christian feminine and maternal God to find its fullest development in fourteenth century England within her own ***Revelations of Divine Love.***

Notes

[1] Joseph E. Milosh, *The Scale of Perfection and the English Mystical Tradition* (Madison: University of Wisconsin Press, 1966), p. 3.

[2] *The Incendium Amoris of Richard Rolle of Hampole,* ed. Margaret Deanesly (Manchester, England: The University Press, 1915), p. xix.

[3] *The Cloud of Unknowing,* ed. Phyllis Hodgson, EETS, OS, No. 218 (1944; rpt. London: Oxford University Press, 1958), p. ix.

[4] *A Book of Showings to the Anchoress Julian of Norwich,* I, 33-34. All further references to this work appear in the text. The Shorter Version of the *Revelations* is found in Vol. I. The Longer Version is in Vol. II.

[5] Julian of Norwich, *A Revelation of Love,* ed. Marion Glasscoe (Exeter: University of Exeter Press, 1976), p. vii.

Ritamary Bradley (essay date 1984)

SOURCE: "Julian of Norwich: Writer and Mystic" in *An Introduction to Medieval Mystics of Europe,* edited by Paul E. Szarmach, State University of New York Press, 1984, pp. 195-216.

[*In the essay that follows, Bradley places Julian's writings within the context of the traditions of Christian mysticism and the canon of English literature.*]

Julian of Norwich is the first known woman of letters in English literature, and one is hard-put to find prose superior to hers in the Middle English period. She belongs, by right, to the mainstream of studies in literature and culture. This survey article undertakes to show that Julian deserves to be rated as a distinguished prose stylist and recognized as a gifted mystic. In support of this reading and in the light of emerging scholarship, I will examine Julian's ***Showings,*** first looking for its literary qualities, and then to its ideas and the account of Julian's experiences as they relate to mysticism. As background I will summarize what is known of Julian's life, and in an afterword take note of some signs of her influence among writers in modern times.

Julian's Life

Since Julian's book is practically the only source for reconstructing her life, it is scarcely a digression to begin with a short biography. (The only other sources are mentions in a few wills, a single contemporary witness, and what little is known of her surroundings and the life style of the anchoress, for whom there were specific rules.)[1] Julian was born in 1342 and died sometime after 1416. In her youth she heard the legend of St. Cecilia, the same story which Chaucer adapted in the Second Nun's Tale. Inspired to seek a deeper knowledge of the Passion of Jesus, Julian meditated on pictures and images of the crucifixion. In a prayer of petition she asked for three gifts from God: to understand his Passion, to suffer physically while still a young woman of thirty, and to have as God's gift three wounds. The first two prayers she left to God's will, but to the third she attached no condition:

> I developed a strong desire to receive three wounds, namely, the wound of true contrition, the wound of genuine compassion, and the wound of sincere longing for God. There was no proviso attached to this third prayer.[2]

After she had forgotten about the first two prayers, she fell into a sickness so severe that she seemed to be at the point of death. Surrounded by her mother and friends, probably in her home, she was visited by a priest who counselled her to look upon the crucifix. This became the occasion for fifteen showings, which included visions of the Passion of Christ. At the end of the day she said to another priest that she had raved and been in delirium. But when the priest took seriously her mention of the visions, she was ashamed that she herself was doubting them. During the night she experienced what seemed to be an attack of the fiend. She survived the ordeal, her illness subsided, and in a final visionshe became certain that her experiences were genuine and to be believed. She ascribed to them a threefold meaning:

> The first quality is the literal meaning of the words as I then received them; the second is the inner significance that I have discovered since; the third is the whole revelation itself, which, from beginning to end—covering the contents of this book—God in his goodness brings to mind, often and freely.[3]

Sometime after the revelations she became an anchoress living in a cell attached to the Church of St. Julian, Norwich, from which she is thought to have taken her name. (It was customary for anchoresses to take the name of the Church where they were enclosed.) It is probable that she was guided by a rule for anchoresses, such as the thirteenth-century *Ancrene Riwle*.[4] As an anchoress she wrote two accounts of her revelations, the second after some twenty years of reflection on what had occurred, moving from a position of insecurity in writing the Short Version, to meditative certainty in the Long Version.[5]

She also became a spiritual guide as a result of her life as an anchoress. Visitors could speak with her through one of the small windows of her room. (The other window opened into the Church, so that she could follow religious services.) One account of her spiritual counsel has survived, in the *Booke of Margery Kempe*. Margery, who sought out Julian in distinguishing the stirrings of grace from the deceptions of the devil, reports that the "anchoress was expert in such things and could give good counsel."[6] There is also internal evidence in the ***Showings*** that Julian meant to serve as a spiritual guide to others. She explains that "it is truly love which moves me to tell it to you, for I want God to be known and my fellow Christians to prosper. . . . "[7] And in another place she says: "I am not trying to tell the wise something they know already, but I am seeking to tell the uninstructed, for their peace and comfort."[8]

Julian in English Letters

Transmission of the Text: But it was not to be easy for Julian's book to reach the audience she envisioned. She herself was aware of one obstacle she faced in making her message known—that, as a woman, she was not likely to be considered expert in theological matters. Scholars are uncertain about the extent of her education, but she pleaded to be heard, against any objections that might arise:

> I am a woman, ignorant, weak and frail. But I know very well that what I am saying I have received by the revelation of him who is the sovereign teacher. . . . But because I am a woman, ought I therefore to believe that I should not tell you of the goodness of God? . . . [9]

The general disregard accorded the writings of women may have worked to keep Julian obscure, since she herself felt she must offer such a defense of her authority.

But another reason for the long delay in giving Julian her rightful place in English letters is rooted in the sparse manuscript tradition, and the difficulties the few remaining copies of her work present to scholars. Only six manuscripts have been located, and of these only two—Amherst (BL Addit. 37790) and the Westminster Cathedral copy of selected chapters—date before the sixteenth century. The short text exists only in Amherst, dating from around 1450. Westminster was not discovered until after World War II, in 1955, and only in the 1960's did the Upholland manuscript, containing excerpts from the ***Showings,*** come to light. It originated in the seventeenth century and is copied in four different hands. There is also a short quotation from Julian in Colwich Abbey MS 18. Long text copies are preserved in Sloane I (BL Sloane 2499), Paris (BN Fonds Anglais 40) of the seventeenth century, and

Sloane II (BL Sloane 3705), judged to be an eighteenth century imitation of a fifteenth century scribal hand. At this time there is still not firm agreement as to which manuscript should be considered the primary one for the long text, and hence there are problems over contested passages. Scholars generally agree though that the short text was written first, closer to the actual experience of the visions, and that the long text, while being faithful to the same facts, adds the insights gained from some twenty years of reflections.[10]

Those primarily responsible for transmitting Julian's text were the English Benedictines, exiled to the continent after the dissolution of the monasteries. The chaplain of the Benedictine nuns in exile at Cambrai, Father Augustine Baker, wrote back to England to Sir Robert Cotton, asking for a share in his rich library of spiritual writings known "in the olde tyme."[11] This request was in large part for the benefit of Dame Gertrude More, great-great granddaughter of Sir Thomas More, martyred chancellor under Henry VIII. These English Benedictines, it is believed, copied the complete versions of the long texts of the **Showings** that have been preserved. In addition, there is evidence that Julian's work was in the nuns' libraries of both the Cambrai and Paris foundations. From the exiled Benedictines also came the first printed text of the **Showings,** in 1670, edited by Dom Serenus Cressy, successor to Father Baker.

For two centuries this printed edition was virtually the only source of information on Julian's work. Then in the twentieth century many learned of Julian through the excellent translation made in 1901 from Sloane I by Grace Warrack, from Edinburgh, "who, suddenly, at the age of 46, produces this amazing book: a solid piece of independent research with excellent footnotes and cross references, a lucid introduction, and, above all, a wonderful feeling for the strengths and rhythms of Julian's prose."[12] Even now Warrack's edition stands as "an excellent introduction which has well stood the test of time, and has been used (not always with due acknowledgement) by many later writers."[13] Through the Cressy and Warrack texts many Catholics, Anglicans, and Protestants rediscovered Julian in the nineteenth and twentieth centuries, and for different and sometimes contradictory reasons, she began to gain an international audience.

The first major university research devoted to Julian is a Leeds University dissertation by Sister Anna Maria Reynolds, who produced a critical edition of the **Showings** in 1956, from all known manuscripts, with introduction, critical notes, and glossary. She edited the short and long version, including the Westminster chapters, and later published the short version in book form.[14] In 1978 Fathers Edmund Colledge and James Walsh completed a critical edition at the University of Toronto. (See bibliographical notes.) In recent years translations of both versions have begun to appear in English, French, German, and Italian.[15]

Language of the Showings

Since Julian was not a scholar she did not have, as Chaucer did, models of discourse drawn from Latin, French, or Italian. True, as has been mentioned, she probably knew the *Ancrene Riwle,* but that work does not provide the theological terms she needed. There is no evidence that she drew to any significant degree on the mystical writings of her time. Instead, she drew on the Scriptures directly, and on the everyday language of Norwich. For example, this is the way she described her vision of the bleeding head of Christ:

> Great drops of blood rolled down from the garland like beads, seemingly from the veins; and they came down a brownish-red colour—for the blood was thick—and as they spread out they became bright red, and when they reached his eyebrows they vanished. . . . They were as fresh and living as though they were real: their abundance like the drops of water that fall from the eaves during a heavy shower, falling so thickly that no one can possibly count them; their roundness as they spread out on his forehead were like the scales of herring.[16]

Certain commonly-used alliterative expressions occur in the **Showings,** but these do not point to any borrowings or specific influences. Among these expressions are "meke and mylde," "wele and wo," and "doubtefull drede." These same alliterative expressions occur in such medieval writings as *The Wohunge of Ure Lauerd, Hali Maidenhead,* and *Sawles Warde* of the thirteenth century, and in the *Lives* of St. Katherine, St. Margaret, and St. Juliana.[17]

Even without extensive knowledge of works in Middle English, however, the reader will find few difficulties in Julian's language, though a few words require defining. "Sensuality and substance," for example, designate, respectively, the human mental structure—all that depends on the body—and the spiritual structure—that which shares in the life of God. These terms relate to the history of humanity: sensuality and substance were broken off from one another by sin, leaving a state of disharmony, but they can achieve unity again through Jesus Christ, who was fully human, and took sensuality, while remaining grounded in the Trinity. "Ground" is used to identify this unity of Christ in the Trinity, in this sense meaning also the ultimate base whereby humanity is linked to God. The "ground of being" is that which knits the human soul to Christ and is therefore the soul's deepest center, the mystic's point of contact with God.

"Kind" or "kindly" is used with overtones from the modern sense, to connote compassion; and with dependence on the medieval sense, to denote an individual species or nature—though it must be remembered that "unmade kind" is God. "Homely" is paired with courtly to suggest familiar, hospitable, being at home with, and is thus in tension with attributes of dignity and restraint associated with knightly conventions. Julian perceived these characteristics as co-existing in God's revelation of himself to his creatures.

Terms used in Christian catechesis, such as the Trinity, the Incarnation, grace, and contrition, occur throughout the text, in senses close to those used in Langland's *Piers Plowman* and other contemporary medieval writings. But Julian taught a specific form of Christian theology, and therefore used some words with a special sense. For example, Adam means, in different contexts, the historical Adam of the Genesis account; Christ as the eternal Adam, first-born of all creatures, and the one in whom all humanity will be recapitulated; and even the total Adam, which is all humanity. And the word sin is used, not generally in a moral, but in an existential sense, connoting, in different parts of the *Showings,* non-being, a turning away from God, the consequence of not seeing God, a monstrosity contrary to human nature, a void where God is not, and all that is not good. Metaphorically sin is named a blindness, diverting one's sight from God, or a sickness. Once defined, these special terms, in their varied senses, add richness to Julian's text, without detracting from its unity of theme.

Rhetoric in the Showings

Julian used the common rhetorical devices employed by her contemporaries,[18] but of first significance is the overall rhetorical focus of her work, which distinguishes her from others of her time. Her text is set apart from other mystical tracts, not so much because of the person speaking, of whom so little is known, but because of the audience addressed. The practice in Julian's time of carefully ranking persons byprofession, position in religious orders or in the Church, or title in society frequently carried over into the life of devotion. The devout tried to achieve measurable progress, labeled by distinct degrees, as in William Langland's *Piers Plowman,* which uses the allegory of Do-Well, Do-Bet, Do-Best. But Julian spoke to all Christians. She spoke to all who are to be saved, men and women, without mention of grades, degrees of holiness, or hierarchical rank. The *Cloud of Unknowing,*[19] by contrast, has for its audience a young man spiritually advanced above the ordinary. Furthermore, the author of that tract cautioned that his book is only for those who have forsaken the active life and have espoused the contemplative life, given over primarily to prayer. Likewise, Richard Rolle's *Fire of Love* is for a special class of exercitants, all of whom must renounce the love of women.[20] But Julian's *Showings* are not alone for anchoresses, but for the whole Church—all who make up the invisible and corporate body whose mem-

bers will reach heaven (for those of the devil's party she has no revelation). She spoke to the person who had turned to God for one day of service or for a lifetime—all will share the bliss of heaven. This concept of equality, of universal love, permeates the treatise.

Furthermore, she meant by "all who are to be saved," not just individuals, no matter how numerous, but humanity corporately and collectively: all are one through their bond in the first-born of all that has been made—Christ—who is, in turn, grounded in the Trinity. Thus Julian is distinguished among her contemporaries by the audience she envisioned for her work.

Julian's treatise lends itself to literary as well as rhetorical analysis. One scholar has discovered, for example, that a musical dialectic pervades the treatise, stemming from concepts of looking, seeing, and beholding.[21] In whatever way one approaches the structure of the *Showings,* it becomes clear that literary devices bond with the underlying concepts and experiences. The most remarkable of these literary devices is an original parable added to the Long Version—the parable of the Lord and the Servant.

Julian as Mystic

The beginning reader of the *Showings* might do well to start with a study of this central parable of the Lord and the Servant and the attendant explication (chaps. 51-54). The total book might then be read in normal sequence. Repeated readings will unveil the essential ideas in Julian's mysticism. The text gives guidance as to the three ways in which Julian received her mystical knowledge:

> All this blessed teaching of our Lord was shown in three ways: by physical sight, by words formed in my intellect, and by spiritual sight. With regard to the physical sight I have related what I have seen as truthfully as I can. For the words I haverepeated them exactly as our Lord showed them to me. About the spiritual sight I have already said a fair amount, but I can never describe it fully. So I am prompted to say more about it, if God will give me grace.[22]

In the following section of this paper, then, I will deal: (1) with what Julian relates directly about her bodily visions and the words formed in her understanding; (2) with the metaphors and parables she employs, including the parable of the Lord and the Servant; and (3) with the overall question of Julian's mysticism.

The Experience of the Showings

Julian presents herself as one being continually taught by Christ, the divine teacher.[23] She learns progressively by attending to the bodily showings, by using her reason—sometimes to question, sometimes to relate one part of the revelations to another part—and also by opening her heart with desire and trust to the mysteries she cannot understand. This seeking, which sometimes breaks out into a beholding of divine wisdom and love, is sustained by persevering prayer.

In bodily visions Julian saw five phases of the Passion of Christ: his head bleeding from the garland of thorns; his face undergoing changes of color; his flesh marked with the scourging and the consequent profuse bleeding; his body drying from lack of moisture as it neared the moment of death; and the cloven heart, from which flowed an abundance of blood. These were only appearances, she insisted, for had the flow of blood been real, it would have saturated the bed. She also saw Christ transfigured in a glorified state.

The words formed in her understanding and the reflections and spiritual showings she reports are integral to all the sixteen showings. In the first revelation (Chap. 1-9), though visually she focuses on the crown of thorns, Julian understands in an interior way that the one who suffers is God and that he endures his pain for all God's people. Further, she knows that it is the Trinity which fills her heart with mystical joy. She thinks of this time of comfort as strength fortifying her for the hour of purifying struggle which she foresees may come. God Incarnate and the Trinity seem to her both homely and courteous. As an example of homely loving, she perceives that God enwraps us—clothes us—in his goodness. In fact, God is the goodness which is in all things as they touch and serve us. More comprehensively, in the vision of a little thing the size of a hazelnut, she sees that God is at work in all things that exist, making them, loving them, sustaining them. She arrives at the truth which Augustine had stressed in the *Confessions:* no one will be at ease or at rest in heart and soul, by seeking sufficiency in things that are made. Only God is rest. Her first explicit teaching about prayer comes also in this showing: prayer is cleaving to God's goodness—that which rightfully moves our desires. This goodness is at work for us in the lowliest of human needs and reaches to the true knowing of God himself.

Perhaps the most important line in the first revelation is: "For where Jesus is spoken of, the Blessed Trinity is always to be understood, as I see it" (Chap. 4).[24] Julian's mysticism takes its character from this belief:

> . . . For Julian the Incarnation "manifests" the Trinity: that is, the relationship between the divinity and the humanity of Christ, in which the Godhead dwells bodily in Christ, manifests the in-dwelling relationship of the Persons of the Godhead to one another. . . . The divine Love which impresses Julian in this vision is . . . evident in the presence of the whole Trinity to humanity, in the person of Christ. This is the Love which brings God to

man . . . his self-revelation, such that Julian herself is able to see the glory of God "without any intermediary."[25]

Yet God's love for us is beyond our knowing: there is no creature who can grasp this immeasurable divine love. The effect of the vision on Julian is that her compassion and charity for all her fellow Christians expands while she seems very little in her own sight. This effect is strengthened by a sight of Mary, the mother of God, as she was as a young girl. Then in a spiritual sight Julian sees in part the wisdom and truth of God reflected in Mary's soul. But even this highest of God's creatures remains entirely other than God himself.

In the second showing (Chap. 10), Julian contemplates the bruised face of Christ and reflects on the love which moved him to take on our broken, helpless condition in order to restore us to the divine likeness: his fair face was bruised and blackened so that our face, wounded by sin, might become fair with God's own likeness. In a section that echoes the spirit of Psalm 68, she sees herself in the depths of the sea, but she finds hope there in the sight of "hills and green dales." These are symbols that God is everywhere, leading to safety and providing sustenance for all those who trust him, however limited their experience of seeeing the glory of God.

Then—in the third revelation (Chap. 11)—Julian sees that God does all things, that all his works are good, ordained to a purpose, undisturbed by chance, and all is rightly accomplished, though, from our perspective, his purpose may seem blocked by evil. At this point she does not see the workings of creatures but only of God; and as for sin, she concludes that it has no substance or positive reality—"no being in kind."

Among the good deeds which God does (fourth revelation, Chap. 12)is giving us the plentiful waters of the earth for our service and bodily comfort. But it is his blood—which is a human substance—that by its power purifies from sin. It is poured out in a cleansing stream on all sinful creatures of good will, bursting the hellish bonds of the fiends, and in Christ's glorified body, praying for us to the Father. Christ's blood is an image for his life, and for his power to give and restore life.

In the fifth revelation (Chap. 13) Julian sees how this power of God frustrates the malice of the fiend, who is, in fact, powerless. (It was this malice of the fiend she had feared would mislead her at the hour of her death). But all the woe and tribulation he has occasioned will be turned into an increase of joy for Christ's lovers.

That joy will reach its fullness in heaven, as the sixth showing portrays (Chap. 14). All service of God will be rewarded eternally. Heaven is like a great feast to which God welcomes all his friends, moving among them in intimate communion, but with a royal demeanor. His fair face is the music of this feast, filling heaven with "a marvellous melody of endless love."

In revelation seven (Chap. 15), Julian finds this heaven in her own soul, which was flooded with gladness and peace, emanating from God's presence. She is thereby taught that even when the absence of God does not result from sin, the pain of that absence must be endured patiently in faith. There are prayers which are appropriate to these alternating states of comfort and desolation. While in peace she protests like St. Paul "that nothing shall separate me from the love of Christ"; and in desolation she cries out with St. Peter, "Lord, save me, I perish."

In the eighth and ninth showings (Chap. 16-23), she learns to choose Jesus for her heaven, even when she sees him only in his suffering state. The highest reality of the Passion is to realize that it is the work of the whole Trinity. Though "only the maiden's son suffered," it is God who suffered: the one-ing with the Godhead gave strength to the humanity of Christ to travail without measure out of love. Since in the Incarnation the Son of God took upon himself all mankind—human nature, body and mind, physical and spiritual humanity—and since he is the "remaking" of that humanity in his Passion, he has lifted human lives into the being of God.[26] He continues to suffer in the people who are one with him. As a further consequence of his bond with humanity, all those whom he leads to heaven are the sign of his victory—his crown. That is the meaning of the second garland of dried blood formed over the crown of thorns: it is his eternal triumph. Under those perspectives Julian continues to contemplate the Godhead in its manifestation in Christ and in its bonding with humankind. About the one-ing with humanity she says: "The whole Trinity was involved in the passionof Christ, giving us an abundance of virtue and grace by him. . . . " (Chap. 23).

Elsewhere Julian speaks of this whole work of the Trinity as nature (the Father), mercy (the Son), and grace (the Holy Ghost);[27] Pelphrey explains how this mystery affects human lives:

> . . . nature, mercy and grace work together, as the expressions of the Father, Son, and Spirit in our lives. In "nature" our capacity for God is established; in "mercy" this capacity is made an actuality, in the person of Christ; by "grace" it becomes true of ourselves . . . for Julian, nature itself turns toward God (for example, in the needs of our bodies, or in fear). In "mercy" God comes to meet humanity as a human being; and in "grace" we are enabled to respond to God.[28]

In the tenth, eleventh, and twelfth showings (Chap. 24-26), Christ further assures Julian of his love for mankind, whom he wills to bring to everlasting peace. Again, he relates to her not only courteously, but as a friend—as brother, savior, parent. As an example of full response to God Mary is shown again, this time not in bodily likeness but as a mirror of the Trinity, which is truth, wisdom, and charity (Chap. 25). The twelfth revelation is a profound mystical experience of Christ glorified.

Then the showings take a somewhat different turn. Revelations thirteen and fourteen (Chap. 27-63) deal with the obstacles on the human side for responding to mercy and grace, namely sin. These same revelations also treat of the means which open the way for receiving grace and comfort, especially prayer.

The problem of sin baffled Julian greatly—her own sin, the sin of mankind collectively, the sin of Adam, the sin of those to be damned. She put many troubling questions to herself and presented them in her prayer: Why was sin allowed? Why did she herself fall again and again? Why was not Adam's sin forestalled? How can it be that God's love never wavers, yet people are often alienated from him by their sin? If God loves us even in our sin, why do we blame ourselves, if he is not angry with us? How could anger be compatible with compassionate love? Even when reassured by the repeated promise that "all will be well," she asked how, then, there can be a hell for the damned, as her Church taught?

The words in her understanding let her comprehend that "sin is behovable"—that is, necessary. The key to the conflict, she learned, is in the first great secret, by which she means a mystery. The first secret is that all men are one man and one man is all men, with all that such a union implies. Our nature is wholly in God. The higher part is grounded and rooted in the Trinity; God is knit to the lower part in the Incarnate Word.

The meeting point of this union makes it possible for God always to love humanity, since he thereby loves Christ. Furthermore, in the perspective of eternity, he loves all that human beings will become, though we see them as they are in moments of time. Though sin is not to be taken lightly, there is no wrath in God—that is, no shifting, unpredictable, human-like displeasure. There is rather loving compassion, which is like what we know in human parents and marriage partners—father, mother, husband, wife.

This secret, though a mystery for us, has been made known for our belief. But there is a second great secret, which is a deed yet to be accomplished, and it will resolve the seeming impossibilities raised in her remaining questions. In some way, yet unknown, all that is good will be transformed—nothing will be lost or left behind—for God is the highest, the lowest, the all:

> God was revealing that he himself would do it: this deed with all its qualities already mentioned. . . . But what this deed was going to be was kept secret from me.[29]

In this context Julian heard again that all will be well, for he who made the greatest evil to be well—that is, Adam's sin—can make all else well. All manner of things will be well, and she herself, and her co-Christians, will see for themselves that all will be well (Chap. 27).

She is counseled not to try further to probe the hidden things of God in this regard. Instead, she is to heed the lesson she learned in the first revelation, that God himself is sufficient for her:

> And as long as we are in this life, whenever in our folly we turn to behold the reproved, tenderly our Lord toucheth us and blissfully claspeth, saying in our soul: "Let be, my love, my most dear child, and attend to me (for I am enough to thee), and take joy in thy Saviour and thy salvation.[30]

This passage also relates to what Julian teaches about prayer in the context of the fourteenth revelation. It is in harmony too with the awareness Julian develops that Christ is mother. This metaphor, along with the parable of the Lord and the Servant which unveils the first secret, are communications which she calls spiritual sights. There is more in them than bodily visions or reason can comprehend.

The fifteenth and sixteenth revelations (Chap. 64-86) present Julian confronted alternately with comfort and with fear. She acknowledges that such is the human condition, as long as we are in this life:

> The more clearly the soul sees the blessed face by grace and love, the more it longs to see it in its fullness. Notwithstanding that our Lord lives in us, and is here with us; notwithstanding that he is nearer to us than tongue and heart can think or tell, the fact remains that we shall never cease from sighs, complaints, or tears—or longing—till we see clearly his blessed face. In that precious, blessed sight, no grief can live, no blessing fail.[31]

Julian's account closes with the final teaching of the **Showings,** received as a spiritual sight:

> From the time that these things were first revealed I had often wanted to know what was our Lord's meaning. It was more than fifteen years after that I

was answered in my spirit's understanding. "You would know our Lord's meaning in this thing? Know it well. Love was his meaning. Who showed it to you? Love. What did he show you? Love. Why did he show it? For love. Hold on to this and you will know and understand love more and more. But you will not know or learn anything else—ever."[32]

The Spiritual Sight in Metaphors and Parables: The spiritual sights are at times described in direct discourse and dialogue. More often they are conveyed through metaphors and parables, or at least amplified by such means.

Some of the metaphors in Julian's work are common to medieval writings, and to mystical writings generally. Among these well-known metaphors are the journey, to signify the spiritual life on earth, spiritual blindness, the ground of being, light and darkness, the city of the soul. Julian also develops concrete analogies from nature, with references to water, blood, rain, thirst, dryness, the seabed, the garden to be cultivated by God's servants, and the treasure hidden in the earth, which stands for humanity in its capacity to grow and flower into something greater than the seed of its common status.

But Julian adds metaphors of her own to this familiar list. Among these is the well-loved reference to the little thing in the palm of her hand, about the size of a hazelnut, which stands for all that has been made. Though this experience teaches her the littleness of creation, it also helps her see that nothing that has been made is to be despised, for it reveals God's goodness. In taking such a position Julian differs from many medieval writers, such as Walter Hilton, who often seemed to despise the flesh.

Julian further affirms how near God is to his creation by images of cloth and clothing. The torn flesh of Christ resembles a cloth about to fall into shreds; and the Church, considered as the body of Christ, because sorrows afflict it, is like a cloth shaken in the wind. Clothing images also amplify the parable of the Lord and the Servant: Julian describes the garments of both Lord and Servant and explains what they signify, both as to kind and color.[33]

Julian also uses familiar metaphors in a new way. An important example is the likening of God to a point:

> . . . I saw God in a point . . . by which I learned that he is in all things . . . at this time the working of creatures was not shown, but only the Lord God in the creature; for he is the mid-point of all things and of all that he does . . ."See: I am God. I am in all things. I never lift my hands from my works, nor ever shall, without end."[34]

Some writers have used the symbol of the point as if it related to a geometrical figure:

> . . . all the radii of a circle are concentrated into a single unity in the center, and this point contains all the straight lines brought together within itself, and unified to one another, and to the one starting point from which they began.[35]

The concept in this form is as old, at least, as the writings of the Pseudo-Dionysius and occurs widely. Dante, for one, sees a point of light—the starting point in God's mind of all that is—radiating out into all that exists.[36] Father William Johnston describes still another variant on the metaphor, which he calls the "still point." It involves:

> . . . vertical thinking, a process in which the mind goes silently down to its own center, revealing cavernous depths ordinarily latent and untouched by the flow of images and concepts that pass across the surface of the mind. It is that mysticism in which one descends to the "still point" or to the ground of the soul, thus finding a type of knowledge that is supra-conceptual and therefore ineffable, a species of super-thinking whereby one grasps the unity of all things. . . . [37]

But Julian's metaphor of the point suggests a more concrete reference than either the geometrical or super-conceptual figures of these others. For her, God is the central point of all, and human life is only a point in him. This concept extends to the idea that God is present to the lowest parts of human needs, even including the body's eliminative functions, for which the body is suited like a fine purse.[38] She may be thinking, then, of needle- or lace-point, which anchoresses made. In such a structure each point (or stitch) is everywhere the same, yet each is really distinct from the pattern which arises from the points. Also this pattern pre-exists in the mind of the worker, who, for a perfect work, never lifts his hands from what he makes. Such a metaphor conveys Julian's teaching that God is in all things, as maker and keeper, yet is really other from what he sustains in being:

> To the same blessed power, wisdom, and love by which he made them are all things being continually led, and our Lord himself will bring them there. In due time, we shall see. . . . The reason for this was shown in the first revelation, and more clearly in the third, where it was said: "I saw the whole Godhead concentrated in a single point."[39]

The metaphor which contains Julian's most intricate theology—those mysteries which she herself struggled with for nearly twenty years—is the great parable of the Lord and the Servant. This story conveys Julian's insights about the first Adam, the cosmic Christ, the Trinity, and the unity of all who are to be saved.[40] The one great reality in the parable is the person of Christ, in whom are mysterious compenetrations of other realities—the Adam of Genesis; the total Adam (all humanity); Christ as the second Adam (and in one sense the first Adam, since to his eternal image all things were made); and Christ, meaning all humanity to be saved. The basic parable weaves into other metaphors: for example, the sinful Adam fell in misery to the earth, but likewise the divine Adam falls on the earth—into human nature in Mary's womb—and makes the garden of the earth spring forth with food and drink for which the Father thirsts and longs, in his unending love for the treasure which was hidden in the earth.

The allegory of the Lord and the Servant, initially referred to in Julian's first revelation,[41] flows easily into the second great metaphor—that of the motherhood of Christ. For the Lord in the parable "rejoices to be our mother," and the deep Wisdom seen in the Trinity "is our mother." Julian then devotes four chapters to explaining how Christ is mother. He is mother because he gives birth to us in creation, in our again-making, and in our dying, a birth to eternal life. He carries out all the functions of motherhood: he nurtures, feeds, chides, rewards, and loves tenderly with more compassion and tenderness than any other mother could exercise.

This striking metaphor, rooted in Scripture, existed in an unbroken tradition from earliest Christian times and had antecedents in Judaism. It fell into disuse only under the impact of systematic theology in the thirteenth century. An ancient Hebrew teaching placed the feminine in the Godhead,[42] and Philo of Alexandria, a Hellenistic Jew who was a primary influence on early Christian exegesis, used maternal names for God. Among Christian exegetes who continued to use such images are Irenaeus, Justin Martyr, Clement of Alexandria, John Chrysostom, Hilary of Poitiers, Jerome, and Ambrose. St. Augustine assimilated what these Latin and Greek Fathers had said, and transmitted the concept through such expressions as "Our Mother, the Wisdom of God." In sermons and commentaries on the Psalms, on Isaiah, and other Old Testament texts, he repeated maternal imagery in several forms: for example, he says that Christ became incarnate because weak human beings could not eat the bread that is God, our Father, until it became milk at the breast of Christ, our Mother. The New Testament event in which Christ compared himself to a hen who desired to gather her chickens under her wings occasioned repeated analogies and was blended with the metaphor from the Song of Moses which portrayed God as the eagle sheltering the fledgeling people of God under her wings.

Echoes of Augustine's metaphors, together with some new variations, occur in an unbroken sequence to the time of Julian's *Showings.* Maternal imagery for God, and sometimes for Christ, occurs in such diverse writers as Cassiodorus, Remigius, Rabanus Maurus, Peter Lombard, Anselm, Bernard of Clairvaux, Albert the Great, and Bonaventure. The image also appears in Thomas Aquinas' gathering of texts from the Fathers, the *Catena Aurea*.[43]

Though there are these many suggestions in earlier writings giving a basis for applying the motherhood image to Christ and the Trinity, Julian worked out the appropriation more fully than any of her predecessors and with some original nuances. For her, Christ is our mother in the order of creation: "We have our being of him, there, where the ground of motherhood beginneth."[44] We are grounded in the Trinity through this motherhood: "And the deep Wisdom of the Trinity is our Mother, in whom we are enclosed."[45] In this same motherhood our sensual being is united to God, redeemed, and restored to harmony with our substance: "... I saw that the second Person, who is our Mother substantially—the same very dear Person is now become our Mother sensually. ... He is our Mother of mercy in taking our sensuality ... in our Mother Christ, we have profit and increase; and in mercy he re-formeth and restoreth us; and by the power of his passion, his death and uprising, oned us to our substance."[46]

Christ's motherhood in the work of grace has its roots in his experience of being formed by a mother—that is, of being a child in the womb and subject to a human mother:

> But now I must say a little more about this "overflowing" as I understand its meaning: how we have been brought back again by the motherhood of mercy and grace to that natural condition which was ours originally when we were made through the motherhood of natural love (kind love)—which love, indeed, has never left us.

> Our Mother by nature and grace—for he would become our Mother in everything—laid the foundation of his work in the Virgin's womb with great and gentle condescension. (This was shown in the first revelation when I received a mental picture of the Virgin's genuine simplicity at the time she conceived.) In other words, it was in this lowly place that God most high, the supreme wisdom of all, adorned and arrayed himself with our poor flesh, ready to function and serve as Mother in all things.[47]

Thus Christ, whom the Scriptures say "learned through suffering," although he was God (Hebrews 5:8), learned motherhood through Mary. He exercised his own motherhood as a service—a word which suggests both the official liturgical service and the lowly service of the mother; and as an office, which is the same word used to designate the functions to which members of

the Church are called and for which they are publicly ordained. What is only implied in these words is made explicit when Julian says, with reference to the Mass and the Eucharist, ongoing workings of grace:

> He might die no more, but that does not stop him working, for he needs to feed us . . . it is an obligation of his dear, motherly love. The human mother will suckle her child with her own milk, but our beloved Mother, Jesus, feeds us with himself, and, with the most tender courtesy, does it by means of the Blessed Sacrament, the precious good of true life. And he keeps us going through his mercy and grace by all the sacraments.[48]

John Clark summarizes what is apparently new and more fully developed in Julian than in any of her known predecessors with reference to this motherhood metaphor:

> It is now recognized that the image of God as "Mother" can claim a continuous tradition, with roots in the Bible and the Fathers; in particular the appropriation of *Sapientia* to Christ opens the way to applying to him some of those texts in the Sapiential books of the Bible which speak of Wisdom, God's agent in the creation and ordering of the world, as a female figure. At the same time, no full antecedent has yet been found for Julian's bold appropriation to Christ of Motherhood in the order of creation as well as of redemption, nor of her explicit development of a fully Trinitarian theology in which Motherhood is consistently appropriated to Christ as Wisdom.[49]

Thus, the metaphor becomes the most comprehensive, integrative, and significant one within Julian's *Showings.*

Is Julian a Mystic?

Those who study Julian's *Showings,* aided by recent research, should be able to grant that she is a writer of the first rank, and that she transmits an appealing message of love, expressed in skilled language, with consistent rhetorical strategies, and effective metaphors. It is also clear, from a survey of the meaning of her visionary experiences, that her book is not merely devotional but profoundly theological. But in what sense, if at all, is Julian a mystic? Are the attributes of mysticism, as commonly described, present in her experience? It seems that they are indeed present, despite the surface simplicity of her treatise.

The core of mysticism in the orthodox Christian tradition is a way of life. The authentic mystic is purified, illuminated, and transformed as the God of love reveals himself in such a manner that the mystic is explicitly conscious of the way of life demanded by God's own self-communication. The goal of the mystic is conscious union with God. The fully matured contemplative is ultimately united with the source of Love in a profound union, in which, nonetheless, God remains God, and the creature remains a creature. Transformed by God's love and wisdom, the Christian mystic discerns more than ever before how the Christ-life affects every dimension of human activity—not only of the individual but of the people of God.[50]

In general terms this view of mysticism applies to Julian. Yet, paradoxically, the very persistence with which she stresses that her way of life is for all who will be saved may distract us from her own path of purification, illumination, and transformation. Likewise, because what was revealed to Julian was not prophecy in the narrow sense but a deeper insight into the truths of faith already proposed for her belief, we may fail to attend adequately to the depth and breadth of God's self-revelation to her. It is useful, then, to review how Julian becomes one with the mystery of divine love, a growth experience comparable to what she invites her co-Christians to seek.

As the record of the two versions of the **Showings** witness, Julian persevered in her search of God from her youth, through the trials recorded in the revelations, and into some twenty years of reflection and prayer after the showings. Hers was a lifetime of purgation and enlightenment. However, unlike many other writers, she did not regard her spiritual journey as a series of progressive steps culminating in perfection. Rather, she saw human life as more like the teeth of a saw, a series of risings and fallings.[51] She reduced meditations, asceticism, and reflections to a single turning of attention to God, with the eye of faith, or with the beholding of confident love:

> If, because of our weakness, we fall back again into our old inertia and spiritual blindness, and experience suffering both spiritual and physical, God's will is for us to know that he has not forgotten us.[52]

Mystics often speak of experiences which they call the dark night, when they seem abandoned and on the verge of extinction. We may look in vain for an explicit example of this experience in the **Showings,** partially because Julian was of a strong, positivedisposition, and experiences of the dark night are in some degree linked to the personality of the individual. Nonetheless, Julian explains that she shared in some way in the deepest desolation of Christ himself, in a mystical death which is followed by joy:

> I understood that in this life (as our Lord sees it)
> We are on his cross

> dying with him in our pains and passion.
> Then suddenly his countenance shall be
>   changed upon us
> and we shall be with him in heaven.
> Between this disposition and the other there
>   will be no
> break in time and then—
> We shall all be brought into joy.[53]

Some awareness of divine transcendence is also part of the mystic's experience and testimony. Julian witnesses to such an awareness repeatedly:

> I had in some measure both touch, sight, and feeling of these three of God's attributes . . . the attributes are these three: Life, love, and light. . . . These three exist in one goodness.[54]

Her awareness of God extended but was not limited to his presence in the human soul:

> Our good Lord showed himself to me in various ways both in heaven and on earth. But the only *place* I saw him occupy was in man's soul. He showed himself on earth in his precious incarnation and his blessed passion. In another way he showed himself—on earth still—when I said, "I saw the whole Godhead as it were in a single point."[55]

It is in the twelfth revelation, an experience to which she refers again and again, that Julian felt the most overwhelming sense of the presence of God, with the resulting joy which flooded her whole being:

> After this our Lord showed himself, in glory even greater than I had seen before—so it seemed to me. By this was I taught that our soul can never rest until it comes to him, and knows him to be the fullness of joy, friendly and considerate, blessed and life indeed. And he said again and again "It is I; it is I; it is I who am most exalted; it is I whom you love; it is I whom you delight in; it is I whom you serve; it is I whom you long for, whom you desire; it is I whom you mean; it is I who am all. It is I whom Holy Church preaches and teaches; it is I who showed myself to you here.". . . . the joy I saw in that revelation surpasses all the heart could wish for or desire.[56]

True, mysticism is not only the hunger of the heart of God, nor is it just an intellectual activity. Rather, it begets an energy that organizes the whole life in an arduous search which transforms the person. Julian speaks of this transformation, applying it not only to the individual, but to corporate humanity:

> This blessed love works in us in two ways. In our lower part there are pains and passions, sympathy, pity, mercy and forgiveness, and so on . . . ; in the higher part are none of these, but altogether the

most tremendous love and marvellous joy. And in this joy all our sufferings are set right . . . he also showed the honor and nobility to which he will bring us through the work of grace in the lower part of our nature, transforming our blameworthiness into eternal worthiness.[57]

Julian's **Showings** thus manifest characteristics found in other figures and writers whom we are ready to call "mystics."[58]

Julian's Influence Today

Though, as stated at the beginning, Julian has not been given her rightful place in English letters, nonetheless traces of her influence exist. T. S. Eliot in *Little Gidding* has familiarized readers with a notable phrase from Julian—"All shall be well"—and has associated this saying with mystical symbolism:

> And all shall be well and
> All manner of thing shall be well
> When the tongues of flame are enfolded
> Into the crowned knot of fire
> And the fire and the rose are one.[59]

Likewise, Aldous Huxley ended the meditative chapter of *Eyeless in Gaza* with an echo of the same saying from Julian: " . . . he thought of what was in store for him. Whatever it might be, he knew that all would be well."[60]

Closer to our own days such popular writers as Annie Dillard and Mary Gordon make Julian known in prose works. Annie Dillard in *Holy the Firm*[61] has a Julie Norwich as a major character, in a prose-poem which presents some images and teachings from the **Showings.** And Mary Gordon in *Final Payments* has her narrator in the midst of a religious crisis discover a prayer card with words from Julian, printed in "the slant, liturgical script that had made its truth seem inevitable":

> He said not thou shalt not be tempted
> He said not thou shalt not be troubled
> He said thou shalt not be overcome.[62]

Among well-known writers on the contemplative life, Thomas Merton has called Julian one of the great theologians of all time—equal to John Henry Newman, superior to John of the Cross and even to Teresa of Avila.[63]

Admittedly, these are small, scattered signs of recognition, and even the scholarship devoted to the **Showings** is recent and in need of supplements. But given these advances in scholarship and a growing interest in mysticism, Julian may soon attain the place she deserves in English letters.

Notes

[1] For the records in wills see Edmund Colledge and James Walsh, critical edition, *A Book of Showings to the Anchoress Julian of Norwich,* 2 vols. (Toronto, 1978), 1, 33-34. See also, F. I. Dunn, "Hermits, Anchorites and Recluses: A Study with Reference to Medieval Norwich," in *Julian and Her Norwich,* ed. Frank Dale Sayer (Norwich, 1973), pp. 18-26; and Ann K. Warren, "The Anchorite in Medieval England 1100-1539," diss. Case Western Reserve, 1980 (available on microfilm).

[2] Chap. 2, tr. Wolters (Baltimore, 1973), p. 64. Unless otherwise indicated, all references in this paper are to the Long Version.

[3] Chap. 3 (tr. Wolters), p. 143.

[4] Tr. M. B. Salu (London, 1955). This guide for anchoresses contains directives for their daily lives, devotions, work, and relations with others.

[5] See B. A. Windeatt, "Julian and Her Audience," *Review of English Studies,* n.s. 28 (1977), 1-17.

[6] William Butler-Bowdon, ed., *The Book of Margery Kempe* (London, 1954), p. 38.

[7] Chap. 6, Short Text (tr. Colledge and Walsh, *Showings*), p. 135.

[8] Chap. 9 (tr. Wolters), p. 75.

[9] Chap. 6, Short Text (Colledge and Walsh, *Showings*), p. 135.

[10] For a fuller history of the manuscripts see Chaps. I-V, Introduction, Part One of critical edition, Colledge and Walsh, pp. 1-33.

[11] T. A. Birrell, "English Catholic Mystics in Non-Catholic Circles—I," *Downside Review,* 94 (1976), 60-81.

[12] Sheila Upjohn, *Mind Out of Time* (Julian Shrine Publications, 1979), p. 6.

[13] Introduction, Colledge and Walsh, Critical Edition, Part One, p. 13.

[14] *A Critical Edition of the Revelations of Julian of Norwich* (1342-c. 1416), prepared from all the known manuscripts, presented as a thesis for the degree of Doctor of Philosophy in the School of English Language and Literature, Leeds Univ., May, 1956: Amherst, pp. 1-52; Westminster, Appendix B., 36 pp.

[15] See Valerie Lagorio and Ritamary Bradley, *The 14th-Century English Mystics: A Comprehensive Annotated Bibliography* (New York, 1981), items 503, 505, 512, 517-19.

[16] Chap. 7 (tr. Wolters), p. 72.

[17] Maisonneuve, Vol. I, 74-75.

[18] See Donald F. Homier, "The Function of Rhetoric in Suggesting Stages of Contemplation in the Vernacular Writings of the Fourteenth Century English Mystics," diss., Northern Illinois Univ., 1975.

[19] The anonymous author of *The Cloud of Unknowing* is an experienced spiritual director whose works come from the latter part of the fourteenth century. A widely-circulated edition is that of Clifton Wolters (Baltimore, 1961) and subsequent re-printings. See the essay by John P. H. Clark below.

[20] Richard Rolle, *The Fire of Love,* ed. Clifton Wolters (Baltimore, 1971), p. 136.

[21] Roland Maisonneuve, "L'Univers Visionnaire de Julian de Norwich."

[22] Chap. 73 (tr. Wolters), pp. 191-92.

[23] Ritamary Bradley, "Christ, the Teacher, in Julian's *Showings:* The Biblical and Patristic Traditions," *The Medieval Mystical Tradition in England,* Papers Read at the Dartington Symposium, 1982 (Exeter, 1982), pp. 127-42.

[24] Tr. Wolters, p. 66.

[25] Brant Pelphrey, *Love Was His Meaning. The Theology and Mysticism of Julian of Norwich* (Salzburg, 1982), p. 105.

[26] Ibid., p. 163.

[27] Chap. 58 (tr. Wolters), p. 166.

[28] Pelphrey, p. 193.

[29] Chap. 36 (tr. Wolters), p. 115.

[30] Chap. 36 (tr. Wolters), p. 106. This is the quotation contained in Colwich Abbey Ms. 18.

[31] Chap. 72 (tr. Wolters), p. 190.

[32] Chap. 86 (tr. Wolters), p. 211-12.

[33] See Ritamary Bradley, "Cloth and Clothing Metaphors in the *Showings* of Julian of Norwich" (to be published in *Mediaevalia*).

[34] Chap. 11 (author's translation from critical edition, Colledge and Walsh), p. 336.

[35] Sr. Anna Maria Reynolds, "Some Literary Influences in the *Revelations* of Julian of Norwich," in *Leeds Studies in English and Kindred Languages,* 7-8 (1952), p. 24.

[36] *Divine Comedy,* Paradiso, Canto 27.

[37] William Johnston, *The Still Point. Reflections on Zen and Christian Mysticism* (New York, 1970), pp. 132-33.

[38] Chap. 6.

[39] Chap. 35 (tr. Wolters). The same idea is expressed again in Chap. 52, p. 152.

[40] For a systematic explication of the teachings underlying this parable, see Thomas Merton, *The New Man* (New York, 1961), pp. 134-37. Merton does not refer in this book to Julian, however.

[41] Chap. 7.

[42] Maisonneuve, Part One, pp. 349-50. See also David Biale, "The God with Breasts: El Shaddai in the Bible," *History of Religions,* 21 (1982), 240-56.

[43] Ritamary Bradley, "Patristic Background of the Motherhood Similitude in Julian of Norwich," *Christian Scholar's Review,* 8 (1978), 101-13. See also Carolyn Walker Bynum, *Jesus as Mother: Studies in the Spirituality of the High Middle Ages* (Berkeley, 1982).

[44] Chap. 59 (tr. Walsh), p. 161.

[45] Chap. 54 (tr. Walsh), p. 150.

[46] Chap. 58 (tr. Walsh), pp. 159-60.

[47] Chap. 60 (tr. Wolters), p. 169.

[48] Chap. 60 (tr. Wolters), p. 170.

[49] John P. H. Clark, "Nature, Grace and the Trinity in Julian of Norwich," *Downside Review,* 100 (1982), 211.

[50] Harvey D. Egan, "Mystical Crosscurrents," *Communio,* 7 (1980), 4-23.

[51] Maisonneuve, Part II, p. 417.

[52] Chap. 64 (tr. Wolters), p. 178.

[53] Chap. 21 (tr. Walsh), p. 82.

[54] Chap. 83 (tr. Wolters), pp. 208-09.

[55] Chap. 81 (tr. Wolters), p. 206.

[56] Chap. 26 (tr. Wolters), pp. 102-03.

[57] Chap. 71 (tr. Wolters), p. 188.

[58] These criteria are based on a standard work on mysticism, Evelyn Underhill, *Mysticism* (New York, 1961), Chap. 4, "The Characteristics of Mysticism," pp. 70-94.

[59] T. S. Eliot, *Collected Poems, 1909-1962* (London, 1970), p. 223.

[60] Aldous Huxley, *Eyeless in Gaza* (New York, 1936), p. 473.

[61] Annie Dillard, *Holy the Firm* (New York, 1977).

[62] Mary Gordon, *Final Payments* (New York, 1978), p. 300.

[63] Thomas Merton, *Conjectures of a Guilty Bystander* (Garden City, 1968), p. 211; and *14th-Century English Mystics Newsletter,* 4 (1978), 2.

Kenneth Leech (essay date 1985)

SOURCE: "Contemplative and Radical: Julian Meets John Ball" in *Julian: Woman of Our Day,* edited by Robert Llewelyn, Darton, Longman and Todd, 1985, pp. 89-101.

[*In the following essay Leech speculates on Julian's attitude toward the social upheaval of her day. He imagines her as the sympathetic supporter of peasants protesting the conditions of their lives.*]

In 1973 a group of people gathered in Norwich, England, to celebrate the 600th anniversary of Julian's **Revelations** and to consider her relevance to the spiritual needs of the twentieth century. At one point in the discussions, a devout evangelical psychiatrist was reflecting on the pastoral value of the contemplative character. How wonderful it would be, he suggested, if the gifts and qualities of the great contemplatives could be brought out of the enclosure and put at the service of those ministering to deeply troubled persons. Suddenly, the room shook as an Anglo-Catholic theologian, known for his somewhat rigid opinions, brought down his fist upon the table. 'No', he announced. 'Julian must stay where she is—in her cell. That is where she belongs.'

No doubt his purpose was to preserve the integrity and authentic witness of the solitary and contemplative life against the possible threats from activism and direct pastoral concerns. In a highly activistic, work-dominated culture (such as ours), in which people are defined by what they *do* rather than by who they *are,* the very existence of solitaries and hermits presents a fundamental test of our belief in the life of prayer. For judged in terms of function and efficiency, judged by the managerial professional model, the solitary is absurd. Something of the perplexity is caught in Phyllis McGinley's poem on St Simeon Stylites. The poem ends:

> And why did Simeon sit like that,
> Without a mantle,
> Without a hat.
> In a holy rage
> For the world to see?
> It puzzled the sage.
> It puzzles me.
> It puzzled many
> A desert father,
> And I think it puzzled the
> Good Lord rather.[1]

Why did Julian sit like that? One thing is clear. Her life of solitude was not a selfish, egocentric withdrawal, a flight of the alone to the alone, but a life of love, warmth and care towards her 'even-Christians'; a life of solidarity with Christ's passion which overflowed in compassion for humanity; a life nourished by a profound optimism about humanity and the world. Like St Antony the first hermit, Julian would have insisted that her life and her death was with her neighbour, and that only those committed to the common life could risk the commitment to life in solitude. No one who is enclosed within the false self, the self-absorbed self, can be a true solitary. The Christian solitary lives and has meaning only within the context of the Christian solidarity, within the living organism of the body of Christ. Julian is part of the common life: that is where she belongs.

The fourteenth century in England was a period of great social upheaval and of intense interior striving, an age of militancy and of mysticism, of upheaval in soil and soul. Externally, it was a time of distress among agricultural labourers, of exploitation of the rural peasants and of the urban poor, of sickness, disease and social violence. It was the age of the Black Death and of the Peasants' Revolt. Among the peasants and others who rose up in 1381, there was a thirst for social justice and for equality, a desire to see the end of serfdom and bondage. While many commentators blamed the rising on those heretics and 'outside agitators' loosely lumped together as 'Lollards'—a term used in a similar way to the current use of the term 'Marxists'—historians such as Rodney Hilton suggest that the social radicalism of the period drew its impetus more from the orthodox Christian tradition and from patristic writers such as St Basil, St Ambrose and St John Chrysostom, whose writings had been rediscovered with enthusiasm.[2]

At the interior level, the fourteenth century marked the climax of a process which had begun several centuries earlier, often referred to as 'the feminization of language', the rebirth of an affective sensitized piety. There was a profound quest for the inner way, combined with a fundamental optimism about the universe, features which are clearly seen in the writings of Julian as of other mystics before her. The flowering of affective spirituality in the period after the twelfth century has been described by Caroline Bynum in her *Jesus as Mother*.

> The affective piety of the high Middle Ages is based on an increasing sense of, first, humankind's creation in the image and likeness of God, and, second, the humanity of Christ as guarantee that what we are is inextricably joined with divinity. Creation and incarnation are stressed more than atonement and judgement.[3]

I will return to these two features in discussing Julian. Yet this deeply human, incarnational tradition was not the only manifestation of spiritual life, for the fourteenth century was also a time when gnosticism, millenarian cults, and a whole range of visionary, apocalyptic and what we would today call theosophical movements flourished within an age of accelerating confusion in both the inner and outer worlds.

This was the context within which Julian practised her life of solitude and contemplation. We know very little about the life of Julian apart from her revelations. However, we do know, from the writings of her contemporary Margery Kempe, that the talkative and tearful Margery visited the solitary Julian, and it is a reasonable guess that others did so too. The Christian tradition, in east and west, contains numerous examples, from the desert Fathers onwards, of solitaries who were spiritual guides to social activists and those in the thick of the world's struggles. So Jim Forest and the Berrigans gained strength and vision during their resistance to the Vietnam war from their friendship with the contemplative prophet Thomas Merton.[4] So, we might conjecture, Julian, sensitive and compassionate soul that she was, could not have remained unaffected by the social upheavals taking place in East Anglia in the later years of the fourteenth century.

Now there was in East Anglia at the same time as Julian another Christian figure of whom we know little: a priest called John Ball. John Ball was one of the leaders of the Peasants' Revolt of 1381 when the rural poor, industrial workers, and a significant number of the lower clergy revolted against the harsh taxation laws, and demanded the ending of serfdom—

and, incidentally, of hierarchy within the Church and clergy. (They chopped off the head of the Archbishop of Canterbury, Simon of Sudbury, and his head can still be seen in the local church of Sudbury in Suffolk!) 'I have come not from heaven but from Essex', announced John Ball. Ball was a hedge priest, a *sacerdos vagans,* a wanderer, and it is therefore open to speculation that his journeyings in East Anglia might have led him beyond his home city of Colchester to Norwich, and to Julian's cell.

What might have happened had the contemplative of Norwich and the radical priest of Essex met? What would they have said to each other, these early representatives of contemplative solitude and liberation theology? What would have been the common ground between the mystic and the militant?

They would, first of all, have shared a belief in the closeness of God in the intimacy of prayer and of human comradeship. As Julian wrote: 'He is the ground, his is the substance, he is very essence of nature, and he is the true Father and the true Mother of natures' (ch. 62). God is closer to us, Julian explains, than we are to our own souls, for he is the ground in which our soul stands. Our human nature (she emphasizes, following the teaching of the Greek Fathers) was joined to God *in its creation* (ch. 57). God is our substance, and is in our sensuality also (ch. 56).

> As the body is clad in the cloth, and the flesh in the skin, and the bones in the flesh, and the heart in the trunk, so are we, soul and body, clad in the goodness of God, and enclosed, groundedand rooted in God. (ch. 6. Paris MS)

In her teaching about the fundamental grounding and rooting of the soul in God by virtue of its creation, Julian, consciously or unconsciously, stands within the theological tradition of Eastern Orthodoxy.[5] Her language recalls that of St Gregory of Nazianzus who stressed the fundamental communion of the whole person with God: or, in the modern period, the writings of Paul Evdokimov who speaks of 'ontological deiformity', the God-shaped character of humankind by virtue of its creation in the image and likeness of God.[6] In *Christ in Eastern Christian Thought*, Fr John Meyendorff stresses that the openness of humanity to God, in Orthodox theology, is not a supernatural gift, but is the very core of human nature.[7] In Julian's words, that nature was joined to God *in its creation*. Humanity as created is struck in the image and likeness of God: it is essentially deiform.

It was this humanity, grounded in God, created for union with God, which Christ assumed at the incarnation. Julian would therefore have greeted John Ball as a brother, struck in the divine image, restored through the incarnation to share the divine life. In contrast to all forms of gnostic spirituality, with their mistrust of the flesh and of the common people, Julian's mysticism was earthy and fleshly, incarnational through and through. In this incarnational, materialistic spirituality, Julian stands as an early and highly significant representative of what can be seen as the dominant theological tradition within Anglicanism. This tradition sees the incarnation not simply as a historic event, an article of belief, but also as a process, a movement—in Lionel Thornton's words, the 'regulative principle' of the Christian conception of God.[8] In this tradition there is no such thing as a 'lower nature', itself a Greek and non-biblical idea. Human nature in its entirety has been raised and restored in Christ. In the words of Charles Gore, writing in 1901, Christian theology 'associates the lower and material nature with the whole process of redemption, and teaches us that not without a material and visible embodiment is the spiritual life to be realized either now or in eternity'.[9]

This incarnational, materialistic foundation of Christian mysticism needs to be emphasized strongly today when, as in the fourteenth century, many people are looking to 'spirituality' as a way out of the pain and complexity of the world. Rarely has such false spirituality been so strongly attacked than it was by Julian's contemporary, the Flemish mystic Jan van Ruysbroeck, in his warning against 'those who practise a false vacancy', and who ignore the common life and the demands of love and justice. They are, says Ruysbroeck, the most evil and most harmful people that live.[10] Spirituality and the contemplative life can never be a purely personal quest for peace and inner harmony. It is intimately involved with the anguish of the world, for it is rooted in the incarnation and the passion of Christ. Nor can it exalt the 'spiritual' above the demands of material life, for it sees (as St Teresa of Avila put it) that God is among the saucepans, a reference perhaps to the prophecy of Zechariah that there will come a time when all the household pots and pans will be labelled 'Holy to the Lord!' (Zech. 14:20-1).

John Ball also stood within a long tradition, central to Christian orthodoxy, which stressed that spiritual reality must have a material embodiment, that spiritual theology and the struggle for social justice were inextricably bound up together through the incarnation. This unity of spiritual and material, of mysticism and politics, of holy and common, was the practical outworking of the early Christological debates. For human nature, orthodoxy insisted against the heretics, must be raised and restored in its entirety. And in fact Christian spirituality is utterly rooted in the historic reality of Christ's incarnation, death and resurrection. In Rowan Williams' words:

> The life of Jesus has sanctified the particular, the 'spare and strange', manifesting God in a con-

ditioned human story. Henceforth it is clear that the locus of God's saving action, his will to be known, loved, encountered, is the world of historical decision, whether individual or corporate. It is not, and cannot be, in a 'privileged' dehistoricized ecstasy or in the mechanisms of the gnostics' spiritual science.[11]

The spiritual necessity of orthodoxy is something which needs to be stated strongly in the face of today's gnostic revival.

John Ball would have agreed with all this, and he would have added that God was intimately and disturbingly present in the poor and downtrodden, in the anger of the oppressed and the broken, in the voices of the unheard. He would have agreed with Leonardo Boff who speaks of Christ's 'sacramental density' among the poor and disadvantaged. In conversation with Julian, he might well have pointed to the terrible oppression and cruelty inflicted upon Christ. For the peasants were images of God, Christ's brothers and sisters, and inasmuch as cruelty and neglect was inflicted on them, it was done to Christ himself. That is a central theological truth which we need to recover in western society where to be poor is seen as little less than criminal. The Christian spiritual tradition includes, at its heart, the prophetic warning against those who grind the faces of the poor, who sell the righteous for a pair of sandals, and who neglect the alien, the orphan and the widow. It is an obligation laid upon the Christian community and its pastors, now as in the fourteenth century, to warn governments and communities of the grave moral and physical dangers of such policies of cruelty and neglect. In the words of the Bishop of Durham, broadcast to the British people in April 1985: 'A society which does such things deliberately and refuses to recognize that that is what it is doing is a society which is tearing itself apart and heading for turbulence and disaster.'[12] The fourteenth century was a time of turbulence and disaster. John Ball warned of woe, and, says the unsympathetic chronicler, it was whispered in the hedgerows and among the common people that John Ball spoke true.

Julian might have reassured him of the abiding and strengthening presence of God in his own troubled and restless heart, as he told her of the great suffering which the naked and wounded Christ was enduring on the roads of eastern England.

Secondly, they would have agreed that, terrible as is the reality of sin, it is not the final word about humanity. Sin, Julian wrote, 'is in opposition to our fair nature'. It is 'unnatural'. 'It belongs to our nature to hate sin' (ch. 63). It is a violation of the divine image in all people. Nature is all good and fair, and grace was sent to save it. Again, Julian is much closer to the Eastern Orthodox tradition with its emphasis on the divine image and the glory of the human than to the Augustinian tradition with its emphasis on human fallenness. This does not mean that Julian was 'soft on sin'. But she would not allow her life or her spirituality to be dominated by the sinfulness of the world, holding rather to the power of grace to perfect and transfigure humanity and the creation itself. It is important to stress how different is her approach from that tendency in much western Christian theology which at times seems to regard original sin as the only Christian doctrine, and which misuses the doctrine as an argument against change. Christian theology is a theology not of imperfection and resignation before imperfection, but of redemption and of overpowering grace. 'You can't change human nature' is a blasphemous denial of the most fundamental Christian belief: that God *has* changed, transformed, healed, transfigured human nature, taken that nature into himself ('humanity into God'), and raised that nature to the glory of heaven. Julian recovered for all time the truth that transforming, perfecting grace, grace which perfects nature and does not destroy it, is a more fundamental reality than sin. Sin is strictly accidental, a pathological distortion of human nature, not a fundamental part of it.

No doubt John Ball would have been told, as those who struggle for a more just and more Godlike world in all ages are told, that humanity is fallen, that a perfect society is impossible, and that a belief in human imperfectibility is the basic Christian doctrine. The combination of a belief in total, even cosmic, depravity with a low view of grace is a recipe for social inaction, indeed for social autism. It cuts the ground away from Christian social action and represents a serious and dangerous perversion of Christian belief. Against the cosmic pessimism of those who exalt sin at the expense of grace, he would point to the fundamental equality of humankind, rooted in the equality and common life of the Holy Trinity. He saw the Holy Trinity as the basis of the new world order. As in the Holy Trinity, so on earth: none is afore or after other, none is greater or less than another. If human beings shared the divine image, then they shared the common life and the inner equality of the divine being.

So, on the 13 July 1381, the feast of Corpus Christi, John Ball preached his memorable sermon on Blackheath in south London, in which he warned: 'Things cannot go well in England, nor ever shall, till all be held common; till there be not bond and free but we all are of one condition.' He rooted that belief in human equality in his understanding of the nature of God, and, significantly, in the account of Adam and Eve, created in the image of God. Were we not all children of these original parents, he asked. Inequality in wealth and status did not exist in Paradise, for

When Adam delved and Eve span,
Who was then the gentleman?

We find John Ball's words and themes picked up later by the radical movements of the English Civil War period, the Levellers, the Diggers and the Fifth Monarchy Men. In language which recalls John Ball's sermon, Gerrard Winstanley speaks of the created order as the 'clothing of God', of the earth as a 'common storehouse', and of Christ's presence among the poor, for 'he takes up his abode in a manger in and amongst the poor in spirit and the despised ones of the earth'.[13]

Julian of Norwich and John Ball shared a high view of human nature and of human potential, a view of humanity as sharing God's image, rooted and enfolded in the divine ground. Humanity is 'fundamentally rooted in God's eternal love'. Like John Ball, Julian saw the divine purpose expressed in the most basic physical functions: in one manuscript she speaks of the process of excretion as the work of God who does not 'disdain to serve us in the simplest natural functions of the body'.[14] Similarly, John Ball rejected the sharp dualism of spirit and matter which sought to protect God from flesh and from the struggles of humanity. Both Julian and John lived at a time when, as in our day, gnostic and occult spiritual movements were undergoing a renaissance. They were thoroughgoing incarnationalists and Christian materialists, believing that what has not been assumed has not been healed. At the heart of their spirituality was the Eucharist, the sacramental manifestation of the common life, the *koin nia*. The Christian Eucharist stands as a permanent protest against private, de-materialized, elitist spirituality, for it roots its mystical vision in the social, physical, common, shared reality of eating and drinking. John Ball and his followers drew radical consequences from the eucharistic sharing: they saw it as a pointer towards a more eucharistic world in which resources were truly offered, consecrated, divided and shared. The Eucharist for them was a living symbol of how human society could be refashioned. They would have agreed with the nineteenth-century Anglican writer Stewart Headlam that those who assist at holy communion are bound to be holy communists.[15]

Finally, Julian and John Ball would have shared that divinely inspired optimism expressed in Julian's memorable words: 'All shall be well, and all shall be well, and all manner of thing shall be well.' Julian might have strengthened John Ball with such words as these. For the future to him must have seemed bleak. He was soon to meet his death, with the peasant rising crushed. Things would not go well in England. Many less optimistic souls would have given up the struggle as hopeless. Neither Julian nor John Ball were fatalists: neither was naive about the easy perfectibility of human beings or human society. Yet both held firmly to an unshakeable conviction that God was in control, that human beings and human society were not doomed, that God was mending his broken creation. This belief that God is at work within human history, within the upheavals and crises of nations and peoples, is the heart of the prophetic tradition. The New Testament symbol for the belief is the Kingdom of God. To discern the ways in which God is bringing in the Kingdom, to discern the signs of the times, to recognize, and cooperate with, the working out of God's purpose within history, is a central task of Christian spirituality. This is why contemplation and prophecy must always go together, for without the contemplative vision, the sun goes down on the prophets. Prophecy and action are born from, and constantly nourished and sustained by, vision. But vision must be vision of reality, involving a deepened awareness of the anguish of the world, and of what is happening to the images of God. Julian of Norwich and John Ball need each other badly. Contemplatives and activists need to hold close to each other, to nourish, to interrogate, to disturb, confront, and sustain each other.

Of course, there is not a shred of evidence that this meeting ever took place. But we do know that over the centuries contemplatives and activists, mystics and militants, seekers after personal and political liberation, have talked with, and gained nourishment and insight from, each other. We know too that Christian spirituality at its best seeks to unite interior and exterior struggles and cares, rooted as it is in the materiality of incarnation, resurrection and Eucharist. We know too that in our own day, among Christians of many traditions, the false polarizing of spirituality and social justice is being overcome, and that the ending of the related false polarity of personal and political remains one of our most urgent theological and pastoral tasks at the end of the twentieth century. Central to this task is the recovery of Christological orthodoxy and of the good news of the Kingdom of God.

For we know also the subtle temptations for spirituality and politics to be driven apart by those who seek a private ecstasy and those who wish to maintain power, untroubled by religious interference. We know that, in our day, 'spirituality' is being marketed as a diversion, a form of inner excitement, a devotional commodity which in no way disturbs, upsets or affects the established order. We know that spirituality can easily become a way of escape from the living God who continues to confront and trouble us in the desperate and anguished faces of the broken and dehumanized people of the back streets. We need to learn from Julian that spirituality must be human, natural, earthy, and joyful: and from John Ball that it must be related to, and tested against, the experiences and sufferings of the common people.

In our own discipleship the encounter must take place between the recognition of the presence of God in the depths of the soul, and the recognition of his presence in the poor and downtrodden; between the awareness of the terrible reality of personal and structural sin, and the awareness of the potential Godlikeness, the 'ontological deiformity', of the human person and the human community; between the recognition of the destructive forces in the world, and of the reality of the Kingdom of God as a sure and certain hope; between the vision of God and the anguish of the world.

If these encounters take place in us, Julian of Norwich and John Ball, the contemplative and the radical prophet, will truly have met.

Notes

[1] Phyllis McGinley, *Times Three* (New York 1975), pp. 46-7.

[2] See Rodney Hilton, *Bond Men Made Free: medieval peasant movements and the English Rising of 1381* (London 1977 edn.). Hilton claims that 'the better they knew the Bible and the writings of the Fathers of the Church the more explosive the mixture of social and religious radicalism was likely to be' (p. 210). Of John Ball, he notes that 'his reported sayings are in the long tradition of Christian social radicalism which goes back to St Ambrose of Milan if not before' (p. 211).

[3] Caroline Walker Bynum, *Jesus as Mother: Studies in the spirituality of the High Middle Ages* (Berkeley, Los Angeles, and London 1982), p. 130.

[4] For some reflections on Merton by his friends, see Paul Wilkes (ed.), *Merton by those who knew him* (San Francisco 1984).

[5] Brant Pelphrey, *Love Was His Meaning: the theology and mysticism of Julian of Norwich* (Salzburg 1982). Pelphrey says that Julian's work 'draws together the important strands of Christian spirituality as it is found in both the western Catholic mystics and in Eastern Orthodoxy' (p. x.).

[6] Paul Evdokimov, *L'Orthodoxie* (Neuchatel 1959), p. 88.

[7] John Meyendorff, *Christ in Eastern Christian Thought* (New York 1975), p. 11.

[8] L. S. Thornton, *The Incarnate Lord* (London 1928), p. 7.

[9] Charles Gore, *The Body of Christ* (London 1901), p. 39.

[10] Jan van Ruysbroeck, *The Book of Supreme Truth*, ch. 4. See also *The Adornment of the Spiritual Marriage,* ch. 66.

[11] Rowan Williams, *The Wound of Knowledge* (London 1979), p. 30.

[12] David Jenkins, 'The God of freedom and the freedom of God', The Hibbert Lecture 1985, *The Listener* (18 April 1985), pp. 14-17.

[13] G. H. Sabine (ed.) *The Works of Gerrard Winstanley* (New York 1941), pp. 190, 251-2, 473-4. See also Christopher Hill, *The World Turned Upside Down: radical ideas during the English Revolution* (London 1972).

[14] *RDL* ch. 6 (Paris MS). Here and elsewhere I have used the translation of E. Colledge and J. Walsh (London and New York 1978).

[15] Stewart Headlam, *The Laws of Eternal Life* (London 1888), p. 52.

Joan M. Nuth (essay date 1991)

SOURCE: "The Work of Grace" in *Wisdom's Daughter: The Theology of Julian of Norwich,* Crossroad, 1991, pp. 148-69.

[*In the following excerpt, Nuth delineates Julian's concept of grace, which she says finds its coherence in Julian's unfailing emphasis on divine love for humanity.*]

Although the Spirit of God is active with the whole trinity in the works of nature and mercy already described, the particular work attributed to the Spirit by Julian is eschatological fulfillment, which she calls the work of grace:

> Grace works with mercy, and especially in two properties, . . . which working belongs to the third person, the Holy Spirit. He works, rewarding and giving. Rewarding is a gift of trust which the Lord makes to those who have labored; and giving is a courteous act which he does freely, by grace, fulfilling and surpassing all that creatures deserve (58:294).

The ultimate gift and reward of the Spirit is heaven, that state of union with God which the blessed will enjoy for all eternity. Julian's strong emphasis upon heaven is proof of her indebtedness to the monastic tradition, where the longing for heaven was the fundamental atmosphere within which monastic culture flourished, an atmosphere that was predominantly eschatological and transcendent.[1] The message of Julian's revelations which urged her to live within the divine perspective with respect to sin and salvation is consistent with such an eschatological tradition.

Future Eschatology: The Bliss of Heaven

In the sixth revelation, Julian's understanding is "lifted up into heaven" where she sees God as the lord of a great feast, "gladdening and consoling" all his friends.[2] As she contemplates this image, she is led to understand that anyone "who has voluntarily served God in any degree on earth" will enjoy "three degrees of bliss" in heaven. The person will experience "honor and thanks from our Lord God," a thanks "so exalted and so honorable" that it is indescribable joy. Furthermore, God will make this thanks public so that "all the blessed in heaven will see the honor of the thanks," increasing the joy and honor experienced by the saved person. Finally, this joy and honor "will last forevermore."[3] Although Julian makes the point that joy will be especially great for those who "voluntarily and freely offer their youth to God," all three degrees of bliss belong to all the saved, whether their service lasted a lifetime or a day (14:203-4).[4]

Later, in the ninth revelation, Julian's understanding is lifted up into heaven again, where she sees "three heavens" reflecting the three persons of the trinity, all in relation to the humanity of Christ. The first heaven reveals the pleasure the Father takes in rewarding the Son for "all the deeds that Jesus has done for our salvation" (22:216). The second heaven is the bliss the Son experiences through the honor he receives from the Father by being awarded the gift of all the saved. The third heaven is the "endless delight" the Holy Spirit takes in the work of salvation (23:218).

The three degrees of bliss experienced by the blessed in heaven correspond to the three heavens of the trinity. Heaven is essentially a sharing in the pleasure and joy of the Father, the honor and bliss of the Son, and the endless delight of the Holy Spirit over the great deed of salvation which has enabled the human race, made in God's image, to become the bliss, the reward, the honor, and the crown of God. Heaven is thus the final fulfillment of the work of the incarnation, through which temporal and earthly reality has been raised up into the mystery of God.

There is a parallel between God's joy, honor, and endless delight and the qualities of might, wisdom, and love by which Julian usually describes the trinity. The Father's joy represents the triumph of God's might, the Son's honor the vindication of God's wisdom, and the Spirit's endless delight the eternity of the love which has guided all to fulfillment. When the blessed in heaven share in the joy, honor, and delight of the trinity over their salvation, they are, in effect, sharing, insofar as it is possible for creatures, in the triumphant might, wisdom, and love of God. They are sharing this through the perfection of those qualities in themselves by which they have always imaged God, the qualities of human might, wisdom, and love, which were blemished by sin but restored and increased by Christ and fulfilled by the Holy Spirit. Heaven means the fulfillment of God's desire "to have the blessed creatures who will be in heaven with him without end like himself in all things" (77:331).

The end of the parable of the lord and the servant crystallizes Julian's understanding of the bliss of heaven. There the servant is no longer dressed in an old, tight-fitting, threadbare, and short tunic, representing the blemished image of God, but in clothing "made lovely by our savior, new, white and bright and forever clean," fairer, even, than the clothing on the lord. Restored human nature, symbolized by Christ's clothing, is "now of a fair and seemly mixture," so marvellous that it is beyond description (51:278).[5] The fact that it is fairer than the original clothing of the lord seems to imply that the works of mercy and grace have added something to God's glory, not to the essence of God, but to the glory given to God through God's works in time.

It is customary to think of heaven as a state of joy for human beings. What is unique about Julian's presentation is her stress on the joy which God experiences there, when all the saved are given to Christ as his reward for suffering on their behalf. The saved are given to Christ as his crown, and the entire trinity rejoices in this: "For it was revealed that we are his crown, which crown is the Father's joy, the Son's honor, the Holy Spirit's delight, and endless marvellous bliss to all who are in heaven" (51:278).[6] Christ takes up his permanent residence in the city prepared for him by the Father, the souls of all the faithful which together comprise the heavenly kingdom, where there is eternal peace, joy, and love.[7] There all the saved enter into the inner life of the trinity, sharing in the very attributes of God.

Heaven means that God's promise, "all will be well," will be fulfilled and understood by all the blessed. Julian is told that this promise includes the fact that "you will see yourself that every kind of thing will be well." She understood this phrase to indicate the "union of all who will be saved in the blessed trinity" (31:229).[8] The nature of this union is more precisely described in the following passage:

> We shall all come into our Lord, knowing ourselves clearly and wholly possessing God, and we shall all be endlessly hidden in God, truly seeing and wholly feeling, and hearing him spiritually and delectably smelling him and sweetly tasting him. And there we shall see God face to face, familiarly and wholly. The creature which is made will see and endlessly contemplate God who is the maker (43:255).[9]

In heaven the blessed will finally see with God's wisdom and will with God's love. Full union with the mind and will of God and the true knowledge of self which accompanies it will be finally achieved.

Jesus promises Julian that heaven also means the cessation of all suffering:

> Suddenly you will be taken out of all your pain, all your sickness, all your unrest and all your woe. And you will come up above, and you will have me for your reward, and you will be filled full of joy and bliss, and you will never again have any kind of pain, any kind of sickness, any kind of displeasure, no lack of will, but always joy and bliss without end (64:306).[10]

But the labor spent on earth dealing with the suffering caused by sin will endure eternally, transformed into honor:

> As we are punished here with sorrow and penance . . . we shall be rewarded in heaven by the courteous love of our almighty God, who does not wish anyone who comes there to lose his labors in any degree. . . . The reward which we shall receive will not be small, but it will be great, glorious and honorable. And so all shame will be turned into honor and joy (39:245).

Julian looks forward to having her most perplexing problems about sin and salvation solved in heaven: "when the judgment is given, and we are all brought up above, we shall then clearly see in God the mysteries which are now hidden from us" (85:341). However, this will cause a bliss "so deep and so high" that, "out of wonder and marvelling" the blessed will be filled with a reverent fear of God, so far surpassing what they have experienced before, "that the pillars of heaven will tremble and quake" (75:327).[11] This is the proper attitude of the creature before God, even in heaven. Although the creature experiences union with the wisdom and love of God, the essential difference between creature and Creator is not dissolved. Indeed, the awareness of this difference, with the reverent fear that accompanies it, increases in heaven with greater knowledge of God:

> For this reverent fear is the fairer courtesy which is in heaven before God's face; and by as much as he will be known and loved, surpassing how he now is, by so much will he be feared, surpassing how he now is. Therefore it must necessarily be that all heaven, all earth will tremble and quake (75:327-28).

God will remain for all eternity the totally other, holy, Incomprehensible Mystery before whom creatures can only bow in adoration.

Realized Eschatology: Anticipation of Heaven

In the monastic tradition, heaven was not solely a future reality to be awaited, but one experienced partially in the present through the life of grace, which was greatly aided by the practice of contemplative prayer. Julian follows this tradition, and is particularly interested in showing how this present anticipation of heaven, this realized eschatology, can provide comfort and solace in the midst of earthly suffering.

While Julian emphasizes particular virtues of the Christian life closely associated with God's work of mercy (as outlined in the last chapter), she also treats those gifts of the Spirit through which all who will be saved receive a foretaste on earth of the sharing in the life of God which they will enjoy in heaven. Once again, the notion of the *imago Dei* dominates Julian's study of growth in the life of grace. The gifts she describes correspond to the attributes of God discussed in Chapter 4: God's immutability finds a parallel in the gift of peace, God's joy in the gift of joy, and God's love in the further increase of love, accompanied by the reverent fear which reflects God's incomprehensibility.

The surest entrance into the enjoyment of these gifts is through contemplative prayer, wherein one is afforded a sight of God suited to one's present need and condition:

> And so we shall by his sweet grace in our own meek continual prayer come into [God] now in this life by many secret touchings of sweet spiritual sights and feelings, measured out to us as our simplicity may bear it. And this is done and will be done by the grace of the Holy Spirit, until the day that we die, still longing for love. . . . But when [God] of his special grace wishes to show himself here, he gives the creature more than its own strength, and measures the revelation according to his own will, and it isprofitable for that time (43:255).

The effect of this sight is to fill the soul with peace, joy, and love.

The Gift of Peace and Rest

For Julian, "God is true rest," and desires "that we should rest in him" (5:184). Therefore God bestows the gift of peace on the willing soul:

> Our good Lord the Holy Spirit, who is endless life dwelling in our soul . . . produces in the soul a peace, and brings it to ease through grace, and makes it obedient and reconciles it to God. And this is . . . the way on which our good Lord constantly leads us, so long as we are in this changeable life (48:261-62).

Julian often describes peace as the absence of the wrath or "contrariness" caused by sin.[12] When filled with God's peace, "we find no contrariness in any kind of hindrance," not even in the things that at other times greatly afflict us (49:265).

The gift of peace and rest in God is a foretaste of the eternity of heaven, a sharing in the immutability of God, for God "will make us as unchangeable as he is when we are there" (49:265). When one contemplates God and God's works under the influence of this gift, one realizes that "all [God's] judgments are easy and sweet," and learns to prefer them to the "blind judgments" of human beings (11:198).[13] One glimpses the "blessed harmony" that always exists between God and God's works, seeing that God "is always fully pleased with himself and with all his works" (35:237). One becomes, in short, as one shall be in heaven: "wholly contented with God and with all his works and with all his judgments, and loving and content with ourselves and with our fellow Christians and with everything which God loves" (49:265).

Resting in the peace of God is an experience of the assurance of salvation, and Julian describes her personal realization of this:

> I was filled full of everlasting surety, powerfully secured without any painful fear. This sensation was so welcome and so spiritual that I was wholly at peace, at ease and at rest, so that there was nothing upon earth which could have afflicted me. . . . And then presently God gave me again comfort and rest for my soul, delight and security so blessedly and so powerfully that there was no fear, no sorrow, no pain, physical or spiritual, that one could suffer which might have disturbed me (15:204-5).

However, this consoling experience was a fleeting one for Julian, alternating with the experience of desolation. She realizedthat peace is the unearned, free gift of the Spirit, yet she also learned that God wants human beings to dispose themselves to receive and retain it:

> For it is God's will that we do all in our power to preserve our consolation, for bliss lasts forevermore, and pain is passing, and will be reduced to nothing for those who will be saved. Therefore it is not God's will that when we feel pain we should pursue it in sorrow and mourning for it, but that suddenly we should pass it over, and preserve ourselves in the endless delight which is God (15:205).

The Gift of Joy

In the first revelation, while Julian is contemplating the suffering Christ, she tells us of her sudden experience of joy; "Suddenly the trinity filled my heart full of the greatest joy, and I understood that it will be so in heaven without end to all who will come there" (4:181). In heaven the blessed share in "the delight which the blessed trinity has in the cruel passion of Christ, once his sorrowful death was accomplished." But it is God's will that this, too, be experienced on earth: "[God] wishes that joy and delight to be our solace and happiness, as it is [God's], until we come to glory in heaven" (1:176). One ought to seek for this gift from God, for God is eager to give it (10:196). Julian records her own prayer:

> Ah, Jesus, let us pay heed to this bliss over our salvation which is in the blessed trinity, and let us desire to have as much spiritual delight by his grace. . . . Let our delight in our salvation be like the joy which Christ has in our salvation, as much as that may be whilst we are here (23:219).

It is especially through contemplation that the soul enters into this joy of God. One first learns to understand God's joy over human salvation:

> Our courteous Lord shows himself to the soul, happily and with the gladdest countenance, welcoming it as a friend. . . . Our soul is honorably received in joy, as it will be when it comes into heaven, as often as it comes by the operation of grace of the Holy Spirit and the power of Christ's passion (40:246).[14]

Then the contemplative begins to share in God's joy, and to recognize it as the gift beyond all others that God wants human beings to possess:

> What can make us to rejoice more in God than to see in him that in us, of all his greatest works, God has joy? . . . [God] wants our hearts to be powerfully lifted above the depths of the earth and all empty sorrows, and to rejoice in him (68:314).[15]

We are invited, in other words, to rejoice in God's joy in us. We can love ourselves, find joy in ourselves, because God loves and rejoices in us. This joy can be ours even in the midst of pain and suffering. While throughout our lives we always have "matter for mourning, because our sin is the cause of Christ's pains," *even more* do we have "constantly matter for joy, because endless love made [Christ] suffer" (52:280; my emphasis). Once again we are reminded of the "much more" of Romans 5.[16]

Contemplative prayer is actually "a right understanding of that fulness of joy which is to come, with true longing and trust" (42:252). As such, it initiates in the contemplative a foretaste of the bliss of heaven, which is "to possess God in the clarity of endless light, truly seeing him, sweetly feeling him, peacefully possessing him in the fulness of joy" (72:320). In the union thus

created, "God rejoices in the creature and the creature in God, endlessly marvelling" (44:256).

The joy received as gift from the Spirit overflows into thanksgiving and praise:

> Thanksgiving is a true inward acknowledgment, we applying ourselves with great reverence and loving fear and with all our powers to the work that our Lord moved us to, rejoicing and giving thanks inwardly. And sometimes the soul is so full of this that it breaks out in words and says: Good Lord, great thanks, blessed may you be (41:250).[17]

This is what the saved experience in the bliss of heaven, "praising and thanking God," saying "with one voice: Lord, blessed may you be."[18] In spite of human foolishness and blindness, this is how God constantly regards humanity, rejoicing in the work of creation which praises God. One can, even now, please God best "by wisely and truly believing it, and rejoicing with him and in him" (85:341).

The Perfection of Love

Julian describes every aspect of the Christian life in terms of its grounding in love. There is a permanence about humanity's love for God, even when one is separated from God through sin, because human creation is always held united to God in the substance of the soul; but that love is also increased and perfected through sensual life in time. Julian uses three terms to describe this love: Uncreated Charity, created charity, and given charity. God is Uncreated Charity, the source of the soul's love for God, in distinction to created charity which is the human soul in God, that is, the natural love by which the human always longs for God, the ineradicable image of God seated in the human will. But given charity is a gift of the Spirit over and above created charity; it perfects and increases the soul's natural love and desire for God. It is "a gift of grace in deeds, in which we love God for himself, and ourselves in God, and all that God loves for God" (84:341).[19] It is the gradual bringing of the whole self, including one's sensuality, into the union with God's will which has been eternally present in one's substance.

It is especially through prayer that the Spirit brings to perfection the union of wills that exists between God and the creature. Eventually, the human will is so much in tune with God's that one can pray for what one desires, confident that it is also pleasing to God: "we may with reverence ask from our lover all that we will, for our natural will is to have God, and God's good will is to have us" (6:186). Consequently, one can have a certain confidence that God will do what one desires. As Christ told Julian:

How could it now be that you would pray to me for anything pleasing to me which I would not very gladly grant to you? For my delight is in your holiness and in your endless joy and bliss in me (24:221).

Prayer is, then, in essence, "a true and gracious, enduring will of the soul, united and joined to our Lord's will by the sweet, secret operation of the Holy Spirit." Through it, God gradually "makes us like to himself in condition as we are in nature" (41:249). This is a foretaste of the union with God's will in love that one will enjoy in heaven. The Christian is made like the servant of the parable, "loving to do his lord's will" (51:267). Like the servant, the Christian realizes deep within the self "a foundation of love, the love which he had for the lord, which was equal to the love which the lord had for him" (51:273). And this love is the presence of the Spirit, who is "Uncreated Charity," bringing into fulfillment the potential of the human to image the love of God.

We have already discussed the emphasis Julian places upon love for others in her theology. Hers is no "private mysticism." Growth into union with the will of God finds expression in love for others. In this union Christians experience "a great and marvellous knowledge of love in God without end," which "makes us to love everything which [God] loves for love of him, and to be well satisfied with him and with all his works" (61:300). This love is what prompted Julian to insist so strongly that the privileges granted her in prayer were meant for all her fellow Christians: "For of all things, contemplating and loving the creator makes the soul to seem less in its own sight, and fills it full with reverent fear and true meekness, and with much love for its fellow Christians" (6:187).

Love and Reverent Fear

The gradual perfection of love drives out fear, especially the fear destructive of trust in God which Julian calls despair or "doubtfulfear."[20] In the seventh revelation, Julian experienced a security in God's love which was completely "without any painful fear" (15:204). When a person opens self to God in love to receive God's "sweet gracious teaching," and knows the comforting presence of God, doubtful fear disappears, and one learns to resist any movement which encourage it (79:334).

The perfection of love in human nature has the same qualities as God's love for humanity, namely courtesy and homeliness.[21] The absence of doubtful fear and the assurance of salvation, which come as the gifts of prayer, allow one to enter into a certain intimacy with God: "For our courteous Lord wants us to be as [homely] with him as heart may think or soul may desire." Yet this homeliness does not wipe out courtesy: "let us

beware that we do not accept this [homeliness] so carelessly as to forsake courtesy. For our Lord himself is supreme [homeliness], and he is as courteous as he is [homely]" (77:331). True love for God never degenerates into presumptive familiarity, but the courtesy that the creature owes the majesty of God is expressed in an attitude of awe which Julian calls "reverent fear."

Though all other forms of fear are driven out by love, reverent fear is increased. It is gentle, like God's attitude of courtesy, but it honors the reality of who God is in all God's transcendent, mysterious otherness. It always accompanies the perfection of love:

> Love and fear are brothers, and they are rooted in us by the goodness of our Creator, and they will never be taken from us without end. It is our nature to love, and we are given grace to love; and it is our nature to fear, and we are given grace to fear. . . . And yet this reverent fear and love are not the same, but they are different in kind and in effect, and neither of them may be obtained without the other (74:324-25).[22]

Love and reverent fear are human responses to different attributes in God:

> It is proper to God's lordship and his fatherhood to be feared, as it is proper to his goodness to be loved; and it is proper to us who are his servants and his children to fear him, for his lordship and fatherhood, as it is proper to us to love him for his goodness (74:325).

Whoever loves God also fears God, and the experience of this on earth is a foreshadowing of the life of heaven:

> The natural attribute of fear which we have in this life by the grace-giving operation of the Holy Spirit will be the same in heaven before God, gentle, courteous, most sweet; and thus in love we shall be [homely] and close to God, and in fear we shall begentle and courteous to God, and both the same, in the same way (74:325).[23]

Julian's notion that reverent fear increases with the perfection of love allows her to describe mystical union with God in a way that forbids any identification between the soul and God. The sense of the essential difference between creature and Creator is enhanced, not diminished, by the perfection of love.

The Saints in Heaven

Julian's description of heaven includes the community of the saints, that "blessed company" completely united in mind and will with God, who rejoice in the salvation of each other as much as they do in their own salvation. They also long, with Christ's love-longing, for the coming to bliss of those still on their earthly sojourn. Therefore Christians receive help from them, and "holy, endless friendship" (6:185).

Julian lived in an age well aware of the companionship of love and concern provided by the blessed in heaven to the church on earth. The intercession of the saints, the veneration of relics, and pilgrimage to sacred shrines were hallmarks of the late Middle Ages.[24] However, undoubtedly aware of the extremes to which such devotions could go, Julian exhibits a cautious attitude towards them.[25] It was much more important for her to enter into companionship with God in prayer than to pray to many saints. In speaking of the purpose of her first revelation, Julian makes the following comment:

> This revelation was given to my understanding to teach our souls wisely to adhere to the goodness of God; and in that same time our habits of prayer were brought to my mind, how in our ignorance of love we are accustomed to employ many inter-mediaries. Then I saw truly that it is more honor to God and more true delight if we faithfully pray to him for his goodness, and adhere to this by grace, with true understanding and steadfast belief, than if we employed all the intermediaries of which a heart may think. For if we employ all these intermediaries, this is too little and it is not complete honor to God; but his goodness is full and complete, and in it is nothing lacking (6:184-85).

Julian intimates that, for many in her day, devotion to the saints had replaced prayer to God, chiefly because God's goodness and love were poorly understood. Through the publication of her revelations, which emphasize God's love so strongly, she hopes to help rectify this.

There is a place for devotion to the saints: "the intermediaries which the goodness of God has ordained to help us are very lovely and many," and it pleases God "that we seek him and honor him through intermediaries," as long as we understand that God is "the goodness of everything." The proper attitude towards the saints is the same that holds for everything else in Julian's understanding of reality. One cannot find rest in anything created, but only in God. Though it may be good and beneficial on occasion to pray to the saints, "the highest form of prayer is to the goodness of God, which comes down to us to our humblest needs." Furthermore, one must always remember that "the chief and principal intermediary is the blessed nature which [Christ] took of the virgin" (6:185). It is through the mediation of Jesus, especially the suffering Jesus, that one is put in touch with the inner life of the trinity.

Julian does consider the saints, however, as concrete evidence for the triumph of God's mercy and grace over sin. With the exception of Mary, the only saints she mentions are those whose sinfulness is well documented, such as David, Mary Magdalen, Peter and Paul, Thomas of India, and John of Beverly (38:242-43).[26] Since the saints once shared human weakness yet now enjoy honor in heaven, sinners can take courage that the same honor will come to them.

Mary: Prototype of the Perfect Christian

Mary is the only saint whom Julian "saw" in her revelations; she gained an inward understanding of "the virtues of her blessed soul, her truth, her wisdom, her love" through which Julian was taught to know herself and reverently to fear God (25:222). Mary functions in Julian's theology as a prototype for human nature. She is the true image of God, one whose own truth [or might], wisdom, and love luminously reflect the trinity.

Julian saw Mary on three occasions: "as she conceived, . . . as she had been under the cross, and . . . as she is now, in delight, honor and joy" (25:223). The first sight emphasizes Mary as the perfect example of human nature as created by God, the second reveals the way she shared in Christ's work of mercy, suffering compassionately with him and for him, and the third presents Mary as the human being perfected by grace, sharing in the three "heavens" of the trinity. All three works of God, nature, mercy, and grace, are seen in their effects upon Mary, the perfect Christian.

At the time of the Incarnation, Mary's attitude towards God's messenger reveals those virtues basic to the creature who realizes the Creator's greatness:

> I saw her . . . [as] a simple, humble maiden, young in years, grown a little taller than a child, of the stature which she had when she conceived. Also God showed me part of the wisdom and the truth of her soul, and in this I understood the reverent contemplation with which she beheld her God, who is her creator, marvelling with great reverence that he was willing to be born of her who was a simple creature created by him. And this wisdom and truth, this knowledge of her creator's greatness and of her own created littleness, made her say very meekly to Gabriel: Behold me here, God's handmaiden (4:182).[27]

Mary is thus the perfection of creaturehood, the true image of God, "greater, more worthy, and more fulfilled, than everything else which God has created," except for the humanity of Christ (4: 182).

When Julian saw Mary at the time of Christ's passion, she was given to understand the nature of her compassion for Christ:

Christ and she were so united in love that the greatness of her love was the cause of the greatness of her pain. For in this I saw a substance of natural love, which is developed by grace, which his creatures have for him, and this natural love was most perfectly and surpassingly revealed in his sweet mother; for as much as she loved him more than all others, her pain surpassed that of all others. For always, the higher, the stronger, the sweeter that love is, the more sorrow it is to the lover to see the body which he loved in pain (18:210).

Mary represents for Julian the perfection of the quality of compassion which she herself had prayed to attain: the grace of being able to "have the mind of Christ" in order to suffer with him. She represents the realism of Julian's approach to suffering. Though suffering is temporary, and will be cause for joy in heaven, it is nevertheless real and painful. It becomes even more painful, not less so, when one grows in love of Christ, because then one sorrows over the sufferings of Christ, whom one loves.

Finally, Julian saw Mary's glorification in heaven:

Just as before I had seen her small and simple, now [Christ] showed her high and noble and glorious and more pleasing to him than all creatures. And so he wishes it to be known that all who take delight in him should take delight in her, and in the delight that he has in her and she in him (25:222-23).

Julian makes an explicit link between Mary in glory and Mary at the foot of the cross. She sees the exalted Mary immediately after the countenance of the Crucified has turned to joy, and he has revealed to her the "three heavens" by which the trinity rejoice over Christ's sufferings, and the joy he takes in his side opened up for love. Then he "looked down on his right, and brought to . . . mind where our Lady stood at the time of his passion" (25:221). Julian does not see the sorrowing mother, but Mary glorious in heaven. Her glory, however, is intimately connected to the suffering she endured in union with the suffering and death of Christ. So it shall be for all the saved.

Julian understood her vision of Mary in glory as a revelation not only of Mary, but of the love God has for her:

Because of the wonderful, exalted and singular love that he has for this sweet maiden, his blessed mother, our Lady St. Mary, he reveals her bliss and joy through the sense of these sweet words, as if he said, do you wish to see how I love her, so that you could rejoice with me in the love which I have in her and she has in me? (25:222).

Mary is therefore the model for the unity of love that exists between creature and God in heaven.

Furthermore, through the love Christ showed towards Mary, Julian understood an even deeper message of love for all who will be saved:

And for greater understanding of these sweet words our good Lord speaks in love to all [humankind] who will be saved, addressing them all as one person, as if he said, do you wish to see in her how you are loved? It is for love of you that I have made her so exalted, so noble, so honorable; and this delights me. And I wish it to delight you (25:222).

Christ's love for all the saved motivated him to enter into Mary's womb, so that he might become "our mother in all things" (60:297). Julian therefore understands the motherhood of Mary towards humanity in terms of the motherhood of Christ:

So our Lady is our mother, in whom we are all enclosed and born of her in Christ, for she who is mother of our savior is mother of all who are saved in our savior; and our savior is our true Mother, in whom we are endlessly born and out of whom we shall never come (57:292).

Mary is the mother of the whole Christ, "perfect humanity," which includes all the saved united to Christ in one renewed human nature (57:292).

Like all those on the path to salvation, Mary enjoyed in her earthly life the intimations of the life of heaven which are the fruits of the Spirit's work. These gifts come most easily and abundantly through prayer, and Mary is the model of the true contemplative:

Our good Lord showed our Lady St. Mary . . . to signify the exalted wisdom and truth which were hers as she contemplated her creator. This wisdom and truth showed her in contemplation how great, how exalted, how mighty and how good was her God. The greatness and nobility of her contemplation of God filled her full of reverent fear; and with this she saw herself so small and so humble, so simple and so poor in comparison with her God that this reverent fear filled her with humility. And founded on this, she was filled with grace and with every kind of virtue, and she surpasses all creatures (7:187).[28]

Except for Christ himself, there is no better example of the fully graced image of God than Mary.

The Possibility of Universal Salvation

Throughout her revelations, Julian reminds us that she is speaking only of those destined for salvation because "God showed me no one else" (9:192). Yet this also causes her some perplexity concerning damnation, about which nothing was revealed. In fact, her revelations seem to come close to preaching *apocatastasis*, or universal salvation, and Julian sees this as being in conflict with official Church teaching.[29] Though no clear revelation about eternal damnation is ever given to her, Julian eventually comes to some conclusions about it.

From the beginning to the end of her revelations, Julian had "two kinds of contemplation," two points of view, from which to consider what was revealed to her. The one supplied by her revelations was "endless continuing love, with certainty of protection and blessed salvation," the notion summed up so often in the phrase "all will be well," and which certainly tended towards *apocatastasis*. The other was "the common teaching of Holy Church" in which, until the time of her revelations, Julian "had been instructed and grounded" and which she had "practiced and understood" (46:258). Julian insists that the new insight supplied by her revelations did not replace the teaching of the church:

> And the contemplation of this [church teaching] did not leave me, for by the revelation I was not moved or led away from it in any way at all; but I was taught in the revelation to love it and rejoice in it, so that I might with the help of our Lord and his grace increase and rise to more heavenly knowledge and a higher loving (44:258-59).

Since both her revelations and church teaching come from God, they cannot contradict one another, but only contextualize and deepen each other.

Nonetheless, church teaching, as Julian understands it, seems incompatible with the tendency towards *apocatastasis* she sees in her revelations:

> And one article of our faith is that many creatures will be damned, such as the angels who fell out of heaven because of pride, who now are devils, and many . . . upon earth who die out of the faith of Holy Church, that is to say those who are pagans and many who have received baptism and who live unchristian lives and so die out of God's love. All these will be eternally condemned to hell, as Holy Church teaches me to believe (32:233).[30]

Julian believes that this teaching is "founded on God's word" which "will be preserved in all things." Indeed, Christ explicitly promises Julian, "I shall preserve my word in everything," but in the same breath also promises, "I shall make everything well." Julian understands this dual promise to mean that she must believe firmly in both church teaching and the more universally salvific promise of her revelations (32:233), and at first she views this as an irreconcilable contradiction. If church teaching were indeed true, it seems to her "impossible that every kind of thing should be well." The only answer she

receives to her perplexity is Christ's statement that "what is impossible to you is not impossible to me" (32:233).[31]

But Julian's speculative mind will not let her rest with this, and she seeks greater clarity. She desires "some sight of hell and of purgatory," not because she wants confirmation of church teaching, but so that she might better understand it. This sight is never granted to her (33:234). Instead, she is reminded of God's attitude towards the devil which had already been revealed in the fifth revelation:

> In God there can be no anger . . . and it is with power and justice, to the profit of all who will be saved, that [God] opposes the damned, who in malice and malignity work to frustrate and oppose God's will. Also I saw our Lord scorn [the devil's] malice and despise him as nothing. . . . For in this God revealed that the devil is damned. . . . I saw that on Judgment Day he will be generally scorned by all who will be saved, of whose salvation he has had great envy. For then he will see that all the woe and tribulation which he has caused them will be changed into the increase of their eternal joy. And all the pain and the sorrow that he wanted to bring them into will go forever with him to hell (13:201-2).

God's making all well could conceivably include the ultimate destruction of the devil along with all the evils he attempted to inflict upon the human race. Julian speculates that the same might be true of people who become enslaved to Satan:

> I understand that every creature who is of the devil's condition in this life and so dies is no more mentioned before God and all his saints than is the devil, notwithstanding that they belong to the human race, whether they have been baptized or not (33:234).[32]

It is not clear what Julian means here. Perhaps God and the saints simply overlook the damned, not taking them seriously since they pose no threat to them. She could, however, be implying that the damned will fall into oblivion, into nothingness, rather than suffer some eternal torment.[33] She certainly receives no pictures of eternal hell-fire. Elsewhere, she equates the pain of hell with despair (17:209). Her revelations remain silent on the subject: "the revelation was shown to reveal goodness, and little mention was made in it of evil" (33:234).

While Julian seems able to entertain the possibility of damnation for certain persons who are truly evil, she questions its application towards the multitudes which seem to be condemned by church teaching. She singles out the Jews for special mention:

But I saw nothing so exactly specified concerning the Jews who put [Christ] to death; and nonetheless I knew in my faith that they were eternally accursed and condemned, except those who were converted by grace (33:234).

"All will be well" continues to seem irreconcilable with the church's judgment on this issue.

Another possible way out of the contradiction between her revelations and church teaching is through the subordination of the particular to the general. At one point Julian asks whether someone she loves will be saved, and she is given no reply. Instead, she is counseled to accept "generally" the lessons she learns about salvation, "for it is more honor to God to contemplate him in all things than in any one special thing" (35:236). If she can learn to act in accordance with this, Julian thinks, "I should not be glad because of any special thing or be greatly distressed by anything at all, for all will be well; for the fulness of joy is to contemplate God in everything" (35:237). By viewing the whole picture, in which God has ordained everything "for the best" and always leads it to that end, one might conceivably be able to include the eternal damnation of particular persons as part of that process.

However, Julian is also taught that the promise "all will be well" specifically includes the particular: "every kind of thing." God takes heed not only of "the noble and great" but also of the "little and small," and God wants us to know "that the smallest thing will not be forgotten" (32:231-32). Contemplating God's activity on behalf of humanity "in general" does not exclude particular individuals (36:240), as is evident in the following passage reminiscent of the gospel parable of the lost sheep:[34]

[Christ] dwells here in us, and rules us, and cares for us in this life, and brings us to his bliss. And so he will do as long as any soul is on earth who will come to heaven; and so much so that if there were no such soul on earth except one, he would be with it, all alone, until he had brought it up into his bliss (80:335-36).

Julian's revelations strongly suggest that the "all" that will be well in God's promise includes "every particular" human being, although this is never stated absolutely.

In further support of this conclusion, the stress throughout Julian's revelations on the goodness of creation, situated within the eternal goodness and power of God, tends towards the absolute:

I saw most truly that [God] never changed his purpose *in any kind of thing,* nor ever will eternally.

For there was nothing unknown to him in his just ordinance before time began, and therefore *all things were set in order,* before anything was made, as it would endure eternally. And *no kind of thing will fail* in that respect, for he has made *everything totally good* (11:198-99; emphasis mine).

This is why sin is ultimately powerless against God's eternal might, wisdom, and goodness.[35]

Julian's revelations lead to the conclusion that it is at least much more probable that everyone will be saved than that some will be damned. Their emphasis upon trust in salvation is so strong, and the absence of anything to the contrary so glaring, that this is likely the conclusion that Julian herself reached, though she does not say so explicitly.

This conclusion is further supported by two other insights which Julian received. First, the full reality of God and God's purposes are finally beyond human understanding in this world, even beyond the teachings of the church, though those are truly God's word. Julian talks about this insight by contrasting God's viewpoint with that of the church in terms of two "portions," two mysteries, and two judgments.

God's will for humanity is contained in two portions, one open and revealed, the other hidden. The open portion contains everything related to "our savior and our salvation." It includes "all who are of good will," that is, all the just who live the sacramental life, and follow the teachings of the church and the inner inspirations of the Holy Spirit:

We are bound to this [open portion] by God, and drawn and counselled and taught, inwardly by the Holy Spirit, and outwardly through the same grace by Holy Church. Our Lord wants us to be occupied in this, rejoicing in him, for he rejoices in us. And the more plentifully we accept from this with reverence and humility, the more do we deserve thanks from him, and the more profit do we win for ourselves (30:228).

The other portion includes "all which is additional to our salvation," which I take to mean God's will for those outside the pale of Christianity and unacquainted with the gospel message of salvation, along with all the aspects of human history that do not appear consistent with Christian doctrine. This is hidden from human understanding in this life:

For this is our Lord's privy counsel, and it is fitting to God's royal dominion to keep his privy counsel in peace, and it is fitting to his servants out of obedience and respect not to wish to know his counsel (30:228).[36]

Julian speaks in a similar fashion of two kinds of mystery:

> One is this great mystery, with all the individual mysteries pertaining to it, and these [God] wishes us to know as hidden until the time that he wishes to reveal them to us plainly. The other is the mysteries which he himself plainly showed in this revelation, for these are mysteries which he wishes to make open and known to us (34:235).

Here Julian's "private" revelations are included with the teachings of the church as part of the open revelation which God wants humans to know.

Julian also speaks of two "judgments," in which her revelations are distinguished from church teaching: the first is "that fair, sweet judgment" which was shown in her revelations, wherein God always looks upon sinners with love; the second is "mixed" human judgment, sometimes "good and lenient," and sometimes "hard and painful." Julian calls the latter the "lower judgment" and equates it with the judgment of the church: "The lower judgment had previously been taught me in Holy Church, and therefore I could not in any way ignore the lower judgment" (45:256-57). The higher judgment, however, comes from God's eternal viewpoint, and while stated as general fact in Julian's revelations, still contains many mysteries hidden within it. The full realization of its meaning will not be available until the end of time.

In all three cases, God's activity towards the world is not limited by the church's understanding and interpretation of God's revelation, even though church teaching is truly God's word. Thereremains a profound mystery surrounding God's dealings with humanity.

The second insight Julian received in support of universal salvation deals with a mysterious deed which God will perform at the end of time:

> There is a deed which the blessed trinity will perform on the last day, as I see it, and what the deed will be and how it will be performed is unknown to every creature who is inferior to Christ, and it will be until the deed is done. . . . This is the great deed ordained by our Lord God from without beginning, treasured and hidden in his blessed breast, known only to himself, through which deed he will make all things well. For just as the blessed trinity created all things from nothing, just so will the same blessed trinity make everything well which is not well (32:232-33).

Julian must mean some further salvific act on the part of God whereby all those presently unconnected with Christianity will somehow be saved at the end of time.[37] She refuses to speculate more specifically about it, because God does not wish her to do so (33:235). God's

love wants human beings to know it will occur, and it is summarized in the promise, "all will be well." Trusting in this promise will allow Christians "to be at ease in our souls and at peace in love, disregarding every disturbance which could hinder our true rejoicing." But God's power and wisdom, also out of love for humanity, "want to conceal it and hide it from us, what it will be and how it will be done" (32:232).

These two insights, working together, allow Julian to make an eventual reconciliation between church teaching and the message of her revelations. Church teaching is the open portion of God's revelation. God allows the possibility of damnation to be one of the teachings which can lead to salvation. Eternal damnation is understood in a way similar to Julian's reflection on mortal sin, which can be interpreted as "deadly" for us, though it is not actually so in God's sight.[38] Church teachings about damnation, like those about mortal sin, are legitimate and necessary; without them human beings would not realize the horror of sin, nor the value of the sacramental life of grace within the church, and they would be tempted to presumption.

But Julian's revelations provide a corrective to this teaching, which she sees as even more important. The fear engendered by any unmitigated teaching about eternal damnation could, in fact, lead many away from salvation and into despair.[39] God's promise that "all will be well," points beyond specific church doctrine to a God utterly more loving and mysterious than humans can understand. The promise that such a loving and generous God will indeed "make allwell" allows God's lovers to take courage and find comfort in the midst of their struggle with evil. The way to salvation is through trust and love, not through painful fear.

Julian eventually came to the conclusion that both ways of looking at salvation are needed:

> It seemed to me that it was necessary to see and to know that we are sinners and commit many evil deeds which we ought to forsake, and leave many good deeds undone which we ought to do, so that we deserve pain, blame and wrath. And despite all this, I saw truly that our Lord was never angry, and never will be. . . . I saw in the same revelation that there are many hidden mysteries which can never be known until the time when God in his goodness has made us worthy to see them (46:259).

With this realization she found a resolution to the apparent contradictions between her revelations and church teaching. She tells us, "I am well satisfied, waiting upon our Lord's will in this great marvel. And now I submit myself to my mother, Holy Church, as a simple child should" (46:259).

Julian does not, strictly speaking, teach a doctrine of universal salvation. For one thing, she allows the possibility that the devil and those enslaved to the powers of evil will sink into nothingness at the end of time. She keeps eternal damnation as a possibility, and admits that church teaching on this subject is legitimate. But she finds it far more important to stress the power of God's love to conquer evil in all its forms and to bring "every kind of thing" into the perfection for which it was created. Since God's love is infinitely more powerful than diabolical or human efforts to perpetrate evil, we can hope that God will effect the salvation even of those whom human judgment deems irrevocably lost.[40] Since God's might, wisdom, and love exceed by far human ability to know, one ought to submit one's understanding to the greater judgment of God. Finally, Julian expresses faith in some eschatological deed, presently beyond human knowledge and understanding, through which God will bring everything into the fulfillment established as God's will from the beginning.

If Julian's teaching can be summed up in one word, that word is love. Her whole effort is to present to her troubled times the picture of a God who loves absolutely the whole creation which is itself an expression of divine love. Eschatological hope is not misplaced when it trusts that this love can bring all into eternal fulfillment. No more fitting conclusion to a discussion of Julian's eschatology can be found than the words with which she herself ends *Showings,* words summing up the meaning of her whole revelatory experience:

> And from the time that it [the showing] was revealed, I desired many times to know in what was our Lord's meaning. And fifteen years after and more, I was answered in spiritual understanding, and it was said: What, do you wish to know your Lord's meaning in this thing? Know it well, love was his meaning. Who reveals it to you? Love. What did he reveal to you? Love. Why does he reveal it to you? For love. Remain in this, and you will know more of the same. But you will never know different, without end.

So I was taught that love is our Lord's meaning. And I saw very certainly in this and in everything that before God made us he loved us, which love was never abated and never will be. And in this love he has done all his works, and in this love he has made all things profitable to us, and in this love our life is everlasting. In our creation we had beginning, but the love in which he created us was in him from without beginning. In this love we have our beginning, and all this shall we see in God without end (86:342-43).

Notes

[1] Leclercq, *The Love of Learning,* 65-86.

[2] Note how this image recalls scriptural passages about the eschatological banquet, such as Mt 22:1-10 and Rev 19:9.

[3] This passage is full of scriptural echoes. For example, the joy and honor of the first heaven recall the reward promised in the beatitudes to those who suffer for righteousness (Mt 5:6, 11-12), the parable of the talents (Mt 25:14-30; Lk 19:11-27) and the parable of the last judgment (Mt 25:31-34), and John 12:26: "if anyone serve me the Father will honor him." The second heaven recalls Ps 90:16 and the joy of all heaven over repentant sinners of Lk 15:7, 10.

[4] Note how this picks up the theme of the parable of the workers in the vineyard (Mt 20:1-16).

[5] This recalls Christ's transfiguration: "and his garments became glistening, intensely white" (Mk 9:3).

[6] The image of the crown symbolizes that Christ, the faithful servant, receives the reward of the just, as in Isaiah 61:10: "he has clothed me with the garments of salvation, he has covered me with the robe of righteousness, as a bridegroom decks himself witha garland," and James 1:12: "Blessed is the man who endures trial, for when he has stood the test he will receive the crown of life which God has promised to those who love him." See also Heb 2:9: "But we see Jesus, who for a little while was made lower than the angels, crowned with glory and honor."

[7] The use of "city" in this context, recalls Rev 21:2-3: "And I saw the holy city, new Jerusalem, coming down out of heaven from God, prepared as a bride adorned for her husband; and I heard a loud voice from the throne saying, 'Behold the dwelling of God is with men. He will dwell with them, and they shall be his people, and God himself will be with them.'" See Leclercq's comments on the symbol of the heavenly Jerusalem (*The Love of Learning,* 66-70, 76-83).

[8] This is the union desired by Jesus in John 17:21: "That they may all be one; even as thou, Father, art in me, and I in thee, that they also may be in us."

[9] This passage provides a clear example of the kind of sensual language frequently used in the Middle Ages for describing the experience of God (cf. Bynum, *Holy Feast,* pp. 150-52). It lists the "spiritual senses," which were often elaborately described in mystical literature (See, for example, Karl Rahner, "The Doctrine of the 'Spiritual Senses' in the Middle Ages," *TI* XVI, 104-34). The end of the passage has scriptural ties; see 1 Cor 13:12: "For now we see in a mirror dimly, but

then face to face" and 1 Jn 3:2: "Beloved, we are God's children now; it does not yet appear what we shall be, but we know that when he appears we shall be like him, for we shall see him as he is."

[10] This is an elaboration on the promise of Rev 21:4: "He will wipe away every tear from their eyes, and death shall be no more, neither shall there be mourning nor crying nor pain any more, for the former things have passed away."

[11] The trembling of the pillars of heaven is a scriptural image: "the pillars of heaven tremble, and are astounded" (Job 26:11); also, in Isaiah's vision of God, "the foundations of the thresholds shook at the voice of him who called" (Is 6:4).

[12] Colledge and Walsh point out that Julian may have in mind here the resurrection appearances of Christ in which peace is offered and fear is dispelled (Mt 28:10; Lk 24:36-38; Jn 20:19-21, 26; C&W, 506.13n).

[13] Note how this parallels Mt 11:28-30, especially "For my yoke is easy and my burden is light."

[14] The "friendly welcoming" recalls the welcome given to the prodigal son in Lk 15:20.

[15] Compare with Col 3:2: "Set your minds on things that are above, not on things that are on earth."

[16] See the discussion of this in Chapter 3 above, pp. 56-57.

[17] This passage could owe its inspiration to Phil 4:4-6: "Rejoice in the Lord always; again I will say, Rejoice. . . . Have no anxiety about anything, but in everything by prayer and supplication with thanksgiving let your requests be made to God," and Heb 12:28: "let us be grateful . . . and let us offer to God acceptable worship, with reverence and awe."

[18] This echoes the phrase "una voce dicentes" of the Preface, the preamble to the prayer of the heavenly host taken from Isaiah 6:3: "Holy, holy, holy is the Lord of hosts." It is also reminiscent of the picture of heaven given at the end of Augustine's *De civitate Dei* (22.30).

[19] Aquinas also distinguishes between Uncreated Charity, which is the Holy Spirit dwelling in us and created charity, whereby we participate in the mutual love between Father and Son (*ST* 2-2. Q23.A2). He also understands charity as a virtue infused into the soul (*ST* 2-2.Q24.A3). See C&W, 727.10n for other references.

[20] Julian is obviously applying the message of 1 John 4:17-18: "In this is love perfected with us, that we may have confidence for the day of judgment. . . . There is no fear in love, but perfect love casts out fear. For fear has to do with punishment, and he who fears is not perfected in love." This thought underlies the teaching of Cassian, Augustine, and Bernard on the "filial fear" of God (cf. Clark, *"Fiducia,"* 101).

[21] See Chapter 4 above, pp. 74-79.

[22] Note here how grace builds on nature. Colledge and Walsh consider this to be one of Julian's finest rhetorical and theological passages. See their comment at 673.20n.

[23] Note the parallel to the thought of Is 11:3: "His delight shall be in the fear of the Lord."

[24] See the discussion of this in Pelikan, 174-84.

[25] Such extremes were brilliantly satirized by Erasmus (cf. *Ten Colloquies,* trans. Craig R. Thompson [Indianapolis: Bobbs-Merrill, 1957]). For a discussion of medieval popular devotions, see Ronald C. Finucane, *Miracles and Pilgrims: Popular Beliefs in Medieval England* (Totowa, NJ: Rowman & Littlefield, 1977).

[26] Julian obviously expects John of Beverly to be known to her readers, but his fame has not extended to the present day. See C&W, 51 and 447.22n for information about him.

[27] The last line of this passage is an obvious paraphrase of Lk 1:38.

[28] Note how this passage expresses the sentiment of the Magnificat (Lk 1:46-55). It also contains an allusion to the angel's greeting of Lk 1:28.

[29] The notion of *Apocatastasis panton* is found in Clement of Alexandria, Origen, and Gregory of Nyssa. It was strongly attacked by Augustine. Julian, so thoroughly Augustinian in other respects, parts from him here, as she does with her teaching on sin. *Apocatastasis* was formally condemned by the Council of Constantinople in 543. Julian was correct in understanding this to be against church teaching (see the discussion of this in Chapter 1 above, pp. 18-22, with respect to the danger of heresy). For a bibliography on *apocatastasis,* see Gotthold Müller, *Apocatastasis Panton: A Bibliography* (Basel: Basler Missionsbuchhandlung, 1969).

[30] Cf. Mt 25:41; Is 14:12-14.

[31] Lk 18:27: "What is impossible with men is possible with God" and par. in Mt 19:26, and Lk 1:37: "For with God nothing will be impossible" (cf. also Gen 18:14; Job 42:2; Jer 32:17).

[32] Note the congruence here with Ps 69:28: "Let them be blotted out of the book of the living; let them not be enrolled among the righteous."

[33] Clark makes this interpretation (*"Fiducia,"* 105).

[34] Lk 15:3-10.

[35] Julian never even considers the solution advanced by Calvin a century and a half later, that God predestines some to damnation. This would be irreconcilable with her understanding of God's love.

[36] Note 1 Cor 2:7: "But we impart a secret and hidden wisdom of God, which God decreed before the ages for our glorification"; Rom 11:33: "O the depth of the riches and wisdom and knowledge of God! How unsearchable are his judgments and how inscrutable his ways!" and Sir 11:4: "For the works of the Lord are wonderful, and his works are concealed from men."

[37] This deed is not to be confused with another deed Julian speaks of which pertains to the future salvation of the individual Christian, referring especially to how God will make human sinfulness the cause of heavenly bliss, something which remains amystery to us in this present life, but which we will understand immediately upon entering heaven. Julian makes a special effort to distinguish this deed from the one mentioned earlier (36:238-40).

[38] See the discussion of this in Chapter 6 above, p. 127.

[39] Julian is trying to counteract the great fear of death and final judgment which permeated the popular religion of her day, made explicit, for instance, in the *Dies Irae* and the *Libera Me* of the Mass for the Dead. This fear is, as Colledge and Walsh note, contrary to her spirit of trust (C&W, 729.11n).

[40] This is similar to Karl Rahner's conclusion about universal salvation. See "The Hermeneutics of Eschatological Assertions," *TI* IV, 338-40. See also John R. Sachs, S.J., "Current Eschatology: Universal Salvation and the Problem of Hell," *Theological Studies* 52:2 (1991):227-54.

Works Cited

A Book of Showings to the Anchoress Julian of Norwich. Edited by Edmund Colledge, O.S.A. and James Walsh, S.J. Toronto: Pontifical Institute of Mediaeval Studies, 1978. . . .

Aquinas, Thomas. *Summa Theologica.* 3 vols. Translated by the Fathers of the English Dominican Province. New York: Benziger Brothers, 1947. . . .

Bynum, Caroline Walker. *Holy Feast and Holy Fast: The Religious Significance of Food to Medieval Women.* Berkeley: University of California Press, 1987. . . .

Clark, John P. H. *"Fiducia* in Julian of Norwich." *Downside Review* 99 (1981): 97-108, 214-29. . . .

Finucane, Ronald C. *Miracles and Pilgrims: Popular Beliefs in Medieval England.* Totowa, NJ: Rowman & Littlefield, 1977. . . .

Leclercq, Jean. *The Love of Learning and the Desire for God.* 2nd ed. Translated by Catharine Misrahi. New York: Fordham University Press, 1974. . . .

Müller, Gotthold. *Apocatastasis Panton: A Bibliography.* Basel: Basler Missionsbuchhandlung, 1969. . . .

Pelikan, Jaroslav. *The Christian Tradition: A History of the Development of Doctrine.* Vol. 3: *The Growth of Medieval Theology (600-1300).* Chicago: University of Chicago Press, 1978. . . .

Rahner, Karl. *Theological Investigations.* 20 vol. New York:Crossroad, 1982/83. . . .

Denise Nowakowski Baker (essay date 1994)

SOURCE: "The Parable of the Lord and Servant and the Doctrine of Original Sin" in *Julian of Norwich's "Showings": From Vision to Book,* Princeton University Press, 1994, pp. 83-106.

[*In the excerpt that follows, Baker examines several of Julian's revelations in detail, focusing on the vision that derived from the biblical parable of the Lord and the Servant. The critic suggests that Julian's interpretation of this vision diverges from traditional emphasis on sin and punishment, and instead uses the story to demonstrate forgiveness and redemption.*]

One of the most striking features of Julian of Norwich's solution to the problem of evil is her refusal to attribute wrath to God. She insists in Revelation Thirteen that God ascribes "no maner of blame to me ne to none that shalle be safe" (13.27.407) ["no kind of blame to me or to anyone who will be saved" (225)]. And she commences Revelation Fourteen by acknowledging that her showings seem to contradict the teachings of the church in regard to God's attitude toward sinners. In rejecting the depiction of God as wrathful, Julian calls into question a central premise of orthodox medieval theodicy. Claiming that "whatever is called evil is either sin or the punishment of sin,"[1] Augustine's solution to the problem of evil concentrates on justifying God's retribution against those who transgress divine injunctions. Invoking a juridical paradigm,

Augustine argues: "Sinners are ordained to punishment. This order is contrary to their nature, and is therefore penalty. But it suits their fault and is therefore just."[2] Drawing on the rhetoric of the Old Testament and the Pauline Epistles, medieval teachings about sin follow Augustine in portraying God as wrathful in his reprisals against the wicked.

The fear of such a wrathful judge pervades the medieval preoccupation with penance. Following the Fourth Lateran Council's decree in 1215 that all the faithful confess their sins at least once a year, the themes of guilt and punishment came to dominate verbal and visual pastoral instruction. A complex ecclesiastical apparatus developed based on "the conviction that God the Creditor kept an exact account of every sin and every debt."[3] Summae for confessors and manuals for penitents, designed to aid in the examination of conscience and the assessment of culpability, proliferated. To the sculptural programs of the virtues and vices developed in the high Middle Ages were added the more macabre images of the dead and dying in the late medieval period.[4] And the relief of the Last Judgment usually found on the tympanum over the west portal of the Gothic cathedral warned the faithful of the horrifying torments that those who die in sin will suffer eternally.[5] Based on a survey of similar evidence, Jean Delumeau concludes, "To thus re-create the image of God as it was proposed by theologians leads to the very heart of a history of mentalities, which reveals a link between the devaluation of a horribly sinful humanity and the rigor of the Supreme Judge."[6]

Although medieval theologians, in contrast to the uneducated laity, recognized that their characterization of God as wrathful was metaphoric, they insisted on the legal paradigm informing the orthodox Augustinian solution to the problem of evil. Augustine himself, explaining that Scripture often uses "words which even the most simple customarily use among themselves," concedes that God punishes without passion. "Because it is very difficult for a man to avenge something without experiencing anger, the authors of Scripture have decided to use the name *wrath* for God's vengeance, although God's vengeance is exercised with absolutely no such emotion."[7] Aquinas, likewise, acknowledges, "In attributing anger to God what is signified is not an emotion but a just judgment and the will to punish sin."[8] While both theologians deny that God feels anger, they nonetheless continue to regard the deity as punitive. The characterization of God as wrathful, despite its figurative status, thus betrays the juridical economy of human transgression and divine retribution informing Augustinian theodicy.

This theology of retribution troubled Julian of Norwich. She was not upset, as might be expected, by a fear of punishment, but rather by the depiction of God as wrathful. Without denying human sinfulness, Julian refuses to attribute to God the malevolence toward sinners that is characteristic of Augustinian theodicy. She admits that her showing seems to contradict the church's teachings and that this contradiction poses a dilemma for her. Referring to the two different perspectives from which humankind is judged, she writes:

> The furst dome, whych is of goddes ryghtfulnes, and that is of his owne hygh endlesse loue, and that is that feyer swete dome that was shewed in alle the feyer revelation in whych I saw hym assign(e) to vs no maner of blame. And though theyse were swete and delectable, 3ytt only in the beholdyng of this I culde nott be fulle esyd, and that was for the dome of holy chyrch, whych I had before vnderstondyn and was contynually in my syght. And therefore by this dome me thought that me behovyth nedys to know my selfe a synner. And by the same dome I vnderstode that synners be sometyme wurthy blame and wrath, and theyse two culde I nott see in god. And therfore my desyer was more than I can or may telle, for the hygher dome god shewed hym selfe in the same tyme, and therfore (m)e behovyd nedys to take it. And the lower dome was lernyd me beforetyme in holy chyrche, and therfore I myght nott by no weye leue the lower dome. (14.45.487-88)

> [The first judgment, which is from God's justice, is from his own great endless love, and that is that fair, sweet judgment which was shown in all the fair revelation in which I saw him assign to us no kind of blame. And though this was sweet and delectable, I could not be fully comforted only by contemplating it, and that was because of the judgment of Holy Church, which I had understood before, and which was continually in my sight. And therefore it seemed to me that by this judgment I must necessarily know myself a sinner. And by the same judgment I understood that sinners sometimes deserve blame and wrath, and I could not see these two in God, and therefore my desire was more than I can or may tell, because of the higher judgment which God himself revealed at the same time, and therefore I had of necessity to accept it. And the lower judgment had previously been taught me in Holy Church, and therefore I could not in any way ignore the lower judgment. (257)]

The discrepancy between her vision and the teachings of the church perplexed Julian. Although the resolution to her dilemma was revealed in "a mervelous example of a lorde and of a seruannt, as I shall sey after, and that full mystely shewed" (14.45.488) ["a wonderful example of a lord and a servant, as I shall tell later, and that was very mysteriously revealed" (257)], she confesses that it took her two decades of reflection to achieve an understanding of its meaning.

The difficulty that Julian must have had in comprehending this example is corroborated by her silence about all but the first three chapters of Revelation Fourteen in the summary of the showings she gives in chapter 1 of the long text; her failure to mention either the parable of the lord and servant or the idea of Jesus as Mother suggests that most of this revelation was composed during her second revision of the short text.[9] Nonetheless, as I will demonstrate in this chapter and the next, Revelation Fourteen completes the teleological theodicy that Julian commences in Revelation Thirteen. In the last ten chapters of Revelation Fourteen, she offers an ontological confirmation of her theodicy by developing an anthropology derived from mystical theology. In chapters 45 through 52 she expresses her disagreement with Augustinian premises about the nature of sin and the character of God's response to it.

The parable of the lord and servant in chapter 51 of Revelation Fourteen is the linchpin of Julian's solution to the problem of evil. Through this parable she offers an alternative to the doctrine of original sin crucial to Augustine's juridical theodicy. Based on his reading of Genesis 3 and Romans 5, Augustine proposes a theory of original sin to account for the depravity of the will that, he believes, renders individuals inevitably wicked but nonetheless culpable. By attributing the eruption of evil in creation to the free acts of rational creatures, angelic and human, who chose to disobey divine injunctions, Augustine and his medieval successors exonerate the all-knowing, all-good, and all-powerful Creator. Because Adam and Eve deliberately transgressed, God justly punishes their descendants, who inherit both guilt and weakness as a result of the original sin.

Julian's parable of the lord and servant revises the prevailing Augustinian reading of Genesis 3 and epitomizes her opposition to retributive theodicy. Augustine's interpretation is primarily etiological; hers, teleological. He reads the narrative as a literal, historical account; she, disregarding many of the details, stresses the typological relationship of Adam to Christ. Augustine emphasizes Adam's freedom in offending God and God's subsequent condemnation of the human race to punishment; Julian emphasizes the atonement made by Christ and God's subsequent gifts of justification and perseverance to the elect. Although both allude to chapter 5 of Paul's Epistle to the Romans, they concentrate on different parts of that text. The bishop of Hippo verifies his teachings on original sin by invoking Rom. 5:12-14; the anchorite of Norwich derives her dual interpretation of the vision of the lord and servant from Rom. 5:15-21. While both regard Adam's sin as a *felix culpa,* Augustine focuses his attention on the last word of the phrase; Julian, on the first. The distinctive metaphors that Augustine and Julian choose to define sin reveal a significant difference in their thinking about evil and in the emphasis of their theodicies. Both consider sin a deviation from the original created order, but Augustine's dominant metaphors for this condition are those of political conflict, whereas Julian's are those of physical separation.

As Elaine Pagels has shown, Augustine consistently discusses the etiology of evil, both historically and psychically, in terms of rebellion.[10] His impotence to resist sin despite his desire to do so he describes as an internal war. "I neither willed with my whole will nor was I wholly unwilling. And so I was at war with myself and torn apart by myself."[11] This *psychomachia,* this war within, is the penalty for an ancestral rebellion against God. "And this strife was against my will; yet it did not show the presence of another mind, but the punishment of my own. Thus it was no more I who did it, but the sin that dwelt in me—the punishment of a sin freely committed by Adam, and I was a son of Adam."[12] Augustine thus attributes his self-estrangement, the disobedience of his own will to his conscious desires, to the original disobedience of Adam to God. Writing of the Fall in *The City of God,* he concludes, "In the punishment of [Adam's] sin the retribution for disobedience is simply disobedience itself. For man's wretchedness is nothing but his own disobedience to himself, so that because he would not do what he could, he now wills to do what he cannot."[13] The *depravatio* that causes personal, actual sin is also the inherited punishment for a primordial, ancestral sin.

Augustine asserts the justice of such an inherited punishment on the grounds that God is just in punishing the rebellion of free agents. "The important point is that through the justice of God, who is our Lord and master and whom we refused to serve as his subjects, our flesh, which had been subject to us, now gives us trouble through its noncompliance, whereas we by our defiance of God have only succeeded in becoming a nuisance to ourselves, and not to God."[14] Although Augustine derives the idea of the inherited weakness or *vitium* from Paul, he presents it in a juridical context alien to the Apostle.[15] His theory of original sin holds not only that human beings commit actual, personal sins because of this inherited propensity, but also that all individuals are equally guilty of the first sin through their seminal identity in Adam. He thus speaks of the legacy of original sin as a defect in human nature and as a moral offense, as *vitium* and as *reatus,* both of which merit punishment.

Although Augustine attempts to legitimize his concept of original guilt by the use of political metaphors of freedom, authority, and rebellion, such legalisms are suspect when applied to the descendants of the act's perpetrator.[16] Nonetheless, ignoring the illogic of these political metaphors in his theodicy, Augustine exempts God from responsibility for evil by arguing that it is just for the all-good, all-knowing, and all-powerful deity to punish the uncompelled transgression of the parents by inflicting on their progeny both moral culpability for the primordial sin and the compulsion to further sin, each eternally damnable.

Augustine's concept of original sin provides the context and contrast for Julian's parable of the lord and servant. In her retelling of Genesis 3, she refuses to attribute disobedience to Adam or wrath to God. She presents the original transgression as an inadvertent separation from God rather than a deliberate act of rebellion. And she shows God's response to be compassionate mercy instead of justified anger. In so transforming the conventional reading of Genesis 3, Julian reveals her familiarity with the notion of the *regio dissimilitudinis,* or land of unlikeness, particularly as presented by the twelfth-century Cistercians, and with the theory of salvation developed by Anselm of Canterbury in *Cur Deus homo.* Representing original sin as a fall into the self, she mitigates the malice assigned to Adam in the Augustinian interpretation. And stressing the typological relationship between Adam and Christ, she nullifies any emphasis on the just wrath of God in response to such a transgression. In contrast to the traditional Augustinian explication of Genesis 3, Julian's does not concentrate on the justness of God's punishment of the initialtransgression but on the promise of a restoration. As in her discussion of the pedagogical effects of actual sin in Revelation Thirteen, she focuses on the teleology or purpose rather than the etiology or cause of original sin.

I

Julian admits that the example of the lord and servant was very difficult for her to comprehend. Presenting it in chapter 51, she attempts to recapitulate the process by which she came to understand its meaning. As she explains, this revelation was manifest in two ways: "That one perty was shewed gostly in bodely lycknesse. That other perty was shewed more gostly withoute bodely lycknes" (14.51.514); ["One part was shown spiritually, in a bodily likeness. The other part was shown more spiritually, without bodily likeness" (267)]. In addition to the two different kinds of showings combined in the example of the lord and servant, Julian identifies three levels of understanding.

> The furst is the begynnyng of techyng that I vnderstode ther in in the same tyme. The secunde is the inwarde lernyng that I haue vnderstonde there in sythen. The thyrd is alle the hole revelation fro the begynnyng to the ende whych oure lorde god of his goodnes bryngyth oftymes frely to the syght of my vnderstondyng. And theyse thre be so onyd, as to my vnderstondyng, that I can nott nor may deperte them. (14.52.519-20)

[The first is the beginning of the teaching which I understood from it at the time. The second is the

inward instruction which I have understood from it since. The third is all the whole revelation from the beginning to the end, which our Lord God of his goodness freely and often brings before the eyes of my understanding. And these three are so unified, as I understand it, that I cannot and may not separate them. (269)]

Although Julian had an immediate comprehension of one level, her full interpretation develops over a period of time. She tries to recapitulate this growth of awareness by presenting the example recursively, moving from the description of the bodily likeness to her immediate response and then to the subsequent interpretation.

Julian begins with a description of the scene she envisioned. Her focus moves from the pair to the servant and then back to the lord. She presents the initial relationship between lord and servant as mutually benevolent: "The servannt stondyth before his lorde, reverently redy to do his lordes wylle. The lorde lokyth vppon his seruannt full louely and swetly and mekely" (14.51.514); ["The servant stands before his lord, respectfully, ready to do his lord's will. The lord looks on his servant very lovingly and sweetly and mildly" (267)]. Then Julian observes the servant in theact of falling. She emphasizes the good will with which he sets out to perform the lord's command and depicts his fall as a consequence of his eagerness to obey.

> [The lord] sendyth hym in to a certeyne place to do his wyll. The servannt nott onely he goyth, but sodenly he stertyth and rynnyth in grett hast for loue to do his lordes wylle. And anon he fallyth in a slade, and takyth ful grett sorow; and than he gronyth and monyth and wallowyth and wryeth, but he may nott ryse nor helpe hym selfe by no manner of weye. (14.51.514-515)

[[The lord] sends him to a certain place to do his will. Not only does the servant go, but he dashes off and runs at great speed, loving to do his lord's will. And soon he falls into a dell and is greatly injured; and then he groans and moans and tosses about and writhes, but he cannot rise or help himself in any way. (267)]

Surprised by the cause of the fall, Julian scrutinizes the servant closely to ensure that she perceives his motivation correctly.

> I merveyled how this seruannt myght thus mekely suffer all this woo; and I behelde with avysement to wytt yf I culde perceyve in hym ony defaute, or yf the lorde shuld assigne in hym any maner of blame; and verely there was none seen, for oonly hys good wyll and his grett desyer was cause of his fallyng. And he was as vnlothfull and as good inwardly as he was when he stode before

his lorde, redy to do his wylle. (14.51.516)

[I was amazed that this servant could so meekly suffer all this woe; and I looked carefully to know if I could detect any fault in him, or if the lord would impute to him any kind of blame; and truly none was seen, for the only cause of his falling was his good will and his great desire. And in spirit he was as prompt and as good as he was when he stood before his lord, ready to do his will. (268)]

As a result of this fall, the servant is no longer able to see the lord nor to recognize his love. Julian identifies seven pains the servant suffers: bruising, bodily heaviness, a consequent feebleness, diminution or blinding of his reason, inability to rise, loneliness, and isolation in a desolate place.

Next Julian turns her attention to the lord. His outward expression shows his ruth and pity for the fallen servant, but his inward expression, as her subsequent understanding has revealed, is one of enjoyment. Recognizing that the servant suffers as a consequence of his good will, the lord promises to reward him "aboue that he shulde haue be yf he had nott fallen, yea, and so ferforth that his fallyng and alle his wo that he hath takyn there by shalle beturnyd in to the hye ovyrpassyng wurschyppe and endlesse blesse" (14.51.518) ["above what he would have been if he had not fallen, yes, and so much that his falling and all the woe that he received from it will be turned into high, surpassing honour and endless bliss" (269)]. After interrupting this initial presentation of what "was shewed gostly in bodely lycknesse" ["was shown spiritually, in a bodily likeness"], Julian returns to focus on other significant details later in chapter 51. She offers more information about the lord's position and appearance (14.51.523-24) and about the servant's position, appearance, and task (14.51.527-32).

Julian indicates that she immediately interprets the scene as an enactment of the original sin, the representative of all human transgressions.

The lorde that satt solemply in rest and in peas, I vnderstonde that he is god. The seruannt that stode before hym, I vnderstode that he was shewed for Adam, that is to sey oone man was shewed that tyme and his fallyng to make there by to be vnderstonde how god beholdyth alle manne and his fallyng. For in the syghte of god alle man is oone man, and oone man is alle man. (14.51.521-22)

[I understood that the lord who sat in state in rest and peace is God. I understood that the servant who stood before him was shown for Adam, that is to say, one man was shown at that time and his fall, so as to make it understood how God regards all men and their falling. For in the sight of God all men are one man, and one man is all men. (270)]

Julian subsequently realizes, however, that the servant is also the typological second Adam, Christ. "In the servant is comprehendyd the seconde person of \??\e trynyte, and in the seruannt is comprehendyd Adam, that is to sey all men" (14.51.532); ["In the servant is comprehended the second person of the Trinity, and in the servant is comprehended Adam, that is to say all men" (274)]. Any analysis of Julian's example of the lord and servant must account for all the details of the scene from this double perspective, as appropriate both to Adam and to Christ. Four issues are particularly significant: the servant's good will in responding to the lord's command, the suffering that results from the servant's fall, the lord's refusal to blame the servant for the fall, and the greater reward the servant receives as a result of his suffering.

As Julian explains, she immediately identifies the lord as God and the servant as Adam, the representative of sinful humanity. Although she acknowledges that Adam and humankind suffer as a consequence of his fall, she insists that his fall was not the result of rebellion or disobedience.

This man was hurte in his myghte and made fulle febyll, and he was stonyd in his vnderstandyng, for he was turnyd fro the beholdyng of his lorde, but his wylle was kepte in gods syght. For his wylle I saw oure lorde commende and aproue, but hym selfe was lettyd and blyndyd of the knowyng of this wyll. And this is to hym grett sorow and grevous dysses, for neyther he seeth clerly his lovyng lorde whych is to hym full meke and mylde, nor he seeth truly what hym selfe is in the syght of his louyng lord. (14.51.522)

[This man was injured in his powers and made most feeble, and in his understanding he was amazed, because he was diverted from looking on his lord, but his will was preserved in God's sight. I saw the lord commend and approve him for his will, but he himself was blinded and hindered from knowing this will. And this is a great sorrow and a cruel suffering to him, for he neither sees clearly his loving lord, who is so meek and mild to him, nor does he truly see what he himself is in the sight of his loving lord. (270-71)]

The originality of Julian's insistence on Adam's good will becomes apparent when her account of the Fall is compared to one that closely resembles it.

In *Cur Deus homo* Anselm of Canterbury also refers to original sin as a metaphoric fall into a pit. Although, as I will demonstrate later in this chapter, Julian invokes Anselm's soteriology in her interpretation of the servant as Christ, her conception of Adam's fall differs from his Augustinian view of original sin. Anselm attributes this fall to the servant's malicious disobedience and insists that he deserves to be punished. The dialogue between Anselm and the interlocutor Boso articulates the major premises of the doctrine of original sin at the heart of retributive theodicy.

> A[nselm]. . . . Suppose that a man enjoins some task on his servant, and charges him not to throw himself into a pit which he [the master] points out to him, out of which he [the servant] cannot possibly escape. But that servant despises the command and the warning of his master and, of his own free will, throws himself into the pit that has been shown him, so that he is unable to carry out his assigned task. Do you think that this inability is worth anything as an excuse for not performing the assigned task?
>
> B[oso]. Not at all. On the contrary, it increases his guilt, since he brought this inability on himself. For he sinned doubly, because he did not do what he was ordered to do, while what he was commanded not to do he did.[17]

Both speakers in the dialogue insist that the servant's fall is the result of his deliberate disobedience of a divine injunction. As a result, the servant is incapable of performing the tasks assigned him, but he is nonetheless morally culpable for his incapacity because his initial offense was voluntary. Anselm thus endorses the Augustinian position that the legacy of original sin is both weakness and guilt. The former does not excuse the latter since Adam freely chose to transgress and all of Adam's descendants are seminally present in him.

The differences between Anselm's example and Julian's strikingly demonstrate her disagreement with the conventional interpretation of Genesis 3. Julian, remarkably, denies that Adam's fall into the pit is deliberate or voluntary. In fact, it results from his efforts to perform the lord's command, not disobey it. Julian provides a clue about what this command entails for Adam when she resumes the description of the bodily likeness later in chapter 51. She sees the servant standing to the left of the lord, dressed as a laborer in a ragged, white garment stained with perspiration. The lord commands the servant to go to earth to seek a treasure.

> And then I vnderstode that he shuld do the grettest labour and the hardest traveyle that is. He shuld be a gardener, deluyng and dykyng and swetyng and turnyng the erth vp and down, and seke the depnesse and water the plantes in tyme. And in this he shulde contynue his traveyle, and make swete flodys to rynne and nobylle plentuousnesse fruyte to spryng, whych he shulde bryng before the lorde, and serve hym therwith to his lykynk. And he shulde nevyr turne ageyne, tyll he had dyghte this mett alle redy, as he knew that it lykyd to the lorde; and than he shulde take thys mett with the dryngke, and bere it full wurschypply before the lorde. (14.51.530-31)

[And then I understood that he was to do the greatest labour and the hardest work there is. He was to be a gardener, digging and ditching and sweating and turning the soil over and over, and to dig deep down, and to water the plants at the proper time. And he was to persevere in his work, and make sweet streams to run, and fine and plenteous fruit to grow, which he was to bring before the lord and serve him with to his liking. And he was never to come back again until he had made all this food ready as he knew was pleasing to the lord; and then he was to take this food, and drink, and carry it most reverently before the lord. (273-74)]

Julian's imagery of productive labor alludes to two events in Genesis: God's bestowal on the newly created Adam of dominion over the earth (Gen. 2:19-20) and his curse on the ground to punish the disobedient Adam (Gen. 3:17-19). Medieval iconography of Adam delving typically represents the second event.[18] Although Julian admits that the cultivation of the land requires hard manual labor, she transforms its punitive implications with her description of the earth's bounty and the lord's pleasure. Julian's celebration of Adam's labor presages the positive attitude toward the human body that she expresses in her analogy of Jesus as Mother later in Revelation Fourteen. It also indicates that she regards the Adamic narrative as a story about creation rather than transgression.

In her interpretation of Genesis 3, Julian invokes the theological commonplace of the fall into a region of unlikeness and thus evokes the anthropology of the *imago Dei* that she develops more thoroughly in chapters 53 through 63 of Revelation Fourteen. "Adam fell fro lyfe to deth, in to the slade of this wrechyd worlde, and aftyr that in to hell" (14.51.533-34); ["Adam fell from life to death, into the valley of this wretched world, and after that into hell" (274)]. The ontological separation indicated by the phrase "fro lyfe to deth" suggests the Neoplatonic implications of this concept as it was developed by Augustine and adapted by the Cistercians and other medieval theologians. Based on the assertion in Gen. 1:27 that humankind is created in the image and likeness of the Trinity, this anthropology regards separation from God as an exile into a land of unlikeness.[19] Most often medieval theologians ascribe this distance from God to either a natural or a moral breach. The natural separation from God results from the difference between Creator and creature. This ontological distance between God and humankind is further increased by a moral separation that occurs as a result of sin. Medieval theologians thus refer to both creation and transgression as a fall into a region of unlikeness.

Although his use of the metaphor is frequent and varied, Bernard of Clairvaux on several occasions refers to Adam's fall as a descent into the region of unlikeness.[20] In his *Sermons on the Song of Songs* (*Sermones super cantica canticorum,* 1135-1153), for example, Bernard associates the region of unlikeness with the exile of Adam and Eve, identifying their sin specifically as a descent from the spiritual to the material realm due to ignorance of their true natures. In sermon 35 Bernard attributes Adam's expulsion to a lack of self-understanding that led him to pride and subsequent bestiality.

> Placed in a position of honor, [Adam] was so intrigued by the dignity of his rank that he did not understand that he was but clay. . . . From then on this fairest of creatures was reduced to the level of the herd; from then on the likeness of God was changed to the likeness of a beast; from then on association with the animals took the place of fellowship with the angels. You see how careful we must be to shun this ignorance that has brought evils by the thousands on the whole human race![21]

In sermon 82 Bernard likewise argues that Eve sinned because she forgot her true spiritual resemblance to God. "Consider Eve, and how her immortal soul of immortal glory was infected by the stain of mortality through her desire for mortal things. Why didshe not spurn mortal and transitory things, when she was immortal, and satisfy herself with the immortal and eternal things which were proper to her?"[22] These two examples reveal the duality of the ontological relationship between Creator and creatures. On the one hand, as in the case of Adam, human beings are dissimilar to their Creator because of their material bodies; God remains trancendent. On the other hand, as in the case of Eve, human beings are similar to their Creator because of their spiritual souls through which the image of God is immanent within them.[23] Through creation and transgression, then, humankind is distanced from God and exiled into the world of matter, the *regio dissimilitudinis.*

The Neoplatonic assumptions informing this concept of an ontological fall into the region of unlikeness are even clearer in Bernard's source, Augustine's *Confessions.* Addressing God, Augustine writes:

> When I first knew thee, thou didst lift me up, that I might see that there was something to be seen, though I was not yet fit to see it. . . . I realized that I was far away from thee in the land of unlikeness, as if I heard thy voice from on high: "I am the food of strong men; grow and you shall feed on me; nor shall you change me, like the food of your flesh into yourself, but you shall be changed into my likeness."[24]

The digestive metaphor Augustine uses to refer to the substantial union between God and humankind reveals the Neoplatonic influence on his thought; this Neoplatonism becomes more explicit in his discussion of

the first chapter of Genesis in the last three books of the *Confessions.*[25] Analyzing Augustine's meditation on Gen. 1:2 in book 11 of the *Confessions,* Gilson explains how Augustine's notion of the region of unlikeness fits into his exemplarist theory of creation, for matter, lacking form, is most dissimilar to God who is absolute form.[26] Although created in the image of God, human beings are dissimilar to their Creator insofar as they consist of body as well as soul. This ontological distance is further increased by their moral offense. Associating the region of unlikeness with matter, Augustine regards both creation and transgression as causes of humankind's exile into this land alien to the spirit.

Julian's discussion of Adam's fall also seems to be informed by Christian Neoplatonism. In claiming that Adam's fall was a descent from life into death, she implies an exemplarist theory of creation, similar to though not necessarily derived from Augustine's, for, as Cousins observes, "from the time of Augustine until the Reformation and even beyond, Christian Neoplatonism was the mainstream philosophical-theological tradition in the spirituality of Western Christianity."[27] Julian interprets the lord's position "syttyng on the erth, bareyn and desert" ["sittingon the ground, barren and waste"] as a sign of this ontological separation between Creator and creature that occurs when the soul is embodied.

> He made mannes soule to be his owne cytte and his dwellyng place, whych is most pleasyng to hym of all his workes. And what tyme man was fallyn in to sorow and payne, he was not all semely to serve of \??\at noble offyce; and therfore oure kynde fader wolde haue dyght hym noon other place but to sytt vppon the erth, abydyng man kynde, which is medlyd with erth, tyll what tyme by his grace hys deerwurthy sonne had brought agayne hys cytte in to the nobyll feyernesse with his harde traveyle. (14.51.525-26)

> [He made man's soul to be his own city and his dwelling place, which is the most pleasing to him of all his works. And when man had fallen into sorrow and pain, he was not wholly proper to serve in that noble office, and therefore our kind Father did not wish to prepare any other place, but sat upon the ground, awaiting human nature, which is mixed with earth, until the time when by his grace his beloved Son had brought back his city into its noble place of beauty by his hard labour. (272)]

As I shall show in my discussion of Julian's anthropology in the next chapter, she also associates this process of embodiment with Jesus' motherhood in creation.

The ontological union involves the Son as well as the Father, for each individual who will be saved has been predestined in Christ from all eternity. Julian alludes to this eternal union between the elect and Christ when she explains Adam's fall.

> When Adam felle godes sonne fell; for the ryght onyng whych was made in hevyn, goddys sonne myght nott be seperath from Adam, for by Adam I vnderstond alle man. Adam fell fro lyfe to deth, in to the slade of this wrechyd worlde, and aftyr that in to hell. Goddys son fell with Adam in to the slade of the meydens wombe, whych was the feyerest doughter of Adam, and that for to excuse Adam from blame in hevyn and in erth; and myghtely he fechyd hym out of hell. (14.51.533-34)

> [When Adam fell, God's Son fell; because of the true union which was made in heaven, God's Son could not be separated from Adam, for by Adam I understand all mankind. Adam fell from life to death, into the valley of this wretched world, and after that into hell. God's Son fell with Adam, into the valley of the womb of the maiden who was the fairest daughter of Adam, and that was to excuse Adam from blame in heaven and on earth; and powerfully he brought him out of hell. (274-75)]

The predestination of humanity in the second person of theTrinity from all eternity necessitates the incarnation of Christ when Adam falls from union with God into the region of unlikeness; Jesus' motherhood in creation incites his motherhood in restoration. Julian's anthropology is thus closely connected to her soteriology. However, before we examine the influence of Anselm of Canterbury's theory of atonement on Julian's interpretation of the Adamic myth, it is important to note how Julian modified the tradition of the region of unlikeness.

In sermon 36 of *On the Song of Songs,* Bernard of Clairvaux presents the consequences of sin, both original and actual, as a fall into a region of unlikeness. A comparison of Julian's list of the pains the servant suffers with this similar account from Bernard epitomizes the difference between her attitude toward the body and his, a difference that I will explore in greater detail in my discussion in the next chapter of Julian's concept of Jesus as Mother. Bernard focuses on the dangers posed by embodiment.

> When a man thus takes stock of himself in the clear light of truth, he will discover that he lives in a region where likeness to God has been forfeited. . . . How can he escape being genuinely humbled on acquiring this true self-knowledge, on seeing the burden of sin that he carries, the oppressive weight of his mortal body, the complexities of earthly cares, the corrupting influence of sensual desires; on seeing his blindness, his worldliness, his weakness, his embroilment in repeated errors; on seeing himself exposed to a thousand dangers, trembling amid a thousand fears,

confused by a thousand difficulties, defenceless before a thousand suspicions, worried by a thousand needs; one to whom vice is welcome, virtue repugnant?[28]

The seven pains the servant suffers as a result of his fall in chapter 51 of *A Book of Showings* bear some resemblance to Bernard's catalog.

> And of all this the most myschefe that I saw hym in was feylyng of comfort, for he culde nott turne his face to loke vppe on his lovyng lorde, whych was to hym full nere, in whom is full comfort; but as a man that was full febyll and vnwyse for the tyme, he entendyd to his felyng and enduryng in woo, in whych woo he sufferyd vij grett paynes. The furst was the soore brosyng that he toke in his fallyng, whych was to hym moch payne. The seconde was the hevynesse of his body. The thyrde was fybylnesse that folowyth of theyse two. The iiij was that he was blyndyd in his reson and stonyd in his mynde so ferforth that allmost he had forgeten his owne loue. The v was that he myght nott ryse. The vj was payne most mervelous to me, and that was that he leye aloone. I lokyd alle about and behelde, and ferre ne nere ne hye ne lowe I saw to hym no helpe. The vijth was that the place whych he ley in was alang, harde and grevous. (14.51.515-16)

> [And of all this, the greatest hurt which I saw him in was lack of consolation, for he could not turn his face to look on his loving lord, who was very close to him, in whom is all consolation; but like a man who was for the time extremely feeble and foolish, he paid heed to his feelings and his continuing distress, in which distress he suffered seven great pains. The first was the severe bruising which he took in his fall, which gave him great pain. The second was the clumsiness of his body. The third was the weakness which followed these two. The fourth was that he was blinded in his reason and perplexed in his mind, so much so that he had almost forgotten his own love. The fifth was that he could not rise. The sixth was the pain most astonishing to me, and that was that he lay alone. I looked all around and searched, and far and near, high and low, I saw no help for him. The seventh was that the place in which he lay was narrow and comfortless and distressful. (267-68)]

Of the seven pains Julian identifies, the middle three have a counterpart in Bernard's catalog in sermon 36: the weight of the mortal body, weakness or feebleness, and blindness. However, while Bernard emphasizes the burdens of sensuality and earthly cares, Julian stresses the servant's isolation and loneliness. She is not as worried as Bernard about the problems posed by the body and the world; instead, she is troubled by the separation from God. Julian articulates the servant's suffering in medical and psychological rather than forensic terms; she focuses on the ontological rather than the moral consequences of Adam's fall.

In contrast to the Augustinian doctrine of original sin, which attributes malevolence to both Adam and his descendants, Julian denies that either disobeys God deliberately. Her definition of personal sin, like her version of the Genesis narrative, emphasizes the consequences of separation from God, not the revolt of the will causing such separation.

> Man is channgeabyll in this lyfe, and by sympylnesse and vncunnyng fallyth in to synne. He is vnmyghty and vnwyse of hym selfe, and also his wyll is ovyr leyde in thys tyme he is in tempest and in sorow and woe. And the cause is blynnes, for he seeth not god; for yf he saw god contynually, he shulde haue no myschevous felyng ne no maner steryng, no sorowyng that servyth to synne. (14.47.496)

> [Man is changeable in this life, and falls into sin through naivete and ignorance. He is weak and foolish in himself, and also his will is over-powered in the time when he is assailed and in sorrow and woe. And the cause is blindness, because he does not see God; for if he saw God continually, he would have no harmful feelings nor any kind of prompting, no sorrowing which is conducive to sin. (260)]

Julian consistently stresses weakness rather than guilt as the legacy of the ancestral transgression. Accordingly, she portrays actual sin as the result of ignorance rather than depravity.

> And therfore we fayle oftymes of the syght of hym, and anon we falle in to oure selfe, and than fynde we felyng of ryght nowght but the contraryous that is in oure selfe, and that of the olde rote of oure furst synne with all that folowyth of oure owne contynuance; and in this we be traveyled and temptyd with felyng of synne and of payne in many dyverse maner, gostely and bodely, as it is knowyn to vs in this lyfe. (14.46.498-99)

> [And therefore often we fail to perceive him, and presently we fall back upon ourselves, and then we find that we feel nothing at all but the opposition that is in ourselves, and that comes from the old root of our first sin, with all that follows from our own persistence; and in this we are belaboured and tempted with the feeling of sin and of pain in many different ways, spiritually and bodily, as is known to us in this life. (261)]

For Augustine, sin causes separation from God; for Julian, sin ensues from such separation. She considers the suffering that results from sin not as a penalty inflicted by a wrathful God, but as the natural consequence of the sinner's violation of his or her "feyer

kynde" (14.63.615) ["fair nature" (304)], the breach of the ontological union between Creator and creature. And whereas Augustine emphasizes the perverse will of Adam's descendants, Julian concentrates on the godly will of the elect, "that nevyr assentyd to synne ne nevyr shall" (14.53.555) ["which never assented to sin nor ever will" (283)].

Moreover, in Julian's parable the lord regards the servant as a compassionate healer rather than a just judge.[29] In contrast to the wrathful God of retributive theodicy, Julian's lord beholds his servant with a "doubyll chere" ["double aspect"]: outwardly of pity and ruth for the servant's suffering, inwardly of joy at the prospect of his eventual restoration (14.51.516-17). This showing confirms Julian's earlier insistence, despite church teaching, that God feels no wrath toward sinners. "And then I saw that oonly payne blamyth and ponyschyth, and oure curteyse lorde comfortyth and socurryth, and evyr he is to the soule in glad chere, lovyng and longyng to bryng vs to his blysse" (14.51.523); ["And then I saw that only pain blames and punishes, and our courteous Lord comforts and succours, and always he is kindly disposed to the soul, loving and longing to bring us to his bliss" (271)]. Julian thus implies that sin is its own punishment and that the conception of God as wrathful is itself a consequence of the blindness that is sin.

Furthermore, Julian provides the theological justification for her refusal to regard God as punitive in her subsequent interpretation of the servant as Christ, the second Adam. As she explains, the lord's outward expression of pity and ruth is directed toward Adam, who falls inadvertently rather than deliberately; his inward expression of joy is directed toward Christ, who rescues Adam and restores him to an even greater reward than that originally intended for him (14.51.524-25). In presenting this second interpretation of the example of the lord and servant, Julian invokes the soteriology or theory of salvation first developed by Anselm of Canterbury in *Cur Deus homo*.

II

As Gillian Evans observes, "Anselm was the first thinker since Augustine to take a comprehensive fresh look at the problem of evil."[30] In *Cur Deus homo* (*Why God Became Man,* 1098) Anselm resolves the contradiction between the conception of divine retribution underlying Augustinian theodicy and the idea of divine mercy informing the theory of redemption. Boso, the interlocutor in the dialogue with Anselm, poses the problem by claiming that unbelievers regard the incarnation and crucifixion of Christ as affronts to God's honor and dignity. Why, they ask, did the Father demand that his Son endure such humiliation and suffering? Repeating the hypothetical words of such a nonbeliever, Boso states the apparent contradiction:

If you say that God, who, according to you, created all things by his commandment, could not do all this by a simple command, you contradict yourselves by making him powerless. Or if you admit that he could have done this, but preferred to act as he did, how can you prove that he is wise, when you assert that he was willing to suffer such unseemly things without any reason? For all the things that you allege depend on his will. For the wrath of God is nothing but his will to punish.[31]

The anthropomorphization of God as wrathful had in some sense, as this hypothetical objection claims, paralyzed divine omnipotence within the constraints of divine vengeance.

Anselm solves this problem by displacing the rhetoric of divine retribution with that of cosmic rectitude. As Jaroslav Pelikan explains:

> Instead of speaking of the "wrath" of God, . . . Anselm spoke of his justice; the justice of God had been violated by the failure of man to render to God what he owed him; the justice of God also made it impossible for God to forgive this sin by mere fiat, for this would have been a violation of the very order in the universe that God had to uphold to be consistent with himself and with his justice. Any scheme of human salvation, therefore, had to be one that would render "satisfaction" to divine justice and leave the "rightness" and moral order intact.[32]

Anselm's doctrine of atonement depends on an understanding of the satisfaction rendered by Christ as a restoration of the moral order rather than an appeasement of an angry God. The fall of Adam had disrupted the moral order and appropriate restitution was necessary for humankind's violation of rectitude. No human being could make this restitution, however, since no one was without sin; only the guiltless God was capable of making amends. Therefore, as Anselm concludes, "the person who is to make this satisfaction must be both perfect God and perfect man, because none but true God can make it, and none but true man owes it."[33] The dual nature of Christ as God and man achieved through the Incarnation resolved the seeming contradiction between divine justice and divine mercy. As God, Christ restored the moral order; as man, he offered expiation for the transgressions of humankind.

Anselm contends that the God-man's act of atonement renders Adam's fall a *felix culpa,* both because of its result and because of its means. First of all, the restoration of humankind exceeds its original creation, "since the former was done to a sinner against his desert, but the latter neither to a sinner nor against his desert." Moreover, Anselm continues, the means by which this restoration is accomplished is also remarkable. "Again, what a great thing it is for God and man to meet in one person, so that, while the integrity of both natures is preserved, the same person is man and God!"[34] Interpreting Rom. 5:19, Anselm develops the typological parallels between Adam and Christ:

> For when death had entered into the human race through man's disobedience, it was fitting that life should be restored through the obedience of man. When the sin which was the cause of our condemnation had its beginning from a woman, it was fitting for the author of our justice and salvation to be born of a woman. Since the devil, when he tempted man, conquered him by the tasting of a tree, it was fitting for him to be conquered by man's bearing of suffering on a tree.[35]

As the second Adam, the God-man satisfies the demands of divine justice at the same time that he demonstrates the immensity of divine mercy.

By the fourteenth century Anselm's argument had become the definitive soteriology of the medieval church.[36] Even though Julian of Norwich may not have known *Cur Deus homo* directly, she invokes concepts similiar to Anselm's in proposing her second interpretation of the showing of the lord and servant. Over the course of time she comes to understand the characteristics of the servant as appropriate for Jesus as well as for Adam. In presenting this subsequent reading, Julian shows that every detail about the servant in the "bodely lycknesse" is also true of Christ because ontologically and morally Christ and humankind are one. Connected with humankind for all eternity through the predestination of the elect in the second person of the Trinity, as will be discussed in the next chapter, Christ falls into the maiden's womb just as Adam falls into this wretched world. Like Adam, Jesus stumbles to earth as he eagerly sets out to do the will of God the Father by taking on a human body. "His stertyng was the godhed, and the rennyng was the manhed; for the godhed sterte fro the fader in to the maydyns wombe, fallyng in to the takyng of oure kynde, and in this fallyng he toke grete soore" (14.51.539-40); ["His rushing away was the divinity, and his running was the humanity; for the divinity rushed from the Father into the maiden's womb, falling to accept our nature, and in this falling he took great hurt" (277)]. Christ, like Adam, is injured by his fall, but Julian clearly identifies these pains as the physical torments of the Passion rather than those of separation from God (14.51.540-42). Using the metaphor of the body as a garment, Julian explains that Christ takes on Adam's flesh and becomes a God-man in order to atone for the sins of humankind. "And thus hath oure good lorde Jhesu taken vppon hym all oure blame; and therfore oure fader may nor wyll no more blame assigne to vs than to hys owne derwurthy son Jhesu Cryst" (14.51.535); ["And so has our good Lord Jesus taken upon him all our blame; and therefore our Father may not, does not wish to assign more blame to us than to his own be-loved Son Jesus Christ" (275)]. Julian's interpretation of the servant as Christ thus conforms to Anselm's atonement theory of salvation.

Although this redemptive relationship between Christ and Adam is the most significant dimension of Julian's example, other details of chapter 51 are also doubly appropriate. Like Adam, for example, Jesus comes to earth to be a gardener; however, his task is metaphoric rather than literal, for the ground he cultivates is the human soul. Julian alludes to the same traditional image that Langland develops in *Piers Plowman* when he places the tree of charity "'in a gardyn . . . what god made hymselue / Amyddes mannes body; . . . / Herte highte the herber that it Inne groweth'";[37] ["in a garden . . . that God made himself / Amid man's body; . . . / The garden that it grows in is called heart"]. Although Julian does not invoke the Devil's rights theory as Langland does, she may have in mind the same metaphoric apples of fallen humanity that Piers/Christ rescues from Satan when she refers to the trea-sure hidden in the garden of the heart as "a mete whych is delicious and plesyng to the lorde" (14.51.530) ["a food which is delicious and pleasing to the lord" (273)]. As Wolfgang Riehle indicates, this familiar metaphor of the soul as a garden was developed from biblical passages such as "the New Testament parable of the treasure hidden in the field (Matt. 13:44), or a verse from the Book of Proverbs which states that whoever searchesfor wisdom as for hidden treasures will find the knowledge of God (Prov. 2:4), but above all the 'hortus conclusus' of the *Song of Songs* (S. of S. 4:12)."[38]

Julian completes her exposition of the showing of the lord and servant by explaining the lord's promise to restore his servant to glory. Again, she insists that this promise applies to both the first and second Adam. Chapter 51 ends with her description of the victorious Christ seated in peace and rest at the right hand of the Father. Alluding to Revelation Nine, she identifies the crown that he wears as those he has redeemed. And chapter 52 explains what this restoration means for Adam and the elect. Thanks to Christ's sacrifice, sin, both original and personal, becomes a *felix culpa,* for those predestined will receive an even greater reward in heaven than the bliss the first parents experienced in paradise (14.52.550).[39] For Julian and her fellow Chris-tians, however, this restoration is yet to come. None-theless, through her final interpretation of the servant (chapter 52), she is able to reconcile the apparent con-tradiction posed earlier in Revelation Fourteen between the inevitability of human sinfulness and God's prom-ise of salvation to the elect.

Julian reveals that she and her fellow Christians, like the servant, also have a dual identity; they are both Adam and Christ.

For the tyme of this lyfe we haue in vs a mervelous medelur both of wele and of woo. We haue in vs oure lorde Jhesu Cryst vp resyn, and we haue in vs the wrechydnesse and the myschef of Adams fallyng. Dyeng by Cryst we be lastynly kept, and by hys gracyous touchyng we be reysed in to very trust of saluacyon. And by Adams fallyng we be so broken in oure felyng on dyverse manner by synne and by sondry paynes, in whych we be made derke and so blynde that vnnethys we can take any comforte. (14.52.546-47)

[During our lifetime here we have in us a marvellous mixture of both well-being and woe. We have in us our risen Lord Jesus Christ, and we have in us the wretchedness and the harm of Adam's falling. Dying, we are constantly protected by Christ, and by the touching of his grace we are raised to true trust in salvation. And we are so afflicted in our feelings by Adam's falling in various ways, by sin and by different pains, and in this we are made dark and so blind that we can scarcely accept any comfort. (279)]

Returning to the theme she developed at the end of Revelation Thirteen, Julian explains how this dual iden-tity of those who will be saved insures that personal sin is indeed a *felix culpa,* for Christ atoned not only for Adam's offense but also for the past and future transgressions of all the elect. Reiterating the meta-phor of falling and rising, she reconciles the apparent contradiction—between the propensity to sin inherited from Adam andthe promise of salvation merited by Christ—by discriminating between venial and mortal sin and by emphasizing the efficacy of the sacrament of penance (14.52.551).

Julian also clarifies how the distinction between two parts of the soul resolves the apparent contradiction between her showings and the church's teachings about God's wrath. At the beginning of chapter 45, she had related this distinction between the higher and lower parts of the soul to the difference between God's ex-cusing and the church's accusing of sinners. "God demyth vs vpon oure kyndely substance, whych is evyr kepte one in hym, hole and safe, without ende; and this dome is of his ryghtfulhede. And man demyth vppon oure channgeable sensualyte, whych semyth now oone and now a nother, after that it takyth of the partyes and shew(yth) outward" (14.45.486); ["God judges us in our natural substance, which is always kept one in him, whole and safe, without end; and this judgment is out of his justice. And man judges us in our change-able sensuality, which now seems one thing and now another, as it derives from parts and presents an ex-ternal appearance" (256)]. In chapter 52 Julian associ-ates these two judgments with the "doubyll chere" ["double aspect"] of the lord. His outward expression of ruth and pity she attributes to two causes: Adam's fall and the suffering Christ endured to atone for it. She also focuses this outward expression on the lower part of the soul, capable of sin and in need of mercy and grace.

> Thus wylle oure good lorde that we accuse oure selfe wylfully, and truly se and know (our fallyng and all the harmes that cum therof, seand and witand that we may never restoren it; and therwith, if we wilfully and truly sen and knowen,) his evyrlastyng loue that he hath to vs and his plentuous mercy. And thus gracyously to se and know both to geder is the meke accusyng that oure good lorde askyth of vs. And hym selfe wurkyth there it is, and this is the lower party of mannys lyfe. (14.52.552-53)

> [So does our good Lord want us willingly to accuse ourselves, and to see truly and know our falling, and all the harms which come from it, seeing and knowing that we can never repair it; and also we willingly and truly see and know the everlasting love which he has for us, and his plentiful mercy. And so by grace to see and know both together is the meek self-accusation which our good Lord asks from us. And he himself works where it is, and this is the lower part of man's life. (281-82)]

The lord's inward expression of love and joy, however, indicates God's exoneration of the higher part of the soul, the substance that is eternally united to its maker. Because humans can see only the outward manifestation of the lower part, or sensuality, it is appropriate for them to blame themselves for sin. But God, who beholds the sensuality united to the substance of thesoul, can excuse human frailty. Bringing her argument full circle from chapter 45, Julian thus resolves the dialectic contradiction between the Augustinian ideology of guilt and her own vision by distinguishing between the limited human perspective and the comprehensive divine one.

Recognizing that Augustine's juridical theodicy reduces the divine nature to deceptive human proportions, Julian rejects the anthropomorphic characterization of a punitive God. Her conclusion to the parable of the lord and servant clarifies her declaration earlier in Revelation Fourteen that wrath is impossible for God because it would violate the divine nature. "I saw verely that oure lorde was nevyr wroth nor nevyr shall. . .

God is that goodnesse that may nott be wroth, for god is nott but goodnes. Our soule is onyd to hym, vnchanngeable goodnesse. And betwen god and oure soule is neyther wrath nor forgevenesse in his syght" (14.46.493); ["I saw truly that our Lord was never angry, and never will be. . . . God is that goodness which cannot be angry, for God is nothing but goodness. Our soul is united to him who is unchangeable goodness. And between God and our soul there is neither wrath nor forgiveness in his sight" (259)]. Avoiding even a metaphorical attribution of anger to God, Julian locates wrath within humans. "For I saw no wrath but on mannes perty, and that forgevyth he in vs. . . . For we by synne and wrechydnesse haue in vs a wrath and a contynuant contraryousnes to pees and to loue" (14.48.500-501); ["For I saw no wrath except on man's side, and he forgives that in us. . . . For we through sin and wretchedness have in us a wrath and a constant opposition to peace and to love" (262)]. Without denying human sinfulness, Julian of Norwich refuses to attribute to God the malevolence toward sinners that is characteristic of Augustinian theodicy. While she affirms her submission to church teachings, she nonetheless presents a solution to the problem of evil that interrogates the retributive premises of orthodox theodicy.

Notes

[1] Augustine, *On the Literal Interpretation of Genesis: An Unfinished Book* 1.3, in Teske, 146; Migne, *PL* 34.221. See also Elaine Pagels, *Adam, Eve, and the Serpent* (New York: Random House, 1988), chapter 6, especially 135.

[2] Augustine, *The Nature of the Good* 7, in *Augustine: Earlier Writings,* trans. John H. S. Burleigh, Library of Christian Classics 6 (Philadelphia: Westminster Press, 1953), 328; for the Latin text, see *De natura boni,* in Migne, *PL* 42.554.

[3] Jean Delumeau, *Sin and Fear: The Emergence of a Western Guilt Culture, Thirteenth-Eighteenth Centuries,* trans. Eric Nicholson (1983; New York: St. Martin's Press, 1990), 203. Delumeau's survey of penitential literature in chapter 7 owes much to Thomas Tentler,*Sin and Confession on the Eve of the Reformation* (Princeton: Princeton University Press, 1977). As Tentler explains, "Sacramental confession was designed to cause guilt as well as cure guilt" (xiii). Gavin Langmuir indicates the methodological limitations of *Sin and Fear* in a review in *Speculum* 67 (1992): 657-59.

[4] Mâle, *Religious Art in France: The Late Middle Ages,* 318-24.

[5] Emile Mâle, *Religious Art in France: The Thirteenth Century,* trans. Marthiel Mathews from the 9th ed. of 1958, Bollingen Series 90, 2 (1898 and 1958; Princeton: Princeton University Press, 1984), 362-84. Mâle shows that the depiction of the torments of the damned becomes even more gruesome in the fourteenth and fifteenth centuries, in the next volume of this work, *Religious Art in France: The Late Middle Ages,* 420-33.

[6] Delumeau, *Sin and Fear,* 293.

[7] Augustine, *Eighty-Three Different Questions,* trans. David Mosher, The Fathers of the Church 70 (Washington, D.C.: Catholic University of America

Press, 1982), 89; for the Latin text, see *De diversis quaestionibus octoginta tribus,* ed. Almut Mutzenbecher, in *Aurelii Augustini opera,* Part 13, 2, Corpus christianorum, Series latina 44A (Turnhout: Brepols, 1975), 83.

[8] Thomas Aquinas, *Summa theologiae* 1a2ae.47, 1, Blackfriars ed., vol. 21, ed. and trans. John Patrick Reid, O.P. (New York: McGraw-Hill, 1964), 115; for the Latin text, see Sancti Thomae Aquinatis, *Opera omnia iussu impensaque,* 6:300.

[9] Colledge and Walsh, "Introduction," *A Book of Showings,* 1:24-25.

[10] Pagels, *Adam, Eve, and the Serpent,* chapter 5.

[11] Augustine, *Confessions* 8.10, in Outler, 172; Verheijen, 127.

[12] Augustine, *Confessions* 8.10, in Outler, 172; Verheijen, 127.

[13] Augustine, *Concerning the City of God against the Pagans* 14.15, trans. Henry Bettenson (Harmondsworth, England: Penguin Books, 1972), 575; for the Latin text, see *De civitate Dei Libri XI-XXII,* ed. Bernard Dombart and Alphonsus Kalb, *Aurelii Augustini opera,* Part 14, 2, Corpus christianorum, Series latina 47 (Turnhout: Brepols, 1955), 437.

[14] Augustine, *The City of God* 14.15, in Bettenson, 576; Dombart and Kalb, 437-38. See also *Confessions* 7.3, in Outler, 136-37; Verheijen, 94-95.

[15] Norman Powell Williams, *The Ideas of the Fall and of Original Sin* (1927; reprint, London: Longmans, Green and Co., 1938), 133.

[16] For further discussion of this free-will defense in Augustinian theodicy, see Hick, *Evil and the God of Love,* 66-75; and Stoeber, *Evil and the Mystics' God,* 14-15.

[17] Anselm, *Why God Became Man* 1.24, in Fairweather, 142; Schmitt, *Opera omnia,* 2:92-93. Bradley also presents this example in *Julian's Way,* 101, but she does not comment on it in the same way that I do.

[18] Louis Réau, *Iconographie de l'art chrétien,* vol. 1, *Iconographie de la Bible* (1956; reprint, Nendeln, Liechtenstein: Kraus Reprints, 1974), 91-92.

[19] Robert Javelet, *Image et ressemblance au douzième siècle de Saint Anselme à Alain de Lille,* 2 vols. (Paris: Éditions Letouzey & Ané, 1967), 1:266-85.

[20] Ibid., 273-76.

[21] Bernard of Clairvaux, *On the Song of Songs II,* 169-70; Leclercq, Talbot, and Rochais, *Opera,* 1:253.

[22] Bernard of Clairvaux, *On the Song of Songs IV,* trans. Irene Edmonds, Cistercian Fathers Series 40 (Kalamazoo, Mich.: Cistercian Publications, 1980), 174; for the Latin text, see Leclercq, Talbot, and Rochais, *Opera,* 2:294.

[23] Javelet, *Image et ressemblance,* 1:276, points out that the medieval theological vocabulary of similitude and dissimilitude corresponds to the modern concepts of immanence and transcendence.

[24] Augustine, *Confessions* 7.10, in Outler, 147; Verheijen, 103-4. Pierre Courcelle, "Tradition Neo-Platonicienne et traditions Chrétiennes de la 'region de dissemblance,'" *Archives d'histoire doctrinale et littéraire du moyen âge* 23 (1957): 5-10, identifies this passage from Augustine's *Confessions* as Bernard's source for the allusion to the region of unlikeness in sermon 36 of *On the Song of Songs.*

[25] Etienne Gilson, "*Regio dissimilitudinis* de Platon à Saint Bernard de Clairvaux," *Mediaeval Studies* 9 (1947): 126, recognizes that Augustine's concept of original sin as a fall into a region of unlikeness has both Neoplatonic and scriptural precedent.

[26] Ibid., 122-23.

[27] Ewert Cousins, "Bonaventure's Mysticism of Language," in *Mysticism and Language,* ed. Steven Katz (New York: Oxford University Press, 1992), 239.

[28] Bernard of Clairvaux, *On the Song of Songs II,* 178; Leclercq, Talbot, and Rochais, *Opera,* 2:7.

[29] Julian's description of the lord as compassionate is another similarity between her examination of original sin and Bernard's sermon 36.

> But if I look up and fix my eyes on the aid of the divine mercy, this happy vision of God soon tempers the bitter vision of myself, and I say to him: "I am disturbed within so I will call you to mind from the land of Jordan." This vision of God is not a little thing. It reveals him to us as listening compassionately to our prayers, as truly kind and merciful, as one who will not indulge his resentment. His very nature is to be good, to show mercy always and to spare. By this kind of experience, and in this way, God makes himself known to us for our good. . . . In this way your self-knowledge will be a step to the knowledge of God; he will become visible to you according as his image is being renewed with you. And you, gazing confidently on the glory of the Lord with unveiled face, will be transformed into that same image with ever increasing brightness, by the work of the Spirit of the Lord.

See Bernard of Clairvaux, *On the Song of Songs II,* 179; Leclercq, Talbot, and Rochais, *Opera,* 2:7-8.

[30] Evans, *Augustine on Evil,* 175.

[31] Anselm, *Why God Became Man* 1.6, in Fairweather, 106-7; Schmitt, *Opera omnia,* 2:54.

[32] Pelikan, *The Christian Tradition,* 3:110.

[33] Anselm, *Why God Became Man* 2.6, in Fairweather, 152; Schmitt, *Opera omnia,* 2:101.

[34] Anselm, *Why God Became Man* 2.16, in Fairweather, 167; Schmitt, *Opera omnia,* 2:117.

[35] Anselm, *Why God Became Man* 1.3, in Fairweather, 104-5; Schmitt, *Opera omnia,* 2:51.

[36] Pelikan, *The Christian Tradition,* 4:23.

[37] *Piers Plowman: The B Version,* ed. George Kane and E. Talbot Donaldson (London: The Athlone Press, 1975), 14.14-15.

[38] Riehle, *The Middle English Mystics,* 161 and 215n.187.

[39] A commonplace of medieval theology, the idea that the elect will exceed the original perfection of Adam ultimately derives from Augustine; see *Admonition and Grace* 12.33, in Murray, 285; Migne, *PL* 44.936. The idea is articulated for the Middle Ages in Anselm of Canterbury's *Why God Became Man,* especially 2.16, in Fairweather, 166-67; Schmitt, *Opera omnia,* 2:117.

Grace M. Jantzen (essay date 1995)

SOURCE: "'Cry out and write': Hysticism and the Struggle for Authority" in *Power, Gender, and Christian Mysticism,* Cambridge University Press, 1995, pp. 157-92.

[*In the following excerpt, Jantzen charts the "reintegration" of body and spirit performed in Julian's revelations—a feature that Jantzen claims breaks with Christian tradition and arises from Julian's experiences as a woman.*]

. . . As the Middle Ages waned, increasing numbers of women learned to read and write, in the vernacular if not in Latin. How Julian of Norwich was educated it is impossible to say. She was born in 1342, probably somewhere in East Anglia or the Midlands. Virtually everything that is known about her comes from her writings. She wrote two accounts of the same set of visions, twenty years apart, the second being much longer than the first. By comparing the two texts, it is possible to see how Julian developed in theological understanding and her spiritual teaching (Jantzen [*Julian of Norwich: Mystic and Theologian*] 1987). We will look again at her visions and her changing perception of herself as a woman in the next chapter. Here, I wish to focus on her theological and spiritual integration, which takes up much that was already present in medieval spirituality but develop it in a unique way.

From the outset, Julian's writing was intended for the comfort and encouragement of her 'even Christians' and for their spiritual assistance. Like Eckhart, she addressed herself not only to clerics or male or female religious, but also to a lay readership; but whereas in his case we have not only the sermons addressed to a lay audience but also more scholarly works, all we have from Julian are the two versions of her book. Furthermore, we would look as fruitlessly to Julian as to Hadewijch [of Antwerp, early thirteenth century] for any systematic exposition of a spiritual path, or steps in spiritual progress: there are none of the 'ladders of contemplation' or 'steps of ascent' which are frequent in male writing. Like other women writers, Julian chose to convey her spiritual teachings by recounting her own spiritual experiences and the insights based on them, rather than by any systematic treatise in spiritual theology.

In some ways, Julian offers a contrast to Hadewijch. Her writings breathe serenity and tranquillity; she speaks of peace and rest in God, not of frenzied desire or ecstatic madness. There is very little erotic imagery in her writings, though she speaks much of the love of God, of God who is 'all love'. Although like Hadewijch she is influenced by the courtly love tradition, Julian speaks of God as 'her courteous Lord', not as her 'Lady Love'; and she never characterises herself as a knight panting after Love and doing great exploits for her sake. None of Julian's writing is presented as poetry. Nevertheless, both Hadewijch and Julian, though very different in context, genre, style and temperament, show similarities to one another and differences from male mystical writers.

The most significant of these is that both Julian and Hadewijch emphasise the body, the physical and sensual and material; and for both of them this bodily reality is integrated into their spirituality in a way which is not true for either the speculative or the affective tradition of male spirituality. Julian's spirituality depends upon a well thought-out anthropology, which takes its starting-point from creation. Julian makes a point of stressing that 'we are double by God's creating, that is to say substantial and sensual' [*Showings,* trans. Edmund Colledge and James Walsh] (1978: 294). This might be taken to signal a division between body and soul, as it would in many medieval writers; but in Julian that is not the case. Sensuality in Julian does involve bodiliness, but it also involves consciousness, the life of the senses and the mind: we are made sensual, she says, 'when our soul is breathed into our body' (286), and Jesus, in sharing our humanity, shares our sensuality. Our substance, on the other hand, is for Julian the essential part of ourselves, which she holds is directly united with God at all times, whether we are aware of it or not. There is a strong parallel here with Eckhart, who also held that the essential self was always connected with God. But whereas Eckhart defined that essential self in terms of the (male) higher intellect, Julian never does so. What she does instead is, when seen against the background of Eckhart's speculative mysticism, nothing short of astonishing.

Julian does not think of God as a remote deity, but, again similar to Eckhart, she thinks of God as the substance or essence of everything that exists. This is particularly true of ourselves. She says,

> It is a great understanding to see and to know inwardly that our soul, which is created, dwells in God in substance, of which substance, through God, we are what we are. And I saw no difference between God and our substance, but, as it were, all God; and stillmy understanding accepted that our substance is in God, that is to say that God is God, and our substance is as creature in God. (285)

She is very near, here, to Eckhart's claims, but seems to be distancing herself from any interpretation of monism, for which he was suspect. But whereas in content her position is similar, it is focused much less abstractly than Eckhart's discussion of God as *esse* or being, and always interwoven with her understanding of human nature.

Julian goes on to say that it is substance and sensuality which form human 'doubleness': the substance is continually united with God, while the sensuality is the locus of independence. Julian elaborates that theme of doubleness in her concept of two wills:

> For in every soul which will be saved there is a godly will which never assents to sin and never will. Just as there is an animal will in the lower part which cannot do any good, so there is a godly will in the higher part, which is so good that it cannot ever will any evil, but always good. (241)

The 'godly will' can be seen as a parallel to Eckhart's apex of the soul, always united with God; but whereas he placed that apex in the intellect, for Julian it is centred in the will. This 'godly will' is a part or aspect of our substance, and it can will only what God wills. The 'animal will' which is incapable of willing what is good is an aspect of our sensuality in its fallen state. It is not to be equated with sensuality as such, and certainly not with physicality, but rather with that tendency toward evil which Julian believed

was part of the sinful condition of humanity inherited from Adam.

This tendency to sin is characterised by Julian not so much as a falling away from God as a fragmentation of the human person, a split between the substance and the sensuality, so that whereas the substance wills only what is good, the sensuality is constantly lapsing into evil. 'And so in our substance we are full and in our sensuality we are lacking', she says. And then she completely subverts both the speculative tradition of Eckhart and the affective tradition of Bernard. Instead of proffering advice or exhortations about how to leave the sensuality behind and progress upwards toward the realm of spirit or substance where only the good is willed, she says, hardly pausing for breath,

> and this lack God will restore and fill by the operation of mercy and grace, plentifully flowing into us from his own natural goodness. (291)

Rather than practising ascetical techniques which will free the higher self, the godly will from the sensuality, Julian looksfor a reintegration of that fragmented sensuality into the substance. Spirituality does not mean leaving part of the self behind, but bringing the whole of the self, sensuality included, into the unity of the love of God in which she believes we are enfolded. It is a breath-taking reversal of Eckhart.

To accomplish the reversal, she looks to Christ, whom she sees as the remedy of the fragmentation between sensuality and substance. In taking flesh, Jesus shared human sensuality, but in such a way that, in him, it was not in conflict with substance. Put another way, Jesus' godly will and his animal will were united in constantly willing the good. This reunification of substance and sensuality in Christ is, according to Julian, the remedy for the split which we experience, as well as the prototype for our reunification and healing. She articulates the doctrine of the two natures of Christ in traditional terms of the death of Christ for human salvation:

> And because of the glorious union which was thus made by God between the soul and the body, mankind had necessarily to be restored from a double death, which restoration could never be until the time when the second person of the Trinity had taken the lower part of human nature, whose highest part was united to him in its first creation. And these two parts were in Christ, the higher and the lower, which are only one soul. The higher part was always at peace with God in full joy and peace. The lower part, which is sensuality, suffered for the salvation of mankind. (287)

Traditional as this might be thus far, Julian then pushes it in the very untraditional direction of affirming that *all* people have two natures, just as Christ did, and that it is precisely because of this that the incarnation is effectual for human salvation.

> And so in Christ our two natures are united, for the Trinity is comprehended in Christ, in whom our higher part is founded and rooted; and our lower part the second person has taken . . . For in the same time that God had joined himself to our body in the maiden's womb, he took our soul, which is sensual, and in taking it, having enclosed us all in himself, he united it to our substance. In this union he was perfect man, for Christ, having joined in himself every man who will be saved, is perfect man. (291)

Christ reunites in himself divine substance and human sensuality, and thereby effects the healing of human fragmentation. All that the person was created to be, including the body and its sensuality, is taken up into the full spiritual life made possible by the incarnation.

Accordingly, we find in Julian's writings no comment about ascetical practices, nothing about chastity, no cautions about sexuality or any other form of bodily need or desire. Instead, she speaks of bodily functions in a completely natural way as an illustration of the extent of divine love:

> A man walks upright, and the food in his body is shut in as if in a well-made purse. When the time of his necessity comes, the purse is opened and then shut again, in most seemly fashion. And it is God who does this, as it is shown when he says that he comes down to us in our humblest needs. For he does not despise what he has made, nor does he disdain to serve us in the simplest natural functions of our body, for love of the son which he created in his own likeness. For as the body is clad in the cloth, and the flesh in the skin, and the bones in the flesh, and the heart in the trunk, so are we, soul and body, clad and enclosed in the goodness of God. (186)

The positive valuation of the body and sensuality means that, rather than being left behind or 'mortified' in spiritual progress, the body is cherished and enfolded in the love of God, and reintegrated in a spiritual whole-making. It is a vastly different perspective from the male traditions we have considered.

Julian's account of spiritual progress is directly related to this. She says that until our substance and sensuality are reunited and we are whole again, we are 'moaning and mourning', distressed at our brokenness. But how and when will they be reunited? There are three answers to this. The first is that it has happened already; 'in Christ our two natures are united', and are united because of his incarnation. The second is that it will not happen until heaven. Only then will the split within ourselves be fully healed. The third is that it can be going on gradually throughout our lives, largely by a

process of our recognising that in Christ the reintegration has already taken place, and living in that growing realisation. Julian's spirituality involves this deepening awareness, gradually increasing in knowledge of God and of our own soul. In some ways this is like Eckhart, who also encourages us to 'become what we are'. Yet in Julian, rather than this involving a *detachment* from (female) sensuality and being in tune with the (male) higher reason, it requires an increasing *integration* of the sensuality and the substance, the godly will. As she puts it,

> And I saw very certainly that we must necessarily be in longing and in penance until the time when we are led so deeply into God that we verily and truly know our own soul . . . For until the time that it is in its full powers, we cannot be all holy; and that is when our sensuality by the power of Christ's Passion can be brought up into the substance . . . (289)

Sensuality is not a barrier or a distraction from spirituality but rather is crucially involved in it.

Like Eckhart, therefore, Julian is full of the importance of self-knowledge, but her emphasis is much more homely: she stresses that we come to the recognition that we are good and beautiful and precious to God, learning to take delight in ourselves as Julian is sure that God takes delight in us.

> For I saw in the same revelation that if the blessed Trinity could have created man's soul any better, any fairer, any nobler than it was created, the Trinity would not have been fully pleased with the creation of man's soul. But because it made man's soul as beautiful, as good, as precious a creature as it could make, therefore the blessed Trinity is fully pleased without end in the creation of man's soul. And it wants our hearts to be powerfully lifted above the depths of the earth and all empty sorrows, and to rejoice in it. (314)

Here is something quite different from what we find in the male traditions. Eckhart also stressed positive self-knowledge, but it was, as we have seen, knowledge of the higher intellect as the god-like apex of the soul. The affective tradition, on the other hand, would emphasise the importance of knowing oneself, not to recognise god-likeness, but to become contrite for one's sinfulness and unworthiness before God: in Bernard's *The Steps of Humility*, for instance, self-knowledge was to lead to penitence and humility. Julian does not deny the need for penitence, but her emphasis falls differently: recognising our beauty and worth will be a source of joy for us just as it is for the Trinity itself. She says that it is of great profit to us to contemplate this, because contemplation of the Trinity who delights in us 'makes the soul which so contemplates like to him who is contemplated, and unites it in rest and peace'

(314). Here once again is the old Platonic theme that the knower becomes like what it knows; but it is turned to a purpose that is very much Julian's own: in taking pleasure in God who takes pleasure in us, we learn to take pleasure in ourselves.

Julian never mentions gender in this discussion. But if her reversal of the traditional theme of self-knowledge is striking, her application of it to herself as a woman, and by implication to other women, is nothing short of audacious. Women, after all, were exhorted in the Bible and throughout patristic and medieval writing to 'learn humility, in all subjection', not to learn to delight in themselves. Since it was through Eve that sin had entered into the world, and since women were still held to be the locus of temptation, especially sexual temptation, the path to holiness for women would be a path of penitence, humility, and self-renunciation. Self-knowledge would be knowledge of oneself as related to Eve, the source of temptation and a snare to men.

Julian does talk about contrition and humility, but never with the overtones of the above paragraph. She is troubled about why God permitted sin; but in all her anxious questioning about sin's nature and origin, she never once links it to women. Contrition is for sin actually committed, and not for a vague sinfulness connected with the very fact of being an embodied, sexual creature, let alone being female. Humility has to do with accepting and receiving the overwhelming love and delight of God in us, not with being ashamed of who and what we are. And surely it must be highly significant that Julian never mentions chastity or virginity. Though she herself, as an anchoress, had almost certainly taken the monastic vow of chastity, it is never raised as an issue in her book, never suggested as part of spiritual progress, in fact, never mentioned at all. In an era when it was taken as a commonplace that sexuality, especially female sexuality, was a hindrance to spiritual progress, and virginity held up to be the ideal, Julian's silence is eloquent.

Coupled with this, Julian offers other pieces of spiritual instruction unusual for women of any age and doubly unusual for her own. One of the most central of these was the admonition not to be unduly distressed by sin and failure. Julian recounts that in one of her visions, 'God brought it to mind that I should sin.' But the reason for which she was reminded of this was not to make her ashamed or fearful, but rather to reassure her of God's protection and mercy whatever happened, so that when she did sin she would not fall into despair (241). Julian agonises about sin, calling it 'the sharpest scourge with which any chosen soul can be struck, which scourge belabours man or woman', until they feel that they are 'not fit for anything but as it were to sink into hell' (244). But she develops the insight that sin and wrongdoing, though serious, are the very things

which teach us most about sensitivity and compassion for ourselves and one another.

In fact, Julian develops an audacious comparison between our sins and the wounds that were inflicted on Jesus at his crucifixion. According to scripture and tradition, those wounds of Jesus, the nail prints in his hands and feet and side, became the badges of honour of the risen Christ: just so, too, the wounds of our sins will be turned into honours, so that it will be far better for us than if we had never sinned at all.

> For [God] regards sin as sorrow and pains for his lovers, to whom for love he assigns no blame. The reward which we shall receive will not be small, but it will be great, glorious and honourable. And so all our shame will be turned into honour and joy. For our courteous Lord does not want his servants to despair because they fall often and grievously; for our falling does not hinder him in loving us. (245)

Again, there is no indication in Julian that this discussion is genered, and we can only speculate about whether she might have had women particularly in mind. Whatever the case, her words carry a weight for women quite different from the shame and blame that women had been taught to assume. According to Julian, disproportionate shame or guilt is not the response God desires (even if there were those in the ecclesiastical structures who might have found it gratifying that women should bear such a weight). Although she was made to understand 'that we cannot in this life keep ourselves completely free from sin', nevertheless the remedy for that sin has already been provided.

> And if we through our blindness and our wretchedness at any time fall, then let us quickly rise, knowing the sweet touch of grace, and willingly amend ourselves according to the teaching of Holy Church, as may fit the grievousness of the sin, and go on our way with God in love, and neither on the one side fall too low, inclining to despair, nor on the other side be too reckless, as though we did not care; but let us meekly recognise our weakness, knowing that we cannot stand for the twinkling of an eye except with the protection of grace, and let us reverently cling to God, trusting only in him. (281)

Thus we can see that in Julian's terms, spiritual progress involves self-knowledge, but that self-knowledge is construed differently than in the other strands of the tradition we have looked at. For her, self-knowledge also means an increasing sense of self-worth, but not one built only upon increasing identification with rationality, but rather with a realism that accepts not only bodiliness but also sinfulness without being crushed by guilt. Her words were written for *all* her 'even Christians', men as well as women; but they must have had a special resonance for women, whose sinfulness and shame was so often highlighted by ecclesiastical preaching and practice and whose self-worth was so regularly undermined. She sums up her encouraging message in a metaphor of knitting, a figure of speech which beautifully conveys her meaning:

> And just as we were to be without end, so we were treasured and hidden in God, known and loved from without beginning. Therefore he wants us to know that the noblest thing which he ever made is mankind, and the fullest substance and the highest power is the blessed soul of Christ. And furthermore, he wants us to know that this beloved soul was preciously knitted to him in its making, by a knot so subtle and so mighty that it united us in God. In this uniting it is made endlessly holy. Furthermore, he wants us to know that all the souls which will be saved in heaven without end are knit in this knot, and united in this union, and made holy in this holiness. (284)

Both Hadewijch and Julian, different as they are in temperament, context and style, offer a spirituality or mysticism of integration which contrasts considerably with their male counterparts. Unlike the speculative tradition, they did not develop a spirituality centring on the mind; and unlike the male affective tradition, they did not use spiritual love as an alternative to bodily love, or see the physical as something to be overcome. Although both of them respected reason, and were no advocates of a mysticism of ignorance, they placed emphasis on love and on the will, which must be united in the growth of spiritual wholeness, based in the flesh, not in its suppression. Hadewijch used passionate and erotic language more than Julian did, but Julian was at least as emphatic about the body and its integration in spirituality. Neither woman saw spiritual development in terms of steps or stages, or used metaphors of ladders or staircases as did many male writers. Their construction of mysticism, their understanding of what spirituality is, was therefore quite different from that of their male counterparts in the tradition of western spirituality. It was, furthermore, an understanding which allowed a good deal of scope for visionary experience, on which female authority could be based; and as we shall see in the next chapter, this became a threat to male dominance in the social construction of mysticism which could not be allowed to go unchecked.

The struggle for power and authority in deciding who should count as a mystic, and the issues of gender within that struggle, are largely ignored by contemporary philosophers of religion, who frequently behave as if there is a single sort of phenomenon known as 'mystical experience' which is available for philosophical scrutiny. As is becoming evident, however, the understanding of the mystical went through major shifts within the western tradition; and those shifts were not innocent. If contemporary philosophers of religion ig-

nore these shifts, and work on the assumption of an 'essence' of mysticism, it is unsurprising if the net result produces more obfuscation than insight. Not only are the philosophical arguments built on dubious argumentation, they are based on dubious morality as well, because an uncritical acceptance of a gender-skewed understanding of mysticism is bound to perpetuate it.

Maria R. Lichtmann (essay date 1996)

SOURCE: "'God fulfylled my bodye': Body, Self, and God in Julian of Norwich" in *Gender and Text in the Later Middle Ages,* edited by Jane Chance, University Press of Florida, 1990, pp. 263-78.

[In the following essay, Lichtmann discerns in Julian's writings radical notions of sensuality and the feminine in divinity; she concludes that Julian "offers us . . . a theology of the body."]

Sometime after she received a series of sixteen "showings" or revelations during the course of a nearly fatal illness, Julian of Norwich became an anchoress, walling herself up in a cell attached to a church in Norwich, England. In such a state of isolation, Julian would seem an odd choice for a visionary with special insight into the nature of the self, of God, and especially of reality. Yet, with her emphasis on neglected aspects of these psychological, theological, and ontological realms, Julian offers us a new, fuller vision than much of the Western tradition to date. This essay argues that the thoroughly embodied character of her experience of Christ and of herself opens her to a more holistic relationship to God, on the basis of which she can originate an actual theology of the body, of God informing her "sensuality." In her consistently positive valuation of the body, Julian manages to overcome centuries of a Neoplatonic-Augustinian dualism of body and soul, matter and spirit, which is pervasive of the Western religious tradition. Julian, in her isolation from social structures of family, church, and even religious community, became liberated from some of their confining implications. Her anchorite existence freed her to accept uncommon insights into the spiritual significance of the body. Further, her trust in her own experience, sometimes at odds with the received authority of the Church, enabled her to unshackle herself from the exclusively patriarchal tradition.

Embodied modes of consciousness affect every aspect of Julian's thought, from her epistemology with its grounding in experiences of the body, to her vocabulary of the self, with its insistence on the sensuality of the self, to her theology of the motherhood of God. Julian's anthropology is radically and consistently incarnational, for it incorporates the spirit left disembodied in more dualist, patriarchal versions of human personhood. Julian rewrites the famous Anthanasian dictum that "God became 'man' in order that 'man' might become God," by allowing God through her illness and her visions to become her body, that is to come into and inscribe her body with illness, so that she in her body might become the incarnation of Christ. The deeply female root metaphors that give life to her theology of divine motherhood—the womb of God, the nurturing blood of Jesus—inscribe and incarnate God with the female body. It is no accident that this theology of the body as already grace-filled derives from a spirituality of reflection on her female experience and subjectivity. The importance of the body as a nonrational vehicle of divine perception has not usually been seen in Julian's work.[1] This paper seeks to address Julian's bodily experience as an epistemology of the Divine that lays the foundation for her full-blown theology of "sensualyte."

Among fourteenth-century English mystics like Richard Rolle and Walter Hilton, Julian is in the forefront in expressing an emphatically incarnational view of Jesus, and an emphatically Christocentric piety. Just as divine and human, spirit and matter (as Holy Spirit and Mary's flesh), came together in the Incarnation, so fleshly humanness was the most appropriate vehicle of the Divine and body the most appropriate receptacle of spirit. The doctrine of incarnation is clearly the source of Julian's affirmation of body. Moreover, for fourteenth-century English mysticism, incarnationalism becomes far more than doctrine, as Jesus' fleshliness is, through the Benedictine tradition's *lectio divina* and scriptural meditations, taken in, embedded in the body. Gospel event becomes flesh again in being lived through at the deepest center of self, the ensouled body. Further, Julian's internalized meditations become externalized once more in the sixteen visions she receives over a day and night in the year 1373.[2] In this process of embodying and then revisualizing the meditations, the visionary becomes participant in the new vision.[3]

Julian's experience of the body—her bodily sickness, her healing, her intensely physical visions of Christ's passion—informs nearly every dimension of her book of ***Shewings*** or ***Revelations.*** From the bodily experiences recorded in the first, short text of her visions comes a plethora of insights in the long text, the fruit of twenty years' reflection on the visions and their meaning. Although we know nothing about Julian's former life before she became an anchoress, we do know from the *Ancrene Riwle,* the Rule for Anchoresses and Anchorites,[4] that meditation on the sufferings and Passion of Christ formed an integral part of the "Devotions" expected of those leading this enclosed life. Julian's meditations reflected and forged a theology of incarnation uncompromising in its attention not only to the humanity but to the very fleshliness of Jesus. This theology, Franciscan and Cistercian in its origins, is assumed, without needing explicit formula-

tion at the time of her visions. But a threefold process is actually at work: Julian's theology of incarnation of Word into flesh is itself incarnated in the bodiliness of her sickness and in her visions, and once that Word is made flesh in her flesh, it renews itself as Word, becoming theology again in her long text's theology of the body, of "sensualyte" as God-informed. Through her illness, her flesh becomes Worded with Christ and Christ's sufferings. Her written text then becomes a hermeneutic of the text written into her body and her visions. And what she reads there is a Christ whose suffering and bleeding are motherly love.

Julian's incarnationalism and embodied knowing form part of a larger feminine awareness and language that are much more pervasive than has usually been seen in her work, since they anticipate and are not limited to the motherhood of God theme. Although I agree to a certain extent with the distinguished medievalist, Dom Jean Leclercq, when he says, "What she develops is not the idea of femininity as opposed to or distinct from masculinity, but that of the motherhood of God as complement to that of his fatherhood,"[5] I believe feminine knowing and being as an ontological principle pervades Julian's writings from beginning to end.[6] The idea of femininity never appears as an idea, disembodied and abstracted from her experiences; yet her work is at every turn grounded in her feminine experience.

Julian is not particularly interested in notions of gender and in differences based on gender, or in describing traits of individual men and women.[7] Differences between men and women did not concern her, and in that sense I agree with Jean Leclercq that she does not offer us a vocabulary of sex. But Julian's notions of motherhood-fatherhood, nature-substance, mercy-grace—and the list could be extended—all encompass a transcendent notion of sexuality: sexual categories raised to an ontological principle for understanding human nature, the world, and God. Jean Leclercq reminds us that sex means "a part, a division, the opposite of totality,"[8] and it is just for this reason that Julian must complete the totality by including the excluded member. Julian's division into sexually charged opposites is in the service of a higher unity. Her sexual opposites are not merely divisive, but are in an ultimately unifying polarity. As William James tells us in his *Varieties of Religious Experience,* mystics have nearly always seen the opposites arraying themselves into such a higher unity.[9] In Julian of Norwich, the priestly assertion in the first chapter of Genesis that "In the image of God he created them, male and female he created them" finds fulfillment in the images both of God and of humanity as both take on their full complement of femininity as well as masculinity. In order to fulfill the image of God, all human beings, whether male or female, must accept the feminine aspect of their natures.

Julian's epistemology of the divine, grounded as it is in the body, breaks through the Western tradition's bias toward reason as the defining aspect of human nature. In her homely but powerfully articulate way, Julian introduces new categories, overturning centuries of rigid adherence to the notion that the soul or mind is the only vehicle for divine perception. Clearly, she does not identify the person with the strictly rational dimension. Feminine awareness as an alternative way of understanding and engaging reality, as an epistemology, appears in Julian's work first by her constant recourse to the depth and concreteness of experience. No matter how theologically abstract her reflections become, they are never merely scholastic but are continually grounded and fed by the experience of her visions. Again and again, she reminds us of the experiential character of her way of knowing by the use of the phrase "I saw."[10]

In her feminine epistemological standpoint, Julian seems to have sensed the necessity of undergoing through experience as a way to gain true wisdom, the wisdom of the mother as she later calls it. To incarnate what had been known only in her theology and meditation, Julian prayed to enhance her own experience of Christ's bodiliness through her desires for three transformative experiences or "graces." Out of the "sloth and weakness" of her early life, *ennui* in modern existentialist terms or *accidia* in medieval ones, Julian desired and prayed intensely for those transforming experiences: to experience more deeply the Passion of Christ, to suffer an intense illness, and to receive the three wounds of contrition, compassion, and ardent longing for God. In each of these transformations, Julian is entrusting her conversion to her body.

Each of these experiences is connected to the others through body as the middle term. The Passion of Christ is taken in bodily, in the sense that it is both perceived as "bodyle syghte" or sensate image and that it is undergone in her own bodily illness. The fruits of these corporeal experiences are her "wounds," which though spiritual, bear the stamp of their bodily origin. Moreover, it is significant that Julian prays for the concrete wounds of bodily sickness rather than the spiritual *blessure d'amour* of Origen. "In this sekenes," she says, "I desyrede to hafe alle manere of paynes, bodelye *and* gastelye, that I schulde have zyf I schulde dye . . ." (1:203). Julian's second desire, for a bodily illness, is received first, since it is the means by which she is to experience the Passion of Christ. Julian's illness acts as a kind of ensoulment for her. Unlike those attempting to escape the prison of body, Julian sees body as the locus of spiritual enlightenment, in other words, as the temple of the Holy Spirit.

It is as if the contemplative senses that until she knows with her body, in her marrow and bones and in every cell, she will have no basis for knowing Christ at all.

Whatever resistances she has to knowing and experiencing God are contained first in the body. Julian's desire for bodily sickness seems to be a means of unlocking those resistances, and unleashing the considerable spiritual resources of the fully embodied consciousness. Both her paralysis and its sudden healing a few days later mark a metaphorical transformation, a death to her old slothful body and a birthing of the newly soulful one. It is significant that Julian's *desire* initiates this spiritual transformation. The intentionality of Julian's bodily suffering powerfully fuses body and soul into one.[11] A suffering that is willed, desired, and actively chosen as was Julian's, as part of a larger context of meaning and purpose, is transformed into something more.

Like Teresa of Avila, Julian goes from living on the surface—an aimless, slothful, frivolous life—to living at the depth and center of her soul. In both mystics, it is curious that images of the soul as a city with Christ sitting in its midst[12]—images of masculine-feminine wholeness and unity in polarity—appear as this deepening and centering take place (68.313).[13] Julian's true center, expressed in this paradoxical metaphor and arrived at through the paradoxical deepening that her wounds bring, is Christ.

Julian's threefold hermeneutic of the visions she receives involves her whole psychophysical nature. "Alle this blyssede techynge of oure lorde god was shewyd to me in thre partyes, that is be bodyle syght, and be words formede in myne vndyrstandynge, and be gastelye syght" (1:224). Nearly all Julian's visions and revelations are in bodily form. As visionary rather than as mystic, she advocates the concrete nature of her experience. Quite explicitly, she says: "I desyrede a bodylye syght, whare yn y myght have more knawynge of bodelye paynes of oure lorde our savyoure and of the compassyonn of oure ladye and of all his trewe loverse. . . . Other syght of gode ne schewynge desyrede I nevere none tylle atte the sawlle were departyd from the bodye. . . . " (1:202). The corporeal nature of her visions enables her to perceive in them seemingly opposing qualities, as her catalogue of adjectives— "quyck and lyuely and hidows and dredfulle and swete and louely" (2:313)—running the opposites together, attests. This reconciliation of opposites in the bodily visions prepares her for her later spiritual insights into the polar nature of God and humanity. Indeed, a visceral reading of her sickness and her visions enables Julian to mediate her revelations through her body now become a vehicle of profound insight and wisdom. Julian perceives a direct relation between her bodily experience and the truth she gains from it, when she says, "this was my menynge [intention], for I wolde aftyr be cawse of that schewynge have the more trewe mynde in the passionn of Cryste" (1:203).

Though she too has inherited the body-soul dualism of

Plato and Paul,[14] but not yet in its full-blown Cartesian form, Julian has come to appreciate a wisdom of the body, even a spirituality of the body. For Julian, the body is first a means to a deepened spiritual experience of a transformative character, and second, in its transformed, ensouled state, a principle of "sensualyte" in which God is present. Both in her experience and in the theology that pours forth from it, the transformed body is the medium through which she comes to know God.

At the end of her nearly fatal but short-lived illness, as her body becomes suddenly healed, she expresses the desire for the first and third graces: "that he walde fulfylle my bodye with mynde of felynge of his blessede passyonn, . . . with compassyonn and aftyrwarde langynge to god" (1:210). A body fulfilled with "mind of feeling" is a newly ensouled body, a body that becomes the medium of her spiritual revelation. Looking back on her original desire from the twenty-year vantage point of the long text, she restates this remarkably holistic sentiment: "my body was fulfylled of felyng and mynd of Cristes passion and his dyeng. And ferthermore with this was a suttell felyng and a prevy inwarde syghte. . . . " (2:569). "Inward sight" and "subtle feeling" capture the holism of embodied thinking and being.

Julian's desire for a deepened experience of Christ's Passion, "to have mynde of Chryste es passionn" (1:203), carries with it a desire to be present with Mary Magdalen and others of Christ's lovers so that she might suffer with Christ. Her faith in the Incarnation must itself be embodied. For, although she "believed firmly" in Christ's pains, as she states, "Nouzt withstondynge alle this trewe be leve I desyrede a bodylye syght . . . ; for I wolde have beene one of thame and suffrede with thame" (1:202). Contemporaneity with Christ and depth of experience are the antidotes for a belief that no longer goes far enough. Julian seeks to move, then, from faith to experience, from mere belief to vision, and from a doctrinal, secondhand knowing to her own inner authority.[15] And the passage from an intellectual, nonintegral faith to a thoroughly grounded experience is through bodiliness, both the bodiliness of the visions and her own bodily experience, her suffering, of them and with them.

It is no accident, then, that her desires for bodily sickness and a body filled with mindful feeling of the Passion of Christ lead naturally to the spiritual "wounds" of compassion and longing for God (i.127).[16] Julian's woundedness allows soul to emerge and guide her life. As the Passion of Christ becomes her passion, in all the meanings of that word, passion leads naturally to compassion. No dissociated sensibility can obtain, for it is her body that is fulfilled with "mind of feeling," a feeling-minded body, an embodied soul, an ensouled body. As Julian draws more deeply on her

bodily experience, she becomes a more integrated and therefore more truly spiritual self. Further, her own integration and its resulting compassion lead to her feeling of one body with her "even Cristens" (2:220).[17] Julian's bodily experience, her sickness and her body wounded with compassion, may well be the link between her suffering, Christ's suffering, and a compassionate feeling of oneness with all other beings. In her long text, Julian emphasizes the human being's material interconnectedness with all the things of earth in her account of creation: "whan god shulde make mannes body, he toke the slyme of the erth, whych is a mater medelyd and gaderyd of alle bodely thynges" (2:558).[18]

Julian's desire for a deeper knowledge of the Passion of Christ is met with a vision of the "the rede blode treklylle downe fro vnder the garlande" (1:210). The sight of profuse bleeding from the crown of thorns, the most persistent recurring image in Julian's visions (see 1:217), is comfort and strength to her (1:211). She compares it to "bountiful waters," to a drink which is "most plentiful," which "blessedly flows over us" and is flowing now in heaven (12.200; 2:342-45). This image "viscerally meditated" over twenty years, is so charged,[19] taboo, and powerful that it resists direct and immediate interpretation, yielding up its import after almost twenty years' reflection. An outpouring of blood so continual that she thought it would soak the bedsheets (1:227) is made even more taboo when we compare its overflowing of boundaries to the necessity for containment of fluidity in Talmudic texts.[20] The metaphor of flowing, powerfully embedded in the seer by the vision of bleeding, reappears in the long text to signify the flowing of the operation of mercy, God's "feminine" side.

The key to Julian's hermeneutics of this vision and of all her visions is that all the theology found in the long text is contained first in the visions. She states this explicitly at the very beginning of the long text: "this is a reuelacion of loue that Jhesu Christ our endles blisse made in xvi shewynges, of which the first is of his precious crownyng of thornes; and ther in was conteined *and* specified the blessed trinitie with the incarnacion and vnithing betweene god and mans sowle. . . . " (2:281). The Word of the suffering Christ inscribed in her body's illness is rewritten to be reinterpreted in and from the visions. The long text completes the three-stage process of theology, embodiment in visions, and new theology. Yet, in another sense there are no stages, no heights, no ascents but a continued *deepening* of her initial knowing.

Throughout the long text, then, Julian's visions and her experience, her body filled full with mind of feeling, are continually culled for the insight they provide into the nature of "sensualyte." Her brief illness appears to operate as a cauterizing experience fusing body and soul in a unity only fully understood in her mature theology of "sensualyte."[21] This term, which begins to appear in the long text, seems to point as much to an event as to an abstract quality for Julian. It is the event of ensoulment, a unifying of body-soul, so that the body can never live again as disspirited "dedlye flesshe," nor the soul as disembodied. Julian lives now in a new wholeness of embodied soul. She is "oned" (united) in her own being as precondition of her "oneing" with Christ. Hers is a true at-onement of spiritual and physical worlds. So, the "vnithing betweene god and mans sowle" (2:281) that the long text's theology articulates began within her.

Corresponding to the body as a heuristic basis for receiving and writing her visions is Julian's richly developed psychology of the self. In her incarnational affirmation of the self as nature and sensuality as well as grace and substance, Julian foregrounds a principle of body much neglected in the patriarchal tradition. She forges a vernacular vocabulary of the self, one that encompasses and transcends the prevailing Augustinian psychology. What is new in Julian's anthropology is that nature and grace, the lower part and higher part of human nature, deserve equal place in the economy of God's salvific action. Although Julian employs hierarchical metaphors of the union of soul and body, she undermines their very hierarchical nature, as when she says: "the lyfe and the vertu that we have in the lower perty is of the hyer. . . . Betwene that one and that other is ryght nought, for it is all one love, which one blessyd loue hath now in vs doubyll/werkyng; . . ." (2:553).[22] Soul and body, to the extent that they can be reified, are penultimate realities, transcended by the all-unifying action of love. Like John Ruysbroeck, who said that nature is the bride of God, Julian can state that "I saw that oure kynde is in god hoole . . . for oure kynde, whych is the hyer party is knytte to god in þe makyng, and god is knytt to oure kynde, whych is the lower party in oure flessch takyng" (2:577-78). She sees that God has made a glorious "oneing" between the soul and the body (2:568), so that each takes help from the other (2:567; 55.287). This oneing has already occurred in Christ, where the higher part of the soul is always at peace with God, and the "lower" part, our sensuality, still is given the high purpose of suffering for the salvation of humankind (55.288; 2:569). The idea of a union of body and soul dominates almost everything she wrote about the human being in the long text.

Developing her new anthropology into a new theology, Julian states explicitly that "God is in our sensualyte . . . for in the same poynt that oure soule is made sensuall, in the same poynt is the citte of god, ordeyned to hym fro without begynnyng" (2:567). God has in Julian's words, "no disdain to serve us in the simplest natural functions that belong to our body" (2:307). Julian even marvels over the fact of defecation (6.186)! And our bodily birthing too is

accomplished by God.[23] As our sensuality becomes a vehicle of the Divine, no aspect of human nature escapes the all-encompassing action of divine love. Employing one of her favorite metaphors, that of clothing, Julian can describe the self in physico-spiritual terms, which defy ancient dualisms; we are, "soule and body, cladde and enclosydde in the goodnes of god" (2:307).

While Julian has greatly enriched the concept of self in her emphasis on its bodily aspects, she never conceives the self apart from God's workings in it. As in Meister Eckhart, to "know thyself" in Julian is to know God: "And when we know and see verely and clerely what oure selfe is, than shalle we verely and clerly see and know oure lorde god in fulhed of joye" (2:490).[24] Thus, it is no surprise that Julian's psychology is symmetrical with her theology and that its constantly reiterated feminine element has anticipated the feminine in God. If body and nature suggest the implicitly "feminine" elements of the self, the feminine aspect of godhead becomes fully explicit in her theology. Whereas there were bubblings up of this theme of divine motherhood among the twelfth-century Cistercians, as Caroline Walker Bynum's study *Jesus as Mother* amply shows, in Julian this theme fairly erupts not only as metaphor but as the literal truth of the divine nature.[25]

But long before her explicit reflection on the mystery of divine motherhood in the long text, Julian has offered a cryptic clue to her later insights in the hazelnut passage found near the beginning of the short text. After God shows her " . . . a lytille thynge, the qwantyte of a haselle nutte . . ." and she asks, "Whate maye this be?" she is answered, "It is alle that ys made" (1:2-13). Her choice in this image is of an object whose worth is anterior to any human reckoning or valuing. Its only value is in being itself, but that value is infinite because it is informed and sustained by God. The hazelnut passage, with its concern for the ordinary, nonutilitarian aspects of being, reveals the kind of love that accepts and protects what is undeveloped and undistinguished—motherly love.[26]

Yet, it is only after Julian's insertion of the completely new lord and servant parable in the long text, a parable that editors Colledge and Walsh see as suppressed in the short text, that her reflections on the maternity of God and Jesus begin to pour out. It is as if along with the parable, which she says was too mysterious for her immediate understanding, she also suppressed her insights into the feminine nature of God as potentially subversive of the overwhelmingly patriarchal teachings of Holy Church. She allowed her vision twenty years of growth in darkness before giving birth full-term to the mature theme of the Motherhood of God. Julian's way offers a paradigm of the feminine mode of patient nurturing of a conception—in her case a vision—

before it is brought to birth. Her term of pregnancy with the full import of her visions was twenty years!

As in her concept of the self, so too in God's being Julian sees the balance of opposites, of motherhood-fatherhood, mercy-grace, as when she says: "Mercy is a pyttefull properte, whych longyth to moderhode in tender loue; and grace is a wurshypfull properte, whych longyth to ryall lordschyppe in the same loue. Mercy werkyth kypyng, sufferyng, quyckyng and helyng, and alle is of tendyrnesse of loue; and grace werkyth with mercy, reysyng, rewarding, endlesly ovyr passyng that oure louyng and our traveyle deseruyth. . . . " (2:502-3).[27] Julian precisely balances the more interior maternal quality of mercy in its quickening and healing with grace, a more "paternal" quality, which acts in an external way to raise and reward. However, in the parable the characters embody the both-and of paradox, as they contain both qualities within themselves. The lord of the lord and servant parable is a type of both mother and father, for he looks with compassion on his servant and later raises him when he falls. What is dichotomized in Julian's discursive language is unified in the parable.

God's mercy and compassion are, therefore, not merely abstract attributes for Julian but are grounded in the full compass of activities of the mother. Jennifer Heimmel points out that all stages of the divine maternity are present in Julian's reflections: "Enclosure and growth within the womb; the trauma of labor and birth; the suckling of the infant and feeding of the child; the care and education of the older child; the setting of examples and disciplining of the child; the washing, healing, forgiving, and comforting of the child as it matures; and the continual loving, touching, and guiding of the child even to the point of its own death which becomes in turn a rebirth and return to the original womb."[28] Nowhere is the divine motherhood more powerfully or paradoxically expressed than in the beautiful images of Mother Jesus bearing us for joy and endless life, nourishing us with him/herself, and comforting us against his/her breast (2:598). Motherhood in Julian's notion of God fairly explodes as it expands to include "kynd [nature], loue, wysdom and knowyng" and in fact the reality of God (2:599).

Julian's notions of the union of opposites in God and the nondualist vision of the self have, I believe, a nonrational bodily origin, reflecting a female capacity, the capacity of the womb, to hold otherness and opposition within itself. She grounds her notions of the human being as a body-soul unity in the bodily image of the womb, which operates on an unconscious but pervasive level in her work. Drawing on the womb's capacity for uniting the opposing elements of being, she unites Christ's incarnation with the creation of humans: "For in that same tyme that god knytt hym to oure body in the meydens wombe, he toke oure sensu-

all soule, in whych takyng, he vs all havyng beclosyd in hym, he onyd it to oure substance" (2:580). The metaphor of the womb underlies Julian's frequent assertions of the coinherence of all beings in God and of God in all beings.[29] God is the womb of all beings as we are the womb of God. In this consists the ground of the Motherhood of God.

Recalling Julian's hermeneutic of her theology in and through her visions, we can see how she reads the image of Christ's flowing blood as containing in inchoate ways the theology of the Motherhood of Christ. Like a mother's menstrual blood and lactating breasts, Christ's blood flows to heal and nurture.[30] Christ is our Mother both substantially *and* sensually, "our Mother in nature in our substantial creation, in whom we are founded and rooted, and he is our Mother of mercy in taking our sensuality" (58.294).

The root metaphors of the womb and the superabundant blood/milk form the unfathomable ground for Julian's theology of the Motherhood of God and Jesus. If God as Mother holds us in the divine maternal womb, then Jesus as Mother flows out to us in an ever-cascading flood of nurture. Our being in the womb of God is eternal for "oure savyoure is oure very moder, in whom we be endlessly borne and nevyr shall come out of hym . . ." (2:580). It is the maternal womb in which paradoxically we are at the same time enclosed and outflowing (2:556-58).

In assessing the distinctness of Julian's writing on and through the body, we can point to Peter Brown's thesis that social asceticism offered the individual a means of social dissent, of opting out of the pressure for marriage and social commitment.[31] On the other hand, Julian's asceticism, unlike that of those saints examined in Caroline Walker Bynum's *Holy Feast and Holy Fast*,[32] does not involve her in an obsession with ascetic practices toward the body. She appears remarkably balanced in seeking almost unconsciously a body-soul concord. Julian does not seek suffering for its own sake. "As to the penance which one takes upon oneself," she says in her long text, "that was not revealed to me. . . . But what was revealed is that we ought to bear and suffer the penance which God himself gives us." (77.330).[33] She appears neither to engage in nor to encourage penitential asceticisms such as fasting, flagellation, and other extreme austerities so popular with other female saints, which Weinstein and Bell tell us are "invariably associated with rejection of [their] sexuality."[34] Even her actual physical illness does not linger nor does she linger in it but it disappears in a sudden healing.[35]

As her illness disappears, it gives way to a torrent of exuberant insights into the goodness of God, culminating in the final insight that the meaning of the whole experience was Love. It was Love she was suffering at the beginning and that suffered her to learn its meaning at the end. Julian's "end is her beginning," as suffering is reconciled and even identified with Love. And the body is the alchemical vessel where the dross of suffering is turned into the gold of love. While her nearly mortal illness involves the ascetic participation of body, its emptying, her visions involve the ecstatic participation of body, its fulfillment.[36] In Julian, the suffering of bodily asceticism turns easily into the joy of ecstatic illumination. In this process, "soul" becomes embodied, and body becomes ensouled, breaking down whatever unnatural divisions might obtain between them. Another bodily experience in the life of a woman, the carrying and birthing of a child, attests to the possibility of the coinherence of suffering and love, the dialectic of suffering and joy.[37]

In conclusion, what Julian offers us is not only a nondualistic epistemology of the body as spirit but a theology of the body, a somatic revelation of God in and as body. In her anthropology, we see how far Julian has come from any trace of Manichean (or in their contemporary version, Catharist) attitudes toward the body or of a Docetic spiritualizing of Christ and the human being. In her incarnational affirmation of the self as God-informed sensuality, Julian foregrounds a principle of the body much neglected in the patriarchal tradition. As she reads the text of her God-inscribed body, she finds her sensuality filled with God and God filled with sensuality. Julian's final reconciliation of opposites reconciles an exclusive psychology and an exclusive theology in God's *all*-encompassing *self*-enclosure. Such radical visions of reality are made possible only by her equally radical ontology of feminine being at the heart of reality. Because the feminine as an ontotheological principle seeks to unite disparate elements, her psychology of the self is God-informed and her metaphysics profoundly personal. Julian's emphasis on the body as vehicle of the Divine, on nature and sensuality as already united to God, and on the motherhood of God deeply enriches the self, God, and reality itself.

Notes

[1] Jantzen, *Julian of Norwich,* deals admirably with the concept of sensuality in Julian's thought but does not see the body as an organ of knowing in Julian. Other studies, like that of Brant Pelphrey, treat Julian as spiritual writer and visionary without the important link to embodiment in her work. Joan Nuth's masterful recent study of Julian, *Wisdom's Daughter,* treats Julian primarily as theologian, and although she is careful to lay out a thoroughgoing theology of nature in Julian, the corporeality of her experience of God is not emphasized.

[2] See Wright, "Birthing Jesus," 23-44, for a discussion

of contemplation as internalization of symbol leading to a subsequent reemergence of the symbol in visions.

[3] Petroff, in *Consolation of the Blessed,* 59-66, classifies these visions as "participatory."

[4] Ackerman and Dahood, eds. and trans. *Ancrene Riwle,* 18, 35, 57, and 63. For example, "Let her meditate, at about midday who can, or some time, on God's cross as much as she can and on his precious torment . . . and say such a prayer as this: We adore you, O Christ. We adore your cross. . . . Hail, holy cross. . . . wood triumphant" (69).

[5] Leclercq, preface to *Julian of Norwich,* trans. Colledge and Walsh, 11.

[6] This notion of an ontological feminine allies itself more readily with dual than with single anthropology feminism, and with "romantic" feminism than with liberal feminism. See Rosemary Radford Ruether's *Sexism and God-Talk* (Boston: Beacon Press, 1983) for discussion of this latter typology.

[7] The only exception occurs when she demurs that she is "a woman, ignorant, weak and frail," but at the same time asks, "But because I am a woman, ought I therefore to believe that I should not tell you of the goodness of God . . ." (Colledge and Walsh, trans., vi.135; Colledge and Walsh, eds., 1:222). (References to the latter [the critical edition] appear with volume and page number; vol. 1 indicates the short text and vol. 2 the long text.) The topos of the frailty of the female gender does not invade her writings as it does those of the twelfth-century prophetess and saint, Hildegard of Bingen. See Newman, *Sister of Wisdom,* especially chap. 1.

[8] Leclercq, preface to *Julian of Norwich,* trans. Colledge and Walsh, 11.

[9] William James, *Varieties of Religious Experience* (New York: New American Library, 1958), 298.

[10] In one of the more striking instances of this emphasis on seeing, she says, "when we see god we hafe that we desyre, and than nedes vs nought to praye" (Colledge and Walsh, eds., 1:261).

[11] Yet it is paradoxical language she uses to express both active and passive aspects of this desire: "there came into my mind with contrition—a free gift from God which I did not seek—a desire of my will to have by God's gift a bodily sickness" (Colledge and Walsh, trans., i.126).

[12] "That wurshypful cytte pat oure lorde Jhesu syttyth in, it is oure sensualyte, in whych he is enclosyd; and oure kyndly substance is beclosyd in Jhesu, with the

blessyd soule of Crist syttyng in rest in the godhed" (2:572).

[13] References to Colledge and Walsh's modern English translation of the short text are in lowercase roman numerals followed by page numbers; to the long text, in arabic numerals followed by page numbers.

[14] In what appears a striking exception to Julian's holistic vision, she sees a body lying on the earth, itself "a devouring pit of stinking mud" (64.306), while out of this loathsome body springs a beautiful child. Here the opposites, the body as mortal flesh and the child as the pure soul, threaten to disengage from their "glorious union." Compare Brant Pelphrey's statement that "in the past [Julian] had conceived of a false separation between flesh and spirit, nature and holiness. Whereas she evidently believed that spirituality means rising above our mortal flesh—our human nature, our sensuality—she now sees that God loves all nature and delights in it," in "Spirituality in Mission: Lessons from Julian of Norwich," *Cross Currents* (Summer 1984): 182. See also Vinje, *Understanding of Love,* 151-62.

[15] For a modern interpretation of such a movement from "received knowledge" to subjective knowing, see Mary Field Belenky, *Women's Ways of Knowing: The Development of Self, Voice, and Mind* (New York: Basic Books, 1986).

[16] Compare Angela of Foligno's saying that: "The sight of the crucified body of the good and beloved Jesus did awaken such compassion that in all my inward parts and my bones and joints did I feel new pain, and I lamented afresh with terrible anguish" (quoted in Petroff, *Consolation,* 210).

[17] "The charyte of god makyth in vs such a vnitie that when it is truly seen no man can parte them selfe from other," she says (2:629).

[18] Compare Bynum's statement that "the woman, by suffering, fused with a cosmic suffering that redeemed the world" (*Holy Feast,* 289); and Petroff's that "The participation in the crucifixion became enormously liberating, for in the crucifixion women saw a powerful male figure saving the world by suffering passively, as women do" (*Consolation,* 66).

[19] Robert Detweiler, in *Breaking the Fall* (New York: Harper and Row, 1989), 123, speaks of a "charged corporeality too forceful to be fully articulated in language."

[20] See Jacob Neusner, *The Oral Torah: The Sacred Books of Judaism, An Introduction* (San Francisco: Harper and Row, 1986), 16-21.

[21] Jantzen *Julian of Norwich,* 143, points out that for Julian sensuality involves the union of soul and body, of consciousness with embodiment.

[22] Jantzen too sees little or no body-soul dualism in Julian: "Julian firmly rejects the idea derived from a one-sided reading of Plato that the body is independent recalcitrant matter, always tending to evil, while the soul is the divine principle always tending toward good" (ibid., 144).

[23] Unlike Margery Kempe, for whom chastity after bearing fourteen children has become an obsessional issue, Julian sees birthing as a divine function, in that Jesus as true Mother carries us, bears us forth, and nourishes us.

[24] See also the corollary of this in chapter 56: "For oure soule is so depe growndyd in god and so endlesly tresoryd that we may nott come to the knowyng ther of tylle we haue furst knowyng of god, which is the maker to whom it is onyd" (2:570).

[25] Bynum, *Jesus as Mother,* 110-69. See, especially on this theme, Bradley, "Motherhood Theme in Julian of Norwich"; Heimmel's *"God Is Our Mother";* and Molinari, *Julian of Norwich,* 169-76.

[26] Ann Belford Ulanov in *The Feminine in Jungian Psychology and in Christian Theology* (Evanston, Illinois: Northwestern University Press, 1971), 198, points up the maternal capacity for accepting the lowest, rejected aspects of being.

[27] Concerning this and the many other passages on divine motherhood belonging to Julian's reflections on the lord and servant parable in the long text, Colledge and Walsh remark, "The working of mercy and grace is the simple countering of evil by goodness; and this belongs to the feminine principle of the *natura creatrix,* the divine creative activity *where the ground of moderhed begynneth"* (Colledge and Walsh, eds., 1:151).

[28] Heimmel, *"God is Our Mother,"* 54-55.

[29] St. Ambrose uses the image of the womb in his conception of God the Father giving birth to the Son (ibid., 20). Guerric of Igny (d. 1157) produces similar images in speaking of God drawing souls "into his very bowels." See his second sermon for Lent, chapter 2, *Sermons* 2:30 (quoted in Bynum, *Jesus as Mother,* 121). Images of the womb and of clothing occupy a prominent place in the visionary speculations of Hildegard of Bingen. See Newman, *Sister of Wisdom,* 71-75, 103. See also the extensive work of the contemporary French feminist Julia Kristeva on the *chora:* "About Chinese Women" and "Stabat Mater" in *The Kristeva Reader,* ed. Toril Moi (New York: Columbia University Press, 1986).

[30] Bynum, in *Jesus as Mother,* makes the late medieval connection between milk and processed blood (132-33).

[31] Peter Brown, "Society and the Body: The Social Meaning of Asceticism in Late Antiquity" (Plenary Address, International Medieval Congress, Kalamazoo, Mich., May 1986). See Brown, *Body and Society.*

[32] Bynum's revaluation of asceticism as "an effort to plumb and to realize all the possibilities of the flesh" (*Holy Feast,* 294) certainly applies to Julian, though her own asceticism seems limited to reclusion.

[33] Although this statement goes a long way to indicate that Julian was not involved in extreme self-inflicted penances, as Bynum pointed out to me at a panel at the American Academy of Religion meeting in New Orleans, 1990, we do not have a biography of Julian to confirm such self-descriptions.

[34] Bell and Weinstein, *Saints and Society,* 234.

[35] Though it reappears briefly after the fifteenth revelation and before the sixteenth.

[36] See Paul Tillich, *Dynamics of Faith* (New York: Harper Torchbooks, 1957), 106.

[37] I am indebted for this notion to a paper given by Roger Corless at the International Medieval Congress, Kalamazoo, Mich., May, 1985.

Selected Bibliography

Ackerman, Robert W., and Roger Dahood, eds. and trans. *Ancrene Riwle.* Part I, Vol. 31. Binghamton, N.Y.: Medieval and Renaissance Texts and Studies, 1984.

Bell, Rudolph, and Donald Weinstein. *Saints and Society: The Two Worlds of Western Christendom.* Chicago: University of Chicago Press, 1982.

Bradley, Ritamary. "The Motherhood Theme in Julian of Norwich." *Fourteenth Century English Mystics Newsletter* 2, no. 4 (1976): 25-30.

Brown, Peter. *The Body and Society: Men, Women and Sexual Renunciation in Early Christianity.* New York: Columbia University Press, 1988.

Bynum, Caroline Walker. *Holy Feast and Holy Fast: The Religious Significance of Food to Medieval Women.* Berkeley: University of California Press, 1987.

————. *Jesus as Mother: Studies in the Spirituality of the High Middle Ages.* Berkeley: University of California Press, 1982.

Colledge, Edmund, and James Walsh, eds. *A Book of Showings to the Anchoress Julian of Norwich.* 2 vols. Toronto: Pontifical Institute of Medieval Studies, 1978.

————. trans. *Julian of Norwich: Showings.* New York: Paulist Press, 1978.

Heimmel, Jennifer P. *"God Is Our Mother": Julian of Norwhich and the Medieval Image of Christian Feminine Divinity.* Salzburg: Institut für Anglistik und Amerikanistik, 1982.

Jantzen, Grace M. *Julian of Norwich: Mystic and Theologian.* New York: Paulist Press, 1988.

Molinari, Paul. *Julian of Norwich: The Teaching of a FourteenthCentury English Mystic.* London: Longman, Green, and Company, 1958.

Newman, Barbara. *Sister of Wisdom.* Berkeley: University of California Press, 1987.

Nuth, Joan M. *Wisdom's Daughter: The Theology of Julian of Norwich.* New York: Crossroad Publishing Co., 1991.

Pelphrey, Brant. "Spirituality in Mission: Lessons from Julian of Norwich." *Cross Currents* (Summer 1984): 171-90.

Petroff, Elizabeth. *Consolation of the Blessed.* New York: Alta Gaia Society, 1979.

Vinje, Patricia Mary. *An Understanding of Love According to the Anchoress Julian of Norwich.* Salzburg: Institut für Anglistik und Amerikanistik.

Wright, Wendy M. "Birthing Jesus: A Salesian Understanding of the Christian Life." *Studia Mystica* 8, no. 1 (Spring 1990): 23-44.

FURTHER READING

Bibliography

Sawyer, Michael E. "Julian of Norwich." In his *A Bibliographical Index of Five English Mystics: Richard Rolle, Julian of Norwich, the Author of "The Cloud of Unknowing," Walter Hilton, Margery Kempe,* pp. 53-68. Pittsburgh: Clifford E. Barbour Library, Pittsburgh Theological Seminary, 1978.

Secondary bibliography.

Biography

Beer, Frances. "Julian of Norwich." In her *Women and Mystical Experience in the Middle Ages,* pp. 130-57.

Woodbridge, Suffolk: The Boydell Press, 1992.

An overview of Julian's life and work with an emphasis on her unique ability to both convey and embody the word of God.

Molinari, Paul. *Julian of Norwich: The Teaching of a 14th Century English Mystic.* London: Longmans, Green and Co., 1958, 214p.

Attempt to create an authoritative "life" of Julian. The book includes detailed examinations of Julian's teachings and writings.

Criticism

Review of *Revelations of Divine Love Recorded by Julian, Anchoress of Norwich, Anno Domini 1373. The Athenaeum,* No. 3857 (28 September 1901): 412.

Brief overview of *Revelations of Divine Love,* concluding that is is unimportant in the history of mysticism.

Baker, A. E. "The Lady Julian of Norwich." In his *Prophets for a Day of Judgement,* pp. 39-55. London: Eyre & Spottiswoode, 1944.

Surveys Julian's mysticism and teaching, focusing on her insistence on the unity between God and the human soul.

Beer, Frances. Introduction to *Julian of Norwich's "Revelations of Divine Love": The Shorter Version,* by Julian of Norwich, pp. 7-37. Middle English Texts, edited by M. Görlach, Vol. 8, Heidelberg: Carl Winter Universitätsverlag, 1978.

Examines the language used in *Revelations* short and long text versions and explores differences between the two texts.

Chambers, P. Franklin. *Juliana of Norwich: An Introductory Appreciation and Interpretive Anthology.* New York: Harper & Brothers, 1955, 224 p.

Historical study of Julian and Norwich in her day; also stresses the relevance of *Revelations* to today's reader.

Colledge, Eric [later Edmund]. *The Medieval Mystics of England.* New York: Charles Scribners' Sons, 1961, 309 p.

Survey of medieval English mysticism which places Julian's work in her contemporary context.

Colledge, Edmund, and James Walsh. Introduction to *"A Book of Showings to the Anchoress Julian of Norwich," Part I: Introduction and the Short Text,* by Julian of Norwich, pp. 1-198. Toronto: Pontifical Institute of Medieval Studies, 1978.

Comprehensive study of the two versions of *Revelations,* focusing on Julian's intellectual formation and her work's theological content.

Jantzen, Grace M. *Julian of Norwich: Mystic and Theologian.* New York: Paulist Press, 1987, 230 p.

An in-depth study of Julian's teachings that seeks to "integrate the findings of scholarship with the interests of contemporary philosophy."

Lawlor, John. "Note on the Revelations of Julian of Norwich." *The Review of English Studies,* n.s. II, No. 7 (July 1951): 255-58.

Argues that the short text was the first and probably the only version of *Revelations* made public in Julian's lifetime.

Lewis, C. S. "Religious Controversy and Translation." In his *English Literature in the Sixteenth Century, Excluding Drama,* pp. 157-221. Oxford: Oxford University Press, Clarendon Press, 1954.

Includes a brief, favorable comparison of Julian's prose style in *Revelations* with that of Sir Thomas More.

Llewelyn, Robert, ed. *Julian: Woman of Our Day.* London: Darton, Longman and Todd, 1985, 144p.

A collection of essays for the general reader that illuminates Julian's work from a variety of perspectives.

Maisonneuve, Roland. "The Visionary Universe of Julian of Norwich: Problems and Methods." In *The Medieval Mystical Tradition in England: Papers Read at the Exeter Symposium,* edited by Marion Glasscoe, pp. 86-98. Exeter: University of Exeter, 1980.

Explores the complex visionary universe that is detailed in the text of Julian's *Revelations.*

Palliser, Margaret Ann. *Christ, Our Mother of Mercy: Divine Mercy and Compassion in the Theology of the Shewings of Julian of Norwich.* Berlin and New York: Walter de Gruyter, 1992, 262 p.

A detailed analysis of *Revelations* that seeks to demonstrate "that Julian's *Shewings* offers a profound theological basis for understanding divine mercy and compassion."

Pelphrey, Brant. *Love Was His Meaning: The Theology and Mysticism of Julian of Norwich.* Salzburg: Institut für Anglistik und Amerikanistik, Universität Salzburg, 1982, 360p.

Provides an overview of the bases of Julian's mysticism and theology, with an emphasis on the the the theme of charity.

Riehle, Wolfgang. *The Middle English Mystics.* Translated by Bernard Standring. London: Routledge & Kegan Paul, 1981, 244p.

Comparative study of the major medieval English mystics' literary expression. Riehl comments on the metaphors for mystical union that appear in the *Revelations* and discusses Julian's personal experience of God.

Warrack, Grace. Introduction to *Revelations of Divine Love Recorded by Julian, Anchoress at Norwich, Anno Domini 1373,* 2d ed., by Julian of Norwich, pp. xvii-lxxviii. London: Methuen & Co., 1907.

    Discusses themes, style, and content of *Revelations.*

Watkin, E. I. "Revelations of Divine Love." *The Catholic World* CXXXI, No. 782 (May 1930): 174-82.

    Discusses love, redemption, and atonement in *Revelations.*

Watson, Nicholas. "The Composition of Julian of Norwich's *Revelations of Love.*" *Speculum: A Journal of Medieval Studies* 68, No. 3 (July 1993): 637-83.

    Takes issue with the scholarly consensus regarding the dating and composition of the two versions of *Revelations,* arguing that the process may have been "more prolonged and hesitant than has been thought."

Additional coverage of Julian's life and career is contained in the following source published by the Gale Group: *Literature Criticism from 1400 to 1800, Vol. 6,* **and** *Dictionary of Literary Biography, Vol. 146: Old and Middle English Literature.*

Matthew Prior

1664-1721

English poet, essayist, and satirist.

INTRODUCTION

Prior is remembered as the author of some of the finest occasional verse in English and for his love poetry. As England's unofficial poet laureate during the reigns of King William III (1689-1702) and Queen Anne (1702--1714), Prior produced poems on momentous occasions and on demand to commemorate a variety of events. Although Prior wrote during the Augustan Age his verse retains the classical allusions of Restoration lyrics. A master of light verse, an accomplished essayist, and a distinguished wit, Prior became wealthy by selling subscriptions to his 1718 edition of *Poems on Several Occasions,* demonstrating to fellow poets that there were alternatives to soliciting the support of a wealthy patron.

Biographical Information

Prior was born in 1664 in Westminster, the only child of six to survive infancy. Prior's parents sent him at age eight to Westminster School. The death of his father three years later forced the boy to leave and begin working. While employed by an uncle, Prior met the Earl of Dorset, who paid for his tuition and returned him to school. In 1683 Prior enrolled in St. John's College in Cambridge, taking a bachelor's degree four years later. Prior achieved fame as an undergraduate with *The Hind and the Panther Transvers'd to the Story of The Country Mouse and the City-Mouse* (1687), a satire written with his friend Charles Montagu ridiculing Poet Laureate John Dryden's *The Hind and the Panther*. In 1690 Lord Dorset secured for him a minor diplomatic post in The Hague, launching him on a career in public office as a Tory. In 1697 Prior was instrumental in securing the signing of the Treaty of Ryswick. Later he played a central role in ending the War of the Spanish Succession by his secret negotiations with the French government. The 1713 Treaty of Utrecht, ending that war, became popularly known as "Matt's Peace." His public life culminated in his being made Plenipotentiary to France in 1712. Following Queen Anne's death in 1714 and the resulting turmoil, Prior was recalled to England. A loyal Tory, Prior was arrested and confined for a year by the newly established Whig government in an unsuccessful attempt to force him to give damaging evidence against his fellow Tory politicians. During this time he wrote

"Alma; or the Progress of the Mind" (1718). After his release, Prior retired to Essex, where he died in 1721.

Major Works

From *The Hind and the Panther Transvers'd* Prior gained a national reputation at the expense of Dryden's poem, which celebrated his recently-acquired Catholic religion; so stinging was Prior's mock-heroic burlesque that reportedly Dryden cried reading it. To comfort William III after the death of Queen Mary, Prior composed "An Ode, Presented to the King, on His Majesty's Arrival in Holland, After the Queen's Death, 1695" (1695). Sometimes considered the best of Prior's occasional or "public" poems, "An Ode" features elaborate construction, sophisticated wordplay, and a careful melding of form and content. Prior's most famous works are contained in his *Poems on Several Occasions,* particularly in the expanded edition of 1718. *Poems on Several Occasions* includes what Prior considered his finest works, including light Anacreontics, bawdy verse narratives, and philosophical poems dealing with such topics as the limitations of human reason. "Paulo Purganti and His Wife: An Honest, but a Simple Pair," "Hans Carvel," and "The Ladle" are structured around sexual humor. The long poem "Solomon on the Vanity of the World" illustrates the assertion in *Ecclesiastes* that "All is vanity." Other notable verses include "Henry and Emma," a sentimental adaptation of the traditional ballad "The Nutbrown Maid," and "Alma," which describes in poetic terms an obscure belief about the location of human mind, soul, and spirit.

Critical Reception

Prior enjoyed an enviable reputation as a poet, wit, and man of letters, and benefited from the devotion of influential literary friends. Some negative critical commentary by his contemporary Samuel Johnson impacted public opinion, but Johnson also praised many of Prior's works. Prior is perhaps most vulnerable to the charge of lack of inventiveness. In his defense, he did not make claims to the contrary and many of his borrowings were openly acknowledged as imitations or adaptations. Prior may have considered his career as a poet to be secondary to his life in politics. Such distinguished critics as F. R. Leavis and R. P. Blackmur have attributed to Prior a significant role in the evolution of a tradition of minor poetry in English. During the twentieth century Prior's work has been the subject of continued study both for it own merits and in order to explore his influence on later writers, including Anne Finch, Thomas Moore, William MakepeaceThackeray, and Oliver Wendell Holmes

PRINCIPAL WORKS

A Satyr on the modern Translators (satire) 1685

Satyr on the Poets. In Imitation of the Seventh Satyr of Juvenal (satire) 1687

The Hind and the Panther Transvers'd to the Story of The Country Mouse and the City-Mouse [with Charles Montagu] (prose and verse) 1687

Poems on Several Occasions (poetry) unauthorized edition, 1707; authorized edition, 1709; revised and enlarged edition, 1718

A Second Collection of Poems on Several Occasions (poetry) 1716

A Supplement to Mr. Prior's Poems (poetry) 1722

The Poetical Works of Matthew Prior (poetry) 1777

Matthew Prior: Dialogues of the Dead, and Other Works in Prose and Verse (poetry and essays) 1907

The Shorter Poems of Matthew Prior (poetry) 1923

The Literary Works of Matthew Prior. 2 vols. (poetry, essays, drama, letters, satire, and fragments) 1959

The Literary Works of Matthew Prior. Enlarged edition. (poetry, essays, drama, letters, satire, and fragments) 1971

CRITICISM

Reverend George Gilfillan (essay date 1858)

SOURCE: "The Life of Matthew Prior," in *The Poetical Works of Matthew Prior,* pp. v-xx. Edinburgh: James Nichol, 1858.

[*In the following excerpt from an introduction to a nineteenth-century edition of Prior's poetry, Gilfillan offers his opinion regarding Prior's most popular and accomplished works.*]

His writings have been accurately and comprehensively divided by Dr Johnson into his **"Tales,"** his **"Occasional Poems," "Alma,"** and **"Solomon."** His **"Tales"** are, so far as the incidents are concerned, in general, borrowed, but the handling is Prior's own. They are sprightly and amusing, and have been compared to the productions of that "fable tree," Fontaine. He that touches pitch must run his chance of being defiled, but Prior carries away less of it from his rather ticklish themes than might have been expected. Should anyone insist that two or three of these stories are blots, he must, at the same time, admit that they are small in size; that they bear no proportion to the mass of his poetry; and that, as compositions, they are too clever and characteristic to be omitted. His **"Occasional Poems"** are of unequal merit. His love verses are often graceful and often very trifling. His translations from Callimachus are called by Johnson "licentious"—*i. e.,* too free in their rendering—and by other critics, stiff and hard. To us they read very much like a portion of Cowper's "Homer," and, like it, are full of a grave and true, if somewhat faint and sluggish, fire. His war poetry is, to a great extent, spoiled by its classical allusions, which are dragged in as by cart-ropes, instead of flowing naturally from the poet's memory or imagination. Johnson calls his "Henry and Emma" a "dull and tedious dialogue," and by doing so has subjected himself to the poetical anathema of Cowper. Certainly, as compared with the ancient ballad of the "Nut-brown Maid," **"Henry and Emma"** is artificial and poor; but this arises not from the subject, but from Prior's treatment of it. There is no task more difficult, and few more invidious, than that of modernising an ancient and favourite poem. It may be doubted if any one save Dryden has fully succeeded in it. Pope, in his "Temple of Fame," certainly has not; nor has Prior, in **"Henry and Emma,"** in which, if the numbers are smoother than in the ancient poem, much of the race, and freshness, and the wild woodland charm, is lost. We cannot but count Johnson's criticism exceedingly prosaic and hypercritical, when he says, "The example of Emma, who resolves to follow an outlawed murderer wherever fear and guilt shall drive him, deserves no imitation; and the experiment, by which Henry tries the lady's constancy, is such as must end either in infamy to her or in disappointment to himself." We suspect none ever thought that the Poet meant to recommend Emma's conduct as a model, and few were likely to follow it even though he had. The story is simply an ingenious artifice, such as Malcolm, in Macbeth, employs in blackening his own character to Macduff; and the object of the Poet is to shew how love, in certain circumstances, spurns the bounds of prudence, and sets "infamy" at defiance.

"Alma" is said, by Johnson, to be imitated from Butler's "Hudibras," although Cowper, on the contrary, says, "They were both favourites of mine, and I often read them, but never saw in them the least resemblance to each other; nor do I now, except that they are composed in the same measure." "Hudibras" has a story, although a very slight one, and one that fades away and is lost in the thick umbrage of the wit and learning. **"Alma"** has none. "Hudibras" laughs at religion—at least, the religion of the Puritans. **"Alma"** turns philosophy into ridicule. Butler has to repress and pack down his enormous mass of learned allusions, while Prior manages, by spreading his knowledge thin, to make it seem greater than in reality it is. "Butler pours out a negligent profusion, certain of the weight, but careless of the stamp. Prior has comparativelylittle, but with this little he makes a fine show." The two poems resemble each other more in their faults than in their merits. Both are often obscure and recondite in their allusions, and sometimes offensively coarse in their language. Next to his **"Tales,"** however, **"Alma"** has been the most popular of Prior's works. It is ever lively, discursive, and entertaining.

We are, perhaps, singular in our opinion; but we cannot help, along with Prior himself, preferring **"Solomon,"** to all his other productions. Heavy in parts, and in construction rather a planless paraphrase than a well-arranged story, with some broken lines and one egregiously absurd passage, in which Solomon is made to predict and describe the glories of Great Britain, it is a grave, high-toned, and majestic poem. Its versifica-

tion is in general rotund and rolling—its moral excellent—and its descriptions terse and graphic. The whole story of Abra is admirable, and has touches of nature in it little inferior to Shakespeare, as in that exquisite line—

"When I called another, Abra came."

In no poem, and in no prose work, we believe, has so much justice ever been done to the character of Israel's "Grand Monarque"—the most splendid of sensualists—the most gorgeous of love poets—the most amiable of despots—the most sententious of moralists—whose magnificent wealth, commercial enterprise, love of peace and of pomp, wondrous wisdom, and, for his age, universal knowledge, errors, and faults, which, like his merits and virtues, were on a colossal scale, and were gilded, though not redeemed, by the gusto with which he entered on them—whose fame, as the builder of the temple and of the forest palace of Lebanon, as the husband of Pharaoh's daughter, as the admired of the magnificent Queen of Sheba—whose memorable estrangement from God, and still more memorable return, recorded by himself in the Book of Ecclesiastes, all taken together, rendered him, if not the most consistent or lovely, certainly the greatest, broadest, and most brilliant of Israel's monarchs; so that in the lustre of the glory of Solomon, that of the deep-hearted David, the holy Hezekiah, and the pious and ardent Josiah, fades and dwindles away. Nowhere, save in his own page, is this extraordinary person pictured in such life-like and vivid colours as in Prior's **"Solomon."**

This production is one of the best of a particular, and we may add, a very ambitious class of poems—those, namely, founded on Scripture history or Scripture song. Such, besides many others, are Cowley's "Davideis," Giles Fletcher's "Christ's Victory," Young's "Paraphrase of the Book of Job," Smart's "David," Moore's and Byron's "Hebrew Melodies," Croly's "Scenes from Scripture," and Thomas Aird's "Nebuchadnezzar," and "Demoniac." These, while all belonging to one class of poetry, and attesting one primal fount of inspiration, vary exceedingly in character; Cowley's poem being at once clumsy and fragmentary, although shewing prodigious powers of misdirected genius, and misapplied learning; Fletcher's being a grand but unequal production—the abortive "Faery Queen" of Christianity; Young's being a translation of the sublime of Hebrew into the elegant of English poetry; Moore's "Hebrew Melodies" being mawkish, and Byron's morbid renderings of their respective originals—while Croly, Aird, Smart, and Prior have all, in different degrees, entered into the soul of the Scripture writers. Croly, in his "Dothan," recalling the very spirit of the scene when the "Lord opened the eyes of the young man, and he saw and behold the mountain was full of horses and chariots of fire round about Elisha;" Aird, walking with emulous foot beside Ezekiel,

> "Whose spirit stumbles on the corner-stones Of realms disjointed, and of broken thrones;"

Smart mating with the magnificent aberrations, as well as the lofty flights of the lord of Adullam's cave—and Prior (as if he had written or read the lost volume, "The Book of the Acts of Solomon,") recalling from the "sepulchre of the kings of Israel," the majestic form of the Great Man to whom "God gave wisdom and understanding exceeding much, and greatness of heart, even as the sand that is by the sea-shore."

Prior's place as a poet, is in the second rank of the Pope and Dryden School—beneath these two masters, but on a level with Swift and Gay. His imagination is fertile but not creative—his language, except in his **"Tales,"** is copious rather than terse—his wit is Swift's, but with the gall diluted; possessing Swift's ease, without his malignant *animus*—he displays the unvarying good sense, coolness, and self-command of a man of the world, rather than the ardour and enthusiasm of a bard, and has been well called the "most natural of artificial poets."

Oswald Doughty (essay date 1922)

SOURCE: "The Augustans: Prior," in *English Lyric in the Age of Reason,* pp. 46-56. London: Daniel O'Connor, 1922.

[*In the following excerpt, Doughty discusses the influence of earlier poets on Prior as well as works by Prior that display a striking modernity.*]

Prior lives to-day, not even by his clever and formerly much admired **Ode sur la Prise de Namur,** but by his light occasional verse. Though Johnson failed to do him justice, Cowper at once stepped into the breach, and admirably defended his idol.[1] "Prior's," says Thackeray, also picking up the glove which Johnson had thrown down, "seem to me amongst the easiest, the richest, the most charmingly humorus of English lyrical poems."[2] Though by his collaboration in *The Country Mouse and the City Mouse* Prior had, according to Spence,[3] reduced the ageing Dryden to tears, he followed in his Pindaric odes, before the close of the seventeenth century, the literary fashion of Cowley and Dryden. He even contributed to Dryden's *Miscellanies,* and in 1693 prepared for the music of Purcell a New Year's *Hymn to the Sun.*

But the singing of hymns, whether in life or in art, was less characteristic of Prior than his diplomatic activities. These led him to join the throng of tender-hearted mourners for the death of Queen Mary, and to swell the universal chorus of anguish by a funeral poem. His burlesque **Ode sur la Prise de Namur,** admirable in its way, was sent by him from The Hague to Tonson, in 1695, and published interleaved with the original ode by Boileau, of which it was a brilliant parody. The recapture of Namur by the English in 1695 enabled Prior to turn the pompous and sycophantic ode of Boileau, celebrating its capture by the French three years before, against the French poet with great effect. With Prior poetry not infrequently went hand in hand with politics, and politics in that benighted age were, it must be admitted, not without occasional material advantages for the politician. To Prior indeed politics brought speedy and substantial prosperity, though fortune was not invariably kind to him. It was during the chief reverse of his career, the two years' imprisonment which began in 1715, that he wrote his **Alma; or, Progress of the Mind.** In his occasional, social verse we find the real, lovable Prior. Within this narrow sphere of society verse, Prior is a master. He crowned the work of Dryden with a grace and delicacy of versification to which the earlier poet never attained; he brought the familiar style in poetry to a high degree of polish; he became the supreme representative of French influence in English poetry.

Poetry to Prior was merely a diversion. He was too wise in the things of this world to turn professional poet and starve in a garret.

> "As to my own part," he says, "I found this impulse [to write verse] very soon, and shall continue to feel it as long as I can think. I remember nothing further in life than that I made Verses. . . . But I had two Accidents in Youth which hindered me from Being quite possessed with the Muse: I was bred in a College where Prose was more in fashion than Verse, and as soon as I had taken my first Degree was sent the King's Secretary to the Hague: There I had enough to do studying French and Dutch and altering my Terentian and Virgilian Style into that of Articles, Conventions, and Memorials: So that Poetry which by the bent of my Mind might have become the Business of my life, was by the happyness of my Education only the Amusement of it."[4]

But Prior clearly saw that poetry, which worshipped as a deity might have angered Fortuna, could, if courted with discretion, become an ally, and win for him a place, if not in the seats of the mighty, at least of some considerable elevation. Consequently, for reasons of policy, as he candidly avows, he made no attempt to write satire, which might have retarded his advance in the world. In his preface to **Poems on Several Occasions,** Prior tells us the work consists of:

> "Public Panegyrics, Amorous Odes, Serious Reflections, or Idle Tales, the Product of his leisure Hours, who had Business enough upon his Hands, and was only a Poet by Accident."

In these poems Prior reveals himself as an eighteenth-century Herrick, both as man and poet. He has the same light, kindly humour, through which runs a suggestion of irony, deepening sometimes until it is touched to darker thought. We sometimes suspect that the tears of laughter have silently changed into the *lacrymœ rerum,* that the jester's heart is less light than his song. We know that, like Herrick, Prior can laugh at himself, as well as at the rest of the world. Both pay homage to Horace; both are "classical," both "pagan." And this community of taste and spirit clearly reveals itself, despite the newer, less gracious poetic dress of the later poet. Prior, unlike Herrick, is the modern, the man of fashion, the coffee-house wit. He has the new polish which Chesterfield and his brethren of the spirit were importing from France. Nevertheless, when Prior sings—

> Her Hair,
> In Ringlets rather dark than fair,
> Does down her Iv'ry Bosom roll
> And hiding Half, adorns the Whole.
> In her high Forehead's fair half-round
> Love sits in open Triumph crown'd:
> He in the Dimple of her Chin,
> In private State by Friends is seen,[5]

he is only echoing with less charm of expression, the spirit which made Herrick sing:

> Then, when I see thy Tresses bound
> Into an Ovall, square, or round;
> And knit in knots far more then I
> Can tell by tongue; or true-love tie:
> Next, when those Lawnie Filmes I see
> Play with a wild civility:
> And all those airie silks to flow,
> Alluring me, and tempting so:
> I must confesse, mine eye and heart
> Dotes less on Nature then on Art.[6]

Both poets delight in the society of women, nor is their devotion confined to a single Julia or Cloe. The more sophisticated ladies of the later age seem to have been less placable than their predecessors, and the same, apparently, may also be said of the two poets.

> When Julia chid, I stood as mute the while,
> As is the fish, or tonguelesse Crocodile,[7]

says the peaceable Herrick; but Prior, with a felicity of phrase and measure which makes the lines a model of the familiar style in verse, replies to his fair accuser:

> To be vext at a Trifle or two that I writ,
>   Your Judgment at once, and my Passion
>   You wrong:
> You take that for Fact, which will scarce be
>   found Wit:

Od's Life! must one swear to the Truth of a Song?[8]

Then he recovers his temper, and tries to soothe Cloe in such delightful stanzas as these:

> What I speak, my fair Cloe, and what I write,
>   shews
>   The Diff'rence there is betwixt Nature and
>   Art:
> I court others in Verse; but I love Thee in
>   Prose:
>   And They have my Whimsies; but thou hast
>   my Heart.

In persuading Cloe, he almost begins to believe this elaborate *apologia* himself, as he continues:

> So when I am weary'd with wand'ring all
>   Day;
>   To Thee, my Delight, in the Evening I
>   come:
> No Matter what Beauties I saw in my Way:
>   They were but my Visits; but Thou art my
>   Home.

Cloe is apparently sufficiently worked upon by this, to accept a story which she does not really believe; whereupon Prior, perhaps himself not sure of its truth or fiction, resumes his usual bantering tone, quotes Horace and Lydia, and concludes with a ludicrous and no doubt intentionally ungrammatical couplet, which is to bring back the smiles to the tear-stained face of Cloe. It is in similar vein that Prior sings:

> The Merchant, to secure his Treasure,
>   Conveys it in a borrow'd Name:
> Euphelia serves to grace my Measure;
>   But Cloe is my real Flame.[9]

And in like manner are ***The Question, to Lisetta,*** and ***Lisetta's Reply.***

Prior also shared Herrick's devotion to the bowl. To both men the bowl is something almost sacred, part of the mystic rites of Bacchus. How cordially would Prior have endorsed Herrick's noble resolve:

> But Ile spend my comming houres,
> Drinking wine, and crown'd with flowres.[10]

But Julia and Cloe would have had to share the banquet. There is the same pseudo-paganism, born of Horace and the Greek Anthology, in the following ***Song*** by Prior:

> If Wine and Musick have the Pow'r,
> To ease the Sickness of the Soul;
> Let *Phœbus* ev'ry String explore;

And Bacchus fill the sprightly Bowl.
Let them their friendly Aid imploy,
To make my Cloe's Absence light;
And seek for Pleasure to destroy
The Sorrows of this live-long Night.

But She to Morrow will return:
Venus be Thou to Morrow great;
Thy Myrtles strow, Thy Odours burn;
And meet Thy Fav'rite Nymph in State.
Kind Goddess, to no other Pow'rs
Let Us to Morrow's Blessings own;
Thy darling Loves shall guide the Hours;
And all the Day be Thine alone.

Similar, too, are Herrick's *Cheat of Cupid* and Prior's **Cupid Mistaken.**

Forthwith his bow he bent,
  And wedded string and arrow,
And struck me, that it went
  Quite through my heart and marrow,

sings the earlier poet, describing Cupid's attack. Prior seeks to bring all the famed smoothness of Waller into his description:

With Skill He chose his sharpest Dart:
  With all his Might his Bow He drew:
Swift to His beauteous Parent's heart
  The too well-guided Arrow flew.

At times the familiar refrain of *Carpe Diem* is the common burden of their song.

For what To-morrow shall disclose,
  May spoil what You To-night propose:
England may change; or Cloe stray:
  Love and Life are for To-day,

Prior exclaims in a quatrain entitled **Quid sit futurum Cras fuge quærere,** just as Herrick had preached the same doctrine in his famous *Gather ye Rose-buds while ye may,* and similar verses.

The inextricably mingled humour and pathos which forms perhaps Prior's greatest charm, finds delightful expression in the verses **For My Own Monument.**

Fierce robbers there are that infest the
  highway,
  So Matt may be kill'd, and his bones never
  found,
False witness at court, and fierce tempests at
  sea,
  So Matt may yet chance to be hang'd, or be
  drown'd.

If his bones lie in earth, roll in sea, fly in air,

To Fate we must yield, and the thing is the
  same,
And if passing thou giv'st him a smile, or a
  tear,
  He cares not—yet pr'ythee be kind to his
  Fame.

Like Herrick, too, Prior sang of children long before children had become a part of the poet's stock-in-trade.

Prior, then, carries into the eighteenth century, in a very real manner, the spirit of Herrick. We find indeed, in the lesser known verses of the earlier poet, the germ of those characteristics of eighteenth-century occasional verse which are usually regarded as belonging to that century alone. It is undoubtedly true that Herrick's greatest qualities as a poet—his tenderness, his love of nature, his childlike simplicity, his delicate cadences of expression—die with him. But though the quaint dress of his thought and feeling is discarded for the more formal, more elaborate brocade of the later age, his lines **Upon a Painted Gentlewoman, On a Perfum'd Lady, Upon Some Women,** and similar productions, are in the same line of development as much Restoration verse, a somewhat milder foretaste of Swift's *Lady's Dressing Room.* It cannot be denied that to proceed from some of the lyrics of Herrick, to the occasional verse of the Restoration and eighteenth century, is merely to turn from what was done in the green tree to its counterpart in the dry.

But if Prior represents a transitional stage in English verse, pointing backward to preceding poets, he also points forward along the road of poetic evolution. There is a strangely modern note, a suggestion of Tennyson's manner in such a stanza as this:

Yet car'd I not, what might presage
  Or withering Wreath, or fleeting Youth:
Love I esteem'd more strong than Age,
  And Time less permanent than Truth.[11]

In his delightful poem **The Female Phaeton,** Prior enters the borderland of Swift's lyrical narrative verse, and points to Cowper. Prior did a number of foolish things in poetry as in life. At times he tries to be conventional and to write odes in the manner of Cowley. But perhaps the most foolish of his poetic transgressions was his attempt to alter the Spenserian stanza, an attempt which was doomed to failure.

Prior's great virtue as a poet is an intense realism. He has too vital a personality to be restrained by the current poetic theories. For him abstractions have no meaning. He demands life with all its colour, noise, change, reality, crudity. In one point Prior was far removed from the typical Augustan, for he preferred passion to stagnation, emotion to reason. He has no sympathy for the "sauntering Jacks and idle Joans" of the world.

> Nor Good, nor Bad, nor Fools, nor Wise;
> They wou'd not learn, nor cou'd advise:
> Without Love, Hatred, Joy, or Fear,
> They led—a kind of—as it were:
> Nor Wish'd, nor Car'd, nor Laugh'd, nor
>   Cry'd:
> And so They liv'd; and so They dy'd.[12]

Prior had no intention of making his own life "a kind of—as it were"; his sympathies are rather with those like his typical heroine **"Jinny the Just,"** who—

> . . . read and Accounted & payd & abated
> Eat and drank, Play'd & Work't, laugh't &
>   Cry'd, lov'd & hated,
> As answer'd the end of her being Created.

This delight in life, in all its aspects, was rank heresy against those principles of the fashionable common-sense philosophy which made reason supreme, and the separation of the elect from common humanity a fundamental rule. That of his own free-will a man should leave the world of wit and fashion to snatch a few moments among humble folks in an ale-house was incomprehensible to the exalted devotees of reason, and the explanation of this practice of Prior was at once found in his humble ancestry. On the score of birth, Lord Strafford declined to act with the poet in negotiating the Treaty of Utrecht. In two poems, *The Old Gentry,* and an *Epitaph Extempore,* Prior replied to such, in verse full of the laughter of his light-hearted scorn:

> Heralds and Statesmen, by your leave,
>   Here lye the Bones of Matthew Prior;
> The Son of Adam and of Eve,
>   Can Bourbon, or Nassau, go higher?[13]

But even for Prior song, woman, and wine could not entirely banish deeper questionings, and at times a touch of fatalism creeps into his verse. There is a deeper note, an undertone of sadness in the lines to his monument already quoted. The same tinge of regret turns his *Parting with Elavia* to darker hues:

> You sigh and weep: the Gods neglect
>   That precious dew your eyes let fall:
> Our joy and grief with like respect
>   They mind; and that is, not at all.
>
> We pray, in hopes they will be kind,
>   As if they did regard our state:
> They hear; and the return we find
>   Is, that no prayers can alter Fate.

Something of this darker mood finds expression, though somewhat weakened by a touch of the sentimental and artificial, in *The Garland.* In this poem the writer tells us how—

> The Pride of ev'ry Grove I chose,
>   The Violet sweet, and Lilly fair,
> The dappl'd Pink, and blushing Rose,
>   To deck my charming Cloe's Hair.

But the flowers fade, and the sentimental Cloe weeps over their decay.

> She sigh'd; She smil'd: and to the Flow'rs
>   Pointing, the Lovely Moralist said:
> See! Friend, in some few fleeting Hours,
>   See yonder, what a Change is made.
>
> Ah Me! the blooming Pride of May,
>   And That of Beauty are but One:
> At Morn Both flourish bright and gay,
>   Both fade at Evening, pale, and gone.

There is too a very modern touch in the following stanza from some lines to **"The Honourable Charles Montagu":**

> Our Hopes, like tow'ring Falcons, aim
>   At Objects in an airy height:
> The little Pleasure of the Game
>   Is from afar to view the Flight.

Is it merely fanciful to see in the following verses

> The ancient Sage, who did so long maintain,
> That Bodies die, but Souls return again,
>   With all the Births and Deaths He had in
>   store,
> Went out Pythagoras, and came no more,[14]

a foretaste in both form and spirit of:

> Myself when young did eagerly frequent
> Doctor and Saint, and heard great Argument
> About it and about; but evermore
> Came out by the same Door as in I went?[15]

Surely too there is the bitterness of personal sorrow, a trace of passing sadness in those verses of Prior which found their way to the heart of Sir Walter Scott[16]:

> The Man in graver Tragic known
> (Tho' his best Part long since was done)
> Still on the Stage desires to tarry:
> And He who play'd the *Harlequin,*
> After the Jest still loads the Scene,
> Unwilling to retire, tho' Weary.[17]

Can it be that the years changed for Prior the emphasis

of those thoughtless verses of his earlier days . . . ?

Notes

[1] Letter to the Rev. Wm. Unwin, January 5, 1782.

[2] *English Humorists,* ed. W. L. Phelps, 1908, p. 152.

[3] *Anecdotes,* ed. S. W. Singer, 1858, p. 47.

[4] *An Essay upon Learning.*

[5] *Her Right Name.*

[6] *Teares are Tongues.*

[7] *Art above Nature: To Julia.*

[8] *Cloe Jealous: A Better Answer.*

[9] *An Ode.*

[10] *On Himselfe.*

[11] *Cloe Jealous.*

[12] *An Epitaph.*

[13] *Epitaph Extempore.*

[14] *Ode to the Memory of Hon. Col. George Villiers.*

[15] Fitzgerald's *Rubaiyát of Omar Khayyám.*

[16] Lockhart's *Life of Scott,* 2nd ed., 1853, pp. 738-9.

[17] Lines written in the beginning of Mezeray's *History of France.*

Richard Morton (essay date 1964)

SOURCE: "Matthew Prior's *Dialogues of the Dead,*" in *Ball State University Forum,* Vol. VIII, No. 3, Summer, 1967, pp. 73-8.

[In the following essay, first presented as a lecture in 1964, Morton contrasts the approach to the dialogue des morts *("dialogue of (or with) the dead") taken by various seventeenth- and eighteenth-century writers with that of Prior in his* Dialogues of the Dead. *Morton focuses particularly on Prior's use of irony, his subtlety, and effective portrayal of setting.]*

"I shall be transported into the company of wise and just gods," said Socrates of his approaching death, "and of dead men greater than those left alive. You may be assured that I expect to find myself amongst good men." Dr. John Arbuthnot has his Bishop Burnet "dream that I am dead, and conversing with the ghosts of emperors, popes and kings." From the Augustans to the present century—

> For I shall meet Sir Philip Sidney . . .
> And other heroes of that kidney—

the immortal and loquacious throngs of Hades have offered themselves to the imagination, and it is small wonder that manywriters have tried to verbalize the wit and wisdom of the dead. Particularly in the seventeenth and eighteenth centuries, in France and in England, the *dialogue des morts* flourished. Among those who wrote in English, Matthew Prior has perhaps the most distinguished name, and his dialogues well deserve A. R. Waller's praise, "among the best of their kind." Prior wrote only four dialogues and in variety and scope he is more limited than his fellow necrodramatists, but his uniquely keen insight into the full potentials of the form gives his pieces a particular appeal and effectiveness.

The dead may be presumed to have neither illusions nor false dignity; Lucian, the classical exponent of the dialogue from Hades, vigorously propounded the cynic theme that human success and achievement are transitory, and he made his dialogues primarily satires against pretension. In his celebrated Dialogue 20 we see the various dead souls crowding into Charon's boat, stripped of their beauty, their wealth, their physical prowess, their trophies, and their luxury. The transported rhetorician must abandon his flowers of rhetoric, and only Menippus is allowed to bring aboard his worldy possessions—frankness, geniality, independence, and laughter. This Lucianic theme is widely continued. Frequent passages in the *Letters from the Dead to the Living* by Tom Brown (one of Dryden's translators of Lucian) attest to the decay of human fortune. We are, for example, shown Semiramis as an alewife:

> and this may serve as a lesson of instruction to you, that when once death has laid his icy paws upon us all other distinctions of fortune and quality immediately vanish. . . .

and numerous other notables appear similarly grovelling in penury.

This fairly obvious satirical device is utilized by Prior—in his opening speech of Oliver Cromwell, who is to discourse with his late, mad porter:

> What a Vicisitude does Death bring to human affairs! No Coronet on my Head, no purple Robe to my back no Scepter in my hand, neither Heralds before nor Guards around me, Justled and Affronted by a hundred Cavalier Ghosts whom I ruined in t'other World.

Yet Lucian himself seems mostly to have exhausted the satirical possibilities of death as disposer of honors. Indeed, his more successful dialogues take place on the way to Hades where the trappings of life are present, though reluctantly being shed. When the vanities of life have been thoroughly purged away, the individuality of the speaker evaporates. The once-great dead become intellectual and spiritual paupers, whose conversations can have no comic potential; there is only the one irony—the discrepancy between the heroic reputation and the impotent ghost. A more viable form for the dialogue shows the dead permitted to retain their status and their baggage: the satire arises more dynamically from the clash between the different sorts and conditions of men flung together in the democracy of the afterlife and maintaining the beliefs and philosophies, or the illusions and eccentricities, of their lives. Such dialogues have potential intellectual subtlety. Little of interest could flow from the consultations of the following characters, to use Tom Brown again:

> Alexander the Great is bully to a guinea-dropper; and Cardinal Mazarin keeps a nine-holes: Mary of Medicis foots stockings, and Katharine, queen of Sweedland, cried "Two bunches a penny card-matches, two bunches a penny"; Henry the Fourth of France carries a raree-show; and Mahomet, mussels; Seneca keeps a fencing-school, and Julius Caesar a two-penny ordinary, etc.

But when we see, in Prior's dialogue between Charles the Emperor and Clenard the Grammarian, the ruler and the scholar still, in death, tranquilly totting up their human conquests, we expect some good entertainment:

> CHARLES: Burgundy with Brabant and Flanders, Castile, Arragon, Germany Possessed: Italy, France, Africa, Greece Attempted.

> CLENARD: Noun Substantive and Adjective, Pronoun, Verb, Participle Declined: Adverb, Conjunction, preposition, Interjection undeclined.

> CHARLES: Into this Model I had cast Europe, how Glorious was the Design?

> CLENARD: How happy was the Division I made of all Greece into five Dialects.

A classic confrontation of human values is clearly about to begin.

In his most Lucianic dialogue, that between Cromwell and the porter, Prior skillfully recognizes and avoids the fruitless theme of naked grandeur. The mad porter explains that while the pretensions of the world are rejected from Hades, their imprints linger on, giving a recognizable identity to the individuals. The dead are shown as acting out not a meaningless series of drudg-

eries as in Tom Brown, but a legitimate, if mimic, continuance of their earthly lives:

> You may find [the Conquerors and Heroes] there with Spartacus, Massenellio, and Jack Cade, making of Dirt pies or playing at Cudgells for it is not absolutely true what the Poets say of Lethé Waters That they make us forget all we have done, they only cool our Passions and calm the heat of Our Mondane Distempers. Every Man acts in Jeast here what He did in the t'other World in Earnest. You may excercise amongst the Heroes without blowing up Citadells and destroying whole Countries, You may study among the Lawgivers without being Stark wild about Ordonnances and Proclamations, etc.

Prior's words, "for it is not absolutely true what the Poets say," are a valid clue to his thoughtful and cautious consideration of the nature of the form he uses. Others, less subtle than Prior at this point, simply let the satire and humor emerge from the shades' retention of their human qualities and distinctions, unchanged by death. Thus, we often meet good satire, but rarely good *dialogue des morts*. Obvious social vices or intellectual claptrap, when revealed after death, have the most palpable air of folly. William King's *Dialogues of the Dead* (1699), for example, are an extended commentary on Bentley and the Phalaris controversy, and the scholar and his minions are shown distracting the dead with their pedantry exactly as on earth they confuse the living. William Wotton, thinly disguised as *Moderno*, retails to a skeptical shade named *Indifferentio* the extent of his researches:

> In the meantime I think I have demonstrated from the ditches, crevices, tadpoles, spiders, divinity, caterpillars, optics, maggots, tobacco, flies, oranges, lemons, cider, coffee and linen rags of the moderns, that THE EXTENT OF KNOWLEDGE IS AT THIS TIME VASTLY GREATER THAN IT WAS IN FORMER TIMES.

In such satire, only the title, "Dialogues of the Dead," lets us know that we are dealing with other than a worldly dispute such as we frequently meet with in the John Bull papers or the memoirs of Martinus Scriblerus.

In the Varronian satire of King, the intellectual disputes of the real world can be dramatized; but these are disputes of a kind familiar (indeed actual) among the living. The unique criterion of Lucian, the *isotimia* of Hades which reduces everything to dust (the bones of Nireus and Thersites undistinguished) is equally unfruitful. But the fully developed dialogue of the dead, when used imaginatively, can bring together habits of mind and attitudes which would, in practice, never come together in the real world. When the shades retain their earthly vanities the dialogues can develop into meaningful confrontations of different points of view and different sets of values. Prior, in the debate between Charles and Clenard, lets each maintain his peculiar eminence as a basic position:

> CLENARD: . . . You would not find so much difference between us Two as you imagine.
>
> CHARLES: Difference? Why I was by Birth Monarch of Nations, by Acquisition and Power Emperor of the West, and by Stratagem and refinement one of the most Cunning Politicians and most renowned Warriors of my time.
>
> CLENARD: And I was the best Grammarian of Mine, very Virtuous as to my Morals, well versed in the *Belles Lettres,* and of an agreable Wit in Conversation.
>
> CHARLES: Why Thou dost not intend I should submit to so Comical a Comparison.

Undeniably, such an unexpected juxtaposition of individuals from different ends of the corridors of power could take place only in the open and eternal society of Hades. In another dialogue Sir Thomas More and the Vicar of Bray meet on equal terms and well laden with maxims of stoicism and compromise to argue for their positions, and, in the longest of Prior's pieces, Montaigne and Locke dispute on the great questions of philosophy.

This is the approach to the *dialogue des morts* of the great French moralists of the period, such as Fénelon or, later, Vauvenargues. They can show a pair of intellectual positions, symbolic frequently of two civilizations, in conflict. Usually a solemn moral purpose is served. Fénelon is avowedly didactic, and his dialogues come equipped with titles sounding in moral virtue:

> "Justice and happiness are only found in fidelity, righteousness and courage," "To oblige the ungrateful is to destroy oneself," "Virtue is worth more than high birth," "Lies and tricks have more effect on the credulous than truth and virtue," etc.

Hardin Craig warned us, many years ago, not to ignore the effect of Erasmus on the European dialogue, and we can sense his impact here, or in the later work of Lord Lyttelton. But, as in some of the admittedly satirical dialogues, so in the openly moral pieces of the French—the authors seem to recognize the juxtaposition of ideas but largely ignore the peculiar nature of the setting. In general, they might be accused of writing, to use Landor's term, "Imaginary Conversations" rather than *dialogues des morts;* we forget, in reading them, the central, motivating fact that the disputants are dead. A parallel might be found in some of the "beast fables" of sophisticated cultures in which we forget that the speakers are after all animals. Prior, at

the beginning of his career, had observed this flaw in Dryden and wittily attacked it in the *Hind and Panther Transvers'd:*

> Gadsokers! Mr. Johnson, does your Friend think I mean nothing but a *Mouse,* by all this? I tell thee, Man. I mean a *Church,* and these young Gentlemen her Sons, signifie *Priests,* Martyrs and *Confessors,* that were hang'd in *Oats's Plot.*

It is a sign of Prior's skill that in his dialogues he never lets the reader forget the vital correlate. Even in the discourse of Locke and Montaigne, which ranges most widely over nonpersonal and abstract considerations, he makes Montaigne's "Contemplation on Death" a centerpiece for commentary. The dialogues of More and the Vicar, and Charles and Clenard are essentially occupied with the nature of death and the due preparation for it; Clenard, speaking of regal pomp, relates it specifically to Charles dead:

> You are launched into the Ocean of Eternity with all your Scutchons and Bandirolls about your Hearse, and probably you may have Four Marble Virtues to Support the Monument you were Speaking of just now.

The "you" meaning Charles' social group turns appositely to "you" meaning Charles himself. The Vicar is able to use the situation to advantage in his argument:

> Admirable Philosophy indeed, in the Practice of which you were Beheaded on Tower Hill at fifty-three, whereas without it I Dyed quietly in my bed at eighty.

Nor does Prior forget the central irony of the situation, the ridiculous meeting in the afterworld. Charles, defeated in argument, begs Clenard not to tell his fellow princes of his shame. More and the Vicar discourse of Laud, pointing out that:

> it is as reasonable for Us to mention a Man that was born Since we Dyed as it is for those in the t'other World to quote an Author that Dyed before They were born.

To point this moral home, Charles and Clenard briefly digress to comment on the poetry of Prior himself. The reader, then, is always aware of the marks of death on the speakers, as the Vicar reminds us with his condolences on More's mishap:

> Oh that ugly Seam, Sir; that remains still
>   about your Neck.
> O Sir a Head Sewed on again never sits well.

The clash of cultures brought together in the fellowship of death, which produces the moral crux in the

French writers, is well utilized by Prior when he elects speakers whose whole visions of humanity conflict, so that the debate between them can be farranging and meaningful. Charles the tyrant debates with Clenard the humane teacher, whose character is, in the Emperor's eyes, unambitious, modest, and insignificant. The saintly Thomas More reveals the selfish pettiness of the Vicar of Bray's inconstancy. Locke's pedantic scholasticism is mocked by the urbane geniality of Montaigne. A danger not always avoided in such dialogues is that well defined by Dr. Johnson in his comment on Lyttelton, "The names of his persons too often enable the reader to anticipate their conversation." The comment would also hold true of Fénelon; Prior avoids blame not so much by the introduction of novel or startling points of view as by his constantly witty dialogue, and by his willingness to write at length, so that the obvious ideas can be scrutinized closely and pointedly. To this extent Prior is skillful. To the extent that one character, representing an apparent ideal, debates with a less admirable interlocutor, Prior's dialogues are conventional.

But Prior goes beyond skillful conventionality in some passages. The Locke-Montaigne confrontation shows that he has a somewhat subtler approach to the dramatic possibilities of the form than his contemporaries—even including Fontenelle who surpasses him in sheer fun. This dialogue is not a plain confrontation of the desirable and the undesirable; though the sympathtic Montaigne seems the obvious victor, Locke is not denied some shrewd hits:

> Speak, Sir, Answer me logically [says Locke after making a splendid rebuttal], You are not used to Pause for a Reply.

> MONTAIGNE: Faith I think he has me a little upon the hipp, with his Logic, where one cannot perfectly Excuse, all one can do is to recriminate.

which he now proceeds to do. Indeed, this debate is at a logical and philosophical rather than a moral level—Prior has no intention of accusing Locke of wickedness, but merely of some foppery. Even the other debates are by no means as one-sided as we might expect. The author works on the reader's too facile acceptance of Clenard and More as the ideals, and lets us see that their opponents can direct sure and thought-provoking responses. As in Book IV of *Gulliver's Travels* the unwary reader is confused by whether Gulliver or the Houyhnhnm or either represents the decent norm, so in these dialogues the writer's irony is apparent in his refusal to accept an easy moral victory for the obvious ethical superior. Clenard, in his enthusiastic zeal for the status of the grammarian, comes at the end of the dialogue to the point of accepting Charles' view of power, and proudly runs through a list of wars and quarrels caused by the verbal quibbles

of the scholars. Surely Prior is exercising his irony here:

> Two Latin prepositions Trans and Cum joined withSubstantiation a word invented by us Scholemen were the Cause of all your troubles in Germany, and the same Contention is stil on foot tho it is now one hundred and fifty Years Since we were discharged from having any part in it.

He retells the famous story of the EINIG-EUIG confusion, noting:

> for the Power of an *n* and a *u* here is the Grandson of Maximilian of Austria, and Mary of Burgundy . . . playing a Trick for which a public Notary in the smallest Imperial District would be Censured, and to say no worse of the matter. The Emperor both as to his Sense and honor depending wholly upon the Grammarian.

Charles is more readily persuaded by this sign of real power in the hands of the grammarians, but the reader must surely demur somewhat. In the debate between More and the Vicar the reader senses that, willy-nilly, practice and the world are on the side of the Vicar:

> MORE: If I were to be Chancellor again, and had all the Livings in the Land to dispose I would not give You one of them.

> VICAR: If all Succeeding Chancellors were of Your Opinion your Livings would want Incumbents, and the Civil Power might send out Press Gangs for Priests to supply the Parishes.

The selections for the incomplete dialogue involving Jane Shore (printed in the apparatus to the majestic Oxford edition of Prior by H. Bunker Wright and Monroe K. Spears) shows again that Prior had thought out some skillful knocks to come from the enemy.

A powerful dramatic device is to let the unsympathetic character have some of the best lines—traditionally a weakness of the *dialogues des morts* as a form has been the failure of the writers to give the wicked shades a fair hearing. Prior's momentary ironic reversals of sympathy accomplish the desirable effect.

From the traditional forms of the *dialogue des morts* Prior absorbs what is meaningful, and he adds insights of his own. Throughout, these dialogues, written late in his life, manifest that sophistication which distinguishes all of his work. He does not deny the power of opinion, as he observes in his essay on that topic:

> We cannot see two People play, but we take part with One, and wish the other Should lose, this without any previous reason or consideration: But

alas! the Bowl takes a stronger Bias, as we more know the Person: If we Love him his Defects are diminished, if we hate him, his faults are Exagerated. We look upon the differentobjects without finding that we have insensibly turned the Tube.

But in his dialogues, regardless of obvious opinion, he takes care to manage his tube with consistency and, when the reader least expects it, he bowls counter to the bias and startles our complacency.

Otis Fellows (essay date 1972)

"Prior's 'Pritty Spanish Conceit'," in *Modern Language Notes,* Vol. 87, No. 6, November, 1972, pp. 3-11.

[*In the following essay, Fellows posits a Spanish source for a poetical concept developed in Prior's* Alma.]

"Dediti ventri et turpissimae parti corporis"
(Sallust, *Bellum Jugurthinum,* Chapter 85)

Matthew Prior's ancestors were, for the most part, farm laborers. His father, however, was a carpenter, and his uncle a prosperous tavern keeper. Upon his father's death, the uncle took young Matthew into his employ as a waiter at the Rhenish Wine Tavern. There the earl of Dorset discovered the boy trying to read Horace. Impressed with the youth's knowledge of Latin and his ready wit, Dorset became his patron and sent him first to Westminster for formal schooling. By the time he received the degree of Bachelor of Arts at Cambridge in 1686, Prior had grown into a tall, thin young man with considerable poise whose bony features already held the promise of what was to be referred to in later years as "ce visage de bois." Such attributes as intelligence, wit, perspicacity, urbanity, diligence and an excellent education allowed him to make a greater mark in the world than might have been expected of a Briton of the day who was considered of lowly birth. Despite Voltaire's rosy picture in the *Letters anglaises* (1733, 1734) of talented members of the third estate in England being fêted and rewarded by a grateful government, this picture was true only in comparison with the situation on the Continent. Certainly recognition of talent among the middle and lower classes in Great Britain was in marked contrast to the condition that then prevailed in France.

It is nevertheless altogether remarkable that Prior held a number of highly responsible government posts and participated in various diplomatic missions under both William III and Queen Anne. In fact, following the Queen's accession, he became the principal architect of the Treaty of Utrecht, known as "Matt's peace." He had already transferred his allegiance to the Tory party

and in so doing was readily accepted by Swift, Pope, Bolingbroke, the future earl ofOxford and others of the same political persuasion and often the same literary interests. From 1712 to 1714 as minister plenipotentiary to France, he cut a fine figure in Paris and at Versailles, spoke exquisite French, and was repeatedly received with cordiality by the aging Louis XIV. He was, in short, on familiar footing with the great and near great both in England and on the Continent. At his death he was remembered as a diplomat and poet of distinction whose final resting place was at the foot of Spenser in Westminster Abbey.

But, because of his humble birth, he had not been able to achieve his ideal, to be Her Majesty's ambassador to the French Court. Moreover, upon the Queen's death, he had been recalled to London and, with the Whigs again in power, refused to betray the confidence of the ousted Tory leaders.

For this, on 9 June 1715, he was confined to the home of the Sergeant-at-Arms of the House of Commons, there to stay for somewhat over a year. During this time, he was allowed no visitors except through permission of the Speaker of the House. Nor was he permitted to carry on written correspondence with the outside world. He was, each evening, though, allowed to walk under guard in the very St. James's Park where, in happier days, he used to stroll with Jonathan Swift and Lord Oxford.

There remain secrets to be unlocked concerning Matthew Prior, man and poet, and his *Alma* in particular. For the past several years, however, there has come to be general agreement on a few aspects of the poem where opinion had once been diverse or where there was no opinion at all. It is now recognized, for instance, that Prior had a considerably higher regard for *Alma* than had been first supposed. Pope, upon reading it for the first time, presumably said: "Your *Alma* is a masterpiece," even though Prior modestly replied that it was but "a loose and hasty scribble."[1] And when Lord Bathhurst, pointing to the paper on which *Alma* was written out, asked him whether he had no further poetry to publish, Prior replied: "A trifle that I wrote in three weeks, not worthy of your attention."[2] Prior could hardly have been serious.

Yet he worked on this exercise in hudibrastic metaphysics and materialistic philosophy throughout a good part of his incarceration. Shortly upon his release from confinement, he distributed *Alma* in manuscript form among friends for their enjoyment[3] and, perhaps, counsel—a clear indication that he himself felt it to be more than a hastily scribbled trifle.

Then too, the conclusion that readers, past and present, prefer the "finished couplets" and "earnestness" of Prior's *Solomon* to the "hasty Hudibrastics" and "burlesque philosophy" of *Alma*[4] can no longer be accepted at full value. Not only distinguished Britons of the age, but also writers of the French Enlightenment—including Voltaire and Diderot—were highly appreciative of the merits of the latter poem; and twentieth-century scholarship has been turning to it with increased frequency as a fascinating challenge.

The long-held view that *Alma* apparently had no plan and was composed on a day-to-day basis as the spirit moved, has been pretty well disposed of in recent criticism, especially that of Monroe K. Spears. In an important and favorably received article, Mr. Spears successfully concludes that he has been "concerned only to show that *Alma* does have a plan, that the plan is an expression of Pyrrhonism, and that the poem of which it is the core is a significant and characteristic application of this philosophy to contemporary thought."[5]

Considerable emphasis has also been given to foreign, especially French, influences on the poetry of Prior, who knew his European literature well. This was afforded initial impetus by a study in German and an unpublished doctoral dissertation in English.[6] But little has been done on Prior's very real influence on European literature.

The chief preoccupation of the present paper, however, is with the English poet's **"Pritty spanish Conceit."** The expression, coined by Prior, appeared in his unfinished essay, *Opinion,* one of the last important products of his pen. There he makes his well-known assertion so often turned to and puzzled over by students of *Alma.* It reads in part: "I have read somewhere a Pritty spanish Conceit, that, as we are Born our Mind comes in at our Toes, so goes upward thro our Leggs to our Middle, thence to our Heart and Breast . . . (*Pr.,* I, 587)."[7]

Readers have been quick to recognize that we have here the substance of lines already composed for *Alma,* and which appear early in the poem:

> My simple *System* shall suppose,
> That ALMA enters at the Toes;
> That then She mounts by just Degrees
> Up to the Ancles, Leggs and Knees:
> Next, as the Sap of Life does rise,
> She lends her Vigor to the Thighs:
> And, all these under-Regions past,
> She nestles somewhere near the Waste:
> Gives Pain or Pleasure, Grief or Laughter;
> As We shall show at large hereafter.
> Mature, if not improv'd by Time
> Up to the Heart She loves to climb.
>
> (*Pr.* I, 477)

But what, precisely, *is* the Spanish source referred to

by Prior? In his 1915 monograph, Frey was obliged to confess: "Eine Spanische Quelle dieses Einfalls ist mir nicht bekannt."[8] "Alma," to be sure, is Spanish for "soul," but forty-four years later the editors of the definitive edition of Prior were forced to echo Frey: "No Spanish source has been discovered."[9] Meanwhile, interested parties, aware of Prior's fondness for Montaigne, were struck by a passage in the Frenchman's essay, *De l'Yvrognerie,* which seemed to be at once the **"Pritty spanish Conceit"** and the central *concetto* in *Alma.* In fact, Charles K. Ewes appeared to be voicing a general concensus of opinion when he categorically stated: "As Professor Barrett has shown, the major conceit of the poem came directly from Montaigne.[10]

The passage in question is familiar to all Prior specialists:

> La chaleur naturelle, disent les bons compaignons, se prent premierement aux pieds: celle là touche l'enfance. De là elle monte à la moyenne region, où elle se plante long temps et y produit, selon moy, les seuls vrais plaisirs de la vie corporelle: les autres voluptez dorment au pris. Sur la fin, à la mode d'une vapeur qui va montant et s'exhalant, ell'arrive au gosier, où elle faict sa derniere pose.

Monroe Spears is persuaded, however, that the above passage could have furnished nothing more than a hint for the poet's "system." He explains with commendable prudence: "Montaigne is speaking of 'chaleur naturelle,' with reference to sensitivity to physical pleasure, and not of the mind or the soul; since he is discussing drunkenness, he makes the throat the final stage." Cautiously but effectively he concludes: "The development of the idea and its contemporary application in *Alma* appear to be entirely Prior's own."[11]

But there is another, and in this instance, contemporary text suggesting a parallel to the basic conceit. It has caused as much ink to flow as has that in Montaigne's essay. And, like *De l'Yvrognerie,* it regards the principle or center of human animation on a materialistic, a physiological basis. It is to be found in Chapter XII of the *Memoirs of Martinus Scriblerus.* The opening sentences of the passage, showing Martinus trying to ascertain the seat of the soul, run as follows: "In this Design of Martin to investigate the Diseases of the Mind, he thought nothing so necessary as an Enquiry after the *Seat* of the *Soul.* . . . Sometimes he was of opinion that it lodg'd in the Brain, sometimes in the Stomach, and sometimes in the Heart."[12] In Chapter XV, Dr. Penny-Feather appears before the Court to present the learned Martinus Scriblerus's ultimate conclusion in the matter: "And after his most diligent enquiries and experiments, he hath been verily persuaded, that the Organ of Generation is the true and only *Seat of the Soul.* That this part is seated in the middle, and near the Center of the whole body, is obvious to your Honour's view (p. 158)."

These extracts from the *Memoirs* are far more in keeping with essential verses in *Alma* than anything in Montaigne's essay. In both instances there is absurdly metaphysical inquiry into the locus of the mind or soul. And in both instances, when the metaphysical is stripped away, the animating principle is held to be located in what both the *Memoirs* (p. 158) and Prior's essay, *Opinion* (*Pr.,* I, 158), call "the middle," that is to say the organs of generation, or those of assimilation and digestion, or both.

The unfinished *Memoirs* are a product of the Scriblerus Club formed around 1713 by such close friends and associates of Prior as Swift, Pope, Gay, Parnell, Lord Oxford and Dr. John Arbuthnot. This satirical work was designed to ridicule all the false tastes in learning of a fictitious scholar, Martinus Scriblerus. It is generally thought that Dr. Arbuthnot, writer of medical works of a high order, composer of one poem and a number of much appreciated satirical pamphlets, was the principal author of this extended satire. The *Memoirs* first saw the light of public day in Pope's *Works* (1741) several years after Arbuthnot's death. There is evidence that, before publication, they were revised, perhaps extensively, by the author of the *Essay on Man.* In consequence, according to a leading authority on Arbuthnot, it is impossible to determine how much of the work was changed or added to after the learned and witty doctor's death.[13]

Whether Arbuthnot or Pope was largely responsible for Chapters XII and XV, one thing is manifest: the burlesque approach to situating the mind or the soul in the body was very much the order of the day. In a letter to Swift dated 26 June 1714, Arbuthnot wrote: "There is an excellent subject of ridicule from some of the German physicians, who set up a sensitive soul as a sort of first minister to the rational. . . . He has under him several other genii, that reside in the particular parts of the body, particularly prince Cardimelech in the heart; Gasteronax in the stomach; and the plastic prince in the organs of generation."[14] And Swift himself, in *The Right of Precedence between Physicians and Civilians Enquir'd into* (Dublin, 1720), declared that, "contrary to vulgar notions," he had always considered the stomach to be not only the seat of honor "but of most great qualities of the mind, as well as of the disorders of the body."

Arbuthnot, Pope and Swift, all three were on intimate terms with the author of *Alma,* all wrote satirically on the seat of the soul or mind, and all lent a helping hand in 1717 and 1718 to see that a subscription edition of Prior's works be launched.[15]

There remains one curious fact, however. In all that has been said about Prior's **"Pritty spanish Conceit"** in relation to Montaigne or to early eighteenth-century satire, no one has, to my knowledge, spoken of a contemporary reference to Prior and any sort of Spanish conceit. Yet such a reference, tenuous though it may be, does exist.

In the *Miscellaneous Works of the Late Dr. Arbuthnot,*[16] there is a mordant satire entitled "The Life and Adventures of Don Bilioso de l'Estomac." It bears the date "Anno 1719," and directly under the satirical piece's title is an epigraph drawn from Prior's *Alma,* but without mention of the poet's name:

> I say, whatever You maintain
> Of ALMA in the Heart or Brain
> The plainest Man alive may tell Ye,
> Her Seat of Empire is the Belly
> From whence She sends out those Supplies
> Which make us either stout or wise.

These lines from the third and concluding canto announce a long, hudibrastic disquisition on the "Belly" as the seat of the mind.

In the satirical essay itself, there are several references to Cervantes' *Don Quixote.* The only one that directly concerns us here, however, arises when the author again turns to what he calls "Dr. W's State of Physick,"[17] and tells the reader: "The Beginning of this ingenious Performance put me in Mind of *Don Quixote*'s good squire *Sancho,* whose favourite Maxim was, that the Belly kept up the Heart, and not the Heart the Belly." To which he adds forthwith: "I won't say the Doctor stole this Notion from that merry Gentleman, because I believe I shall prove presently that the Author of *Don Quixote* was also the Author of the State of Physick."

There are, as might be expected, a number of references in *Don Quixote* to the "estómago" or to the "tripas." But the author of *Don Bilioso* had in mind Sancho's statement: "Tripas llevan corazón, que no corazón a tripas" (Part ii, Chapter 47 of the novel). The saying appeared at the beginning of the eighteenth century in Peter Motteux's warmly received translation as: "'Tis the Belly keeps up the Heart, and not the Heart the Belly."

The various Tory wits, including Swift, Pope and Arbuthnot, were much taken with *Don Quixote,* and their *Memoirs of Martinus Scriblerus* were to be written in the manner of Cervantes. In his edition of the *Memoirs,* Professor Kerby-Miller has this to say: "The general influence of Cervantes on the central project of the club is clear and it seems not unlikely that *Don Quixote* came to mind more than once during, at least, the first planning stage.Cervantes was a favorite author of Swift and probably of several other Scriblerians; and there are some resemblances between the two works (pp. 68-9)." Prior's good friend Dr. Arbuthnot may not, after all, have written *Don Bilioso*.[18] Nevertheless, he or someone claiming to be Arbuthnot and also claiming that the satire had been written in 1719, deliberately linked Prior's long, involved diatribe on the "Belly" with Sancho's proverb, but Arbuthnot or the possibly anonymous author of *Don Bilioso* may have had excellent reason to associate *Alma* with Sancho Panza's sententious statement. There was nothing original about Sancho's proverb, it was as old as man himself. But it may have been the impetus for Prior's real Spanish conceit, a down-to-earth maxim on which, during his long months of imprisonment, he could embroider his more complexly metaphysical conceit that begins with:

My simple *System* shall suppose,
That ALMA enters at the Toes.

Prior, like all good satirists of the age—Swift, Pope, Arbuthnot in England, Voltaire and Diderot in France—was something of a *mystificateur;* doubtless it was a necessary adjunct to daring satire. Prior, both through temperament and practice, would have been far closer to Sancho's earthy maxim than to the neo-Aristotelian theory that the mind extends throughout the body or the still more modish Cartesian-scientific dualism of the period with its forced appeal to rationalism. Prior would have quite understood Sancho Panza, but he would have appreciated still more—and the second and third cantos of *Alma* suggest as much—Sallust's dictum that serves as epigraph to the paper at hand to the effect that we are all "slaves to the belly and the most shameful parts of the body." And he would have appreciated it with an understanding smile.

The present writer is still as convinced as he was a few years ago when he wrote that in the debate between Mat and Richard, it is the latter who says that the mind's seat of empire is the belly, and that it is sig-nificant that Richard should have the last thirty lines, which are in praise of happiness, or at least contentment. It remains his considered judgment that, in the end, "the pragmatic Richard is closer to Prior's position than Mat, and Prior's poem succeeds only as Mat's system fails, as indeed all systems must fail that employ only the modest agent of human reason for metaphysical speculation. Thus, Mat's system—the reconciling product of intellectual pyrotechnics that are not only magnificent but absurd—collapses before the awesome prospect of Richard's discontented Belly."[19]

Notes

[1] Owen Ruffhead, *The Life of Alexander Pope, Esq.* (London, 1769), p. 482.

[2] Matthew Prior, *Selected Poems.* Ed. Austin Dobson (London, 1889), p. lvii.

[3] Cf. Charles K. Ewes, *Matthew Prior, Poet and Diplomatist* (New York, 1939), p. 369.

[4] This is the considered opinion of Charles K. Ewes, *op. cit.,* p. 361.

[5] "The Meaning of Matthew Prior's *Alma,*" *Journal of English Literary History,* xiii (1946), 290.

[6] Reference is to Englebert Frey's *Der Einfluss der englischen, französischen, italienischen und lateinischen Literatur auf die Dichtungen Matthew Priors* (Strassburg, 1915) and to Wilfred P. Barrett's *Matthew Prior and His Literary Relations with France* (University of Cambridge, 1931, microfilm).

[7] References to Prior's writings, here indicated by *"Pr.,"* come from *The Literary Works of Matthew Prior.* Ed. H. Bunker Wright and Monroe K. Spears (Oxford, 1959), 2 vols.

[8] *Op. cit.,* pp. 29-30. To this he added: "Vielleicht wollte Prior seiner Leser durch diese Andeutung nur auf eine falsche Fahrte bringen." The suggestion is echoed by Ewes, who writes: "But Prior either had forgotten his source or was deliberately hoaxing his reader." *Op. cit.,* p. 360.

[9] *Op. cit.,* II, 1008.

[10] *Op. cit.,* p. 360. The article referred to is by Wilfred O. Barrett, and entitled, "Matthew Prior's Use of Montaigne," *Modern Language Review,* xxvii (1932), 454-8. Barrett's discovery had been forestalled, however, as early as 1798, for which see H. B. Wright's article, "William Jackson on Prior's USE of Montaigne," *Modern Language Review,* xxx (1936), 203-5.

[11] *Loc. cit.,* p. 279.

[12] *Memoirs of the Extraordinary Life, Works, and Discoveries of Martinus Scriblerus.* Ed. Charles Kerby-Miller (New Haven, 1950), p. 137.

[13] See Lester M. Beattie, *John Arbuthnot, Mathematician and Satirist* (New York, 1935), pp. 266 and *passim.,* as well as the Kerby-Miller edition to the *Memoirs,* pp. 57-67.

[14] G. A. Aitken, *Life and Works of John Arbuthnot* (Oxford, 1892), p. 65.

[15] For this last detail, see Ewes, *op. cit.,* p. 364.

[16] "Glasgow, Printed for James Carlile, 1751" in two volumes.

[17] For the satirical pamphlet *in toto*, see *Miscellaneous Works,* I, 182-91.

[18] See Lester M. Beattie, *op. cit.,* the section entitled "Irresponsible Attributions."

[19] "Metaphysics and the *Bijoux indiscrets:* Diderot's Debt to Prior," *Studies in Voltaire and the Eighteenth Century,* lvi (1967), 523.

John Higby (essay date 1974)

"Idea and Art in Prior's *Dialogues of the Dead,*" in *Englightenment Essays,* Vol. V, No. 2, Summer, 1974, pp. 62-9.

[*In the essay below, Higby eschews comparisons with Prior's contemporaries who also wrote dialogue of the dead in order to examine what Prior's work in this subgenre reveals about his intellect and artistic gift.*]

Matthew Prior's **Dialogues of the Dead** are like the young woman who is admired by all but courted by none. Since their first publication well over a half century ago, they have been favorably but always briefly treated by Prior's biographers and by some of the more comprehensive literary histories. But apart from one or two short studies, little has been published in the way of criticism, certainly less than one might expect in view of the general enthusiasm among readers familiar with them.

The neglect of these dialogues, especially of their substance, may stem in part from the curiosity of their form. Those who have seen fit to comment on them have tended to be concerned with Prior's place among writers of dialogues of the dead at the expense of examination of his literary art or of his expression of a temper of mind not uncommon in his age. The following remarks will be directed to some of the neglected areas of criticism, and since the art of the **Dialogues** depends in considerable degree on Prior's intellectual bent, one should probably begin with a word about it.

Prior, like Swift to name another of his time, or Dryden and Fielding in adjacent times, was a man of letters in a rationalist age who mistrusted the systems that rationalism produced. In a series of scholarly essays published in the 1940's Monroe K. Spears argued that Prior was a Pyrrhonist and that as such he was in th-ecamp of Montaigne. Pyrrhonism is a form of skepticism developed by Pyrrho of Elis, who lived in the late fourth and early third centuries B. C. Pyrrho held that it was impossible to come at any incontrovertible knowledge of the nature of things and that tranquillity of mind could be obtained only by not troubling about matters which man could not understand in any final

way. Men who are skeptical on ultimate questions are also apt to be circumspect in their regard of mundane affairs. Montaigne certainly was, as the discursiveness of his essays affirms, and so was his eighteenth century admirer, Matthew Prior.

The two contenders in each of Prior's dialogues, however, are fairly sure of themselves, and their attitudes are polarized. In no dispute does a speaker substantially change his position. The arguments are dialectical in a loose rather than classical sense: that is, the speakers do not go forward together, abandoning certain positions in favor of sounder ones discovered dialectically, but maintain single postures throughout, which they modify only to the extent that they restate their positions to refute the objections of their opponents. At the end of each dialogue the disputants are still at odds, nor can the reader resolve the debate by deciding himself who has "won." Either contender in any dialogue can be considered the winner depending on how one views the world--except that in any single dialogue the arguments presented on either side have both strong points and flaws, and the strong points of either appeal to the experience of most men.

Yet Prior does not create absurd predicaments, for the values of one speaker in each dialogue, subjective though they may be, are preferable. That they are so is made clear by the satiric treatment of the less sympathetic opponent. It is by literary technique that Prior shows us what we ought to admire when objective judgments prove unworkable. Through his comic art he indicates that if there are no absolute standards of human conduct, the relation of one standard to another can at least be submitted to humanistic evaluation. One certainly warms more to Prior's Sir Thomas More than to his Vicar of Bray.

Whom the reader likes better or admires more in any one of the **Dialogues** has little to do, however, with how that person fares against his opponent on pragmatic grounds. Where the sympathetic figure seems to have an edge in the argument--and sometimes the reverse appears to be the case--it is slight, too slight to give the reader in search of simple resolutions any comfort. Prior exposes comic failings in the figures for whom he feels less sympathy, but he is too honest to reward virtue regularly. Like Fielding in *Tom Jones,* he feels that virtue as the path to happiness and vice to misery is "A very wholesome and comfortable doctrine, and to which we have one objection, namely, that it isnot true."

It should be noted at the outset that certain resemblances are apparent among the characters juxtaposed in the **Dialogues.** In all of them Prior opposes a man who had made peace with the world of material things and the powers over them to another who in some way has been less fortunate in his relation to the material world but those values undercut the position of his more comfortable opponent. The pattern is not overly simple; in the dialogue between Locke and Montaigne, for example, one's sympathy gravitates toward Montaigne, who in many respects enjoyed a higher place in the material world than did Locke. But Montaigne is shown to be less in harmony with current philosophical trends, particularly as they were materialistic and positivistic, so that he is at a disadvantage, from an eighteenth century point of view, in arguing these matters.

Quite simply, Prior's less admirable contenders are able to present some formidable arguments in their own behalf. Men who live in a world of power and material things can hardly deny their importance; to wish matters otherwise is, in a sense, to wish the world away. Nor does Prior direct his comic abilities at his materialists alone. They are more comic, more subject to satire, but even Montaigne shows a foible or two. Whether as skeptical Pyrrhonist, man of the world, or man of letters, Prior is too candid to create dialogues wherein unsympathetic materialism and power are opposed to sympathetic, humane skepticism, always at the expense of the former.

The first of the *Dialogues,* between Charles V (of the Holy Roman Empire, Charles I of Spain) and his contemporary, the grammarian Nicholas Clenard (Cleynaerts), is perhaps the most equivocal. Its subject is the relativity of greatness, and Charles V, the person of material wealth and power in the dispute, is crowded into more than one uncomfortable corner as he discusses with Clenard the influence that each exerted in the world and the felicity accompanying such influence. Clenard, on the other hand, is forced to admit that greatness in this world is usually tied to power and its exercise. Beginning with the premise that his power as a schoolmaster was nearly as great as the power of a king and far less troublesome, he gradually comes to argue the influence of grammarians in political matters, showing how a word or phrase can sometimes change the fate of a great man or nation. The analysis of greatness in this dialogue is finally reduced to a consideration of the relative importance of the word and the deed to the condition of men.

If Clenard seems to have the better of Charles in the argument, one must remember that not only is he using his own weapons but that he argues chiefly for equality, not superiority. The object is not toprove Clenard a greater man, nor in all respects a happier man, than Charles, but to show that here is a way of looking at things which renders the grammarian the equal of the monarch. Of course there is another way of looking at things that makes the argument silly, and since both points of view are relative in themselves and to one another, this dialogue seems undeniably Pyrrhonistic.

That there can be no final solution to the problem which Charles and Clenard debate is suggested through an aside by the king when, badly unsettled by the force of Clenard's mental agility, he says, "This Fellow presses me hard, and I grow weary of his company. I'l e'en draw down my main Argument, my great Battering Piece upon him, and Strike him Dead at once." The reader should not let the humor in this passage obscure the fact that Charles could do what he threatens. That both men speak in the land of the dead has no significance; since greatness belongs to the world of the living, the whole argument is impossible unless we assume that each man can exercise his particular greatness within the framework of the dispute. Clenard has no more--indeed, less—defense against Charles's "great Battering Piece" than the king has against verbal prowess. There can be no final evaluation of the relative greatness of words and deeds because there can be no meaningful opposition of them. The only judgment that can be made is a humanistic one. The agents either of words or deeds can be great or trivial men in relation to their worldly professions or apart from them.

All that can be said emphatically in Clenard's favor is that he is the more skilled dialectician. What makes this first dialogue equivocal is the uncharacteristically even division of comic treatment between the two speakers. If the emperor is pompous, the grammarian is feisty. Perhaps an explanation of Prior's neutrality is to be found in Clenard's pretensions to greatness. His mental agility is amusing, but he uses it to serve his vanity and in doing so sacrifices admiration that he might otherwise command. When Clenard tells Charles "You Heros . . . always overshoot the Mark", he fails to see that a grammarian who wishes to establish himself as a great man is guilty of the same fault. That the man of words might desire fame is understandable, but fame and greatness are not quite the same thing, and there is something distasteful in Clenard's presumption and self-satisfaction regarding the latter. Even if the man of words is as great as the man of deeds, he must be so only by not pursuing greatness. The vanity of such a pursuit will tend to corrode those things which elevate the grammarian on humanistic grounds. His greatness must be something with which he himself is not preoccupied.

Prior's second dialogue, between Locke and Montaigne, is deceptive. Those who have felt that Locke is unfairly and unfavorably treated have failed to recognize that Prior is not so much biased against his fellow Englishman as he is in sympathy with the humane approachto knowledge of Montaigne. Notwithstanding opinions that Prior could not cope with epistemology or that he simply was opposed to system-makers, the view of the present writer is that this dialogue reveals not only an understanding of the empiricist's thought but a recognition of its skeptical implications. Prior's obvious preference for Montaigne is based not on opposition to

Locke's system nor on the trenchancy of Montaigne's observations in debate (they are trenchant and more discursive than Locke's, but people do not win sympathy merely by being clever or verbose). Rather, in a world where skepticism is natural to many reflective men, Prior preferred the skepticism of the humanist to that implied by logician. Montaigne could help one to live among men; Locke could not.

Particularly interesting is an exchange that occurs shortly after the men have settled down to their argument:

> Locke. How this Gascon runs away with things. I do not say I have the exact *Criterion veritatis,* but I search it. I don't pretend to Infallibility, but as much as I can I endeavor to avoid Error, and since it is only by my understanding that I can judge of other things, it is proper in order to that end that I make that understanding first Jodge of it self.

> Montaigne. There is a Je ne-scay quoy in those words that affords me but little Satisfaction. But you Metaphysicians think with too much Subtilty to be pleased with what is natural.

What troubles Montaigne is his clouded recognition that he is arguing with a man who is after the same thing, an understanding of one's self against a backdrop of the world, and that means, not the end, separate him from Locke. Down through the twentieth century no one has been able to reconcile humanism and empiricism, mankind and his science, perfectly.

But whatever the true value of his thought, Locke emerges as a comic figure in this dialogue through an unsympathetic presentation of those elements in his work which most smack of pedantry. Almost without exception his speeches are uttered with a seriousness that is not more than once or twice touched with wit or genial humanity. His incapacity to rise to a jest is made all the more conspicuous by Montaigne's clever opposition. his assertion that "in one word I do not write to the Vulgar" suggests that his inquiry into the nature of human experience has deprived him of the ability to partake of it, while at the same time Montaigne emerges as a man who is intimately in touch with the world, spiritually if not socially.

Prior makes Montaigne wander in dialogue (he does roughly four-fifths of the talking) as the Frenchman does in his essays,but always to good purpose. Having made peace with the things he cannot know, Montaigne addresses himself to those that he can, declaring his source of knowledge to be "the great Miror of the World, where I saw the Universal face of nature, and the Images of all Objects that the Eye can possibly take in." Offering Locke some axioms in return for those the empiricist has delivered at the beginning of the debate, Montaigne continues with a lengthy piling-up of epigrams which form no coherent pattern except by the applicability of them all to human issues. He is not altogether ready to leave off when he makes an annoying discovery: "Would you have any more, Mr. Lock, Mort de ma Vie, Why You are fast asleep! Man."

Locke's inattention to Montaigne is based on two objections: his ideas form no logical train, and they are derivative. The Frenchman's defense against the first objection is satisfactory: "Method! our Life is too short for it. The general rules even of Morality are commonly too long and tedious. How many Scholars have been Debauched before they have gone through Aristotle's Precepts upon Temperance . . ." The second objection creates more trouble. Locke uses Montaigne's own declaration that not the externals surrounding a man but what is within him constitutes his true nature (*Essais,* Book I, Chapter 62) to argue "that if Plato, Plutarch, Cicero, Seneca, Horace and Virgil should reclaim his own, Montaign hath writ no Book." Montaigne stumbles for a moment but then escapes by observing that assimilative humanism looks out upon the world rather than in. In the largest sense, though not necessarily the most obvious, Prior's sympathetic characters are always more circumspect, and their circumspection renders them more to be admired than their opponents.

Before any evaluation of the dialogue between Sir Thomas More and the Vicar of Bray can be undertaken, it is necessary to determine just what is being debated, a problem more difficult than it first appears. At surface level, the Vicar seems to be the archetypal trimmer, whose comic vacillations are sharply contrasted with the firm-minded idealism of More. It is then possible to rescue the Vicar from the role of straw man by pointing to the necessity for his compromises if he was to continue living in the world, something Sir Thomas failed to do after 1535. From thence it could be argued that sympathy is possible either for idealistic tenacity or practical compromise in political or ecclesiastical affairs, and that our admiration for Sir Thomas More is based on a humanistic portrayal of character contrasts, particularly since Prior's treatment of character is a conspicuous part of his literary technique in this dialogue.

But too many things are brought into play during the debate to permit a simple resolution of its meaning. For example, no appraisal that ignores its religious implications can be completelysatisfactory, though to open the subject is possibly to repeat Pandora's mistake. Sir Thomas More's orthodoxy and his constancy are things that Prior might have admired, perhaps, but his own orthodoxy was fideistic; the skepticism he felt in other matters he also felt toward religion, so that for him religious orthodoxy was a matter of faith, not an intellectual acceptance of coherent dogma. Since Prior's religious practice was almost certainly not based on an intense conviction of religious truth, and since his skepticism rendered him conservative in other matters, it seems plausible that Prior regarded orthodoxy, at least his own, as a position in harmony with the secular tradition that supported it. In other works, he would not have regarded all modifications of one's religious position, particularly those required by secular authority, as "unorthodox" trimming.

Prior was, during much of his career, in circumstances not unlike those of his opponents in this dialogue. As a diplomat he was in service to the government, subject to its demands, and as a diplomat he was keenly aware of the necessity for compromise. It must be something other than the Vicar of Bray's compromises that makes him comic. On grounds of religious practice or its relation to political service, there are reasons to believe that Prior would have been as much in sympathy with the Vicar as with More.

Yet comic treatment is confined to the Vicar of Bray, and More is the only figure in any of Prior's dialogues to escape a comic touch. There should be some satisfactory explanation for this variance in treatment. One should also note that steadfastness does not belong to Sir Thomas alone. The Vicar's determination to hold his living against attacks by "Missals and Common Prayer, Acts of Parliament opposed to Decrees of the Church, Mortuair'es in the Legates Courts, and Praemunire's in Westminster-Hall" may be comic enough, but he also says that in preaching "Sometimes indeed I ventured a little against Pluralities or Nonresidence . . . , and neither of these cases affected my Self." Whatever his faults, the Vicar remained within his parish, so that we have juxtaposed in the combatants fidelity to the spiritual world and fidelity to a small part of the material world. To a man of Prior's conservative bent, the latter fidelity is not without merit.

The great difference in treatment of these two men arises not so much from the end they pursue as the means by which they pursue it. Service to conflicting worlds is the dilemma of both, and it is in the nature of their service that they differ. The dialogue between More and the Vicar of Bray finally reduces itself to a statement about conscience and the practical effects of conscience, ethical conduct. Prior could understand both More's firmness of mind and the Vicar's need to compromise, but the blithe spirit the Vicar exhibits in justifying his doctrinal meanderings makes him the most amusing of all Prior's dialogical characters. The basis forsympathy in this dialogue is the sincerity with which More measured himself against authority and the insincerity of the Vicar's similar actions.

The relevance of Prior's dialogue between More and the Vicar to the practical world, the greater significance of a dialogue about conscience to ordinary men than the earlier ones about greatness and knowledge, gives the piece an underlying seriousness that might escape notice because of the presence of the highly amusing Vicar. Its seriousness is disturbing, however, because Prior is unable to resolve the issue of conscience and its importance despite his undoubtable admiration for More. Conscience itself is not invulnerable to the probings of the skeptical mind, and Prior is unable to show the reader how a deeply conscientious man can direct his actions to meet the demands of the world. The dialogue seems to suggest that the dictates of strong conscience are sometimes so severe as to be of little value unless the one who holds them is willing to relinquish his humanity to death. Such a relinquishment may possbily be the most positive affirmation of strength of conscience, but it is not particularly helpful to those who must go on living. More is noble but unworldy; the Vicar is comic but in harmony with his world. Where a man should put himself between them is left to the conscience of the reader.

In the final dialogue, between Cromwell and his Porter, it is the disputants themselves that seem to interest Prior. To be sure they argue their self-estimates by reference to the things they think they represented, but what really matters is the inability of these men to communicate effectively because of the aberrations in both their minds. Prior manages these contenders so as to make clear that he considers Cromwell fully as mad as his legendary prophet-porter. The dialogue approaches skeptically the question of sanity; the problem it poses is whether there can be any completely satisfactory communication of the mental life, and the implication it develops is that sanity itself is an elusive state since to determine its nature the mental life, the internal life, must be communicable in terms not only mutually acceptable but similarly understood by the communicants. The highly individual state of mind cannot effectively be shared. Being well deceived within the norm creates no problems, for the norm is unlikely to be questioned by ordinary men, but extraordinary men, but the Lord Protectors or prophets, have private visions which cannot be communicated. The conflicts between them cannot be resolved, and the sanity of their individual views cannot be evaluated.

As in his other dialogues, Prior hints at an acceptable standard for human conduct, sane or insane, based on a humanistic position. The madness of any man is to be judged by its effects. If the effects are harmful, the madness is harmful; if no harmful effects ensue, the madness should be indulged. Cromwell's actionsdisquieted millions and gave himself no peace. His power made him so vulnerable to opposition that he "durst not Stir out without a Coat of Maile under [his] clothes, not Sleep a nights without a pair of Pistols Loaded by [his] Bedside." The Porter, far from harming anyone, "proclaimed to that World the Raptures and Pleasures I enjoyed in endeavoring to Convert it."

Prior's last dialogue is quite probably his most skeptical, for it goes beyond the themes of the earlier pieces that there are no unassailable standards of greatness or knowledge or conscience to suggest that the private vision of any man with regard to these or other matters is incommunicable and that sanity itself can be judged only subjectively. Despite the less finished artistry of this final debate, it is critical as a summary of them all, which Prior may have intended to constitute an artistic whole.

It seems significant that each of the first three dialogues is progressively more important than the one preceding it in terms of humanistic evaluation, not only of the issues themselves but of the people who debate the issues. Greatness is not as important as knowledge by humanistic standards, nor is knowledge as important as conscience and its proactical effects in daily living. Furthermore, comic treatment of the characters seems to make a similar and related pattern. In the first dialogue, between Charles V and Clenard, Prior is most equivocal toward the disputants, giving both his figures easily recognized comic attributes. In the second, between Locke and Montaigne, Locke is more exposed to comic attack than is Montaigne, whom Prior undoubtedly admired, though the Frenchman is not altogether spared. In the third, Sir Thomas More escapes comic treatment completely; the Vicar of Bray, though he develops strong arguments, remains unadmirable because his character is clearly comic. The final dialogue, with its theme of the elusiveness and incommunicability of sanity itself, appears to form a Pyrrhonistic commentary on those which precede it and ties them all into an artistic whole, unfinished only because the dialogue between Cromwell and his Porter was never polished to the degree that the earlier debates were.

The textual evidence that Prior may have written his fourth dialogue to unite and conclude the first three is especially interesting. To begin with, Wright and Spears affirm in their edition of the *Literary Works* that there is "an exceptionally complete series of manuscripts" for the first three, and though they elsewhere suggest that Prior "had not finished work on them at the time of his death," their account indicates that he had taken considerable pains to polish them. The first set of manuscripts for these three dialogues is found in a volume designated L21, one of the volumes of the Longleat Collection owned by the Marquis of Bath. Other manuscripts for them are contained in L25 and L26, volumes from the same collection. In the earlier manuscripts of L21 the dialogues do not fall in the order necessary to the greatness—knowledge—conscience pattern that has been suggested, but they do in both L25 and L26. Copies of the dialogue between Cromwell and his Porter are found in L26 and L26 but not in L21, which would seem to give evidence that Prior began work on it later than on the others, particularly since some rough notes for it are contained in a manu-

script designated L29, which contains Prior's commonplace book for 1720 and 1721, and since the "News of the Day" in the earlier dialogue between Locke and Montaigne refers to events during April, 1719, indicating rather clearly that other dialogues were in progress before 1720. Most important, some rough notes for dialogues that were planned but never executed are contained in L21, so that there is reason to believe that Prior passed over other dialogical ideas conceived earlier to write his conversation between Cromwell and his Porter, which, as has been noted, appears to contain a summarizing statement with regard to the first three.

Two reasons for Prior's attempt to develop an artistic whole in his first four dialogues, in spite of an earlier projection of several more, seem plausible. First he may have known that one of his dialogical progenitors, Fenelon, had published a few of his pieces years before the collected edition of them appeared, so that he had a precedent for developing—and even publishing if he desired—a part of his larger project by itself. Second, Prior knew during the period when he was writing his dialogues that his health was failing, and he may have seized on the idea for his final debate in an attempt to finish his work while he was still able to do so.

In any event, it must be admitted that the work--even the smaller project embraced by the four written dialogues--was not really complete at his death. The dialogue between Cromwell and his Porter, its importance in itself and to the pattern of the series nothwithstanding, is not as finished as its companion pieces. A defense of it on artistic grounds is hardly possible if the standard of achievement is to be the other dialogues, nor have the foregoing comments been intended as a complete defense, but rather as an indication that Prior had a plan in mind possessing both thematic and artistic integrity, and that any failure in his final dialogue should be considered not a failure of his ability but more probably of his allotted time to write.

Ronald Rower (essay date 1978)

SOURCE: "Pastoral Wars: Matthew Prior's Poems to Cloe," in *Ball State University Forum*, Vol. XIX, No. 2, Spring, 1968, pp. 39-49.

[*In the following essay, Rower explains that, while Prior's early poems are typical of the Restoration, his later lyrics addressed to Cloe feature an enlarged context in which he achieves previously unattained levels of characterization and realism.*]

There is no love poetry of the English Augustan Age quite like Matthew Prior's. With the possible exception of Swift, whose *Cadenus and Vanessa* and birthday poems to Stella[1] are not totally unlike Prior's love poems in their subtle delineations of a relationship between a man and a woman, Prior alone, of all his contemporaries, went beyond the trivial limits established for the genre of amorous lyric in the Restoration. Perhaps the only other nondramatic writing of the earlier part of the eighteenth century that gives a comparable sense of realistic relationships between emotionally involved people may be found, not in imaginative literature at all, but in such private correspondence as, for example, Swift's *Journal to Stella,*[2] Richard Steele's hurried notes to "Dear Prue,"[3] or Prior's own letters to Elizabeth Singer.[4] For the special quality of Prior's mature love poetry is that, in spite of its nymphs and shepherds, Cupids and lyres, it suggests the complex interaction characteristic of human beings conducting their affairs in the real world.

Prior's earliest love poems belong to that slightest of genres, the Restoration love lyric. The writers of Restoration lyrics restricted themselves to materials, topics, and styles that were remarkably uniform and superficial. The action of their poems is commonly set in a vague Arcadian landscape, where lovers participate in the traditional stage business of the literary pastoral: tending (or more often neglecting) sheep, plucking lyres, gathering nosegays, and reclining under trees. The themes are the timeless, commonplace ones of nonplatonic love: carpe diem, absent love, constant and inconstant love, love requited and unrequited. Under the conventional, even obligatory, aegis of Cupid and Venus, swains and shepherdesses meet, attempt conquests, vow, quarrel, part, praise, complain, and often, die. Prior's early lyrics capture very well indeed the fluent elegance of the Restoration mode, but they are virtually indistinguishable from scores of poems by such authors as Dryden, Dorset, Etherege, Congreve, and Rochester, to name only some of them.[5]

Sometime after 1703, however, Prior replaced the Celias, Morellas, Delias, Phillises, Leonoras, and Dorindas, and all the other undifferentiated nymphs to whom he addressed his early love songs, with one charming girl named Cloe. Cloe became the sole literary mistress of the rest of his career, the subject and recipient of more than a score of poems written over the next fifteen years. With her permanent installation profound changes take place in Prior's love poems. Because the thematic stress of the Restoration love song focuses on the rhetorical skills of the "singer," its swains and shepherdesses require virtually no characterization at all. In a lament, the lover must only be melodiously heartbroken, the nymph only beautiful and obdurate. In one of the very best of Prior's early poems, **"While Blooming Youth,"** the speaker is simply eager and tender, his girl merely "Celia" and reluctant.[6] The characters are interchangeable with all the others in con-

ventional seduction poems. But as the same lover continues to celebrate the same nymph in Prior's later songs, both become more individualized. The poems to Cloe, although ostensibly concerned with much the same topics as those of the tradition from which they develop, come to focus on the personalities of the particular couple whose relationship they describe. Through this change of focus, Cloe and her lover become deeply characterized, and the poems themselves embrace a range of themes and attitudes quite beyond the scope of the Restoration lyric. The Cloe poems employ the whole spectrum of Restoration materials and styles: the song stanzas, the themes and conventions, the artificial diction, the pastoral and mythological machinery; they have the same urbane, casual air, the same offhand tone that never insists on itself. But while the Restoration lyric is quite literally and completely defined by these elements (the lovers in a Restoration song are, in effect, on the inside and can see no farther than the edge of their limited Arcadian landscape), the Cloe poems include the same elements within a larger context. Cloe and her lover play in pastoral settings, but they know that their real lives lie outside it. The result is that the Cloe poems achieve and utilize a realism that the Restoration lyric never attained.

Although the Cloe poems taken all together make up a single informal sequence, they fall into two distinct groups. The earlier group, published in 1709 in Prior's first collection of *Poems on Several Occasions,* includes **"An Ode"** ("The Merchant, to secure . . ."), **"To Cloe Weeping," "To Mr. Howard,"** the prologue to **"Henry and Emma,"** and the first five of seven poems concerning Cloe's relationship with Cupid and Venus. The later group, collected with the earlier in the second *Poems on Several Occasions* (1718), contains two more Cupid and Cloe poems, **"A Lover's Anger,"** and a set of eight poems that tell the story of Cloe's jealousy of a younger rival. In the earlier poems Cloe's primary role is the traditional one of the lady who is celebrated; she exists to be addressed by the speaker whose poems, much like those of Sidney's Astrophel, express his personality, his sensibilities and attitudes. These earlier poems are songs of courtship in which the poet says those timeless, conventional things designed to capture a woman's heart: that she is divinely beautiful; that, of course, he loves her dearly, that she is the whole inspiration of his art; that she exerts tremendous power, not only over the hearts of men, but over nature itself, for when she weeps, the world weeps in sympathy (I. 270-71). In short, Cloe is a poet's mistress par excellence. She gets no chance to reply to her lover's praises, but her acceptance of all the conventions is implied in the poet's freedom to pile hyperbole upon outrageous hyperbole. The whole sequence of Cloe poems concerns itself constantly with the ambiguity of the division between the natural and the artificial; and since it is a real ambiguity, a real confusion, for the lover as well as for his nymph, it never does get resolved.

The first Cloe poem, **"The Merchant to Secure,"** is directly concerned with this problem of distinguishing nature and art. It opens with an explanation of the lover's employment of the traditional device of safeguarding the identity of the beloved lady by pretending to woo a different woman:

> The Merchant, to secure his Treasure,
> Conveys it in a borrow'd Name:
> EUPHELIA serves to grace my Measure;
> But CLOE is my real Flame.

> [I. 259. 1-4]

The speaker really loves Cloe, but he has borrowed Euphelia so that no one will know—Euphelia is a softer, more "poetic" name anyway, one that better graces at least an iambic measure. There seems to be no problem here; the speaker is giving away a trade secret, and, in fact, is betraying Cloe, but his account is quite straightforward.

But in describing an occasion on which he has followed this practice, he reveals his own difficulty with the device. He, Cloe, and Euphelia had all obviously been seated in Euphelia's closet:

> My softest Verse, my darling Lyre
> Upon EUPHELIA'S Toylet lay;
> When CLOE noted her Desire,
> That I should sing, that I should play.

> My Lyre I tune, my Voice I raise;
> But with my Numbers mix my Sighs:
> And whilst I sing EUPHELIA'S Praise,
> I fix my Soul on CLOE'S Eyes.

> Fair CLOE blush'd: EUPHELIA frown'd:
> I sung and gaz'd: I play'd and trembl'd:
> And VENUS to the LOVES around
> Remark'd, how ill We all dissembl'd.

> [ll. 5-16]

On the one hand, the poem celebrates the triumph of real emotion over artificiality. Not all the stage properties of theconvention, the pastoral names, the classical instrument, the conventional deities (painted on the walls and ceiling, perhaps)[7] can keep out real passion. If it is conventional enough to sigh while singing—and it is certainly artificial literally to sing—neither Cloe nor Euphelia should want to be seen blushing or frowning under the circumstances. But they cannot help themselves, any more than the speaker can keep from trembling: true emotion will reveal itself. The player cannot remain uninvolved in the game that he arranges,

and as soon as he is involved, it is not really a game any longer.

At the same time, however, the speaker has demonstrated his nonchalant skill in manipulating the conventions of situation, character, and amorous accessories. He has used all the ingredients in the mixture but has subversively declined to follow the directions on the label. He establishes the artificiality of the mode at the very beginning, and when he seems to be most powerless to prevent life from dominating art, he employs as the spokeswoman of reality as artificial a creation as the tradition owns. He makes the real work against the artificial in such a way as to confound the distinction between truth and fiction, sincerity and dissembling. By the end, there is theoretically no way of telling what is art and what nature at all.

The problem of distinguishing the real from the artificial moves into the background in the series of poems in which the lover does not appear in the action, and Cloe is the companion of Cupid. Uninvolved himself, the lover is able to retain better control over the fiction. The topic of all but one of the Cupid and Cloe poems[8] is the whimsical apotheosis of Cloe. In plot each is a little joke constructed for one of two endings: either that Cloe's eyes are more potent than Cupid's darts, or that her beauty makes her indistinguishable from Venus. In **"Love Disarm'd"** (I. 271-72) Cupid is trapped in the "Heav'n" of Cloe's breast and is forced to give up his arrows. He becomes a harmless pet (like Lesbia's sparrow) while Cloe "gives Grief, or Pleasure; spares, or kills" (l. 50) in his place. Even though Cupid, in **"Cupid and Ganymede"** (I. 272-74), loses all his darts at dice, he knows that the supply is easily replenished with "keener Shafts from CLOE'S Eye" (l. 71). In **"Mercury and Cupid"** (I. 442-43), when Mercury delivers Jove's command that Cupid surrender his quiver, he is frightened away by Cupid's threat to shoot Jove with a bolt from Cloe's eye. In **"Cupid Mistaken"** (I. 276-77), Cupid shoots his own mother thinking she is Cloe, while Venus, in **"Venus Mistaken"** (I. 277), believes a portrait of Cloe to be of herself. Cloe's divine beauty confuses Apollo too. In **"Cloe Hunting"** (I. 278) he thinks that the nymph is his sister, the virgin goddess Cynthia.

Obviously, the poet could hardly have chosen more conventional material for these poems. The deification of the mistress, the wounding shafts from her eyes, the ubiquitous Cupid and Venus, had all been commonplaces long before Prior's time. It is no wonder that Samuel Johnson, feeling justifiably that the machinery of classical mythology and the conventions of amorous praise were all worn out, and failing to discern the particular uses to which Prior adapted these clichés, thought the poems despicable, dictated neither by nature or by passion, lacking gallantry and tenderness.[9]

Such charges, however, are irrelevant to the poems, which transcend the banality of their elements by focusing on the delicate whimsy of their setting and on the game Cloe is made to play in it. The poems celebrate the activities of Cloe's private life, the one she leads apart from her mortal, ironic lover whose presence would shatter the small, delicate universe that he has created for her. She is depicted as a powerful deity from a summery, erotic world. As Cupid tells Apollo in **"Cloe Hunting":**

> . . . in This Nymph, My Friend, My Sister
>   know:
> She draws My Arrows, and She bends My
>   Bow:
> Fair THAMES She Haunts, and ev'ry neigh-
>   b'ring Grove
> Sacred to soft Recess, and gentle Love.

[ll. 13-16]

To assign such a role to Cloe is literally to flatter her extravagantly and conventionally. In context, however, the poems turn out to be elaborate tongue-in-cheek teasings of the nymph. Her companions are much diminished. Cupid is a captivating urchin with no more sense of responsibility than a puppy; Venus has consummate beauty but absolutely no dignity at all. The variety of love belonging to such deities is treated as something only comic and sensual, and the world of such love is shown to be charming, decorative, and tiny. This world is located in that no-place that is the traditional setting for love poetry in the Augustan age. And unlike so much love poetry of any age, where the passage of time is brandished like a whip, time has no function in the earlier Cloe poems either. The implication there is that the poet cares, however ironically, only about courting his mistress; it would not matter if the courtship lasted forever. However much she is teased in them, the earlier poems protect Cloe by giving her a world in which no one is more important than she and in which she is immortal.

The later Cloe poems, those written between 1709 and 1718, continue Prior's comedy of the ingenuous nymph and her worldly lover and his satire on the amorous pastoral, but they do so with substantially greater power than the earlier ones. Through three intimately related shifts, in time scale, setting, and mode of action, the late poems are able to express wider range of emotional nuance, with greater verisimilitude of tone and subtler implications of theme than had the earlier poems. In the late poems, the presence of the amorous pastoral becomes incidental. Its materials are used, but they are much less the focal point. The pastoral love poem is present in the late Cloe poems because it is on the minds of the characters who inhabit the poems: a lover who happens to be an ironist and a poet, and his mistress, who happens to have conventional notions about how a love affair should work. The subject of the late poems is the relationship between the two protagonists.

The late poems, moreover, are firmly located in a world of time and space. In them, the lover is still pretending to court Cloe, but the courtship becomes one that is appropriate to an established, in fact, rather cozily settled, love affair, rather than to the pursuit of a still unyielding lady. The couple are past the stage of wooing, the stage at which the Restoration lyric, as well as most love poetry, always remains. The later Cloe and her lover are quite aware of the passing of time, not only of the progress of their lifetimes but of the time that slips by as afternoons are dawdled away while the world goes about its business. And even where their scenery is most pastoral, the late Cloe poems always make explicit the connection to the realistic, everyday world of streets and houses and rooms. The very settings of the late poems call the pastoral ideal into question.

The themes of the later Cloe poems are organized around a series of conflicts between the artificial world of amorous tradition, for which Cloe is the innocent advocate, and the real world of time, which her lover constantly invokes. It is a conflict, as the lover says, "betwixt Nature and Art," (**"A Better Answer,"** I. 451. l. 14) but also between fidelity and fickleness, beauty and decay, security and desertion, youth and age. Cloe longs for the artificial, since only within its orientation does she feel secure and valuable. She always argues from its viewpoint. Her lover, on the other hand, insists that she acknowledge the world of time. He says not that time will pass, the traditional threat of the carpe diem poet, but that quite a lot has passed already, that her youth and beauty—and consequently her powers over him—are threatened by decay. The threat of the loss of youth and the power to please and command, of mortality itself, is handled lightly; and at the end of the sequence, the lover takes pains to assure his mistress that it was all a literary joke, that in reality he loves her faithfully. But his evocation of mortality is strong, and its claim for attention gives the late Cloe poems overtones of sadness. They continuously explore the delicate, tantalizing relationship between the controllable realm of fiction and the world of ordinary mortal existence, which is subject to no one's ideal impositions. In this set of tensions, between tenderness and cruelty, between the subversively ironic expressed in the same gesture as the benevolently affirming, between the artificial and the real, the love poems of Prior's mature years acquire their particular, inimitable strength and charm.

The general situation of the late Cloe poems is one in which the lover speaks through the mask of a conventional poet-swain who, in turn, sings the praises of an ideal pastoral mistress named Cloe. The "real" Cloe

associates herself with the pastoral Cloe; and the sequence of poems explores the possibilities of the disparity between the impossible fictitious shepherdess and
the real girl who thinks that her lover and the swain
are one.

Cloe's allegiance to the pastoral mode and the nature
of her lover's allegiance to her are the subjects of the
first two poems, **"A Lover's Anger"** (I. 441) and **"On
Beauty. A Riddle"** (I. 444-45). **"A Lover's Anger"**
starts out as a nonpastoral account of an incident that
occurred one day when the poet's mistress had kept
him waiting for two hours:

> As CLOE came into the Room t'other Day,
> I peevish began; Where so long cou'd You
>   stay?
> In your Life-time You never regarded your
>   Hour:
> You promis'd at Two; and (pray look Child)
>   'tis Four.
> A Lady's Watch needs neither Figures nor
>   Wheels:
> 'Tis enough, that 'tis loaded with Baubles
>   and Seals.
> A Temper so heedless no Mortal can bear—
> Thus far I went on with a resolute Air.

[ll. 1-8]

This is not, of course, the pastoral swain who is speaking; such a setting and action belong to the mundane
world. The couple meet in a room on a specific occasion, "t'other Day" at four o'clock, rather than in a
glade at some undeterminable time. Peevishness is not
an acceptable emotion in a swain, and the anapaestic
couplet is perhaps the least suitable in the world for a
shepherd's complaint. The speaker's stance, in short,
is completely unpastoral. One does not assail a shepherdess, as he does Cloe, for lacking an adult's sense
of responsibility. It annoys him that women wear watch-
es, the symbol of a world where appointments are
important, merely as an item of feminine adornment.
But just as he is working up to a good general indictment of her character ("a Temper so heedless . . ."),
Cloe self-righteously cuts him off:

> Lord bless Me! said She; let a Body but
>   speak:
> Here's an ugly hard Rose-Bud fall'n into
>   my Neck:
> It has hurt Me, and vext Me to such a
>   Degree—
> See here; for You never believe Me; pray
>   see,
> On the left Side my Breast what a Mark
>   it has made.
> So saying, her Bosom She careless
>   display'd.

> That Seat of Delight I with Wonder
>   survey'd;
> And forgot ev'ry Word I design'd to have
>   said.

[ll. 9-16]

Cloe inhabits two worlds simultaneously in **"A
Lover's Anger."** Her diction is homely and unliterary,
but her excuse is absolutely pastoral: she gives an explanation that is appropriate to one mode of existence
in another, apparently inappropriate, one. Only in an
Arcadian world, where the time of day is rarely an
issue (but where one would not wear a watch decorat-
ed with seals), can nymphs be injured by falling rose-
buds. At the same time, there is a witty, ambiguous
hint of female tactics, appropriate to both worlds, in
Cloe's "careless" (l. 14) displaying of her breasts.
The lover's attitude toward Cloe and the situation is
quite complex. He speaks peevishly at first (l. 2), but
in chiding her with only an "Air" of resolution (l. 8),
he suggests that he was not really angry. He forgets
what he had intended to say primarily because of her
sexual attractiveness; yet her pastoral masquerade is
obviously an equal source of delight to him. Cloe makes
the pastoral world accessible to the lover, and as a
couple, they make the two worlds almost completely
dissolve into one.

The implicit lovers' game played in **"A Lover's Anger"** gives way in the next poem to an explicit one. In
"On Beauty" the lover sets Cloe a riddle which she
must answer or "forfeit . . . One precious Kiss." Cloe
has no trouble guessing the answer, for the lover gives
her with whimsical thoroughness almost a score of easy
clues.

Beauty is

> . . . the first Off-spring of the Graces;
> Bears diff'rent Forms in diff'rent Places;
> Acknowledg'd fine, where-e'er beheld;
> Yet fancy'd finer, when conceal'd.
> 'Twas FLORA's Wealth, and CIRCE's Charm;
> PANDORA's Box of Good and Harm:
> 'Twas MAR's Wish, ENDYMION's Dream;
> APPELLES' Draught, and OVID's Theme.

[ll. 3-10]

The speaker alludes to the amorous involvements of
Theseus, Paris, Jason, Mark Antony, Tarquin, Alexander, Hercules, and Apollo, ending his list with three
instances of Jove's infatuation with mortal women (ll.
11-34).

When, at this point, Cloe smiles and says that the
answer is easy to guess, her lover goes on to apply the
lesson to himself. For this same beauty, he says,

. . . I leave,
Whate'er the World thinks Wise or Grave,
Ambition, Business, Friendship, News,
My useful Books, and serious Muse.
For THIS I willingly decline
The Mirth of Feasts, and Joys of Wine;
And chuse to sit and talk with Thee,
(As Thy great Orders may decree)
Of Cocks and Bulls, of Flutes and Fiddles,
Of Idle Tales, and foolish Riddles.

[ll. 39-48]

"On Beauty" is, of course, partly a gallant compliment to Cloe: she is as beautiful, implies her lover, as the famous temptresses of classical history and myth. But for the first time, the lover also unequivocally states what his other poems imply: that in terms of this world, paying homage to Cloe is an act of trifling, of amusement. His attentions to Cloe, in person and in verse, are distractions from his role as man of the world and serious poet. He is very willing to trifle and is totally charmed with her. Nonetheless, his devotion to her is thoroughly self-conscious.

"On Beauty" is the first poem in a sequence of eight concerning Cloe's distress over the literary treatment that she receives in her lover's verse. After "On Beauty" come four poems (I. 445-48) that make Cloe fear that the poet has become interested in another woman because he thinks that Cloe is aging. The poet praises Cloe in "The Question, to Lisetta," but in the next poem, "Lisetta's Reply," Lisetta claims that the poet's homage to Cloe unsuccessfully disguises his real interest in herself. In "The Garland" Cloe is depicted as tearfully discovering that beauty and life are transitory things; in "The Lady who offers her Looking-Glass to Venus" an unnamed woman admits that her beauty has faded. In the sixth poem, "Cloe Jealous" (I. 448-49), Cloe who hasread all five and thinks that they indicate the true state of her lover's feelings toward her, comments on the situation. In the last two poems of the sequence, "Anwer to Cloe Jealous" and "A Better Answer" (I. 450-51), the poet replies to Cloe's complaint.

In "On Beauty" Cloe and her poet-lover remain firmly located in the real world, but beginning with "The Question, to Lisetta," the lover joins the nymph in the vales of Arcady, only to threaten her with a rival. "The Question, to Lisetta" and "Lisetta's Reply" make up the two halves of a pastoral dialogue. A swain addresses to Lisetta a series of rhetorical questions about his good fortune in possessing Cloe, who is beautiful, just, attentive, appreciative of his poetic skills, sympathetic, and grateful, and very possibly not very much like the "real" Cloe, the Cloe who speaks in "Cloe Jealous," at all. In the last two lines of the poem, the swain summarizes and pauses for a reply:

In Love am I not fully blest?
LISETTA, pr'ythee tell the rest.

[ll. 12-13]

Lisetta's answer is rather surprising. Cloe may love the swain perfectly, she replies, but his song to her is false; his actions show that Lisetta is, in fact, the one for whom he yearns:

. . . When You and She to Day
Far into the Wood did stray,
And I happen'd to pass by;
Which way did You cast your Eye?
But when your Cares to Her You sing,
Yet dare not tell Her whence they spring;
Does it not more afflict your Heart,
That in those Cares She bears a Part?
When you the Flow'rs for CLOE twine,
Why do You to Her Garland join
The meanest Bud that falls from Mine?

[ll. 3-13]

Lisetta cruelly implies that Cloe is now, in effect, the "Euphelia" of the very first Cloe poem, "The Merchant to Secure"; that is, the poet now sings Cloe's praise, but fixes his thoughts on Lisetta. "Simplest of Swains!" she concludes,

the World may see,
Whom CLOE loves, and Who loves Me.

[ll. 14-15]

As will be seen, Cloe herself takes the obvious hint from the Lisetta poems and combines it with what she thinks the next poems imply. In "The Garland," the swain and Cloe play at poetic philosophizing. He gives her, one morning, a garland made of the loveliest flowers that grow in literary landscapes:

The Pride of ev'ry Grove I chose,
The Violet sweet, and Lilly fair,
The dappl'd Pink, and blushing Rose,
To deck my charming CLOE's Hair.

[ll. 1-4]

Cloe wears the wreath on her brow all through the day, gracing it so sweetly that "ev'ry Nymph and Shepherd" are moved to say that the flowers look more beautiful in her hair than "glowing in their Native Bed" (ll. 9-12). By nightfall, however, the blossoms have withered, and Cloe weeps to discover this. Her swain knows very well what is troubling her, but dissembling his knowledge, he asks her the reason for her tears. With a sigh and a smile, the "lovely Moralist" points to the garland:

See! Friend, in some few fleeting Hours,
See yonder, what a Change is made.

[ll. 27-28]

Then, in faultless quatrains, she mournfully speaks with epigrammatic preciseness:

Ah Me! the blooming Pride of MAY,
And That of Beauty are but One:
At Morn Both flourish bright and gay,
Both fade at Evening, pale, and gone.

At Dawn poor STELLA danc'd and sung;
The am'rous Youth around Her bow'd:
At Night her fatal Knell was rung;
I saw, and kiss'd Her in her Shrowd.

Such as She is, who dy'd to Day;
Such I, alas! may be to Morrow:
Go, DAMON, bid Thy Muse display
The Justice of thy CLOE's Sorrow.

[ll. 29-40]

"The Lady who offers her Looking-Glass to Venus" is a woman's farewell to youth, a final prayer to the goddess she has served as priestess. It is only a quatrain in length:

VENUS, take my Votive Glass:
Since I am not what I was;
What from this Day I shall be,
VENUS, let Me never see.

The lady cannot serve Venus any longer because the image of the goddess that she has worshipped—the reflection of her own face in her mirror—has decayed; she is no longer fit for the rites of love. Her looking-glass is a poignant offering. She would rather not see herself once youth and beauty have fled.

There is obviously no consistency of characterization throughout these first five poems. The shepherd named "Damon" in **"The Garland"** feels very differently about his mistress than does the swain who is perhaps secretly in love with Lisetta. The "Cloe" who guesses the riddle is not necessarily the same as the "Cloe" who has a rival, or the one who sees the garland as an emblem. However, in **"Cloe Jealous"** the nymph shows that she has assumed that all the Cloes, as well as the woman who gives up her looking glass, are intended to refer to her. The poem opens with Cloe in tears, and sulkily refusing to tell her lover what has caused them:

i

Forbear to ask Me, why I weep;
Vext CLOE to her Shepherd said:

Tis for my Two poor stragling Sheep
Perhaps, or for my Squirrel dead.

[ll. 1-4]

But immediately, in a long, distressed apophasis, she reveals everything:

ii

For mind I what You late have writ?
Your subtle Questions, and Replies;
Emblems, to teach a Female Wit
The Ways, where changing CUPID flies.

iii

Your Riddle, purpos'd to rehearse
The general Pow'r that Beauty has:
But why did no peculiar Verse
Describe one Charm of CLOE's Face?

iv

The Glass, which was at VENUS' Shrine,
With such Mysterious Sorrow laid:
The Garland (and You call it Mine)
Which show'd how Youth and Beauty fade.

Cloe is not, of course, unjustified in assuming that she is the woman portrayed in the first five poems. In her fear, she assembles the inferences into a threatening syllogism: the poet has loved her because of her beauty; her beauty has faded with the passing of time; therefore the poet now loves someone else. Her vulnerability is reflected by the turbulent mixture of emotions with which she reacts to this deduction: bruised pride, fear, chagrin, a sense of outraged rectitude. Her pride would prompt her to remain silent or to pretend indifference, but she cannot resist enumerating every item in her bill of grievances, to make the extent of her heartsickness absolutely clear to her lover, in order to excite in him as much solicitude or remorse as possible.

In other words, jealousy is quite explicitly not the sole basis of Cloe's distress in **"Cloe Jealous."** The poem records the nymph's response to the intrusion of the real world onto her consciousness. Time and age are making themselves known in the pastoral world of truth and love that her lover's "dubious Verse" had commemorated and sustained. Her complaint challenges what is in effect the irrelevance in real life of the idea that she will outlive time through her lover's poetry; what he will learn from her tombstone is that her death will have refuted his whole poetic universe. Two realities are in conflict. For Cloe, "Beauty is Truth, Truth Beauty" no longer; she is unwilling to continue to suspend disbelief.

Although the poet does not cease teasing Cloe in his two answers to her, both poems show that he is deeply disturbed by her repudiation of the fictional world that he had created. In **"Answer to Cloe Jealous, in the same Stile. The Author sick"** he addresses her in the pose of a dying swain:

III

From Jealousy's tormenting Strife
For ever by Thy Bosom free'd:
That nothing may disturb Thy Life,
Content I hasten to the Dead.

IV

Yet when some better-fated Youth
Shall with his am'rous Parly move Thee;
Reflect One Moment on His Truth,
Who dying Thus, persists to love Thee.

The subtitle shows what his gambit is. He answers Cloe "in the same Stile" as her complaint, but while affirming that he loves her, he refuses to consider the issue of her decay. Instead, he invents his own decay and insists that all her disquiet comes from jealousy, a pretense that ignores, of course, much of the substance of Cloe's reaction in the preceding poem.

Likewise, in **"A Better Answer"** the poet continues to beg the question even while pretending to take it up:

I

Dear Cloe, how blubber'd is that pretty
  Face?
Thy Cheek all on Fire, and Thy Hair all
  uncurl'd:
Pr'ythee quit this Caprice; and (as Old
  FALSTAF says)
Let us e'en talk a little like Folks of This
  World.

. . . . .

VI

So when I am weary'd with wand'ring all
  Day;
To Thee my Delight in the Evening I
  come:
No Matther what Beauties I saw in my Way:
They were but my Visits; but Thou art my
  Home.

VII

Then finish, Dear CLOE, this Pastoral War;
And let us like HORACE and LYDIA agree:

For Thou art a Girl as much brighter than
  Her,
As He was a Poet sublimer than Me.

This is a better answer in that it seeks to reestablish the poetic world that Cloe had felt was so threatened. The poet attempts to do so by gently chiding her naïveté, by suggesting that they talk in adult, realistic terms, "like Folks of This World," about the problems that she has raised, but by converting her real questions into something more controllable. The "prosy" anapaestic meter, colloquial diction, and half-bullying downrightness of **"A Better Answer"** are part of the speaker's attempt to restore himself and Cloe to the secure domestic world from which they started. By his insisting that the game is over, and by acknowledging that he has been speaking fiction all along but is telling the truth now, the poet claims a final repudiation of the pretending and masquerading of love poetry, of the artifice that has miscarried.

But, of course, there can be no relinquishing of art. Although **"A Better Answer"** does not sound very much like a conventional love poem (even though it is very loving), it is still a poem—a work of artifice. In **"The Merchant, to Secure,"** the lyre-strumming lover could not keep real love outside his self-conscious arrangement of amorous conventions. Now, in the very last of the Cloe poems, the lover has no way of avoiding art even as he pretends to use none. He explains the very distinction between nature and art through an extended simile that uses the god of poets, Apollo himself. And while the poem presumably serves to dry Cloe's tears, its very bluffness reassuring her that the "Pastoral War" is over, the poet has not ceased to play games with her. The reference to Horace and Lydia in the last stanza alludes to Horace's "reconciliation ode" (*Odes,* III. 9), in which the Roman poet demonstrates that the disenchanted Lydia's objections to reunion are no more than defensive talk. Lydia declares herself gladly and unconditionally willing to redevote herself to the poet provided only that he offers to take her back. Unless Cloe knew her Horace, which does not seem very likely, she would not have discovered in this last, affectionate compliment to her that though she may have forced him to change his rhetorical stance, her lover's heart and sense of whimsy were practically the same.

The Cloe poems are impressive examples of Prior's talent for depicting with warmth and understanding the intimate, somewhat childish, but central concerns of ordinary people. If passion is a praiseworthy element of love poetry, in none of his love poems does Prior depict strong passion. Yet, as Maynard Mack has pointed out, none of the elaborate fooling of the Cloe poems quite obscures an affection that is "as clear-sighted as it is deeply human."[10] But even beyond this, they place over against the ideals through which life expresses some of its hopes for itself—ideals of pastoral innocence and true love—the emotional subterfuges and rationalizations through which people try to reconcile themselves to their sense of their own finiteness and impotence.

Notes

[1] *The Poems of Jonathan Swift,* ed. Harold Williams, 3 vols. (Oxford: Clarendon Press, 1937), II, 686-714, 720ff. "Cadenus and Vanessa" (1713) may be indebted to Prior's "Cupid and Cloe" poems for its handling of mythological characters.

[2] Ed. Harold Williams, 2 vols. (Oxford: The Clarendon Press, 1948).

[3] *The Correspondence of Richard Steele,* ed. Rae Blanchard (London: Oxford Univ. Press, 1941), p. 189ff.

[4] For substantial extracts from the letters see H. Bunker Wright, "Matthew Prior and Elizabeth Singer," *Philological Quarterly,* 24 (1945), 71-82.

[5] There is, unfortunately, no space in this study to characterize in detail either the Restoration amorous lyric or Prior's contributions to it. Good selections of lyrics may be found in *Restoration Verse,* ed. William Kerr (London: Macmillan, 1930) and in the more recent *Penguin Book of Restoration Verse,* ed. Harold Love (Harmondsworth: Penguin, 1968). Informative accounts of many of the features of the Restoration lyric are contained in the introduction to the latter volume and in John Harold Wilson, *The Court Wits of the Restoration* (Princeton, N.J.: Princeton Univ. Press, 1948), pp. 85-108. For Prior's own work in the genre see H. Bunker Wright and Monroe K. Spears, eds., *The Literary Works of Matthew Prior,* 2 vols. (Oxford: Clarendon Press, 1959), I, 104-106, 110-12, 183, 196, 197-99, 700-15. (For the dating of this last group of lyrics, see Commentary on *"Stephonnetta Why,"* [*Works,* II, 1034].)

[6] *Works,* I, 119-42. Quotes are from 2nd ed. 1971 Oxford Univ. Press.

[7] As suggested by Mark Van Doren, *Introduction to Poetry* (New York: The Dryden Press, 1951), pp. 17-18.

[8] "The Dove" (1717), *Works,* I, 432-37. In this poem, which marks the transition between the earlier and later Cloe poems, Cloe is the victim of Cupid's mischievousness, and the action is set in London, although a highly stylized one.

[9] *Lives of the English Poets,* ed. George Birkbeck Hill, 3 vols. (Oxford: Clarendon Press, 1905), II, 202.

[10] "Matthew Prior: et Multa Prior Arte . . . ," *Sewanee Review,* 68(1960), 171.

Frances Mayhew Rippy (essay date 1986)

SOURCE: "The Major Impact of a Minor Poet," in *Matthew Prior,* Boston: Twayne Publishers, 1986, pp. 119-34.

[*In the following essay, Rippy summarizes Prior's contributions to British literature and describes his influence on Jonathan Swift, Alexander Pope, Samuel Johnson, and other writers.*]

This study began by asking the question raised by Prior's impressive monument in the Poets' Corner of Westminster Abbey: in what sense may a so-called minor poet have made a major contribution to literature? Matthew Prior's contribution to British literature was a major one in at least four senses.

First, Prior produced a respectable body of literary work, in prose and verse, including effective and influential works in a number of genres: serious and mocking full-length philosophical poems, imitations of classical sources, a long amorous dialogue, tales, *vers de société,* epigrams, epitaphs, lyrics, songs. A number of his shorter lyrics, mixing laughter and tears, are still often quoted and frequently anthologized.

Second, through the impressive financial success of the 1718 subscription edition of his ***Poems on Several Occasions,*** Prior established a direct connection between practicing writer and reading public without dependence upon an intervening patron. Earlier similar successful financial ventures had been made by Dryden with a translation of Virgil and by Pope with translations of Homer, but in both cases the subscribers themselves would have been hard put to say whether they were pledging their guineas to Virgil or to Dryden, to Homer or to Pope. Prior's 1718 edition was not a translation but a collection of his own work; subscribers were buying Prior. The edition was thus, in its conspicuous financial success, a milestone in literary history.

Third, in an age often treated as if it were monolithically dedicated in poetry to the heroic couplet, Prior wrote competently and well in at least six different line or two-line patterns: iambic pentameter in both heroic couplet and blank verse, octosyllabics both lyric and comic, and anapaests in trimeter and tetrameter, the last two of which he brought to a height they had never reached before. He arranged these lines, moreover, into avariety of stanzaic patterns besides couplets and blank verse—a modified Spenserian stanza, Horatian and Pindaric odes, quatrains, triplets, sestets—using the last three groupings as effectively as they had ever been employed in English, and in an astonishing variety of tones and approaches. He led the way for a Spenserian revival in the eighteenth century, and his other forms reminded the poets who followed him in the eighteenth century that there always existed workable alternatives to the heroic couplet form. Dr. Johnson, a reluctant witness for the defense, stated that it was Prior's variety that had given him his great reputation.

Last, Prior's writing exercised a marked influence upon the writings of the three most important literary figures of the eighteenth century—Swift, Pope, and Johnson—and upon a number of lesser figures in Great Britain and America throughout the eighteenth and nineteenth centuries.

Prior's Influence upon Jonathan Swift

Prior and Swift had become friends as early as 1704,[1] for a letter from Dr. Francis Atterbury to Robert Harley, first Earl of Oxford, in that year indicates that Prior was in possession of either the proofs or an advanced copy of one of Swift's books.[2] Prior appears repeatedly in Swift's *Journal to Stella,* the first mention being in the entry for 15 October 1710.[3] Swift and Prior were both members of the Brothers Club, which met in London every Thursday.[4] Swift refers frequently to their dining, drinking, jesting, walking, quarreling, punning, reading their poetry, or planning political maneuvers together while Prior was in London. Later, when Prior began to be sent on secret missions to France, he and Swift corresponded.[5] Prior arrived in Paris on 17 August 1712, and did not live in London for any lengthy period again until March 1715. Meanwhile, Swift returned to Ireland on 16 August 1714, and did not come back to England until March 1726, over four years after Prior's death. Thus, the last portion of their friendship was conducted exclusively by letter, yet the warmth of affection seems never to have cooled. Swift subscribed for four copies of Prior's 1718 **Poems on Several Occasions** and expended great amounts of time and effort in raising and collecting subscriptions to this edition, an activity that he continued even after Prior's death.[6]

From Gaulstown, Swift wrote to Archbishop King on 28 September 1721: "I am just now told from some newspapers, that one of the King's enemies, and my excellent friend, Mr. Prior, is dead; I pray God deliver me from many such trials. I am neither old nor philosopher enough to be indifferent at so great a loss; and therefore I abruptly conclude. . . . "[7] On 25 January 1722, Adrian Drift, Prior's amanuensis and close friend, wrote to Swift from Prior's home in Duke Street, Westminster, of a ring "which you will be pleased to accept and wear in memory of Mr. Prior, whom you so dearly loved. . . . "[8] On 3 February 1722, Swift replied to Drift that he would be "very thankful of a memorial of Mr. Prior, though I need nothing to make

me remember him with all regard due to his merits, and whose friendship I so highly esteemed."[9] When on 19 February 1729, Swift drew up his list of twenty-two acquaintances, "Men famous for their learning, wit, or great employments or quality, who are dead," Prior's name was included.[10]

Swift's friendship for Prior and his high opinion of him as diplomat and as poet exercised a profound influence on Swift's own poetry. F. Elrington Ball, the foremost twentieth-century critic of Swift's poetry, sees Prior as a chief influence on Swift's verse from 1710 on, teaching him "art and ease." Ball adds: "Of the power of Prior, to whom Cowper, Thackeray, and Dobson unite in giving pre-eminence in familiar verse, to impart such qualities, there cannot be question. Of the situation and disposition of Swift to receive them there can be as little doubt."[11] Sir Harold Williams in his more recent edition of Swift's poems states that "the unhappiness of Swift's life" was partially caused by the fact that his poetry fell short of that of his friends, Pope, Prior, and Gay, that Pope was his superior in verse while "Gay and Prior had a more lyrical gift."[12]

Occasional anonymous poems, such as "The Fable of the Widow and Her Cat," were attributed by some critics to Prior, some to Swift, and some to the two men jointly.[13] Swift loved Prior as a man, deferred to him as a diplomat, and learned from him as a poet. Swift was writing tetrameter lines and *vers de société* before the two men became friends, but Prior taught him to write them more gracefully and elegantly. Though the influence persisted throughout the last thirty years of Swift's lifetime, it was particularly marked in the period 1710-12, when the two politician-poets were frequently and intimately associated. Ball cites evidence of Prior's influence upon three of Swift's best poems of this period: two Horatian imitations (of the Epistle *Quinque dies* and the Satire *Hoc erat*) and the famous 900-line *Cadenus and Vanessa.* Even years later, when Prior's only contact with Swift was through letters, Swift, in the last four stanzas of "The Bubble," takes a statement that Prior had written him in prose about the South Sea speculation and expands it in verses influenced by Prior's own poetry.[14] Prior's greatest gift to Swift as a poet, however, was not so much of specific lines, concepts, and echoes as it was of tone and style. Prior taught Swift a courtliness and ease of familiar verse that he had not hitherto mastered; it was a gift that Swift never forgot, either to practice or to repay.

Prior's Influence upon Alexander Pope

With Alexander Pope, a generation younger than Prior and Swift, indebtedness to Prior was much deeper and more specific.[15] Few poets have had a better opportunity to analyze another man's poetry from many sides than Pope did to study Prior's. Pope was young and avidly reading during Prior's period of greatest fame and survived Prior by twenty-three years, long enough to consider all his works. Pope and Prior had many mutual friends; they were also personally acquainted and for five years moved in some of the same circles. In preparing the 1718 subscription edition of Prior's **Poems on Several Occasions** and, in 1723, the projected posthumous edition of Prior's works, Pope read, in print or in manuscript, almost everything extent of Prior's—an unusually full grouping, for Prior had, as Pope later told Spence, "kept every thing by him, even to all his school exercises."[16]

The result of this close literary association between Prior and Pope was that the young Pope decided, more or less consciously, to make use of Prior in the same sense that, on a larger scale, he made use of Dryden. With each, he was focusing attention on a figure whose unusual merit both he and the public conceded without question. He formulated for himself a detailed analysis of the poetical virtues and limitations of each: his forte, his contributions, the relative merits of his individual pieces. Then, at certain key points, he set out first to emulate and then to surpass him. Later, he merely borrowed from him phrases or ideas that were particularly apt for his own purposes.[17]

Pope's earliest open competition with Prior on a literary theme came in versions of the "Adriani Morientis," the valedictory to his soul attributed to the dying Roman Emperor Hadrian in the second century A.D. Fontenelle, Prior's dinner companion in France, had published a French version of the poem in 1683; Prior's English version of the poem—**"POOR little, pretty, flutt'ring Thing"**—was included in the 1703/4 Dryden edition of *Miscellany Poems* and later, revised, in the 1718 **Poems on Several Occasions,** which Pope assisted in bringing out. On 12 June 1713, Pope wrote to John Caryll, senior, from London, enclosing Prior's poem and two by himself—"The Same by Another Hand" ("Ah, fleeting spirit! wandering fire") and "christiani Morientis Ad Animam."[18] The first Pope poem is heavily influenced by Prior's; the second, an expanded and Christianized version, is most influenced by Thomas Flatman's "A Thought of Death." Caryll preferred the Christianized version, but for most modern readers Prior has won this particular competition. His version seems both closest to the spirit of Hadrian and most satisfactory as a poem in itself. Pope's versions seem elevated in diction but not improved.[19]

Four years later (in 1717) Pope again put himself into deliberate competition with a successful Prior poem, at least if we are to believe James Ralph and Richard Savage. In *Sawney. An Heroic Poem. Occasion'd by the Dunciad,* Ralph had written that Prior's **Henry and Emma** had "charm[ed] the finest Tastes" and that Pope had, in aneffort to compete with its success, created

Eloisa to Abelard, with its "enamour'd, raging, longing Nun. . . . "[20] Pope retorted that Prior had himself praised *Eloisa to Abelard* in his *Alma,*[21] but he never replied to the specific charge that he was attempting to outdo Prior with his *Eloisa.* The Pennsylvania-born Ralph had come to London with Benjamin Franklin in 1724 and was little better than a Grub Street hack; more significant testimony comes from Richard Savage, who had worked closely with Pope on the *Dunciad* itself and on its prefatory prose material as well. Sutherland has called Savage Pope's chief link with Grub Street during this period and his chief informant.[22] Savage later told Dr. Johnson that Pope's poem had been motivated by Prior's, for Johnson wrote in his "Life of Pope" that "Of the *Epistle from Eloisa to Abelard,* I do not know the date. His first inclination to attempt a composition of that tender kind arose, as Mr. Savage told me, from his perusal of Prior's **Nut-brown Maid.** How much he has surpassed Prior's work it is not necessary to mention, when perhaps it may be said with justice, that he has excelled every composition of the same kind."[23] Though modern critics of Pope have not been inclined to take Savage's testimony seriously,[24] there is considerable external and internal evidence of Pope's indebtedness to Prior in this poem. **Henry and Emma** had first appeared in 1708, when Pope was twenty, and had gained instant popularity; moreover, it was to reappear in the 1718 **Poems on Several Occasions,** which Pope was helping to bring out. It was also a great favorite of Lady Mary Wortley Montagu, who exercised such a strong personal influence in Pope's maturing years that he liked to imagine himself in love with her, as he hints strongly at the close of *Eloisa to Abelard.* Lady Mary, as we have seen, was such an enthusiastically untiring admirer of **Henry and Emma** that she could recite the entire 773 lines by heart, even when she was old.[25] At least four times, lines from **Henry and Emma** are echoed in other poems by Pope—in *The Rape of the Lock, Windsor Forest, The Dunciad,* and *Of the Characters of Women;* there are also a number of less plainly marked parallels between **Henry and Emma** and other Pope poems.[26] **Henry and Emma** was thus a highly successful poem by a renowned poet, and Pope may well have hoped to outdo Prior at his own game while profiting from the popularity that Prior had helped to build for the high-flown rhetoric of bitterly tested love.

Both **Henry and Emma** and *Eloisa to Abelard* are extended pieces of elegant amorous verse, concerning a pair of lovers already familiar to the English reading public. Thus the task of each poet was not to inform his readers of an amorous dilemma, but rather to present that dilemma with a pointedness and a polish that it had never before received—to tell what had oft been told before, but never so intricately, to exploit what Professor Tillotson has called an Ovidian geometry of amorous situation.[27] In both pairs of lovers the total attention is ultimately focused on the woman, the man playing not only a subsidiary part but an essentially unsympathetic one. Ineach instance the woman is subjected to a peculiarly sharp torment, in which a choice that at one point seems to be between love and reputation becomes no choice at all—at least, one in which sexual love is not an alternative. Emma finally is told by Henry that she must either part from him or follow him into the woods only to act as servant to his new love. Eloisa is repeatedly forced to remember that she is no longer free to choose whether she may love Abelard illicitly or not; the attack upon him has made it impossible for him to love her sexually at all. The only choice that the future can offer her, as Professor Tillotson has remarked, is complete acquiescence to her vows as a nun or death.[28] Thus in both poems the amorous dilemma is so painful that the woman contemplates with melancholy pleasure the prospect of her own death, somewhat comforted by the consciousness that she is to become a heroine of stories in future ages.

There are other resemblances in the structure of the two poems. Both poets use their fiction in order to plead a personal amorous cause of their own: Prior to Cloe (probably Anne Durham, as Professor Wright has shown[29]); Pope, more obliquely, to Lady Mary Wortley Montagu.[30] Both poems are also essentially speeches, the main body of Prior's piece being a dialogue between Henry and Emma, and of Pope's a reply to Abelard's letter in a manner that seems to be spoken rather than written.

Eloisa to Abelard incorporates at least two modified passages from Prior's **"Celia to Damon,"**[31] but its greatest verbal debt to Prior comes from ***Henry and Emma.*** Of the eleven distinct parallels between the two poems, over half occur in the first third of *Eloisa to Abelard* (the first 122 lines), although there was no reason in the structure or subject matter of *Eloisa to Abelard* for Pope to resemble Prior less as his poem progressed. As Pope's poem grew under his hand, he seems to have become more confident of his own rhetoric and less dependent upon the Prior poem. Some of the more striking parallels are merely fitted into convenient places in Pope's poem, but others are altered by Pope in a manner that illuminates his poetical intention as contrasted with Prior's.[32]

Pope's *Eloisa to Abelard* owes much to sources other than Prior's **Henry and Emma,** particularly to English versions of amorous epistles. Professors Root and Tillotson have established clearly that Pope was writing *Eloisa to Abelard* in the tradition of the heroic epistle, with his greatest single debt being to John Hughes's 1713 translation of the letters of Abélard and Héloïse.[33] Pope's debt to Prior, however, is also significant. Pope probably owed to him the original incentive for writing a female amorous declamation that would outdo the popularity of **Henry and Emma.** He owed to him some

of the variations in general structure of the poem that differentiate it from Hughes's version of the letters, particularly the personal coda, considered by Tillotson "original,for an epistle,"[34] though corresponding in purpose exactly to Prior's personal prologue. Finally, he owed to Prior the verbal patterns of certain phrases, lines, and passages, which in *Eloisa to Abelard* frequently serve a new purpose but retain something of their Prior form.

As an effort to excel Prior at his own poetical game, *Eloisa to Abelard* is much more successful than Pope's *Adriani Morientis* had been four years earlier. Most modern readers would prefer *Eloisa to Abelard* to **Henry and Emma,** and even in Pope's own age Eloisa began to overshadow Emma. *Eloisa to Abelard* is more concise (half the length of **Henry and Emma**). Its ordeal has greater dramatic melancholy: Eloisa's dilemma is real; Emma's test is merely a trick known in advance by the audience. The rhetoric is more appropriate to the situation of Eloisa, who has had years in which to contemplate the various nuances of her amorous dilemma, whereas Emma is suddenly surprised by hers and should be active rather than verbal.

Another of Prior's long poems, ***Solomon on the Vanity of the World,*** heavily influenced another of Pope's major poems, the *Essay on Man,* written over a decade after *Eloisa to Abelard.* **Solomon** achieved a highly favorable response in its own century, being twice translated into Latin verse (by William Dobson and by George Bally) and once into German (by Simon Grynaeus).[35] Sixty years after the death of Prior, John Wesley praised **Solomon,** concluding "Now what has Mr. *Pope* in all his eleven Volumes, which will bear any comparison with this?"[36] On another occasion, Wesley described **Solomon** as "one of the noblest poems in the English tongue. . . . "[37] Earlier in 1782, the year that Wesley's essay appeared, William Cowper had called **Solomon** "the best poem, whether we consider the subject of it or the execution, that [Prior] ever wrote."[38] Pope himself apparently did not like the poem; he turned aside Prior's direct question about his opinion of **Solomon** by praising **Alma** instead.[39] Nevertheless, Pope's own *Essay on Man* is heavily indebted to **Solomon,** as it also owes lines to Prior's **"On Exodus iii. 14"** and his **"Essay on Opinion."**[40]

There are some forty verbal parallels between Prior's **Solomon** and Pope's *Essay on Man.* These generally occur in passages concerned with brief and painful human existence, with the search for happiness, with man's reason and his passions, or with the animal kingdom. Prior and Pope also resemble each other in their treatment of two of the poetical-philosophical figures popular throughout the eighteenth century: the Great Chain of Being and the Ages of Man.

A comparison of Prior's **Solomon** and Pope's *Essay*

on Man clarifies the nature, limitations, and merits of each piece as a philosophical poem. Prior's ideas in **Solomon** appear only in certain sections of the *Essay on Man,* but in these sections theresemblances are strong. That is, parts of the *Essay on Man* are very much like the Pyrrhonistic, pessimistic, sceptical philosophy of **Solomon,** but other parts are much more optimistic and sound much more like Shaftesbury than like Prior.[41] Pope, in order to vindicate the ways of God to Man, looked closely at the worst aspects of human existence, then endeavored to explain reasonably how and why they were ultimately right. So long as Pope is examining the moral and physical evils of this world, he and Prior run closely parallel; but as soon as he begins to explain why these partial evils produce universal good, he and Prior diverge sharply. The only solution that Prior's **Solomon** can offer to human suffering is fideism—an acceptance by faith of a difficult universe and an inscrutable God. Pope, on the contrary, attempts to establish reasonably that those things that appear to be evil and unjust to man are not so when viewed in the whole scheme of things.

Because Prior's **Solomon** refuses to accept any rational way out, insisting that all things in this world are vanity and dust, it is both philosophically more consistent and poetically more tedious than Pope's *Essay on Man.* Dr. Johnson wrote in criticism of **Solomon** that "The event of every experiment is foreseen, and therefore the process is not much regarded."[42] Because we know in advance that knowledge or pleasure or power will not long satisfy Solomon, we are held to the reading not by the interest of the framework of plot that Prior has provided but by the phrasing and individual ideas. Though these deserve more attention than the nineteenth or twentieth centuries have paid them, perhaps verbal purity and ideological precision are not enough to sustain over 2600 lines of verse. Prior's single theme of Pyrrhonistic philosophical belief, which he refused to relinquish in favor of any optimistic rational solution, has nevertheless continued to impress those who do manage to read through **Solomon.** George Saintsbury maintained that "If he had not Pope's intense craftsmanship, Prior . . . has something of the 'behind the veil' touch that Pope never even hints at."[43] This "something . . . behind the veil" in Prior's **Solomon** is the philosophical consistency that forced him to eschew any Shaftesburian hope of human benevolence and the rational rightness of the present universe and to retain instead the position of unresolved doubt which led Professor Spears to call him "a harbinger of future dissatisfactions."[44]

Pope in the *Essay on Man* views the suffering and injustice of this world quite as clearly as does Prior and often in much the same terms. Yet, having taken this full look at the worst, Pope endeavors to establish by reason what Christian mystics sometimes perceive extrarationally: that all suffering and evil are part of a divine plan that will bring a unity of good from this apparent multiplicity of evil. Pope's difficulty is that he is trying to vindicate the ways of God to man by the very reason that he has elsewhere in the same poem asserted to be weak, fallible,presumptuous, and misleading. Thus the *Essay on Man* seems to shift back and forth between two incompatible positions—the Pyrrhonistic doctrine that man's reason is unable to cope with either the problem of God or that of the natural universe and the Deistic concept that man can do a fairly efficient job of dealing rationally with both.

The distance between Prior's and Pope's ultimate position is shown by their differing use of a similar figure to embody the human predicament. Prior in **Solomon,** 3:697, speaks of human existence as "Lab'rynths," as Pope calls it in the *Essay on Man,* 1:6, "A mighty maze!" Either figure suggests a complex puzzle, but one with a builder and a plan. Pope sets out to find this plan, asserting some ten lines later (1:16) that he intends to "vindicate the ways of God to Man." But Prior, painfully aware that he is neither Daedalus nor Theseus, never feels that he can see the plan of the labyrinth and instead finds himself (3:696-97) "unable to explain / The secret Lab'rynths of Thy Ways to Man. . . . "[45]

Twice Pope imitated a Horatian ode already Anglicized by Prior. Both men imitated Horace's Satires, II, vi, which contained the account of the country mouse and the city mouse, Prior in **The Hind and the Panther Transvers'd,** Pope in the octosyllabic *An Imitation of the Sixth Satire of the Second Book of Horace.* In each case, the poet had a collaborator (Prior had Charles Montagu, Pope had Jonathan Swift), but the lines telling the story of the city mouse and the country mouse are believed by most critics to have been written by Prior and by Pope. The relevant lines in Pope's poem begin

> Our Friend Dan *Prior* told, (you know)
> A Tale extreamly *a propos:*
> Name a Town Life, and in a trice,
> He had a Story of *two Mice.*[46]

Despite this friendly reference to Prior, Pope's version of the same story owes to Prior's **Hind and the Panther Transvers'd** at most only three small details.[47] What the *Imitation of the Sixth Satire of the Second Book of Horace* may actually demonstrate is that both Swift and Pope learned from Prior's colloquial use of octosyllabics but that each man adapted his learning to his own gifts. Swift's colloquialism is straightforward and flexible; Pope's is brilliant, balanced, and perhaps a little rigid.

Both Prior and Pope translated Horace's Ode I, iv, which Ben Jonson had also translated. Jonson's version was called "Ode the First. The Fourth Booke. To

Venus"; Prior's is "**Cantata. Set by Monsieur Galliard**" (1716); Pope's is "The First Ode of the Fourth Book of Horace" (1737). In general Pope's version is more like Jonson's than like Prior's, for Prior is not simply translating but iswriting words to be set to music, divided into five parts for recitative and arias.[48]

The methods of Jonson, Prior, and Pope with this same Horatian ode offer an illuminating contrast. Jonson is cautious, fairly literal, somewhat rough, and powerful. Prior takes his material where it pleases him and suits it to his own purposes, creating a Restoration love-lyric that resembles Horace's farewell to love only in general outline. Pope follows Horace rather closely, though not so closely as Jonson, substituting for Roman geographical and amorous details equivalents more familiar to English thought or acceptable to English taste. Pope's version is as polished, easy, and elegant as Prior's but much closer to his Horatian original. In general, Jonson modifies Horace to make a more powerful metaphor; Prior, to simplify and generalize; and Pope, to polish and "modernize."

The influence of one poet on the next is slight; each seems to have worked primarily with the Horatian original. Prior shows no indebtedness to Jonson; Pope possibly owes to Jonson his verse form, but little else, and he owes to Prior only a single line ("Ah sound no more thy soft alarms"), the addition of Chloe, and the change of the beloved "wanton boy," Ligurinus, to a more acceptable girl (a shift explicit in Prior and implicit in Pope).[48]

The problem of Pope's more general indebtedness to Prior is an intriguing one. When Edward Harley in 1723 asked Pope to read through all of Prior's manuscripts with a view toward editing and bringing out a comprehensive edition, Pope replied, "I now not only desire, but want, & long, to read the Remains of Mr Prior. My Respect for him living extends to his memory; & give me leave to say, In this I resemble your Lordship, that it dies not with his person."[49] Twice in the *Dunciad* Pope coupled Prior's name with those of major contemporary literary figures (Congreve, Addison, Swift) as the models of good writing against which the dunces were weighed in the balance and found wanting. In his last two years of life, when he was projecting a dictionary "that might be authoritative for our English writers," Pope listed Prior as one of the nine "that might serve as authorities for poetical language. . . . "[50] Three of these—Dryden, Swift, and Prior—were drawn from the Restoration-Augustan period, but Swift was restricted to being an authority for burlesque language only. Prior and Dryden had no such restrictions.

The question then becomes what Pope—who set out to become England's first "correct" poet—learned in general from Prior, one of his projected dictionary "authorities for poetical language." As an assistant in planning the 1718 ***Poems on Several Occasions*** and as the chief editor of the projected posthumous edition of Prior's works, Pope had dealt either casually or closely with almosteverything that Prior had written. Moreover, Pope had an extraordinary literary memory for lines of poetry read years before[51] and a sharply sensitive personal recollection of the friends of his youth.[52] In general, then, it is likely that Pope learned from Prior—or intensified because of Prior's tutelage—what Charles Kenneth Eves has called "that rococo style which pointed directly to the *Rape of the Lock.*"[53] Prior's deft placing of the floridly ornamental mantle of style upon subjects deliberately too small for it may have foreshadowed that same mixture of high style and low subject in Pope. The matter of a delicate and easy tone, which also has been suggested as a skill perfected by Prior and passed along to Pope, is another facet of the same question of style. To a young man aiming, like Pope, to become England's first correct poet, Prior had much to teach of tone and style.

In addition to teaching Pope a delicacy and ease of perfect light verse tone, Prior improved the heroic couplet which was to become Pope's masterpiece. Robert Southey commented that "For improving [the heroic couplet], too much has been ascribed to Waller, and not enough to Prior. From Prior, Pope adopted some of the most conspicuous artifices of his verse."[54] Nevertheless, though Prior improved the heroic couplet which Pope was to perfect, it was probably in matters of lightness, delicacy, and ease of tone that Prior had the most profound influence upon Pope.

Prior's Influence upon Samuel Johnson

Though the third great literary figure of the eighteenth century, Samuel Johnson, disapproved of Prior and damaged his poetical reputation by a very unfriendly and unsympathetic "Life of Prior," he also learned from Prior in his own writings, particularly in *Rasselas,* which is heavily indebted to Prior's ***Solomon.*** Both works are elegant, serious narratives in which a young prince is attempting to make a choice of life, only to find one pathway after another leading to a dead end— or a minotaur. In both works the prince acts a little and talks and listens a great deal. Ian Jack has pointed out that both works employ a "remote, vague, and Oriental" setting, are heavily indebted to the Bible, and are basically "Christian satires on the lot of Man."[55] Though Johnson found ***Solomon*** tedious—"Tediousness is the most fatal of all faults. . . . "[56]—he also found it a mine of useful observations, a number of which he incorporated into *Rasselas* and into *The Vanity of Human Wishes.* All three works stand squarely, as Jack has pointed out, in the tradition of Christian pessimism, but Prior's specific three-fold division in ***Solomon*** of areas to be examined—knowledge, pleasure, and power—finds specific parallels in those questions that Rasselas and Imlac and Nekayah and Pekuah raise in *Rasselas* and in those goods that the poet finds it vain and dangerous to wish for in *The Vanity of Human Wishes.*

Prior taught the English poets of the eighteenth century more than matters of style and subject. Along with Dryden and Pope, he also taught them that it was possible for a practicing poet to support himself handsomely from his writings without dependency upon patrons if he would deal directly, in a businesslike fashion, with his reading public. All three poets used the subscription method to secure advances while they worked upon projects and hence to support themselves rather well with funds drawn directly from their potential readers. Prior died a wealthy man not because of his diplomatic career, which often proved a financial disaster, but because of the 1718 *Poems on Several Occasions.*

Prior's Influence upon Other Writers

Prior's poetry also exerted a discernible influence upon lesser poets of the eighteenth and nineteenth centuries, in England and in five other countries. Anne Finch, the preromantic Countess of Winchilsea, frequently mentioned Prior in her poems, in the most notable instance, a thirteen-line section of "The Nymph whose Virginheart thy charms have taught," calling Prior her Teacher and Master.[57]

William Cowper reacted against Johnson's censure of Prior, and J. W. H. Atkins has praised Cowper as a corrective "with exquisite taste" to Johnson, who had condemned Prior's use of classical fable as insincere and missed Prior's "most subtle quality."[58] Oswald Doughty has shown the influence of Prior upon Cowper's light verse: "in it he continued Prior's vein of humour, though with less subtlety than Prior showed at his best, while he possessed also Prior's facility in rhyme and rhythm, when writing in the 'familiar style.'"[59]

In this same period Prior's poetry was prized by three of the Wesleys: Samuel the younger, John, and Charles. John Wesley in his journal, letters, and sermons quoted from Prior some sixty times, more than from any other poet of that century and more than from any other poet of any age except Milton. In 1779 he printed *Henry and Emma* whole in the *Arminian Magazine.* Sixteen times the Wesleys' hymns incorporate phrases borrowed from Prior,[60] the most familiar being the third line of "Jesus, Lover of My Soul"—"While the nearer waters roll"—a direct borrowing from Prior's *Solomon.* Samuel J. Rogal explains the Wesleys' continued interest in Prior thus: "Either firsthand or by way of the printed page, the brothers discovered in this Augustan poet a model of perfection for eighteenth-century man: the scholar, the poet, the statesman whose

Tory principles anchored him firmly to the trinity of God, king, and nation, and whose sense of loyalty allowed him to endure harassment and even persecution from an overzealous Whig ministry."[61] Henry Bett argues that Prior also taught the Wesleys "Something of the freedom of their versification. . . . "[62]

Prior likewise exerted a strong influence on a number of German poets of the eighteenth and nineteenth centuries. Wieland's *Musarion* was inspired by Prior's *Alma*[63]; Friedrich von Hagedorn was praised as the "deutsch Prior"[64]; Spiridion Wukadinovic has shown that in Germany Prior also influenced Uz, J. N. Götz, Herder, J. G. Struckmann, Fr. Justin Bertuch, and Gleim.[65]

The Scottish pastoral poet Allan Ramsay (1686-1758) wrote his best pastoral occasional poem[66] in "Robert, Richy, and Sandy: A Pastoral on the Death of Matthew Prior"; in the poem Prior is praised as a satirist, wit, teller of poetic tales, and love poet, in whose work, "Nae word stood wrang."[67] Ramsay's most scholarly biographer, Burns Martin, has, in fact, called Prior one of the two strongest contemporary influences upon Ramsay's work, a model for his attempts at *vers de société.*[68]

In Ireland the nineteenth-century lyricist Thomas More owed a considerable debt to the earlier light verse of Prior, a debt pointed out by William Thackeray, and in nineteenth-century England, Prior's influence fell almost exclusively upon the Victorian writers of familiar verse, Thackeray among them. Thackeray defended Prior against the strictures of Dr. Johnson, calling his lyrics "amongst the easiest, the richest, the most charmingly humorous of English lyrical poems."[69] Brander Matthews named Prior the master of Praed and of Locker-Lampson, classifying all three poets as among the ten great writers of English *vers de société.*[70] Still another Victorian writer of polished, elegant verse, heavily influenced by classical models, William Johnson Cory, paid tribute to Prior in 1877 in a revision of his collection *Ionica* by titling his translation of a Greek mirror-epigram "In Honour of Matthew Prior."[71] Cory's lyrics plainly show the influence of Prior.

In nineteenth-century America, Prior's influence is most apparent in the familiar verse of Oliver Wendell Holmes, who wrote to Locker-Lampson from Boston, 14 January 1873, that "My mother was brought up on the literature of Queen Anne's men & used to quote Pope & I am afraid sometimes Prior without knowing the length to which his vivacities sometimes went, I am quite certain."[72] Holmes shows in his own verse a marked influence from Prior, though not from his bawdier poems.

Thus, throughout the eighteenth century Prior exerted a broad and significant influence upon British and

German poets writing in many different forms: long philosophical poems either serious or half-mocking, Horatian imitations, tales, lyrics. Though his influence was still plainly discernible in Britain, Germany, and the United States throughout the nineteenth century, it was felt almost exclusively, especially in the English-speaking countries, in the one genre of *vers de société.* Because the twentieth century does not prize any of the forms in which Prior excelled, he has had little to teach it thus far, though he and similar writers may yet offer a particularly attractive alternative to irregular and obscure verse or to the laceratingly personal confessional poem.

Prior willed to those poets who followed him his immediate inheritance from the Restoration: gifts of lyricism and levity, of octosyllabics and anapaests. Like Swift, though not a rebel against Augustan poetic practices, by his use of other verse forms and other tones, he retained for poets the precedent of a nonpentameter, non-iambic verse in various moods. It is in this role that he had his major impact as a minor poet.

Even more than most poets, Prior lived in an age of transition. Just as he managed quietly to pass from the Whig to the Tory party when it became apparent that the country that he wished to serve had changed its allegiance, so he passed smoothly from the Restoration to the Augustan mode of verse when the muse whom he wished to serve shifted her taste. Horace Walpole commented that Prior as a politician "left his party, but not his friends"; so too in poetry Prior managed to retain (without any show of nostalgia) some of the Restoration language, lyricism, and levity, along with certain verse-forms popular during that earlier period. When Pope commented to Spence that Sir John Suckling, Sir John Mennes, and Matthew Prior all belonged to the same school of poetry, he was grouping three men whose style was often burlesque, anti-Petrarchan, familiar, and colloquial, expressing its easy informality in varied metrical patterns. It is to a considerable degree because of Prior that this school of poetry continued as a current within the mainstream of Augustan elegantly formal poetry, written in heroic couplets and highly serious in its estimate of itself. It is likely, moreover, that Prior's major significance in the late twentieth century is that he offers certain alternatives—in genre, tone, polish, style, approach—to the chief types of poetry that we currently practice. He may justly continue to claim that elaborate tomb in Westminster Abbey, at the feet of Spenser, on the grounds that what he meant to English poets in the eighteenth and nineteenth centuries he may once again come to mean to us.

Notes

1. The most detailed study of Prior's relationship to Swift has been made by James Alfred Koger, "The Personal and Literary Relationship of Matthew Prior and Jonathan Swift" (Ph.D. diss., Rice University, 1971).

2. Historical Manuscripts Commission, *Report on the Manuscripts of His Grace the Duke of Portland. Preserved at Welbeck Abbey* (London: Eyre & Spottiswoods, 1897), 4:155. L. G. Wickham Legg conjectures that this book shown by Prior was probably *A Tale of a Tub. Matthew Prior: A Study of His Public Career and Correspondence* (Cambridge: University Press, 1921), 127, n.2.

3. Swift, *Journal to Stella,* 59.

4. Allen, *Clubs of Augustan London,* 78.

5. The first extant letter from Prior to Swift was written from Paris, 8 April 1713. Ball, ed., *Correspondence of Jonathan Swift,* 2:18-19.

6. For a detailed account of Swift's share in this subscription edition, see Rippy, "Matthew Prior and Alexander Pope," 154-59.

7. Ball, ed., *Correspondence of Jonathan Swift,* 3:103.

8. Ibid., 6:235.

9. Ibid., 236.

10. The list was first printed in Sir Walter Scott's "Life of Swift," in *The Works of Jonathan Swift, D.D.* (Edinburgh: Archibald Constable & Co., 1814), 1:359, later reprinted in appendix 17 to Ball, ed., *Correspondence of Jonathan Swift,* 5:465-66. For documentation of Swift's high opinion of Prior as politician, see Rippy, "Matthew Prior and Alexander Pope," 6-7.

11. F. Elrington Ball, *Swift's Verse: An Essay* (London: John Murray, 1929), 102-3.

12. Williams, ed., "Introduction," in *The Poems of Jonathan Swift,* 1:xiv-xv.

13. Ball, *Swift's Verse,* 124.

14. Westminster, 28 February 1721. "I am tired with politics and lost in the South Sea: the roaring of the Waves and the madness of the people were justly putt together. . . . " Williams, ed., *Correspondence of Jonathan Swift,* 2:378. Ball (*Swift's Verse,* 160-61) argues that the Prior letter produced the four stanzas in the Swift poem; Williams believes that the Swift poem produced the Prior letter (*Poems of Jonathan Swift,* 1:250).

[15] For a full treatment of this question of the literary influence of Prior upon Pope, see Rippy, "Matthew Prior and Alexander Pope."

[16] 211, Joseph Spence, *Observations, Anecdotes, and Characters of Books and Men Collected from Conversation,* ed. James M. Osborn (Oxford: Clarendon Press, 1966), 1:91.

[17] For a discussion of four Prior epigrams that linked him in some fashion with Pope, see Rippy, "Matthew Prior and Alexander Pope," 376-405.

[18] Sherburn ed., *Correspondence of Alexander Pope,* 1:179. Pope's contributions to the *Adriani* imitations are complicated by his love of mystification, for he redated and readdressed letters, substituted one version of the poem for an earlier one, and even wrote footnotes conjecturing about his own editorial practices. Norman Ault has unraveled many of the details of Pope's devious readjustments of fact and chronology in "The 'Hadrian' Poems," in *New Light on Pope with Some Additions to His Poetry Hitherto Unknown* (London: Methuen & Co., 1949), 60-67.

[19] For a full discussion of these versions of the *Adriani Morientis,* see Rippy, "Matthew Prior and Alexander Pope," 406-32.

[20] Ralph, *Sawney,* 11-12.

[21] James Sutherland, ed., *The Dunciad,* vol. 5 of *The Twickenham Edition of the Poems of Alexander Pope,* gen. ed. John Butt (London: Methuen & Co., 1943), 28.

[22] Ibid., xxv-xxvi. See also Sir Leslie Stephen, *Alexander Pope,* English Men of Letters Series (London: Macmillan & Co., 1880), 126.

[23] Johnson, "Pope," in *Lives of the English Poets,* 3:105.

[24] See Robert Kilburn Root, *The Poetical Career of Alexander Pope* (Princeton: Princeton University Press, 1938), 235, and Geoffrey Tillotson, ed., *The Rape of the Lock and Other Poems,* vol. 2 of *The Twickenham Edition of the Poems of Alexander Pope* (London: Methuen & Co., 1940), 397. Tillotson's appendix N (pp. 397-98) is devoted to a consideration of *Eloisa to Abelard* and *Henry and Emma.*

[25] Elton, *A Survey of English Literature 1730-1780,* 1:63-64.

[26] For a full enumeration of these parallels and a more detailed discussion of the relationship of *Henry and Emma* to *Eloisa to Abelard,* see Rippy, "Matthew Prior and Alexander Pope," 433-65.

[27] Tillotson, ed., *The Rape of the Lock and Other Poems,* 281.

[28] Ibid., 285.

[29] Wright, "Matthew Prior's Cloe and Lisetta," 9-23.

[30] See Tillotson, ed., *The Rape of the Locak and Other Poems,* 291-93.

[31] Prior's ll. 9-10 become Pope's 11. 59-60; Prior's ll. 41-44 become Pope's ll. 45-48. See Rippy, "Matthew Prior and Alexander Pope," 454-55.

[32] For a detailed itemization and discussion of these verbal parallels, see ibid., 456-63.

[33] Root, *The Poetical Career of Alexander Pope,* 94-99; Tillotson, ed., *The Rape of the Lock and Other Poems,* 275-88.

[34] Tillotson, ed., *The Rape of the Lock and Other Poems,* 288.

[35] For a fuller discussion of the reputation of *Solomon,* see chapter four.

[36] Wesley, "Thoughts on the Character and Writing of Mr. Prior," 600-3, 660-65.

[37] *The Works of the Rev. John Wesley,* 6:433.

[38] Letter to the Rev. William Unwin, 5 January 1782, in Hayley, ed., *Life and Letters of William Cowper,* 1:232.

[39] Ruffhead, *Life of Alexander Pope,* 482n.

[40] For a full discussion and itemization of the indebtedness of the *Essay on Man* to Prior's various works, see Rippy, "The Ways of God to Man': Prior's *Solomon* and Pope's *Essay on Man,*" in "Matthew Prior and Alexander Pope," 466-92.

[41] See two articles by William E. Alderman, "Shaftesbury and the Doctrine of Benevolence in the Eighteenth Century," *Transactions of the Wisconsin Academy* 26 (1931):137-59; "Shaftesbury and the Doctrine of Optimism," *Transactions of the Wisconsin Academy* 28 (1933):297-305.

[42] Johnson, "Prior," in *Lives of the English Poets,* 2:207.

[43] George Saintsbury, *The Peace of the Augustans: A Survey of Eighteenth Century Literature as a place of Rest and Refreshment* (London: Oxford University Press, 1946), 57.

[44] Spears, "Matthew Prior's Attitude Toward Natural Science," 506.

[45] Comparing these two passages in the *Essay on Man* and *Solomon*, Professor Spears concludes: "Against the dominant rationalism and optimism of his age, Prior upholds an Anglican Fideism; he is, in a sense, a tragic figure, for without the calm certainty of faith he remains a Fideist manqué." "Matthew Prior's Religion," 180.

[46] Ll. 153-56, John Butt ed., *Imitations of Horace with An Epistle to Dr. Arbuthnot and the Epilogue to the Satires,* vol. 4 of *The Twickenham Edition of the Poems of Alexander Pope,* gen. ed. John Butt (London: Methuen & Co., 1939), 259.

[47] For an identification and discussion of these details and of the broader question of Prior and Pope as Horatian imitators, see Rippy, "'I Have Taken Horace's Design': Prior, Pope, and Four Horatian Imitations," in "Matthew Prior and Alexander Pope," 493-516.

[48] In two instances, Pope's Horatian imitations draw lines directly from Prior pieces other than his reworkings of Horace. In his *Letter to Monsieur Boileau Despreaux: Occasion'd by the Victory at Blenheim, 1704,* Prior had written:

> amongst our selves, with too much Heat,
> We sometimes wrangle, when We should debate;
> (A consequential ILL which Freedom draws;
> A bad Effect, but from a Noble Cause:)

(11.191-94, *LW,* 1:226)

Pope makes the same specific observations upon the same English political situation in "The First Epistle of the Second Book of Horace, Imitated":

> But Britain, changeful as a Child at play,
> Now calls in Princes, and now turns away.
> Now Whig, now Tory, what we lov'd we hate;
> Now all for Pleasure, now for Church and State:
> Now for Prerogative, and now for Laws:
> Effects unhappy! from a Noble Cause.

(ll. 155-60, Butt ed., *Imitations of Horace,* 209)

In the second instance, Pope borrowed a contrast from Prior's manuscript prose and turned it into a line of poetry. Pope had praised Prior's four manuscript *Dialogues of the Dead* to Spence, recalling the precise content of each, including "another between Montaigne and Locke on a most regular and a very loose way of thinking.... " (Spence, *Observations, Anecdotes, and Characters of Books and Men,* 1:92). Into his "First

Epistle of the First Book of Horace Imitated," a decade later (1737), Pope incorporated the lines:

> But ask not, to what Doctors I apply?
> Sworn to no Master, of no Sect am I:
> As drives the storm, at any door I knock.
> And house with Montagne now, or now with Lock.

(ll. 23-26, in Butt, ed., *Imitations of Horace,* 281)

[49] Letter of 24 August 1723, in Sherburn, ed., *Correspondence of Alexander Pope,* 2:193.

[50] Item #390, Spence, *Observations, Anecdotes, and Characters of Books and Men,* 1:171.

[51] Samuel Johnson wrote of Pope: " . . . he is said to have had great strength and exactness of memory. That which he had heard or read was not easily lost; and he had before him not only what his own meditation suggested, but what he had found in other writers that might be accommodated to his present purpose." Johnson, "Pope," in *Lives of the English Poets,* 3:217.

[52] Pope wrote to Swift on 30 December 1736: " . . . I find my heart harden'd and blunt to new impressions, it will scarce receive or retain affections of yesterday; and those friends who have been dead these twenty years, are more present to me now, than these I see daily." Sherburn, ed., *Correspondence of Alexander Pope,* 4:51.

[53] Eves, *Matthew Prior: Poet and Diplomatist,* 181-82.

[54] Robert Southey, "Preface," in *Specimens of the Later English Poets* (London: Longman, Hurst, Rees & Orme, 1807), 1:xxix-xxx.

[55] Jack, "The 'Choice of Life' in Johnson and Prior," *Journal of English and Germanic Philology* 49 (October 1950):523-30. J. W. Johnson, "Rasselas and His Ancestors," *Notes and Queries* 204 (May 1959):185-88, cautions that "Johnson certainly received hints for *Rasselas* from reading Prior's *Solomon* . . . but despite striking similarities . . . there are several important differences between the 'plots', tone, and implications of the two works."

[56] Johnson, "Prior," *Lives of the English Poets,* 2:206.

[57] Samuel Humphreys, "Some Account of the Author: Memoirs of the Life of Mr Prior," in *Poems on Several Occasions. By Matthew Prior, Esq;* 4th ed. (London: C. Hitch & J. Hodges, 1754), 2:lxxii.

[58] J. W. H. Atkins, *English Literary Criticism: 17th and 18th Centuries* (London: Methuen, 1951), 323.

[59] Doughty, "The Poet of the 'Familiar Style,'" 5.

[60] Henry Bett, *The Hymns of Methodism,* 3d ed. (London: Epworth Press, 1945), 154-60.

[61] Samuel J. Rogal, *John and Charles Wesley,* Twayne's English Authors Series, no. 368. (Boston: Twayne Publishers, 1983), 102.See also two works by T. B. Shepherd: "John Wesley and Matthew Prior," *London Quarterly and Holborn Review,* July 1937, 368-73, and *Methodism and the Literature of the Eighteenth Century* (London: Epworth Press, 1940).

[62] Bett, *Hymns of Methodism,* 159.

[63] Johan S. Egilsrud, *Le "Dialogue des morts" dans les littératures française, allemande et anglaise (1664-1789)* (Paris: L'Entente linotypiste, 1934), 140.

[64] Spiridion Wukadinovic, *Prior in Deutschland* (Graz: K. K. Unicweaitäts-Buchdruckerei und Verlags-Buchhandlung 'Styria," 1895), in Anton E. Schoenbach and Bernhard Seuffert, *Grazer Studien zur deutschen Philologie,* 4:7.

[65] Ibid., passim.

[66] Burns Martin, *Allan Ramsay, A Study of His Life and Works* (Cambridge: Harvard University Press, 1931), 68.

[67] L. 103, in Burns Martin, ed., *The Works of Allan Ramsay* (Edinburgh and London: A. Fullarton & Co., [1851]), 2:176.

[68] Martin comments further, "we need hardly add that the Scot never achieved the polish and urbanity of his master." Ibid., 59.

[69] "Prior, Gay, and Pope," in *The English Humourists of the Eighteenth Century,* ed. by Derek Stanford (London: Grey Walls Press, 1949), 164. For specific instances of Thackeray's indebtedness to Prior, see William P. Trent, "Thackeray's Verse," in *Longfellow and Other Essays* (New York: Thomas Y. Crowell & Co., 1910), 182.

[70] Brander Matthews, "Familiar Verse," in *Gateways to Literature and Other Essays* (New York: Charles Scribner's Sons, 1912), 163-64.

[71] William Johnson Cory, *Ionica,* introduction and notes by Arthur C. Benson, Sesame Library (London: George Allen & Unwin, n.d.), 218.

[72] Letter quoted in full in Augustine Birrell, *Frederick Locker-Lampson: A Character Sketch* (New York: Charles Scribner's Sons, 1920), 96.

Nicolas H. Nelson (essay date 1988)

"Dramatic Texture and Philosophical Debate in Prior's *Dialogues of the Dead,*" in *Studies in English Literature 1500-1900,* Vol. 28, No. 3, Summer, 1988, pp. 427-41.

[*In this essay Nelson supplies an overview of what he considers Prior's unique contributions to the "dialogues of (or with) the dead" literary form.*]

Since ancient times, the dialogue has proven itself one of the most versatile of all the forms of literature. One offshoot of this form, the dialogue of the dead, has had, however, a much less fertile literary history.[1] The three most eminent writers of this more restricted form are probably Lucian, Fontenelle, and Fénelon, but there is another who merits, and is beginning to receive, a wider recognition. In the final years of his life, Matthew Prior composed several dialogues of the dead that have received high praise from their few commentators. K. N. Colvile declares that they are "among the very best of their kind ever written in any tongue,"[2] and Frederick Keener, in the most comprehensive and illuminating discussion of this genre, says that "they do not pale when set beside acknowledged masterpieces of eighteenth-century literature."[3] Since they were first published only in 1907 and since only four of them were written (of which one is unfinished), these dialogues have received relatively little scholarly attention. Two aspects of these works in particular, I believe, could use further exploration: the nature of Prior's thought, his central philosophical values, and the various techniques he uses to dramatize these ideas. In this paper I propose to show how Prior blends the different uses of such dialogues, from satire to a discussion of ethics, into dramatic confrontations between two personalities with radically conflicting ways of looking at the world. To understand Prior's distinctive contribution to this form, we need to look briefly at the three writers mentioned above before turning to the Englishman's writings.

Writing in the second century of the Christian era, Lucian is generally credited with originating the dialogue of the dead, and he placed it firmly in the satiric tradition. Lucian depicts mythological or historical figures who discover, to their chagrin, that death obliterates all worldly distinctions and that their earthly obsessions no longer matter. He ridicules those who cling to their possessions or to their physical beings after death, though he makes little effort to render human personality in his conversations. A typical example occurs in the debate between Nireus and Thersites about which one is better looking. They appeal the decision to Menippus the Cynic, Lucian's satiric mouthpiece, whose decision underscores their absurdity: "Bones are all alike. The only

way of distinguishing your skull from Thersites',"
he tells Nireus, "is that yours wouldn't take much crack-
ing; it's fragile—not very masculine." And at the end
of this brief dialogue Menippus sums up: "There aren't
any distinctions in Hades; everybody's equal."[4]
Thus Lucian initiates one of the central themes of the
dialogue of the dead, the leveling power of death.
Lucian's attack on man's pretensions is harsh and cynical, since, as Bryan Reardon has observed, his "merciless rationality never reaches any but negative conclusions. Lucian knows all the answers; and they are
all 'No'."[5]

Closer to Prior in time if not in spirit are the French
dialogists of the late seventeenth and early eighteenth
centuries, Fontenelle and Fénelon. Fontenelle first established himself as a writer with his dialogues published in 1683, in which he mixes ancient and modern
characters in urbane, witty, and often ironic explorations of the vagaries of human nature or the paradoxical quality of life. Like Lucian's, they are brief discussions of general ideas, but they lack his strongly
marked satiric impulse. One of the characters commonly acts as the instructor of the other as they probe
the subtleties of their topic. Socrates, for example,
explains to Montaigne that the nature of man is essentially constant throughout history: "La politesse ou la
grossièreté, la science ou l'ignorance, le plus ou le
moins d'une certaine naïveté, le génie sérieux ou ba-
din, ce ne sont là que les dehors de l'homme, et tout
cela change; mais le coeur ne change point, et tout
l'homme est dans le coeur."[6] But there are few moments of high tension or sharp intellectual debate in
these conversations, which, for the most part, remain
smooth, polite, and clever, and without much passion
or personality.

At the end of the seventeenth century, Fénelon adopted
the dialogue of the dead for the instruction of his prince-
pupil, the Duke of Burgundy. His conversations naturally have a strong didactic element, with their goal of
showing the future king of France the proper values
and attitudes of a wise and benevolent monarch. In
one of these, Achilles confesses to the centaur Chiron
in the afterlife that he was an impetuous young
man whose passion got the better of him, as youth
is prone to allow: "la jeunesse," he remarks, "serait
charmante si on pouvait la rendre modérée et capable
de réfexions." Chiron replies, however, that this will
only be possible if one learns "de se craindre soi-même,
de croire les gens sages, de les appeler à son secours,
de profiter de ses fautes passées pour prévoir celles
qu'il faut éviter à l'avenir, et d'invoquer souvent
Minerve dont la sagesse est au-dessus de la valeur
emportée de Mars."[7] Moral judgments permeate these
dialogues as Fénelon lays bare for his young student
the shocking ignorance or misguided intentions of
past leaders and civilizations. In commenting on
recent French history, for example, Fénelon has

Richelieu condemn Mazarin for being weak, timid,
secretive, and lacking in principle. The Italian, Richelieu declares, is responsible for undermining the morality of the French: "vous avez corrompu le fond de
leurs moeurs, vous avez rendu la probité gauloise et
ridicule."[8]

Such are the major dialogists of the dead before Prior.
The Englishman, despite the few dialogues he wrote,
manages to strike a new and distinctive note in this
tradition, by combining the satire, irony, and didacti-
cism of his predecessors with a greater sense of the
dramatic, together with a fuller exploration of the philosophical issues in question.

In his dialogues Prior depicts historical characters who
engage in serious discussions of issues and ideas, defending their lives according to their conception of man
and the world. Philosophy comes alive through personality; the human clash is elevated by the debate about
general principles. Though not all of the dialogues are
equally successful, they point to a more theatrical approach to the form than found in the past. Before detailing some of the dramatic aspects of these dialogues,
we must look carefully at Prior's central ideas.

Critics have generally identified Prior as a philosophical skeptic. Forty years ago, in a series of seminal
articles on Prior, Monroe Spears, though acknowledging Prior's fideism, made Pyrrhonism the key to his
religious thought. Prior, Spears declared, "is, throughout his work, a consistent exponent of Pyrrhonism and
a disciple of Montaigne," and he cites the Locke-
Montaigne dialogue for an important piece of evidence.
Montaigne's "chief argument" in Prior's dialogue,
Spears says, is "the basic Pyrrhonist one against the
possibility of any knowledge of absolute truth beyond the uncertain realm of sense-impressions."[9]
Recently, John Higby and Frederick Keener have con-
curred with this judgment, though Keener speaks more
generally of "Prior's distinctive blend of skepticism
and energy, disillusionment and generosity."[10] Prior's
skepticism has, in effect, become a critical commonplace.

But I believe we have accepted this designation too
easily. True Pyrrhonist or skeptical doctrines are less
evident in Prior's dialogues, or his work as a whole,
than we are given to believe. Many years ago, C. K.
Eves, Prior's biographer, pointed out that Prior wrote
a number of religious poems throughout his career,
some of which were among his favorites, and that he
"was as loyal a Church of England man as he was a
patriotic Englishman. For the natural religion of many
of his contemporaries or for irreligion, he had neither
patience nor understanding."[11] It is difficult to believe
that a man who can casually refer to Christ as "our
Savior" in his own commonplace book at this time
(1720-21) could be a true skeptic.[12]

435

A TREATY of PEACE, &c.

Concluded at *UTRECHT* the $\frac{31}{11}$ Day of $\frac{March}{April}$ 1713.

HEREAS it has pleafed Almighty GOD, for the Glory of His Name, and for the Univerfal Welfare, fo to Direct the Minds of Kings, for the Healing, now in His own Time, the Miferies of the Wafted World, that they are difpofed towards one another with a Mutual Defire of making PEACE: Be it therefore known to All and Singular, whom it may Concern, That under this Divine Guidance, the Moft Serene and Moft Potent Princefs and Lady *ANNE*, by the Grace of GOD, Queen of *Great-Britain, France*, and *Ireland* ; and the Moft Serene and Moft Potent Prince and Lord *Lewis* XIV. by the Grace of GOD, the Moft Chriftian King ; Confulting, as well the Advantage of their Subjects, as Providing (as far as Mortals are able to do) for the Perpetual Tranquility of the whole Chriftian World, have refolv'd at laft to put an End to the WAR, which was unhappily Kindled, and has been obftinately carried on above thefe Ten Years ; being both Cruel and Deftructive, by reafon of the Frequency of Battles, and the Effufion of Chriftian Blood. And for Promoting this Their Royal Purpofe, of Their own proper Motion, and from that Paternal Care which they Delight to Ufe towards Their Own Subjects, and the Publick Weal of *Chriftendom*, have Nominated and Appointed the moft Noble, Illuftrious, and Excellent Lords, Their Royal Majefties refpective Ambaffadors Extraordinary and Plenipotentia-

F f 2   ries,

Facsimile of the first page of the Treaty of Utrech, popularly known as "Matt's Peace" because of Prior's negotiations to end the War of the Spanish Succession.

Nor do his dialogues support a skeptical or libertine interpretation. Montaigne himself, in Prior's dialogue, refers disparagingly to the founder of Greek skepticism in discussing a contemporary philosopher: "Descartes in the middle of the Joy he felt when he was certain he doubted of every thing and only knew his own Ignorance, was just in the same piteous estate where Pyrrho found himself two thousand years before" (1:633). In the passage from the Locke-Montaigne dialogue that Spears cites to support his claim for Prior's Pyrrhonism, Montaigne's purpose is to demonstrate the fallibility of man's sensory knowledge, thus undermining Locke's philosophy. Arguments against the validity of sense impressions are not unique to skepticism, nor does Montaigne assert that certain knowledge does not exist. From his other comments it is clear that he believes there is plenty of knowledge and wisdom about life available to man if he will only open his eyes a little more. Moreover, some other characteristics of skepticism are missing from Montaigne's arguments. The goal of the skeptic was, according to Long, "freedom from disturbance,"[13] since it was impossible to determine any absolute truth. Montaigne neither argues for such tranquility of mind nor does he exhibit it. And, finally, a proper skeptic would suspend judgment on any question and refuse to discriminate between good and evil for the same reason that he values imperturbability: ultimate reality can never be known for certain. On the contrary, Prior's Montaigne, like the real one, is positive, cheerful, dogmatic, and fully engaged with life. He is a vigorous Gascon with a Gallic wit and a rapid-fire mind. There is very little of the true skeptical philosopher about him or his arguments.

If Prior is not a skeptic, what is he? His own philosophy is difficult to characterize because it is unsystematic and eclectic. Like Montaigne, he draws on a variety of sources, both classical and Christian, for his themes. He is a traditional moralist who harks back to Horatian moderation as an antidote for the excessive zeal or enthusiasm with which human beings generally pursue their selfish goals. He sees clearly the limits of our reason and knowledge, and he roundly condemns our inclination to presumption and pretense. He wants us to know ourselves and our limitations better and not to impose ourselves on others as we strive to realize our ambitions or our happiness. Prior's dialogues affirm the values of simplicity, honesty, and moderation, in part by satirizing the human tendency to self-righteousness and an inflated sense of self-worth. Humility, restraint, and tolerance are key words in Prior's lexicon, or implicit assumptions in his satiric mode. Like Swift, he chooses not to depict humanity's spiritual condition, focusing instead on the ethical dimension of our behavior. Prior's ideas are scarcely original, but they are threaded throughout his dialogues, providing a continuous basis for judging what is being said.

As many have pointed out, one of Prior's characters appears to speak for the author in each of his dialogues, though he may not embody absolute truth or represent the perfection of humanity. This character, in the course of the dialogue, instructs the other one not only in ideas but also in feelings and sensitivity, though hehimself may show some failings or weaknesses of character along the way. Aristotle's Golden Mean furnishes one of the truths that Prior's characters keep returning to in their discussions. Montaigne is perhaps Prior's chief exponent of this idea, especially when he summarizes some of his own axioms on life in opposition to Locke. "There is no pleasure," Montaigne asserts, "so just and Lawfull but is blamable if used in Intemperance or Excess" (1:627). "Valor," too, according to Montaigne, "has its Limits as well as the other Virtues, and foolhardiness is as great a Vice as Cowardise" (1:627). Even the concept of courtesy includes the possibility of excess: "I have seen," Montaigne remarks, "People impertinent by too much good Manners, and troublesome with the greatest Decorum" (1:627).

Prior's other dialogues contain a similar concern with virtue as a mean. The Vicar of Bray suggests to Thomas More that virtue itself requires restraint, and quotes some verses from a "Freind" (actually Prior himself) that were originally composed for *Alma:*

> Your Conscience like a Firy Horse
> Shou'd never know His native force
> Ride him but with a Moderate Rein
> And stroke him down with Worldly gain;
> Bring him by Management and Art
> To every thing that made him Start;
> And strive by just degrees to Settle
> His native warmth and height of mettle.
>
> (1:653)

Occasionally, this theme is adapted directly from Horace, whose poetry Prior admired and imitated. Nicolas Clenard, a learned and lively professor of languages, in his conversation with Charles V, former Emperor of the Holy Roman Empire, cites Horace's first satire from Book I to support his contention that moderation should guide our attitudes and actions in life, in contrast to the hauteur that Charles displayed. As Clenard translates Horace's famous lines on this theme:

> One equal bound there is, one Stated line,
> Which shou'd the Justice of our Act confine:
> There Right resides, what goes beyond is Wrong:
> Grows idly vast, and trails absurdly long.
>
> (1:603)

Clenard further advises Charles that "Reason should Direct your view, but Ambition dazles it, So you never attain your Desires, because you neversufficiently consider what will satisfy them" (1:603). The grammarian proceeds to condemn heroic virtue, which, according to him, once it transcends "the measure of Nature from Sublime turns to Ridiculous" (1:603). All of this sounds very much like Aristotle's discussion of virtue in his *Ethics,* where he says that virtue "is a mean between two kinds of vice, one of excess and the other of deficiency; and also for this reason, that whereas these vices fall short of or exceed the right measure in both feelings and actions, virtue discovers the mean and chooses it."[14] Like Horace, then, who based his satires on the idea of the "happy medium,"[15] Prior centers his dialogues on the same commonplace, though he gives it his own dress and style.

Because of its wide-ranging nature, the Locke-Montaigne dialogue, especially in Montaigne's axioms for life, summarizes most of Prior's central themes. Throughout Montaigne's long monologue, he emphasizes simplicity in life, integrity, and tolerance. "To be honest is the end and Design of our Life" he declares (1:627), though the difficulty of this modest goal is clearly implied. Another statement about the purpose of life suggests an even more limited end: "Our chief Business in life is to learn to bear the ills of it" (1:627). Life, Montaigne implies, will furnish enough suffering for us without our creating more problems for ourselves through imaginary anxieties or a crusading zeal. We should learn to accept ourselves and our conditions, and not seek out greener pastures elsewhere. But human beings are eternally restless: "we are always beyond our selves, fear, Desire, hope, throw us forward into futurity, and take away our sense of what is to amuse us, with what shal be, and that too possibly when we cannot perceive it" (1:627). Because of our restlessness we find it difficult to live peaceably in a community: "Have you composed your own Manners, and lived as you ought to do with Your Neighbors? You have done more than he who has written Volumes or taken Cities" (1:627). Even in education restraint is the key: "As to Science," Montaigne asserts, "Plants may be Killed with too plentifull Nourishment, and Lamps Extinguisht by too great a supply of Oyle; We may have so much Science that it may confound our Judgment" (1:628). To find stability in life we must recognize that many apparently desirable goals are illusions, such as the lives of the "great," who suffer from many serious "Inconveniences and hindrances" (1:628) by being constantly in the public eye. Finally, Prior paraphrases Montaigne's thoughts on death, where he tries to moderate ournatural fear of it and to lessen the importance we attach to life: "Comfort Your self, You have good Company in the way. A thousand Men and ten thousand Animals Dye in the very same moment with You" (1:628). In such maxims carefully selected from Montaigne's essays, Prior inculcates the virtues of temperance and modesty, of limited goals and realistic visions, and, in doing so, sounds a good deal more like a traditional moralist than a philosophical skeptic.

Similar sentiments occur in Prior's other dialogues. One common theme is that happiness may be found in any station of life. Clenard makes this point to Charles after the Emperor has wondered how people of inferior rank can possibly be considered as happy as their superiors: "Every Wise Man has [an equal share of happiness] . . . for . . . he must form it himself, and this is soon done, when the necessarys of Life very few and easy to come at, almost within every Mans reach are once acquired" (1:606). Cromwell's porter, too, defends his life in a prison cell after the Lord Protector expresses his astonishment that anyone could be happy there, especially one who was judged to be mad. Simplicity of desire, the porter remarks, mocks all of Cromwell's "Splendor and Magnificence, Gardens Parks and Palaces." After all, the porter notes: "I had every thing which I desired or wanted, My Potage well dressed, my Straw fresh and my Coverlet Clean, Whilst in the midst of the Plunder of Three Nations You were always in Necessity, and every Week laying New Taxes upon an opprest People For the Support of an awkward ill founded Greatness" (1:657). The simple life of a madman in his cell was certainly not Prior's literal ideal, but it favorably contrasts with Cromwell's extravagant and immoral attempts as self-glorification. Simplicity also appears in the Vicar of Bray's disarmingly plain answer to Thomas More's question about his goal in life: "Why," the Vicar replies, "to teach my Parish and Receive my Tythes" (1:644). To the extent that he retains his integrity, the Vicar is right. His modesty acts as a satiric counterpoint to More's self-righteousness.

As these examples show, the defense of the simple life leads naturally to some of Prior's most telling blows against social pretense and snobbery. Clenard's description of Charles V's exploits as a conqueror reduces them to an immoral spectacle: "Now of the Hundred thousand Men, with whom You went Dub a Dub, and Tantara rara thrô the World Nineteen parts in Twenty were only Machines, meer Instruments of War, made use of to fill Trenches, or stop Breaches, played off by whole Battallions, Food for Powder, as Sir John Falstaff calls it, in the English Play" (1:601). A number of such passages appear in this dialogue as Clenard's satiric imagination catches fire when he denounces Charles's abuse of his power and his contemptuous attitude toward the common people. In a statement that does much to discredit his own judgment, Thomas More exhibits a similar attitude toward the people when he exclaims: "the Mass of Mankind is a Multitude of Such Animals as this Vicar, the Burden of the Earth, who only feed upon it without endeavoring to deserve the Bread it affords them, Wretches, who in having done nothing have done ill" (1:654-55). Sympathy for the common man is one of Prior's most constant and most endearing themes.

Another snobbery that Prior ridicules is the intellectual, with Locke being the chief target. Locke opens the dialogue musing upon his very important role in the history of philosophy: "Is it not wonderfull," he remarks, "that after what Plato and Aristotle, Descartes and Malbranch have written of Human understanding, it should be reserved to Me to give the most clear, and Distinct Account of it?" (1:615). Montaigne, of course, cannot allow such vanity to go by without laughing at it, but he also levels some serious as well as satiric criticisms at the Englishman's philosophy. In particular, he attacks Locke's use of language, especially his penchant for giving circular or meaningless definitions. In a parody of Locke's method, Montaigne imagines the following interchange:

> I hold a Stone in my hand, and ask you what it is, You tell me 'tis a body, I ask you what is a Body, You reply it is a Substance; I am troublesome enough once more to ask You what is a Substance, you look graver imediately, and inform me that it is something whose Essence consists in Extension in such a manner as to be capable of receiving it, in Longitude, Latitude, and Profundity.

(1:618)

Intellectual pretense joins with social snobbery when Locke scorns the effort to write "to the Vulgar" as he defends the difficulty of his philosophy. Montaigne counters that common readers are "the only People that should be writ to," pointing out that many of the greatest writers either came from the "Vulgar" themselves or wrote for them: "Esop and Epictetus had more Sense than their Masters. Sophocles shewed his Tragedies to his Maid. Since our time Racine, said, he doubted of the Success of his Phaedra till his Coachman told him he liked the Character of Hypolitus, and Boileau, addresses one of his Epistles to Antoine his Fav'rite Gardiner" (1:624). Montaigne concludes his debate with Locke by showing how impractical the Englishman's philosophy is when applied to everyday life. He imagines Locke's servant trying to carry out the simplest command from his master ("You may go down and Sup, Shut the Door" [1:635]) by analyzing it in Lockean terms. Such a process effectively reduces the command to nonsense, confusing the servant and embroiling him with his fellow servants. Wisdom is clearly not served by such a method of reasoning.

In ridiculing Locke's search for truth, Prior does not adopt the premise that it is impossible ever to know anything for sure, as a good Pyrrhonist would. Rather, through Montaigne and his other spokesmen, he shows how selfishness, pride, and presumption cloud our vision and obstruct the search for wisdom, and how simplicity, integrity, and moderation could provide a positive set of norms and attitudes for guiding our lives toward a reasonable measure of happiness and fulfill-

ment. The dialogue form enables Prior to present such values indirectly without preaching, but they emerge nonetheless clearly and distinctly. The personalities Prior sets in conflict, especially his favored speakers, defend their lives and their ideas vigorously and often eloquently, with the result that these dialogues are unusually lively and dramatic. It is to this human side of the dialogues, with its theatrical aspect, that I now wish to turn.

Each dialogue opens with a sudden and apparently accidental meeting of the two characters in the afterlife. No exposition of situation or setting introduces the discussion, but the issues in the debate emerge clearly in the opening statements. In a kind of reverie, Charles V reviews his conquests on earth: "Burgundy with Brabant and Flanders, Castile, Arragon, Germany Possessed: Italy, France, Africa, Greece Attempted" (1:599). Hearing this, Clenard, without an introduction, recites his own achievements as if in mockery: "Noun Substantive and Adjective, Pronoun, Verb, Participle Declined: Adverb, Conjonction, preposition Interjection undeclined" (1:599). Thus Prior pits the warrior against the intellectual, the active life against the contemplative, to the detriment of the proud conqueror. We have already noted Locke's complacent dream of his place in the history of philosophy being shattered by Montaigne's pointed challenges, but there is also the Vicar of Bray's fond farewell to his parish that is upset by Thomas More's rebuke for his reluctance to go to his eternal home. From the start, then, Prior's characters square off in abrupt confrontations over their lives and values, with one of them challenging the other to philosophical debate.

Other dramatic techniques heighten the characterization in the dialogues and increase the tension between the debaters. Monologues not only enable one of the speakers to develop his ideas at length, but they also more fully reveal him as an individual. Clenard's speeches tend to turn into monologues because he is a "Word-Man" as Charles notes (1:605) and because he is defending a difficult position. The power of language is rarely accorded much recognition in contrast to the power of the sword, yet Clenard maintains that "Swords Conquer some, but words Subdue all Men" (1:611). These arguments, which Charles is unable to counter effectively, reinforce Clenard's central theme, though we see that he too goes overboard in his assertions. Like Clenard, Montaigne loves to amplify and embroider his ideas, not only to win the debate but also to show his wit and to indulge his love of invention and expression. We sense the joy in his verbal powers as his recital of various axioms for life extends to over two pages. When he finally stops to look up for a moment, he discovers that Locke has fallen asleep. On waking up, Locke naturally ridicules Montaigne's garrulous, rambling treatment of his ideas, a criticism sometimes made of the *Essays,* yet despite this comic incident, Montaigne's arguments are not seriously undermined but only given a human context. In the other two dialogues monologues are less in evidence since no personality dominates them as do Clenard and Montaigne in theirs.

Another dramatic device Prior uses effectively, though sparingly, in the dialogues is the aside. The speaker of the aside is generally in the process of losing the argument, and it enables us to see into his feelings about the course of the discussion. After Clenard concludes his long diatribe on the power of language, Charles comments to himself with a typical image: "I'l e'en draw down my main Argument, my great Battering Piece upon him, and Strike him Dead at once" (1:612). Charles's confidence is, however, seriously misplaced, since he cannot repel Clenard's verbal assault so easily. A variation of the aside occurs when Thomas More, true to his character, moralizes on the foolish Vicar's worries about his curate outliving him: "Strange Illusion! of which even Death has not cured this Wretch, We join Ideas which in Nature have no Coherence: Our fear of Death gives us not sufficient leizure to consider what Death it self is" (1:648). More goes on to speak of the Vicar in the third person as if he were not there in front of him: "What was it to this Vicar who should enjoy that Benefice from which Death has given him an Eternal Quietus. Yet with Regret he considers who shall possess the Tythes when he shal neither have Mouth to Receive or Stomach to Digest the produce" (1:648). No doubt More is right about the Vicar's silly concerns, yet the interesting element is More's contempt for people of lesser intellectual capacity than his own. The aside, then, momentarily interrupts the flow of the discussion to allow a sudden perspective on it that often suffuses it with dramatic irony.

Prior uses language effectively to heighten our sense of two personalities in conflict over basic issues. It is considerably more varied than the language of Fontenelle and Fénelon, ranging from the highly formal to the colloquial or idiomatic. The colloquial expressions of some of his most educated speakers stand out, with such words as "Od zooks," "Pough, hang it," and "Egad" cropping up rather frequently. Even the Emperor Charles flavors his comments with a "prythee Man" (1:609) and "hark You" (1:615) that imitate an actual conversation taking place. Montaigne's language is naturally spiced with French exclamations like "Mort de ma Vie" (1:629) and "foy de Gentilhomme" (1:617), as well as a number of idiomatic English phrases such as "Who the Devil" (1:618), "come in for a Snack with my Landlord" (1:633), and "knock Your heart out" (1:638). He also uses contractions like "'tis," "'em," and "t'other," and coins some words like "Ergoismes" (1:631) and "Sectators" (1:619). Characters occasionally employ nicknames for their opponents that contribute to the satirical tone of the dialogue. Cromwell's

porter calls the great man "Noll" to his face, Clenard refers to the Emperor as "Neighbor Charles," and More speaks of the Vicar as a "Drole." The Vicar is consistently respectful toward Sir Thomas, but he does call two of Henry VIII's queens "Old Kate" and "Nanny Bullen" (1:645). This informal language clearly gives us the impression of a vivid, almost realistic conversation taking place before us.

Language is also wittily employed in these dialogues, especially by Prior's favored speakers. Clenard, for instance, often introduces satiric analogies to deflate Charles's self-importance, as when he asks if Charles has never noticed "a large Ship going out of Port . . . with her Sails all spread, and her Streamers flying? . . . yet how soon her Bulk diminishes to the Eye of those that stand upon the Shoar 'till as the distance increases She becomes quite lost" (1:608). Applying this directly to Charles's career on earth, Clenard mocks his dependence upon the writer for his future reputation:

> You are launched into the Ocean of Eternity with all your Scutchons and Bandirolls about your Hearse, and probably you may have Four Marble Virtues to Support the Monument you were Speaking of just now. But alas, the Funeral Pomp is soon diminishd worn out and forgotten: Age and Accident deface the Tomb, And, it is only one of Us Scholars that must take an Account of Your true Worth, and transmit its safe to succeeding Generations.
>
> (1:608)

In his defense Charles asserts that men of words are the parasites of men of action, but his language lacks the expressiveness of Clenard's and thus fails in persuasive power.

The wittiest of Prior's characters is undoubtedly Montaigne. His speeches are filled with analogies, metaphors, similes, and imagery, much as his actual essays were, giving them an energy and an appeal that Locke cannot hope to match. When he ridicules Locke's penchant for defining terms without discussing his topic in a substantive fashion, Montaigne declares: "You seem, in my poor apprehension, to go to and fro upon a Philosophical Swing like a Child upon a wooden Horse always in motion but without any Progress, and to Act as if a Man instead of Practising his Trade should spend all his Life in Naming his Tools" (1:620-21). And when he defends his apparently confused method of treating his own subjects, Montaigne asserts that he is simply following the mode of Nature herself: "Is it not the variety it self that pleases while it instructs?" he asks. After all, "If all your Lillies were Collected together in one bed next your House, then all your Roses in an other, and all your Sun flowers in a Third, Who would admire the Beauty of your Garden?"

(1:630). In answering Montaigne's critique of his lack of substance, Locke briefly introduces his own figure ("if a Man does not leap Hedge and Ditch, in your Opinion, he stands stock stil" [1:621]), but he is soon overwhelmed by a profusion of images and arguments from the Frenchman.

The other dialogues offer fewer imaginative passages than these because of the characters involved, yet the ones that do exist help reveal character or convey Prior's point of view. The Vicar of Bray, though a rather simple and uncomplicated man, exposes More's rigid moral approach to life after he hears some of the saint's hardhitting maxims: "you mix't too much Gall with your Ink," the Vicar declares, "Egad with these Maximes of Your's you would raise both Court and Country against You, and if You had as many heads as there are Loops upon Your Gown You might run a fair risk to have 'em all cut off" (1:655). The Vicar speaks the truth here and more effectively because of his figurative language. More himself, as Prior depicts him, is not a very imaginative character, but when he does employ some figures, they are more bitter than most, as in the passage quoted above where he calls the common people "Animals" who are the "Burden of the Earth." Cromwell's porter is inherently not very imaginative, yet even he can introduce his own metaphors, as when he describes his master's own madness in despoiling his enemies of their property: "You find others," he tells Cromwell, "bitt with the same Tarantula who Second your fury pertake of the Plunder and justify your error. Yee all herd together, and it is a very hard thing to catch one of You" (1:661-62). Without this witty, imaginative language, Prior's characters, and hence his dialogues, would lack much of their interest and persuasiveness.

A final ingredient in these dialogues as miniature human dramas remains to be considered, that is, the range of emotion expressed. Prior's characters defend their convictions and attack their opponents with vigor and sometimes passion. Abrupt changes of tone occur, as characters react to one another in the flow of the exchange. All of the emotions we would expect are here, from the consternation of an emperor at being challenged by a lowly scholar to the haughty dogmatism of Cromwell. Montaigne himself plays most of the notes on the scale of feeling except perhaps those of deep anger or bitterness. There are, however, other feelings present that we would not anticipate and that lend a human richness to these conversations. Thus the Emperor Charles, by the end of his discussion with Clenard, is so frustrated with the professor that he breaks off any further debate, yet he solicits Clenard's help in concealing their talk because of its potential embarrassment for him. "Pray," he begs Clenard, "dont take the least Notice to any of my Fellow Princes of the Discourse we have had" (1:615). Fear of shame humanizes this haughty prince. The Vicar of Bray is remarkably mild and gentle throughout his dialogue until the last sentence when he allows himself a pointed thrust at Sir Thomas: "Thou Great Chancellor of England, without a head, Adieu" (1:655). Sarcasm humanizes the saintly Vicar. When Cromwell's porter describes the effect the execution of Charles I had upon him, we cannot help being struck by the depth of his disillusionment: "I imitated You, I looked upon You as my Idol till running from your Door with my Staff in my hand one thirtieth of January, I Shal never forget the Day, I saw You order your Master to be brought out of the Window, and Murthered at his own Palace Gate. I confess when You cut off the Kings head you turned mine into the bargain" (1:657). Though this dialogue may have the appearance of being Prior's most Lucianic work,[16] the porter's unusual sensitivity gives it a pathos not found in the Greek author. Prior thus enriches the human side of his dialogues with these diverse and unexpected emotions.

Each of the dialogues ends with the two characters going their separate ways without having found any common ground of agreement. The reader, I believe, knows which one has had the better of the argument, though he also knows that neither has an exclusive option on the truth. Even Montaigne has to admit the justice of Locke's comment that many of his best ideas are taken from other writers. Prior, in other words, achieves a richer characterization in his dialogues, a greater "negative capability," than most other dialogists of the dead. Without sacrificing his central theme of Horatian moderation, Prior depicts a scene of conflicting personalities whose views and characters are unchanged since their earthly careers. The fusion of mimetic, satiric, and philosophical elements into a coherent dramatic scene is a remarkable achievement. It is a pity Prior had so little time to pursue his work in this genre.

Notes

[1] The land of the dead was used as the setting for a large number of literary works from the Renaissance down to modern times, as Benjamin Boyce has shown in "News from Hell," *PMLA* 58 (1943):402-37. As a distinct form, however, the dialogue of the dead appears only sporadically since Prior's time, from Lord Lyttleton's *Dialogues* (1760) to W. S. Landor's *Imaginary Conversations* (1824-29; 1853), George Santayana's *Dialogues in Limbo* (1925), and Steve Allen's television series "Meeting of Minds" (published in book form in 1978).

[2] K. N. Colvile, "Dialogues of the Dead," *Quarterly Review* 267 (1936): 312.

[3] Frederick M. Keener, *English Dialogues of the Dead: A Critical History, An Anthology, and a*

Check List (New York: Columbia Univ. Press, 1973), p. 55.

[4] Lucian, *Selected Works,* trans. Bryan Reardon. The Library of Liberal Arts (Indianapolis: Bobbs-Merrill, 1965), p. 45.

[5] Bryan Reardon, Introduction to Lucian, *Selected Works* (Indianapolis: Bobbs-Merrill, 1965), p. xxix.

[6] Bernard le Bovier de Fontenelle, *Nouveaux Dialogues des Morts,* ed. Donald Schier (Chapel Hill: Univ. of North Carolina Press, 1965), pp. 65-66.

[7] François de Salignac Fénelon, *Oeuvres,* ed. Jacques Le Brun. Bibliothèque de la Pléiade (Paris: Gallimard, 1983, p. 285.

[8] Fénelon, p. 493.

[9] Monroe K. Spears, "The Meaning of Matthew Prior's *Alma,*" *ELH* 12 (1946): 285.

[10] Frederick Keener, *English Dialogues of the Dead: A Critical History, An Anthology and a Check List* (New York: Columbia Univ. Press, 1973), p. 69. John Higby, "Idea and Art in Prior's *Dialogues of the Dead,*" *Enlightenment Essays* 5 (1974): 62-69.

[11] Charles Kenneth Eves, *Matthew Prior: Poet and Diplomatist* (New York: Columbia Univ. Press, 1939), p. 207; see also p. 404.

[12] See Matthew Prior, *The Literary Works,* ed. H. Bunker Wright and Monroe K. Spears, 2nd edn., 2 vols. (Oxford: Clarendon Press, 1971), 1:1011. All references to Prior's dialogues and other writings are to this edition.

[13] A. A. Long, *Hellenistic Philosophy: Stoics, Epicureans, Sceptics* (New York: Scribner, 1970), p. 79.

[14] Aristotle, *The Ethics: The Nichomachean Ethics,* trans. J. A. K. Thomson, rev. Hugh Tredennick (Harmondsworth and New York: Penguin, 1976), p. 102.

[15] Niall Rudd, *The Satires of Horace* (Cambridge: Cambridge Univ. Press, 1966), p. 23.

[16] Richard Morton, "Matthew Prior's *Dialogues of the Dead,*" *Ball State University Forum* 8 (1967): 74.

Arthur S. Williams (essay date 1989)

"Making 'Intrest and freedom agree': Matthew Prior and the Ethics of Funeral Elegy," in *Studies in English Literature 1500-1900,* Vol. 29, No. 3, Summer, 1989, pp. 431-45.

[*In the following essay the critic suggests that Prior's personal and professional values and beliefs made him reluctant to write an elegy on the death of Queen Mary in 1694.*]

Queen Mary's death in December 1694 called forth the British muse. While the likes of Dennis, Walsh, Stepney, Congreve, and Steele rose—or sank—to the literary occasion, the diplomat and poet Matthew Prior remained conspicuously silent for more than two months after Mary's funeral. As the leading English poet in public life and unofficial "laureate" of William III's reign, Prior experienced pressure to elegize the late queen, and his hesitation is surprising considering his position and taste for occasional verse.[1] Although several scholars have remarked upon this episode, its implications for understanding Prior's career as a whole have never been explored.[2] By defining what he would and would not write under duress, Prior's reluctance to compose an elegy for Queen Mary helps to clarify his poetic values, while circumstances informing his behavior evoke ethical issues related to those of his philosophical verse and prose. Viewed alongside later ethical works, Prior's responses to Queen Mary's death and funeral suggest continuity among aspects of his life, thought, and expression difficult to reconcile in literary criticism.

In some ways typical of the thirty years following William III's succession, Prior's career raises questions concerning the value he accorded to poetry.[3] Neither hack nor belletrist, he never served officially as laureate and, except for scattered political squibs, rarely took up the satirist's lance. Broad learning and worldly experience enriched his intellectual and human perspective but qualified his poetic role and probably his sense of poetry's importance. Mixing literature with diplomacy and courtiership with philosophy, his career exemplifies the marriage of politics and literature, action and contemplation, in late seventeenth and early eighteenth-century England. Such variety calls for spacious principles of evaluation and analysis, but studies of Prior's life and writing have been hemmed in by disciplinary boundaries. For the biographer he is above all a shrewd but beleaguered diplomat; for the historian of ideas, a seventeenth-century skeptic and "harbinger of future dissatisfactions"; for the prosodist, a master of the anapest and octosyllabic couplet; for the modern critic, a practitioner of elegant *vers de société.*[4] So many varied perspectives are not readily subsumed under a broad intellectual framework, and truly comprehensive appreciation of Prior's career may lie beyond the reach of individual scholarly arts.

Economic factors, however, provide one unifying element. As his first modern biographer was aware, the question of "ways and means" touched Prior's existence at many levels, sharpening his instincts for survival, quickening his moral sense, and often informing his utterance.[5] Events surrounding Queen Mary's funeral, which occurred during his financially troubled tenure at The Hague, help illustrate the effect of poverty on Prior's moral and intellectual life.[6] Straitened circumstances as well as grief affected his reaction to the Queen's death and prompted him to examine the motives informing his attitudes and expression. In a climate of grief, poverty, ethical self-consciousness, and concern for the nation, the funeral elegy became a focus of Prior's mixed motives and emotions.

The immediate problem occasioned by Mary's death was how to reconcile sincerity of feeling and expression with unwelcome demands of patronage and solicited publication, and letters and poems of the period witness Prior's efforts to give his emotions meaningful form. The larger issue of reconciling ideals with material realities, however, was to be an enduring concern of Prior's career, one dramatized in poems and philosophical prose written near the end of his life. **"The Turtle and the Sparrow,"** a metrical tale chronologically and thematically related to Prior's dialogues in prose, explores the possibility of sincere elegiac poetry—and of disinterested emotion generally—and sheds a retrospective light on Prior's reluctance to elegize the late queen. Viewed alongside documents of 1694-95, **"The Turtle and the Sparrow"** appears a fictionalized recapitulation of themes of interest to Prior during his period of mourning for Queen Mary, a final denial of prospects for sincere feeling and expression in an imperfect word that involved the poet in moral ambiguity.

Queen Mary died 28 December 1694, and the distraught King William postponed her funeral until 5 March.[7] Events surrounding Mary's death and funeral illustrate forces at work in Prior's career. As a talented poet then serving as Lord Dursley's secretary at The Hague, he was expected to furnish a poem in the queen's memory. At first Prior demurred, remarking caustically upon the poor quality of the funeral verse then appearing in Holland. "We have had nothing new," he wrote to the Earl of Dorset, "but volumes of bad poetry upon a blessed queen. I have not put my mite into this treasury of nonsense, having been too truly afflicted by the subject to say anything about it."[8] On this occasion Prior apparently found silence more decorous than poetry as an observance of Mary's death, a stance Lord Dorset seems to have countenanced.

But matters were not to rest here. By the last decades of the seventeenth century, public poetry had become a quasi-official obligation of preferment, one which Prior's political masters expected him to fulfill. Two who exacted verse from Prior in the 1690s were James Vernon, private secretary to the Duke of Shrewsbury, and Sir William Trumbull, a Secretary of State under

William III and in retirement a friend of the youthful Pope.[9] When Prior attempted to discharge his responsibility toward the late queen by designing a medal with a Horatian inscription in her memory, Vernon chastized him: "If you think this will acquit you from the expectations people have of a poem from you, you will be mistaken, for they say you are not to come off with a posey and a shred of Horace."[10]

Proving more influential than Vernon, Trumbull succeeded where the former apparently failed. Prior ultimately consented to furnish a poem—though not the funeral elegy expected of him—and responded to Trumbull's entreaties with deference toward the aristocratic patron combined with disdain for the bookseller Joseph Tonson: "Sir," writes Prior, "I yield the question, and have a poem on the stocks to be given to his majesty at his arrival here, and since that cur [Tonson] instigated the writing of it, I hope it may be unsold, and contribute to the breaking of him."[11]

The poem in question—**"To the King, An Ode on His Majesty's Arrival in Holland, After the Queen's Death"**—appeared in May 1695, two months after Mary's funeral (2:869). The epigraph, from Horace's Ode 1.4, gives traditional expression to the problem-atic nature of elegy, invoking Melpomene's aid in controlling—and thus giving form to—boundless grief.[12] The poem itself witnesses Prior's effort to engage the limitations of artistic form suggested in the epigraph. Having donned Horace's mantle, he casts his poem in iambic-tetrameter quatrains, creating in the opening lines a dignified elegiac tone:

> At Mary's Tomb, (sad, sacred Place!)
>   The Virtues shall their Vigils keep:
> And every Muse, and every Grace
>   In solemn State shall ever weep.
>
> (lines 1-4)

This beginning, however, soon proves misleading, for in the fifth quatrain the tone shifts abruptly from elegiac to hortatory:

> But let the King dismiss his Woes,
>   Reflecting on his fair Renown;
> And take the Cypress from his Brows,
>   To put his wonted Lawrels on.
>
> (lines 17-20)

The poem continues in this vein, with Prior urging the king to resume his offensive against the French. In finally taking up his pen, he had awaited an occasion—King William's arrival in Holland—that justified a mode of expression that avoids the machinery and alters the tone of funeral elegy.

Like his other responses to Mary's death cited here, Prior's 1695 ode to William III is in one sense evasive, its elegiac opening serving as point of departure for an appeal to William III. His initial silence and effort to substitute a medal for a poem have within two months of Mary's funeral given way to a martial ode that answers to the occasion but leaves the issue of funeral elegy largely in abeyance. Evidently Prior had found the prospect of writing elegy uncongenial, though he is never explicit about the causes of his reserve. Although a number of factors probably contributed, the most revealing touch upon aesthetic and ethical issues emanating in part from Prior's status as a dependent poet.

To seek the grounds of his diffidence is to explore layers of sensibility, loyalty, civic humanism, and self-interest that helped shape Prior's public poetry. Sexual attitudes might have been one contributing factor. Frances Mayhew Rippy has recently noted that Prior likely derived more powerful inspiration from the "warrior king" William III than from his Stuart consort Mary. Prior's characteristic attitude toward women is one of worldly—and witty—condescension, a note scarcely adaptable to funeral elegy.[13] Though no stranger to occasional poetry in either the honorific or the pastoral mode, on this occasion Prior may have found himself thwarted by his feminine subject.

Circumstances surrounding the observance of Mary's death also seem to have posed objections. Three months elapsed between Mary's death and funeral, a protracted time of mourning incompatible with vigorous pursuit of national policy. As both diplomat and poet, Prior demonstrated instincts for decisive, unambiguous action by an unfettered monarch, a trait illustrated in the Horatian ode of 1695. The lassitude accompanying King William's grief was potentially threatening to England's efforts against Louis XIV, and Prior used his role as unofficial laureate to counteract the debilitating effects of personal and public malaise.

Sufficient in themselves to account for his avoidance of elegy, Prior's putative sexism, personal loyalty to William III, and public spirit merge with social, literary, and ethical factors in shaping his literary responses to Queen Mary's death. As previously observed, Prior's aristocratic biases were apparently at odds with the literary demands of preferment over the issue of writing an elegy on the late queen. As a protégé of the Earl of Dorset, a former Restoration wit who had survived to become William III's Lord Chamberlain, Prior was conditioned by literary training and social upbringing to resist the overtly commercial aspects of publication.[14] His reaction to Sir William Trumbull's entreaties mingle respect for the patron with contempt for the "cur" publisher and, by inference, for the entrepreneur's role in soliciting verse on so unhappy an occasion. Presumably the public-spirited message of the ode Prior finally offered for print helped to offset in his mind the grubbier aspects of its publication.

Even more fundamental objections appear to have resided in pastoral elegy itself. When Prior writes to Dorset of being "too truly afflicted" to write poetry, his remark seems aimed at the artificiality of pastoral poetry. Among the most formalized of poetic kinds, pastoral transforms warm emotion into cold art, thus inviting charges of insincerity.[15] His remarks suggest that Prior found contrived expression utterly incompatible with authentic grief experienced on the occasion of Mary's death. In a letter to Lord and Lady Lexington penned a few days before Mary's funeral, he reiterates his claim that grief accounts for his not writing poetry: "I am as yet so afflicted for the death of our dear mistress, that I cannot express it in bad verse, as all the world here does; all that I have done was today on Scheveling Sands, with the point of my sword." He encloses the following chaste lines:

> Number the sands extended here;
> So many Mary's virtues were:
> Number the drops that yonder roll;
> So many griefs press William's soul.[16]

Prior's epigram enclosed in a familiar letter contrasts with the fustian then appearing in print, suggesting that only minimal, unadorned expression shared privately was consistent with genuine grief.[17] The apparent distaste for commercial publication informing Prior's remarks to Trumbull here joins with a general skepticism toward poetic artifice adding another layer of motive to Prior's evasion of funeral elegy.

We can be skeptical in turn, however, as to the real springs of Prior's emotion, which were not clear even to him. Although an inauspicious occasion for sublime poetry, Queen Mary's death nonetheless did furnish Prior opportunity to reflect upon the possible origins of his own grief. Mary's passing had deprived him of a small sinecure, and in a letter to Lord and Lady Lexington Prior complains of his fate: "I have written nothing but nonsense, which is a present I humbly offer some of my correspondents, but it is not very proper for you. Upon this occasion I have lost my senses and £100 a year, which is something for a philosopher of my circumstances." Poverty, Prior suggests, renders him insusceptible to philosophic consolation. He goes on to explore the sources of his emotion: "I am so much in earnest in this sad affair that people think I am something very considerable in England, that have such a regard to the public, and it makes me cry afresh when they ask me in what country my lands are. Whether this proceeds from loyalty or interest God knows, but I have truly cried a basin full."[18]

Prior's tone here, as elsewhere in his letters, is not fullyintelligible, partially because it emanates from a psychological and ethical muddle.[19] As a loyal subject he probably did mourn for the queen, and the loss of his sinecure occasioned hardship. Though merely suggestive, the reference to "loyalty" and "interest" as possible sources of emotion implies that poverty and social insecurity had created in Prior a state of mind that rendered unselfish motives hard to distinguish from selfish ones. The letter to Lord and Lady Lexington, along with others of the period, is valuable because it suggests how socio-economic factors influenced the consciousness of an English poet in the era of political patronage.[20]

Rather than entirely visceral, however, such utterances seem partially conditioned by learning, for learning and experience played complementary roles in shaping Prior's attitudes. Prior's well-known intellectual affinities sanction the idea that circumstances shape thoughts and feelings. His most important debt in this regard is to Montaigne.[21] Like Montaigne, Prior stresses the influence of the body on the mind, distrusts philosophical systems, and relies heavily on ordinary experience. Evocative of Montaigne's *Essais,* Prior's prose treatises convey a sense of life's plenitude, portraying intellect amidst its human surroundings rather than in isolation. The essay **"Opinion,"** for example, remarks upon the "many external Objects" which "have an influence" upon the mind. Although his language sometimes becomes vaguely Lockean, Prior's notion of the mind's relationship to experience comprehends more than sensory impressions *per se.* Among several "external Objects" influencing thought, he broadly includes the "too frequent Excitation or Disuse of any Passion from the Neighbourhood, or abcence of its Object, The Favour of Fortune or the hand of Adversity" (1:592). In thus noting mind's responsiveness to the vicissitudes ("fortune" and "adversity") of complex human experience, Prior takes issue with the Stoic Epictetus, shifting ground by conflating epistemology with ethics: "Our Opinion for all what EPICTETUS says must be directed by something without us, for Opinion it self is really nothing else but the effect of that impression, which an External or Intellectual object makes upon our Thoughts" (1:594).[22]

Here, again, Prior's thinking seems to reflect personal experience, even if that experience is itself shaped by learning. If the mind of man is never free of external influences, Prior's own mind habitually inquires into the worldly circumstances that affect its attitudes. In December 1694, for example, he wrote to Trumbull from The Hague complaining of financial neglect by the ministry in England: "Necessity, Sir, has as little manners as it has law, and when one is really starving, 'tis in vain to be told one is impertinent. . . . There is a great correspondence between the stomach and the heart: one is out of humor when one is hungry; and it is time to think what friends I have at Whitehall when Famine sits triumphant on the cheeks of my two footmen and the ribs of my two horses."[23] "Correspondence" between "stomach" and "heart," "interest" and "loyalty," intellect and environment are recurring,

analogous themes of Prior's letters, poetry, and philosophical prose, the comico-philosophical fusion of body and mind in **"Alma"** being entirely consistent with the material and ethical concerns of a dependent life.[24]

Self-interest is a motive closely associated with such dependence. Among the sources of human "opinion" outlined in Prior's treatise, it plays a central, if imprecisely defined, role. Connected with the mind's capacity for self-preservation, self-interest responds to the "beauty of deformity of the Images placed before it" [the mind], those conceptions that attract the mind or repel it. Abandoning the optical metaphor, Prior goes on in homelier terms to describe self-interest as a predisposition to judge things as harmful or hurtful: "This in plainer English is before we judge of things we are already determined to shun what we think hurtful, and to embrace what we esteem Good, so that under the Denomination of profit or pleasure we always pursue our Interest, or gratify our Vanity, and this single thought thrown into different forms gives us all that ROCHFOCAULT ever writ" (1:594-95).

Self-interest certainly helped motivate Prior's diplomatic career, as well as his poetry, often written under straitened circumstances with an eye toward improving his worldly prospects. Speaking of poetry as an "Amusement," not the "business" of his life, he adds, "and in this too, having the Prospect of some little Fortune to be made, and Friendship to be cultivated with the great Men, I did not launch much out into Satyr," much too dangerous a venture to provide a secure basis for worldly success (1:583). Poetry, then, early became a means of cultivating "the assistance and countenance of Men in favour" and panegyric his characteristic mode of poetic address.[25]

Even Prior's panegyrics, however, are often more than self-serving exercises. In addition to self-interest, he attached high value to patriotism, remarking in his "Preface" to *Solomon* that "I had rather be thought a good English-man than the best Poet, or greatest Scholar that ever wrote" (1:309). Public spirit is one saving grace of the panegyrics, helping to mute the personal hopes implicit in most honorific forms and very explicit in some of Prior's public verse.[26] Along with the utilitarian functions of poetry in his career, furthermore, Prior paradoxically sustained an idealistic sense of the poet's calling. Whereas "every Man is obliged to speak and write prose," he writes in the *"Heads for a Treatise upon Learning,"* "as to Poetry I mean the writing of Verses, it is another thing, I would advise no Man to attempt it except he cannot help it, and if he cannot it is in vain to disswade him from it" (1:583). The distinction between poetry andprose is a recurring theme in Prior's works, which often assign poetry the higher value. **"An Ode, Humbly Inscrib'd to the Queen"** (1706), a poem commemorating the Duke of Malborough's victory at Blenheim, speaks of Horace's having redeemed "fair actions from degrading Prose" (line 7) in Augustus's reign, an achievement Prior seeks to emulate in Queen Anne's. "Prose, and other Human Things may take what Turn they can," he explains in the "Postscript" to the 1718 edition of his *Poems,* "but Poetry, which pretends to have something of Divinity in it, is to be more permanent" (1:440). In the much earlier **"An Ode in Imitation of . . . Horace"** (1692), which glances at the corrupt practices of French court poets, heroic "virtue" and "verse" combine to resist time's depredations:

> Virtue to Verse the real Lustre gives,
> Each by the others mutual Friendship lives:
> The Heros Acts Sustain the Poets Thought,
> *Aeneas* suffer'd and *Achilles* fought,
> Or *Virgils* Majesty, and *Homers* rage
> In vain had strove to Vanquish Envious Age.
>
> (lines 108-13)

Patriotism, loyalty, permanence, divinity, virtue—these are the personal ideals and enabling literary fictions which, even in the absence of "a central poetic conception," lend a dignity unattainable in prose to public themes and achievements.[27]

Such sentiments, however, do not represent a stable or ultimate position as to the relative value of poetry and prose in Prior's works. Capable of dignifying public acts, "poetry" becomes for Prior highly suspect in the sphere of private emotions, where "prose" connotes not "the mundane" but "the true." **"A Better Answer"** (1718) undermines a beautiful cycle of pastoral love lyrics by denying authenticity to verse while locating emotional truth in human speech and "Prose":

> What I speak, my fair CLOE, and what I
>   write, shews
> The Diff'rence there is betwixt Nature and
>   Art:
> I court others in Verse; but I love Thee in
>   Prose:
> And They have my Whimsies; but Thou hast
>   my Heart.
>
> (lines 13-16)[28]

While rendering the term "love poetry" virtually an oxymoron, this passage nonetheless finds grounds for such poetry in verse that approximates human speech. Though more difficult, the problems of elegy were in some respects analogous to those of Prior's love poetry and represent a bridge between his public and private verse. The death of a queen called for dignified public expression, but no poetic fiction could adequately represent grief, which, belonging to the world of **"Prose"** and **"Human Things,"** was solvent to literary artifice. Poverty, furthermore, conspired to render Prior's emotions ambiguous, contributing in turn to his

evasive but fundamentally conscientious responses to Mary's death.

However elusive in the real world, the ideal of pure emotion and its corresponding poetic expression nonetheless remained a feature of Prior's thought. Elegy resounds in the imaginary garden of **"The Turtle and the Sparrow"** (1720), a poem once erroneously thought to be associated with Prince George's death in 1708 (2:986). Among the last of his fourteen metrical tales, **"The Turtle and the Sparrow"** belongs to a period of philosophical reflection at the end of Prior's life. As a dialogue in verse, it resembles in both form and content the four prose dialogues completed during the same period—works which dramatize intellectual and ethical conflicts reminiscent of Prior's career.[29] Evocative of **"A Dialogue between the Vicar of Bray, and Sir Thomas More," "The Turtle and the Sparrow"** dramatizes an encounter between a passionate and idealistic wife (the aggrieved Turtle) and a prudent, calculating, essentially corrupt antagonist (the Sparrow), and thus belongs to the eighteenth-century debate concerning the appropriate roles of reason and passion in human life.[30] The fable's ethical issues, furthermore, carry specifically literary significance. Prior's turtle is an elegist, her cry modeled on Bion's lament for Adonis, and, like poems and letters already cited, **"The Turtle and the Sparrow"** explores the motives of elegiac poetry.

Although the preamble assures that "SPARROWS and TURTLES" "Can think as well as You or I" (lines 9-10), the obvious fiction of the beast fable initially distances the poem from the human world. Within the fable's imaginary kingdom, turtles are poets, and Turturella's lament for the dead "COLUMBO" invokes the tradition of funeral elegy:

> My hopes are lost, my Joys are fled,
> Alas! I weep COLUMBO dead:
>
>   . . . . .
>
> Sing, Philomel, his Funeral Verse,
> Yee pious Redbreasts, deck his Herse.
>
> (lines 13-18)

Although her self-interested allusion to lost "hopes" and "Joys" (line 13) gives reason for pause, Turturella insists upon the purity of her emotion and calls upon the sparrow to join in her lament:

> And hast Thou lov'd and can'st Thou hear
> With piteous heart a Lover's care?
> Come then, with me thy Sorrows join,
> And ease my Woes by telling Thine:
> For thou, poor Bird, perhaps may'st moan
> Some PASSERELLA dead and gone.
>
> (lines 73-78)

A reluctant elegist, however, the Sparrow regards Turturella's behavior as both imprudent and ethically suspect. Poetry, he argues, "neither Suits the Place nor time" (line 80). The reasons are practical:

> That Fowlers hand, whose cruel Care,
> For Dear COLUMBO set the Snare,
> The Snare again for Thee may set;
> Two Birds may perish in one Nett.
>
> (lines 81-84)

When the Turtle ignores the Sparrow's argument, he questions her motives:

> When Widdows use this Canting strain
> They seem Resolv'd to wedd again.
>
> (lines 89-90)

Counseling that "sorrow shou'd to prudence yield" (line 86), the Sparrow at this stage appears to offer a legitimate counter-perspective on the limits of self-sacrifice and grief, much as Prior himself had counseled King William to "dismiss his Woes" in the 1695 ode. In refusing to give up her "BION-style" (line 182), the Turtle's behavior seems excessive and self-indulgent, if not downright perverse. When the Sparrow pragmatically recommends a second marriage, the Turtle demurs:

> No, SPARROW, No,
> Let me indulge my pleasing Woe:
> Thus Sighing, Coeing, ease my pain;
> But never wish nor Love again.
>
> (lines 166-69)

If, at such moments within the poem, the aggrieved Turtle clearly protests too much, the Sparrow's rationalizing behavior soon appears even more suspect. Prudence quickly yields to corruption during the Sparrow's lengthy account of his six marriages (lines 197-419). Unlike the Turtle, whose grief bars consolation and thwarts practicality, the Sparrow leans to an opposite extreme, too easily dismissing the loss of his second wife. Prior's octosyllabic couplets echo the click of the Sparrow's self-interested calculation:

> Well, rest her bones, quoth I, she's
>   gone:
> But must I therefore lye alone?
> What, am I to her Memory ty'd?
> Must I not live, because She dy'd?
> And thus I Logically said,
> ('Tis good to have a Reas'ning head)
> Is this my Wife, *probatur*, Not;
> For Death dissolv'd the Mariage Knot.
>
> (lines 245-52)

During the Sparrow's libertine narrative, the poem gradually moves from the idealized realm of the turtle-

poet to a recognizably human, courtly world where self-interest taints all passions. The marriage bond itself represents for the Sparrow a mere commodity in the quest for worldly advantage:

> Cuckoo! Cuckoo! that Echo'd word
> Offends the Ear of Vulgar Bird;
> But those of finer Tast have found
> There's nothing in't beside the sound.
>
> (lines 315-18)

Sentiments like these earn the Sparrow a rebuke from the Turtle, momentarily restored to moral superiority. His cynicism and self-interest "defile" the "Sacred Groves" (line 422) of "Faithful Loves" and unsullied expression, earning him banishment "To Cities and to Courts" (line 434) whence his sentiments derive:

> There all thy wretched Arts employ,
> Where Riches triumph over Joy.
> Where Passion does with Int'rest Barter,
> And HYMEN holds by MAMMON's Charter.
>
> (lines 436-39)

If the Sparrow's confusion of "Passion" and "Int'rest" ties him to the world of men, the Turtle's display of loyalty distances her from it at the end of the poem. Circumstances surrounding the poem—including the birthday of six-year-old Margaret Harley—called for an exemplary model, and the coda provides it (1:987). Addressing a "Dearest Daughter of Two dearest Friends" (line 442), Prior urges the "Immortal Charms" of "constant Virtue" and bids her "Imitate the TURTLES Fame" (line 453). This verbal gesture seems intended to mute lingering doubts about the Turtle, doubts which survive as the sordid residue of an imperfect world that implicates even the poet himself.

Accomplished only through rhetorical sleight-of-hand, the Turtle's moral victory over the cynical sparrow is highly tenuous, the fable's attempt to suspend disbelief incomplete and unconvincing. The human world, where motives are suspect and poetry disingenuous, encroaches upon the Turtle's pastoral shades, allowing moral ambiguity to overshadow the poetic fiction of untainted passion. This overshadowing of idealism by moral ambiguity figures aspects of Prior's career, one that mingled the practical with the ideal and, on the occasion of Queen Mary's death, emotion with self-interest. Sufficient for panegyric, civic and literary ideals proved unable to legitimize funeral elegy, a poetic form rendered especially problematic by poverty and the poet's regret at losing a sinecure. Prior's much later inability to provide a convincing exemplary model of perfect grief in a fable written for Margaret Harley provides distant commentary upon his own ambiguous feelings and avoidance of elegiac verse in the real kingdom of William III.

Notes

¹ For discussion of Prior's "laureate" role see Frances Mayhew Rippy, *Matthew Prior,* Twayne's English Authors Series no. 418 (Boston: Twayne, 1986), pp. 44-56.

² Charles Kenneth Eves, *Matthew Prior: Poet and Diplomatist,* Columbia Univ. Studies in English and Comparative Literature No. 144 (New York: Columbia Univ. Press, 1939), pp. 93-96. Ronald Eugene Rower, "Matthew Prior: A Critical Study" (Ph.D. diss., Columbia Univ., 1968), pp. 91 and 102. *The Literary Works of Matthew Prior,* ed. H.B. Wright and Monroe K. Spears, 2nd edn., 2 vols. (Oxford: Clarendon Press, 1971), 2:868-69. (All references to Prior's works are from this edition, cited hereafter as *"Literary Works."* All citations of prose are by volume and line. Line numbers for poetry will be given in the text.) Rippy, pp. 48-50.

³ On Prior's representativeness see William Stebbing, *Some Verdicts of History Reviewed* (London: John Murray, 1887), p. 88. For an interesting modern assessment, see Pat Rogers, *The Augustan Vision* (New York: Barnes and Noble, 1974), pp. 116-21.

⁴ The best biography is by Eves, cited above. For discussion of Prior and modern discontents, see Monroe K. Spears, "Matthew Prior's Attitude toward Natural Science," *PMLA* 63 (June 1948) :485-507. George Saintsbury, *A History of English Prosody from the Twelfth Century to the Present Day,* 3 vols. (London: Macmillan, 1906-1910), 2:423-35, discusses Prior's use of the anapest and octosyllabic couplet. Admiration for Prior's social verse is expressed by Oswald Doughty, "The Poet of the 'Familiar Style'," *ES* 7 (February 1925): 5-10. Maynard Mack endorses Prior's lyrics in "Matthew Prior: *Et Multa Prior Arte . . . ,"* *Collected in Himself: Essays Critical, Biographical, and Bibliographical on Pope and Some of His Contemporaries* (Newark: Univ. of Delaware Press, 1982), pp. 81-89; rpt. from *SR* 68 (1960): 165-75. For additional views of Prior see Rippy, pp. 154-61.

⁵ Francis Bickley, *The Life of Matthew Prior* (London: Pitman, 1914), p. 47.

⁶ See Eves, pp. 57-67, for an account of Prior's financial difficulties at The Hague.

⁷ See Nesca A. Robb, *William of Orange: A Personal Portrait,* 2 vols. (New York: St. Martin's Press, 1966), 2:354-66.

⁸ Historical Manuscripts Commission, *Calendar of the Manuscripts of the Marquis of Bath,* 3 (*Prior Papers*):49. Cited in *Literary Works,* 2:868.

⁹ "Trumbull, Sir William" and "Vernon, James," *DNB,* 1949-50 edn. For Trumbull's friendship with Pope, see George Sherburn, *The Early Career of Alexander Pope* (Oxford: Clarendon Press, 1934), pp. 41-42.

¹⁰ *Prior Papers,* p. 50. Cited in *Literary Works,* 2:869.

¹¹ *H.M.C. Downshire,* 1:465. Cited in *Literary Works,* 2:869.

¹² *Literary Works,* 1:130.

¹³ Rippy, p. 49.

¹⁴ According to J. W. Saunders, Prior later found subscription "a decorous half-way house between the amateurism he could not afford and the professionalism he abhorred." *The Profession of English Letters* (London: Routledge & Kegan Paul; Toronto: Univ. of Toronto Press, 1964), p. 134.

¹⁵ See Samuel Johnson's strictures against "Lycidas" in *Lives of the English Poets,* intro. L. Archer Hind, 2 vols. (London: J.M. Dent; New York: E.P. Dutton, 1954), 2:95-96.

¹⁶ *The Lexington Papers,* ed. H. Manners Sutton, 1851, p. 63. Cited in *Literary Works,* 2:868.

¹⁷ In his distrust of elegiac fictions, Prior demonstrates a trait also observed in one of his literary models, Edmund Spenser. See Peter M. Sacks, *The English Elegy: Studies in the Genre from Spenser to Yeats* (Baltimore and London: Johns Hopkins Univ. Press, 1985), pp. 38-63.

¹⁸ *The Lexington Papers,* p. 46, cited in Eves, p. 94. Eves notes the "strange mingling of self-interest and grief" in Prior's behavior.

¹⁹ See H.B. Wright's comments on Prior's letters to Elizabeth Singer, "Matthew Prior and Elizabeth Singer," *PQ* 24 (1945): 81.

²⁰ According to W.B. Coley, social dependency "entered into the very mind of the writer and gave him a certain kind of matter and a castof thought." "Notes toward a 'Class Theory' of Augustan Literature: The Example of Fielding," *Literary Theory and Structure: Essays in Honor of William K. Wimsatt,* ed. Frank Brady, John Palmer, and Martin Price (New Haven and London: Yale Univ. Press, 1973), p. 131.

²¹ See W.P. Barrett, "Matthew Prior's 'Alma'," *MLR* 27 (October 1932): 454-58.

²² See Monroe K. Spears, "Some Ethical Aspects of Matthew Prior's Poetry," *SP* 45 (1948): 606-29.

[23] *Prior Papers,* p. 39.

[24] See Monroe K. Spears, "The Meaning of Matthew Prior's 'Alma'," *ELH* 13 (1946): 266-90.

[25] "Things Relative to Myself About and after the Treaty of Ryswick," cited in Bickley, p. 85.

[26] W.J. Courthope, *A History of English Poetry,* 6 vols. (London: Macmillan, 1911), 5:28. For a negative view of Prior's panegyrics, see Mack, p. 82.

[27] My understanding of "fiction" as "something we know does not exist, but which helps us to make sense of and to move in the world" comes from Frank Kermode, *The Sense of an Ending* (London and New York: Oxford Univ. Press, 1966), p. 37. For the absence of unifying patterns in Prior's political verse see Rower, "Matthew Prior," p. 96.

[28] See Ronald Eugene Rower, "Pastoral Wars: Matthew Prior's Poems to Cloe," *Ball State University Forum* 19 (Spring 1978):3 9-49.

[29] For suggestions concerning the relationship between life and thought in Prior's prose dialogues, see John Higby, "Ideas and Art in Prior's Dialogues of the Dead," *Enlightenment Essays* 5 (Summer 1974): 62-69.

[30] For discussion see Spears, "Some Ethical Aspects of Matthew Prior's Poetry," cited above. Spears does not mention "The Turtle and the Sparrow."

Nicolas H. Nelson (essay date 1992)

SOURCE: "The English Horace in Defense of Literature: Matthew Prior's Early Satires," in *Papers on Language & Literature,* Vol. 28, No. 1, Winter, 1992, pp. 19-37.

[*In the following essay, Nelson traces the development of Prior's satires, which began as expressions of personal invective and evolved into more considered satiric commentary on human types rather than specific individuals and often included elements of self-deprecation.*]

By the early eighteenth century, Matthew Prior had already acquired the title of the "English Horace" because of his evident attraction to the great Latin poet of antiquity and occasional imitation of his work (Goad 90).[1] Since that time, this identification has generally been accepted without qualification, so that Prior's poetry is still commonly described in Horatian terms, as being easy, elegant, and urbane. George Sherburn perhaps best summarizes this approach to Prior the poet in *The Literary History of England,* where he

claims that Prior "became perhaps the ideal neo-classicist, writing with both lightness and a noble urbanity, with elegant ease and a deft and imaginative use of classical patterns, yet he captured the mood and felicity of both Horace and Anacreon" (909). While this is not an inaccurate description of some of Prior's verse, we do a disservice to Prior if we fail to recognize another side to him and his poetry, a side that can scarcely be subsumed under the rubric of "elegant ease." His early satires, on the contrary, reveal a poet with a much stronger, more caustic voice than is usually acknowledged. This mode of invective, however, is soon complicated by other tones and voices. Prior's growth as a satirist shows him developing a sophistication and complexity that lead to the fine poems of his middle and later years.

Prior began his career in the early 1680s in quite a different tradition from that of Horace. Rochester, Oldham, the Earl of Dorset (Prior's patron), Dryden, and others were circulating or publishing satires characterized by a freedom and vehemence that have rarely been equalled (Lord 107-08). Instead of the restrained and elegant mode, we find a bold, slashing, and occasionally passionate voice, at least in Prior's satires, which has more to do with Juvenal than Horace.[2] Lampoon and invective were commonplace among the greatest writers of the time, so it is natural that a young man who wanted to make a name for himself should write in the same vein. The decade of the 1680s was, of course, a tumultuous one, with the country verging on civil war at its outset and undergoing a revolution at its end. Politics and religion were divisive subjects, and the poetry of the time reflects this explosive atmosphere. Although Prior is not particularly political, his poetry is colored by his connection with the Earl of Dorset and his later allegiance to William III. Any account of Prior's poetic career must deal with his beginning in the punitive satiric mode popular at the time, a mode that was inevitably tied to the social conflict that split the country. Even as a young poet, we will see, he was not afraid to name names and to make cutting personal attacks.[3]

His first satires were written in 1685 while he was still an undergraduate at Cambridge. One of these, **"A Satyr on the Modern Translators,"** was sent in a letter to Dr. Humphrey Gower, who was then Master of St. John's College, Cambridge, where Prior was a student. Prior's purpose, he declares in his letter, is to

> let our translators know that Rome and Athens are our territories; that our Laureate might in good manners have left the version of Latin authors to those who had the happiness to understand them; that we accuse not others, but defend ourselves, and would only shew that these corruptions of our tongue proceed from him [Dryden] and his tribe, which he unjustly casts upon the clergy.
>
> (Prior 2: 823)[4]

The occasion that prompted Prior's poem was the publication of three volumes of classical translations and English poetry gathered by Dryden and Jacob Tonson from 1680-85.[5] Prior believed that the Poet Laureate and other translators were stepping outside their literary expertise to the detriment of English letters. He lashes out at the distortions and errors of these translations, rejecting Dryden's theory of paraphrase and refusing to be intimidated by the reputation and social standing of the translators. For his epigraph Prior takes a line from Horace's *Epistles, "Odi imitatores servum pecus"* 'O you mimics, you slavish herd,' (1.19.19) with the *Odi* apparently added by Prior to clarify the anger behind the line. Responding to criticism of his poetry that it was warmed-over Greek imitation, Horace fired the charge back at his critics. Occasionally, Horace himself was not very "Horatian." Prior picked up this lead, however, and amplified it in his own satire.

Prior opens his attack with a satiric account of the reasons for the appearance of these miscellanies. The unification of the theaters, he declares, has thrown some writers out of work, so they desperately need a new source of income:

> Those who with nine months toil had spoil'd
>   a Play,
> In hopes of Eating at a full Third day,
> Justly despairing longer to sustain
> A craving Stomach from an empty Brain,
> Have left Stage-practice, chang'd their old
>   Vocations,
> Atoning for bad Plays, with worse transla-
>   tions. . . .
>
>   (1:19; 7-12)

Dryden particularly is singled out for some scathing remarks on his versions of the Latin poems:

> When *Virgil's* height is lost, when *Ovid*
>   soars,
> And in Heroics *Canace* deplores
> Her Follies, louder than her Father roars,
> I'd let him take *Almanzor* for his Theme;
> In lofty Verse make *Maximin* blaspheme,
> Or sing in softer Airs St. Katherine's Dream . . .
> But when not satisfy'd with Spoils at home,
> The Pyrate wou'd to foreign Borders roam;
> May he still split on some unlucky Coast,
> And have his Works, or Dictionary lost;
> That he may know what *Roman* Authors
>   mean,
> No more than does our blind Translatress
>   *Behn*.
>
>   (59-64; 73-78)

Prior's chief concern here, as in some later satires, is with the despoiling of the classics, the violation of

their sense and style merely to serve the mercenary purposes of the modern poets. His metaphor of the pirate is especially apt and effective. In the last line of the passage above, Prior uses Dryden's own statement in the Preface to *Ovid's Epistles* that Aphra Behn "understood not Latine . . ." (Prior 2: 824, n.78) to underscore the ignorance of these interlopers.

Dryden's collaborators in these translations come in for some equally harsh treatment. The Earl of Mulgrave, Thomas Rymer, Thomas Creech, John Ogilby, and Behn all are assailed for their gross errors, inaccuracies, and absurdities in rendering the Latin authors. Despite his title and eminence, Mulgrave is depicted as a totally inept translator, dependent on the already ridiculed Dryden for his language and ideas:

> My Lord I thought so generous would prove,
> To scorn a Rival in affairs of Love:
> But well he knew his teeming pangs were
>   vain,
> Till Midwife *Dryden* eas'd his labouring
>   Brain;
> And that when part of *Hudibras's* Horse
> Jogg'd on, the other would not hang an Arse;
> So when fleet *Jowler* hears the joyfull halloo,
> He drags his sluggish Mate, and *Tray* must
>   follow.
> But how could this learn'd brace employ their
>   time?
> One construed sure, while th'other pump'd for
>   Rhime. . . .
>
>   (31-40)

Prior's combination of literary and animal imagery effectively reduces these prominent writers to foolish adventurers who have strayed outside their proper field of expertise. No wonder that Prior later disavowed all connection with this poem, as well as his **"Satyr upon Poets,"** when he had become a friend of Mulgraveand somewhat reconciled to Dryden (Prior 2: 823). As for "painfull" Creech, whose 1682 version of Lucretius had been widely admired, Prior suggests that he would have done better not to have continued his translating efforts:

> Had he stopt here—But ruin'd by Success,
> With a new Spawn he fill'd the burthen'd
>   Press,
> Till, as his Volumes swell'd, his Fame grew
>   less.
> So Merchants flattered with increasing Gain,
> Still tempt the falshood of the doubtfull Main;
> So the first running of the lucky Dice,
> Does eager Bully to new Bets intice;
> Till fortune urges him to be undone,
> And *Ames-Ace* loses what kind *Sixes* wone.
>
>   (125-33)

Likening Creech to both a greedy merchant and a gambling fool, Prior maintains the theme of mercenary motives driving these writers to fields of endeavor beyond their abilities. Prior's heroic couplet, although not a match for Butler's octosyllable for learned farce and rhyming ridicule, is nevertheless an effective vehicle for embodying his satiric purpose. For a young man, Prior's command over his verse form and his imagery is quite remarkable. But, most of all, his gift for a bold, slashing, and serious satire is already apparent.[6]

In another poem of the same year, this one sent to Francis Turner, Bishop of Ely, Prior adopts the "advice-to-the-painter" form common in the time to use for political satire. Here he comments on the short-lived 1685 rebellion against James II led by the Duke of Monmouth and the Earl of Argyle.[7] Using this "advice" format, Marvell and others had vigorously attacked the regime of Charles II, but Prior employs the form here not only to defend the monarchy from the aggressions of a pretender but also to defend the integrity of art. His weapon is satire, of course, less strident and more sophisticated than most previous "painter" poems, but still displaying an interesting sympathy for the rebel. He describes in detail the new portrait of the Duke and his activities that should be painted to replace the old one that was given to the university when Monmouth became chancellor of Cambridge in 1674. The first portrait had been ordered burned by university authorities after Monmouth led the invasion to depose James II. Prior reserves his harshest attacks for Monmouth's allies and associates, such as Robert Ferguson, a dissenting minister who served as chaplain to the rebel army and whom Prior char-acterizes as "The Wretch that hates (like his Arguile) the Crown, / The Wretch that (like our Oates) defames the Gown . . ." (1:9; 43-44). Ferguson, Prior suggests, is a sinister figure whose malignant hatred of the principal English institutions is comparable to that of one of the most infamous men of his time, Titus Oates.

Another of Monmouth's associates whom Prior attacks is Forde Grey, Baron Grey of Werk, who was commander of the rebel cavalry at Sedgemoor, where they suffered their final defeat. Grey's cowardice at the battle comes in for some scathing remarks:

> Then near the Pageant Prince, (alass! too
>   nigh,)
> Draw Gray with a Romantic constancy,
> "Resolv'd to conquer or resolv'd to—
>   fly."
> And let there in his guilty Face appear
> The Rebel's malice and the Cowards fear,
> That future ages in thy Piece may see,
> Not his Wife falser to his bed, then to his
>   party He.
>
>   (49-55)

Not only did he betray his friends at the battle, he later betrayed them to the government at the trial of the rebels. Prior treats him with deserved contempt and sarcasm. In addition, Prior berates the city of Taunton for welcoming Monmouth to England and aiding him in the early stages of the rebellion, he lashes out against Holland's support for the rebels, and he ridicules the Duke's army itself, which was urged into battle by Ferguson's zealous rhetoric:

> Excited thus by their Camp-preist's long
>   prayer,
> Their Countries curses, and their own despair,
> Whilst Hell combines with it's black offspring
>   night,
> To hide their Treach'ry, or Secure their flight,
> The watchfull Troops with cruell hast come
>   on,
> Then shout, look terrible, discharge, and run.
>
>   (65-70)

Such a portrait as Prior recommends will obviously use much stronger colors than the original, but mainly black.

Prior's attack on the Duke, on the other hand, is muted, like Dryden's in *Absalom and Achitophel*. Monmouth is, he suggests, a "misled, aspiring, wretched Man" (13), whose "Pride and Sorrow" (92) struggle for supremacy in his divided heart. The Duke is thus "the great, pittied, stubborn Traytour" (90), whose family grieves at his refusal to accept clerical offers of grace if he would only recant. The poem closes with an admonition to the painter not to employ the full resources of his art to evoke compassion for Monmouth, since he might very well succeed:

> Now close the dismal Scene, conceal the
>   rest—
> —That the sad Orphan's Eyes can teach us
>   best,
> Thy guilty Art might raise our ill-plac'd grief
>   too high
> And make us whilst We pitty Him, forgett our
>   Loyalty.
>
>   (111-14)

Such a mixed portrait of this pretender to the throne probably reflects the continuing popularity of the Duke even after his execution for treason. Prior shows that he can easily and skillfully modulate from the harshly satiric to the pathetic in his verse when he wishes. Here partisanship and invective are momentarily transcended by a broader sympathy, a trait that few political poems of the time displayed. His brief foray into political poetry thus reveals the approach that guided much of the rest of his career: strong support for the established power structure, a powerful attack on opponents of the government, and yet a recognition of the valuable qualities that may exist in certain in-dividual antagonists. Rather than being radical or subversive, Prior's personal and public satire expresses clearly and directly the feelings that many of his countrymen must have shared. His central premise is that art, like literature, must tell the exact truth about its subject and not succumb to partisan passion.

In Prior's next satire, the **"Satyr upon the Poets"** (probably written in the spring of 1687), he imitates, very loosely, the first ninety-seven lines of Juvenal's seventh satire, which he expands into 218.[8] It seems likely that Prior was attracted to this poem because of Juvenal's concern with the wretched state of the arts in Rome in his time. Like Juvenal, Prior deals with the failure of the patronage system and the subsequent hardship for serious writers. Unlike Juvenal, Prior focuses exclusively on the fate of creative writers in his time; the Latin poet ranges more broadly over professional writers as a class, from historians to rhetoricians.[9] His imitation, if we can call it that, significantly alters the targets of the ridicule to include incompetent and mercenary poets as well as patrons. There is, then, little specific interplay between Prior's satire and Juvenal's, other than the theme of neglect and misery among writers.

The treatment of patrons by the two poets is also quite different. Although he begins with the possibility that the emperor may lend his support, Juvenal dwells at length on the impossibility of any intelligent private patronage. He suggests not only that the current nobility scorn writers, but that they will do anything to avoid having to give support to the poets, including writing poetry themselves. As a result, writers are forced either into a penurious independence, which makes great art impossible, or into a debased relationship that requires them to flatter their masters' absurd works. Prior, in contrast, opens his poem by addressing his patron, the Earl of Dorset, in very personal and complimentary terms:

> All my Endeavours, all my Hopes depend
> On you, the Orphans, and the Muses Friend:
> The only great good Man, who will declare
> Virtue, and Verse the Objects of your Care,
> And prove a Patron in the worst of times. . . .
>
> (1:28; 1-5)

More than conventional praise, these lines establish that the ideal can be a reality, when the right person is involved. Juvenal briefly mentions Maecenas, the Roman patron who took care of Horace and Virgil, but he makes clear that such wise benevolence has long since been abandoned. At the end of his poem Prior returns to address his Maecenas, thanking Dorset for his help and acknowledging his great personal debt to him: "for O! to you / My Song, my Thought, my very Soul is due" (206-07). Juvenal, on the other hand, never re-

turns to the possibility that Caesar may prove to be a munificent patron, concluding his poem with the portrait of a harassed, ill-respected schoolteacher, who will be lucky to make as much from a pupil in one year as a jockey will in a single race. Dorset thus serves to mitigate the Juvenalian satire on English society that Prior sets forth, though it is also clear that one lone man cannot make up for the general indifference.

In the body of the poem Prior follows Juvenal more closely when he inveighs against the failure of patronage in his time. His chief example is the Earl of Mulgrave, one of those eminent persons who should be a patron, but who has become a poet himself and expects praise from his dependents. He

> Damns the dull Poems of the Scribling Town,
> Applauds your Writing, and Esteems his own:
> Whil'st thou in Complaisance oblig'd must sit
> To extol his Judgment, and admire his Wit;
> And wrapt with his Essay on Poetry,
> Swear *Horace* writ not half so strong as he,
> But that we're partial to Antiquity.
>
> (91-97)

Such vanity and hypocrisy are destructive of any fruitful relationship and thus of any great writing, which requires material and psychological support, freely offered and sensitively given. Juvenal emphasized that great poetry is impossible in poverty: "When Horace cried 'Rejoice' / His stomach was comfortably full" (165). But the best way to ensure that you have a full stomach, he suggests, is to please the most powerful people behind the throne—certain actors, dancers, and other crowd-pleasers. In England the worst example of public neglect that Prior cites is Thomas Otway. At one time Otway had been much appreciated, but neglect caused his death from "slow starvation" just two years before Prior was writing (Prior 2:830). His lines on Otway are a powerful indictment:

> There was a time When *Otway* Charm'd the Stage;
> *Otway* the Hope, the Sorrow of our Age!
> When the full Pitt with pleas'd attention hung,
> Wrap'd with each Accent from *Castalio's* Tongue:
> With what a Laughter was his Soldier read!
> How Mourn'd they, when his *Jaffier* Struck and Bled!
> Yet this best Poet, tho with so much ease,
> He never drew his pen, but sure to please . . .
> He had of's many Wants, much earlier dy'd,
> Had not kind Banker *Betterton* supply'd. . . .
>
> (155-62; 165-66)

Such a passage as this, without precedent in Juvenal, reveals Prior at his best in a generous tribute to a contemporary poet and playwright. No more dramatic example of the failure of the patronage system need be offered than this, yet Otway's fate creates a pathos that significantly complicates the tone of the satire.

Most of the poem is invective, as Prior ridicules some of his fellow poets, who, he suggests, are not really poets in any case and should not expect public support. Some of these are prominent:

> *Shadwell* and starving *Tate* I scorn to Name;
> Poets of all Religions are the same:
> Recanting *Settle,* brings the tuneful Ware,
> Which wiser *Smithfield* damn'd to *Sturbridge*
>   Fair:
> Protests his Tragedies and Lybels fail
> To yield him Paper, penny Loaves and Ale;
> And bids our Youth, by his Example fly
> The love of Politicks, and Poetry.
>
> (10-17)

These are partisan poets who have involved themselves in a variety of causes and made their art subservient to their politics, religion, or self-interest. They would do better to appeal directly to a popular audience with ballads, songs, shows, and salves to be sold on the street. Their end is sad to contemplate: old age and infirmities, poverty, loneliness, and a bitter death. No comparable passage appears in Juvenal's poem, yet this is surely central to Prior's concern: poets themselves must share the blame for their unhappy condition, since they have sold their literary labors to the highest bidder and compromised their integrity. Prior's "imitation" of Juvenal's seventh satire, in sum, becomes a substantially original poem that reflects his own continuing concerns and values. He may "confuse" us somewhat in his mixture of praise and blame for poets, public, and patrons (Kupersmith 138), but at the same time he reveals his skill at writing both vigorous personal satire and forceful invective against the state of the arts in England.

Up to this point Prior's satires had all remained in manuscript,though they had probably circulated among his friends and acquaintances. In the summer of 1687, however, the first published work that brought him public attention appeared, ***The Hind and the Panther Transvers'd,*** a satire written in collaboration with his friend Charles Montagu.[10] This work was, of course, another attack on Dryden, who had published an allegorical defense of his conversion to Roman Catholicism shortly before. With their work Prior and Montagu established themselves as rising young wits with a taste for sharp ridicule. To launch their attack they adopted an already popular burlesque of Dryden, *The Rehearsal,* with the characters Bayes (Dryden), and Johnson and Smith (spokesmen for the authors). In addition, Prior and Montagu employ Horace's fable of the country mouse and the city mouse, recently imitated by Abraham Cowley, to parody the beast fable form that Dryden had used for his allegory. According to

Earl Miner, this satire was the "best-known and least polemical" (Dryden 3: 327) of the various attacks on the Poet Laureate after the publication of *The Hind and the Panther.* According to tradition, Dryden wept to see how two young writers treated him after he had been "civil" to them (Winn 428).

In ***The Hind and the Panther Transvers'd*** Bayes greets his old friends in a hostile manner, shunning their invitation to share a pint with them because of his new faith. Indeed, Bayes prepares to draw his sword if Johnson and Smith appear antagonistic toward his new religion. They are, naturally, confounded by his aggressiveness, but calm his fears and urge him to join them for the sake of old times. So he does, and after describing his new outlook, Bayes brings out a story he has recently written to explain and defend his conversion. It is based on Horace's fable, but it goes, he declares, far beyond anything Horace did:

> Now whereas *Horace* keeps to the dry naked
>   story, I
> have more copiousness than to do that, I'gad.
>   Here, I
> draw you general *Characters,* and describe all
>   the
> *beasts* of the *Creation;* there, I launch out into
> long *Digressions,* and leave my *Mice* for
>   twenty
> Pages together; then I fall into *Raptures,* and
> make the finest *Soliloquies,* as would ravish
>   you.
>
> (1:39; 79-84)

With his enormous ego and his tricks of speech like "I'gad," this Bayes does indeed sound like the central character in *The Rehearsal.* He also loves to point out his own poetic conceits, such as the line *"Was least deform'd because Reform'd the least,"* of which he declares: "There's *De* and *Re* as good I'gad as ever was" (320-21). His pride in silly wordplay is matched by his desire to explain the obvious (cf. 441-43), by his inability to catch the irony directed at him by his friends (as in 252), and by his egregious delight in the power and point of his religious allegory. Dryden could not help but be hurt by an attack that treated hisvery personal "confession of faith" (Fujimura 407) with such sarcasm and mockery.

The first four lines of Bayes's poem about the mice, which parody Dryden's famous opening lines, effectively establish the diminished level of discourse common in Restoration satire:

> *A milk-white* Mouse *immortal and unchang'd,*
> *Fed on soft Cheese, and o're the* Dairy *rang'd;*
> *Without, unspotted; innocent within,*
> *She fear'd no danger, for she knew no* Ginn.
>
> (90-93)

When Johnson remarks that "soft Cheese is a little too coarse Diet for an *immortal Mouse*" (94-95), Bayes admits that he should have found more ethereal food to give his divine creature, but he "could not readily find it in the Original,"—that is, Homer—thus exposing his ignorance of Greek. At the same time, these lines implicate Dryden's tendency to treat his mice as both real and divine or allegorical, a fault Prior and Montagu particularly deplore. In their Preface to *The Hind and the Panther Transvers'd,* they ridicule Dryden's *"new way of telling a story, and confounding the* Moral *and the* Fable *together"* (Prior 1: 36), so that the story alternates between the two levels without coherence. Another example occurs when Bayes has his mice eat their way out of the back of a hackney coach, so they won't have to pay the fare. Smith comments that a Templar would not normally be able to do this, but Bayes replies that these are, after all, mice. Much of Prior and Montagu's satire, then, is directed at Dryden's failure to create a proper fable rather than at his moral or spiritual failures.

In their parody Prior and Montagu often follow Dryden's verse closely, italicizing those words they actually quote from his poem and altering others to bring out an absurdity or contradiction. Skillful compression or expansion enables them to reduce Dryden's complex narrative to ridiculous simplicity. A typical example occurs when the two parodists imitate Dryden's version of the creation and fall of man. In his fable Dryden tries to justify James's recent shift to a policy of toleration for Dissenters and Catholics, so he identifies mercy as a central ingredient in the human mind, along with reason. The Creator he portrays as a blacksmith:

> The Smith divine, as with a careless beat,
> Struck out the mute creation at a heat:
> But, when arriv'd at last to humane race,
> The god-head took a deep consid'ring space:
> And, to distinguish man from all the rest,
> Unlock'd the sacred treasures of his breast:
> And mercy mix'd with reason did impart;
> One to his head, the other to his heart:
> Reason to rule, but mercy to forgive:
> The first is law, the last prerogative.
>
> (3:130; 253-62)[11]

At the same time, Dryden depicts God as a baker, who molds humanity from clay, adding some milk to soften the mixture so that humans will find satisfaction in being "kind as kings upon their coronation day" (271):

> Thus kneaded up with milk, the new made
>   man
> His kingdom o'er his kindred world began:
> Till knowledge misapply'd, misunderstood,
> And pride of Empire sour'd his balmy bloud.
>
> (274-77)

Picking up these images, Prior and Montagu collapse them into one incoherent one:

> But he work'd hard to Hammer out our Souls,
> He blew the Bellows, and stir'd up the Coals;
> Long time he thought and could not on a
>   sudden
> *Knead up with* unskim'd *Milk* this Reas'ning
>   Pudding:
> Tender, and mild within its Bag it lay
> *Confessing still the softness of its Clay,*
> And kind as Milk-Maids on their Wedding-
>   Day.
>
> (281-87)

The mixed metaphor of the passage, the change in human makeup from clay to pudding, and the absurd picture of the original fetus all contribute to the wonderful farce of the parody. Prior and Montagu continue their mockery by extrapolating these images into human history to identify where we eventually went wrong:

> Till *Pride of Empire, Lust,* and hot Desire
> Did over-boile him, like too great a Fire,
> And, understanding grown, *misunderstood,*
> Burn'd Him to th'Pot, and sour'd his curdled
>   Blood.
>
> (288-91)

Dryden's serious argument is thereby reduced to a ridiculous culinary blunder, by extending the original metaphors to their nonsensical, if literal, consequences. While James's policy of toleration is called into question, the central thrust of the attack is Dryden's lack of command over his medium, his failure as a poet.

Furthermore, Prior and Montagu ridicule Bayes's pride in the *"Majestick turn of Heroick Poesy"* (405), which he claims to have given his poem, echoing Dryden's own words in his preface (3:122).They mock Bayes's use of language when he tries to distinguish between "doomed" and "fated." Bayes claims, anticipating Humpty-Dumpty, that he can use words as he wants since he is their boss: "sure I that made the Word, know best what I meant by it" (112-13). Prior and Montagu further suggest that Dryden sets himself up as literary dictator or poetic Pope, allowing no one to question his judgment (526-36). They burlesque Dryden's simile of tradition as a staircase, which, they suggest, sends their wits soaring as they climb up the stairs to the coffee house (571-80). Bayes's taste for the morality found in "the *delectable History of Reynard the Fox*" is parodied along with his difficulty in understanding Milton's poetry, so "that a Man must sweat to read Him" (391-92). *The Hind and the Panther Transvers'd,* then, is serious literary satire, carried out with precision and wit, and its notable achievement did not go un-recognized.

Two other poems culminate Prior's early satiric phase. The first, **"A Session of the Poets"** (most of it probably written in 1688), takes up a popular poetic genre, the "sessions" poem, to comment on the literary scene. Following an earlier poem by Rochester, Prior imagines Apollo reviewing various candidates for the office of Poet Laureate, which James II must fill because, the poet declares, he has replaced so many of his other ministers. Each candidate appears before the god to argue his case, with Dryden leading the way by defending his record for having written well and often in support of the king. Apollo dismisses his claim:

> They that set you at work let 'em e'en pay
>   you for't.
> Whats Religion to Us, tis well known that
>   many
> Have manag'd the Place well without having
>   Any.
>
> (1:63; 15-17)

Other claimants offer their credentials, from Sir Francis Fane and his plays, to Edmund Waller, Aphra Behn, Thomas Shadwell, and the other writers Prior had already attacked. Most of them, like Elkanah Settle, are simply insulted or sneered at by Apollo:

> With a bundle of Poetry Settle was there
> Some brought from the Play-House, and some
>   from the Fair.
> But Apollo assur'd him, He never wou'd
>   Chuse
> The Lawrel from such Demi Poets as those
> Who write Treason in Verse, and recant but in
>   Prose.
>
> (78-82)

As writers, some might be acceptable, like Waller or Sedley, but they are dismissed for other reasons—Waller for not having been punished because of his writing (like Dryden in the Rose Alley ambush) and Sedley for having an independent fortune. Rarely does Prior's poem rise above this kind of abuse or superior dismissal.

Perhaps the most interesting part of the poem is the introduction, where James II is compared to an aggressive player in a fashionable card game:

> Since the King like a venterous Gamster at
>   Loo
> Threw by his old Courtiers, and took in for
>   New
> Till by shuffling and drawing the cards were
>   so mix't

> That those which Won this deal were laid
>   aside next
> The Sons of the Muses began to repine
> That who e'er was turn'd out John Dryden
>   kept in
> So, Numerous and Noisy to Phoebus they
>   came
> To ask why of All the Knaves he shou'd be
>   Pam.
>
> (1-8)

Politics continues to disturb the literary scene; but other than these lines, imaginative railing is scarcely employed and the poem breaks off as one more group of writers comes on stage to be reviewed by Apollo. Prior never finished the poem and never published it, with good reason; but it demonstrates his serious concern about literature at this time of social and political turmoil and his condemnation of both individual writers and partisan conflict. Perhaps his failure in this poem arises from his inability to find an object of pathos or praise in the situation that would enable him to transcend a genre not especially suited to him.

Another poem, **"Epistle, to Lord—"** (probably written in 1687 to Lord Dorset in response to Dorset's praise of *The Hind and the Panther Transvers'd*), reveals a striking shift in Prior's approach to satire: it deals with types rather than individuals and incorporates self-irony into the satiric texture. Prior opens with traditional praise of Dorset's comprehensive genius and goodness. Not only is Dorset generous, noble, and the leading poet of his day "since great Strephons death" (7), but he is also a genuinely good man with "A real Judgment, and a Solid Mind / Expert to use these blessings in their kind, / As Prudence dictates, and as God design'd" (1:57; 13-15). Dorset has been given great gifts and knows how to use them, Prior declares, thus establishing his central theme that one's life should focus on fulfilling special powers or aptitudes.

The rest of the poem is taken up with the failure of this ideal. Prior takes his theme from Horace's *Epistles* 1:14 that all people have at least one good quality or talent in their lives (the faculty of reason, artistic powers, martial prowess), but few know how to use it wisely or effectively, generally hoping to shine in other ways or inappropriate fields. As Prior puts it, "Not that Men want, but use their parts amiss" (47). He surveys a broad spectrum of types who exemplify this failing, from the sailor who tries to become a "Spark" to the peaceful youth who parades around the city with a long sword analyzing military defeats as if he were an expert. One of the major examples of such a misguided desire is the poetic translator who chooses the most difficult work possible to show his skill, but with only ludicrous results:

No Ancient Piece, much harder than the rest,
That by Translation scorns to be exprest,
But all those People who to Phillis chime,
And make *admiring* and *desiring* Rhime,
With Emu'lous Labour turn and tumble it,
And heads forthwith are scratch'd, and nailes
 are bitt.

          (52-57)

The awkward last line of this passage comically mocks the poor poet struggling to find ways of expressing the complex original, but only emerging with the banal and commonplace, if indeed with anything. Prior thus returns to the theme of mistranslation that occupied him previously in his **"Satyr upon Translators"**; but unlike the earlier poem, only two real names appear in this poem, Pulton and Higden, minor writers whose brief mention sets off the general satire of the rest. Moreover, the tone of the attack here is significantly different from previous satires, whose punitive force has turned into an amused acceptance at the foolishness of flawed human nature.[12]

The most unusual and interesting parts of the poem, very briefly introduced but nevertheless striking, are those where Prior turns the satire back on himself. The first instance occurs with reference to writers who pretend to be more than they really are:

Is there another, with such moderate Sence
It just suffices not to give offence?
Tis odds but he shal Print his Poetry,
Tho such perhaps as *Higden* writes or I. . . .

          (85-88)

Though only a passing remark, such self-deprecation is not very convincing. The ending of the poem provides a more effective and authentic example of this new note:

I met [a] Youth, and truly, far from spight,
Told him his Tallent never was to fight—
He frown'd, and said, *"Nor yours perhaps to
Write!"*

          (134-36)

As the poem's conclusion this self-mockery offers a dramatic shift in Prior's normal satiric mode, away from the sharp and sometimes vitriolic abuse found in his other satires. Prior clearly owes this new note to Horace, but the contrast with his other satires shows how unusual the self-deprecating mode is for him.

Our "English Horace," then, emerges as much less Horatian in his early satires than we might expect, given his reputation. From the Restoration mode of invective, Prior moved to more complex and varied approaches that he eventually developed into such poems as **"Paulo Purganti and His Wife," "Jinny the Just,"** and ***Alma.*** Early in his career, however, writing in the shadow of Rochester, Dryden, and Oldham, Prior's targets were specific, often eminent individuals whom he treats with contempt and derision. In light of Prior's own precarious station in life, his boldness in engaging and challenging some of the finest satirists of the time is impressive. As tone and mode vary from one work to the next, evolving (though not in a strict linear fashion) toward a mixed and balanced complexity, one theme remains constant: the deplorable state of literature in his time.

Prior was not completely happy with invective, perhaps because it was not suitable to his own poetic genius, and perhaps because the temper of the nation was changing as well. Whatever the cause, Prior moved toward a less aggressive satire, gradually incorporating more pathos, praise, or bemused tolerance. Nevertheless, even in his later poetry Prior often includes a sharp bite or cutting thrust that surely owes something to his earlier interest and skill in using the poetic lash.

Notes

[1] Goad, however, believes that Prior's Horatian qualities are less than Addison's; Prior, she believes, lacks Horace's "depth of feeling" and "breadth of vision" (97).

[2] The importance of Juvenal as a model for the Restoration satirist has been thoroughly documented by Howard Weinbrot in chapter 1 of *Pope.*

[3] The statement that Prior's "characteristic mode of poetic address" is "panegyric" (Williams 438) seems quite off the mark, especially for his early poetry where punitive satire plays an important role.

[4] All citations of Prior's poetry and prose are from the standard edition of his works by Wright and Spears. I am much indebted to their excellent annotations. The first reference to each work gives volume, page, and line numbers; subsequent references cite only lines.

[5] These volumes include *Ovid's Epistles* (1680), *Miscellany Poems* (1684), and *Sylvae* (1685). Prior naturally singled Dryden out because the Poet Laureate wrote prefaces to two of these volumes (*Ovid's Epistles* and *Sylvae*) and included a number of his own English poems and translations. Raman Selden shows that Dryden's "liberal" theory of translation, which he outlined in the preface to *Ovid's Epistles,* was not universally accepted at the time and that a more literalist view had its proponents ("Juvenal" 481). Dryden himself freely admitted that he had significantly altered the original in his versions: "I have both added and omitted, and even sometimes very boldly made such expositions of my Authors, as no Dutch commen-

tator will forgive me" (*Works* 3: 3-4). Dryden's editors have noted these frequent changes, including the occasional additions of lines that have no basis in the Latin (see, e.g. *Works* 1: 338-39). Thus, there is some factual basis for Prior's attack.

[6] The few critics, however, who have commented on Prior's early satires do not find much to praise. Rachel Trickett declares that these poems do "not reflect much credit on him" and that he seemed to have a "vicious dislike of Dryden" (142). Eric Rothstein, more plausibly, finds in Prior's work "a good sample of volleys in the continuing paper war that marks the period . . ." (181). Frances Mayhew Rippy finds the "Satyr on the modern Translators" harsh and "somewhat uncivil" (70), while crediting the "Satyr on the Poets" with an attack on England that exposes some of the "social ills underlying individual faults" (71). William Kupersmith judges the "Satyr on Poets" to be "both a poor imitation of Juvenal's seventh satire and unattractive as an original poem" because Prior attempts "to write satire and panegyric simultaneously . . ." (138).

[7] Monmouth led a small invasion force to England from Holland, landing at Lyme Regis on 11 June 1685. He was captured after his army was defeated at Sedgemoor on July 6 and executed on July 15. "Archibald Campbell, ninth Earl of Argyle, unsuccessfully attempted to rally Scotland to Monmouth's standard in May, and was taken prisoner on 18 June. He was executed on 1 July" (Prior 2: 818).

[8] Brooks, Weinbrot (*Formal Strain*), and Kupersmith discuss the relevant background for the imitation, which became a distinct genre in the Restoration. Brooks suggests that "it was by Oldham that Thomas Wood, Henry Higden, and Matthew Prior were inspired in writing four imitations of Juvenal published between 1683 and 1694" (137-38), and notes that Prior in his "Satyr upon the Poets" quotes Oldham's imitation of Juvenal's seventh satire, thus following his lead. Kupersmith, more accurately I believe, comments that Prior's poem is a "very free adaptation with no real attempt at keeping a running parallel between the original and the Imitation . . ." and that it "reminds one of Rochester and Scroope rather than of Oldham and Wood, whose stricter and more sophisticated technique gives the reader the additional pleasure of seeing the interplay between the original and the Imitation" (133). Prior, I believe, creates his own voice and sets forth his own personal themes.

[9] Not long before Prior, John Oldham had done a version of this satire using the ghost of Spenser to deplore the wretched conditionin which poets were forced to live by public neglect and indifference. Spenser was the classic exemplar of the neglected poet, and his ghost cites the similar cases of Cowley, Waller, and Butler that occurred in the Restoration. Spenser concludes his diatribe against the contemporary world

by acknowledging that he will undoubtedly never convince Oldham to give up his devotion to poetry and that Oldham will no doubt end up in misery. It is a very bleak vision with even less hope than Juvenal found in Rome, where the new emperor (Hadrian) appeared to be ready to offer some support to the arts. Prior offers comparatively more hope, since he has a patron who supports letters wisely and generously. Still, the picture Prior paints of his society is largely negative.

[10] Prior had previously published a few Latin and English poems, but they had not attracted any particular notice.

[11] All references to Dryden's *Works* are to the California edition. The first reference to each work gives volume, page, and line numbers; subsequent references cite only lines.

[12] Such milder satire was typical of the epistle, as Howard Weinbrot points out in *The Formal Strain* (93).

Works Cited

Brooks, Harold F. "The 'Imitation' in English Poetry, Especially in Formal Satire, before the Age of Pope." *Review of English Studies* 25 (1949): 124-40.

Dryden, John. *The Works of John Dryden.* Vol. 1: *Poems 1649-1680.* Ed. Edward Niles Hooker et al. Berkeley: U of California P, 1956. Vol. 3: *Poems 1685-1692.* Ed. Earl Miner et al. Berkeley: U of California P, 1969.

Fujimura, Thomas H. "The Personal Drama of John Dryden's *The Hind and the Panther.*" *PMLA* 87 (May 1972): 406-16.

Goad, Caroline. *Horace in the English Literature of the Eighteenth Century.* New Haven: Yale UP, 1918.

Horace. *Horace: Satires, Epistles and 'Ars Poetica.'* Trans. H. Rushton Fairclough. Loeb Classical Library. Cambridge: Harvard UP, 1961.

Juvenal. *The Sixteen Satires.* Trans. Peter Green. Rev. ed. Harmondsworth: Penguin, 1974.

Kupersmith, William. *Roman Satirists in Seventeenth-Century England.* Lincoln: U of Nebraska P, 1985.

Lord, George deForest. *Classical Presences in Seventeenth-Century English Poetry.* New Haven: Yale UP, 1987.

Prior, Matthew. *The Literary Works of Matthew Prior.* Ed. H. Bunker Wright and Monroe K. Spears. 2nd ed. 2 vols. Oxford: Clarendon P, 1971.

Rippy, Frances Mayhew. *Matthew Prior*. Boston: Twayne, 1986.

Rothstein, Eric. *Restoration and Eighteenth-Century Poetry 1660-1780*. Routledge History of English Poetry 3. Boston: Routledge, 1981.

Selden, Raman. *English Verse Satire 1590-1765*. London: Allen & Unwin, 1985.

————. "Juvenal and Restoration Modes of Translation." *Modern Language Review* 68 (1973): 481-93.

Sherburn, George. "Restoration and Eighteenth-Century Literature." *A Literary History of England*. Ed. Albert C. Baugh. New York: Appleton, 1948. 699-1108.

Trickett, Rachel. *The Honest Muse: A Study in Augustan Verse*. Oxford: Clarendon P, 1967.

Weinbrot, Howard D. *Alexander Pope and the Traditions of Formal Verse Satire*. Princeton: Princeton UP, 1982.

————. *The Formal Strain: Studies in Augustan Imitation and Satire*. Chicago: U of Chicago P, 1969.

Williams, Arthur S. "Making 'Intrest and freedom agree': Matthew Prior and the Ethics of Funeral Elegy." *SEL* 29 (1989): 431-45.

Winn, James Anderson. *John Dryden and His World*. New Haven: Yale UP, 1987.

Linda E. Merians (essay date 1992)

SOURCE: "Matthew Prior's Correspondence," in *Studies on Voltaire and the Eighteenth Century*, Vol. 304, 1992, pp. 932-33.

[*In the following essay, Merians contends that Prior deliberately adopted a style of letter-writing incorporating metaphor and persona. She also explores possible personal, professional, and political reasons for Prior's deliberate adoption of this mode of correspondence.*]

The purpose of my paper is to demonstrate how Matthew Prior used his public and private correspondence to become the last English poet-courtier who successfully promoted and maintained himself by linking his poetry and his political friendships. Past commentators on Prior's letters have not regarded them as (literary) documents that could shed light on his poetry, and as a result have dismissed them as simple letters of flattery written by a struggling young diplomat. This approach is wrong-headed because it fails to take into account how Prior deliberately devised literary strategies in his letters that would help him to gain the favour of the noblemen in the court of King William III. Unlike any of his contemporaries in similar circumstances, Prior managed to solve the dilemma faced by any ambitious but unconnected young diplomatist: how could he write formal letters and dispatches which would satisfy his professional obligations but would also be familiar enough to win him the friends and patrons he so desperately needed without being branded an impertinent flatterer?

The first decade of Prior's professional career, from 1690 to 1700, was spent overseas, when he served as secretary to the English envoy at The Hague, secretary of the embassy at The Hague, secretary to the English plenipotentiaries at the Ryswick peace treaty negotiations, and secretary of the English embassy in Paris. As a secretary, Prior was, of course, expected to be a consistent and skilful writer. He realised, however, that dry and precise prose would not on its own win him the friends he sought nor would it bring him any special recognition from the monarch. It took him just a couple of years to discover an appropriate style for his official correspondence, one that would lend his letters a tone and pace usually reserved for familiar letters.

In order to achieve an 'easy' tone in his letters, Prior looked to his light occasional verse as opposed to his heavy panegyrics. From them he adapted his use of metaphor in such a way as to allow distinct *personae* to emerge in his letters. Each *persona* was shaped and determined by his relationship with the particular man to whom he was writing, and thus every letter communicated a sense and a context of their relationship. Prior's self-serving hope was that his noblemen 'friends' would not fail to do him the service that an aristocrat could easily deny a social inferior. On a parallel level of meaning, the use of *personae* also helped Prior to create a partially fictive appearance, one that was not necessarily restrained by the history of the personal relationship or by social protocol. Thus, Prior did not have to employ the hyperbolic language that other courtiers were bound to use. Indeed, in this regard Prior's letters have a unique style and sound. His strategy was a daring one, but it succeeded far more often than it failed. By 1697 Prior was held in high estimation by King William and most, if not all, of his important counsellors, and as a result he received the choicest appointments available to men of his rank and experience.

Over the course of his career, Prior, like anyone, had periods of triumph and failure, and his letters and literary works record these moments. An interesting pattern emerges if we look at the totality of his correspondence, which amounts to over 3000 letters written to or by him between 1685 and 1721. We see that Prior consistently employed metaphor and *persona* in his letters, which suggests that he was quite aware of its beneficial effect, and that an extraordinarily high percentage of his correspondents were enchanted and entertained by his somewhat unorthodox style of letter-writing. All this is to say that Prior's letters helped to bring him what he hoped they would; that is, when he died in 1721 he was rich and (in)famous.

Those of us who are students of eighteenth-century British literature know that the assuming of *personae* (for example, Mr Spectator, Isaac Bickerstaffe, and Martinus Scriblerus) and the assigning of *personae* (for example, Cibber as the Prince of Dulness) was a particular trait of Restoration and early eighteenth-century writers. Whether devised to increase one's personal stature or to offer political satire, the *personae* often show the author at his or her inventive best. Unlike writers who preceded or succeeded them, English Augustan writers enjoyed experimenting with the idea of 'selves', knowing full well that their pens afforded them a flexibility that the rest of British society did not have. On paper they could be anybody they wanted to be. Indeed, as Prior's letters show, in his case the mask made the man.

H. Bunker Wright and Deborah Kempf Wright (essay date 1992)

SOURCE: "An Autobiographical Ballad by Matthew Prior," in *The British Library Journal,* Vol. 18, No. 2, Autumn, 1992, pp. 163-70.

[*In the following essay, Wright and Wright describe and discuss a previously unpublished ballad by Prior.*]

In the most recent edition of Prior's works, the editors asserted their confidence that, while Prior was a parliamentary prisoner, he composed a poem reflecting some of the circumstances of his confinement and his first acquaintance with Elizabeth Cox, the mistress of his later years.[1] However, the only vestige of such a poem known to the editors was a set of nine untitled stanzas that Joseph Moser had contributed to *The European Magazine* in 1803.[2] Since Moser explained that the poem had come to him through its recitation by a relative who had learned it from Prior when she was a child, and since he confessed that he could 'only recollect a few verses . . . , and those perhaps not quite correct', the editors were obliged to relegate this fragment to a place among 'works of doubtful authenticity'.[3]

This situation is now, however, remedied by the discovery in the British Library of a text of undoubted authenticity, which extends the poem from nine to eighteen stanzas. This manuscript, Harl. 6907, has for over two hundred years rested unrecognized among the papers the British Museum acquired at its founding from the heirs of Edward Harley, second Earl of Oxford. It is a fair copy in the hand of Prior's secretary, Adrian Drift, who together with Harley was co-executor of the poet's will. Both before and after Prior's death in 1721, Drift was occupied in making copies of Prior's works which constitute a large portion of the Prior papers that went to Harley in accordance with that will. The presence, therefore, of Drift's transcript of this poem among the manuscripts that belonged to Harley justifies its unconditional acceptance into Prior's works and its publication here in its fullest expanded form, only half of which has previously been printed, and that from a defective text.

A principal reason for this manuscript's having been heretofore overlooked is that it was preserved with the antiquarian collection purchased for the British Museum in 1753, not a likely location for such a ballad to appear. On the contrary, one would have expected to find it with the private papers of the Harley family that included the largest body of manuscripts of Prior's literary works. These were not sold to the Museum, but were transferred to Bulstrode by Harley's daughter, the Duchess of Portland, whence many of them were later taken to Longleat House by his granddaughter.[4]

Having arrived at the Museum in an unlikely collection, the five unbound leaves of the ballad then passed through hands that gave them so little attention they not only failed to recognize Drift's distinctive hand, they also missed the identification of the speaker as 'Mr: P . . . r' and the date '1715' as relating the situation of the speaker to Prior's circumstances in that year. As a consequence, the manuscript was catalogued anonymously as 'A few Sheets containing a Ballad, made in 1715'.[5] Then its obscurity was rendered more secure by its being bound into a slim volume in which it is preceded by two other short manuscripts entirely unrelated to it: Harl. MSS. 393 and 4659.

In order to fit Harl. 6907 into this small quarto binding, the first three sheets have been folded up from the bottom and then in from the right side; the fourth sheet has been cut off at the bottom and folded in from the side; the fifth sheet (blank) has been cut off at both bottom and side. When unfolded, to what appears to be the original size, each of the first three leaves makes a folio leaf of high-quality paper bearing the watermark of 'A RIBERONNE'. The poem is inscribed on the rectos of the first four leaves, their versos and both pages of the fifth leaf being left blank. The folio numbers 1, 2, 3, 4 have been pencilled in by a later hand.

At the top of the first page are several library identification numbers, including the Harleian MS. number '6907' and three numbers of uncertain origin: two press marks (probably Harley's) '161.A.8' and '\m?\A' and what appears to be an early item number '126'. With the exception of the numerals of either foreign or uncertain origin, all the writing in Harl. 6907, from the title to the final flourish, was unmistakably inscribed by Adrian Drift in his most formal italic hand, the hand he regularly used for creating a calligraphic fair copy of a written text. It shows no corrections or erasures, with a possible exception in the last stanza; and there is nothing to identify the manuscript from which the secretary was copying. It could have been a Prior holograph that he asked Drift to copy for presentation to Robert Harley, or one that Drift found after the poet's death and copied for Edward Harley. There is even the possibility that Drift's copytext was not derived from any manuscript written by Prior, but from a recorded memory of Prior's recitation of the verses—either Drift's own memory or someone else's. Even if that is all Drift had, his text of the poem carries greater authority than Moser's second-hand recollection because Drift set it down at least sixty-seven years closer to Prior's lifetime.[6]

The date '1715' on the first page of Drift's manuscript is so placed it may have been intended not as a part of the title but as a dating of the situation described in the ballad and perhaps of its composition as well. When Prior returned to England in 1715 after years in Paris, he found that the Whigs, who had come into power after the death of Queen Anne and the downfall of the Tories, who were responsible for the peace with France, condemned him and the Tories for achieving the Treaty of Utrecht. In particular, the Secret Committee of the Parliament was eager to impeach and convict the Earl of Oxford for being a traitor to the nation. The Committee sought to squeeze from Prior evidence of the Tories' having acted in a way favourable to the French. Its failure to obtain such evidence caused it to order Prior's parliamentary confinement without any specific charge. The Serjeant at Arms, Thomas Wybergh, was to arrange for him to remain captive in a private house under observation by John Hollingshead. The only freedom allowed Prior during this period, 9 June 1715 to 26 June 1716, was the privilege of evening walks in the company of Wybergh.[7] It is his confinement and his evening privileges that the two texts of the ballad describe.[8]

According to Harl. 6907, this poem is entitled **'A Ballad, To the Tune of a Begging we will go'**.[9] To indicate the refrain, Drift has simply written 'And a begging &cª' at the end of each stanza. Moser's version, however, plays variations, chiefly between 'I' and 'you', on the lines 'Since a prisoner I must lie, must lie; / Since a prisoner I must lie'. These lines would, of course, be sung to the tune of 'A Begging We Will Go'; and they serve as a constant reminder of the poet's unhappy situation. The essential elements of that situation are delineated in the nine-stanza version of the poem. The house where Prior is detained is in Brownlow Street; its owner is 'witty Jack' (John Hollingshead). Prior wastes the mornings of his imprisonment in sleep, but studies his books all afternoon. The Serjeant at Arms arrives at night; and when he has no news of Prior's hoped-for release, they repair to Betty Cox's tavern where Prior can wash away his grief. At the inn greetings are exchanged, drinks are prepared, one final drink is demanded so that a toast can be drunk to Nan, and payment of the bill is deferred until tomorrow when Betty will call on Prior at home, where she is sure to find him 'Since a prisoner you must lie, must lie; / Since a prisoner you must lie'.

The fuller text expands the poem in several ways, while maintaining the basic structure and chronology of the shorter version. Five of the additional stanzas are middle stanzas which elaborate the scene at the tavern. Stanza three describes the occasional walk in the fields, apparently the fields around St. Giles's Church in which parish the house in Brownlow Street was located.[10] It also laments the absence of Nannet. Nannet and the poet's confinement from her are mentioned in stanza one as well, which provides a suitable opening for the poem, summarizing the narrator's plight and establishing the context for the remaining verses. The references to Nannet, as she is also called in stanza fourteen, are important in clarifying the identity of the woman. Moser mistakenly identified the 'Nan' of his version as Queen Anne. H. Bunker Wright has already argued that she must have been Anne Durham, who preceded Betty Cox as Prior's mistress.[11] The additional references to Nannet, describing the poet's sense of personal grief that he cannot be with her, substantiate that view.

The fuller version's stanza four, corresponding with Moser's stanza two, clarifies a point often misunderstood. Both versions have the Serjeant coming at night, but Moser's line 'When home the Sergeant comes at night' tends to confuse the Serjeant with Hollingshead. Drift's transcript does not have the reference to 'home'; and although his line is irregular in metre (as are other lines in both texts), it maintains the verifiable distinction between 'witty Jack' Hollingshead and the Serjeant, Wybergh.

The remaining two new stanzas are the last stanzas of the poem. They continue Betty Cox's farewell to her 'Friend'. The penultimate stanza is important first for its ironic jab at Lord Coningsby, an especially unfriendly member of the Secret Committee who declared Prior's confinement to be necessary 'for the Safety of the Nation'.[12] This stanza is important, secondly, for its hope for 'a Speedy Prorogation'. It was the prorogation of Parliament on 26 June 1716 that finally brought about Prior's release.[13] The poem concludes, then, with Betty's admonition, 'Pray never seek a Wife'. The reader, with hindsight, sees the irony of the warning, coming as it does from the woman who would be Prior's last mistress and who, being widowed about one month before Prior's death, apparently was ambitious to be his wife.[14] Prior's own fearful attitude toward marriage may be reflected here; and he may enjoy the irony of having a woman, married herself, take the long-suffering man's view of the situation. However we interpret that aspect of the last stanza, the stanza provides one final intriguing question in the line 'The Serjeant has You for a Year'. The term of Prior's confinement, not specified at its imposition, was just over one year when the prorogation of Parliament ended it. Does the reference to 'a Year' in the custody of the Serjeant at Arms indicate that Prior wrote this poem in 1716, after his release; or is 'Year' merely a good rhyme for 'Clear' and, coincidentally, accurate as well? The poem is written from the perspective of the prisoner, not the released man; and it seems likely that composition occurred over the entire period of Prior's confinement. Whether he continued to work on it after his release it is impossible to say, but we do know that he did not think enough of the ballad to include it in his *Poems on Several Occasions* (1718). A product of imprisonment and no doubt boredom, it chronicles a period of his life that perhaps he came to feel was not worth celebrating. We, however, can be grateful for the ballad's survival, especially in the fuller version in Harl. 6907, precisely because it does celebrate that pivotal time.

Drift's Text

A Ballad. (1715.)
To the Tune of a Begging we will go.

That, I'm an humble Pris'ner
  You in my Song will find,
From house and home, & Man & Maid,
  And from Nannet Confind.
    And a begging &c:ª

The Serjeant took me by the back,
  And high for Brownloe Street;
There to Converse with witty Jack,
  And with his Spouse so sweet.
    And a begging &cª

Sometimes we Walk into the Fields
  To take a little Air,
But what care I what Nature yields
  If Nannet is not there.
    And a begging &cª

I lye Abed all Morning,
  'Till five on Books I muse,
The Serjeant comes at Night
  But, Gods-bud, he knows no News.
    And a begging &cª

No News say I, why what a pox
  Must I lie here for ever?
Then let Us go to Betty C. .
  And wash Grief from our Liver.
    And a begging &cª

Here here let Martha light You,
  Will, Will, make up the Fire:
Your Servant Mrs: Betty,
  Your Servant Mr: P . . . r.
    And a begging &cª

See here, sweet Madam C. ., I add,
  How low my Hatt I move,
What not One Curtzey to be had
  For Mony nor for Love.
    And a begging &cª

Says She, pshaw pshaw, to such as You
  My Knee it never bends,
Curtseys to Customers are due,
  And You are only Friends.
    And a begging &cª:

She spoils the Fire with such a Grace,
  Who can her Charms withstand,
With a little pritty smudl'd face,
  And a Poker in her Hand.
    And a begging &cª:

And now, She says, To-night at Ten
  Ye all to bed shal go.
Betty, my Child, what dost thou mean
  Thou'lt say so till tis Two.
    And a Begging &cª:

But our Cares go to the Devil;
  And we begin to live,
When the smiling slender Sybill,
  Takes her Pitcher, and her Sieve.
    And a begging &cª:

To make the Drink that chears our breast
  The Mystic Drugs are chosen,
The least of Lemmons are the Best,
  And Eleven make the Dosen.
    And a begging &cª.

We neither Scale nor Measure try
  To make our Mixture right,
The mingling Goddess has an Eye
  As just as it is bright,
    And a begging &cª

Go, Betty, make the t'other Bowl
  It is not Midnight yet,
Nay, nay, I'll have it by my Soul
  For We have not drank Nannet.
    And a begging &cª:

Now, Bess, the Reck'ning must be paid
   Else thou must beg or borrow,
Leave that To-night, the Gypsy said,
   I'll call on You To-Morrow.
      And a begging &cᵃ

But tell Me pritty Neighbor
   At what a Clock You'l come,
Said She, what need I name the Hour
   You'l be all-day at Home.
      And a begging &cᵃ

'Till Noon, I know, in Bed you lye
   (God save this happy Nation)
Praying for good Lord Coningsby,
   And a Speedy Prorogation.
      And a begging &cᵃ

Now good, Sir, hear when once Y'are Clear
   Pray never seek a Wife,
The Serjeant has You for a Year,
   She takes You in for Life
      And a begging &cᵃ:

Moser's Text

   The Sergeant tapp'd me on the back,
      Then hie for Brownlow-street;
   There to converse with witty Jack,
      And with his spouse so sweet:
   Since a prisoner I must lie, must lie;
      Since a prisoner I must lie.

                 . . . . .

   We doze away the morn so bright,
      From noon on books we muse:
   When home the Sergeant comes at night,
      Ads'bud he brings no news!
   So a prisoner I must lie, must lie;
      So a prisoner I must lie.

   No news! I cry! Why? What the pox,
      Must I stay here for ever?
   Do let me go to Betty Cox,
      And wash grief from my liver,
   Since a prisoner I must lie, must lie;
      Since a prisoner I must lie.

                 . . . . .

                 . . . . .

   Here light the candles, Hetty,
      And, William, stir the fire:
   Your servant, Mistress Betty:
      I am yours, Mr. Prior!
   Tho' a prisoner you must lie, must lie;
      Tho' a prisoner you must lie.

   When I attempt to ope the bar,
      My hat I humbly move.
   With scorn she cries, "You come not here
      For money nor for love,"
   Since a prisoner you must lie, must lie;
      Since a prisoner you must lie.

   To make the bowl that cheers the heart
      The choicest drugs are chosen:
   "Little lemons are most tart,"
      And eleven to the dozen!
   Since a prisoner I must lie, must lie;
      Since a prisoner I must lie.

                 . . . . .

   Come, Betty, fill another bowl.
      "Lard, Sir! the watch is set!"
   Nay! nay, I'll have it, by my soul!
      I have not drank *Nan* yet:
   Since a prisoner I must lie, must lie;
      Since a prisoner I must lie.

   So now the reck'ning must be paid,
      I must either *tick* or borrow.
   "No matter, Sir," the Gypsey said,
      "I'll call on you to morrow!
   Since a prisoner you must lie, must lie;
      Since a prisoner you must lie."

   But tell me, pretty neighbour,
      At what o'clock you'll come?
   "I cannot lose my labour,
      "You'll be all day *at home,*"
   Since a prisoner you must lie, must lie;
      Since a prisoner you must lie.

Notes

¹ H. Bunker Wright and Monroe K. Spears (eds.), *The Literary Works of Matthew Prior* (Oxford, 1971), pp. 1071-2.

² 'Vestiges, Collected and Recollected', xliii, pp. 9-13.

³ *Literary Works,* pp. 785-6. Moser's text had previously been reprinted under the title 'Song in Prison' in R. B. Johnson (ed.), *The Poetical Works of Matthew Prior,* vol. ii (London, 1892), p. 384, together with Moser's unreliable annotations. The credibility of Moser's account of the oral transmission of the stanzas is discussed in H. Bunker Wright, 'Matthew Prior's Cloe and Lisetta', *Modern Philology,* xxxvi (Aug. 1938), pp. 17-19.

⁴ In due course, the Bulstrode papers went to Welbeck Abbey and then, in the mid-twentieth century, to the British Museum as the Portland Loan (Loan 29). In 1987 ownership was transferred to the British Library,

and the papers became the Portland Papers (Add MSS. 70001-70523). The papers that went to Longleat House remain there in the possession of the Marquess of Bath.

5 *A Catalogue of the Harleian Manuscripts in the British Museum,* vol. iii (1808), p. 447.

6 Drift died in 1737 according to J. L. Chester (ed.), *The Marriage, Baptismal, and Burial Registers of the Abbey of St. Peter, Westminster* (1876), p. 348.

7 *Calendar of Treasury Papers, 1714-1719* (1883; repr. 1974), pp.374-5, 454. For Prior's own account of his examination by the Secret Committee, see *The History of His Own Time,* 2nd ed. (London, 1740), pp. 416-35.

8 We display transcripts of both texts side by side, with parallel stanzas opposite each other in the double-column format. Where Moser indicated gaps in *his* recollection with rows of asterisks, we include those asterisks.

9 This tune was a popular ballad setting during Prior's lifetime. See W. Chappell (ed.), *Popular Music of the Olden Time,* vol. i (London, n.d.), pp. 345-7.

10 Wright, 'Prior's Cloe and Lisetta', p. 17 n. 45.

11 Ibid., p. 18.

12 Prior, *History of His Own Time,* p. 435.

13 *Calendar of Treasury Papers, 1714-1719,* pp. 374-5, 454.

14 Wright, 'Prior's Cloe and Lisetta', pp. 15-16.

Nicolas H. Nelson (essay date 1993)

SOURCE: "Narrative Transformations: Prior's Art of the Tale," in *Studies in Philology,* Vol. XC, No. 4, Fall, 1993, pp. 442-61.

[*In the following essay, Nelson examines four of Prior's verse tales, comparing them to their sources, and explains how their adaptations benefitted from Prior's "refinements in narrator, theme, and characterization."*]

In 1968 Bertrand Bronson published an imaginative dialogue between Matthew Prior and Samuel Johnson called "On Choosing Fit Subjects for Verse; or, Who Now Reads Prior?"[1] In their discussion Prior blames Johnson for his low current reputation as a writer, suggesting that it has never recovered from some of Johnson's statements in the *Lives of the Poets.* Johnson, on the other hand, defends himself by recalling several of his original comments in which he praised Prior's

poetry, particularly the tales. These, he noted, were significant achievements, despite the existence in them of some "improprieties," which detract from such narratives as **"Hans Carvel," "The Ladle,"** and **"Paulo Purganti and his Wife,"** though without seriously undermining their literary value. Johnson singles out **"Protogenes and Apelles"** for special praise, declaring that it is the "one most unexceptionably superior example of[Prior's] skill" in the tale, a form in which he says "you have seldom been equalled in our tongue, and seldom perhaps in any other."[2] Bronson then has Johnson identify the general qualities that distinguish these poems "in supreme degree: humor, sophistication, wit, and sociability." And he mentions the importance for Prior of a "small, homogeneous, literate society [which] was the indispensable condition for such a precarious and delicate balance as [Prior] contrived to sustain in these tales."[3] Thus, Bronson focuses our attention on the positive aspects of Johnson's discussion of Prior's poetry, with particular emphasis on his tales for which Prior was much admired in his own time.

With such appreciation as this from two eminent critics one might wonder why these tales have not been more discussed. Why, indeed, have they often been left out of the anthologies and ignored in discussions of eighteenth-century poetry?[4] Various causes are undoubtedly at work, but we must admit that the "improprieties" themselves have probably contributed to this neglect, though this would scarcely seem to be an objection a modern reader might raise. Prior is, perhaps, not extreme enough for our taste, offering as he does a smiling, witty, and often wry account of human foibles rather than a savage condemnation of human evil or a bleak look at a meaningless universe. The bawdy joke that furnishes the climax in two of these tales may diminish their impact and significance, but this does not negate the powers he displays in narrating his tales and in creating character, dialogue, and scene. Prior borrows some of his plot elements, to be sure, but he remakes his sources and generates his own themes and values. His revisions of his sources are quite thorough. In doing so he expands the role of the narrator in the story, increases the complexity of the characters and their interrelationships, and treats his human figures with an unusual combination, at least for the time, of satire and sympathy. Despite a relatively simple surface, then, the art of these tales is complex and multifaceted, and will repay a closer look than has hitherto been made. I shall concentrate on the four tales that Johnson identified as especially effective, but many of my remarks will apply to several of his other narrative poems, all of which, I believe, put him on a par with his better recognized contemporaries, Swift and Gay.

The earliest of these tales, **"Hans Carvel"** (1701), is in some respects the least attractive. Prior found it in

La Fontaine's *contes* in a rudimentary version and specifically noted its source in the title as **"Monsieur De la Fontaine's Hans Carvel, Imitated."** As the editors of Prior's works point out, "it is, however, a very free imitation, greatly expanded."[5] Prior was, of course, fluent in French, having lived in France as a diplomat for several years (1697-99), so he was quite familiar with its literature as well as some of the writers. He himself has been called the "English La Fontaine,"[6] though he imitates the French poet in only a very fewpoems; nevertheless, he has something of La Fontaine's gift for combining "seriousness and playfulness."[7] La Fontaine's tale, drawn from Rabelais, runs to only forty-eight lines. In it he recounts the conventional story of an old man who, foolishly, marries a beautiful young woman who is not about to curtail her worldly activities after her marriage. Hans, fearing for his forehead, attempts to convince her of the danger and even sinfulness of her ways, but to no avail. One night the devil appears to him in a dream and promises to solve his problem with a magic ring. All Hans has to do is wear this ring and his troubles are gone. When Hans awakes, he finds that his finger, is, as La Fontaine puts it, "où vous savez."[8]

Apart from the story itself, there is little additional characterization or description. Prior, on the other hand, expands both of these aspects of the tale and enriches its theme. He does this, in the first place, by portraying Hans's young wife in much greater detail. La Fontaine has little to say about her.[9] Prior, in contrast, creates a typical London coquette who is enthralled with shopping, sleeping late, dressing long, and attending the theater. She displays something of a philosophical bent, too, when she maintains that she is not responsible for anything she might do:

> She made it plain, that Human Passion
> Was order'd by Predestination;
> That, if weak Women went astray,
> Their Stars were more in Fault than They.

> (1:184; ll. 9-12)

The irony of her use of a form of Calvinistic justification for her actions, especially when she aligns it with the power of the stars, is obvious. In hoping to correct her behavior Hans gives her various moral and spiritual works, all of which

> Stood unmolested on the Shelf.
> An untouch'd Bible grac'd her Toilet:
> No fear that Thumb of Her's should spoil it.

> (ll. 58-60)

Like Pope's Belinda, her confusion of spiritual and worldly values is manifest. The pristine condition of the books and the words like "unmolested" and "grac'd"

that Prior employs to describe them comment ironically on the moral and spiritual quality of the young woman's behavior. A related quality is her love of the theater:

> Whole Tragedies She had by Heart;
> Enter'd into ROXANA's Part:
> To Triumph in her Rival's Blood,
> The Action certainly was good.
> How like a Vine young AMMON curl'd!
> Oh that dear Conqu'ror of the World!
> She pity'd BETTERTON in Age,
> That ridicul'd the God-like Rage.

> (ll. 13-20)

Her passionate, sensual nature is evident in her appreciation of this play and, in setting the action in London with Lee's *The Rival Queens* (1677), a popular play about the life and death of Alexander the Great, Prior creates a woman who takes on a more fully realized existence than in the French version, though still an obvious stereotype. Her empathy with Roxana, who murdered her rival Statira, and her obvious delight in Alexander's physical attraction, underscore her very worldly interests.[10] She does have an almost animal vitality that has a certain charm, like Chaucer's Alison, yet we also understand why her husband is worried.

Hans, too, is characterized more fully than in La Fontaine's version. Instead of the flat figure of the jealous elderly husband, Prior gives us a man who speaks to his wife in tones of distress, anger, bewilderment, and desperation. Hans urges her to reflect on the truisms of morality, such as

> The Comforts of a Pious Life:
> . . . how Transient Beauty was;
> That All must die, and Flesh was Grass:
> He bought Her Sermons, Psalms, and
>   Graces;
> And doubled down the useful Places.

> (ll. 48-52)

These commonplaces have no effect, of course, so Hans, confused and upset, has recourse to "Spells." The only remedy left, he decides, is to call on the devil for help. And he does this by rationalizing as his wife had for her own questionable activities. Prior's Hans, in contrast to La Fontaine's, absolves himself of any guilt in advance for what he is doing:

> Tis but to hinder something Worse.
> The End must justifie the Means:
> He only Sins who Ill intends:
> Since therefore 'tis to Combat Evil;
> 'Tis lawful to employ the Devil.

> (ll. 66-70)

As an example of special pleading this speech is a model of its kind. When the devil appears, he is contrasted with his description in the popular literature and superstitions of the time, the one used to frighten children into good behavior; this one, the narrator notes, seems "Like a grave Barrister at Law" (l. 78). In fact, Hans fails to recognize him, so Satan identifies himself. Their subsequent dialogue is a small masterpiece of wit and irony, a mockery of polite discourse. Hans begins by apologizing for not recognizing him:

> Sir, your Slave:
> I did not look upon your Feet:
> You'll pardon Me:—Ay, now I see't:
> And pray, Sir, when came You from Hell?
> Our Friends there, did You leave Them well?
> All well: but pr'ythee, honest HANS,
> (Says SATAN) leave your Complaisance:
> The Truth is this: I cannot stay
> Flaring in Sun-shine all the Day:
> For, *entre Nous,* We Hellish Sprites,
> Love more the Fresco of the Nights;
> And oft'ner our Receipts convey
> In Dreams, than any other Way.
>
> (ll. 82-94)

Here we are in the fashionable world of the eighteenth century listening to the conversation of two fine, if rather pretentious, gentlemen. No such scene occurs in La Fontaine. Satan's urgent desire to help and Hans's ridiculous acceptance of it are delightfully rendered. So, as the devil has instructed, Hans has a dinner party that night at which he drinks heavily and is eventually carried off to bed by his servants. His dream and the ensuing discovery of the nature of the "ring" complete his humiliation.

The role of the narrator in this poem is not as prominent as it becomes in Prior's later poems. He makes only a few asides and comments on the action and the characters. He cites a proverb (deftly altered to fit the poetic line) when Hans thinks of using Satan to straighten up his wife's behavior: "For name Him and He's always near" (l. 72). He offers a brief ironic remark when he describes Hans, asleep and snoring, and his wife in bed after the party:

> In Bed then view this happy Pair;
> And think how HYMEN Triumph'd there.
>
> (ll. 121-22)

In his later tales Prior more fully develops the narrator's function, where he uses him to introduce the story and occasionally to provide a moral for it. Here Prior remains relatively close to the point of the tales in his source; later he will significantly alter the theme, primarily through his narrator. **"Hans Carvel,"** then, is Prior's enriched version of a conventional tale enlivened with freshly imagined characters and some amusing dialogue, though such additions scarcely redeem the bawdy joke at the end.

"The Ladle" (1704), though similar to **"Hans"** in its ribaldry, offers some further refinements in narrator, theme, and characterization. The story is adapted from the familiar tale of Baucis and Philemon as found in Ovid's *Metamorphoses* (8.626-724) and recently translated by Dryden for his *Fables*. The pious but poor couple, it will be recalled, are rewarded for their goodness and hospitality by Jupiter and Mercury, who visit the earth incognito and find no one else willing to share their substance with them. Angered by the rudeness and lack of charity they have encountered among the rest of the population, the gods flood the earth, saving only the modest house of the old couple, which is then transformed into a temple with them as priests. Moreover, in accordance with their wishes, Baucis and Philemon are allowed to die at the same time so neither will outlive the other. This is a tale told in Ovid's poem by the worthy Lelex to demonstrate the power and justice of the gods and to rebuke the scoffing unbelief of Pirithous. Prior, however, uses only the general outline of this story of divine retribution, focusing less upon the kindness and humility of his old people than upon the nature of their wishes and the way these are expressed.[11] He also adapts the ending of the tale to one he apparently found in another source, Edmund Gayton's *Pleasant Notes upon Don Quixot* (1654),[12] in which the ladle plays a significant part. This creates another amusing ending, but the whole poem offers a good deal more than jest.

One of Prior's chief additions to the story is a prominent narrator who contributes a long prologue and a moral at the end. Although Samuel Johnson declared that the prologue was "neither necessary nor pleasing, neither grave nor merry,"[13] it does, nevertheless, focus our attention on the theme of the gods' visit and uses contemporary terms in which to discuss it, thus bringing the story into Prior's own world. The issue is the credibility of such divine visits to this world, as it appears to a sophisticated modern observer. The narrator begins,

> The Scepticks think, 'twas long ago,
> Since Gods came down *Incognito,*
> To see Who were Their Friends or Foes,
> And how our Actions fell or rose:
> That since They gave Things their Beginning;
> And set this Whirligig a Spinning;
> Supine They in their Heav'n remain,
> Exempt from Passion, and from Pain:
> And frankly leave us Human Elves,
> To cut and shuffle for our selves:
> To stand or walk, to rise or tumble,
> As Matter, and as Motion jumble.
>
> (1:202; ll. 1-12)

These skeptics clearly represent a version of the deists and their idea of a creator who was, for some of them at least, simply a passive observer of the human world. A debate was then raging in England over the deists and freethinkers, like Charles Blount, John Toland, and Anthony Collins, and their skeptical doctrines.[14] The narrator, of course, does not seriously enter this debate, but describes it from a mock-objective point of view, indicating that it is impossible to determine which side is right. He concludes that we may take whatever position pleases us, which, for the purposes of the story, will be that the gods do make such visits. The narrator's comments on the contentious nature of this dispute underscore its ridiculous side:

> These Points, I say, of Speculation
> (As 'twere to save or sink the Nation)
> Men idly learned will dispute,
> Assert, object, confirm, refute:
> Each mighty angry, mighty right,
> With equal Arms sustains the Fight;
> 'Till now no Umpire can agree 'em:
> So both draw off, and sing *Te Deum*.
>
> (ll. 37-44)

The narrator mocks such self-righteous, futile disputation as well as the role of the gods in protecting their mythological heroes in fashionable painters like Veronese and Caracci, whose large paintings, he playfully suggests (ll. 13-36), inflate the gods' power and care for their favorites on the earth.[15] Art is a subject that Prior introduces into several of his tales, here clearly treating poets and painters who create such grandiose works glorifying the classical gods with some irony.

The moral of the story given by the narrator at the end (and in the 1709 edition of Prior's poetry set off by italics) transforms the central theme.[16] In it the restless and generally misguided human quest for happiness becomes the focus, instead of Lelex's piety and the divine rewards for goodness. The narrator offers a penetrating critique of humanity's perennial desire to find ultimate satisfaction in more and more material or social goods, or whatever it is we believe we lack:

> This Commoner has Worth and Parts,
> Is prais'd for Arms, or lov'd for Arts:
> His Head achs for a Coronet:
> And Who is Bless'd that is not Great?
>   Some Sense, and more Estate, kind Heav'n
> To this well-lotted Peer has giv'n:
> What then? He must have Rule and Sway:
> And all is wrong, 'till He's in Play.
>   The Miser must make up his Plumb,
> And dares not touch the hoarded Sum:
> The sickly Dotard wants a Wife,
> To draw off his last Dregs of Life.
>
> (ll. 149-60)

From the upper classes to the lower, people create their own unhappiness through an insatiable need to discover the final answer to their search, the one thing needful to complete their felicity. This sounds Johnsonian, and a connection between the two writers has indeed been suggested.[17]

To build toward this idea Prior revised the story to give it a more contemporary, realistic dress. As in Ovid's tale, the gods arrive to find a farm where all seems well. The soil is prosperous, and the people are hospitable and industrious. Prior's gods, however, do not test the hospitality of their neighbors, nor, unlike the Ovidian originals, is his couple perfectly happy together. In fact, over the years they have experienced the usual domestic problems:

> The honest Farmer and his Wife,
> To Years declin'd from Prime of Life,
> Had struggl'd with the Marriage Noose;
> As almost ev'ry Couple does:
> Sometimes, My Plague! sometimes, My
>   Darling!
> Kissing to Day, to Morrow snarling;
> Jointly submitting to endure
> That Evil, which admits no Cure.
>
> (ll. 79-86)[18]

Using the half-line of the tetrameter couplet within which to focus the conflicts and contradictions of his ordinary humans, Prior plays off his realistic vision of marriage against the ideal one found in Ovid's tale. Such a jarring relationship, he implies, is inevitable within this human institution made up of imperfect beings. A stoical acceptance of our fate is the only solution.

Prior introduces further changes in the dinner the old couple prepare for the gods. Instead of dwelling at length on the homely fare they provide like Ovid, he depicts a more courtly and sophisticated scene, with less emphasis on its material nature.[19] The gods greet the old couple as if they were in fashionable society without, of course, any warrant in the original:

> Jove made his Leg, and kiss'd the Dame:
> Obsequious HERMES did the same.
> Jove kiss'd the Farmer's Wife, You say.
> He did—but in an honest way:
> Oh! not with half that Warmth and Life,
> With which He kiss'd AMPHITRYON's Wife.
>
> (ll. 99-104)

The incongruity of manner and setting is the source of much of the ironic humor along with the narrator's allusion to Jove's amorous liaison with Alcmena (which produced Hercules). Their conversation at the dinner is also a model of contemporary discussion of politics and social reform, as they "Fight o'er the Wars; reform the State: / A thousand knotty Points they clear" (ll. 96-97). Like the debate over the gods visiting the earth, such a discussion clearly leads nowhere. Although Prior loses some of the charm of Ovid's rustic meal and home in these alterations, he gains in keeping the narrator firmly in control and in maintaining a tone of playful irony. Prior's version, obviously, is quite a different poem from Ovid's.

Human folly dominates the ending of Prior's poem as he adapts the surprise that he found in Gayton and draws from it psychological and moral conclusions. After being received so kindly and hospitably, the gods give the couple three wishes for immediate fulfillment with no limitation on the content. The wife, after thanking the gods for their goodness, blurts out that she would like "A Ladle for our Silver Dish" (l. 135), exposing her thoughtlessness as well as her trivial and selfish materialism. The husband proves to be just as thoughtless, exclaiming in response to her foolish wish, that he would like to see the ladle "in [her] A[rse]" (l. 140). Both wishes are promptly fulfilled, so that the third must be used to remove the ladle. Such, Prior suggests, is the foolishness of human nature that, when it has happiness within its grasp, it will inevitably allow opportunity to go unrealized. The narrator draws the final moral then in the last ten lines of the poem, after detailing the various ways people let their obsessions rule their lives and bring about their own unhappiness:

> Against our Peace We arm our Will:
> Amidst our Plenty, *Something* still
> For Horses, Houses, Pictures, Planting,
> To Thee, to Me, to Him is wanting.
> That cruel *Something* unpossess'd
> Corrodes, and levens all the rest.
> That *Something,* if We could obtain,
> Would soon create a future Pain:
> And to the Coffin, From the Cradle,
> 'Tis all a WISH, and all a LADLE.
>
> (ll. 161-70)

The elegiac tone for the fatal flaw in human nature that creates "all our woe" raises the level of the poem beyond the simple jest to a serious plane that manages to incorporate the humor without negating it. Comedy, satire, and seriousness fuse to produce light verse that transforms itself into something weightier without losing all of its charm.

"Paulo Purganti and His Wife: An Honest, but a Simple Pair" (1708) treats one of Prior's favorite subjects, the life of a couple and, in particular, their sexual relationship. No specific source for this tale has been identified, though La Fontaine's "Le Calendrier des Vieillards" (*Contes*, II, 8)[20] provides some parallels. La Fontaine, however, focuses on the conventional theme of the foolish old man who takes a young wife without being able to satisfy her physical needs. The old man, a judge in Italy, uses the large number of holy days to excuse himself from his marriage duties, and says that most other days may be unlucky or unpropitious for such activities. After his wife is captured by a pirate and learns about physical pleasure from him, she refuses to return to her husband, who soon dies from heartbreak. Prior's plot is quite different, since his central figure is an eminent doctor who uses his medical knowledge to suggest that his wife must be ill and in a fever when her desire becomes too importunate. Of course he is unable to withstand his wife's assault and eventually must give in, despite all the learned and moral barriers he raises in his defense. Prior, thus, does not use the disparity in age theme or the religious pretext in his tale.[21] Its appeal comes from a greater exploration of character, particularly the woman's, as well as from a more original theme.

The doctor's wife is initially described as a very proper woman who has strong feelings about sexual virtue and propriety, both within marriage and without. She herself is chaste and faithful, and has little sympathy or tolerance for others' sins:

> On marry'd Men, that dare be bad,
> She thought no Mercy should be had;
> They should be hang'd, or starv'd, or
>   flead,
> Or serv'd like ROMISH Priests in SWEDE.—
> In short, all Lewdness She defy'd:
> And stiff was her Parochial Pride.
>
> Yet in an honest Way, the Dame
> Was a great Lover of That same;
> And could from Scripture take her Cue,
> That Husbands should give Wives their
>   Due.
>
> (1:261; ll. 47-56)

Without being a religious hypocrite the woman is still a striking and amusing anomaly because of the strength of her own sexual desire. Moreover, she supervises her husband's diet with great care, allowing him certain foods like "Oysters, Eggs, and Vermicelli" (65),[22] but denying anything like wine and coffee, which may, it is hinted, weaken his sexual appetite. The doctor, too, is individualized through his speech and his actions. When resisting his wife's advances, he proves a skillful actor:

> The Doctor feign'd a strange Surprise:
> He felt her Pulse: he view'd her Eyes:
> That beat too fast: These rowl'd too
>   quick:
> She was, He said, or would be Sick:
> He judg'd it absolutely good,

That She should purge and cleanse her
    Blood.

(ll. 103-8)

Again Prior effectively manages the half-line of the couplet to suggest the urgent pace of the speech and action of the increasingly desperate doctor. In order to fend off his wife whose persistence is remarkable, the doctor brings to bear the authority of his learning with scholastic seriousness:

He rang'd his Tropes, and preach'd up
    Patience;
Back'd his Opinion with Quotations,
Divines and Moralists; and run ye on
Quite thro' from SENECA to BUNYAN.

(ll. 138-41)

All is to no avail, naturally, in this unequal combat between the forces of nature and the eloquence of learning.

Once again Prior employs a narrator to enrich his tale. The first thirty-eight lines of the poem are his as he introduces the central concerns of the story. This prologue Samuel Johnson declared was "of more value than the Tale,"[23] probably because of the imaginative way in which Prior develops the ironic contrast between the "letter of the law" and the wife's sensual nature. He begins broadly philosophical:

Beyond the fix'd and settl'd Rules
Of Vice and Virtue in the Schools,
Beyond the Letter of the Law,
Which keeps our Men and Maids in Awe,
The better Sort should set before 'em
A Grace, a Manner, a Decorum;
Something, that gives their Acts a Light;
Makes 'em not only just, but bright.

(ll. 1-8)[24]

The narrator proceeds to take up the same question in painting as an analogy to general human conduct, comparing one who lacks such "Grace" to a painter who draws well and according to rule, but who lacks the "*Je ne scay quoy* of Beauty" (l. 26) that will give his work the distinction of great art.[25] In real life, the narrator declares, though the popular preachers may not expose or identify such "Error," it will be brought to light and punished by the satiric wits, such as Wycherley and Congreve. Prior thus links his own art to that of the Restoration comic dramatists, a connection that is clearly appropriate. In the course of the story, the narrator adds further asides and comments on the action, referring to various classic and modern writers from Plutarch to Bunyan. He particularly uses historians like Livy and Philippe de Commines to lend a mock-serious tone to the battle between the doctor and his wife.[26] He also cites two

contemporary doctors to support his view of his wife's disease:

For a Distemper of this Kind,
(BLACKMORE and HANS are of my Mind)
If once it youthful Blood infects,
And chiefly of the Female Sex;
Is scarce remov'd by Pill or Potion;
What-e'er might be our Doctor's Notion.

(ll. 113-18)[27]

Such comments not only bring the action into modern England, but also lend it a certain universality by giving it a pseudo-scientific aura. Finally, near the end of the poem, the narrator remarks in a self-conscious intrusion that he must not digress or prolong the action too much:

Reduce, my Muse, the wand'ring Song:
A Tale should never be too long.

(ll. 150-51)

Without the witty, learned narrator, this tale would lose much of its richness, humor, and significance. Through him, we are given an amusing account of a conventional stereotype, the sexually insatiable woman married to a good, but rather passive and limitedintellectual who finds it impossible to resist the advances of his wife. Prior's version thus constitutes a largely original treatment of a common theme.

The final tale to be considered here, **"Protogenes and Apelles,"** comes from another Latin source, Pliny's *Natural History* (XXXV, 36:81-83). Horace Walpole celebrated the superiority of Prior's version of this story of two Greek painters. Walpole declares that Prior reveals a superior artistic sensibility in comparison with Pliny's account of the rivalry "between two Dutch performers" (i.e., Protogenes and Apelles) who vie at drawing lines finer and straighter than the other. "But the English poet," Walpole asserts,

who could distinguish the emulation of genius from nice experiments about splitting hairs, took the story into his own hands, and in a less number of trials, and with bolder execution, comprehended the whole force of painting, and flung drawing, colouring, and the doctrine of light and shade into the noble contention of those two absolute masters.[28]

Prior's expansion of the story, as Walpole accurately notes, broadens its significance for art as well as for human behavior. In Pliny's account the two artists compete at drawing one line on top of the other to show how precise each can be. After Apelles draws the first, Protogenes adds a second line much finer and in a different color. Apelles, however, is able to put on a third line in another color, forcing Protogenes to admit defeat. Prior, on the other hand, has Apelles draw a circle at first as his signature to let the other artist know he is in Rhodes. Protogenes then, when he returns home, adds color and shade to the circle to give it solidity and texture. Apelles acknowledges his rival's great ability and proclaims their joint mastery of drawing and painting to the glory of "the Arts of GREECE!" (1:465; l. 84). Neither is said to have won the competition; both are masters in their field.

As usual, Prior employs a narrator to interpret his tale. In the prologue the narrator identifies the historical setting of the story in artistic terms as coming before the barbarity of "GOTHIC Forms" and "Monkish Rhimes / Had jangl'd their fantastic Chimes" (ll. 3-6—even while using rhyme, of course). This epoch was a kind of golden age of art "When Poets wrote, and Painters drew, / As Nature pointed out the View" (ll. 1-2). The specific Greek island where the action takes place provides the narrator with the occasion for another satiric aside. It is "on the flow'ry Lands of RHODES" where

> Those Knights had fix'd their dull Abodes,
> Who knew not much to paint or write,
> Nor car'd to pray, nor dar'd to fight.
>
> (ll. 7-10)

The Middle Ages thus provides a contrast to the civilization that came before it in Greece, and, by implication, to Prior's own age. These were the dark ages that cared not for the arts or even for the religion to which they were supposedly dedicated. From such comments we know that we are in the presence of a witty, sophisticated narrator. Occasionally he interjects a comment on the action of the poem, as he does when he describes the housemaid who answers Apelles's ring at Protogenes's door:

> If Young or Handsom, Yea or No,
> Concerns not Me, or Thee to know.
>
> (ll. 27-28)

Such an interruption, of course, reminds us of the very thing he pretends to want to dismiss. When the maid invites Apelles to return at tea time to see her master, the narrator anticipates an objection a skeptical reader might make:

> Tea, says a Critic big with Laughter,
> Was found some twenty Ages after:
> Authors, before they write, shou'd read:
> 'Tis very true; but We'll proceed.
>
> (ll. 45-48)

He notes the anachronism, but insouciantly dismisses its importance and proceeds with his story without bothering to argue in his own defense. At the conclusion, then, the narrator draws the moral. It is not what

one might expect:

> That the distinguish'd Part of Men,
> With Compass, Pencil, Sword, or Pen,
> Shou'd in Life's Visit leave their Name,
> In Characters, which may proclaim
> That They with Ardor strove to raise
> At once their Arts, and Countrey'sPraise:
> And in their Working took great Care,
> That all was Full, and Round, and Fair.
>
> (ll. 95-102)

Such a meaning is, of course, without precedent in Pliny. Prior leaves us with an image that not only echoes the circle Apelles drew and that Protogenes embellished, but also suggests the significance of personal fulfillment and self-realization in the arts as well as, more generally, in life. Thus, Prior's story takes on far broader implications than the original.

Perhaps the most interesting addition Prior makes to his source is in character development and interaction. The encounter between the maid or "Governante" and Apelles becomes the central focus of the action, not, as we might expect, the confrontation between the two artists. Protogenes only appears indirectly when the maid quotes his words to Apelles. She and the artist from Co (modern-day Kos) engage in a revealing and amusing interchange in which Prior conveys a remarkably rich sense of character and feeling in very few lines. When the maid tells Apelles that Protogenes is not at home, she reveals herself to be a wonderful combination of garrulity, politeness, and respectful modesty:

> I hope, Sir, You intend to stay,
> To see our VENUS: 'tis the Piece
> The most renown'd throughout all GREECE,
> So like th'Original, they say:
> But I have no great Skill that Way.
>
> (ll. 36-40)

Indeed, Prior puts a great deal more emphasis on her than is warranted either by his source or by the story itself. He seems to delight in drawing her portrait and dramatizing this encounter. When she takes the board with Apelles's circle on it to keep for her master to see, she promises,

> I shall not fail to tell my Master:
> And, Sir, for fear of all Disaster,
> I'll keep it my own self: Safe bind,
> Says the old Proverb, and Safe find.
> So, Sir, as sure as Key or Lock—
> Your Servant Sir—at Six a Clock.
>
> (ll. 61-66)

As a personality, she is as lively and interesting as the great artist Apelles, whose speech and behavior offer a subtle contrast with hers.[29] When she invites him to tea, he immediately accepts:

> Fair Maiden, yes:
> Reach me that Board. No sooner spoke
> But done. With one judicious Stroke,
> On the plain Ground APELLES drew
> A Circle regularly true:
> And will you please, Sweet-heart, said He,
> To shew your Master this from Me?
> By it He presently will know,
> How Painters write their names at CO.
>
> (ll. 50-58)

Concise, familiar, decisive, and proud, Apelles is a living character in his own right, speaking and acting in his own idiom and for his own motives. Prior's presentation of these mixed characters, who are neither perfect nor evil nor absurd, as they interact in an ordinary situation is a tribute to his literary powers as well as to his sympathetic understanding of common and uncommon people. In this brief encounter between artist and maid, man and woman, Prior renders, in almost gratuitous fashion with no larger point or purpose, a delicate and nuanced portrait of a modestly dramatic scene, where the interaction itself with its sparks of human feeling takes on greater import than the subject of their conversation. The two artists never actually meet in the poem or discuss their artistic theories other than indirectly through their sketches. Art, clearly, takes second place to human relationships. For a witty and sometimes sharp satirist, Prior often found in the undistinguished as well as the distinguished, and their intersection, a genuine source of interest, admiration, and amusement.

These tales are, of course, not the only poems in which Prior reveals his powers as a narrative poet, others, like **"Jinny the Just"** (1708) and **"An Epitaph"** (1718), having long been recognized as among his finest. But the four tales discussed here reveal most clearly several characteristic themes and techniques that came to be associated with his most appealing work: a sophisticated narrator who comments urbanely on the action, vivid characters who engage in amusing and revealing dialogues, and a broad tone of acceptance for the mixed condition of human life. He seems to have been an instinctively dramatic poet who loved to explore and expose the ordinary and commonplace behind the unusual. In addition, Prior transplants his borrowed stories into English society, playing with the clash of time or culture that results. He thus gives a contemporary English twist to a rich tradition drawn from the French, Italian, and Latin literatures that he knew well. Moreover, the poise between delight and ridicule, between amused tolerance and incisive exposure, that we find in Prior's later poetry reflects his growth toward a fuller appreciation for the complexity of human nature. The longer he wrote, the less

interested he was in stock characters and action, and the more concerned he came to be with depicting the amusing contradictions of human behavior without losing a sense of the intrinsic interest of even the most commonplace life. Prior, I believe, stands near the beginning of the spread of the democratizing spirit that increasingly empathized with common humanity. His poetry is not by any means revolutionary, but its wide-ranging sympathy for many people at different levels in society reflects some of that new spirit. It is a sympathy, however, that never loses its keen sense of realism. As a result, his wit, characters, dialogue, and reworking of older literature create a delightful narrative poetry that is worthy of our continuing attention and recognition. Samuel Johnson first noted Prior's achievement in the verse tale, and it would be our loss, as Bertrand Bronson implies, to ignore it.

Notes

[1] Published in *Facets of the Enlightenment: Studies in English Literature and Its Contexts* (Berkeley and Los Angeles: University of California Press, 1968), 26-44.

[2] Ibid., 43, 40.

[3] Ibid., 42. These points are not found in Johnson's discussion of Prior's tales in the *Lives of the Poets.*

[4] None of the four tales makes it into *The New Oxford Book of Eighteenth Century Verse,* ed. Roger Lonsdale (Oxford: Oxford University Press, 1984), nor does Margaret Doody discuss any of them in her excellent study *The Daring Muse: Augustan Poetry Reconsidered* (Cambridge: Cambridge University Press, 1985). A good many years ago John W. Draper surveyed eighteenth-century tales and mentioned Prior's work in this genre, citing "The Ladle" in particular as an example of concision in such narratives ("The Metrical Tale in Eighteenth-Century England," *PMLA* 52 [1937]: 396).

[5] H. Bunker Wright and Monroe K. Spears eds., *The Literary Works of Matthew Prior,* 2nd ed., 2 vols. (Oxford: Clarendon Press, 1971), 2:880. All quotations of Prior's poetry are taken from this edition, which will be cited hereafter as *Works.* The first reference to each poem gives volume, page, and line numbers; subsequent references cite only lines.

[6] Veronica Bassil, "The Faces of Griselda: Chaucer, Prior, and Richardson," *TSLL* 26 (Summer 1984): 162; see also, Charles K. Eves, *Matthew Prior: Poet and Diplomatist* (New York: Columbia University Press, 1939), 217.

[7] John C. Lapp, *The Esthetics of Negligence: La Fontaine's Contes* (Cambridge: Cambridge University Press, 1971), 172. Lapp does not think much of La

Fontaine's version of this story either, calling it "this rather unrewarding anecdote" (p. 137) taken from Rabelais.

8 La Fontaine, *Contes et Nouvelles,* ed. Edmond Pilon et Fernand Dauphin (Paris: Garnier Frères, 1958), 114.

9 La Fontaine merely says she is "du bon poil, ardente, et belle / Et propre à l'amoureux combat" (*Contes,* 113).

10 In the clinging ivy image Hans's wife echoes Statira's description of Alexander's sensual appeal:

> From every pore of him a perfume falls,
> He kisses softer than a southern wind,
> Curls like a vine, and touches like a god.
> (I.ii.42-44)

It is also true that *The Rival Queens* had by this time become the object of a good deal of mockery: "by the late 1690's most references [to the play] are humorous" (P. J. Vernon, Introduction to *The Rival Queens* [Lincoln: University of Nebraska Press, 1970], xvii). Accordingly, many of Prior's readers would undoubtedly have understood the humor in this ironic allusion.

11 Swift wrote another version of this story after Prior's, which may have influenced him. Pat Rogers believes that the "folk element in style and allusion [in Swift's poem] derives from Prior's free treatment of the same story in *The Ladle* (1704). Swift's opening lines answer directly to the start of *The Ladle*" (Jonathan Swift, *The Complete Poems* [New Haven and London: Yale University Press, 1983], 633). Swift's poem, however, is quite different from Prior's version, changing Ovid's story into a religious satire.

In his "Observations on Ovid's Metamorphoses," a collection of notes that Prior may have intended to form into an essay before his untimely death, he mentions the parallels between this story and the biblical story of Lot and the two angels (*Works* 1:666). In this regard Prior appears to have been following George Sandys's moralized commentary on the *Metamorphoses* (see *Ovid's 'Metamorphosis': Englished, Mythologized, and Represented in Figures,* ed. Karl K. Hulley and Stanley T. Vandersall [Lincoln: University of Nebraska Press, 1970], 393). From such a note we can see the seriousness with which Prior interpreted classical poetry, so we should not be surprised that his own can be serious as well.

12 Wright and Spears print the relevant passage from Gayton (*Works* 2:889).

13 *Lives of the Poets,* 2 vols., The World's Classics (London: Oxford University Press, 1906; repr. 1967), 2:14.

14 Dryden, the Boyle lecturers, and others had attacked the deists from the late seventeenth century, and the controversy ran well into the eighteenth century. Phillip Harth has called this debate the "longest and most heated religious controversy of the eighteenth century" (*Contexts of Dryden's Thought* [Chicago: University of Chicago Press, 1968], 61). Samuel Clarke, who was Boyle lecturer in 1704 and 1705, criticized the deists and Leibnitz in particular for advocating the notion that the universe was "a great machine, going on without the interposition of God, as a clock continues to go without the assistance of a clockmaker" (quoted by Franklin L. Baumer, *Religion and the Rise of Scepticism* [New York: Harcourt Brace, 1960], 86). Such a metaphor, Baumer notes, was "quite common in intellectual circles by the late seventeenth century" (79).

15 *Works* 1:203. Of course both Veronese and the Carracci (especially Annibale) were among the most admired painters of the time (see Jean H. Hagstrum, *The Sister Arts: The Tradition of Literary Pictorialism and English Poetry From Dryden to Gray* [Chicago: University of Chicago Press, 1958], 163-65). Prior himself had a small sketch by Veronese, and Pope included both these artists among the six that he and Jervas should see in their imaginary voyage to Italy ("Epistle to Mr. Jervas" [1716]), the other four being Raphael, Guido Reni, Titian, and Correggio. Prior does not mean seriously to disparage Veronese and Carracci, but in a lightly mocking way to suggest that even the greatest painters depend upon a kind of inflation of their subject through mythological allusion and images.

16 Frances Mayhew Rippy notes the seriousness of the moral by relating it to Prior's "Serious Reflections" and *Soloman.* She points out that this moral is "distinctively his, as it often is in his serious meditations upon the vanity and frivolity of human wishes" (*Matthew Prior* [Boston: Twayne, 1986], 78-79).

17 Ian Jack, "The 'Choice of Life' in Johnson and Matthew Prior," *JEGP* 49 (1950): 523-30. Jack, however, focuses only on Johnson's debt in *The Vanity of Human Wishes* to Prior's *Soloman or the Vanity of the World* (1718).

18 In contrast to Prior, Ovid emphasizes the perfectly loving and harmonious nature of their relationship:

> There *Baucis* and *Philemon* liv'd, and there
> Had liv'd long marry'd, and a happy Pair:
> Now old in Love, though little was their
>   Store,
> Inur'd to Want, their Poverty they bore,
> Nor aim'd at Wealth, professing to be poor.
> For Master or for Servant here to call,
> Was all alike, where only Two were All.

Command was none, where equal Love was
   paid,
Or rather both commanded, both obey'd.

(Trans. John Dryden, *The Poems of John Dryden,* ed.
James Kinsley, 4 vols. [Oxford: Clarendon Press, 1958],
4:1566; ll. 32-40).

[19] Prior's narrator pointedly remarks on his refusal to
describe meals and banquets in elaborate detail in contrast to that usually found "In Epic sumptuous" (l. 109).
Ovid dwells at length on the specific food Baucis and
Philemon offer the gods, from the cabbage and bacon
to the olives, cherries, endive, radishes, etc. In other
words, they have put out all they have for their guests
without knowing who the gods are, going so far as to
try to seize their only goose, the "watchdog" of their
property, to make a more substantial meal. The goose
is too quick for them, of course, escaping to the protection of the strangers. At this point the gods reveal
who they are and proceed to reward Baucis and Philemon for their generosity.

[20] La Fontaine took his story from Boccaccio (*De-
cameron,* II, 10), keeping quite close to his source and
making a "plea for the rights of nature," according to
Lapp, *Esthetics of Negligence,* 72.

[21] These themes were central to La Fontaine's story.
Because of the manifest differences between Prior's
version and the French writer's, Wright and Spears
conclude that "there is nothing to suggest that [Prior]
was indebted to La Fontaine or Boccaccio" (*Works*
2:903).

[22] These foods appear in P. V. Taberner's extensive list
of aphrodisiacs in Appendix 1 of his *Aphrodisiacs:
The Science and the Myth* (Philadelphia: University
of Pennsylvania Press, 1985), 257-62. They also appear in Byron's *Don Juan* (Canto 2, st. 170), where
he describes the flowering of love between Juan and
Haidee:

> While Venus fills the heart, (without heart,
>   really,
>   Love, though good always, is not quite so
>   good,)
> Ceres presents a plate of vermicelli,—
>   For Love must be sustained like flesh and
>   blood,—
> While Bacchus pours out wine, or hands a
>   jelly:
> Eggs, oysters, too, are amatory food;
> But who is their purveyor from above
> Heaven knows,—it may be Neptune, Pan, or
>   Jove.

>   (*Don Juan,* ed. Leslie A. Marchand
>   [Boston: Houghton Mifflin,
>   1958], 97).

[23] *Lives of the Poets* 2:14.

[24] The epigraph, drawn from Cicero's *On Moral Obligation,* should have already alerted the reader to the
serious intentions in the poem. The passage comes from
Cicero's discussion of decorum or propriety in human
behavior, a comprehensive virtue in Cicero's terms that
includes "considerateness and self-control" together
with "temperance, complete subjection of all the passions, and moderation in all things," and it is "insep-
arable from moralgoodness" (*De Officis,* Trans. Walter
Miller, Loeb Classical Library [Cambridge, Mass.:
Harvard University Press, 1961], 97). Prior's poem is
not philosophical, of course, but it clearly is more than
fluff.

[25] This passage may remind us of Pope's similar remarks in the "snatch a Grace beyond the Reach of Art"
passage in *An Essay on Criticism* (written ca. 1709), ll.
141-60. Like Prior, Pope fuses art and morality. Pope
himself cites Quintilian, 2.13.6-7, to justify his praise
of deviations from the rules. Samuel Holt Monk has
documented the long tradition of commentators before
Pope who had discussed the necessity for such a grace,
or deviation from the rules, in order to achieve an
effect beyond the mechanical or coldly perfect ("A
Grace Beyond the Reach of Art," *JHI* 5 [1944]: 131-
50; repr. in *Essential Articles for the Study of Alexander Pope,* ed. Maynard Mack, rev. ed. [Hamden,
Conn.: Archon Bks., 1968], 38-62). Apelles, Monk
points out, was the prototype of grace and ease in
painting from Pliny down to the Renaissance (40-41).

[26] Commines's *Memoirs* cover primarily the reigns of
Louis XI (1461-83) and Charles VIII (1483-98), both
of whom he served as an adviser. His book is an
important contribution to our understanding of early
modern France. Both he and Livy wrote extensively
about the warfare involved in their histories.

[27] Sir Richard Blackmore, although the butt of many
wits' scorn because of his tedious epics like *Prince
Arthur* (1695) and *King Arthur* (1697) as well as his
Satyr Against Wit (1700), was nevertheless a well-
known and respected physician who attended both King
William and Queen Anne. Sir Hans Sloane, was, of
course, a distinguished physician, scientist, and collec-
tor, who served as secretary and later president of the
Royal Society. If Blackmore's name might evoke some
sense of mockery, Sloane's would not.

[28] Quoted by Wright and Spears, *Works* 2:958 (from
Walpole's Introduction to *Aedes Walpolianae* [1752]).

[29] Charles Eves links her (and others like her in Prior's
poetry) with the "sprightly nymphs of charming im-
pertinence [who] proclaim themselves true sisters
to the Olivias, the Melanthes, the Millamants, [and]
the Florimels of Restoration comedy" (*Matthew Prior,*

p. 376). Prior certainly drew on the Restoration drama-tists for his character portraits, though he usually displays greater sympathy for his subjects than they do.

James L. Thorson (essay date 1993)

SOURCE: "Matthew Prior's 'An Epitaph'," in *The Explicator,* Vol. 51, No. 2, Winter, 1993, pp. 84-9.

[*In the following essay, Thorson offers a close analy-sis of "An Epitaph."*]

> *Stet quicunque volet potens*
> *Aulae culmine lubrico, &c.* Senec.

[The epigraph: "Let who will stand firm upon the slip-pery pinnacle of princely power." Seneca, *Thyestes* 391-92.]

> Interr'd beneath this Marble Stone,
> Lie Saunt'ring Jack, and Idle Joan.
> While rolling Threescore Years and One
> Did round this Globe their Courses run;
> If Human Things went Ill or Well;
>   5
> If changing Empires rose or fell;
> The Morning past, the Evening came,
> And found this Couple still the same.
> They Walk'd and Eat, good Folks: What then?
> Why then They Walk'd and Eat again:
>   10
> They soundly slept the Night away:
> They did just Nothing all the Day:
> And having bury'd Children Four,
> Wou'd not take Pains to try for more.
> Nor Sister either had, nor Brother:
>   15
> They seem'd just Tally'd for each other.
>   Their Moral and Oeconomy
> Most perfectly They made agree:
> Each Virtue kept it's proper Bound,
> Nor Trespass'd on the other's Ground.
>   20
> Nor Fame, nor Censure They regarded:
> They neither Punish'd, nor Rewarded.
> He car'd not what the Footmen did:
> Her Maids She neither prais'd, nor chid:
> So ev'ry Servant took his Course;
>   25
> And bad at First, They all grew worse.
> Slothful Disorder fill'd His Stable;
> And sluttish Plenty deck'd Her Table.
> Their Beer was strong; Their Wine was *Port;*
> Their Meal was large; Their Grace was short.
>   30
> They gave the Poor the Remnant-meat,
> Just when it grew not fit to eat.

> They paid the Church and Parish-Rate;
> And took, but read not the Receit:
> For which They claim'd their *Sunday*'s due,
>   35
> Of slumb'ring in an upper Pew.
>   No Man's Defects sought They to know;
> So never made Themselves a Foe.
> No Man's good Deeds did They commend;
> So never rais'd Themselves a Friend.
>   40
> Nor cherish'd They Relations poor:
> That might decrease Their present Store:
> Nor Barn nor House did they repair:
> That might oblige Their future Heir.
>   They neither Added, nor Confounded:
>   45
> They neither Wanted, nor Abounded.
> Each *Christmas* They Accompts did clear;
> And wound their Bottom round the Year.
> Nor Tear, nor Smile did They imploy
> At News of Public Grief, or Joy.
>   50
> When Bells were Rung, and Bonfires made;
> If ask'd, They ne'er deny'd their Aid:
> Their Jugg was to the Ringers carry'd
> Who ever either Dy'd or Marry'd
> Their Billet at the Fire was found;
>   55
> Who ever was depos'd, or Crown'd.
>   Nor Good, nor Bad, nor Fools, nor Wise;
> They wou'd not learn, nor cou'd advise:
> Without Love, Hatred, Joy, or Fear,
> They led—a kind of—as it were:
>   60
> Nor Wish'd, nor car'd, nor Laugh'd, nor
>   Cry'd:
> And so They liv'd; and so They dy'd.

>   1718

Matthew Prior has, from his own time to today, en-joyed a literary reputation as a writer of some very pleasing light poems. Samuel Johnson was to object that "[h]is numbers are such as mere diligence may attain; they seldom offend the ear, and seldom soothe it; they commonly want airiness, lightness, and fa-cility: what is smooth is not soft. His verses always roll, but they seldom flow." Joseph Addison, though writing before "An Epitaph" was published, damn-ed him with faint praise, conceding that Prior had "a happy talent of doggerel, where he writes on a known subject: where he tells us in plain intelligible language." I contend that both of these assessments of his poetic achievement are wrong and that Pope may well have anticipated Prior's achievement in **"An Epitaph"** when he wrote, in *An Essay on Criti-cism,*

> True ease in writing comes from art, not
>   chance,

As those move easiest who have learned to
  dance.
'Tis not enough no harshness gives offense,
The sound must seem an echo to the sense.

I will focus my argument particularly on the last verse
paragraph of **"An Epitaph"** but will need to present
some analysis of the poem in general, as well as its
position in literary history, before turning to that last,
most brilliant part of this gently satiric poem.

The poem is a participant in a literary and philosophical argument that had been going on for a long time.
It concerns the classical concept of *otium,* and Prior
was probably responding to John Pomfret's *The Choice*
(1700), a poem that presented the popular ideas associated with otium to a large English audience of the
period. Samuel Johnson was later to say of Pomfret's
poem, "Perhaps no composition in our language has
been oftener perused." Published anonymously in 1700,
it went through numerous editions and stimulated much
speculation. It built on the Renaissance tradition of
popular poems, such as "In Praise of a Contented Mind"
(often known by its first line, "My mind to me a kingdom is"), though the idea goes back to classical times,
most notably the work of one of Prior's idols, Horace.
Put most simply, otium is a preference for the simple
country life of retirement over the sophisticated life of
the city or the court. Pomfret's version of the ideal is
also often known as a typical "neoclassical" poem, as
it stresses the value of the via media and restraint of
the passions, even including romantic love. It is clear
that Prior is responding to the detached ideal of otium
presented by Pomfret by presenting his idea of what a
retired country life might be like.

Prior, who had lost his diplomatic post and was imprisoned after the death of Queen Anne and the subsequent ejection of the Tory government in 1714, had a
jaundiced view of the pleasures of retirement, and that
is the primary theme of the poem. It first appeared in
the 1718 edition of ***Poems on Several Occasions,*** a
folio volume published by subscription, which, with
the energetic promotion of Jonathan Swift, Alexander
Pope, John Gay, and other Tory writers and politicians, allowed Prior to retire in relative financial security (though he may not have been confident of this
financial success when he wrote the poem). As Brean
Hammond has recently noted,

> Subscription publishing is now generally recognized
> to be a form of patronage: a hybrid form that called
> for co-operation between private patrons, who
> lobbied friends to subsidize the author prior to
> publication, and bookseller, who agreed to bear
> printing costs on this basis.[1]

The success of this effort, and the direct patronage of
Lord Edward Harley, managed to allow the last year

and a half of Prior's life (1720-21) to be spent in that
pleasant country retirement rejected by **"An Epitaph."**

"An Epitaph" takes the position that the restriction of
the passions suggested by *The Choice* and other exem-
plars of otium would result not in a gentle, happy retired life but, rather, in no lifeat all. Though "Saunt'ring
Jack and Idle Joan" are married, their sex life is not
wildly passionate: "And having buried children four, /
Would not take pains to try for more." These two lines,
along with most of the first verse paragraph (lines 1-
16), establish the metrical standard for the poem, the
iambic tetrameter rhymed couplet. It is this metrical
ground on which variations, particularly of the caesuras, will be played in order to establish an important
part of the meaning of the poem. The form, of course,
has a varied history but would probably have reminded
readers in the second decade of the eighteenth century
of Samuel Butler's *Hudibras,* the satirical poem of the
previous century, which was still popular, as well as
the poetry of Prior's friend Jonathan Swift, which was
often written in the same verse form. Butler's form
was so noticeable that it was called "the Hudibrastic,"
but usually when it exhibited some of the comic characteristics of double rhymes and false sight rhymes
that Butler used so often in his long satiric poem. We
know that Prior was familiar with *Hudibras,* as he
reveals a close knowledge of it in his **"Journey to
Copt-Hall,"** written probably in 1689, though not
published until 1907.[2] The rhymes in the first verse
paragraph of **"An Epitaph"** are quite regular, and none
of them is a double or false sight rhyme, the forms that
were utilized by Butler (and elsewhere by Prior) for
comic effect. It should be recalled that Sir Roger de
Coverley of *The Spectator* admired Butler's false sight
rhyme "And Pulpit, Drum Ecclesiastic / Was beat with
fist, instead of a stick" (*Hudibras* 1.1. 11-12). This
couplet is probably the best single example of the
metrical games that I am talking about, though other
examples abound.

After Prior introduces his passive protagonists, Jack
and Joan, in this first verse paragraph, he points out
that the fictive "marble stone" under which they lie
tells a simple tale of a long ("threescore years and
one") and in Prior's poem, at least, exceedingly dull
life of rural retirement. The second through fifth verse
paragraphs (17-56) use some of the techniques of the
Theophrastan character popular in the seventeenth century to set up Jack and Joan as ideal character types by
giving concrete examples of their conduct. Moral and
economic terms are the focus of the second verse paragraph, with relations with neighbors and servants the
subject matter.

The short third verse paragraph summarily dismisses
their church duties, which they discharge, like all things,
with a minimum of effort and attention. This might
be contrasted with Sir Roger de Coverley's proper

attention to his church duties in *The Spectator* for Monday, July 11, 1711. Sir Roger is generally a figure of gentle fun for Addison and Steele, who gently ridicule the Tory squire for his old-fashioned habits and characteristics, but in this essay, often titled "Sir Roger at Church," his actions are seen as worthy of unstinted praise. To the essayists, a life ofcountry retirement is an opportunity for good Christian actions, whereas Prior sees such a life as allowing the minimal efforts ("slumbering in an upper pew") of Jack and Joan.

The couplet of lines 47-48, "Each Christmas they accompts did clear, / And wound their bottom round the year," is about the only one that may cause trouble to modern readers. Most anthologies note that the "bottom" of this passage is a ball of thread that was used to tie up papers to be saved but not used any longer. Prior had used the same phrase in a letter to Lord Jersey, his sometime patron, on August 26, 1699, as he prepared to leave Paris from one of his diplomatic missions: "I have wound up my bottom, I have liquored my boots, and my foot is in the stirrup: that is I leave Paris tomorrow,"[3] The *OED* lists this meaning as "15. A clew or nucleus on which to wind thread; also a skein or ball of thread" and shows several usages in this sense from the fifteenth through the eighteenth centuries.

It is, however, in the last verse paragraph that Prior's artistry comes to the fore and his metrical form most clearly expresses his anti-otium meaning. I will quote it in its entirely:

> Nor good, nor bad, nor fools, nor wise;
> They would not learn, nor could advise:
> Without love, hatred, joy, or fear,
> They led—a kind of—as it were:
>   60
> Nor wished, nor cared, nor laughed, nor cried
> And so they lived: and so they died.

The first line uses three caesuras of equal duration to divide the line into four equal negative parts of two syllables each. The first two are opposite abstract ideas, and the last two are less abstract human characters. The constant breaking of the line after each two syllables indicates the jerkiness of the thought process when considering Jack and Joan, such passive, thoughtless, indifferent people. The next line extends the syntax and the meter slightly, both negatively, as the speaker of the poem notes what they would and could not do in parallel, dividing the paired predicates to the subject "They" by a medial caesura. The third line of the verse paragraph utilizes three caesuras again, though now the two middle elements in the line are even shorter than in the first, one and two syllables respectively. The strong couplet form causes the reader to expect closure in the second line of each couplet, and it is this expectation that Prior brilliantly foils in line 60. The

parallel of line 59 with the first line of this verse paragraph is not exact, as line 59 begins with the three-syllable unit "Without love," which can best be scanned as an iamb followed by a single stressed syllable. This variation should alert the reader to the potential for further change in the second half of the couplet, but Prior's change is so radical that thereader finds his or her tongue stumbling over the dashes, which impede the flow and almost stop it completely to imitate the thought processes of Jack and Joan. The retired country life, so highly prized by Pomfret and other proclaimers of the ideal of otium, has led them into a kind of mental paralysis exemplified by the stuttering dance of the syllables around the dashes: "They led—a kind of—as it were." The complete breakdown of thought into ambling, incomplete, incoherent utterances is brilliantly mimicked by the verses' own stumbling cadence and syntax.

After this brilliant line, Prior returns to a metrical echo of the first couplet of this verse paragraph, with three caesuras dividing the penultimate line into four equal iambs. The final line is divided into two equal and parallel grammatical units, contrasting their lives and their deaths around a final, strong caesura. The rhetorical emphasis on "died" is especially strong because of the masculine rhyme on the last word of the poem and the final verse paragraph. Prior's theme, that retiring to the country is not an ideal but, to a thoughtful person, a sentence of mental and moral death is beautifully exemplified here.

Notes

[1] Brean S. Hammond, "'A Poet, and a Patron, and Ten Pound': John Gay and Patronage," *John Gay and the Scriblerians,* ed. Peter Lewis and Nigel Wood (New York: St. Martins, 1988) 29. Hammond suggests that Gay may have seen Prior as a role model (30-31).

[2] Noted by Frances Mayhew Rippy in *Matthew Prior,* (Boston: Twayne, 1986) 10.

[3] Charies Kenneth Eves, *Matthew Prior: Poet and Diplomatist* (New York: Columbia UP, 1939) 139.

Faith Gildenhuys (essay date 1995)

SOURCE: "Convention and Consciousness in Prior's Love Lyrics," in *Studies in English Literature 1500-1900,* Vol. 35, No. 3, Summer, 1995, pp. 437-55.

[In the following essay, Gildenhuys examines the function of consciousness in Prior's love poetry.]

Critics have always had a difficult time "placing" Matthew Prior's achievement, but, in general, they have chosen to see him as the tail end of the seventeenth-century tradition of love poetry. In his famous essay, "The Metaphysical Poets," T. S. Eliot observes that "'courtly' poetry is derivative from Jonson, who borrowed liberally from the Latin; it expires in the next century with the sentiment and witticism of Prior." In the same essay, of course, Eliot makes his famous remark that "[i]n the seventeenth century a dissociation of sensibility set in, from which we have never recovered," a divorce of thought and feeling for which he felt that Milton and Dryden in particular were responsible.[1] It is a curious accident that Eliot employs "sensibility" to refer to an attitude that he felt had disappeared before, apparently, the word itself begins to occur in the language, at least according to the OED, and with significantly different meanings than those apparently lying behind Eliot's statement. In his stimulating study of the artistic expression of affective love in the eighteenth century, Jean H. Hagstrum begins by pointing out that "sensibility" "became [in the middle of that period] a central term of complex and multiple signification covering such meanings as perceptibility by the senses, the readiness of an organ to respond to sensory stimuli, mental perception, the power of the emotions, heightened emotional consciousness, and the quickness of feeling."[2] Hagstrum sees the notion of sensibility as combining erotic love and the ideal in a particularly civilized, "tenderized," fashion peculiar to that century. If one looks at Prior's love poetry through the lens of sensibility, rather than its breakdown, it appears less like the end of a tradition than in the vanguard of changing attitudes toward love.

Love poetry is what Prior is primarily remembered for. *The New Oxford Book of Eighteenth-Century Verse* (1984), edited by Roger Lonsdale, devotes thirteen pages to Matthew Prior's poetry. The emphasis is on Prior's light lyrics, and Lonsdale's selection remains very similar to that of David Nichol Smith in his 1926 original *Oxford Book of Eighteenth-Century Verse*.[3] He has chosen four of the same poems—all to or about women—a different excerpt from *Solomon,* and added several lyrics and a burlesque imitation, "Daphne and Apollo," from Ovid. One might say that Prior's reputation is "secure," if not indeed petrified. This is the case despite the fact that, between the 1926 edition and Lonsdale's, Prior's poetry was collected in 1959 in a meticulously edited Oxford edition. Moreover, a good biography by Matthew Eves appeared in 1939 and the philosophical bases of his work were throughly examined in a series of four articles by Monroe K. Spears in the late 1940s.[4]

It may be ironic that Prior is remembered for verses that delight in human emotion when in *Solomon* he concludes "that the passions should be sternly suppressed."[5] but it is not surprising. The Prior of public pronouncement who appears to share in "the gloom of the Tory satirists" is out of sympathy with the more modern affirmation of ordinary life reflected in his light

verse. However, the playfulness and apparent deferral of judgment which are the sourceof so much of the charm of the love lyrics may arise from the awareness of the contingency of human life which finds straightforward assertion in his "serious" poetry. In response to the perception that life is miserable, Prior "gain[s] temporary relief from misery . . . through diverting [his] thoughts, whether concerned with present or future, to other things."[6]

> Ev'n a Romance, a Tune, a Rhime
> Help Thee to Pass the tedious Time,
> Which else would on thy Hand remain:
> Tho' flown, it ne'er looks back again.
> And Cards are dealt, and Chess-boards brought,
> To ease the Pain of Coward-Thought.
>
> (*Alma,* canto 3, lines 484-9)

It may be that Samuel Johnson was responding to what he perceived as moral flippancy when he said in his "Life of Prior": "If Prior's poetry be generally considered his praise will be that of correctness and industry, rather than of compass of comprehension or activity of fancy. He never made any effort of invention: his greater pieces are only tissues of common thoughts; and his smaller, which consist of light images or single conceits, are not always his own."[7] Although this is an unsympathetic assessment, even Prior's admirers are inclined to agree with its outlines, if not its implied censure. For example, George Wiley Sherburn's praise implicitly acknowledges Prior's lack of "invention" while extolling what Johnson seems to have dismissed as cleverness: "[Prior] became perhaps the ideal neoclassicist, writing with both lightness and a noble urbanity, with elegant ease and a deft and imaginative use of classical mythology unequalled in the century. He avoided the pedantry involved in minute attention to classical patterns, yet he captured the mood and felicity of both Horace and Anacreon."[8] Maynard Mack fends off over-eager interpreters: "No one can fail to admire these effects, but to dwell on them is to run the risk of making the poem smaller, and other, than it is."[9]

But surely some credit must be given to the popularity of Prior's poetry which began early and continued throughout the eighteenth century. He felt impelled to publish a volume of his poetry in 1709 when much of it began to appear in an unauthorized edition by Edmund Curll. Fifty-three lyrics, three ballads, and two longer poems were set to music during his lifetime and after.[10] Prior and his supporters (Swift was tireless) obtained more subscribers for his elaborate folio edition of his work (1717) than subscribed to Pope's translations.[11] Lady Mary Wortley memorized all six hundred lines of his **"Henry and Emma,"** and Prior allusions are credited by Samuel Richardson in *Clarissa* not only to Lovelace but to Sally Martin, one of the "women below the stairs."[12] And, although Samuel Johnson may have had reservations about his poetry,

William Cowper admired Prior and had a sincere appreciation of the difficulty of the "familiar style" and Prior's mastery of it.[13]

The problem of assessing Prior's accomplishment is complicated by his apparently self-deprecating approach to poetry, an attitude which appears thematically as a comfortable skepticism and often formally as burlesque. The poetic forms, as Eliot's comparison with Jonson makes clear, and the classical allusions force the reference point steadily into the past, while the tone is rueful, almost dismissive. Because the forms are conventional, most critics, following Johnson, have assumed that the sentiments are derivative as well. But it may be that Prior's claim on our attention lies elsewhere. As James Sutherland remarks of Gay, it is difficult to achieve "the right critical attitude to minor poets" if critics place "a disproportionate emphasis on values: the critic who is preoccupied with the question of values is in danger of discounting any writer who has not got an impressive balance at the bank."[14] An exception is Bonamy Dobrée, who finds in Prior that "[t]he sentiment may not be very deep; but you know that what Prior did feel he felt and expressed with absolute sincerity . . . He is never sentimental, and behind many of his poems there is a vague, half-caught sense of something else stirring; something faintly but persistently suggests awareness of a world beyond."[15] What appears to some as a faded emotion is, I believe, an expression of sensibility, that delicacy and tenderness characteristic of the complex of emotions which replaced passionate love in the new age of intimacy and affection.

A recent critic, Ronald Rower, has perceptively discussed "Prior's talent for depicting with warmth and understanding the intimate, somewhat childish, but central concerns of ordinary people." Tracing Prior's Cloe and her poet-lover as they move from the pastoral setting of one poem to the next, Rower highlights Prior's interest in the "conflicts between the artificial world of amorous tradition, for which Cloe is the innocent advocate, and the real world of time, which her lover constantly invokes."[16] As Rower notes, the recurrent characteristics of Prior's lyrics are his use of anacreontic and marginally pastoral imagery that accompany his concern with love: Cupid flies, Damon sighs, Cloe weeps, and the Fates are unkind; a sympathetic nature echoes lovers' plights with fading flowers and stormy skies. In a number of these poems, the conventional elements provide the major interest and Prior's skill is devoted to deploying them with lucidity and precision. Their mildly witty conclusions demonstrate Prior's mastery of the genre, but, for the most part, these poems seem to counterfeit emotion. By the eighteenth century the ability of these conventions to suggest innocent rapture is all but eradicated by their familiarity. The metonymies no longer have much resonance. The myth, which was originally used to elevate the lovers is, itself, in this application reduced to the domestic level through the intrusion of the colloquial and familiar into the classical setting. Prior's more interesting poetry is written with a freer, more casual use of the conventional motifs, which recognizes their lineage in seventeenth-century aristocratic attitudes toward love and the Restoration parody and debasement of those attitudes. It is the attitude toward love, rather than toward Cloe, as Rower suggests, that changes.

The poems in *Lyric Poems,* a volume of Prior's verse with musical settings first published in 1741, after his death, have a "marked 'Restoration' flavour" about them. They may well have been composed around the turn of the century, a product of his early maturity.[17] Of the twenty-four poems, fifteen are concerned with persuasions to love, the cruel mistress, or physical separations from her. These themes have in common the potential for exploring the reaction of the lover to the conflict between his desire and the threats to its fulfillment presented by the mistress's indifference or the passage of time. The conventional response to this conflict is imminent death, as in the earl of Rochester's "My dear Mistress has a heart":

> But my jealous heart would break
> Should we live one day asunder.[18]

The point of view is normally the speaker's, who yearns for the total and uncomplicated fulfillment of his erotic desires. The displacement of these desires through pastoral and anacreontic conventions idealizes them and creates the illusion that they can be equated with a return to a prelapsarian innocence. If, however, the woman attains a physical presence, these desires tend to appear lustful and the lyric to become satiric, as in much of Restoration verse.

Although the opening lines of Prior's lyrics general-ly prepare the reader for the standard seduction or lament, the female partner is acknowledged as something more than the stimulus of desire or the impediment to the fulfillment of it. Despite the appearance of familiar allusions for idealizing romantic love, Prior appears to be less interested in focusing on the anguish engendered by unfulfilled passion than in that love capable of being subjected to common sense. "To Phillis" reflects a skepticism about love's ability to provide transcendence, while maintaining a recognition of its erotic and emotional appeal.

> PHILLIS *since we have both been kind,*
> *And of each other had our fill,*
> *Tell me, what Pleasure you can find;*
> *In forcing Nature 'gainst her will.*
>
> 2
>
> *'Tis true, you may with Art and Pain,*
> *Keep in some Glowings of Desire;*

But still, those Glowings, which remain,
    Are only Ashes of the Fire.

3

Then let us free each others Soul,
    And laugh at the dull constant Fool,
Who would Love's liberty controul,
    And teach us how to whine by Rule.

4

Let us no Impositions set,
    Or clogs upon each others Heart;
But as for Pleasure first we met;
    So now for Pleasure let us part.

5

We both have spent our Stock of Love,
    So consequently should be free,
Thirsis expects you in yon Grove,
    And pretty Chloris stays for me.

(lines 1-20)

Love lyrics generally rely on our recognition of the alogical and resistless impulse of love to provide poetic movement. Typically the use of pastoral and anacreontic allusion serves to relocate the lovers from city to country, thus stripping them of the rationality of the quotidian and allowing them to luxuriate in pure emotion: "Come live with me and be my love." Prior's poem preserves the appearance of love thus simplified while applying quite a different, and strictly rational, argument from nature. Both the invocation of nature and the imagery invoke the ghost of the conventional *carpe diem,* which also makes itself felt in the stock phrases such as "Glowings of Desire" and "free each others Soul." At the same time, the colloquial diction—"had our fill," "whine by Rule"—underscores the familiarity and, more significantly, the mutuality of the lovers' relationship, setting into perspective the limits of purely romantic love. Prior's poem, although revealing the fragility of the romantic vision, does not invert it or annihilate it altogether; Prior exposes, rather, the extent to which it is governed by its human context. Prior also internalizes the constraints on love; they are no longer centered in some external impediment but appear under the control of the lovers themselves.

In adopting the form and style of the conventional love lyric, Prior alludes to a courtly ideal as well as to the pastoral notion of innocent desire. The pastoral and the courtly share the propensity to hypostatize romantic passion, but there is some difference in the role of the loved one implied in their use. A pastoral poem tends to focus on the lover's emotion, whereas courtly elements tend to be employed in praising the object of the emotion. It is true of both, however, that the female is invested with permanent qualities whereas the male lover's emotion may be subjected to change. "Ladies don't move": when they do, the illusion of romantic love is overtaken by a sense of the familiar and the domestic.

When Prior's lyrics play at the margins of passion, his transformation of the conventions becomes more apparent. The simplest rendering of a changed perspective is represented in two of the poems appearing in both Oxford anthologies that are addressed to young girls. **"To a Child of Quality of Five Years Old, the Author suppos'd Forty,"** explores the contrast between the child's attractive innocence and the poet's response to it as filtered through the conventions of romance which she does not understand: "all the House my Passion reads, / In Papers round her Baby's Hair" (lines 14-5). His impossible infatuation is modified by a witty turn in the final stanza:

For as our diff'rent Ages move,
    'Tis so ordain'd, wou'd Fate but mend it,
That I shall be past making Love,
    When she begins to comprehend it.

(lines 25-8)

The intensity of the passion is qualified through the shift in focus to the reality of aging. The human desire for transcendence through love shimmers in the reference to Fate and is met by a detached reasonableness. But if the acceptance of man's limited nature is tinged with melancholy, as in much of Prior's poetry, its articulation is ruefully humorous (intensified by the double rhyme), as if consciousness itself is some partial solace in the face of a world of irresolvable contradictions and wayward Fates. The piquancy of **"To a Child of Quality"** arises from the interaction of the speaker's "consciousness" and the supposedly uncontrollable passion of love. Love is conventionally a fatal and overmastering force, but, when subjected to consciousness, sexual excitement is modified by the awareness of virtue and becomes touchingly displaced in the curling papers for doll babies' hair. **"A Letter to the Honorable Lady Mrs: Margaret Candish Harley,"**[19] also written in Prior's characteristic tetrameter couplets, admonishing "My noble, lovely, little Peggy" (line 1) to be a good girl, is more economical. The emotion generated by the poem emerges from the implicit contrast between the simplicity of the child and the intimidating aristocratic title that she must eventually live up to, and the poet's wistful affection for her innocence is rooted in his awareness of the inevitability of adulthood.

Both poems appeal to our sense of the sentimental, as the word refers to "refined, tender emotions with an erotic coloration." The poems also embody "sentiment," that close eighteenth-century relative of "sensibility," which "came to refer specifically to the gentle, tender, loyal, courteous emotions, precisely those most amenable to domestic needs and desires."[20] These adjectives all covertly acknowledge the element of emotional exchange involved in affection and intimacy. Thus eros is modified by rueful whimsy and wit when its object becomes recognizably someone other than a simple embodiment of masculine desire.

The delicacy of emotion, the sentiment, arises from the consciousness in the speaker of the distance between himself and the object of his affections, and his respect for it. And conscious restraint, along with sensibility, may help to explain why Prior's verse was so in tune with the eighteenth-century cast of mind. As Hagstrum points out, at this time the word "conscious" developed a variety of meanings, uniting "feeling with" and "knowing with," creating a sense of intimacy: "Shared knowledge, one supposes, can theoretically be neutral enough; but the very fact that a secret is kept and shared tends to make the mutual knowledge tremble with fear or glow with emotion. The secret can eat like the canker worm . . . but [it] can also titillate."[21] Knowledge and intimacy combine to associate consciousness with the awareness of both virtue and guilt, especially of a sexual nature, and in turn it becomes linked with sensibility and its physical manifestation, the blush.

The exploration of adult love that incorporates awareness is more interesting and more complex. Prior portrays men and women as equally aware of the multiple roles women might play in romantic relationships. Not surprisingly, the romantic conflict is revealed to be more than a "will-she, won't-she" situation, and, in fact, develops a plot. As with women in eighteenth-century romance narrative, women in Prior's verse begin to be characterized as not only the object of male passion but also by their potential to transform men either through status or virtue.[22] The development of "consciousness" is not accidentally accompanied by the change in women's roles as reflected in these plots of love.

"An Ode" (1709) provides one of the best examples of Prior's apprehension of the intersection of feeling and knowing and romantic passion:

I.

    The Merchant, to secure his Treasure,
      Conveys it in a borrow'd Name:
    EUPHELIA serves to grace my Measure;
      But CLOE is my real Flame.

II.

    My softest Verse, my darling Lyre
      Upon EUPHELIA's Toylet lay;
    When CLOE noted her Desire,
      That I should sing, that I should play.

III.

    My Lyre I tune, my Voice I raise;
      But with my Numbers mix my Sighs:
    And whilst I sing EUPHELIA's Praise,
      I fix my Soul on CLOE's Eyes.

IV.

    Fair CLOE blush'd: EUPHELIA frown'd:
      I sung and gåz'd: I play'd and trembl'd:
    And VENUS to the LOVES around
      Remark'd, how ill We all dissembl'd.

                    (lines 1-16)

The theme of romantic love is once again conveyed by the anacreontic conventions: the Greek names, the lyre, the blushes and sighs. Venus becomes more of a duenna than a tutelary deity. The insufficiency of the conventions of amorous poetry to carry the burden of love is underscored by the simile of the merchant, which frames the poem, and by its conclusion. The merchant, as part of the "real" world, suggests that it is not transcendent passion being displayed here, but a much more conscious, even manipulative, social transaction. The lover is exploiting Cloe's jealousy through the attention he pays to Euphelia in order to ensure Cloe's love. Her blush acknowledges the mediation of love by a third person.[23] The awareness of another's involvement in the romance changes the nature of desire, when the rivals reinforce their own obsessions through imagining the feelings of the other. Desire, as René Girard has pointed out,[24] can be less a matter of straightforward sexual passion, becoming more a complicated, perhaps indefinable, mix of possessive jealousy, exhibitionism, and eroticism.

The intimations of desire, rather than the real thing, arise in large part from the deliberate mythologizing of the actors in the poem, as the conclusion reveals. The women are dressing up in their pastoral costumes and the lover has his lyre, as if for a fancy dress ball. The eighteenth-century penchant for costumes in portraits is well known. The public masquerade also achieved its moment of greatest popularity in the eighteenth century, and Terry Castle has suggested its significance for erotic love: "The mask signified a certain physical detachment from the situation, and by implication a moral detachment also. At the same time, by a somewhat Proustian logic the mask was thought to heighten the desire of one's partner. The mask mystified the object of desire; it symbolized the absence or withholding of connection. It was a kind of stylized evasion—a formal sign of resistance to full human exchange."[25] The anacreontic gestures in Prior's poem, revealed to be at odds with the people assuming them, are very like masquerade costumes in that they are consciously assumed in order to elicit an amorous response, without, perhaps, the wearers having to assume the responsibility for the con-sequences. The gap between the masks and the wearers is exposed in the last lines, which wittily reveal how inadequately the wearers fill their roles.

Prior's flirtatious poem, **"To the Author of Love and Friendship: A Pastoral,"** written in response to a pastoral dialogue by Elizabeth Singer, shows the ways in which such poetic masquerading can be used to manipulate a subtle mix of amorous emotions. The Sylvia of Singer's poem declares herself devoted to her female friend Aminta, thereby evading the demands of a heterosexual relationship. Prior's poem is an attempt to assert his emotional control; it exploits the mask of the pastoral to profess an innocent esteem for the friend which will thus enmesh Sylvia in a relationship with him, willy-nilly:

> O! let me in AMINTA's Praises join:
> Her's my Esteem shall be, my Passion Thine.
> . . . . .
>
> My Heart shall own the Justice of Her Cause;
> And Love himself submit to Friendship's
>   Laws.
>
> (lines 3-10)

The poem also invokes a range of other responses: grief—if Sylvia should love another—generosity, and shared sorrow, which are validated by the pastoral context. All these emotions involve consciousness and sensibility, of feeling with as well as for the other person. And they open up any number of possible storylines for the future of the relationship. But to the extent that these emotions echo those of the loved female, they exist in and for themselves, without consummation.[26]

The sensibility that is developed through the interaction of consciousness and desire in the masquerade is also at the center of Prior's Cloe-Lisetta poems, a sequence of amorous lyrics first appearing in *Poems on Several Occasions* (1718).[27] They are loosely organized around the challenge of a new mistress (Lisetta) to the poet's current one (Cloe). Each poem appears to have closure according to the conventions governing the lyric, while Prior introduces a plot by carrying through the ramifications of a situation to the next poem. In the end, the poems are less concerned with dramatizing the conflict between the two women than with the growing awareness of the limits of the romantic myth. The sequence moves from a more or less straightforward use of conventional descriptive romantic rhetoric to a realistic reassessment of its place in understanding the vicissitudes of human love. Much of the pleasure of the last poem, the frequently anthologized **"A Better Answer,"** derives from its place at the end of the sequence after various alternative perspectives have been explored.[28]

The series begins with **"On Beauty: A Riddle,"** in which Prior exercises all his ingenuity in rhetorical amplification to describe Cloe with as many classical similes as he can. That it does not become labored or boring is a tribute to Prior's skillful management of the line, especially in his use of trochaic substitution and the variations in the placement of the caesura, while maintaining the conversational flow of the verse. The self-conscious artifice involved becomes central to the playfulness at the close of the poem:

> For THIS [Beauty] I willingly decline
> The Mirth of Feasts, and Joys of Wine;

> And chuse to sit and talk with Thee,
> (As Thy great Orders may decree)
> Of Cocks and Bulls, of Flutes and Fiddles,
> Of Idle Tales, and foolish Riddles.

The mythological apparatus is reduced to cocks and bulls and foolish riddles with the same sophistication which informs the initial lengthy comparisons. Continuity is sustained by the speaker's drawing our attention to his cleverness in manipulating the mythology with virtuosity while remaining perceptive enough to recognize its artificiality. The wit resides in the development of a second perspective from the poetic craft employed in generating the first.

In the two following poems, Prior absorbs his double perspective into the dramatic fabric with the introduction of Lisetta (**"The Question, to Lisetta"**), whom the speaker attempts to persuade through a series of rhetorical questions that his fidelity to Cloe is natural:

> In Love am I not fully blest?
> LISETTA, pr'ythee tell the rest.
>
> (lines 12-3)

In **"Lisetta's Reply"** the new mistress mocks the single vision implied by such fidelity:

> When You the Flow'rs for CLOE twine,
> Why do You to Her Garland join
> The meanest Bud that falls from Mine?
> Simplest of Swains! the World may see,
> Whom CLOE loves, and Who loves Me.
>
> (lines 10-5)

Lisetta triumphs by exposing the way in which conventional emblems, presented as images of an idealized and permanent love, are in fact subject to the vagaries of the lover's feelings. The wit of the poem depends on the gently ironic interplay between the two ways of regarding them.

"The Garland" and **"The Lady who offers her Looking Glass to Venus"** are more serious reflections on the transient nature of love. Although both poems can stand alone, they are more interesting for their place within the sequence. **"The Garland"** is a re-working of pastoral motifs, which explores the correspondence between natural change and human life and incorporates awareness of this correspondence into the dramatic fabric of the poem. It is less an assertion of the enduring truth of time's role in life than a study of Cloe's growing realization of it. Prior shifts the emphasis from the standard *carpe diem* theme to focus on the role of consciousness in coming to terms with time's pressures. The last two stanzas seem bathetic and self-indulgent in comparison to the delicacy and tact with which the pastoral is handled in the first part of the poem. They can best be understood as an ironic commentary on both the speaker, Cloe, and on the convention itself. When Cloe utters the simple truth, unadorned by pastoral imagery,

> Such as She is, who dy'd to Day;
> Such I, alas! may be to Morrow,
>
> (lines 37-8)

Prior exposes the limits of usefulness of the conventional romantic motifs. The pastoral is an inherently self-conscious mode: "The pastoral poet is, after all, a city man, not a country man; consequently, he looks at rustic life with a characteristic admixture of sentimentality and comic irony."[29] Prior appeals to the recognition of this mixture to provide a rueful comment on Cloe's attitude toward romantic love.

Such a reading is borne out by **"The Lady who offers her Looking Glass to Venus,"** an epigrammatic quatrain of some emotional power:

> VENUS, take my Votive Glass:
>   Since I am not what I was;
> What from this Day I shall be,
>   VENUS, let Me never see.
>
> (lines 1-4)

According to Wright and Spears, "Dr. Johnson pointed out . . . Prior's source was an epigram attributed to Plato in the *Greek Anthology*" or one of a number of imitations.[30] Prior's version gains in suggestiveness by omitting direct reference to the loss of lovers, mentioned in the original epigram. Among other matters that Cloe may not wish to consider in giving up her mirror to Venus may be the realization that love is not the intense and simple emotion that the pastoral convention would have it. Here, as in the preceding poems of the series, Prior has subjected the conventions to critical scrutiny by dramatizing their consequences in a complex and changing world.

Prior dramatizes a vexed Cloe's consciousness that the conventional may conceal as well as reveal the truth of love in **"Cloe Jealous."** Her awareness is conveyed through references to each of the poems in the series:

> Emblems, to teach a Female Wit
>   The Ways, where changing CUPID flies.
>
> (lines 7-8)

But the belief in true love dies hard:

> Yet car'd I not, what might presage
>   Or withering Wreath, or fleeting Youth:
> Love I esteem'd more strong than Age,
>   And Time less permanent than Truth.
>
> (lines 33-6)

And yet death seems to provide her with the only adequate dramatization of her conviction:

> The secret Wound with which I bleed
>   Shall lie wrapt up, ev'n in my Herse.
>
> (lines 41-2)

The author's **"Answer to Cloe Jealous, in the same Stile. The Author Sick,"** is a pointed indulgence in the anguish of unrequited passion:

> From Jealousy's tormenting Strife
>   For ever be Thy Bosom free'd:
> That nothing may disturb Thy Life,
>   Content I hasten to the Dead.
>
> (lines 9-12)

Prior allows the overstatement of "content" and "hasten" to provide the ironic commentary on the artificiality of the attitude.

A more human, if more humdrum, response to the complexities of love is put forward by **"A Better Answer."** In it Prior dismisses all that is artificial in passion and asserts the importance of a realistic approach.

> What I speak, my fair CLOE, and what I write, shews
>   The Diff'rence there is betwixt Nature and Art:
> I court others in Verse; but I love Thee in Prose:
>   And They have my Whimsies; but Thou hast my Heart.
>
> (lines 13-6)

The poem explores the extent to which the artifice of passion and the passion itself were so cunningly mingled in the earlier poems of the series and reveals how the conventions can be emblems of vanity:

> Then finish, Dear CLOE, this Pastoral War;
>   And let us like HORACE and LYDIA agree:
> For Thou art a Girl as much brighter than Her,
>   As He was a Poet sublimer than Me.
>
> (lines 25-8)

In this concluding stanza we see once again the convention resuscitated to support a revised version of the romantic situation, one that goes beyond the frozen simplicities of pastoral form to include both mutuality and mutability. And the wit of the poem feeds upon the difference between the conventions and colloquial language. As well, the verse mocks the lyrical iambic tetrameters in its galloping anapestic pentameters.

Like a number of Restoration precursors, Prior's lyrics

often begin by inverting the pastoral convention for satiric purposes. However, the best of Prior's love lyrics, in their revision of the pastoral, demonstrate more than the limitations of the desire they portray. The awareness of convention is extended to include the lovers themselves; as a result, the women are no longer simply objects of romantic passion but acquire responses of their own beyond simple acquiescence or flight. Their passion, too, is exposed as being as susceptible as men's to self-indulgence and destructiveness, as in **"Cloe Jealous."** Passion is replaced by "sensibility" and understanding the other.

This domesticating of love through the introduction of the woman as subject has other implications as well, the most apparent being the suppression of erotic desire as a major component of love. When "dying for love" ceases to be a serious consequence, its covert meaning of sexual consummation is shifted from its central position. Sexual desire remains vestigially embedded in the conventions, but even so it undergoes a transformation through awareness, and it appears that the roles assumed by participants are appropriated, as in a masquerade, to induce the illusion of the mystery in love.

Prior's major achievement is in exploiting the potential of conventional modes as vehicles for exploring the function of consciousness in love. The double perspective, inherent in the assumption of pastoral forms, for example, provided earlier poets with a means of enacting in morally neutral territory fantasies of desire which masked the consequences of the emotion with a veil of innocence. This use of pastoral and its obverse in Restoration inversions of it limit the double perspective to reader and poet. Prior, by embedding the doubleness within the poems themselves, uses these conventions to comment on the impossibility of such desire as well as on the human yearning for it. The delicate balance required to contain both interpretations is sustained in **"A Better Answer."** There, the participants are still role-playing to the end, though now they are Horace and Lydia, rather than Damon and Cloe.

The impossibility of pure desire to survive the light of day is apparent not only in the relationship of lover and mistress, but also through the introduction of a rival mistress whose presence intensifies the emotional complexity of desire through the addition of envy and imitation. Although the implications are not fully explored in these poems, giving women an active role exposes their essential passivity in the plot of romantic love. In **"Daphne and Apollo,"** for example, Prior gives Daphne the role of the romantic aggressor, turning the poem into a lightly satiric commentary on the feminine desire for security as opposed to male lust. Daphne, in response to Apollo's plea to "let me woo thee as thou wou'd'st be woo'd," replies:

First therefore don't be so extreamly rude
Don't tear the Hedges down and tread the
 Clover
Like a Hobgoblin rather than a Lover
Next to my Fathers Grotto sometimes come.

. . . . .

As any Maid or Footman comes or goes
Pull off your Hatt and ask how Daphne does:
These sort of Folks will to each other tell
That you respect me.

(lines 42-53)

As with similar eighteenth-century burlesques of Ovid, the humor arises in the shift from a focus on the marvelous to the homely and familiar. Instead of the terrified object of Apollo's lust, in Prior's hands Daphne becomes the housewife attending to domestic details. Finally, she proposes marriage, at which point Apollo is effectively rendered speechless, "by Ratts alas the Manuscript is eat" (line 91). It would seem that the traditions of the amorous lyric can accommodate only a male aggressor.

Although applying the notion of "domestic" to his amatory verse appears to belittle Prior's poetry, it is in fact appropriate to see him as a part of the growing eighteenth-century interest in women as subjects rather than simply objects of male passion. His use of anacreontic and pastoral conventions is more than a nostalgic appeal to outworn fashions,[31] as it becomes a subtle means of exploring the contradictions and limitations of the myths of masculine desire. Perhaps the fact that Prior's best lyrics aresuggestive of reciprocal relationships in love accounts for their continuing appeal. Perhaps the fact that they are only suggestive can be attributed to the lyric poem's inability to accommodate the implications of that vision.

Notes

1 T. S. Eliot, "The Metaphysical Poets," in *Selected Prose* (London: Penguin, 1953), pp. 111-20, 111, 117.

2 Jean H. Hagstrum, *Sex and Sensibility: Ideal and Erotic Love from Milton to Mozart* (Chicago: Univ. of Chicago Press, 1980), p. 9.

3 Roger Lonsdale, ed., *The New Oxford Book of Eighteenth-Century Verse* (Oxford: Oxford Univ. Press, 1984), pp. 47-60. David Nichol Smith, ed., *The Oxford Book of Eighteenth-Century Verse* (Oxford: Oxford Univ. Press, 1926), pp. 15-31.

4 H. Bunker Wright and Monroe K. Spears, eds., *The Literary Works of Matthew Prior*, 2 vols. (Oxford: Clarendon Press, 1959). Charles Kenneth Eves, *Matthew Prior: Poet and Diplomatist*, Columbia

University Studies in English and Comparative Literature 144 (New York: Columbia Univ. Press, 1939). Monroe K. Spears, "The Meaning of Matthew Prior's *Alma*," *ELH* 13, 4 (December 1946): 266-90; Spears, "Matthew Prior's Religion," *PQ* 27, 2 (April 1948): 159-80; Spears, "Matthew Prior's Attitude toward Natural Science," *PMLA* 63, 2 (June 1948): 485-507; Spears, "Some Ethical Aspects of Matthew Prior's Poetry," *SP* 45, 4 (October 1948): 606-29. All Prior quotations are taken from the 2d edn. of *The Literary Works* (ed. H. Bunker Wright and Monroe K. Spears, 2 vols. [Oxford: Clarendon Press, 1971]) and will be indicated by line number in the text or as *Works* in the notes.

[5] Spears, "Ethical Aspects," p. 619.

[6] Spears, "Ethical Aspects," p. 623. The passage from *Alma* is also quoted by Spears (p. 624).

[7] Samuel Johnson, "Matthew Prior," in *Lives of the English Poets,* ed. George Birkbeck Hill, 3 vols. (Oxford: Oxford Univ. Press, 1968), 2:180-211, 207.

[8] George Wiley Sherburn, "The Restoration and the Eighteenth Century," in *A Literary History of England,* ed. Albert C. Baugh, 2d edn. (New York: Appleton-Century-Crofts, 1967), pp. 699-1108, 909.

[9] Maynard Mack, "Matthew Prior: *et multa prior arte,*" *SR* 68, 1 (Winter 1960): 165-76, 173.

[10] Majl Ewing, "Musical Settings of Prior's Lyrics in the EighteenthCentury," *ELH* 10, 2 (June 1943): 159-71.

[11] Frances Mayhew Rippy, *Matthew Prior,* Twayne's English Authors Series 418 (Boston: Twayne, 1986), p. 36.

[12] Sally Martin quotes "Hans Carvel" in Letter 333 and Lovelace quotes from "A Ladle" in Letter 453 (Samuel Richardson, *Clarissa; or The History of a Young Lady,* ed. Angus Ross [London: Penguin, 1985], pp. 1061, 1309).

[13] Oswald Doughty, "The Poet of the 'Familiar Style,'" *ES* 7, 1 (February 1925): 5-10, 8.

[14] James Sutherland, "John Gay," in *Pope and His Contemporaries: Essays Presented to George Sherburn,* ed. James L. Clifford and Louis A. Landa (Oxford: Oxford Univ. Press, 1949), pp. 201-14, 213-4.

[15] Bonamy Dobrée, *English Literature in the Early Eighteenth Century* (Oxford: Oxford Univ. Press, 1959), pp. 165-6.

[16] Ronald Rower, "Pastoral Wars: Matthew Prior's Poems to Cloe," *Ball State University Forum* 19, 2 (Spring 1978): 39-49, 49, 43-4.

[17] Wright and Spears, in the commentary to *Works,* note that one of the poems included in *Lyric Poems* had been previously published with the date 1701. This fact, plus internal evidence, leads them to believe that "the whole group of songs may well have been written at about the same time" (2:1034).

[18] John Wilmot, earl of Rochester, "My dear Mistress has a heart," in *The Complete Poems,* ed. David M. Vieth (New Haven: Yale Univ. Press, 1968), p. 12, lines 15-6.

[19] Prior, *Works,* 1:527.

[20] Hagstrum, *Sex and Sensibility,* pp. 7, 10.

[21] Jean H. Hagstrum, "Towards a Profile of *Conscious—* and *Unconscious—*in Eighteenth-Century Literature," in *Eros and Vision: The Restoration to Romanticism* (Evanston IL: Northwestern Univ. Press, 1989), pp. 3-27, 14.

[22] Michael McKeon, *The Origins of the English Novel, 1600-1740* (Baltimore: Johns Hopkins Univ. Press, 1987), pp. 255-65, and Ruth Perry, *Women, Letters, and the Novel* (New York: AMS Press, 1980), chap. 6, touch on this aspect of the romances, which were extremely popular in the eighteenth century.

[23] Rower feels that the blush is a sign of emotional sincerity:"true emotion will reveal itself" (p. 41), but he is more interested in the theme of truth versus fiction, with which he sees the lovers grappling, than in the permutations of love dramatized in their situation.

[24] René Girard, "Triangular Desire," in *Deceit, Desire, and the Novel: Self and Other in Literary Structure,* trans. Yvonne Freccero (Baltimore: Johns Hopkins Univ. Press, 1961), pp. 1-52.

[25] Terry Castle, *Masquerade and Civilization: The Carnivalesque in Eighteenth-Century English Culture and Fiction* (Stanford: Stanford Univ. Press, 1986), p. 39.

[26] Sterne's *Sentimental Journey* is perhaps the purest dramatization of the masculine conscious sensibility and it is completely plotless. See Janet Todd for a brief discussion of the absence of plots for "men of feeling" (*Sensibility: An Introduction* [London: Methuen, 1986], pp. 88-90). Narcissism may be one way of resolving the dilemma that heterosexuality represents for sensibility, as Hagstrum suggests in "Eros and Psyche: Some Versions of Romantic Love and Delicacy" (*Eros and Vision,* pp. 71-92).

[27] Wright and Spears include the poem "Her Right

Name" in the series on the grounds that Cloe's "right name" is Nancy, as set out in this poem. Although there may be sound biographical reasons for this, "Her Right Name" does not fit with Prior's use of convention in the rest of the series and I have chosen to exclude it.

[28] Rower, in his assessment of this sequence, also discusses the diverse perspectives in these poems, but, although he begins by saying that there is "obviously no consistency of characterization throughout [the] first five poems," he discovers in the Cloe of "Cloe Jealous" a "turbulent mixture of emotions," arising from her consciousness of her portrayal in the preceding poems, as if such consistency can finally be deduced (pp. 47, 48).

[29] Patrick Cullen, *Spenser, Marvell, and Renaissance Pastoral* (Cambridge MA: Harvard Univ. Press, 1970), p. 10.

[30] Prior, *Works,* 2:948-9.

[31] Rippy lists the qualities of Prior's lyrics: "simplicity, balance, artful repetition, the dressing of familiar material in a familiar guise, without sacrificing polish and elegance, the proper, easy placement of every word, and touches of unobtrusive originality." She comments that they link Prior "as closely to the Renaissance and Restoration as to his Augustan fellows" (p. 66).

Matthew M. Davis (essay date 1997)

SOURCE: "'The Most Fatal of All Faults': Samuel Johnson on Prior's *Solomon* and the Need for Variety," in *Papers on Language & Literature,* Vol. 33, No. 4, Fall, 1997, pp. 422-37.

[In the following essay, Davis examines the negative aspects of Samuel Johnson's The Life of Prior, *in particular focusing on Johnson's assessment that much of Prior's work is tedious. Although the piece focuses on Johnson, it provides insightful analyses of his views on Prior's works.]*

As literary critics we are always tempted to blur the categories of instruction and pleasure, to conclude that a work of literature is aesthetically excellent simply because we find it ideologically excellent. Perhaps no literary critic has ever managed to keep these two categories completely separate: our aesthetic judg-ments are always partially informed by our ideological beliefs. But the influence of ideological beliefs on aesthetic judgment is a matter of degree. Some critics are virtually incapable of detecting faults in works which flatter their own ideological principles; others are more willing to "divide against themselves"

and concede the aesthetic shortcomings of their ideological favorites.

In this essay I wish to argue that Samuel Johnson falls into the second category. Johnson's remarks on Matthew Prior's *Solomon* provide a striking proof that Johnson was not automatically pleased with a work of literature which confirmed his own world view. It would be hard to find a poem that is closer to Johnson's ideological views than Prior's *Solomon,* and yet Johnson does not allow this ideological affinity to overpower his aesthetic sense. He praises Prior's poem for its instructive excellence, but he damns it for its aesthetic shortcomings, especially its tediousness and lack of variety. Johnson's comments on *Solomon* are interesting in their own right, but they also provide a key which can help us understand a number of his other critical verdicts, as well as his approach to criticism in general.

As the title suggests, Prior's *Solomon on the Vanity of the World* (1708) has a great deal in common with Johnson's *Vanity of Human Wishes* (1749).[1] Both are Christian philosophical poems, heavily influenced by *Ecclesiastes* and the Preacher's lament that "All is vanity." Both are written in heroic couplets, and both offer sweeping surveys of life. Johnson "Survey[s] Mankind from *China* to *Peru*" (2) and concludes that man "Shuns fancied Ills, or chases airy Good" (10). Prior's Solomon "considers Man through the several Stages and Conditions of Life" (Argument to Book III) and concludes that "We pursue false Joy, and suffer real Woe" (I.13).

There are also a number of remarkable local similarities between these two poems. Johnson examines the trials and tribulations of eminent men and gives five English examples: Wolsey, Villiers, Harley, Wentworth, and Hyde (99-134). Solomon does the same, but he gives five Biblical examples: Adam, Noah, Abraham, Moses, and David (III.347-466). Both Johnson and Solomon conclude that "no Rank, no Station, no Degree" can escape the "contagious Taint of Sorrow" (III.249-50).

Johnson observes that wealth cannot buy peace of mind: "Wealth heap'd on Wealth, nor Truth nor Safety buys, / The Dangers gather as the Treasures rise" (27-28). Solomon likewise finds that wealth is not "the potent Sire of Peace" he had hoped it would be (III.245). The philosopher-king builds elaborate mansions and palaces, but he finds that "all the various Luxe of costly Pride" (II.14) cannot drive away unhappiness:

> To my new Courts sad Thought did still
> repair;
> And round my gilded Roofs hung hov'ring
> Care.

In vain on silken Beds I sought Repose;
And restless oft' from purple Couches
　　rose.

　　　　　　　　　　　　(II.53-56)

Many men seek military glory, but Johnson recognizes that military triumphs generally benefit individuals rather than nations:

The festal Blazes, the triumphal Show,
The ravish'd Standard, and the captive Foe,
The Senate's Thanks, the Gazette's pompous
　　Tale,
With Force resistless o'er the brave prevail. . .

Yet Reason frowns on War's unequal Game,
Where wasted Nations raise a single Name,
And mortgag'd States their Grandsires Wreaths
　　regret
From Age to Age in everlasting Debt.
　　　　　　　　(175-78, 185-88)

Solomon describes how the victorious general returns from war "with Conquest on his Brow," "Captive Generals" tied to his chariot, and "Joyful Citizens" echoing his victories (III.291-95). But Solomon also recognizes the darker side of this triumphal show, and of military aggression in general:

The Wretches he brings back, in Chains relate,
What may To-morrow be the Victor's Fate.
The Spoils and Trophies born before Him,
　　show
National Loss, and Epidemic Woe,
Various Distress, which He and His may
　　know.

　　　　　　　　　　(III.298-302)

It is natural to wish for a long life, but Johnson reminds his readers that an old man is generally a sick man: "Unnumber'd Maladies his Joints invade, / Lay Siege to Life and press the dire Blockade" (283-84). Solomon asks, "Why seek We Brightness from the Years to come?" (III.98) He reminds us that in our old age we will suffer from "slow Disease, and subtil Pain . . . / The Gout's fierce Rack, the burning Feaver's Rage, / The sad Experience of Decay . . . and Age" (III.136,142-43).

When senility sets in, Johnson explains, nature and the rhythm of the seasons will delight us no more:

In vain their Gifts the bounteous Seasons
　　pour,
The Fruit Autumnal, and the Vernal Flow'r,
With listless Eyes the Dotard views the Store,
He views, and wonders that they please no
　　more.

　　　　　　　　　　　(261-64)

Solomon describes the same withering away of nature's delights:

The verdant Rising of the flow'ry Hill,
The Vale enamell'd, and the Crystal Rill,
The Ocean rolling, and the shelly Shoar,
Beautiful Objects, shall delight no more;
When the lax'd Sinews of the weaken'd Eye
In watr'y Damps, or dim Suffusion lye.

　　　　　　　　　　(III.158-63)

Nor will music appease the dotard. Johnson:

Approach, ye Minstrels, try the soothing
　　Strain,
Diffuse the tuneful Lenitives of Pain:
No Sounds alas would touch th' impervious
　　Ear,
Though dancing Mountains witness'd *Orpheus*
　　near.

　　　　　　　　　　(267-70)

And Solomon:

Nought shall the Psaltry, and the Harp
　　avail,
The pleasing Song, or well repeated Tale,
When the quick Spirits their warm March
　　forbear;
And numbing Coldness has unbrac'd the Ear.
　　　　　　　　　　(III.154-57)

Johnson notes that even the best retirement has its share of woe:

But grant, the Virtues of a temp'rate Prime
Bless with an Age exempt from Scorn or
　　Crime;
An Age that melts with unperceiv'd
　　Decay,
And glides in modest Innocence away . . .
Yet ev'n on this her Load Misfortune
　　flings,
To press the weary Minutes flagging
　　Wings:
New Sorrow rises as the Day returns,
A Sister sickens, or a Daughter mourns.
Now Kindred Merit fills the sable Bier,
Now lacerated Friendship claims a Tear.
　　　　　　　　(291-94, 299-304)

Solomon makes precisely the same point:

But be the Terror of these Ills suppress'd:
And view We Man with Health and Vigor
　　blest. . . .
Hap'ly at Night He does with Horror shun
A widow'd Daughter, or a dying Son
　　　　. . .
The next Day, and the next he must attend

His Foe triumphant, or his buried Friend.
In ev'ry Act and Turn of Life he feels
Public Calamities, or Household Ills.
                    (III.185-86, 192-93, 196-99)

At the end of *The Vanity of Human Wishes* Johnson
urges his reader to abandon vain dreams and pray for
the good things in life:

Pour forth thy Fervours for a healthful Mind,
Obedient Passions, and a Will resign'd;
For Love, which scarce collective Man can
        fill;
For Patience sov'reign o'er transmuted Ill;
For Faith, that panting for a happier Seat,
Counts Death kind Nature's Signal of Retreat.
                                        (359-64)

At the end of Prior's poem, an angel appears to
Solomon and tells him to make the happiness he has
not found:

Thy Hope of Joy deliver to the Wind:
Suppress thy Passions; and prepare thy Mind
            . . .
Go forth: Be strong: With Patience, and with
        Care
Perform, and Suffer: To Thy self severe,
Gracious to Others, Thy Desires suppress'd,
Diffus'd Thy Virtues, First of Men, be Best.
                            (III.723-24, 867-72)

Both poets conclude by urging resignation to the will
of God. Johnson makes the point in a couplet: "Im-
plore his Aid, in his Decisions rest, / Secure whate'er
he gives, he gives the best" (355-56). The more verbose Prior supplies a triplet: "Thy sum of Life must
His Decrees fulfill: / What derogates from His Command, is Ill; / And that alone is Good, which centers
in His Will"(III.843-45).

Given these similarities, it is hardly surprising that
Johnson should conclude that *Solomon* contains "much
knowledge and much thought . . . many passages, to
which [the reader] may recur for instruction or delight:
many from which the poet may learn to write, and
the philosopher to reason" (*Lives* II: 207). What is
surprising, however, is Johnson's negative view of
Prior's poem as an aesthetic whole. In his *Life of Dryden*
Johnson insists that "It is not by comparing line
with line that the merit of great [lengthy] works is
to be estimated, but by their general effects and ultimate result" (I: 454). Although he concedes that individual passages of *Solomon* may please, Johnson
denies that the general effect or ultimate result is
pleasing.

Johnson gives two reasons why Prior's poem fails to
please. The first has to do with Prior's versification. In

the *Life of Milton* Johnson explains why he believes
rhyme is vital in English verse:

The musick of the English heroick line strikes the
ear so faintly that it is easily lost, unless all the
syllables of every line co-operate together: this
co-operation can be only obtained by the preseva-
tion of every verse unmingled with another as a
distinct system of sounds, and this distinctness
is obtained and preserved by the artifice of rhyme.
(I: 192)

Here Johnson imagines that rhyme will prevent one
line from "mingling" its sounds with the next, but in
Solomon rhyme does not serve this function, for Prior
has admitted what Johnson calls "broken" or "interrupted" lines:

In his preface to *Solomon* he proposes some im-
provements [to the heroic couplet], by extending the sense from one couplet to another, with a
variety of pauses. This he has attempted, but without success; his interrupted lines are unpleasing,
and his sense as less distinct is less striking. (II:
209)

Anyone who glances back at the excerpts from *Solomon* which I have quoted above will see what Johnson
has in mind. Whereas Johnson's couplets are generally
end-stopped, Prior more frequently carries the sense
across a rhyme. In general, the results are not particularly satisfying. Enjambment robs the rhymes of much
of their emphasis, and Prior loses the succinctness and
detachability of the couplet without gaining the flow
of blank verse. His sense is indeed "less distinct," and
his couplets are certainly less memorable: when was
the last time you heard someone quote a couplet from
Solomon?

However, Johnson insists that the most devastating
weakness of *Solomon* has to do not with versification,
but with organization and disposition. In *The Life of
Dryden* Johnson explains that "Works of imagination
excel by their allurement and delight; by their power
of attracting and detaining the attention" (I: 454).
Johnson thinks that Prior's *Solomon* fails to do this.
Prior "perceived . . . many excellences" in his poem,
but he "did not discover that it wanted that without
which all others are of small avail, the power of engaging and alluring curiosity" (II: 206). Johnson insists
that the wisdom of *Solomon* is vitiated first and foremost by tediousness:

The tediousness of this poem proceeds not from the
uniformity of the subject, for it is sufficiently
diversified, but from the continued tenour of the
narration; in which Solomon relates the successive vicissitudes of his own mind, without the
intervention of any other speaker or the mention of

lines of narration with almost no dialogue; *Paradise Regained* contains 2070 lines of dialogue with almost no action. In both cases the lack of variety causes the reader to lose momentum.

Butler's *Hudibras* is another instructive poem made tedious by a superabundance of dialogue. In *Hudibras,* Butler not only champions Johnson's beloved Royalists but also adds much to "the general stock of practical knowledge." However, Butler's poem is less pleasing than it might have been because there is too much talk and not enough action:

> I believe every reader regrets the paucity of events, and complains that in the poem of *Hudibras,* as in the history of Thucydides, there is more said than done. The scenes are too seldom changed, and the attention is tired with long conversation. (*Lives* I: 211)

Cowley's *Davideis* is full of "wit and learning," but the reader of Cowley's poem is "never delighted" (*Lives* I: 55). When Cowley decided to leave this poem unfinished, Johnson deadpans, "posterity lost more instruction than delight" (I: 54). Why does *The Davideis* fail to please? Johnson says it is because Cowley's abortive epic contains little that can "reconcile impatience or attract curiosity" (I: 51). The poet expends all of his energy on a "tedious" accumulation of conceits and digressions. He describes everything at excessive length. When he describes the Angel Gabriel, for instance, he cannot "let us go till he [has] related where Gabriel first got his skin, and *then* his mantle, *then* his lace, and *then* his scarfe" (I: 53, emphasis added).

Dryden's *Absalom and Achitophel* supports "the king's friends," *i.e.* the Tories, and attacks "the faction which, by lord Shaftesbury's incitement, set the duke of Monmouth at its head," *i.e.* the Whigs(*Lives* I: 373). Few poems could have been more gratifying to Johnson's own Tory political views. And yet strong political affinity does not keep Johnson from recognizing a certain tediousness in the poem:

> The subject had likewise another inconvenience: it admitted little imagery or description, and a long poem of mere sentiments [opinions] easily becomes tedious; though all the parts are forcible and every line kindles new rapture, the reader, if not relieved by the interposition of something that soothes the fancy, grows weary of admiration, and defers the rest. (I: 437)

So far we have been discussing poems, but Johnson believes that plays may also suffer from tediousness. In dramatic performances, he argues, dialogue is the essential thing; anything else is likely to become tedious very quickly. Johnson does not find Shakespeare's plays tedious throughout. In fact, as we have seen, he thinks they are generally paragons of variety. However, Johnson does object to the passages of extended narrative which crop up occasionally in Shakespeare:

> In narration he affects a disproportionate pomp of diction and a wearisome train of locution, and tells an incident imperfectly in many words, which might have been more plainly delivered in few. Narration in dramatick poetry is naturally tedious, as it is unanimated and inactive, and obstructs the progress of the action; it should therefore always be rapid, and enlivened by frequent interruption. Shakespeare found it an encumbrance, and instead of lightening it by brevity, endeavoured to recommend it by dignity and splendour. (*Yale* VII: 73)

Johnson thinks that the tedious passages in Shakespeare are blissfully rare, but he insists that Milton's masque *Comus* is tedious from start to finish. There is no question that *Comus* is an instructive work. It is written, Johnson notes approvingly, "in the praise and defense of virtue" (*Lives* I: 167). However, it is "tediously instructive." Johnson finds *Comus* windy and monotonous, from the opening speech on:

> The discourse of the Spirit is too long, an objection that may be made to almost all of the following speeches; they have not the spriteliness of a dialogue animated by reciprocal contention, but seem rather declamations deliberately composed and formally repeated on a moral question. The auditor therefore listens as to a lecture, without passion, without anxiety.[7]

Throughout the masque, Johnson insists, "there is something wanting to allure attention" (I: 169). Even the most "animated" scene, the dispute between the lady and Comus, needs "a brisker reciprocation of objections and replies."[8]

In his criticisms of **Solomon,** *Paradise Regained, Hudibras, The Davideis, Absalom and Achitophel,* and *Comus* Johnson divides against himself. He concedes the instructive excellence of these works, but he questions their aesthetic excellence. What's more, in each of these cases it is the absence of variety, or the presence of tediousness, which Johnson cites as critical. On the other hand, it is the presence of variety and the consequent absence of tediousness which make Pope's *Windsor Forest*, Dryden's critical prefaces, and Shakespeare's plays such pleasing works.

There is a consistency in Johnson's comments on tediousness and variety which should lead us to question those critics who insist that Johnson's approach to criticism is haphazard and unprincipled. Paul Fussell insists that Johnson's critical thinking recognizes "hardly any fixed principles," and that "his literary sensibility . . . is really madly irrational, un-systematic, impulsive, and untidy" (60). Harold Bloom has recently advanced a similar view. He contends that Johnson is hostile to "rules, principles, [and] methods." According to Bloom, Johnson's criticism proves that "there is no method except oneself" (2).

The passages which I have examined suggest that Fussell and Bloom have overstated their case. It is true that Johnson was no friend to the neoclassical "rules." It is also true that his criticism cannot be reduced to a simple "method," like painting by numbers. How-ever, as we have seen, certain patterns and principles *do* emerge in Johnson's criticism. When it comes to the need for variety, Johnson is neither "madly irra-tional" nor "impulsive." Rather, he is reasonable, consistent, and principled. Not only in his comments on Prior's **Solomon** but throughout his criticism Johnson insists that variety is the most vital of all aesthetic principles and tediousness the most fatal of all faults.

Notes

[1] Ian Jack notes several parallel passages in his arti-cle, but he does not cite any of those which I cite below. In general his emphasis is on stylistic simi-larities rather than ideological ones. All citations to Johnson's *Vanity* are by line number and are tak-en from the Fleeman edition. All citations to Pri-or's *Solomon* are by book and line number and are taken from Volume I of the Wright and Spears edition.

[2] *Lives* II: 207. There is a certain irony in this verdict, for Prior had written in his Preface to *Solomon* that, as precepts, "however true in Theory, or useful in Prac-tice, would be but dry and tedious in verse . . . I found it necessary to form some Story."

[3] Boswell, IV: 338. For more examples of Newtonian similes, see *Adventurer* 45 (*Yale* II: 359-60), *Idler* 1 (*Yale* II: 5), and Boswell, IV: 105-07. For commentary on Johnson and Newton, see Wiltshire, 161 and Jack-son, 393-94.

[4] *Lives* II: 206. Here and elsewhere, Johnson declines to exalt authors above other human beings, as some romantic writers would do after him. Rather, Johnson insists that authors partake of flawed human nature just like everybody else. See also *Rambler* 207 (*Yale* V: 313).

[5] For a fine discussion of Johnson's views on tedious-ness and boredom in daily life, see Spacks, 31-55.

[6] *Yale* VIII: 873. See also Johnson's comments on the *Henry IV* plays (VII: 522-23), *The Merry Wives of Windsor* (VII: 341), *Midsummer Night's Dream* (VII: 160), and *The Tempest* (VII: 135).

[7] *Lives* I: 168. By likening *Comus* to a lecture, Johnson places Milton's masque in the unfortunate company of James Thomson's play *Sophonisba*. At the premiere of Thomson's play, "It was observed . . . that nobody was much affected, and that the company rose as from a moral lecture" (*Lives* II: 288).

[8] Johnson made a similar comment on Hester Chapone's play *The Father's Revenge*, which he read in manu-script: "It seems to want that quickness of reciproca-tion which characterises the English drama, and is not always sufficiently fervid or animated." (*Letters* IV: 251).

Works Cited

Bate, W. Jackson. *The Achievement of Samuel Johnson.* Chicago: U of Chicago P, 1955.

Bloom, Harold. Introduction. *Dr. Samuel Johnson and James Boswell.* New York: Chelsea House, 1986.

Boswell, James. *The Life of Johnson.* Ed. George Birk-beck Hill and L. F. Powell. 6 vols. Oxford: Clarendon, 1934-50.

Fussell, Paul. *Samuel Johnson and the Life of Writing.* New York: Norton, 1986.

Jack, Ian. "The Choice of Life in Johnson and Prior." *Journal of English and Germanic Philology* 49 (1950): 523-30.

Jackson, H. J. "The Immoderation of Samuel John-son." *University of Toronto Quarterly* 59 (1990): 382-98.

Johnson, Samuel. *Dictionary of the English Language.* 4th ed. 2vols. London, 1774.

———. *Letters of Samuel Johnson.* Ed. Bruce Red-ford. 5 vols. Princeton: Princeton UP, 1992-94.

———. *Lives of the English Poets.* Ed. George Birk-beck Hill. 3 vols. Oxford: Clarendon, 1905.

———. *Samuel Johnson: The Complete English Poems.* Ed. D. J. Fleeman. New Haven: Yale UP, 1982.

———. *The Yale Edition of the Works of Samuel Johnson.* 16 vols. New Haven: Yale UP, 1958.

Prior, Matthew. *The Literary Works of Matthew Prior.* Ed. H. Bunker Wright and Monroe K. spears. 2 vols. Oxford: Clarendon, 1971.

Spacks, Patricia Meyer. *Boredom: The Literary History of a State of Mind*. Chicago: U of Chicago P, 1995.

Wiltshire, John. *Samuel Johnson and the Medical World: The Doctor and the Patient*. Cambridge: Cambridge UP, 1991.

FURTHER READING

Bibliography

Godshalk, William Leigh. "Prior's Copy of Spenser's 'Works' 1679." *The Papers of the Bibliographical Society of America* 61, No. 1 (January-March, 1967): 52-5.

> Examines the marginalia and underlinings in Prior's volume of Spenser's *Works*.

Wright, H. Bunker. "Ideal Copy and Authoritative Text: The Problem of Prior's *Poems on Several Occasions* (1718)." *Modern Philology* XLIX, No. 4 (May, 1952): 234-41.

> Discusses the findings of an exhaustive comparison of different copies of *Poems on Several Occasions* and explains why most are imperfect.

Wright, H. Bunker and P. J. Croft. "Matthew Prior's Last Manuscript: 'Predestination'." *The British Library Journal* 11, No. 2 (Autumn, 1985): 99-112.

> Discusses the discovery of Prior's own manuscript of "Predestination." The article reproduces several pages of the manuscript in Prior's handwriting.

Biography

Bickley, Francis. *The Life of Matthew Prior*. 1914. Reprint. Folcraft, Penn.: Folcroft Press, 1970, 295 p.

> The first full-length biography of Prior. Prior's literary career is only briefly discussed.

Eves, Charles Kenneth. *Matthew Prior: Poet and Diplomatist*. 1939. Reprint. New York: Octagon, 1971, 436 p.

> Critically acclaimed as finest Prior biography.

Johnson, Samuel. "Prior." In his *Lives of the English Poets*, 2: 180-211. Edited by George Birkbeck Hill. Oxford: Clarendon Press, 1905.

> Classic biographical sketch of Prior, including some critical commentary.

Legg, L. G. Wickham. *Matthew Prior: A Study of His Public Career and Correspondence*. Cambridge: Cambridge University Press, 1921, 348 p.

> The standard study of Prior's public life.

Wright, H. Bunker. "Prior Knowledge." *The Scriblerian* VI, No. 2 (Spring, 1974): 68-70.

> Discusses the merits of three twentieth-century biographies: by Francis Bickley, L. G. Wickham Legg, and Charles Kenneth Eves.

Criticism

Croft, P. J. "'Mr. Prior' and Alexander Pope." *The Review of English Studies* XXXIII, No. 129 (February, 1982): 52-8.

> Examines a four-line epigram and a couplet associated with Prior and Pope. The critic disputes the contention that Prior authored the epigram and uses it to support an argument for adding the couplet to Pope's unofficial verse canon.

Doughty, Oswald. "The Poet of the 'Familiar Style'." *English Studies* VII, No. 1-6 (1925): 5-10.

> Considers William Cowper's praise of Prior and the merit of several of Prior's verses.

Jack, Ian. "The 'Choice of Life' in Johnson and Matthew Prior." *The Journal of English and Germanic Philology* XLIX, No. 4 (October, 1950): 523-30.

> Offers evidence that Samuel Johnson was heavily influenced by both the substance and style of Prior's *Solomon* when he wrote both *Rasselas* and *The Vanity of Human Wishes*.

Kline, Richard B. "Matthew Prior and 'Dear Will Nuttley': An Addition to the Canon." *Philological Quarterly* XLVII, No. 2 (April, 1968): 157-63.

> Provides background for a character sketch Prior incorporated in a letter. The text of the letter is included.

Meier, T. K. "Prior's Adaptation of 'The Nutbrown Maid'." *Moderna Sprak* LXVIII, No. 4 (1974): 331-36.

> Examines the extent to which Prior's *Henry and Emma* succeeds as an adaptation of the folk ballad "The Nutbrown Maid."

Rippy, Frances Mayhew. "Matthew Prior as the Last Renaissance Man." In *Studies in Medieval, Renaissance, American Literature*, 120-31. Edited by Betsy F. Colquitt. Fort Worth: Texas Christian University Press, 1971.

> Claims Prior "embodied in himself and in his writings many of the qualities which still seem to us peculiarly Renaissance. . . . " The author uses common sources to demonstrate Prior's indebtedness to Greek and Latin models.

Williams, Arthur S. "Panegyric Decorum in the Reigns of William III and Anne." *The Journal of British Studies* XXI, No. 1, (Fall, 1981): 56-67.

> Contends that Prior broke from the "conventions of Whig panegyric as his political sympathies shifted toward an extreme Tory faction. . . . " The essay offers a critical examination of Prior's heroic verse.

Wright, H. Bunker. "Matthew Prior and Elizabeth Singer." *The Philological Quarterly* XXIV, No. 1 (January, 1945): 71-82.

> Analyzes Prior's relationship with Elizabeth Singer. Nine letters from Prior to Singer are examined and form the basis of the study.

Wright, H. Bunker and Monroe K. Spears. Introduction to *The Literary Works of Matthew Prior,* Volume I, xxvii-liii. Edited by Bunker and Spears. Oxford: Clarendon Press, 1959.

> Describes the three major collections of Prior manuscripts, the criteria used by the editors to determine the authenticity of questionable works, lists principal collected editions, and discusses the history of Prior's canon.

Additional coverage of Prior's life and work is contained in the following sources published by The Gale Group: *Literature Criticism from 1400 to 1800, Vol. 4,* **and** *Dictionary of Literary Biography, Vol. 95.*

Gerrard Winstanley

1609-1676

English political writer

INTRODUCTION

Writing during the turbulent years immediately after the English Revolution, Winstanley, seized the opportunity to propose an alternative form of government to replace the recently dismantled monarchy. While some radical groups sought a more equitable society and advocated religious freedom, Winstanley, in *The Law of Freedom in a Platform* (1652) developed a program for a communist utopia. The combination of Winstanley's unorthodox political beliefs and his radical political agenda have marked him as a progressive thinker whose ideas in some ways presaged those of later communist revolutionaries.

Biographical Information

Born into a middle-class Puritan family in Wigan, Winstanley followed family tradition and entered the clothing industry. He traveled to London where he was apprenticed to a clothier. Before the Civil War, Winstanley established his own business and was married. The war destroyed Winstanley's business, as it had many others. Retiring to the Surrey countryside, Winstanley worked as a hired laborer and, between 1648 and 1652, wrote and published pamphlets promoting the causes of economic, social, political, and religious freedom. Between 1649 and 1650 he organized two communities based on the principle that the land was the "common treasury" of the people of England. He and his followers, termed "Diggers" because of their agrarian practices, appropriated and farmed commonly held land in Walton and Cobham, but the communities failed, largely due to opposition by local landholders. In 1652, Winstanley wrote *The Law of Freedom in a Platform,* in which he outlines the means by which a communist commonwealth may be achieved (although he did not use the term "communist" in his writings). Informed by the failures of the Digger communities, this pamphlet emphasizes the interim role of the state in the establishment of an ideal commonwealth. This focus on external government rather than individual moral responsibility marks an apparent shift in Winstanley's views, and is the focus of much critical debate. Winstanley never published another work after *The Law of Freedom,* and aside from a few references to him in contemporary records, he very nearly disappears from the historical record until his death in 1676.

Major Works

Much of Winstanley's written work, including such early pamphlets as *The Mysterie of God* (1648), are concerned with his views on God and religion. Winstanley rejected many traditional core doctrines, including belief in the historic Christ, the role of the clergy as mediators between God and worshippers, and the superiority of the Scriptures over the ability of every individual to experience and understand the sacred. As Winstanley discusses in pamphlets such as *The New Law of Righteousness* (1649), it is this core of inherent godliness that he believed would rise up in every person, given proper philosophical enlightenment. When this occurred, people would break free from the oppression imposed by private ownership of land, and the inequities inherent in this system would then dissolve. After writing pamphlets defending the Digger communities and exposing the attacks suffered by the Diggers at the hands of private landholders, Winstanley wrote *The Law of Freedom in a Platform* in 1652. Drawing on what he learned from the failures of the Digger communities, he elaborated the means by which a communist commonwealth could be established. In this pamphlet, Winstanley focuses on the possibility that the reordering of society will positively influence the motivations and conduct of all people. *The Law of Freedom* also advocates an economy without money; reemphasizes that private property is the source of oppression; and maintains that the state plays a necessary role in creating the conditions required for the realization of a socialist utopia.

Critical Reception

Critical debate surrounding Winstanley's works is heavily concerned with the relevance of his theology to his political agenda and with the apparent shift in Winstanley's thought from an emphasis on an internal theological motivation for reformation to a focus on external regulation of morality. In analyzing these issues, George H. Sabine argues that Winstanley's use of Biblical language and imagery in his writings was typical of his time and reflected what other writers on the extreme left wing of the Puritan Revolution expressed. Sabine further contends that Winstanley's beliefs, such as his conviction in the superiority of the "inner light" over the Scripture and his anti-clerical views, demonstrate that Winstanley had made a complete break with "any doctrinal or theological standard of religion." For Winstanley, Sabine contends, religion referred to a moral way of life. The commonwealth outlined by Winstanley was seen by its creator as morally superior to a monarchy because of its basis in principles of community and cooperation rather than on competition and individual acquisition. Winstanley's *The Law of Freedom* focuses on individual moral change through social and institutional reorganization. However, Winstanley maintained his belief in the development of the inner being as the key to bringing about a utopia of fairness. *The Law of Freedom* still advocates sharing land, labor, and goods; the outlawing of a money-based economy; and the end of class exploitation. While some critics suggest that Winstanley had become a rationalist and a materialist by the time he wrote *The Law of Freedom,* Winstanley's views on the role and nature of God had not fundamentally changed by 1652. Winstanley viewed "Reason" not as a replacement for God, but as a name for God that accurately expresses the way God works through humankind. Andrew Bradstock contends that Winstanley's theological position never shifted radically. Bradstock states that even though Winstanley rejected many traditional beliefs, he did not reject Christianity altogether. Bradstock emphasizes the similarity of some of Winstanley's beliefs to those of contemporary Quakers, Fifth Monarchists, and modern day Liberation Theologians. In his discussion of *The Law of Freedom*'s focus on law and punishment, Michael Rogers also maintains that Winstanley did not undergo a major shift in his thinking. He argues that Winstanley remained optimistic that when individuals rejected private property, the causes of crime would disappear. By 1652, Rogers suggests, when *The Law of Freedom* was written, Winstanley had come to believe that this process of transformation would take longer than he originally thought and that a democratized legal code could be used to institu-tionalize Reason until people could be free of the constraints of "kingly government" and private property.

PRINCIPAL WORKS

The Breaking of the Day of God (pamphlet) 1648

The Mysterie of God (pamphlet) 1648

Truth Lifting Up Its Head Above Scandal (pamphlet) 1648

The New Law of Righteousness (pamphlet) 1649

The True Levellers Standard Advanced (pamphlet) 1649

Fire in the Bush (pamphlet) 1650

An Humble Request (pamphlet) 1650

The Law of Freedom in a Platform (pamphlet) 1652

CRITICISM

George H. Sabine (essay date 1941)

SOURCE: An Introduction to *The Works of Gerrard Winstanley,* edited by George H. Sabine, Russell & Russell, 1941, pp. 1-70.

[*In the following excerpt, Sabine reviews Winstanley's evolving religious and political convictions and agenda.*]

Winstanley's Religious Argument

Winstanley nowhere set out in logical order an outline of the religious convictions which, as he believed, led inevitably to communism as their social corollary. This was in part due to the fact that his writings are pamphlets, written as occasion demanded, and in part to the fact that his convictions were in process of formation, not in the stage of being logically systematized. It is quite clear that he would have regarded this last stage, if he had reached it, as a mark of degeneration and not of progress. Winstanley's communism belonged to the class of prophetical writing, with no delusions about a "scientific" proof—the contemporary analogue would have been a theological proof—of the validity of human aspirations. Nevertheless, it is not difficult to arrange in a logical order the chief headings of his argument, which is in fact not very complicated. The propositions are repeated again and again throughout his works. After the revelation recorded in **The New Law of Righteousnes,** which turned his interest definitely toward the social implications of his religion, his train of thought is complete, though he varied the presentation of his case somewhat to adapt it to the audience he was addressing. **The Law of Freedom,** which was published a year and a half after the attempt to cultivate the common land had failed, is somewhat different from the works produced in the course of the controversy. Here Winstanley is trying to set out a rounded communist constitution that he hoped might commend itself to Cromwell. As his reliance on statesmanship has perforce grown, so his millenarian hopes have correspondingly shrunk. But even with this change of interest and purpose, there is no change of the convictions that lay behind Winstanley's communism.

The premise from which Winstanley's thought began, often stated but never argued, was his belief that the events of the Puritan Revolution were part of a tremendous change that was altering the whole status of human life. It is to be a real reformation, affecting to their roots all the relationships of men in society. As such it has a cosmic rather than a national significance, though it has the latter too. England, he hopes—speaking in the congenial chiliastic imagery of *Revela-*

tion and the *Book of Daniel*—will be the tenth part of the city Babylon that falls off first from the Beast. In the troubles that accompany and follow the Civil Wars, and more especially in the contempt and persecution visited upon the sectaries, he sees the rage of the evil powers, in man and the world, against the power of spiritual reformation, which in the end is certain to overcome them. The sectaries, therefore, have a quite extraordinary significance; the persecution of the "mechanick preachers" is part of the persecution which the synagogue visited upon the equally humble disciples of Jesus, and which the world, the flesh, and the devil always visit upon the saints. The subtle craft, the unparalleled hypocrisy, and the cruelty expressed against the saints (i.e., the sectaries) are an expression of the angels of darkness let loose in the spirits of men. The bright appearing of God in the saints, casting down all forms and customs of the beast (i.e., religious law) is what torments the world today. For the saints are about to partake of the glory of the city of God. The present is a transitional stage—the dividing of time—between one cosmic era and another, in which the rule of divine love will finally be consummated on earth. Hence a true reformation concerns not the church alone but will extend to government and all the social relationships on which government depends. Magistrates will "love and delight to be executing justice for the good and safety of the commonwealth". God has cast England into the fire: hence the troubles of the times and hence also the greatness of the triumph that awaits the spirit of love and truth.

Winstanley's language, it should be observed, was more extraordinary than the idea he had to express. Millenarian hopes and imagery are a normal accompaniment of every revolution. They are expressed in the figures of speech which, in the circumstances, come easiest to the pen—the New Jerusalem, democratic liberty and equality, or the classless society. However expressed, they represent the religious aspect of the revolution: the symbols that serve to release men's energies, that wear the guise of ultimate ends, and that always remove farther into the future when one tries to approach them. In Puritan England there was no effort to disguise the fact that these symbols were religious, and their natural imagery came from the Bible. In some degree most men, and by no means the most visionary, shared ideas like those that Winstanley expressed. Cromwell's letters show that he habitually regarded himself as acting under the guidance of God to accomplish the designs of Providence. In the course of the discussion in the Army Council with the Levellers he said:

> I am one of those whose heart God hath drawn out to wait for some extraordinary dispensations, according to those promises that he hath held forth of things to be accomplished in the later times, and I cannot but think that God is beginning of them.[1]

Milton's pamphlets, especially those on the reform of the church, include many passages holding out extravagant hopes of the regeneration, both of church and of government, that is impending in England. The Fifth Monarchy movement produced a great outcropping of works that set forth the chiliastic hopes from which that movement grew, though such ideas were not wanting at any time after 1642.[2] As usual it was the groups on the extreme left wing of the revolution that abounded most in millenarian expectations. In this respect, then, Winstanley was merely typical, both of his time and also of the place that he occupied in the Puritan Revolution.

It is characteristic of Winstanley, and also of others who were most given to these expectations, that they looked for the literal and, so to speak, the physical realization of the Kingdom of God on earth. It is a mere trick of self-seeking priests, he thought, to fob men off with hopes of a better life beyond the grave, or with "spiritual" meanings of Scriptural promises, instead of urging them to create the New Jerusalem here and now. Flesh judges it right that some should be poor and others rich and powerful, but in the light of equity and reason it is right that all should have freedom and subsistence. It dishonors the Maker that there should be oppressing tyrants, especially among Christians who make a verbal profession of love while in action they deny it. Fleshly dominion of one over all shall cease, and the eye of flesh shall see it. The visions of the Apocalypse thus become literal prophecies of that which is about to be. The saving distinction which Calvinists usually drew between the realms of nature and grace was quite obliterated. In 1647 the Baptist Thomas Collier preached a sermon at Army Headquarters which in part might have been uttered by Winstanley.

> It's true that we have had, and still have, exceeding low and carnal thoughts of heaven, looking on it as a glorious place above the firmament, out of sight, and not to be enjoyed till after this life. But God himself is the Saints' kingdom, their enjoyment, their glory. Where God is manifesting himself, there is his and the Saints' kingdom, and that is in the Saints.

In the new Heaven and the new earth that will thus arise, "The nations shall become the nations of Christ, and the government shall be in the hands of the saints."[3]

It was not the case, however, that Winstanley belonged with the Fifth Monarchy Men in the implications that he attached to a government in the hands of the saints. The rule of the saints became a synonym for government that was censorious, meddlesome, illiberal, and reactionary, devoted to establishing on earth not the kingdom of love but the dominance of a church, a dogma, and a discipline. This is the character that messianism in politics has always tended to assume, and the character that Puritanism often did assume. So far as can be judged of a man who never had to take the responsibility for any actual rule, Winstanley had no leanings whatever in this direction. In his *Law of Freedom* there is no suggestion that he wished to give the suffrage to the saints, meaning thereby persons of one religious profession as distinct from another. He was saved, I think, by the completeness with which he had broken away from any doctrinal or theological standard of religion. He believed, naively no doubt, that a life of Christian love was about to transform the whole economic and political organization of society, but he expected also a complete transformation of human nature. He did not believe that some, already in possession of the light, could force it on others. The all-sufficiency of the mystical experience, carried to its logical conclusion, destroyed church and clergy, and with them tests of orthodoxy and rationalized systems of the supernatural. The result, though it seems paradoxical, was something that might almost be described as secularism tinged with a religious motivation.

The second premise of Winstanley's religious argument, and the one which was central to all that he had to say, was his belief in the Light, or the Christ within—a divinely given insight or intuition working a moral reformation—as the essential part of religion. So much has already been said on this point that there is little need to add more; there is no limit to the number of citations that could be given from Winstanley's works, if there were any object in multiplying them. In contrast with "experimental" religion he places the "imaginary power"—parallel with John Everard's contrast of religious action with "notions and speculations"—by which Winstanley means school divinity, especially Calvinist theology, and all that he conceived to flow from it. There was of course nothing distinctive merely in the belief that religious experience is unique; Christians of every group agreed to that, and even a man so hard-headed as Ireton might assert that, "Everyone hath a spirit within him." But for Winstanley, and for the mystics and the Quakers, the experience becomes all in all. It supersedes the whole system of doctrine built up by inference from Scripture: the supposed truths of metaphysics and cosmology, the plan of church-government, and the ethical rules supposed to be demonstrable by piecing together Biblical texts. In a word it did away with all that made the clergy a learned profession, and Quakerism merely drew the logical conclusion when it abolished the distinction between clergy and laity. To this Winstanley added another inference when he argued that the abolition of the clergy implied also a thoroughgoing change in social organization. The "imaginary power", according to Winstanley, had four branches: the preaching "universative" power, the kingly power, the power of lawyers, and the art of buying and selling. Of these the clergy is the chief, and all fall if it falls. The universal power of love which rules in the creation, if once it is given first

place in human life, must reform all human relationships and hence both the economic and political organization of society.

If Winstanley had been a speculative metaphysician, he would have been a pantheist. Some such conception is characteristic of mysticism, which of necessity sets aside any such rigid conception of God's personality as is required by theism. God is an indwelling power in nature and in man. Winstanley, in the address which precedes *Truth Lifting up its Head,* expressly adopts the word "Reason" in place of God, because the latter suggests a being apart from nature and from man, a being whose action is imagined to be far away or long ago, rather than an omnipresent power whose action is immediately felt. It would certainly be an error to infer that this implied any rationalistic (in the sense of non-religious) intention on Winstanley's part. Reason is, for him, merely a neutral word for "the incomprehensible spirit" from which the creation flowed and which continually works in it, "that living power of light that is in all things". He often calls it also "universal love". It manifests itself in the unconscious teleology of all living things, but especially in man by leading him to govern his actions according to justice, wisdom, and righteousness; if reason rules in a man, he will never trespass against his fellow-creature. There was plenty of authority for such a use of the word in the mystical tradition which Winstanley somehow tapped. The opposite of reason for him is "imagination", the false idea of separateness from God and one's fellows, that issues in covetousness and self-seeking, and fills men with fears, doubts, wars, divisions, and lust. From imagination proceeds the letter that killeth; from reason or love proceeds the spirit that maketh alive.

The struggle between reason and imagination—the higher and the lower natures—which every man experiences in his own being, is but a part of the cosmic struggle between light and darkness, God and the Devil, that goes on continually in the world. This struggle, and the final victory of light, is a standard theme of mystical experience, as it is with Winstanley and George Fox and as it was with Jakob Boehme. To this way of thinking it is more than an analogy, for there is a literal identification of reason with God, and of evil inclinations with the devil. The cosmic drama is reenacted in every man and is continually repeated in human society. Both God and the devil are literally within the soul. Winstanley is quite explicit in saying that it was the discovery of this fact that first set him free from the fears and anxieties, the dread of the supernatural that had assailed him, which forms an almost normal antecedent to the state of mystical exaltation. It is accordingly characteristic of this conception that it pictures history as successive stages in the struggle, or as "risings-up" of the spirit against the flesh. Winstanley tries his hand more than once at periodizing history, especially the Scriptural story and the history of the church, in the light of this idea, as Saltmarsh had done in his *Sparkles of Glory* and as many others did. It ought to be noted that the idea behind this reading of history is essentially millenarian. It in no way implies progress or a gradual development but the contrary. The "outpourings" of the spirit come when "the time has been fulfilled" and they invariably lead up to a perfect stage in which the light will be fully triumphant, a new heaven and a new earth.

In the case of Winstanley the identification of inner and outer, of evil in man and evil in nature, was carried in his earlier pamphlets to the most naive extreme. In *The New Law of Righteousnes* he supposed that the corruption of the flesh in evil men literally infected the whole of nature. Their decaying bodies, after they were dead and buried, corrupted the plants and through them imparted the poison of evil to the beasts that fed upon the plants. The very elements, and all bodies that are composed of them, are disordered by man's rejection of the spirit. In *The Mysterie of God* he supposed that when the spirit recovers its sway in man, as he expects that it is about to do, all the creatures other than man will be dissolved, since there will be no further need for food. It seems pretty clear that this conception of the close sympathetic relation between man and nature played a considerable part in the beginning of his communism. From the first of the Digger manifestoes, *The True Levellers Standard Advanced,* it appears that he confidently expected the reestablishing of the rule of community and love among men to increase automatically the fertility of the barren land. In fact, without such a belief, his communism was hardly workable, since it implied that a large part of the English population would be fed from the produce of land that had not previously been arable. This mystical element in Winstanley's thought had become less prominent when he wrote *The Law of Freedom;* in that work he assumes the existence of a considerable amount of nationalized land got from the confiscated estates of the King, the royalists, and the clergy.

In Winstanley's rather simple-minded metaphysics, then, the visible world is quite literally the garment of God, and God is the moving spirit in the world, manifested in the sun, moon, and stars, in plants and animals, but especially in human history. This universal power is present in every man and is able completely to transform human nature. All that is required is that men should be aware, directly and immediately, of the light that is within them and, being aware, should follow its dictates. This for Winstanley is the essence of all religion, its only necessary condition and its all-sufficient condition. It is, however, not an easy condition, for not only the temptations of the flesh but also the forms and outward observances that imagination creates stand between men and the direct apprehension of truth and righteousness. It does not appear that Winstanley thought of this experience as a transcendent vision,

momentarily attained, which sometimes lifts the mystic into another world. Like the Quakers he thought of it rather as an experience repeatedly enjoyed and continuously affording strength and guidance in quite everyday affairs. The beginning of religion is the knowledge that there is within one the capacity for such experience and guidance; the practice of religion consists in having habitual recourse to it, and everything else belongs among things indifferent.

> When men suck content from creatures, as from men's learning, gifts, customs, prayers, or forms of worship, and think they shall never have comfort unless they enjoy these outward helps, this is to prefer the broken cisterns before the fountains. . . . He cannot meditate nor understand till God come into him; he cannot speak till God give utterance; he feels his heart barren of understanding, of love, of peace; he feels and sees nothing in him but only a thirsting soul after God, whom his secret thoughts tell him is able to satisfy him, if he please but to manifest himself. . . . The experience and writings of prophets, apostles, and saints are dry shells to me and cannot comfort, unless God, whom my soul breathes after, give to me likewise some experiences of his love, as he gave to them, and then I shall have joy; yea, and my joy then will be fulfilled, and not till then.[4]

All Winstanley's reflection upon the religious and social problems of his day, which eventuated in his communism, was little more than an effort to carry through, relentlessly and to their final conclusions, the implications of this fundamental insight. These implications were devastating for all existing forms of faith and ecclesiastical institution, and also, as he came to believe, for all existing political and economic institutions, since he supposed that the latter must stand or fall with the former. In truth, his procedure, though simple-minded and without much grasp of the complexities of the phenomena he was trying to deal with, was surprisingly logical and thorough-going. Without trying to reproduce the many repetitions and digressions into which he fell, I shall summarize his chief deductions relative to the authority of Scripture, the nature of the church, and the position of the clergy.

Winstanley's belief in the sufficiency of an experimental religion, consistently carried out, made a clean sweep of the mythology of the Christian tradition, and more particularly of Protestant bibliolatry. By placing the whole religious drama within the setting of the human mind, the mystics quite destroyed the external or, so to speak, the physical existence of those entities upon which all doctrinal forms of Christianity depended. Christ and the Devil, Winstanley says over and over again, are not forces outside human nature; they are the impulsions and inclinations, respectively, of good and evil—the flesh and the spirit—which every man experiences as the controlling motives of his own action. The Devil is not "a middle power between God and me, but it is the power of my proud flesh". And "the power of the perfect law taking hold thereupon threw me under sorrow and sealed up my misery, and this is utter darkness".[5] Heaven and hell are therefore literally within the soul, not places far off. Similarly, Christ is the regenerating power of goodness within every man, not the historical character who lived long ago in Palestine.

> And therefore if you expect or look for the resurrection of Jesus Christ, you must know that the spirit within the flesh is the Jesus Christ, and you must see, feel, and know from himself his own resurrection within you, if you expect life and peace by him.[6]

> So that you do not look for a God now, as formerly you did, to be [in] a place of glory beyond the sun, moon, and stars, nor imagine a divine being you know not where, but you see him ruling within you, and not only in you, but you see him to be the spirit and power that dwells in every man and woman; yea, in every creature, according to his orb, within the globe of the creation.[7]

In the second place, the belief in the all-sufficiency of direct experience destroyed the importance of a literal interpretation of Scripture. For Winstanley Scripture was valuable as a record of experiences enjoyed by spiritually minded men in other times and places. To the Scripture stories, such for example as the story of the Gadarine swine, he attached, especially in his earlier writings, a considerable symbolic importance as typifying spiritual truths. After the first two or three of his pamphlets, his inclination to look for far-fetched symbolic meanings in them seems to have decreased, and at no time did he attach much importance to their literal truth. More and more he reserved elaborate citations of Scriptural authority for arguments addressed to those who presumably regarded this as an effective kind of proof, such as the paper addressed to John Platt which he inserted in *An Humble Request.* In order to be rightly interpreted or even recognized it requires the same kind of immediate experience that enabled its authors to write it. It is at the most an aid, not a substitute, and Winstanley clearly looked forward to a time when "none shall need to turn over books and writings to get knowledge". This distinction between the "experimental" knowledge of religion and "hearsay" knowledge from reading or from hearing a teacher was made habitually by George Fox.

> I told him [Cromwell] that all Christendom (so-called) had the Scriptures, but they wanted the power and Spirit that those had who gave forth the Scriptures; and that was the reason they were not in fellowship with the Son, nor with the Father, nor with the Scriptures, nor with one another.[8]

This willingness to dispense with the literal interpretation of Scripture was enough by itself to put Winstanley outside the main intellectual current of Puritanism. Presbyterians, Independents, and Baptists differed from one another in the deductions, with reference either to doctrine or to church-government, which they drew from Scripture, but they were quite in agreement on two points, first, that Scripture contained, either directly or by implication, a complete body of doctrine and practice, and second, that no doctrine or practice was binding upon Christians unless it were justified by the authority of Scripture. The differences between these groups of Puritan Protestants, therefore, were in a sense intellectually superficial. They might have been healed by the development of a sufficiently complete and a sufficiently learned system of theological science, something that these bodies all professed to look forward to. The superiority of Calvinism over other forms of Protestant theology lay in the fact that it went about as far as it was humanly possible to go in constructing this kind of system. On the other hand, the form of religious faith represented by Winstanley and the Quakers was a forthright challenge to the whole principle of Biblical theology. It flatly denied that there was any such system of learned doctrine, or that it would be significant if it could be constructed. The whole theological project ends in nothing except "imaginary, book-studying, university divinity", as Winstanley calls it, a mass of dark interpretations and glosses upon the Scriptural records of an experience which, taken by itself, is self-sufficient and self-explanatory.

The implications of this position for scholarship and for public education will have to be examined later in connection with Winstanley's views of such matters in his *Law of Freedom.* Here it is necessary only to refer briefly to its implications with reference to the church and the clergy. From Winstanley's point of view the true church is exclusively a spiritual body, the whole company of the saints who have experienced salvation and have been morally regenerated by the inward operation of reason or the law of righteousness. No outward organization is required, and it needs no visible marks or signs to distinguish it from the world. It has no doctrinal tests, and certainly no mandate from magistrates to teach any creed or apply any discipline. It requires no rites or ordinances or set forms of worship, and if any congregation uses such forms, they have at the most only a symbolic meaning which might equally well be expressed in other ways, or indeed might equally well remain without formal expression. Winstanley set forth most fully his views upon the ordinances of religion in *Truth Lifting up its Head above Scandals,* where he defended himself against the charge of denying such ordinances altogether. Here it seems apparent that he had dispensed with every form of religious service except the meeting and communion of like-minded persons, and perhaps the "prophesying" of those whom the spirit might move. He expressly denies that baptism, except in the mystical sense of baptism by the spirit, is essential. Preaching from texts or from "imaginary beliefs" is worse than useless. Prayer, if it is "a declaration of the heart", is permissible, but words are "the remotest part of prayer"; its essence consists in acting righteously and in the "reasonings of the heart", that is, in reflection and self-examination. The observance of set days, as of the Sabbath, is a formality, and the notion that a whole parish can be called a church is a grotesque misunderstanding of the term. These views are, of course, substantially identical with those of George Fox and with the practice of the Quakers. But Winstanley's emphasis is on the negations. I believe it to be true to say that he saw no need even for that minimum of organization by which Fox preserved the Quakers as a recognizable religious body.

From this view of the church it follows that the clergy, as a distinct class of professionally trained persons, simply disappears. There is no place for it, since every man must experience the revelation of the inner light for himself. Moreover, there is no secular training which appreciably contributes to the attainment of such an experience: it is *sui generis* and therefore quite different from any form of worldly skill or learning. Hence the conventional requirements for ordination, and the university training designed to fulfill those requirements, are of no value in preparing men to teach spiritual truths. Like the Baptists generally, Winstanley repeatedly insists that the founder of Christianity and his apostles were simple, uneducated men—fishermen, tent-makers, and publicans—unskilled in those arts and sciences which have become the mainstay of university education. In this he exactly agreed with William Dell, who said:

> It is one of the grossest errors that ever reigned under Antichrist's kingdom to affirm that universities are the fountain of ministers of the Gospel, which do only proceed out of Christ's flock.[9]

For Winstanley, what he calls the "preaching universative power" is not only an error; it is part of a general conspiracy by the "zealous professors" of organized religion to keep down those risings of the spirit in the poor and despised ones of the earth that threaten their titles and their special privileges. It would be quite impossible to exaggerate the violence of Winstanley's anti-clericalism. The "ecclesiastical bastardly power got in fornication with the kings of the earth" he sometimes describes as an invention of secular rulers to support their tyrannous power, but more often he represents kings themselves as the dupes of cunning priests. In *The Law of Freedom* he does not hesitate to classify the clergy with those who practice witchcraft.

Thus for Winstanley the church as an organization, the clergy as a distinct class, and theology as a learned profession all disappear before a conception of religion that strips it of all sacerdotal and institutional elements. By what may seem at first sight a paradox, the very universality of religious experience in the life of the saint gives to Winstanley's personal philosophy a tone of secularism. Religion has for him no necessary connotation of supernaturalism, though it depends throughout upon an idealist or spiritualist conception of nature and man. Even personal immortality has ceased to be a matter of moment to him. He obviously believed that nothing is known about it; he had become convinced, no doubt both by experience and observation, that the omnipresent fear of damnation among the Puritans was a fruitful source of mental disorder; he believed that the hope of heaven had been used with cynical premeditation to turn men's thoughts away from tyranny and exploitation and to prevent them from applying the suitable remedies in this world for their ills and wrongs. In short, religion was for him a way of life, not a ceremonial, a profession, or a metaphysic. And as a way of life, though it required a continuous recourse to mystical communion with God, it did not exclude the application of intelligence or science to any problem either of individual or of social life.

In concluding this section, it is necessary to say something about the ethical implications that Winstanley attached to his religious beliefs. This is difficult because Winstanley certainly would not have understood a distinction between religion and ethics nor the possibility of one without the other. On the other hand, he undoubtedly did believe that the differences between himself and other religious groups of his time had the most important ethical consequences. His communism was neither more nor less than the expression of that belief. There is nothing harder, however, than to say precisely how religious beliefs pass over into moral conduct, for the transition is not made by logic and often is not such as an outside observer would infer that it ought to be. Philosophers have said that Calvinist predestination ought to have sapped the sources of individual initiative and vigorous action, but anyone who has studied the seventeenth-century Calvinists knows that it had the opposite effect. Similarly, a mystic ought, by conventional standards, to be visionary and incompetent, but the Quakers certainly were far from that. Even in Winstanley's case, though his communistic society was visionary, it was no mean accomplishment under the circumstances to keep the experiment going for a year and to spread his case before the public as he did. In moral matters it is a kind of logic of the emotions that connects belief with action.

Winstanley's ethics, like that of the Quakers, had a quality which might be called, for want of better terms, quietism or pacifism. It does not appear that Winstanley was literally a pacifist, in the sense that he thought it wrong to bear arms. He was undoubtedly a pacifist, however, so far as concerned the realization of his communism. God, he says, puts no weapons into the hands of his saints to fight against reproaches, oppression, poverty, and temptation. The Levellers will not conquer by the sword, for Christ, who is the head Leveller, fights only with the sword of love, and this in the end will throw down all government and ministry that is lifted up by the imagination. In the end, Christ, the law of universal love, will reign, and this will be true magistracy, the light of truth, reason, humility, and peace. Like George Fox—and this was the root of Quaker pacifism—Winstanley distrusted the efficacy of force to accomplish any permanent moral results, and this was altogether in accord with the belief that morality begins with a change of heart. Hence the root of moral regeneration is a kind of passivity, submissiveness to the better impulse that will rise if it be given the chance, a silence and a waiting until the wiser thought and action ripens.

> Tell a man that he hath no knowledge and no faith of God, and his heart swells presently and thinks you wrong him; tell him his own human learning and workings is abomination to the Lord and that he must lay aside his beloved actings and wait only upon God for knowledge and faith, and his heart swells and cannot endure to hear of waiting upon God: and truly God is more honored by our waiting than by the multitude of our self-actings. . . . For the flesh grudges to give God his liberty to do with his own what he will, and the flesh would have something in itself; it hath a secret grudging to acknowledge all wisdom, faith, and life must be given of God, and that his actings can get nothing.[10]

This sense of waiting and receiving, I have no doubt, is an authentic moral experience, quite apart from Winstanley's antiquated terminology. There is a type of mind, as William James has said, that finds itself able to tap unsuspected sources of energy by dipping below the surface-play of consciousness. It was very different, however, from the typical moral experience that lay behind Calvinism—as different as Winstanley's religion was from Presbyterianism or Independency. Calvinism, I think, was a quasi-military ethics in which the fundamental virtues were conceived to be obedience and loyalty to the commands of the sovereign ruler of the world. The attribute of that ruler which Calvinists were most inclined to stress was not love but power or possibly justice. The relationship was rigidly personal. It required the unswerving devotion and the strict responsibility of every man to his divine superior, and perhaps for that very reason it implied his equality with all the other servants of God. Its moral effect was to steel men in the fight against evil, to discipline their energies and harden their endurance, sometimes to the point of harshness and cruelty. It was a form of moral individualism that stressed the virtues of enterprise and activity and self-assertion". Hence the

political affinity of Calvinist ethics, when it showed itself as a radical movement in the Puritan Revolution, was with the democratic radicalism of the main body of the Levellers, of which the best extant record is the debates in the Army Council at Putney. For the social philosophy of democratic radicalism was built upon the postulate of inalienable natural rights, among which the right to own property acquired by one's exertions was not the least. From such a social philosophy communism was necessarily excluded.

It would be quite wrong to imply that the moral quietism or passivity of Winstanley and the Quakers carried with it a lack of vigor or pertinacity. In their case mysticism was neither a doctrine of moral defeat, an escape from a too harsh reality, nor a withdrawal from effective action on the level of everyday affairs. This ethics too may be called individualism, since every man must find out for himself the secret of his own being, without benefit of institutions or of clergy. But the secret that he discovers is not his self-sufficiency but rather his dependence upon subconscious powers that take possession of him and act through him. The relationship is not a personal one of loyalty to an omnipotent ruler, but one of reliance upon forces greater than himself that he nevertheless finds in himself. The outcome of moral reflection is felt not as self-assertion but rather as self-abnegation. Hence the fundamental fact of social ethics is not individual enterprise and self-preservation but rather the preservation of community and the responsibility of the strong for the weak. This Winstanley called the law of universal love. In all but words he thus arrived at the formula of all the utopian socialisms: From each according to his powers; to each according to his needs.

Winstanley differed from Fox and the Quakers chiefly in believing that this consciousness of human brotherhood must at once become the principle of a new form of community. For him true religion required the immediate creation of a society that substituted community and mutual aid for individualism and competition. He could not content himself with a religious experience that ended with a change of a personal morality, nor imagine a moral reform that did not include the elimination of poverty and the removal of political oppression. Both these, he believed, grew from the single root of self-love and covetousness, or individual aggressiveness, which issued in the tyranny of kings and rulers, the monopoly of the means of production by the landlords, the clerical pretensions of the hireling preachers, and the chicanery of lawyers, who played jackal to kings, landlords, and clergy alike. Because these had all one root Winstanely could not envisage a political reform which was not at the same time economic, or a form of civil liberty that could coexist with poverty and economic dependence. Hence he looked to the English Revolution, pledged by Parliament and the people to a "real reformation", to make the earth a common treasury and England a community in which the king of righteousness should rule in every heart.

Winstanley's Political Argument

When Winstanley sets out a formal outline of his argument for communism, he sometimes speaks of a three-fold proof: by direct revelation, by the citation of Scripture, and by reason. The religious beliefs behind his trust in the inner Light have been described in the preceding section. Winstanley's offer to prove his case by the authority of Scripture was never, in my opinion, more than the acceptance of what was at the time a conventional form of argument. In his **Letter to the Lord Fair fax** he said that the issues raised had to be settled not by Scripture but by the law in men's hearts. The third line of proof, that based upon reason and equity, was borrowed by Winstanely from the pattern of argumentation built up for the Levellers by writers such as Lilburne, Overton, and Walwyn. In a measure it was second-hand—an effort, so to speak, to talk in the political vernacular—though certainly not insincere. Winstanely must of course have known about the Leveller agitation that had been going on since 1647, but there is nothing in his early pamphlets to show that he was concerned with it. His use of stereotyped Leveller arguments was not in itself either interesting or important. The question is, how far he perceived the differences of principle that separated his communism from the democratic radicalism of the Leveller program. The answer, I think, is that both sides were surprisingly clear-headed about the contrast. Lilburne repudiated Winstanely in his *Legal Fundamentall Liberties,* and Winstanely marked off his communist group as the "True Levellers".

In asserting that equity and right reason are the foundation of all morally binding laws Winstanley was merely taking a position that in one way or another is taken by every party which backs a revolutionary reform. The Levellers had used the argument again and again, in attacking one abuse or another, that no law can be really binding unless it is just and equitable. Richard Overton, for example, in the *Remonstrance* which he addressed to Parliament in 1646, had demanded a general revision of English Law in the light of reason:

> Ye know, the laws of this nation are unworthy a free people and deserve from first to last to be considered and seriously debated and reduced to an agreement with common equity and right reason, which ought to be the form and life of every government.[11]

With this Winstanley of course agreed, as he agreed in regarding the Revolution as the occasion for a complete overhauling of English law and institutions. But in calling himself a "true Leveller" he recorded the judgment that the political reforms sought by Lilburne and his party were superficial. Winstanley often says that the object of the Revolution is to restore men's "birthright", and like the Levellers, he does not trouble to distinguish at all sharply between the birthright of an Englishman and the rights of man. Sometimes the Digger manifestoes assert that the object of their movement is to recover for Englishmen their right to use the land of England. Sometimes they claim the "creation-right" of every man to gain his living from the earth, which by the law of righteousness is a common treasury for all human beings. In these respects Winstanley's social philosophy agreed with that of the Levellers in appealing to a fundamental law of equity lying behind the positive law.

This resemblance, however, is superficial, since no revolutionist could fail to assert the justice of what he desired. Behind the resemblance there was a fundamental difference between Winstanley and the Levellers. Winstanley was clearly aware that he could not effectively claim a right to subsistence as an individual liberty. The Levellers, on the other hand, were in principle democrats. The purpose of their philosophy was to erect barriers against the incursions of bad law and bad government into those private rights which they considered fundamental to human liberty. Hence their plan of reform included bills of rights embodied in a written constitution which Parliament was expressly forbidden to change. Among the disabilities that they proposed to lay on Parliament was that of "abolishing propriety".[12] In general the Levellers thought of reform as equalizing civil and political liberties, abolishing monopoly, and opening up opportunity to equal competition. For them natural law meant individual rights, and natural equity meant that all men individually should be protected in the exercise of their rights.

Winstanley's conception of social reform was quite different. It is true that he objected to the private ownership of land because it permitted a few men to monopolize what justly belonged to all, but he had no notion of correcting the injustice by increasing the number of landowners, or by making private ownership possible to everyone. His communism was an effort to envisage a different kind of social system. His argument is that the common land is communally owned. Ideally his plan implied that land and all the means of production should be nationalized, and this is certainly the end he looked forward to, though he was opposed to the violent expropriation of private owners. The "creation-right" to subsistence, therefore, was a communal and not an individual right. Accordingly, Winstanley could not possibly identify equity with individual liberty. In **The Law of Freedom,** where he gave the most carefully planned statement of his theory, he based his communism upon the difference between two types of society, the monarchy and the commonwealth.

In substance this amounted to the contrast between an individualist, acquisitive, competitive society and a cooperative society. Reduced to a single sentence Winstanley's argument is simply that the latter is morally superior because it grows from the better impulses of human nature. It is not built upon individual enterprise but upon mutual aid and protection.

The political argument that Winstanley perhaps uses most frequently is drawn from the Solemn League and Covenant—the oath taken in 1643 by Parliament and people "to amend our lives and each one to go before another in the example of a real reformation". This might seem like an *ad hoc* argument, unless it be remembered that Winstanley never conceived of any social or political reform that did not have its origin in a religious transformation. Obviously his interpretation of the Covenant had nothing whatever to do with the actual political purposes of that document when it was framed. He took it as creating nothing less than a solemn personal obligation on every subscriber to effect a real reformation in England, with all that was implied by that expression. To Winstanley's mind it meant nothing less than an effort to realize "the pure law of righteousness". He acknowledged the obligation in his own conduct: apparently his refusal to employ a lawyer when he was sued for damages at Kingston was based on the belief that the administration of the law as it existed was an iniquitous institution which could not be supported by anyone who meant to amend his life in the interest of a real reformation. It was clearly the intention of the Digger community to boycott the courts and the magistracy as being unsuitable to a Christian society, just as they renounced the use of force as an unchristian way of gaining their ends. They say that they are willing to answer for any unlawful act that they commit, but they will not appeal to the courts for protection even against the unlawful acts of their assailants. In presenting his communistic platform to Cromwell Winstanley, of course, abandoned this attitude. At the same time he still believed the strongest argument for his communism to be the contention that it was implied in the express intent of the nation to effect a true reformation. If this were honestly meant, he urged, there was no place to stop short of a completely Christian society in which covetousness, the root of all inequality, was altogether grubbed up. All bad government, all war and all misery, Winstanley believed, arise from the acquisitiveness which is chiefly represented by the private ownership of land. Hence there can be no real reformation unless the land is restored to its rightful condition as a common treasury for all men. True religion, he says, is to make restitution of the land.

Often, however, Winstanley gives to the Covenant a much more specific meaning than this: he construes it as a contract between Parliament and the common people for prosecuting the war against the King to recover England's fundamental liberties. Parliament, he says, persuaded the people to take up arms by the promise that each should enjoy his right; some gave military service, some gave free quarter to troops, and all gave taxes. Parliament, Winstanley assumes, represents specifically the gentry and the clergy; their legislation shows that they mean to look after the interests of those classes. The question is whether they will "cozen" the poor commoners of their part of the bargain. Of all liberties the most fundamental is access to the land. This the gentry already enjoy in their enclosures, and Winstanley is willing to leave them in possession. But to complete the bargain the common people ought to have the common land, since this is the very least that can be given in recognition of their "creation-right". Everyone, Winstanley says, desires and struggles for land—gentry, clergy, and commons alike. Hence there can be no talk of restoring the fundamental liberties of Englishmen unless all are given the right to use the land of England. The most interesting part of the argument is its frank assumption that English government is controlled by a class in its own interest, even though Parliament legally represents the nation. The only question is whether the class in control means to live up to the contract implied in the National Covenant or whether the gentry mean to pursue their own interests at the cost of being "covenant-breakers". There is in Winstanley's writing a good deal that would now be called "class-consciousness", but he invariably repudiates the use of force as a way of securing the commoners' rights.

Winstanley addressed another argument to Parliament based not upon the Covenant but upon the legislation passed after the execution of the King declaring that monarchy was abolished and that England was a "free commonwealth". This formed, I believe, Winstanley's most important political argument, since it turned upon his belief that there are two opposed kinds of society and consequently two kinds of government. The "kingly power" is based upon greed and force, and therefore corresponds with private ownership of the land, while "true commonwealth-government" is based upon cooperation and therefore corresponds with making the land a "common treasury". Winstanley's argument amounts to showing that Parliament has contradicted itself. By its own act it has "cast out the kingly power", but it has also passed an act "to uphold the old law". By the latter he meant the act authorizing the courts to continue administering the law in force when the King died, but issuing writs in the name of the Keepers of the Liberty of England instead of the King. This, Winstanley argued, is absolutely illogical, if it does not cloak a hypocritical design to change the possessor of the kingly power without changing the thing itself. For the "old law" was merely the will of the Norman conqueror, and Charles's title to the throne was merely as the successor to William. Hence, if the kingly power were really cast out, the whole fabric of legal tyranny ought to go with it. The Civil Wars, he argued, had been fought not to remove the King but to reform a tyrannous system. This identification of tyranny with the Norman Power was a common form of Leveller argument. Winstanley merely adopted it. It had been fully developed by Overton in his *Remonstrance* in 1646 and by John Hare in several pamphlets published in 1647. In fact it was merely one phase of an argument that was common to all the anti-royalist parties and not to the Levellers alone: the mythical presumption that there had once been a free constitution in England which it was the purpose of the Civil War to restore.

Winstanley, however, made his own use of the Leveller argument against the Norman Power. At the conquest, Winstanley supposes, William turned the English out of their land and put his own soldiers in their place. In general, he thinks, all private ownership of land rests on cunning, robbery, and violence; the Norman conquest was merely the case that most concerns England. The lords of manors are the successors of William's "colonels", and the freeholders of the Norman common soldiers. They are merely the beneficiaries of a successful theft, and in consequence they are wholly lacking in title to their land, if the kingly power were really to be cast out. But the power of the landowners has two accessory supporters. These are the lawyers and the clergy. Both, Winstanley thinks, were set up by William to bolster his power. The lawyers were a deliberately created engine of oppression, made possible by keeping the law in French and Latin, and employed to twist its meaning by cunning and chicanery to the interest of the landowning gentry, who alone have money to pay them.

> England is a prison; the varities of subtleties in the laws preserved by the sword are the bolts, bars, and doors of the prison; the lawyers are the jailors; and poor men are the prisoners.[13]

The privileges of the clergy also were designed expressly to support the conqueror's yoke. William gave them tithes "to preach him up"; they persuaded the people to fancy

> That true freedom lay in hearing them preach, and to enjoy that heaven which, they say, every man who believes their doctrine shall enjoy after he is dead. And so [they] tell us of a heaven and hell after death, which neither they nor we know what will be, so that the whole world is at a loss in the true knowledge thereof.[14]

According to Winstanley, therefore, the casting out of the kingly power, if carried out completely, would carry with it the lords of manors, tithing priests, bad laws and bad judges, and cunning lawyers.

Over against this representation of kingly government under the Norman yoke Winstanley places government in a free commonwealth, which Parliament has declared England to be. In his controversial tracts he nowhere undertakes to describe this kind of government or to make clear the contrast in principle which distinguished monarchy and commonwealth. This, however, is his point of departure in *The Law of Freedom,* and there can be no doubt that the distinction between the two types of society is the logical foundation upon which his communism ought to rest. In the controversial tracts he contents himself with arguing that Parliament's pledge is not fulfilled so long as the "old law" remains in force or so long as the landlords are permitted to retain both their enclosures and control of the commons as well. So long as the "creation-right" of access to the land is denied, there can be no pretense that law and government are really based upon equity and reason. The English are not a free people until the poor have the right at least to plant and sow the common land. Equally, he added later, Parliament ought to see to it that the confiscated estates, the king's lands, and the lands of bishops and deans, are not permitted to fall into the hands of private owners but are kept for the use of the poor. The outline of what Winstanley thought would constitute a true commonwealth he sketched out for Cromwell, hoping as so many utopians in the seventeenth century hoped, that that hard-headed man of God would use his limitless power to bring the millennium into existence.

Winstanley's Communist Commonwealth

Some eighteen months after the final failure of the communist venture at Cobham, Winstanley was moved, as he says, "to pick together" as many of his scattered papers as he could find, in one more effort to realize his idea of a true commonwealth. What had happened to him in the interval is unknown. If the authorities had thought it worth while to press the indictment returned against the Diggers, he may have served a jail sentence. When he reopened the question of communism by publishing *The Law of Freedom,* he evidently thought it wise to divorce the national project which he now offered to Cromwell from the unfortunate experiment that had failed in Surrey, for he nowhere referred to the latter. He speaks of his book as "intended for your view above two years ago", which is hard to credit, since he would scarcely have written and laid aside an elaborate appeal to Cromwell at the very time when he was issuing a continuous series of less elaborate appeals to Fairfax, to the army, and to Parliament. It is likely enough that Winstanley had long planned a more complete exposition of his ideas about a true commonwealth, separating them from the controversies connected with his attempt to cultivate the commons. In the winter of 1651 it was an obvious expedient to address the work to Cromwell, but I doubt whether this step would have been indicated until after the Battle of Worcester.

The outcome of the digging at Cobham had demonstrated the impossibility of cultivating the common land by communistic groups, so long as the legal power of the landlords over the unenclosed land remained intact, and it was obvious also that a fundamental change in the law could be made only by a national government free from the forces that had dominated Parliament. Accordingly Winstanley was led to add another to the list of national utopias of which Harrington's *Oceana,* published four years later, was the most famous. The immediate occasion of the work, he says, was a suggestion of Hugh Peters, that government and law ought to be accommodated to Scripture.[15] The general purport of the book is identical with that of the controversial tracts that Winstanley had published in 1649 and 1650. The kingly oppressor, he says, has been cast out but his powers and the abuses inherent in them are still intact: the clergy and their tithes, the lawyers and the Norman law, the monopoly of the land by the lords of manors. By creation-right the land belongs to all, and no man becomes rich by his own labors but only by being able to appropriate the labor of other men. Winstanley now undertakes to show, by experience, by Scripture, and by history, that all war and all civil disturbances arise from the struggle to gain possession and control of the land. He therefore appeals to Cromwell to cast out oppression and to realize true commonwealth-government by making England a communistic society. He still professes to confine the program of communist tillage to the common and the nationalized land, and he still rejects the idea of expropriating the landlords, but it is very hard to see how he thought the two systems could have persisted side by side. Whatever interest his "platform" possesses lies in its being the outline for a wholly communist society.

Though the general purpose is the same, there is a change of emphasis in *The Law of Freedom.* Winstanley seems to rely less upon a millenarian hope that the spirit will move men to bring in true commonwealth, and more upon the possibility that changing the organization of society will affect their motives and conduct. In one rather surprising passage he avows this kind of change.

> I speak now in relation between the oppressor and the oppressed; the inward bondages I meddle not with in this place, though I am assured that if it be rightly searched into, the inward bondages of the mind, as covetousness, pride, hypocrisy, envy, sorrow, fears, desperation, and madness are all occasioned by the outward bondage that one sort of people lay upon another.[16]

In his desire to see progress made Winstanley even says that some parts of his platform might be put into effect though communism were not adopted.[17] It is not likely that these passages imply any real change in Winstanley's convictions but he had clearly undergone a change of mood, induced by experience and by the failure of his year's agitation for the communal tilling of the common land. The millenarian expectations appropriate to the first stage of his revolutionary activity had given place to a soberer consideration of ways and means and a greater willingness to rely on changes in law and institutions.

In the opening three chapters of his book Winstanley undertakes to set forth the principles upon which he conceives the government of a true commonwealth to rest. This is evidently the result of an attempt to develop more affirmatively ideas that had remained implicit in his controversial tracts. In these his condemnation of the "kingly power" had been clearer than the idea of a commonwealth to which the kingly power stood opposed. In *The Law of Freedom* Winstanley developed the contrast more systematically. Government is a way of "ordering the earth and the manners of mankind" by law, and its purpose ought to be to enable men to live peaceably in freedom and plenty. There are, however, two different ways of ordering the earth— by private ownership and "the cheating art of buying and selling" and by communal ownership without buying and selling. There are therefore two kinds of government, kingly government and commonwealth, and two kinds of law. Kingly government, because it depends on private ownership, depends also on war and conquest, upon the dominion of some men over others through force and fraud, and upon lawyers and the clergy as the twin agencies of covetousness and subtlety necessary for that kind of government. Commonwealth, because it does away with buying and selling, is able to abolish the abuses and oppressions that go with them; it gives a lawful livelihood to the poor as well as to the rich, and its law arises from equity, reason, and righteousness.

In his third chapter Winstanley traces the two forms of government back to two antagonistic principles in human nature. These he calls common preservation— the tendency in a man to seek the good of others as well as himself—and self-preservation. True magistracy, as distinguished from the false magistracy of force, springs from the impulse to common preservation. In origin it begins with the family, in which the superior experience and wisdom of the father are applied to the protection and nourishment of his dependents. Adam, Winstanley says, was the first ruler, and the necessity of planting the earth to gain a common livelihood was his law. The fundamental law of a commonwealth, governed with a view to the common preservation, is that the strong should help and protect the weak and the foolish. The false magistrate is one who favors the rich and the strong; the true magistrate is one who casts out "self-ended" interests and protects the peace and liberties of the common people. The first is the root of all civil wars and revolutions; the second is the root of right government and peace. Essentially, therefore, Winstanley's contrast of kingly government and commonwealth is the contrast between acquisitiveness and competition on the one hand and cooperation and mutual aid on the other, the opposition upon which all communistic utopias have depended.

Having thus set forth the underlying principle of a commonwealth, Winstanley goes on to specify what might be called its chief political device. Like most of the early theorists of democracy he has been captivated by the idea of popular elections and short terms of office. In a commonwealth, he says, all officers are elected and hold office for a single year. He gives the familiar arguments to show that power long and continuously held corrupts the officials who have it, while frequent change keeps them faithful to the public interest and gives political experience to more persons. This part of Winstanley's argument probably shows an affinity with the political ideas of the Levellers. Like the Levellers also, and in contrast with what might have been expected of a person with millenarian tendencies, he shows no inclination to restrict political power to the saints. No one is excluded from the suffrage by his plan except persons whose interests attach them obviously to the Royalist side in the Civil Wars. He expresses himself as against even a moral qualification for voting, and against a religious qualification for officeholding, though "uncivil livers" ought not to be elected to office. For obvious reasons those who have profited by buying confiscated estates are to be excluded from a plan of government that aims at nationalizing this land for the use of the poor.

The fourth chapter of *The Law of Freedom,* which is the longest section of Winstanley's platform of government, is an elaborate effort to outline the officers required in a communistic commonwealth. True to the ideas that commonwealth begins with and grows from the family, he enumerates the father of a family as the first officer in the plan, each such person being responsible for the education of his dependents, for directing their labor, and for seeing that they are brought up in a useful trade. Beyond the family there are local officers—those responsible for each town, city, or parish—county officers, and national officers. The local officers in Winstanley's plan are of two kinds: the peacemakers, whose duty is mainly to keep the peace, and the overseers, whose duties are mainly industrial. The peacemakers appear to be modeled on the justices of the peace, except that they are arbitrators rather than judges. The settlement of local disputes by arbitration was a part of the Levellers' plan for the reform of local government, designed of course to circumvent the delays, costs, and technicalities of proceedings in the regular courts. The overseers are of four types, (1) those whose duty it is to protect the private property

that in Winstanley's communistic scheme still belongs to each family; (2) those who oversee the practice of each trade and the system of apprenticeship by which the youth are to be educated in the trades; (3) those who oversee the common storehouses into which all goods are brought except those produced for immediate consumption; and (4) men over sixty years of age, who have a kind of roving commission to oversee everybody and everything. It is clear that Winstanley based the idea of his overseers upon a guild-system of production; he speaks with high commendation of the London companies and the oversight of production which they were supposed to exercise. The local officers include also a soldier, who is a kind of marshal to execute and enforce the orders of officers and courts, an executioner, and a task-master. The last has the custody and supervision of those who refuse to conform to the general plan, for like all communistic schemes, Winstanley's platform has to provide that those who do not work at the recognized occupations not only shall not eat, but also shall not have their freedom or the custody of their persons.

The essential institution of county government in Winstanley's plan is the county court, held four times a year like the Quarter Sessions, and consisting of a judge and of the peacemakers and overseers from the towns and parishes of the county. Here again Winstanley took a leaf from the Levellers' book. The judges are to be rigidly interdicted from interpreting the law but are to pronounce only its bare letter. This has been a perennial ideal of radicals whose purpose is to simplify the law and its procedure, and who see in judicial legislation a chief cause of legal formality and technicality.[18] Above the county courts in Winstanley's plan is Parliament, which he describes as the highest court, having supervision of all other courts and officers, with power to remedy all grievances. Nothing is said on the subject, but I assume that Winstanley would abolish the courts at Westminster, as the extreme Levellers proposed to do. Parliament is to be composed of representatives chosen annually from the cities, towns, and counties. Winstanley shows, however, no great confidence in parliaments: he proposes that legislation, after it is passed, shall not take effect for a month, in order that the people may have a chance to register their objections. He did not adopt the Leveller plan of limiting the legislative power with a written constitution. The most positive duty of Parliament in Winstanley's plan is very naturally to direct the planting of the "commonwealth land", which consists of the common and of all the land recovered from the church, the king, and the royalists. This land is to be permanently nationalized, but he does not undertake to frame rules by which it is to be administered.

The same applies generally to Winstanley's account of the economic organization of a society that has abolished buying and selling, which he deals with in the latter part of his fifth chapter. Apart from the overseers in his roster of officers, there is not much that can properly be called an outline of a communistic economy. His plan is that all crops when harvested, and all goods when manufactured, are to go into public storehouses, some wholesale and some retail, and are to be dispensed without price, upon the request of anyone who needs them, either for his own consumption or as raw material for further processing. Winstanley had not reflected on the fact that the price-system which results from buying and selling goods does regulate production and that there would still have to be some kind of regulation, even in an economy that was purely cooperative. Buying and selling seemed to him nothing but a "cheating art", that gives an iniquitous advantage to the cunning and unscrupulous, an estimate which may very well have had its roots in the personal humiliation of his bankruptcy.[19] By its abolition he expected that it would be possible to uproot covetousness and oppression. For the regulation of the system he relied upon criminal penalties against idleness, waste, and the failure to practice a useful trade. For its direction he depended upon the overseers, who are supposed not only to know the best processes for producing goods but also what goods are needed and in what quantities. Winstanley emphasized the duty of the overseers to encourage the discovery of new knowledge and its application to the arts and crafts. Inventors, he says, ought to be signally honored, and all useful discoveries ought to be made known at once to the whole country. Nevertheless, as was perhaps natural for a small tradesman in the seventeenth century, he still thought of industry as dominated by custom and as controlled by self-regulating crafts. For this reason his plan for a communistic society contained little in the way of economic analysis.

The most interesting parts of Winstanley's plan of government are those in which he sketches his ideas of public education. The first part of his fifth chapter is devoted to this subject. Both heads of families and the overseers of arts and trades are required to see that all children are instructed in morals and in useful trades, in languages and in the arts and sciences. It appears clear that Winstanley intends education to be extended to all citizens of the commonwealth. This is not, however, the point which he mainly stresses. What he thinks chiefly desirable is to avoid the creation of a class of professional scholars, educated only in book-learning, in reading and lazy contemplation, like his ancient enemies, the lawyers and the clergy. Every member of a commonwealth, therefore, ought to learn a useful trade or art and ought also to know something of languages, sciences, and history. The arts Winstanley describes as knowledge in practice, laborious and not traditional knowledge. He divides them into five classes: husbandry, with all the supplemental and derivative arts which have to do with the growing and utilization

of crops that come from the soil; the arts that have to do with the production and processing of minerals; the arts that concern the care of domestic animals and the use of all the products derived from them; the arts that concern the growth and utilization of timber; and, finally, arts that depend upon the stars, among which he mentions astronomy, astrology, and navigation. Winstanley's commonwealth has a completely secularized education centered in the practical applications of knowledge.

He proposes also that popular education in secular subjects shall altogether replace the religious teaching of the church. In his outline of officers for the commonwealth the two whose work is most carefully described are the parish minister and the postmaster. The minister is a parish officer elected, like all other officers, for a single year. One day in seven is to be free from labor, but this has no religious significance. On this day the people meet in their parishes, partly that they may become acquainted with one another but chiefly for purposes of general public education. The minister has the direction of this but he has no monopoly of teaching, such as has been claimed by the ordained clergy. The teaching consists largely of reading from the laws of the commonwealth, but not expounding or interpreting them, and of lectures on public affairs. To supply material for the latter Winstanley provides another group of officers, the postmasters. The postmasters in each parish gather the local news and report it to the capital, where the reports are compiled and printed and a copy sent to each parish for publication at the weekly meetings. In addition to this kind of reading and lectures, Winstanley would have lectures on the arts and sciences, sometimes in English and sometimes in foreign languages, and also on moral subjects like the nature of man and the benefits of liberty. In all this, however, there is nothing that can be called religious instruction of a doctrinal sort. In Winstanley's commonwealth there is literally no church and no clergy, since he identified the practice of that profession with witchcraft.

> He who professes the service of a righteous God by preaching and prayer, and makes a trade to get the possessions of the earth, shall be put to death for a witch and a cheater.[20]

So far as his own views were concerned, Winstanley had clearly reached the conclusion that no sort of public worship was necessary. It does not appear what rights he would have extended to those who did not agree with him, which is curious, in view of his very emphatic endorsement of religious toleration in his earlier works. I suppose, though I am not certain, that he would have permitted churches whose membership was voluntary, so long as they relinquished any form of compulsory public maintenance.

Winstanley's secularizing of education was derived directly from his ideas about religion. By making religion exclusively an inner revelation and worship exclusively communion with God, he had divorced it from any relationship to learning, and had abolished any distinction between different branches of knowledge in respect of their relation to religion. This had a twofold effect: on the one hand it destroyed the study of divinity as a branch of learning and on the other it raised all the arts and sciences to the dignity formerly claimed by theology. To know the secrets of nature, he says, is to know the works of God. This is a knowledge by experience as much as that "experimental" knowledge of the spirit upon which he had insisted in his religious tracts. Hence the pursuit of useful knowledge in the arts and sciences is itself almost an act of worship. The very omnipresence of God in nature and of the inner light in human experience brought Winstanley to a completely secular idea of education and scholarship. In this he went squarely against all the prevailing ideas of Puritan education, though his conclusion was the culmination of ideas inherent in Puritanism itself: Again and again throughout the first half of the seventeenth century the Puritan clergy had attacked the remnants of medievalism in the English universities. Their object was to displace the ancient curriculum, based on scholastic metaphysics and dialectic, and to replace it with studies more suitable for the training of pulpit orators and pastors.[21] Thus rhetoric, moral philosophy, and the ancient languages became the essential parts of the course of study. Always, however, there was the assumption that the clergy formed a learned profession, with a body of demonstrated truth (usually thought to be Calvinist theology) at their back. All classes of Puritan clergy, Presbyterian and Independent, poured contempt on the "mechanick preachers" who leaped into notoriety with the spread of the Baptist and other sects.

The small group of Puritan mystics to whom Winstanley was allied, when they broke with the prevailing idea of the clergy, had necessarily to abandon the idea that education ought to be directed to training clergymen. If a religious teacher required before everything else an intuition of spiritual truth, he could hardly be expected to get this from a study of Greek and Hebrew. In almost identical words John Saltmarsh and George Fox denied that university teaching could make a clergyman.[22] William Dell, who as Master of Caius College, Cambridge, had an educational position of some importance, went on to propose the secularizing of university studies:

> If the Universities will stand upon an human and civil account, as schools of good learning for the instructing and educating youth in the knowledge of the tongues, and of the liberal arts and sciences, thereby to make them useful and serviceable to the commonwealth . . . and will be content to shake hands with their ecclesiastical and anti-Christian

> interest, then let them stand during the good pleasure of God; but if they will still exalt themselves above themselves, and place themselves on Christ's very throne, as if they had ascended upon high to lead captivity captive and to give gifts to men for the work of the ministry . . . then let them in the name of Christ descend into that darkness out of which they first sprang.[23]

In his *Right Reformation of Learning, Schools, and Universities*[10] Dell outlined a system of publicly supported elementary schools for England, with high schools for teaching the languages, arts, and sciences in all the larger cities. Like Winstanley he favored the teaching of a trade with the study of books.

Winstanley's ideas about education, therefore, were not peculiar to him but were shared by those whom he most resembled in his religious ideas. Like Dell he looked toward an education open to the generality of the population, an education in subjects useful to the commonwealth and closer to experience and the practice of the useful arts. But with these men the high value that they set on knowledge at first hand grew not from any usual kind of empirical philosophy but from the peculiar form of mysticism embodied in their religious experience. It was the knowledge of the inner light which, in the first instance, they contrasted with verbal learning and the building up of vast systems of unverifiable inferences. The very type and model of this kind of hair-splitting was for them the attempts of literal-minded Puritans to spin out a whole body of belief and practice from the texts of Scripture. In the case of Winstanley that which cuts off clericalism at its root is the fact that the divinity in which the clergy are trained and which they are supposed to practice is an "imaginary" science. It is false in its learned pretensions and, what is worse, it is pernicious in its social consequences. In the end Winstanley became convinced that it was unwholesome both mentally and morally, a result of semi-pathological fears and a cause of hysteria. The passage in his **Law of Freedom** in which he condemns the "divining doctrine" is certainly the most remarkable he ever wrote. It must have grown from much observation of the darker side of religious fanaticism, and it must constitute one of the most extraordinary indictments of Puritanism that was written in the seventeenth century.

> There is a threefold discovery of falsehood in this doctrine.

> For, first, it is a doctrine of a sickly and weak spirit, who hath lost his understanding in the knowledge of the creation, and of the temper of his own heart and nature, and so runs into fancies, either of joy or sorrow.

> And if the passion of joy predominate, then he fancies to himself a personal God, personal angels,

and a local place of glory which he saith he and all who believe what he saith shall go to, after they are dead.

And if sorrow predominate, then he fancies to himself a personal devil and a local place of torment that he shall go to after he is dead, and this he speaks with great confidence.

Or, secondly, this is the doctrine of a subtle running spirit, to make an ungrounded wise man mad, that he might be called the more excellent man in knowledge, for many times when a wise understanding heart is assaulted with this doctrine of a God, a devil, a heaven, and a hell, salvation and damnation after a man is dead, his spirit being not strongly grounded in the knowledge of the creation nor in the temper of his own heart, he strives and stretches his brains to find out the depth of that doctrine and cannot attain to it. For indeed it is not knowledge but imagination. And so, by poring and puzzling himself in it, loses that wisdom he had, and becomes distracted and mad. And if the passion of joy predominate, then he is merry and sings and laughs, and is ripe in the expressions of his words, and will speak strange things, but all by imagination. But if the passion of sorrow predominate, then he is heavy and sad, crying out, He is damned, God hath forsaken him, and he must go to hell when he die, he cannot make his calling and election sure. And in that distemper many times a man doth hang, kill, or drown himself. So that this divining doctrine, which you call spiritual and heavenly things, torments people always when they are weak, sickly, and under any distemper. Therefore it cannot be the doctrine of Christ the Savior.

For my own part, my spirit hath waded deep to find the bottom of this divining spiritual doctrine; and the more I searched, the more I was at a loss; and I never came to quiet rest, and to know God in my spirit, till I came to the knowledge of the things in this book. And let me tell you, They who preach this divining doctrine are the murderers of many a poor heart who is bashful and simple and that cannot speak for himself but that keeps his thoughts to himself.

Or, thirdly, This doctrine is made a cloak of policy by the subtle elder brother to cheat his simple younger brother of the freedoms of the earth. . . . So that this divining spiritual doctrine is a cheat. For while men are gazing up into heaven, imagining after a happiness, or fearing a hell after they are dead, their eyes are put out, that they see not what is their birthright, and what is to be done by them here on earth while they are living. This is the filthy dreamer and the cloud without rain.

And indeed the subtle clergy do know that, if they can but charm the people by this their divining doctrine to look after riches, heaven, and glory when they are dead, then they shall easily be the inheritors of the earth and have the deceived people to be their servants.[24]

Here was a new note in the secularism which spread over political thought and indeed over all thought after the Restoration. It grew not from philosophic rationalism, or from a skeptical indifference to religion, or from the repugnance of political-minded men to clericalism. On the contrary it sprang from an unusually intense and sincere form of religious experience and from the very essence of Protestantism. It was as genuinely a part of the Pauline tradition in Christianity as those elements which Calvinist Puritans liked better to emphasize. It was, as William James said of Quakerism, "a religion of veracity", the creation of men who had faced the fundamental unreasonableness of the world and of their own natures and, without benefit of clergy, had found serenity and the power to work, the widest scope possible for the exercise of intelligence, and a sense of human brotherhood that lifts the non-rational above the brutalities of irrationalism.

Notes

[1] A. S. P. Woodhouse, *Puritanism and Liberty,* p. 103; *The Clarke Papers,* Vol. I, pp. 378 f.

[2] A number of typical passages are quoted by Louise F. Brown, *Baptists and Fifth Monarchy Men,* Washington, 1912, pp. 14 ff.

[3] The sermon is reprinted in A. S. P. Woodhouse's *Puritanism and Liberty,* Appendix, p. 390.

[4] *The Breaking of the Day of God,* 1648, pp. 51 f.

[5] *The Saints Paradice* (edition of 85 pp.), pp. 21-23.

[6] *Ibid.,* p. 54.

[7] *Ibid.,* pp. 55 f.

[8] *Journal,* edited by R. M. Jones, Vol. I, p. 214.

[9] *The Stumbling-Stone, wherein the University is Reproved,* 1653; *Christ's Spirit,* Germantown, Penna., 1760, p. 155.

[10] *The Breaking of the Day of God,* 1648, pp. 72 f.

[11] The pamphlet is reprinted in William Haller's *Tracts on Liberty in the Puritan Revolution,* New York, 1934, Vol. III, p. 351; the passage quoted is on p. 365.

[12] The Leveller petition of September 11, 1648; reprinted by A. S. P. Woodhouse, *Puritanism and Liberty,* p. 340. The Second Agreement of the People,

Article VII, contained a list of matters upon which Parliament was not to act, Woodhouse, *ibid.,* p. 361.

[13] *A New-Yeers Gift,* p. 10 (bracketed paging).

[14] *The Law of Freedom,* p. 20 (bracketed paging).

[15] Presumably in the Committee appointed January 20, 1651, to suggest to Parliament revisions of the laws. Peters appears to have been the *enfant terrible* of the Committee. See Bulstrode Whitelocke's *Memorials,* pp. 520, 521, 523, 528.

[16] P. 18 (bracketed paging).

[17] P. 72 (bracketed paging).

[18] John Lilburne proposed the following on judicial reform, as a petition to the first Parliament to be elected pursuant to the adoption of the Agreement of the People: "That the next Representative be most earnestly pressed for the ridding of this kingdom of those vermin and caterpillars, the lawyers, the chief bane of this poor nation; to erect a court of justice in every hundred in the nation, for the ending of all differences arising in that hundred, by twelve men of the same hundred annually chosen by freemen of that hundred, with express and plain rules in English, made by the Representative or supreme authority of the nation, for them to guide their judgments by." Reprinted by A. S. P. Woodhouse, *Puritanism and Liberty,* p. 366.

[19] There is possibly a note of bitterness in Winstanley's occasional references to his reduction to the status of a day-laborer, "which I was never brought up to". See p. 67 (bracketed paging).

[20] P. 86 (bracketed paging).

[21] The subject is discussed with special reference to Milton in William Haller's *The Rise of Puritanism,* New York, 1938, pp. 297 ff.

[22] "It is not a University, a Cambridge or Oxford, a pulpit or a black gown or cloak, that makes one a true minister of Jesus Christ." Saltmarsh's *Divine Right of Presbytery,* 1646. "The Lord opened unto me that being bred at Oxford or Cambridge was not enough to fit and qualify men to be ministers of Christ, and I wondered at it because it was the common belief of people." Fox's *Journal,* Vol. I, p. 75.

[23] *The Stumbling-Stone, wherein the University is Reproved,* 1653; cited from a reprint entitled *Christ's Spirit,* Germantown, Penna., 1760, pp. 155 f.

[10] *Select Works,* p. 578.

[24] Pp. 60 ff. (bracketed paging).

H. N. Brailsford (essay date 1961)

SOURCE: "The True Levellers" in *The Levellers and the English Revolution,* edited by Christopher Hill, The Cresset Press, 1961, pp. 657-70.

In the following essay, Brailsford traces possible influences on Winstanley's thought, discussing his religious ideas and his political philosophy.

On Sunday, 1 April, 1649, a band of a dozen landless men with their families camped on St George's Hill, near Walton-on-Thames, and proceeded to dig and manure the common.[1] Their leader, William Everard, had served in the New Model Army, until his radicalism caused him to be cashiered: but this was to be for him and his comrades a peaceful, albeit revolutionary act. The 'True Levellers', as they called themselves, had lost their faith alike in the men of property who dominated the Long Parliament, and in the Grandees who commanded the Army. But with unflagging courage they meant with their spades to open yet another campaign for freedom. They would by direct action make good their natural right to use the earth and enjoy its fruits: they would undo the Norman Conquest and challenge the slavery of property, which had oppressed Englishmen through six centuries. They sang, as they dug in company, a naïve chorus:

> *You noble Diggers all, stand up now, stand*
> *up now,*
> *You noble Diggers all, stand up now,*
> *The waste land to maintain, seeing Cavaliers*
> *by name*
> *Your digging does disdain and persons all*
> *defame.*

The song, of which the tune may have been better than the verse, went on to defy by turns the gentry, the lawyers and the clergy. 'The club is all their law . . . but they no vision saw.' The Diggers meant 'to conquer them by love' for 'freedom is not won neither by sword nor gun'. A century had passed since the Saints had used those weapons at Münster in vain. Once more, this time in England, the broken bodies of peasants manured the fields that others owned. The Diggers, with a faith that no disillusionment could quench, would attempt a new way to establish 'community'. They were the pioneers: presently, as they believed, five thousand of their proletarian comrades would join them in digging the waste lands. But their movement was also the culmination of the long guerrilla struggle against enclosure (see Chapter XXI). The True Levellers fought the last bloodless battle in this war, which differed from the obscure skirmishes that preceded it in this— that these rebels were inspired by a simple but clearcut communist theory and had worked out a tactic by which they believed they could end the usurpations of property and establish a classless society. For the first time they made articulate the instinctive belief of every peasantry that God gave the earth to his children (to use the Diggers' phraseology) as their 'common treasury'.

The story of this spirited enterprise is soon told. The Diggers were men of courage, whose faith gave them a stubborn perseverance against impossible odds. First at St George's Hill, and afterwards at Cobham, they challenged the rights of two lords of the manor, not merely by squatting on the commons and cultivating them, but also by defiantly felling timber. They succeeded in causing considerable alarm to the Council of State, and troops of horse were twice sent to repress them. Twice their doings brought them into court. Fairfax, with his usual courtesy, listened to what they had to say, but the lords of the manor were less tolerant and twice their hired men, helped by the troopers, broke up the Diggers' settlement, destroyed the cottages they had built and turned the cattle into the growing corn. Their numbers grew, none the less, from twelve men to fifty: they managed to raise corn on eleven acres of waste land, not to mention other crops, and they kept up their defiance of the landlords, the Army and the law for rather more than a year. Their missionaries, meanwhile, were touring England in carts and preaching their gospel as they went. They had some success. Their example was followed at Cox Hall, in Kent, and at Wellingborough, Northamptonshire. There, as a broadsheet published for the Diggers in 1650 tells us, there were, in one parish alone, 1,169 persons dependent on alms. They had petitioned the Justices in vain to be set to work, but nothing was done for them. The itinerant Diggers organised them and they set to work 'to dig up, manure and sow corn upon the common and waste ground called Bareshank, belonging to the inhabitants of Wellingborough'. They evidently met with a good deal of sympathy in the town and some farmers gave them seed, but they, too, were suppressed; which is not surprising since their broadsheet, which their leaders had the courage to sign, boldly proclaimed the right of all to the use and enjoyment of the land.

Fortunately for posterity, there was among the Diggers a man of rare talent and originality, Gerrard Winstanley, who has left behind him in his voluminous writings a record of the faith and beliefs with which he inspired this movement. Though Everard may have been its leader in the early days of its adventure, it is probable that Winstanley inspired it from the start and certain that he soon took over the leadership. During its hectic year of activity he poured forth pamphlets in which he addressed by turns the Army, the City of London and the Parliament. In these, in simple but vigorous English, in the language of the Bible and of daily life, he gave a straight-forward narrative of what the Diggers had done and suffered and set forth the principles on which they acted. Of his life very little is known. He was born at Wigan in 1609 and doubtless had a gram-

mar school education and no more. He then went up to London, where he was in business in some branch of the cloth or linen trade. Like many others, he was ruined in the Civil War and withdrew to the country, somewhere in the Thames Valley, where friends gave him a lodging: in return, he took charge of their cattle. Here he had leisure to think, and during 1648 he published no less than four pamphlets in which, without touching on politics, he set forth his daring theological opinions, which evolved rapidly through a pantheistic mysticism to a position that can only be described, if we may use modern terms, as agnostic and secularist. He bravely signed his name to them, though the least unorthodox of them exposed him to the grim penalties of the Long Parliament's Blasphemy Act. They went into several editions, but he escaped the fate that overtook some less audacious heretics even under Cromwell's relatively tolerant rule.

Suddenly, in this year, his interest turned to politics and he wrote the most characteristic of his books, *The New Law of Righteousness,* which is in reality a Communist Manifesto written in the dialect of its day. Throughout the next year, 1649-50, he was the life and pen of the Diggers' adventure. When that failed, after writing *Fire in the Bush,* a defence of his ideas addressed to the churches, he published in 1652 the most mature of his books, *The Law of Freedom in a Platform.* It was dedicated, in an eloquent and plain-spoken address, to Cromwell, whom it summoned to lay the foundations of a communist commonwealth. The sketch of a classless society that follows is a deeply interesting blend of the radical democracy professed by the main body of the Levellers with the communism of More's *Utopia* and a secularism that was Winstanley's own. Like More, he advocated an economy without money, organised round public storehouses. To these each should carry the products of his work and from them each should satisfy his needs. Though the book lacks the literary and imaginative grace of More's work, it is in the history of socialist thought the more significant of the two, since it sprang from a proletarian movement and proposed a strategical plan by which communism could actually be realised. This was the last of Winstanley's writings, and all that we know of the rest of his life is that in 1660 he was living at Cobham and had evidently become more prosperous, since he was able to file a suit in Chancery to clear up his financial affairs. The traditional belief that he joined the Quakers is mistaken, though he had much in common with them. Of his death we have no record.

How did Winstanley come by his ideas? There is nothing to suggest that he read widely. He quotes no book except the Bible and never mentions *Utopia,* though he must have read it carefully. Once he exclaims 'England is a prison', which may be an echo of Hamlet. Once, and only once, he quotes a Latin line. He tells us that in his early years he listened attentively to sermons and was 'dipped' as a Baptist. There we have the first important clue. Communist thought in the sixteenth century had two chief sources, the persecuted left wing of the Bohemian Hussites and the Anabaptist movement, whose doctrines were preached underground in England by the persecuted Family of Love (see Chapter II). This tradition, of which the main stream was pacifist, filtered through most of the more radical sects of the Commonwealth period, kept alive by word of mouth. There is one outstanding passage in Winstanley which echoes almost *verbatim* a revolutionary sermon by Münzer, the German peasants' leader—though it is unlikely that Winstanley had ever heard of him.

The other decisive formative influence was the controversial literature of the Leveller movement, though Winstanley never refers to it. It is probable that he came in contact with the Levellers of the Chilterns and the Thames Valley, who published *Light Shining in Buckinghamshire* and *More Light Shining in Buckinghamshire*. Winstanley cannot have been the author, for the crude style of the pamphlets is not his; but he may well have had a share in drafting them. . . .

Winstanley, then, was no lonely theorist, but if we could have asked him where he got his communism he would have mentioned neither the Anabaptist tradition nor the Leveller movement. It came to him by direct revelation from God. Three times, as he tells us, in trance and out of trance, he heard a Voice which uttered these three commands:

> Work together; eat bread together; declare this all abroad.

> Israel shall neither take hire, nor give hire.

> Whosoever labours the earth for any person or persons, that are lifted up to rule over others, and doth not look upon themselves as equal to others in the creation: the hand of the Lord shall be upon that labourer: I the Lord have spoken it and I will do it.

In obedience to this Voice he went to work with the first pioneers on St George's Hill. For the benefit of others, who had not yet learned in silence and patience to listen to the Voice of the Spirit within, Winstanley would argue his case, if need be from Scripture, but preferably from history and experience. Fundamentally, his argument was ethical. He assumes throughout, as men have done from the earliest days of the cult of ancestors, that mankind is naturally, was originally, or was by God's ordinance and promise, a family of equals.

This was the commonplace of every peasant movement from the days of John Ball downwards. But Winstanley saw much more than this and he contrives to analyse the society round him with a shrewdness unusual

in mystics. The only difficulty in understanding him comes from the simplicity of his language. He has no technical terms and it is only when we translate his Biblical idiom into modern phraseology that we realise how much he understood. More clearly than any of the instinctive communists who preceded him, he saw the source of all exploitation and of most of the misery round him in the private appropriation of the means of life, which, in the green England of his day, meant the land. When men take to 'buying and selling the earth', as he puts it, 'saying *This is mine* . . . [they] restrain other fellow-creatures from seeking nourishment from their mother earth. . . . So that he that had no land was to work for those, for small wages, that called the land theirs; and thereby some are lifted up into the chair of tyranny and others trod under the foot-stool of misery, as if the earth were made for a few; not for all men.' Again and again he declares that labour is the source of all wealth and that no man ever grew rich save by appropriating the fruits of others' work. 'No man can be rich, but he must be rich either by his own labours, or by the labours of other men helping him. If a man have no help from his neighbour, he shall never gather an estate of hundreds and thousands a year. If other men help him to work, then are those riches his neighbours' as well as his; for they be the fruits of other men's labours as well as his own.'

Winstanley perceived that this institution of 'particular propriety' was inevitably the source of all oppressions and all wars. 'All the strivings,' he writes, 'that is in mankind is for the earth', and again of those who own land he says 'that they or their fathers got it by the sword'. Property can be maintained only by the sword, or by the law which originally sanctioned the feudal claims of 'the Norman bastard's' officers. He saw, too, and said plainly, that economic inequality degrades those who must submit to it and infects them with a consciousness of their predestined inferiority. The enslaved worker, as he puts it, 'looks upon himself as imperfect, and so is dejected in his spirit'.

Winstanley's revolutionary strategy was prescribed by 'the Voice of the Spirit within him'—or, as we should say, by his sub-conscious self, clarifying, it may be, the confused discussions he had held with the Levellers of the Chilterns. In one passage he says, as Rousseau did, that no man should retain more land than he can till with his own hands. But his ideal was not peasant ownership. He aimed at 'community', which meant for him both team work and eating at a common table. He saw two ways of reaching this. Landless men were to join together to dig the waste lands. But even more emphatically he insisted on making an end of all hired service. In plain words, he summoned the workers to withdraw their labour from employment on the land. This was, as he saw it, more than a general strike: the strikers would find permanent work in cultivating the commons for themselves. This may sound to our ears more simple-minded than it was. Did he really forget that the Council of State had Fairfax and his dragoons behind it? But he believed, as well he might, that revolution was on the march, and he knew that many a troop of these same dragoons was on the verge of mutiny. But to grasp Winstanley's approach to communism we must try to understand his whole *Weltanschauung*.

The difficulty in grasping Winstanley's view of the universe and human society is that his thought was in flux and underwent a rapid development. His voluminous writing was all done, much of it rapidly, in four years: he had little sense for form or order in his compositions and often seems to be thinking aloud. His was an intuitive mind rather than a trained intellect, and his ideas reach us most clearly in single phrases or sentences which often have a poetical colour. In his early religious pamphlets he had not yet reached his own distinctive position, which may have come to him in his talks with William Everard. In the first of these he argues for 'universalism', at that date a most dangerous heresy: he will not believe that any soul can be eternally damned: there will be a final delivery, by God's mercy, even of the wicked from hell. In his later writings he abandoned any belief in hell. It was in the daring pamphlet *Truth Lifting Up Its head Above Scandals* (1648) that he first outlined his theological opinions by way of defending Everard, who had been thrown into gaol at Kingston for blasphemy. In this, as in all his subsequent works, Winstanley throws over the idea of a personal God, reduces to very narrow limits the significance of an historical Christ, and offers us in their stead the pantheistic conception of an ordered cosmos. These, needless to say, were not his words—he rarely used an abstract term—but they render his meaning fairly in modern phraseology.

Let us try, first of all, to reach his positive beliefs. He first startles us by telling us that he proposes 'to use the word Reason instead of the word God' in his writings. He objects that when men tell him that 'God is the chief Maker and Governor, and that the chief Maker and Governor is God', he is 'lost in this wheel that turns round'. This seems to mean that he cannot distinguish God from the universe. For him Reason is 'that living power of light that is in all things'. The Spirit Reason 'lies in the bottom of love, of justice, of wisdom'; 'it doth govern and preserve all things . . . for Reason guides them in order and leads them to their end, which is not to preserve a part, but the whole creation'. Again, he tells us that Reason 'hath a regard to the whole creation and knits every creature into a oneness'.

This, it may be, is poetry rather than metaphysics. So, too, are many of his happier sayings. Thus he tells us that 'the whole creation is the clothing of God'. But what he is trying to say is quite clear. In flashes of

insight, before Newton wrote his *Principia,* he had grasped the idea of the order and unity of the universe. God for him was this order and 'the incomprehensible spirit Reason', of which he might have said what Wordsworth said of Duty: 'Thou dost preserve the stars from wrong.'

How much did he mean by this identification of God with the cosmos? The test must be sought in the negative side of his thinking. There he did not flinch. 'What other knowledge have you of God,' he asks, 'but what you have within the circle of the creation?' In one passage he even speaks of 'The law of nature (or God)', as Spinoza used to write *'Deus sive Natura'.* To these must be added the many passages that amount to a denial of a personal God. 'Neither are you to look for God in a place of glory beyond the sun, but within yourself and in every man . . . He that looks for a God outside himself and worships a God at a distance worships he knows not what.'

This did not prevent him from using the word God fairly often, for he did not stick to his resolution to use only the word Reason. Even more often he uses the name Christ, and declares more than once that Christ is 'the true and faithful Leveller'. Elsewhere he speaks of 'Christ, or the spreading power of light'. He gives this name, with no thought of its historical connotations, to the spirit of love, order and reason that dwells in the heart of all men—and even, as he expressly insists, of the beasts. Again and again he repeats that men cannot be 'saved by believing that a man lived and died long ago at Jerusalem'—and he insists that Christ is 'not a man at a distance, but the wisdom of the Father'. Always he rejects from his theology any 'outward Christ'—a word we may fairly translate by 'historical'. He defines Him as 'a meek spirit drawn up to live in the light of Reason', which is his way of sublimating the story of the Resurrection. The passage implies quite clearly that any man may become such a 'meek spirit'. He goes on to deny the physical resurrection and ascension pretty bluntly: the Apostles cannot have seen Christ 'arise and ascend' to God in heaven, for God is in no 'particular place' but 'in every place and in every creature'. Again and again, in one phrase or another, in all his books he declares that 'heaven is not a local place of glory at a distance': a good man has 'heaven within himself'. Neither are we bound to believe that there is 'a local place of hell': 'as yet none ever came from the dead to tell men on earth, and till then men ought to speak no more than they know'. In his last book his agnosticism about the after-life is even more outspoken: he is not sure of man's personal survival after death. 'After the man is dead' he may be scattered 'into his essences of fire, water, earth and air of which he is compounded'. He recommends to us the example of 'wise-hearted Thomas', who believed nothing but what he saw reason for. Elsewhere he sweeps away the whole body of

Hebrew and Christian mythology as 'the deceit of imagination and fleshly wisdom and learning; it teaches you to look altogether upon a history without you of things that were done 6,000 years ago and of things that were done 1,649 years ago'. He is never weary of tilting at the Bibliolatry of the Puritan divines, and likes to remind them that they have no better ground than 'tradition' for trusting the 'copies of the Scriptures in their universities' and that there are 'many translations and interpretations, which differ much one from another'. He could, none the less, quote these Scriptures copiously when they suited his purpose.

It is proper to stress this negative side of Winstanley's thought, since in the Puritan England of the seventeenth century it was all but unique. None the less, in his own individual way, his was a deeply religious mind. One belief he retained with intense conviction, which he shared with the whole of the Puritan left—the Second Coming of Christ. It is true that he sublimates it almost beyond recognition. It is no sudden miracle that he means. He was as far as possible from expecting, as General Harrison and the Fifth Monarchy sect did, that the Saints will conquer the earth, with the Lord of Hosts ordering their ranks. What he did believe was that 'Christ, or the spreading power of light', will penetrate men's minds so that they will cease to covet and oppress, and 'community' will be realised without recourse to the sword. When that happens 'the whole creation will laugh in righteousness' and even the waste commons will blossom. It will make an end of government as we have known it in the past: 'the state', as Marx put it, 'will wither away.' 'You soldiers may see the end of your trade.' With his sharp consciousness of class, he loves to quote the Biblical prophecies which assure this triumph to 'the despised ones of the earth' and bid the rich men 'weep and howl'. He predicts that this revolution will be accomplished 'ere many years wheel about'. It is a law of human nature that every revolution must attain this certainty before it risks its all. Men got it in that century from the Book of Revelation as they get it in ours from the Marxist interpretation of history. If we could delve into the deeper strata of Winstanley's consciousness we might discover that he got it as much from observation as from prophecy. He had seen the mighty hurled from their seats. A king's head had fallen in Whitehall before he flung his challenge at property. The revolution he desired was to come through a change wrought by 'the Spirit Reason' in men's hearts. But that in no way deterred him from devising a shrewd tactic to hasten the process of conversion.

The positive side of Winstanley's creed was an unshaken faith in the 'inner light', which he shared with the Anabaptists before him and his contemporaries, the first Quakers. Like them, he held that the spirit of Reason and Love will reveal itself to a mind that waits in patience and silence. To dismiss this conviction of

his as a pre-scientific way of saying that the mind has its sub-conscious processes would be a superficial misunderstanding. He meant much more than this. The self-discipline he prescribed consisted of 'righteous actions and patient silence'. The mind must cease to dwell on outward objects; it must strip itself of covetousness and acquisitiveness, which lead inevitably to oppression; it must practise the golden rule towards its fellow-men and also towards the cattle; it must aim at universal love, which is for him the whole basis of 'community' (i.e. communism). In a long definition of prayer he dismisses words as unimportant and stresses only conduct and the rule of 'waiting with a meek and quiet spirit'. A man who lives thus will discover that he has 'a teacher within himself', for he is brought 'into community with the globe'. To grasp his meaning we have only to remember that it is Reason, or God, that 'knits every creature into a oneness'. By right conduct and patient waiting we overcome our finitude and become conscious of our part in the cosmos: then, and then only, it will reveal itself to us and speak to us. This doctrine of the 'inner light' is often interpreted as the extremest expression of Protestant individualism. As Winstanley understands it, it is, on the contrary, an inference from his mystical pantheism. The ordered whole of the universe becomes conscious and vocal in a mind that lives according to Reason.

From this doctrine of the inner light, Winstanley drew the extremest consequences without flinching. The Scriptures may be useful, but the inner light is a superior authority, and it alone can interpret them. He boldly sweeps away all organised religion, churches, Independent meetings, and all the sacraments, including marriage, baptism and funeral rites. 'What is the end of all this but to get money?' He will not use what the Puritans called the means of grace. 'That which you call means doth harden your hearts.' He pours his scorn on the universities which claim 'to own the writings of the Apostles'. He despises the hired clergy: 'you go on selling words for money to blind people you have deceived'. 'Men must leave off teaching one another' and speak only from 'the original light within'. A strong consciousness of class colours all he writes about the universities and the clergy. 'A ploughman that was never bred in their universities' may know more of the truth: the first prophets and apostles were shepherds and fishermen.

This contempt for the hired clergy was a common attitude among the Levellers and far outside their ranks: Milton shared it. But Winstanley, in his anti-clericalism, went much deeper. He compares the 'imaginary' science of the 'divines'—their 'divining doctrine', as he calls it—to witchcraft, and broadens his assault into an attack on all supernatural religion, with its by-products of melancholia and hysteria. What is even more important, he saw that organised religion had become the instrument of the owning class. One outstanding passage from *The Law of Freedom* deserves to be quoted in full:

> There is a threefold discovery of falsehood in this doctrine.
>
> For first it is a doctrine of a sickly and weak spirit, who hath lost his understanding in the knowledge of the creation . . . and so runs into fancies either of joy or sorrow.
>
> And if the passion of joy predominate, then he fancies to himself a personal God, personal angels and a local place of glory, which, he saith, he and all who believe what he saith shall go to after they are dead.
>
> And if sorrow predominate, then he fancies to himself a personal devil and a local place of torment that he shall go to after he is dead, and this he speaks with great confidence.
>
> Or, secondly, this is the doctrine of a subtle running spirit to make an ungrounded wise man mad. . . . For many times when a wise understanding heart is assaulted with this doctrine of a God, a devil, a heaven and a hell, salvation and damnation after a man is dead, his spirit being not strongly grounded in the knowledge of the creation nor in the temper of his own heart, he strives and stretches his brains to find out the depth of that doctrine and cannot attain to it. For, indeed, it is not knowledge but imagination. And so, by poring and puzzling himself in it, loses that wisdom he had, and becomes distracted and mad. And if the passion of joy predominate, then he is merry and sings and laughs, and is ripe in the expression of his words, and will speak strange things; but all by imagination. But if the passion of sorrow predominate, then he is heavy and sad, crying out, He is damned; God had forsaken him and he must go to hell when he die; he cannot make his calling and election sure. And in that distemper many times a man doth hang, kill or drown himself. So that this divining doctrine which you call spiritual and heavenly things, torments people always when they are weak, sickly and under any distemper. . . .
>
> Or, thirdly, this doctrine is made a cloak of policy by the subtle elder brother to cheat his simple younger brother of the freedoms of the earth. For saith the elder brother, 'The earth is mine, and not yours, brother; and you must not work upon it, unless you will hire it of me: and you must not take the fruits of it, unless you will buy them of me, by that which I pay you for your labour: for if you should do otherwise, God will not love you, and you shall not go to heaven when you die, but the devil will have you and you must be damned in hell. . . . You must believe what is written and

> what is told you; and if you will not believe, your damnation will be the greater'. . . .
>
> Well, the younger brother being weak in spirit, and having not a grounded knowledge of the creation, nor of himself, is terrified, and lets go his hold in the earth, and submits himself to be a slave to his brother for fear of damnation in hell after death, and in hopes to get heaven thereby after he is dead; and so his eyes are put out, and his reason is blinded.
>
> So that this divining spiritual doctrine is a cheat; for while men are gazing up to heaven, imagining after a happiness, or fearing a hell after they are dead, their eyes are put out that they see not what is their birthrights, and what is to be done by them here on earth while they are living: This is the filthy dreamer, and the cloud without rain.
>
> And indeed the subtle clergy do know, that if they can but charm the people by this their divining doctrine, to look after riches, heaven and glory when they are dead, that then they shall easily be the inheritors of the earth, and have the deceived people to be their servants.

Thus, two centuries before Marx, Winstanley, in the simplest of plain English, dared to say that 'religion is the opium of the people', and not only did he write it, he thrust it under Cromwell's eyes.

In this last book of his, though he was sketching an ideal community, Winstanley has his feet firmly on the earth. His mood of exaltation has passed and the long internal conflict in his mind between the tradition in which he was reared and the rationalism he won by wrestling, ends in the complete victory of his new outlook. He was, after all, the contemporary of the pioneers who were soon to found the Royal Society, but it may have been from More that he derived the enthusiasm for experimental science that glows on so many pages of *The Law of Freedom.* He was impatient with universities because, as he said, they were busy only with words and traditions. He now proposes to organise research into all the secrets of nature, largely with a practical purpose. The only titles of honour he would bestow are to go to inventors. He suggests that the postmaster of his commonwealth shall conduct a weekly gazette, to which correspondents in every district shall contribute not merely news of local happenings, especially where help or relief is needed, but, above all, reports of the discovery of 'any secret in nature, or new invention in any art or trade, or in the tillage of the earth'.

The most significant detail in his picture of an ideal community is his sketch of Sunday, for it is entirely his own. It is 'very rational and good,' he writes, that 'one day in seven be still set apart' for fellowship and rest. Under the charge of a 'minister' (a layman, of course) elected annually, each parish is to hold its meetings. For these he will have no ritual of any kind. The minister may read aloud the laws of the commonwealth, which are to be few, simple and brief, and also the reports on 'the affairs of the whole land' contained in the postmaster's gazette. Then are to follow 'speeches' or 'discourses' on history and the sciences, among which he mentions especially botany and astronomy:

'Likewise men may come to see into the nature of the fixed and wandering stars, those great powers of God in the heavens above; and hereby men will come to know the secrets of nature and creation, within which all true knowledge is wrapped up.'

Other lectures may deal with the nature of man. He stipulates that others, beside the minister, shall speak, as the latter may arrange: but 'everyone who speaks of any herb, plant, art or nature of mankind is required to speak nothing by imagination, but what he hath found out by his own industry and observation in trial'. In plain words, experimental science was Winstanley's substitute for the dogmatism of the chapels and churches. Another touch is significant: he suggests that some of the lectures should be given in foreign languages: from the days of the Hussites downwards, communists had always an international outlook. 'By this means,' he sums up, 'in time men shall attain to the practical knowledge of God truly; that they may serve him in spirit and truth, and this knowledge will not deceive a man.'

Truly, we are an ungrateful and forgetful nation. Never, though its population counted less than five millions, has England produced in thought and action so many daring pioneers as in these days of the Commonwealth, when men staked their all for an idea, and lived with an intensity their descendants have never touched. Among them, buried though he is in oblivion, Gerrard Winstanley ranks high, as much by his startling courage as by the clarity of his intellectual vision.

Note

[1] [As explained in the Editorial Note, this chapter was not written by Brailsford for this book. It is reprinted from an article which he wrote for *The Plain View* (July 1945), published by The Ethical Union. This article has been slightly abbreviated, in order to avoid repetitions; the first two paragraphs were extracted from Brailsford's original Chapter II.—Ed.]

Richard T. Vann (essay date 1965)

SOURCE: "The Later Life of Gerrard Winstanley," *Journal of the History of Ideas,* Vol. XXVI, No. 1, January-March, 1965, pp. 133-36.

[*In the following essay, Vann reviews the scant evidence available regarding the later years of Winstanley's life, examining the way in which the few known facts may support or contradict the portrait of Winstanley painted by the pamphlets he wrote in the late 1640s and early 1650s.*]

The Digger Gerrard Winstanley published his last pamphlet in 1652. Almost three centuries passed before his collected works were edited by George H. Sabine and made the subject of a book by D. W. Petegorsky.[1] But neither Sabine nor Petegorsky could do much to dispel the obscurity cloaking the life of Winstanley after his retirement as a pamphleteer. The only glimpse of Winstanley was in 1660, when he appeared as a plaintiff in chancery and as a "tithe-gatherer of propriety" in the pages of a hostile pamphlet. In 1948 Wilhelm Schenk could comment that "the known facts about Winstanley's life are tantalisingly meagre and it is extremely unlikely, after the patient researches of Petegorsky and Sabine, that any more will be discovered in the future."[2]

This prediction has proven to be unduly pessimistic. Recently discovered evidence allows us a fuller picture of Winstanley's later life, no longer as polemicist and communist theorist, but as corn-chandler, Quaker, and litigant.

After the final dispersal of the Digger community in Surrey, Winstanley spent the late summer and autumn of 1650 as steward to the eccentric prophetess Lady Eleanor Douglas on her estate at Pirton, Hertfordshire. From a letter found in the Huntington Library we know that Winstanley had to defend himself from a charge of dishonesty in the keeping of his accounts. Characteristically, Winstanley interpreted his relationship to Lady Eleanor as one of seeking her conversion rather than commerce: "I came not under your rooffe to earn money like a slave. It is the convertion of your spirit to true Nobilities, which is falne in the earth, not the weight of your purse that I looke after." But his services had gone beyond the spiritual, for as he reminds her, "I was your Saviour in this last Somer's crop in getting the sequestracon taken of [off] your estate, and you freely promised before Ellin to give me 20£." Not only had this promise not been fulfilled, but the "prophetesse Melchisedecke" had appeared suddenly "like a theeff in the night" to audit Winstanley's accounts, and apparently they had a violent falling-out.[3]

Winstanley may have continued his activities as a steward, since in 1660 he was attacked for taking tithes by the Ranter Laurence Claxton. In his *The Lost Sheep Found, or the Prodigal Returned to his Father's House,* Claxton claims to have detected vanity in Winstanley's proceedings as a Digger, and charges him on page 27 with an ignominious, though not unexpected retreat from his principles:

> I made it appear to *Gerrard Winstanley* there was a self-love and vain-glory nursed in his heart, that if possible, by digging to have gained people to him, by which his name might become great among the poor Commonality of the Nation, as afterwards in him appeared a most shameful retreat from *Georges-Hill,* with a spirit of pretended universality, to become a real Tithe-gatherer of propriety; so what by these things in others, and the experience of my own heart, I saw all that men spoke or acted, was a lye. . . . [4]

Claxton's veracity is questionable, but since any steward of an estate with impropriated tithes would be involved in tithe-collection there may well be some basis for his attack.

But much the best evidence for Winstanley's later life lies in the documents of two actions brought by him in chancery. One is his complaint of October 1660 against Robert Western, Francis Barnes, and Edward Lewies; the other is an action brought 23 June 1675 by Winstanley and his wife, her two sisters, and their husbands, against Ferdinando Gorges and John Holland, guardian of the infant Thomas Coningsby.[5]

Winstanley's dispute with Western, Barnes, and Lewies arose out of his former dealings in cloth-trading with Richard Alsworth of London. Winstanley, who was a member of the Merchant Taylors' company, had been in debt to Alsworth by almost £500 when he left off trading in 1643, but he claimed that he had since discharged all his obligations. Unfortunately Winstanley's books had been lost or defaced during the Civil War, and he had never bothered to obtain any "acquittance, receipte or discharge" from Alsworth for the money paid him. Now Alsworth's executors were pressing for payment of a note which they claimed to be in Winstanley's own handwriting, acknowledging a debt of £114 15s. 3d, which Winstanley had promised to pay from a debt of £114 owed him by one Philip Peake of Dublin. Winstanley had already been arrested for the debt and put under subpoena into chancery.[6] His complaint asked that Alsworth's books be examined so that the repayment could be verified.

Since Alsworth's executors thought Winstanley could repay 114 pounds, it appears that his financial situation must have improved since 1650, when he spoke of the unaccustomed necessity to do daily labor for his bread. It also appears that Winstanley had been accustomed to fairly large and far-flung transactions. This impression is amply confirmed by proceedings involving his wife and her sisters, the daughters of one Gabriel Stanley. Winstanley here claimed that Ferdinando Gorges owed him £1,850 by an indenture of 10 April

1666 and that he had also promised a £200 annuity to the three sisters. These sums were to be paid out of the revenues of Hampton Court manor in Herefordshire. However, Winstanley admits that he gave the "writings" for Hampton Court estate to Gorges after the latter had made a sustained effort to wheedle them from him. He even describes himself as a "plain illiterate Man as hee the sd. Mr. Gorges well knew." Winstanley was using the word in its contemporary sense of "simple" or "unsophisticated," as Gorges retorted that "the Comp¹ts are all of them Literate person and write faire and intelligeable hands." Gorges, in this response of 30 May 1676, singled out Winstanley and Fisher as "persons of indigent and low fortunes."

There is no further record of the suit, for Winstanley died on 10 September 1676. The record of his death has been found in burial registers kept by the Westminster Monthly Meeting of the Quakers.[7] Winstanley, whose occupation is given as "corn chandler," was aged about 62, according to the Friends' register. He had two sons by his wife Elizabeth: Gerrard, born about 1665 and dying 20 August 1683 and Clement, born about 1670 and dying 2 October 1684. Elizabeth subsequently remarried Giles Tutchbury (also Tutchberry and Tichbury), a cooper, at the Bull and Mouth meeting of London Friends.

One great remaining puzzle about Winstanley's life is the void between 1660 and 1675. It is, of course, possible that the man who filed suit in the latter year and died a Quaker in 1676 was not the Digger. No other references to Winstanley in Quaker records have been discovered, nor has any burial record of Susan, Gerrard Winstanley's first wife. On the other hand, the name is uncommon. It does not occur at all in those contemporary London parish registers which have been printed (almost one-third of those surviving). This would make it seem unlikely that there were in London two men of this name, both about the same age.

More pertinent is the well-known similarity between the religious thought of Winstanley and that of the early Friends.[8] As Carlyle remarked of Winstanley's interview with Fairfax, during which he refused to remove his hat, "The germ of Quakerism and much else is curiously visible here."[9] On the basis of the consonance of Winstanley's *The Saint's Paradise,* which they thought to have been written in 1658, and contemporary Quaker tracts, G. P. Gooch and Eduard Bernstein supposed that Winstanley must have become a Friend. *The Saint's Paradise* has since been correctly dated as 1648,[10] but this mistaken date does not affect the community of ideas shared by Winstanley and the Friends—a community too close merely to be explained as "the result of the general environment of the period."[11]

Certainty on this question (if it can ever be attained) and further knowledge of Winstanley's later life must probably depend on more serendipity. Friends' records, printed London parish registers, and the indexes to the London probate registries and to chancery plaintiffs have been thoroughly examined. But even if nothing more is found, if we accept the probability that all our present evidence pertains to the same person, we can sketch in more fully the picture of the man who was the spokesman for the short-lived Digger movement.

It is a picture puzzlingly at variance with what one would expect. His entrance into the grain trade, for example, is doubly surprising in view both of his denunciation of trade in the fruits of the earth and of the widespread popular detestation of corn-dealers.[12] Although it may be held that Winstanley produced a "proletarian ideology," he followed the classic bourgeois pattern of a gentleman's son from Lancashire who came to London and joined one of the city companies.[13] Perhaps he atoned for his interest in commerce by his subsequent incompetence in pursuing it. His ineptitude in business is consistent, and after his forced leaving of the cloth trade, his dispute over his accounts with Lady Eleanor Douglas, his failure to obtain important receipts and his self-confessed simple-mindedness in handing over vital documents, it is not surprising that at the end of his life his fortune was "indigent and low." The experiment in Digger communism would seem to have come between the ruin of a career as a Merchant Tailor and the scarcely propitious beginning of one as a steward and corn-trader. These few facts about his life seem to invite the interpretation of the radical as one who turns on a system in which he personally has failed. But it is doubtful that such fragments of a biography can explain Winstanley, much less explain him away. After all it is only worthwhile collecting them because of what he wrote and did in a few months of the Commonwealth of England. His historical justification, if he finds one, will be not of works but of faith.

Notes

[1] See *The Works of Gerrard Winstanley, with an Appendix of Documents Relating to The Digger Movement,* edited by George H. Sabine (Ithaca, 1941), and D. W. Petegorsky, *Left-Wing Democracy in the English Civil War* (1940). Sabine wrote without reference to the work of Petegorsky, which gives a somewhat more detailed account of Winstanley's life.

[2] *The Concern for Social Justice in the Puritan Revolution* (1948), 97.

[3] This letter was discovered and edited by Paul H. Hardacre for the *Huntington Library Quarterly,* XXII, 4 (1959), 345-49.

[4] Quoted by Andrew Brink in *Friends' Historical Society Journal,* 49, 3 (1960), 179-80. See also Petegorsky, 229-30.

[5] Winstanley's complaint against Western, Barnes, and Lewies is C.9/412/269 and their replies are C.6/44/101 and C.5/415/123 in Chancery Proceedings, Public Record Office. The complaint of Gerrard Winstanley and Elizabeth his wife, William Fisher and Anne his wife, and John Hicks and Elizabeth his wife is C.5/581/55; the responses are C.6/244/96 and C.5/581/55. Sabine, 6, and Petegorsky, 123, did not know of the second suit and quote only Winstanley's complaint from the various documents of the first one.

[6] Winstanley's affluence then was perhaps not so great as is suggested by H. N. Brailsford, who says in *The Levellers and the English Revolution* (1961), 659, that Winstanley in 1660 "had evidently become more prosperous, since he was able to file a suit in Chancery to clear up his financial affairs."

[7] Richard T. Vann, "From Radicalism to Quakerism: Gerrard Winstanley and Friends," *Friends' Historical Society Journal,* 49, 1 (1959), 41-46.

[8] This is discussed in greater detail in *Friends' Historical Society Journal,* 49, 1 (1959), 41-46.

[9] Quoted in Lewis H. Berens, *The Digger Movement in the Days of the Commonwealth* (2nd ed., 1961), 38.

[10] Sabine, 91, and Petegorsky, Appendix I, 248.

[11] Petegorsky, 248.

[12] Max Beloff, *Public Order and Popular Disturbances 1660-1714* (Oxford, 1938), 73.

[13] His father was a mercer in Wigan and, to judge from the honorific "Mr." that preceded the record of his burial in the Wigan parish register, was a man of social prominence.

James Farr (essay date 1983)

SOURCE: "Technology in the Digger Utopia" in *Dissent and Affirmation: Essays in Honor of Mulford Q. Sibley,* edited by Arthur L. Kolleberg, J. Donald Moon, and Daniel R. Sabia, Jr., Bowling Green University Popular Press, 1983, pp. 118-31.

[*In the following essay, Farr studies the "problem of technology" in Winstanley's utopian political program. Farr demonstrates that Winstanley supported technological advancements, but only those determined to be responsible, humane, and beneficial to the utopian commonwealth.*]

During the bold and heady days which followed in the wake of the first English Revolution, Gerrard Winstanley the Digger wrote and published "the first socialist utopia formed in the hopes of becoming a party program."[1] *The Law of Freedom in a Platform* was Winstanley's last work and its design of utopian laws and institutions captured the spirit of Digger ideology—socialism, democracy, and pacifism. These were daring visions for the mid-seventeenth century, a time known for its daring visions. Amidst the great lights of his age—from Hobbes to Harrington, Bacon to Newton—Winstanley's "candle" burns bright still.

Winstanley and the Diggers were dead two and a half centuries before they received attention commensurate with their historical significance.[3] In this essay I shall investigate the problem of technology in Winstanley's utopian political thought. As did most of his contemporaries, Winstanley praised technological advance. Yet much more than they, he grasped the need to submit technology to constant democratic scrutiny in order that it remain responsible, humane, and part of the "common treasury for all."

The general story-line into which I am placing the Digger utopia is an important and familiar one, thanks to the work of Mulford Sibley.[4] In one of a number of fine analyses, Professor Sibley has suggested that utopias fall into one of three general patterns as regards technology: (1) whole-hearted acceptance; (2) radical rejection; and (3) selective implementation.[5] On balance, Winstanley's utopian platform falls into the third category. However, the Digger utopia also displays certain features common to utopias of the first two types. It is as if in Winstanley we find the ambivalence on technology which has marked human history from the very beginning. In broad outline, then, I shall narrate in some detail one episode in the history of utopian political thought in terms of the problem of technology. I write this also with a conviction that we still require utopian thinking, and that any such thinking must come to grips with technology. I believe, moreover, that only a socialist utopia committed to egalitarian participation in all areas of life and to an educational system which promotes virtue, not merely skills, can begin to deal humanely and effectively with the pervasive problem of technology. Winstanley and the Diggers—among others—helped us to see that in seventeenth century revolutionary England; a select band of contemporary thinkers—Mulford Sibley foremost among them—help us to see that today.

Winstanley's Utopian Political Thought

Utopian speculation was one of the visionary products thrown up by the turmoil of the English Revolution. Creative energies previously censored and obstructed by despotic government were suddenly unleashed. These energies assumed many practical and literary forms—including utopias, constitutions, and communities. The Digger communities, of which there were several,[6] were but more radical versions of the Puritan design to establish a City on the Hill. Puritans and Diggers alike believed that congregations of saints (differently understood) could make the world anew by their very example. In print and pulpit model constitutions were also drafted and debated—a phenomenon all the more remarkable in a land never to know a written constitution. The most important was the Leveller's *Agreement of the People.* Many English writers chose the format of utopian literature which Sir Thomas More had rescued from antiquity and given new life a century earlier. More's *Utopia* became a model for Francis Bacon in *New Atlantis,* as for Campanella in *City of the Sun.* The utopias of the 1640s and 1650s were as diverse and contradictory as the times which produced them. Their titles display that curious mixture of solemnity and Puritan sobriety on the one hand, with unbridled fancy and exotic imagination on the other. One hears the turmoil of those times in *The Christian Commonwealth* and *A Way Propounded,* and again in *Macaria, Oceana, Nova Solyma,* and *Olbia.*

In the midst of this ferment Winstanley wrote and published his own utopia "in a platform." Having remained silent during the chaos of the civil war, Winstanley finally spoke in 1648 by producing three sectarian and millenarian pamphlets. Winstanley's thought took an even more radical turn in the *New Law of Righteousness.* Revealed to him "in a trance," the new law bade all men and women to "work together. Eat bread together; declare this all abroad" /190/. True to his revelation, Winstanley soon organized a community of Diggers—or "true Levellers," as they called themselves—at St. George's Hill in Surrey. The Diggers were mainly impoverished commoners forced off the land by inclosures and hard-pressed by a decade of bad harvests.[7] In the *True Leveller's Standard Advanced,* Winstanley next proclaimed the Diggers' intention to make the earth a "common treasury" for all. Not surprisingly, the Diggers soon attracted the hostility of the local landowners. Within a year the community was harassed out of existence, even after relocating to Cobham Heath. All the while Winstanley protested furiously. In a number of remarkable pamphlets documenting the Digger hopes and travails, Winstanley appealed to the principal agents of the Revolution: the House of Commons, the Army and Lord Fairfax, the City of London, the Clergy and Lawyers, indeed "all Englishmen." But alas, all were deaf. And so in 1650 Winstanley once again fell silent.

The Law of Freedom in a Platform broke Winstanley's silence one final time. The work is without question among the most important theoretical contributions of the revolutionary period. As a work of political theory, the *Law of Freedom* falls somewhere between two genres: the fictional utopia and the model constitution. The platform is classically utopian in that it measures the immense distance between the possible and the actual. However, Winstanley foregoes the literary fiction standard to many other English utopias of his day. In the *Law of Freedom* we find no idealized account of Utopia, Oceana, Arcadia, Macaria, Bensalem, Olbia, or even the Land of Cokayne. Rather, Winstanley offered his platform as something of a rough blueprint or as the materials out of which a working commonwealth could be crafted: "Tho this Platform be like a peece of Timber rough hewd, yet the discreet workman may take it, and frame a handsome building out of it" /510/. But the vision of such a bold new political architecture makes it an implausible candidate for an actual constitution. Seventeenth century England was just not ready. The fact that certain laws and institutions could be implemented characterizes a draft plan like Winstanley's; but so does it characterize a fictional utopia. The agrarian law described in *Oceana* was Harrington's hope for England's reformation; and the Royal Society of 1662 modelled itself on Bacon's Saloman's House. So the dividing line between a fictional utopia and a model constitution is very fine indeed. What must be recognized is that the connection between utopian speculation and political theory aimed at institutional change is very close—a connection which is likely to be missed if one overemphasizes the idealism of utopia, as expressed in its being a "good place" located literally "nowhere," or if one contrasts "utopian" with "real" or "scientific."

Utopias like Winstanley's platform for true commonwealth deal essentially with institutions and, as such, are "eminently practical," as Mulford Sibley reminds us.[8] But utopian institutions also reflect political theories of the more systematic and critical kind. Utopias, in short, perform theoretical, critical and practical functions. In performing these functions utopias reflect their times, and idealize a world lost or one anticipated. Winstanley's utopia is no exception and his institutions reflect the socialist, pacifist, and democratic character of Digger philosophy.

The *Law of Freedom* continues and develops Digger ideology. But two related changes of emphasis take place. First, the earlier emphasis on individual moral regeneration as the key to a real reformation is more or less replaced by an emphasis on social and institutional change. Social and institutional relations are now taken to be causes of individual moral change.

> I speak now in relation between Oppressor and oppressed; the inward bondages I meddle not with in this place, though I am assured that if it be rightly searched into, the inward bondages of the mind, as covetousness, pride, hypocrisy, envy, sorrows, fears, desperation, and madness, are all occasioned by the outward bondage, that one sort of people lay upon another.

Winstanley, we might say, exteriorizes the problem of utopia and freedom. A second change accompanies the first. More than any previous Digger pamphlet, the *Law of Freedom* concerns itself with laws and the external regulation of behavior. There must now be "suitable laws for every occasion and almost for every action that men do" /582/. The *Law of Freedom* is, we might say, Winstanley's most "Puritan" work. Law—not just love—must make true commonwealth.

These changes notwithstanding, the *Law of Freedom* is a decidedly Digger platform. Land, labor, and goods are shared as part of the "common treasury for all." There are laws to prevent idleness—aimed no doubt at the idle rich, as much as at beggars. "Every one shall be brought up in Trades and Labors," and consequently "all Trades shall be maintained with more improvement, to the enriching of the commonwealth" /526/. Storehouses for common collection and distribution are established for food, raw materials, and finished products. After all, what is freedom but the "free enjoyment of the earth" /520/, and the earth itself but a "common storehouse" /252/? "As every one works to advance the Common Stock, so everyone shall have a free use of any commodity in the Storehouse . . . without buying and selling" /583/. Indeed buying and selling would be outlawed, as would money. Reversing Midas, gold and silver would be transformed into ordinary "dishes and other necessities" /595/. On the basis of this economic transformation, all institutions of English society would be changed. "There shall be no Tyrant Kings, Lords of Manor, Tything Priests, Oppressing Lawyers, exacting Landlords, nor any such pricking bryar" /535/.

Winstanley's socialism is Janus-faced. It looks back to the peasant communalism of the middle ages and foward to the proletarian movements of the next three centuries. True commonwealth is populated, as it were, by Joachimites and Anabaptists, Chartists and Wobblies. The simplicity of life and needs is surely pre-modern, as is Winstanley's view of small-scale science and technology. But Winstanley's overall vision is in many ways historically precocious, not medieval at all. Many medieval utopists had made utopia heaven, and heaven utopia. Winstanley, on the contrary, is forthright in his this-worldliness. Why, he asks, must "the poor people . . . be content with their poverty" with a "promise of a Heaven hereafter? . . . But why may we not have our Heaven here (that is, a comfortable livelihood in the earth)?" /409/. More importantly, he stresses the primacy of labor and production over distribution. This allows him to grasp a crucial point about exploitation. In history as a whole Winstanley discovers that "the difference between Lords of Manors and the poor, about the commons land, is the greatest controversie that hath rise up these 600 years past" /420/. But it wasn't just land, but labor which was at the heart of this exploitation.

> The Inferior Tenants and Laborers bears all the burdens in laboring the Earth . . . : and yet the Gentry, who oppress them, and that live idle upon their labors, carry away all the comfortable livelihood of the earth /507/.

> All rich men live at ease, feeding and clothing themselves by the labors of other men, not by their own. . . . Rich men receive all they have from the labourers hand, and what they give, they give away other men's labours, not their own /512f/.

The materialist interpretation of history and the theory of surplus value may well be a long time coming, but Winstanley has here already grasped the root of the matter.

Winstanley designed his utopia, then, to rectify class exploitation. But he was well aware that his vision was wholly out of step with the England of 1652. He must have sensed that his readers would have thought his ideas to be extravagantly anachronistic at best; and at worst only institutionalizable by armed force. So Winstanley came up with an ingenious suggestion. He claimed only to want the "ancient commons and waste lands" /513/ and such property as was donated by willing owners. "And for others, who are not willing, let them stay in the way of buying and selling, which is the Law of the Conqueror, till they be willing" /513/. In short, Winstanley offered an interim program for a dual commonwealth. A true commonwealth could coexist alongside the property-sanctifying one already in existence.[9] In this way the commoners could have the commons land, and the landlords their enclosures.

In sketching this visionary program, Winstanley thereby bolstered his pacifism: "I do not say, nor desire, that every one shall be compelled to practise this Commonwealth's Government" /513/. Rather, as Gandhi and the utopian socialists would later, Winstanley hoped that good example would ultimately persuade gentry and freeholders to surrender private property and gain a community. Here Winstanley echoes the pacifism which consistently and nobly marked the Diggers' conduct even amidst much harm and physical abuse. To soldiers and bullies he proclaimed: "We abhor fighting for Freedom . . . : and do thou uphold it by the sword we will not; we will conquer by Love and Patience, or else we count it no Freedom" /378/.

It merits observing, however, that in the *Law of Freedom* Winstanley appears to compromise his pacifism to some degree by legislating capital punishment for extreme crimes. Puzzling at the possible inconsistency here, Mulford Sibley suggests Winstanley's possible motive: "Perhaps his harsh discipline is in part a reaction to what Winstanley regards as the centuries of

exploitation to which the people of England have been subjected: he expects the exploiters to resist."[10] This may also account for Winstanley's justification of popular defence by "force of arms . . . against any Invasion, Rebellion, or Resistance" /539/. Even with these surprising twists in mind, however, Winstanley still trusts that his platform alone "will turn swords into ploughshares, and settle such a peace in the Earth, as Nations shall learn War no more" /513/.

The *Law of Freedom* also expresses a democratic creed. The fact that Winstanley's utopian political theory is both socialist *and* democratic is especially noteworthy because other socialist utopias, like Plato's or Campanella's or debatably More's, are exceedingly non-democratic. Winstanley's plan for universal manhood suffrage was far ahead of the limited franchise proposed by the Levellers—the only other remote contenders for the title of democrats during the English Revolution. Winstanley retained Parliament as the supreme and sole "Head of Power" /562/ and demanded that Members of Parliament be elected yearly for single terms to ensure democratic accountability. All other public officials would also be elected annually, including ministers, bureaucrats, postmasters, justices, and military officers. More generally, a democratic and participatory way of life (and not just democratic political institutions) invigorate the Digger utopia. There would be no lawyers; judges would pronounce "the bare letter of the law" /554/; and the law would be in English, not French, Latin, or legalese (as it remains today). In this way, all commonwealthmen would know the law and be able to speak for themselves in court. Even Sunday meetings were democratic. During gatherings any individual could speak, not just ministers. All of God's children had the light within. God was no doubt a democrat; Christ was the "Head Leveller" /390/.

Finally, the single most important democratic mechanism of the *Law of Freedom* was the continuous referendum on all acts of Parliament. This alone would insure that all "new laws must be by the Peoples' consent and knowledge" /559/. Whenever Parliament proposes a law it must "make a public Declaration thereof to the people of the Land . . . ; and if no Objections come in from the people within one month, they may then take the people's silence as a consent thereto" /559/. Winstanley did not elaborate on the details, nor did he suggest how deadlocked Parliaments might move ahead in the face of public dissent. He clearly envisioned a more enlightened and informed electorate whose sense of democracy would come increasingly with the practice of it. So too their concern for the public good. The Quaker principle of consensus seems to guide Winstanley here—as indeed do many other Quaker principles, like pacifism, the seeking after truth, and the belief that religious experience is an "inward light and power of life within"

/234/. Consensus on public issues should result as long as "common interest" and not "particular interest" informs the peoples' choices /559/.

Science and Technology in the Digger Utopia

Winstanley's utopian political theory, to say the least, was an amazing achievement, especially given its origins. Three years after the conclusion of a nasty, brutish, and protracted civil war, whose true victors were the rural gentry and the urban bourgeoisie, Winstanley crafts a platform for a socialist, democratic, and peaceful commonwealth. Surely he dissembled not when he claimed never to have learned his first principles in books. But if one listens closely, one can hear the tumult of voices which characterized the excitement, novelty, and fecundity of seventeenth-century political debate.

Winstanley engaged his age and had new things to say about the role of science and technology in utopia, as well. Seventeenth century utopians, particularly Bacon, Campanella, and Hartlib, were almost possessed by the new experimental science. Indeed the connection between utopia and science was particularly strong. For example, the Royal Society founded in 1662—which Sibley rightly marks as "the symbolic initiation of the new age" of science and technology—was inspired and even patterned after Saloman's House in *New Atlantis*.[11] The utopians, and the educational reformers generally, believed that science served two masters: it glorified God, whose works it discovered and marvelled at; and it benefitted Man by useful technological invention. God, science, and human technology formed a new trinity in the saintly but practical minds of the seventeenth century.

Our Digger philosopher shared this general enthusiasm for science. Although Winstanley was never in the front ranks of scientific speculation, nor became Lord Chancellor as did Bacon, nor founder of a scientific college as did Hartlib, the *Law of Freedom* is of premier importance precisely because it tells us so much about the popularization of science at a time when popular scientific education was virtually nonexistent, and when science was still hedged around by astrology, magic, and traditional religion.

Despite his enthusiasm, however, Winstanley never glorified science and technology. Indeed he limited them in true commonwealth to preserve democratic and socialist institutions. It is for this reason that, on balance, I would place the Digger utopia in the third of Sibley's three types of utopian appropriation of technology:

(1) whole-hearted acceptance of complex technology, without limits, as a key to the good life; (2)

radical distrust of technological development; and (3) the adoption of some forms of technology and the rejection of others.[12]

The third—"selective implementation"—type best captures Winstanley's intentions. But the fit is perhaps not perfect, and indeed we find hints of the first two types as well. The *Law of Freedom* is something of a complicated document which records man's historic ambivalence on technology.

True commonwealthmen breathe the new air of science. This was not to spite God, as moderns might suppose, but to praise Him: "To know the secrets of Nature, is to know the works of God; and to know the works of God within the Creation, is to know God Himself, for God dwels in every visible work or body" /565/. The pantheism and plebeian materialism which pervades such a view makes for a curious union of mysticism and rationalism. From mystical trances Winstanley uttered revelations of "the great Creator Reason" /251/. Indeed in praising God and coming to know Him, we can only approach Him rationally and experimentally through His works in nature, through "motion or growth . . . the stars and planets . . . grass, plants, fishes, beasts, birds, and mankind. . . . To reach God beyond the Creation is a knowledge beyond the line or capacity of man to attain" /565/. So it is that like the Quakers, of whom he might be numbered,[13] Winstanley praised "experimental religion" /40ff/. Such views made for a certain skepticism, as well. It was not just doubting but "wise-hearted Thomas to believe nothing but what / there is/ reason for" /523/. Puritan divines, naturally enough, found these views heretical, even atheistic. But Winstanley was not unnerved by such charges. Indeed he returned the slander.

> The subtle clergy can but charm the people. . . . Their divining Spiritual Doctrine is a cheat; for while men are gazing up to Heaven, imagining after a Happiness, or fearing a Hell, after they are dead, their eyes are put out, that they see not what is their birthrights, and what is to be done by them here on earth while they are living /569/.

Even Hobbes' sneers at the "kingdom of Darkness" in *Leviathan* were more generous.

Digger eyes are cast upon God then when they seek "experimental knowledge in the things which are" /564/. It is "in every Trade, Art, and Science," therefore, that men "finde out the Secrets of the Creation" /577/. In short, the technological inventions appropriate to humanly-scaled Trades and Arts are "knowledge in the practice, and it is good" /579/. Technological innovation is positively encouraged in the Digger utopia and the democratic spirit pervades the encouragement:

In the managing of any trade, let no young wit be
crushed in his invention, for if any man desire to
make a new tryall of his skill in any Trade or
Science, the overseers shall not hinder him, but
incourage him therein; that so the spirit of knowledge
may have his full growth in man, to find out the
secret in every Art /579f/.

Such activity is not only to be encouraged, but rewarded. "Let every one who finds out a new invention have
a deserved honor given him" /580/.

Winstanley cleverly redesigned two traditional offices
—the ministry and the post office—to ensure the
success of a scientific and democratic polity. There
was no love lost between our Digger philosopher and
Anglican and Puritan divines, for reasons we have partly seen. But Winstanley would keep a new model
ministry in true commonwealth, not, it should be emphasized, to enforce any particular religious doctrine
nor even to have a civil religion. Rather, a Sabbath day
organizer was crucial for the solidarity so essential
to a communitarian society. The people must "meet
together to see one anothers faces, and beget or preserve fellowship in friendly love" /562/. The minister's
role was minimal. He or she read both the "law of
the Commonwealth" and "the affairs of the whole
land as it is brought in by the Post-master" /562/.
But since wits need exercising the minister may also
give speeches or sermons on a delimited range of
topics, sometimes on history and government, "sometimes on the nature of Mankind" /563/. But most importantly, "speeches may be made, of all Arts and
Science, some one day, some another; As in Physick,
Chryrurgery, Astrology, Astronomy, Navigation, Husbandry, and such like" /563/. Speechmakers, much less
sermonizers, as we all know from experience, are infamous for holding forth. So Winstanley, the unabashed
true Leveller, would have the minister stand down on
demand.

> He who is the chosen Minister for that year to read,
> shall not be the only man to make sermons or
> speeches: but every one who hath any experience,
> and is able to speak of any art or language, or of the
> Nature of the Heavens above, or of the Earth below,
> shall have free liberty to speak when they offer
> themselves /564/.

The only criterion which Winstanley demands is a simple, but scientific one:

> And every one who speaks of any Herb, Plant, Art,
> or Nature of Mankind is required to speak nothing
> by imagination, but what he hath found out by his
> own industry and observation in tryal /564/.

In this way, ordinary scientific and technical knowledge speaks from the hearts and minds of ordinary

men and women; and the old ministers—who are but
"Witches and Cheats" /597/—can no longer fool the
plain-hearted people with their mysteries and incanta-
tions.

The postmasters also serve the cause of Digger science
and technology. Besides the likely task of providing
"speedy knowledge," the postmasters were to perform
a somewhat unlikely task. "If any through industry of
understanding have found out any Secret in Nature, or
new invention in any Art or Trade, or in the Tillage of
the Earth" /571/ then the postmasters were to spread
this news, too. Casting patents to the wind, the postmasters were to help fertilize the land with knowledge.
"When other parts of the land hear of it, many thereby
will be encouraged to employ their Reason and industry to do the like, that so in time there will not be any
Secret in Nature, which now lies hid" /571/. The obvious point is that Winstanley was using and reforming
the postal service to secure both democratic and scientific results. Indeed it has even been argued that "Winstanley was slightly ahead of actual developments in
the postal service of England. . . . It was not until
Oliver Cromwell's Post Office Act of 1657 that a
comprehensive system with a postmaster general was
established."[14] Although it is doubtful that it was Cromwell's inspiration, it would be ironic, nay tragic, if the
candle Winstanley set forth before the Lord Protector's
door illuminated the way not to true commonwealth,
but to a postal system.

Surely it is no exaggeration, then, to say that in the
Law of Freedom we find "one of the most magnificent
panegyrics of rational science, with its feet on the
earth, to be found in the whole of seventeenth century
English literature."[15] Neither Bacon nor Hartlib, nor
Hobbes nor Boyle, outdo Winstanley on this score.
Our Digger philosopher made science and technology
part of everyday life—in the trades, in the pulpit,
in the mailbox. It would be wrong, however, to conclude from Winstanley's panegyric that his utopia
whole-heartedly embraces complex technology. Despite some shared elements with Bacon and Hartlib,
the Digger utopia is not a full-fledged instance of
Sibley's first category. There is the obvious point that
Winstanley set his sights on a relatively simple and
small-scale technology. But much more importantly,
utopians who whole-heartedly accept technology characteristically commit themselves to one or all of four
further points.

First, their commitment to technology entails specialized education for, and sometimes rule by, a narrow
elite. This, for example, was Bacon's view, whose
fellows of Saloman's House were uniquely well-
educated in New Atlantis and were consequently self-
perpetuating scientist guardians of both technology
and polity. Secondly, most utopias of whole-hearted
acceptance develop a domineering, even imperialistic,

attitude towards nature. Again Bacon is paradigmatic. He argued that by technology we "control" nature and make her "submit to our experiments," thus "enlarging the bounds of human empire to the effecting of all things possible."[16] Thirdly, in Sibley's words, technology is understood to be "the key to the good life." That is, causally, and perhaps ethically, technological innovation makes for the good life. The more technology, the better our lives. Finally, utopians of this kind never provide mechanisms of popular oversight. Technology is granted a life of its own. When introduced it is developed without consideration to consequences. And if unwanted consequences develop, it is simply assumed that still newer technology will arrive to relieve us. More technology means more technology.

Winstanley will have none of these. First, his view of education was democratic and anti-elitist. As such, Winstanley's views were "strikingly modern in comparison with the traditional concepts of his day."[17] Education in true commonwealth would be universal and life-long. Winstanley would have shared the belief of Mulford Sibley's own latter-day utopians that "true rule implies education in its broadest sense."[18] Winstanley conceived of education as both practical and humanistic, and he refused to allow a class of scholars to remain idle while others worked. That was the principal failure of the educational system under "kingly government" where scholarly idleness in the universities was like "the standing ponds of stinking waters" /238/. Winstanley's vision is the antithesis of the elitism and narrow intellectualism which pervades Bacon's Saloman's House, or even John Milton's proposals for education. "Let no young wit be crushed" was the motto of Digger pedagogy.

Secondly, Winstanley would have winced at Bacon's boasts of "human empire" over nature. By contrast, Winstanley spoke of scientific knowledge enhancing the "beauty of our Commonwealth" and providing "nourishment and preservation" and "enjoyment of the earth" /519f, 571/. Moreover, he implies that only those forms of technology which preserve the beauty and enjoyment of the earth should be engaged in, since he limits trades to those "which mankind should be brought up in" /577/. That is, Winstanley proposes an ethic about our relationship with nature which should not be violated by technological progress. In this regard he shares some of the views of later utopians who were decidedly anti-technological. In William Morris' *News From Nowhere,* for example, just as in the ***Law of Freedom,*** money is not used, goods and services are exchanged solely on the basis of human need, and the spiritual union with nature is valued as part of life itself.[19] In this somewhat ambivalent way, the Digger utopia is built upon some of the very premises which later utopians would use to radically reject complex technology.

Thirdly, Winstanley actually reverses the relationship between technology and the good life which characterizes those utopians who accept technology whole-heartedly. The latter regard technology as the causal and ethical key to the good life. But this puts the matter on its head, Winstanley would say. In his platform he sets the matter aright:

> When men are sure of food and raiment, their reason will be ripe, and ready to dive into the secrets of the Creation, that they may learn to see and know God . . . in all his works; for fear of want, and care to pay Rent to Taskmakers, hath hindered many rare inventions /580/.

Only a just society can provide the good life, and the freedom which is that life. Science and technology are not its producers, but one of its products.

Finally and most importantly, Winstanley's parliamentary referendum subjects technological implementation to popular discussion and democratic decision-making. The referendum was designed to ensure democracy in this as in all other matters. Since there must be "laws for every occasion" /528/, Parliament (by implication) must legislate on matters of technological implementation which affect the "common treasury." As with the medievals, so with Winstanley: "Whatever touches all, must be judged by all." In the month between Parliament's proposing a law and its final passage, the people must be informed and their support solicited. The burden of proof would lie with those MPs who favored the law supporting technological change. After all, the people need not provide alternatives when they use their veto. During this month, the public, counselled by partisans of change as well as by partisans of preservation, would register their final say. Obviously for the referendum to achieve its democratic goals a minimal scientific education would be required of all. This, as we have seen, Winstanley sought to institute. Moreover, extra-technological concerns could surely guide new legislation. Winstanley's abiding concern for the "poor oppressed people" made him favor technological innovation which reduced unnecessary toil, but not when it displaced people from their work, or when it made them dependent on the changing technical composition of work. Neither Luddites nor romantics, the Diggers nonetheless would not have technological growth at any cost.

Surely, modifications in the Digger plan would be required for the complexities introduced by larger populations, more complex technology, and the like. But the important point is that in the Digger utopia the spirit exists, and with modification so too the mechanism, to keep technology under democratic rein and to ensure its service for human needs. It is this spirit which makes the Digger utopia a unique seventeenth century utopia of selective technology.

Winstanley was, if nothing else, a visionary. Sadly, not all his visions were uplifting. Despite his efforts to stem the tide, he knew that science, technology, and knowledge itself, when not harnessed to a vision of justice, equity, and true freedom, bring about their opposites. This Winstanley felt deeply, and perhaps with a sense of resignation. **The Law of Freedom** begins with a hopeful buoyancy that knowledge in the form of his platform might, like a candle, light the way to the good life. But alas, not all knowledge is of this kind. What begins with hopeful buoyancy ends in a lament: "Knowledge, why didst thou come, to wound, and not to cure?" Winstanley's parting poem could be hung over our age, as well as his:

> Here is the righteous Law, Man, wilt thou it
>   maintain?
> It may be, is, as hath still, in the world been
>   slain.
> Truth appears in Light, Falsehood rules in
>   Power;
> To see these things to be, is cause of grief
>   each hour.
> Knowledge, why didst thou come, to wound,
>   and not to cure?
> I sent not for thee, thou didst me inlure.
> Where knowledge does increase, there sorrows
>   multiply.
> To see the great deceit which in the World
>   doth lie.
> Man saying one thing now, unsaying it anon,
> Breaking all's Engagements, when deeds for
>   him are done.
> O power where are thou, that must mend
>   things amiss?
> Come change the heart of Man, and make him
>   truth to Kiss:
> O death where art thou? wilt thou not tidings
>   send?
> I fear thee not, thou art my loving friend.
> Come take this body, and scatter it in the
>   Four,
> That I may dwell in One, and rest in peace
>   once more.

Notes

1 George Sabine, ed., *The Works of Gerrard Winstanley* (Ithaca: Cornell University Press, 1941), p. 5.

2 Parenthetical references in the text are to Sabine's edition of Winstanley's works *(ibid.)*. I also follow Sabine in leaving Winstanley's seventeenth century English in its original form.

3 The best full-length study of Winstanley is by David Petegorsky, *Left-Wing Democracy in the English Civil War* (London: Victor Gollanz, 1940). Besides a number of articles (some of which are cited below),

Sabine's introduction is particularly important, as is Christopher Hill's to his edition of Winstanley's works, *The Law of Freedom and Other Essays* (Middlesex: Harmondsworth, 1973). Also see Hill's *The World Turned Upside Down* (New York: Viking Press, 1972), ch. 7. Histories of political thought often fail to deal with Winstanley and the Diggers. The exceptions are important: Perez Zagorin, *A History of Political Thought in the English Revolution* (London: Routledge and Kegan Paul, 1954); and Mulford Sibley, *Political Ideas and Ideologies* (New York: Harper and Row, 1970).

4 Mulford Sibley, *Technology and Utopian Thought* (Minneapolis: Burgess, 1971); and *Nature and Civilization: Some Implications for Politics* (Itasca: F. E. Peacock, 1977).

5 *Nature and Civilization,* pp. 171ff.

6 For areas of Digger influence see Keith Thomas "Another Digger Broadside," *Past and Present,* 42 (1969). With the discovery of this pamphlet those areas proved to be greater than previously thought.

7 Thomas, p. 58, has suggested the broader background against which to understand the Diggers of 1649: "The whole Digger movement can plausibly be regarded as the culmination of a century of unauthorized encroachment upon the forests and wastes by squatters and local commoners, pushed on by land shortage and the pressure of population."

8 *Nature and Civilization,* p. 254.

9 For a longer discussion of the importance of this feature of Winstanley's program see J.C. Davis, "Gerrard Winstanley and the Restoration of True Magistracy," *Past and Present,* 70 (1976).

10 *Political Ideas and Ideologies,* p. 369.

11 *Technology and Utopian Thought,* p. 20.

12 *Nature and Civilization,* p. 171.

13 The ideological connection between Winstanley's ideas and the early Quakers has frequently been noted. Some have sought a more material connection between them, suggesting that Winstanley once was a Quaker, or became one sometime after 1652. See the articles by R.T. Vann, "From Radicalism to Quakerism: Gerrard Winstanley and Friends," *Friends Historical Society Journal,* XLIX (1959); "Diggers and Friends—A Further Note," *ibid,* L (1961); and "The Later Life of Gerrard Winstanley," *Journal of the History of Ideas,* XXVI (1965).

14 Nell Eurich, *Science in Utopia* (Cambridge: Harvard University Press, 1967), p. 314.

[15] Hill, *The Law of Freedom and Other Essays,* p. 46.

[16] Bacon in *Ideal Commonwealths,* edited by Henry Morley (New York: The Colonial Press, 1901), p. 129.

[17] R.L. Greaves, "Gerrard Winstanley and Educational Reform in Puritan England," *British Journal of Educational Studies,* XVII (1969), p. 169.

[18] *Nature and Civilization,* p. 273.

[19] See discussion in *ibid,* p. 183.

Christopher Hill (essay date 1986)

SOURCE: "Winstanley and Freedom" in *Freedom and the English Revolution: Essays in History and Literature,* edited by R. C. Richardson and G. M. Ridden, Manchester University Press, 1986, pp. 151-68.

[*In the following essay, Hill argues that the freedom Winstanley sought for his countrymen included economic, social, and religious freedom. Hill examines the implications behind such beliefs and demonstrates that Winstanley attempted to appeal to the people of England through his use of the common vernacular in his writings.*]

Gerrard Winstanley was born in Wigan in 1609, into a middle-class puritan family of clothiers. He came to London, was apprenticed to a clothier, married and set up in business just before the Civil War. The war, severing communications between London and Lancashire, ruined him; he retired to the Surrey countryside where he herded other men's cows as a hired labourer.

The 1640s were years of religious and political turmoil—the Civil War, leading to the defeat of the King; Levellers in London; and the Army arguing for a republic and a wide extension of the parliamentary franchise. In 1647 the Army seized the King, hitherto a prisoner of Parliament, and in January 1649 he was tried and executed as a traitor to the people of England. An MP for Wigan was one of the regicides. The House of Lords was abolished, and England was proclaimed a Commonwealth. Millenarian expectations ran high: almost anything seemed possible, including the return of King Jesus as successor to King Charles. There was a ferment of political and religious discussion.

But the forties were also years of great economic hardship for the lower classes. Over the century before 1640 wages had halved. The years between 1620 and 1650, Professor Bowden has said, were among the most terrible the English lower classes have ever endured. The economic disruption of the war, leading to unem-ployment, was accompanied by exceptionally high taxation, billeting and free quartering of soliders, and plunder. On top of all this there was a series of exceptionally bad harvests, famine and disease. The problem of the poor was acute. Rioting crowds seized corn. Men were said to lie starving in the London streets.

In the years 1648-9 a spate of pamphlets was published advocating use of confiscated church, crown and royalist lands to provide for the poor, and even fresh land confiscations; there were those who suggested expropriating the rich and establishing a communist society. Many predicted the second coming of Jesus Christ, and foresaw a thousand-year rule of the saints in which a materialist utopia would be established on earth—egalitarian, just to the poor at the expense of the rich. So Winstanley, who brooded deeply over these matters in his poverty, was not alone. But he was the only thinker we know of to break through to a systematically worked-out theory of communism which could be put into immediate effect. More's *Utopia,* published in 1516, had been in Latin, and More rejected with horror any idea of making it accessible to ordinary people by translating it into English. But Winstanley wrote, at a time of acute social and political crisis, in the vernacular, and appealed to the common people of England to take action to establish a communist society. 'Action is the life of all', he wrote; 'and if thou dost not act thou dost nothing'.[1]

It started, as so much seventeenth-century thinking did, with a vision, in which Winstanley received the messages 'Work together, Eat bread together', 'Let Israel go free: . . . Israel shall neither give nor take hire'. Winstanley decided he must 'go forth and declare it in my action' by organising 'us that are called the common people to manure and work upon the common lands'.[2] This was two months after the execution of Charles I. Winstanley, with a handful of poor men, established a colony on St. George's Hill, near Cobham, to take symbolic ownership of the uncultivated common and waste lands. It lasted a year.

Winstanley wrote a series of pamphlets defending the Digger colony and calling on others to imitate their example. At least ten more colonies were established. In the process Winstanley elaborated a quite original theory of communism. It is not possible to do full justice to the theory as a whole since we are concerned with Winstanley and freedom; but freedom was crucial to his thinking. It had indeed been crucial for the revolutionaries from the start. 'Liberty and property' was the slogan of the moderates; 'back to Anglo-Saxon freedom' the cry of the radicals. The word 'liberty' was hopelessly ambiguous. The close association of liberty and property in orthodox Parliamentary discourse is not fortuitous, for the Latin word *'libertas',* like the French word *'franchise',* came very close to meaning a property right: a 'liberty' is something you can exclude others from. To these Norman words Winstanley preferred the more plebeian Anglo-Saxon 'freedom'. Throwing off the Norman Yoke, as John Hare argued in a pamphlet published in 1647, involved a linguistic as well as a political revolution. There was no agreement on what liberty was, or should be.

'All men have stood for freedom', wrote Winstanley;

> and now the common enemy is gone, you are all like men in a mist, seeking for freedom and know not where nor what it is . . . And those of the richer sort of you that see it are ashamed and afraid to own it, because it comes clothed in a clownish garment . . . Freedom is the man that will turn the world upside down, therefore no wonder he hath enemies.[3]

He summed up in *The Law of Freedom* (1652): 'The great searching of heart in these days is to find out where true freedom lies, that the commonwealth of England might be established in peace'.[4] (A few years earlier Edward Hyde, in exile, had observed from a more conservative viewpoint that 'though the name of liberty be pleasant to all kinds of people, yet all men do not understand the same thing by it'.)[5]

Winstanley listed four current versions of freedom; and the ordr in which he discusses them is perhaps significant:

> 1 'Free use of trading, and to have all patents, licences [i.e. monopolies] and restrictions removed;' freedom for business men;

> 2 Freedom of conscience, no constraints 'from or to any form of worship'; the sort of freedom the sects called for;

> 3 'It is true freedom to have community with all women, and to have liberty to satisfy their lusts'— Ranter libertinism;

> 4 absolute freedom of property, for landlords and their eldest sons—the freedom the gentry most wanted.

Curiously, there is no mention of constitutional liberty. None of these, Winstanley thought, are 'the true foundation freedom which settles a commonwealth in peace'.[6]

So Winstanley was aware that his concept of freedom differed from that of most Parliamentarians. He insisted on economic freedom for the poor as well as the rich, on social as well as religious freedom. 'If thou consent to freedom to the rich in the City, and givest freedom to the freeholders in the country and to priests and lawyers and lords of manors . . . and yet allowest

the poor no freedom, thou art there a declared hypocrite'. All men had a 'creation birth-right' of access to cultivate the land.[7] In his final pamphlet, published in 1652 after the defeat of the Diggers, Winstanley was quite specific: 'True freedom lies where a man receives his nourishment and preservation, and that is in the use of the earth . . . A man had better to have no body than to have no food for it . . . True commonwealth's freedom lies in the free enjoyment of the earth'.[8] Living in a preponderantly agrarian society, Winstanley uses 'the land', 'the earth', to signify property in general; but he knew from his own experience in Wigan and London that England was already becoming an industrial country, and he had interesting things to say about a state monopoly of foreign trade and the abolition of commercial secrets.

In 1646 the Leveller John Lilburne had asserted that 'the poorest that lives hath as true a right to give a vote as well as the richest and greatest'.[9] The Levellers were agitating for a wide extension of the parliamentary franchise. Next year there were debates at Putney in the Army Council between generals, elected representatives of junior officers and of the rank and file, as well as some London Levellers—a remarkable occasion. Discussing the parliamentary franchise, Colonel Rainborough echoed Lilburne in memorable words:—'the poorest he that is in England has a life to live as the greatest he, and therefore . . . the poorest man in England is not at all bound in a strict sense to that government that he hath not had a voice to put himself under'. This led to a long debate with Commissary-General Ireton, who argued that 'liberty cannot be provided for in a general sense if property be preserved'. If the right to a vote derived from 'the right of nature', then 'by the same right of nature' a man 'hath the same right in any goods he sees, . . . to take and use them for his sustenance'. Natural right leads to communism: 'constitution founds property'.[10]

This argument nonplussed the Levellers at Putney, because most of them wanted to retain the institution of private property. William Walwyn was believed to be a theoretical communist, and the boundary line between Levellers and True Levellers (Diggers) was never clearly drawn. But Lilburne and other Levellers leaders repudiated the communism of the Diggers.[11] Many of them were prepared to exclude servants and paupers from the franchise. Winstanley, on the other hand, insisted uncompromisingly that 'the common people' are 'part of the nation'; 'without exception, all sorts of people in the land are to have freedom', not just 'the gentry and clergy'.[12]

Winstanley alone grasped Ireton's theoretical nettle. He agreed that a natural right to accumulate property was incompatible with liberty. 'There cannot be a universal liberty till this universal community be established.'[13] 'I would have an eye to property', Ireton had insisted.[14] Winstanley preferred liberty. For him the introduction of private property—and he speaks especially of property in land—had been the Fall of Man. 'In the beginning of time the great Creator Reason made the earth to be a common treasury'; and all men were equal, none ruling over another. But covetousness overcame Reason and equality together. 'When self-love began to arise in the earth, then man began to fall.'[15] 'When mankind began to quarrel about the earth and some would have all and shut out others, forcing them to be servants: this was man's fall.'[16] 'Murdering property' was founded on theft; and the state was set up to protect the property of the plunderers: 'You hold that cursed thing by the power of the sword'. Property is the devil, and to support it is 'rebellion and high treason against the King of Righteousness'.[17] Buying and selling, hiring wage labour, the laws regulating the market, are all part of the Fall.

So long as private property survives, 'so long the creation lies under bondage'. The government that maintains private property is 'the government of . . . self-seeking Antichrist', 'the government of high-waymen'.[18] Exploitation, not labour, is the curse of fallen man. Property and wage labour, Winstanley thought, must be abolished before all can enjoy freedom.

The Levellers and many in the Army argued that Parliament's victory in the Civil War over the Norman Yoke of King and landlords ought to lead to the establishment of political democracy. Winstanley held that it must lead to a restoration of economic equality. 'Everyone upon the recovery of the [Norman] conquest ought to return into freedom again without respecting persons . . . Surely all sorts, both gentry in their enclosures, commonalty in their commons, ought to have their freedom, not compelling one to work for another?' 'The laws that were made in the days of the kings . . . give freedom' only 'to the gentry and clergy; all the rest are left servants and bondmen to those taskmasters'. 'If the common people have no more freedom in England but only to live among their elder brothers [landlords] and work for them for hire, what freedom then can they have in England more than we can have in Turkey or France?'[19]

This would necessitate wholesale change. 'All laws that are not grounded upon equity and reason, not giving a universal freedom to all but respecting persons, ought . . . to be cut off with the King's head'.[20] What Winstanley called 'kingly power' had survived the King: 'that top bough is lopped off the tree of tyranny, and kingly power in that one particular is cast out. But alas, oppression is a great tree still, and keeps off the sun of freedom from the poor commons still'.[21] 'Everyone talks of freedom, but there are but few that act for freedom, and the actors for freedom are oppressed by the talkers and verbal professors of freedom.'[22]

Winstanley thus insisted that formal political liberty was inadequate unless accompanied by economic freedom, by equality. When J. C. Davis says that 'to Winstanley the only freedom that mattered was freedom from economic insecurity', he is, I think, quite wrong.[23] Winstanley said, indeed, that 'free enjoyment' of the earth 'is true freedom';[24] and that heaven is a 'comfortable livelihood in the earth'. 'There cannot be a universal liberty till this community be established.'[25] But freedom for Winstanley meant intellectual as well as economic freedom, meant the rule of Reason, the beginning of civilised life for all. 'When men are sure of food and raiment, their reason will be ripe, and ready to dive into the secrets of the creation.'[26] He foresaw a commonwealth in which science would flourish. Hitherto 'fear of want and care to pay rent to task-masters hath hindered many rare inventions'. In a free commonwealth, men would be encouraged to 'employ their reason and industry'; inventions would benefit all, not just the inventor. Kingly power had 'crushed the spirit of knowledge'; now it could 'rise up in its beauty and fullness'.[27] His belief in the possibilities of democratically controlled science is one of the most attractive features of Winstanley's thought.

In his final pamphlet, Winstanley declared that 'all the inward bondages of the mind, as covetousness, pride, hypocrisy, envy, sorrows, fears, desperation and madness, are all occasioned by the outward bondage that one sort of people lay upon another'.[28] 'No true freedom can be established for England's peace . . . but such a one as hath respect to the poor as well as the rich.' But economic freedom is the beginning, not the end. 'Freedom', he declared, 'is Christ in you and among you'.[29]

For Winstanley, Christ was not a person. The Biblical stories are allegories, not history. 'Whether there was any such outward things or no', he remarked nonchalantly, 'it matters not much'.[30] In a pamphlet written in his pre-communist phase, Winstanley explained that he preferred to use the word Reason rather than God, because he had been 'held in darkness' by the word God.[31] Reason is 'the great Creator', not a personal God beyond the skies but the law of the universe which will ultimately prevail among all men and women. For Winstanley, the Second Coming is 'the rising up of Christ in sons and daughters'—Christ, the spirit of Reason entering the hearts of all men and women, 'comes to set all free'. Freedom 'is Christ in you'.[32]

And what will Reason tell us? 'Is thy neighbour hungry and naked today, do thou feed him and clothe him; it may be thy case to-morrow, and then he will be ready to help thee.'[33] Reason is co-operation, and the rising of Reason in all men and women will lead to recognition of the necessity of a communist society.

The ethos of existing society was the negation of co-operation, of sharing. Here Winstanley drew on his own rudimentary version of the labour theory of value:

> No man can be rich, but he must be rich either by his own labours, or by the labours of other men helping him. If a man have no help from his neighbours, he shall never gather an estate of hundreds and thousands a year. If other men help him to work, then are those riches his neighbours' as well as his; for they be the fruit of other men's labours as well as his own . . . Rich men receive all they have from the labourer's hand, and what they give, they give away other men's labours, not their own.[34]

Men and women will be truly free when Reason 'knits every creature together into a oneness, making every creature to be an upholder of his fellow, and so everyone is an assistant to preserve the whole'.[35] 'To live in the enjoyment of Christ . . . will bring in true community and destroy murdering property.'[36] 'True freedom . . . lies in the community in spirit and community in the earthly treasury; and this is Christ . . . spread abroad in the creation'.[37] 'This commonwealth's freedom will unite the hearts of Englishmen together in love, so that if a foreign enemy endeavour to come in we shall all with joint consent rise up to defend our inheritance, and shall be true to one another. Whereas now the poor . . . say . . ."We can as well live under a foreign enemy working for day wages as under our own brethren, with whom we ought to have equal freedom" '.[38]

Every man subject to Reason's law becomes a Son of God. His ruler is within, whether it is called conscience, or love, or Reason, or Christ. After the Second Coming, when Reason has risen in sons and daughters, 'the ministration of Christ in one single person is to be silent and draw back' before the righteousness and wisdom in every person.[39] Religion will wither away.

But kingly power proved stronger than the Christ within. After the destruction of his communist colony in 1650, a less optimistic Winstanley asked why 'Most people are so ignorant of their freedom, and so few fit to be chosen commonwealth's officers?' His answer was that 'the old kingly clergy . . . are continually distilling their blind principles into the people and do thereby nurse up ignorance in them.'[40] He had a virulent anti-clericalism worthy of Milton. It made Winstanley almost anticipate Marx's 'opium of the people'.

> 'While men are gazing up to heaven, imagining after a happiness or fearing a hell after they are dead, their eyes are put out, that they see not what is their birthrights, and what is to be done by them here on earth while they are living . . . And indeed the subtle clergy do know that if they can but charm the

people . . . to look after riches, heaven and glory when they are dead, that then they shall easily be the inheritors of the earth and have the deceived people to be their servants. This . . . was not the doctrine of Christ'.[41]

'The upshot of all your universities and public preachers . . . is only to hinder Christ from rising', 'a cloak of policy' to cheat the poor of 'the freedom of the earth'. Only when the clergy have been deprived of their privileged position will each of us be free to 'read in your own book, your heart'.[42]

The 'murdering God of this world', 'the author of the creatures' misery', who defends property and ensures that the clergy get their tithes, is covetousness. Any external God must be rejected: the Diggers would 'neither come to church, nor serve their God'. The true God is within, and each man has 'his God'.[43]

Winstanley originally evisaged the transition to a communist society in ingeniously simple and peaceful terms. The example of the Digger community inspired ten or more similar communities in central and southern England. Winstanley believed that 'the work of digging' is 'freedom or the appearance of Christ in the earth'.[44] 'For the voice is gone out, freedom, freedom, freedom'.[45] The rising of Christ in men and women would be irresistible, starting from the lowest classes. 'The people shall all fall off from you, and you shall fall on a sudden like a great tree that is undermined at the root.' The poor would take over and begin to cultivate the commons and wastes everywhere.[46] Then a universal withdrawal of wage labour would be organised. The gentry would find themselves possessed of large estates which they were unable to cultivate. In time, they too would be influenced by the rising of Christ in them, would see that the only rational course was for them to throw the lands they could not farm themselves into the common stock and share in the advantages of a communist society. Winstanley even envisaged facilitating the transition by giving them specially favourable compensatory terms.

It was deliciously simple; but it failed to allow for the continued existence of 'kingly power' even after the abolition of kingship. Landlords, lawyers, clergy, all stood together to preserve the *status quo* and their privileged position. So, by the time he published *The Law of Freedom* in 1652, the experience of harassment, persecution, and finally violent suppression, had finally convinced Winstanley that Christ would be prevented from rising by lords of manors, priests, lawyers, and their state. *The Law of Freedom* was dedicated to Oliver Cromwell: 'you have power . . . to act for common freedom if you will: I have no power'.[47] Whether or not Winstanley really hoped that Cromwell would help to set up a communist state in England, he was right in thinking that it could not be done without the support of the revolutionary Army. And Oliver had not yet adopted the conservative posture he found appropriate after 1653.

Previously Winstanley had attacked all forms of state authority and punishment. 'What need have we of imprisoning, whipping or hanging laws to bring one another into bondage?' To execute a murderer is to commit another murder.[48] But now the title of his pamphlet, *The Law of Freedom: Or, True Magistracy Restored,* shows a new recognition that the state will have to be used if kingly power is to be overcome. Winstanley looks forward to a transitional period in which 'it is the work of a Parliament to break the tyrants' bonds, to abolish all their oppressing laws, and to give orders, encouragements and directions unto the poor oppressed people of the land'. Then 'the spirit of universal righteousness dwelling in mankind' and 'now rising up' would be able to take over.[49] 'In time . . . this commonwealth's government . . . will be the restorer of long lost freedom to the creation.' But till then, landlords, priests and lawyers must be curbed; so must be the 'rudeness of the people' from which the Diggers had suffered. Christ, 'the true and faithful Leveller', 'the spirit and power of universal love' 'or the law written in the heart',[50] would not rise in all men and women as quickly as Winstanley had hoped. Meanwhile the law of the commonwealth must 'preserve peace and freedom'.[51] The battle had still to be fought, education and political education carried on (a subject on which Winstanley is very interesting). Choices had to be made. 'There is but bondage and freedom', he wrote, 'particular interest or common interest'.[52]

For some especially grave offences, the death penalty would have to be retained as a deterrent during the transitional period: and it is interesting to see what these offences were. They were murder, 'buying and selling' (which 'killed Christ' and hindered his resurrection), taking money as a lawyer ('the power of lawyers is the only power that hinders Christ from rising') or as a priest; and rape.[53]

But Winstanley was well aware that "freedom gotten by the sword is an established bondage to some part or other of the creation'.[54] 'Tyranny is tyranny . . . in a poor man lifted up by his valour as in a rich man lifted up by his lands.'[55] Experience had taught Winstanley that a standing army separate from the people could swiftly lose its political ideals. Instead he wanted government by a really representative Parliament and magistrates, elected annually and responsible to 'their masters, the people, who chose them'. The ultimate check was that the people retained arms in their hands and had a right of insurrection.[56] Winstanley rejected in advance the theory of forcing men to be free, of dictatorship in the interests of democracy, which has defaced some later communist practice.

Winstanley's ideas were unprecedented. What is astonishing is the sophistication of his analysis, the distance he covered in the years from 1649 to 1652. At Putney, Rainborough and the Levellers could find no answer to Ireton's 'Liberty cannot be provided for in a general sense if property be preserved'. Basing political democracy on natural rights would leave no logical argument against a natural right to equality of property: the right to property derived from substantive laws, not natural rights. This was conventional wisdom by Ireton's day. Thomas Hedley had said in the Parliament of 1610 that property existed not by the law of nature but by municipal law.[57] But then, how did the state which passed these substantive laws get its authority?

Forty years later, Locke thought he had solved the problem. A right to property arises in the state of nature, anterior to the state. 'As much land as a man tills, plants, improves and can use the product of, so much is his property. He by his labour does, as it were, enclose it from the common.'[58] All men by mutual agreement then set up a state to guarantee their property: all men were property-owners. Locke's theory is all very well as an explanation of the *origins* of property, avoiding the danger of giving all men a natural right to it. But how had gross inequalities of property developed? Could they be justified? Locke attributed them to the invention of money, which allowed some men to amass more property than they needed to sustain life; and the state protected them in their unequal ownership in the interests of law and order, of social peace. But what about those with no property at all? Locke seems always to have been uneasy about this part of his argument, insisting that the poor had a *right* to subsistence in time of dearth and to maintenance in old age. What kind of right?[59]

Unlike the Levellers, Winstanley was able to answer this position, adumbrated by Ireton before being worked out by Locke. Money, buying and selling land, led to inequality. That was for Winstanley the Fall of Man. 'Thereby . . . man was brought into bondage and became a greater slave to such of his own kind than the beasts of the field were to him . . . The earth . . . was hedged into enclosures by the teachers and rulers, and the others were made servants and slaves.' Property ever since has been held 'by the power of the sword'; even if the present owners 'did not kill or thieve', yet their ancestors had done so.[60] This state of affairs can be reversed only by abolishing buying and selling which, Winstanley agreed with Locke, was the source of inequality. 'This will destroy all government and all our ministry', Winstanley imagined someone objecting; and he replied 'it is very true'.[61] It meant a total overthrow of kingly power and a reconstruction of society and the state on the basis of communal property. There was no other solution. It was a difficult programme, which could be put into effect only when

Christ—the power of Reason—had risen in all men and women. Then there would be a decent society.

Winstanley seems to have had an equally effective answer to Hobbes. *Leviathan* was not published until 1651, but in 1650 Winstanley seems to be answering Hobbist arguments. He was hardly likely to have read Hobbes in Latin, but Hobbism was in the air; the economic and political situation gave rise to Hobbist theories, in others as well as in Hobbes.[62] Hobbes based the state on an original contract which all men had entered into to escape from the state of nature. In his state the competitive drives of individualistic men all roughly equal in physical strength, and enjoying equal individual rights, inevitably produced anarchy until they agreed to elevate a sovereign with, in the last resort, absolute authority. Winstanley agreed with much of Hobbes's analysis, but drew different conclusions. If you abolish competitive individualist property relations, you abolish the problem. Property was not created by sinful human nature but vice versa; so only the abolition of property could get rid of the coercive state and the preachers of sin, both of which had come into existence to protect property. Winstanley saw that Hobbes's system was based on challengeable psychological assumptions: 'This same power in man that causes divisions and war is called by some the state of nature, which every man brings into the world with him'.[63] Winstanley rejected the competitive spirit which Hobbes pushed back from his own society into the state of nature as something universal. Winstanley had a rival psychology. 'Look upon the child that is new-born, or till he grows up to some few years; he is innocent, harmless, humble, patient, gentle, easy to be entreated, not envious.' He is corrupted by the competitive world in which he grows up.[64] But Reason governs the universe; when Reason rules in man he lives 'in community with . . . the spirit of the globe'. Man stands in need of others, and others stand in need of him. He 'dares not trespass against his fellow-creature, but will do as he would be done unto'.[65]

This strikes us as a fairly obvious criticism of the competitive psychology on which Hobbes's philosophy was based. But in the seventeenth century Hobbes seemed more difficult to refute on that plane. For his psychology was that of the almost universally accepted Calvinism, and was reinforced by the pressures of early capitalist society. Only someone who had emancipated himself from the ethos of that society (and from Calvinism) could attack Hobbes at what then seemed his strongest point.

One further point on Winstanley's refutation of Hobbes: 'Winstanley', says Dr Eccleshall, 'rejected, more fully and explicitly than any previous writer, the assumption that human nature was a fixed datum of which the established political system was the natural and invariable counterpart. Human nature . . . was an

historical artefact', and was 'historically modifiable' as social relationships changed.[66] In his recognition that you *can* change human nature, Winstanley, unlike Hobbes and Locke, was in the modern world.

In the context of what mattered in the seventeenth century, a word on Filmer and patriarchialism seems necessary. His argument, that the authority of kings derives by direct descent from Adam and is therefore absolute over all subjects, seems puerile to modern readers; yet Locke felt it necessary to answer him seriously, and historians have pointed out what strong roots patriarchialism had in that society where (not to mention the Bible) the household was also the workplace (family farms, family businesses) and the father was responsible for the conduct and discipline of his apprentices and servants, no less than of his children. The father of a family indeed wielded over his dependants all the powers of the state except that of life and death. He could flog, fine and imprison his dependants. (Pepys locked up one of his maids in a cellar for the night). He was also responsible for their education, technical training, religious and moral behaviour. In the countryside, where the vast mass of the population lived, with no police force, no state educational system or social services, the authority of the head of the household could be highly beneficial as well as on occasion tyrannical. Recall too the deference still shown to fathers. In this society, where symbols mattered, Quaker sons who kept their hats on and thou'd their fathers had a painful time of it. The commandment, Honour thy father and thy mother, was regularly used in sermons and treatises discussing political obligation. As late as 1700, Mary Astell argued from the example of 1688 that if monarchial tyranny in the state was wrong, male tyranny in the family must be wrong too.[67]

The household plays an important part in the community which Winstanley sketched in **The Law of Freedom**. But he totally rejected the political conclusions which Filmer drew from the authority of heads of households. Authority for Winstanley is based on the social functions which the father performs and acceptance of them by his dependants. The only justification of authority is 'common preservation . . . a principle in everyone to seek the good of others as himself without respecting persons'. For a magistrate to put self-interest above the common interest 'is the root of the tree of tyranny', which 'is the cause of all wars and troubles'. 'A true commonwealth's officer is to be . . . chosen . . . by them who are in necessity and judge him fit for that work', just as 'a father in a family is a commonwealth's officer because the necessity of young children chose him by joint consent'. The chain of authority goes upwards from the family to the parish or town, each of which is governed by elected officers, to MPs—all to be chosen annually. The implied contract is 'Do you see our laws observed for our preservation and peace, and we will assist and protect you'. And these words 'assist' and 'protect' imply the rising up of the people by force of arms to defend their laws and officers against 'any invasion, rebellion or resistance', or any who 'are fallen from true magistracy'[68]—for example, by trying to restore private property. So the paternalism of the society, which Filmer used to justify absolute monarchy, becomes for Winstanley an argument for communities in his ideal state to defend their rights.

Only one of his contemporaries seems to have entered directly into controversy with Winstanley. This was Anthony Ascham. In 1648 he published *A Discourse Wherein is examined What is particularly lawfull during the Confusions and Revolutions of Government.* In the following year, after the execution of Charles I, an expanded version appeared under the title *Of the Confusions and Revolutions of Governments.* This included a new chapter called 'The Originall of Property'. 'Some authors of this age', Ascham said, 'by a new art of levelling, think nothing can be rightly mended or reformed unless the whole piece ravel out to the very end, and that all intermediate greatness betwixt kings and them should be crumbled even to dust'. Such men say 'the law enslaves one sort of people to another. The clergy and gentry have got their freedom, but the common people are still servants to work for the other'. 'I wonder not so much at this sort of arguing', Ascham continued patronisingly, 'as to find that they who have such sort of arguments in their mouths should have spades in their hands'.[69] The reference to the Diggers could hardly be more explicit.

Ascham's arguments against Winstanley are rather disappointing. He was critical of what he took to be the Digger's primitivism. In Hobbist vein he argued that the state of nature would have been a state of perpetual war. It was inequality that 'perfectly bred dominion, and that [bred] property'. Men are bound by the contract which got them out of this state of nature and legitimised private property. Significantly perhaps, in view of Locke's later argument, Ascham followed his chapter on property with another inserted chapter 'Of the Nature of Money'. Property, Ascham thought, had good as well as evil consequences: 'that some faultlessly lead indigent lives in a state is no argument of tyranny in property, but of the ill use of it'. The rich 'are unhappier than the poor', who do not suffer from diseases like gout and the stone.[70] It is possible that he wrote this chapter in rather a hurry!

My claims for Winstanley are being pitched high, setting him up against in some respects the greatest political thinkers to emerge from the fertile soil of the English Revolution—the Levellers, Hobbes, Filmer, Ascham, Locke. One remains—James Harrington. Both Winstanley and Harrington recognised the economic basis of society and of political change. Russell Smith speculated seventy years ago that Harrington might even have been influenced by Winstanley. It is an interesting coincidence that Richard Goodgroom, who signed one of the Digger manifestoes in 1649, wrote a tract (probably in 1654) which incorporates many of the ideas elaborated in Harrington's *Oceana* two years later.[71]

Harrington argued that the land transfers of the century before 1640 necessitated a commonwealth—by which he meant a state ruled by property-owners, who alone constitute 'the people'. 'Robbers or Levellers', servants and paupers, cannot be free and so are excluded from the franchise, and representation in Harrington's ideal state would be titled to favour the well-to-do. Harrington himself disliked anything like the oligarchy which complete freedom for capitalist development was to produce in eighteenth-century England. He thought to safeguard against oligarchy by two devices: an agrarian law—no one to inherit more than £2000 per annum—and secret ballot to prevent the domination of elections by money.

Harrington dedicated *Oceana* to Oliver Cromwell in 1656, when it seemed as little likely that the Lord Protector would establish an 'equal commonwealth' as it was likely in 1652, when Winstanley dedicated **The Law of Freedom** to him, that he would establish a communist society. In this sense, both writers were utopians. Harringtonianism was very influential in the later seventeenth and eighteenth centuries, when England was (in Harringtonian terms) not a monarchy but a commonwealth headed by a price. Harrington was interpreted as arguing that the men of property *ought* to rule, thus justifying the Whig oligarchy; and his prediction that a commonwealth would be far more effective than absolute monarchy 'for increase', for aggressive colonial expansion, proved well founded.[72]

Complete freedom for private property was incompatible with Harrington's 'equal commonwealth'—as Winstanley could have told him. Winstanley rejected Harrington's starting point no less than he did that of Hobbes, from whom Harrington no doubt derived it. For Harrington, reason taught self-interest, not co-operation. (Primary allegiance is due to ourselves, Ascham thought).[73] Whether Winstanley's system would have proved any more workable than Harrington's is debatable; unlike Cromwell, Winstanley was never tested by having to exercise power;[74] but at least he had faced head on the intellectual problems which made Harrington's 'equal commonwealth' utopian.

Winstanley is arguably the most intellectually respectable and consistent of the great political theorists who emerged from the English Revolution. (Milton cannot be included in this context, since he was not an original political thinker). Central to Winstanley's vision was his argument that 'there cannot be a universal liberty till this universal community be established'.[75] True freedom and true equality can be guaranteed only when 'community . . . called Christ or universal love' rises unimpeded in sons and daughters and casts out 'property, called the devil or covetousness'.[76]

Winstanley failed; but his writings justify the words he prefixed to one of his Digger pamphlets:

> When these clay bodies are in grave, and children stand in place, This shows we stood for truth and peace and freedom in our days.[77]

Notes

[1] G. Winstanley, *The Law of Freedom and Other Writings,* Cambridge, 1983, pp. 127-8. See G. E. Aylmer, 'The religion of Gerrard Winstanley' in J. F. McGregor and B. Reay (eds.), *Radical Religion in the English Revolution,* Oxford, 1984; C. Hill, 'The Religion of Gerrard Winstanley', *Past and Present Supplement 5,* 1978; K. V. Thomas (ed.), 'A Declaration . . . [from] Iver, *Past and Present,* 42, 1969; D. W. Petegorsky, *Left-Wing Democracy in the English Civil War,* London, 1940.

[2] G. H. Sabine (ed.), *The Works of Gerrard Winstanley,* New York, 1941, pp. 190, 194, 199.

[3] Winstanley, *The Law of Freedom,* p. 128.

[4] *Ibid.,* p. 294.

[5] Edward Hyde's Commonplace Book, 1646-7, quoted by F. Raab, *The English Face of Machiavelli, A Changing Interpretation, 1500-1700,* London, 1964, p. 148.

[6] Winstanley, *The Law of Freedom,* p. 294.

[7] *Ibid.,* pp. 129, 306.

[8] *Ibid.,* p. 295.

[9] Lilburne, *The Charters of London,* 1646, quoted in D. M. Wolfe (ed.), *leveller Manifestoes of the Puritan Revolution,* New York, 1944, p. 14.

[10] A. S. P. Woodhouse (ed.), *Puritanism and Liberty,* London, 1938, pp. 53, 58, 69, 73. (2nd. ed., London, 1950, reprinted 1973.)

[11] See my *The World Turned Upside Down,* Harmondsworth, 1975, p. 119.

[12] Winstanley, *The Law of Freedom,* pp. 182, 116.

[13] Sabine, *op. cit.,* p. 199.

[14] Woohouse, *op. cit.,* p. 57.

[15] Winstanley, *op. cit.,* pp. 77-8, 193.

[16] Sabine, *op. cit.,* p. 424.

[17] Winstanley, *op. cit.,* pp. 85, 99, 120-1, 141, 222, 266-8; Sabine, *op. cit.,* p. 201.

[18] Winstanley, *op. cit.,* pp. 244, 306-7.

[19] Sabine, *op. cit.,* pp. 287-8.

[20] *Ibid.,* p. 288.

[21] Winstanley, *op. cit.,* p. 166.

[22] *Ibid.,* p. 129.

[23] J. C. Davis, 'Gerrard Winstanley and the restoration of true magistracy', *Past and Present,* 70, 1976, pp. 78, 92.

[24] Winstanley, *op. cit.,* p. 296.

[25] Sabine, *op. cit.,* p. 199.

[26] Winstanley, *op. cit.,* pp. 365-6.

[27] *Ibid.,* pp. 355-6.

[28] *Ibid.,* p. 296.

[29] *Ibid.,* pp. 128-9.

[30] *Ibid.,* p. 232.

[31] Sabine, *op. cit.,* p. 105.

[32] Winstanley, *op. cit.,* pp. 216, 128; Sabine, *op. cit.,* pp. 114-15, 162, 204-5, 225.

[33] Winstanley, *The Saints Paradice,* 1648?, p. 123.

[34] Winstanley, *Law of Freedom,* p. 287.

[35] Sabine, *op. cit.,* p. 105.

[36] Winstanley, *op. cit.,* p. 222.

[37] *Ibid.,* p. 129.

[38] Sabine, *op. cit.,* p. 414.

[39] Winstanley, *op. cit.,* pp. 222, 227; Sabine, *op. cit.,* p. 162.

[40] Winstanley, *op. cit.,* p. 324.

[41] *Ibid.,* pp. 353-4.

[42] Sabine, *op. cit.,* pp. 238-42, 213-14.

[43] Winstanley, *op. cit.,* pp. 138, 144, 196-8, 225-6, 271-2, 307-8, 310, 379; Sabine *op. cit.,* pp. 197, 434.

[44] Thomas, *op. cit.,* pp. 57-60; Sabine, *op. cit.,* p. 437.

[45] Winstanley, *op. cit.,* p. 217.

[46] *Ibid.,* p. 203.

[47] *Ibid.,* p. 285.

[48] Sabine, *op. cit.,* p. 193, 283; cf. p. 197, and Winstanley, *op. cit.,* p. 192.

[49] Winstanley, *op. cit.,* pp. 340, 312.

[50] *Ibid.,* pp. 199, 203-4, 312.

[51] *Ibid.,* p. 222.

[52] *Ibid.,* p. 342.

[53] *Ibid.,* pp. 171, 366, 383, 388; Sabine, *op. cit.,* p. 238.

[54] Winstanley, *op. cit.,* p. 190.

[55] Sabine, *op. cit.,* p. 198.

[56] Winstanley, *op. cit.,* pp. 318-20.

[57] E. R. Forster (ed.), *Proceedings in Parliament, 1610,* New Haven, Conn., 1966, II, pp. 189, 194-6.

[58] Locke, *Two Treatises,* ed. P. Laslett, Cambridge, 1967, Second Treatise, p. 325.

[59] Locke's views are usefully summarised in J. Dunn, *Locke,* Oxford, 1984, especially pp. 29-41. They were perhaps not altogether original. Aquinas described appropriation as a dictate of natural reason and denied that uncorrupted reason dictated communal ownership (Beryl Smalley, '*Quaestiones* of Simon of Henton's in R. W. Hunt, W. A. Pantin, and R. W. Southern (eds.), *Studies in Medieval History Presented to F. M. Powicke,* Oxford, 1948, p. 219.).

[60] Winstanley, *op. cit.,* pp. 77-8, 99.

[61] *Ibid.,* p. 243.

[62] Cf. *The World Turned Upside Down,* appendix I; Q. Skinner, 'Conquest and Consent: Thomas Hobbes and the Engagement Controversy', in G. E. Aylmer (ed.), *The Interregnum: The Quest for Settlement, 1646-1660,* London, 1972.

[63] Winstanley, *op. cit.,* p. 268. cf. p. 309.

[64] *Ibid.,* p. 269.

[65] Sabine, *op. cit.,* pp. 109-12; Winstanley, *The Saints Paradice,* p. 123.

[66] R. Eccleshall, *Order and Reason in Politics: Theories of Absolute and Limited Monarchy in Early Modern England,* Oxford, 1978, pp. 174-6.

[67] Mary Astell, *Some Reflections upon Marriage,* 1706, preface. The work was first published in 1700. For Filmer, see Laslett's Introduction to *Patriarcha and other Political Works of Sir Robert Filmer,* Oxford, 1949.

[68] Winstanley, *op. cit.,* pp. 314-20.

[69] Ascham, *Of the Confusions,* pp. 18-19.

[70] *Ibid.,* pp. 20-5. Ascham was assassinated in 1650 by royalist exiles when he was acting as agent for the parliamentary Commonwealth in Madrid.

[71] H. F. R. Smith, *Harrington and his Oceana,* Cambridge, 1914. For Goodgroom see J. G. A. Pocock (ed.), *Political Works of James Harrington,* Cambridge, 1977, pp. 11-12, 58.

[72] See my *The Experience of Defeat: Milton and Some Contemporaries,* London, 1984, ch. 10, section 5.

[73] Ascham, *Of the Confusions,* pp. 106-7.

[74] See Roger Howell on Cromwell, pp. 25-44, above.

[75] Sabine, *op. cit.,* p. 199.

[76] Winstanley, *op. cit.,* p. 268.

[77] *Ibid.,* p. 125.

Bibliography

J. Alsop, 'Gerrard Winstanley's later life', *Past and Present,* 82, 1979.

G. E. Aylmer, '*Englands Spirit Unfoulded, or an Incouragement to take the Engagement:* a newly discovered pamphlet by Gerrard Winstanley', *Past and Present,* 40, 1968.

G. E. Aylmer, 'The religion of Gerrard Winstanley' in J. F. McGregor and B. Reay (eds.), *Radical Religion in the English Revolution,* Oxford, 1984.

C. H. George, 'Gerrard Winstanley: a critical retrospect' in C. R. Cole and M. E. Moody (eds.), *The*

Dissenting Tradition: Essays for Leland Carlson, Athens, Ohio, 1975.

P. H. Hardacre, 'Gerrard Winstanley in 1650', *Huntington Library Quarterly,* XXII, 1958-59.

T. W. Hayes, *Winstanley the Digger: A Literary Analysis of Radical Ideas in the English Revolution,* Cambridge, Mass., 1979.

C. Hill, 'The religion of Gerrard Winstanley', *Past and Present Supplement 5,* 1978.

C. Hill, *The World Turned Upside Down,* London, 1972.

O. Lutaud, *Winstanley: Socialisme et Christianisme sous Cromwell,* Paris, 1976.

D. W. Petegorsky, *Left-Wing Democracy in the English Civil War,* London, 1940.

G. H. Sabine (ed.), *The Works of Gerrard Winstanley,* New York, 1941.

D. C. Taylor, *Gerrard Winstanley in Elmbridge,* Elmbridge, Surrey, 1982.

K. Thomas, 'Another Digger broadside', *Past and Present,* 42, 1969.

K. Thomas, 'The date of Gerrard Winstanley's *Fire in the Bush*', *Past and Present,* 42, 1969.

G. Winstanley, *The Law of Freedom and Other Writings,* Cambridge, 1983.

P. Zagorin, *A History of Political Thought in the English Revolution,* London, 1954.

Nicola Baxter (essay date 1988)

SOURCE: "Gerrard Winstanley's Experimental Knowledge of God (The Perception of the Spirit and the Acting of Reason)," *The Journal of Ecclesiastical History,* Vol. 39, No. 2, April, 1988, pp. 184-201.

[*In the following essay, Baxter examines Winstanley's religious pamphlets in a study of Winstanley's use of words, language, and concepts.*]

This essay is an attempt to find out what Winstanley meant by certain terms, using close textual analysis. Extensive work has already been done in locating Winstanley in political, theological and, as far as possible, intellectual terms. This will receive only cursory treatment here. A scholarly tradition can be traced from Bernstein, through Petergorsky and Margaret James to Christopher Hill, which places Winstanley at the beginning of the development of materialist socialism although, it is suggested, his ideas proved to be a false start and went underground for a century or more.[1] This view derives from his later works, especially *The Law of Freedom,* with its practical design of tilling the land communally, and sees his mysticism either as a cloak for revolutionary aims or as an undeveloped stage in his thought which he later left behind and which is thus of secondary importance. Work has been done, sometimes by the same scholars, to map out the tenets of his religious beliefs in the context of contemporary radical Puritanism, considering whether he was, for instance, a mortalist, a universalist or a millenarian, and how far he was any of these. For such doctrinal identification one can look to W. S. Hudson, the cooperative study of L. Mulligan, J. K. Graham and J. Richards and to Christopher Hill, for all of these have compared and contrasted his beliefs with those of Seekers, Ranters, Fifth Monarchists and Quakers.[2] Hill himself, however, has pointed out the difficulties of placing Winstanley in a particular group because of the fluidity of the borders between one sect and another; sects sharing certain beliefs while differing in others and changing character internally with changing political circumstances.

It is dangerous to try and trace Winstanley's ideas to literary sources, since he was not himself an intellectual. However, a recent work by T. W. Hayes shows how he was unconsciously continuing a tradition of poet-prophets by dealing originally with established sources of language and imagery.[3] His imagery was biblical and his language was apocalyptic; his use and treatment of them can be compared with Joachim of Fiore and the Anabaptists and Zwickau Prophets of a century earlier. Out of these materials he forged his own symbolism, elaborating the myth of the Norman Yoke by synthesising biblical 'myth' (as he saw it) with historical 'fact'; these constructions, inspired by an inner light and a belief in a utopia, reveal him as a creative artist. Hayes states in his preface that he believes an analysis of language and imagery to be the key to the content of the religious or political thought of a writer. This approach comes nearest to this writer's intention, since the aim of this paper is not to label Winstanley's thought definitively, but to observe patterns running through the works. By studying his terms, key words will emerge that seem to reflect the development of his ideas and thus uncover the unifying principles in his thought.

Gerrard Winstanley was born in 1609 in Lancashire.[4] It is known that he was a cloth merchant in London at the beginning of the Civil War, and that around 1643 his business, like many others, went bankrupt. He was forced to accept the hospitality of friends in Cobham, Surrey, where, until 1649, he seems to have made a precarious living pasturing neighbours' cattle.

His first pamphlet was *The Mysterie of God,* issued shortly before *The Breaking of the Day of God* (20 May 1648), both of which coincided with the outbreak of the Second Civil War and interpreted the national troubles in religious terms as a struggle between the flesh and the spirit.[5] The two preceding years had witnessed tremendous uncertainty and insecurity in the country, politically, socially and economically. The king had been defeated, but he was hardly treated as an enemy, and the victors were made up of diverse religious and social groupings who were almost as much opposed to each other as to the king. The bad harvest of 1647, the lack of evidence of change in their fortunes and the continuation of heavy taxes carried over from the war, left the common people understandably dissatisfied. In October, the Levellers voiced their disappointment in the form of the Putney Debates, but they received no real answers to demands made in the light of what they had been promised and the principles on which they believed the war had been fought. Winstanley wrote two more theological pamphlets in 1648, *The Saints Paradise* and *Truth Lifting up its Head Above Scandal.*[6] By the time he came to write *The New Law of Righteousness* (26 January 1649), in which he put forward the idea of communistic tilling of the earth, the king had been declared guilty of treason;[7] he was executed at the end of the month. Winstanley's new plan of action was paralleled by the renewed efforts of the Levellers at this time to press for the civil rights of the individual. Over the next few months it became apparent that their radical constitutional demands would not be met, and they were finally crushed by Cromwell.

This final failure of the Levellers may have made Winstanley more convinced that alternative action was necessary. On 20 April, *The True Levellers Standard Advanced* was published as the manifesto of the Diggers: God had directed Winstanley in a revelation to till the soil communally; and now, with like-minded individuals he set about doing this in Surrey, according to the Spirit, with the aim of gaining a living by the planting and reaping of their own crops.[8] While the digging continued and the community grew in number (as local opposition likewise increased), numerous pamphlets appeared justifying their action, defending their right to the common land and publicising the ill-treatment they had received at the hands of English law. By April 1650, the economic experiment had failed because of sabotage and legal action. In March 1650, *Fire in the Bush* had been published, an elaboration of Winstanley's theology which may have been a last-minute attempt to win sympathy by explaining the purpose behind their action.[9] The next pamphlet to appear was *The Law of Freedom in a Platform* in 1652.[10] Written probably a year before, this elaborated a political programme for the institution of a Commonwealth in England and is very different in character

from the earlier pamphlets, suggesting to some scholars that Winstanley had become a rationalist and a materialist.[11]

It seems worthwhile to look first at how Winstanley thought words worked, that is, how they come to be valid conveyors of meaning. Examples can be taken from a cross-section of his pamphlet; it is not necessary to pursue the particular issue raised in the context of his overall argument for the moment. Winstanley, as a self-conscious writer, is aware of the games that can be played with words. His writing is full of puns and he takes what might be called poetic licence in changing the spelling of words to emphasise the point he is trying to make; as he writes, Divines becomes Day-vines, David Davider and Adam A-dam. To define a word by another word, he wishes to say, is as futile as worrying about how a word is spelt as neither helps towards understanding. Yet learned clergy and professors use mere words as absolutes to quell curiosity and silence questioning: 'The People demands, What is the Gospel? You say, it is the Scriptures. The People replies again; How can these Scriptures be called the everlasting Gospel, seeing it is torn in peeces daily amongst your selves, by various translations, inferences and conclusions?'[12] Words, written and spoken, must be made subject to 'spiritual judging' or 'tryall'[13] if they are to ring true or be authentic in usage.

In one of the prefaces to *Truth Lifting up its Head* Winstanley explains why he will henceforward call God by the name of Reason. It is to break the circle of words that form men's conceptions since Reason suggests an actual quality:

> If I demand of you, who made all things? And you answer God. If I demand what is God? You answer the spirituall power; that as he made; so he governs and preserves all things, so the sum of all is this, God is the chief Maker or Governor and this Maker and Governor is God: Now I am lost in this wheel that runs round and lies under darkness.[14]

'Maker' and 'Governor' are just nouns, external labels which do not tell what is involved in the act of making or governing. Winstanley's own reply to the same question entails describing the process by which an absolute is translated into the sphere of experience:

> Reason is that living power of light that is in all things: It is the salt that savours all things . . . It lies in the bottom of love, of justice, of wisdome; for if the Spirit Reason did not uphold and moderate these they would be madnesse; nay they could not be called by their names; for Reason guides them in order, and leads them to their right end, which is not to preserve a part, but the whole creation.[15]

Reason is not to be understood as a definitive name or an abstract term, but as a condition or state of reasonableness, and people must therefore identify how the Spirit works in them before naming God for themselves. 'Every one must give him a name according to that spirituall power that they feel and see rules in them, carrying them forth in action to preserve their fellow creatures.'[16]

The word 'God' had acquired a mystique. For this reason, Winstanley abandoned it in favour of a word which better expressed his experience of that spiritual power which was God; men should no longer rest upon 'words without knowledge'. Winstanley's criticism of the clergy was often founded on their veneration of Scripture as if the words themselves represented God's power when, in fact, 'they are dry shells until God gives experience of his love such as the prophets had'.[17] People must 'therefore learne to put a difference between the Report, and the thing Reported of. The spirit that made flesh is he that is reported of. The writings and words of Saints is the report.'[18] To speak Scripture is not to witness the Spirit for the only test of its presence is if it moves a man actually to 'live of the gospel', which churchmen often fail to do. 'Well, your word Divinity darkens knowledge; you talk of a body of Divinity and of Anatomyzing Divinity: O fine language! But when it comes to triall, it is but a husk without the kernell; words without life . . . and the spirit is not in your service, for your publique service stinks before him . . . Love and righteous acting within the Creation is not to be found in your hands.'[19]

For Winstanley, pious words are empty of meaning unless the speaker has experienced the Spirit within, for the Spirit does not move through words: it moves individuals. Discerning good from bad spirits was a tradition in Christianity, and the chaos and confusion of the Civil War period made it an issue of immediate concern to everyone in the land and, collectively, to both sides, for all believed themselves to be acting in God's name. Many of the specific grievances brought up at the Putney Debates resolved into discussion about where the Spirit lay, for the Spirit in man was a guarantee of an objective good or righteousness not swayed by self-interest.[20] The problem was to identify the Spirit. Cromwell suggested that it could be recognised by the 'appearance of meekness and gentleness . . . and a desire to do good to all, and to destroy none that can be saved'.[21] These criteria would not have satisfied Winstanley, however, for whom the Spirit was known by the actual bringing about of justice in the world.

In Winstanley's work, the word 'Spirit' is often accompanied by the word 'Reason' as in 'the Spirit Reason', or in the sentence 'The Spirit or Father is pure Reason'. They are often used synonymously and

they have in common certain attributes; they are life-giving and life-preserving and are found within men. However, a distinction can be made which throws a light on Winstanley's concept of God. Winstanley did not believe in the separation of God, the Holy Spirit and Christ. Similarly, just as he uses the words 'Christ' and 'God' almost synonymously since Christ as an historical figure is not necessary to man's salvation, Reason and Spirit seem to represent two aspects of God. These two aspects of God correspond to the stages which constitute the individual's experience or knowledge of Him. One is the simple sensation of God and the other is the carrying forward of the effects of that sensation to others. The Oxford Dictionary defines the Spirit of God as 'active essence, essential power of Deity, conceived as a creative, animating or inspiring influence'. For Winstanley, it was all this, but he would have described it in more palpable terms. G. F. Nuttall has made an extensive study of the place of the Spirit in radical Puritanism and shows how it was conceived of as a physical reality, so that one might rather say that it was perceived—'a spiritual perception analogous to physical perception of the senses'.[22] This is why it was talked of as light or heat, for this objective reality distinguished it from man's reason. Uneducated people (of whom Richard Baxter said, 'their knowledge is more sensible and experimental and beneficial to them') were thus deemed more suitable candidates for witness to the Spirit, since discursive powers inhibited immediate and intuitive apprehension.[23] Experience of the Spirit was the touchstone of faith, and the touchstone of this experience was sensual perception.

In his earliest pamphlets Winstanley still uses the word 'God' and has not yet drawn the distinction in God between Spirit and Reason. Where he talks about 'God' in the examples that follow, he might later use the word 'Spirit'. He tells how he was converted from his old form of worship and that he did not arrive at his present state of mind by his own intellectual powers: 'This I know, first, by my own experience. Though I lay under bondage to the Serpent, I saw no bondage until God caused me to see that I was dead in sin . . . I could not deny self until God pulled me out of selfish striving and gave me peace.'[24] Winstanley here stresses his passivity in the course of the change, as his will had to be put aside for God to work in him. His guarantee that this was the Spirit and not his reason is that he felt an outside agent at work in him. He refers to this experience elsewhere as 'experimental persuasions in me . . . of God's own working'.[25] Likewise, when defending the divine origin of his communist revelation, 'I understood it from thy teaching first within me'.[26] It is for this reason that Winstanley looks to the common people as a vehicle of God's Spirit working in the world: they are more responsive to sensible stimuli. 'God's teaching shall never cease, for it gives a feeling experience to the heart which can never be forgot. This alone overcomes the self-conceit and evil inclinations of the flesh. Not the Apostles' writings but the spirit that dwelt in them and inspired their hearts gives life and peace.'[27]

By the time he wrote *Fire in the Bush* (1650), he had arrived at his mature descriptive language. Now he talks of the Spirit as an inward friend. Although it is within him, it is apart from him, having the status of 'other', so that he can see it as he would see something that was really outside his body: 'Oh that I could see and feele Love . . . and peace live and rule in power in me . . . if all my outward friends and objects forsooke me; yet if I had familiar friendship, with that sweet spirit within, I should have peace enough.'[28] The Spirit is felt and, to this extent, the individual plays a passive role; but friendship implies an active relationship where both move towards each other. From the effects worked in him by the Spirit he has peace, that is, he is peaceful in himself. The work of the Spirit is extended in a second stage of the experience of God, making the individual peaceable. He is now disposed to peace, working to bring about peace in others, as the Spirit has done in him.

The word 'communion' is never far from the word 'Spirit'. It is constituted of two similar but distinct parts, union and communion: the former represents that part of the experience of God in which the individual perceives the Spirit within him, the latter the extension of the Spirit's work in one's relations with others. A man who has the Spirit within is united to it and joined with it, and he partakes of the benefits of the Spirit and love lives in him. But when he lives in love, that is, practises love towards others, he is in active communion with the Spirit in others: 'Souls have no peace until they have community with the Spirit within them, but when they feel the spirit of righteousness governing their flesh, they begin to know God and they will be brought into community with the whole globe.'[29] Community is a stronger version of unity, suggesting not simply juxtaposition but active participation and a shared social life. The Spirit is not a static presence but a dynamic power which operates in the individual, engendering a motion which he will continue. If a man is open to the workings of the Spirit within, he will be inclined to replicate the process in his relations with others who also have the Spirit working in them. The more people who have or recognise the Spirit in themselves the more love becomes an effective mover. 'Thus men will knit together in one body and will cease to teach, for everyone will be taught of the Father.'[30]

Many other radical Puritans, especially Quakers, used another word to express the same idea as community. 'Tenderness' implies 'openness to the workings of God's Spirit within and consequent sensitiveness to the Spirit's workings in others also, according to their measure'.[31] In fact, a sign of the Spirit within was awareness of it in others, and this, in turn, was signified by spontaneous acts of charity and justice towards others. The acting out of love (living in charity) is a sign of someone who is already sharing in the gifts of the Spirit. The receiving of the Spirit and the administering of its benefits to others are virtually simultaneous: man moved to act in love expresses in outward form the inner work of the Spirit.

There was opposition to those who lived by the dictates of the Spirit since it was seen as a licence for anarchy, each man being his own governor and seeking his own ends to the inevitable disadvantage of others. But for Winstanley, precisely the opposite is true, since acts of charity are evidence of the Spirit whereas self-love is a mark of the workings of man's reason. Winstanley's Reason—which is expressed in actions inspired by the Spirit—is almost the opposite of man's reason. Within, God is felt as the Spirit. In relations with others, He is known through the carrying out of reasonable acts which link one man to another. Like the Spirit, reason was often invoked as a criterion for the justice or rightness of an act, but this also was sometimes difficult to identify. To some, reason was man's intellectual power, God given, to be used with His aid: with God's grace to guide it, all men's reason would reach the same ends. This idea of 'right reason' was used by Milton as the basis for his argument for freedom from censorship in *Areopagitica*. The discussion also pervades the debates at Putney where reason was sometimes seen as a touchstone in this way.[32] It was also seen, however, as a possible barrier to God's will, for, if man tried to work out what was right by his own standards, he lacked the larger perspective to see beyond his own interests.[33] If Winstanley's Reason was not man's reasoning then neither was it any kind of rationalist theology. In fact it referred not so much to rationality as to reasonableness, or righteousness. Christopher Hill says that Reason is Winstanley's new name for God, but goes on to discuss it as if man's reason is his new God, as if the concept had changed instead of the word. Winstanley did indeed write that Reason is the highest name that can be given to the Father. Taken on its own, this could sound as if he meant that Reason exists independently of the Father. According to Hill's paraphrase of Winstanley, 'in a non-exploitative society Reason might have a chance of rising in men and women, on the basis of their own social experience, and of being universally accepted as a guide to conduct'.[34] Translated into modern, secular speech this is what Winstanley said, but such literalism neglects to define his terms.

In his essay on reason in the seventeenth century, Hill aims to show how 'right reason' became a social concept of usefulness. While this comes close to Winstanley's notion of Reason being socially defined, he would have found it overly reliant on man's own estimation of what was good for him.[35] Reason does not replace

God: it is merely another name for Him since it comes nearer to expressing what His power constitutes and how it works through man to the benefit of all mankind. It is not something man can arrive at on his own. 'The further you dive into Reason, the more incomprehensive hee will appear; for he is infinite in wisdom, and mighty in power, past finding out by flesh, till the flesh be made to see light in his light.'[36] Reason (God) is outside man but works through him as a spirit of righteousness, making him act reasonably; 'and the same Spirit that made the Globe, dwels in man to Govern the Globe; so that the flesh of man being subject to Reason, his Maker, hath him to be his Teacher and Ruler within himself'.[37] Although Spirit and Reason are interchangeable as words, Winstanley is describing two parts of one process: the act of creation and the residing of the Creator in the Creation to work in it. The Spirit felt internally is seen outwardly as Reason.

> But now the Spirit Reason, which I call God [i.e. which is what I call God], the Maker and Ruler of all things, is that spirituall power, that guides all men's reasoning in right order, and to a right end: for the Spirit Reason, does not preserve one creature and destroy another; as many times mens reasoning doth . . . but it hath a regard to the whole creation; and knits every creature together into a oneness; making every creature to be an upholder of his fellow; and so every one is an assistant to preserve the whole.[38]

Only God, outside Creation, can understand the whole in relation to its parts and is therefore able to move through it for the preservation of all.

Truth Lifting up its Head addresses the question, how one should know if one's God is the Father and if one is witness to His Spirit. He describes a two-sided sensation: when the Spirit is first perceived within and is at once recognisable in others. 'When thou art, by that spirit, made to see him, rule and governe, not onely in them, but in the whole creation: so that thou feels and sees that the spirituall power that governes in thee, hath a community in thee with the whole globe . . . Now thou mayst call him God warrantably, for thou knowst him to be the might governour.'[39] A man moved by the Spirit is made subject to God's will; and the righteous acts acknowledge that this is the 'wisdom of the Father' channelled through man: 'When flesh becomes subject to the reason (King of righteousness) within it, it can never act unrighteously . . . but it does as it would be done by.'[40] Man's part in this process is not wholly passive, however, since he has, in the first place, to relinquish his will and open his heart to God's ruling.

The Spirit within man links him through Reason to the Spirit in other men. The Spirit is tested against the same in others, and the practice of Reason in the community is a sign of the Spirit's presence in its members: in these two ways it is experienced and tried. Without the Spirit, man has no native guide to help him interpret what is beyond himself. The result is the predominance of man's reason, which Winstanley calls 'unexperienced Imagination' since it is not correcting itself according to an objective standard.[41] He also calls reasoning the 'powers of the flesh', which echoes Cromwell's warning against mistaking carnal imagination and carnal reasonings for faith. Imagination—far from Coleridge's later idea of it, but akin to his definition of fancy—is suspect since it colours what is actually seen and heard; for this reason, the Quakers referred to it as 'notions'. As the Spirit is recognized by external, reasonable acts which help others, so the work of the flesh is characterised by deeds that serve the individual and bypass the welfare of the community.[42] This wilful individualism results from inclinations that arise when the Spirit is not felt within; it is shown in the desire to own objects and in exaggerated fears not grounded in reality. The two go hand in hand, since insecurity engineers a desire to possess things, and possessiveness leads to jealousy and suspicion.

> They that live upon outward objects are filled with inward trouble . . . they dare not live in the life of free community, or universall Love; least others jeare, hate, and trouble them; or least they come to want food and rayment; for Imagination thinks, if they love and succour others, yet others will not love them againe; These know not the Spirit, they live without [exteriorly] upon the Earth.[43]

This selfish power is a product of the combination of man's natural inclinations and the temptations placed before him.[44] There has been much debate about whether, for Winstanley, the external object creates the desire to have it, or whether the desire is already in man's heart. He implies both on different occasions, which is why proponents of both views may be literally correct. Taken overall, his terms admit no contradiction.

In ***Fire in the Bush,*** Winstanley gives a full account of his version of man's fall, which daily enacts the Original Fall. Man's primary sin is self-love, a desire to promote himself above others and be equal with God. Before this happens, however, he is in an innocent state, living instinctively by his five pure senses. However before the Spirit is his, he cannot judge what is good or bad and wants whatever is placed before him. At this stage, man is leading a good life in the image of God, yet lacks the strength and life of God: 'It is wise, but not wisdome it selfe; it is just but not Justice; it is loving but not Love it selfe. It rejoyces, but is not Joy it selfe . . . '.[45] Winstanley, as before, notes the difference between a passive state, in which the imprint of God is received, and the active disposition, in which His will is realised in actual deed. In this receptive condition, still untried by experience, man is open to temptation since the heart will take the imprint of whatever is before it: 'The outward objects of riches, honours, being set before the living soul, Imaginary covetousnesse, which is the absence of true Light, moves the man to close with those objects, and to seeke content without [outside] him.'[46] This move towards objects is the reaction of an inward disposition with external stimuli. The two-way process is described by Winstanley as a 'league';[47] as in the friendship with the Spirit, it is a case of being influenced by something and then responding actively to it.

Elsewhere he makes clearer his belief that no external object can affect a man unless a corresponding impulse exists within him:

> Now I desire any man to show by experience, any other Devill, or darker power, than these two, that is, The objects without, and the powers of the curse within, joyning in consent together, to enslave the . . . innocencie of the five Sences . . . While these two joyne together and meet in consent, Mankinde enters into sorrow . . . But when the power of Lust is killed within, by the blessing . . . then outward objects troubles not, nor enslaves the man.[48]

Winstanley breaks up the phrase 'joyning in consent together' into its two constituent parts: 'joyne together' echoes a union, a weaker form of communion which is suggested by the more active 'meet in consent'. Man has to consent to the temptation before it can have any power over him; the presence of the Spirit within gives him the freedom to ignore it.

The period after man's fall into the sin of self-love, and before his restoration, is marked by the Dominance of Imagination. The misguidedness is the result of seeking enjoyment from outside objects. However, the restoration is characterised by God's entering the creation, and it is this stage in Winstanley's theology which has led some historians to see him as a materialist. This would not appear to be the case if his early and late theology are reconciled and his understanding of outward forms as declarations of an inner power is borne in mind.

According to Winstanley, man's restoration is characterised by Christ's rising within man and God's manifesting himself in Creation. However, this does not mean that outside objects will become the reference point for knowledge of good or evil. Christopher Hill, again paraphrasing Winstanley, describes the manifestation of God as follows: 'Given the spirit of Christ within, man needs no other preachers than "the objects of the creation", the material world.'[49] The full quotation, however, paints a significantly different picture:

'And your Preachers shal be all the objects of the Creation, through which the Father wil convey himself unto you, and manifest himself before you: these shal be your outward Preachers. And the same word of power speaking it, and to your hearts, causing your hearts to open to his voyce, shall be your Teacher within.'[50] The Spirit within does not merely give access to knowledge imparted by objects, it also teaches the heart directly. Nor are the objects themselves preachers, even once the Spirit has opened man to material objects, for they are merely shells of the Spirit within them. The Father is manifested in this way, but a manifestation is something different from the thing manifested.

The terms in which the manifestation is described reveal something about what Winstanley meant by it. He calls it alternatively a description, a declaration, 'the breakings forth of that glorious power that is seated within and manifested abroad' and 'what proceeds out of himself'.[51] All these suggest the outward form of an inner power, or a moment of its surfacing, but not the vital essence of that power. He talks of God filling Creation. That does not mean that created matter equals the sum of God, but rather implies that God is an infinite source of power that cannot be used up.[52] Similarly, Christ dwelling in man does not mean that, in total, Christ will amount to man, but merely that he is using him as a medium. Another metaphor used is that of breathing: God will 'make the earth subject to himself and fill all with his holy breathing'.[53] While this implies that he will reside in and breathe through man, it also means that he must remain a power beyond man as well, breathing new life into him. The manifestation is almost always presented from a double perspective, so that something is seen from both sides simultaneously. 'The Spirit in this great mystery of truth being manifested in flesh, burns up that drosse out of the Creation and draws in all things back again into himself and declares himself to be the alone wisdom and power of Righteousnesse, *that rules, dwels, that governs and preserves both in and over the whole Creation.*'[54] He seems to be saying, quite deliberately, that God can be both immanent and transcendent, as when he talks of God's revelation 'in us, and to us',[55] and he stresses that the immanent God is as traditional as the God without: 'It is the same report that the Pen-men of Scriptures gave for the everlasting Gospel, "God with us" or "God manifest in flesh". The Father exalted above all, and in all; for the Prophets and Apostles declare these two things.'[56] The terms are not mutually exclusive; God is outside us, near us, and also in us. Winstanley's dialectic has been studied by T. W. Hayes, who notes how he combines references to internal and external forces whenever he gives causal explanations.[57] Hill also notes this dialectical way of thinking, but his comments often fail to show an awareness of the distinction Winstanley makes between source and final expression. He interprets

Winstanley as saying that 'matter is God'.[58] He seems to take the word 'Creation' to mean 'matter', but the two are not necessarily the same. By 'Creation' Winstanley chiefly means mankind, in part animals and in part 'creature-objects', a term which includes intangibles such as 'victories' and 'prosperity'.[59] He would not, anyway, have said that the creation is God since he distinguished it as God's clothing, so it is created by Him for His use.

In *The Law of Freedom,* Winstanley puts forward a practicable political programme in which he appears to be nearer to being a materialist as he states that, 'to know the secrets of nature, is to know the Works of God'. While his emphasis has changed, it is still necessary to qualify statements made by Hill to the effect that this shows a respect for natural science; Winstanley was not observing the individual properties of natural objects, but observing rather the power that ran through all of them.[60] Reason, or God, was never an abstraction for Winstanley, but a vital energy giving life to all things, 'for God is an active Power, not an imaginary Fancy'. He says, too, that there is a limit to what we can know of God in this life, until we become spiritualised and joined with Him. 'To reach God beyond the Creation, or to know what he will be to a man, after the man is dead . . . is a Knowledge beyond the line, or capacity of man to attain while he lives in his compounded body.'[61] While God will manifest Himself in outside objects, He is working through them as a power, exhibited as a process of how one thing is related to another.[62] He is the law of behaviour that moves them and is observable as such. 'To see him in the Sun, Moon, Stars, Clouds, Grasse, Trees, Cattle, and all the Earth, how he hath sweetly caused every one of these to give in assistance to preserve each other Creature: or rather how he Himself in these gives forth preservation and protection from one another, and so unites the whole Creation together, by the unity of himself.'[63] Seeing God in the creation is similar to seeing Him in the Scriptures or in the historical Christ, which are only descriptions: God is perceived outside the self, in how He works, but He is not felt working within. 'And when any attains to see Christ in these outward discoveries, it is full of sweet delight, but this settles no true peace; for that delight that is fetching in from things at a distance from us, may be lost againe, and return into its proper seat againe.'[64] It is better thus, living 'on the Creation' as man does when he lives by Imagination, for he is now living upon the Spirit in Creation.

This is still not the most direct experience of Him. To think that seeing the Spirit of God, exhibited as Reason, in exterior objects is seeing God himself, is like believing that He dwells in the blue sky and that Christ lived and died two thousand years ago. It is still knowledge of the Spirit within which provides experience of God, since this is to 'know feelingly'.

But now to see the King sitting in his banqueting-house, to see the Law of Rightiousnesse and peace ruling and dwelling in the heart, and to be refreshed with those sweet-smelling spices, the discoveries of the Father's love within; This is the Word of God; This is sweeter than the honey-comb, for this is to see him near at hand, even within the heart ruling and resting there.[65]

Only when the Spirit is perceived sensually within (sweet), can Reason be seen in other things or people: 'All creatures teats are to be dried up, that the soul can suck no refreshing milk from them, before the Lord teach it knowledge.'[66] However, too large a separation should not be made between the initial, inward sensation of knowing the Spirit and the experience of seeing it in others, for the 'bridging' is immediate and spontaneous. Winstanley writes that Christ will 'manifest himself to be the indweller of the five senses'. In this capacity, the Spirit acts as a connecting line between man and outside objects, rather than being in one or the other, or first in one and then in the other. Knowledge of the Spirit within 'unblocks' the senses, making possible a correspondence with the Spirit that already exists in other people or objects.

The exchange with the outside world is thus not strictly an exchange, since 'other' no longer exists when there is direct, instinctive communion with the Spirit in others, and that Spirit is the same as one's own. Recognition of the Spirit in others completes knowledge of it in oneself. 'This holy breathing is the Kingdom of Heaven within you, when he rules within you and the Kingdom of Heaven without you likewise, when you see the same glory rule in others, in which you rejoyce.'[67] 'The Kingdom of Heaven within you' is inclusive, and partly made up, of seeing the Kingdom of Heaven in others. Observing Reason as a working principle in natural phenomena is not so direct, since man is not himself subject to it. The restoration of mankind has to be seen as a reciprocal exchange: God comes into creation, not to be reduced to matter, but to charge the world with his life-giving spirit. Man is taken up to a higher spiritual plane, enabling a more direct relationship with God, through the Spirit in himself and by contact with the same in others. God entering creation and man dwelling in God are merely two ways of saying the same thing, that a oneness or re-integration of Spirit has been established between God and man, and man and man. Those who have the right relation with God can meet their fellows in the light of that knowledge.

Then man is drawne up into himself againe; or new 'Jerusalem', which is the spirit of truth, comes down to Earth, to fetch Earth up to live in that life . . . that is a life above objects . . . This is the life, that will bring in true community; and destroy murdering propriety. Now mankinde enters into the garden of God's rest, and lives for ever . . . This

Seed is he (Love/Reason) that leads mankinde into Truth, making every one to seeke the preservation and peace of others, as of themselves; This teaches man inwardly to know the nature and necessity of every body, and to administer to every body accordingly.[68]

Matter seems almost to be transcended, allowing direct communication and free-flowing traffic between Spirits, without the resistance or interference of substance which traps and particularises things.

When Winstanley talks of 'a new heaven and a new earth', he is not saying that heaven is something attained after death. Rather, it is marked by a transition into a new realm of experience: Heaven is not a place in the sky, not a paradise on earth as we know it, but the endowment of a special intuitive sense once the Spirit has entered the individual and united him with the Spirit in others. What takes place is thus a return to man's state before the Fall, when relations were based on implicit understanding through direct spiritual communication and conducted on the principle of mutual help. 'In the beginning of time the whole Creation lived in man, and man lived in his Maker, the Spirit of Righteousness and peace . . . Then . . . there was a sweet communion of Love in the creation: and as the Spirit was a common Treasurie of Unitie and peace within, so the Earth was a common Treasurie of Delight for the preservation of their bodies without.'[69] The creatures did not literally live in man, nor man in his Maker; this is just a way of saying that no creature was opposed to another, and man was not alienated from God. It is as if all shared the same body and worked together as members of it.

Community was what existed before the Fall—before self-love and covetousness—but not with absolute equality for, as Winstanley points out, man ruled creatures and was ruled by God. It was the acknowledgement of this order that brought about spiritual harmony. This was what Winstanley was trying to regain when he set about tilling the land communally—unity of spirit among men which reflected their subjection to God. That Winstanley was also responding to immediate economic circumstances is not in question: the venture was undertaken to alleviate material hardship caused by the disruption of two wars, and he himself was earning a precarious living off the land. This practical motive for the digging has been dealt with elsewhere. There was another, equally important, motive, to restore community of spirit. Generally, the historiography of the digging has either regarded it as an 'economically necessary step' or seen as a sign or symbol.[70] Hill grants that it was a 'symbolic challenge', but the diggers were not, in fact, aiming to be provocative: their only worldly concern was the simple need to feed themselves; their action was not intended as a mere political gesture. W. S. Hudson offers an

alternative and more substantial version of the symbolic line of interpretation, but he also makes too great a distinction between the sign of what is to come and the action whose immediate end is material realisation. He sees the digging as an eschatological sign 'demanding attention to a message from the Lord'; its purpose 'was not to do something but to say something'.[71] Those who declared the revelation by action were proclaiming the will of God by obeying His command, and assuring believers (and warning non-believers) that God would fulfil this promise in the future and Himself establish a communion of Saints. Such a sign gave inner peace to the individual who declared it.[72]

This misleading separation of saying and doing in Hudson's interpretation is similar to his separation of life on earth and life after death. Only after this life would God establish a communion of Saints. Community here on earth could be no more than a foundation, an interim Holy Commonwealth by which God makes men ready to accept His Commonwealth. Practising Christian love was a rehearsal. Winstanley has said, throughout his writing, that two parts complete the Blessing: peace received from the Spirit, and the fulfilment of peace coming with the practice of the Law of Love. It is not an individualistic Salvation, since attention to the Spirit within draws the individual automatically to the Spirit in others. Any approach to the significance of the digging should therefore bear in mind Winstanley's habit of synthesising opposites. A sign is empty if it is not expressed in deed, and words are hollow that are not carried over into action; sign and deed, word and act are reconciled, made consistent by the same power moving through both. Winstanley refers to his action as a declaration, and, as he also calls words declarations of something inward, the principle can be followed through. He declared his revelation in writing to put forth the Spirit, the thing declared, into a form accessible to others. 'The words of a man's mouth are the declaration of the spirit or power within; and are created by the spirit, and so hold forth as a creature to the creation.'[73] He wrote pamphlets, not for the sake of creating dissension (although aware that they might do so), but for the benefit of those who also knew the Spirit within: 'Some may have their joy fulfilled in seeing a conjecture of experience between me and them.'[74] His writing, although only a declaration of the Spirit within, does not serve merely to point to the presence of the Spirit. A declaration is not addressed to a void but to receptive ears and hearts. Being witness to the Spirit in others completes the work of the Spirit within. The establishment of sympathy between hearts lays the foundation for community: 'I only hold forth to my fellow creature, man . . . that others from me, and I from them may be witnesses each to other, of our Maker how he shines forth in his own light, through each other to the profit of the Creation.'[75] Nevertheless, to talk of the Spirit is not enough on its own. The 'manifestation of a righteous heart shall be known' by the application of what is professed. 'They that do worship the Father, shall worship him by walking righteously in the Creation, in the strength of the Law of Love and equity one to another.'[76] Winstanley always stresses man as part of creation, living among men and acting in this social condition. He places the direct and personal relationship between the individual and God in the context of man's living with man; thus communion with one's neighbours is an extension of familiarity with God, since He dwells also in them.

Words declare the Spirit and action reinforces that declaration; this is the first function of the digging and gives peace to the individual who has obeyed the Spirit. But this 'peace in the Spirit' is, for Winstanley, a prelude to the time when 'the spirit of the poor, shall be drawn forth . . . to act materially this Law of Righteousnesse', when others show that they have also received the Spirit's message by declaring it in their action: 'his new Law, that is to be writ in every man's heart, and acted by every man's hand . . . that they may serve him together, in community of spirit, and in community of the earthly treasure'.[77] As more people practise the Law of Righteousness, so more spiritual channels are made clear for communion, since doors are opened to each others' hearts. Love is an objective reality felt inwardly as the Spirit which impels love to be directed towards others; its kinetic nature means that the outward practice realises the love within. The absence of righteous acting is a sign that the Spirit is not present in individuals. Such action brings in community of spirit, and with it community of earth, these being one community in two branches. They come in together, each making the other a closed possibility. Even though the diggers plant the crops themselves, they rely on God's blessing to make the crop a good one: 'And they . . . wait upon him, saying, do thine own work.'[78] But their action is not a distinct introduction to God's work since they are already acting in the knowledge of His Spirit.

It is significant that the words of the revelation 'Eat bread together' have obvious overtones of Holy Communion. English Protestants normally believed that, in receiving communion, they were not doing something 'merely symbolic', but actually receiving nourishment and life from Christ. In a similar way the action of digging was not, for Winstanley, 'just' a symbolic act and not just a practical one. It was justified, not in the mere act of obedience to the Spirit, nor in the visible harvest, but in spiritual 'nourishment' gained by digging together in a state of spiritual communion. The Spirit's work in man was completed when it opened him to a knowledge of the Spirit in others, and the act of digging showed outwardly in whom the Spirit lay.

Justice cannot be done to Winstanley and his works unless they are approached on the level of the language he employed. To translate his ideas into modern, secular language changes the concepts themselves. Equally, to isolate Winstanley's words, and interpret them literally, is to lose the spirit of his whole argument. A uniformity must be found in his use of certain terms and a continuity in his way of thinking, so that details of inconsistency do not stand in the way of an appreciation of the habits of mind and ways of conceiving and interpreting the world which are displayed through the writing. Winstanley believed in the Spirit as an aspect of God because he felt it within him as a physical presence or sensation, and he understood all outward forms as the declaration of an infinite being. Thus he was never a thorough-going materialist. His God existed within him, as the Spirit, and outside of him, as the Creator who brought justice to creation by working as Reason in man's relation to man. One knew or experienced God internally and externally, and this simultaneity of perception is shown in the dialectical pattern of his thought. What has been interpreted as political radicalism in his action of digging was, for him, primarily a fellowship of spirits, an extension of the Spirit within united with the Spirit in one's neighbours. Like the mystical idea of oneness which had held him back from Puritan individualism, his feeling for the reality of symbolic communion suggests a rather traditional sensibility.

Notes

[1] E. Bernstein, *Cromwell and Communism,* London 1961; D. W. Petergorsky, *Left-wing Democracy in the English Civil War,* London 1940; W. James, *Social Problems and Policy during the Puritan Revolution;* C. Hill (ed.), *The Law of Freedom and Other Writings,* Harmondsworth 1973.

[2] W. S. Hudson, 'The economic and social thought of Gerrard Winstanley', *Journal of Modern History* xvii (1946), 1-21; L. Mulligan, J. K. Graham and J. Richards, 'Winstanley: a case for the man as he said he was', this JOURNAL xxviii (1977), 57-75; C. Hill, 'The religion of Gerrard Winstanley,' Past and Present, Supp. v (1978).

[3] T. W. Hayes, *Winstanley the Digger,* Harvard 1978.

[4] For biographical details see *The Works of Gerrard Winstanley* (hereinafter cited as *Works*), ed. G. H. Sabine, New York 1941, introduction.

[5] Ibid. 81-3, 87-90. Both pamphlets are reproduced in abstract only, as is a third pamphlet of 1648, *The Saints Paradise,* in ibid. 93-6. The remaining pamphlets are reproduced in full.

[6] For *Truth Lifting up its Head,* see ibid. 97-146.

[7] Ibid. 147-245.

[8] Ibid. 249-66.

[9] Ibid. 443-97.

[10] Ibid. 499-602.

[11] A lot of work has been done to discover whether Winstanley returned to practising a trade and died a Quaker, which would show that his 'materialist' phase was a temporary one and that he became a pacifist, see R. T. Vann, 'The later life of Gerrard Winstanley', *Journal of the History of Ideas* xxvi (1965), 133-6; James Alsop, 'Gerrard Winstanley's later life', *Past and Present* lxxvii (1979), 73-81.

[12] *Truth*, 100.

[13] Ibid. 101.

[14] Ibid. 104.

[15] Ibid. 104-5.

[16] Ibid. 105.

[17] *The Breaking of The Day of God*, abstracted in *Works*, 87-90, esp. at p. 88.

[18] *Truth*, 124.

[19] *The New Law of Righteousness*, in *Works*, 147-245, esp. at p. 242.

[20] See the remarks of General Ireton reproduced in *Puritanism and Liberty, being the Army Debates (1647-9) from the Clarke Manuscripts with Supplementary Documents in Puritanism*, ed. A. S. P. Woodhouse, London 1950, 21.

[21] Quoted in ibid. 106.

[22] G. F. Nuttall, *The Holy Spirit in Puritan Faith and Experience*, London 1947, 38.

[23] *Puritanism and Liberty*, 59-60.

[24] *Mystery of God*, 81-2.

[25] *Breaking of The Day*, 89.

[26] *A Watchword to the City of London*, 315-39 esp. at pp. 328-9.

[27] *The Saints Paradise* in *Works*, 93-4.

[28] In *Works*, 459.

[29] *Paradice*, abstract in *Works*, 93.

[30] Ibid.

[31] Nuttall, *Holy Spirit*, 115.

[32] Col. Rainborough, quoted in Woodhouse, *Puritanism and Liberty*, 55.

[33] Capt. J. Clarke quoted in ibid. 38.

[34] Hill, 'Religion', 37-9.

[35] C. Hill, 'Reason and reasonableness', in C. Hill (ed.), *Change and Continuity in Seventeenth-century England*, London 1974.

[36] *Truth*, 199.

[37] *The True Levellers Standard Advanced* (1649), in *Works*, 247-66 esp. at p. 251.

[38] *Truth*, 105.

[39] Ibid. 108.

[40] *Paradice*, 96.

[41] *Fire in The Bush*, in *Works*, 462; cf. Lawrence Clarkson, 'A single eye all light, no darkness', in Norman Cohn. *The Pursuit of the Millennium*, London 1957, 113.

[42] *Fire*, 456.

[43] Ibid. 458.

[44] Ibid. 494.

[45] Ibid. 481.

[46] Ibid. 489.

[47] Ibid. 485.

[48] Ibid. 495.

[49] C. Hill, *The World Turned Upside Down: radical ideas during the English Revolution*, Harmondsworth, 1982, 140.

[50] *New Law*, 224-5.

[51] Ibid. 216, 217.

[52] *The Law of Freedom*, in *Works*, 501-602 esp. at p. 565.

[53] *New Law*, 229.

[54] Ibid. 162-3 (my emphasis).

[55] *True Levellers,* 256.

[56] *New Law,* 169.

[57] Hayes, *Winstanley the Digger,* 15.

[58] Hill, *World Turned Upside Down,* 150.

[59] *New Law,* 231.

[60] Hill, op. cit. 142.

[61] *Law of Freedom,* 565.

[62] See also G. Rupp, *Patterns of Reformation,* London 1969, part iii, ch. xxi (Thomas Müntzer, Hans Huth and the 'Gospel of All Creatures').

[63] *New Law,* 231.

[64] Ibid. 165.

[65] Ibid. 221.

[66] Ibid. 226.

[67] Ibid. 229.

[68] *Fire,* 453.

[69] *New Law,* 155. *A New-Years Gift for the Parliament and Armie,* in *Words,* 353-96 esp. at p. 376.

[70] Hill, *World Turned Upside Down,* 131.

[71] Hudson, 'Economic and social thought', 8, 21.

[72] 'The peace they experienced in their hearts was the final justification of the digging', ibid. 11.

[73] *Truth,* 134.

[74] *New Law,* 243-4.

[75] Ibid. 155.

[76] Ibid. 185.

[77] Ibid. 195.

[78] *New-Years Gift.* 369.

Andrew Bradstock (essay date 1991)

SOURCE: "Sowing in Hope: The Relevance of Theology to Gerrard Winstanley's Political Programme," *The Seventeeenth Century,* Vol. VI, No. 2, Autumn, 1991, pp. 189-204.

[*In the following essay, Bradstock maintains that Winstanley's "radically unorthodox" theology contributed significantly to the development of the Digger communist platform—contrary, Bradstock contends, to what many modern critics allow.*]

Since Gerrard Winstanley's writings first became a subject for serious study at the end of the nineteenth century, one question which has regularly exercised his interpreters is how far his political philosophy is shaped by or grounded upon theological premises, and exactly what those premises are. The question is both an interesting and an important one, since it reaches right to the heart of the Diggers' whole project to cultivate the common land and restore a true commonwealth on English soil. We can state the question in the form of two propositions. Did Winstanley's religious beliefs provide the main conceptual framework for his understanding of the world, and underpin his political and economic programme, as a cursory glance at his writings might suggest? Or can the religious language he uses be viewed as incidental or even cosmetic flourishes, sops, maybe, to the milieu in which he lived, such that his political philosophy could be restated, without alteration to its substance, in wholly secular language? This essay seeks to assess the validity of these two positions, and concludes that, radically unorthodox though Winstanley's theology certainly was, it did play a far more significant role in shaping the Digger's praxis than many of his latter-day admirers have been prepared to acknowledge.

One of the stoutest defences of Winstanley as a fundamentally theological thinker, whose religious convictions remained central to his political activity throughout the digging experiment and beyond, has been made by the Australian scholars Mulligan, Graham and Richards.[1] They do not dispute that Winstanley, in stressing the immanence of God, rejected much traditional theology, but caution against leaping from there to the assumption that he gave up theology altogether: it was rather the case that he adopted an '*alternative* theology'. Indeed, it is dangerous to try to see Winstanley as a 'secular revolutionary', they argue, since this can only be done by 'making allowances' for his language in a manner advocated, for example, by Christopher Hill. For modern readers to gain a correct understanding of Winstanley it is essential that they accept the Digger's own explanation of his terms, and not impose their own 'secular and rationalistic meanings' on his language.[2] Further, they argue, Winstanley's theological position remained more or less constant throughout his digging career: even though his last work, *The Law of Freedom in a Platform,* suggests a 'shift in emphasis' in Winstanley's thinking, the theological beliefs to be found in *Truth Lifting up its Head,* which was written six months prior to the digging, remained central to his thought throughout the remainder of his literary career.[3]

Other scholars have reached broadly similar conclusions. George H. Sabine, for example, who edited the first complete collection of Winstanley's writings,[4] considers that, with the publication of **The New Law of Righteousnes** (three months after **Truth Lifting . . .**) his 'train of thought is complete'; and even though **The Law of Freedom,** published some eighteen months after the digging experiment failed, is 'somewhat different' from the tracts written during the experiment itself, it represents only a 'change of emphasis', not 'of the convictions that lay behind Winstanley's communism'.[5]

Elmen[6] is another who recognizes a 'transition' in Winstanley, with the author of the more mystical early tracts becoming concerned increasingly with 'practical communism', but, like Mulligan *et al* and Sabine, he considers this merely a 'change in emphasis' which does not undermine the 'unity of his position'. Indeed, Elmen argues, the motivation behind the digging, and the degree of certainty Winstanley had about its ultimate success, cannot be understood apart from reference to his religious beliefs: 'Because his views were fundamentally theological, Winstanley hopefully undertook a task which economic considerations alone would have told him was impossible: the communization of the English land'.[7] Woodhouse,[8] Hudson[9] and Schenk[10] have also noted the centrality of Winstanley's theology to his programme. The main driving force behind the Diggers, Woodhouse argues, was a 'desire to establish the reign of righteousness', and their 'view of secular life', 'interpretation of the past', and 'vision of the future' are dominated by 'the direct inferences from their religious thought'.[11] According to Hudson, Winstanley 'had begun his propagandist career as an exponent of a chiliastic mysticism', and 'he retained this emphasis to the end'. Following Woodhouse he notes that theological concerns were Winstanley's main preoccupation, but draws the rather surprising conclusion that the Digger was not a 'practical reformer' but represented a 'nonpolitical variation' of the 'general eschatological expectation' of his time.[12] For Schenk a preoccupation with mystical theology is also discernable throughout Winstanley's writing career, and even those of his views which may appear to us to be 'modern' are not unconnected with his religious beliefs, which, we may infer from his writings, were 'the mainspring of all his thought'.[13]

On two central assumptions these writers are united: first, that Winstanley's theology played a central role in his thinking throughout his literary career; and secondly, that no *fundamental* shift in his thinking can be detected between the publication of his early 'mystical' writings in 1648, and that of the blueprint for his communist utopia, *The Law of Freedom,* four years later. However, the approach more commonly adopted by those who want to give less weight to Winstanley's theology is to delineate stages in his literary career during which his thinking underwent major transition. Thus, whilst they might accept the first assumption above in respect of Winstanley's early tracts, they reach the virtually unanimous conclusion that by the time the digging began, and certainly by the time it was over, the theological impulses which might originally have prompted Winstanley into action could no longer be said to be a major motivating factor.

This line of reasoning has surfaced regularly in Winstanley scholarship ever since the rediscovery of his writings towards the end of the last century. For example, the Marxist writer Eduard Bernstein, who is usually credited with having made that initial rediscovery, observes that in **The Law of Freedom** the author, 'dropping all mysticism. . . . propounds a complete social system based on communistic principles'.[14] Strachey, another early commentator, considers that, like everyone of his generation, Winstanley originally came to social and economic questions through theology and the Bible. By the time of **The Law of Freedom,** however, his 'mystical, Quakerish views' had been abandoned in favour of a 'magnificently expressed materialism'.[15] Zagorin makes a similar point: in **The Law of Freedom,** he writes, Winstanley's philosophy 'complete[s] the circuit along which its inner logic had impelled it. Inspired still by a deeply felt religion of conduct, he passed, nevertheless, to a substantially rationalist-materialist position'.[16] Davis also observes Winstanley undergoing a major shift in his last pamphlet, exchanging a position of passive hope in God to produce a new social order, for the more robust tactic of advocating an 'exploitation' of the state 'to fashion a better society'. The subtitle of **The Law of Freedom**—'True Magistracy Restored'—suggests, to Davis, the true nature of this shift: 'Winstanley drops both his millenarianism and his anarchism and concerns himself with the remodelling of the state by men. Cromwell, not Christ, is to be the agent of the change'.[17] David W. Petegorsky, in his extended analysis of Winstanley, asserts that although the Digger never lost his 'profound spirituality', the 'theological framework' which originally underpinned his ideas gradually became redundant. In the end his argument comes to rest upon a foundation 'wholly secular in its nature' even if 'primarily spiritual in its original inspiration'. In **The Law of Freedom** his position is 'an almost purely materialistic one'. The turning point in Winstanley's life, suggests Petegorsky, was that period which immediately preceded the digging, from autumn 1648 to spring 1649, during which he underwent a rapid transition from 'rational theology' to 'practical communism'. Humanity's struggle, which once Winstanley had seen in spiritual terms as 'the clash of good and evil within man', now became a struggle 'between economic classes', the wealthy who wanted to retain their privileges, and the poor who demanded that they be shared.[19]

A more extreme position with regard to the transition in Winstanley's thought is taken by Juretic.[20] For him, any talk of a mere shift in Winstanley's thinking, whether at the point of the digging or during the preparation of *The Law of Freedom,* is gross understatement. What was actually the case, Juretic argues, was that once the digging experiment got under way on St George's Hill in April 1649, Winstanley's ideas became 'rapidly secularized', so that by the time *The True Levellers Standard Advanced,* the first Digger tract, was written, the 'millenarian underpinning' of the pre-Digger tracts 'began to disappear'. Then, 'it was only a matter of time for him to discard completely his mystical beliefs. . . . Mysticism failed to provide him with solutions to the political problems Winstanley encountered while farming the commons'.[21] The way to a correct understanding of Winstanley does not therefore lie in trying to find a link between the pre-Digger and the Digger, but in recognizing that the real concrete political experience he endured during the digging project transformed him to such an extent, from mystical millenarian to full-blown secularist, that it is possible to speak of 'two Winstanleys'. We must not try to see Winstanley's writings as a 'monolithic whole', nor assume that 'religious impulses' were the foundation for his thinking and praxis: the key to Winstanley's 'socialistic concepts' lies, not in his early mystical writings, but in his 'political experiences while defending his settlement on St George's Hill'.[22]

If this general thesis is accepted, that Winstanley at some point lost the religious impulses which originally motivated him, the question still remains of how to account for his continued use of theological terminology and Biblical idiom in his later writings. Strikingly, the conclusion reached by virtually all defenders of this thesis is that the inclusion of religious language in these writings can be explained simply by reference to the times in which he lived: it serves, in other words, either to lend added weight or authority to conclusions he reached on straightforwardly rational grounds; to make his arguments more comprehensible to his readers by using the popular idiom of the day; or, since he was writing under the shadow of the Blasphemy Ordinance of 1648, to provide his subversive and heretical message with a cloak of respectability. Thus Bernstein, for example, writes of the Diggers' pamphlets being 'couched in somewhat mystical phraseology, which manifestly serves as a cloak to conceal the revolutionary designs of the authors',[23] and Petegorsky of the 'theological garb' in which so frequently Winstanley's ideas were clothed.[24] For Hill, 'Winstanley drew on Bible stories largely because he thought they would help his contemporaries to understand him: he used

them as poetic imagery'.[25] The Bible was used to illustrate 'conclusions at which [he] had arrived by rational means'.[26] Juretic also considers that Winstanley was merely following convention in seeking 'Biblical justification' for his conclusions, and finds the inclusion of the majority of scripture references irrelevant to his overall argument. Although Winstanley wanted to keep his faith in the Bible, he writes, 'the mass of his exegetical citations were vague, general statements signifying nothing'.[27]

This is not a view held only by Marxist critics, for Maurice Ashley makes a similar point when, during a discussion of the Fifth Monarchy Men, he suggests that if we 'ignore their biblical texts (as we are invited to ignore those of . . . Winstanley) . . . there are your seventeenth-century Jacobins or Bolsheviks'.[28] Even Sabine, who appears overall to take a conservative position with regard to Winstanley's theology, concludes, *à propos* of the proofs the latter advances to support his communist position, that his offer to defend his case by invoking the authority of Scripture was only an 'acceptance of what was at the time a conventional form of argument'.[29]

James[30] offers a slightly more nuanced variation of the 'comprehensibility' argument. Winstanley, she argues, began from both rational *and* theological premises: he 'examined existing institutions in the light of Nature and Reason and found them evil'. He was clear that the inequality and exploitation he saw and experienced had not always existed, and that there had been a Golden Age after Creation when men and women exercised dominion over the beasts of the field but not over one another. However, James concludes, 'it was unlikely that arguments drawn from the rarefied heights of Nature and Reason would prove a popular battlecry', and so, in effect, to give his case a more ready appeal, Winstanley contemporized biblical concepts by making them merely metaphors for the actual episodes in English history, in particular the Norman conquest, which had brought about the present evil state of affairs: 'In the appeal to all Englishmen to unite in destroying the Norman power, the abstract was made concrete, and the theory of a Golden Age and Fall was given decent English clothing'.[31]

What conclusions may be drawn from this discussion? Perhaps the first and most obvious point to make concerns the straightforward impossibility of being able to say with any degree of certainty what the real source of Winstanley's inspiration was at any given time. We may draw certain inferences from both his language and his actions, but to seek to establish a 'real' motivation behind them must of necessity be beyond the bounds of possibility. It must be acknowledged, therefore, that the mere fact that Winstanley's use of religious terminology appears to diminish as he becomes more politically radicalized, and seems to look more and more like a convenient disguise for a materialist philosophy when it *is* employed, does not necessarily say anything about his 'subjective' assessment of himself as a Christian.[32] It may also be true, as Petegorsky has suggested, that Winstanley's decision to republish his five earliest tracts in collected form while the digging was still in progress is a sign that he saw his political position at that time as a 'logical development' of the ideas in those tracts, rather than a contradiction or rebuttal of them.[33] Hill also notes that Winstanley's preface to this collection 'contains a salutary reminder that he did not reject these writings', though, Hill adds, 'his thought had in many respects passed beyond them'.[34]

A second point to note is the tendency among some interpreters of Winstanley to perceive his rejection of *traditional* Christianity as a rejection of Christianity altogether. The clearest statement of this position is made by Zagorin who argues, in respect of **The Law of Freedom,** that, despite the presence of Christian terminology, the religion expressed in that tract is no longer Christian. Winstanley, he writes,

> had eliminated a transcendent God, an historic Christ, creed, dogma, and church, and retained naught but the ethical inspiration of the gospel. And even this he did not allow to operate, in the traditional way, as the spirit of charity and love that was to be shown despite the existence of slavery and coercion which man's fall had made inevitable. Instead, the gospel ethic was for him the imperative compelling the remodelling of institutions in the image of reason.[35]

Hill also appears to adopt this position—though he stops short of actually saying Winstanley's theology was not Christian—when he points to Winstanley's thinking being 'in opposition to traditional Christianity' and to the 'profound difference between the content of his ideas and that of traditional Christianity' such that 'his thinking was struggling towards concepts which were to be more precisely if less poetically formulated by later, non-theological materialisms'.[36]

What these comments reveal, I believe, are two false assumptions which seriously weaken the argument that Winstanley was (or became) a secular thinker. The first is that the particular interpretation of Christianity generally termed 'traditional' may serve as a yardstick against which to measure, and by implication reject, the claim of other formulations; and the second that Winstanley's tendency towards a more reductionist and pantheistic theological position amounts to a rejection of Christianity itself rather than one interpretation of it, that propounded by the church of his day. Thus Winstanley's rejection of a transcendent God,

historic Christ, and creed, dogma and church, is, for Zagorin, a rejection of Christianity itself, whereas in fact Winstanley can be located in that small but vocal tradition which, albeit from its fringes but nevertheless from within the professing Christian church itself, has continually set out to challenge perceived conservative and reactionary interpretations of the faith, positing instead an alternative reading of the gospel stressing themes of protest against injustice and hope for a radically new social order in the shape of the Kingdom or Reign of God. From Lollards to Hussites, through Müntzer and the 'radical Reformation' in Germany, and Quakers, Ranters and Fifth Monarchists in England—and even down to Liberation Theologians of the present day—voices echoing the self-same themes with which Zagorin has difficulty in Winstanley—divine immanence, universalism, iconoclasm, communitarianism and even revolution—have persistently been audible within the Christian church.[37] These would hardly comprehend Zagorin's shock that Winstanley should find the 'ethical inspiration of the gospel' an 'imperative compelling the remodelling of institutions in the image of reason', nor for that matter his assumption that there is an apparent incompatibility between the 'blazing chiliastic expectancy of the religious radical who daily looks for Jesus' second coming to inaugurate a reign of righteousness' and the hope for a 'rationalistic communism, abounding in plans and projects', let alone his contention that to move from the former to the latter is to pass beyond orthodoxy to heresy.[38] At the root of Zagorin's difficulty with Winstanley is a conception of Christianity as a static rather than developing faith, and a tendency to mistake one culturally-related manifestation of it for its totality.

Another problem with Zagorin's position is that it does not fully appreciate Winstanley as a person of his time. Winstanley lived in an age in which religion permeated every area of life, the Bible shaped the way people thought, and the church was central to the life of the community. In such a climate most people, whether educated or not, accepted unquestioningly fundamental religious doctrines.[39] So interwoven was religion into the fabric of society, and so intermixed with political, economic and social questions, that, as Elmen has suggested, 'it would not have occurred to any of [Winstanley's] contemporary critics or friends to wonder whether the ownership of land'—the central issue on the Diggers' agenda—'was a proper concern for the theological mind'.[40] The Bible's relevance to all areas of life, including the political, economic and social, was accepted far more unproblematically then than is the case today. Thus as Hill rightly suggests,

> it is perhaps irrelevant to ask whether Winstanley 'believed' the Christian myths, or whether he used them only as a convenient mode of expression, a

metaphor. The question imposes twentieth-century assumptions on him. This was the idiom in which men thought.[41]

Yet to see Winstanley against the background of his own time is also to understand why he could not for *political* reasons accept what might appear to Zagorin and others to be a more conventional or traditional form of Christianity. For this was the Christianity preached by the clergy of the established church, whose motives for so preaching it, Winstanley was clear, were both to promote support for the *status quo,* and their not uncomfortable position within it. The political task assigned to this theology in his own day gave Winstanley reason enough, quite apart from any misgivings he had on rational grounds, to reject it outright.

For Winstanley the whole theological system of the church was oppressive for the ordinary people to whom it was preached. The clergy encouraged belief in a God 'out there' which, although Winstanley rejected on the grounds that knowledge about such entities was 'beyond the line or capacity of man to attain to while he lives in his compounded body', he did the more so because he saw how the clergy contrived to make God appear punitive and capricious, one who approved the unfair distribution of the earth originally given as a common treasury, and, significantly, one who 'appointed the people to pay Tythes to the Clergy'.[42] Both God and Christ, Winstanley considered, were held by the priests 'at-a-distance' so that they could then be mediated to the people only through them. The clergy also preached an historic Fall, through which all men and women individually are sinners, and by thus evoking feelings of insufficiency and fear in their hearers, who sought to restore their identity by relating to objects outside themselves, particularly the God- and Christ-at-a-distance, the clergy made the people even more dependent upon them. With the addition of a heaven in the next life as a reward for subservience to them, or hell as punishment, the system by which the clergy reinforced their authority and power over the people was complete. 'By this divined Hell after death', wrote Winstanley, 'they preach to keep both King and people in aw to them'. The clergy persuaded people to think

> That true Freedom lay in hearing them preach, and to enjoy that Heaven which they say, every man who beleeves their doctrine, shall enjoy after he is dead: And so tell us of a Heaven and Hell after death, which neither they nor we know what wil be . . .[43]

For Winstanley these 'heavenly and spiritual things' served only to destroy the true knowledge of God and spoil the individual's peace. The clergy actually prevented Christ from rising in his people, and instead led them into what he called 'Imagination', a unnecessary feeling of incompleteness, fear and uncertainty which kept them in subjection to the church and the authorities. For Winstanley this was the antithesis of true religion, and he rejected it wholesale.

In place of this alienating form of religion Winstanley stressed the immanence of God, who could be known by all without the 'aid' of the professional beneficed clergy. Humankind, he taught, need not be bowed down by Imagination: 'Every single man, Male and Female, is a perfect Creature of himself', and has the creator dwelling in him 'to be his Teacher and Ruler within himself'.[44] The individual was therefore able to judge all things by experience, which was more important than the whole edifice of doctrine and church government built up on biblical texts. Such line of thinking eliminated, too, any need for a learned clergy. Winstanley often preferred to use the word 'Reason' instead of 'God', because it emphasized his immanence and stood in contrast to the Imagination from which he would redeem his sons and daughters as he rose in them and brought them together into community. The term may have signified for Winstanley something more akin to a 'spirit' or 'force' than a 'personal' God, but it removed the 'otherness' which the clergy had invested in the term.[45] In fact, however, as Hill has said, the question of an antithesis between immanence and transcendence appears never to have concerned Winstanley, and he could unproblematically hold in tension the notion that ' "the same spirit that made the globe" is "the indweller in the five senses of hearing, seeing, tasting, smelling and feeling" '.[46] Creation was for Winstanley *ex deo,* not *ex nihilo.*[47]

Christ, too, was no longer remote but within the individual, and Winstanley saw Christ in every person, and every person in Christ. As he says in ***The Law of Freedom,*** all who have shown themselves to be 'Promoters of Common Freedom, whether they be members in Church fellowship or not . . . all are one in Christ'.[48] Heaven and hell are present states: heaven is humankind and hell describes the conditions men and women have created for themselves on earth. Winstanley left open the question whether there may be a physical heaven or hell, but did hold the highly unorthodox belief that all humankind would be saved. Sin, in Winstanley, is the whole system of buying and selling with its resultant inequality and domination by landowners and priests. Antichrist, traditionally interpreted as the Pope or the Church, and the Fall, are also to be understood in terms of property relations, the former being property itself, and the latter having occurred once selfish desires began to manifest themselves, and not, as usually held, the other way around. 'When Mankinde began to buy and sell, then did he fall from this Innocency'.[49] Finally, Christ's second coming will be the establishment of a communitarian society on earth, and the entering into all men and women of Christ's spirit as they awaken to the rule of Reason within them and embrace the principle of community life lost since the Fall. In summary Winstanley rejects quite explicitly the whole theological system of the church, but not, *pace* Zagorin, Christianity itself; his own theological formulations are rather, I suggest, an attempt to keep the essentials of the faith and recast them in a non-alienating form, to recover what he believed to be the original message of Christianity which the church, through time, had distorted and submerged.

There is yet another problem with attempts to see Winstanley as an essentially secular thinker, namely his continued adherence to some form of millennial hope, even, it would appear, up until the time of writing **The Law of Freedom.** Clearly there is little question that such a hope was influential in originally inspiring the digging venture.[50] In **The True Levellers Standard Advanced** Winstanley suggests than an apocalyptic vision in the Book of Daniel is to be realized in his own day,[51] and two pages later that 'all the Prophecies, Visions, and Revelations of Scriptures, of Prophets, and Apostles. . . . doth all seat themselves in this Work of making the Earth a Common Treasury',[52] a work, as he was told in a trance, assigned to him and the diggers on St George's Hill. Thus 'all the Prophesies of Scriptures and Reason are Circled here in this Community'.[53] These, he was clear, were the last days:

> the righteous Father suffered himself . . . to be suppressed for a time, times and dividing of time, or for 42 months, or for three dayes and half, which are all but one and the same term of time: And the world is now come to the half day.[54]

As we have noted, Winstanley's millennium did not involve a literal physical return of Jesus Christ as King, as many believed the Bible taught, but rather the restoration of community as Christ began to rise in his sons and daughters. Nevertheless, it is not sufficient to say that his reformulation of the Second Coming in this way is an example of the use of Biblical imagery to conceal an essentially political hope, for a belief that the millennium was now to begin appears, in fact, to have been the one single hope which sustained the digging project in the face of all opposition and hardship. 'We have another encouragement that this work shall prosper', Winstanley wrote at the outset,

> Because we see it to be the fulness of Time: For whereas the Son of Man, the *Lamb,* came in the Fulness of Time . . . Even so now in this Age of the World, that the Spirit is upon his Resurrection, it is likewise the Fulness of Time in a higher measure.[55]

We noted earlier Elmen's assertion that it was Winstanley's theological perspective which motivated him to undertake a task which purely economic considerations would have suggested was an impossibility. Sabine notes a reference in **The True Levellers**

Standard Advanced where Winstanley appears to expect that, with the restoration of community life, barren commons and waste ground would once more became fertile, and comments that 'without such a belief, his communism was hardly workable, since it implied that a large part of the English population would be fed from the produce of land that had not previously been arable'.[56] Clearly Winstanley saw the outbreak of digging in 1649, at St George's Hill and subsequently at a number of other locations, as a sign that the millennium was imminent, that Christ was beginning to rise in men and women, and this would have encouraged him to think that the venture must of necessity meet with success and be taken up by more and more people until the transformation of the earth was complete. In practical terms this would most likely mean that, infilled with a renewed sense of community, the common people would revolt against property, refuse to sell their labour, and generate a situation in which no one would own more land than they could themselves cultivate, thus making most privately-enclosed land the common possession of all.

That Winstanley's millenarianism sustained his political hopes, not only through but even beyond the digging venture, is suggested by the recurrence of themes from Daniel and Revelation in his last work, **The Law of Freedom in a Platform,** written in the wake of the Diggers' enforced removal from Cobham Heath (whither they had resorted following expulsion from St George's Hill). This writing, which takes the form of a detailed outline of a radically new socio-economic order which Winstanley hopes can be constructed on the ashes of the old 'kingly power', stands apart from his earlier tracts in many respects, not least in so far as it recognizes that Christ's work of transforming people and drawing them together into community may be a somewhat more gradual process than anticipated in, say, **The New Law of Righteousnes.** In **The Law of Freedom** Winstanley also goes to greater lengths to demonstrate how his new society may be implemented: Cromwell, to whom it is dedicated, not Christ, this time appears to hold the key. Yet millenarian hopes are not discarded: God, 'the Spirit of the whole Creation . . . is about the Reformation of the World', he writes in his foreword;[57] or, we might say, is *still* about this reformation. 'This Kingly Power is the old Heaven, and the old Earth, that must pass away', he asserts in Chapter 2, whereas the new 'Commonwealth's Government' will be 'Sion', 'Jerusalem', and the 'holy Mountain of the Lord God our Righteousness and Peace'.[58] These images Winstanley borrows from the unambiguously apocalyptic writer Micah, and they are joined by others from the Apocalypse and the Book of Daniel. Kingly power and government is 'the great Man of Sin', 'the great Antichrist, and Mystery of Iniquity', 'the Devil', and 'the Power and Government of the Beast', soon to be cast down;[59] covetousness is 'the great red Dragon, the god of this world', from whom the groaning creation waits to be delivered;[60] and the deceitful and oppressing 'Divinity' taught by the clergy is 'the language of the Mystery of Iniquity and Antichrist', and 'that great City Babylon . . . which hath filled the whole Earth with her sorcery, and deceived all people, so that the whole world wondered after this Beast'. 'How is it faln', Winstanley concludes, 'and how is her Judgment come upon her in one hour?'[61] But perhaps more significantly Winstanley still appears to believe that Christ is rising in his sons and daughters, if at a rather slower pace than he anticipated earlier: 'But surely Light is so broke out, that it will cover the Earth, so that the Divinity Charmers shall say, The people will not hear the voyce of our charming, charm we never so wisely,' he writes as he concludes his discourse on these false preachers.[62] Indeed, the fact that a commonwealth has been declared in England, though the even greater work of establishing it on right principles is still to be done, is a sign that 'the spirit of universal Righteousness' is rising up in men and women. 'We may hope' that 'these be the days of his resurrection to power', Winstanley writes, 'because the name of *Commonwealth* is risen and established in *England* by a Law'.[63] The work of consolidating the Commonwealth's Government is also vital, Winstanley argues, not only because a failure in this regard will deny people the peace, plenty and freedom which they desire, but because it would 'shew our Government to be gone no further but to the half day of the Beast, or the dividing of Time, of which there must be an over-turn'.[64]

It may be plausible also to suggest that, had Winstanley's millenarianism not been genuine—had he, in other words, truly been a secular thinker—he could arguably have produced a more revolutionary programme than he did, since by placing a religious interpretation on the political struggle in which he was engaged he failed to see it in a true historical perspective. His millenarianism, in other words, made it 'unnecessary' for him to demonstrate how it was possible for his programme to be realized, and therefore it was destined to remain only as what it was, namely an idea superimposed on to his particular situation but not historically related to it. He anticipated, as Turner has said, 'in the form of a communist *myth,* a stage of social development—communism—which would become possible only on the basis of the achievements of the bourgeois revolution to which [he was] in fact *opposed*'.[65] The significance of this should not be underrated, for although it is Winstanley's eschatology that forces us to classify his programme as in practice reactionary and not revolutionary, the line between the two definitions is thin. Winstanley's analysis was undoubtedly revolutionary in that it was rooted in the 'material activity and the material intercourse of men' in a way in which Marx would have recognized; yet his hopes for the fulfilment of his political programme were grounded, not in the real world, but in a belief

that its time had come. Thus his ideas, not having came historically to term, 'fell stillborn from the womb'.[66]

One final weakness in the argument propounded by some, particularly Marxist, interpreters of Winstanley, that he was essentially a secular thinker, arises from their *a priori* understanding of religion as either, in Maguire's words, 'a set of abstract platitudes, at best useless . . . [or] . . . in so far as it says anything about the social and political reality of its time', not religion at all.[67] For such thinkers—for whom perhaps the *locus classicus* is Engels' analysis of Thomas Müntzer in *The Peasant War in Germany*—even when one encounters a culture which is deeply religious (as in the case of Müntzer and Winstanley), and which gives rise to revolutionary programmes couched in language which reflects that culture, such language may be seen as at best superfluous and metaphorical, or, at worst, a means of misrepresenting political struggles in the guise of theological ones. Thus according to Engels, the class struggles in which Müntzer and Luther were engaged could be understood quite adequately without reference to the theological differences between them:

> Although the class struggles of that day were clothed in religious shibboleths, and though the interests, requirements, and demands of the various classes were concealed behind a religious screen, this changed nothing and is easily explained by the conditions of the time.[68]

Thus the presence of religious language in the revolutionary programme of a Müntzer or a Winstanley is politically insignificant: tautologous, abstract, metaphorical and non-cognitive; and this being the case, where such programmes *do* say something about reality, nothing is added by the use of theological terminology in the presentation.

Reasoning of this sort, I believe, lies behind some of the attempts to sift out the 'theological' from the 'political' in Winstanley, in order the more easily to play down the former. Petegorsky, as we have noted, refers to the 'theological garb' in which Winstanley's ideas were frequently clothed;[69] George to 'the almost ornamental, certainly at best tangential, relation of the Bible' to his thought;[70] and Aylmer to the way in which Winstanley 'uses millenarian images and scriptural texts to convey his sense of immediacy and crisis'.[71] But it is Hill who perhaps pursues the point farther than most. In his introduction to the volume of Winstanley's writings he edited in 1973,[72] he begins by suggesting that, since Winstanley wrote before the Industrial Revolution, 'some of his insights may be of interest to those in the Third World today who face the transition from an agrarian to an industrial society'.[73] Winstanley, in other words, may be read as a modern. If one were to raise the obvious objection that the situation in some parts of the developing world differs from the one

67 John Maguire, 'Gospel or Religious Language?: Engels on the Peasant War', *New Blackfriars,* 54 (1973), 350.

68 Frederick Engels, *The Peasant War in Germany* (Moscow, 1956), p. 42 (first German edition 1850).

69 Petegorsky, p. 206.

70 C. H. George, 'Gerrard Winstanley: A Critical Retrospect', in *The Dissenting Tradition: Essays for Leland H. Carlson,* edited by C. Robert Cole and Michael E. Moody (Athens, Ohio, 1975), p. 214.

71 G. E. Aylmer, 'The Religion of Gerrard Winstanley', in *Radical Religion in the English Revolution,* edited by J. F. McGregor and B. Reay (Oxford, 1984), p. 95.

72 Hill, *Winstanley: The Law of Freedom* . . .

73 Ibid., p. 10.

74 Ibid., pp. 19, 55.

75 Hill, *The Religion* . . . , p. 57.

John Gurney (essay date 1994)

SOURCE: "Gerrard Winstanley and the Digger Movement in Walton and Cobham," *The Historical Journal,* Vol, 37, No. 4, December, 1994, pp. 775-802.

[*In the following essay, Gurney refers to Winstanley's pamphlets and other contemporary documents to discuss the levels of general societal acceptance received by the Digger communities Winstanley established in Surrey.*]

Although much has been written in recent years about the life of Gerrard Winstanley,[1] our knowledge of those who joined him in the Digger venture of 1649-50 remains extremely limited. Surprisingly little attention has been paid to the Digger movement in recent studies of popular protest, and there has been a tendency to emphasize the Diggers' lack of popular appeal and their apparent failure to gain the support of the local tenantry. In the absence of detailed studies of the Surrey Diggers and their opponents, it has proved difficult to test the validity of the widely-held view that Winstanley and his followers were, unlike the Diggers of Iver in Buckinghamshire, outsiders who met with considerable hostility from the inhabitants of the communities in which they tried to organize, and were defeated as much by popular opposition as by the campaigns waged against them by local landowners.[2] The suggestion that the Diggers were unwelcome intruders has important implications, not only for the study of the

Digger movement itself, but also for what it tells us about the links between social conflict and popular radicalism, and about the receptiveness of rural communities to the spread of radical ideas during the English revolution. It can be argued that there was in fact not one, but two responses to the Diggers in Surrey, and that historians have failed to distinguish adequately between the Diggers' contrasting experiences in the two parishes of Walton and Cobham. Although there was determined local opposition to the Diggers in Walton, a parish with a long tradition of hostility towards outsiders, it would seem that Winstanley was able to draw on Cobham's very different traditions in order to gain a degree of support for his venture from among the inhabitants of the latter parish.

I

Evidence of intense local hostility is certainly to be found in early newsbook reports of the digging on St George's Hill. Frequent references were made in newsbooks published in April and May 1649 to the assaults carried out by 'the Country people' in their repeated attempts to drive the Diggers off the hill.[3] These reports must of course be treated with caution, and it is clear that the interest shown by the London press reflected the high levels of political uncertainty in the spring of 1649, and the widespread fears of Leveller and royalist conspiracy against the newly-installed republican regime.[4] The Diggers, having chosen to call themselves 'True Levellers', were easily, and no doubt conveniently, confused by their opponents with the mainstream Leveller movement, and it is not surprising that hostile observers should seek to emphasize the local opposition to their activities in Walton.[5] Press reports about the Diggers' activities became much less frequent with the decline of the Leveller challenge in the summer of 1649.[6]

The newsbook accounts of popular opposition did, however, receive corroboration from Winstanley himself in the pamphlets issued by the Diggers while they remained on St George's Hill. Winstanley's readiness to acknowledge the deep hostility aroused by the Diggers is indeed striking, given that these pamphlets were designed primarily to advance the Diggers' cause. Winstanley did not attempt to deny the early hostility shown by 'the rude multitude', and, although he tried to persuade Fairfax in May that the country people 'that were offended at first, begin now to be moderate, and to see the righteousnesse in our work',[7] he was soon complaining about further attacks on the Diggers, including the ritualized protest of 11 June, when four Diggers were beaten by 'men in womens apparell . . . with every one a staffe or club'.[8]

St George's Hill lay in the parish of Walton-upon-Thames, and it would seem that the attacks and petty harassment experienced there were organized predominantly by members of Walton's yeoman elite rather than leading local landowners.[9] The Diggers were said to have been released by justices of the peace on the first two occasions they were attacked by local inhabitants;[10] direct gentry involvement in the campaign against them did not become evident until prosecutions were initiated on behalf of Francis Drake in Kingston's court of Record in June 1649, after the Diggers had challenged the landlords' right to take wood from the commons and had declared their intention of selling wood to provide funds for the colony.[11] The resort to legal action may have served to reduce the risk of coninued rioting by the people of Walton as well as to rid the parish of the Diggers.

It was a Walton yeoman, the county committee official Henry Sanders, who first alerted the council of state to the Diggers' activities on St George's Hill.[12] John Taylor and William Starr, who were accused by Winstanley of organizing attacks on the Diggers, including the assault of 11 June, were also members of Walton's middling sorts.[13] William Starr was a prosperous freeholder and resident of Painshill, which lay close to St George's Hill on the borders of Walton and Cobham.[14] He was of sufficient social standing to serve as high constable of Elmbridge hundred in 1648.[15] Two John Taylors were resident in the parish in 1649, both of them sons of Robert Taylor of Walton.[16] The Taylors appear to have been committed supporters of parliament during the Civil War; members of the family contributed generously on the propositions,[17] and some served in the parliamentary forces.[18] John Taylor senior was active in the implementation of parliament's assessment ordinances in Walton. He was appointed as one of the assessors for the weekly assessment in the parish in May 1643,[19] and later served as an assessor for the monthly assessment.[20]

II

Winstanley's recognition of middling sorts involvement in the organization of anti-Digger protests is evident in the Walton Digger pamphlets. While consistent emphasis was placed in these pamphlets on the fundamental antagonism in society between the landowning gentry and the poor, and on the pressing need for the earth to 'be set free from intanglements of Lords and Landlords', Winstanley voiced an added concern about the 'violent bitter people that are Free-holders'.[21] He had paid scant attention to the middling sorts in general, or to freeholders in particular, in *The new law of righteousnes,* when he denounced those who continued to exploit and oppress the poor. In *The true levellers standard advanced,* which was published after the Diggers had experienced the first attacks on their colony, freeholders were cast as the Norman Bastard's common soldiers;[22] when Fairfax visited the colony in May, Winstanley complained to the lord general about the continuing opposition of 'covetous Free-holders,

that would have all the Commons to themselves, and that would uphold the Norman Tyranny over us'.[23] In the second Digger tract, landlords and freeholders were addressed together as those who 'make the most profit of the Commons, by your overstocking of them with Sheep and Cattle', while 'the poor that have the name to own the Commons have the least share therein'.[24] 'This fury in the free-holders', Winstanley complained after the attack led by Starr and Taylor, 'declares plainly, that they got their Lands, both they and their Fathers, by murder, violence, and theft, and they keep it by the same power'.[25]

Winstanley's insistence that the Diggers had no intention of invading or expropriating private property has often been noted,[26] and it is probable that his frequent reiteration of this principle in the Walton pamphlets reflected his desire to appease those 'elder brothers and Free-holders' who were responsible for the harassment on St George's Hill.[27] The Diggers, Winstanley maintained, 'will neither meddle with Corn, Cattell, nor inclosure Land, but only in the Commons'.[28] Winstanley and Everard had assured the lord general of their peaceable intentions when they were summoned before him on 20 April, and Winstanley repeated these assurances during Fairfax's visit in May.[29] Winstanley's earlier, confident prediction of the imminent and complete destruction of private property was much less visible in such pamphlets as *A letter to the lord Fairfax and his councell of war,* when he complained of the continuing hostility of the Walton yeomanry, and expressed his hope that

> these our angry neighbours, whom we never wronged, nor will not wrong, will in time see their furious rashnesse to be their folly, and become moderate, to speak and carry themselves like men rationally, and leave off pushing with their hornes like beasts.[30]

In *The new law of righteousnes* and, to a lesser extent in *The true levellers standard advanced,* Winstanley appears to have anticipated, as Christopher Hill has argued, a speedy transition to a system of communal cultivation, with only a temporary survival of private property; the power of Reason and the withdrawal of wage labour would soon bring about the surrender of estates which could not adequately be worked by family labour.[31] In the later St George's Hill pamphlets, Winstanley was clearly aware of the need to reassure his local opponents that their lands and enclosures were safe, and that two systems of landholding could exist in relative harmony, the poor cultivating the commons and the gentry and freeholders their enclosed lands, 'not burthening one another in this land of our Nativity'.[32] Although Winstanley continued to hope that his opponents would eventually be induced to give up their lands, it is apparent that this became less important to him in the short term than the need to ensure the survival of the Digger colony.[33] The desire to achieve some form of compromise is also evident in the absence from the Digger pamphlets published in June, July and August 1649, of the demand that labourers should refuse to work for hire. This demand, which had been such an important part of the Digger programme in April, would have seemed at least as threatening to the middling sorts of the locality as it was to the gentry.[34]

III

Henry Sanders's report to the council of state, with its emphasis on the 'very great prejudice to the Towne' caused by the digging, provided a clear expression of local concerns about the Diggers' activities.[35] The inhabitants of Walton had for several years been involved in struggles to prevent incursions on to their commons by outsiders. Pressure on the commons had grown during the late sixteenth century, as local farmers took advantage of the absence of any stint to engage in large-scale stock rearing for the profitable London market.[36] Walton's commons had also attracted squatters and cottagers, and during the 1580s it was claimed that 'dyvers cottages' had recently been built on Walton Heath by people who were not tenants of the manor, but who had access to the waste 'without stynt yf they have any thing to putt uppon yt'.[37] Piecemeal enclosure of the waste and common fields in Walton also took place during the sixteenth century, as when William Hammond of Apps Court enclosed a large part of the common arable fields to the north-east of the village of Walton,[38] and when owners of cattle pastured in Lakefield near St George's Hill divided up and enclosed the field to prevent 'quarrelles and bralles' breaking out among the servants employed to graze the cattle.[39]

The potential for conflict was increased by the tradition of intercommoning with neighbouring manors and parishes, and by Walton Heath's lack of precise boundaries.[40] In 1650, the parliamentary surveyors of Walton Leigh found it impossible to trace the boundaries of the commons and wastes belonging to the two manors of Walton and Walton Leigh, they having been 'never severed or divided'.[41] Earlier surveyors had noted that in the case of the commons shared by the parishes of Walton and Weybridge, the liberties 'cannot be sett downe directly by neyther of the parishes'.[42] Tenants of the manor of Walton entered into legal actions in 1587 and 1590 against Robert Benne, the occupier of Apps Court, who had taken advantage of the ill-defined common rights to pasture his cattle on Walton Heath.[43] Incursions of this kind were to continue during the seventeenth century; as late as 1664, the astrologer William Lilly was involved in a lawsuit with the lord of the manor of Esher, whose sheep Lilly had impounded on Walton common in his capacity as churchwarden of 'that distracted parish'.[44]

IV

In Walton-upon-Thames the Diggers were treated as outsiders by inhabitants who had considerable experience of dealing with threats to their commons, and who lost no time before organizing to drive them off St George's Hill. The Diggers probably were genuine outsiders here; few Walton residents appear to have joined in the digging. Attempts to identify individual Diggers are of course extremely hazardous, and only tentative conclusions can be drawn. The names of at least seventy Surrey Diggers are known; many had common surnames,[45] and it would be too risky to claim, for instance, that the Smiths and Taylors who are known to have lived in Walton in 1649 were necessarily those who signed Digger manifestoes. Winstanley sought to appeal especially to the landless poor, whose names are least likely to feature in surviving records, and the digging no doubt attracted people who had no connection with the locality.[46] Many of these may have spent only a short time with the Diggers: 43 Diggers signed no more than one pamphlet, including 32 of those who put their names to *A declaration of the poor oppressed people of England,* the pamphlet containing the largest collection of Digger names.[47]

Only two Diggers can be said with any degree of certainty to have come from Walton. One was Richard Maidley or Medley, whose son was buried in Walton in December 1640, and who had two children baptized there in 1642 and 1643.[48] In October 1649 he was prosecuted in Kingston court by two Walton gentlemen, William Tucker and Augustine Phillips, and in November by Sir Gregory Norton, the regicide MP for Midhurst in Sussex.[49] Norton was at this time the state's tenant at Oatlands park,[50] and had been appointed to the Surrey Bench in September 1649, perhaps in an attempt to make up for the lack of experienced JPs in an area where the Diggers were active.[51] Both Sir Anthony Vincent of Stoke d'Abernon and Francis Drake of Walton, two prominent local landowners who had direct contact with the Diggers, had been removed from the Bench when it was remodelled at the beginning of the year.[52] Richard Maidley was one of the Diggers indicted at the Lent assizes of 1650, and he remained with the colony until it was destroyed in mid-April.[53]

The other Walton Digger was Henry Bickerstaffe, who stood surety for Winstanley in Kingston court in June 1649, and was the one Digger imprisoned by the court.[54] He had become acquainted with Winstanley before the start of the Digger venture, and had acted with him in February 1649 as arbitrator for the Kingston separatist John Fielder, in an action for false imprisonment brought by Fielder against two former Kingston bailiffs, Richard Lidgold and John Childe.[55] Bickerstaffe is perhaps the best documented Digger besides Winstanley, and their careers have much in common. He was, like Winstanley, a freeman of a major City livery company; he appears to have been unable to establish himself successfully in business, and he moved from London to Walton a few years before the start of the digging.[56]

Henry Bickerstaffe was a younger son of Robert Bickerstaffe of Walton, who died in 1640.[57] The Bickerstaffes possessed freehold and copyhold lands in both Walton and Cobham, their chief holding being the ninety-eight acre crown estate of Painshill farm and Cobham Bridge on the borders of the two parishes.[58] Robert Bickerstaffe is known to have refused to lend on the privy seal loans of 1625, and he was later listed as a knighthood defaulter in Surrey.[59] He was for several years involved in a protracted and sometimes violent land dispute with his neighbour James Starr, the father of the Diggers' assailant William Starr. James Starr was said in 1621 to have been 'much ympoverished' by the numerous suits brought against him by Bickerstaffe; the latter was also alleged to have assaulted Starr when he was barred from taking wood from the disputed lands.[60]

Robert Bickerstaffe's estates were inherited in 1640 by his son Anthony, a liveryman in the Skinners' company and a resident of the parish of Christchurch Newgate Street.[61] He was a friend of the presbyterian minister William Jenkyn, and during the Civil War became an active supporter of the presbyterian party in City politics.[62] He put his name to the City petition of 18 November 1645 in favour of increasing the prospective powers of London's presbyterian elders,[63] and in June 1647 he was one of the treasurers appointed to disburse £10,000 due to be paid to private soldiers as part of parliament's programme for disbanding the army.[64]

Henry Bickerstaffe served a seven-year apprenticeship to his brother Anthony from 20 February 1626, being admitted to the freedom of the Skinners' company on 11 April 1633.[65] It is unlikely that he succeeded in setting up in business on his own, since the company registers do not record the names of any apprentices bound by him during the 1630s.[66] His address was unknown to the company when in 1641 he was listed as a poll tax defaulter.[67] He was almost certainly living in Walton by the end of 1639, when his son Edward was born.[68] After the death of his father, Henry Bickerstaffe remained in Walton, and appears to have taken over the management of the lands inherited by his brother Anthony, who continued to reside in London.[69] There are no references to Anthony Bickerstaffe in surviving Walton and Cobham parish records of the 1640s, nor in civil war accounts and assessments for Surrey. Although Anthony Bickerstaffe was listed as the farmer of the Painshill estate in 1643, it was Henry who paid the Bickerstaffes' wartime assessments in Walton.[70]

Henry Bickerstaffe was a member of the jury which found in January 1642 that the whole of Surrey lay outside the boundaries of Windsor forest and was no longer subject to forest law.[71] He contributed 10s towards the relief of Irish protestants in 1642, and lent silver plate valued at £514s.8d. on the propositions.[72] He was appointed an assessor for the first three months' weekly assessment in Walton, and in August 1643 he paid £3 for his fifth and twentieth part to the earl of Essex's commissioners in Kingston;[73] in October he contributed £1 towards the raising of horses for Sir William Waller in Surrey's middle division.[74] During the following summer he shared with his neighbour William Starr the cost of listing a soldier, John Tinsley, for service against Basing house.[75]

Bickerstaffe signed only the first Digger pamphlet, and may therefore have left the colony soon after his arrest and trial in June 1649.[76] He had become a Kingston resident by December 1650,[77] but he did not sever his links with Walton: during the 1650s he continued to collect rents in Walton and Cobham, both for Anthony Bickerstaffe and for the latter's son James.[78] In September 1661, twelve years after his imprisonment in the town, Henry Bickerstaffe of Kingston entered a bond with the corporation to become keeper of the town gaol.[79]

V

It would be wrong to judge the Diggers' relations with the local community solely on the evidence of their treatment in Walton. The nature of their local reception can only properly be understood if the differences between their experiences in Walton and Cobham are fully recognized. The Diggers had arrived in Cobham by 24 August 1649, and were to remain in the parish until the following April; it is possible, therefore, that they spent roughly twice as long on Cobham's Little Heath as they did on St George's Hill.[80] The move to Cobham did not lead to any immediate resumption of newsbook reports of attacks on the colony, and Winstanley made no new complaints about popular opposition or protests. In spite of the meetings of 'Knights, Gentlemen and rich Freeholders' at the White Lion, and the installation of a lecturer in Cobham's parish church 'to drive off the Diggers',[81] it seems that the Diggers were able to enjoy a relatively peaceful stay on Little Heath until October, when the council of state was encouraged to renew the appeal to Fairfax and the Surrey justices to disperse Winstanely and his followers.[82]

The campaign against the digging was revived in earnest in the autumn and winter of 1649, with arrests being made in mid-October and further prosecutions initiated in Kingston's Court of Record in October, November and December.[83] Two Digger houses were pulled down by soldiers at the end of November, and plans were made to indict fifteen Diggers at the assizes.[84] It is now clear that presentments were also drawn up against four Diggers—John Hayman, Anthony Wrenn, Daniel Freeland and Henry Barton—for having erected cottages in Cobham with less than four acres of land attached, contrary to the statute of 1589.[85]

The tone of the pamphlets issued by the Diggers after the resumption of the attacks in Cobham was markedly different from that of the later St George's Hill tracts. The Diggers' hostility towards landlords was intensified in the Cobham pamphlets, with much less emphasis being placed on the oppressive role of freeholders.[86] Particularly striking was the direct challenge issued to landlords in *An appeale to all Englishmen* and *Englands spirit unfoulded,* in which support for the commonwealth was linked by Winstanley to the demand that copyhold tenants should renounce their obedience to lords of manors.[87] With the declared opposition of the army and parliament to 'all Kingly and Lordly entanglements', landlords could no longer legally

> compell their Tenants of Copy-holds, to come to their Court-Barons, nor to be of their Juries, nor take an Oath to be true to them, nor to pay fines, heriots, quit-rent, nor any homage, as formerly, while the King and Lords were in their power.

Tenants would be indemnified against their landlords, and be 'protected by the Laws and Engagement of the Land'.[88]

The change of emphasis in the Digger writings must in part have reflected Winstanley's belief that the renewed attacks were organized by the local gentry, rather than the middling sorts, and were carried out by 'their fearfull tenants'; 'the poor tenants . . . durst do no other, because their Land-lords and Lords looked on, for fear they should be turned out of service, or their livings'.[89] By appealing to copyholders to throw off their obligations to landlords, Winstanley could hope to undermine the power of his chief opponents and persuade their tenants that they were free to resist pressure to attack the colony. His appeal to tenants also contained an unmistakable threat: although Winstanley had declared in June 1649 that the Diggers were ready to 'answer to all the Laws of the Land as Defendents, but not as Plaintiffs', he was now prepared to warn that charges could be brought against those who conspired with the gentry to 'uphold or bring in the Kingly and Lordly Power again'.[90] Such people were guilty of breaking the engagement; they would forfeit all legal protection and stand 'lyable to answer for this offence, to their great charge and trouble if any will prosecute against them'.[91]

The Diggers' most active opponent in Cobham was

undoubtedly John Platt, the rector of West Horsley, who had only recently come into possession of the manor of Cobham through his marriage to Margaret Gavell.[92] 'The fury of Parson Plat', Winstanley complained, 'exceedes the fury of any other Lord of Mannor'.[93] Platt has often been portrayed as a persistent opponent of the Diggers in both Walton and Cobham, but there is no evidence that he took an active part in the campaign against them before they moved to Little Heath; no mention was made of him by Winstanley in the St George's Hill pamphlets.[94] Platt was accused by Winstanley of being responsible for the destruction of Digger houses in November, of making false allegations against the Diggers to the lord general and council of state, and of persuading the latter to send soldiers to Cobham.[95] He was also accused of taking the leading role in the final attack in April 1650.[96]

The other major landowner identified by Winstanley as being active in the campaign against the Diggers in Cobham was Sir Anthony Vincent, lord of the neighbouring manor of Stoke d'Abernon.[97] Both Vincent and Platt appear to have been particularly concerned about the threat posed by the Diggers to their timber rights; the Diggers are known to have taken wood from Stoke common, and Winstanley claimed in April 1650 that Platt had promised to leave their houses alone if they 'would not cut the wood upon the Common'.[98] It is likely that Winstanley was referring to Vincent when he suggested that some of the Diggers' opponents 'were alwayes Cavaleers, and had a hand in the Kentish riseing, and were cheife promoters of the offensive Surry petition'.[99] Vincent had lent £100 on the propositions in 1642,[100] but he withdrew from involvement in Surrey's parliamentarian administration after the summer of 1643, and was to come under suspicion due to his wife's royalism.[101] His son and heir, Sir Francis Vincent, was involved in the earl of Holland's rising in 1648, and was faced with a composition fine of £800, the highest charged in Surrey.[102]

Also active in the campaign was Thomas Sutton, the impropriator of the Cobham living, who belonged to a minor Cobham gentry family.[103] He had already clashed with Winstanley and Henry Bickerstaffe, having joined John Downe of Cobham in February 1649 as an arbitrator for Richard Lidgold and John Childe in their dispute with John Fielder.[104] Sutton was a member of Surrey's assize grand jury, and was, in the 1640s, one of the wealthier inhabitants of the parish.[105]

VI

The most detailed description of the final assault on the Digger colony, in which six Digger homes were destroyed, was provided by Winstanley in his pamphlet *An humble request.*[106] John Platt was said to have been accompanied by fifty men, including several hired men and 'most of' Sir Anthony Vincent's tenants and servants, as well as Thomas Sutton and William Starr.[107] The landlords' coercion of their tenants was again emphasized by Winstanley:

> many of those that came were threatened by Vincent his chief men, to be turned out of their Livings, if they came not, so that this is not an act of the tenants by free consent, but the Gentlemen hired others to do it.[108]

An humble request has long been our sole source of information about the final assault, but it is now possible to check Winstanley's account against other surviving evidence. It is clear that a group of Diggers sought to carry out the threat to prosecute their opponents, by trying to bring an indictment at the assizes against those responsible for the destruction of the Digger houses.[109] Their draft bills, which were rejected by the grand jury at the Croydon assizes in July 1650, are important in that they confirm the date of the colony's destruction, provide us with further possible Digger names, and list twenty of those accused of participating in the attack. The date of the dedicatory address of *An humble address,* 9 April 1650, has led to some confusion when attempts have been made to identify the precise date of the assault. The draft indictments confirm that the attack took place on 19 April, which suggests that Winstanley had begun *An humble address* some days before the attack, and added his narrative of the incident to the pamphlet after the completion of the dedicatory address and eleven pages of the text.[110]

The twenty men named in the draft bills were said to have destroyed the houses of Thomas Adams, Henry Barton, Daniel Freeland and Robert Sawyer, all known Diggers.[111] Barton and Freeland were among the group of Diggers presented for having built cottages with less than four acres of land, and this may have provided their opponents with the pretext for destroying their homes.[112] The witnesses to the attack were the Diggers Richard Maidley and John Palmer, and also Elizabeth Barton, Jane Edsarr, Matthew Mills and one Lowry; Winstanley's name is absent from the documents.[113]

John Platt's name headed the list of accused, which also included the familiar names of Thomas Sutton, Edward Sutton and William Starr. At least seven of the accused were from Stoke d'Abernon, including William Davey senior and junior, Henry and Edward Bird, Thomas Shore, Thomas Lee and John Poore.[114] Davey was described in *An humble request* as 'Sir Anthony Vincents Servant', and Poore may have been the servant John Power to whom Vincent left £10 in his will.[115] Thomas Lee was described as a poor man in 1644, when his name was included in a list of defaulters on the two-month weekly assessment.[116] John Goose, Thomas Parrish, Robert Melsham and William Honyard can all be identified as Cobham residents.[117] It is likely

that more than one John Goose was living in Cobham in 1650, but one at least had fought for the king during the Civil War: he petitioned successfully for a pension in 1663, claiming that he had been wounded in the service of Charles I and was 'att present very sicke and weake haveinge a wife and six Children and like to perish for want of reliefe'.[118]

By no means all those who joined Platt and the Suttons could be described as 'poor enslaved Tenants' or hired men. Thomas Parrish, for instance, was to serve as high constable of Elmbridge hundred in 1651, as William Starr had done in 1648.[119] Robert Melsham was to become constable of Cobham in 1665.[120] Parrish was appointed as an assessor for the weekly assessment in 1643, and both he and Thomas Shore of Stoke were later involved in the collection of the monthly assessment.[121] Parrish was described in contemporary documents as a yeoman, and lent £1 on the propositions; he was a juror at Cobham's manor court in 1647 and 1648.[122]

Some members of Cobham's parish elite were, therefore, involved in the final assault on the Digger colony. This evidence may provide a corrective to Winstanley's description of the attack, but it should not detract from the overriding impression that it was the local gentry who took the initiative in organizing opposition to the Diggers in Cobham. The middling sorts of Cobham were much more divided in their response to the Diggers than Walton's inhabitants had been, and there is no evidence here of a community united in its determination to resist an external threat. Most importantly, several locals joined the digging and would appear to have been among Winstanley's most active supporters.

Henry Sanders claimed in April 1649 that the Diggers who set to work on St George's Hill were 'all living att Cobham'.[123] It has been known for several years that Winstanley was resident in Cobham in 1649, having moved there from London after the collapse of his business in 1643.[124] He was still living in the parish of St Olave Jewry when he took the covenant on 8 October 1643,[125] but he had presumably settled in Cobham by 20 December, when the committee at Kingston ordered the high constables of Elmbridge hundred to warn parochial assessors to set rates for the two months' weekly assessment, on which Winstanley was charged as a Cobham inhabitant.[126] Winstanley's home was in the tithing of Church Cobham, and, despite his severe financial difficulties, he was still being described as a gentleman in Cobham's court rolls in 1648.[127]

Sanders also mentioned 'one Stewer and Colten' in his report to the council of state.[128] Thomas Starr, who signed four Digger manifestoes, and was prosecuted in Kingston court in June 1649 and indicted at the Southwark assizes of April 1650, was a shoemaker and resident of Church Cobham.[129] He was baptized in Cobham in December 1615, the fourth son of Edmund Starr, a clothworker who died in May 1638.[130] Thomas Starr was listed in 1647 and 1648 as a defaulter at the manorial court.[131] Winstanley described him in 1649 as 'a poore man not worth ten pounds', but by 1663 he was rated as having six hearths.[132] Two years later, in 1665, he was to be presented at the Guildford quarter sessions for refusing to assist Cobham's constable in breaking up a quaker meeting at the house of Ephraim Carter, a Cobham butcher.[133]

John Coulton was another Cobham inhabitant who put his name to four Digger pamphlets in 1649 and 1650.[134] He was a yeoman who came from a long-established Cobham family, and was a prominent member of the village community.[135] He lent £2 on the propositions, was appointed an assessor for the weekly assessment in May 1643, and collected taxes in Cobham during the Civil War for the garrison at Farnham.[136] He appears to have served with the county forces at the siege of Basing in 1644, and in the following year he joined with Thomas Sutton, John Downe and John Goldwire in compiling Cobham's parish accounts.[137] Coulton was a juror at the manorial court in 1647 and 1648.[138] When he died in 1652, he left legacies worth £117 to his children and grandchildren. His will was witnessed by his 'freind Jerrard Winstanly', who was also nominated as one of the overseers.[139]

Henry Barton, John Hayman, Daniel Freeland and Samuel Webb were, like Gerrard Winstanley and Thomas Starr, listed as defaulters at Cobham's manorial court in 1648.[140] Henry Barton lived in Street Cobham, and two of his sons were baptized in the parish in 1640 and 1643.[141] John Hayman, also of Street Cobham, married Constance Jackson in Cobham in June 1642; three of their children were baptized in 1643, 1660 and 1663.[142] In 1658 Hayman witnessed the signing of the will of Francis Stint the elder, a Cobham husbandman.[143] He had three hearths in 1663, and died in 1675.[144] Barton signed three Digger pamphlets and Hayman put his name to four.[145] The names Barton and Hayman were both Cobham quaker surnames: in 1674, for instance, the birth of Constance Hayman of Cobham was recorded in the registers of the Kingston quaker meeting, and a widow Barton of Cobham was buried as a quaker in 1672.[146]

Mary and Daniel, the children of Daniel Freeland of Church Cobham, were baptized in 1642 and 1643.[147] In 1657 Daniel son of widow Freeland was bound by the parish as an apprentice to Lawrence Johnson, a Cobham victualler who had been presented at the assizes in 1653 for keeping a disorderly alehouse.[148] Johnson was to join John Hayman in 1658 as a witness to Francis Stint's will.[149] Widow Freeland was in receipt of parish relief in 1662, and in the hearth tax assessments of 1664 she was listed as possessing only

one hearth; she died in December 1664.[150] Samuel Webb had a son baptized in Cobham in November 1642, and in 1648 was living in Cobham Downside.[151]

It is important to emphasize again the problems involved in trying to identify individual Diggers; no complete run of court rolls has survived for the manor of Cobham, and the parish registers exist only in eighteenth-century transcripts. The lack of any settled minister during the 1640s led to there being gaps in the original registers, and these gaps were only partially filled by later incumbents. The churchwardens' records are also incomplete.[152] Winstanley's accounts of the Digger movement provide few references to the place of origin of the Diggers; on only one occasion did he refer explicitly to the local origin of some of them, when he described the evictions of Digger families in April 1650:

> Thereupon at the Command of this Parson Plat, they set fire to six houses, and burned them down, and burned likewise some of their housholdstuffe, and wearing Clothes, throwing their beds, stooles, and housholdstuffe, up and down the Common, not pittying the cries of many little Children, and their frighted Mothers, *which are Parishioners borne in the Parish.*[153]

It is, however, possible that a provisional list of Diggers with Cobham connections should also include the names of John Palmer,[154] John South, John South junior,[155] Thomas South[156] and Anthony Wrenn.[157] John Palmer the Digger signed five of the Digger pamphlets; he was one of those indicted at the Southwark assizes, and was a witness to the destruction of the colony.[158] John South put his name to four pamphlets and was, like Palmer, a member of the Digger colony in both Walton and Cobham; John South junior, Thomas South and Anthony Wrenn appear to have joined the colony only after the move to Cobham.[159] Thomas Edcer or Edsaw, who signed four Digger pamphlets, may also have been a local inhabitant, and have come from a family long-settled in Stoke d'Abernon. Children of Thomas Edsaw of Stoke were baptized in 1656 and 1663. In 1664 he had one hearth and was exempted from the hearth tax.[160]

If some at least of these identifications are correct, it does show that an important core group of local people was involved in the digging in Cobham, as is known to have been the case in the Iver Digger community in Buckinghamshire. This may help to explain the absence in Cobham of the levels of popular opposition seen in Walton, where attacks took place as soon as the Diggers started their work on St George's Hill; it may also account for the apparent reluctance of some tenants to carry out their landlords' orders to pull down Digger homes. The Cobham Diggers included not only landless labourers and cottagers but also at least one member of the middling sorts; again, the pattern is similar to that of Iver.[161] It is evident that many of the local Diggers were able to return to the neighbourhood after the collapse of the digging, and after the Diggers' brief stay at Lady Eleanor Davies's estate at Pirton in Hertfordshire.[162] Although fifteen of them were indicted for riot and trespass at the Southwark assizes in 1650, they seem to have escaped effective prosecution even after their return to their homes.[163] Warrants were issued regularly at subsequent assizes for the production of the Diggers before the courts; these warrants were still being issued in 1652, and as late as 1653 in the case of Winstanley.[164] Winstanley had presumably returned to Cobham by June 1652, when he witnessed John Coulton's will in the company of William Remnant and John Fuller, two members of Cobham's village establishment who had not been involved in the digging.[165]

VII

There can of course be no single explanation for the existence of some local support for Winstanley's digging venture, but it may be significant that Cobham lacked a regular minister after William King left to become rector of Ashtead in 1644.[166] John Goldwire, an ordained minister and schoolmaster who lent £20 on the propositions in Cobham, was described as minister when in 1645 he helped to compile the parish accounts, but by March 1646 he had moved to the rectory of Millbrook in Hampshire.[167] The small size of the Cobham living, worth only £9 13s. 4d. per annum, would have made it difficult to find a permanent successor to King; the living was, as John Aubrey later complained, only a 'poor mean pittance'.[168] The possibility that Winstanley was able, during the later 1640s, to develop his revolutionary ideas and build up a local following without hindrance from a settled minister, should therefore not be discounted. The decision to appoint a lecturer in Cobham when the Diggers moved to little Heath certainly suggests that their opponents feared Winstanley's local influence, and believed that it would be unwise to allow the Diggers' propaganda to go unchallenged in the parish.[169]

It is not known when Winstanley first emerged as a radical thinker; attempts to trace Winstanley's intellectual development are invariably hampered by the fact that he published nothing before 1648. It is clear, however, that he had already gained some experience of political activity by the time he moved to Cobham, having attended meetings of the St Olave Jewry vestry on at least eight occasions.[170] At a meeting held on 4 January 1642, he had shown his support for the reform movement in the City by opposing the decision of the majority to resist moves to restore to general assemblies of the wardmote the power to choose members of common council; these moves would have led to a significant increase in popular participation in the

common council elections.[171] Winstanley may also have come into contact with radical ideas before he left London. Anti-episcopal riots are known to have taken place in the parish church in May 1642, and there is a distinct possibility that Christopher Feake, the future fifth monarchist, was employed as a lecturer in St Olave's while Winstanley was still resident in the parish and active as a member of the vestry.[172]

Radical religious views were certainly being expressed openly in Kingston by the summer of 1644, within a year of Winstanley's move to Cobham. The Kingston chamberlains' accounts for 1643-4 record that 25s. was spent by the town on 'carrying . . . Anabaptists to the parliament two sevrall tymes'; in August 1644 further payments were made by the county committee for sending an 'Anabaptist' to London.[173] When Richard Byfield, minister of Long Ditton and friend of Kingston's presbyterian vicar Edmund Staunton, sought to expose the 'evils and pernicious Errours . . . that infest our Church', in sermons preached at the town's lecture in February 1645, he made particular reference to the 'diseasedness of the Congregation of Kingston'. Among Byfield's principal targets were the 'Sensuall Separatists . . . that walke after their lusts; Mockers, that jugling with the Scriptures broach bruitish-damnable Tenets'. Mortalist and pacifist views were, he claimed, being circulated, and he complained of those who tried to bring their listeners 'into astonishment, and a trance upon the conceit of the great power of God in them, and some inspirations of the Holy Ghost'; 'they conceive they have a great light, and a new light'. Such people hoped to 'alleviate the threats of Gods word with vain words, and to promise liberty; and turn Gods grace into wantonnesse'. The 'new disturbers' disgraced 'the publique and solemn Assemblies, . . . troubling them by barbarous confusion' with their revelations and false doctrines, 'and if they may not have liberty to speak in the Publick Assemblies . . . they will deny their Presence to the Publick, and fling dishonour upon them all they can'.[174]

It is likely that Byfield's anger was directed in part against the radical separatist group that had been founded in 1644 by the Kingston miller John Fielder. Members of the group were arrested at meetings in the town in January and March 1645; their activities aroused much popular hostility, and 'uproars and tumults' were said to have taken place when they were attacked by crowds of apprentices, soldiers and watermen.[175] Winstanley had met Fielder by February 1649 at the latest, but in view of the close links between Cobham and Kingston, and Winstanley's own disputes with the Kingston authorities, it is indeed possible that he had links with the town's separatists before he acted on Fielder's behalf at the 1649 Lent assizes; Kingston's radical milieu may well have provided an important setting for the development of his ideas.[176] The town's first quaker meeting, which later developed out of Fielder's group, certainly drew adherents from the rural parishes of Kingston and Elmbridge hundreds, including Cobham and Walton.[177]

Winstanley and Henry Bickerstaffe were not the only Surrey Diggers to have links with John Fielder, and it is evident that contacts between the Diggers and Kingston's separatists were maintained after the start of the digging in April 1649. Urian Worthington, a member of Fielder's circle who was arrested at one of their prayer meetings in 1645, became a Digger and put his name to *A declaration from the poor oppressed people of England*.[178] He was the son of John Worthington, a husbandman of Thorpe,[179] and he was later to become a convert to quakerism.[180] Peter Gosse, a Kingston heelmaker who had been imprisoned with Fielder and Worthington in 1645, and whose house had been used for the group's meetings, stood surety for Richard Maidley when the latter was prosecuted by Sir Gregory Norton in Kingston court in November 1649.[181]

VIII

Local support for the Diggers may also have been connected with Cobham's marked traditions of social conflict. The manor of Cobham, a former possession of Chertsey abbey, had passed into the hands of Robert Gavell in 1566 and was to remain with his family until 1708.[182] During the later sixteenth century the Gavell family became involved in a long and protracted series of disputes with their tenants. In a case brought in the court of Requests by William Wrenn, a Cobham husbandman, Robert Gavell was accused of overturning manorial customs and of infringing his tenants' rights, by seeking to extract more rent than was customarily paid, and by spoiling the timber on Wrenn's copyhold. He was also charged with attempting to escape the payment of tax by shifting the burden on to his tenants, laying 'a hevy burden uppon the poorer tennants contrarye to the Ancient usage, equitie and Consciens'.[183]

Actions against Robert Gavell and his son Francis were resumed in the court of Chancery during the 1590s by tenants seeking to halt the continued assault on manorial custom.[184] The Gavells were certainly in need of tapping the increasing wealth of the peasantry; Francis Gavell's debts, for instance, were estimated at £3,000 when he died in 1610.[185] Cobham's tenants claimed that the Gavells were attempting to abandon the custom of fixed entry fines of not more than two years' rent, in favour of arbitrary fines, and were exacting uncertain fines for licence to demise copyholds. The tenants also sought to uphold their right to take timber growing on their copyhold lands, not only for repairing but also for new-building their tenements.[186]

Some of Cobham's most substantial tenants, including Anthony Bickerstaffe and James Sutton, were involved in these attempts to defend the copyholders' rights, but one tenant in particular was singled out by the Gavells as a leading instigator of the actions. William King was accused of having 'espetially contrived' the tenants' 'surmised and new found customes', and of having caused his landlords 'diverse iniuryes' by keeping unlicensed rabbit warrens on his holdings.[187] An attempt to evict him in 1593 was thwarted when he succeeded in obtaining a court order for the Gavells to allow him quiet possession of his copyhold until the dispute was settled.[188] King was the son-in-law of the Gavells' opponent William Wrenn, and had succeeded to his disputed copyhold lands; he was also the grandfather of Susan King, who was to marry Gerrard Winstanley in 1640.[189] Cobham's tenants had, therefore, long experience of conflict with the lords of the manor, and the family into which Winstanley married had played a leading role in the tenants' campaigns to defend their customary rights.

Further exploitation of Cobham's manorial resources evidently took place during the 1630s, after the death in 1633 of Francis Gavell. His kinsmen the Vincents of Stoke d'Abernon held courts in Cobham until Vincent Gavell came of age, and in 1638 Sir Francis and Sir Anthony Vincent had to be ordered by the court of Wards to stop felling timber and fishing in the ponds belonging to the manor of Cobham.[190]

IX

The Digger movement emerged in 1649 against a background of hardship and scarcity in the aftermath of civil war.[191] Cobham's parish accounts, which were drawn up in 1645 on the orders of Surrey's sub-committee of accounts, give a vivid impression of the high costs sustained by the parishioners during the war. It was claimed in these accounts that up to £2,208 10s. 1d. had been spent in the parish in taxes, free quarter and voluntary contributions between November 1640 and Michaelmas 1645, including £138 3s. 6d. in taxes in lieu of provisions for Waller's army, and £1,079 3s. 8d. in free quarter. In addition to the 14 horses listed by Cobham residents for the service of parliament, 29 horses, worth an estimated £139 5s. 4d., were said to have been seized by parliament's soldiers during the war.[192] Parish accounts must of course be used with caution, but it would appear that Cobham's free quarter expenses were among the highest recorded in Surrey: they were only slightly lower than the estimated £1,125 spent by the inhabitants of the populous and heavily-charged parish of Egham by the spring of 1645, and were certainly higher than the costs incurred by most east and mid-Surrey parishes.[193] The inhabitants of many Surrey parishes complained in their accounts of the burdens of free quarter, and of the 'most extravagant abusiveness of Souldiers',[194] but Cobham's accounts are unique in their reference to parishioners who were forced to 'forsake there habitations' as a result of these pressures.[195]

Cobham's parish accounts are unusually detailed, but they fail to provide a complete picture of wartime burdens; there is no mention, for instance, of royalist plunder, which took place in the vicinity of Cobham in November 1642 and was still seen as a daily threat in the area as late as November 1643.[196] In addition, parish accounts could not take notice of the increase in free quartering that followed the army's march on London in 1647. In parts of the county the costs of free quarter were said in December 1647 to have doubled, and in some cases trebled, since the army's arrival, and tenants were again said to be abandoning their holdings.[197]

The resilience of local communities during the Civil War and revolution has been emphasized in recent studies, and historians have rightly been warned against exaggerating the breakdown of order.[198] It is apparent, however, that in many areas the pressures of war and high taxation contributed to a noticeable exacerbation of social conflict and to the accentuation of divisions within the community.[199] Conflict between landlords and tenants over the payment of rent and abatements for tax, and over disputed manorial customs and timber use-rights, certainly took place in Surrey during the 1640s, as did disputes between taxpayers and local officials.[200] The belief that poorer inhabitants had been left with a disproportionate share of the costs of war was to be voiced frequently by Winstanley and his fellow Diggers.[201] Winstanley's appreciation of the unfair distribution of burdens at a local level was expressed most clearly when he complained that in 'many parishes, two or three of the great ones bears all the sway, in making Assessments, over-awing Constables, and other Officers':

> And when time was to quarter Souldiers, they would have a hand in that, to ease themselves, and over-burden the weaker sort; and many times make large sums of money over and above the Justices Warrant in Assessments, and would give no accompt why, neither durst the inferior people demand an accompt, for he that spake should be sure to be crushed the next opportunity . . . we see one great man favored another, and the poor oppressed have no relief.[202]

It is possible that he was writing from experience. The inclusion of Winstanley's name on a list of taxpayers in Kingston and Elmbridge hundreds who had failed to pay their share of the two-month weekly assessment in 1644 may, as has recently been suggested, indicate that he could not afford to pay the 5*s.* 4*d.* he was said to owe.[203] It may be more likely, however, that he was a victim of the inefficiency of Surrey's county committee, which was notorious for its breaking spectacle of seeing so many hanged every Sessions as they are'; 'all poor People by their righteous labours shall be relieved, and freed from Poverty and Straits'.[219]

In drawing on traditional arguments of popular protest, Winstanley went well beyond the limitations of this tradition. In the Digger pamphlets, traditional themes became subsumed within new currents of political and religious radicalism: the demand for compensation for wartime sufferings merged with the demand for freedom, and there was a new emphasis on the contractual obligations of the victorious parliament. The common people had bought their freedom with their 'Money, in Taxes, Free-Quarter, and Bloudshed'; they had made a 'firme bargan and contract' with parliament. 'We that are the common People are brought almost to a morsell of bread, therefore we demand our bargain, which is freedom, with you in this Land of our Nativity.'[220] Winstanley's ability to attract a measure of support in Cobham for the Digger venture owed much to his successful appropriation of the traditional language of popular protest for radical ends; it also demonstrated most clearly how far—given the right local conditions—the radical ideas which circulated during the later 1640s could find a receptive audience in rural communities as well as in urban areas and the army.

Notes

[1] R. T. Vann, 'The later life of Gerrard Winstanley', *Journal of the History of Ideas,* XXVI (1965); 'From radicalism to quakerism: Gerrard Winstanley and Friends', *Journal of the Friends' Historical Society,* XLIX (1959); J. S. Alsop, 'Gerrard Winstanley's later life', *Past and Present,* LXXXII (1979); 'Gerrard Winstanley: religion and respectability', *Historical Journal,* XXVIII, 3 (1985); 'Ethics in the marketplace: Gerrard Winstanley's London bankruptcy, 1643', *Journal of British Studies,* XXVIII (1989); R. J. Dalton, 'Gerrard Winstanley: the experience of fraud 1641', *Historical Journal,* XXXIV, 4 (1991).

[2] See, for example, H. E. Malden (ed.), *The Victoria county history of Surrey (V. C. H. Surrey),* I (London, 1902), 422; Malden, *A history of Surrey* (London, 1900), pp. 252-4, based largely on Whitelocke's account of local opposition: Bulstrode Whitelocke, *Memorials of the English affairs* (Oxford, 1853), III, 23. Local opposition is emphasized in J. S. Morrill and J. D. Walter, 'Order and disorder in the English revolution', in *Order and disorder in early modern England, 1500-1714,* ed. Anthony Fletcher and John Stevenson (Cambridge, 1985), p. 160. See also Buchanan Sharpe, 'Popular protest in seventeenth-century England', in *Popular culture in seventeenth-century England,* ed. Barry Reay (London, 1985), pp. 299-300, for the suggestion that the Digger programme conflicted with the interests of rural cottagers, and Brian Manning, 'The peasantry and the English revolution', *Journal of Peasant Studies,* II (1975), 155, for the view that the overwhelming mass of peasants would be antagonized by such schemes; cf. Manning, *The English people and*

the English revolution (Harmondsworth, 1978), pp. 315-16; Ronald Hutton, *The British Republic* (London, 1990), pp. 31-2. For the Iver Diggers, see Keith Thomas, 'Another Digger broadside', *Past and Present,* XLII (1969), 57-68.

[3] British Library (B.L.), E 529(18): *A perfect diurnall of some passages in parliament* (16-23 April 1649), pp. 2448, 2450; E 529(22): *The kingdomes faithfull and impartiall scout* (20-7 April); E 529(24) *A perfect summary of an exact dyarie* (23-30 April); E 552(7): *A modest narrative of intelligence* (21-8 April); E 556(29): *Mercurius republicus* (22-9 May), p. 5. Whitelocke's account was, of course, drawn from these reports.

[4] D. W. Petegorsky, *Left-wing democracy in the English Civil War* (London, 1940), pp. 162-8.

[5] Ibid. pp. 165-7; Olivier Lutaud, *Winstanley: socialisme et christianisme sous Cromwell* (Paris, 1976), pp. 177-8; Christopher Hill, *The world turned upside down* (Harmondsworth, 1975), p. 118; cf. B.L. E 551(15): *Mercurius pragmaticus (for Charles II)* (17-24 April 1649). Whitelocke referred to the Diggers as Levellers: Add. MS 37,344 (Bulstrode Whitelocke's annals), fos. 283, 286. Aubrey later assumed that the 'great Meeting of Levellers' on St George's Hill had been 'headed and encourag'd by John Lilburn': John Aubrey, *The natural history and antiquities of the county of Surrey* (London, 1718-19), III, 95.

[6] Lutaud, *Winstanley,* p. 178. For later reports during the summer, see for example B.L. E 532(4): *The moderate messenger* (23-30 July 1649); E 566(4): *Moderate intelligencer* (19-26 July).

[7] G. H. Sabine (ed.), *The works of Gerrard Winstanley* (Ithaca, 1941), pp. 282, 392; B.L. E 530(24): *The speeches of the lord generall Fairfax . . . to the Diggers* (1649).

[8] Sabine, *Works,* pp. 295-8.

[9] Ibid. pp. 295, 392; cf. Clive Holmes, 'Drainers and fenmen', in Fletcher and Stevenson, *Order and disorder,* pp. 166-95 for middling-sort leadership of riots in the fens.

[10] Sabine, *Works,* pp. 14, 392.

[11] Surrey County Record Office (S.R.O.), Royal Borough of Kingston archives, KE1/1/14 (Kingston court of Record book 1645-54), 23 June 1649; Sabine, *Works,* pp. 18, 272-4, 301, 319-35.

[12] *The Clarke papers,* ed. C. H. Firth, II (London, Camden Society, 1894), 210-11.

[13] Sabine, *Works,* pp. 295-6, 331, 392.

[14] For Starr, see P.R.O., E317/41/44 (parliamentary survey of Painshill and Cobham Bridge, March 1650) and 55 (survey of Walton Leigh, March 1650); E134/19 Jas I/T2 (James Starr *vs.* Robert Bickerstaffe); SP28/180 (unfol.), Walton-upon-Thames parish accounts (abstracts); Greater London Record Office (G.L.R.O.), DW/PA/7/14 (will of William Starr of Walton, 1661); Guildford Muniment Room (G.M.R.), PSH/COB/1/1 (Cobham parish registers), pp. 24, 47, 52.

[15] P.R.O., ASSI 35/89/5 (Assizes, home circuit, indictments and other documents: Kingston, Sep. 1648).

[16] P.R.O., Prob. 11/118, fo. 264 (will of Richard Taylor of Walton, carpenter, 1 Oct. 1611). The two John Taylors are described in the will as his second and third sons. The elder son was a carpenter and the younger a bricklayer: Prob. 11/272, fo. 346v (will of John Taylor of Walton, carpenter, 6 Feb. 1657); Guildhall Library, London (G.L.), 9051/6, fo. 143v (will of Richard Taylor, citizen and carpenter of London, 9 Sep. 1624); S.R.O., 2381/1/1 (Walton parish registers, 1639-53), p. 5; *Kingston-upon-Thames register of apprentices 1563-1713,* ed. Anne Daly (Kingston: Surrey Record Society, 1974), p. 23.

[17] John Taylor's brother Samuel left £10 to parliament in his will 'for the good of the Kingdome': G.L.R.O., DW/PA/7/13, fo. 308 (will of Samuel Taylor son of Richard Taylor, 14 Sep. 1643); P.R.O., SP28/180, Walton parish accounts (abstracts); S.R.O., 2381/1/1, p. 4.

[18] G.L.R.O., DW/PA/7/13, fo. 308, for John Taylor the bricklayer, 'now a souldier'; P.R.O., SP28/35, fo. 356 (schedule of soldiers at Basing and owners of arms, Elmbridge hundred, June 1644), for William and Mark Taylor of Walton (the latter served on behalf of Thomas Knight, Samuel Taylor's father-in-law).

[19] P.R.O. SP28/35, fo. 359 (list of parochial assessors appointed in Kingston and Elmbridge hundreds, May 1643).

[20] SP28/291 (unfol.), certificate of Walton assessors 11 March 1650.

[21] Sabine, *Works,* pp. 259, 315-16.

[22] Ibid. p. 259.

[23] Ibid. p. 282; cf. p. 506.

[24] Ibid. p. 273.

[25] Ibid. pp. 296, 330.

[26] Christopher Hill, *Religion and politics in seventeenth century England* (Brighton, 1986), p. 206; Hill,

Winstanley: the law of freedom and other writings (Cambridge, 1983), pp. 39-40; Thomas, 'Another Digger broadside', p. 64; J. C. Davis, 'Gerrard Winstanley and the restoration of true magistracy', *Past and Present,* LXX (1976), 79.

[27] Sabine, *Works,* pp. 272, 282-6, 296, 301, 305-7, 326.

[28] Ibid. p. 296.

[29] B.L. E 551(9): *A modest narrative of intelligence* (14-21 April 1649), p. 23; Sabine, *Works,* pp. 266, 282-3.

[30] Ibid. p. 282; cf. Hill, *Religion and politics,* p. 219.

[31] Sabine, *Works,* pp. 191-2, 194, 196-7, 199-200, 205-6, 208, 258, 262-6; Hill, *Religion and politics,* pp. 204, 218-19, 220.

[32] Sabine, *Works,* pp. 305, 326.

[33] Ibid. pp. 285-6, for example.

[34] Ibid. pp. 190-1, 194, 262; cf. Timothy Kenyon, *Utopian communism and political thought in early modern England* (London, 1989), pp. 165-6, 176, 178; Davis, 'Restoration of true magistracy', pp. 81-3; Hill, *Religion and politics,* pp. 206, 220.

[35] *Clarke papers,* II, 210.

[36] P.R.O., E134/29,30 Eliz/M17 (Henry Dogwell et al. *vs.* Robert Benne), deposition of John Greentree of Walton; E134/32 Eliz/E14 (Robert Alexander et al. *vs.* Robert Benne), deposition of Thomas Downes of Cobham.

[37] P.R.O., E134/29,30 Eliz/M17, depositions of Robert Dally of Walton and William Greentree of Hersham in Walton; E134/32 Eliz/E14, deposition of William Taylor of Walton. The right of all inhabitants to use the commons was already being questioned by at least one tenant in 1587: E134/29,30 Eliz/M17, deposition of John Hellys of Walton; cf. S.R.O., 442 (abstracts of court rolls, nine manors, 1606-16), fo. 42v, for later attempts to curb the influx of migrants and cottagers in Walton.

[38] P.R.O., E134/32 Eliz/E14, depositions of John Frye of Apps in Walton and Robert Stackford of West Molesey.

[39] P.R.O., E134/9 Jas I/H7 (Robert Bickerstaffe et al. *vs.* James Starr). By 1650, much of Lakefield had been turned over to arable: E317/41/44, p. 6.

[40] P.R.O., LR2/197, fos. 6-9 (survey of Oatlands and Weybridge, 2 Jas I); LR2/197, fos. 192-5v (survey of Walton Leigh, 2 Jas I); E317/40/38 (parliamentary survey of East Molesey, Feb. 1651); E134/29,30 Eliz/M17, depositions of William Greentree and Robert Dally.

[41] P.R.O., E317/41/55, pp. 10, 12.

[42] P.R.O., LR2/197, fo. 8v.

[43] P.R.O., E134/29,30 Eliz/M17; E134/32 Eliz/E14.

[44] William Lilly, *History of his life and times* (ed. E. Ashmole, London, 1715), p. 94.

[45] R. T. Vann, 'Diggers and quakers - a further note', *Journal of the Friends' Historical Society,* L (1962), 65.

[46] Sabine, *Works,* pp. 260-1; *Clarke papers,* II, 211. St George's Hill lay close to the busy London to Portsmouth road.

[47] Sabine, *Works,* p. 277. 29 of these 32 are not mentioned in other Digger related documents.

[48] S.R.O., 2381/1/1, pp. 2, 3, 4.

[49] S.R.O., Kingston archives, KE1/1/14, 27 Oct., 17 Nov. 1649.

[50] P.R.O., SP18/16/140 (certificate of parliamentary surveyors, Surrey, 1651).

[51] P.R.O., C231/6 (crown office docquet book 1642-60), p. 166. Oatlands palace lay in the parish of Weybridge, but much of the park lay in Walton, and bordered Walton Heath close to St George's Hill: LR2/197, fos. 6-9; LR2/297, fos. 105-12, 113-18 (parliamentary surveys of Oatlands house and park, June 1650).

[52] P.R.O., C231/6, p. 141.

[53] P.R.O., ASSI 35/91/4 (home circuit: gen., Lent 1650), m. 40.

[54] S.R.O., Kingston archives, KE1/1/14, 23 June 1649; Sabine, *Works,* pp. 319, 327.

[55] B.L. E 787(34): John Fielder, *The humble petition and appeal of John Fielder of Kingston miller, to the parliament of the common-wealth of England* (London, 1651), p. 5; cf. L. F. Solt, 'Winstanley, Lilburne, and the case of John Fielder', *Huntington Library Quarterly,* XLV, 2 (1982), for a detailed description of the case.

[56] For Winstanley's career before 1649, see especially

Alsop, 'Ethics in the marketplace'; Dalton, 'Experience of fraud'.

[57] G.L.R.O., DW/PA/7/13, fo. 95 (will of Robert Bickerstaffe of Walton, gentleman, 8 Sep. 1640); G.M.R., PSH/COB/1/1, p. 42. (Robert Bickerstaffe is mistakenly referred to as Henry in the 18th century transcripts of the parish register.)

[58] P.R.O., E317/41/44; LR2/197, fo. 193v; SC12/15/43 (Walton, Weybridge, Esher and Oatlands rental [22 Jas I]); C10/468/162 (John Povey *vs.* James and William Bickerstaffe, John and Margaret Platt, Robert Gavell, and Henry Baldwin, 1661); C5/592/2 (Rebecca Bickerstaffe *vs.* William Bickerstaffe, 1662); C2/CHAS I/B170/46 (Rebecca *vs.* William Bickerstaffe).

[59] P.R.O., SP16/11/21 (Sir George More to the privy council, 5 Dec 1625); E401/2586 (loan assessment, Surrey); E178/7284 (schedule of knighthood defaulters).

[60] P.R.O., E134/19 Jas I/T2, depositions of George Gyldon of Kingston and Elizabeth Dalton Weybridge; E134/9 Jas I/H7.

[61] Skinners' Hall, London, Skinners' company register of apprenticeships and freedoms 1601-94, fos. 48, 83, 194 (I am grateful to the clerk of the Skinners' company for permission to consult records held at Skinners' Hall); P.R.O., E179/251/22 (poll tax assessments, by company, 1641), fo. 261v; G.L.R.O., DW/PA/7/13, fo. 95.

[62] P.R.O., Prob. 11/248, fos. 393v-5 (will of Antony Bickerstaffe of Christ Church parish London, citizen and Skinner, 19 May 1654); Jenkyn was an executor of the will and was left 20s. for preaching a sermon.

[63] Corporation of London Record Office (C.L.R.O.), Journal of the court of common council, 40, fo. 153v; Michael Mahony, 'Presbyterianism in the City of London, 1645-1647', *Historical Journal*, XXII, I (1979), 105, III; Tai Liu, *Puritan London* (Newark, New Jersey, 1986), p. 95.

[64] *Commons Journal* (*C.J.*), v, 216; B.L. 669 fo. 11 (30); *Five orders and ordinances of parliament for payment of soldiers* (London, 1647). The Walton Bickerstaffes were closely related to the royalist Hayward Bickerstaffe of Godstone, for whom see P.R.O., SP23/186/890-900 (composition papers, Hayward Bickerstaffe); SP28/218 (unfol.), breviate of Surrey sequestrations; Prob. 11/207, fo. 101 (will of Hayward Bickerstaffe of Godstone, 15 May 1647); E317/41/44, pp. 7-8; *Lords Journal* (*L.J.*), v, 686; vi, 53.

[65] Skinners' Hall, register 1601-94, ff. 87, 108v; C.L.R.O., CF1/25/131v (Henry Bickerstaffe, certificate of freedom, 11 April 1633).

[66] For apprentices taken on by Anthony Bickerstaffe in the years 1635-46, see Skinners' Hall, register 1601-94, fos. 117, 124, 145v, 154, 155.

[67] P.R.O., E179/251/22, fo. 222v; T. C. Dale (ed.), *The members of the City companies in 1641* (London, 1935), p. 18. (I am grateful to Robert Dalton for this reference.)

[68] G.M.R., PSH/COB/1/1, p. 39. His son was baptized at Cobham on 1 Jan. 1640; as residents of Painshill, the Bickerstaffes attended Cobham church rather than the more distant church of Walton: pp. 10, 15, 36, 42, 45.

[69] Anthony Bickerstaffe's home was in Newgate market: P.R.O., E317/41/44, p. 9.

[70] P.R.O., SP28/177 (unfol.), answers of farmers, fee-farmers and others, Kingston, 21 Nov. 1643.

[71] *Forresta de Windsor in com. Surrey. The meers, meets, limits and bounds of the forrest of Windsor, in the county of Surrey* London, 1646), p. 13.

[72] P.R.O., SP28/179 (unfol.), accounts of John Redferne; SP28/180 (unfol.), Walton parish accounts (abstracts), in which the sum of £4 12s6d. is given; *Surrey contributors to the relief of protestant refugees from Ireland, 1642,* ed. C. Webb (London: East Surrey Family History Society, 1981).

[73] P.R.O., SP28/35, fo. 359; SP28/180 (unfol.), Walton parish accounts (abstracts). He collected taxes in Walton for the Farnham garrison in 1645; SP28/177 (unfol.), accounts of Sackford Gunson.

[74] P.R.O., SP28/179 (unfol.), accounts of Sir John Dingley; SP28/180 (unfol.), Walton parish accounts (abstracts).

[75] P.R.O., SP28/35, fo. 357; SP28/180 (unfol.), Walton parish accounts (abstracts). Starr had witnessed Robert Bickerstaffe's will: G.L.R.O., DW/PA/7/13, fo. 95; the dispute between the two families may therefore have been settled by 1640.

[76] Sabine, *Works,* p. 266.

[77] S.R.O., Kingston parish registers (typescripts), p. 205.

[78] P.R.O., C9/243/14 (James Bickerstaffe *vs.* Henry Bickerstaffe et al., 1659), complaint of James Bickerstaffe, answers of Henry Bickerstaffe, Robert and Winifred Trolliffe and John Fleming; cf. C33/211, fos.

40v, 128, 550. Anthony Bickerstaffe bought Painshill of the state in April 1650; E121/4/8 (certificates of the sale of crown lands, Surrey).

[79] S.R.O., Kingston archives, KB/13/3/4 (Kingston gaolers' bonds). Another gaoler was appointed less than 6 months later: KB/13/3/5.

[80] Sabine, *Works,* pp. 18, 317, 331, 337. The Diggers were still present on St George's Hill when a petition was presented to parliament on 24 July: B.L. E 532(4): *The moderate messenger* (23-30 July 1649); E 566(4): *Moderate intelligencer* (19-26 July).

[81] Sabine, *Works,* pp. 326, 331, 336.

[82] B. L. Egerton MS, 2618, fo. 38 (council of state to Fairfax, 10 Oct. 1649); P.R.O., SP25/94, pp. 477-8 (council of state to Surrey justices, 10 Oct.).

[83] S.R.O., Kingston archives, KE1/1/14, 29 Oct., 17 Nov., 1 Dec. 1649; B.L. E 575(22): *A brief relation* (16 Oct. 1649); E 575(27): *Mercurius elenticus* (15-22 Oct.); Sabine, *Works,* pp. 19, 360.

[84] P.R.O., ASSI 35/91/4, m. 40; *Clarke papers,* II, 216; Sabine, *Works,* pp. 365-7.

[85] P.R.O., ASSI 35/91/10 (home circuit; gen., summer 1650), mm. 149, 151. The date given on the presentments was 1 March.

[86] Sabine, *Works,* pp. 385, 387, for later references to freeholders.

[87] Ibid. pp. 407-15; *Englands spirit unfoulded, or an incouragement to take the Engagement* (1650), ed. G. E. Aylmer, *Past and Present,* XL (1968), 9-15; Hill, *Law of freedom,* pp. 38-9; Hill, *Religion and politics,* p. 218.

[88] Sabine, *Works,* pp. 407, 412; Hill, *Religion and politics,* pp. 205-6.

[89] Sabine, *Works,* pp. 367-8; cf. pp. 434-5.

[90] Ibid. pp. 296, 412.

[91] Ibid. p. 412; Aylmer (ed.), *Englands spirit unfoulded,* p. 13.

[92] T. E. C. Walker, 'Cobham's manorial history', *Surrey Archaeological Collections (S.A.C.),* LVIII (1961), 41. Platt was not resident in Cobham; the manor house was leased to Captain John Inwood of Walton.

[93] Sabine, *Works,* p. 435.

[94] P.R.O. SP18/42/144 (Jerrard Winstanley and John Palmer to the council of state, n.d. [Dec. 1649]); *Clarke papers,* II 217, for the Diggers' first mention of Platt.

[95] Ibid. p. 217; Sabine, *Works,* pp. 362, 365-6, 393.

[96] Ibid. pp. 433-7.

[97] Ibid. pp. 434-6. Sabine's suggestion that this was in fact Sir Francis Vincent is based on an error in O. Manning and W. Bray, *History and antiquities of the county of Surrey* (1804-14; reprint Wakefield, 1970), II, 724-5, in which the date of Sir Anthony's death is given as 1642. The error was repeated in Sabine's source, *V.C.H. Surrey,* III (London, 1911), 286. Vincent did not die until 1656: P.R.O., Prob. 11/260, fo. 379 (will of Sir Anthony Vincent of Stoke d'Abernon, 29 May 1654); W. Bruce Bannerman (ed.), *The parish registers of Stoke d' Abernon* (London, 1911), p. 34.

[98] Sabine, *Works,* pp. 392, 433; Hill, *World turned upside down,* p. 131; Walker, 'Cobham', p. 49.

[99] *Clarke papers,* II, 216, 218.

[100] P.R.O., SP28/177 (unfol.), accounts of Henry Hastings.

[101] P.R.O., SP28/214 (unfol.), accounts of Henry Wilcock; cf. SP28/244 (unfol.), warrants of JPs to high constables of Elmbridge hundred, 21 April, 1 May, 6 May 1643; SP16/497/85 (assessment commissioners' warrant to high constables of Elmbridge hundred, 16 May 1643). He remained active as a JP: ASSI 35/88/6 (home circuit, gen., autumn 1647); ASSI 35/89/5.

[102] P.R.O., SP19/86/57 (Surrey compositions, Holland's rising).

[103] Sabine, *Works,* pp. 433, 435. For the Sutton family, see Walker, 'Manorial history', pp. 48, 71, 75; Alsop, 'Religion and respectability', pp. 707-8.

[104] Fielder, *Petition and appeal,* p. 5.

[105] P.R.O., Prob. 11/227, fo. 134v (will of Thomas Sutton of Cobham, gent, 2 Sep. 1650); SP28/179 (unfol.), Cobham parish accounts; SP28/244 (unfol.), county committee warrant to Sackford Gunson, 7 Nov. 1644; ASSI 35/92/8 (Kingston, July 1651); ASSI 35/93/5 (Southwark, March 1652); ASSI 35/93/7 (Kingston, July 1652); ASSI 35/94/7 (Southwark, March 1653).

[106] Sabine, *Works,* pp. 419-47.

[107] Ibid. pp. 433-5.

[108] Ibid. pp. 435-6.

[109] P.R.O., ASSI 35/91/10, mm. 119-22.

[110] Sabine, *Works,* pp. 420-1, 433-7. Easter day was 14 April; Winstanley claimed that the attack took place on 'Fryday in Easter week', i.e. the 19th.

[111] Ibid. pp. 266, 277, 413-14, 440; *Clarke papers,* II, 217; P.R.O., ASSI 35/91/4, m. 40; S.R.O., Kingston archives, KE1/1/14, 23 June 1649.

[112] Above, note 85.

[113] Barton, Edsarr, Mills and Lowry are not mentioned elsewhere as Diggers or Digger sympathisers; only male Diggers signed Digger manifestoes.

[114] P.R.O., SP28/244 (unfol.), county committee warrant to high constables of Elmbridge hundred, 29 Nov. 1643; Bannerman, *Stoke parish registers,* pp. 3, 33, 46; *Surrey hearth tax 1664* (ed. C. A. F. Meekings, Kingston, Surrey Record Society, 1940), pp. 27, 46, 135. In the draft indictments, the accused were all said to be of Cobham, the scene of the alleged offence.

[115] Sabine, *Works,* p. 434; P.R.O., Prob. 11/260, fo. 378v.

[116] P.R.O., SP28/245 (unfol.), accounts of Augustine Phillips.

[117] S.R.O., Acc. 317/566/IX (Cobham court rolls, 1647 and 1648); Acc. 2610/11/8/33 (Cobham manor court book, 1624-31), pp. 35, 39, 53; G.M.R., PSH/COB/1/1, pp. 10, 18, 19, 25-6, 45, 48-9, 92-3; P.R.O., SC12/22/34 (schedule of quit-rents, Cobham, 1626); G.L.R.O., DW/PA/7/10, fo. 144 (will of John Melsham the elder of Cobham, yeoman, 6 Nov. 1620).

[118] *Surrey quarter sessions records: order book and sessions rolls 1663-1666* (ed. D. L. Powell and H. Jenkinson, Kingston, Surrey Record Society, 1938), p. 3; cf. G.M.R., PSH/COB/5/1 (Cobham church book 1588-1839), accounts for 1662, 1663, 1667, 1669, 1670, for receipts by Goose of parish relief.

[119] P.R.O., ASSI 35/92/8; above, note 15.

[120] *Quarter sessions records 1663-6,* p. 72.

[121] P.R.O., SP28/35, fo. 359; SP28/159 (unfol.), schedule of assessments, Surrey, middle division, 1645-6; SP28/177 (unfol.), Stoke d'Abernon parish accounts; SP28/178 (unfol.), accounts of Sackford Gunson; SP28/179 (unfol.), Cobham parish accounts.

[122] P.R.O., SP28/179 (unfol.), accounts of Henry Hastings and John Redferne; S.R.O., Acc. 317/566/IX.

[123] *Clarke Papers,* 11, 210.

[124] Petegorsky, *Left-wing democracy,* p. 124; Alsop, 'Later life', pp. 73-5. The most detailed accounts of his business failure are Alsop, 'Ethics in the marketplace' and Dalton, 'Experience of fraud'.

[125] G.L., MS 4415/1 (St Olave Jewry vestry minutes), fo. 118.

[126] P.R.O., SP28/178 (unfol.), county committee warrant to high constables of Elmbridge hundred, 20 Dec. 1643; SP28/245 (unfol.), accounts of Augustine Phillips.

[127] S.R.O., Acc. 317/566/IX; Sabine, *Works,* pp. 328-34; Walker, 'Manorial history', p. 70.

[128] *Clarke papers,* 11, 210.

[129] S.R.O., Acc. 317/566/IX; ASSI 35/91/4, m. 40; S.R.O., Kingston archives, KE1/1/14, 23 June 1649; Sabine, *Works,* pp. 266, 277, 414, 440.

[130] G.L.R.O., DW/PA/7/12, fo. 495 (will of Edmund Starr of Cobham, clothworker, 26 May 1638); G.M.R., PSH/COB/1/1, pp. 5, 7, 11, 16, 39.

[131] S.R.O., Acc. 317/566/IX.

[132] Sabine, *Works,* p. 328.

[133] *Quarter sessions records 1663-6,* p. 241.

[134] Sabine, *Works,* pp. 266, 277, 414; *Clarke papers,* 11, 217.

[135] For Coulton and his family, see S.R.O., Acc. 2610/11/8/33, pp. 35, 39, 53; Acc. 317/566/VIII (Cobham court rolls, 1613-23); Acc. 317/566/IX; G.M.R., PSH/COB/1/1, pp. 5, 7, 16, 17, 19, 26, 28, 31, 35, 44, 52, 55; PSH/COB/5/1, accounts for 1629-30; P.R.O., SC2/204/43 (Cobham court rolls, 5 Eliz. 12 Jas I); SC12/22/34; Daly (ed.), *Kingston apprentices,* p. 48.

[136] P.R.O. SP28/35, fo. 359; SP28/177 (unfol.), accounts of Sackford Gunson; SP28/179 (unfol.), accounts of Henry Hastings and John Redferne.

[137] P.R.O., SP28/35, fo. 356; SP28/179 (unfol.), Cobham parish accounts.

[138] S.R.O., Acc. 317/566/IX.

[139] P.R.O., Prob. 11/224, fo. 307v (will of John Coulton of Cobham, yeoman, 15 June 1652). The will was proved 14 Sep. 1652.

[140] S.R.O., Acc. 317/566/IX.

[141] G.M.R., PSH/COB/1/1, pp. 41, 45; S.R.O., Acc. 317/566/IX.

[142] G.M.R., PSH/COB/1/1, pp. 44, 54, 57.

[143] P.R.O., Prob. 11/298, fo. 300 (will of Francis Stint the elder of Cobham, husbandman, 24 April 1658). Nathaniel Coulton, John Coulton's nephew, was one of the overseers.

[144] P.R.O., E179/257/30 (Surrey hearth tax returns, 1663); G.M.R., PSH/COB/1/1, p. 75.

[145] Sabine, *Works,* pp. 277, 413-4, 440; *Clarke papers,* 11, 217.

[146] P.R.O., RG6/956 (Kingston quaker registers, 1658-1779), p. 7; RG6/1240 (registers, 1649-73), p. 3.

[147] G.M.R., PSH/COB/1/1, pp. 44, 45.

[148] G.M.R., PSH/COB/5/1, accounts for 1657; P.R.O., ASSI 35/94/12 (home circuit; gen., summer 1653), m. 121; ASSI 35/99/7 (Southwark, March 1658). Also charged with Johnson was Thomas Ward of Cobham. A Thomas Ward stood surety for Henry Bickerstaffe in Kingston court in June 1649 (S.R.O., KE1/1/14). On 12 April 1650, at the height of the campaign against the Diggers, Thomas Ward of Cobham was informed against for having fought for the king in the Civil War: P.R.O., SP19/22, p. 37. Thomas Ward of Kingston was awarded a royalist pension in 1663: *Surrey quarter sessions records: order book and sessions rolls 1661-3,* ed. D. L. Powell and H. Jenkinson (Kingston: Surrey Record Society, 1935), p. 70.

[149] P.R.O., Prob. 11/298, fo. 300.

[150] G.M.R., PSH/COB/1/1, p. 60; PSH/COB/5/1, accounts for 1662; Meekings, *Surrey hearth tax,* p. 60; G.L.R.O., DW/PC/1/1, fo. 53v (will of Mary Freeland of Cobham, Feb. 1665).

[151] G.M.R., PSH/COB/1/1, p. 44; S.R.O., Acc. 317/566/IX.

[152] Details of baptisms from 1644 were not registered until 1656; records of marriages and burials were not collected; G.M.R., PSH/COB/1/1, pp. 1, 47.

[153] Sabine, *Works,* p. 434 (my italics).

[154] Possibly the illegitimate son of Julian Palmer, baptized in Cobham Nov. 1611 (G.M.R., PSH/COB/1/1, p. 5), or the son of John Palmer of Cobham, blacksmith, apprenticed in 1626 to William Stedwell of Kingston, baker: Daly (ed.), *Kingston apprentices,* p. 36. A Cobham resident was fined in 1630 for receiving a John Palmer as an inmate in his cottage: S.R.O.,

Acc. 2610/11/8/33, p. 37. John Palmer of Cobham had two hearths in 1664, and was exempted from the hearth tax: Meekings, *Surrey hearth tax,* p. 116.

[155] In 1664 'Ould South' of Cobham had one hearth (exempt). He was in receipt of parish relief in 1668 (Old South), and in 1669 and 1670 (John South): G.M.R., PSH/COB/5/1. John South was buried in 1672: PSH/COB/1/1, p. 71.

[156] He married Phoebe Coulton, whose grandfather Robert was the brother of John Coulton the Digger, in 1658. Their children were baptized in 1659, 1663, 1666, 1669 and 1674: G.M.R., PSH/COB/1/1, pp. 53-4, 58, 61, 66, 74; G.L.R.O., DW/PC/5/1665/Coulton, Robert (will of Robert Coulton of Burwood in Walton, husbandman, 24 Feb. 1665); DW/PC/5/1665/Coulton, Joseph (will of Joseph Coulton of Cobham the elder, 23 Jan. 1665). Thomas South had 2 hearths in 1663 and was in receipt of relief in 1674: P.R.O., E179/257/30; G.M.R., PSH/COB/5/1.

[157] Anthony Wrenn was, until 1649, occupier of a warren house leased from George Evelyn of Wotton: Walker, 'Cobham's manorial history', p. 76; D. C. Taylor, 'Old Mistral, Cobham: a sixteenth-century warrener's house identified', *S.A.C.* LXXIX (1989), 119. David Taylor also identifies Wrenn as a Digger.

[158] Sabine, *Works,* pp. 266, 277, 413, 440; *Clarke papers,* II, 217; P.R.O., SP18/42/144; ASSI 35/91/4, m. 40; ASSI 35/91/10, mm. 119-22.

[159] Sabine, *Works,* pp. 266, 277, 413, 440; *Clarke papers,* II, 217.

[160] Bannerman, *Stoke parish registers,* pp. 4, 6, 7; Meekings, *Surrey hearth tax,* p. 52.

[161] Thomas, 'Another Digger broadside', pp. 649-50.

[162] For which, see P. H. Hardacre, 'Gerrard Winstanley in 1650', *Huntington Library Quarterly,* XXII, 4 (1959).

[163] P.R.O., ASSI 35/91/4, m. 40. These included Winstanley, Barton, Starr, Palmer, Edsaw, Bickerstaffe and Maidley.

[164] P.R.O., ASSI 35/91/5 (Croydon, July 1650); ASSI 35/92/7 (Southwark, March 1651); ASSI 35/92/8; ASSI 35/93/5; ASSI 35/94/8 (Croydon, July 1653).

[165] P.R.O., Prob. 11/224, fo. 307v; S.R.O., Acc. 317/566/IX.

[166] G.M.R., PSH/COB/1/1, p. 47; T. E. C. Walker, 'Cobham incumbents and curates'; *S.A.C.* LXXI (1977), 209; A. G. Matthews, *Walker revised* (Oxford, 1948), p. 310.

[167] P.R.O., SP28/179 (unfol.), accounts of Henry Hastings and John Redferne; Cobham parish accounts; Webb, *Ireland;* A. G. Matthews, *Calamy revised* (Oxford, 1934), p. 226; cf. Dalton. 'Experience of fraud', p. 977. It is not clear whether he was ever formally instituted as vicar of Cobham.

[168] Aubrey, *History of Surrey,* III, 126; Manning and Bray, *History,* I, CXIX.

[169] Sabine, *Works,* p. 326.

[170] G.L., MS 4415/1, fos. 101-5v, 109v. Winstanley first attended on 30 Apr. 1641, and the last occasion was 19 Jan. 1643; 14 meetings are known to have taken place during this period.

[171] G.L., MS 4415/1, fo. 104; cf. V. Pearl, *London and the outbreak of the puritan revolution* (Oxford, 1961), pp. 54-6.

[172] Tai Liu, *Puritan London,* p. 108; G.L., MS 4415/1, fo. 101v, for Feake; Keith Lindley, 'London and popular freedom in the 1640s', in *Freedom and the English revolution,* ed R. C. Richardson and G. M. Ridden (Manchester, 1986), p. 139.

[173] S.R.O., Kingston archives, KD5/1/2 (Kingston chamberlains' accounts, 1638-1710), p. 63; P.R.O., SP28/244 (unfol.), county committee warrant to Sackford Gunson, 15 Aug. 1644.

[174] B.L. E 278(20): Richard Byfield, *Temple-defilers defiled* (1645), passim; cf. Richard Mayo, *The life and death of Edmund Staunton* (London, 1673), pp. 11-12, for Staunton's problems with 'wrangling persons' in Kingston.

[175] Fielder, *Petition and appeal,* pp. 1-5, 13-17, 20-3; P.R.O., SP24/61 (unfol.), Lidgold *vs.* Fielder, petition of Richard Lidgold and John Childe to committee of indemnity, 3 May 1650; Solt, 'Winstanley, Lilburne, Fielder', pp. 120, 127.

[176] Sabine, *Works,* p. 99.

[177] S.R.O., Kingston archives, KE2/7/3; KE2/7/4/; KE2/7/12 (papers relating to the arrest and conviction of sectaries, 1664 and 1670); P.R.O., RG6/956; RG6/1240; Joseph Besse, *A collection of the sufferings of the people called quakers* (London, 1753), 1, 698, 707.

[178] Fielder, *Petition and appeal,* p. 2; Sabine, *Works,* p. 277.

[179] G.L.R.O., DW/PA/7/9, fo. 265v (will of Urian Worthington of New Windsor, Berks, yeoman, 20 April 1615); DW/PA/7/10, fo. 94 (will of John Worthington of Thorpe, husbandman, n.d., proved Nov. 1619).

[180] *Quarter sessions records 1663—6,* p. 176; Besse, *Sufferings,* 1, 699; Van, 'Diggers and quakers', p. 66.

[181] S.R.O., Kingston archives, KE1/1/14, 17 Nov. 1649. Gosse also later became a quaker.

[182] *V.C.H. Surrey,* III, 443-4; Walker, 'Manorial history', pp. 48-50.

[183] P.R.O., REQ 2/34/23 (William Wrenn *vs.* Robert Gavell); REQ 2/157/503 (Wrenn *vs.* Gavell, papers 1579-94); REQ 2/159/192 (Wrenn *vs.* Gavell, depositions 1577).

[184] P.R.O., REQ 2/159/13 (Anthony Bickerstaffe et al. *vs.* Robert and Francis Gavell, Chancery depositions 1594); SP15/33/74 (William King et al. *vs.* Robert and Francis Gavell, Chancery bill and related documents). (Anthony Bickerstaffe was the father of Robert Bickerstaffe of Walton.)

[185] P.R.O., SP15/40/48(1) (note of Francis Gavell's debts and legacies).

[186] P.R.O., REQ 2/159/13; SP15/33/74.

[187] P.R.O., SP15/33/74, answer of Robert and Francis Gavell.

[188] P.R.O., SP46/19/212 (draft order, court of Kings Bench, 21 Nov. 1593).

[189] P.R.O., REQ 2/159/13, depositions of James Smyth and James Hypkin of Cobham, labourers, 1594; Prob. 11/320, fo. 103 (will of William King, 6 June 1664); Alsop, 'Religion and respectability', p. 707.

[190] S.R.O., 2610/1/38/22 (court of Wards order, 1638); Walker, Manorial history', p. 49.

[191] For the economic and social background, see especially Hill, *World turned upside down,* pp. 107-8; Hill, *Law of freedom,* pp. 22-6; cf. Thomas, 'Another Digger broadside', p. 58; Sabine, *Works,* pp. 263, 265, 414-15, 431-2, 650.

[192] P.R.O., SP28/179 (unfol.), Cobham parish accounts. Taxes paid before the outbreak of war amounted to £96 11*s.* 10*d.* wartime assessments to £464 17*s.* 8*d.* (including the second moiety of the £400,000 tax, which was not raised in Surrey until 1643), and the excise to £142 8*d.*

[193] P.R.O., SP28/178 (unfol.), Egham parish accounts (n.d., April or May 1645). Tooting's inhabitants had spent only £120 13*s.* 3*d.* in free quarter by Feb. 1645; Woodmansterne's bill was just over £40: SP28/178, Tooting parish accounts; SP28/180 (unfol.), Woodmansterne parish accounts (abstracts).

[194] The quote is form John Platt and his West Horsley parishioners: P.R.O., SP28/177 (unfol.), West Horsley parish accounts (Nov. 1645).

[195] P.R.O., SP28/179 (unfol.), Cobham parish accounts; Dalton, 'Experience of fraud', p. 976. These were inhabitants of Street Cobham, which lay on the Portsmouth road.

[196] P.R.O., SP19/98/90A (certif. of committee for the safety of Surrey on behalf of Capt. John Inwood of Walton, 6 May 1645); SP28/11, fo. 170 (petition of [Elizabeth Hammond] of Chertsey, n.d.); SP28/177 (unfol.), answers of farmers, fee-farmers and others, 21 Nov. 1643; Byfleet parish accounts; Chertsey parish accounts; SP28/178 (unfol.), Egham parish accounts; SP28/180 (unfol.), Walton parish accounts (abstracts); *Calendar of the proceedings of the committee for advance of money 1642-56,* ed. M. A. E. Green (London, 1888), p. 40. Francis Drake's house in Walton was plundered: B. L. Harl. MS 164 (Parliamentary diary of Sir Simonds D'Ewes), fos. 290-290v.

[197] House of Lords Record Office (H.L.R.O.), main papers 1647, 20 Nov., petition of John Turner; 19 Nov., Sir Thomas Fairfax to Robert Scawen; P.R.O., SP24/47 (unfol.), petition of 'the farmers of Surrey' to Fairfax; *V.C.H. Surrey,* 1, 413-14.

[198] Morrill and Walter, 'Order and disorder', passim.

[199] cf. A. Hughes, *Politics, society and civil war in Warwickshire, 1620-1660* (Cambridge, 1987), pp. 265-6, for the exacerbation of social tensions in Warwicks.

[200] Examples of conflict in Surrey during the 1640s are discussed in J. R. Gurney, 'The county of Surrey and the English revolution' (unpublished D.Phil. thesis, University of Sussex, 1991), pp. 238-45.

[201] For example, Sabine, *Works,* pp. 256, 259, 260, 263-4, 282, 286, 303, 305, 667, 672; *Clarke papers,* II, 215; Aylmer (ed.), *Englands spirit unfoulded,* p. 12; cf. B.L. E 252(30): *A perfect diurnall of some passages in parliament* (22-9 April 1644); E 518(18): *A perfect diurnall* 9-16 Aug. 1647); E 518(20); *Perfect occurrences of every day iournall in parliament* (Aug. 1647); J. Rushworth, *Historical collections* (London, 1721), VII, 77, for the expression of similar complaints by others.

[202] Sabine, *Works,* p. 506.

[203] Dalton, 'Experience of fraud', p. 975; Gurney, 'County of Surrey', p. 245. The list is in P.R.O., SP28/245 (unfol.).

[219] Sabine, *Works,* pp. 263, 414-15; cf. pp. 263, 431-2.

[220] Ibid. pp. 256, 286; P.R.O., SP18/42/144; cf. Aylmer (ed.), *Englands spirit unfoulded,* p. 13; Sabine, *Works,* pp. 285, 415.

Michael Rogers (essay date 1996)

SOURCE: "Gerrard Winstanley on Crime and Punishment," *The Sixteenth Century Journal,* Vol. XXVII, No. 3, Fall, 1996, pp. 735-47.

[*In the following essay, Rogers analyzes the emphasis of* The Law of Freedom in a Platform *(1652) on crime, law, and punishment. Rogers comments specifically on the apparent shift in Winstanley's thought from a belief in individual moral responsibility to a focus on the state's role in governing morality.*]

Scholars have long recognized the importance of legal themes in Gerrard Winstanley's last writing, *The Law of Freedom in a Platform* (1652). This detailed work devotes its final chapter not only to a general discussion of law but also to the specific criminal code appropriate to a communist commonwealth. Here the reader finds a lengthy list of crimes paired with punishments ranging from private rebukes to public execution. In addition, scattered throughout chapter 4, Winstanley takes up the elections, qualifications, and duties of judges and law enforcement officials. It is fair to say that crime and punishment constitute one of the crucial themes in *Law of Freedom.* Yet Winstanley's pre-1652 writings reveal a man far less interested in law and crime; in the pamphlets produced during the year of "digging" between 1649 and 1650 Winstanley focused his attention on other issues.

Oddly, the changes in Winstanley's legal thought have not received thorough historical analysis. Instead, much commentary on his views on crime and punishment, influenced by political science debate, has centered around an anachronistic attempt to determine whether or not the Digger leader was a seventeenth-century "socialist totalitarian." As early as 1957 the political scientist Walter F. Murphy emphasized the coercive side of *Law of Freedom*'s utopian society, with its plethora of enforcement officials and laws designed to correct "standard human frailties." He concluded that it would be "hard to imagine a better example of a primitive police state than the True Commonwealth."[1] In the late 1970s and early 1980s, the historian J. C. Davis further developed this approach to Winstanley's legal thought. Professor Davis posited a radical disjuncture between the "early" and "later" Winstanley. In the works of 1649 and 1650, Winstanley believed in a society made ideal by the moral perfecting of individuals, which meant that government's role remained limited to keeping order.[2] Yet by the time he composed *Law of Freedom,* Professor Davis lamented, the Digger writer had abandoned this for a completely different social model, which Davis characterized as "a utopian reliance on a dynamic secular state and its agencies. . . . "[3] For Davis, the crucial change in Winstanley's thought came with his acceptance of original sin by 1652. By then Winstanley realized that original sin was imbedded in human beings and led inevitably to self-interest; hence, "the scope of law had to be totalitarian," and had to regulate every aspect of life because the state remained locked in eternal combat with human nature. Therefore, in *Law of Freedom* Winstanley elaborated a complex legal system, with harsh corporal punishments to enforce its penal code.[4] Davis insisted that in practice this not only would have led to "judicial slavery," flogging, "judicial violence and torture," and capital punishment, but also to a "Big Brother" state in which common human shortcomings such as gossip, hypocrisy, and idleness would have been punished as civil offenses. Further, Davis noted that whereas Winstanley's earlier works denied the necessity of lawyers, *Law of Freedom* embraced the notion of "every man his own lawyer"; for Davis, Winstanley's utopia would swarm with contentious citizen-attorneys. Thus, by 1652 law was integral to the total system of indoctrination and social discipline that Winstanley now recognized as necessary to shape and mold people to the needs of the state.[5] Even in his controversial 1986 work on the Ranters, Davis continued to insist that Christopher Hill and others sympathetic to the Diggers' aims ought to admit that Winstanley "became more repressive than the formulations of *The World Turned Upside Down* allowed."[6]

Other historians have followed this line of thought. In 1988, Austin Woolrych seconded Davis' judgment of Hill, pointing to the "severely authoritarian regulations and penalties proposed in *The Law of Freedom*. . . ." A year earlier, Robert Zaller complained that although Winstanley's earlier works, alone among the writings of legal reformers during the Revolution, absolutely rejected the death penalty, *Law of Freedom* prescribed it for a host of offenses. This fact, plus Winstanley's general embrace of eye-for-an-eye punishments in his last work, prompted Zaller to lament that the Digger leader's earlier "dream of a spontaneous brotherhood was replaced by the arid formulas of a utopia," and that Winstanley "seemed to fall back on a scarcely convincing conflation of the Mosaic code and the Sermon on the Mount. . . . "[7]

Timothy Kenyon's *Utopian Communism and Political Thought in Early Modern England* (1989) is to date the best of the studies inspired by political science debate and takes issue with Davis' analysis. Kenyon underscored Winstanley's consistent optimism about people's restoration to spiritual wholeness. More important is Kenyon's analysis of the means by which that spiritual restoration was to take place, for he insisted that Winstanley focused on the crucial role of social institutions in molding individuals freed from

the spiritual destructiveness of the Fall. Although Winstanley viewed several social institutions (the household, education, apprenticeship, etc.) as vital, Kenyon argued that a comprehensive legal system "constitutes the minimum and rudimentary provision in Winstanley's scheme for the restoration of Man."[8] This code would in general serve as a guide to action for all members of Winstanley's utopia. Thus, for Kenyon, *Law of Freedom*'s legal system constituted merely one (albeit a crucial one) among many institutional parameters vital to the lifelong process of spiritual restoration of individuals. Winstanley, Kenyon concluded, clearly recognized the usefulness of legal restraints, since only slowly and fitfully would people progress toward an understanding of cooperation; coercive law had to be ready to respond to the inevitable lapses in rational behavior.[9]

Among all the scholars of Winstanley's thought on criminal justice, Christopher Hill has come closest to placing those ideas solidly within the mid-seventeenth-century context. In 1978 he published a major assessment of Winstanley's thought, which, among other things, directly challenged Murphy's and Davis' views. Professor Hill first rejected the idea of a dramatically different "early" as opposed to "later" Winstanley, maintaining that Winstanley consistently supported punishing unrighteous behavior in civil matters.[10]

More importantly, Hill analyzed *Law of Freedom* within the matrix of real political events of the late 1640s and early 1650s. To begin, Hill reminded readers that in Winstanley's early works, written during the optimism felt by many radicals at the dawn of the Commonwealth, he expected a swift and peaceful transition to communist society, as "Reason" or "Christ" rose within all people and they came to realize that common cultivation was the solution to England's problems. But the disappointments and ultimate defeat of the Diggers by 1650 taught Winstanley important lessons reflected in *Law of Freedom,* most notably that communist society would be a long time in coming. Thus, in the meantime, in the transitional period between "kingly government" (regimes that support private property) and that glorious future (that is, in the period dealt with by *Law of Freedom*), people would need the guidance of law. Only state authority could curb the power of the "Norman" and "antichristian" gentry and clergy and thereby disentangle people's minds from the mystification wrought by "Kingly power." Hill thus insisted that Winstanley came to understand the need to institutionalize Reason by means of an elaborate law code.[11]

Hill also found unrealistic Davis' interpretation of Winstanley's state as a totalitarian one, constantly at war with "human nature" due to original sin. Such a view, he argued, ignores Winstanley's expectation that Christ would indeed rise in every person, even if it would take longer than he initially expected. In addition, Hill asked whether, given the cruelty and disease endemic to seventeenth-century prisons, there existed any practical alternative to corporal punishment and forced labor? He pointed to the fact that whipping and burning in the hand were considered minor by contemporaries such as John Bunyan.[12]

Students of Winstanley's legal thought find themselves tempted to put this debate at the center of their analyses. Yet, despite Professor Hill's laudable sabotage of the anachronistic "socialist totalitarian" model, such a temptation should be resisted, for there remain two things that scholars must do before a full portrait of Winstanley's legal mind can emerge. First, we must extensively analyze both the theoretical and practical aspects of criminal justice not only in *Law of Freedom* but also in Winstanley's earlier writings; this provides a clearer picture of the evolution of his ideas. Second, and more importantly, we need to interpret Winstanley's opinions on crime and punishment within the heady world of radical (and even moderate) legal reform schemes that erupted during the Interregnum.[13] As we shall see, Winstanley's theoretical-historical perspective on law remained unique. Nevertheless, like many Leveller writers before and Quaker and Fifth Monarchist authors after him, he advocated decentralization of the court system, popular legal education, self-representation, and other measures that would have democratized the legal system.[14] Any thorough historical study of Winstanley's legal thought must operate within that context.

The Writings of 1649 and 1650: Theoretical Dimensions

Winstanley's pre-1652 writings on legal matters focused on the evils of private property ownership and the unjust law enforcement system that supported it. This does not mean that he failed to discuss criminal activity and punishments; however, his views on religion and history made him optimistic that, as individuals rejected private property, the root causes of crime largely would melt away. We must therefore examine briefly the theoretical context of his thought on law and crime.

Unlike the Levellers, whose analysis of the history of law rarely extended back further than Anglo-Saxon times,[15] Winstanley examined the origins of law both before and after the Fall of Adam. Prior to the Fall, all laws were rooted in "common preservation," which meant that individuals sought the good of others without respect of persons. Winstanley adapted traditional natural law doctrine to his own ends when he declared that "the Law of Necessity, that the Earth should be planted for the common preservation and peace of his household, was the righteous Rule and Law to Adam," whose people also had that law inscribed in their hearts.[16] Thus, before the Fall, God made the earth a common treasury, a communist paradise without social or property-based distinctions;[17] law was based on each person's innate respect and concern for others.

With Adam's transgression, however, human society changed and along with it law. As covetousness arose in the hearts of some, "one branch of mankind began to lift up himself above another," stealing the use of the earth and killing. So, "thieves and murderers, upheld by preaching witches and deceivers," came to govern and to establish laws which upheld their conquest and oppression. Gradually, therefore, the common people were subjugated by enslaving laws handed down from one generation of conquerors to another in order to justify murder and theft.[18]

Naturally enough, Winstanley used the Norman Yoke myth to fit England into this pattern of world history. "And the last enslaving Conquest which the Enemy got over Israel, was the *Norman* over *England,*" he duly noted, which introduced not only kings, lords, and freeholders, but also judges, justices, bailiffs, and the "binding and restraining laws" which have subjugated the English ever since.[19] Winstanley thus believed that all laws since 1066 buttressed the Norman enslavement of the English to this "Kingly power." "This Kingly power is covetousness in his branches," Winstanley wrote early in 1650, "or the power of self-love, ruling in one or in many men over others, and enslaving those who in the Creation are their equals." Whether it assumed the form of royal prerogative or "state Priviledge of Parliament," Winstanley argued that "Kingly power" had always denied the soil to one part of the human race. Every monarch since the Conqueror had confirmed the old "Norman" laws, and even the best of them (for example, the Magna Carta) bound the people to their masters, for the clergy and gentry are free, Winstanley complained, while the people must work for them just as the Israelites labored for the Egyptians.[20]

So, when Winstanley turned to an analysis of English positive law, he worked within the world-historical context of "Kingly power's" use of the legal system to secure the privileges of private property. Winstanley and the Diggers saw property as a fundamental evil, "the cause of all wars, bloud-shed, theft, and enslaving Laws, that hold the people under miserie." If out of want the poor should steal, the hypocrisy of English law was revealed in all its nakedness; the rich thieves, the bribe-taking lawyers, and court officers cheated people of their property with impunity while the poor faced the gallows. Thus, Winstanley believed that the "particular propriety of mine and thine" was the root cause of both crime and unjust punishments. "It tempts people to doe an evil action," Winstanley wrote early in 1649, "and then kils them for doing of it: Let all judge if this be not a great devil."[21]

Winstanley's second major point about positive law was that the execution of Charles I, the last of the "Norman" kings, did not automatically sweep away "Kingly Law and Power." Nonetheless, in 1650 Winstanley took heart in the acts abolishing the House of Lords and establishing a commonwealth, for he saw them as freeing the people from obedience to laws that originated in "Kingly power," including laws enforcing tenurial relations.[22] In his optimism about the spread of Reason, Winstanley warned that the Diggers sought no mere return to pre-Norman laws; unlike the Levellers, he advocated a far more radical restitution, the "pure Law of righteousness before the Fall . . . unto which all things are to be restored."[23] He was sure that soon the "law of common preservation" would reign in all people's hearts, thus returning England to that law of righteousness.

Crime and Punishment

So, to Winstanley private property was the single most important cause of criminal behavior. Moreover, in his early pamphlets he remained hopeful that as communism gradually took hold, that is, as Christ or Reason rose within individual men and women, crime and punishment would virtually disappear. Nonetheless, he did make a few statements about criminal activity and its suppression.

To begin, even at the height of his optimism about the inner transformation of individuals, Winstanley did not envision a world completely without coercion or magistrates. In **Truth Lifting up its Head Above Scandals** (1649), he embraced the rather traditional Christian view of the magistrate as "a terror to all unrighteousness" in anyone who might "walk unrighteously towards his fellow creature in civil matters." It is clear that Winstanley expected some crime, although he primarily believed that it would assume the form of attempts to reestablish property ownership. Perhaps as a result, in the writings of 1649 and 1650, he fiercely rejected prisons as well as corporal and capital punishment; all three were outgrowths of the "sharp Laws of Bondage" imposed by the Normans. The only punishment he deemed appropriate was to work on the land, marked as a servant of the state by the special clothing which, he believed, was the mark of fools in ancient Israel. This would continue until such time as the spirit within made the offender aware of the error of attempting to rise above others by reintroducing private property.[24]

The Law of Freedom In a Platform: Theory of Law

Law of Freedom retained the theory of history Winstanley had developed in the pre-1652 writings. Moreover, as he did in those pamphlets from 1649 and 1650, Winstanley sought to ground his communist legal system in the "Spirit of universal Righteousness dwelling in Mankinde, now rising up to teach every one to do to another as he would have another do to him." Continuing to define fundamental law in a revolutionary way, Winstanley warned all officials, including members of Parliament, of their obligation to ensure that the people enjoy their "creation-Freedoms in the Earth" (that is, their right to communist ownership of the land), "for the Necessity of common preservation and peace is the Fundamental Law both to Officers and the People."[25] In short, Winstanley still believed law had to be based on a spirit of righteousness within, a spirit which taught people the importance of economic cooperation and the Golden Rule.

If Winstanley still sought a spiritual justification for his legal system, he conceptualized the actual operation of the law much more concretely than he did in his earlier writings. Broadly speaking, he viewed law as creating the institutional parameters within which his definition of the Golden Rule could flourish, for by 1652 he had concluded that "Reason" was only very slowly rising within the hearts of his countrymen. Therefore, one purpose of the law was to establish a communist economy by forbidding commercial transactions and by setting up communal cultivation and distribution. These economic changes Winstanley termed "commonwealths government" and "commonwealths freedom"; their establishment "fulfills the righteous law of Christ, *Do as you would be done by:* for that law of Christ can never be performed, till you establish Commonwealths freedom."[26] Private property constituted the main institutional obstacle to the Golden Rule, and its removal had to take priority over any other matter.

The other function of law according to **Law of Freedom** was the restraint and correction of people's behavior, something far less emphasized in the earlier pamphlets. Winstanley believed that law was needed not only because of "unreasonable ignorance" (that is, the desire for private property) but because of "ignorant and rude fancy in man," such as the notion that community of property implies community of women, obviously a rebuke to Ranters. What Winstanley had realized by 1652 was that although the tyranny of "Kingly" governments provoked a desire for a commonwealth, still, as he put it, "the spirit in Mankinde is various within it self." Thus, some people were still idle, foolish, rash, and covetous. This variety indicated to him that the spirit of Christ had not yet entered into the hearts of enough people and that the law itself would have to function both as a communist standard of action and as a preserver of peace.[27]

If the laws were to function efficiently in Winstanley's ideal commonwealth, two things became absolutely essential. One was effective law enforcement; consequently, he proposed a vast array of elected state officials and overseers to implement his new legal code.

"And the Reason of all this," he noted, "is that many eyes being watchfull, the Laws may be obeyed, for to preserve Peace."[28] Second, like the Quakers and Fifth Monarchy Men who wrote about the law after him, Winstanley insisted that the people must know the law. "If there were good Laws," he wrote, "and the People be ignorant of them, it would be as bad for the Commonwealth as if there were no Laws at all." Noting how Moses had ordered the law to be read once a week to the people, he proposed a form of popular legal education; the elected minister of each parish would read the law publicly four times per year, "for the Laws of a Land hath the power of freedom and bondage, life and death in its hand . . . and he is the best prophet that acquaints men therewith."[29]

Crime and Punishment

Because Winstanley intended to use the law to bring human behavior in line with "commonwealths freedom," *Law of Freedom* prescribed an assortment of punishments, ranging from private and public rebukes to the death penalty, for a host of offenses. A detailed examination of Winstanley's proposed punishments reveals not only the shifts in his views on the nature of communist society but also the extent to which his earlier opinions on crime had changed by 1652.

Winstanley never overcame the dislike of prisons so prominently featured in his earlier writings. He specifically noted in *Law of Freedom* that there should be no imprisonment in noncapital cases, even for holding the accused before trial. The cruelty of prisons was one justification for this, although Winstanley also concerned himself with another vital issue: remorse. He hoped that if the offender lived at home while awaiting trial he would come to see his errors. With his neighbors close by to see his changed ways, the judge could justify mitigation of the sentence, "for it is amendment not destruction that Common-wealths Law requires."[30]

If Winstanley maintained his earlier distaste for prisons, his opinions on the death penalty changed dramatically, for the list of capital crimes in *Law of Freedom* is actually fairly long. The first broad category concerns attempted escape while in state custody. Winstanley believed that an offender who fled after promising to appear before a court should be executed immediately after capture. He also advocated the death penalty for escape while serving a sentence of deprivation of freedom under the supervision of a state taskmaster, that is, bondage to the state.[31] Another type of capital offense was engaging in commercial transactions of various kinds. Winstanley particularly opposed the commodification of legal services, and he noted that anyone who attempted to administer the law for gain should die as a traitor to the commonwealth; like a few moderate legal reformers and many radicals, he staunchly stood for self-representation.[32] He also believed that persons who tried to buy or sell land or its fruits should be put to death as "traytors to the peace of the *Common-wealth* because it brings in Kingly bondage again and is the occasion of all quarrels and oppressions." Likewise, those who sought, through conspiracy or force, to re-introduce private property would suffer the death penalty. Treason (armed insurrection) and rape were the final capital offenses in his ideal legal code.[33]

Like many radical and other legal thinkers of the 1640s and 1650s, Winstanley prescribed a host of corporal punishments for less serious crimes.[34] For Winstanley, the most fundamental principle was eye-for-an-eye justice administered by the state executioner; "and the reason is, that men may be tender of one anothers bodies, doing as they would be done by."[35] This perfectly illustrates how Winstanley sought to use the law to bring forth adherence to a principle (his view of the Golden Rule) that in his earlier works he had hoped would take hold "naturally" as the spirit of Reason spread through all people. Another form of corporal punishment Winstanley advocated was branding, the use of which the Leveller Richard Overton had urged in 1647. The person who stubbornly continued to claim ownership of land would be placed "upon a stool, with those words [that is, concerning ownership] written in his forehead, before all the Congregation."[36]

Whipping was yet another physical punishment, sometimes prescribed for the second and third offenses of freemen who habitually lied, intimidated, and berated their neighbors,[37] although Winstanley most often advocated it for individuals already under some form of bondage to the state. Those who disobeyed the taskmasters or spoke against the law would be subject to short rations, a coarse diet, and whipping, "for a rod is prepared for the fools back, till such time as their proud hearts do bend to the Law."[38] Scholars such as Colin Davis, who find Winstanley's criminal code uniquely objectionable because of its sanction of "judicial violence and torture," would do well to recall attitudes toward corporal punishment evinced by the Hale Commission of 1652. Dominated by lawyers and recognized as the quintessential voice of moderate law reform during the Interregnum, this body recommended that perjurers have their ears cut off, their nostrils slit, and their hands burned with red hot irons; afterward, they would be sent to a house of correction.[39]

Crucial to Winstanley's ideas about proper punishment in his ideal society was bondage to the state, something advocated by many radical and moderate reformers, ranging from Hugh Peters to the Fifth Monarchy Men.[40] Winstanley usually prescribed it for a one-year period. Sometimes he held that it should be used straightaway in first convictions for a particular crime, such as striking a government officer, enticing a person to buy or sell, hiring labor, offering to work for wages, or persistently denying that all property should be held in common.[41] More commonly Winstanley advocated labor service as a last resort, after private and public reproaches had failed. Idlers would draw a private warning by the overseers for the first offense, a public rebuke for the second, and twelve months' labor service under a taskmaster for the third. The same sequence of punishments would apply to the head of a family who neglected to maintain the tools necessary for agricultural production.[42]

Winstanley also recommended labor service for official negligence of duty, specifically for two agents of the state, waiters (workers in the storehouses and small shops), and overseers. After one private warning, a waiter found negligent would be taken before a judge and sentenced to work in the fields under a taskmaster, "for he who may live in freedom and will not, is to taste servitude." Overseers too would be subject to a private warning by a judge for allowing idleness among the working population; a second offense would result in his expulsion from office and his falling back into the ranks of "young people and servants to be a worker."[43]

Labor service also appeared among Winstanley's proposals to deal with problems arising from interpersonal relationships but again only after private and public warnings for first and second offenses. Liars and promoters of dissension among their neighbors would receive a three-month sentence for their third conviction and a permanent loss of freedom for a fourth. If a witness could prove the charge, a person found guilty of verbal intimidation a fourth time would serve for twelve months, as would anyone convicted of lordly domination of others. Wife stealing was another crime that Winstanley believed deserved a twelve-month sentence of forced labor, at least for the second conviction.[44]

Winstanley laid out the manner in which these "laboring servants" to the Commonwealth were to be supervised. Offenders would be under the watch of a taskmaster, who would use his own judgment in assigning appropriate work. White woolen garments were to be the special "badge" of these people as they worked on public projects or as laboring assistants to the freemen. Winstanley also provided that, at the termination of their sentences, the offenders be restored to their freedom only if they "give open testimony of their humility and diligence, and their care to observe the Laws of the Commonwealth. . . ."[45]

Even among the radical reformers of the 1640s and 1650s Gerrard Winstanley was a unique legal theorist because his call for a restoration of prelapsarian law grew out of an extraordinary perspective on world and English history. Moreover, although virtually all radicals employed some form of natural law theory to justify their reform proposals,[46] only Winstanley's interpretation of the "Law of God" sanctioned—indeed commanded—a criminal code supportive of a communist society. Law reform and economic change had to advance hand in hand.

Winstanley's thought on crime and punishment, especially in ***Law of Freedom,*** is also marked by realism. Given the Diggers' experiences with a coercive state in defense of private property, Winstanley realistically insisted that his communist society required a new criminal code in order to combat the selfishness that accompanied capitalist property relations.[47] As an early materialist, Winstanley correctly realized that true freedom, the rising of the spirit of Christ, of Reason, could not take place without institutionalizing cooperation by means of the law. Timothy Kenyon's insistence on Winstanley's many-faceted institutional approach to spiritual restoration properly underscores the importance of such a code.[48]

Finally, and most importantly, we must recognize that despite these distinctive features of Winstanley's legal thought, he was very much part of the vibrant law reform tradition that poured forth in the 1640s and 1650s. As I have indicated earlier, he shared many democratizing legal ideas and proposals with the Levellers, Quakers, and Fifth Monarchy Men, not to mention moderate reformers. Among these numbered popular legal education, the right of self-representation, decentralization of the courts,[49] and election of judges and other legal officials. His commitment to a democratically controlled legal system extended even further, for he also endorsed popular approval of reformed laws[50] and the informal adjudication of disputes; moreover, he intended punishments to be corrective, not punitive.[51]

I think it should at last be clear that Winstanley did not make the radical aboutface from a "spiritual" individualist to a "totalitarian" collectivist that Colin Davis and others have suggested. Rather, Winstanley's thought on crime and punishment reflects both the popular, radical tradition of law reform in the revolutionary era and realistic lessons in common cultivation and state power learned in the Digger colonies. All in all, it was a unique and humane legal vision.

Notes

[1] Walter F. Murphy, "The Political Philosophy of Gerrard Winstanley," *Review of Politics* 19 (1957): 257.

[2] J.C. Davis, "Gerrard Winstanley and the Restoration of True Magistracy," *Past and Present,* 70 (1976): 86, 91; J.C. Davis, *Utopia and the Ideal Society: A Study of English Utopian Writing, 1516-1701* (Cambridge: Cambridge UP, 1981), 192.

[3] Davis, "Winstanley and True Magistracy," 92.

[4] Davis, "Winstanley and True Magistracy," 84-85, 86; Davis, *Utopia and the Ideal Society,* 190-191, 193, 199.

[5] Davis, "Winstanley and True Magistracy," 89-90, 92-93.

[6] J.C. Davis, *Fear, Myth, and History: The Ranters and Their History* (Cambridge: Cambridge UP, 1986), 133 n.

[7] Austin Woolrych, "Revising Stuart Britain: Towards a New Synthesis?" *Historical Journal* 31 (1988): 450; Robert Zaller, "The Debate on Capital Punishment during the English Revolution," *American Journal of Legal History* 31 (1987): 141-142.

[8] Timothy Kenyon, *Utopian Communism and Political Thought in Early Modern England* (London: Pinter, 1989), 203-205, 205 n.

[9] Kenyon, *Utopian Communism,* 209-210, 217.

[10] Christopher Hill, *The Religion of Gerrard Winstanley,* Past and Present Supplement, 5 (Oxford: Past and Present Society, 1978), 38.

[11] Hill, *Religion of Winstanley,* 24, 41-45, 49; Christopher Hill, "Gerrard Winstanley and Freedom," in *A Nation of Change and Novelty: Radical Politics, Religion and Literature in Seventeenth-Century England* (London: Routledge, 1990), 124-125; originally published in *Freedom and the English Revolution,* ed. R.C. Richardson and G.M. Ridden (Manchester: Manchester UP, 1986).

[12] Hill, *Religion of Winstanley,* 41-42.

[13] For the overall law reform context, see Donald Veall, *The Popular Movement for Law Reform, 1640-1660* (Oxford: Clarendon, 1970); Nancy Matthews, *William Sheppard: Cromwell's Law Reformer* (Cambridge: Cambridge UP, 1985); and Stuart Prall, *The Agitation for Law Reform during the Puritan Revolution* (The Hague: Nijhoff, 1966). For radical law reform in particular, see Michael Rogers, "Law Reform and Legal Thought among English Radicals, 1645-1660" (Ph.D. diss., Northern Illinois U, 1988).

[14] Popular legal education and self-representation in radical thought is discussed below. For Leveller and Fifth Monarchist proposals to decentralize the court system, see Rogers, "Law Reform and Legal Thought," 138-151, 203-205, 448-450, 464-465. For Quaker ideas on decentralization, see Michael Rogers, "Quakerism and the Law in Revolutionary England," *Canadian Journal of History* 22 (1987): 167.

[15] Pauline Gregg, *Free-born John: A Biography of John Lilburne* (London: George Harrap, 1961), 208; Christopher Hill, "The Norman Yoke," in *Puritanism and Revolution* (New York: Schocken, 1964), 78; Robert B. Seaberg, "The Norman Conquest and the Common Law: The Levellers and the Argument from Continuity," *Historical Journal* 24 (1981): 800-801; David Wooten, "Leveller Democracy and the Puritan Revolution," in *The Cambridge History of Political Thought, 1450-1700,* ed. J. H. Burns (Cambridge: Cambridge UP, 1991), 427-428.

[16] Gerrard Winstanley, *The Law of Freedom in a Platform* (London, 1652), rptd. in *The Works of Gerrard Winstanley,* ed. George H. Sabine (Ithaca: Cornell UP, 1941; reprint, New York: Russell & Russell, 1965), 536-537. (All subsequent citations of Winstanley's writings are to Sabine's edition, hereafter cited as *Works.*) Although best expressed in *Law of Freedom,* this view was also common in the pre-1652 pamphlets.

[17] Gerrard Winstanley, *A Watch-Word to the City of London and the Armie* (London, 1649), rptd. in *Works,* 323.

[18] Gerrard Winstanley, *The True Levellers Standard Advanced* (London, 1649), rptd. in *Works,* 254-255; Winstanley, *Watch-Word,* 323-324.

[19] Winstanley, *True Levellers,* 259.

[20] Gerrard Winstanley, *A New-yeers Gift for the Parliament and Armie* (London, 1650), rptd. in *Works,* 354-355; idem, *A Letter to the Lord Fairfax and his councell of war* (London, 1649), rptd. in *Works,* 286-287; idem, *An Appeal to the House of Commons* (London, 1649), rptd. in *Works,* 303.

[21] Gerrard Winstanley, *A Declaration from the Poor Oppressed People of England* (London, 1649), rptd. in *Works,* 276; idem, *New-yeers Gift,* 388; idem, *The New Law of Righteousness* (London, 1649), rptd. in *Works,* 201.

[22] Gerrard Winstanley, *An Appeale to all Englishmen* (London, 1650), rptd. in *Works,* 410-411, 413.

[23] Winstanley, *Letter to Fairfax,* 292; idem, *New Law of Righteousness,* 191, 205, 225.

[24] Gerrard Winstanley, *Truth lifting up its head above scandals* (London, 1649), rptd. in *Works,* 130; idem, *New-Yeers Gift,* 355-356; idem, *New Law of Righteousness,* 197-198.

[25] Winstanley, *Law of Freedom,* 534, 561.

[26] Winstanley, *Law of Freedom,* 585.

[27] Winstanley, *Law of Freedom,* 515, 526, 535-536.

[28] Winstanley, *Law of Freedom,* 552. For Winstanley's franchise and the annual election of state officers, including judges, see idem, *Law of Freedom,* 538-539, 540, 548, 555-556.

[29] Winstanley, *Law of Freedom,* 562-563, 591. Winstanley believed it important that no person suffer death at the hands of the state on account of ignorance of the law. For Quaker proposals to educate people about the law see the following: George Fox, *To the Parliament . . . Fifty-nine Particulars* (London: Thomas Simmons, 1659), 4; P[aul] M[oon], *Some Passages and Proceedings in Court* (1657), in George Fox, *An Instruction to Judges and Lawyers* (London: Thomas Simmons, 1657), 37; Edward Burrough, *A Declaration to all the World of our Faith* (London, 1658), rptd. in his *The Memorable Works of a Son of Thunder and Consolation,* ed. Ellis Hookes (London, 1672), 442; and George Fox, *Instruction to Judges and Lawyers,* 8. For a similar proposal by an author very popular among Fifth Monarchists, see John Brayne, *The Authority of God Over Men in the Law* (London: Richard Moon, 1654), 5, 9. Both Fox and Brayne followed Winstanley in harkening back to the practices of Moses's day.

[30] Winstanley, *Law of Freedom,* 553.

[31] Winstanley, *Law of Freedom,* 553-554.

[32] Winstanley, *Law of Freedom,* 554, 591. Actually, Winstanley had argued for self-representation well before 1652; see, for example, his 1649 tract *Appeal to the House of Commons,* 311. On the moderate reformers Hugh Peters and William Sprigge, see Veall, *Popular Movement for Law Reform,* 119, 121. For Leveller opinion on self-representation see John Lilburne, *The Just Mans Justification* (London, 1646), 11, and *An Agreement of the Free People of England* (London, 1649), rptd. in *Leveller Manifestoes of the Puritan Revolution,* ed. Don M. Wolfe (New York: Nelson, 1944; reprint, New York: Humanities Press, 1967), 406. For the Quakers, see Fox, *Fifty-Nine Particulars,* 4; Fox, *Instruction to Judges and Lawyers,* 19; and George Fox, *The law of God the rule of law-makers* (London: Giles Calvert, 1658), 5 [misprint for 3]. For the Fifth Monarchists, see John Brayne, *The New Earth* (London: Richard Moon, 1653), 7, "Epistle Dedicatory," 2d page; William Medley, *A Standard Set Up* (London, 1657), 18, and Bernard Capp, *The Fifth Monarchy Men* (London: Faber and Faber, 1972), 159.

[33] Winstanley, *Law of Freedom,* 594-595, 597, 599.

[34] The radicals' views often echoed the widespread belief of the ruling classes in stiff corporal punishments for the lower classes, although most wanted to ensure that criminals of every social standing answered

for their misdeeds with the rod. For commonplace opinions on punishments, see Veall, *Popular Movement for Law Reform,* 28, and Zaller, "Debate on Capital Punishment," 132, 138-139. For some continental examples of class bias in the application of corporal punishment, see Ruth Pike, "Crime and Criminals in Sixteenth-Century Seville," *Sixteenth Century Journal* 6 (1975): 6, 16-18.

[35] Winstanley, *Law of Freedom,* 591.

[36] Winstanley, *Law of Freedom,* 595. For Overton's views, see his *An Appeale from the Degenerate Representative Body of the Commons of England* (London, 1647), rptd. in *Leveller Manifestoes,* ed. Don M. Wolfe, 193.

[37] Winstanley, *Law of Freedom,* 592.

[38] Winstanley, *Law of Freedom,* 553, 598.

[39] Veall, *Popular Movement for Law Reform,* 134. On the influence of lawyers on the Hale Commission, see Mary Cottrell, "Interregnum Law Reform: The Hale Commission of 1652," *English Historical Review* 83 (1968): 690-692, 694-695, and Veall, *Popular Movement for Law Reform,* 83.

[40] See Zaller, "Debate on Capital Punishment," 132-133, for bondage to the state as a common moderate alternative to death for theft. For Leveller views on this issue, see Overton, *Appeale,* 193; Samuel Chidley, *A Cry Against a Crying Sin* (London, 1652), rptd. in *The Harleian Miscellany; or, A Collection of Scarce, Curious, and Entertaining Pamphlets and Tracts,* 12 vols. (London: R. Dutton, 1808-1811), 6:283; and Zaller, "Debate on Capital Punishment," 133-135. For examples of Quaker endorsement of bondage to the state, see Edward Billing, *A Mite of Affection* (London, 1659), 3; Richard Farnworth, *Gods Covenanting with his People* (London: Giles Calvert, 1653); 38, 42-43; and George Fox, *To the Protector and Parliament* (London: Giles Calvert, 1658), 13; Fifth Monarchist opinion can be found in William Aspinwall, *The Legislative Power is Christs* (London: Livewell Chapman, 1656), 31; Brayne, *New Earth,* 55; and the anonymous *Door of Hope* (London, 1660), 5. Some Fifth Monarchist and Quaker authors did not specify whether convicts would be kept in bondage to the state or to private citizens, but all of them clearly supported the "sale" of criminals as an alternative to death for theft.

[41] Winstanley, *Law of Freedom,* 592, 594-595. Winstanley favored public commendations for persons who, after being enticed to engage in commercial transactions, resisted and reported the offense to an overseer.

[42] Winstanley, *Law of Freedom,* 592-593. Winstanley's concern that farm families keep the proper implements

reveals the importance he placed on agriculture as the economic basis of his communist commonwealth.

[43] Winstanley, *Law of Freedom,* 551, 593-594.

[44] Winstanley, *Law of Freedom,* 592, 599.

[45] Winstanley, *Law of Freedom,* 553-554, 597-598.

[46] Rogers, "Law Reform and Legal Thought," 468-478.

[47] Gerald Aylmer, "The Religion of Gerrard Winstanley," in *Radical Religion in the English Revolution,* ed. J. F. McGregor and Barry Reay (Oxford: Oxford UP, 1984), 110-111, has criticized Davis' thesis about Winstanley's embrace of coercive state authority. Aylmer stresses, quite correctly, that by the time *Law of Freedom* appeared, Winstanley had realized that a coercive state had defeated the Digger movement; hence, he realistically insisted on a radically new state and legal system for the new society he envisioned.

[48] Hill, *Religion of Winstanley,* 28-29; Kenyon, *Utopian Communism,* 203.

[49] Winstanley, *Law of Freedom,* 545-546, 555-556.

[50] Winstanley, *Law of Freedom,* 558-559.

[51] This point was underscored by Christopher Hill as early as 1972; see Hill, *The World Turned Upside Down: Radical Ideas During the English Revolution* (New York: Viking, 1972), 108, and idem, *Religion of Winstanley,* 42.

FURTHER READING

Biography

Alsop, J. D. "Ethics in the Marketplace: Gerrard Winstanley's London Bankruptcy, 1643." *Journal of British Studies* 28, No. 2 (April 1989): 97-119.

> Studies the contemporary documents regarding the failure of Winstanley's business in 1643 and speculates on the relationship between Winstanley's bankruptcy and his later contempt for all forms of commerce.

———. "A High Road to Radicalism? Gerrard Winstanley's Youth." *The Seventeenth Century* IX, No. 1 (Spring 1994): 11-24.

> Reviews the facts available about Winstanley's life, particularly those concerned with his birth and early years. Alsop suggests that many scholars have presumed with no substantive basis that Puritanism was a strong formative influence on the youthful Winstanley.

Criticism

Aylmer, G. E. "The Religion of Gerrard Winstanley." In *Radical Religion in the English Revolution,* edited by J. F. McGregor and B. Reay, pp. 91-119. Oxford: Oxford University Press, 1984.

> Analyzes the development of Winstanley's thought, from his early religious writings, through his espousal of a communal way of life, the subsequent failure of the Digger communities, and to his "most elaborate programme for a new society." Additionally, Aylmer comments on Winstanley's historical significance.

Barg, M. A. "Gerrard Winstanley—Thinker, Revolutionary and Prophet." In *The English Revolution of the 17th Century Through Portraits of Its Leading Figures,* pp. 288-356. Moscow: Progress Publishers, 1990.

> Offers a detailed overview of Winstanley's religious and political philosophies as evidenced in his writings. Barg reviews what is known about Winstanley's life.

Bradstock, Andrew. "Part Two: Gerrard Winstanley." In *Faith in the Revolution: The Political Theologies of Muntzer and Winstanley,* pp. 69-138. London: Society for Promoting Christian Knowledge, 1997.

> An introduction to Winstanley's life and writings, a discussion of his theological and political convictions, and a study of Winstanley as a Christian revolutionary.

Dalton, R. J. "Gerrard Winstanley: The Experience of Fraud in 1641." *The Historical Journal* 34, No. 4 (1991): 973-84.

> Cites evidence that in 1641 Winstanley was a victim of fraud, and argues that this experience "was undoubtedly the single most influential of Winstanley's life: without it he might never have developed his communist ideology." Dalton goes on to maintain that this event, coupled with the bankruptcy Winstanley suffered two years later, combined to propel him to publish his developing radical views.

Haskin, Dayton. "Studies in the Poetry of Vision: Spenser, Milton, and Winstanley." *Thought: A Review of Culture and Idea* 56, No. 221 (June 1981): 226-39.

> Review essay discussing several books published in 1979, one of which includes a full-length study of Winstanley's works and which argues that Winstanley should be considered a "visionary poet in a line that stretches from Langland to Blake."

Hill, Christopher. "Levellers and True Levellers." In *The World Turned Upside Down: Radical Ideas during the English Revolution,* pp. 86-120. London: Temple Smith, 1972.

> Examines the activities of the Levellers and the group led by Winstanley, the Diggers, or True Levellers. Hill studies these groups within the context of the political events taking place in London during the late 1640s and 1650s.

Petegorsky, David W. *Left-Wing Democracy in the English Civil War: A Study of the Social Philosophy of Gerrard Winstanley.* London: V. Gollancz, 1940, 254 p.

The first full-length study of Winstanley's life and thought.

Rogers, John. "Marvell, Winstanley, and the Natural History of the Green Age." In *The Matter of Revolution: Science, Poetry, and Politics in the Age of Milton,* pp. 39-69. Ithaca, N.Y.: Cornell University Press, 1996.

Identifies an understanding of Winstanley's ideology as beneficial to a full comprehension of Andrew Marvell's pastoral poems.

Literature
Criticism from
1400 to 1800

Cumulative Indexes

How to Use This Index

The main references

Calvino, Italo
1923–1985 .... CLC **5, 8, 11, 22, 33, 39,
73; SSC 3**

list all author entries in the following Gale Literary Criticism series:

BLC = *Black Literature Criticism*
CLC = *Contemporary Literary Criticism*
CLR = *Children's Literature Review*
CMLC = *Classical and Medieval Literature Criticism*
DA = *DISCovering Authors*
DAB = *DISCovering Authors: British*
DAC = *DISCovering Authors: Canadian*
DAM = *DISCovering Authors: Modules*
     DRAM: *Dramatists Module;* *MST*: *Most-Studied Authors Module;*
     MULT: *Multicultural Authors Module;* *NOV*: *Novelists Module;*
     POET: *Poets Module;* *POP*: *Popular Fiction and Genre Authors Module*
DC = *Drama Criticism*
HLC = *Hispanic Literature Criticism*
LC = *Literature Criticism from 1400 to 1800*
NCLC = *Nineteenth-Century Literature Criticism*
PC = *Poetry Criticism*
SSC = *Short Story Criticism*
TCLC = *Twentieth-Century Literary Criticism*
WLC = *World Literature Criticism, 1500 to the Present*

The cross-references

See also CANR 23; CA 85-88;
    obituary CA116

list all author entries in the following Gale biographical and literary sources:

AAYA = *Authors & Artists for Young Adults*
AITN = *Authors in the News*
BEST = *Bestsellers*
BW = *Black Writers*
CA = *Contemporary Authors*
CAAS = *Contemporary Authors Autobiography Series*
CABS = *Contemporary Authors Bibliographical Series*
CANR = *Contemporary Authors New Revision Series*
CAP = *Contemporary Authors Permanent Series*
CDALB = *Concise Dictionary of American Literary Biography*
CDBLB = *Concise Dictionary of British Literary Biography*
DLB = *Dictionary of Literary Biography*
DLBD = *Dictionary of Literary Biography Documentary Series*
DLBY = *Dictionary of Literary Biography Yearbook*
HW = *Hispanic Writers*
JRDA = *Junior DISCovering Authors*
MAICYA = *Major Authors and Illustrators for Children and Young Adults*
MTCW = *Major 20th-Century Writers*
NNAL = *Native North American Literature*
SAAS = *Something about the Author Autobiography Series*
SATA = *Something about the Author*
YABC = *Yesterday's Authors of Books for Children*

Literary Criticism Series
Cumulative Author Index

20/1631
See Upward, Allen

A/C Cross
See Lawrence, T(homas) E(dward)

Abasiyanik, Sait Faik 1906-1954
See Sait Faik
See also CA 123

Abbey, Edward 1927-1989 **CLC 36, 59**
See also CA 45-48; 128; CANR 2, 41; MTCW 2

Abbott, Lee K(ittredge) 1947- **CLC 48**
See also CA 124; CANR 51; DLB 130

Abe, Kobo 1924-1993**CLC 8, 22, 53, 81; DAM NOV**
See also CA 65-68; 140; CANR 24, 60; DLB 182; MTCW 1, 2

Abelard, Peter c. 1079-c.1142 **CMLC 11**
See also DLB 115, 208

Abell, Kjeld 1901-1961 **CLC 15**
See also CA 111

Abish, Walter 1931- **CLC 22**
See also CA 101; CANR 37; DLB 130

Abrahams, Peter (Henry) 1919- **CLC 4**
See also BW 1; CA 57-60; CANR 26; DLB 117; MTCW 1, 2

Abrams, M(eyer) H(oward) 1912- **CLC 24**
See also CA 57-60; CANR 13, 33; DLB 67

Abse, Dannie 1923- **CLC 7, 29; DAB;DAM POET**
See also CA 53-56; CAAS 1; CANR 4, 46, 74; DLB 27; MTCW 1

Achebe, (Albert) Chinua(lumogu) 1930-**C L C 1, 3, 5, 7, 11, 26, 51, 75; BLC 1; DA; DAB; DAC; DAM MST, MULT, NOV;WLC**
See also AAYA 15; BW 2, 3; CA 1-4R; CANR 6, 26, 47; CLR 20; DLB 117; MAICYA; MTCW 1, 2; SATA 38, 40; SATA-Brief 38

Acker, Kathy 1948-1997 **CLC 45, 111**
See also CA 117; 122; 162; CANR 55

Ackroyd, Peter 1949- **CLC 34, 52**
See also CA 123; 127; CANR 51, 74; DLB 155; INT 127; MTCW 1

Acorn, Milton 1923- **CLC 15; DAC**
See also CA 103; DLB 53; INT 103

Adamov, Arthur 1908-1970 **CLC 4, 25; DAM DRAM**
See also CA 17-18; 25-28R; CAP 2; MTCW 1

Adams, Alice (Boyd) 1926-1999**CLC 6, 13, 46; SSC 24**
See also CA 81-84; 179; CANR 26, 53, 75; DLBY 86; INT CANR-26; MTCW 1, 2

Adams, Andy 1859-1935 **TCLC 56**
See also YABC 1

Adams, Brooks 1848-1927 **TCLC 80**
See also CA 123; DLB 47

Adams, Douglas (Noel) 1952- **CLC 27, 60; DAM POP**
See also AAYA 4; BEST 89:3; CA 106; CANR 34, 64; DLBY 83; JRDA; MTCW1

Adams, Francis 1862-1893 **NCLC 33**

Adams, Henry (Brooks) 1838-1918 **TCLC 4, 52; DA; DAB; DAC; DAM MST**

See also CA 104; 133; CANR 77; DLB 12, 47, 189; MTCW 1

Adams, Richard (George) 1920-**CLC 4, 5, 18; DAM NOV**
See also AAYA 16; AITN 1, 2; CA 49-52; CANR 3, 35; CLR 20; JRDA; MAICYA; MTCW 1, 2; SATA 7, 69

Adamson, Joy (-FriederikeVictoria) 1910-1980 **CLC 17**
See also CA 69-72; 93-96; CANR 22; MTCW 1; SATA 11; SATA-Obit 22

Adcock, Fleur 1934- **CLC 41**
See also CA 25-28R; CAAS 23; CANR 11, 34, 69; DLB 40

Addams, Charles (Samuel) 1912-1988**CLC 30**
See also CA 61-64; 126; CANR 12, 79

Addams, Jane 1860-1945 **TCLC 76**

Addison, Joseph 1672-1719 **LC 18**
See also CDBLB 1660-1789; DLB 101

Adler, Alfred (F.) 1870-1937 **TCLC 61**
See also CA 119; 159

Adler, C(arole) S(chwerdtfeger) 1932-**CLC 35**
See also AAYA 4; CA 89-92; CANR 19, 40; JRDA; MAICYA; SAAS 15; SATA 26, 63, 102

Adler, Renata 1938- **CLC 8, 31**
See also CA 49-52; CANR 5, 22, 52; MTCW 1

Ady, Endre 1877-1919 **TCLC 11**
See also CA 107

A. E. 1867-1935 **TCLC 3, 10**
See also Russell, George William

Aeschylus 525B.C.-456B.C. **CMLC 11; DA; DAB; DAC; DAM DRAM, MST; DC 8; WLCS**
See also DLB 176

Aesop 620(?)B.C.-564(?)B.C. **CMLC 24**
See also CLR 14; MAICYA; SATA 64

Affable Hawk
See MacCarthy, Sir(Charles Otto) Desmond

Africa, Ben
See Bosman, Herman Charles

Afton, Effie
See Harper, Frances Ellen Watkins

Agapida, Fray Antonio
See Irving, Washington

Agee, James (Rufus) 1909-1955 **TCLC 1, 19; DAM NOV**
See also AITN 1; CA 108; 148; CDALB 1941-1968; DLB 2, 26, 152; MTCW 1

Aghill, Gordon
See Silverberg, Robert

Agnon, S(hmuel) Y(osef Halevi) 1888-1970 **CLC 4, 8, 14; SSC 30**
See also CA 17-18; 25-28R; CANR 60; CAP 2; MTCW 1, 2

Agrippa von Nettesheim, Henry Cornelius 1486-1535 **LC 27**

Aguilera Malta, Demetrio 1909-1981
See also CA 111; 124; DAM MULT, NOV; DLB 145; HLCS 1; HW 1

Agustini, Delmira 1886-1914
See also CA 166; HLCS 1; HW 1, 2

Aherne, Owen
See Cassill, R(onald) V(erlin)

Ai 1947- **CLC 4, 14, 69**
See also CA 85-88; CAAS 13; CANR 70; DLB 120

Aickman, Robert (Fordyce) 1914-1981 **C L C 57**
See also CA 5-8R; CANR 3, 72

Aiken, Conrad (Potter) 1889-1973**CLC 1, 3, 5, 10, 52; DAM NOV, POET; PC 26; SSC 9**
See also CA 5-8R; 45-48; CANR 4, 60; CDALB 1929-1941; DLB 9, 45, 102; MTCW 1, 2; SATA 3, 30

Aiken, Joan (Delano) 1924- **CLC 35**
See also AAYA 1, 25; CA 9-12R; CANR 4, 23, 34, 64; CLR 1, 19; DLB 161; JRDA; MAICYA; MTCW 1; SAAS 1; SATA 2, 30, 73; SATA-Essay 109

Ainsworth, William Harrison 1805-1882 **NCLC 13**
See also DLB 21; SATA 24

Aitmatov, Chingiz (Torekulovich) 1928-**C L C 71**
See also CA 103; CANR 38; MTCW 1; SATA 56

Akers, Floyd
See Baum, L(yman) Frank

Akhmadulina, Bella Akhatovna 1937- **C L C 53; DAM POET**
See also CA 65-68

Akhmatova, Anna 1888-1966**CLC 11, 25, 64; DAM POET; PC 2**
See also CA 19-20; 25-28R; CANR 35; CAP 1; MTCW 1, 2

Aksakov, Sergei Timofeyvich 1791-1859 **NCLC 2**
See also DLB 198

Aksenov, Vassily
See Aksyonov, Vassily (Pavlovich)

Akst, Daniel 1956- **CLC 109**
See also CA 161

Aksyonov, Vassily (Pavlovich) 1932-**CLC 22, 37, 101**
See also CA 53-56; CANR 12, 48, 77

Akutagawa, Ryunosuke 1892-1927 **TCLC 16**
See also CA 117; 154

Alain 1868-1951 **TCLC 41**
See also CA 163

Alain-Fournier **TCLC 6**
See also Fournier, Henri Alban
See also DLB 65

Alarcon, Pedro Antonio de 1833-1891**NCLC 1**

Alas (y Urena), Leopoldo (Enrique Garcia) 1852-1901 **TCLC 29**
See also CA 113; 131; HW 1

Albee, Edward (Franklin III) 1928-**CLC 1, 2, 3, 5, 9, 11, 13, 25, 53, 86, 113; DA; DAB; DAC; DAM DRAM, MST; DC 11;WLC**
See also AITN 1; CA 5-8R; CABS 3; CANR 8, 54, 74; CDALB 1941-1968; DLB 7; INT CANR-8; MTCW 1, 2

Alberti, Rafael 1902- **CLC 7**

See also CA 85-88; CANR 81; DLB 108; HW 2

Albert the Great 1200(?)-1280 · **CMLC 16**
See also DLB 115

Alcala-Galiano, Juan Valera y
See Valera y Alcala-Galiano, Juan

Alcott, Amos Bronson 1799-1888 **NCLC 1**
See also DLB 1

Alcott, Louisa May 1832-1888 **NCLC 6, 58; DA; DAB; DAC; DAM MST, NOV; SSC 27; WLC**
See also AAYA 20; CDALB 1865-1917; CLR 1, 38; DLB 1, 42, 79; DLBD 14; JRDA; MAICYA; SATA 100; YABC 1

Aldanov, M. A.
See Aldanov, Mark (Alexandrovich)

Aldanov, Mark (Alexandrovich) 1886(?)-1957 **TCLC 23**
See also CA 118

Aldington, Richard 1892-1962 **CLC 49**
See also CA 85-88; CANR 45; DLB 20, 36, 100, 149

Aldiss, Brian W(ilson) 1925- **CLC 5, 14, 40; DAM NOV**
See also CA 5-8R; CAAS 2; CANR 5, 28, 64; DLB 14; MTCW 1, 2; SATA 34

Alegria, Claribel 1924-**CLC 75; DAM MULT; HLCS 1; PC 26**
See also CA 131; CAAS 15; CANR 66; DLB 145; HW 1; MTCW 1

Alegria, Fernando 1918- **CLC 57**
See also CA 9-12R; CANR 5, 32, 72; HW 1, 2

Aleichem, Sholom **TCLC 1, 35; SSC 33**
See also Rabinovitch, Sholem

Aleixandre, Vicente 1898-1984
See also CANR 81; HLCS 1; HW 2

Alepoudelis, Odysseus
See Elytis, Odysseus

Aleshkovsky, Joseph 1929-
See Aleshkovsky, Yuz
See also CA 121; 128

Aleshkovsky, Yuz **CLC 44**
See also Aleshkovsky, Joseph

Alexander, Lloyd (Chudley) 1924- **CLC 35**
See also AAYA 1, 27; CA 1-4R; CANR 1, 24, 38, 55; CLR 1, 5, 48; DLB 52; JRDA; MAICYA; MTCW 1; SAAS 19; SATA 3, 49, 81

Alexander, Meena 1951- **CLC 121**
See also CA 115; CANR 38, 70

Alexander, Samuel 1859-1938 **TCLC 77**

Alexie, Sherman (Joseph, Jr.) 1966- **CLC 96; DAM MULT**
See also AAYA 28; CA 138; CANR 65; DLB 175, 206; MTCW 1; NNAL

Alfau, Felipe 1902- **CLC 66**
See also CA 137

Alger, Horatio, Jr. 1832-1899 **NCLC 8**
See also DLB 42; SATA 16

Algren, Nelson 1909-1981**CLC 4, 10, 33; SSC 33**
See also CA 13-16R; 103; CANR 20, 61; CDALB 1941-1968; DLB 9; DLBY 81, 82; MTCW 1, 2

Ali, Ahmed 1910- **CLC 69**
See also CA 25-28R; CANR 15, 34

Alighieri, Dante
See Dante

Allan, John B.
See Westlake, Donald E(dwin)

Allan, Sidney
See Hartmann, Sadakichi

Allan, Sydney

See Hartmann, Sadakichi

Allen, Edward 1948- **CLC 59**

Allen, Fred 1894-1956 **TCLC 87**

Allen, Paula Gunn 1939-**CLC 84; DAM MULT**
See also CA 112; 143; CANR 63; DLB 175; MTCW 1; NNAL

Allen, Roland
See Ayckbourn, Alan

Allen, Sarah A.
See Hopkins, Pauline Elizabeth

Allen, Sidney H.
See Hartmann, Sadakichi

Allen, Woody 1935- **CLC 16, 52; DAM POP**
See also AAYA 10; CA 33-36R; CANR 27, 38, 63; DLB 44; MTCW 1

Allende, Isabel 1942- **CLC 39, 57, 97; DAM MULT, NOV; HLC 1; WLCS**
See also AAYA 18; CA 125; 130; CANR 51, 74; DLB 145; HW 1, 2; INT 130; MTCW 1, 2

Alleyn, Ellen
See Rossetti, Christina (Georgina)

Allingham, Margery (Louise) 1904-1966**CLC 19**
See also CA 5-8R; 25-28R; CANR 4, 58; DLB 77; MTCW 1, 2

Allingham, William 1824-1889 **NCLC 25**
See also DLB 35

Allison, Dorothy E. 1949- **CLC 78**
See also CA 140; CANR 66; MTCW 1

Allston, Washington 1779-1843 **NCLC 2**
See also DLB 1

Almedingen, E. M. **CLC 12**
See also Almedingen, Martha Edith von
See also SATA 3

Almedingen, Martha Edith von 1898-1971
See Almedingen, E. M.
See also CA 1-4R; CANR 1

Almodovar, Pedro 1949(?)-**CLC 114; HLCS 1**
See also CA 133; CANR 72; HW 2

Almqvist, Carl Jonas Love 1793-1866 **NCLC 42**

Alonso, Damaso 1898-1990 **CLC 14**
See also CA 110; 131; 130; CANR 72; DLB 108; HW 1, 2

Alov
See Gogol, Nikolai (Vasilyevich)

Alta 1942- **CLC 19**
See also CA 57-60

Alter, Robert B(ernard) 1935- **CLC 34**
See also CA 49-52; CANR 1, 47

Alther, Lisa 1944- **CLC 7, 41**
See also CA 65-68; CAAS 30; CANR 12, 30, 51; MTCW 1

Althusser, L.
See Althusser, Louis

Althusser, Louis 1918-1990 **CLC 106**
See also CA 131; 132

Altman, Robert 1925- **CLC 16, 116**
See also CA 73-76; CANR 43

Alurista 1949-
See Urista, Alberto H.
See also DLB 82; HLCS 1

Alvarez, A(lfred) 1929- **CLC 5, 13**
See also CA 1-4R; CANR 3, 33, 63; DLB 14, 40

Alvarez, Alejandro Rodriguez 1903-1965
See Casona, Alejandro
See also CA 131; 93-96; HW 1

Alvarez, Julia 1950- **CLC 93; HLCS 1**
See also AAYA 25; CA 147; CANR 69; MTCW 1

Alvaro, Corrado 1896-1956 **TCLC 60**

See also CA 163

Amado, Jorge 1912- **CLC 13, 40, 106; DAM MULT, NOV; HLC 1**
See also CA 77-80; CANR 35, 74; DLB 113; HW 2; MTCW 1, 2

Ambler, Eric 1909-1998 **CLC 4, 6, 9**
See also CA 9-12R; 171; CANR 7, 38, 74; DLB 77; MTCW 1, 2

Amichai, Yehuda 1924- **CLC 9, 22, 57, 116**
See also CA 85-88; CANR 46, 60; MTCW 1

Amichai, Yehudah
See Amichai, Yehuda

Amiel, Henri Frederic 1821-1881 **NCLC 4**

Amis, Kingsley (William) 1922-1995**CLC 1, 2, 3, 5, 8, 13, 40, 44; DA; DAB; DAC; DAM MST, NOV**
See also AITN 2; CA 9-12R; 150; CANR 8, 28, 54; CDBLB 1945-1960; DLB 15, 27, 100, 139; DLBY 96; INT CANR-8; MTCW 1, 2

Amis, Martin (Louis) 1949- **CLC 4, 9, 38, 62, 101**
See also BEST 90:3; CA 65-68; CANR 8, 27, 54, 73; DLB 14, 194; INT CANR-27; MTCW 1

Ammons, A(rchie) R(andolph) 1926-**CLC 2, 3, 5, 8, 9, 25, 57, 108; DAM POET; PC 16**
See also AITN 1; CA 9-12R; CANR 6, 36, 51, 73; DLB 5, 165; MTCW 1, 2

Amo, Tauraatua i
See Adams, Henry (Brooks)

Amory, Thomas 1691(?)-1788 **LC 48**

Anand, Mulk Raj 1905- **CLC 23, 93; DAM NOV**
See also CA 65-68; CANR 32, 64; MTCW 1, 2

Anatol
See Schnitzler, Arthur

Anaximander c. 610B.C.-c. 546B.C.**CMLC 22**

Anaya, Rudolfo A(lfonso) 1937- **CLC 23; DAM MULT, NOV; HLC 1**
See also AAYA 20; CA 45-48; CAAS 4; CANR 1, 32, 51; DLB 82, 206; HW 1; MTCW 1, 2

Andersen, Hans Christian 1805-1875**NCLC 7, 79; DA; DAB; DAC; DAM MST, POP; SSC 6; WLC**
See also CLR 6; MAICYA; SATA 100; YABC 1

Anderson, C. Farley
See Mencken, H(enry) L(ouis); Nathan, George Jean

Anderson, Jessica (Margaret) Queale 1916- **CLC 37**
See also CA 9-12R; CANR 4, 62

Anderson, Jon (Victor) 1940- **CLC 9; DAM POET**
See also CA 25-28R; CANR 20

Anderson, Lindsay (Gordon) 1923-1994**CLC 20**
See also CA 125; 128; 146; CANR 77

Anderson, Maxwell 1888-1959**TCLC 2; DAM DRAM**
See also CA 105; 152; DLB 7; MTCW 2

Anderson, Poul (William) 1926- **CLC 15**
See also AAYA 5; CA 1-4R; CAAS 2; CANR 2, 15, 34, 64; CLR 58; DLB 8; INT CANR-15; MTCW 1, 2; SATA 90; SATA-Brief 39; SATA-Essay 106

Anderson, Robert (Woodruff) 1917-**CLC 23; DAM DRAM**
See also AITN 1; CA 21-24R; CANR 32; DLB 7

Anderson, Sherwood 1876-1941 **TCLC 1, 10, 24; DA; DAB; DAC; DAM MST, NOV; SSC 1; WLC**

6, 9, 13, 15, 25, 41, 77; DAM POET; PC 26
See also CA 5-8R; CANR 9, 37, 66; DLB 5, 165; DLBY 81; INT CANR-9; MTCW 1, 2

Ashdown, Clifford
See Freeman, R(ichard) Austin

Ashe, Gordon
See Creasey, John

Ashton-Warner, Sylvia (Constance) 1908-1984 CLC 19
See also CA 69-72; 112; CANR 29; MTCW 1, 2

Asimov, Isaac 1920-1992 CLC 1, 3, 9, 19, 26, 76, 92; DAM POP
See also AAYA 13; BEST 90:2; CA 1-4R; 137; CANR 2, 19, 36, 60; CLR 12; DLB 8; DLBY 92; INT CANR-19; JRDA; MAICYA; MTCW 1, 2; SATA 1, 26, 74

Assis, Joaquim Maria Machado de
See Machado de Assis, Joaquim Maria

Astley, Thea (Beatrice May) 1925- CLC 41
See also CA 65-68; CANR 11, 43, 78

Aston, James
See White, T(erence) H(anbury)

Asturias, Miguel Angel 1899-1974 CLC 3, 8, 13; DAM MULT, NOV; HLC 1
See also CA 25-28; 49-52; CANR 32; CAP 2; DLB 113; HW 1; MTCW 1, 2

Atares, Carlos Saura
See Saura (Atares), Carlos

Atheling, William
See Pound, Ezra (Weston Loomis)

Atheling, William, Jr.
See Blish, James (Benjamin)

Atherton, Gertrude (Franklin Horn) 1857-1948 TCLC 2
See also CA 104; 155; DLB 9, 78, 186

Atherton, Lucius
See Masters, Edgar Lee

Atkins, Jack
See Harris, Mark

Atkinson, Kate CLC 99
See also CA 166

Attaway, William (Alexander) 1911-1986CLC 92; BLC 1; DAM MULT
See also BW 2, 3; CA 143; CANR 82; DLB 76

Atticus
See Fleming, Ian (Lancaster); Wilson, (Thomas) Woodrow

Atwood, Margaret (Eleanor) 1939-CLC 2, 3, 4, 8, 13, 15, 25, 44, 84; DA; DAB; DAC; DAM MST, NOV, POET; PC 8; SSC 2; WLC
See also AAYA 12; BEST 89:2; CA 49-52; CANR 3, 24, 33, 59; DLB 53; INT CANR-24; MTCW 1, 2; SATA 50

Aubigny, Pierre d'
See Mencken, H(enry) L(ouis)

Aubin, Penelope 1685-1731(?) LC 9
See also DLB 39

Auchincloss, Louis (Stanton) 1917-CLC 4, 6, 9, 18, 45; DAM NOV; SSC 22
See also CA 1-4R; CANR 6, 29, 55; DLB 2; DLBY 80; INT CANR-29; MTCW 1

Auden, W(ystan) H(ugh) 1907-1973CLC 1, 2, 3, 4, 6, 9, 11, 14, 43; DA; DAB; DAC; DAM DRAM, MST, POET; PC 1;WLC
See also AAYA 18; CA 9-12R; 45-48; CANR 5, 61; CDBLB 1914-1945; DLB 10, 20; MTCW 1, 2

Audiberti, Jacques 1900-1965 CLC 38; DAM DRAM
See also CA 25-28R

Audubon, John James 1785-1851 NCLC 47

Auel, Jean M(arie) 1936- CLC 31, 107; DAM POP
See also AAYA 7; BEST 90:4; CA 103; CANR 21, 64; INT CANR-21; SATA 91

Auerbach, Erich 1892-1957 TCLC 43
See also CA 118; 155

Augier, Emile 1820-1889 NCLC 31
See also DLB 192

August, John
See De Voto, Bernard (Augustine)

Augustine 354-430CMLC 6; DA; DAB; DAC; DAM MST; WLCS
See also DLB 115

Aurelius
See Bourne, Randolph S(illiman)

Aurobindo, Sri
See Ghose, Aurabinda

Austen, Jane 1775-1817 NCLC 1, 13, 19, 33, 51; DA; DAB; DAC; DAM MST, NOV; WLC
See also AAYA 19; CDBLB 1789-1832; DLB 116

Auster, Paul 1947- CLC 47
See also CA 69-72; CANR 23, 52, 75; MTCW 1

Austin, Frank
See Faust, Frederick (Schiller)

Austin, Mary (Hunter) 1868-1934 TCLC 25
See also CA 109; 178; DLB 9, 78, 206

Autran Dourado, Waldomiro Freitas 1926-
See Dourado, (Waldomiro Freitas) Autran
See also CA 179

Averroes 1126-1198 CMLC 7
See also DLB 115

Avicenna 980-1037 CMLC 16
See also DLB 115

Avison, Margaret 1918- CLC 2, 4, 97; DAC; DAM POET
See also CA 17-20R; DLB 53; MTCW 1

Axton, David
See Koontz, Dean R(ay)

Ayckbourn, Alan 1939- CLC 5, 8, 18, 33, 74; DAB; DAM DRAM
See also CA 21-24R; CANR 31, 59; DLB 13; MTCW 1, 2

Aydy, Catherine
See Tennant, Emma (Christina)

Ayme, Marcel (Andre) 1902-1967 CLC 11
See also CA 89-92; CANR 67; CLR 25; DLB 72; SATA 91

Ayrton, Michael 1921-1975 CLC 7
See also CA 5-8R; 61-64; CANR 9, 21

Azorin CLC 11
See also Martinez Ruiz, Jose

Azuela, Mariano 1873-1952 TCLC 3; DAM MULT; HLC 1
See also CA 104; 131; CANR 81; HW 1, 2; MTCW 1, 2

Baastad, Babbis Friis
See Friis-Baastad, Babbis Ellinor

Bab
See Gilbert, W(illiam) S(chwenck)

Babbis, Eleanor
See Friis-Baastad, Babbis Ellinor

Babel, Isaac
See Babel, Isaak (Emmanuilovich)

Babel, Isaak (Emmanuilovich) 1894-1941(?) TCLC 2, 13; SSC 16
See also CA 104; 155; MTCW 1

Babits, Mihaly 1883-1941 TCLC 14
See also CA 114

Babur 1483-1530 LC 18

Baca, Jimmy Santiago 1952-

See also CA 131; CANR 81; DAM MULT; DLB 122; HLC 1; HW 1, 2

Bacchelli, Riccardo 1891-1985 CLC 19
See also CA 29-32R; 117

Bach, Richard (David) 1936- CLC 14; DAM NOV, POP
See also AITN 1; BEST 89:2; CA 9-12R; CANR 18; MTCW 1; SATA 13

Bachman, Richard
See King, Stephen (Edwin)

Bachmann, Ingeborg 1926-1973 CLC 69
See also CA 93-96; 45-48; CANR 69; DLB 85

Bacon, Francis 1561-1626 LC 18,32
See also CDBLB Before 1660; DLB 151

Bacon, Roger 1214(?)-1292 CMLC 14
See also DLB 115

Bacovia, George TCLC 24
See also Vasiliu, Gheorghe

Badanes, Jerome 1937- CLC 59

Bagehot, Walter 1826-1877 NCLC 10
See also DLB 55

Bagnold, Enid 1889-1981 CLC 25;DAM DRAM
See also CA 5-8R; 103; CANR 5, 40; DLB 13, 160, 191; MAICYA; SATA 1, 25

Bagritsky, Eduard 1895-1934 TCLC 60

Bagrjana, Elisaveta
See Belcheva, Elisaveta

Bagryana, Elisaveta 1893-1991 CLC 10
See also Belcheva, Elisaveta
See also CA 178; DLB 147

Bailey, Paul 1937- CLC 45
See also CA 21-24R; CANR 16, 62; DLB 14

Baillie, Joanna 1762-1851 NCLC 71
See also DLB 93

Bainbridge, Beryl (Margaret) 1933-CLC 4, 5, 8, 10, 14, 18, 22, 62; DAM NOV
See also CA 21-24R; CANR 24, 55, 75; DLB 14; MTCW 1, 2

Baker, Elliott 1922- CLC 8
See also CA 45-48; CANR 2, 63

Baker, Jean H. TCLC 3, 10
See also Russell, George William

Baker, Nicholson 1957- CLC 61;DAM POP
See also CA 135; CANR 63

Baker, Ray Stannard 1870-1946 TCLC 47
See also CA 118

Baker, Russell (Wayne) 1925- CLC 31
See also BEST 89:4; CA 57-60; CANR 11, 41, 59; MTCW 1, 2

Bakhtin, M.
See Bakhtin, Mikhail Mikhailovich

Bakhtin, M. M.
See Bakhtin, Mikhail Mikhailovich

Bakhtin, Mikhail
See Bakhtin, Mikhail Mikhailovich

Bakhtin, Mikhail Mikhailovich 1895-1975 CLC 83
See also CA 128; 113

Bakshi, Ralph 1938(?)- CLC 26
See also CA 112; 138

Bakunin, Mikhail (Alexandrovich) 1814-1876 NCLC 25, 58

Baldwin, James (Arthur) 1924-1987CLC 1, 2, 3, 4, 5, 8, 13, 15, 17, 42, 50, 67, 90; BLC 1; DA; DAB; DAC; DAM MST, MULT, NOV, POP; DC 1; SSC 10, 33; WLC
See also AAYA 4; BW 1; CA 1-4R; 124; CABS 1; CANR 3, 24; CDALB 1941-1968; DLB 2, 7, 33; DLBY 87; MTCW 1, 2; SATA 9; SATA-Obit 54

Ballard, J(ames) G(raham) 1930-CLC 3, 6, 14, 36; DAM NOV, POP; SSC 1

See also AAYA 3; CA 5-8R; CANR 15, 39, 65;
DLB 14, 207; MTCW 1, 2; SATA 93

Balmont, Konstantin (Dmitriyevich) 1867-1943
TCLC 11
See also CA 109; 155

Baltausis, Vincas
See Mikszath, Kalman

Balzac, Honore de 1799-1850 **NCLC 5, 35, 53;**
DA; DAB; DAC; DAM MST, NOV; SSC
5; WLC
See also DLB 119

Bambara, Toni Cade 1939-1995 **CLC 19, 88;**
BLC 1; DA; DAC; DAM MST, MULT;
SSC 35; WLCS
See also AAYA 5; BW 2, 3; CA 29-32R; 150;
CANR 24, 49, 81; CDALBS; DLB 38;
MTCW 1, 2

Bamdad, A.
See Shamlu, Ahmad

Banat, D. R.
See Bradbury, Ray (Douglas)

Bancroft, Laura
See Baum, L(yman) Frank

Banim, John 1798-1842 **NCLC 13**
See also DLB 116, 158, 159

Banim, Michael 1796-1874 **NCLC 13**
See also DLB 158, 159

Banjo, The
See Paterson, A(ndrew) B(arton)

Banks, Iain
See Banks, Iain M(enzies)

Banks, Iain M(enzies) 1954- **CLC 34**
See also CA 123; 128; CANR 61; DLB 194;
INT 128

Banks, Lynne Reid **CLC 23**
See also Reid Banks, Lynne
See also AAYA 6

Banks, Russell 1940- **CLC 37, 72**
See also CA 65-68; CAAS 15; CANR 19, 52,
73; DLB 130

Banville, John 1945- **CLC 46, 118**
See also CA 117; 128; DLB 14; INT 128

Banville, Theodore (Faullain) de 1832-1891
NCLC 9

Baraka, Amiri 1934- **CLC 1, 2, 3, 5, 10, 14, 33,**
115; BLC 1; DA; DAC; DAM MST, MULT,
POET, POP; DC 6; PC 4; WLCS
See also Jones, LeRoi
See also BW 2, 3; CA 21-24R; CABS 3; CANR
27, 38, 61; CDALB 1941-1968; DLB 5, 7,
16, 38; DLBD 8; MTCW 1, 2

Barbauld, Anna Laetitia 1743-1825 **NCLC 50**
See also DLB 107, 109, 142, 158

Barbellion, W. N. P. **TCLC 24**
See also Cummings, Bruce F(rederick)

Barbera, Jack (Vincent) 1945- **CLC 44**
See also CA 110; CANR 45

Barbey d'Aurevilly, Jules Amedee 1808-1889
NCLC 1; SSC 17
See also DLB 119

Barbour, John c. 1316-1395 **CMLC 33**
See also DLB 146

Barbusse, Henri 1873-1935 **TCLC 5**
See also CA 105; 154; DLB 65

Barclay, Bill
See Moorcock, Michael (John)

Barclay, William Ewert
See Moorcock, Michael (John)

Barea, Arturo 1897-1957 **TCLC 14**
See also CA 111

Barfoot, Joan 1946- **CLC 18**
See also CA 105

Barham, Richard Harris 1788-1845 **NCLC 77**

See also DLB 159

Baring, Maurice 1874-1945 **TCLC 8**
See also CA 105; 168; DLB 34

Baring-Gould, Sabine 1834-1924 **TCLC 88**
See also DLB 156, 190

Barker, Clive 1952- **CLC 52; DAM POP**
See also AAYA 10; BEST 90:3; CA 121; 129;
CANR 71; INT 129; MTCW 1, 2

Barker, George Granville 1913-1991 **CLC 8,**
48; DAM POET
See also CA 9-12R; 135; CANR 7, 38; DLB
20; MTCW 1

Barker, Harley Granville
See Granville-Barker, Harley
See also DLB 10

Barker, Howard 1946- **CLC 37**
See also CA 102; DLB 13

Barker, Jane 1652-1732 **LC 42**

Barker, Pat(ricia) 1943- **CLC 32, 94**
See also CA 117; 122; CANR 50; INT 122

Barlach, Ernst 1870-1938 **TCLC 84**
See also CA 178; DLB 56, 118

Barlow, Joel 1754-1812 **NCLC 23**
See also DLB 37

Barnard, Mary (Ethel) 1909- **CLC 48**
See also CA 21-22; CAP 2

Barnes, Djuna 1892-1982 **CLC 3, 4, 8, 11, 29;**
SSC 3
See also CA 9-12R; 107; CANR 16, 55; DLB
4, 9, 45; MTCW 1, 2

Barnes, Julian (Patrick) 1946- **CLC 42; DAB**
See also CA 102; CANR 19, 54; DLB 194;
DLBY 93; MTCW 1

Barnes, Peter 1931- **CLC 5, 56**
See also CA 65-68; CAAS 12; CANR 33, 34,
64; DLB 13; MTCW 1

Barnes, William 1801-1886 **NCLC 75**
See also DLB 32

Baroja (y Nessi), Pio 1872-1956 **TCLC 8; HLC**
1
See also CA 104

Baron, David
See Pinter, Harold

Baron Corvo
See Rolfe, Frederick (William Serafino Austin
Lewis Mary)

Barondess, Sue K(aufman) 1926-1977 **CLC 8**
See also Kaufman, Sue
See also CA 1-4R; 69-72; CANR 1

Baron de Teive
See Pessoa, Fernando (Antonio Nogueira)

Baroness Von S.
See Zangwill, Israel

Barres, (Auguste-) Maurice 1862-1923 **TCLC**
47
See also CA 164; DLB 123

Barreto, Afonso Henrique de Lima
See Lima Barreto, Afonso Henrique de

Barrett, (Roger) Syd 1946- **CLC 35**

Barrett, William (Christopher) 1913-1992
CLC 27
See also CA 13-16R; 139; CANR 11, 67; INT
CANR-11

Barrie, J(ames) M(atthew) 1860-1937 **TCLC**
2; DAB; DAM DRAM
See also CA 104; 136; CANR 77; CDBLB
1890-1914; CLR 16; DLB 10, 141, 156;
MAICYA; MTCW 1; SATA 100; YABC 1

Barrington, Michael
See Moorcock, Michael (John)

Barrol, Grady
See Bograd, Larry

Barry, Mike

See Malzberg, Barry N(athaniel)

Barry, Philip 1896-1949 **TCLC 11**
See also CA 109; DLB 7

Bart, Andre Schwarz
See Schwarz-Bart, Andre

Barth, John (Simmons) 1930- **CLC 1, 2, 3, 5, 7,**
9, 10, 14, 27, 51, 89; DAM NOV; SSC 10
See also AITN 1, 2; CA 1-4R; CABS 1; CANR
5, 23, 49, 64; DLB 2; MTCW 1

Barthelme, Donald 1931-1989 **CLC 1, 2, 3, 5, 6,**
8, 13, 23, 46, 59, 115; DAM NOV; SSC 2
See also CA 21-24R; 129; CANR 20, 58; DLB
2; DLBY 80, 89; MTCW 1, 2; SATA 7;
SATA-Obit 62

Barthelme, Frederick 1943- **CLC 36, 117**
See also CA 114; 122; CANR 77; DLBY 85;
INT 122

Barthes, Roland (Gerard) 1915-1980 **CLC 24,**
83
See also CA 130; 97-100; CANR 66; MTCW
1, 2

Barzun, Jacques (Martin) 1907- **CLC 51**
See also CA 61-64; CANR 22

Bashevis, Isaac
See Singer, Isaac Bashevis

Bashkirtseff, Marie 1859-1884 **NCLC 27**

Basho
See Matsuo Basho

Basil of Caesaria c. 330-379 **CMLC 35**

Bass, Kingsley B., Jr.
See Bullins, Ed

Bass, Rick 1958- **CLC 79**
See also CA 126; CANR 53; DLB 212

Bassani, Giorgio 1916- **CLC 9**
See also CA 65-68; CANR 33; DLB 128, 177;
MTCW 1

Bastos, Augusto (Antonio) Roa
See Roa Bastos, Augusto (Antonio)

Bataille, Georges 1897-1962 **CLC 29**
See also CA 101; 89-92

Bates, H(erbert) E(rnest) 1905-1974 **CLC 46;**
DAB; DAM POP; SSC 10
See also CA 93-96; 45-48; CANR 34; DLB 162,
191; MTCW 1, 2

Bauchart
See Camus, Albert

Baudelaire, Charles 1821-1867 **NCLC 6, 29,**
55; DA; DAB; DAC; DAM MST, POET;
PC 1; SSC 18; WLC

Baudrillard, Jean 1929- **CLC 60**

Baum, L(yman) Frank 1856-1919 **TCLC 7**
See also CA 108; 133; CLR 15; DLB 22; JRDA;
MAICYA; MTCW 1, 2; SATA 18, 100

Baum, Louis F.
See Baum, L(yman) Frank

Baumbach, Jonathan 1933- **CLC 6, 23**
See also CA 13-16R; CAAS 5; CANR 12, 66;
DLBY 80; INT CANR-12; MTCW 1

Bausch, Richard (Carl) 1945- **CLC 51**
See also CA 101; CAAS 14; CANR 43, 61; DLB
130

Baxter, Charles (Morley) 1947- **CLC 45, 78;**
DAM POP
See also CA 57-60; CANR 40, 64; DLB 130;
MTCW 2

Baxter, George Owen
See Faust, Frederick (Schiller)

Baxter, James K(eir) 1926-1972 **CLC 14**
See also CA 77-80

Baxter, John
See Hunt, E(verette) Howard, (Jr.)

Bayer, Sylvia
See Glassco, John

Baynton, Barbara 1857-1929 **TCLC 57**

Beagle, Peter S(oyer) 1939- **CLC 7,104**
See also CA 9-12R; CANR 4, 51, 73; DLBY 80; INT CANR-4; MTCW 1; SATA 60

Bean, Normal
See Burroughs, Edgar Rice

Beard, Charles A(ustin) 1874-1948 **TCLC 15**
See also CA 115; DLB 17; SATA 18

Beardsley, Aubrey 1872-1898 **NCLC 6**

Beattie, Ann 1947-**CLC 8, 13, 18, 40, 63; DAM NOV, POP; SSC 11**
See also BEST 90:2; CA 81-84; CANR 53, 73; DLBY 82; MTCW 1, 2

Beattie, James 1735-1803 **NCLC 25**
See also DLB 109

Beauchamp, Kathleen Mansfield 1888-1923
See Mansfield, Katherine
See also CA 104; 134; DA; DAC; DAM MST; MTCW 2

Beaumarchais, Pierre-Augustin Caronde 1732-1799 **DC 4**
See also DAM DRAM

Beaumont, Francis 1584(?)-1616**LC 33; DC 6**
See also CDBLB Before 1660; DLB 58, 121

Beauvoir, Simone (Lucie Ernestine Marie Bertrand) de 1908-1986**CLC 1, 2, 4, 8, 14, 31, 44, 50, 71; DA; DAB; DAC; DAM MST, NOV; SSC 35; WLC**
See also CA 9-12R; 118; CANR 28, 61; DLB 72; DLBY 86; MTCW 1, 2

Becker, Carl (Lotus) 1873-1945 **TCLC 63**
See also CA 157; DLB 17

Becker, Jurek 1937-1997 **CLC 7, 19**
See also CA 85-88; 157; CANR 60; DLB 75

Becker, Walter 1950- **CLC 26**

Beckett, Samuel (Barclay) 1906-1989 **CLC 1, 2, 3, 4, 6, 9, 10, 11, 14, 18, 29, 57, 59, 83; DA; DAB; DAC; DAM DRAM, MST, NOV; SSC 16; WLC**
See also CA 5-8R; 130; CANR 33, 61; CDBLB 1945-1960; DLB 13, 15; DLBY 90; MTCW 1, 2

Beckford, William 1760-1844 **NCLC 16**
See also DLB 39

Beckman, Gunnel 1910- **CLC 26**
See also CA 33-36R; CANR 15; CLR 25; MAICYA; SAAS 9; SATA 6

Becque, Henri 1837-1899 **NCLC 3**
See also DLB 192

Becquer, Gustavo Adolfo 1836-1870
See also DAM MULT; HLCS 1

Beddoes, Thomas Lovell 1803-1849 **NCLC 3**
See also DLB 96

Bede c. 673-735 **CMLC 20**
See also DLB 146

Bedford, Donald F.
See Fearing, Kenneth (Flexner)

Beecher, Catharine Esther 1800-1878 **NCLC 30**
See also DLB 1

Beecher, John 1904-1980 **CLC 6**
See also AITN 1; CA 5-8R; 105; CANR 8

Beer, Johann 1655-1700 **LC 5**
See also DLB 168

Beer, Patricia 1924- **CLC 58**
See also CA 61-64; CANR 13, 46; DLB 40

Beerbohm, Max
See Beerbohm, (Henry) Max(imilian)

Beerbohm, (Henry) Max(imilian) 1872-1956 **TCLC 1, 24**
See also CA 104; 154; CANR 79; DLB 34, 100

Beer-Hofmann, Richard 1866-1945**TCLC 60**
See also CA 160; DLB 81

Begiebing, Robert J(ohn) 1946- **CLC 70**
See also CA 122; CANR 40

Behan, Brendan 1923-1964 **CLC 1, 8, 11, 15, 79; DAM DRAM**
See also CA 73-76; CANR 33; CDBLB 1945-1960; DLB 13; MTCW 1, 2

Behn, Aphra 1640(?)-1689 **LC 1, 30, 42; DA; DAB; DAC; DAM DRAM, MST, NOV, POET; DC 4; PC 13; WLC**
See also DLB 39, 80, 131

Behrman, S(amuel) N(athaniel) 1893-1973 **CLC 40**
See also CA 13-16; 45-48; CAP 1; DLB 7, 44

Belasco, David 1853-1931 **TCLC 3**
See also CA 104; 168; DLB 7

Belcheva, Elisaveta 1893- **CLC 10**
See also Bagryana, Elisaveta

Beldone, Phil "Cheech"
See Ellison, Harlan (Jay)

Beleno
See Azuela, Mariano

Belinski, Vissarion Grigoryevich 1811-1848 **NCLC 5**
See also DLB 198

Belitt, Ben 1911- **CLC 22**
See also CA 13-16R; CAAS 4; CANR 7, 77; DLB 5

Bell, Gertrude (Margaret Lowthian) 1868-1926 **TCLC 67**
See also CA 167; DLB 174

Bell, J. Freeman
See Zangwill, Israel

Bell, James Madison 1826-1902 **TCLC 43; BLC 1; DAM MULT**
See also BW 1; CA 122; 124; DLB 50

Bell, Madison Smartt 1957- **CLC 41, 102**
See also CA 111; CANR 28, 54, 73; MTCW 1

Bell, Marvin (Hartley) 1937-**CLC 8, 31; DAM POET**
See also CA 21-24R; CAAS 14; CANR 59; DLB 5; MTCW 1

Bell, W. L. D.
See Mencken, H(enry) L(ouis)

Bellamy, Atwood C.
See Mencken, H(enry) L(ouis)

Bellamy, Edward 1850-1898 **NCLC 4**
See also DLB 12

Belli, Gioconda 1949-
See also CA 152; HLCS 1

Bellin, Edward J.
See Kuttner, Henry

Belloc, (Joseph) Hilaire (Pierre Sebastien Rene Swanton) 1870-1953 **TCLC 7, 18; DAM POET; PC 24**
See also CA 106; 152; DLB 19, 100, 141, 174; MTCW 1; YABC 1

Belloc, Joseph Peter Rene Hilaire
See Belloc, (Joseph) Hilaire (Pierre Sebastien Rene Swanton)

Belloc, Joseph Pierre Hilaire
See Belloc, (Joseph) Hilaire (Pierre Sebastien Rene Swanton)

Belloc, M. A.
See Lowndes, Marie Adelaide (Belloc)

Bellow, Saul 1915-**CLC 1, 2, 3, 6, 8, 10, 13, 15, 25, 33, 34, 63, 79; DA; DAB; DAC; DAM MST, NOV, POP; SSC 14; WLC**
See also AITN 2; BEST 89:3; CA 5-8R; CABS 1; CANR 29, 53; CDALB 1941-1968; DLB 2, 28; DLBD 3; DLBY 82; MTCW 1, 2

Belser, Reimond Karel Maria de 1929-
See Ruyslinck, Ward
See also CA 152

Bely, Andrey **TCLC 7; PC 11**
See also Bugayev, Boris Nikolayevich
See also MTCW 1

Belyi, Andrei
See Bugayev, Boris Nikolayevich

Benary, Margot
See Benary-Isbert, Margot

Benary-Isbert, Margot 1889-1979 **CLC 12**
See also CA 5-8R; 89-92; CANR 4, 72; CLR 12; MAICYA; SATA 2; SATA-Obit 21

Benavente (y Martinez), Jacinto 1866-1954 **TCLC 3; DAM DRAM, MULT; HLCS 1**
See also CA 106; 131; CANR 81; HW 1, 2; MTCW 1, 2

Benchley, Peter (Bradford) 1940- **CLC 4, 8; DAM NOV, POP**
See also AAYA 14; AITN 2; CA 17-20R; CANR 12, 35, 66; MTCW 1, 2; SATA 3, 89

Benchley, Robert (Charles) 1889-1945**T C L C 1, 55**
See also CA 105; 153; DLB 11

Benda, Julien 1867-1956 **TCLC 60**
See also CA 120; 154

Benedict, Ruth (Fulton) 1887-1948 **TCLC 60**
See also CA 158

Benedict, Saint c. 480-c. 547 **CMLC 29**

Benedikt, Michael 1935- **CLC 4, 14**
See also CA 13-16R; CANR 7; DLB 5

Benet, Juan 1927- **CLC 28**
See also CA 143

Benet, Stephen Vincent 1898-1943 **TCLC 7; DAM POET; SSC 10**
See also CA 104; 152; DLB 4, 48, 102; DLBY 97; MTCW 1; YABC 1

Benet, William Rose 1886-1950 **TCLC 28; DAM POET**
See also CA 118; 152; DLB 45

Benford, Gregory (Albert) 1941- **CLC 52**
See also CA 69-72, 175; CAAE 175; CAAS 27; CANR 12, 24, 49; DLBY 82

Bengtsson, Frans (Gunnar) 1894-1954**T C L C 48**
See also CA 170

Benjamin, David
See Slavitt, David R(ytman)

Benjamin, Lois
See Gould, Lois

Benjamin, Walter 1892-1940 **TCLC 39**
See also CA 164

Benn, Gottfried 1886-1956 **TCLC 3**
See also CA 106; 153; DLB 56

Bennett, Alan 1934-**CLC 45, 77; DAB; DAM MST**
See also CA 103; CANR 35, 55; MTCW 1, 2

Bennett, (Enoch) Arnold 1867-1931 **TCLC 5, 20**
See also CA 106; 155; CDBLB 1890-1914; DLB 10, 34, 98, 135; MTCW 2

Bennett, Elizabeth
See Mitchell, Margaret (Munnerlyn)

Bennett, George Harold 1930-
See Bennett, Hal
See also BW 1; CA 97-100

Bennett, Hal **CLC 5**
See also Bennett, George Harold
See also DLB 33

Bennett, Jay 1912- **CLC 35**
See also AAYA 10; CA 69-72; CANR 11, 42, 79; JRDA; SAAS 4; SATA 41, 87; SATA-Brief 27

Bennett, Louise (Simone) 1919-**CLC 28; BLC 1; DAM MULT**
See also BW 2, 3; CA 151; DLB 117

Benson, E(dward) F(rederic) 1867-1940
    TCLC 27
    See also CA 114; 157; DLB 135, 153
Benson, Jackson J. 1930-   **CLC 34**
    See also CA 25-28R; DLB 111
Benson, Sally 1900-1972   **CLC 17**
    See also CA 19-20; 37-40R; CAP 1; SATA 1,
    35; SATA-Obit 27
Benson, Stella 1892-1933   **TCLC 17**
    See also CA 117; 155; DLB 36, 162
Bentham, Jeremy 1748-1832   **NCLC 38**
    See also DLB 107, 158
Bentley, E(dmund) C(lerihew) 1875-1956
    TCLC 12
    See also CA 108; DLB 70
Bentley, Eric (Russell) 1916-   **CLC 24**
    See also CA 5-8R; CANR 6, 67; INT CANR-6
Beranger, Pierre Jean de 1780-1857**NCLC 34**
Berdyaev, Nicolas
    See Berdyaev, Nikolai (Aleksandrovich)
Berdyaev, Nikolai (Aleksandrovich) 1874-1948
    TCLC 67
    See also CA 120; 157
Berdyayev, Nikolai (Aleksandrovich)
    See Berdyaev, Nikolai (Aleksandrovich)
Berendt, John (Lawrence) 1939-   **CLC 86**
    See also CA 146; CANR 75; MTCW 1
Beresford, J(ohn) D(avys) 1873-1947 **TCLC 81**
    See also CA 112; 155; DLB 162, 178, 197
Bergelson, David 1884-1952   **TCLC 81**
Berger, Colonel
    See Malraux, (Georges-)Andre
Berger, John (Peter) 1926-   **CLC 2, 19**
    See also CA 81-84; CANR 51, 78; DLB 14, 207
Berger, Melvin H. 1927-   **CLC 12**
    See also CA 5-8R; CANR 4; CLR 32; SAAS 2;
    SATA 5, 88
Berger, Thomas (Louis) 1924-**CLC 3, 5, 8, 11,
    18, 38; DAM NOV**
    See also CA 1-4R; CANR 5, 28, 51; DLB 2;
    DLBY 80; INT CANR-28; MTCW 1, 2
Bergman, (Ernst) Ingmar 1918- **CLC 16, 72**
    See also CA 81-84; CANR 33, 70; MTCW 2
Bergson, Henri (-Louis) 1859-1941 **TCLC 32**
    See also CA 164
Bergstein, Eleanor 1938-   **CLC 4**
    See also CA 53-56; CANR 5
Berkoff, Steven 1937-   **CLC 56**
    See also CA 104; CANR 72
Bermant, Chaim (Icyk) 1929-   **CLC 40**
    See also CA 57-60; CANR 6, 31, 57
Bern, Victoria
    See Fisher, M(ary) F(rances) K(ennedy)
Bernanos, (Paul Louis) Georges 1888-1948
    TCLC 3
    See also CA 104; 130; DLB 72
Bernard, April 1956-   **CLC 59**
    See also CA 131
Berne, Victoria
    See Fisher, M(ary) F(rances) K(ennedy)
Bernhard, Thomas 1931-1989 **CLC 3, 32, 61**
    See also CA 85-88; 127; CANR 32, 57; DLB
    85, 124; MTCW 1
Bernhardt, Sarah (Henriette Rosine) 1844-1923
    TCLC 75
    See also CA 157
Berriault, Gina 1926- **CLC 54, 109; SSC 30**
    See also CA 116; 129; CANR 66; DLB 130
Berrigan, Daniel 1921-   **CLC 4**
    See also CA 33-36R; CAAS 1; CANR 11, 43,
    78; DLB 5
Berrigan, Edmund Joseph Michael, Jr. 1934-

1983
    See Berrigan, Ted
    See also CA 61-64; 110; CANR 14
Berrigan, Ted   **CLC 37**
    See also Berrigan, Edmund Joseph Michael, Jr.
    See also DLB 5, 169
Berry, Charles Edward Anderson 1931-
    See Berry, Chuck
    See also CA 115
Berry, Chuck   **CLC 17**
    See also Berry, Charles Edward Anderson
Berry, Jonas
    See Ashbery, John (Lawrence)
Berry, Wendell (Erdman) 1934- **CLC 4, 6, 8,
    27, 46; DAM POET**
    See also AITN 1; CA 73-76; CANR 50, 73; DLB
    5, 6; MTCW 1
Berryman, John 1914-1972**CLC 1, 2, 3, 4, 6, 8,
    10, 13, 25, 62; DAM POET**
    See also CA 13-16; 33-36R; CABS 2; CANR
    35; CAP 1; CDALB 1941-1968; DLB 48;
    MTCW 1, 2
Bertolucci, Bernardo 1940-   **CLC 16**
    See also CA 106
Berton, Pierre (Francis Demarigny) 1920-
    CLC 104
    See also CA 1-4R; CANR 2, 56; DLB 68; SATA
    99
Bertrand, Aloysius 1807-1841   **NCLC 31**
Bertran de Born c. 1140-1215   **CMLC 5**
Besant, Annie (Wood) 1847-1933   **TCLC 9**
    See also CA 105
Bessie, Alvah 1904-1985   **CLC 23**
    See also CA 5-8R; 116; CANR 2, 80; DLB 26
Bethlen, T. D.
    See Silverberg, Robert
Beti, Mongo   **CLC 27; BLC 1; DAM MULT**
    See also Biyidi, Alexandre
    See also CANR 79
Betjeman, John 1906-1984 **CLC 2, 6, 10, 34,
    43; DAB; DAM MST, POET**
    See also CA 9-12R; 112; CANR 33, 56; CDBLB
    1945-1960; DLB 20; DLBY 84; MTCW 1,
    2
Bettelheim, Bruno 1903-1990   **CLC 79**
    See also CA 81-84; 131; CANR 23, 61; MTCW
    1, 2
Betti, Ugo 1892-1953   **TCLC 5**
    See also CA 104; 155
Betts, Doris (Waugh) 1932- **CLC 3, 6, 28**
    See also CA 13-16R; CANR 9, 66, 77; DLBY
    82; INT CANR-9
Bevan, Alistair
    See Roberts, Keith (John Kingston)
Bey, Pilaff
    See Douglas, (George) Norman
Bialik, Chaim Nachman 1873-1934 **TCLC 25**
    See also CA 170
Bickerstaff, Isaac
    See Swift, Jonathan
Bidart, Frank 1939-   **CLC 33**
    See also CA 140
Bienek, Horst 1930-   **CLC 7, 11**
    See also CA 73-76; DLB 75
Bierce, Ambrose (Gwinett) 1842-1914(?)
    **TCLC 1, 7, 44; DA; DAC; DAM MST; SSC
    9; WLC**
    See also CA 104; 139; CANR 78; CDALB
    1865-1917; DLB 11, 12, 23, 71, 74, 186
Biggers, Earl Derr 1884-1933   **TCLC 65**
    See also CA 108; 153
Billings, Josh
    See Shaw, Henry Wheeler

Billington, (Lady) Rachel (Mary) 1942- **C L C
43**
    See also AITN 2; CA 33-36R; CANR 44
Binyon, T(imothy) J(ohn) 1936-   **CLC 34**
    See also CA 111; CANR 28
Bioy Casares, Adolfo 1914-1999**CLC 4, 8, 13,
    88; DAM MULT; HLC 1; SSC 17**
    See also CA 29-32R; 177; CANR 19, 43, 66;
    DLB 113; HW 1, 2; MTCW 1, 2
Bird, Cordwainer
    See Ellison, Harlan (Jay)
Bird, Robert Montgomery 1806-1854**NCLC 1**
    See also DLB 202
Birkerts, Sven 1951-   **CLC 116**
    See also CA 128; 133; 176; CAAS 29; INT 133
Birney, (Alfred) Earle 1904-1995**CLC 1, 4, 6,
    11; DAC; DAM MST, POET**
    See also CA 1-4R; CANR 5, 20; DLB 88;
    MTCW 1
Biruni, al 973-1048(?)   **CMLC 28**
Bishop, Elizabeth 1911-1979 **CLC 1, 4, 9, 13,
    15, 32; DA; DAC; DAM MST, POET; PC
    3**
    See also CA 5-8R; 89-92; CABS 2; CANR 26,
    61; CDALB 1968-1988; DLB 5, 169;
    MTCW 1, 2; SATA-Obit 24
Bishop, John 1935-   **CLC 10**
    See also CA 105
Bissett, Bill 1939-   **CLC 18; PC 14**
    See also CA 69-72; CAAS 19; CANR 15; DLB
    53; MTCW 1
Bissoondath, Neil (Devindra) 1955-**CLC 120;
    DAC**
    See also CA 136
Bitov, Andrei (Georgievich) 1937-   **CLC 57**
    See also CA 142
Biyidi, Alexandre 1932-
    See Beti, Mongo
    See also BW 1, 3; CA 114; 124; CANR 81;
    MTCW 1, 2
Bjarme, Brynjolf
    See Ibsen, Henrik (Johan)
Bjoernson, Bjoernstjerne (Martinius) 1832-
    1910   **TCLC 7, 37**
    See also CA 104
Black, Robert
    See Holdstock, Robert P.
Blackburn, Paul 1926-1971   **CLC 9, 43**
    See also CA 81-84; 33-36R; CANR 34; DLB
    16; DLBY 81
Black Elk 1863-1950 **TCLC 33;DAM MULT**
    See also CA 144; MTCW 1; NNAL
Black Hobart
    See Sanders, (James) Ed(ward)
Blacklin, Malcolm
    See Chambers, Aidan
Blackmore, R(ichard) D(oddridge) 1825-1900
    TCLC 27
    See also CA 120; DLB 18
Blackmur, R(ichard) P(almer) 1904-1965
    CLC 2, 24
    See also CA 11-12; 25-28R; CANR 71; CAP 1;
    DLB 63
Black Tarantula
    See Acker, Kathy
Blackwood, Algernon (Henry) 1869-1951
    TCLC 5
    See also CA 105; 150; DLB 153, 156, 178
Blackwood, Caroline 1931-1996**CLC 6, 9, 100**
    See also CA 85-88; 151; CANR 32, 61, 65; DLB
    14, 207; MTCW 1
Blade, Alexander
    See Hamilton, Edmond; Silverberg, Robert

Bowers, Edgar 1924- **CLC 9**
See also CA 5-8R; CANR 24; DLB 5

Bowie, David **CLC 17**
See also Jones, David Robert

Bowles, Jane (Sydney) 1917-1973 **CLC 3, 68**
See also CA 19-20; 41-44R; CAP 2

Bowles, Paul (Frederick) 1910- **CLC 1, 2, 19, 53; SSC 3**
See also CA 1-4R; CAAS 1; CANR 1, 19, 50, 75; DLB 5, 6; MTCW 1, 2

Box, Edgar
See Vidal, Gore

Boyd, Nancy
See Millay, Edna St. Vincent

Boyd, William 1952- **CLC 28, 53, 70**
See also CA 114; 120; CANR 51, 71

Boyle, Kay 1902-1992 **CLC 1, 5, 19, 58, 121; SSC 5**
See also CA 13-16R; 140; CAAS 1; CANR 29, 61; DLB 4, 9, 48, 86; DLBY 93; MTCW 1, 2

Boyle, Mark
See Kienzle, William X(avier)

Boyle, Patrick 1905-1982 **CLC 19**
See also CA 127

Boyle, T. C. 1948-
See Boyle, T(homas) Coraghessan

Boyle, T(homas) Coraghessan 1948- **CLC 36, 55, 90; DAM POP; SSC 16**
See also BEST 90:4; CA 120; CANR 44, 76; DLBY 86; MTCW 2

Boz
See Dickens, Charles (John Huffam)

Brackenridge, Hugh Henry 1748-1816 **NCLC 7**
See also DLB 11, 37

Bradbury, Edward P.
See Moorcock, Michael (John)
See also MTCW 2

Bradbury, Malcolm (Stanley) 1932- **CLC 32, 61; DAM NOV**
See also CA 1-4R; CANR 1, 33; DLB 14, 207; MTCW 1, 2

Bradbury, Ray (Douglas) 1920- **CLC 1, 3, 10, 15, 42, 98; DA; DAB; DAC; DAM MST, NOV, POP; SSC 29; WLC**
See also AAYA 15; AITN 1, 2; CA 1-4R; CANR 2, 30, 75; CDALB 1968-1988; DLB 2, 8; MTCW 1, 2; SATA 11, 64

Bradford, Gamaliel 1863-1932 **TCLC 36**
See also CA 160; DLB 17

Bradley, David (Henry), Jr. 1950- **CLC 23, 118; BLC 1; DAM MULT**
See also BW 1, 3; CA 104; CANR 26, 81; DLB 33

Bradley, John Ed(mund, Jr.) 1958- **CLC 55**
See also CA 139

Bradley, Marion Zimmer 1930- **CLC 30; DAM POP**
See also AAYA 9; CA 57-60; CAAS 10; CANR 7, 31, 51, 75; DLB 8; MTCW 1, 2; SATA 90

Bradstreet, Anne 1612(?)-1672 **LC 4, 30; DA; DAC; DAM MST, POET; PC 10**
See also CDALB 1640-1865; DLB 24

Brady, Joan 1939- **CLC 86**
See also CA 141

Bragg, Melvyn 1939- **CLC 10**
See also BEST 89:3; CA 57-60; CANR 10, 48; DLB 14

Brahe, Tycho 1546-1601 **LC 45**

Braine, John (Gerard) 1922-1986 **CLC 1, 3, 41**
See also CA 1-4R; 120; CANR 1, 33; CDBLB 1945-1960; DLB 15; DLBY 86; MTCW 1

Bramah, Ernest 1868-1942 **TCLC 72**
See also CA 156; DLB 70

Brammer, William 1930(?)-1978 **CLC 31**
See also CA 77-80

Brancati, Vitaliano 1907-1954 **TCLC 12**
See also CA 109

Brancato, Robin F(idler) 1936- **CLC 35**
See also AAYA 9; CA 69-72; CANR 11, 45; CLR 32; JRDA; SAAS 9; SATA 97

Brand, Max
See Faust, Frederick (Schiller)

Brand, Millen 1906-1980 **CLC 7**
See also CA 21-24R; 97-100; CANR 72

Branden, Barbara **CLC 44**
See also CA 148

Brandes, Georg (Morris Cohen) 1842-1927 **TCLC 10**
See also CA 105

Brandys, Kazimierz 1916- **CLC 62**

Branley, Franklyn M(ansfield) 1915- **CLC 21**
See also CA 33-36R; CANR 14, 39; CLR 13; MAICYA; SAAS 16; SATA 4, 68

Brathwaite, Edward (Kamau) 1930- **CLC 11; BLCS; DAM POET**
See also BW 2, 3; CA 25-28R; CANR 11, 26, 47; DLB 125

Brautigan, Richard (Gary) 1935-1984 **CLC 1, 3, 5, 9, 12, 34, 42; DAM NOV**
See also CA 53-56; 113; CANR 34; DLB 2, 5, 206; DLBY 80, 84; MTCW 1; SATA 56

Brave Bird, Mary 1953-
See Crow Dog, Mary (Ellen)
See also NNAL

Braverman, Kate 1950- **CLC 67**
See also CA 89-92

Brecht, (Eugen) Bertolt (Friedrich) 1898-1956 **TCLC 1, 6, 13, 35; DA; DAB; DAC; DAM DRAM, MST; DC 3; WLC**
See also CA 104; 133; CANR 62; DLB 56, 124; MTCW 1, 2

Brecht, Eugen Berthold Friedrich
See Brecht, (Eugen) Bertolt (Friedrich)

Bremer, Fredrika 1801-1865 **NCLC 11**

Brennan, Christopher John 1870-1932 **TCLC 17**
See also CA 117

Brennan, Maeve 1917-1993 **CLC 5**
See also CA 81-84; CANR 72

Brent, Linda
See Jacobs, Harriet A(nn)

Brentano, Clemens (Maria) 1778-1842 **NCLC 1**
See also DLB 90

Brent of Bin Bin
See Franklin, (Stella Maria Sarah) Miles (Lampe)

Brenton, Howard 1942- **CLC 31**
See also CA 69-72; CANR 33, 67; DLB 13; MTCW 1

Breslin, James 1930-1996
See Breslin, Jimmy
See also CA 73-76; CANR 31, 75; DAM NOV; MTCW 1, 2

Breslin, Jimmy **CLC 4, 43**
See also Breslin, James
See also AITN 1; DLB 185; MTCW 2

Bresson, Robert 1901- **CLC 16**
See also CA 110; CANR 49

Breton, Andre 1896-1966 **CLC 2, 9, 15, 54; PC 15**
See also CA 19-20; 25-28R; CANR 40, 60; CAP 2; DLB 65; MTCW 1, 2

Breytenbach, Breyten 1939(?)- **CLC 23, 37;**

DAM POET
See also CA 113; 129; CANR 61

Bridgers, Sue Ellen 1942- **CLC 26**
See also AAYA 8; CA 65-68; CANR 11, 36; CLR 18; DLB 52; JRDA; MAICYA; SAAS 1; SATA 22, 90; SATA-Essay 109

Bridges, Robert (Seymour) 1844-1930 **TCLC 1; DAM POET**
See also CA 104; 152; CDBLB 1890-1914; DLB 19, 98

Bridie, James **TCLC 3**
See also Mavor, Osborne Henry
See also DLB 10

Brin, David 1950- **CLC 34**
See also AAYA 21; CA 102; CANR 24, 70; INT CANR-24; SATA 65

Brink, Andre (Philippus) 1935- **CLC 18, 36, 106**
See also CA 104; CANR 39, 62; INT 103; MTCW 1, 2

Brinsmead, H(esba) F(ay) 1922- **CLC 21**
See also CA 21-24R; CANR 10; CLR 47; MAICYA; SAAS 5; SATA 18, 78

Brittain, Vera (Mary) 1893(?)-1970 **CLC 23**
See also CA 13-16; 25-28R; CANR 58; CAP 1; DLB 191; MTCW 1, 2

Broch, Hermann 1886-1951 **TCLC 20**
See also CA 117; DLB 85, 124

Brock, Rose
See Hansen, Joseph

Brodkey, Harold (Roy) 1930-1996 **CLC 56**
See also CA 111; 151; CANR 71; DLB 130

Brodskii, Iosif
See Brodsky, Joseph

Brodsky, Iosif Alexandrovich 1940-1996
See Brodsky, Joseph
See also AITN 1; CA 41-44R; 151; CANR 37; DAM POET; MTCW 1, 2

Brodsky, Joseph 1940-1996 **CLC 4, 6, 13, 36, 100; PC 9**
See also Brodskii, Iosif; Brodsky, Iosif Alexandrovich
See also MTCW 1

Brodsky, Michael (Mark) 1948- **CLC 19**
See also CA 102; CANR 18, 41, 58

Bromell, Henry 1947- **CLC 5**
See also CA 53-56; CANR 9

Bromfield, Louis (Brucker) 1896-1956 **TCLC 11**
See also CA 107; 155; DLB 4, 9, 86

Broner, E(sther) M(asserman) 1930- **CLC 19**
See also CA 17-20R; CANR 8, 25, 72; DLB 28

Bronk, William (M.) 1918-1999 **CLC 10**
See also CA 89-92; 177; CANR 23; DLB 165

Bronstein, Lev Davidovich
See Trotsky, Leon

Bronte, Anne 1820-1849 **NCLC 71**
See also DLB 21, 199

Bronte, Charlotte 1816-1855 **NCLC 3, 8, 33, 58; DA; DAB; DAC; DAM MST, NOV; WLC**
See also AAYA 17; CDBLB 1832-1890; DLB 21, 159, 199

Bronte, Emily (Jane) 1818-1848 **NCLC 16, 35; DA; DAB; DAC; DAM MST, NOV, POET; PC 8; WLC**
See also AAYA 17; CDBLB 1832-1890; DLB 21, 32, 199

Brooke, Frances 1724-1789 **LC 6, 48**
See also DLB 39, 99

Brooke, Henry 1703(?)-1783 **LC 1**
See also DLB 39

Brooke, Rupert (Chawner) 1887-1915 **TCLC**

2, 7; DA; DAB; DAC; DAM MST, POET; PC 24; WLC
See also CA 104; 132; CANR 61; CDBLB 1914-1945; DLB 19; MTCW 1, 2

Brooke-Haven, P.
See Wodehouse, P(elham) G(renville)

Brooke-Rose, Christine 1926(?)-   **CLC 40**
See also CA 13-16R; CANR 58; DLB 14

Brookner, Anita 1928- **CLC 32, 34, 51; DAB; DAM POP**
See also CA 114; 120; CANR 37, 56; DLB 194; DLBY 87; MTCW 1, 2

Brooks, Cleanth 1906-1994   **CLC 24, 86, 110**
See also CA 17-20R; 145; CANR 33, 35; DLB 63; DLBY 94; INT CANR-35; MTCW 1, 2

Brooks, George
See Baum, L(yman) Frank

Brooks, Gwendolyn 1917- **CLC 1, 2, 4, 5, 15, 49; BLC 1; DA; DAC; DAM MST, MULT, POET; PC 7; WLC**
See also AAYA 20; AITN 1; BW 2, 3; CA 1-4R; CANR 1, 27, 52, 75; CDALB 1941-1968; CLR 27; DLB 5, 76, 165; MTCW 1, 2; SATA 6

Brooks, Mel   **CLC 12**
See also Kaminsky, Melvin
See also AAYA 13; DLB 26

Brooks, Peter 1938-   **CLC 34**
See also CA 45-48; CANR 1

Brooks, Van Wyck 1886-1963   **CLC 29**
See also CA 1-4R; CANR 6; DLB 45, 63, 103

Brophy, Brigid (Antonia) 1929-1995 **CLC 6, 11, 29, 105**
See also CA 5-8R; 149; CAAS 4; CANR 25, 53; DLB 14; MTCW 1, 2

Brosman, Catharine Savage 1934-   **CLC 9**
See also CA 61-64; CANR 21, 46

Brossard, Nicole 1943-   **CLC 115**
See also CA 122; CAAS 16; DLB 53

Brother Antoninus
See Everson, William (Oliver)

The Brothers Quay
See Quay, Stephen; Quay, Timothy

Broughton, T(homas) Alan 1936-   **CLC 19**
See also CA 45-48; CANR 2, 23, 48

Broumas, Olga 1949-   **CLC 10, 73**
See also CA 85-88; CANR 20, 69

Brown, Alan 1950-   **CLC 99**
See also CA 156

Brown, Charles Brockden 1771-1810 **NCLC 22, 74**
See also CDALB 1640-1865; DLB 37, 59, 73

Brown, Christy 1932-1981   **CLC 63**
See also CA 105; 104; CANR 72; DLB 14

Brown, Claude 1937- **CLC 30; BLC 1; DAM MULT**
See also AAYA 7; BW 1, 3; CA 73-76; CANR 81

Brown, Dee (Alexander) 1908- **CLC 18, 47; DAM POP**
See also AAYA 30; CA 13-16R; CAAS 6; CANR 11, 45, 60; DLBY 80; MTCW 1, 2; SATA 5

Brown, George
See Wertmueller, Lina

Brown, George Douglas 1869-1902 **TCLC 28**
See also CA 162

Brown, George Mackay 1921-1996 **CLC 5, 48, 100**
See also CA 21-24R; 151; CAAS 6; CANR 12, 37, 67; DLB 14, 27, 139; MTCW 1; SATA 35

Brown, (William) Larry 1951-   **CLC 73**

See also CA 130; 134; INT 133

Brown, Moses
See Barrett, William (Christopher)

Brown, Rita Mae 1944- **CLC 18, 43, 79; DAM NOV, POP**
See also CA 45-48; CANR 2, 11, 35, 62; INT CANR-11; MTCW 1, 2

Brown, Roderick (Langmere) Haig-
See Haig-Brown, Roderick (Langmere)

Brown, Rosellen 1939-   **CLC 32**
See also CA 77-80; CAAS 10; CANR 14, 44

Brown, Sterling Allen 1901-1989 **CLC 1, 23, 59; BLC 1; DAM MULT, POET**
See also BW 1, 3; CA 85-88; 127; CANR 26; DLB 48, 51, 63; MTCW 1, 2

Brown, Will
See Ainsworth, William Harrison

Brown, William Wells 1813-1884   **NCLC 2; BLC 1; DAM MULT; DC 1**
See also DLB 3, 50

Browne, (Clyde) Jackson 1948(?)-   **CLC 21**
See also CA 120

Browning, Elizabeth Barrett 1806-1861 **NCLC 1, 16, 61, 66; DA; DAB; DAC; DAM MST, POET; PC 6; WLC**
See also CDBLB 1832-1890; DLB 32, 199

Browning, Robert 1812-1889 **NCLC 19, 79; DA; DAB; DAC; DAM MST, POET; PC 2; WLCS**
See also CDBLB 1832-1890; DLB 32, 163; YABC 1

Browning, Tod 1882-1962   **CLC 16**
See also CA 141; 117

Brownson, Orestes Augustus 1803-1876 **NCLC 50**
See also DLB 1, 59, 73

Bruccoli, Matthew J(oseph) 1931- **CLC 34**
See also CA 9-12R; CANR 7; DLB 103

Bruce, Lenny   **CLC 21**
See also Schneider, Leonard Alfred

Bruin, John
See Brutus, Dennis

Brulard, Henri
See Stendhal

Brulls, Christian
See Simenon, Georges (Jacques Christian)

Brunner, John (Kilian Houston) 1934-1995 **CLC 8, 10; DAM POP**
See also CA 1-4R; 149; CAAS 8; CANR 2, 37; MTCW 1, 2

Bruno, Giordano 1548-1600   **LC 27**

Brutus, Dennis 1924- **CLC 43; BLC 1; DAM MULT, POET; PC 24**
See also BW 2, 3; CA 49-52; CAAS 14; CANR 2, 27, 42, 81; DLB 117

Bryan, C(ourtlandt) D(ixon) B(arnes) 1936- **CLC 29**
See also CA 73-76; CANR 13, 68; DLB 185; INT CANR-13

Bryan, Michael
See Moore, Brian

Bryant, William Cullen 1794-1878 **NCLC 6, 46; DA; DAB; DAC; DAM MST, POET; PC 20**
See also CDALB 1640-1865; DLB 3, 43, 59, 189

Bryusov, Valery Yakovlevich 1873-1924 **TCLC 10**
See also CA 107; 155

Buchan, John 1875-1940   **TCLC 41; DAB; DAM POP**
See also CA 108; 145; DLB 34, 70, 156; MTCW 1; YABC 2

Buchanan, George 1506-1582   **LC 4**
See also DLB 152

Buchheim, Lothar-Guenther 1918-   **CLC 6**
See also CA 85-88

Buchner, (Karl) Georg 1813-1837 **NCLC 26**

Buchwald, Art(hur) 1925-   **CLC 33**
See also AITN 1; CA 5-8R; CANR 21, 67; MTCW 1, 2; SATA 10

Buck, Pearl S(ydenstricker) 1892-1973 **CLC 7, 11, 18; DA; DAB; DAC; DAM MST, NOV**
See also AITN 1; CA 1-4R; 41-44R; CANR 1, 34; CDALBS; DLB 9, 102; MTCW 1, 2; SATA 1, 25

Buckler, Ernest 1908-1984   **CLC 13; DAC; DAM MST**
See also CA 11-12; 114; CAP 1; DLB 68; SATA 47

Buckley, Vincent (Thomas) 1925-1988 **CLC 57**
See also CA 101

Buckley, William F(rank), Jr. 1925- **CLC 7, 18, 37; DAM POP**
See also AITN 1; CA 1-4R; CANR 1, 24, 53; DLB 137; DLBY 80; INT CANR-24; MTCW 1, 2

Buechner, (Carl) Frederick 1926- **CLC 2, 4, 6, 9; DAM NOV**
See also CA 13-16R; CANR 11, 39, 64; DLBY 80; INT CANR-11; MTCW 1, 2

Buell, John (Edward) 1927-   **CLC 10**
See also CA 1-4R; CANR 71; DLB 53

Buero Vallejo, Antonio 1916-   **CLC 15, 46**
See also CA 106; CANR 24, 49, 75; HW 1; MTCW 1, 2

Bufalino, Gesualdo 1920(?)-   **CLC 74**
See also DLB 196

Bugayev, Boris Nikolayevich 1880-1934 **TCLC 7; PC 11**
See also Bely, Andrey
See also CA 104; 165; MTCW 1

Bukowski, Charles 1920-1994 **CLC 2, 5, 9, 41, 82, 108; DAM NOV, POET; PC 18**
See also CA 17-20R; 144; CANR 40, 62; DLB 5, 130, 169; MTCW 1, 2

Bulgakov, Mikhail (Afanas'evich) 1891-1940 **TCLC 2, 16; DAM DRAM, NOV; SSC 18**
See also CA 105; 152

Bulgya, Alexander Alexandrovich 1901-1956 **TCLC 53**
See also Fadeyev, Alexander
See also CA 117

Bullins, Ed 1935- **CLC 1, 5, 7; BLC 1; DAM DRAM, MULT; DC 6**
See also BW 2, 3; CA 49-52; CAAS 16; CANR 24, 46, 73; DLB 7, 38; MTCW 1, 2

Bulwer-Lytton, Edward (George Earle Lytton) 1803-1873   **NCLC 1, 45**
See also DLB 21

Bunin, Ivan Alexeyevich 1870-1953 **TCLC 6; SSC 5**
See also CA 104

Bunting, Basil 1900-1985   **CLC 10, 39, 47; DAM POET**
See also CA 53-56; 115; CANR 7; DLB 20

Bunuel, Luis 1900-1983   **CLC 16, 80; DAM MULT; HLC 1**
See also CA 101; 110; CANR 32, 77; HW 1

Bunyan, John 1628-1688   **LC 4; DA; DAB; DAC; DAM MST; WLC**
See also CDBLB 1660-1789; DLB 39

Burckhardt, Jacob (Christoph) 1818-1897 **NCLC 49**

Burford, Eleanor
See Hibbert, Eleanor Alice Burford

Burgess, Anthony CLC 1, 2, 4, 5, 8, 10, 13, 15, 22, 40, 62, 81, 94; DAB
See also Wilson, John (Anthony) Burgess
See also AAYA 25; AITN 1; CDBLB 1960 to Present; DLB 14, 194; DLBY 98; MTCW 1

Burke, Edmund 1729(?)-1797 **LC 7, 36; DA; DAB; DAC; DAM MST; WLC**
See also DLB 104

Burke, Kenneth (Duva) 1897-1993 **CLC 2, 24**
See also CA 5-8R; 143; CANR 39, 74; DLB 45, 63; MTCW 1, 2

Burke, Leda
See Garnett, David

Burke, Ralph
See Silverberg, Robert

Burke, Thomas 1886-1945 **TCLC 63**
See also CA 113; 155; DLB 197

Burney, Fanny 1752-1840 **NCLC 12, 54**
See also DLB 39

Burns, Robert 1759-1796 **LC 3, 29, 40; DA; DAB; DAC; DAM MST, POET; PC 6; WLC**
See also CDBLB 1789-1832; DLB 109

Burns, Tex
See L'Amour, Louis (Dearborn)

Burnshaw, Stanley 1906- **CLC 3, 13, 44**
See also CA 9-12R; DLB 48; DLBY 97

Burr, Anne 1937- **CLC 6**
See also CA 25-28R

Burroughs, Edgar Rice 1875-1950 **TCLC 2, 32; DAM NOV**
See also AAYA 11; CA 104; 132; DLB 8; MTCW 1, 2; SATA 41

Burroughs, William S(eward) 1914-1997 **CLC 1, 2, 5, 15, 22, 42, 75, 109; DA; DAB; DAC; DAM MST, NOV, POP; WLC**
See also AITN 2; CA 9-12R; 160; CANR 20, 52; DLB 2, 8, 16, 152; DLBY 81, 97; MTCW 1, 2

Burton, Sir Richard F(rancis) 1821-1890 **NCLC 42**
See also DLB 55, 166, 184

Busch, Frederick 1941- **CLC 7, 10, 18, 47**
See also CA 33-36R; CAAS 1; CANR 45, 73; DLB 6

Bush, Ronald 1946- **CLC 34**
See also CA 136

Bustos, F(rancisco)
See Borges, Jorge Luis

Bustos Domecq, H(onorio)
See Bioy Casares, Adolfo; Borges, Jorge Luis

Butler, Octavia E(stelle) 1947- **CLC 38, 121; BLCS; DAM MULT, POP**
See also AAYA 18; BW 2, 3; CA 73-76; CANR 12, 24, 38, 73; DLB 33; MTCW 1, 2; SATA 84

Butler, Robert Olen (Jr.) 1945- **CLC 81; DAM POP**
See also CA 112; CANR 66; DLB 173; INT 112; MTCW 1

Butler, Samuel 1612-1680 **LC 16, 43**
See also DLB 101, 126

Butler, Samuel 1835-1902 **TCLC 1, 33; DA; DAB; DAC; DAM MST, NOV; WLC**
See also CA 143; CDBLB 1890-1914; DLB 18, 57, 174

Butler, Walter C.
See Faust, Frederick (Schiller)

Butor, Michel (Marie Francois) 1926- **CLC 1, 3, 8, 11, 15**
See also CA 9-12R; CANR 33, 66; DLB 83; MTCW 1, 2

Butts, Mary 1892(?)-1937 **TCLC 77**

See also CA 148

Buzo, Alexander (John) 1944- **CLC 61**
See also CA 97-100; CANR 17, 39, 69

Buzzati, Dino 1906-1972 **CLC 36**
See also CA 160; 33-36R; DLB 177

Byars, Betsy (Cromer) 1928- **CLC 35**
See also AAYA 19; CA 33-36R; CANR 18, 36, 57; CLR 1, 16; DLB 52; INT CANR-18; JRDA; MAICYA; MTCW 1; SAAS 1; SATA 4, 46, 80; SATA-Essay 108

Byatt, A(ntonia) S(usan Drabble) 1936- **C L C 19, 65; DAM NOV, POP**
See also CA 13-16R; CANR 13, 33, 50, 75; DLB 14, 194; MTCW 1, 2

Byrne, David 1952- **CLC 26**
See also CA 127

Byrne, John Keyes 1926-
See Leonard, Hugh
See also CA 102; CANR 78; INT 102

Byron, George Gordon (Noel) 1788-1824 **NCLC 2, 12; DA; DAB; DAC; DAM MST, POET; PC 16; WLC**
See also CDBLB 1789-1832; DLB 96, 110

Byron, Robert 1905-1941 **TCLC 67**
See also CA 160; DLB 195

C. 3. 3.
See Wilde, Oscar

Caballero, Fernan 1796-1877 **NCLC 10**

Cabell, Branch
See Cabell, James Branch

Cabell, James Branch 1879-1958 **TCLC 6**
See also CA 105; 152; DLB 9, 78; MTCW 1

Cable, George Washington 1844-1925 **T C L C 4; SSC 4**
See also CA 104; 155; DLB 12, 74; DLBD 13

Cabral de Melo Neto, Joao 1920- **CLC 76; DAM MULT**
See also CA 151

Cabrera Infante, G(uillermo) 1929- **CLC 5, 25, 45, 120; DAM MULT; HLC 1**
See also CA 85-88; CANR 29, 65; DLB 113; HW 1, 2; MTCW 1, 2

Cade, Toni
See Bambara, Toni Cade

Cadmus and Harmonia
See Buchan, John

Caedmon fl. 658-680 **CMLC 7**
See also DLB 146

Caeiro, Alberto
See Pessoa, Fernando (Antonio Nogueira)

Cage, John (Milton, Jr.) 1912-1992 **CLC 41**
See also CA 13-16R; 169; CANR 9, 78; DLB 193; INT CANR-9

Cahan, Abraham 1860-1951 **TCLC 71**
See also CA 108; 154; DLB 9, 25, 28

Cain, G.
See Cabrera Infante, G(uillermo)

Cain, Guillermo
See Cabrera Infante, G(uillermo)

Cain, James M(allahan) 1892-1977 **CLC 3, 11, 28**
See also AITN 1; CA 17-20R; 73-76; CANR 8, 34, 61; MTCW 1

Caine, Mark
See Raphael, Frederic (Michael)

Calasso, Roberto 1941- **CLC 81**
See also CA 143

Calderon de la Barca, Pedro 1600-1681 **L C 23; DC 3; HLCS 1**

Caldwell, Erskine (Preston) 1903-1987 **CLC 1, 8, 14, 50, 60; DAM NOV; SSC 19**
See also AITN 1; CA 1-4R; 121; CAAS 1; CANR 2, 33; DLB 9, 86; MTCW 1, 2

Caldwell, (Janet Miriam) Taylor (Holland) 1900-1985 **CLC 2, 28, 39; DAM NOV, POP**
See also CA 5-8R; 116; CANR 5; DLBD 17

Calhoun, John Caldwell 1782-1850 **NCLC 15**
See also DLB 3

Calisher, Hortense 1911- **CLC 2, 4, 8, 38; DAM NOV; SSC 15**
See also CA 1-4R; CANR 1, 22, 67; DLB 2; INT CANR-22; MTCW 1, 2

Callaghan, Morley Edward 1903-1990 **CLC 3, 14, 41, 65; DAC; DAM MST**
See also CA 9-12R; 132; CANR 33, 73; DLB 68; MTCW 1, 2

Callimachus c. 305B.C.-c.240B.C. **CMLC 18**
See also DLB 176

Calvin, John 1509-1564 **LC 37**

Calvino, Italo 1923-1985 **CLC 5, 8, 11, 22, 33, 39, 73; DAM NOV; SSC 3**
See also CA 85-88; 116; CANR 23, 61; DLB 196; MTCW 1, 2

Cameron, Carey 1952- **CLC 59**
See also CA 135

Cameron, Peter 1959- **CLC 44**
See also CA 125; CANR 50

Camoens, Luis Vaz de 1524(?)-1580
See also HLCS 1

Camoes, Luis de 1524(?)-1580
See also HLCS 1

Campana, Dino 1885-1932 **TCLC 20**
See also CA 117; DLB 114

Campanella, Tommaso 1568-1639 **LC 32**

Campbell, John W(ood, Jr.) 1910-1971 **C L C 32**
See also CA 21-22; 29-32R; CANR 34; CAP 2; DLB 8; MTCW 1

Campbell, Joseph 1904-1987 **CLC 69**
See also AAYA 3; BEST 89:2; CA 1-4R; 124; CANR 3, 28, 61; MTCW 1, 2

Campbell, Maria 1940- **CLC 85; DAC**
See also CA 102; CANR 54; NNAL

Campbell, (John) Ramsey 1946- **CLC 42; SSC 19**
See also CA 57-60; CANR 7; INT CANR-7

Campbell, (Ignatius) Roy (Dunnachie) 1901-1957 **TCLC 5**
See also CA 104; 155; DLB 20; MTCW 2

Campbell, Thomas 1777-1844 **NCLC 19**
See also DLB 93; 144

Campbell, Wilfred **TCLC 9**
See also Campbell, William

Campbell, William 1858(?)-1918
See Campbell, Wilfred
See also CA 106; DLB 92

Campion, Jane **CLC 95**
See also CA 138

Campos, Alvaro de
See Pessoa, Fernando (Antonio Nogueira)

Camus, Albert 1913-1960 **CLC 1, 2, 4, 9, 11, 14, 32, 63, 69; DA; DAB; DAC; DAM DRAM, MST, NOV; DC 2; SSC 9; WLC**
See also CA 89-92; DLB 72; MTCW 1, 2

Canby, Vincent 1924- **CLC 13**
See also CA 81-84

Cancale
See Desnos, Robert

Canetti, Elias 1905-1994 **CLC 3, 14, 25, 75, 86**
See also CA 21-24R; 146; CANR 23, 61, 79; DLB 85, 124; MTCW 1, 2

Canfield, Dorothea F.
See Fisher, Dorothy (Frances) Canfield

Canfield, Dorothea Frances
See Fisher, Dorothy (Frances) Canfield

Canfield, Dorothy

See Fisher, Dorothy (Frances) Canfield
Canin, Ethan 1960-   **CLC 55**
    See also CA 131; 135
Cannon, Curt
    See Hunter, Evan
Cao, Lan 1961-   **CLC 109**
    See also CA 165
Cape, Judith
    See Page, P(atricia) K(athleen)
Capek, Karel 1890-1938   **TCLC 6, 37; DA;**
    DAB; DAC; DAM DRAM, MST, NOV; DC
    1; WLC
    See also CA 104; 140; MTCW 1
Capote, Truman 1924-1984**CLC 1, 3, 8, 13, 19,**
    34, 38, 58; DA; DAB; DAC; DAM MST,
    NOV, POP; SSC 2; WLC
    See also CA 5-8R; 113; CANR 18, 62; CDALB
    1941-1968; DLB 2, 185; DLBY 80, 84;
    MTCW 1, 2; SATA 91
Capra, Frank 1897-1991   **CLC 16**
    See also CA 61-64; 135
Caputo, Philip 1941-   **CLC 32**
    See also CA 73-76; CANR 40
Caragiale, Ion Luca 1852-1912   **TCLC 76**
    See also CA 157
Card, Orson Scott 1951-**CLC 44, 47, 50; DAM**
    POP
    See also AAYA 11; CA 102; CANR 27, 47, 73;
    INT CANR-27; MTCW 1, 2; SATA 83
Cardenal, Ernesto 1925-   **CLC 31; DAM**
    MULT, POET; HLC 1; PC 22
    See also CA 49-52; CANR 2, 32, 66; HW 1, 2;
    MTCW 1, 2
Cardozo, Benjamin N(athan) 1870-1938
    TCLC 65
    See also CA 117; 164
Carducci, Giosue (Alessandro Giuseppe) 1835-
    1907   **TCLC 32**
    See also CA 163
Carew, Thomas 1595(?)-1640   **LC 13**
    See also DLB 126
Carey, Ernestine Gilbreth 1908-   **CLC 17**
    See also CA 5-8R; CANR 71; SATA 2
Carey, Peter 1943-   **CLC 40, 55, 96**
    See also CA 123; 127; CANR 53, 76; INT 127;
    MTCW 1, 2; SATA 94
Carleton, William 1794-1869   **NCLC 3**
    See also DLB 159
Carlisle, Henry (Coffin) 1926-   **CLC 33**
    See also CA 13-16R; CANR 15
Carlsen, Chris
    See Holdstock, Robert P.
Carlson, Ron(ald F.) 1947-   **CLC 54**
    See also CA 105; CANR 27
Carlyle, Thomas 1795-1881   **NCLC 70; DA;**
    DAB; DAC; DAM MST
    See also CDBLB 1789-1832; DLB 55; 144
Carman, (William) Bliss 1861-1929 **TCLC 7;**
    DAC
    See also CA 104; 152; DLB 92
Carnegie, Dale 1888-1955   **TCLC 53**
Carossa, Hans 1878-1956   **TCLC 48**
    See also CA 170; DLB 66
Carpenter, Don(ald Richard) 1931-1995**C L C**
    41
    See also CA 45-48; 149; CANR 1, 71
Carpenter, Edward 1844-1929   **TCLC 88**
    See also CA 163
Carpentier (y Valmont), Alejo 1904-1980**CLC**
    8, 11, 38, 110; DAM MULT; HLC 1; SSC
    35
    See also CA 65-68; 97-100; CANR 11, 70; DLB
    113; HW 1, 2

Carr, Caleb 1955(?)-   **CLC 86**
    See also CA 147; CANR 73
Carr, Emily 1871-1945   **TCLC 32**
    See also CA 159; DLB 68
Carr, John Dickson 1906-1977   **CLC 3**
    See also Fairbairn, Roger
    See also CA 49-52; 69-72; CANR 3, 33, 60;
    MTCW 1, 2
Carr, Philippa
    See Hibbert, Eleanor Alice Burford
Carr, Virginia Spencer 1929-   **CLC 34**
    See also CA 61-64; DLB 111
Carrere, Emmanuel 1957-   **CLC 89**
Carrier, Roch 1937-**CLC 13, 78; DAC; DAM**
    MST
    See also CA 130; CANR 61; DLB 53; SATA
    105
Carroll, James P. 1943(?)-   **CLC 38**
    See also CA 81-84; CANR 73; MTCW 1
Carroll, Jim 1951-   **CLC 35**
    See also AAYA 17; CA 45-48; CANR 42
Carroll, Lewis   **NCLC 2, 53; PC 18; WLC**
    See also Dodgson, Charles Lutwidge
    See also CDBLB 1832-1890; CLR 2, 18; DLB
    18, 163, 178; DLBY 98; JRDA
Carroll, Paul Vincent 1900-1968   **CLC 10**
    See also CA 9-12R; 25-28R; DLB 10
Carruth, Hayden 1921- **CLC 4, 7, 10, 18, 84;**
    PC 10
    See also CA 9-12R; CANR 4, 38, 59; DLB 5,
    165; INT CANR-4; MTCW 1, 2; SATA 47
Carson, Rachel Louise 1907-1964   **CLC 71;**
    DAM POP
    See also CA 77-80; CANR 35; MTCW 1, 2;
    SATA 23
Carter, Angela (Olive) 1940-1992 **CLC 5, 41,**
    76; SSC 13
    See also CA 53-56; 136; CANR 12, 36, 61; DLB
    14, 207; MTCW 1, 2; SATA 66; SATA-Obit
    70
Carter, Nick
    See Smith, Martin Cruz
Carver, Raymond 1938-1988 **CLC 22, 36, 53,**
    55; DAM NOV; SSC 8
    See also CA 33-36R; 126; CANR 17, 34, 61;
    DLB 130; DLBY 84, 88; MTCW 1, 2
Cary, Elizabeth, Lady Falkland 1585-1639
    LC 30
Cary, (Arthur) Joyce (Lunel) 1888-1957
    TCLC 1, 29
    See also CA 104; 164; CDBLB 1914-1945;
    DLB 15, 100; MTCW 2
Casanova de Seingalt, Giovanni Jacopo 1725-
    1798   **LC 13**
Casares, Adolfo Bioy
    See Bioy Casares, Adolfo
Casely-Hayford, J(oseph) E(phraim) 1866-1930
    TCLC 24; BLC 1; DAM MULT
    See also BW 2; CA 123; 152
Casey, John (Dudley) 1939-   **CLC 59**
    See also BEST 90:2; CA 69-72; CANR 23
Casey, Michael 1947-   **CLC 2**
    See also CA 65-68; DLB 5
Casey, Patrick
    See Thurman, Wallace (Henry)
Casey, Warren (Peter) 1935-1988   **CLC 12**
    See also CA 101; 127; INT 101
Casona, Alejandro   **CLC 49**
    See also Alvarez, Alejandro Rodriguez
Cassavetes, John 1929-1989   **CLC 20**
    See also CA 85-88; 127; CANR 82
Cassian, Nina 1924-   **PC 17**
Cassill, R(onald) V(erlin) 1919-   **CLC 4, 23**

See also CA 9-12R; CAAS 1; CANR 7, 45; DLB
    6
Cassirer, Ernst 1874-1945   **TCLC 61**
    See also CA 157
Cassity, (Allen) Turner 1929-   **CLC 6, 42**
    See also CA 17-20R; CAAS 8; CANR 11; DLB
    105
Castaneda, Carlos (Cesar Aranha) 1931(?)-
    1998   **CLC 12, 119**
    See also CA 25-28R; CANR 32, 66; HW 1;
    MTCW 1
Castedo, Elena 1937-   **CLC 65**
    See also CA 132
Castedo-Ellerman, Elena
    See Castedo, Elena
Castellanos, Rosario 1925-1974**CLC 66; DAM**
    MULT; HLC 1
    See also CA 131; 53-56; CANR 58; DLB 113;
    HW 1; MTCW 1
Castelvetro, Lodovico 1505-1571   **LC 12**
Castiglione, Baldassare 1478-1529   **LC 12**
Castle, Robert
    See Hamilton, Edmond
Castro (Ruz), Fidel 1926(?)-
    See also CA 110; 129; CANR 81; DAM MULT;
    HLC 1; HW 2
Castro, Guillen de 1569-1631   **LC 19**
Castro, Rosalia de 1837-1885   **NCLC 3, 78;**
    DAM MULT
Cather, Willa
    See Cather, Willa Sibert
Cather, Willa Sibert 1873-1947 **TCLC 1, 11,**
    31; DA; DAB; DAC; DAM MST, NOV;
    SSC 2; WLC
    See also AAYA 24; CA 104; 128; CDALB 1865-
    1917; DLB 9, 54, 78; DLBD 1; MTCW 1, 2;
    SATA 30
Catherine, Saint 1347-1380   **CMLC 27**
Cato, Marcus Porcius 234B.C.-149B.C.
    CMLC 21
    See also DLB 211
Catton, (Charles) Bruce 1899-1978 **CLC 35**
    See also AITN 1; CA 5-8R; 81-84; CANR 7,
    74; DLB 17; SATA 2; SATA-Obit 24
Catullus c. 84B.C.-c. 54B.C.   **CMLC 18**
    See also DLB 211
Cauldwell, Frank
    See King, Francis (Henry)
Caunitz, William J. 1933-1996   **CLC 34**
    See also BEST 89:3; CA 125; 130; 152; CANR
    73; INT 130
Causley, Charles (Stanley) 1917-   **CLC 7**
    See also CA 9-12R; CANR 5, 35; CLR 30; DLB
    27; MTCW 1; SATA 3, 66
Caute, (John) David 1936-**CLC 29;DAM NOV**
    See also CA 1-4R; CAAS 4; CANR 1, 33, 64;
    DLB 14
Cavafy, C(onstantine) P(eter) 1863-1933
    TCLC 2, 7; DAM POET
    See also Kavafis, Konstantinos Petrou
    See also CA 148; MTCW 1
Cavallo, Evelyn
    See Spark, Muriel (Sarah)
Cavanna, Betty   **CLC 12**
    See also Harrison, Elizabeth Cavanna
    See also JRDA; MAICYA; SAAS 4; SATA 1,
    30
Cavendish, Margaret Lucas 1623-1673**LC 30**
    See also DLB 131
Caxton, William 1421(?)-1491(?)   **LC 17**
    See also DLB 170
Cayer, D. M.
    See Duffy, Maureen

See also Chopin, Katherine
See also CDALB 1865-1917; DLB 12, 78
Chopin, Katherine 1851-1904
See Chopin, Kate
See also CA 104; 122; DAC; DAM MST, NOV
Chretien de Troyes c. 12th cent.-   **CMLC 10**
See also DLB 208
Christie
See Ichikawa, Kon
Christie, Agatha (Mary Clarissa) 1890-1976
CLC 1, 6, 8, 12, 39, 48, 110; DAB; DAC; DAM NOV
See also AAYA 9; AITN 1, 2; CA 17-20R; 61-64; CANR 10, 37; CDBLB 1914-1945; DLB 13, 77; MTCW 1, 2; SATA 36
Christie, (Ann) Philippa
See Pearce, Philippa
See also CA 5-8R; CANR 4
Christine de Pizan 1365(?)-1431(?)   **LC 9**
See also DLB 208
Chubb, Elmer
See Masters, Edgar Lee
Chulkov, Mikhail Dmitrievich 1743-1792**LC 2**
See also DLB 150
Churchill, Caryl 1938-   **CLC 31, 55;DC 5**
See also CA 102; CANR 22, 46; DLB 13; MTCW 1
Churchill, Charles 1731-1764   **LC 3**
See also DLB 109
Chute, Carolyn 1947-   **CLC 39**
See also CA 123
Ciardi, John (Anthony) 1916-1986 **CLC 10, 40, 44; DAM POET**
See also CA 5-8R; 118; CAAS 2; CANR 5, 33; CLR 19; DLB 5; DLBY 86; INT CANR-5; MAICYA; MTCW 1, 2; SAAS 26; SATA 1, 65; SATA-Obit 46
Cicero, Marcus Tullius 106B.C.-43B.C.
CMLC 3
See also DLB 211
Cimino, Michael 1943-   **CLC 16**
See also CA 105
Cioran, E(mil) M. 1911-1995   **CLC 64**
See also CA 25-28R; 149
Cisneros, Sandra 1954- **CLC 69, 118; DAM MULT; HLC 1; SSC 32**
See also AAYA 9; CA 131; CANR 64; DLB 122, 152; HW 1, 2; MTCW 2
Cixous, Helene 1937-   **CLC 92**
See also CA 126; CANR 55; DLB 83; MTCW 1, 2
Clair, Rene   **CLC 20**
See also Chomette, Rene Lucien
Clampitt, Amy 1920-1994   **CLC 32;PC 19**
See also CA 110; 146; CANR 29, 79; DLB 105
Clancy, Thomas L., Jr. 1947-
See Clancy, Tom
See also CA 125; 131; CANR 62; INT 131; MTCW 1, 2
Clancy, Tom   **CLC 45, 112; DAM NOV, POP**
See also Clancy, Thomas L., Jr.
See also AAYA 9; BEST 89:1, 90:1; MTCW 2
Clare, John 1793-1864 **NCLC 9; DAB; DAM POET; PC 23**
See also DLB 55, 96
Clarin
See Alas (y Urena), Leopoldo (Enrique Garcia)
Clark, Al C.
See Goines, Donald
Clark, (Robert) Brian 1932-   **CLC 29**
See also CA 41-44R; CANR 67
Clark, Curt
See Westlake, Donald E(dwin)

Clark, Eleanor 1913-1996   **CLC 5, 19**
See also CA 9-12R; 151; CANR 41; DLB 6
Clark, J. P.
See Clark, John Pepper
See also DLB 117
Clark, John Pepper 1935-   **CLC 38; BLC 1; DAM DRAM, MULT; DC 5**
See also Clark, J. P.
See also BW 1; CA 65-68; CANR 16, 72; MTCW 1
Clark, M. R.
See Clark, Mavis Thorpe
Clark, Mavis Thorpe 1909-   **CLC 12**
See also CA 57-60; CANR 8, 37; CLR 30; MAICYA; SAAS 5; SATA 8, 74
Clark, Walter Van Tilburg 1909-1971**CLC 28**
See also CA 9-12R; 33-36R; CANR 63; DLB 9, 206; SATA 8
Clark Bekederemo, J(ohnson) P(epper)
See Clark, John Pepper
Clarke, Arthur C(harles) 1917-**CLC 1, 4, 13, 18, 35; DAM POP; SSC 3**
See also AAYA 4; CA 1-4R; CANR 2, 28, 55, 74; JRDA; MAICYA; MTCW 1, 2; SATA 13, 70
Clarke, Austin 1896-1974   **CLC 6, 9;DAM POET**
See also CA 29-32; 49-52; CAP 2; DLB 10, 20
Clarke, Austin C(hesterfield) 1934-**CLC 8, 53; BLC 1; DAC; DAM MULT**
See also BW 1; CA 25-28R; CAAS 16; CANR 14, 32, 68; DLB 53, 125
Clarke, Gillian 1937-   **CLC 61**
See also CA 106; DLB 40
Clarke, Marcus (Andrew Hislop) 1846-1881
NCLC 19
Clarke, Shirley 1925-   **CLC 16**
Clash, The
See Headon, (Nicky) Topper; Jones, Mick; Simonon, Paul; Strummer, Joe
Claudel, Paul (Louis Charles Marie) 1868-1955
TCLC 2, 10
See also CA 104; 165; DLB 192
Claudius, Matthias 1740-1815   **NCLC 75**
See also DLB 97
Clavell, James (du Maresq) 1925-1994**CLC 6, 25, 87; DAM NOV, POP**
See also CA 25-28R; 146; CANR 26, 48; MTCW 1, 2
Cleaver, (Leroy) Eldridge 1935-1998**CLC 30, 119; BLC 1; DAM MULT**
See also BW 1, 3; CA 21-24R; 167; CANR 16, 75; MTCW 2
Cleese, John (Marwood) 1939-   **CLC 21**
See also Monty Python
See also CA 112; 116; CANR 35; MTCW 1
Cleishbotham, Jebediah
See Scott, Walter
Cleland, John 1710-1789   **LC 2, 48**
See also DLB 39
Clemens, Samuel Langhorne 1835-1910
See Twain, Mark
See also CA 104; 135; CDALB 1865-1917; DA; DAB; DAC; DAM MST, NOV; DLB 11, 12, 23, 64, 74, 186, 189; JRDA; MAICYA; SATA 100; YABC 2
Cleophil
See Congreve, William
Clerihew, E.
See Bentley, E(dmund) C(lerihew)
Clerk, N. W.
See Lewis, C(live) S(taples)
Cliff, Jimmy   **CLC 21**

See also Chambers, James
Cliff, Michelle 1946-   **CLC 120; BLCS**
See also BW 2; CA 116; CANR 39, 72; DLB 157
Clifton, (Thelma) Lucille 1936- **CLC 19, 66; BLC 1; DAM MULT, POET; PC 17**
See also BW 2, 3; CA 49-52; CANR 2, 24, 42, 76; CLR 5; DLB 5, 41; MAICYA; MTCW 1, 2; SATA 20, 69
Clinton, Dirk
See Silverberg, Robert
Clough, Arthur Hugh 1819-1861   **NCLC 27**
See also DLB 32
Clutha, Janet Paterson Frame 1924-
See Frame, Janet
See also CA 1-4R; CANR 2, 36, 76; MTCW 1, 2
Clyne, Terence
See Blatty, William Peter
Cobalt, Martin
See Mayne, William (James Carter)
Cobb, Irvin S(hrewsbury) 1876-1944   **TCLC 77**
See also CA 175; DLB 11, 25, 86
Cobbett, William 1763-1835   **NCLC 49**
See also DLB 43, 107, 158
Coburn, D(onald) L(ee) 1938-   **CLC 10**
See also CA 89-92
Cocteau, Jean (Maurice Eugene Clement) 1889-1963**CLC 1, 8, 15, 16, 43; DA; DAB; DAC; DAM DRAM, MST, NOV; WLC**
See also CA 25-28; CANR 40; CAP 2; DLB 65; MTCW 1, 2
Codrescu, Andrei 1946- **CLC 46, 121; DAM POET**
See also CA 33-36R; CAAS 19; CANR 13, 34, 53, 76; MTCW 2
Coe, Max
See Bourne, Randolph S(illiman)
Coe, Tucker
See Westlake, Donald E(dwin)
Coen, Ethan 1958-   **CLC 108**
See also CA 126
Coen, Joel 1955-   **CLC 108**
See also CA 126
The Coen Brothers
See Coen, Ethan; Coen, Joel
Coetzee, J(ohn) M(ichael) 1940- **CLC 23, 33, 66, 117; DAM NOV**
See also CA 77-80; CANR 41, 54, 74; MTCW 1, 2
Coffey, Brian
See Koontz, Dean R(ay)
Coffin, Robert P(eter) Tristram 1892-1955
TCLC 95
See also CA 123; 169; DLB 45
Cohan, George M(ichael) 1878-1942**TCLC 60**
See also CA 157
Cohen, Arthur A(llen) 1928-1986 **CLC 7, 31**
See also CA 1-4R; 120; CANR 1, 17, 42; DLB 28
Cohen, Leonard (Norman) 1934- **CLC 3, 38; DAC; DAM MST**
See also CA 21-24R; CANR 14, 69; DLB 53; MTCW 1
Cohen, Matt 1942-   **CLC 19; DAC**
See also CA 61-64; CAAS 18; CANR 40; DLB 53
Cohen-Solal, Annie 19(?)-   **CLC 50**
Colegate, Isabel 1931-   **CLC 36**
See also CA 17-20R; CANR 8, 22, 74; DLB 14; INT CANR-22; MTCW 1
Coleman, Emmett

See Reed, Ishmael
Coleridge, M. E.
See Coleridge, Mary E(lizabeth)
Coleridge, Mary E(lizabeth) 1861-1907 **TCLC 73**
See also CA 116; 166; DLB 19, 98
Coleridge, Samuel Taylor 1772-1834 **NCLC 9, 54; DA; DAB; DAC; DAM MST, POET; PC 11; WLC**
See also CDBLB 1789-1832; DLB 93, 107
Coleridge, Sara 1802-1852 **NCLC 31**
See also DLB 199
Coles, Don 1928- **CLC 46**
See also CA 115; CANR 38
Coles, Robert (Martin) 1929- **CLC 108**
See also CA 45-48; CANR 3, 32, 66, 70; INT CANR-32; SATA 23
Colette, (Sidonie-Gabrielle) 1873-1954 **TCLC 1, 5, 16; DAM NOV; SSC 10**
See also CA 104; 131; DLB 65; MTCW 1, 2
Collett, (Jacobine) Camilla (Wergeland) 1813-1895 **NCLC 22**
Collier, Christopher 1930- **CLC 30**
See also AAYA 13; CA 33-36R; CANR 13, 33; JRDA; MAICYA; SATA 16, 70
Collier, James L(incoln) 1928- **CLC 30; DAM POP**
See also AAYA 13; CA 9-12R; CANR 4, 33, 60; CLR 3; JRDA; MAICYA; SAAS 21; SATA 8, 70
Collier, Jeremy 1650-1726 **LC 6**
Collier, John 1901-1980 **SSC 19**
See also CA 65-68; 97-100; CANR 10; DLB 77
Collingwood, R(obin) G(eorge) 1889(?)-1943 **TCLC 67**
See also CA 117; 155
Collins, Hunt
See Hunter, Evan
Collins, Linda 1931- **CLC 44**
See also CA 125
Collins, (William) Wilkie 1824-1889 **NCLC 1, 18**
See also CDBLB 1832-1890; DLB 18, 70, 159
Collins, William 1721-1759 **LC 4, 40; DAM POET**
See also DLB 109
Collodi, Carlo 1826-1890 **NCLC 54**
See also Lorenzini, Carlo
See also CLR 5
Colman, George 1732-1794
See Glassco, John
Colt, Winchester Remington
See Hubbard, L(afayette) Ron(ald)
Colter, Cyrus 1910- **CLC 58**
See also BW 1; CA 65-68; CANR 10, 66; DLB 33
Colton, James
See Hansen, Joseph
Colum, Padraic 1881-1972 **CLC 28**
See also CA 73-76; 33-36R; CANR 35; CLR 36; MAICYA; MTCW 1; SATA 15
Colvin, James
See Moorcock, Michael (John)
Colwin, Laurie (E.) 1944-1992 **CLC 5, 13, 23, 84**
See also CA 89-92; 139; CANR 20, 46; DLBY 80; MTCW 1
Comfort, Alex(ander) 1920- **CLC 7; DAM POP**
See also CA 1-4R; CANR 1, 45; MTCW 1
Comfort, Montgomery
See Campbell, (John) Ramsey
Compton-Burnett, I(vy) 1884(?)-1969 **CLC 1,**

3, 10, 15, 34; DAM NOV
See also CA 1-4R; 25-28R; CANR 4; DLB 36; MTCW 1
Comstock, Anthony 1844-1915 **TCLC 13**
See also CA 110; 169
Comte, Auguste 1798-1857 **NCLC 54**
Conan Doyle, Arthur
See Doyle, Arthur Conan
Conde (Abellan), Carmen 1901-
See also CA 177; DLB 108; HLCS 1; HW 2
Conde, Maryse 1937- **CLC 52, 92; BLCS; DAM MULT**
See also Boucolon, Maryse
See also BW 2; MTCW 1
Condillac, Etienne Bonnot de 1714-1780 **LC 26**
Condon, Richard (Thomas) 1915-1996 **CLC 4, 6, 8, 10, 45, 100; DAM NOV**
See also BEST 90:3; CA 1-4R; 151; CAAS 1; CANR 2, 23; INT CANR-23; MTCW 1, 2
Confucius 551B.C.-479B.C. **CMLC 19; DA; DAB; DAC; DAM MST; WLCS**
Congreve, William 1670-1729 **LC 5, 21; DA; DAB; DAC; DAM DRAM, MST, POET; DC 2; WLC**
See also CDBLB 1660-1789; DLB 39, 84
Connell, Evan S(helby), Jr. 1924- **CLC 4, 6, 45; DAM NOV**
See also AAYA 7; CA 1-4R; CAAS 2; CANR 2, 39, 76; DLB 2; DLBY 81; MTCW 1, 2
Connelly, Marc(us Cook) 1890-1980 **CLC 7**
See also CA 85-88; 102; CANR 30; DLB 7; DLBY 80; SATA-Obit 25
Connor, Ralph **TCLC 31**
See also Gordon, Charles William
See also DLB 92
Conrad, Joseph 1857-1924 **TCLC 1, 6, 13, 25, 43, 57; DA; DAB; DAC; DAM MST, NOV; SSC 9; WLC**
See also AAYA 26; CA 104; 131; CANR 60; CDBLB 1890-1914; DLB 10, 34, 98, 156; MTCW 1, 2; SATA 27
Conrad, Robert Arnold
See Hart, Moss
Conroy, Pat
See Conroy, (Donald) Pat(rick)
See also MTCW 2
Conroy, (Donald) Pat(rick) 1945- **CLC 30, 74; DAM NOV, POP**
See also Conroy, Pat
See also AAYA 8; AITN 1; CA 85-88; CANR 24, 53; DLB 6; MTCW 1
Constant (de Rebecque), (Henri) Benjamin 1767-1830 **NCLC 6**
See also DLB 119
Conybeare, Charles Augustus
See Eliot, T(homas) S(tearns)
Cook, Michael 1933- **CLC 58**
See also CA 93-96; CANR 68; DLB 53
Cook, Robin 1940- **CLC 14; DAM POP**
See also BEST 90:2; CA 108; 111; CANR 41; INT 111
Cook, Roy
See Silverberg, Robert
Cooke, Elizabeth 1948- **CLC 55**
See also CA 129
Cooke, John Esten 1830-1886 **NCLC 5**
See also DLB 3
Cooke, John Estes
See Baum, L(yman) Frank
Cooke, M. E.
See Creasey, John
Cooke, Margaret

See Creasey, John
Cook-Lynn, Elizabeth 1930- **CLC 93; DAM MULT**
See also CA 133; DLB 175; NNAL
Cooney, Ray **CLC 62**
Cooper, Douglas 1960- **CLC 86**
Cooper, Henry St. John
See Creasey, John
Cooper, J(oan) California (?)- **CLC 56; DAM MULT**
See also AAYA 12; BW 1; CA 125; CANR 55; DLB 212
Cooper, James Fenimore 1789-1851 **NCLC 1, 27, 54**
See also AAYA 22; CDALB 1640-1865; DLB 3; SATA 19
Coover, Robert (Lowell) 1932- **CLC 3, 7, 15, 32, 46, 87; DAM NOV; SSC 15**
See also CA 45-48; CANR 3, 37, 58; DLB 2; DLBY 81; MTCW 1, 2
Copeland, Stewart (Armstrong) 1952- **CLC 26**
Copernicus, Nicolaus 1473-1543 **LC 45**
Coppard, A(lfred) E(dgar) 1878-1957 **TCLC 5; SSC 21**
See also CA 114; 167; DLB 162; YABC 1
Coppee, Francois 1842-1908 **TCLC 25**
See also CA 170
Coppola, Francis Ford 1939- **CLC 16**
See also CA 77-80; CANR 40, 78; DLB 44
Corbiere, Tristan 1845-1875 **NCLC 43**
Corcoran, Barbara 1911- **CLC 17**
See also AAYA 14; CA 21-24R; CAAS 2; CANR 11, 28, 48; CLR 50; DLB 52; JRDA; SAAS 20; SATA 3, 77
Cordelier, Maurice
See Giraudoux, (Hippolyte) Jean
Corelli, Marie 1855-1924 **TCLC 51**
See also Mackay, Mary
See also DLB 34, 156
Corman, Cid 1924- **CLC 9**
See also Corman, Sidney
See also CAAS 2; DLB 5, 193
Corman, Sidney 1924-
See Corman, Cid
See also CA 85-88; CANR 44; DAM POET
Cormier, Robert (Edmund) 1925- **CLC 12, 30; DA; DAB; DAC; DAM MST, NOV**
See also AAYA 3, 19; CA 1-4R; CANR 5, 23, 76; CDALB 1968-1988; CLR 12, 55; DLB 52; INT CANR-23; JRDA; MAICYA; MTCW 1, 2; SATA 10, 45, 83
Corn, Alfred (DeWitt, III) 1943- **CLC 33**
See also CA 179; CAAE 179; CAAS 25; CANR 44; DLB 120; DLBY 80
Corneille, Pierre 1606-1684 **LC 28; DAB; DAM MST**
Cornwell, David (John Moore) 1931- **CLC 9, 15; DAM POP**
See also le Carre, John
See also CA 5-8R; CANR 13, 33, 59; MTCW 1, 2
Corso, (Nunzio) Gregory 1930- **CLC 1, 11**
See also CA 5-8R; CANR 41, 76; DLB 5, 16; MTCW 1, 2
Cortazar, Julio 1914-1984 **CLC 2, 3, 5, 10, 13, 15, 33, 34, 92; DAM MULT, NOV; HLC 1; SSC 7**
See also CA 21-24R; CANR 12, 32, 81; DLB 113; HW 1, 2; MTCW 1, 2
Cortes, Hernan 1484-1547 **LC 31**
Corvinus, Jakob
See Raabe, Wilhelm (Karl)
Corwin, Cecil

See Kornbluth, C(yril) M.

Cosic, Dobrica 1921-   **CLC 14**
See also CA 122; 138; DLB 181

Costain, Thomas B(ertram) 1885-1965 **C L C
30**
See also CA 5-8R; 25-28R; DLB 9

Costantini, Humberto 1924(?)-1987 **CLC 49**
See also CA 131; 122; HW 1

Costello, Elvis 1955-   **CLC 21**

Costenoble, Philostene
See Ghelderode, Michel de

Cotes, Cecil V.
See Duncan, Sara Jeannette

Cotter, Joseph Seamon Sr. 1861-1949 **T C L C
28; BLC 1; DAM MULT**
See also BW 1; CA 124; DLB 50

Couch, Arthur Thomas Quiller
See Quiller-Couch, SirArthur (Thomas)

Coulton, James
See Hansen, Joseph

Couperus, Louis (Marie Anne) 1863-1923
TCLC 15
See also CA 115

Coupland, Douglas 1961-**CLC 85; DAC; DAM
POP**
See also CA 142; CANR 57

Court, Wesli
See Turco, Lewis (Putnam)

Courtenay, Bryce 1933-   **CLC 59**
See also CA 138

Courtney, Robert
See Ellison, Harlan (Jay)

Cousteau,Jacques-Yves 1910-1997   **CLC 30**
See also CA 65-68; 159; CANR 15, 67; MTCW
1; SATA 38, 98

Coventry, Francis 1725-1754   **LC 46**

Cowan, Peter (Walkinshaw) 1914- **SSC 28**
See also CA 21-24R; CANR 9, 25, 50

Coward, Noel (Peirce) 1899-1973**CLC 1, 9, 29,
51; DAM DRAM**
See also AITN 1; CA 17-18; 41-44R; CANR
35; CAP 2; CDBLB 1914-1945; DLB 10;
MTCW 1, 2

Cowley, Abraham 1618-1667   **LC 43**
See also DLB 131, 151

Cowley, Malcolm 1898-1989   **CLC 39**
See also CA 5-8R; 128; CANR 3, 55; DLB 4,
48; DLBY 81, 89; MTCW 1, 2

Cowper, William 1731-1800   **NCLC 8;DAM
POET**
See also DLB 104, 109

Cox, William Trevor 1928-   **CLC 9, 14, 71;
DAM NOV**
See also Trevor, William
See also CA 9-12R; CANR 4, 37, 55, 76; DLB
14; INT CANR-37; MTCW 1, 2

Coyne, P. J.
See Masters, Hilary

Cozzens, James Gould 1903-1978**CLC 1, 4, 11,
92**
See also CA 9-12R; 81-84; CANR 19; CDALB
1941-1968; DLB 9; DLBD 2; DLBY 84, 97;
MTCW 1, 2

Crabbe, George 1754-1832   **NCLC 26**
See also DLB 93

Craddock, Charles Egbert
See Murfree, Mary Noailles

Craig, A. A.
See Anderson, Poul (William)

Craik, Dinah Maria (Mulock) 1826-1887
NCLC 38
See also DLB 35, 163; MAICYA; SATA 34

Cram, Ralph Adams 1863-1942   **TCLC 45**

See also CA 160

Crane, (Harold) Hart 1899-1932 **TCLC 2, 5,
80; DA; DAB; DAC; DAM MST, POET;
PC 3; WLC**
See also CA 104; 127; CDALB 1917-1929;
DLB 4, 48; MTCW 1, 2

Crane, R(onald) S(almon) 1886-1967**CLC 27**
See also CA 85-88; DLB 63

Crane, Stephen (Townley) 1871-1900 **T C L C
11, 17, 32; DA; DAB; DAC; DAM MST,
NOV, POET; SSC 7; WLC**
See also AAYA 21; CA 109; 140; CDALB 1865-
1917; DLB 12, 54, 78; YABC 2

Cranshaw, Stanley
See Fisher, Dorothy (Frances) Canfield

Crase, Douglas 1944-   **CLC 58**
See also CA 106

Crashaw, Richard 1612(?)-1649   **LC 24**
See also DLB 126

Craven, Margaret 1901-1980   **CLC 17;DAC**
See also CA 103

Crawford, F(rancis) Marion 1854-1909**TCLC
10**
See also CA 107; 168; DLB 71

Crawford, Isabella Valancy 1850-1887**N C L C
12**
See also DLB 92

Crayon, Geoffrey
See Irving, Washington

Creasey, John 1908-1973   **CLC 11**
See also CA 5-8R; 41-44R; CANR 8, 59; DLB
77; MTCW 1

Crebillon, Claude Prosper Jolyot de (fils) 1707-
1777   **LC 1, 28**

Credo
See Creasey, John

Credo, Alvaro J. de
See Prado (Calvo), Pedro

Creeley, Robert (White) 1926-**CLC 1, 2, 4, 8,
11, 15, 36, 78; DAM POET**
See also CA 1-4R; CAAS 10; CANR 23, 43;
DLB 5, 16, 169; DLBD 17; MTCW 1, 2

Crews, Harry (Eugene) 1935- **CLC 6, 23, 49**
See also AITN 1; CA 25-28R; CANR 20, 57;
DLB 6, 143, 185; MTCW 1, 2

Crichton, (John) Michael 1942-**CLC 2, 6, 54,
90; DAM NOV, POP**
See also AAYA 10; AITN 2; CA 25-28R; CANR
13, 40, 54, 76; DLBY 81; INT CANR-13;
JRDA; MTCW 1, 2; SATA 9, 88

Crispin, Edmund   **CLC 22**
See also Montgomery, (Robert) Bruce
See also DLB 87

Cristofer, Michael 1945(?)-   **CLC 28; DAM
DRAM**
See also CA 110; 152; DLB 7

Croce, Benedetto 1866-1952   **TCLC 37**
See also CA 120; 155

Crockett, David 1786-1836   **NCLC 8**
See also DLB 3, 11

Crockett, Davy
See Crockett, David

Crofts, Freeman Wills 1879-1957   **TCLC 55**
See also CA 115; DLB 77

Croker, John Wilson 1780-1857   **NCLC 10**
See also DLB 110

Crommelynck, Fernand 1885-1970   **CLC 75**
See also CA 89-92

Cromwell, Oliver 1599-1658   **LC 43**

Cronin, A(rchibald) J(oseph) 1896-1981**C L C
32**
See also CA 1-4R; 102; CANR 5; DLB 191;
SATA 47; SATA-Obit 25

Cross, Amanda
See Heilbrun, Carolyn G(old)

Crothers, Rachel 1878(?)-1958   **TCLC 19**
See also CA 113; DLB 7

Croves, Hal
See Traven, B.

Crow Dog, Mary (Ellen) (?)-   **CLC 93**
See also Brave Bird, Mary
See also CA 154

Crowfield, Christopher
See Stowe, Harriet (Elizabeth) Beecher

Crowley, Aleister   **TCLC 7**
See also Crowley, Edward Alexander

Crowley, Edward Alexander 1875-1947
See Crowley, Aleister
See also CA 104

Crowley, John 1942-   **CLC 57**
See also CA 61-64; CANR 43; DLBY 82; SATA
65

Crud
See Crumb, R(obert)

Crumarums
See Crumb, R(obert)

Crumb, R(obert) 1943-   **CLC 17**
See also CA 106

Crumbum
See Crumb, R(obert)

Crumski
See Crumb, R(obert)

Crum the Bum
See Crumb, R(obert)

Crunk
See Crumb, R(obert)

Crustt
See Crumb, R(obert)

Cruz, Victor Hernandez 1949-
See also BW 2; CA 65-68; CAAS 17; CANR
14, 32, 74; DAM MULT, POET; DLB 41;
HLC 1; HW 1, 2; MTCW 1

Cryer, Gretchen (Kiger) 1935-   **CLC 21**
See also CA 114; 123

Csath, Geza 1887-1919   **TCLC 13**
See also CA 111

Cudlip, David R(ockwell) 1933-   **CLC 34**
See also CA 177

Cullen, Countee 1903-1946**TCLC 4, 37; BLC
1; DA; DAC; DAM MST, MULT, POET;
PC 20; WLCS**
See also BW 1; CA 108; 124; CDALB 1917-
1929; DLB 4, 48, 51; MTCW 1, 2; SATA 18

Cum, R.
See Crumb, R(obert)

Cummings, Bruce F(rederick) 1889-1919
See Barbellion, W. N. P.
See also CA 123

Cummings, E(dward) E(stlin) 1894-1962**CLC
1, 3, 8, 12, 15, 68; DA; DAB; DAC; DAM
MST, POET; PC 5; WLC**
See also CA 73-76; CANR 31; CDALB 1929-
1941; DLB 4, 48; MTCW 1, 2

Cunha, Euclides (Rodrigues Pimenta) da 1866-
1909   **TCLC 24**
See also CA 123

Cunningham, E. V.
See Fast, Howard (Melvin)

Cunningham, J(ames) V(incent) 1911-1985
CLC 3, 31
See also CA 1-4R; 115; CANR 1, 72; DLB 5

Cunningham, Julia(Woolfolk) 1916- **CLC 12**
See also CA 9-12R; CANR 4, 19, 36; JRDA;
MAICYA; SAAS 2; SATA 1, 26

Cunningham, Michael 1952-   **CLC 34**
See also CA 136

Cunninghame Graham, R(obert) B(ontine)
1852-1936   **TCLC 19**
  See also Graham, R(obert) B(ontine)
    Cunninghame
  See also CA 119; DLB 98

Currie, Ellen 19(?)-   **CLC 44**

Curtin, Philip
  See Lowndes, Marie Adelaide (Belloc)

Curtis, Price
  See Ellison, Harlan (Jay)

Cutrate, Joe
  See Spiegelman, Art

Cynewulf c. 770-c. 840   **CMLC 23**

Czaczkes, Shmuel Yosef
  See Agnon, S(hmuel) Y(osef Halevi)

Dabrowska, Maria (Szumska) 1889-1965 **CLC 15**
  See also CA 106

Dabydeen, David 1955-   **CLC 34**
  See also BW 1; CA 125; CANR 56

Dacey, Philip 1939-   **CLC 51**
  See also CA 37-40R; CAAS 17; CANR 14, 32,
    64; DLB 105

Dagerman, Stig (Halvard) 1923-1954 **TCLC 17**
  See also CA 117; 155

Dahl, Roald 1916-1990 **CLC 1, 6, 18, 79; DAB; DAC; DAM MST, NOV, POP**
  See also AAYA 15; CA 1-4R; 133; CANR 6,
    32, 37, 62; CLR 1, 7, 41; DLB 139; JRDA;
    MAICYA; MTCW 1, 2; SATA 1, 26, 73;
    SATA-Obit 65

Dahlberg, Edward 1900-1977   **CLC 1, 7, 14**
  See also CA 9-12R; 69-72; CANR 31, 62; DLB
    48; MTCW 1

Daitch, Susan 1954-   **CLC 103**
  See also CA 161

Dale, Colin   **TCLC 18**
  See also Lawrence, T(homas) E(dward)

Dale, George E.
  See Asimov, Isaac

Dalton, Roque 1935-1975
  See also HLCS 1; HW 2

Daly, Elizabeth 1878-1967   **CLC 52**
  See also CA 23-24; 25-28R; CANR 60; CAP 2

Daly, Maureen 1921-   **CLC 17**
  See also AAYA 5; CANR 37; JRDA; MAICYA;
    SAAS 1; SATA 2

Damas, Leon-Gontran 1912-1978   **CLC 84**
  See also BW 1; CA 125; 73-76

Dana, Richard Henry Sr. 1787-1879 **NCLC 53**

Daniel, Samuel 1562(?)-1619   **LC 24**
  See also DLB 62

Daniels, Brett
  See Adler, Renata

Dannay, Frederic 1905-1982   **CLC 11; DAM POP**
  See also Queen, Ellery
  See also CA 1-4R; 107; CANR 1, 39; DLB 137;
    MTCW 1

D'Annunzio, Gabriele 1863-1938 **TCLC 6, 40**
  See also CA 104; 155

Danois, N. le
  See Gourmont, Remy (-Marie-Charles) de

Dante 1265-1321   **CMLC 3, 18; DA; DAB; DAC; DAM MST, POET; PC 21; WLCS**

d'Antibes, Germain
  See Simenon, Georges (Jacques Christian)

Danticat, Edwidge 1969-   **CLC 94**
  See also AAYA 29; CA 152; CANR 73; MTCW
    1

Danvers, Dennis 1947-   **CLC 70**

Danziger, Paula 1944-   **CLC 21**

  See also AAYA 4; CA 112; 115; CANR 37; CLR
    20; JRDA; MAICYA; SATA 36, 63, 102;
    SATA-Brief 30

Da Ponte, Lorenzo 1749-1838   **NCLC 50**

Dario, Ruben 1867-1916   **TCLC 4; DAM MULT; HLC 1; PC 15**
  See also CA 131; CANR 81; HW 1, 2; MTCW
    1, 2

Darley, George 1795-1846   **NCLC 2**
  See also DLB 96

Darrow, Clarence (Seward) 1857-1938 **TCLC 81**
  See also CA 164

Darwin, Charles 1809-1882   **NCLC 57**
  See also DLB 57, 166

Daryush, Elizabeth 1887-1977   **CLC 6, 19**
  See also CA 49-52; CANR 3, 81; DLB 20

Dasgupta, Surendranath 1887-1952 **TCLC 81**
  See also CA 157

Dashwood, Edmee Elizabeth Monica de la Pas-
  ture 1890-1943
  See Delafield, E. M.
  See also CA 119; 154

Daudet, (Louis Marie) Alphonse 1840-1897
  NCLC 1
  See also DLB 123

Daumal, Rene 1908-1944   **TCLC 14**
  See also CA 114

Davenant, William 1606-1668   **LC 13**
  See also DLB 58, 126

Davenport, Guy (Mattison, Jr.) 1927- **CLC 6, 14, 38; SSC 16**
  See also CA 33-36R; CANR 23, 73; DLB 130

Davidson, Avram (James) 1923-1993
  See Queen, Ellery
  See also CA 101; 171; CANR 26; DLB 8

Davidson, Donald (Grady) 1893-1968 **CLC 2, 13, 19**
  See also CA 5-8R; 25-28R; CANR 4; DLB 45

Davidson, Hugh
  See Hamilton, Edmond

Davidson, John 1857-1909   **TCLC 24**
  See also CA 118; DLB 19

Davidson, Sara 1943-   **CLC 9**
  See also CA 81-84; CANR 44, 68; DLB 185

Davie, Donald (Alfred) 1922-1995 **CLC 5, 8, 10, 31**
  See also CA 1-4R; 149; CAAS 3; CANR 1, 44;
    DLB 27; MTCW 1

Davies, Ray(mond Douglas) 1944- **CLC 21**
  See also CA 116; 146

Davies, Rhys 1901-1978   **CLC 23**
  See also CA 9-12R; 81-84; CANR 4; DLB 139,
    191

Davies, (William) Robertson 1913-1995 **CLC 2, 7, 13, 25, 42, 75, 91; DA; DAB; DAC; DAM MST, NOV, POP; WLC**
  See also BEST 89:2; CA 33-36R; 150; CANR
    17, 42; DLB 68; INT CANR-17; MTCW 1,
    2

Davies, W(illiam) H(enry) 1871-1940 **TCLC 5**
  See also CA 104; 179; DLB 19, 174

Davies, Walter C.
  See Kornbluth, C(yril) M.

Davis, Angela (Yvonne) 1944- **CLC 77; DAM MULT**
  See also BW 2, 3; CA 57-60; CANR 10, 81˙

Davis, B. Lynch
  See Bioy Casares, Adolfo; Borges, Jorge Luis

Davis, B. Lynch
  See Bioy Casares, Adolfo

Davis, Harold Lenoir 1894-1960   **CLC 49**
  See also CA 178; 89-92; DLB 9, 206

Davis, Rebecca (Blaine) Harding 1831-1910
  TCLC 6
  See also CA 104; 179; DLB 74

Davis, Richard Harding 1864-1916 **TCLC 24**
  See also CA 114; DLB 12, 23, 78, 79, 189;
    DLBD 13

Davison, Frank Dalby 1893-1970   **CLC 15**
  See also CA 116

Davison, Lawrence H.
  See Lawrence, D(avid) H(erbert Richards)

Davison, Peter (Hubert) 1928-   **CLC 28**
  See also CA 9-12R; CAAS 4; CANR 3, 43; DLB
    5

Davys, Mary 1674-1732   **LC 1, 46**
  See also DLB 39

Dawson, Fielding 1930-   **CLC 6**
  See also CA 85-88; DLB 130

Dawson, Peter
  See Faust, Frederick (Schiller)

Day, Clarence (Shepard, Jr.) 1874-1935
  TCLC 25
  See also CA 108; DLB 11

Day, Thomas 1748-1789   **LC 1**
  See also DLB 39; YABC 1

Day Lewis, C(ecil) 1904-1972 **CLC 1, 6, 10; DAM POET; PC 11**
  See also Blake, Nicholas
  See also CA 13-16; 33-36R; CANR 34; CAP 1;
    DLB 15, 20; MTCW 1, 2

Dazai Osamu 1909-1948   **TCLC 11**
  See also Tsushima, Shuji
  See also CA 164; DLB 182

de Andrade, Carlos Drummond 1892-1945
  See Drummond de Andrade, Carlos

Deane, Norman
  See Creasey, John

Deane, Seamus (Francis) 1940-   **CLC 122**
  See also CA 118; CANR 42

de Beauvoir, Simone (Lucie Ernestine Marie Bertrand)
  See Beauvoir, Simone (Lucie Ernestine Marie
    Bertrand) de

de Beer, P.
  See Bosman, Herman Charles

de Brissac, Malcolm
  See Dickinson, Peter (Malcolm)

de Chardin, Pierre Teilhard
  See Teilhard de Chardin, (Marie Joseph) Pierre

Dee, John 1527-1608   **LC 20**

Deer, Sandra 1940-   **CLC 45**

De Ferrari, Gabriella 1941-   **CLC 65**
  See also CA 146

Defoe, Daniel 1660(?)-1731   **LC 1, 42; DA; DAB; DAC; DAM MST, NOV; WLC**
  See also AAYA 27; CDBLB 1660-1789; DLB
    39, 95, 101; JRDA; MAICYA; SATA 22

de Gourmont, Remy(-Marie-Charles)
  See Gourmont, Remy (-Marie-Charles) de

de Hartog, Jan 1914-   **CLC 19**
  See also CA 1-4R; CANR 1

de Hostos, E. M.
  See Hostos (y Bonilla), Eugenio Maria de

de Hostos, Eugenio M.
  See Hostos (y Bonilla), Eugenio Maria de

Deighton, Len   **CLC 4, 7, 22, 46**
  See also Deighton, Leonard Cyril
  See also AAYA 6; BEST 89:2; CDBLB 1960 to
    Present; DLB 87

Deighton, Leonard Cyril 1929-
  See Deighton, Len
  See also CA 9-12R; CANR 19, 33, 68; DAM
    NOV, POP; MTCW 1, 2

Dekker, Thomas 1572(?)-1632   **LC 22; DAM**

See also DLB 115

Eckmar, F. R.
See de Hartog, Jan

Eco, Umberto 1932- **CLC 28, 60; DAM NOV, POP**
See also BEST 90:1; CA 77-80; CANR 12, 33, 55; DLB 196; MTCW 1, 2

Eddison, E(ric) R(ucker) 1882-1945 **TCLC 15**
See also CA 109; 156

Eddy, Mary (Ann Morse) Baker 1821-1910 **TCLC 71**
See also CA 113; 174

Edel, (Joseph) Leon 1907-1997 **CLC 29, 34**
See also CA 1-4R; 161; CANR 1, 22; DLB 103; INT CANR-22

Eden, Emily 1797-1869 **NCLC 10**

Edgar, David 1948- **CLC 42;DAM DRAM**
See also CA 57-60; CANR 12, 61; DLB 13; MTCW 1

Edgerton, Clyde (Carlyle) 1944- **CLC 39**
See also AAYA 17; CA 118; 134; CANR 64; INT 134

Edgeworth, Maria 1768-1849 **NCLC 1,51**
See also DLB 116, 159, 163; SATA 21

Edison, Thomas 1847-1931 **TCLC 96**

Edmonds, Paul
See Kuttner, Henry

Edmonds, Walter D(umaux) 1903-1998 **C L C 35**
See also CA 5-8R; CANR 2; DLB 9; MAICYA; SAAS 4; SATA 1, 27; SATA-Obit 99

Edmondson, Wallace
See Ellison, Harlan (Jay)

Edson, Russell **CLC 13**
See also CA 33-36R

Edwards, Bronwen Elizabeth
See Rose, Wendy

Edwards, G(erald) B(asil) 1899-1976 **CLC 25**
See also CA 110

Edwards, Gus 1939- **CLC 43**
See also CA 108; INT 108

Edwards, Jonathan 1703-1758 **LC 7; DA; DAC; DAM MST**
See also DLB 24

Efron, Marina Ivanovna Tsvetaeva
See Tsvetaeva (Efron), Marina (Ivanovna)

Ehle, John (Marsden, Jr.) 1925- **CLC 27**
See also CA 9-12R

Ehrenbourg, Ilya (Grigoryevich)
See Ehrenburg, Ilya (Grigoryevich)

Ehrenburg, Ilya (Grigoryevich) 1891-1967 **CLC 18, 34, 62**
See also CA 102; 25-28R

Ehrenburg, Ilyo (Grigoryevich)
See Ehrenburg, Ilya (Grigoryevich)

Ehrenreich, Barbara 1941- **CLC 110**
See also BEST 90:4; CA 73-76; CANR 16, 37, 62; MTCW 1, 2

Eich, Guenter 1907-1972 **CLC 15**
See also CA 111; 93-96; DLB 69, 124

Eichendorff, Joseph Freiherrvon 1788-1857 **NCLC 8**
See also DLB 90

Eigner, Larry **CLC 9**
See also Eigner, Laurence (Joel)
See also CAAS 23; DLB 5

Eigner, Laurence (Joel) 1927-1996
See Eigner, Larry
See also CA 9-12R; 151; CANR 6; DLB 193

Einstein, Albert 1879-1955 **TCLC 65**
See also CA 121; 133; MTCW 1, 2

Eiseley, Loren Corey 1907-1977 **CLC 7**
See also AAYA 5; CA 1-4R; 73-76; CANR 6;

DLBD 17

Eisenstadt, Jill 1963- **CLC 50**
See also CA 140

Eisenstein, Sergei (Mikhailovich) 1898-1948 **TCLC 57**
See also CA 114; 149

Eisner, Simon
See Kornbluth, C(yril) M.

Ekeloef, (Bengt) Gunnar 1907-1968 **CLC 27; DAM POET; PC 23**
See also CA 123; 25-28R

Ekelof, (Bengt) Gunnar
See Ekeloef, (Bengt) Gunnar

Ekelund, Vilhelm 1880-1949 **TCLC 75**

Ekwensi, C. O. D.
See Ekwensi, Cyprian (Odiatu Duaka)

Ekwensi, Cyprian (Odiatu Duaka) 1921- **C L C 4; BLC 1; DAM MULT**
See also BW 2, 3; CA 29-32R; CANR 18, 42, 74; DLB 117; MTCW 1, 2; SATA 66

Elaine **TCLC 18**
See also Leverson, Ada

El Crummo
See Crumb, R(obert)

Elder, Lonne III 1931-1996 **DC 8**
See also BLC 1; BW 1, 3; CA 81-84; 152; CANR 25; DAM MULT; DLB 7, 38, 44

Elia
See Lamb, Charles

Eliade, Mircea 1907-1986 **CLC 19**
See also CA 65-68; 119; CANR 30, 62; MTCW 1

Eliot, A. D.
See Jewett, (Theodora) Sarah Orne

Eliot, Alice
See Jewett, (Theodora) Sarah Orne

Eliot, Dan
See Silverberg, Robert

Eliot, George 1819-1880 **NCLC 4, 13, 23, 41, 49; DA; DAB; DAC; DAM MST, NOV; PC 20; WLC**
See also CDBLB 1832-1890; DLB 21, 35, 55

Eliot, John 1604-1690 **LC 5**
See also DLB 24

Eliot, T(homas) S(tearns) 1888-1965 **CLC 1, 2, 3, 6, 9, 10, 13, 15, 24, 34, 41, 55, 57, 113; DA; DAB; DAC; DAM DRAM, MST, POET; PC 5; WLC**
See also AAYA 28; CA 5-8R; 25-28R; CANR 41;CDALB 1929-1941; DLB 7, 10, 45, 63; DLBY 88; MTCW 1, 2

Elizabeth 1866-1941 **TCLC 41**

Elkin, Stanley L(awrence) 1930-1995 **CLC 4, 6, 9, 14, 27, 51, 91; DAM NOV, POP; SSC 12**
See also CA 9-12R; 148; CANR 8, 46; DLB 2, 28; DLBY 80; INT CANR-8; MTCW 1, 2

Elledge, Scott **CLC 34**

Elliot, Don
See Silverberg, Robert

Elliott, Don
See Silverberg, Robert

Elliott, George P(aul) 1918-1980 **CLC 2**
See also CA 1-4R; 97-100; CANR 2

Elliott, Janice 1931- **CLC 47**
See also CA 13-16R; CANR 8, 29; DLB 14

Elliott, Sumner Locke 1917-1991 **CLC 38**
See also CA 5-8R; 134; CANR 2, 21

Elliott, William
See Bradbury, Ray (Douglas)

Ellis, A. E. **CLC 7**

Ellis, Alice Thomas **CLC 40**
See also Haycraft, Anna

See also DLB 194; MTCW 1

Ellis, Bret Easton 1964- **CLC 39, 71, 117; DAM POP**
See also AAYA 2; CA 118; 123; CANR 51, 74; INT 123; MTCW 1

Ellis, (Henry) Havelock 1859-1939 **TCLC 14**
See also CA 109; 169; DLB 190

Ellis, Landon
See Ellison, Harlan (Jay)

Ellis, Trey 1962- **CLC 55**
See also CA 146

Ellison, Harlan (Jay) 1934- **CLC 1, 13, 42; DAM POP; SSC 14**
See also Jarvis, E. K.
See also AAYA 29; CA 5-8R; CANR 5, 46; DLB 8; INT CANR-5; MTCW 1, 2

Ellison, Ralph (Waldo) 1914-1994 **CLC 1, 3, 11, 54, 86, 114; BLC 1; DA; DAB; DAC; DAM MST, MULT, NOV; SSC 26;WLC**
See also AAYA 19; BW 1, 3; CA 9-12R; 145; CANR 24, 53; CDALB 1941-1968; DLB 2, 76; DLBY 94; MTCW 1, 2

Ellmann, Lucy (Elizabeth) 1956- **CLC 61**
See also CA 128

Ellmann, Richard (David) 1918-1987 **CLC 50**
See also BEST 89:2; CA 1-4R; 122; CANR 2, 28, 61; DLB 103; DLBY 87; MTCW 1, 2

Elman, Richard (Martin) 1934-1997 **CLC 19**
See also CA 17-20R; 163; CAAS 3; CANR 47

Elron
See Hubbard, L(afayette) Ron(ald)

Eluard, Paul **TCLC 7, 41**
See also Grindel, Eugene

Elyot, Sir Thomas 1490(?)-1546 **LC 11**

Elytis, Odysseus 1911-1996 **CLC 15, 49, 100; DAM POET; PC 21**
See also CA 102; 151; MTCW 1, 2

Emecheta, (Florence Onye) Buchi 1944- **C L C 14, 48; BLC 2; DAM MULT**
See also BW 2, 3; CA 81-84; CANR 27, 81; DLB 117; MTCW 1, 2; SATA 66

Emerson, Mary Moody 1774-1863 **NCLC 66**

Emerson, Ralph Waldo 1803-1882 **NCLC 1, 38; DA; DAB; DAC; DAM MST, POET; PC 18; WLC**
See also CDALB 1640-1865; DLB 1, 59, 73

Eminescu, Mihail 1850-1889 **NCLC 33**

Empson, William 1906-1984 **CLC 3, 8, 19, 33, 34**
See also CA 17-20R; 112; CANR 31, 61; DLB 20; MTCW 1, 2

Enchi, Fumiko (Ueda) 1905-1986 **CLC 31**
See also CA 129; 121; DLB 182

Ende, Michael (Andreas Helmuth) 1929-1995 **CLC 31**
See also CA 118; 124; 149; CANR 36; CLR 14; DLB 75; MAICYA; SATA 61; SATA-Brief 42; SATA-Obit 86

Endo, Shusaku 1923-1996 **CLC 7, 14, 19, 54, 99; DAM NOV**
See also CA 29-32R; 153; CANR 21, 54; DLB 182; MTCW 1, 2

Engel, Marian 1933-1985 **CLC 36**
See also CA 25-28R; CANR 12; DLB 53; INT CANR-12

Engelhardt, Frederick
See Hubbard, L(afayette) Ron(ald)

Enright, D(ennis) J(oseph) 1920- **CLC 4, 8, 31**
See also CA 1-4R; CANR 1, 42; DLB 27; SATA 25

Enzensberger, Hans Magnus 1929- **CLC 43**
See also CA 116; 119

Ephron, Nora 1941- **CLC 17, 31**

See also CA 73-76; CANR 45

Gelber, Jack 1932- **CLC 1, 6, 14, 79**
See also CA 1-4R; CANR 2; DLB 7

Gellhorn, Martha (Ellis) 1908-1998 **CLC 14, 60**
See also CA 77-80; 164; CANR 44; DLBY 82, 98

Genet, Jean 1910-1986**CLC 1, 2, 5, 10, 14, 44, 46; DAM DRAM**
See also CA 13-16R; CANR 18; DLB 72; DLBY 86; MTCW 1, 2

Gent, Peter 1942- **CLC 29**
See also AITN 1; CA 89-92; DLBY 82

Gentile, Giovanni 1875-1944 **TCLC 96**
See also CA 119

Gentlewoman in New England, A
See Bradstreet, Anne

Gentlewoman in Those Parts, A
See Bradstreet, Anne

George, Jean Craighead 1919- **CLC 35**
See also AAYA 8; CA 5-8R; CANR 25; CLR 1; DLB 52; JRDA; MAICYA; SATA 2, 68

George, Stefan (Anton) 1868-1933**TCLC 2, 14**
See also CA 104

Georges, Georges Martin
See Simenon, Georges (Jacques Christian)

Gerhardi, William Alexander
See Gerhardie, William Alexander

Gerhardie, William Alexander 1895-1977 **CLC 5**
See also CA 25-28R; 73-76; CANR 18; DLB 36

Gerstler, Amy 1956- **CLC 70**
See also CA 146

Gertler, T. **CLC 34**
See also CA 116; 121; INT 121

Ghalib **NCLC 39, 78**
See also Ghalib, Hsadullah Khan

Ghalib, Hsadullah Khan 1797-1869
See Ghalib
See also DAM POET

Ghelderode, Michel de 1898-1962**CLC 6, 11;. DAM DRAM**
See also CA 85-88; CANR 40, 77

Ghiselin, Brewster 1903- **CLC 23**
See also CA 13-16R; CAAS 10; CANR 13

Ghose, Aurabinda 1872-1950 **TCLC 63**
See also CA 163

Ghose, Zulfikar 1935- **CLC 42**
See also CA 65-68; CANR 67

Ghosh, Amitav 1956- **CLC 44**
See also CA 147; CANR 80

Giacosa, Giuseppe 1847-1906 **TCLC 7**
See also CA 104

Gibb, Lee
See Waterhouse, Keith (Spencer)

Gibbon, Lewis Grassic **TCLC 4**
See also Mitchell, James Leslie

Gibbons, Kaye 1960- **CLC 50, 88;DAM POP**
See also CA 151; CANR 75; MTCW 1

Gibran, Kahlil 1883-1931 **TCLC 1, 9; DAM POET, POP; PC 9**
See also CA 104; 150; MTCW 2

Gibran, Khalil
See Gibran, Kahlil

Gibson, William 1914- **CLC 23; DA; DAB; DAC; DAM DRAM, MST**
See also CA 9-12R; CANR 9, 42, 75; DLB 7; MTCW 1; SATA 66

Gibson, William (Ford) 1948- **CLC 39, 63; DAM POP**
See also AAYA 12; CA 126; 133; CANR 52; MTCW 1

Gide, Andre (Paul Guillaume) 1869-1951 **TCLC 5, 12, 36; DA; DAB; DAC; DAM MST, NOV; SSC 13; WLC**
See also CA 104; 124; DLB 65; MTCW 1, 2

Gifford, Barry (Colby) 1946- **CLC 34**
See also CA 65-68; CANR 9, 30, 40

Gilbert, Frank
See De Voto, Bernard (Augustine)

Gilbert, W(illiam) S(chwenck) 1836-1911 **TCLC 3; DAM DRAM, POET**
See also CA 104; 173; SATA 36

Gilbreth, Frank B., Jr. 1911- **CLC 17**
See also CA 9-12R; SATA 2

Gilchrist, Ellen 1935-**CLC 34, 48; DAM POP; SSC 14**
See also CA 113; 116; CANR 41, 61; DLB 130; MTCW 1, 2

Giles, Molly 1942- **CLC 39**
See also CA 126

Gill, Eric 1882-1940 **TCLC 85**

Gill, Patrick
See Creasey, John

Gilliam, Terry (Vance) 1940- **CLC 21**
See also Monty Python
See also AAYA 19; CA 108; 113; CANR 35; INT 113

Gillian, Jerry
See Gilliam, Terry (Vance)

Gilliatt, Penelope (Ann Douglass) 1932-1993 **CLC 2, 10, 13, 53**
See also AITN 2; CA 13-16R; 141; CANR 49; DLB 14

Gilman, Charlotte (Anna) Perkins (Stetson) 1860-1935 **TCLC 9, 37; SSC 13**
See also CA 106; 150; MTCW 1

Gilmour, David 1949- **CLC 35**
See also CA 138, 147

Gilpin, William 1724-1804 **NCLC 30**

Gilray, J. D.
See Mencken, H(enry) L(ouis)

Gilroy, Frank D(aniel) 1925- **CLC 2**
See also CA 81-84; CANR 32, 64; DLB 7

Gilstrap, John 1957(?)- **CLC 99**
See also CA 160

Ginsberg, Allen 1926-1997**CLC 1, 2, 3, 4, 6, 13, 36, 69, 109; DA; DAB; DAC; DAM MST, POET; PC 4; WLC**
See also AITN 1; CA 1-4R; 157; CANR 2, 41, 63; CDALB 1941-1968; DLB 5, 16, 169; MTCW 1, 2

Ginzburg, Natalia 1916-1991**CLC 5, 11, 54, 70**
See also CA 85-88; 135; CANR 33; DLB 177; MTCW 1, 2

Giono, Jean 1895-1970 **CLC 4, 11**
See also CA 45-48; 29-32R; CANR 2, 35; DLB 72; MTCW 1

Giovanni, Nikki 1943- **CLC 2, 4, 19, 64, 117; BLC 2; DA; DAB; DAC; DAM MST, MULT, POET; PC 19; WLCS**
See also AAYA 22; AITN 1; BW 2, 3; CA 29-32R; CAAS 6; CANR 18, 41, 60; CDALBS; CLR 6; DLB 5, 41; INT CANR-18; MAICYA; MTCW 1, 2; SATA 24, 107

Giovene, Andrea 1904- **CLC 7**
See also CA 85-88

Gippius, Zinaida (Nikolayevna) 1869-1945
See Hippius, Zinaida
See also CA 106

Giraudoux, (Hippolyte) Jean 1882-1944 **TCLC 2, 7; DAM DRAM**
See also CA 104; DLB 65

Gironella, Jose Maria 1917- **CLC 11**
See also CA 101

Gissing, George (Robert) 1857-1903**TCLC 3, 24, 47**
See also CA 105; 167; DLB 18, 135, 184

Giurlani, Aldo
See Palazzeschi, Aldo

Gladkov, Fyodor (Vasilyevich) 1883-1958 **TCLC 27**
See also CA 170

Glanville, Brian (Lester) 1931- **CLC 6**
See also CA 5-8R; CAAS 9; CANR 3, 70; DLB 15, 139; SATA 42

Glasgow, Ellen (Anderson Gholson) 1873-1945 **TCLC 2, 7; SSC 34**
See also CA 104; 164; DLB 9, 12; MTCW 2

Glaspell, Susan 1882(?)-1948**TCLC 55; DC 10**
See also CA 110; 154; DLB 7, 9, 78; YABC 2

Glassco, John 1909-1981 **CLC 9**
See also CA 13-16R; 102; CANR 15; DLB 68

Glasscock, Amnesia
See Steinbeck, John (Ernst)

Glasser, Ronald J. 1940(?)- **CLC 37**

Glassman, Joyce
See Johnson, Joyce

Glendinning, Victoria 1937- **CLC 50**
See also CA 120; 127; CANR 59; DLB 155

Glissant, Edouard 1928- **CLC 10, 68; DAM MULT**
See also CA 153

Gloag, Julian 1930- **CLC 40**
See also AITN 1; CA 65-68; CANR 10, 70

Glowacki, Aleksander
See Prus, Boleslaw

Gluck, Louise (Elisabeth) 1943-**CLC 7, 22, 44, 81; DAM POET; PC 16**
See also CA 33-36R; CANR 40, 69; DLB 5; MTCW 2

Glyn, Elinor 1864-1943 **TCLC 72**
See also DLB 153

Gobineau, Joseph Arthur (Comte) de 1816-1882 **NCLC 17**
See also DLB 123

Godard, Jean-Luc 1930- **CLC 20**
See also CA 93-96

Godden, (Margaret) Rumer 1907-1998 **C L C 53**
See also AAYA 6; CA 5-8R; 172; CANR 4, 27, 36, 55, 80; CLR 20; DLB 161; MAICYA; SAAS 12; SATA 3, 36; SATA-Obit 109

Godoy Alcayaga, Lucila 1889-1957
See Mistral, Gabriela
See also BW 2; CA 104; 131; CANR 81; DAM MULT; HW 1, 2; MTCW 1, 2

Godwin, Gail (Kathleen) 1937-**CLC 5, 8, 22, 31, 69; DAM POP**
See also CA 29-32R; CANR 15, 43, 69; DLB 6; INT CANR-15; MTCW 1, 2

Godwin, William 1756-1836 **NCLC 14**
See also CDBLB 1789-1832; DLB 39, 104, 142, 158, 163

Goebbels, Josef
See Goebbels, (Paul) Joseph

Goebbels, (Paul) Joseph 1897-1945 **TCLC 68**
See also CA 115; 148

Goebbels, Joseph Paul
See Goebbels, (Paul) Joseph

Goethe, Johann Wolfgang von 1749-1832 **NCLC 4, 22, 34; DA; DAB; DAC; DAM DRAM, MST, POET; PC 5; WLC**
See also DLB 94

Gogarty, Oliver St. John 1878-1957**TCLC 15**
See also CA 109; 150; DLB 15, 19

Gogol, Nikolai (Vasilyevich) 1809-1852**NCLC 5, 15, 31; DA; DAB; DAC; DAM DRAM,**

MST; DC 1; SSC 4, 29; WLC
See also DLB 198

Goines, Donald 1937(?)-1974 CLC 80; BLC 2;
DAM MULT, POP
See also AITN 1; BW 1, 3; CA 124; 114; CANR
82; DLB 33

Gold, Herbert 1924-   CLC 4, 7, 14, 42
See also CA 9-12R; CANR 17, 45; DLB 2;
DLBY 81

Goldbarth, Albert 1948-   CLC 5, 38
See also CA 53-56; CANR 6, 40; DLB 120

Goldberg, Anatol 1910-1982   CLC 34
See also CA 131; 117

Goldemberg, Isaac 1945-   CLC 52
See also CA 69-72; CAAS 12; CANR 11, 32;
HW 1

Golding, William (Gerald) 1911-1993 CLC 1,
2, 3, 8, 10, 17, 27, 58, 81; DA; DAB; DAC;
DAM MST, NOV; WLC
See also AAYA 5; CA 5-8R; 141; CANR 13,
33, 54; CDBLB 1945-1960; DLB 15, 100;
MTCW 1, 2

Goldman, Emma 1869-1940   TCLC 13
See also CA 110; 150

Goldman, Francisco 1954-   CLC 76
See also CA 162

Goldman, William (W.) 1931-   CLC 1,48
See also CA 9-12R; CANR 29, 69; DLB 44

Goldmann, Lucien 1913-1970   CLC 24
See also CA 25-28; CAP 2

Goldoni, Carlo 1707-1793 LC 4; DAM DRAM

Goldsberry, Steven 1949-   CLC 34
See also CA 131

Goldsmith, Oliver 1728-1774 LC 2, 48; DA;
DAB; DAC; DAM DRAM, MST, NOV,
POET; DC 8; WLC
See also CDBLB 1660-1789; DLB 39, 89, 104,
109, 142; SATA 26

Goldsmith, Peter
See Priestley, J(ohn) B(oynton)

Gombrowicz, Witold 1904-1969 CLC 4, 7, 11,
49; DAM DRAM
See also CA 19-20; 25-28R; CAP 2

Gomez de la Serna, Ramon 1888-1963 CLC 9
See also CA 153; 116; CANR 79; HW 1, 2

Goncharov, Ivan Alexandrovich 1812-1891
NCLC 1, 63

Goncourt, Edmond (Louis Antoine Huot) de
1822-1896   NCLC 7
See also DLB 123

Goncourt, Jules (Alfred Huot) de 1830-1870
NCLC 7
See also DLB 123

Gontier, Fernande 19(?)-   CLC 50

Gonzalez Martinez, Enrique 1871-1952
TCLC 72
See also CA 166; CANR 81; HW 1, 2

Goodman, Paul 1911-1972   CLC 1, 2, 4, 7
See also CA 19-20; 37-40R; CANR 34; CAP 2;
DLB 130; MTCW 1

Gordimer, Nadine 1923- CLC 3, 5, 7, 10, 18, 33,
51, 70; DA; DAB; DAC; DAM MST, NOV;
SSC 17; WLCS
See also CA 5-8R; CANR 3, 28, 56; INT CANR-
28; MTCW 1, 2

Gordon, Adam Lindsay 1833-1870 NCLC 21

Gordon, Caroline 1895-1981 CLC 6, 13, 29, 83;
SSC 15
See also CA 11-12; 103; CANR 36; CAP 1;
DLB 4, 9, 102; DLBD 17; DLBY 81; MTCW
1, 2

Gordon, Charles William 1860-1937
See Connor, Ralph

See also CA 109

Gordon, Mary (Catherine) 1949- CLC 13, 22
See also CA 102; CANR 44; DLB 6; DLBY
81; INT 102; MTCW 1

Gordon, N. J.
See Bosman, Herman Charles

Gordon, Sol 1923-   CLC 26
See also CA 53-56; CANR 4; SATA 11

Gordone, Charles 1925-1995 CLC 1, 4; DAM
DRAM; DC 8
See also BW 1, 3; CA 93-96; 150; CANR 55;
DLB 7; INT 93-96; MTCW 1

Gore, Catherine 1800-1861   NCLC 65
See also DLB 116

Gorenko, Anna Andreevna
See Akhmatova, Anna

Gorky, Maxim 1868-1936 TCLC 8; DAB; SSC
28; WLC
See also Peshkov, Alexei Maximovich
See also MTCW 2

Goryan, Sirak
See Saroyan, William

Gosse, Edmund (William) 1849-1928 TCLC 28
See also CA 117; DLB 57, 144, 184

Gotlieb, Phyllis Fay (Bloom) 1926-   CLC 18
See also CA 13-16R; CANR 7; DLB 88

Gottesman, S. D.
See Kornbluth, C(yril) M.; Pohl, Frederik

Gottfried von Strassburg fl. c.1210- CMLC 10
See also DLB 138

Gould, Lois   CLC 4, 10
See also CA 77-80; CANR 29; MTCW 1

Gourmont, Remy (-Marie-Charles) de 1858-
1915   TCLC 17
See also CA 109; 150; MTCW 2

Govier, Katherine 1948-   CLC 51
See also CA 101; CANR 18, 40

Goyen, (Charles) William 1915-1983 CLC 5, 8,
14, 40
See also AITN 2; CA 5-8R; 110; CANR 6, 71;
DLB 2; DLBY 83; INT CANR-6

Goytisolo, Juan 1931-   CLC 5, 10, 23; DAM
MULT; HLC 1
See also CA 85-88; CANR 32, 61; HW 1, 2;
MTCW 1, 2

Gozzano, Guido 1883-1916   PC 10
See also CA 154; DLB 114

Gozzi, (Conte) Carlo 1720-1806 NCLC 23

Grabbe, Christian Dietrich 1801-1836 NCLC
2
See also DLB 133

Grace, Patricia Frances 1937-   CLC 56
See also CA 176

Gracian y Morales, Baltasar 1601-1658 LC 15

Gracq, Julien   CLC 11, 48
See also Poirier, Louis
See also DLB 83

Grade, Chaim 1910-1982   CLC 10
See also CA 93-96; 107

Graduate of Oxford, A
See Ruskin, John

Grafton, Garth
See Duncan, Sara Jeannette

Graham, John
See Phillips, David Graham

Graham, Jorie 1951-   CLC 48, 118
See also CA 111; CANR 63; DLB 120

Graham, R(obert) B(ontine) Cunninghame
See Cunninghame Graham, R(obert) B(ontine)
See also DLB 98, 135, 174

Graham, Robert
See Haldeman, Joe (William)

Graham, Tom

See Lewis, (Harry) Sinclair

Graham, W(illiam) S(ydney) 1918-1986 C L C
29
See also CA 73-76; 118; DLB 20

Graham, Winston (Mawdsley) 1910- CLC 23
See also CA 49-52; CANR 2, 22, 45, 66; DLB
77

Grahame, Kenneth 1859-1932 TCLC 64; DAB
See also CA 108; 136; CANR 80; CLR 5; DLB
34, 141, 178; MAICYA; MTCW 2; SATA
100; YABC 1

Granovsky, Timofei Nikolaevich 1813-1855
NCLC 75
See also DLB 198

Grant, Skeeter
See Spiegelman, Art

Granville-Barker, Harley 1877-1946 TCLC 2;
DAM DRAM
See also Barker, Harley Granville
See also CA 104

Grass, Guenter (Wilhelm) 1927- CLC 1, 2, 4, 6,
11, 15, 22, 32, 49, 88; DA; DAB; DAC;
DAM MST, NOV; WLC
See also CA 13-16R; CANR 20, 75; DLB 75,
124; MTCW 1, 2

Gratton, Thomas
See Hulme, T(homas) E(rnest)

Grau, Shirley Ann 1929-   CLC 4, 9; SSC 15
See also CA 89-92; CANR 22, 69; DLB 2; INT
CANR-22; MTCW 1

Gravel, Fern
See Hall, James Norman

Graver, Elizabeth 1964-   CLC 70
See also CA 135; CANR 71

Graves, Richard Perceval 1945-   CLC 44
See also CA 65-68; CANR 9, 26, 51

Graves, Robert (von Ranke) 1895-1985 C L C
1, 2, 6, 11, 39, 44, 45; DAB; DAC; DAM
MST, POET; PC 6
See also CA 5-8R; 117; CANR 5, 36; CDBLB
1914-1945; DLB 20, 100, 191; DLBD 18;
DLBY 85; MTCW 1, 2; SATA 45

Graves, Valerie
See Bradley, Marion Zimmer

Gray, Alasdair (James) 1934-   CLC 41
See also CA 126; CANR 47, 69; DLB 194; INT
126; MTCW 1, 2

Gray, Amlin 1946-   CLC 29
See also CA 138

Gray, Francine du Plessix 1930-   CLC 22;
DAM NOV
See also BEST 90:3; CA 61-64; CAAS 2;
CANR 11, 33, 75, 81; INT CANR-11;
MTCW 1, 2

Gray, John (Henry) 1866-1934   TCLC 19
See also CA 119; 162

Gray, Simon (James Holliday) 1936- CLC 9,
14, 36
See also AITN 1; CA 21-24R; CAAS 3; CANR
32, 69; DLB 13; MTCW 1

Gray, Spalding 1941- CLC 49, 112; DAM POP;
DC 7
See also CA 128; CANR 74; MTCW 2

Gray, Thomas 1716-1771 LC 4, 40; DA; DAB;
DAC; DAM MST; PC 2; WLC
See also CDBLB 1660-1789; DLB 109

Grayson, David
See Baker, Ray Stannard

Grayson, Richard (A.) 1951-   CLC 38
See also CA 85-88; CANR 14, 31, 57

Greeley, Andrew M(oran) 1928-   CLC 28;
DAM POP
See also CA 5-8R; CAAS 7; CANR 7, 43, 69;

Gustafson, James M(oody) 1925-   **CLC 100**
See also CA 25-28R; CANR 37
Gustafson, Ralph (Barker) 1909-   **CLC 36**
See also CA 21-24R; CANR 8, 45; DLB 88
Gut, Gom
See Simenon, Georges (Jacques Christian)
Guterson, David 1956-   **CLC 91**
See also CA 132; CANR 73; MTCW 2
Guthrie, A(lfred) B(ertram), Jr. 1901-1991
    CLC 23
See also CA 57-60; 134; CANR 24; DLB 212;
SATA 62; SATA-Obit 67
Guthrie, Isobel
See Grieve, C(hristopher) M(urray)
Guthrie, Woodrow Wilson 1912-1967
See Guthrie, Woody
See also CA 113; 93-96
Guthrie, Woody   **CLC 35**
See also Guthrie, Woodrow Wilson
Gutierrez Najera, Manuel 1859-1895
See also HLCS 2
Guy, Rosa (Cuthbert) 1928-   **CLC 26**
See also AAYA 4; BW 2; CA 17-20R; CANR
14, 34; CLR 13; DLB 33; JRDA; MAICYA;
SATA 14, 62
Gwendolyn
See Bennett, (Enoch) Arnold
H. D.   **CLC 3, 8, 14, 31, 34, 73; PC 5**
See also Doolittle, Hilda
H. de V.
See Buchan, John
Haavikko, Paavo Juhani 1931-   **CLC 18, 34**
See also CA 106
Habbema, Koos
See Heijermans, Herman
Habermas, Juergen 1929-   **CLC 104**
See also CA 109
Habermas, Jurgen
See Habermas, Juergen
Hacker, Marilyn 1942-   **CLC 5, 9, 23, 72, 91;**
    DAM POET
See also CA 77-80; CANR 68; DLB 120
Haeckel, Ernst Heinrich (Philipp August) 1834-
1919   **TCLC 83**
See also CA 157
Hafiz c. 1326-1389   **CMLC 34**
Hafiz c. 1326-1389(?)   **CMLC 34**
Haggard, H(enry) Rider 1856-1925 **TCLC 11**
See also CA 108; 148; DLB 70, 156, 174, 178;
MTCW 2; SATA 16
Hagiosy, L.
See Larbaud, Valery (Nicolas)
Hagiwara Sakutaro 1886-1942 **TCLC 60; PC
18**
Haig, Fenil
See Ford, Ford Madox
Haig-Brown, Roderick (Langmere) 1908-1976
    CLC 21
See also CA 5-8R; 69-72; CANR 4, 38; CLR
31; DLB 88; MAICYA; SATA 12
Hailey, Arthur 1920-**CLC 5; DAM NOV, POP**
See also AITN 2; BEST 90:3; CA 1-4R; CANR
2, 36, 75; DLB 88; DLBY 82; MTCW 1, 2
Hailey, Elizabeth Forsythe 1938-   **CLC 40**
See also CA 93-96; CAAS 1; CANR 15, 48;
INT CANR-15
Haines, John (Meade) 1924-   **CLC 58**
See also CA 17-20R; CANR 13, 34; DLB 212
Hakluyt, Richard 1552-1616   **LC 31**
Haldeman, Joe (William) 1943-   **CLC 61**
See also CA 53-56; CAAS 25; CANR 6, 70,
72; DLB 8; INT CANR-6
Hale, Sarah Josepha (Buell) 1788-1879 **NCLC**

75
See also DLB 1, 42, 73
Haley, Alex(ander Murray Palmer) 1921-1992
    CLC 8, 12, 76; BLC 2; DA; DAB; DAC;
    DAM MST, MULT, POP
See also AAYA 26; BW 2, 3; CA 77-80; 136;
CANR 61; CDALBS; DLB 38; MTCW 1, 2
Haliburton, Thomas Chandler 1796-1865
    NCLC 15
See also DLB 11, 99
Hall, Donald (Andrew, Jr.) 1928- **CLC 1, 13,
37, 59; DAM POET**
See also CA 5-8R; CAAS 7; CANR 2, 44, 64;
DLB 5; MTCW 1; SATA 23, 97
Hall, Frederic Sauser
See Sauser-Hall, Frederic
Hall, James
See Kuttner, Henry
Hall, James Norman 1887-1951   **TCLC 23**
See also CA 123; 173; SATA 21
Hall, Radclyffe
See Hall, (Marguerite) Radclyffe
See also MTCW 2
Hall, (Marguerite) Radclyffe 1886-1943
    TCLC 12
See also CA 110; 150; DLB 191
Hall, Rodney 1935-   **CLC 51**
See also CA 109; CANR 69
Halleck, Fitz-Greene 1790-1867   **NCLC 47**
See also DLB 3
Halliday, Michael
See Creasey, John
Halpern, Daniel 1945-   **CLC 14**
See also CA 33-36R
Hamburger, Michael (Peter Leopold) 1924-
    CLC 5, 14
See also CA 5-8R; CAAS 4; CANR 2, 47; DLB
27
Hamill, Pete 1935-   **CLC 10**
See also CA 25-28R; CANR 18, 71
Hamilton, Alexander 1755(?)-1804 **NCLC 49**
See also DLB 37
Hamilton, Clive
See Lewis, C(live) S(taples)
Hamilton, Edmond 1904-1977   **CLC 1**
See also CA 1-4R; CANR 3; DLB 8
Hamilton, Eugene (Jacob) Lee
See Lee-Hamilton, Eugene (Jacob)
Hamilton, Franklin
See Silverberg, Robert
Hamilton, Gail
See Corcoran, Barbara
Hamilton, Mollie
See Kaye, M(ary) M(argaret)
Hamilton, (Anthony Walter) Patrick 1904-1962
    CLC 51
See also CA 176; 113; DLB 191
Hamilton, Virginia 1936-   **CLC 26; DAM
MULT**
See also AAYA 2, 21; BW 2, 3; CA 25-28R;
CANR 20, 37, 73; CLR 1, 11, 40; DLB 33,
52; INT CANR-20; JRDA; MAICYA;
MTCW 1, 2; SATA 4, 56, 79
Hammett, (Samuel) Dashiell 1894-1961 **C L C
3, 5, 10, 19, 47; SSC 17**
See also AITN 1; CA 81-84; CANR 42; CDALB
1929-1941; DLBD 6; DLBY 96; MTCW 1,
2
Hammon, Jupiter 1711(?)-1800(?)   **NCLC 5;
BLC 2; DAM MULT, POET; PC 16**
See also DLB 31, 50
Hammond, Keith
See Kuttner, Henry

Hamner, Earl (Henry), Jr. 1923-   **CLC 12**
See also AITN 2; CA 73-76; DLB 6
Hampton, Christopher (James) 1946- **CLC 4**
See also CA 25-28R; DLB 13; MTCW 1
Hamsun, Knut   **TCLC 2, 14, 49**
See also Pedersen, Knut
Handke, Peter 1942-**CLC 5, 8, 10, 15, 38; DAM
DRAM, NOV**
See also CA 77-80; CANR 33, 75; DLB 85, 124;
MTCW 1, 2
Hanley, James 1901-1985   **CLC 3, 5, 8, 13**
See also CA 73-76; 117; CANR 36; DLB 191;
MTCW 1
Hannah, Barry 1942-   **CLC 23, 38, 90**
See also CA 108; 110; CANR 43, 68; DLB 6;
INT 110; MTCW 1
Hannon, Ezra
See Hunter, Evan
Hansberry, Lorraine (Vivian) 1930-1965 **CLC
17, 62; BLC 2; DA; DAB; DAC; DAM
DRAM, MST, MULT;DC 2**
See also AAYA 25; BW 1, 3; CA 109; 25-28R;
CABS 3; CANR 58; CDALB 1941-1968;
DLB 7, 38; MTCW 1, 2
Hansen, Joseph 1923-   **CLC 38**
See also CA 29-32R; CAAS 17; CANR 16, 44,
66; INT CANR-16
Hansen, Martin A(lfred) 1909-1955 **TCLC 32**
See also CA 167
Hanson, Kenneth O(stlin) 1922-   **CLC 13**
See also CA 53-56; CANR 7
Hardwick, Elizabeth (Bruce) 1916- **CLC 13;
DAM NOV**
See also CA 5-8R; CANR 3, 32, 70; DLB 6;
MTCW 1, 2
Hardy, Thomas 1840-1928 **TCLC 4, 10, 18, 32,
48, 53, 72; DA; DAB; DAC; DAM MST,
NOV, POET; PC 8; SSC 2; WLC**
See also CA 104; 123; CDBLB 1890-1914;
DLB 18, 19, 135; MTCW 1, 2
Hare, David 1947-   **CLC 29, 58**
See also CA 97-100; CANR 39; DLB 13;
MTCW 1
Harewood, John
See Van Druten, John (William)
Harford, Henry
See Hudson, W(illiam) H(enry)
Hargrave, Leonie
See Disch, Thomas M(ichael)
Harjo, Joy 1951-**CLC 83; DAM MULT; PC 27**
See also CA 114; CANR 35, 67; DLB 120, 175;
MTCW 2; NNAL
Harlan, Louis R(udolph) 1922-   **CLC 34**
See also CA 21-24R; CANR 25, 55, 80
Harling, Robert 1951(?)-   **CLC 53**
See also CA 147
Harmon, William (Ruth) 1938-   **CLC 38**
See also CA 33-36R; CANR 14, 32, 35; SATA
65
Harper, F. E. W.
See Harper, Frances Ellen Watkins
Harper, Frances E. W.
See Harper, Frances Ellen Watkins
Harper, Frances E. Watkins
See Harper, Frances Ellen Watkins
Harper, Frances Ellen
See Harper, Frances Ellen Watkins
Harper, Frances Ellen Watkins 1825-1911
    **TCLC 14; BLC 2; DAM MULT, POET;
PC 21**
See also BW 1, 3; CA 111; 125; CANR 79; DLB
50
Harper, Michael S(teven) 1938-   **CLC 7, 22**

See Tynan, Katharine

Hinojosa(-Smith), Rolando (R.) 1929-
See Hinojosa-Smith, Rolando
See also CA 131; CAAS 16; CANR 62; DAM MULT; DLB 82; HLC 1; HW 1, 2; MTCW 2

Hinojosa-Smith, Rolando 1929-
See Hinojosa(-Smith), Rolando (R.)
See also CAAS 16; HLC 1; MTCW 2

Hinton, S(usan) E(loise) 1950- **CLC 30, 111; DA; DAB; DAC; DAM MST, NOV**
See also AAYA 2; CA 81-84; CANR 32, 62; CDALBS; CLR 3, 23; JRDA; MAICYA; MTCW 1, 2; SATA 19, 58

Hippius, Zinaida **TCLC 9**
See also Gippius, Zinaida (Nikolayevna)

Hiraoka, Kimitake 1925-1970
See Mishima, Yukio
See also CA 97-100; 29-32R; DAM DRAM; MTCW 1, 2

Hirsch, E(ric) D(onald),Jr. 1928- **CLC 79**
See also CA 25-28R; CANR 27, 51; DLB 67; INT CANR-27; MTCW 1

Hirsch, Edward 1950- **CLC 31, 50**
See also CA 104; CANR 20, 42; DLB 120

Hitchcock, Alfred (Joseph) 1899-1980**CLC 16**
See also AAYA 22; CA 159; 97-100; SATA 27; SATA-Obit 24

Hitler, Adolf 1889-1945 **TCLC 53**
See also CA 117; 147

Hoagland, Edward 1932- **CLC 28**
See also CA 1-4R; CANR 2, 31, 57; DLB 6; SATA 51

Hoban, Russell (Conwell) 1925- **CLC 7, 25; DAM NOV**
See also CA 5-8R; CANR 23, 37, 66; CLR 3; DLB 52; MAICYA; MTCW 1, 2; SATA 1, 40, 78

Hobbes, Thomas 1588-1679 **LC 36**
See also DLB 151

Hobbs, Perry
See Blackmur, R(ichard) P(almer)

Hobson, Laura Z(ametkin) 1900-1986**CLC 7, 25**
See also CA 17-20R; 118; CANR 55; DLB 28; SATA 52

Hochhuth, Rolf 1931- **CLC 4, 11, 18; DAM DRAM**
See also CA 5-8R; CANR 33, 75; DLB 124; MTCW 1, 2

Hochman, Sandra 1936- **CLC 3, 8**
See also CA 5-8R; DLB 5

Hochwaelder, Fritz 1911-1986**CLC 36; DAM DRAM**
See also CA 29-32R; 120; CANR 42; MTCW 1

Hochwalder, Fritz
See Hochwaelder, Fritz

Hocking, Mary (Eunice) 1921- **CLC 13**
See also CA 101; CANR 18, 40

Hodgins, Jack 1938- **CLC 23**
See also CA 93-96; DLB 60

Hodgson, William Hope 1877(?)-1918 **TCLC 13**
See also CA 111; 164; DLB 70, 153, 156, 178; MTCW 2

Hoeg, Peter 1957- **CLC 95**
See also CA 151; CANR 75; MTCW 2

Hoffman, Alice 1952- **CLC 51;DAM NOV**
See also CA 77-80; CANR 34, 66; MTCW 1, 2

Hoffman, Daniel (Gerard) 1923-**CLC 6, 13, 23**
See also CA 1-4R; CANR 4; DLB 5

Hoffman, Stanley 1944- **CLC 5**
See also CA 77-80

Hoffman, William M(oses) 1939- **CLC 40**

See also CA 57-60; CANR 11, 71

Hoffmann, E(rnst) T(heodor) A(madeus) 1776-1822 **NCLC 2; SSC 13**
See also DLB 90; SATA 27

Hofmann, Gert 1931- **CLC 54**
See also CA 128

Hofmannsthal, Hugo von 1874-1929**TCLC 11; DAM DRAM; DC 4**
See also CA 106; 153; DLB 81, 118

Hogan, Linda 1947- **CLC 73;DAM MULT**
See also CA 120; CANR 45, 73; DLB 175; NNAL

Hogarth, Charles
See Creasey, John

Hogarth, Emmett
See Polonsky, Abraham (Lincoln)

Hogg, James 1770-1835 **NCLC 4**
See also DLB 93, 116, 159

Holbach, Paul Henri Thiry Baron 1723-1789 **LC 14**

Holberg, Ludvig 1684-1754 **LC 6**

Holden, Ursula 1921- **CLC 18**
See also CA 101; CAAS 8; CANR 22

Holderlin, (Johann Christian) Friedrich 1770-1843 **NCLC 16; PC 4**

Holdstock, Robert
See Holdstock, Robert P.

Holdstock, Robert P. 1948- **CLC 39**
See also CA 131; CANR 81

Holland, Isabelle 1920- **CLC 21**
See also AAYA 11; CA 21-24R; CANR 10, 25, 47; CLR 57; JRDA; MAICYA; SATA 8, 70; SATA-Essay 103

Holland, Marcus
See Caldwell, (Janet Miriam) Taylor (Holland)

Hollander, John 1929- **CLC 2, 5, 8, 14**
See also CA 1-4R; CANR 1, 52; DLB 5; SATA 13

Hollander, Paul
See Silverberg, Robert

Holleran, Andrew 1943(?)- **CLC 38**
See also CA 144

Hollinghurst, Alan 1954- **CLC 55, 91**
See also CA 114; DLB 207

Hollis, Jim
See Summers, Hollis (Spurgeon, Jr.)

Holly, Buddy 1936-1959 **TCLC 65**

Holmes, Gordon
See Shiel, M(atthew) P(hipps)

Holmes, John
See Souster, (Holmes) Raymond

Holmes, John Clellon 1926-1988 **CLC 56**
See also CA 9-12R; 125; CANR 4; DLB 16

Holmes, Oliver Wendell, Jr. 1841-1935**TCLC 77**
See also CA 114

Holmes, Oliver Wendell 1809-1894 **NCLC 14**
See also CDALB 1640-1865; DLB 1, 189; SATA 34

Holmes, Raymond
See Souster, (Holmes) Raymond

Holt, Victoria
See Hibbert, Eleanor Alice Burford

Holub, Miroslav 1923-1998 **CLC 4**
See also CA 21-24R; 169; CANR 10

Homer c. 8th cent. B.C.- **CMLC 1, 16; DA; DAB; DAC; DAM MST, POET; PC 23; WLCS**
See also DLB 176

Hongo, Garrett Kaoru 1951- **PC 23**
See also CA 133; CAAS 22; DLB 120

Honig, Edwin 1919- **CLC 33**
See also CA 5-8R; CAAS 8; CANR 4, 45; DLB

5

Hood, Hugh (John Blagdon) 1928-**CLC 15, 28**
See also CA 49-52; CAAS 17; CANR 1, 33; DLB 53

Hood, Thomas 1799-1845 **NCLC 16**
See also DLB 96

Hooker, (Peter) Jeremy 1941- **CLC 43**
See also CA 77-80; CANR 22; DLB 40

hooks, bell **CLC 94; BLCS**
See also Watkins, Gloria
See also MTCW 2

Hope, A(lec) D(erwent) 1907- **CLC 3, 51**
See also CA 21-24R; CANR 33, 74; MTCW 1, 2

Hope, Anthony 1863-1933 **TCLC 83**
See also CA 157; DLB 153, 156

Hope, Brian
See Creasey, John

Hope, Christopher (David Tully) 1944- **CLC 52**
See also CA 106; CANR 47; SATA 62

Hopkins, Gerard Manley 1844-1889 **NCLC 17; DA; DAB; DAC; DAM MST, POET; PC 15; WLC**
See also CDBLB 1890-1914; DLB 35, 57

Hopkins, John (Richard) 1931-1998 **CLC 4**
See also CA 85-88; 169

Hopkins, Pauline Elizabeth 1859-1930**TCLC 28; BLC 2; DAM MULT**
See also BW 2, 3; CA 141; CANR 82; DLB 50

Hopkinson, Francis 1737-1791 **LC 25**
See also DLB 31

Hopley-Woolrich, Cornell George 1903-1968
See Woolrich, Cornell
See also CA 13-14; CANR 58; CAP 1; MTCW 2

Horatio
See Proust, (Valentin-Louis-George-Eugene-) Marcel

Horgan, Paul (George Vincent O'Shaughnessy) 1903-1995 **CLC 9, 53;DAM NOV**
See also CA 13-16R; 147; CANR 9, 35; DLB 212; DLBY 85; INT CANR-9; MTCW 1, 2; SATA 13; SATA-Obit 84

Horn, Peter
See Kuttner, Henry

Hornem, Horace Esq.
See Byron, George Gordon (Noel)

Horney, Karen (Clementine Theodore Danielsen) 1885-1952 **TCLC 71**
See also CA 114; 165

Hornung, E(rnest) W(illiam) 1866-1921 **TCLC 59**
See also CA 108; 160; DLB 70

Horovitz, Israel (Arthur) 1939-**CLC 56; DAM DRAM**
See also CA 33-36R; CANR 46, 59; DLB 7

Horvath, Odon von
See Horvath, Oedoen von
See also DLB 85, 124

Horvath, Oedoen von 1901-1938 **TCLC 45**
See also Horvath, Odon von
See also CA 118

Horwitz, Julius 1920-1986 **CLC 14**
See also CA 9-12R; 119; CANR 12

Hospital, Janette Turner 1942- **CLC 42**
See also CA 108; CANR 48

Hostos, E. M. de
See Hostos (y Bonilla), Eugenio Maria de

Hostos, Eugenio M. de
See Hostos (y Bonilla), Eugenio Maria de

Hostos, Eugenio Maria
See Hostos (y Bonilla), Eugenio Maria de

Jensen, Laura (Linnea) 1948-   **CLC 37**
See also CA 103
Jerome, Jerome K(lapka) 1859-1927**TCLC 23**
See also CA 119; 177; DLB 10, 34, 135
Jerrold, Douglas William 1803-1857**NCLC 2**
See also DLB 158, 159
Jewett, (Theodora) Sarah Orne 1849-1909
TCLC 1, 22; SSC 6
See also CA 108; 127; CANR 71; DLB 12, 74;
SATA 15
Jewsbury, Geraldine (Endsor) 1812-1880
NCLC 22
See also DLB 21
Jhabvala, Ruth Prawer 1927-**CLC 4, 8, 29, 94;**
DAB; DAM NOV
See also CA 1-4R; CANR 2, 29, 51, 74; DLB
139, 194; INT CANR-29; MTCW 1, 2
Jibran, Kahlil
See Gibran, Kahlil
Jibran, Khalil
See Gibran, Kahlil
Jiles, Paulette 1943-   **CLC 13, 58**
See also CA 101; CANR 70
Jimenez (Mantecon), Juan Ramon 1881-1958
TCLC 4; DAM MULT, POET; HLC 1; PC
7
See also CA 104; 131; CANR 74; DLB 134;
HW 1; MTCW 1, 2
Jimenez, Ramon
See Jimenez (Mantecon), Juan Ramon
Jimenez Mantecon, Juan
See Jimenez (Mantecon), Juan Ramon
Jin, Ha 1956-   **CLC 109**
See also CA 152
Joel, Billy   **CLC 26**
See also Joel, William Martin
Joel, William Martin 1949-
See Joel, Billy
See also CA 108
John, Saint 7th cent. -   **CMLC 27**
John of the Cross, St. 1542-1591   **LC 18**
Johnson, B(ryan) S(tanley William) 1933-1973
CLC 6, 9
See also CA 9-12R; 53-56; CANR 9; DLB 14,
40
Johnson, Benj. F. of Boo
See Riley, James Whitcomb
Johnson, Benjamin F. of Boo
See Riley, James Whitcomb
Johnson, Charles (Richard) 1948-**CLC 7, 51,**
65; BLC 2; DAM MULT
See also BW 2, 3; CA 116; CAAS 18; CANR
42, 66, 82; DLB 33; MTCW 2
Johnson, Denis 1949-   **CLC 52**
See also CA 117; 121; CANR 71; DLB 120
Johnson, Diane 1934-   **CLC 5, 13, 48**
See also CA 41-44R; CANR 17, 40, 62; DLBY
80; INT CANR-17; MTCW 1
Johnson, Eyvind (Olof Verner) 1900-1976
CLC 14
See also CA 73-76; 69-72; CANR 34
Johnson, J. R.
See James, C(yril) L(ionel) R(obert)
Johnson, James Weldon 1871-1938 **TCLC 3,**
19; BLC 2; DAM MULT, POET; PC 24
See also BW 1, 3; CA 104; 125; CANR 82;
CDALB 1917-1929; CLR 32; DLB 51;
MTCW 1, 2; SATA 31
Johnson, Joyce 1935-   **CLC 58**
See also CA 125; 129
Johnson, Judith (Emlyn) 1936-   **CLC 7, 15**
See also CA 25-28R, 153; CANR 34
Johnson, Lionel (Pigot) 1867-1902 **TCLC 19**

See also CA 117; DLB 19
Johnson, Marguerite (Annie)
See Angelou, Maya
Johnson, Mel
See Malzberg, Barry N(athaniel)
Johnson, Pamela Hansford 1912-1981**CLC 1,**
7, 27
See also CA 1-4R; 104; CANR 2, 28; DLB 15;
MTCW 1, 2
Johnson, Robert 1911(?)-1938   **TCLC 69**
See also BW 3; CA 174
Johnson, Samuel 1709-1784   **LC 15, 52; DA;**
DAB; DAC; DAM MST; WLC
See also CDBLB 1660-1789; DLB 39, 95, 104,
142
Johnson, Uwe 1934-1984   **CLC 5, 10, 15, 40**
See also CA 1-4R; 112; CANR 1, 39; DLB 75;
MTCW 1
Johnston, George (Benson) 1913-   **CLC 51**
See also CA 1-4R; CANR 5, 20; DLB 88
Johnston, Jennifer 1930-   **CLC 7**
See also CA 85-88; DLB 14
Jolley, (Monica) Elizabeth 1923-**CLC 46; SSC**
19
See also CA 127; CAAS 13; CANR 59
Jones, Arthur Llewellyn 1863-1947
See Machen, Arthur
See also CA 104
Jones, D(ouglas) G(ordon) 1929-   **CLC 10**
See also CA 29-32R; CANR 13; DLB 53
Jones, David (Michael) 1895-1974**CLC 2, 4, 7,**
13, 42
See also CA 9-12R; 53-56; CANR 28; CDBLB
1945-1960; DLB 20, 100; MTCW 1
Jones, David Robert 1947-
See Bowie, David
See also CA 103
Jones, Diana Wynne 1934-   **CLC 26**
See also AAYA 12; CA 49-52; CANR 4, 26,
56; CLR 23; DLB 161; JRDA; MAICYA;
SAAS 7; SATA 9, 70, 108
Jones, Edward P. 1950-   **CLC 76**
See also BW 2, 3; CA 142; CANR 79
Jones, Gayl 1949-   **CLC 6, 9; BLC 2; DAM**
MULT
See also BW 2, 3; CA 77-80; CANR 27, 66;
DLB 33; MTCW 1, 2
Jones, James 1921-1977   **CLC 1, 3, 10, 39**
See also AITN 1, 2; CA 1-4R; 69-72; CANR 6;
DLB 2, 143; DLBD 17; DLBY 98; MTCW 1
Jones, John J.
See Lovecraft, H(oward) P(hillips)
Jones, LeRoi   **CLC 1, 2, 3, 5, 10, 14**
See also Baraka, Amiri
See also MTCW 2
Jones, Louis B. 1953-   **CLC 65**
See also CA 141; CANR 73
Jones, Madison (Percy, Jr.) 1925-   **CLC 4**
See also CA 13-16R; CAAS 11; CANR 7, 54;
DLB 152
Jones, Mervyn 1922-   **CLC 10, 52**
See also CA 45-48; CAAS 5; CANR 1; MTCW
1
Jones, Mick 1956(?)-   **CLC 30**
Jones, Nettie (Pearl) 1941-   **CLC 34**
See also BW 2; CA 137; CAAS 20
Jones, Preston 1936-1979   **CLC 10**
See also CA 73-76; 89-92; DLB 7
Jones, Robert F(rancis) 1934-   **CLC 7**
See also CA 49-52; CANR 2, 61
Jones, Rod 1953-   **CLC 50**
See also CA 128
Jones, Terence Graham Parry 1942- **CLC 21**

See also Jones, Terry; Monty Python
See also CA 112; 116; CANR 35; INT 116
Jones, Terry
See Jones, Terence Graham Parry
See also SATA 67; SATA-Brief 51
Jones, Thom 1945(?)-   **CLC 81**
See also CA 157
Jong, Erica 1942-   **CLC 4, 6, 8, 18, 83; DAM**
NOV, POP
See also AITN 1; BEST 90:2; CA 73-76; CANR
26, 52, 75; DLB 2, 5, 28, 152; INT CANR-
26; MTCW 1, 2
Jonson, Ben(jamin) 1572(?)-1637   **LC 6, 33;**
DA; DAB; DAC; DAM DRAM, MST,
POET; DC 4; PC 17; WLC
See also CDBLB Before 1660; DLB 62, 121
Jordan, June 1936-**CLC 5, 11, 23, 114; BLCS;**
DAM MULT, POET
See also AAYA 2; BW 2, 3; CA 33-36R; CANR
25, 70; CLR 10; DLB 38; MAICYA; MTCW
1; SATA 4
Jordan, Neil (Patrick) 1950-   **CLC 110**
See also CA 124; 130; CANR 54; INT 130
Jordan, Pat(rick M.) 1941-   **CLC 37**
See also CA 33-36R
Jorgensen, Ivar
See Ellison, Harlan (Jay)
Jorgenson, Ivar
See Silverberg, Robert
Josephus, Flavius c. 37-100   **CMLC 13**
Josipovici, Gabriel 1940-   **CLC 6, 43**
See also CA 37-40R; CAAS 8; CANR 47; DLB
14
Joubert, Joseph 1754-1824   **NCLC 9**
Jouve, Pierre Jean 1887-1976   **CLC 47**
See also CA 65-68
Jovine, Francesco 1902-1950   **TCLC 79**
Joyce, James (Augustine Aloysius) 1882-1941
TCLC 3, 8, 16, 35, 52; DA;DAB; DAC;
DAM MST, NOV, POET; PC 22; SSC 3,
26; WLC
See also CA 104; 126; CDBLB 1914-1945;
DLB 10, 19, 36, 162; MTCW 1, 2
Jozsef, Attila 1905-1937   **TCLC 22**
See also CA 116
Juana Ines de la Cruz 1651(?)-1695   **LC 5;**
HLCS 1; PC 24
Judd, Cyril
See Kornbluth, C(yril) M.; Pohl, Frederik
Julian of Norwich 1342(?)-1416(?)   **LC 6, 52**
See also DLB 146
Junger, Sebastian 1962-   **CLC 109**
See also AAYA 28; CA 165
Juniper, Alex
See Hospital, Janette Turner
Junius
See Luxemburg, Rosa
Just, Ward (Swift) 1935-   **CLC 4, 27**
See also CA 25-28R; CANR 32; INT CANR-
32
Justice, Donald (Rodney) 1925-   **CLC 6, 19,**
102; DAM POET
See also CA 5-8R; CANR 26, 54, 74; DLBY
83; INT CANR-26; MTCW 2
Juvenal c. 60-c. 13   **CMLC 8**
See also Juvenalis, Decimus Junius
See also DLB 211
Juvenalis, Decimus Junius 55(?)-c. 127(?)
See Juvenal
Juvenis
See Bourne, Randolph S(illiman)
Kacew, Romain 1914-1980
See Gary, Romain

Kesey, Ken (Elton) 1935- **CLC 1, 3, 6, 11, 46, 64; DA; DAB; DAC; DAM MST, NOV, POP; WLC**
 See also AAYA 25; CA 1-4R; CANR 22, 38, 66; CDALB 1968-1988; DLB 2, 16, 206; MTCW 1, 2; SATA 66

Kesselring, Joseph (Otto) 1902-1967 **CLC 45; DAM DRAM, MST**
 See also CA 150

Kessler, Jascha (Frederick) 1929- **CLC 4**
 See also CA 17-20R; CANR 8, 48

Kettelkamp, Larry (Dale) 1933- **CLC 12**
 See also CA 29-32R; CANR 16; SAAS 3; SATA 2

Key, Ellen 1849-1926 **TCLC 65**

Keyber, Conny
 See Fielding, Henry

Keyes, Daniel 1927- **CLC 80; DA; DAC; DAM MST, NOV**
 See also AAYA 23; CA 17-20R; CANR 10, 26, 54, 74; MTCW 2; SATA 37

Keynes, John Maynard 1883-1946 **TCLC 64**
 See also CA 114; 162, 163; DLBD 10; MTCW 2

Khanshendel, Chiron
 See Rose, Wendy

Khayyam, Omar 1048-1131 **CMLC 11; DAM POET; PC 8**

Kherdian, David 1931- **CLC 6, 9**
 See also CA 21-24R; CAAS 2; CANR 39, 78; CLR 24; JRDA; MAICYA; SATA 16, 74

Khlebnikov, Velimir **TCLC 20**
 See also Khlebnikov, Viktor Vladimirovich

Khlebnikov, Viktor Vladimirovich 1885-1922
 See Khlebnikov, Velimir
 See also CA 117

Khodasevich, Vladislav (Felitsianovich) 1886-1939 **TCLC 15**
 See also CA 115

Kielland, Alexander Lange 1849-1906 **TCLC 5**
 See also CA 104

Kiely, Benedict 1919- **CLC 23, 43**
 See also CA 1-4R; CANR 2; DLB 15

Kienzle, William X(avier) 1928- **CLC 25; DAM POP**
 See also CA 93-96; CAAS 1; CANR 9, 31, 59; INT CANR-31; MTCW 1, 2

Kierkegaard, Soren 1813-1855 **NCLC 34, 78**

Kieslowski, Krzysztof 1941-1996 **CLC 120**
 See also CA 147; 151

Killens, John Oliver 1916-1987 **CLC 10**
 See also BW 2; CA 77-80; 123; CAAS 2; CANR 26; DLB 33

Killigrew, Anne 1660-1685 **LC 4**
 See also DLB 131

Kim
 See Simenon, Georges (Jacques Christian)

Kincaid, Jamaica 1949- **CLC 43, 68; BLC 2; DAM MULT, NOV**
 See also AAYA 13; BW 2, 3; CA 125; CANR 47, 59; CDALBS; DLB 157; MTCW 2

King, Francis (Henry) 1923- **CLC 8, 53; DAM NOV**
 See also CA 1-4R; CANR 1, 33; DLB 15, 139; MTCW 1

King, Kennedy
 See Brown, George Douglas

King, Martin Luther, Jr. 1929-1968 **CLC 83; BLC 2; DA; DAB; DAC; DAM MST, MULT; WLCS**
 See also BW 2, 3; CA 25-28; CANR 27, 44; CAP 2; MTCW 1, 2; SATA 14

King, Stephen (Edwin) 1947- **CLC 12, 26, 37, 61, 113; DAM NOV, POP; SSC 17**
 See also AAYA 1, 17; BEST 90:1; CA 61-64; CANR 1, 30, 52, 76; DLB 143; DLBY 80; JRDA; MTCW 1, 2; SATA 9, 55

King, Steve
 See King, Stephen (Edwin)

King, Thomas 1943- **CLC 89; DAC; DAM MULT**
 See also CA 144; DLB 175; NNAL; SATA 96

Kingman, Lee **CLC 17**
 See also Natti, (Mary) Lee
 See also SAAS 3; SATA 1, 67

Kingsley, Charles 1819-1875 **NCLC 35**
 See also DLB 21, 32, 163, 190; YABC 2

Kingsley, Sidney 1906-1995 **CLC 44**
 See also CA 85-88; 147; DLB 7

Kingsolver, Barbara 1955- **CLC 55, 81; DAM POP**
 See also AAYA 15; CA 129; 134; CANR 60; CDALBS; DLB 206; INT 134; MTCW 2

Kingston, Maxine (Ting Ting) Hong 1940- **CLC 12, 19, 58, 121; DAM MULT, NOV; WLCS**
 See also AAYA 8; CA 69-72; CANR 13, 38, 74; CDALBS; DLB 173, 212; DLBY 80; INT CANR-13; MTCW 1, 2; SATA 53

Kinnell, Galway 1927- **CLC 1, 2, 3, 5, 13, 29; PC 26**
 See also CA 9-12R; CANR 10, 34, 66; DLB 5; DLBY 87; INT CANR-34; MTCW 1, 2

Kinsella, Thomas 1928- **CLC 4, 19**
 See also CA 17-20R; CANR 15; DLB 27; MTCW 1, 2

Kinsella, W(illiam) P(atrick) 1935- **CLC 27, 43; DAC; DAM NOV, POP**
 See also AAYA 7; CA 97-100; CAAS 7; CANR 21, 35, 66, 75; INT CANR-21; MTCW 1, 2

Kinsey, Alfred C(harles) 1894-1956 **TCLC 91**
 See also CA 115; 170; MTCW 2

Kipling, (Joseph) Rudyard 1865-1936 **TCLC 8, 17; DA; DAB; DAC; DAM MST, POET; PC 3; SSC 5; WLC**
 See also CA 105; 120; CANR 33; CDBLB 1890-1914; CLR 39; DLB 19, 34, 141, 156; MAICYA; MTCW 1, 2; SATA 100; YABC 2

Kirkup, James 1918- **CLC 1**
 See also CA 1-4R; CAAS 4; CANR 2; DLB 27; SATA 12

Kirkwood, James 1930(?)-1989 **CLC 9**
 See also AITN 2; CA 1-4R; 128; CANR 6, 40

Kirshner, Sidney
 See Kingsley, Sidney

Kis, Danilo 1935-1989 **CLC 57**
 See also CA 109; 118; 129; CANR 61; DLB 181; MTCW 1

Kivi, Aleksis 1834-1872 **NCLC 30**

Kizer, Carolyn (Ashley) 1925- **CLC 15, 39, 80; DAM POET**
 See also CA 65-68; CAAS 5; CANR 24, 70; DLB 5, 169; MTCW 2

Klabund 1890-1928 **TCLC 44**
 See also CA 162; DLB 66

Klappert, Peter 1942- **CLC 57**
 See also CA 33-36R; DLB 5

Klein, A(braham) M(oses) 1909-1972 **CLC 19; DAB; DAC; DAM MST**
 See also CA 101; 37-40R; DLB 68

Klein, Norma 1938-1989 **CLC 30**
 See also AAYA 2; CA 41-44R; 128; CANR 15, 37; CLR 2, 19; INT CANR-15; JRDA; MAICYA; SAAS 1; SATA 7, 57

Klein, T(heodore) E(ibon) D(onald) 1947-

CLC 34
 See also CA 119; CANR 44, 75

Kleist, Heinrich von 1777-1811 **NCLC 2, 37; DAM DRAM; SSC 22**
 See also DLB 90

Klima, Ivan 1931- **CLC 56; DAM NOV**
 See also CA 25-28R; CANR 17, 50

Klimentov, Andrei Platonovich 1899-1951
 See Platonov, Andrei
 See also CA 108

Klinger, Friedrich Maximilian von 1752-1831 **NCLC 1**
 See also DLB 94

Klingsor the Magician
 See Hartmann, Sadakichi

Klopstock, Friedrich Gottlieb 1724-1803 **NCLC 11**
 See also DLB 97

Knapp, Caroline 1959- **CLC 99**
 See also CA 154

Knebel, Fletcher 1911-1993 **CLC 14**
 See also AITN 1; CA 1-4R; 140; CAAS 3; CANR 1, 36; SATA 36; SATA-Obit 75

Knickerbocker, Diedrich
 See Irving, Washington

Knight, Etheridge 1931-1991 **CLC 40; BLC 2; DAM POET; PC 14**
 See also BW 1, 3; CA 21-24R; 133; CANR 23, 82; DLB 41; MTCW 2

Knight, Sarah Kemble 1666-1727 **LC 7**
 See also DLB 24, 200

Knister, Raymond 1899-1932 **TCLC 56**
 See also DLB 68

Knowles, John 1926- **CLC 1, 4, 10, 26; DA; DAC; DAM MST, NOV**
 See also AAYA 10; CA 17-20R; CANR 40, 74, 76; CDALB 1968-1988; DLB 6; MTCW 1, 2; SATA 8, 89

Knox, Calvin M.
 See Silverberg, Robert

Knox, John c. 1505-1572 **LC 37**
 See also DLB 132

Knye, Cassandra
 See Disch, Thomas M(ichael)

Koch, C(hristopher) J(ohn) 1932- **CLC 42**
 See also CA 127

Koch, Christopher
 See Koch, C(hristopher) J(ohn)

Koch, Kenneth 1925- **CLC 5, 8, 44; DAM POET**
 See also CA 1-4R; CANR 6, 36, 57; DLB 5; INT CANR-36; MTCW 2; SATA 65

Kochanowski, Jan 1530-1584 **LC 10**

Kock, Charles Paul de 1794-1871 **NCLC 16**

Koda Shigeyuki 1867-1947
 See Rohan, Koda
 See also CA 121

Koestler, Arthur 1905-1983 **CLC 1, 3, 6, 8, 15, 33**
 See also CA 1-4R; 109; CANR 1, 33; CDBLB 1945-1960; DLBY 83; MTCW 1, 2

Kogawa, Joy Nozomi 1935- **CLC 78; DAC; DAM MST, MULT**
 See also CA 101; CANR 19, 62; MTCW 2; SATA 99

Kohout, Pavel 1928- **CLC 13**
 See also CA 45-48; CANR 3

Koizumi, Yakumo
 See Hearn, (Patricio) Lafcadio (Tessima Carlos)

Kolmar, Gertrud 1894-1943 **TCLC 40**
 See also CA 167

Komunyakaa, Yusef 1947- **CLC 86, 94; BLCS**
 See also CA 147; DLB 120

Lampman, Archibald 1861-1899 **NCLC 25**
See also DLB 92

Lancaster, Bruce 1896-1963 **CLC 36**
See also CA 9-10; CANR 70; CAP 1; SATA 9

Lanchester, John **CLC 99**

Landau, Mark Alexandrovich
See Aldanov, Mark (Alexandrovich)

Landau-Aldanov, Mark Alexandrovich
See Aldanov, Mark (Alexandrovich)

Landis, Jerry
See Simon, Paul (Frederick)

Landis, John 1950- **CLC 26**
See also CA 112; 122

Landolfi, Tommaso 1908-1979 **CLC 11, 49**
See also CA 127; 117; DLB 177

Landon, Letitia Elizabeth 1802-1838 **NCLC 15**
See also DLB 96

Landor, Walter Savage 1775-1864 **NCLC 14**
See also DLB 93, 107

Landwirth, Heinz 1927-
See Lind, Jakov
See also CA 9-12R; CANR 7

Lane, Patrick 1939- **CLC 25;DAM POET**
See also CA 97-100; CANR 54; DLB 53; INT 97-100

Lang, Andrew 1844-1912 **TCLC 16**
See also CA 114; 137; DLB 98, 141, 184; MAICYA; SATA 16

Lang, Fritz 1890-1976 **CLC 20, 103**
See also CA 77-80; 69-72; CANR 30

Lange, John
See Crichton, (John) Michael

Langer, Elinor 1939- **CLC 34**
See also CA 121

Langland, William 1330(?)-1400(?) **LC 19; DA; DAB; DAC; DAM MST, POET**
See also DLB 146

Langstaff, Launcelot
See Irving, Washington

Lanier, Sidney 1842-1881 **NCLC 6;DAM POET**
See also DLB 64; DLBD 13; MAICYA; SATA 18

Lanyer, Aemilia 1569-1645 **LC 10, 30**
See also DLB 121

Lao-Tzu
See Lao Tzu

Lao Tzu fl. 6th cent. B.C.- **CMLC 7**

Lapine, James (Elliot) 1949- **CLC 39**
See also CA 123; 130; CANR 54; INT 130

Larbaud, Valery (Nicolas) 1881-1957**TCLC 9**
See also CA 106; 152

Lardner, Ring
See Lardner, Ring(gold) W(ilmer)

Lardner, Ring W., Jr.
See Lardner, Ring(gold) W(ilmer)

Lardner, Ring(gold) W(ilmer) 1885-1933 **TCLC 2, 14; SSC 32**
See also CA 104; 131; CDALB 1917-1929; DLB 11, 25, 86; DLBD 16; MTCW 1, 2

Laredo, Betty
See Codrescu, Andrei

Larkin, Maia
See Wojciechowska, Maia (Teresa)

Larkin, Philip (Arthur) 1922-1985**CLC 3, 5, 8, 9, 13, 18, 33, 39, 64; DAB; DAM MST, POET; PC 21**
See also CA 5-8R; 117; CANR 24, 62; CDBLB 1960 to Present; DLB 27; MTCW 1, 2

Larra (y Sanchez de Castro), Mariano Josede 1809-1837 **NCLC 17**

Larsen, Eric 1941- **CLC 55**

See also CA 132

Larsen, Nella 1891-1964 **CLC 37; BLC 2; DAM MULT**
See also BW 1; CA 125; DLB 51

Larson, Charles R(aymond) 1938- **CLC 31**
See also CA 53-56; CANR 4

Larson, Jonathan 1961-1996 **CLC 99**
See also AAYA 28; CA 156

Las Casas, Bartolome de 1474-1566 **LC 31**

Lasch,Christopher 1932-1994 **CLC 102**
See also CA 73-76; 144; CANR 25; MTCW 1, 2

Lasker-Schueler, Else 1869-1945 **TCLC 57**
See also DLB 66, 124

Laski, Harold 1893-1950 **TCLC 79**

Latham, Jean Lee 1902-1995 **CLC 12**
See also AITN 1; CA 5-8R; CANR 7; CLR 50; MAICYA; SATA 2, 68

Latham, Mavis
See Clark, Mavis Thorpe

Lathen, Emma **CLC 2**
See also Hennissart, Martha; Latsis, Mary J(ane)

Lathrop, Francis
See Leiber, Fritz (Reuter, Jr.)

Latsis, Mary J(ane) 1927(?)-1997
See Lathen, Emma
See also CA 85-88; 162

Lattimore, Richmond (Alexander) 1906-1984 **CLC 3**
See also CA 1-4R; 112; CANR 1

Laughlin, James 1914-1997 **CLC 49**
See also CA 21-24R; 162; CAAS 22; CANR 9, 47; DLB 48; DLBY 96, 97

Laurence, (Jean) Margaret (Wemyss) 1926-1987 **CLC 3, 6, 13, 50, 62; DAC; DAM MST; SSC 7**
See also CA 5-8R; 121; CANR 33; DLB 53; MTCW 1, 2; SATA-Obit 50

Laurent, Antoine 1952- **CLC 50**

Lauscher, Hermann
See Hesse, Hermann

Lautreamont, Comte de 1846-1870**NCLC 12; SSC 14**

Laverty, Donald
See Blish, James (Benjamin)

Lavin, Mary 1912-1996**CLC 4, 18, 99; SSC 4**
See also CA 9-12R; 151; CANR 33; DLB 15; MTCW 1

Lavond, Paul Dennis
See Kornbluth, C(yril) M.; Pohl, Frederik

Lawler, Raymond Evenor 1922- **CLC 58**
See also CA 103

Lawrence, D(avid) H(erbert Richards) 1885-1930 **TCLC 2, 9, 16, 33, 48, 61, 93; DA; DAB; DAC; DAM MST, NOV, POET; SSC 4, 19; WLC**
See also CA 104; 121; CDBLB 1914-1945; DLB 10, 19, 36, 98, 162, 195; MTCW 1, 2

Lawrence, T(homas) E(dward) 1888-1935 **TCLC 18**
See also Dale, Colin
See also CA 115; 167; DLB 195

Lawrence of Arabia
See Lawrence, T(homas) E(dward)

Lawson, Henry (Archibald Hertzberg) 1867-1922 **TCLC 27; SSC 18**
See also CA 120

Lawton, Dennis
See Faust, Frederick (Schiller)

Laxness, Halldor **CLC 25**
See also Gudjonsson, Halldor Kiljan

Layamon fl. c. 1200- **CMLC 10**
See also DLB 146

Laye, Camara 1928-1980 **CLC 4, 38; BLC 2; DAM MULT**
See also BW 1; CA 85-88; 97-100; CANR 25; MTCW 1, 2

Layton, Irving (Peter) 1912-**CLC 2, 15; DAC; DAM MST, POET**
See also CA 1-4R; CANR 2, 33, 43, 66; DLB 88; MTCW 1, 2

Lazarus, Emma 1849-1887 **NCLC 8**

Lazarus, Felix
See Cable, George Washington

Lazarus, Henry
See Slavitt, David R(ytman)

Lea, Joan
See Neufeld, John (Arthur)

Leacock, Stephen (Butler) 1869-1944**TCLC 2; DAC; DAM MST**
See also CA 104; 141; CANR 80; DLB 92; MTCW 2

Lear, Edward 1812-1888 **NCLC 3**
See also CLR 1; DLB 32, 163, 166; MAICYA; SATA 18, 100

Lear, Norman (Milton) 1922- **CLC 12**
See also CA 73-76

Leautaud, Paul 1872-1956 **TCLC 83**
See also DLB 65

Leavis, F(rank) R(aymond) 1895-1978**CLC 24**
See also CA 21-24R; 77-80; CANR 44; MTCW 1, 2

Leavitt, David 1961- **CLC 34;DAM POP**
See also CA 116; 122; CANR 50, 62; DLB 130; INT 122; MTCW 2

Leblanc, Maurice (Marie Emile) 1864-1941 **TCLC 49**
See also CA 110

Lebowitz, Fran(ces Ann) 1951(?)-**CLC 11, 36**
See also CA 81-84; CANR 14, 60, 70; INT CANR-14; MTCW 1

Lebrecht, Peter
See Tieck, (Johann) Ludwig

le Carre, John **CLC 3, 5, 9, 15, 28**
See also Cornwell, David (John Moore)
See also BEST 89:4; CDBLB 1960 to Present; DLB 87; MTCW 2

Le Clezio, J(ean) M(arie) G(ustave) 1940- **CLC 31**
See also CA 116; 128; DLB 83

Leconte de Lisle, Charles-Marie-Rene 1818-1894 **NCLC 29**

Le Coq, Monsieur
See Simenon, Georges (Jacques Christian)

Leduc, Violette 1907-1972 **CLC 22**
See also CA 13-14; 33-36R; CANR 69; CAP 1

Ledwidge, Francis 1887(?)-1917 **TCLC 23**
See also CA 123; DLB 20

Lee, Andrea 1953- **CLC 36; BLC 2; DAM MULT**
See also BW 1, 3; CA 125; CANR 82

Lee, Andrew
See Auchincloss, Louis (Stanton)

Lee, Chang-rae 1965- **CLC 91**
See also CA 148

Lee, Don L. **CLC 2**
See also Madhubuti, Haki R.

Lee, George W(ashington) 1894-1976**CLC 52; BLC 2; DAM MULT**
See also BW 1; CA 125; DLB 51

Lee, (Nelle) Harper 1926- **CLC 12, 60; DA; DAB; DAC; DAM MST, NOV; WLC**
See also AAYA 13; CA 13-16R; CANR 51; CDALB 1941-1968; DLB 6; MTCW 1, 2; SATA 11

Lee, Helen Elaine 1959(?)- **CLC 86**

9, 102; DLBD 1; MTCW 1, 2

Lewis, (Percy) Wyndham 1882(?)-1957 **TCLC 2, 9; SSC 34**
See also CA 104; 157; DLB 15; MTCW 2

Lewisohn, Ludwig 1883-1955 **TCLC 19**
See also CA 107; DLB 4, 9, 28, 102

Lewton, Val 1904-1951 **TCLC 76**

Leyner, Mark 1956- **CLC 92**
See also CA 110; CANR 28, 53; MTCW 2

Lezama Lima, Jose 1910-1976 **CLC 4, 10, 101; DAM MULT; HLCS 2**
See also CA 77-80; CANR 71; DLB 113; HW 1, 2

L'Heureux, John (Clarke) 1934- **CLC 52**
See also CA 13-16R; CANR 23, 45

Liddell, C. H.
See Kuttner, Henry

Lie, Jonas (Lauritz Idemil) 1833-1908(?) **TCLC 5**
See also CA 115

Lieber, Joel 1937-1971 **CLC 6**
See also CA 73-76; 29-32R

Lieber, Stanley Martin
See Lee, Stan

Lieberman, Laurence (James) 1935- **CLC 4, 36**
See also CA 17-20R; CANR 8, 36

Lieh Tzu fl. 7th cent. B.C.-5th cent. B.C. **CMLC 27**

Lieksman, Anders
See Haavikko, Paavo Juhani

Li Fei-kan 1904-
See Pa Chin
See also CA 105

Lifton, Robert Jay 1926- **CLC 67**
See also CA 17-20R; CANR 27, 78; INT CANR-27; SATA 66

Lightfoot, Gordon 1938- **CLC 26**
See also CA 109

Lightman, Alan P(aige) 1948- **CLC 81**
See also CA 141; CANR 63

Ligotti, Thomas (Robert) 1953- **CLC 44; SSC 16**
See also CA 123; CANR 49

Li Ho 791-817 **PC 13**

Liliencron, (Friedrich Adolf Axel) Detlevvon 1844-1909 **TCLC 18**
See also CA 117

Lilly, William 1602-1681 **LC 27**

Lima, Jose Lezama
See Lezama Lima, Jose

Lima Barreto, Afonso Henriquede 1881-1922 **TCLC 23**
See also CA 117

Limonov, Edward 1944- **CLC 67**
See also CA 137

Lin, Frank
See Atherton, Gertrude (Franklin Horn)

Lincoln, Abraham 1809-1865 **NCLC 18**

Lind, Jakov **CLC 1, 2, 4, 27, 82**
See also Landwirth, Heinz
See also CAAS 4

Lindbergh, Anne (Spencer) Morrow 1906- **CLC 82; DAM NOV**
See also CA 17-20R; CANR 16, 73; MTCW 1, 2; SATA 33

Lindsay, David 1878-1945 **TCLC 15**
See also CA 113

Lindsay, (Nicholas) Vachel 1879-1931 **TCLC 17; DA; DAC; DAM MST, POET; PC 23; WLC**
See also CA 114; 135; CANR 79; CDALB 1865-1917; DLB 54; SATA 40

Linke-Poot
See Doeblin, Alfred

Linney, Romulus 1930- **CLC 51**
See also CA 1-4R; CANR 40, 44, 79

Linton, Eliza Lynn 1822-1898 **NCLC 41**
See also DLB 18

Li Po 701-763 **CMLC 2**

Lipsius, Justus 1547-1606 **LC 16**

Lipsyte, Robert (Michael) 1938- **CLC 21; DA; DAC; DAM MST, NOV**
See also AAYA 7; CA 17-20R; CANR 8, 57; CLR 23; JRDA; MAICYA; SATA 5, 68

Lish, Gordon (Jay) 1934- **CLC 45; SSC 18**
See also CA 113; 117; CANR 79; DLB 130; INT 117

Lispector, Clarice 1925(?)-1977 **CLC 43; HLCS 2; SSC 34**
See also CA 139; 116; CANR 71; DLB 113; HW 2

Littell, Robert 1935(?)- **CLC 42**
See also CA 109; 112; CANR 64

Little, Malcolm 1925-1965
See Malcolm X ·
See also BW 1, 3; CA 125; 111; CANR 82; DA; DAB; DAC; DAM MST, MULT; MTCW 1, 2

Littlewit, Humphrey Gent.
See Lovecraft, H(oward) P(hillips)

Litwos
See Sienkiewicz, Henryk (Adam Alexander Pius)

Liu, E 1857-1909 **TCLC 15**
See also CA 115

Lively, Penelope (Margaret) 1933- **CLC 32, 50; DAM NOV**
See also CA 41-44R; CANR 29, 67, 79; CLR 7; DLB 14, 161, 207; JRDA; MAICYA; MTCW 1, 2; SATA 7, 60, 101

Livesay, Dorothy (Kathleen) 1909- **CLC 4, 15, 79; DAC; DAM MST, POET**
See also AITN 2; CA 25-28R; CAAS 8; CANR 36, 67; DLB 68; MTCW 1

Livy c. 59B.C.-c. 17 **CMLC 11**
See also DLB 211

Lizardi, Jose Joaquin Fernandez de 1776-1827 **NCLC 30**

Llewellyn, Richard
See Llewellyn Lloyd, Richard Dafydd Vivian
See also DLB 15

Llewellyn Lloyd, Richard Dafydd Vivian 1906-1983 **CLC 7, 80**
See also Llewellyn, Richard
See also CA 53-56; 111; CANR 7, 71; SATA 11; SATA-Obit 37

Llosa, (Jorge) Mario (Pedro) Vargas
See Vargas Llosa, (Jorge) Mario (Pedro)

Lloyd, Manda
See Mander, (Mary) Jane

Lloyd Webber, Andrew 1948-
See Webber, Andrew Lloyd
See also AAYA 1; CA 116; 149; DAM DRAM; SATA 56

Llull, Ramon c. 1235-c. 1316 **CMLC 12**

Lobb, Ebenezer
See Upward, Allen

Locke, Alain (Le Roy) 1886-1954 **TCLC 43; BLCS**
See also BW 1, 3; CA 106; 124; CANR 79; DLB 51

Locke, John 1632-1704 **LC 7, 35**
See also DLB 101

Locke-Elliott, Sumner
See Elliott, Sumner Locke ·

Lockhart, John Gibson 1794-1854 **NCLC 6**
See also DLB 110, 116, 144

Lodge, David (John) 1935- **CLC 36; DAM POP**
See also BEST 90:1; CA 17-20R; CANR 19, 53; DLB 14, 194; INT CANR-19; MTCW 1, 2

Lodge, Thomas 1558-1625 **LC 41**

Lodge, Thomas 1558-1625 **LC 41**
See also DLB 172

Loennbohm, Armas Eino Leopold 1878-1926
See Leino, Eino
See also CA 123

Loewinsohn, Ron(ald William) 1937- **CLC 52**
See also CA 25-28R; CANR 71

Logan, Jake
See Smith, Martin Cruz

Logan, John (Burton) 1923-1987 **CLC 5**
See also CA 77-80; 124; CANR 45; DLB 5

Lo Kuan-chung 1330(?)-1400(?) **LC 12**

Lombard, Nap
See Johnson, Pamela Hansford

London, Jack **TCLC 9, 15, 39; SSC 4; WLC**
See also London, John Griffith
See also AAYA 13; AITN 2; CDALB 1865-1917; DLB 8, 12, 78, 212; SATA 18

London, John Griffith 1876-1916
See London, Jack
See also CA 110; 119; CANR 73; DA; DAB; DAC; DAM MST, NOV; JRDA; MAICYA; MTCW 1, 2

Long, Emmett
See Leonard, Elmore (John, Jr.)

Longbaugh, Harry
See Goldman, William (W.)

Longfellow, Henry Wadsworth 1807-1882 **NCLC 2, 45; DA; DAB; DAC; DAM MST, POET; WLCS**
See also CDALB 1640-1865; DLB 1, 59; SATA 19

Longinus c. 1st cent. - **CMLC 27**
See also DLB 176

Longley, Michael 1939- **CLC 29**
See also CA 102; DLB 40

Longus fl. c. 2nd cent. - **CMLC 7**

Longway, A. Hugh
See Lang, Andrew

Lonnrot, Elias 1802-1884 **NCLC 53**

Lopate, Phillip 1943- **CLC 29**
See also CA 97-100; DLBY 80; INT 97-100

Lopez Portillo (y Pacheco), Jose 1920- **CLC 46**
See also CA 129; HW 1

Lopez y Fuentes, Gregorio 1897(?)-1966 **CLC 32**
See also CA 131; HW 1

Lorca, Federico Garcia
See Garcia Lorca, Federico

Lord, Bette Bao 1938- **CLC 23**
See also BEST 90:3; CA 107; CANR 41, 79; INT 107; SATA 58

Lord Auch
See Bataille, Georges

Lord Byron
See Byron, George Gordon (Noel)

Lorde, Audre (Geraldine) 1934-1992 **CLC 18, 71; BLC 2; DAM MULT, POET; PC 12**
See also BW 1, 3; CA 25-28R; 142; CANR 16, 26, 46, 82; DLB 41; MTCW 1, 2

Lord Houghton
See Milnes, Richard Monckton

Lord Jeffrey
See Jeffrey, Francis

Lorenzini, Carlo 1826-1890
See Collodi, Carlo

See also MAICYA; SATA 29, 100

Lorenzo, Heberto Padilla
See Padilla (Lorenzo), Heberto

Loris
See Hofmannsthal, Hugo von

Loti, Pierre   **TCLC 11**
See also Viaud, (Louis Marie) Julien
See also DLB 123

Lou, Henri
See Andreas-Salome, Lou

Louie, David Wong 1954-   **CLC 70**
See also CA 139

Louis, Father M.
See Merton, Thomas

Lovecraft, H(oward) P(hillips) 1890-1937
TCLC 4, 22; DAM POP; SSC 3
See also AAYA 14; CA 104; 133; MTCW 1, 2

Lovelace, Earl 1935-   **CLC 51**
See also BW 2; CA 77-80; CANR 41, 72; DLB
125; MTCW 1

Lovelace, Richard 1618-1657   **LC 24**
See also DLB 131

Lowell, Amy 1874-1925   **TCLC 1, 8; DAM
POET; PC 13**
See also CA 104; 151; DLB 54, 140; MTCW 2

Lowell, James Russell 1819-1891   **NCLC 2**
See also CDALB 1640-1865; DLB 1, 11, 64,
79, 189

Lowell, Robert (Traill Spence, Jr.) 1917-1977
**CLC 1, 2, 3, 4, 5, 8, 9, 11, 15, 37; DA; DAB;
DAC; DAM MST, NOV; PC 3;WLC**
See also CA 9-12R; 73-76; CABS 2; CANR 26,
60; CDALBS; DLB 5, 169;MTCW 1, 2

Lowenthal, Michael (Francis) 1969-**CLC 119**
See also CA 150

Lowndes, Marie Adelaide (Belloc) 1868-1947
TCLC 12
See also CA 107; DLB 70

Lowry, (Clarence) Malcolm 1909-1957**TCLC
6, 40; SSC 31**
See also CA 105; 131; CANR 62; CDBLB
1945-1960; DLB 15; MTCW 1, 2

Lowry, Mina Gertrude 1882-1966
See Loy, Mina
See also CA 113

Loxsmith, John
See Brunner, John (Kilian Houston)

Loy, Mina   **CLC 28; DAM POET; PC 16**
See also Lowry, Mina Gertrude
See also DLB 4, 54

Loyson-Bridet
See Schwob, Marcel (Mayer Andre)

Lucan 39-65   **CMLC 33**
See also DLB 211

Lucas, Craig 1951-   **CLC 64**
See also CA 137; CANR 71

Lucas, E(dward) V(errall) 1868-1938 **TCLC
73**
See also CA 176; DLB 98, 149, 153; SATA 20

Lucas, George 1944-   **CLC 16**
See also AAYA 1, 23; CA 77-80; CANR 30;
SATA 56

Lucas, Hans
See Godard, Jean-Luc

Lucas, Victoria
See Plath, Sylvia

Lucian c. 120-c. 180   **CMLC 32**
See also DLB 176

Ludlam, Charles 1943-1987   **CLC 46,50**
See also CA 85-88; 122; CANR 72

Ludlum, Robert 1927-**CLC 22, 43; DAM NOV,
POP**
See also AAYA 10; BEST 89:1, 90:3; CA 33-

36R; CANR 25, 41, 68; DLBY 82; MTCW
1, 2

Ludwig, Ken   **CLC 60**

Ludwig, Otto 1813-1865   **NCLC 4**
See also DLB 129

Lugones, Leopoldo 1874-1938   **TCLC 15;
HLCS 2**
See also CA 116; 131; HW 1

Lu Hsun 1881-1936   **TCLC 3; SSC 20**
See also Shu-Jen, Chou

Lukacs, George   **CLC 24**
See also Lukacs, Gyorgy (Szegeny von)

Lukacs, Gyorgy (Szegeny von) 1885-1971
See Lukacs, George
See also CA 101; 29-32R; CANR 62; MTCW 2

Luke, Peter (Ambrose Cyprian) 1919-1995
CLC 38
See also CA 81-84; 147; CANR 72; DLB 13

Lunar, Dennis
See Mungo, Raymond

Lurie, Alison 1926-   **CLC 4, 5, 18, 39**
See also CA 1-4R; CANR 2, 17, 50; DLB 2;
MTCW 1; SATA 46

Lustig, Arnost 1926-   **CLC 56**
See also AAYA 3; CA 69-72; CANR 47; SATA
56

Luther, Martin 1483-1546   **LC 9, 37**
See also DLB 179

Luxemburg, Rosa 1870(?)-1919   **TCLC 63**
See also CA 118

Luzi, Mario 1914-   **CLC 13**
See also CA 61-64; CANR 9, 70; DLB 128

Lyly, John 1554(?)-1606**LC 41; DAM DRAM;
DC 7**
See also DLB 62, 167

L'Ymagier
See Gourmont, Remy (-Marie-Charles) de

Lynch, B. Suarez
See Bioy Casares, Adolfo; Borges, Jorge Luis

Lynch, B. Suarez
See Bioy Casares, Adolfo

Lynch, David (K.) 1946-   **CLC 66**
See also CA 124; 129

Lynch, James
See Andreyev, Leonid (Nikolaevich)

Lynch Davis, B.
See Bioy Casares, Adolfo; Borges, Jorge Luis

Lyndsay, Sir David 1490-1555   **LC 20**

Lynn, Kenneth S(chuyler) 1923-   **CLC 50**
See also CA 1-4R; CANR 3, 27, 65

Lynx
See West, Rebecca

Lyons, Marcus
See Blish, James (Benjamin)

Lyre, Pinchbeck
See Sassoon, Siegfried (Lorraine)

Lytle, Andrew (Nelson) 1902-1995   **CLC 22**
See also CA 9-12R; 150; CANR 70; DLB 6;
DLBY 95

Lyttelton, George 1709-1773   **LC 10**

Maas, Peter 1929-   **CLC 29**
See also CA 93-96; INT 93-96; MTCW 2

Macaulay, Rose 1881-1958   **TCLC 7, 44**
See also CA 104; DLB 36

Macaulay, Thomas Babington 1800-1859
NCLC 42
See also CDBLB 1832-1890; DLB 32, 55

MacBeth, George (Mann) 1932-1992**CLC 2, 5,
9**
See also CA 25-28R; 136; CANR 61, 66; DLB
40; MTCW 1; SATA 4; SATA-Obit 70

MacCaig, Norman (Alexander) 1910-**CLC 36;
DAB; DAM POET**

See also CA 9-12R; CANR 3, 34; DLB 27

MacCarthy, Sir (Charles Otto) Desmond 1877-
1952   **TCLC 36**
See also CA 167

MacDiarmid, HughCLC 2, 4, 11, 19, 63; PC 9
See also Grieve, C(hristopher) M(urray)
See also CDBLB 1945-1960; DLB 20

MacDonald, Anson
See Heinlein, Robert A(nson)

Macdonald, Cynthia 1928-   **CLC 13, 19**
See also CA 49-52; CANR 4, 44; DLB 105

MacDonald, George 1824-1905   **TCLC 9**
See also CA 106; 137; CANR 80; DLB 18, 163,
178; MAICYA; SATA 33, 100

Macdonald, John
See Millar, Kenneth

MacDonald, John D(ann) 1916-1986 **CLC 3,
27, 44; DAM NOV, POP**
See also CA 1-4R; 121; CANR 1, 19, 60; DLB
8; DLBY 86; MTCW 1, 2

Macdonald, John Ross
See Millar, Kenneth

Macdonald, Ross   **CLC 1, 2, 3, 14, 34, 41**
See also Millar, Kenneth
See also DLBD 6

MacDougal, John
See Blish, James (Benjamin)

MacEwen, Gwendolyn (Margaret) 1941-1987
CLC 13, 55
See also CA 9-12R; 124; CANR 7, 22; DLB
53; SATA 50; SATA-Obit 55

Macha, Karel Hynek 1810-1846   **NCLC 46**

Machado (y Ruiz), Antonio 1875-1939**T C L C
3**
See also CA 104; 174; DLB 108; HW 2

Machado de Assis, Joaquim Maria 1839-1908
TCLC 10; BLC 2; HLCS 2; SSC 24
See also CA 107; 153

Machen, Arthur   **TCLC 4; SSC 20**
See also Jones, Arthur Llewellyn
See also DLB 36, 156, 178

Machiavelli, Niccolo 1469-1527**LC 8, 36; DA;
DAB; DAC; DAM MST; WLCS**

MacInnes, Colin 1914-1976   **CLC 4, 23**
See also CA 69-72; 65-68; CANR 21; DLB 14;
MTCW 1, 2

MacInnes, Helen (Clark) 1907-1985 **CLC 27,
39; DAM POP**
See also CA 1-4R; 117; CANR 1, 28, 58; DLB
87; MTCW 1, 2; SATA 22; SATA-Obit 44

Mackenzie, Compton (Edward Montague)
1883-1972   **CLC 18**
See also CA 21-22; 37-40R; CAP 2; DLB 34,
100

Mackenzie, Henry 1745-1831   **NCLC 41**
See also DLB 39

Mackintosh, Elizabeth 1896(?)-1952
See Tey, Josephine
See also CA 110

MacLaren, James
See Grieve, C(hristopher) M(urray)

Mac Laverty, Bernard 1942-   **CLC 31**
See also CA 116; 118; CANR 43; INT 118

MacLean, Alistair (Stuart) 1922(?)-1987**C L C
3, 13, 50, 63; DAM POP**
See also CA 57-60; 121; CANR 28, 61; MTCW
1; SATA 23; SATA-Obit 50

Maclean, Norman (Fitzroy) 1902-1990 **C L C
78; DAM POP; SSC 13**
See also CA 102; 132; CANR 49; DLB 206

MacLeish, Archibald 1892-1982**CLC 3, 8, 14,
68; DAM POET**
See also CA 9-12R; 106; CANR 33, 63;

CDALBS; DLB 4, 7, 45; DLBY 82; MTCW
1, 2

MacLennan, (John) Hugh 1907-1990 **CLC 2,
14, 92; DAC; DAM MST**
See also CA 5-8R; 142; CANR 33; DLB 68;
MTCW 1, 2

MacLeod, Alistair 1936-**CLC 56; DAC; DAM
MST**
See also CA 123; DLB 60; MTCW 2

Macleod, Fiona
See Sharp, William

MacNeice, (Frederick) Louis 1907-1963 **C L C
1, 4, 10, 53; DAB; DAM POET**
See also CA 85-88; CANR 61; DLB 10, 20;
MTCW 1, 2

MacNeill, Dand
See Fraser, George MacDonald

Macpherson, James 1736-1796   **LC 29**
See also Ossian
See also DLB 109

Macpherson, (Jean) Jay 1931-   **CLC 14**
See also CA 5-8R; DLB 53

MacShane, Frank 1927-   **CLC 39**
See also CA 9-12R; CANR 3, 33; DLB 111

Macumber, Mari
See Sandoz, Mari(e Susette)

Madach, Imre 1823-1864   **NCLC 19**

Madden, (Jerry) David 1933-   **CLC 5, 15**
See also CA 1-4R; CAAS 3; CANR 4, 45; DLB
6; MTCW 1

Maddern, Al(an)
See Ellison, Harlan (Jay)

Madhubuti, Haki R. 1942-**CLC 6, 73; BLC 2;
DAM MULT, POET; PC 5**
See also Lee, Don L.
See also BW 2, 3; CA 73-76; CANR 24, 51,
73; DLB 5, 41; DLBD 8; MTCW 2

Maepenn, Hugh
See Kuttner, Henry

Maepenn, K. H.
See Kuttner, Henry

Maeterlinck, Maurice 1862-1949   **TCLC 3;
DAM DRAM**
See also CA 104; 136; CANR 80; DLB 192;
SATA 66

Maginn, William 1794-1842   **NCLC 8**
See also DLB 110, 159

Mahapatra, Jayanta 1928-   **CLC 33;DAM
MULT**
See also CA 73-76; CAAS 9; CANR 15, 33, 66

Mahfouz, Naguib (Abdel Aziz Al-Sabilgi)
1911(?)-
See Mahfuz, Najib
See also BEST 89:2; CA 128; CANR 55; DAM
NOV; MTCW 1, 2

Mahfuz, Najib   **CLC 52, 55**
See also Mahfouz, Naguib (Abdel Aziz Al-
Sabilgi)
See also DLBY 88

Mahon, Derek 1941-   **CLC 27**
See also CA 113; 128; DLB 40

Mailer, Norman 1923-**CLC 1, 2, 3, 4, 5, 8, 11,
14, 28, 39, 74, 111; DA; DAB; DAC; DAM
MST, NOV, POP**
See also AITN 2; CA 9-12R; CABS 1; CANR
28, 74, 77; CDALB 1968-1988; DLB 2, 16,
28, 185; DLBD 3; DLBY 80, 83; MTCW 1,
2

Maillet, Antonine 1929- **CLC 54, 118; DAC**
See also CA 115; 120; CANR 46, 74, 77; DLB
60; INT 120; MTCW 2

Mais, Roger 1905-1955   **TCLC 8**
See also BW 1, 3; CA 105; 124; CANR 82; DLB

125; MTCW 1

Maistre, Joseph de 1753-1821   **NCLC 37**

Maitland, Frederic 1850-1906   **TCLC 65**

Maitland, Sara (Louise) 1950-   **CLC 49**
See also CA 69-72; CANR 13, 59

Major, Clarence 1936-**CLC 3, 19, 48; BLC 2;
DAM MULT**
See also BW 2, 3; CA 21-24R; CAAS 6; CANR
13, 25, 53, 82; DLB 33

Major, Kevin (Gerald) 1949-   **CLC 26; DAC**
See also AAYA 16; CA 97-100; CANR 21, 38;
CLR 11; DLB 60; INT CANR-21; JRDA;
MAICYA; SATA 32, 82

Maki, James
See Ozu, Yasujiro

Malabaila, Damiano
See Levi, Primo

Malamud, Bernard 1914-1986**CLC 1, 2, 3, 5,
8, 9, 11, 18, 27, 44, 78, 85;DA; DAB; DAC;
DAM MST, NOV, POP; SSC 15;WLC**
See also AAYA 16; CA 5-8R; 118; CABS 1;
CANR 28, 62; CDALB 1941-1968; DLB 2,
28, 152; DLBY 80, 86; MTCW 1, 2

Malan, Herman
See Bosman, Herman Charles; Bosman, Herman
Charles

Malaparte, Curzio 1898-1957   **TCLC 52**

Malcolm, Dan
See Silverberg, Robert

Malcolm X   CLC 82, 117; BLC 2; WLCS
See also Little, Malcolm

Malherbe, Francois de 1555-1628   **LC 5**

Mallarme, Stephane 1842-1898 **NCLC 4, 41;
DAM POET; PC 4**

Mallet-Joris, Francoise 1930-   **CLC 11**
See also CA 65-68; CANR 17; DLB 83

Malley, Ern
See McAuley, James Phillip

Mallowan, Agatha Christie
See Christie, Agatha (Mary Clarissa)

Maloff, Saul 1922-   **CLC 5**
See also CA 33-36R

Malone, Louis
See MacNeice, (Frederick) Louis

Malone, Michael (Christopher) 1942-**CLC 43**
See also CA 77-80; CANR 14, 32, 57

Malory, (Sir) Thomas 1410(?)-1471(?)**LC 11;
DA; DAB; DAC; DAM MST; WLCS**
See also CDBLB Before 1660; DLB 146; SATA
59; SATA-Brief 33

Malouf, (George Joseph) David 1934-**CLC 28,
86**
See also CA 124; CANR 50, 76; MTCW 2

Malraux, (Georges-)Andre 1901-1976**CLC 1,
4, 9, 13, 15, 57; DAM NOV**
See also CA 21-22; 69-72; CANR 34, 58; CAP
2; DLB 72; MTCW 1, 2

Malzberg, Barry N(athaniel) 1939-   **CLC 7**
See also CA 61-64; CAAS 4; CANR 16; DLB 8

Mamet, David (Alan) 1947-**CLC 9, 15, 34, 46,
91; DAM DRAM; DC 4**
See also AAYA 3; CA 81-84; CABS 3; CANR
15, 41, 67, 72; DLB 7; MTCW 1, 2

Mamoulian, Rouben (Zachary) 1897-1987
CLC 16
See also CA 25-28R; 124

Mandelstam, Osip (Emilievich) 1891(?)-1938(?)
TCLC 2, 6; PC 14
See also CA 104; 150; MTCW 2

Mander, (Mary) Jane 1877-1949   **TCLC 31**
See also CA 162

Mandeville, John fl. 1350-   **CMLC 19**
See also DLB 146

Mandiargues, Andre Pieyre de   CLC 41
See also Pieyre de Mandiargues, Andre
See also DLB 83

Mandrake, Ethel Belle
See Thurman, Wallace (Henry)

Mangan, James Clarence 1803-1849**NCLC 27**

Maniere, J.-E.
See Giraudoux, (Hippolyte) Jean

Mankiewicz, Herman (Jacob) 1897-1953
TCLC 85
See also CA 120; 169; DLB 26

Manley, (Mary) Delariviere 1672(?)-1724 **L C
1, 42**
See also DLB 39, 80

Mann, Abel
See Creasey, John

Mann, Emily 1952-   **DC 7**
See also CA 130; CANR 55

Mann, (Luiz) Heinrich 1871-1950   **TCLC 9**
See also CA 106; 164; DLB 66, 118

Mann, (Paul) Thomas 1875-1955 **TCLC 2, 8,
14, 21, 35, 44, 60; DA; DAB; DAC; DAM
MST, NOV; SSC 5; WLC**
See also CA 104; 128; DLB 66; MTCW 1, 2

Mannheim, Karl 1893-1947   **TCLC 65**

Manning, David
See Faust, Frederick (Schiller)

Manning, Frederic 1887(?)-1935   **TCLC 25**
See also CA 124

Manning, Olivia 1915-1980   **CLC 5, 19**
See also CA 5-8R; 101; CANR 29; MTCW 1

Mano, D. Keith 1942-   **CLC 2, 10**
See also CA 25-28R; CAAS 6; CANR 26, 57;
DLB 6

Mansfield, Katherine **TCLC 2, 8, 39; DAB; SSC
9, 23; WLC**
See also Beauchamp, Kathleen Mansfield
See also DLB 162

Manso, Peter 1940-   **CLC 39**
See also CA 29-32R; CANR 44

Mantecon, Juan Jimenez
See Jimenez (Mantecon), Juan Ramon

Manton, Peter
See Creasey, John

Man Without a Spleen, A
See Chekhov, Anton (Pavlovich)

Manzoni, Alessandro 1785-1873   **NCLC 29**

Map, Walter 1140-1209   **CMLC 32**

Mapu, Abraham (ben Jekutiel) 1808-1867
NCLC 18

Mara, Sally
See Queneau, Raymond

Marat, Jean Paul 1743-1793   **LC 10**

Marcel, Gabriel Honore 1889-1973   **CLC 15**
See also CA 102; 45-48; MTCW 1, 2

March, William 1893-1954   **TCLC 96**

Marchbanks, Samuel
See Davies, (William) Robertson

Marchi, Giacomo
See Bassani, Giorgio

Margulies, Donald   **CLC 76**

Marie de France c. 12th cent. - **CMLC 8; PC
22**
See also DLB 208

Marie de l'Incarnation 1599-1672   **LC 10**

Marier, Captain Victor
See Griffith, D(avid Lewelyn) W(ark)

Mariner, Scott
See Pohl, Frederik

Marinetti, Filippo Tommaso 1876-1944**TCLC
10**
See also CA 107; DLB 114

Marivaux, Pierre Carlet de Chamblain de 1688-

1763 **LC 4; DC 7**
Markandaya, Kamala **CLC 8, 38**
See also Taylor, Kamala (Purnaiya)
Markfield, Wallace 1926- **CLC 8**
See also CA 69-72; CAAS 3; DLB 2, 28
Markham, Edwin 1852-1940 **TCLC 47**
See also CA 160; DLB 54, 186
Markham, Robert
See Amis, Kingsley (William)
Marks, J
See Highwater, Jamake (Mamake)
Marks-Highwater, J
See Highwater, Jamake (Mamake)
Markson, David M(errill) 1927- **CLC 67**
See also CA 49-52; CANR 1
Marley, Bob **CLC 17**
See also Marley, Robert Nesta
Marley, Robert Nesta 1945-1981
See Marley, Bob
See also CA 107; 103
Marlowe, Christopher 1564-1593 **LC 22, 47;**
DA; DAB; DAC; DAM DRAM, MST; DC
1; WLC
See also CDBLB Before 1660; DLB 62
Marlowe, Stephen 1928-
See Queen, Ellery
See also CA 13-16R; CANR 6, 55
Marmontel, Jean-Francois 1723-1799 **LC 2**
Marquand, John P(hillips) 1893-1960**CLC 2,**
10
See also CA 85-88; CANR 73; DLB 9, 102;
MTCW 2
Marques, Rene 1919-1979 **CLC 96; DAM**
MULT; HLC 2
See also CA 97-100; 85-88; CANR 78; DLB
113; HW 1, 2
Marquez, Gabriel (Jose) Garcia
See Garcia Marquez, Gabriel (Jose)
Marquis, Don(ald Robert Perry) 1878-1937
TCLC 7
See also CA 104; 166; DLB 11, 25
Marric, J. J.
See Creasey, John
Marryat, Frederick 1792-1848 **NCLC 3**
See also DLB 21, 163
Marsden, James
See Creasey, John
Marsh, (Edith) Ngaio 1899-1982 **CLC 7, 53;**
DAM POP
See also CA 9-12R; CANR 6, 58; DLB 77;
MTCW 1, 2
Marshall, Garry 1934- **CLC 17**
See also AAYA 3; CA 111; SATA 60
Marshall, Paule 1929- **CLC 27, 72; BLC 3;**
DAM MULT; SSC 3
See also BW 2, 3; CA 77-80; CANR 25, 73;
DLB 157; MTCW 1, 2
Marshallik
See Zangwill, Israel
Marsten, Richard
See Hunter, Evan
Marston, John 1576-1634**LC 33;DAM DRAM**
See also DLB 58, 172
Martha, Henry
See Harris, Mark
Marti (y Perez), Jose (Julian) 1853-1895
NCLC 63; DAM MULT; HLC 2
See also HW 2
Martial c. 40-c. 104 **CMLC 35;PC 10**
See also DLB 211
Martin, Ken
See Hubbard, L(afayette) Ron(ald)
Martin, Richard

See Creasey, John
Martin, Steve 1945- **CLC 30**
See also CA 97-100; CANR 30; MTCW 1
Martin, Valerie 1948- **CLC 89**
See also BEST 90:2; CA 85-88; CANR 49
Martin, Violet Florence 1862-1915 **TCLC 51**
Martin, Webber
See Silverberg, Robert
Martindale, Patrick Victor
See White, Patrick (Victor Martindale)
Martin du Gard, Roger 1881-1958 **TCLC 24**
See also CA 118; DLB 65
Martineau, Harriet 1802-1876 **NCLC 26**
See also DLB 21, 55, 159, 163, 166, 190; YABC
2
Martines, Julia
See O'Faolain, Julia
Martinez, Enrique Gonzalez
See Gonzalez Martinez, Enrique
Martinez, Jacinto Benavente y
See Benavente (y Martinez), Jacinto
Martinez Ruiz, Jose 1873-1967
See Azorin; Ruiz, Jose Martinez
See also CA 93-96; HW 1
Martinez Sierra, Gregorio 1881-1947**TCLC 6**
See also CA 115
Martinez Sierra, Maria (de la O'Le Jarraga)
1874-1974 **TCLC 6**
See also CA 115
Martinsen, Martin
See Follett, Ken(neth Martin)
Martinson, Harry (Edmund) 1904-1978 **C L C**
14
See also CA 77-80; CANR 34
Marut, Ret
See Traven, B.
Marut, Robert
See Traven, B.
Marvell, Andrew 1621-1678 **LC 4, 43; DA;**
DAB; DAC; DAM MST, POET; PC 10;
WLC
See also CDBLB 1660-1789; DLB 131
Marx, Karl (Heinrich) 1818-1883 **NCLC 17**
See also DLB 129
Masaoka Shiki **TCLC 18**
See also Masaoka Tsunenori
Masaoka Tsunenori 1867-1902
See Masaoka Shiki
See also CA 117
Masefield, John (Edward) 1878-1967**CLC 11,**
47; DAM POET
See also CA 19-20; 25-28R; CANR 33; CAP 2;
CDBLB 1890-1914; DLB 10, 19, 153, 160;
MTCW 1, 2; SATA 19
Maso, Carole 19(?)- **CLC 44**
See also CA 170
Mason, Bobbie Ann 1940-**CLC 28, 43, 82; SSC**
4
See also AAYA 5; CA 53-56; CANR 11, 31,
58; CDALBS; DLB 173; DLBY 87; INT
CANR-31; MTCW 1, 2
Mason, Ernst
See Pohl, Frederik
Mason, Lee W.
See Malzberg, Barry N(athaniel)
Mason, Nick 1945- **CLC 35**
Mason, Tally
See Derleth, August (William)
Mass, William
See Gibson, William
Master Lao
See Lao Tzu
Masters, Edgar Lee 1868-1950 **TCLC 2, 25;**

DA; DAC; DAM MST, POET; PC 1;
WLCS
See also CA 104; 133;CDALB 1865-1917; DLB
54; MTCW 1, 2
Masters, Hilary 1928- **CLC 48**
See also CA 25-28R; CANR 13, 47
Mastrosimone, William 19(?)- **CLC 36**
Mathe, Albert
See Camus, Albert
Mather, Cotton 1663-1728 **LC 38**
See also CDALB 1640-1865; DLB 24, 30, 140
Mather, Increase 1639-1723 **LC 38**
See also DLB 24
Matheson, Richard Burton 1926- **CLC 37**
See also CA 97-100; DLB 8, 44; INT 97-100
Mathews, Harry 1930- **CLC 6, 52**
See also CA 21-24R; CAAS 6; CANR 18, 40
Mathews, John Joseph 1894-1979 **CLC 84;**
DAM MULT
See also CA 19-20; 142; CANR 45; CAP 2;
DLB 175; NNAL
Mathias, Roland (Glyn) 1915- **CLC 45**
See also CA 97-100; CANR 19, 41; DLB 27
Matsuo Basho 1644-1694 **PC 3**
See also DAM POET
Mattheson, Rodney
See Creasey, John
Matthews, Brander 1852-1929 **TCLC 95**
See also DLB 71, 78; DLBD 13
Matthews, Greg 1949- **CLC 45**
See also CA 135
Matthews, William (Procter, III) 1942-1997
CLC 40
See also CA 29-32R; 162; CAAS 18; CANR
12, 57; DLB 5
Matthias, John (Edward) 1941- **CLC 9**
See also CA 33-36R; CANR 56
Matthiessen, Peter 1927-**CLC 5, 7, 11, 32, 64;**
DAM NOV
See also AAYA 6; BEST 90:4; CA 9-12R;
CANR 21, 50, 73; DLB 6, 173; MTCW 1, 2;
SATA 27
Maturin, Charles Robert 1780(?)-1824**N C L C**
6
See also DLB 178
Matute (Ausejo), Ana Maria 1925- **CLC 11**
See also CA 89-92; MTCW 1
Maugham, W. S.
See Maugham, W(illiam) Somerset
Maugham, W(illiam) Somerset 1874-1965
CLC 1, 11, 15, 67, 93; DA; DAB; DAC;
DAM DRAM, MST, NOV; SSC 8; WLC
See also CA 5-8R; 25-28R; CANR 40; CDBLB
1914-1945; DLB 10, 36, 77, 100, 162, 195;
MTCW 1, 2; SATA 54
Maugham, William Somerset
See Maugham, W(illiam) Somerset
Maupassant, (Henri Rene Albert) Guy de 1850-
1893**NCLC 1, 42; DA; DAB; DAC; DAM**
MST; SSC 1; WLC
See also DLB 123
Maupin, Armistead 1944-**CLC 95;DAM POP**
See also CA 125; 130; CANR 58; INT 130;
MTCW 2
Maurhut, Richard
See Traven, B.
Mauriac, Claude 1914-1996 **CLC 9**
See also CA 89-92; 152; DLB 83
Mauriac, Francois (Charles) 1885-1970 **C L C**
4, 9, 56; SSC 24
See also CA 25-28; CAP 2; DLB 65; MTCW 1,
2
Mavor, Osborne Henry 1888-1951

See Bridie, James
See also CA 104

Maxwell, William (Keepers, Jr.) 1908-**CLC 19**
See also CA 93-96; CANR 54; DLBY 80; INT
93-96

May, Elaine 1932-   **CLC 16**
See also CA 124; 142; DLB 44

Mayakovski, Vladimir (Vladimirovich) 1893-
1930   **TCLC 4, 18**
See also CA 104; 158; MTCW 2

Mayhew, Henry 1812-1887   **NCLC 31**
See also DLB 18, 55, 190

Mayle, Peter 1939(?)-   **CLC 89**
See also CA 139; CANR 64

Maynard, Joyce 1953-   **CLC 23**
See also CA 111; 129; CANR 64

Mayne, William (James Carter) 1928-**CLC 12**
See also AAYA 20; CA 9-12R; CANR 37, 80;
CLR 25; JRDA; MAICYA; SAAS 11; SATA
6, 68

Mayo, Jim
See L'Amour, Louis (Dearborn)

Maysles, Albert 1926-   **CLC 16**
See also CA 29-32R

Maysles, David 1932-   **CLC 16**

Mazer, Norma Fox 1931-   **CLC 26**
See also AAYA 5; CA 69-72; CANR 12, 32,
66; CLR 23; JRDA; MAICYA; SAAS 1;
SATA 24, 67, 105

Mazzini, Guiseppe 1805-1872   **NCLC 34**

McAuley, James Phillip 1917-1976   **CLC 45**
See also CA 97-100

McBain, Ed
See Hunter, Evan

McBrien, William Augustine 1930-   **CLC 44**
See also CA 107

McCaffrey, Anne (Inez) 1926-**CLC 17; DAM
NOV, POP**
See also AAYA 6; AITN 2; BEST 89:2; CA 25-
28R; CANR 15, 35, 55; CLR 49; DLB 8;
JRDA; MAICYA; MTCW 1, 2; SAAS 11;
SATA 8, 70

McCall, Nathan 1955(?)-   **CLC 86**
See also BW 3; CA 146

McCann, Arthur
See Campbell, John W(ood, Jr.)

McCann, Edson
See Pohl, Frederik

McCarthy, Charles, Jr. 1933-
See McCarthy, Cormac
See also CANR 42, 69; DAM POP; MTCW 2

McCarthy, Cormac 1933- **CLC 4, 57, 59, 101**
See also McCarthy, Charles, Jr.
See also DLB 6, 143; MTCW 2

McCarthy, Mary (Therese) 1912-1989**CLC 1,
3, 5, 14, 24, 39, 59; SSC 24**
See also CA 5-8R; 129; CANR 16, 50, 64; DLB
2; DLBY 81; INT CANR-16; MTCW 1, 2

McCartney, (James) Paul 1942- **CLC 12, 35**
See also CA 146

McCauley, Stephen (D.) 1955-   **CLC 50**
See also CA 141

McClure, Michael (Thomas) 1932-**CLC 6, 10**
See also CA 21-24R; CANR 17, 46, 77; DLB
16

McCorkle, Jill (Collins) 1958-   **CLC 51**
See also CA 121; DLBY 87

McCourt, Frank 1930-   **CLC 109**
See also CA 157

McCourt, James 1941-   **CLC 5**
See also CA 57-60

McCourt, Malachy 1932-   **CLC 119**

McCoy, Horace(Stanley) 1897-1955**TCLC 28**

See also CA 108; 155; DLB 9

McCrae, John 1872-1918   **TCLC 12**
See also CA 109; DLB 92

McCreigh, James
See Pohl, Frederik

McCullers, (Lula) Carson (Smith) 1917-1967
**CLC 1, 4, 10, 12, 48, 100; DA; DAB; DAC;
DAM MST, NOV; SSC 9, 24;WLC**
See also AAYA 21; CA 5-8R; 25-28R; CABS
1, 3; CANR 18; CDALB 1941-1968; DLB
2, 7, 173; MTCW 1, 2; SATA 27

McCulloch, John Tyler
See Burroughs, Edgar Rice

McCullough, Colleen 1938(?)- **CLC 27, 107;
DAM NOV, POP**
See also CA 81-84; CANR 17, 46, 67; MTCW
1, 2

McDermott, Alice 1953-   **CLC 90**
See also CA 109; CANR 40

McElroy, Joseph 1930-   **CLC 5, 47**
See also CA 17-20R

McEwan, Ian (Russell) 1948-   **CLC 13, 66;
DAM NOV**
See also BEST 90:4; CA 61-64; CANR 14, 41,
69; DLB 14, 194; MTCW 1, 2

McFadden, David 1940-   **CLC 48**
See also CA 104; DLB 60; INT 104

McFarland, Dennis 1950-   **CLC 65**
See also CA 165

McGahern, John 1934- **CLC 5, 9, 48;SSC 17**
See also CA 17-20R; CANR 29, 68; DLB 14;
MTCW 1

McGinley, Patrick (Anthony) 1937- **CLC 41**
See also CA 120; 127; CANR 56; INT 127

McGinley, Phyllis 1905-1978   **CLC 14**
See also CA 9-12R; 77-80; CANR 19; DLB 11,
48; SATA 2, 44; SATA-Obit 24

McGinniss, Joe 1942-   **CLC 32**
See also AITN 2; BEST 89:2; CA 25-28R;
CANR 26, 70; DLB 185; INT CANR-26

McGivern, Maureen Daly
See Daly, Maureen

McGrath, Patrick 1950-   **CLC 55**
See also CA 136; CANR 65

McGrath, Thomas (Matthew) 1916-1990**CLC
28, 59; DAM POET**
See also CA 9-12R; 132; CANR 6, 33; MTCW
1; SATA 41; SATA-Obit 66

McGuane, Thomas (Francis III) 1939-**CLC 3,
7, 18, 45**
See also AITN 2; CA 49-52; CANR 5, 24, 49;
DLB 2, 212; DLBY 80; INT CANR-24;
MTCW 1

McGuckian, Medbh 1950-   **CLC 48; DAM
POET; PC 27**
See also CA 143; DLB 40

McHale, Tom 1942(?)-1982   **CLC 3, 5**
See also AITN 1; CA 77-80; 106

McIlvanney, William 1936-   **CLC 42**
See also CA 25-28R; CANR 61; DLB 14, 207

McIlwraith, Maureen Mollie Hunter
See Hunter, Mollie
See also SATA 2

McInerney, Jay 1955-**CLC 34, 112;DAM POP**
See also AAYA 18; CA 116; 123; CANR 45,
68; INT 123; MTCW 2

McIntyre, Vonda N(eel) 1948-   **CLC 18**
See also CA 81-84; CANR 17, 34, 69; MTCW
1

McKay, Claude   **TCLC 7, 41; BLC 3; DAB;PC
2**
See also McKay, Festus Claudius
See also DLB 4, 45, 51, 117

McKay, Festus Claudius 1889-1948
See McKay, Claude
See also BW 1, 3; CA 104; 124; CANR 73; DA;
DAC; DAM MST, MULT, NOV, POET;
MTCW 1, 2; WLC

McKuen, Rod 1933-   **CLC 1, 3**
See also AITN 1; CA 41-44R; CANR 40

McLoughlin, R. B.
See Mencken, H(enry) L(ouis)

McLuhan, (Herbert) Marshall 1911-1980
CLC 37, 83
See also CA 9-12R; 102; CANR 12, 34, 61;
DLB 88; INT CANR-12; MTCW 1, 2

McMillan, Terry (L.) 1951- **CLC 50, 61, 112;
BLCS; DAM MULT, NOV, POP**
See also AAYA 21; BW 2, 3; CA 140; CANR
60; MTCW 2

McMurtry, Larry (Jeff) 1936-**CLC 2, 3, 7, 11,
27, 44; DAM NOV, POP**
See also AAYA 15; AITN 2; BEST 89:2; CA 5-
8R; CANR 19, 43, 64; CDALB 1968-1988;
DLB 2, 143; DLBY 80, 87; MTCW 1, 2

McNally, T. M. 1961-   **CLC 82**

McNally, Terrence 1939-   **CLC 4, 7, 41, 91;
DAM DRAM**
See also CA 45-48; CANR 2, 56; DLB 7;
MTCW 2

McNamer, Deirdre 1950-   **CLC 70**

McNeal, Tom   **CLC 119**

McNeile, Herman Cyril 1888-1937
See Sapper
See also DLB 77

McNickle, (William) D'Arcy 1904-1977 **C L C
89; DAM MULT**
See also CA 9-12R; 85-88; CANR 5, 45; DLB
175, 212; NNAL; SATA-Obit 22

McPhee, John (Angus) 1931-   **CLC 36**
See also BEST 90:1; CA 65-68; CANR 20, 46,
64, 69; DLB 185; MTCW 1, 2

McPherson, James Alan 1943- **CLC 19, 77;
BLCS**
See also BW 1, 3; CA 25-28R; CAAS 17;
CANR 24, 74; DLB 38; MTCW 1, 2

McPherson, William (Alexander) 1933- **C L C
34**
See also CA 69-72; CANR 28; INT CANR-28

Mead, George Herbert 1873-1958   **TCLC 89**

Mead, Margaret 1901-1978   **CLC 37**
See also AITN 1; CA 1-4R; 81-84; CANR 4;
MTCW 1, 2; SATA-Obit 20

Meaker, Marijane (Agnes) 1927-
See Kerr, M. E.
See also CA 107; CANR 37, 63; INT 107;
JRDA; MAICYA; MTCW 1; SATA 20,61, 99

Medoff, Mark (Howard) 1940-   **CLC 6, 23;
DAM DRAM**
See also AITN 1; CA 53-56; CANR 5; DLB 7;
INT CANR-5

Medvedev, P. N.
See Bakhtin, Mikhail Mikhailovich

Meged, Aharon
See Megged, Aharon

Meged, Aron
See Megged, Aharon

Megged, Aharon 1920-   **CLC 9**
See also CA 49-52; CAAS 13; CANR 1

Mehta, Ved (Parkash) 1934-   **CLC 37**
See also CA 1-4R; CANR 2, 23, 69; MTCW 1

Melanter
See Blackmore, R(ichard) D(oddridge)

Melies, Georges 1861-1938   **TCLC 81**

Melikow, Loris
See Hofmannsthal, Hugo von

See also CA 104; DLB 15

Mitchell, Joni 1943-   **CLC 12**
See also CA 112

Mitchell, Joseph (Quincy) 1908-1996 **CLC 98**
See also CA 77-80; 152; CANR 69; DLB 185;
DLBY 96

Mitchell, Margaret (Munnerlyn) 1900-1949
TCLC 11; DAM NOV, POP
See also AAYA 23; CA 109; 125; CANR 55;
CDALBS; DLB 9; MTCW 1, 2

Mitchell, Peggy
See Mitchell, Margaret (Munnerlyn)

Mitchell, S(ilas) Weir 1829-1914   **TCLC 36**
See also CA 165; DLB 202

Mitchell, W(illiam) O(rmond) 1914-1998 **CLC 25; DAC; DAM MST**
See also CA 77-80; 165; CANR 15, 43; DLB 88

Mitchell, William 1879-1936   **TCLC 81**

Mitford, Mary Russell 1787-1855   **NCLC 4**
See also DLB 110, 116

Mitford, Nancy 1904-1973   **CLC 44**
See also CA 9-12R; DLB 191

Miyamoto, (Chujo) Yuriko 1899-1951 **T C L C 37**
See also CA 170, 174; DLB 180

Miyazawa, Kenji 1896-1933   **TCLC 76**
See also CA 157

Mizoguchi, Kenji 1898-1956   **TCLC 72**
See also CA 167

Mo, Timothy (Peter) 1950(?)-   **CLC 46**
See also CA 117; DLB 194; MTCW 1

Modarressi, Taghi (M.) 1931-   **CLC 44**
See also CA 121; 134; INT 134

Modiano, Patrick (Jean) 1945-   **CLC 18**
See also CA 85-88; CANR 17, 40; DLB 83

Moerck, Paal
See Roelvaag, O(le) E(dvart)

Mofolo, Thomas (Mokopu) 1875(?)-1948
TCLC 22; BLC 3; DAM MULT
See also CA 121; 153; MTCW 2

Mohr, Nicholasa 1938-**CLC 12; DAM MULT; HLC 2**
See also AAYA 8; CA 49-52; CANR 1, 32, 64;
CLR 22; DLB 145; HW 1, 2; JRDA; SAAS 8; SATA 8, 97

Mojtabai, A(nn) G(race) 1938- **CLC 5, 9, 15, 29**
See also CA 85-88

Moliere 1622-1673**LC 10, 28; DA; DAB; DAC; DAM DRAM, MST; WLC**

Molin, Charles
See Mayne, William (James Carter)

Molnar, Ferenc 1878-1952   **TCLC 20;DAM DRAM**
See also CA 109; 153

Momaday, N(avarre) Scott 1934- **CLC 2, 19, 85, 95; DA; DAB; DAC; DAM MST, MULT, NOV, POP; PC 25; WLCS**
See also AAYA 11; CA 25-28R; CANR 14, 34,
68; CDALBS; DLB 143, 175; INT CANR-
14; MTCW 1, 2; NNAL; SATA 48; SATA-
Brief 30

Monette, Paul 1945-1995   **CLC 82**
See also CA 139; 147

Monroe, Harriet 1860-1936   **TCLC 12**
See also CA 109; DLB 54, 91

Monroe, Lyle
See Heinlein, Robert A(nson)

Montagu, Elizabeth 1720-1800   **NCLC 7**

Montagu, Mary (Pierrepont) Wortley 1689-1762   **LC 9; PC 16**
See also DLB 95, 101

Montagu, W. H.
See Coleridge, Samuel Taylor

Montague, John (Patrick) 1929- CLC 13, 46
See also CA 9-12R; CANR 9, 69; DLB 40;
MTCW 1

Montaigne, Michel (Eyquem) de 1533-1592
LC 8; DA; DAB; DAC; DAM MST; WLC

Montale, Eugenio 1896-1981**CLC 7, 9, 18; PC 13**
See also CA 17-20R; 104; CANR 30; DLB 114;
MTCW 1

Montesquieu, Charles-Louis de Secondat 1689-1755   **LC 7**

Montgomery, (Robert) Bruce 1921-1978
See Crispin, Edmund
See also CA 104

Montgomery, L(ucy) M(aud) 1874-1942
TCLC 51; DAC; DAM MST
See also AAYA 12; CA 108; 137; CLR 8; DLB
92; DLBD 14; JRDA; MAICYA; MTCW 2;
SATA 100; YABC 1

Montgomery, Marion H., Jr. 1925-   **CLC 7**
See also AITN 1; CA 1-4R; CANR 3, 48; DLB 6

Montgomery, Max
See Davenport, Guy (Mattison, Jr.)

Montherlant, Henry (Milon) de 1896-1972
CLC 8, 19; DAM DRAM
See also CA 85-88; 37-40R; DLB 72; MTCW 1

Monty Python
See Chapman, Graham; Cleese, John
(Marwood); Gilliam, Terry (Vance); Idle,
Eric; Jones, Terence Graham Parry; Palin,
Michael (Edward)
See also AAYA 7

Moodie, Susanna (Strickland) 1803-1885
NCLC 14
See also DLB 99

Mooney, Edward 1951-
See Mooney, Ted
See also CA 130

Mooney, Ted   **CLC 25**
See also Mooney, Edward

Moorcock, Michael (John) 1939-**CLC 5, 27, 58**
See also Bradbury, Edward P.
See also AAYA 26; CA 45-48; CAAS 5; CANR
2, 17, 38, 64; DLB 14; MTCW 1, 2; SATA 93

Moore, Brian 1921-1999**CLC 1, 3, 5, 7, 8, 19, 32, 90; DAB; DAC; DAM MST**
See also CA 1-4R; 174; CANR 1, 25, 42, 63;
MTCW 1, 2

Moore, Edward
See Muir, Edwin

Moore, G. E. 1873-1958   **TCLC 89**

Moore, George Augustus 1852-1933**TCLC 7; SSC 19**
See also CA 104; 177; DLB 10, 18, 57, 135

Moore, Lorrie   **CLC 39, 45, 68**
See also Moore, Marie Lorena

Moore, Marianne (Craig) 1887-1972**CLC 1, 2, 4, 8, 10, 13, 19, 47; DA; DAB; DAC; DAM MST, POET; PC 4; WLCS**
See also CA 1-4R; 33-36R; CANR 3, 61;
CDALB 1929-1941; DLB 45; DLBD 7;
MTCW 1, 2; SATA 20

Moore, Marie Lorena 1957-
See Moore, Lorrie
See also CA 116; CANR 39

Moore, Thomas 1779-1852   **NCLC 6**
See also DLB 96, 144

Mora, Pat(ricia) 1942-

See also CA 129; CANR 57, 81; CLR 58; DAM
MULT; DLB 209; HLC 2; HW 1, 2; SATA 92

Morand, Paul 1888-1976   **CLC 41;SSC 22**
See also CA 69-72; DLB 65

Morante, Elsa 1918-1985   **CLC 8, 47**
See also CA 85-88; 117; CANR 35; DLB 177;
MTCW 1, 2

Moravia, Alberto 1907-1990**CLC 2, 7, 11, 27, 46; SSC 26**
See also Pincherle, Alberto
See also DLB 177; MTCW 2

More, Hannah 1745-1833   **NCLC 27**
See also DLB 107, 109, 116, 158

More, Henry 1614-1687   **LC 9**
See also DLB 126

More, Sir Thomas 1478-1535   **LC 10, 32**

Moreas, Jean   **TCLC 18**
See also Papadiamantopoulos, Johannes

Morgan, Berry 1919-   **CLC 6**
See also CA 49-52; DLB 6

Morgan, Claire
See Highsmith, (Mary) Patricia

Morgan, Edwin (George) 1920-   **CLC 31**
See also CA 5-8R; CANR 3, 43; DLB 27

Morgan, (George) Frederick 1922-   **CLC 23**
See also CA 17-20R; CANR 21

Morgan, Harriet
See Mencken, H(enry) L(ouis)

Morgan, Jane
See Cooper, James Fenimore

Morgan, Janet 1945-   **CLC 39**
See also CA 65-68

Morgan, Lady 1776(?)-1859   **NCLC 29**
See also DLB 116, 158

Morgan, Robin (Evonne) 1941-   **CLC 2**
See also CA 69-72; CANR 29, 68; MTCW 1;
SATA 80

Morgan, Scott
See Kuttner, Henry

Morgan, Seth 1949(?)-1990   **CLC 65**
See also CA 132

Morgenstern, Christian 1871-1914   **TCLC 8**
See also CA 105

Morgenstern, S.
See Goldman, William (W.)

Moricz, Zsigmond 1879-1942   **TCLC 33**
See also CA 165

Morike, Eduard (Friedrich) 1804-1875**NCLC 10**
See also DLB 133

Moritz, Karl Philipp 1756-1793   **LC 2**
See also DLB 94

Morland, Peter Henry
See Faust, Frederick (Schiller)

Morley, Christopher (Darlington) 1890-1957
TCLC 87
See also CA 112; DLB 9

Morren, Theophil
See Hofmannsthal, Hugo von

Morris, Bill 1952-   **CLC 76**

Morris, Julian
See West, Morris L(anglo)

Morris, Steveland Judkins 1950(?)-
See Wonder, Stevie
See also CA 111

Morris, William 1834-1896   **NCLC 4**
See also CDBLB 1832-1890; DLB 18, 35, 57,
156, 178, 184

Morris, Wright 1910-1998**CLC 1, 3, 7, 18, 37**
See also CA 9-12R; 167; CANR 21, 81; DLB
2, 206; DLBY 81; MTCW 1, 2

Morrison, Arthur 1863-1945   **TCLC 72**

See also CA 120; 157; DLB 70, 135, 197

Morrison, Chloe Anthony Wofford
  See Morrison, Toni

Morrison, James Douglas 1943-1971
  See Morrison, Jim
  See also CA 73-76; CANR 40

Morrison, Jim   **CLC 17**
  See also Morrison, James Douglas

Morrison, Toni 1931-CLC **4, 10, 22, 55, 81, 87;**
    BLC 3; DA; DAB; DAC; DAM MST,
    MULT, NOV, POP
  See also AAYA 1, 22; BW 2, 3; CA 29-32R;
    CANR 27, 42, 67; CDALB 1968-1988; DLB
    6, 33, 143; DLBY 81; MTCW 1, 2; SATA 57

Morrison, Van 1945-   **CLC 21**
  See also CA 116; 168

Morrissy, Mary 1958-   **CLC 99**

Mortimer, John (Clifford) 1923- CLC **28, 43;**
    DAM DRAM, POP
  See also CA 13-16R; CANR 21, 69; CDBLB
    1960 to Present; DLB 13; INT CANR-21;
    MTCW 1, 2

Mortimer, Penelope (Ruth) 1918-   **CLC 5**
  See also CA 57-60; CANR 45

Morton, Anthony
  See Creasey, John

Mosca, Gaetano 1858-1941   **TCLC 75**

Mosher, Howard Frank 1943-   **CLC 62**
  See also CA 139; CANR 65

Mosley, Nicholas 1923-   **CLC 43, 70**
  See also CA 69-72; CANR 41, 60; DLB 14, 207

Mosley, Walter 1952- CLC **97; BLCS; DAM**
    MULT, POP
  See also AAYA 17; BW 2; CA 142; CANR 57;
    MTCW 2

Moss, Howard 1922-1987 CLC **7, 14, 45, 50;**
    DAM POET
  See also CA 1-4R; 123; CANR 1, 44; DLB 5

Mossgiel, Rab
  See Burns, Robert

Motion, Andrew (Peter) 1952-   **CLC 47**
  See also CA 146; DLB 40

Motley, Willard (Francis) 1909-1965 CLC **18**
  See also BW 1; CA 117; 106; DLB 76, 143

Motoori, Norinaga 1730-1801   **NCLC 45**

Mott, Michael (Charles Alston) 1930-CLC **15,**
    34
  See also CA 5-8R; CAAS 7; CANR 7, 29

Mountain Wolf Woman 1884-1960   **CLC 92**
  See also CA 144; NNAL

Moure, Erin 1955-   **CLC 88**
  See also CA 113; DLB 60

Mowat, Farley (McGill) 1921-CLC **26; DAC;**
    DAM MST
  See also AAYA 1; CA 1-4R; CANR 4, 24, 42,
    68; CLR 20; DLB 68; INT CANR-24; JRDA;
    MAICYA; MTCW 1, 2; SATA 3, 55

Mowatt, Anna Cora 1819-1870   **NCLC 74**

Moyers, Bill 1934-   **CLC 74**
  See also AITN 2; CA 61-64; CANR 31, 52

Mphahlele, Es'kia
  See Mphahlele, Ezekiel
  See also DLB 125

Mphahlele, Ezekiel 1919-   CLC **25; BLC 3;**
    DAM MULT
  See also Mphahlele, Es'kia
  See also BW 2, 3; CA 81-84; CANR 26, 76;
    MTCW 2

Mqhayi, S(amuel) E(dward) K(rune Loliwe)
    1875-1945TCLC **25; BLC 3;DAM MULT**
  See also CA 153

Mrozek, Slawomir 1930-   **CLC 3, 13**
  See also CA 13-16R; CAAS 10; CANR 29;

MTCW 1

Mrs. Belloc-Lowndes
  See Lowndes, Marie Adelaide (Belloc)

Mtwa, Percy (?)-   **CLC 47**

Mueller, Lisel 1924-   **CLC 13, 51**
  See also CA 93-96; DLB 105

Muir, Edwin 1887-1959   **TCLC 2, 87**
  See also CA 104; DLB 20, 100, 191

Muir, John 1838-1914   **TCLC 28**
  See also CA 165; DLB 186

Mujica Lainez, Manuel 1910-1984   **CLC 31**
  See also Lainez, Manuel Mujica
  See also CA 81-84; 112; CANR 32; HW 1

Mukherjee, Bharati 1940-CLC **53, 115; DAM**
    NOV
  See also BEST 89:2; CA 107; CANR 45, 72;
    DLB 60; MTCW 1, 2

Muldoon, Paul 1951-CLC **32, 72;DAM POET**
  See also CA 113; 129; CANR 52; DLB 40; INT
    129

Mulisch, Harry 1927-   **CLC 42**
  See also CA 9-12R; CANR 6, 26, 56

Mull, Martin 1943-   **CLC 17**
  See also CA 105

Muller, Wilhelm   **NCLC 73**

Mulock, Dinah Maria
  See Craik, Dinah Maria (Mulock)

Munford, Robert 1737(?)-1783   **LC 5**
  See also DLB 31

Mungo, Raymond 1946-   **CLC 72**
  See also CA 49-52; CANR 2

Munro, Alice 1931-   CLC **6, 10, 19, 50, 95;**
    DAC; DAM MST, NOV; SSC 3; WLCS
  See also AITN 2; CA 33-36R; CANR 33, 53,
    75; DLB 53; MTCW 1, 2; SATA 29

Munro, H(ector) H(ugh) 1870-1916
  See Saki
  See also CA 104; 130; CDBLB 1890-1914; DA;
    DAB; DAC; DAM MST, NOV; DLB 34, 162;
    MTCW 1, 2; WLC

Murdoch, (Jean) Iris 1919-CLC **1, 2, 3, 4, 6, 8,**
    11, 15, 22, 31, 51; DAB; DAC; DAM MST,
    NOV
  See also CA 13-16R; CANR 8, 43, 68; CDBLB
    1960 to Present; DLB 14, 194; INT CANR-
    8; MTCW 1, 2

Murfree, Mary Noailles 1850-1922   **SSC 22**
  See also CA 122; 176; DLB 12, 74

Murnau, Friedrich Wilhelm
  See Plumpe, Friedrich Wilhelm

Murphy, Richard 1927-   **CLC 41**
  See also CA 29-32R; DLB 40

Murphy, Sylvia 1937-   **CLC 34**
  See also CA 121

Murphy, Thomas (Bernard) 1935-   **CLC 51**
  See also CA 101

Murray, Albert L. 1916-   **CLC 73**
  See also BW 2; CA 49-52; CANR 26, 52, 78;
    DLB 38

Murray, Judith Sargent 1751-1820 NCLC **63**
  See also DLB 37, 200

Murray, Les(lie) A(llan) 1938-CLC **40; DAM**
    POET
  See also CA 21-24R; CANR 11, 27, 56

Murry, J. Middleton
  See Murry, John Middleton

Murry, John Middleton 1889-1957 TCLC **16**
  See also CA 118; DLB 149

Musgrave, Susan 1951-   **CLC 13, 54**
  See also CA 69-72; CANR 45

Musil, Robert (Edler von) 1880-1942 T C L C
    12, 68; SSC 18
  See also CA 109; CANR 55; DLB 81, 124;

MTCW 2

Muske, Carol 1945-   **CLC 90**
  See also Muske-Dukes, Carol (Anne)

Muske-Dukes, Carol (Anne) 1945-
  See Muske, Carol
  See also CA 65-68; CANR 32, 70

Musset, (Louis Charles) Alfred de 1810-1857
    NCLC 7
  See also DLB 192

Mussolini, Benito (Amilcare Andrea) 1883-1945
    TCLC 96
  See also CA 116

My Brother's Brother
  See Chekhov, Anton (Pavlovich)

Myers, L(eopold) H(amilton) 1881-1944
    TCLC 59
  See also CA 157; DLB 15

Myers, Walter Dean 1937-   CLC **35; BLC 3;**
    DAM MULT, NOV
  See also AAYA 4, 23; BW 2; CA 33-36R;
    CANR 20, 42, 67; CLR 4, 16, 35; DLB 33;
    INT CANR-20; JRDA; MAICYA; MTCW 2;
    SAAS 2; SATA 41, 71, 109; SATA-Brief 27

Myers, Walter M.
  See Myers, Walter Dean

Myles, Symon
  See Follett, Ken(neth Martin)

Nabokov, Vladimir (Vladimirovich) 1899-1977
    CLC **1, 2, 3, 6, 8, 11, 15, 23, 44, 46, 64;**
    DA; DAB; DAC; DAM MST, NOV; SSC
    11; WLC
  See also CA 5-8R; 69-72; CANR 20; CDALB
    1941-1968; DLB 2; DLBD 3; DLBY 80, 91;
    MTCW 1, 2

Nagai Kafu 1879-1959   **TCLC 51**
  See also Nagai Sokichi
  See also DLB 180

Nagai Sokichi 1879-1959
  See Nagai Kafu
  See also CA 117

Nagy, Laszlo 1925-1978   **CLC 7**
  See also CA 129; 112

Naidu, Sarojini 1879-1943   **TCLC 80**

Naipaul, Shiva(dhar Srinivasa) 1945-1985
    CLC **32, 39; DAM NOV**
  See also CA 110; 112; 116; CANR 33; DLB
    157; DLBY 85; MTCW 1, 2

Naipaul, V(idiadhar) S(urajprasad) 1932-
    CLC **4, 7, 9, 13, 18, 37, 105; DAB; DAC;**
    DAM MST, NOV
  See also CA 1-4R; CANR 1, 33, 51; CDBLB
    1960 to Present; DLB 125, 204, 206; DLBY
    85; MTCW 1, 2

Nakos, Lilika 1899(?)-   **CLC 29**

Narayan, R(asipuram) K(rishnaswami) 1906-
    CLC **7, 28, 47, 121; DAM NOV; SSC 25**
  See also CA 81-84; CANR 33, 61; MTCW 1,
    2; SATA 62

Nash, (Frediric) Ogden 1902-1971   CLC **23;**
    DAM POET; PC 21
  See also CA 13-14; 29-32R; CANR 34, 61; CAP
    1; DLB 11; MAICYA; MTCW 1,2; SATA 2,
    46

Nashe, Thomas 1567-1601(?)   **LC 41**
  See also DLB 167

Nashe, Thomas 1567-1601   **LC 41**

Nathan, Daniel
  See Dannay, Frederic

Nathan, George Jean 1882-1958   **TCLC 18**
  See also Hatteras, Owen
  See also CA 114; 169; DLB 137

Natsume, Kinnosuke 1867-1916
  See Natsume, Soseki

See also CA 104

Natsume, Soseki 1867-1916   **TCLC 2, 10**
See also Natsume, Kinnosuke
See also DLB 180

Natti, (Mary) Lee 1919-
See Kingman, Lee
See also CA 5-8R; CANR 2

Naylor, Gloria 1950-**CLC 28, 52; BLC 3; DA;
DAC; DAM MST, MULT, NOV, POP;
WLCS**
See also AAYA 6; BW 2, 3; CA 107; CANR 27,
51, 74; DLB 173; MTCW 1, 2

Neihardt, John Gneisenau 1881-1973**CLC 32**
See also CA 13-14; CANR 65; CAP 1; DLB 9,
54

Nekrasov, Nikolai Alekseevich 1821-1878
NCLC 11

Nelligan, Emile 1879-1941   **TCLC 14**
See also CA 114; DLB 92

Nelson, Willie 1933-   **CLC 17**
See also CA 107

Nemerov, Howard (Stanley) 1920-1991**CLC 2,
6, 9, 36; DAM POET; PC 24**
See also CA 1-4R; 134; CABS 2; CANR 1, 27,
53; DLB 5, 6; DLBY 83; INT CANR-27;
MTCW 1, 2

Neruda, Pablo 1904-1973**CLC 1, 2, 5, 7, 9, 28,
62; DA; DAB; DAC; DAM MST, MULT,
POET; HLC 2; PC 4; WLC**
See also CA 19-20; 45-48; CAP 2; HW 1;
MTCW 1, 2

Nerval, Gerard de 1808-1855**NCLC 1, 67; PC
13; SSC 18**

Nervo, (Jose) Amado (Ruiz de) 1870-1919
TCLC 11; HLCS 2
See also CA 109; 131; HW 1

Nessi, Pio Baroja y
See Baroja (y Nessi), Pio

Nestroy, Johann 1801-1862   **NCLC 42**
See also DLB 133

Netterville, Luke
See O'Grady, Standish (James)

Neufeld, John (Arthur) 1938-   **CLC 17**
See also AAYA 11; CA 25-28R; CANR 11, 37,
56; CLR 52; MAICYA; SAAS 3; SATA 6,
81

Neville, Emily Cheney 1919-   **CLC 12**
See also CA 5-8R; CANR 3, 37; JRDA;
MAICYA; SAAS 2; SATA 1

Newbound, Bernard Slade 1930-
See Slade, Bernard
See also CA 81-84; CANR 49; DAM DRAM

Newby, P(ercy) H(oward) 1918-1997 **CLC 2,
13; DAM NOV**
See also CA 5-8R; 161; CANR 32, 67; DLB
15; MTCW 1

Newlove, Donald 1928-   **CLC 6**
See also CA 29-32R; CANR 25

Newlove, John (Herbert) 1938-   **CLC 14**
See also CA 21-24R; CANR 9, 25

Newman, Charles 1938-   **CLC 2, 8**
See also CA 21-24R

Newman, Edwin (Harold) 1919-   **CLC 14**
See also AITN 1; CA 69-72; CANR 5

Newman, John Henry 1801-1890   **NCLC 38**
See also DLB 18, 32, 55

Newton, (Sir)Isaac 1642-1727   **LC 35, 52**

Newton, Suzanne 1936-   **CLC 35**
See also CA 41-44R; CANR 14; JRDA; SATA
5, 77

Nexo, Martin Andersen 1869-1954 **TCLC 43**

Nezval, Vitezslav 1900-1958   **TCLC 44**
See also CA 123

Ng, Fae Myenne 1957(?)-   **CLC 81**
See also CA 146

Ngema, Mbongeni 1955-   **CLC 57**
See also BW 2; CA 143

Ngugi, James T(hiong'o)   **CLC 3, 7, 13**
See also Ngugi wa Thiong'o

Ngugi wa Thiong'o 1938-   **CLC 36; BLC 3;
DAM MULT, NOV**
See also Ngugi, James T(hiong'o)
See also BW 2; CA 81-84; CANR 27, 58; DLB
125; MTCW 1, 2

Nichol, B(arrie) P(hillip) 1944-1988 **CLC 18**
See also CA 53-56; DLB 53; SATA 66

Nichols, John (Treadwell) 1940-   **CLC 38**
See also CA 9-12R; CAAS 2; CANR 6, 70;
DLBY 82

Nichols, Leigh
See Koontz, Dean R(ay)

Nichols, Peter (Richard) 1927- **CLC 5, 36, 65**
See also CA 104; CANR 33; DLB 13; MTCW
1

Nicolas, F. R. E.
See Freeling, Nicolas

Niedecker, Lorine 1903-1970   **CLC 10, 42;
DAM POET**
See also CA 25-28; CAP 2; DLB 48

Nietzsche, Friedrich (Wilhelm) 1844-1900
TCLC 10, 18, 55
See also CA 107; 121; DLB 129

Nievo, Ippolito 1831-1861   **NCLC 22**

Nightingale, Anne Redmon 1943-
See Redmon, Anne
See also CA 103

Nightingale, Florence 1820-1910   **TCLC 85**
See also DLB 166

Nik. T. O.
See Annensky, Innokenty (Fyodorovich)

Nin, Anais 1903-1977 **CLC 1, 4, 8, 11, 14, 60;
DAM NOV, POP; SSC 10**
See also AITN 2; CA 13-16R; 69-72; CANR
22, 53; DLB 2, 4, 152; MTCW 1, 2

Nishida, Kitaro 1870-1945   **TCLC 83**

Nishiwaki, Junzaburo 1894-1982   **PC 15**
See also CA 107

Nissenson, Hugh 1933-   **CLC 4, 9**
See also CA 17-20R; CANR 27; DLB 28

Niven, Larry   **CLC 8**
See also Niven, Laurence Van Cott
See also AAYA 27; DLB 8

Niven, Laurence Van Cott 1938-
See Niven, Larry
See also CA 21-24R; CAAS 12; CANR 14, 44,
66; DAM POP; MTCW 1, 2; SATA 95

Nixon, Agnes Eckhardt 1927-   **CLC 21**
See also CA 110

Nizan, Paul 1905-1940   **TCLC 40**
See also CA 161; DLB 72

Nkosi, Lewis 1936-   **CLC 45; BLC 3; DAM
MULT**
See also BW 1, 3; CA 65-68; CANR 27, 81;
DLB 157

Nodier, (Jean) Charles (Emmanuel) 1780-1844
NCLC 19
See also DLB 119

Noguchi, Yone 1875-1947   **TCLC 80**

Nolan, Christopher 1965-   **CLC 58**
See also CA 111

Noon, Jeff 1957-   **CLC 91**
See also CA 148

Norden, Charles
See Durrell, Lawrence (George)

Nordhoff, Charles (Bernard) 1887-1947
TCLC 23

See also CA 108; DLB 9; SATA 23

Norfolk, Lawrence 1963-   **CLC 76**
See also CA 144

Norman, Marsha 1947-**CLC 28; DAM DRAM;
DC 8**
See also CA 105; CABS 3; CANR 41; DLBY
84

Normyx
See Douglas, (George) Norman

Norris, Frank 1870-1902   **SSC 28**
See also Norris, (Benjamin) Frank(lin, Jr.)
See also CDALB 1865-1917; DLB 12, 71, 186

Norris, (Benjamin) Frank(lin, Jr.) 1870-1902
TCLC 24
See also Norris, Frank
See also CA 110; 160

Norris, Leslie 1921-   **CLC 14**
See also CA 11-12; CANR 14; CAP 1; DLB 27

North, Andrew
See Norton, Andre

North, Anthony
See Koontz, Dean R(ay)

North, Captain George
See Stevenson, Robert Louis (Balfour)

North, Milou
See Erdrich, Louise

Northrup, B. A.
See Hubbard, L(afayette) Ron(ald)

North Staffs
See Hulme, T(homas) E(rnest)

Norton, Alice Mary
See Norton, Andre
See also MAICYA; SATA 1, 43

Norton, Andre 1912-   **CLC 12**
See also Norton, Alice Mary
See also AAYA 14; CA 1-4R; CANR 68; CLR
50; DLB 8, 52; JRDA; MTCW 1; SATA 91

Norton, Caroline 1808-1877   **NCLC 47**
See also DLB 21, 159, 199

Norway, Nevil Shute 1899-1960
See Shute, Nevil
See also CA 102; 93-96; MTCW 2

Norwid, Cyprian Kamil 1821-1883 **NCLC 17**

Nosille, Nabrah
See Ellison, Harlan (Jay)

Nossack, Hans Erich 1901-1978   **CLC 6**
See also CA 93-96; 85-88; DLB 69

Nostradamus 1503-1566   **LC 27**

Nosu, Chuji
See Ozu, Yasujiro

Notenburg, Eleanora (Genrikhovna) von
See Guro, Elena

Nova, Craig 1945-   **CLC 7, 31**
See also CA 45-48; CANR 2, 53

Novak, Joseph
See Kosinski, Jerzy (Nikodem)

Novalis 1772-1801   **NCLC 13**
See also DLB 90

Novis, Emile
See Weil, Simone (Adolphine)

Nowlan, Alden (Albert) 1933-1983 **CLC 15;
DAC; DAM MST**
See also CA 9-12R; CANR 5; DLB 53

Noyes, Alfred 1880-1958   **TCLC 7;PC 27**
See also CA 104; DLB 20

Nunn, Kem   **CLC 34**
See also CA 159

Nye, Robert 1939-   **CLC 13, 42;DAM NOV**
See also CA 33-36R; CANR 29, 67; DLB 14;
MTCW 1; SATA 6

Nyro, Laura 1947-   **CLC 17**

Oates, Joyce Carol 1938-**CLC 1, 2, 3, 6, 9, 11,
15, 19, 33, 52, 108; DA; DAB; DAC; DAM**

MST, NOV, POP; SSC 6;WLC
See also AAYA 15; AITN 1; BEST 89:2; CA 5-8R; CANR 25, 45, 74; CDALB 1968-1988; DLB 2, 5, 130; DLBY 81; INT CANR-25; MTCW 1, 2

O'Brien, Darcy 1939-1998 **CLC 11**
See also CA 21-24R; 167; CANR 8, 59

O'Brien, E. G.
See Clarke, Arthur C(harles)

O'Brien, Edna 1936- **CLC 3, 5, 8, 13, 36, 65, 116; DAM NOV; SSC 10**
See also CA 1-4R; CANR 6, 41, 65; CDBLB 1960 to Present; DLB 14; MTCW 1, 2

O'Brien, Fitz-James 1828-1862 **NCLC 21**
See also DLB 74

O'Brien, Flann **CLC 1, 4, 5, 7, 10, 47**
See also O Nuallain, Brian

O'Brien, Richard 1942- **CLC 17**
See also CA 124

O'Brien, (William) Tim(othy) 1946- **CLC 7, 19, 40, 103; DAM POP**
See also AAYA 16; CA 85-88; CANR 40, 58; CDALBS; DLB 152; DLBD 9; DLBY 80; MTCW 2

Obstfelder, Sigbjoern 1866-1900 **TCLC 23**
See also CA 123

O'Casey, Sean 1880-1964 **CLC 1, 5, 9, 11, 15, 88; DAB; DAC; DAM DRAM, MST; WLCS**
See also CA 89-92; CANR 62;CDBLB 1914-1945; DLB 10; MTCW 1, 2

O'Cathasaigh, Sean
See O'Casey, Sean

Ochs, Phil 1940-1976 **CLC 17**
See also CA 65-68

O'Connor, Edwin (Greene) 1918-1968**CLC 14**
See also CA 93-96; 25-28R

O'Connor, (Mary) Flannery 1925-1964 **C L C 1, 2, 3, 6, 10, 13, 15, 21, 66, 104; DA; DAB; DAC; DAM MST, NOV; SSC 1, 23;WLC**
See also AAYA 7; CA 1-4R; CANR 3, 41; CDALB 1941-1968; DLB 2, 152; DLBD 12; DLBY 80; MTCW 1, 2

O'Connor, Frank **CLC 23; SSC 5**
See also O'Donovan, Michael John
See also DLB 162

O'Dell, Scott 1898-1989 **CLC 30**
See also AAYA 3; CA 61-64; 129; CANR 12, 30; CLR 1, 16; DLB 52; JRDA; MAICYA; SATA 12, 60

Odets, Clifford 1906-1963**CLC 2, 28, 98; DAM DRAM; DC 6**
See also CA 85-88; CANR 62; DLB 7, 26; MTCW 1, 2

O'Doherty, Brian 1934- **CLC 76**
See also CA 105

O'Donnell, K. M.
See Malzberg, Barry N(athaniel)

O'Donnell, Lawrence
See Kuttner, Henry

O'Donovan, Michael John 1903-1966**CLC 14**
See also O'Connor, Frank
See also CA 93-96

Oe, Kenzaburo 1935- **CLC 10, 36, 86; DAM NOV; SSC 20**
See also CA 97-100; CANR 36, 50, 74; DLB 182; DLBY 94; MTCW 1, 2

O'Faolain, Julia 1932- **CLC 6, 19, 47, 108**
See also CA 81-84; CAAS 2; CANR 12, 61; DLB 14; MTCW 1

O'Faolain, Sean 1900-1991 **CLC 1, 7, 14, 32, 70; SSC 13**
See also CA 61-64; 134; CANR 12, 66; DLB

15, 162; MTCW 1, 2

O'Flaherty, Liam 1896-1984**CLC 5, 34; SSC 6**
See also CA 101; 113; CANR 35; DLB 36, 162; DLBY 84; MTCW 1, 2

Ogilvy, Gavin
See Barrie, J(ames) M(atthew)

O'Grady, Standish (James) 1846-1928 **T C L C 5**
See also CA 104; 157

O'Grady, Timothy 1951- **CLC 59**
See also CA 138

O'Hara, Frank 1926-1966 **CLC 2, 5, 13, 78; DAM POET**
See also CA 9-12R; 25-28R; CANR 33; DLB 5, 16, 193; MTCW 1, 2

O'Hara, John (Henry) 1905-1970**CLC 1, 2, 3, 6, 11, 42; DAM NOV; SSC 15**
See also CA 5-8R; 25-28R; CANR 31, 60; CDALB 1929-1941; DLB 9, 86; DLBD 2; MTCW 1, 2

O Hehir, Diana 1922- **CLC 41**
See also CA 93-96

Ohiyesa 1858-1939
See Eastman, Charles A(lexander)
See also CA 179

Okigbo, Christopher (Ifenayichukwu) 1932-1967 **CLC 25, 84; BLC 3; DAM MULT, POET; PC 7**
See also BW 1, 3; CA 77-80; CANR 74; DLB 125; MTCW 1, 2

Okri, Ben 1959- **CLC 87**
See also BW 2, 3; CA 130; 138; CANR 65; DLB 157; INT 138; MTCW 2

Olds, Sharon 1942- **CLC 32, 39, 85; DAM POET; PC 22**
See also CA 101; CANR 18, 41, 66; DLB 120; MTCW 2

Oldstyle, Jonathan
See Irving, Washington

Olesha, Yuri (Karlovich) 1899-1960 **CLC 8**
See also CA 85-88

Oliphant, Laurence 1829(?)-1888 **NCLC 47**
See also DLB 18, 166

Oliphant, Margaret (Oliphant Wilson) 1828-1897 **NCLC 11, 61; SSC 25**
See also DLB 18, 159, 190

Oliver, Mary 1935- **CLC 19, 34, 98**
See also CA 21-24R; CANR 9, 43; DLB 5, 193

Olivier, Laurence (Kerr) 1907-1989 **CLC 20**
See also CA 111; 150; 129

Olsen, Tillie 1912-**CLC 4, 13, 114; DA; DAB; DAC; DAM MST; SSC 11**
See also CA 1-4R; CANR 1, 43, 74; CDALBS; DLB 28, 206; DLBY 80; MTCW 1, 2

Olson, Charles (John) 1910-1970**CLC 1, 2, 5, 6, 9, 11, 29; DAM POET; PC 19**
See also CA 13-16; 25-28R; CABS 2; CANR 35, 61; CAP 1; DLB 5, 16, 193; MTCW 1, 2

Olson, Toby 1937- **CLC 28**
See also CA 65-68; CANR 9, 31

Olyesha, Yuri
See Olesha, Yuri (Karlovich)

Ondaatje, (Philip) Michael 1943-**CLC 14, 29, 51, 76; DAB; DAC; DAM MST**
See also CA 77-80; CANR 42, 74; DLB 60; MTCW 2

Oneal, Elizabeth 1934-
See Oneal, Zibby
See also CA 106; CANR 28; MAICYA; SATA 30, 82

Oneal, Zibby **CLC 30**
See also Oneal, Elizabeth
See also AAYA 5; CLR 13; JRDA

O'Neill, Eugene (Gladstone) 1888-1953**TCLC 1, 6, 27, 49; DA; DAB; DAC; DAM DRAM, MST; WLC**
See also AITN 1; CA 110; 132; CDALB 1929-1941; DLB 7; MTCW 1, 2

Onetti, Juan Carlos 1909-1994 **CLC 7, 10; DAM MULT, NOV; HLCS 2;SSC 23**
See also CA 85-88; 145; CANR 32, 63; DLB 113; HW 1, 2; MTCW 1, 2

O Nuallain, Brian 1911-1966
See O'Brien, Flann
See also CA 21-22; 25-28R; CAP 2

Ophuls, Max 1902-1957 **TCLC 79**
See also CA 113

Opie, Amelia 1769-1853 **NCLC 65**
See also DLB 116, 159

Oppen, George 1908-1984 **CLC 7, 13,34**
See also CA 13-16R; 113; CANR 8, 82; DLB 5, 165

Oppenheim, E(dward) Phillips 1866-1946 **TCLC 45**
See also CA 111; DLB 70

Opuls, Max
See Ophuls, Max

Origen c. 185-c. 254 **CMLC 19**

Orlovitz, Gil 1918-1973 **CLC 22**
See also CA 77-80; 45-48; DLB 2, 5

Orris
See Ingelow, Jean

Ortega y Gasset, Jose 1883-1955 **TCLC 9; DAM MULT; HLC 2**
See also CA 106; 130; HW 1, 2; MTCW 1, 2

Ortese, Anna Maria 1914- **CLC 89**
See also DLB 177

Ortiz, Simon J(oseph) 1941- **CLC 45; DAM MULT, POET; PC 17**
See also CA 134; CANR 69; DLB 120, 175; NNAL

Orton, Joe **CLC 4, 13, 43; DC 3**
See also Orton, John Kingsley
See also CDBLB 1960 to Present; DLB 13; MTCW 2

Orton, John Kingsley 1933-1967
See Orton, Joe
See also CA 85-88; CANR 35, 66; DAM DRAM; MTCW 1, 2

Orwell, George **TCLC 2, 6, 15, 31, 51; DAB; WLC**
See also Blair, Eric (Arthur)
See also CDBLB 1945-1960; DLB 15, 98, 195

Osborne, David
See Silverberg, Robert

Osborne, George
See Silverberg, Robert

Osborne, John (James) 1929-1994**CLC 1, 2, 5, 11, 45; DA; DAB; DAC; DAM DRAM, MST; WLC**
See also CA 13-16R; 147; CANR 21, 56; CDBLB 1945-1960; DLB 13; MTCW 1, 2

Osborne, Lawrence 1958- **CLC 50**

Osbourne, Lloyd 1868-1947 **TCLC 93**

Oshima, Nagisa 1932- **CLC 20**
See also CA 116; 121; CANR 78

Oskison, John Milton 1874-1947 **TCLC 35; DAM MULT**
See also CA 144; DLB 175; NNAL

Ossian c. 3rd cent. - **CMLC 28**
See also Macpherson, James

Ossoli, Sarah Margaret (Fuller marchesa d') 1810-1850
See Fuller, Margaret
See also SATA 25

Ostrovsky, Alexander 1823-1886**NCLC 30, 57**

Otero, Blas de 1916-1979 **CLC 11**
See also CA 89-92; DLB 134
Otto, Rudolf 1869-1937 **TCLC 85**
Otto, Whitney 1955- **CLC 70**
See also CA 140
Ouida **TCLC 43**
See also De La Ramee, (Marie) Louise
See also DLB 18, 156
Ousmane, Sembene 1923- **CLC 66; BLC 3**
See also BW 1, 3; CA 117; 125; CANR 81;
MTCW 1
Ovid 43B.C.-17 **CMLC 7; DAM POET; PC 2**
See also DLB 211
Owen, Hugh
See Faust, Frederick (Schiller)
Owen, Wilfred (Edward Salter) 1893-1918
TCLC 5, 27; DA; DAB; DAC; DAM MST,
POET; PC 19; WLC
See also CA 104; 141; CDBLB 1914-1945;
DLB 20; MTCW 2
Owens, Rochelle 1936- **CLC 8**
See also CA 17-20R; CAAS 2; CANR 39
Oz, Amos 1939-**CLC 5, 8, 11, 27, 33, 54; DAM**
NOV
See also CA 53-56; CANR 27, 47, 65; MTCW
1, 2
Ozick, Cynthia 1928- **CLC 3, 7, 28, 62; DAM**
NOV, POP; SSC 15
See also BEST 90:1; CA 17-20R; CANR 23,
58; DLB 28, 152; DLBY 82; INT CANR-
23; MTCW 1, 2
Ozu, Yasujiro 1903-1963 **CLC 16**
See also CA 112
Pacheco, C.
See Pessoa, Fernando (Antonio Nogueira)
Pacheco, Jose Emilio 1939-
See also CA 111; 131; CANR 65; DAM MULT;
HLC 2; HW 1, 2
Pa Chin **CLC 18**
See also Li Fei-kan
Pack, Robert 1929- **CLC 13**
See also CA 1-4R; CANR 3, 44, 82; DLB 5
Padgett, Lewis
See Kuttner, Henry
Padilla (Lorenzo), Heberto 1932- **CLC 38**
See also AITN 1; CA 123; 131; HW 1
Page, Jimmy 1944- **CLC 12**
Page, Louise 1955- **CLC 40**
See also CA 140; CANR 76
Page, P(atricia) K(athleen) 1916- **CLC 7, 18;**
DAC; DAM MST; PC 12
See also CA 53-56; CANR 4, 22, 65; DLB 68;
MTCW 1
Page, Thomas Nelson 1853-1922 **SSC 23**
See also CA 118; 177; DLB 12, 78; DLBD 13
Pagels, Elaine Hiesey 1943- **CLC 104**
See also CA 45-48; CANR 2, 24, 51
Paget, Violet 1856-1935
See Lee, Vernon
See also CA 104; 166
Paget-Lowe, Henry
See Lovecraft, H(oward) P(hillips)
Paglia, Camille (Anna) 1947- **CLC 68**
See also CA 140; CANR 72; MTCW 2
Paige, Richard
See Koontz, Dean R(ay)
Paine, Thomas 1737-1809 **NCLC 62**
See also CDALB 1640-1865; DLB 31, 43, 73,
158
Pakenham, Antonia
See Fraser, (Lady) Antonia (Pakenham)
Palamas, Kostes 1859-1943 **TCLC 5**
See also CA 105

Palazzeschi, Aldo 1885-1974 **CLC 11**
See also CA 89-92; 53-56; DLB 114
Pales Matos, Luis 1898-1959
See also HLCS 2; HW 1
Paley, Grace 1922- **CLC 4, 6, 37; DAM POP;**
SSC 8
See also CA 25-28R; CANR 13, 46, 74; DLB
28; INT CANR-13; MTCW 1, 2
Palin, Michael (Edward) 1943- **CLC 21**
See also Monty Python
See also CA 107; CANR 35; SATA 67
Palliser, Charles 1947- **CLC 65**
See also CA 136; CANR 76
Palma, Ricardo 1833-1919 **TCLC 29**
See also CA 168
Pancake, Breece Dexter 1952-1979
See Pancake, Breece D'J
See also CA 123; 109
Pancake, Breece D'J **CLC 29**
See also Pancake, Breece Dexter
See also DLB 130
Panko, Rudy
See Gogol, Nikolai (Vasilyevich)
Papadiamantis, Alexandros 1851-1911 **T C L C**
29
See also CA 168
Papadiamantopoulos, Johannes 1856-1910
See Moreas, Jean
See also CA 117
Papini, Giovanni 1881-1956 **TCLC 22**
See also CA 121
Paracelsus 1493-1541 **LC 14**
See also DLB 179
Parasol, Peter
See Stevens, Wallace
Pardo Bazan, Emilia 1851-1921 **SSC 30**
Pareto, Vilfredo 1848-1923 **TCLC 69**
See also CA 175
Parfenie, Maria
See Codrescu, Andrei
Parini, Jay (Lee) 1948- **CLC 54**
See also CA 97-100; CAAS 16; CANR 32
Park, Jordan
See Kornbluth, C(yril) M.; Pohl, Frederik
Park, Robert E(zra) 1864-1944 **TCLC 73**
See also CA 122; 165
Parker, Bert
See Ellison, Harlan (Jay)
Parker, Dorothy (Rothschild) 1893-1967**C L C**
15, 68; DAM POET; SSC 2
See also CA 19-20; 25-28R; CAP 2; DLB 11,
45, 86; MTCW 1, 2
Parker, Robert B(rown) 1932-**CLC 27; DAM**
NOV, POP
See also AAYA 28; BEST 89:4; CA 49-52;
CANR 1, 26, 52; INT CANR-26; MTCW 1
Parkin, Frank 1940- **CLC 43**
See also CA 147
Parkman, Francis, Jr. 1823-1893 **NCLC 12**
See also DLB 1, 30, 186
Parks, Gordon (Alexander Buchanan) 1912-
CLC 1, 16; BLC 3; DAM MULT
See also AITN 2; BW 2, 3; CA 41-44R; CANR
26, 66; DLB 33; MTCW 2; SATA 8, 108
Parmenides c. 515B.C.-c.450B.C. **CMLC 22**
See also DLB 176
Parnell, Thomas 1679-1718 **LC 3**
See also DLB 94
Parra, Nicanor 1914- **CLC 2, 102; DAM**
MULT; HLC 2
See also CA 85-88; CANR 32; HW 1; MTCW
1
Parra Sanojo, Ana Teresa de la 1890-1936

See also HLCS 2
Parrish, Mary Frances
See Fisher, M(ary) F(rances) K(ennedy)
Parson
See Coleridge, Samuel Taylor
Parson Lot
See Kingsley, Charles
Partridge, Anthony
See Oppenheim, E(dward) Phillips
Pascal, Blaise 1623-1662 **LC 35**
Pascoli, Giovanni 1855-1912 **TCLC 45**
See also CA 170
Pasolini, Pier Paolo 1922-1975 **CLC 20, 37,**
106; PC 17
See also CA 93-96; 61-64; CANR 63; DLB 128,
177; MTCW 1
Pasquini
See Silone, Ignazio
Pastan, Linda (Olenik) 1932- **CLC 27; DAM**
POET
See also CA 61-64; CANR 18, 40, 61; DLB 5
Pasternak, Boris (Leonidovich) 1890-1960
CLC 7, 10, 18, 63; DA; DAB; DAC; DAM
MST, NOV, POET; PC 6; SSC 31;WLC
See also CA 127; 116; MTCW 1, 2
Patchen, Kenneth 1911-1972 **CLC 1, 2, 18;**
DAM POET
See also CA 1-4R; 33-36R; CANR 3, 35; DLB
16, 48; MTCW 1
Pater, Walter (Horatio) 1839-1894 **NCLC 7**
See also CDBLB 1832-1890; DLB 57, 156
Paterson, A(ndrew) B(arton) 1864-1941
TCLC 32
See also CA 155; SATA 97
Paterson, Katherine (Womeldorf) 1932-**C L C**
12, 30
See also AAYA 1; CA 21-24R; CANR 28, 59;
CLR 7, 50; DLB 52; JRDA; MAICYA;
MTCW 1; SATA 13, 53, 92
Patmore, Coventry Kersey Dighton 1823-1896
NCLC 9
See also DLB 35, 98
Paton, Alan (Stewart) 1903-1988 **CLC 4, 10,**
25, 55, 106; DA; DAB; DAC; DAM MST,
NOV; WLC
See also AAYA 26; CA 13-16; 125; CANR 22;
CAP 1; DLBD 17; MTCW 1, 2; SATA 11;
SATA-Obit 56
Paton Walsh, Gillian 1937-
See Walsh, Jill Paton
See also CANR 38; JRDA; MAICYA; SAAS 3;
SATA 4, 72, 109
Patton, George S. 1885-1945 **TCLC 79**
Paulding, James Kirke 1778-1860 **NCLC 2**
See also DLB 3, 59, 74
Paulin, Thomas Neilson 1949-
See Paulin, Tom
See also CA 123; 128
Paulin, Tom **CLC 37**
See also Paulin, Thomas Neilson
See also DLB 40
Paustovsky, Konstantin (Georgievich) 1892-
1968 **CLC 40**
See also CA 93-96; 25-28R
Pavese, Cesare 1908-1950 **TCLC 3; PC 13;**
SSC 19
See also CA 104; 169; DLB 128, 177
Pavic, Milorad 1929- **CLC 60**
See also CA 136; DLB 181
Pavlov, Ivan Petrovich 1849-1936 **TCLC 91**
See also CA 118
Payne, Alan
See Jakes, John (William)

Paz, Gil
See Lugones, Leopoldo
Paz, Octavio 1914-1998 **CLC 3, 4, 6, 10, 19, 51, 65, 119; DA; DAB; DAC; DAM MST, MULT, POET; HLC 2; PC 1;WLC**
See also CA 73-76; 165; CANR 32, 65; DLBY 90, 98; HW 1, 2; MTCW 1, 2
p'Bitek, Okot 1931-1982 **CLC 96; BLC 3; DAM MULT**
See also BW 2, 3; CA 124; 107; CANR 82; DLB 125; MTCW 1, 2
Peacock, Molly 1947- **CLC 60**
See also CA 103; CAAS 21; CANR 52; DLB 120
Peacock, Thomas Love 1785-1866 **NCLC 22**
See also DLB 96, 116
Peake, Mervyn 1911-1968 **CLC 7, 54**
See also CA 5-8R; 25-28R; CANR 3; DLB 15, 160; MTCW 1; SATA 23
Pearce, Philippa **CLC 21**
See also Christie, (Ann) Philippa
See also CLR 9; DLB 161; MAICYA; SATA 1, 67
Pearl, Eric
See Elman, Richard (Martin)
Pearson, T(homas) R(eid) 1956- **CLC 39**
See also CA 120; 130; INT 130
Peck, Dale 1967- **CLC 81**
See also CA 146; CANR 72
Peck, John 1941- **CLC 3**
See also CA 49-52; CANR 3
Peck, Richard (Wayne) 1934- **CLC 21**
See also AAYA 1, 24; CA 85-88; CANR 19, 38; CLR 15; INT CANR-19; JRDA; MAICYA; SAAS 2; SATA 18, 55, 97
Peck, Robert Newton 1928- **CLC 17; DA; DAC; DAM MST**
See also AAYA 3; CA 81-84; CANR 31, 63; CLR 45; JRDA; MAICYA; SAAS 1; SATA 21, 62; SATA-Essay 108
Peckinpah, (David) Sam(uel) 1925-1984 **C L C 20**
See also CA 109; 114; CANR 82
Pedersen, Knut 1859-1952
See Hamsun, Knut
See also CA 104; 119; CANR 63; MTCW 1, 2
Peeslake, Gaffer
See Durrell, Lawrence (George)
Peguy, Charles Pierre 1873-1914 **TCLC 10**
See also CA 107
Peirce, Charles Sanders 1839-1914 **TCLC 81**
Pellicer, Carlos 1900(?)-1977
See also CA 153; 69-72; HLCS 2; HW 1
Pena, Ramon del Valle y
See Valle-Inclan, Ramon (Maria) del
Pendennis, Arthur Esquir
See Thackeray, William Makepeace
Penn, William 1644-1718 **LC 25**
See also DLB 24
PEPECE
See Prado (Calvo), Pedro
Pepys, Samuel 1633-1703 **LC 11; DA; DAB; DAC; DAM MST; WLC**
See also CDBLB 1660-1789; DLB 101
Percy, Walker 1916-1990 **CLC 2, 3, 6, 8, 14, 18, 47, 65; DAM NOV, POP**
See also CA 1-4R; 131; CANR 1, 23, 64; DLB 2; DLBY 80, 90; MTCW 1, 2
Percy, William Alexander 1885-1942 **TCLC 84**
See also CA 163; MTCW 2
Perec, Georges 1936-1982 **CLC 56, 116**
See also CA 141; DLB 83
Pereda (y Sanchez de Porrua), Jose Maria de

1833-1906 **TCLC 16**
See also CA 117
Pereda y Porrua, Jose Maria de
See Pereda (y Sanchez de Porrua), Jose Maria de
Peregoy, George Weems
See Mencken, H(enry) L(ouis)
Perelman, S(idney) J(oseph) 1904-1979 **C L C 3, 5, 9, 15, 23, 44, 49; DAM DRAM; SSC 32**
See also AITN 1, 2; CA 73-76; 89-92; CANR 18; DLB 11, 44; MTCW 1, 2
Peret, Benjamin 1899-1959 **TCLC 20**
See also CA 117
Peretz, Isaac Loeb 1851(?)-1915 **TCLC 16; SSC 26**
See also CA 109
Peretz, Yitzhok Leibush
See Peretz, Isaac Loeb
Perez Galdos, Benito 1843-1920 **TCLC 27; HLCS 2**
See also CA 125; 153; HW 1
Peri Rossi, Cristina 1941-
See also CA 131; CANR 59, 81; DLB 145; HLCS 2; HW 1, 2
Perrault, Charles 1628-1703 **LC 3, 52**
See also MAICYA; SATA 25
Perry, Brighton
See Sherwood, Robert E(mmet)
Perse, St.-John
See Leger, (Marie-Rene Auguste) Alexis Saint-Leger
Perutz, Leo(pold) 1882-1957 **TCLC 60**
See also CA 147; DLB 81
Peseenz, Tulio F.
See Lopez y Fuentes, Gregorio
Pesetsky, Bette 1932- **CLC 28**
See also CA 133; DLB 130
Peshkov, Alexei Maximovich 1868-1936
See Gorky, Maxim
See also CA 105; 141; DA; DAC; DAM DRAM, MST, NOV; MTCW 2
Pessoa, Fernando (Antonio Nogueira) 1888-1935 **TCLC 27; DAM MULT; HLC 2; PC 20**
See also CA 125
Peterkin, Julia Mood 1880-1961 **CLC 31**
See also CA 102; DLB 9
Peters, Joan K(aren) 1945- **CLC 39**
See also CA 158
Peters, Robert L(ouis) 1924- **CLC 7**
See also CA 13-16R; CAAS 8; DLB 105
Petofi, Sandor 1823-1849 **NCLC 21**
Petrakis, Harry Mark 1923- **CLC 3**
See also CA 9-12R; CANR 4, 30
Petrarch 1304-1374 **CMLC 20; DAM POET; PC 8**
Petronius c. 20-66 **CMLC 34**
See also DLB 211
Petrov, Evgeny **TCLC 21**
See also Kataev, Evgeny Petrovich
Petry, Ann (Lane) 1908-1997 **CLC 1, 7, 18**
See also BW 1, 3; CA 5-8R; 157; CAAS 6; CANR 4, 46; CLR 12; DLB 76; JRDA; MAICYA; MTCW 1; SATA 5; SATA-Obit 94
Petursson, Halligrimur 1614-1674 **LC 8**
Peychinovich
See Vazov, Ivan (Minchov)
Phaedrus c. 18B.C.-c. 50 **CMLC 25**
See also DLB 211
Philips, Katherine 1632-1664 **LC 30**
See also DLB 131
Philipson, Morris H. 1926- **CLC 53**

See also CA 1-4R; CANR 4
Phillips, Caryl 1958- **CLC 96; BLCS; DAM MULT**
See also BW 2; CA 141; CANR 63; DLB 157; MTCW 2
Phillips, David Graham 1867-1911 **TCLC 44**
See also CA 108; 176; DLB 9, 12
Phillips, Jack
See Sandburg, Carl (August)
Phillips, Jayne Anne 1952- **CLC 15, 33; SSC 16**
See also CA 101; CANR 24, 50; DLBY 80; INT CANR-24; MTCW 1, 2
Phillips, Richard
See Dick, Philip K(indred)
Phillips, Robert (Schaeffer) 1938- **CLC 28**
See also CA 17-20R; CAAS 13; CANR 8; DLB 105
Phillips, Ward
See Lovecraft, H(oward) P(hillips)
Piccolo, Lucio 1901-1969 **CLC 13**
See also CA 97-100; DLB 114
Pickthall, Marjorie L(owry) C(hristie) 1883-1922 **TCLC 21**
See also CA 107; DLB 92
Pico della Mirandola, Giovanni 1463-1494 **LC 15**
Piercy, Marge 1936- **CLC 3, 6, 14, 18, 27, 62**
See also CA 21-24R; CAAS 1; CANR 13, 43, 66; DLB 120; MTCW 1, 2
Piers, Robert
See Anthony, Piers
Pieyre de Mandiargues, Andre 1909-1991
See Mandiargues, Andre Pieyre de
See also CA 103; 136; CANR 22, 82
Pilnyak, Boris **TCLC 23**
See also Vogau, Boris Andreyevich
Pincherle, Alberto 1907-1990 **CLC 11, 18; DAM NOV**
See also Moravia, Alberto
See also CA 25-28R; 132; CANR 33, 63; MTCW 1
Pinckney, Darryl 1953- **CLC 76**
See also BW 2, 3; CA 143; CANR 79
Pindar 518B.C.-446B.C. **CMLC 12;PC 19**
See also DLB 176
Pineda, Cecile 1942- **CLC 39**
See also CA 118
Pinero, Arthur Wing 1855-1934 **TCLC 32; DAM DRAM**
See also CA 110;.153; DLB 10
Pinero, Miguel (Antonio Gomez) 1946-1988 **CLC 4, 55**
See also CA 61-64; 125; CANR 29; HW 1
Pinget, Robert 1919-1997 **CLC 7, 13, 37**
See also CA 85-88; 160; DLB 83
Pink Floyd
See Barrett, (Roger) Syd; Gilmour, David; Mason, Nick; Waters, Roger; Wright, Rick
Pinkney, Edward 1802-1828 **NCLC 31**
Pinkwater, Daniel Manus 1941- **CLC 35**
See also Pinkwater, Manus
See also AAYA 1; CA 29-32R; CANR 12, 38; CLR 4; JRDA; MAICYA; SAAS 3; SATA 46, 76
Pinkwater, Manus
See Pinkwater, Daniel Manus
See also SATA 8
Pinsky, Robert 1940- **CLC 9, 19, 38, 94, 121; DAM POET; PC 27**
See also CA 29-32R; CAAS 4; CANR 58; DLBY 82, 98; MTCW 2
Pinta, Harold
See Pinter, Harold

Price, (Edward) Reynolds 1933-**CLC 3, 6, 13, 43, 50, 63; DAM NOV; SSC 22**
See also CA 1-4R; CANR 1, 37, 57; DLB 2; INT CANR-37

Price, Richard 1949- **CLC 6, 12**
See also CA 49-52; CANR 3; DLBY 81

Prichard, Katharine Susannah 1883-1969 **CLC 46**
See also CA 11-12; CANR 33; CAP 1; MTCW 1; SATA 66

Priestley, J(ohn) B(oynton) 1894-1984**CLC 2, 5, 9, 34; DAM DRAM, NOV**
See also CA 9-12R; 113; CANR 33;CDBLB 1914-1945; DLB 10, 34, 77, 100, 139; DLBY 84; MTCW 1, 2

Prince 1958(?)- **CLC 35**

Prince, F(rank) T(empleton) 1912- **CLC 22**
See also CA 101; CANR 43, 79; DLB 20

Prince Kropotkin
See Kropotkin, Peter (Aleksieevich)

Prior, Matthew 1664-1721 **LC 4**
See also DLB 95

Prishvin, Mikhail 1873-1954 **TCLC 75**

Pritchard, William H(arrison) 1932-**CLC 34**
See also CA 65-68; CANR 23; DLB 111

Pritchett, V(ictor) S(awdon) 1900-1997 **C L C 5, 13, 15, 41; DAM NOV; SSC 14**
See also CA 61-64; 157; CANR 31, 63; DLB 15, 139; MTCW 1, 2

Private 19022
See Manning, Frederic

Probst, Mark 1925- **CLC 59**
See also CA 130

Prokosch, Frederic 1908-1989 **CLC 4, 48**
See also CA 73-76; 128; CANR 82; DLB 48; MTCW 2

Propertius, Sextus c. 50B.C.-c.16B.C. **C M L C 32**
See also DLB 211

Prophet, The
See Dreiser, Theodore (Herman Albert)

Prose, Francine 1947- **CLC 45**
See also CA 109; 112; CANR 46; SATA 101

Proudhon
See Cunha, Euclides (Rodrigues Pimenta) da

Proulx, Annie
See Proulx, E(dna) Annie

Proulx, E(dna) Annie 1935- **CLC 81;DAM POP**
See also CA 145; CANR 65; MTCW 2

Proust, (Valentin-Louis-George-Eugene-) Marcel 1871-1922 **TCLC 7, 13, 33; DA; DAB; DAC; DAM MST, NOV; WLC**
See also CA 104; 120; DLB 65; MTCW 1, 2

Prowler, Harley
See Masters, Edgar Lee

Prus, Boleslaw 1845-1912 **TCLC 48**

Pryor, Richard (Franklin Lenox Thomas) 1940-**CLC 26**
See also CA 122; 152

Przybyszewski, Stanislaw 1868-1927**TCLC 36**
See also CA 160; DLB 66

Pteleon
See Grieve, C(hristopher) M(urray)
See also DAM POET

Puckett, Lute
See Masters, Edgar Lee

Puig, Manuel 1932-1990**CLC 3, 5, 10, 28, 65; DAM MULT; HLC 2**
See also CA 45-48; CANR 2, 32, 63; DLB 113; HW 1, 2; MTCW 1, 2

Pulitzer, Joseph 1847-1911 **TCLC 76**
See also CA 114; DLB 23

Purdy, A(lfred) W(ellington) 1918- CLC 3, 6, 14, 50; DAC; DAM MST, POET**
See also CA 81-84; CAAS 17; CANR 42, 66; DLB 88

Purdy, James (Amos) 1923- **CLC 2, 4, 10, 28, 52**
See also CA 33-36R; CAAS 1; CANR 19, 51; DLB 2; INT CANR-19; MTCW 1

Pure, Simon
See Swinnerton, Frank Arthur

Pushkin, Alexander (Sergeyevich) 1799-1837 **NCLC 3, 27; DA; DAB; DAC; DAM DRAM, MST, POET; PC 10; SSC 27;WLC**
See also DLB 205; SATA 61

P'u Sung-ling 1640-1715 **LC 49; SSC 31**

Putnam, Arthur Lee
See Alger, Horatio, Jr.

Puzo, Mario 1920-1999 CLC 1, 2, 6, 36, 107; DAM NOV, POP**
See also CA 65-68; CANR 4, 42, 65; DLB 6; MTCW 1, 2

Pygge, Edward
See Barnes, Julian (Patrick)

Pyle, Ernest Taylor 1900-1945
See Pyle, Ernie
See also CA 115; 160

Pyle, Ernie 1900-1945 **TCLC 75**
See also Pyle, Ernest Taylor
See also DLB 29; MTCW 2

Pyle, Howard 1853-1911 **TCLC 81**
See also CA 109; 137; CLR 22; DLB 42, 188; DLBD 13; MAICYA; SATA 16, 100

Pym, Barbara (Mary Crampton) 1913-1980 **CLC 13, 19, 37, 111**
See also CA 13-14; 97-100; CANR 13, 34; CAP 1; DLB 14, 207; DLBY 87; MTCW 1, 2

Pynchon, Thomas (Ruggles, Jr.) 1937-**CLC 2, 3, 6, 9, 11, 18, 33, 62, 72; DA; DAB; DAC; DAM MST, NOV, POP; SSC 14;WLC**
See also BEST 90:2; CA 17-20R; CANR 22, 46, 73; DLB 2, 173; MTCW 1, 2

Pythagoras c. 570B.C.-c.500B.C. **CMLC 22**
See also DLB 176

Q
See Quiller-Couch, SirArthur (Thomas)

Qian Zhongshu
See Ch'ien Chung-shu

Qroll
See Dagerman, Stig (Halvard)

Quarrington, Paul (Lewis) 1953- **CLC 65**
See also CA 129; CANR 62

Quasimodo, Salvatore 1901-1968 **CLC 10**
See also CA 13-16; 25-28R; CAP 1; DLB 114; MTCW 1

Quay, Stephen 1947- **CLC 95**

Quay, Timothy 1947- **CLC 95**

Queen, Ellery **CLC 3, 11**
See also Dannay, Frederic; Davidson, Avram (James); Lee, Manfred B(ennington); Marlowe, Stephen; Sturgeon, Theodore (Hamilton); Vance, John Holbrook

Queen, Ellery, Jr.
See Dannay, Frederic; Lee, Manfred B(ennington)

Queneau, Raymond 1903-1976 **CLC 2, 5, 10, 42**
See also CA 77-80; 69-72; CANR 32; DLB 72; MTCW 1, 2

Quevedo, Francisco de 1580-1645 **LC 23**

Quiller-Couch, Sir Arthur(Thomas) 1863-1944 **TCLC 53**
See also CA 118; 166; DLB 135, 153, 190

Quin, Ann (Marie) 1936-1973 **CLC 6**

See also CA 9-12R; 45-48; DLB 14

Quinn, Martin
See Smith, Martin Cruz

Quinn, Peter 1947- **CLC 91**

Quinn, Simon
See Smith, Martin Cruz

Quintana, Leroy V. 1944-
See also CA 131; CANR 65; DAM MULT; DLB 82; HLC 2; HW 1, 2

Quiroga, Horacio (Sylvestre) 1878-1937 **TCLC 20; DAM MULT; HLC 2**
See also CA 117; 131; HW 1; MTCW 1

Quoirez, Francoise 1935- **CLC 9**
See also Sagan, Francoise
See also CA 49-52; CANR 6, 39, 73; MTCW 1, 2

Raabe, Wilhelm (Karl) 1831-1910 **TCLC 45**
See also CA 167; DLB 129

Rabe, David (William) 1940- **CLC 4, 8, 33; DAM DRAM**
See also CA 85-88; CABS 3; CANR 59; DLB 7

Rabelais, Francois 1483-1553**LC 5; DA; DAB; DAC; DAM MST; WLC**

Rabinovitch, Sholem 1859-1916
See Aleichem, Sholom
See also CA 104

Rabinyan, Dorit 1972- **CLC 119**
See also CA 170

Rachilde 1860-1953 **TCLC 67**
See also DLB 123, 192

Racine, Jean 1639-1699 **LC 28; DAB; DAM MST**

Radcliffe, Ann (Ward) 1764-1823**NCLC 6, 55**
See also DLB 39, 178

Radiguet, Raymond 1903-1923 **TCLC 29**
See also CA 162; DLB 65

Radnoti, Miklos 1909-1944 **TCLC 16**
See also CA 118

Rado, James 1939- **CLC 17**
See also CA 105

Radvanyi, Netty 1900-1983
See Seghers, Anna
See also CA 85-88; 110; CANR 82

Rae, Ben
See Griffiths, Trevor

Raeburn, John (Hay) 1941- **CLC 34**
See also CA 57-60

Ragni, Gerome 1942-1991 **CLC 17**
See also CA 105; 134

Rahv, Philip 1908-1973 **CLC 24**
See also Greenberg, Ivan
See also DLB 137

Raimund, Ferdinand Jakob 1790-1836**NCLC 69**
See also DLB 90

Raine, Craig 1944- **CLC 32, 103**
See also CA 108; CANR 29, 51; DLB 40

Raine, Kathleen (Jessie) 1908- **CLC 7, 45**
See also CA 85-88; CANR 46; DLB 20; MTCW 1

Rainis, Janis 1865-1929 **TCLC 29**
See also CA 170

Rakosi, Carl 1903- **CLC 47**
See also Rawley, Callman
See also CAAS 5; DLB 193

Raleigh, Richard
See Lovecraft, H(oward) P(hillips)

Raleigh, Sir Walter 1554(?)-1618 **LC 31, 39**
See also CDBLB Before 1660; DLB 172

Rallentando, H. P.
See Sayers, Dorothy L(eigh)

Ramal, Walter
See de la Mare, Walter (John)

Ramana Maharshi 1879-1950 **TCLC 84**
Ramoacn y Cajal, Santiago 1852-1934 **T C L C 93**
Ramon, Juan
See Jimenez (Mantecon), Juan Ramon
Ramos, Graciliano 1892-1953 **TCLC 32**
See also CA 167; HW 2
Rampersad, Arnold 1941- **CLC 44**
See also BW 2, 3; CA 127; 133; CANR 81; DLB 111; INT 133
Rampling, Anne
See Rice, Anne
Ramsay, Allan 1684(?)-1758 **LC 29**
See also DLB 95
Ramuz, Charles-Ferdinand 1878-1947 **T C L C 33**
See also CA 165
Rand, Ayn 1905-1982 **CLC 3, 30, 44, 79; DA; DAC; DAM MST, NOV, POP; WLC**
See also AAYA 10; CA 13-16R; 105; CANR 27, 73; CDALBS; MTCW 1, 2
Randall, Dudley (Felker) 1914-**CLC 1; BLC 3; DAM MULT**
See also BW 1, 3; CA 25-28R; CANR 23, 82; DLB 41
Randall, Robert
See Silverberg, Robert
Ranger, Ken
See Creasey, John
Ransom, John Crowe 1888-1974 **CLC 2, 4, 5, 11, 24; DAM POET**
See also CA 5-8R; 49-52; CANR 6, 34; CDALBS; DLB 45, 63; MTCW 1, 2
Rao, Raja 1909- **CLC 25, 56; DAM NOV**
See also CA 73-76; CANR 51; MTCW 1, 2
Raphael, Frederic (Michael) 1931-**CLC 2, 14**
See also CA 1-4R; CANR 1; DLB 14
Ratcliffe, James P.
See Mencken, H(enry) L(ouis)
Rathbone, Julian 1935- **CLC 41**
See also CA 101; CANR 34, 73
Rattigan, Terence (Mervyn) 1911-1977**CLC 7; DAM DRAM**
See also CA 85-88; 73-76; CDBLB 1945-1960; DLB 13; MTCW 1, 2
Ratushinskaya, Irina 1954- **CLC 54**
See also CA 129; CANR 68
Raven, Simon (Arthur Noel) 1927- **CLC 14**
See also CA 81-84
Ravenna, Michael
See Welty, Eudora
Rawley, Callman 1903-
See Rakosi, Carl
See also CA 21-24R; CANR 12, 32
Rawlings, Marjorie Kinnan 1896-1953**T C L C 4**
See also AAYA 20; CA 104; 137; CANR 74; DLB 9, 22, 102; DLBD 17; JRDA; MAICYA; MTCW 2; SATA 100; YABC 1
Ray, Satyajit 1921-1992 **CLC 16, 76; DAM MULT**
See also CA 114; 137
Read, Herbert Edward 1893-1968 **CLC 4**
See also CA 85-88; 25-28R; DLB 20, 149
Read, Piers Paul 1941- **CLC 4, 10, 25**
See also CA 21-24R; CANR 38; DLB 14; SATA 21
Reade, Charles 1814-1884 **NCLC 2, 74**
See also DLB 21
Reade, Hamish
See Gray, Simon (James Holliday)
Reading, Peter 1946- **CLC 47**
See also CA 103; CANR 46; DLB 40

Reaney, James 1926- **CLC 13; DAC;DAM MST**
See also CA 41-44R; CAAS 15; CANR 42; DLB 68; SATA 43
Rebreanu, Liviu 1885-1944 **TCLC 28**
See also CA 165
Rechy, John (Francisco) 1934- **CLC 1, 7, 14, 18, 107; DAM MULT; HLC 2**
See also CA 5-8R; CAAS 4; CANR 6, 32, 64; DLB 122; DLBY 82; HW 1, 2; INT CANR-6
Redcam, Tom 1870-1933 **TCLC 25**
Reddin, Keith **CLC 67**
Redgrove, Peter (William) 1932- **CLC 6, 41**
See also CA 1-4R; CANR 3, 39, 77; DLB 40
Redmon, Anne **CLC 22**
See also Nightingale, Anne Redmon
See also DLBY 86
Reed, Eliot
See Ambler, Eric
Reed, Ishmael 1938-**CLC 2, 3, 5, 6, 13, 32, 60; BLC 3; DAM MULT**
See also BW 2, 3; CA 21-24R; CANR 25, 48, 74; DLB 2, 5, 33, 169; DLBD 8; MTCW 1, 2
Reed, John (Silas) 1887-1920 **TCLC 9**
See also CA 106
Reed, Lou **CLC 21**
See also Firbank, Louis
Reeve, Clara 1729-1807 **NCLC 19**
See also DLB 39
Reich, Wilhelm 1897-1957 **TCLC 57**
Reid, Christopher (John) 1949- **CLC 33**
See also CA 140; DLB 40
Reid, Desmond
See Moorcock, Michael (John)
Reid Banks, Lynne 1929-
See Banks, Lynne Reid
See also CA 1-4R; CANR 6, 22, 38; CLR 24; JRDA; MAICYA; SATA 22, 75
Reilly, William K.
See Creasey, John
Reiner, Max
See Caldwell, (Janet Miriam) Taylor (Holland)
Reis, Ricardo
See Pessoa, Fernando (Antonio Nogueira)
Remarque, Erich Maria 1898-1970 **CLC 21; DA; DAB; DAC; DAM MST, NOV**
See also AAYA 27; CA 77-80; 29-32R; DLB 56; MTCW 1, 2
Remington, Frederic 1861-1909 **TCLC 89**
See also CA 108; 169; DLB 12, 186, 188; SATA 41
Remizov, A.
See Remizov, Aleksei (Mikhailovich)
Remizov, A. M.
See Remizov, Aleksei (Mikhailovich)
Remizov, Aleksei (Mikhailovich) 1877-1957 **TCLC 27**
See also CA 125; 133
Renan, Joseph Ernest 1823-1892 **NCLC 26**
Renard, Jules 1864-1910 **TCLC 17**
See also CA 117
Renault, Mary **CLC 3, 11, 17**
See also Challans, Mary
See also DLBY 83; MTCW 2
Rendell, Ruth (Barbara) 1930- **CLC 28, 48; DAM POP**
See also Vine, Barbara
See also CA 109; CANR 32, 52, 74; DLB 87; INT CANR-32; MTCW 1, 2
Renoir, Jean 1894-1979 **CLC 20**
See also CA 129; 85-88

Resnais, Alain 1922- **CLC 16**
Reverdy, Pierre 1889-1960 **CLC 53**
See also CA 97-100; 89-92
Rexroth, Kenneth 1905-1982 **CLC 1, 2, 6, 11, 22, 49, 112; DAM POET; PC 20**
See also CA 5-8R; 107; CANR 14, 34, 63; CDALB 1941-1968; DLB 16, 48, 165, 212; DLBY 82; INT CANR-14; MTCW 1, 2
Reyes, Alfonso 1889-1959 **TCLC 33;HLCS 2**
See also CA 131; HW 1
Reyes y Basoalto, Ricardo Eliecer Neftali
See Neruda, Pablo
Reymont, Wladyslaw (Stanislaw) 1868(?)-1925 **TCLC 5**
See also CA 104
Reynolds, Jonathan 1942- **CLC 6, 38**
See also CA 65-68; CANR 28
Reynolds, Joshua 1723-1792 **LC 15**
See also DLB 104
Reynolds, Michael Shane 1937- **CLC 44**
See also CA 65-68; CANR 9
Reznikoff, Charles 1894-1976 **CLC 9**
See also CA 33-36; 61-64; CAP 2; DLB 28, 45
Rezzori (d'Arezzo), Gregorvon 1914-1998 **CLC 25**
See also CA 122; 136; 167
Rhine, Richard
See Silverstein, Alvin
Rhodes, Eugene Manlove 1869-1934**TCLC 53**
Rhodius, Apollonius c. 3rd cent.B.C.- **C M L C 28**
See also DLB 176
R'hoone
See Balzac, Honore de
Rhys, Jean 1890(?)-1979 **CLC 2, 4, 6, 14, 19, 51; DAM NOV; SSC 21**
See also CA 25-28R; 85-88; CANR 35, 62; CDBLB 1945-1960; DLB 36, 117, 162; MTCW 1, 2
Ribeiro, Darcy 1922-1997 **CLC 34**
See also CA 33-36R; 156
Ribeiro, Joao Ubaldo (Osorio Pimentel) 1941- **CLC 10, 67**
See also CA 81-84
Ribman, Ronald (Burt) 1932- **CLC 7**
See also CA 21-24R; CANR 46, 80
Ricci, Nino 1959- **CLC 70**
See also CA 137
Rice, Anne 1941- **CLC 41;DAM POP**
See also AAYA 9; BEST 89:2; CA 65-68; CANR 12, 36, 53, 74; MTCW 2
Rice, Elmer (Leopold) 1892-1967 **CLC 7, 49; DAM DRAM**
See also CA 21-22; 25-28R; CAP 2; DLB 4, 7; MTCW 1, 2
Rice, Tim(othy Miles Bindon) 1944- **CLC 21**
See also CA 103; CANR 46
Rich, Adrienne (Cecile) 1929-**CLC 3, 6, 7, 11, 18, 36, 73, 76; DAM POET; PC 5**
See also CA 9-12R; CANR 20, 53, 74; CDALBS; DLB 5, 67; MTCW 1, 2
Rich, Barbara
See Graves, Robert (von Ranke)
Rich, Robert
See Trumbo, Dalton
Richard, Keith **CLC 17**
See also Richards, Keith
Richards, David Adams 1950- **CLC 59; DAC**
See also CA 93-96; CANR 60; DLB 53
Richards, I(vor) A(rmstrong) 1893-1979**C L C 14, 24**
See also CA 41-44R; 89-92; CANR 34, 74; DLB 27; MTCW 2

See also CA 85-88; CANR 34; DLB 65; MTCW
1

Romero, Jose Ruben 1890-1952   TCLC 14
See also CA 114; 131; HW 1

Ronsard, Pierre de 1524-1585   LC 6; PC 11

Rooke, Leon 1934-   CLC 25, 34;DAM POP
See also CA 25-28R; CANR 23, 53

Roosevelt, Franklin Delano 1882-1945T C L C
93
See also CA 116; 173

Roosevelt,Theodore 1858-1919   TCLC 69
See also CA 115; 170; DLB 47, 186

Roper, William 1498-1578   LC 10

Roquelaure, A. N.
See Rice, Anne

Rosa, Joao Guimaraes 1908-1967   CLC 23;
HLCS 1
See also CA 89-92; DLB 113

Rose, Wendy 1948-CLC 85; DAM MULT; PC
13
See also CA 53-56; CANR 5, 51; DLB 175;
NNAL; SATA 12

Rosen, R. D.
See Rosen, Richard (Dean)

Rosen, Richard (Dean) 1949-   CLC 39
See also CA 77-80; CANR 62; INT CANR-30

Rosenberg, Isaac 1890-1918   TCLC 12
See also CA 107; DLB 20

Rosenblatt, Joe   CLC 15
See also Rosenblatt, Joseph

Rosenblatt, Joseph 1933-
See Rosenblatt, Joe
See also CA 89-92; INT 89-92

Rosenfeld, Samuel
See Tzara, Tristan

Rosenstock, Sami
See Tzara, Tristan

Rosenstock, Samuel
See Tzara, Tristan

Rosenthal, M(acha) L(ouis) 1917-1996 C L C
28
See also CA 1-4R; 152; CAAS 6; CANR 4, 51;
DLB 5; SATA 59

Ross, Barnaby
See Dannay, Frederic

Ross, Bernard L.
See Follett, Ken(neth Martin)

Ross, J. H.
See Lawrence, T(homas) E(dward)

Ross, John Hume
See Lawrence, T(homas) E(dward)

Ross, Martin
See Martin, Violet Florence
See also DLB 135

Ross, (James) Sinclair 1908-1996   CLC 13;
DAC; DAM MST; SSC 24
See also CA 73-76; CANR 81; DLB 88

Rossetti, Christina (Georgina) 1830-1894
NCLC 2, 50, 66; DA; DAB; DAC; DAM
MST, POET; PC 7; WLC
See also DLB 35, 163; MAICYA; SATA 20

Rossetti, Dante Gabriel 1828-1882 NCLC 4,
77; DA; DAB; DAC; DAM MST, POET;
WLC
See also CDBLB 1832-1890; DLB 35

Rossner, Judith (Perelman) 1935-CLC 6, 9, 29
See also AITN 2; BEST 90:3; CA 17-20R;
CANR 18, 51, 73; DLB 6; INT CANR-18;
MTCW 1, 2

Rostand, Edmond (Eugene Alexis) 1868-1918
TCLC 6, 37; DA; DAB; DAC; DAM
DRAM, MST; DC 10
See also CA 104; 126; DLB 192; MTCW 1

Roth, Henry 1906-1995   CLC 2, 6, 11, 104
See also CA 11-12; 149; CANR 38, 63; CAP 1;
DLB 28; MTCW 1, 2

Roth, Philip (Milton) 1933-CLC 1, 2, 3, 4, 6, 9,
15, 22, 31, 47, 66, 86, 119; DA; DAB; DAC;
DAM MST, NOV, POP; SSC 26; WLC
See also BEST 90:3; CA 1-4R; CANR 1, 22,
36, 55; CDALB 1968-1988; DLB 2, 28, 173;
DLBY 82; MTCW 1, 2

Rothenberg, Jerome 1931-   CLC 6, 57
See also CA 45-48; CANR 1; DLB 5, 193

Roumain, Jacques (Jean Baptiste) 1907-1944
TCLC 19; BLC 3; DAM MULT
See also BW 1; CA 117; 125

Rourke, Constance (Mayfield) 1885-1941
TCLC 12
See also CA 107; YABC 1

Rousseau, Jean-Baptiste 1671-1741   LC 9

Rousseau, Jean-Jacques 1712-1778LC 14, 36;
DA; DAB; DAC; DAM MST; WLC

Roussel, Raymond 1877-1933   TCLC 20
See also CA 117

Rovit, Earl (Herbert) 1927-   CLC 7
See also CA 5-8R; CANR 12

Rowe, Elizabeth Singer 1674-1737   LC 44
See also DLB 39, 95

Rowe, Nicholas 1674-1718   LC 8
See also DLB 84

Rowley, Ames Dorrance
See Lovecraft, H(oward) P(hillips)

Rowson, Susanna Haswell 1762(?)-1824
NCLC 5, 69
See also DLB 37, 200

Roy, Arundhati 1960(?)-   CLC 109
See also CA 163; DLBY 97

Roy, Gabrielle 1909-1983 CLC 10, 14; DAB;
DAC; DAM MST
See also CA 53-56; 110; CANR 5, 61; DLB 68;
MTCW 1; SATA 104

Royko, Mike 1932-1997   CLC 109
See also CA 89-92; 157; CANR 26

Rozewicz, Tadeusz 1921-   CLC 9, 23;DAM
POET
See also CA 108; CANR 36, 66; MTCW 1, 2

Ruark, Gibbons 1941-   CLC 3
See also CA 33-36R; CAAS 23; CANR 14, 31,
57; DLB 120

Rubens, Bernice (Ruth) 1923-   CLC 19, 31
See also CA 25-28R; CANR 33, 65; DLB 14,
207; MTCW 1

Rubin, Harold
See Robbins, Harold

Rudkin, (James) David 1936-   CLC 14
See also CA 89-92; DLB 13

Rudnik, Raphael 1933-   CLC 7
See also CA 29-32R

Ruffian, M.
See Hasek, Jaroslav (Matej Frantisek)

Ruiz, Jose Martinez   CLC 11
See also Martinez Ruiz, Jose

Rukeyser, Muriel 1913-1980CLC 6, 10, 15, 27;
DAM POET; PC 12
See also CA 5-8R; 93-96; CANR 26, 60; DLB
48; MTCW 1, 2; SATA-Obit 22

Rule, Jane (Vance) 1931-   CLC 27
See also CA 25-28R; CAAS 18; CANR 12; DLB
60

Rulfo, Juan 1918-1986   CLC 8, 80; DAM
MULT; HLC 2; SSC 25
See also CA 85-88; 118; CANR 26; DLB 113;
HW 1, 2; MTCW 1, 2

Rumi, Jalal al-Din 1297-1373   CMLC 20

Runeberg, Johan 1804-1877   NCLC 41

Runyon, (Alfred) Damon 1884(?)-1946T C L C
10
See also CA 107; 165; DLB 11, 86, 171; MTCW
2

Rush, Norman 1933-   CLC 44
See also CA 121; 126; INT 126

Rushdie, (Ahmed) Salman 1947- CLC 23, 31,
55, 100; DAB; DAC; DAM MST, NOV,
POP; WLCS
See also BEST 89:3; CA 108; 111; CANR 33,
56; DLB 194; INT 111; MTCW 1, 2

Rushforth, Peter (Scott) 1945-   CLC 19
See also CA 101

Ruskin, John 1819-1900   TCLC 63
See also CA 114; 129; CDBLB 1832-1890;
DLB 55, 163, 190; SATA 24

Russ, Joanna 1937-   CLC 15
See also CANR 11, 31, 65; DLB 8; MTCW 1

Russell, George William 1867-1935
See Baker, Jean H.
See also CA 104; 153; CDBLB 1890-1914;
DAM POET

Russell, (Henry) Ken(neth Alfred) 1927-C L C
16
See also CA 105

Russell, William Martin 1947-   CLC 60
See also CA 164

Rutherford, Mark   TCLC 25
See White, William Hale
See also DLB 18

Ruyslinck, Ward 1929-   CLC 14
See also Belser, Reimond Karel Maria de

Ryan, Cornelius (John) 1920-1974   CLC 7
See also CA 69-72; 53-56; CANR 38

Ryan, Michael 1946-   CLC 65
See also CA 49-52; DLBY 82

Ryan, Tim
See Dent, Lester

Rybakov, Anatoli (Naumovich) 1911-1998
CLC 23, 53
See also CA 126; 135; 172; SATA 79; SATA-
Obit 108

Ryder, Jonathan
See Ludlum, Robert

Ryga, George 1932-1987CLC 14; DAC; DAM
MST
See also CA 101; 124; CANR 43; DLB 60

S. H.
See Hartmann, Sadakichi

S. S.
See Sassoon, Siegfried (Lorraine)

Saba, Umberto 1883-1957   TCLC 33
See also CA 144; CANR 79; DLB 114

Sabatini, Rafael 1875-1950   TCLC 47
See also CA 162

Sabato, Ernesto (R.) 1911-CLC 10, 23; DAM
MULT; HLC 2
See also CA 97-100; CANR 32, 65; DLB 145;
HW 1, 2; MTCW 1, 2

Sa-Carniero, Mario de 1890-1916 TCLC 83

Sacastru, Martin
See Bioy Casares, Adolfo

Sacastru, Martin
See Bioy Casares, Adolfo

Sacher-Masoch, Leopold von 1836(?)-1895
NCLC 31

Sachs, Marilyn (Stickle) 1927-   CLC 35
See also AAYA 2; CA 17-20R; CANR 13, 47;
CLR 2; JRDA; MAICYA; SAAS 2; SATA 3,
68

Sachs, Nelly 1891-1970   CLC 14, 98
See also CA 17-18; 25-28R; CAP 2; MTCW 2

Sackler, Howard (Oliver) 1929-1982 CLC 14

See also CA 61-64; 108; CANR 30; DLB 7

Sacks, Oliver (Wolf) 1933- CLC 67
See also CA 53-56; CANR 28, 50, 76; INT CANR-28; MTCW 1, 2

Sadakichi
See Hartmann, Sadakichi

Sade, Donatien Alphonse Francois, Comte de 1740-1814 NCLC 47

Sadoff, Ira 1945- CLC 9
See also CA 53-56; CANR 5, 21; DLB 120

Saetone
See Camus, Albert

Safire, William 1929- CLC 10
See also CA 17-20R; CANR 31, 54

Sagan, Carl (Edward) 1934-1996CLC 30, 112
See also AAYA 2; CA 25-28R; 155; CANR 11, 36, 74; MTCW 1, 2; SATA 58; SATA-Obit 94

Sagan, Francoise CLC 3, 6, 9, 17, 36
See also Quoirez, Francoise
See also DLB 83; MTCW 2

Sahgal, Nayantara (Pandit) 1927- CLC 41
See also CA 9-12R; CANR 11

Saint, H(arry) F. 1941- CLC 50
See also CA 127

St. Aubin de Teran, Lisa 1953-
See Teran, Lisa St. Aubin de
See also CA 118; 126; INT 126

Saint Birgitta of Sweden c. 1303-1373CMLC 24

Sainte-Beuve, Charles Augustin 1804-1869 NCLC 5

Saint-Exupery, Antoine (Jean Baptiste Marie Roger) de 1900-1944 TCLC 2, 56; DAM NOV;WLC
See also CA 108; 132; CLR 10; DLB 72; MAICYA; MTCW 1, 2; SATA 20

St. John, David
See Hunt, E(verette) Howard, (Jr.)

Saint-John Perse
See Leger, (Marie-Rene Auguste) Alexis Saint-Leger

Saintsbury, George (Edward Bateman) 1845-1933 TCLC 31
See also CA 160; DLB 57, 149

Sait Faik TCLC 23
See also Abasiyanik, Sait Faik

Saki TCLC 3; SSC 12
See also Munro, H(ector) H(ugh)
See also MTCW 2

Sala, George Augustus NCLC 46

Salama, Hannu 1936- CLC 18

Salamanca, J(ack) R(ichard) 1922-CLC 4, 15
See also CA 25-28R

Salas, Floyd Francis 1931-
See also CA 119; CAAS 27; CANR 44, 75; DAM MULT; DLB 82; HLC 2; HW 1, 2; MTCW 2

Sale, J. Kirkpatrick
See Sale, Kirkpatrick

Sale, Kirkpatrick 1937- CLC 68
See also CA 13-16R; CANR 10

Salinas, Luis Omar 1937- CLC 90; DAM MULT; HLC 2
See also CA 131; CANR 81; DLB 82; HW 1, 2

Salinas (y Serrano), Pedro 1891(?)-1951 TCLC 17
See also CA 117; DLB 134

Salinger, J(erome) D(avid) 1919-CLC 1, 3, 8, 12, 55, 56; DA; DAB; DAC; DAM MST, NOV, POP; SSC 2, 28; WLC
See also AAYA 2; CA 5-8R; CANR 39; CDALB 1941-1968; CLR 18; DLB 2, 102, 173;

MAICYA; MTCW 1, 2; SATA 67

Salisbury, John
See Caute, (John) David

Salter, James 1925- CLC 7, 52, 59
See also CA 73-76; DLB 130

Saltus, Edgar (Everton) 1855-1921 TCLC 8
See also CA 105; DLB 202

Saltykov, Mikhail Evgrafovich 1826-1889 NCLC 16

Samarakis, Antonis 1919- CLC 5
See also CA 25-28R; CAAS 16; CANR 36

Sanchez, Florencio 1875-1910 TCLC 37
See also CA 153; HW 1

Sanchez, Luis Rafael 1936- CLC 23
See also CA 128; DLB 145; HW 1

Sanchez, Sonia 1934- CLC 5, 116; BLC 3; DAM MULT; PC 9
See also BW 2, 3; CA 33-36R; CANR 24, 49, 74; CLR 18; DLB 41; DLBD 8;MAICYA; MTCW 1, 2; SATA 22

Sand, George 1804-1876NCLC 2, 42, 57; DA; DAB; DAC; DAM MST, NOV; WLC
See also DLB 119, 192

Sandburg, Carl (August) 1878-1967CLC 1, 4, 10, 15, 35; DA; DAB; DAC; DAM MST, POET; PC 2; WLC
See also AAYA 24; CA 5-8R; 25-28R; CANR 35; CDALB 1865-1917; DLB 17, 54; MAICYA; MTCW 1, 2; SATA 8

Sandburg, Charles
See Sandburg, Carl (August)

Sandburg, Charles A.
See Sandburg, Carl (August)

Sanders, (James) Ed(ward) 1939- CLC 53; DAM POET
See also CA 13-16R; CAAS 21; CANR 13, 44, 78; DLB 16

Sanders, Lawrence 1920-1998CLC 41; DAM POP
See also BEST 89:4; CA 81-84; 165; CANR 33, 62; MTCW 1

Sanders, Noah
See Blount, Roy (Alton), Jr.

Sanders, Winston P.
See Anderson, Poul (William)

Sandoz, Mari(e Susette) 1896-1966 CLC 28
See also CA 1-4R; 25-28R; CANR 17, 64; DLB 9, 212; MTCW 1, 2; SATA 5

Saner, Reg(inald Anthony) 1931- CLC 9
See also CA 65-68

Sankara 788-820 CMLC 32

Sannazaro, Jacopo 1456(?)-1530 LC 8

Sansom, William 1912-1976 CLC 2, 6; DAM NOV; SSC 21
See also CA 5-8R; 65-68; CANR 42; DLB 139; MTCW 1

Santayana, George 1863-1952 TCLC 40
See also CA 115; DLB 54, 71; DLBD 13

Santiago, Danny CLC 33
See also James, Daniel (Lewis)
See also DLB 122

Santmyer, Helen Hoover 1895-1986 CLC 33
See also CA 1-4R; 118; CANR 15, 33; DLBY 84; MTCW 1

Santoka, Taneda 1882-1940 TCLC 72

Santos, Bienvenido N(uqui) 1911-1996 CLC 22; DAM MULT
See also CA 101; 151; CANR 19, 46

Sapper TCLC 44
See also McNeile, Herman Cyril

Sapphire
See Sapphire, Brenda

Sapphire, Brenda 1950- CLC 99

Sappho fl. 6th cent. B.C.- CMLC 3; DAM POET; PC 5
See also DLB 176

Saramago, Jose 1922- CLC 119;HLCS 1
See also CA 153

Sarduy, Severo 1937-1993CLC 6, 97; HLCS 1
See also CA 89-92; 142; CANR 58, 81; DLB 113; HW 1, 2

Sargeson, Frank 1903-1982 CLC 31
See also CA 25-28R; 106; CANR 38, 79

Sarmiento, Domingo Faustino 1811-1888
See also HLCS 2

Sarmiento, Felix Ruben Garcia
See Dario, Ruben

Saro-Wiwa, Ken(ule Beeson) 1941-1995 C L C 114
See also BW 2; CA 142; 150; CANR 60; DLB 157

Saroyan, William 1908-1981CLC 1, 8, 10, 29, 34, 56; DA; DAB; DAC; DAM DRAM, MST, NOV; SSC 21; WLC
See also CA 5-8R; 103; CANR 30; CDALBS; DLB 7, 9, 86; DLBY 81; MTCW 1, 2; SATA 23; SATA-Obit 24

Sarraute, Nathalie 1900-CLC 1, 2, 4, 8, 10, 31, 80
See also CA 9-12R; CANR 23, 66; DLB 83; MTCW 1, 2

Sarton, (Eleanor) May 1912-1995 CLC 4, 14, 49, 91; DAM POET
See also CA 1-4R; 149; CANR 1, 34, 55; DLB 48; DLBY 81; INT CANR-34; MTCW 1, 2; SATA 36; SATA-Obit 86

Sartre, Jean-Paul 1905-1980CLC 1, 4, 7, 9, 13, 18, 24, 44, 50, 52; DA; DAB; DAC; DAM DRAM, MST, NOV; DC 3; SSC 32; WLC
See also CA 9-12R; 97-100; CANR 21; DLB 72; MTCW 1, 2

Sassoon, Siegfried (Lorraine) 1886-1967CLC 36; DAB; DAM MST, NOV, POET; PC 12
See also CA 104; 25-28R; CANR 36; DLB 20, 191; DLBD 18; MTCW 1, 2

Satterfield, Charles
See Pohl, Frederik

Saul, John (W. III) 1942-CLC 46; DAM NOV, POP
See also AAYA 10; BEST 90:4; CA 81-84; CANR 16, 40, 81; SATA 98

Saunders, Caleb
See Heinlein, Robert A(nson)

Saura (Atares), Carlos 1932- CLC 20
See also CA 114; 131; CANR 79; HW 1

Sauser-Hall, Frederic 1887-1961 CLC 18
See also Cendrars, Blaise
See also CA 102; 93-96; CANR 36, 62; MTCW 1

Saussure, Ferdinand de 1857-1913 TCLC 49

Savage, Catharine
See Brosman, Catharine Savage

Savage, Thomas 1915- CLC 40
See also CA 126; 132; CAAS 15; INT 132

Savan, Glenn 19(?)- CLC 50

Sayers, Dorothy L(eigh) 1893-1957 TCLC 2, 15; DAM POP
See also CA 104; 119; CANR 60; CDBLB 1914-1945; DLB 10, 36, 77, 100; MTCW 1, 2

Sayers, Valerie 1952- CLC 50, 122
See also CA 134; CANR 61

Sayles, John (Thomas) 1950- CLC 7, 10, 14
See also CA 57-60; CANR 41; DLB 44

Scammell, Michael 1935- CLC 34
See also CA 156

Scannell, Vernon 1922- CLC 49

See also CA 5-8R; CANR 8, 24, 57; DLB 27;
SATA 59
Scarlett, Susan
See Streatfeild, (Mary) Noel
Scarron
See Mikszath, Kalman
Schaeffer, Susan Fromberg 1941- **CLC 6, 11,
22**
See also CA 49-52; CANR 18, 65; DLB 28;
MTCW 1, 2; SATA 22
Schary, Jill
See Robinson, Jill
Schell, Jonathan 1943-   **CLC 35**
See also CA 73-76; CANR 12
Schelling, Friedrich Wilhelm Josephvon 1775-
1854   **NCLC 30**
See also DLB 90
Schendel, Arthur van 1874-1946   **TCLC 56**
Scherer, Jean-Marie Maurice 1920-
See Rohmer, Eric
See also CA 110
Schevill, James (Erwin) 1920-   **CLC 7**
See also CA 5-8R; CAAS 12
Schiller, Friedrich 1759-1805   **NCLC 39, 69;
DAM DRAM**
See also DLB 94
Schisgal, Murray (Joseph) 1926-   **CLC 6**
See also CA 21-24R; CANR 48
Schlee, Ann 1934-   **CLC 35**
See also CA 101; CANR 29; SATA 44; SATA-
Brief 36
Schlegel, August Wilhelmvon 1767-1845
NCLC 15
See also DLB 94
Schlegel, Friedrich 1772-1829   **NCLC 45**
See also DLB 90
Schlegel, Johann Elias (von) 1719(?)-1749**L C
5**
Schlesinger, Arthur M(eier), Jr. 1917-**CLC 84**
See also AITN 1; CA 1-4R; CANR 1, 28, 58;
DLB 17; INT CANR-28; MTCW 1, 2; SATA
61
Schmidt, Arno (Otto) 1914-1979   **CLC 56**
See also CA 128; 109; DLB 69
Schmitz, Aron Hector 1861-1928
See Svevo, Italo
See also CA 104; 122; MTCW 1
Schnackenberg, Gjertrud 1953-   **CLC 40**
See also CA 116; DLB 120
Schneider, Leonard Alfred 1925-1966
See Bruce, Lenny
See also CA 89-92
Schnitzler, Arthur 1862-1931**TCLC 4; SSC 15**
See also CA 104; DLB 81, 118
Schoenberg, Arnold 1874-1951   **TCLC 75**
See also CA 109
Schonberg, Arnold
See Schoenberg, Arnold
Schopenhauer, Arthur 1788-1860   **NCLC 51**
See also DLB 90
Schor, Sandra (M.) 1932(?)-1990   **CLC 65**
See also CA 132
Schorer, Mark 1908-1977   **CLC 9**
See also CA 5-8R; 73-76; CANR 7; DLB 103
Schrader, Paul (Joseph) 1946-   **CLC 26**
See also CA 37-40R; CANR 41; DLB 44
Schreiner, Olive (Emilie Albertina) 1855-1920
TCLC 9
See also CA 105; 154; DLB 18, 156, 190
Schulberg, Budd (Wilson) 1914-   **CLC 7, 48**
See also CA 25-28R; CANR 19; DLB 6, 26,
28; DLBY 81
Schulz, Bruno 1892-1942**TCLC 5, 51; SSC 13**

See also CA 115; 123; MTCW 2
Schulz, Charles M(onroe) 1922-   **CLC 12**
See also CA 9-12R; CANR 6; INT CANR-6;
SATA 10
Schumacher, E(rnst) F(riedrich) 1911-1977
CLC 80
See also CA 81-84; 73-76; CANR 34
Schuyler, James Marcus 1923-1991**CLC 5, 23;
DAM POET**
See also CA 101; 134; DLB 5, 169; INT 101
Schwartz, Delmore (David) 1913-1966**CLC 2,
4, 10, 45, 87; PC 8**
See also CA 17-18; 25-28R; CANR 35; CAP 2;
DLB 28, 48; MTCW 1, 2
Schwartz, Ernst
See Ozu, Yasujiro
Schwartz, John Burnham 1965-   **CLC 59**
See also CA 132
Schwartz, Lynne Sharon 1939-   **CLC 31**
See also CA 103; CANR 44; MTCW 2
Schwartz, Muriel A.
See Eliot, T(homas) S(tearns)
Schwarz-Bart, Andre 1928-   **CLC 2, 4**
See also CA 89-92
Schwarz-Bart, Simone 1938-   **CLC 7;BLCS**
See also BW 2; CA 97-100
**Schwitters, Kurt (Hermann Edward Karl
Julius)** 1887-1948   **TCLC 95**
See also CA 158
Schwob, Marcel (Mayer Andre) 1867-1905
TCLC 20
See also CA 117; 168; DLB 123
Sciascia, Leonardo 1921-1989   **CLC 8, 9, 41**
See also CA 85-88; 130; CANR 35; DLB 177;
MTCW 1
Scoppettone, Sandra 1936-   **CLC 26**
See also AAYA 11; CA 5-8R; CANR 41, 73;
SATA 9, 92
Scorsese, Martin 1942-   **CLC 20, 89**
See also CA 110; 114; CANR 46
Scotland, Jay
See Jakes, John (William)
Scott, Duncan Campbell 1862-1947 **TCLC 6;
DAC**
See also CA 104; 153; DLB 92
Scott, Evelyn 1893-1963   **CLC 43**
See also CA 104; 112; CANR 64; DLB 9, 48
Scott, F(rancis) R(eginald) 1899-1985**CLC 22**
See also CA 101; 114; DLB 88; INT 101
Scott, Frank
See Scott, F(rancis) R(eginald)
Scott, Joanna 1960-   **CLC 50**
See also CA 126; CANR 53
Scott, Paul (Mark) 1920-1978   **CLC 9, 60**
See also CA 81-84; 77-80; CANR 33; DLB 14,
207; MTCW 1
Scott, Sarah 1723-1795   **LC 44**
See also DLB 39
Scott, Walter 1771-1832   **NCLC 15, 69; DA;
DAB; DAC; DAM MST, NOV, POET; PC
13; SSC 32; WLC**
See also AAYA 22; CDBLB 1789-1832; DLB
93, 107, 116, 144, 159; YABC 2
Scribe, (Augustin) Eugene 1791-1861 **N C L C
16; DAM DRAM; DC 5**
See also DLB 192
Scrum, R.
See Crumb, R(obert)
Scudery, Madeleine de 1607-1701   **LC 2**
Scum
See Crumb, R(obert)
Scumbag, Little Bobby
See Crumb, R(obert)

Seabrook, John
See Hubbard, L(afayette) Ron(ald)
Sealy, I. Allan 1951-   **CLC 55**
Search, Alexander
See Pessoa, Fernando (Antonio Nogueira)
Sebastian, Lee
See Silverberg, Robert
Sebastian Owl
See Thompson, Hunter S(tockton)
Sebestyen, Ouida 1924-   **CLC 30**
See also AAYA 8; CA 107; CANR 40; CLR 17;
JRDA; MAICYA; SAAS 10; SATA 39
Secundus, H. Scriblerus
See Fielding, Henry
Sedges, John
See Buck, Pearl S(ydenstricker)
Sedgwick, Catharine Maria 1789-1867**N C L C
19**
See also DLB 1, 74
Seelye, John (Douglas) 1931-   **CLC 7**
See also CA 97-100; CANR 70; INT 97-100
Seferiades, Giorgos Stylianou 1900-1971
See Seferis, George
See also CA 5-8R; 33-36R; CANR 5, 36;
MTCW 1
Seferis, George **CLC 5, 11**
See also Seferiades, Giorgos Stylianou
Segal, Erich (Wolf) 1937-   **CLC 3, 10; DAM
POP**
See also BEST 89:1; CA 25-28R; CANR 20,
36, 65; DLBY 86; INT CANR-20; MTCW 1
Seger, Bob 1945-   **CLC 35**
Seghers, Anna **CLC 7**
See also Radvanyi, Netty
See also DLB 69
Seidel, Frederick (Lewis) 1936-   **CLC 18**
See also CA 13-16R; CANR 8; DLBY 84
Seifert, Jaroslav 1901-1986   **CLC 34, 44, 93**
See also CA 127; MTCW 1, 2
Sei Shonagon c. 966-1017(?)   **CMLC 6**
Sejour, Victor 1817-1874   **DC 10**
See also DLB 50
Sejour Marcou et Ferrand, Juan Victor
See Sejour, Victor
Selby, Hubert, Jr. 1928-**CLC 1, 2, 4, 8; SSC 20**
See also CA 13-16R; CANR 33; DLB 2
Selzer, Richard 1928-   **CLC 74**
See also CA 65-68; CANR 14
Sembene, Ousmane
See Ousmane, Sembene
Senancour, Etienne Pivert de 1770-1846
NCLC 16
See also DLB 119
Sender, Ramon (Jose) 1902-1982**CLC 8; DAM
MULT; HLC 2**
See also CA 5-8R; 105; CANR 8; HW 1;
MTCW 1
Seneca, Lucius Annaeus c. 1-c. 65 **CMLC 6;
DAM DRAM; DC 5**
See also DLB 211
Senghor, Leopold Sedar 1906- **CLC 54; BLC
3; DAM MULT, POET; PC 25**
See also BW 2; CA 116; 125; CANR 47, 74;
MTCW 1, 2
Senna, Danzy 1970-   **CLC 119**
See also CA 169
Serling, (Edward) Rod(man) 1924-1975 **C L C
30**
See also AAYA 14; AITN 1; CA 162; 57-60;
DLB 26
Serna, Ramon Gomez de la
See Gomez de la Serna, Ramon
Serpieres

See Stael-Holstein, Anne Louise Germaine
Necker Baronn
See also DLB 119

**Stael-Holstein, Anne Louise Germaine Necker
Baronn** 1766-1817 **NCLC 3**
See also Stael, Germaine de
See also DLB 192

Stafford, Jean 1915-1979 **CLC 4, 7, 19, 68; SSC
26**
See also CA 1-4R; 85-88; CANR 3, 65; DLB 2,
173; MTCW 1, 2; SATA-Obit 22

Stafford, William (Edgar) 1914-1993 **CLC 4,
7, 29; DAM POET**
See also CA 5-8R; 142; CAAS 3; CANR 5, 22;
DLB 5, 206; INT CANR-22

Stagnelius, Eric Johan 1793-1823 **NCLC 61**

Staines, Trevor
See Brunner, John (Kilian Houston)

Stairs, Gordon
See Austin, Mary (Hunter)

Stairs, Gordon
See Austin, Mary (Hunter)

Stalin, Joseph 1879-1953 **TCLC 92**

Stannard, Martin 1947- **CLC 44**
See also CA 142; DLB 155

Stanton, Elizabeth Cady 1815-1902 **TCLC 73**
See also CA 171; DLB 79

Stanton, Maura 1946- **CLC 9**
See also CA 89-92; CANR 15; DLB 120

Stanton, Schuyler
See Baum, L(yman) Frank

Stapledon, (William) Olaf 1886-1950 **TCLC
22**
See also CA 111; 162; DLB 15

Starbuck, George (Edwin) 1931-1996 **CLC 53;
DAM POET**
See also CA 21-24R; 153; CANR 23

Stark, Richard
See Westlake, Donald E(dwin)

Staunton, Schuyler
See Baum, L(yman) Frank

Stead, Christina (Ellen) 1902-1983 **CLC 2, 5,
8, 32, 80**
See also CA 13-16R; 109; CANR 33, 40;
MTCW 1, 2

Stead, William Thomas 1849-1912 **TCLC 48**
See also CA 167

Steele, Richard 1672-1729 **LC 18**
See also CDBLB 1660-1789; DLB 84, 101

Steele, Timothy (Reid) 1948- **CLC 45**
See also CA 93-96; CANR 16, 50; DLB 120

Steffens, (Joseph) Lincoln 1866-1936 **TCLC
20**
See also CA 117

Stegner, Wallace (Earle) 1909-1993 **CLC 9, 49,
81; DAM NOV; SSC 27**
See also AITN 1; BEST 90:3; CA 1-4R; 141;
CAAS 9; CANR 1, 21, 46; DLB 9, 206;
DLBY 93; MTCW 1, 2

Stein, Gertrude 1874-1946 **TCLC 1, 6, 28, 48;
DA; DAB; DAC; DAM MST, NOV, POET;
PC 18; WLC**
See also CA 104; 132; CDALB 1917-1929;
DLB 4, 54, 86; DLBD 15; MTCW 1, 2

Steinbeck, John (Ernst) 1902-1968 **CLC 1, 5, 9,
13, 21, 34, 45, 75; DA; DAB; DAC; DAM
DRAM, MST, NOV; SSC 11; WLC**
See also AAYA 12; CA 1-4R; 25-28R; CANR
1, 35; CDALB 1929-1941; DLB 7, 9, 212;
DLBD 2; MTCW 1, 2; SATA 9

Steinem, Gloria 1934- **CLC 63**
See also CA 53-56; CANR 28, 51; MTCW 1, 2

Steiner, George 1929- **CLC 24; DAM NOV**

See also CA 73-76; CANR 31, 67; DLB 67;
MTCW 1, 2; SATA 62

Steiner, K. Leslie
See Delany, Samuel R(ay, Jr.)

Steiner, Rudolf 1861-1925 **TCLC 13**
See also CA 107

Stendhal 1783-1842 **NCLC 23, 46; DA; DAB;
DAC; DAM MST, NOV; SSC 27; WLC**
See also DLB 119

Stephen, Adeline Virginia
See Woolf, (Adeline) Virginia

Stephen, Sir Leslie 1832-1904 **TCLC 23**
See also CA 123; DLB 57, 144, 190

Stephen, Sir Leslie
See Stephen, Sir Leslie

Stephen, Virginia
See Woolf, (Adeline) Virginia

Stephens, James 1882(?)-1950 **TCLC 4**
See also CA 104; DLB 19, 153, 162

Stephens, Reed
See Donaldson, Stephen R.

Steptoe, Lydia
See Barnes, Djuna

Sterchi, Beat 1949- **CLC 65**

Sterling, Brett
See Bradbury, Ray (Douglas); Hamilton,
Edmond

Sterling, Bruce 1954- **CLC 72**
See also CA 119; CANR 44

Sterling, George 1869-1926 **TCLC 20**
See also CA 117; 165; DLB 54

Stern, Gerald 1925- **CLC 40, 100**
See also CA 81-84; CANR 28; DLB 105

Stern, Richard (Gustave) 1928- **CLC 4, 39**
See also CA 1-4R; CANR 1, 25, 52; DLBY 87;
INT CANR-25

Sternberg, Josef von 1894-1969 **CLC 20**
See also CA 81-84

Sterne, Laurence 1713-1768 **LC 2, 48; DA;
DAB; DAC; DAM MST, NOV; WLC**
See also CDBLB 1660-1789; DLB 39

Sternheim, (William Adolf) Carl 1878-1942
TCLC 8
See also CA 105; DLB 56, 118

Stevens, Mark 1951- **CLC 34**
See also CA 122

Stevens, Wallace 1879-1955 **TCLC 3, 12, 45;
DA; DAB; DAC; DAM MST, POET; PC
6; WLC**
See also CA 104; 124; CDALB 1929-1941;
DLB 54; MTCW 1, 2

Stevenson, Anne (Katharine) 1933- **CLC 7, 33**
See also CA 17-20R; CAAS 9; CANR 9, 33;
DLB 40; MTCW 1

Stevenson, Robert Louis (Balfour) 1850-1894
**NCLC 5, 14, 63; DA; DAB; DAC; DAM
MST, NOV; SSC 11; WLC**
See also AAYA 24; CDBLB 1890-1914; CLR
10, 11; DLB 18, 57, 141, 156, 174; DLBD
13; JRDA; MAICYA; SATA 100; YABC 2

Stewart, J(ohn) I(nnes) M(ackintosh) 1906-
1994 **CLC 7, 14, 32**
See also CA 85-88; 147; CAAS 3; CANR 47;
MTCW 1, 2

Stewart, Mary (Florence Elinor) 1916- **CLC 7,
35, 117; DAB**
See also AAYA 29; CA 1-4R; CANR 1, 59;
SATA 12

Stewart, Mary Rainbow
See Stewart, Mary (Florence Elinor)

Stifle, June
See Campbell, Maria

Stifter, Adalbert 1805-1868 **NCLC 41; SSC 28**

See also DLB 133

Still, James 1906- **CLC 49**
See also CA 65-68; CAAS 17; CANR 10, 26;
DLB 9; SATA 29

Sting 1951-
See Sumner, Gordon Matthew
See also CA 167

Stirling, Arthur
See Sinclair, Upton (Beall)

Stitt, Milan 1941- **CLC 29**
See also CA 69-72

Stockton, Francis Richard 1834-1902
See Stockton, Frank R.
See also CA 108; 137; MAICYA; SATA 44

Stockton, Frank R. **TCLC 47**
See also Stockton, Francis Richard
See also DLB 42, 74; DLBD 13; SATA-Brief
32

Stoddard, Charles
See Kuttner, Henry

Stoker, Abraham 1847-1912
See Stoker, Bram
See also CA 105; 150; DA; DAC; DAM MST,
NOV; SATA 29

Stoker, Bram 1847-1912 **TCLC 8; DAB; WLC**
See also Stoker, Abraham
See also AAYA 23; CDBLB 1890-1914; DLB
36, 70, 178

Stolz, Mary (Slattery) 1920- **CLC 12**
See also AAYA 8; AITN 1; CA 5-8R; CANR
13, 41; JRDA; MAICYA; SAAS 3; SATA 10,
71

Stone, Irving 1903-1989 **CLC 7; DAM POP**
See also AITN 1; CA 1-4R; 129; CAAS 3;
CANR 1, 23; INT CANR-23; MTCW 1, 2;
SATA 3; SATA-Obit 64

Stone, Oliver (William) 1946- **CLC 73**
See also AAYA 15; CA 110; CANR 55

Stone, Robert (Anthony) 1937- **CLC 5, 23, 42**
See also CA 85-88; CANR 23, 66; DLB 152;
INT CANR-23; MTCW 1

Stone, Zachary
See Follett, Ken(neth Martin)

Stoppard, Tom 1937- **CLC 1, 3, 4, 5, 8, 15, 29,
34, 63, 91; DA; DAB; DAC; DAM DRAM,
MST; DC 6; WLC**
See also CA 81-84; CANR 39, 67; CDBLB
1960 to Present; DLB 13; DLBY 85; MTCW
1, 2

Storey, David (Malcolm) 1933- **CLC 2, 4, 5, 8;
DAM DRAM**
See also CA 81-84; CANR 36; DLB 13, 14, 207;
MTCW 1

Storm, Hyemeyohsts 1935- **CLC 3; DAM
MULT**
See also CA 81-84; CANR 45; NNAL

Storm, Theodor 1817-1888 **SSC 27**

Storm, (Hans) Theodor (Woldsen) 1817-1888
NCLC 1; SSC 27
See also DLB 129

Storni, Alfonsina 1892-1938 **TCLC 5; DAM
MULT; HLC 2**
See also CA 104; 131; HW 1

Stoughton, William 1631-1701 **LC 38**
See also DLB 24

Stout, Rex (Todhunter) 1886-1975 **CLC 3**
See also AITN 2; CA 61-64; CANR 71

Stow, (Julian) Randolph 1935- **CLC 23, 48**
See also CA 13-16R; CANR 33; MTCW 1

Stowe, Harriet (Elizabeth) Beecher 1811-1896
**NCLC 3, 50; DA; DAB; DAC; DAM MST,
NOV; WLC**
See also CDALB 1865-1917; DLB 1, 12, 42,

Tutuola, Amos 1920-1997**CLC 5, 14, 29; BLC 3; DAM MULT**
See also BW 2, 3; CA 9-12R; 159; CANR 27, 66; DLB 125; MTCW 1, 2

Twain, Mark TCLC 6, 12, 19, 36, 48, 59; SSC 34; WLC
See also Clemens, Samuel Langhorne
See also AAYA 20; CLR 58; DLB 11, 12, 23, 64, 74

Tyler, Anne 1941- **CLC 7, 11, 18, 28, 44, 59, 103; DAM NOV, POP**
See also AAYA 18; BEST 89:1; CA 9-12R; CANR 11, 33, 53; CDALBS; DLB 6, 143; DLBY 82; MTCW 1, 2; SATA 7, 90

Tyler, Royall 1757-1826 **NCLC 3**
See also DLB 37

Tynan, Katharine 1861-1931 **TCLC 3**
See also CA 104; 167; DLB 153

Tyutchev, Fyodor 1803-1873 **NCLC 34**

Tzara, Tristan 1896-1963 **CLC 47; DAM POET; PC 27**
See also CA 153; 89-92; MTCW 2

Uhry, Alfred 1936- **CLC 55; DAM DRAM, POP**
See also CA 127; 133; INT 133

Ulf, Haerved
See Strindberg, (Johan) August

Ulf, Harved
See Strindberg, (Johan) August

Ulibarri, Sabine R(eyes) 1919-**CLC 83; DAM MULT; HLCS 2**
See also CA 131; CANR 81; DLB 82; HW 1, 2

Unamuno (y Jugo), Miguel de 1864-1936 **TCLC 2, 9; DAM MULT, NOV; HLC 2; SSC 11**
See also CA 104; 131; CANR 81; DLB 108; HW 1, 2; MTCW 1, 2

Undercliffe, Errol
See Campbell, (John) Ramsey

Underwood, Miles
See Glassco, John

Undset, Sigrid 1882-1949**TCLC 3; DA; DAB; DAC; DAM MST, NOV; WLC**
See also CA 104; 129; MTCW 1, 2

Ungaretti, Giuseppe 1888-1970**CLC 7, 11, 15**
See also CA 19-20; 25-28R; CAP 2; DLB 114

Unger, Douglas 1952- **CLC 34**
See also CA 130

Unsworth, Barry (Forster) 1930- **CLC 76**
See also CA 25-28R; CANR 30, 54; DLB 194

Updike, John (Hoyer) 1932-**CLC 1, 2, 3, 5, 7, 9, 13, 15, 23, 34, 43, 70; DA; DAB; DAC; DAM MST, NOV, POET, POP; SSC 13, 27; WLC**
See also CA 1-4R; CABS 1; CANR 4, 33, 51; CDALB 1968-1988; DLB 2, 5, 143; DLBD 3; DLBY 80, 82, 97; MTCW 1, 2

Upshaw, Margaret Mitchell
See Mitchell, Margaret (Munnerlyn)

Upton, Mark
See Sanders, Lawrence

Upward, Allen 1863-1926 **TCLC 85**
See also CA 117; DLB 36

Urdang, Constance (Henriette) 1922-**CLC 47**
See also CA 21-24R; CANR 9, 24

Uriel, Henry
See Faust, Frederick (Schiller)

Uris, Leon (Marcus) 1924- **CLC 7, 32; DAM NOV, POP**
See also AITN 1, 2; BEST 89:2; CA 1-4R; CANR 1, 40, 65; MTCW 1, 2; SATA 49

Urista, Alberto H. 1947-
See Alurista

See also CA 45-48; CANR 2, 32; HLCS 1; HW 1

Urmuz
See Codrescu, Andrei

Urquhart, Jane 1949- **CLC 90; DAC**
See also CA 113; CANR 32, 68

Usigli, Rodolfo 1905-1979
See also CA 131; HLCS 1; HW 1

Ustinov, Peter (Alexander) 1921- **CLC 1**
See also AITN 1; CA 13-16R; CANR 25, 51; DLB 13; MTCW 2

U Tam'si, Gerald Felix Tchicaya
See Tchicaya, Gerald Felix

U Tam'si, Tchicaya
See Tchicaya, Gerald Felix

Vachss, Andrew (Henry) 1942- **CLC 106**
See also CA 118; CANR 44

Vachss, Andrew H.
See Vachss, Andrew (Henry)

Vaculik, Ludvik 1926- **CLC 7**
See also CA 53-56; CANR 72

Vaihinger, Hans 1852-1933 **TCLC 71**
See also CA 116; 166

Valdez, Luis (Miguel) 1940- **CLC 84; DAM MULT; DC 10; HLC 2**
See also CA 101; CANR 32, 81; DLB 122; HW 1

Valenzuela, Luisa 1938- **CLC 31, 104; DAM MULT; HLCS 2; SSC 14**
See also CA 101; CANR 32, 65; DLB 113; HW 1, 2

Valera y Alcala-Galiano, Juan 1824-1905 **TCLC 10**
See also CA 106

Valery, (Ambroise) Paul (Toussaint Jules) 1871-1945 **TCLC 4, 15; DAM POET; PC 9**
See also CA 104; 122; MTCW 1, 2

Valle-Inclan, Ramon (Maria) del 1866-1936 **TCLC 5; DAM MULT; HLC 2**
See also CA 106; 153; CANR 80; DLB 134; HW 2

Vallejo, Antonio Buero
See Buero Vallejo, Antonio

Vallejo, Cesar (Abraham) 1892-1938**TCLC 3, 56; DAM MULT; HLC 2**
See also CA 105; 153; HW 1

Valles, Jules 1832-1885 **NCLC 71**
See also DLB 123

Vallette, Marguerite Eymery
See Rachilde

Valle Y Pena, Ramon del
See Valle-Inclan, Ramon (Maria) del

Van Ash, Cay 1918- **CLC 34**

Vanbrugh, Sir John 1664-1726 **LC 21; DAM DRAM**
See also DLB 80

Van Campen, Karl
See Campbell, John W(ood, Jr.)

Vance, Gerald
See Silverberg, Robert

Vance, Jack **CLC 35**
See also Kuttner, Henry; Vance, John Holbrook
See also DLB 8

Vance, John Holbrook 1916-
See Queen, Ellery; Vance, Jack
See also CA 29-32R; CANR 17, 65; MTCW 1

Van Den Bogarde, Derek Jules Gaspard Ulric Niven 1921-1999
See Bogarde, Dirk
See also CA 77-80; 179

Vandenburgh, Jane **CLC 59**
See also CA 168

Vanderhaeghe, Guy 1951- **CLC 41**

See also CA 113; CANR 72

van der Post, Laurens (Jan) 1906-1996**CLC 5**
See also CA 5-8R; 155; CANR 35; DLB 204

van de Wetering, Janwillem 1931- **CLC 47**
See also CA 49-52; CANR 4, 62

Van Dine, S. S. **TCLC 23**
See also Wright, Willard Huntington

Van Doren, Carl (Clinton) 1885-1950 **TCLC 18**
See also CA 111; 168

Van Doren, Mark 1894-1972 **CLC 6, 10**
See also CA 1-4R; 37-40R; CANR 3; DLB 45; MTCW 1, 2

Van Druten, John (William) 1901-1957**TCLC 2**
See also CA 104; 161; DLB 10

Van Duyn, Mona (Jane) 1921- **CLC 3, 7, 63, 116; DAM POET**
See also CA 9-12R; CANR 7, 38, 60; DLB 5

Van Dyne, Edith
See Baum, L(yman) Frank

van Itallie, Jean-Claude 1936- **CLC 3**
See also CA 45-48; CAAS 2; CANR 1, 48; DLB 7

van Ostaijen, Paul 1896-1928 **TCLC 33**
See also CA 163

Van Peebles, Melvin 1932- **CLC 2, 20; DAM MULT**
See also BW 2, 3; CA 85-88; CANR 27, 67, 82

Vansittart, Peter 1920- **CLC 42**
See also CA 1-4R; CANR 3, 49

Van Vechten, Carl 1880-1964 **CLC 33**
See also CA 89-92; DLB 4, 9, 51

Van Vogt, A(lfred) E(lton) 1912- **CLC 1**
See also CA 21-24R; CANR 28; DLB 8; SATA 14

Varda, Agnes 1928- **CLC 16**
See also CA 116; 122

Vargas Llosa, (Jorge) Mario (Pedro) 1936- **CLC 3, 6, 9, 10, 15, 31, 42, 85; DA; DAB; DAC; DAM MST, MULT, NOV;HLC 2**
See also CA 73-76; CANR 18, 32, 42, 67; DLB 145; HW 1, 2; MTCW 1, 2

Vasiliu, Gheorghe 1881-1957
See Bacovia, George
See also CA 123

Vassa, Gustavus
See Equiano, Olaudah

Vassilikos, Vassilis 1933- **CLC 4, 8**
See also CA 81-84; CANR 75

Vaughan, Henry 1621-1695 **LC 27**
See also DLB 131

Vaughn, Stephanie **CLC 62**

Vazov, Ivan (Minchov) 1850-1921 **TCLC 25**
See also CA 121; 167; DLB 147

Veblen, Thorstein B(unde) 1857-1929 **TCLC 31**
See also CA 115; 165

Vega, Lope de 1562-1635 **LC 23; HLCS 2**

Venison, Alfred
See Pound, Ezra (Weston Loomis)

Verdi, Marie de
See Mencken, H(enry) L(ouis)

Verdu, Matilde
See Cela, Camilo Jose

Verga, Giovanni (Carmelo) 1840-1922**TCLC 3; SSC 21**
See also CA 104; 123

Vergil 70B.C.-19B.C. **CMLC 9; DA; DAB; DAC; DAM MST, POET; PC 12; WLCS**
See also Virgil

Verhaeren, Emile (Adolphe Gustave) 1855-1916 **TCLC 12**

NOV, POP
See also AITN 1; CA 1-4R; 132; CAAS 1; CANR 1, 27; INT CANR-27; MTCW 1, 2

Wallant, Edward Lewis 1926-1962 **CLC 5, 10**
See also CA 1-4R; CANR 22; DLB 2, 28, 143; MTCW 1, 2

Wallas, Graham 1858-1932 **TCLC 91**

Walley, Byron
See Card, Orson Scott

Walpole, Horace 1717-1797 **LC 49**
See also DLB 39, 104

Walpole, Hugh (Seymour) 1884-1941 **TCLC 5**
See also CA 104; 165; DLB 34; MTCW 2

Walser, Martin 1927- **CLC 27**
See also CA 57-60; CANR 8, 46; DLB 75, 124

Walser, Robert 1878-1956 **TCLC 18; SSC 20**
See also CA 118; 165; DLB 66

Walsh, Jill Paton **CLC 35**
See also Paton Walsh, Gillian
See also AAYA 11; CLR 2; DLB 161; SAAS 3

Walter, Villiam Christian
See Andersen, Hans Christian

Wambaugh, Joseph (Aloysius, Jr.) 1937- **CLC 3, 18; DAM NOV, POP**
See also AITN 1; BEST 89:3; CA 33-36R; CANR 42, 65; DLB 6; DLBY 83; MTCW 1, 2

Wang Wei 699(?)-761(?) **PC 18**

Ward, Arthur Henry Sarsfield 1883-1959
See Rohmer, Sax
See also CA 108; 173

Ward, Douglas Turner 1930- **CLC 19**
See also BW 1; CA 81-84; CANR 27; DLB 7, 38

Ward, E. D.
See Lucas, E(dward) V(errall)

Ward, Mary Augusta
See Ward, Mrs. Humphry

Ward, Mrs. Humphry 1851-1920 **TCLC 55**
See also DLB 18

Ward, Peter
See Faust, Frederick (Schiller)

Warhol, Andy 1928(?)-1987 **CLC 20**
See also AAYA 12; BEST 89:4; CA 89-92; 121; CANR 34

Warner, Francis (Robert le Plastrier) 1937- **CLC 14**
See also CA 53-56; CANR 11

Warner, Marina 1946- **CLC 59**
See also CA 65-68; CANR 21, 55; DLB 194

Warner, Rex (Ernest) 1905-1986 **CLC 45**
See also CA 89-92; 119; DLB 15

Warner, Susan (Bogert) 1819-1885 **NCLC 31**
See also DLB 3, 42

Warner, Sylvia (Constance) Ashton
See Ashton-Warner, Sylvia (Constance)

Warner, Sylvia Townsend 1893-1978 **CLC 7, 19; SSC 23**
See also CA 61-64; 77-80; CANR 16, 60; DLB 34, 139; MTCW 1, 2

Warren, Mercy Otis 1728-1814 **NCLC 13**
See also DLB 31, 200

Warren, Robert Penn 1905-1989 **CLC 1, 4, 6, 8, 10, 13, 18, 39, 53, 59; DA; DAB; DAC; DAM MST, NOV, POET; SSC 4; WLC**
See also AITN 1; CA 13-16R; 129; CANR 10, 47; CDALB 1968-1988; DLB 2, 48, 152; DLBY 80, 89; INT CANR-10; MTCW 1, 2; SATA 46; SATA-Obit 63

Warshofsky, Isaac
See Singer, Isaac Bashevis

Warton, Thomas 1728-1790 **LC 15; DAM POET**

See also DLB 104, 109

Waruk, Kona
See Harris, (Theodore) Wilson

Warung, Price 1855-1911 **TCLC 45**

Warwick, Jarvis
See Garner, Hugh

Washington, Alex
See Harris, Mark

Washington, Booker T(aliaferro) 1856-1915 **TCLC 10; BLC 3; DAM MULT**
See also BW 1; CA 114; 125; SATA 28

Washington, George 1732-1799 **LC 25**
See also DLB 31

Wassermann, (Karl) Jakob 1873-1934 **TCLC 6**
See also CA 104; 163; DLB 66

Wasserstein, Wendy 1950- **CLC 32, 59, 90; DAM DRAM; DC 4**
See also CA 121; 129; CABS 3; CANR 53, 75; INT 129; MTCW 2; SATA 94

Waterhouse, Keith (Spencer) 1929- **CLC 47**
See also CA 5-8R; CANR 38, 67; DLB 13, 15; MTCW 1, 2

Waters, Frank (Joseph) 1902-1995 **CLC 88**
See also CA 5-8R; 149; CAAS 13; CANR 3, 18, 63; DLB 212; DLBY 86

Waters, Roger 1944- **CLC 35**

Watkins, Frances Ellen
See Harper, Frances Ellen Watkins

Watkins, Gerrold
See Malzberg, Barry N(athaniel)

Watkins, Gloria 1955(?)-
See hooks, bell
See also BW 2; CA 143; MTCW 2

Watkins, Paul 1964- **CLC 55**
See also CA 132; CANR 62

Watkins, Vernon Phillips 1906-1967 **CLC 43**
See also CA 9-10; 25-28R; CAP 1; DLB 20

Watson, Irving S.
See Mencken, H(enry) L(ouis)

Watson, John H.
See Farmer, Philip Jose

Watson, Richard F.
See Silverberg, Robert

Waugh, Auberon (Alexander) 1939- **CLC 7**
See also CA 45-48; CANR 6, 22; DLB 14, 194

Waugh, Evelyn (Arthur St. John) 1903-1966 **CLC 1, 3, 8, 13, 19, 27, 44, 107; DA; DAB; DAC; DAM MST, NOV, POP; WLC**
See also CA 85-88; 25-28R; CANR 22; CDBLB 1914-1945; DLB 15, 162, 195; MTCW 1, 2

Waugh, Harriet 1944- **CLC 6**
See also CA 85-88; CANR 22

Ways, C. R.
See Blount, Roy (Alton), Jr.

Waystaff, Simon
See Swift, Jonathan

Webb, (Martha) Beatrice (Potter) 1858-1943 **TCLC 22**
See also Potter, (Helen) Beatrix
See also CA 117; DLB 190

Webb, Charles (Richard) 1939- **CLC 7**
See also CA 25-28R

Webb, James H(enry), Jr. 1946- **CLC 22**
See also CA 81-84

Webb, Mary (Gladys Meredith) 1881-1927 **TCLC 24**
See also CA 123; DLB 34

Webb, Mrs. Sidney
See Webb, (Martha) Beatrice (Potter)

Webb, Phyllis 1927- **CLC 18**
See also CA 104; CANR 23; DLB 53

Webb, Sidney (James) 1859-1947 **TCLC 22**

See also CA 117; 163; DLB 190

Webber, Andrew Lloyd **CLC 21**
See also Lloyd Webber, Andrew

Weber, Lenora Mattingly 1895-1971 **CLC 12**
See also CA 19-20; 29-32R; CAP 1; SATA 2; SATA-Obit 26

Weber, Max 1864-1920 **TCLC 69**
See also CA 109

Webster, John 1579(?)-1634(?) **LC 33; DA; DAB; DAC; DAM DRAM, MST; DC 2; WLC**
See also CDBLB Before 1660; DLB 58

Webster, Noah 1758-1843 **NCLC 30**
See also DLB 1, 37, 42, 43, 73

Wedekind, (Benjamin) Frank(lin) 1864-1918 **TCLC 7; DAM DRAM**
See also CA 104; 153; DLB 118

Weidman, Jerome 1913-1998 **CLC 7**
See also AITN 2; CA 1-4R; 171; CANR 1; DLB 28

Weil, Simone (Adolphine) 1909-1943 **TCLC 23**
See also CA 117; 159; MTCW 2

Weininger, Otto 1880-1903 **TCLC 84**

Weinstein, Nathan
See West, Nathanael

Weinstein, Nathan von Wallenstein
See West, Nathanael

Weir, Peter (Lindsay) 1944- **CLC 20**
See also CA 113; 123

Weiss, Peter (Ulrich) 1916-1982 **CLC 3, 15, 51; DAM DRAM**
See also CA 45-48; 106; CANR 3; DLB 69, 124

Weiss, Theodore (Russell) 1916- **CLC 3, 8, 14**
See also CA 9-12R; CAAS 2; CANR 46; DLB 5

Welch, (Maurice) Denton 1915-1948 **TCLC 22**
See also CA 121; 148

Welch, James 1940- **CLC 6, 14, 52; DAM MULT, POP**
See also CA 85-88; CANR 42, 66; DLB 175; NNAL

Weldon, Fay 1931- **CLC 6, 9, 11, 19, 36, 59, 122; DAM POP**
See also CA 21-24R; CANR 16, 46, 63; CDBLB 1960 to Present; DLB 14, 194; INT CANR-16; MTCW 1, 2

Wellek, Rene 1903-1995 **CLC 28**
See also CA 5-8R; 150; CAAS 7; CANR 8; DLB 63; INT CANR-8

Weller, Michael 1942- **CLC 10, 53**
See also CA 85-88

Weller, Paul 1958- **CLC 26**

Wellershoff, Dieter 1925- **CLC 46**
See also CA 89-92; CANR 16, 37

Welles, (George) Orson 1915-1985 **CLC 20, 80**
See also CA 93-96; 117

Wellman, John McDowell 1945-
See Wellman, Mac
See also CA 166

Wellman, Mac 1945- **CLC 65**
See also Wellman, John McDowell; Wellman, John McDowell

Wellman, Manly Wade 1903-1986 **CLC 49**
See also CA 1-4R; 118; CANR 6, 16, 44; SATA 6; SATA-Obit 47

Wells, Carolyn 1869(?)-1942 **TCLC 35**
See also CA 113; DLB 11

Wells, H(erbert) G(eorge) 1866-1946 **TCLC 6, 12, 19; DA; DAB; DAC; DAM MST, NOV; SSC 6; WLC**
See also AAYA 18; CA 110; 121; CDBLB 1914-1945; DLB 34, 70, 156, 178; MTCW 1, 2; SATA 20

Literary Criticism Series
Cumulative Topic Index

This index lists all topic entries in Gale's *Classical and Medieval Literature Criticism, Contemporary Literary Criticism, Literature Criticism from 1400 to 1800, Nineteenth-Century Literature Criticism,* and *Twentieth-Century Literary Criticism.*

Topic Index

Topic Index

　　　　　　　　　　　　　　　LITERARY CRITICISM SERIES

Young Playwrights Festival
1988—CLC 55: 376-81
1989—CLC 59: 398-403
1990—CLC 65: 444-8

LC Cumulative Nationality Index

Nationality Index

LC Cumulative Title Index

Title Index

Title Index

Title Index

Title Index

Title Index

Title Index

Title Index

Title Index

Title Index

ISBN 0-7876-3267-8

90000